1,000 Places To See

IN THE UNITED STATES & CANADA

Before You Die™

by **PATRICIA SCHULTZ**

WORKMAN PUBLISHING, NEW YORK

AN IMPORTANT NOTE
TO READERS

Though every effort has been made to ensure the accuracy and timeliness of the travel information contained in this book, such information can change at any time. Readers should be sure to check websites and to call ahead for confirmation when making any travel plans. The author, editors, and publisher cannot be held responsible for travel conditions that may differ from those described in this book. And if you discover any out-of-date or incorrect information in the book, we would very much appreciate it if you would let us know at info@workman.com.

Library of Congress Cataloging-in-Publication Data is available.

ISBN 978-0-7611-8943-5 (pb); 978-0-7611-8989-3 (hc)

Design by Paul Hanson and Orlando Adiao

Workman books are available at special discount when purchased in bulk for premiums and sales promotions as well as for fund-raising or educational use. Special editions or book excerpts also can be created to specification. For details, contact the Special Sales Director at the address below or send an email to specialmarkets@workman.com.

Workman Publishing Co., Inc.
225 Varick Street
New York, NY 10014-4381

workman.com

WORKMAN is a registered trademark of Workman Publishing Co., Inc.

Printed in China

First Printing, updated edition: January 2017
10 9 8 7 6 5 4 3 2 1

The whole object of travel

is not to set foot on foreign land;

it is at last to set foot on

one's own country as a foreign land.

—GILBERT K. CHESTERTON

In loving memory

of the two finest parents of all time,

Leonard and Mary Schultz

ACKNOWLEDGMENTS

One thousand thank-yous is not enough.

It's impossible to overstate my gratitude to Workman Publishing for the opportunity to create a companion travel book that I hoped would match the spirit and breadth of the first *1,000 Places to See Before You Die*, and then to let me update it when confronted with the countless changes that occur on a daily basis.

At the helm of the veritable village it took to create this 1,200-plus-page tome was the late Peter Workman, wise and ever infallible: How did he know that a book whose title touched upon dying would galvanize so many people to get off the couch and live? I am honored that Peter believed I was up to the challenge and coaxed another list of a thousand favorites out of me. I am happy that he recognized that our own great country and its northern neighbor and their countless beauties deserve the same attention previously showered upon the globe.

Only a writer will understand that he or she is but the smallest of pieces in a far larger and more complex jigsaw puzzle. The well-oiled and creatively organized Workman Publishing family always saw the big picture. While I was off roaming the continent, hunting down 1,000 destinations, they were back home making sense of my scribblings, whipping them into the handsome book you now hold in your hands.

This cast of disparate characters and talents shared the Herculean task of making this book happen on time— with a tweak, nudge, polish, hone, query, and edit along the way. Front and center I must thank my editor Margot Herrera, who gives new meaning to the expression "sunny disposition" and whose unflappable nature worked as the glue that kept this project together. Cut from the same cloth is her assistant extraordinaire, Evan Griffith, who managed to convince me that he lived to make my life easier.

Paul Hanson's design sensibility, first applied to the original edition, was kept fresh and exciting in this sibling book, expertly assisted by his colleague Orlando Adiao. Other indispensable team members include Barbara Peragine and Genevieve Crane, who so ably typeset the book; Claire McKean, keeper of the schedule; production editor Kim Daly, who dotted all i's and crossed all t's; photo researcher Michael Dimascio, who pored over oceans of images in order to make the right match; and production supervisor Doug Wolff, who oversaw the book's printing.

Workman's editor-in-chief, Suzie Bolotin, has been unwavering in her support, most appreciated during those bumpy patches and moments of short-lived despair. Pat Upton and Jenny Mandel, in licensing and special sales, and the publicity and marketing team of Selina Meere, Jessica Weiner, and Lauren Southard are determined that this new edition will enjoy much of the recognition of its predecessor.

I am profoundly grateful to two fellow travelers who were indispensable in the book's completion: Anitra Brown, placed next to me by fate on the inaugural sailing of the *Queen Mary 2* many years ago, who became a fast and famous friend of indefatigable assistance in making many of these chapters happen, and Bill McCrae, the quintessential travel authority of a dying breed, whose love for explora-tion and learning and inherent sense of perfection and pride is something I aspire to.

Profound thanks to my sister, Rosalyn Vross, for putting up with me for all these years; to her husband, Ed, my go-to guy for military history, Alaska info, and all things field-and-stream–related; and to their children, Star, Corey and Brittany, who are my children too and who, I hope, have vicariously enjoyed coming along for the ride. And to my Aunt Dorothy and my late Aunt Kitty, whom I aspire to be like when I grow up.

And at the end of the day, it is the quiet support of my friends that allows me to tolerate the eight-day weeks and deadline-fueled weekends, who patiently listen when I bemoan how much I miss my life, and are unsurprisingly packed and ready to go when I come up for air and mention the need for a travel fix. Teddy Sitter is confirmation that there is nothing in life so precious as an old friend, and shares with me every vicissitude brought on by my life and work, its successes and wealth of blessings. I'd like to give a special shout-out to Elizabeth Ragagli, who encour-ages me to do un-Patricia-like things such as snowshoeing in Jackson Hole when I am more inclined to check out the great indoors ("Does this hotel have a spa?"), and to Anita Flannery, who plays Thelma to my Louise (or perhaps it's the other way around) during jaunts through the breathtaking canyons of Utah and downtown Manhattan.

Maya Angelou once said you can judge people by how they handle tangled Christmas tree lights and lost luggage. Nick Stringas laughs at lost luggage, wrong turns, and canceled flights—always with a smile the size of Montana—reminding me that there's no such thing as a bad trip.

CONTENTS

INTRODUCTION · x

REDISCOVERING MY OWN BACKYARD *x*

A FEW NUTS AND BOLTS *xiv*

THE UNITED STATES · 1

CANADA • 971

INDEXES · 1073

INTRODUCTION

Rediscovering My Own Backyard

Did the world really need another "short list" of a thousand places to add to the excitement and anxiety of "so much to see, so little time"? Wasn't it enough that my previous book, *1,000 Places to See Before You Die*, was already keeping folks awake at night,

ticking off must-see destinations as if for some grand travel sweepstakes or in a race against time? (Taj Mahal? Did that. Masai Mara? Check. Transylvania? Next year.) After having focused on the planet's abundance of riches, I found myself returning time and again to the notion of a similar book about travel in the U.S.A. and Canada: But would these two countries alone supply me with enough diversity and possibilities? Could the 150-plus U.S.A. and Canada entries I included in my first book be expanded to one thousand, all promising the same kind of specialness that had previously stopped me in my tracks while wandering around the globe? Would I echo Dorothy and declare there's no place like home?

These are the questions that stayed with me in the nascent days of this book's conception. Having tried my best to capture the magic of the world and its untold offerings in *1,000 Places to See*

You are holding the third edition of *1,000 Places to See in the United States & Canada Before You Die.*

I'm lucky enough to work with a publisher who believes in keeping books up to date—even one of this tome's size and detail. Not only do we make corrections with every reprint, but every few years we update the book entirely from head to toe, a Herculean task that is akin to painting a bridge—where no sooner does one finish the job, than it is time to start all over again. We encourage you to contact us (info@workman.com) with any suggested changes or additions to the text based on your own exploration of this magnificent continent. Thank you in advance!

Before You Die, I was heartened by the number of travelers—both rookies and veterans, here and abroad—who embraced the book and poured their carpe-diem energies and pent-up cravings into putting it to good use. My own energies and curiosity were telling me there was an encore waiting in the wings: It was time to turn my international attentions home.

My philosophy of travel has always been based on removing myself from what is comfortable and safe, on seeking out experiences that broaden my horizons and enrich me in ways superficial and profound. That simple concept had always seemed most intoxicating when experienced far from home, but why not apply it to my own backyard? Especially when my backyard is the U.S.A. and Canada—with a great and diversified landmass and rich mosaic of heritages, the pickings don't get any better than these.

North America was by no means terra incognita to me: I had been crisscrossing it ever since I can remember, long ago lured by the possibilities it promised. I prided myself on not being one of the masses Calvin Trillin described when he wrote, "Americans drive across this country like someone is chasing them." I break for photo ops, for kids pouring out of school, to smell the camellias, listen to the church carillon, and for any handmade sign that says "Pick it yourself" or "Homemade here." I've even risen above it in hot-air balloons to sail at a bird's pace and see it from God's perspective.

My meanderings began way back when my sister, Roz, and I were relegated to the back seat of the family station wagon for long summer trips to the Jersey Shore (except for that one year when the gas tank fell off and we never made it past the end of the driveway). One wouldn't consider our modest "are we there yet?" road trips extravagant cross-country journeys, but explain that to a 6-year-old. The anticipation alone was enough to keep me awake the night before, and to this day any passing vignette of countryside framed by the car window awakens in me that same childlike flutter of discovery. We would strike off, leaving behind the predictability of our everyday lives in the small riverside city of Beacon, New York, where we walked to school, left our doors unlocked, and helped shovel out our neighbors after a snowstorm. Our mother's extended Italian family supplied an exuberant and enlightening insight into the inimitable notion of America as melting pot. My Teutonic father was a private man who was 90 years old before he mentioned that one of his parents was part Native American. When I asked why he had never told us before, he answered "You never asked." Together they introduced me to this country where everything that smelled of America was appreciated and good, and we never had to look much beyond North Walnut Street for affirmation.

Beacon didn't have many claims to fame apart from its location on a particularly beautiful bend in the Hudson River and our most illustrious resident, Pete Seeger. Of his incredible repertoire of American folk songs, the one I loved best was one he borrowed from Woody Guthrie and made his own:

This land is your land,
This land is my land.
From California, to the
New York island.
From the redwood forests
To the Gulf Stream waters.
This land was made for you and me.

Glimpsed from this idyllic spot on the Hudson, the potential of America the Beautiful beckoned: How could I not take the opportunity to explore this land Pete Seeger promised was mine, heeding the call of the open road? I decided to dive into this great country of ours—and dip into the wealth that is Canada, our remarkable neighbor to the North—and a new book was on its way.

In the course of my research, I roamed landscapes old and new, some first seen during teenage road trips, revisited now with fresh eyes. Having skied the Alps of Europe, I found our Rockies every bit

as majestic. After time spent absorbing the joys of small villages and cities from France to Scotland, I experienced the historic quarter of Montreal and the old fishing towns of Nova Scotia with a newfound appreciation. I discovered the kinship between chaotic and vibrant Hong Kong and Manhattan, both fueled by ambition and divided into neighborhoods where anything can happen, and almost always does.

States and cities that had never figured on my short list of places I simply had to see, surprised me with their beauty, traditional ways, and proud history. Here are just a few of the eye-openers: the inspiring talent that rolls in from the range for the Cowboy Poetry Gathering in Lewistown, Montana; the beauty of the Oregon Coast (why is it that California gets all the attention?); the unabashed fun of the Dallas State Fair (where I discovered the decadent pleasure of deep-fried everything); the Shenandoah Valley in Virginia, whose display of hardwood trees turning crimson and gold might possibly trump autumn in New England; the safari-like excitement of viewing the polar bears of Churchill in Manitoba; and standing in awe beneath the swirling nocturnal show of the aurora borealis in Fairbanks, Alaska. The romance and grandeur and excitement that I had found elsewhere on the globe were here in spades at every turn, and all for the price of a tank (or two or three) of gas.

For a dose of patriotism, there is nothing more moving than a contemplative walk through the fields of Gettysburg, or Vicksburg, or Antietam, or the quintessentially American thrill of a hike up to Lady Liberty's torch. Dig in at Maine's annual Lobster Festival or browse the small Norman Rockwell Museum in Stockbridge, Massachusetts, for a concentration of all-Americana, the same feeling that stirs me when driving through any crossroads caught in time, dissected by a 1950s Main Street with a shiny chrome diner at its center—a quiet blink-and-you'll-miss-it slice of small-town U.S.A. in the middle of nowhere.

Adventure is where you find it. It needn't be on the other side of the globe or in an ancient medina, but it sure isn't on your couch. There is no limit to the world of possibilities if you nurture your curiosity and keep your eyes open. And look closely, for the most special moments may not be at the Mount Rushmores or the Grand Canyons, although these monumental icons figure high on most travelers' life lists. But so should a visit to Kentucky's serene Shaker Village of Pleasant Hill, or a sighting of the wild horses that still roam the pristine shores of Cumberland Island off the coast of Georgia. What's more, remember that rather than a carefully planned itinerary, it's often serendipity that leads you to our greatest national treasure—the people who make up this great continent, from the gracious couple who run that B&B you stumbled upon in Hannibal (ask for the room where Mark Twain slept) to the rowdy family who spontaneously included you in Grandpa's 80th birthday celebration in that smoky barbeque dive in Plano, Texas.

Back in the days of our massive expansion, Horace Greeley urged America to "Go west, young man." But also go north and south and east while you're at it. Make sure you stop everywhere in between, too, eschewing the interstates for the two-lane highways—and never pass up the homemade pie. Hit the road before you hit the remote, indulge your wanderlust, and you'll wind up agreeing with T. S. Eliot, who wrote:

> *And the end of all our exploring*
> *Will be to arrive where we started*
> *And know the place for the first time.*

Creating this book—and scouring it from cover to cover for this new update—has been challenging, enlightening, and humbling as I discovered time and again the country that is my home. My goal was to shed light on its most wonderful places—both world-famous and unsung—and to get you on your way to discovering them. I join my fellow Beaconite Pete Seeger in singing the high praises of this land that was made for you and me.

A Few Nuts and Bolts

Whether you're using this book to plan your travel or are just doing a little armchair adventuring, it'll help to know some of the general philosophy behind the entries—how they're organized, what level of detail

I've included, what some of the terminology refers to. At the end, I've also included some information on traveling between the U.S.A. and Canada.

Many entries describe a single particular experience—visiting the Heard Museum in Phoenix, Arizona, perhaps the premier collection of Native American art and culture in the country; catching a game at Boston's venerable Fenway Park, the oldest major league ballpark in America; walking in the footsteps of Franklin Delano Roosevelt at his Hudson Valley home and the country's first presidential library in Hyde Park, New York.

Sometimes, though, it just made more sense geographically—or in the simple attempt to create the best experience possible—to combine two, sometimes more, destinations within a single entry. Enjoying Maryland's Talbot County on the Chesapeake's Eastern Shore means visiting small maritime museums and historical lighthouses, then feasting at the dive-y Crab Claw in St. Michaels and overnighting at the 1710 Robert Morris Inn in stuck-

in-time Oxford. And exploring New Hampshire's Lake Region can mean a cruise on Lake Winnipesaukee, and an afternoon at the Antique & Classic Boat Show in Meredith, later falling asleep to the sound of loons at the Manor on Golden Pond on the banks of quiet Squam Lake. The California entry about the Pacific Coast Highway literally brims with all the must-stops and photo ops along America's Dream Drive.

The Sections of the Book

For the purposes of this book, I've divided the United States into nine regions, which are then further subdivided geographically into states grouped from the East Coast to West Coast and beyond:

- New England
- Mid-Atlantic
- The Southeast
- Mississippi Valley
- The Midwest
- Great Plains
- Four Corners and the Southwest

- WEST COAST
- ALASKA AND HAWAII

Canada is loosely divided in half:

- EASTERN CANADA
- WESTERN CANADA

Within these divisions, entries are further divided alphabetically by state or province (see the table of contents for a quick reference), with each one's entries further organized alphabetically by town or city or by the destination itself (Yellowstone National Park, for example, falls at the end of the Wyoming section).

At the back of the book, you'll find a general index and ten special indexes that allow you to find information by type of entry: golf, beaches, scenic drives, museums, and so on, with a specific Take the Kids index for suggested family holidays.

Organizing the Listings

Following the text that describes each of the 1,000 places, I've included practical information that will help you in planning your trip—but remember, since travel information is eternally subject to change, you should always confirm by phone or a quick Google search before you leave home. Here's a run-through of what you'll see within the entries.

WHERE

Most of the practical information sections open with the entry's distance from a major city, and list the phone number and web address. For space

reasons we have included only the street address of those places listed in the entry name; for all others described in text, call or check the website. Contact information for the local tourist office for general information about the area is usually included as well.

HOW

Although rarely mentioned in the text, I sometimes recommend outfitters or operators that offer tours, treks, white-water rafting, and other package or customized travel to the particular destination. Occasionally these are listed by what they offer, for example, KAYAKING or SURFING.

WHERE TO STAY

Hotels, inns, and B&Bs listed under this head may have not been discussed in the entry text but merit a mention here, as they are reliable choices located near the topic of the entry, and are of at least good to very good quality.

COST

As prices are in continual flux, these are meant to provide you with a working indication of expense, rather than a precise to-the-dollar quote. I have listed prices for all hotels, restaurants, theater and event tickets, and package trips discussed in the book, based on the following parameters. I have not included the usual costs for museums, parks, or fares for ferries and the like; they are generally moderate and not surprising. Nor, for the most part, have I included children's prices.

Hotels. Listed hotel costs are per double room, unless noted. Certain kinds of hotels (such as dude ranches or destination spas) commonly quote their rates on a per person, per day, and generally double-occupancy basis and are listed as such. Where applicable, hotel info includes peak and off-peak prices.

Trips/Packages/Excursions. Organized trip costs are usually given in total, per person, based on double occupancy, with notes on what is included in the rate (how many nights of accommodations, meals, transportation, amenities, etc.). Note that "Cost" does not include airfare unless otherwise stated.

Restaurants. Meal prices listed are per person and represent the average cost of a meal without wine. When the restaurant offers a special tasting menu (multiple courses) or a fixed-price menu for which it is known, I've usually listed these as well.

WHEN

I've noted which days and/or seasons each entry is open. For hotels and sites, WHEN does not appear if the establishment is open daily or year-round. Single-day holiday closings (such as for Christmas) have not been noted, nor have short seasonal closings that

may change from year to year—such as when some small restaurants or B&Bs close for a week or two off-season, or a wilderness resort closes during late-spring "mud season." Because so many restaurants have varied schedules, I haven't included WHEN for these. Please call ahead or check their website.

Be especially sure to contact hotels, restaurants, and target attractions in advance if traveling during holiday months or off-season months in areas that may receive little or no traffic.

BEST TIMES

For almost every entry, I've listed the best time or times to visit, taking into account weather, festivals, sports and leisure opportunities, and other significant events. When no BEST TIMES are listed—as is often the case with hotels, restaurants, and museums—the implication is "year-round."

Travel Documents

All U.S. and Canadian citizens are required to show a passport for all travel between the countries. If you don't already have one, leave ample time for the process of procuring a passport: To get a start, U.S. citizens should go to the website travel.state.gov. Canadians can go to passport canada.gc.ca.

THE UNITED STATES

NEW ENGLAND ·
MID-ATLANTIC ·
THE SOUTHEAST ·
MISSISSIPPI VALLEY ·
THE MIDWEST ·
GREAT PLAINS ·
FOUR CORNERS AND
THE SOUTHWEST ·
WEST COAST ·
ALASKA AND HAWAII

UNITED STATES

MAINE — Augusta

NEW HAMPSHIRE — Concord

VERMONT — Montpelier

MASSACHUSETTS — Boston, Portland

RHODE ISLAND — Providence

CONNECTICUT — Hartford

NEW YORK — Albany, Buffalo, New York

PENNSYLVANIA — Harrisburg, Pittsburgh, Philadelphia

NEW JERSEY — Trenton

DELAWARE — Dover

MARYLAND — Annapolis, Baltimore

Washington D.C.

WEST VIRGINIA — Charleston

VIRGINIA — Richmond

NORTH CAROLINA — Raleigh, Charlotte

SOUTH CAROLINA — Columbia, Charleston

GEORGIA — Atlanta, Savannah

FLORIDA — Tallahassee, Jacksonville, Tampa, Miami

OHIO — Columbus, Cleveland

KENTUCKY — Frankfort, Louisville

TENNESSEE — Nashville, Memphis

ALABAMA — Montgomery, Mobile

MISSISSIPPI — Jackson

LOUISIANA — Baton Rouge, New Orleans

MICHIGAN — Lansing, Detroit

INDIANA — Indianapolis

ILLINOIS — Springfield, Chicago

WISCONSIN — Madison

MINNESOTA — St. Paul, Minneapolis, Duluth

IOWA — Des Moines

MISSOURI — Jefferson City, St. Louis, Kansas City

ARKANSAS — Little Rock

NORTH DAKOTA — Bismarck, Fargo

SOUTH DAKOTA — Pierre, Sioux Falls

NEBRASKA — Lincoln, Omaha

KANSAS — Topeka, Wichita

OKLAHOMA — Oklahoma City, Tulsa

TEXAS — Austin, Dallas, Houston, San Antonio, Amarillo, El Paso

MONTANA — Helena, Billings, Missoula

WYOMING — Cheyenne

COLORADO — Denver, Colorado Springs

NEW MEXICO — Santa Fe, Albuquerque

IDAHO — Boise City, Coeur d'Alene

UTAH — Salt Lake City

ARIZONA — Phoenix, Tucson

NEVADA — Carson City, Reno, Las Vegas

WASHINGTON — Olympia, Seattle, Spokane

OREGON — Salem, Portland

CALIFORNIA — Sacramento, San Francisco, Los Angeles, San Diego

ALASKA — Juneau, Anchorage

HAWAII — Honolulu

CANADA

MEXICO

ATLANTIC OCEAN

PACIFIC OCEAN

Gulf of Mexico

Gulf of California

Rocky Mountains

Appalachian Mts.

Mississippi River

Missouri River

Rio Grande

Colorado River

Red River

Pecos River

Grand Tetons

Great Salt Lake

Mt. Whitney

L. Superior

L. Huron

L. Michigan

L. Erie

L. Ontario

N · E · S · W

Miles 0 300

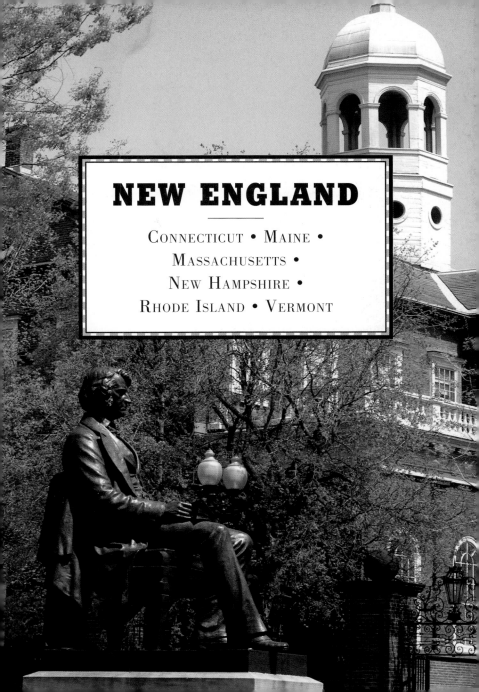

NEW ENGLAND

CONNECTICUT • MAINE •
MASSACHUSETTS •
NEW HAMPSHIRE •
RHODE ISLAND • VERMONT

CHESTER & EAST HADDAM

Connecticut

F ew Connecticut areas better retain the look of yesteryear than the lower Connecticut River valley, particularly the neighboring Victorian villages of East Haddam and Chester. East Haddam (population 9,000)

developed during the 19th-century shipbuilding era, and it still contains countless imposing Victorian structures, including the painstakingly restored Goodspeed Opera House, a magnificent four-story Second Empire building on the banks of the Connecticut River. The opera house boomed for its first few decades but fell on hard times by the middle of the 20th century and nearly faced the wrecking ball. Preservationists stepped in, and now the 398-seat Goodspeed shows three top-quality musicals annually.

Just downriver the curious Gillette Castle anchors the 184-acre state park created by eccentric 19th-century thespian and Connecticut son William Gillette, famous for his Sherlock Holmes portrayal. The elaborate—some say bombastic—20-room fieldstone castle was built between 1914 and 1919 for a then-astounding $1 million. The actor died in 1937, and in 1943 Connecticut purchased it from the executors. You can tour the ambitiously restored bluff-top structure, or stroll along Gillette's 3-mile-long narrow-gauge railroad. Trains no longer operate, but you can hike along the rail bed and admire the handsome stone rail station. It's a wonderful place for a picnic and an afternoon spent exploring the area's myriad nature trails.

Nearby Chester is a delightful spot for its shopping and dining. A smattering of art galleries fill the quaint, walkable downtown of this village perched along a section of the Connecticut River that the Nature Conservancy has called one of "the last great

places on earth." Foodies laud the excellent Restaurant L&E, a classic French bistro, which occupies an unpretentious and intimate dining room. It's satisfying and refreshingly unfussy food, and the service is faultless, too.

WHERE: 30 miles southeast of Hartford. *Visitor info:* Tel 860-787-9640; centerofct .com. **GOODSPEED OPERA HOUSE:** East Haddam. Tel 860-873-8668; goodspeed.org. *Cost:* tickets from $36. *When:* season runs late Apr–Nov; tours June–Oct on Sat. **GILLETTE CASTLE:** East Haddam. Tel 860-526-2336; ct.gov/deep/gillette. *When:* late May–mid-Oct, grounds open year-round. **RESTAURANT L&E:** Chester. Tel 860-526-5301; restaurant french75bar.com. *Cost:* dinner $50. **BEST TIMES:** early Feb for Chester Winter Carnivale, with an outdoor ice-carving competition and gallery receptions (visitchester.com); late Aug for the Chester Fair (chesterfair.org); early Sept for Chester Lobster Festival.

Overlooking the Connecticut River, the Gillette Castle took 20 men 5 years to complete.

The Apex of American Impressionism

CONNECTICUT'S
ART TRAIL

Connecticut

C onnecticut celebrates its important role in the American Impressionist art movement with its own Art Trail. A highlight is Old Lyme, a quiet 19th-century arts colony at the mouth of the Connecticut River.

Here in the late 19th century Miss Florence Griswold—a patroness of the arts—routinely hosted such American Impressionist talents as Henry Ward Ranger, Willard Metcalf, and Childe Hassam. Her 1817 Late Georgian mansion is now a museum; many of the hostess's visiting artists painted directly on the walls and doors of the interior, and their works are visible today.

Within walking distance of the museum, the Bee and Thistle Inn is housed in an imposing yellow 1756 Colonial with a gambrel roof and is set among beautiful gardens and tree-shaded lawns. The ten rooms are handsomely furnished, and the inn's well-regarded kitchen serves simple, contemporary American fare, including a perfectly prepared herb-grilled hanger steak with truffle-smashed new potatoes, grilled asparagus, and white balsamic reduction.

The Connecticut Art Trail links 18 museums and various attractions around the state, including the Bruce Museum in Greenwich, where the Cos Cob Art Colony thrived between the 1890s and 1920s. Metcalf, Hassam, and painters Elmer Livingston MacRae, and John Twachtman all practiced their craft in Greenwich, and their works fill the Bruce Museum, along with paintings by Degas and Seurat.

Just west of Hartford in leafy Farmington, the Hill-Stead Museum is best known for its French Impressionist paintings by Monet, Degas, and Manet, as well as two renowned paintings by American artist Mary Cassatt (who lived in Connecticut at various times). The Hill-Stead occupies a 1901 mansion co-designed (with architectural firm McKim, Mead & White) and formerly owned by Theodate Pope Riddle, who left the property to be run as a museum with all its original art and furnishings (including some precious Chinese porcelains and Japanese woodblock prints). A restored sunken garden originally laid out by famed landscape architect Beatrix Farrand occupies nearly an acre.

A final major stop on the trail is the New Britain Museum of American Art, established in 1903. Housed inside a stunning contemporary limestone building, the collection numbers nearly 12,000 works, including many by Connecticut luminaries such as Hassam, Cassatt, Metcalf, and J. Alden Weir (who is celebrated at the Weir Farm National Historic Site in Wilton; see p. 9).

WHERE: Old Lyme is 42 miles southeast of Hartford. *Visitor info:* Tel 800-863-6569 or 860-444-2206; mystic.org or ctarttrail.org. **FLORENCE GRISWOLD MUSEUM:** Old Lyme. Tel 860-434-5542; florencegriswoldmuseum.org. *When:* closed Mon. **BEE AND THISTLE INN:** Old Lyme. Tel 860-434-1667; beeandthistleinn.com. *Cost:* from $115 (off-peak), from $180 (peak); dinner $40. **BRUCE MUSEUM:** Greenwich. Tel 203-869-0376; brucemuseum.org. *When:* closed Mon. **HILL-STEAD MUSEUM:** Farmington.

Tel 860-677-4787; hillstead.org. *When:* closed Mon. **New Britain Museum:** Tel 860-229-0257; nbmaa.org. **Best time:** late July for Old Lyme's Midsummer Festival, which takes place in part at the Florence Griswold Museum (oldlymemidsummerfestival.com).

Down by the Seashore

Connecticut's Seafood Institutions

Connecticut

I t's not difficult to find no-frills restaurants serving lobster and scallops along the Connecticut shoreline—and wherever you go, you can count on freshness. But some venues assume legendary reputations. Take Abbott's Lobster in the

Rough, an old-fashioned seasonal fish shanty in tiny Noank, 3 miles southwest of Mystic Seaport (see p. 15). All summer, this BYOB restaurant overlooking Long Island Sound pulls in hungry fans of seafood, most of whom have patiently waited on the inevitably long lines. You order when you walk in and then wait for your number to be called. In the meantime, scour the grassy lawn beside the restaurant for a free picnic table. The traditional lobster dinners are de rigueur—choose your lobster, which is then steamed and served with drawn butter, potato chips, and coleslaw. There is plenty more on the menu, all of it tantalizingly good: quarter-pound hot lobster rolls, oysters on the half shell, clear-broth clam chowder, and velvety New York–style cheesecake.

In Madison, along the central Connecticut shoreline, Lenny and Joe's Fish Tale has been serving armies of shellfish lovers since it opened in 1979—a football-field-size parking lot attests to its popularity. Two more restaurants—one 8 miles east in Westbrook, the other 20 miles west in New Haven—dish up the same fresh food. Together, these fish joints attract more than 15,000 customers on a typical summer weekend. Favorite choices from the lengthy menu include seafood platters heaped with fried whole clams and Atlantic sea scallops. Not all the best seafood joints in Connecticut are along the coast. The funky Blue Oar restaurant in Haddam sits just beyond the railroad tracks by a marina along the Connecticut River. It dishes up fresh lobster rolls, steamed mussels, grilled salmon, New England clam chowder, and the like. There's also plenty of nonaquatic fare, including some fairly inventive nightly specials. Dining is on a casual porch or picnic tables, and the food is prepared on a gas grill. It's BYOB, and cash only. The restaurant has remained one of the state's better-kept secrets over the years, its reputation spread by word of mouth.

Abbott's Lobster in the Rough: Noank. Tel 860-536-7719; abbottslobster .com. *Cost:* dinner $25. *When:* May–mid-Oct. **Lenny and Joe's Fish Tale:** Madison. Tel 203-245-7289; Westbrook: Tel 860-669-0767; New Haven: Tel 203-691-6619; ljfishtale.com. *Cost:* dinner $25. **The Blue Oar:** Haddam. Tel 860-345-2994; blueoarct .wix.com. *Cost:* dinner $30. **Best times:** last weekend in May for Lobsterfest in Mystic Seaport; mid-Aug for Milford Oyster Festival (milfordoysterfestival.org); early Sept for Norwalk's Oyster Festival.

The Perfect American Small Town and the State's Oldest Inn

ESSEX

Connecticut

A dignified, Revolutionary War–era spirit lingers in Essex, a mint-condition one-traffic-light village on the Connecticut River, where early colonial and federal houses tell of the town's shipbuilding heyday. On Main Street, white picket fences frame many landmark buildings, a mix of grand private homes and specialty stores.

You can learn about the town's seafaring heritage at the waterfront Connecticut River Museum, which sits 5 miles north of where the river empties into Long Island Sound. It comprises an 1878 steamboat warehouse filled with ship models and maritime artifacts, including a full-scale replica of America's first submarine, *The Turtle*, built during the Revolutionary War. Train buffs will enjoy touring the lower Connecticut River valley while dining in vintage 1920s Pullman cars, or riding the Essex Steam Train north to Deep River, where passengers can either return to Essex by train or continue aboard a three-deck Mississippi-style riverboat to East Haddam (see p. 5).

One of the most celebrated buildings in Essex is the Griswold Inn, the oldest continuously operating inn in Connecticut. Opened in 1776, the "Gris" is most famous for its Tap Room, originally the town's schoolhouse, built in 1735. A potbellied stove sits at its center, and its wood-paneled walls are lined with maritime memorabilia and original Currier & Ives prints. Much of the inn's buzz (not to mention Dixieland jazz and banjo music) emanates from here. Overnighters can hang their hats in any of the handsome guest rooms; many lodgers stay for the weekend just to partake of the inn's Sunday Hunt brunch, an enormous affair said to have been initiated by the British, who commandeered the inn during the War of 1812.

It's just a few minutes' drive inland to tiny Ivoryton's classic Copper Beech Inn, which occupies the former homestead of one of the community's most esteemed merchants. The 7 acres of gardens are stunning, and many of the 22 guest rooms and luxury suites boast soaring cathedral ceilings and deep tubs. Most of the rooms are in a handsomely restored carriage house, with just four in the Main House, also the site of a well-known restaurant.

You may experience a moment of century adjustment if you're in the area mid-July, when nearby Deep River hosts its annual Fife & Drum Muster, said to be the oldest and largest in America. More than 70 units play their hearts out as they march down Main Street during the event's three-hour parade of uber-Americana.

WHERE: 37 miles southeast of Hartford. *Visitor info:* Tel 860-787-9640; centerofct .com. **CONNECTICUT RIVER MUSEUM:** Tel 860-767-8269; ctrivermuseum.org. *When:* closed

An antique car is parked outside the Griswold Inn, which has been in operation since 1776.

Mon. **Essex Steam Train:** Tel 860-767-0103; essexsteamtrain.com. *When:* mid-May–Oct. **Griswold Inn:** Tel 860-767-1776; griswold inn.com. *Cost:* from $115; Tap Room dinner $35, Sunday Hunt brunch $23. **Copper Beech Inn:** Ivoryton. Tel 888-809-2056 or 860-767-0330; copperbeechinn.com. *Cost:* from $179 (off-peak), from $279 (peak); dinner $60. **Best times:** mid-Feb for the Eagle Cruises (ctriverquest.com); mid-July for the Deep River Fife & Drum Muster; Christmas holidays.

Artistic Enclaves in Manhattan's Verdant Backyard

Fairfield County

Connecticut

The countrified but urbane enclaves of Ridgefield and Westport, 15 miles apart in tony Fairfield County, have long enjoyed popularity among artists, actors, and writers. These two upscale towns are celebrated for their artistic attractions and downtowns abundant with galleries, fine restaurants, and elegant shops.

Despite its proximity to Manhattan, Ridgefield feels a bit like one of the grand colonial New England towns in northwestern Connecticut's Litchfield Hills (see p. 14). Mature shade trees line Main Street, a wide showcase of storefront businesses and venerable mansions. Don't miss the town's seminal Aldrich Contemporary Art Museum, one of the country's few noncollecting contemporary art museums. It features changing exhibits of cutting edge art by emerging and midcareer artists. Behind the museum is a fine 2-acre sculpture garden.

Downtown Ridgefield may be known for its snazzy restaurants, but the local legend is a modest hot-dog stand called Chez Lenard, which doles out such heavenly fare as Le Hot Dog Garniture Suisse (topped with cheese fondue blended with white wine and kirsch). Later, dress up for dinner at Bernard's, situated in one of the dignified clapboard houses that illustrate the town's centuries-old roots. On Ridgefield's border with the town of Wilton, you'll find the only National Park dedicated to American painting, the 60-acre Weir Farm National Historic Site. It was

The long-standing Westport Country Playhouse has featured many theater luminaries.

acquired by Impressionist landscape artist J. Alden Weir.

It's 12 miles southeast from the farm to Westport, perhaps best known to many as the longtime home of the late actor Paul Newman and his widow, actress Joanne Woodward, who were closely associated with the acclaimed Westport Country Playhouse, a supreme small-town theater (Olivia de Haviland, Paul Robeson, and Jane Fonda are among the alums). Many of the first-rate dramas and comedies that originated in this converted barn moved on to greater fame on Broadway.

Where: Ridgefield is 65 miles southwest of Hartford. *Visitor info:* Tel 800-663-1273 or 860-567-4506; visitwesternct.com. **Aldrich**

CONTEMPORARY ART MUSEUM: Ridgefield. Tel 203-438-4519; aldrichart.org. *When:* closed Tues. **CHEZ LENARD:** Ridgefield. Tel 203-431-1313; chezlenard.com. *Cost:* lunch $5. **BERNARD'S:** Ridgefield. Tel 203-438-8282; bernardsridgefield.com. *Cost:* dinner $75. **WEIR FARM:** Wilton. Tel 203-834-1896; nps.gov/wefa. **WESTPORT COUNTRY**

PLAYHOUSE: Tel 888-927-7529 or 203-227-4177; westportplayhouse.org. *Cost:* tickets from $40. **BEST TIMES:** late Jan for Taste of Ridgefield food and music festival; mid-June for annual Hidden Garden Tour in Westport; Dec for Antiquarius (the Greenwich Antiques Show) at the Bush-Holly House (greenwich history.org).

Casinos in the Country

FOXWOODS & MOHEGAN SUN

Connecticut

A little bit of Vegas glam has been sprinkled upon the casino resorts of Foxwoods and Mohegan Sun, two of the most appealing mega-gaming properties on the East Coast. Together they have transformed a sleepy

swath of southeastern Connecticut into a hugely popular leisure destination. Even if you're not a slots fan or poker aficionado, consider immersing yourself in high rollers' perks: indulgent spas, toney restaurants, challenging golf courses, first-rate entertainment, and plush hotel rooms. Just 10 miles apart near the small city of Norwich, the two rivals have spawned a series of expansions and renovations as each vies to outdazzle the other.

Operated by the Mohegan tribe, the Mohegan Sun is anchored by a shiny 34-story

Foxwoods offers multiple gaming opportunities and eating options.

hotel tower that soars high over the Thames River. Open 24/7, its massive casino is alive with pulsing lights and clattering bells and whistles, and a huge race book where you can wager on horses. Abundant top-of-the-line shops and restaurants are a big draw, as is a 10,000-seat sports and concert arena, and the luxurious Elemis Spa, where guests can opt for a pro-collagen quartz facial or a lime and ginger salt glow. Among several outstanding restaurants, celeb chef Todd English's Tuscany may be the most popular, with an elegant dining room graced by a soaring waterfall and a menu of Italian classics, including osso bucco with spring pea risotto and Benton's bacon.

Foxwoods, owned by the formerly obscure but now fabulously wealthy Mashantucket Pequot tribe, kicked off Connecticut's casino craze when it opened in 1992 (Mohegan Sun followed four years later). The attractive resort underwent a massive expansion, spending over $700 million to add new hotel rooms, restaurants, gaming areas, and other features. You'll find an enormous gaming space, a concert hall, four contemporary hotels, the fanciest being the Grand Pequot Tower, and a quiet country inn. The resort's Lake of the Isles golf course offers 36 scenic holes of challenging play amid ancient forests and beside lakes and streams, and a 100-shop outlet mall to invest all the recent winnings.

Foxwoods also operates the superb Mashantucket Pequot Museum and Research Center, set beneath a 185-foot observation tower on a ridge near the casino. High-tech, high-quality interactive exhibits tell the story of the Mashantucket Pequot Tribal Nation.

WHERE: 45 miles southeast of Hartford. *Visitor info:* Tel 860-701-9113; mystic.org. **MOHEGAN SUN:** Uncasville. Tel 888-226-7711; mohegansun.com. *Cost:* rooms from $189; dinner at Todd English's Tuscany $50. **FOXWOODS:** Mashantucket. Tel 800-369-9663; foxwoods.com. *Cost:* rooms at Grand Pequot Tower from $249. **MASHANTUCKET PEQUOT MUSEUM:** Mashantucket. Tel 800-411-9671; pequotmuseum.org. **BEST TIMES:** late Aug, when Foxwoods hosts the Schemitzun Powwow (schemitzun.com); Oct for peak foliage.

Old Money Meets Urban Revival

CONNECTICUT'S GOLD COAST

Greenwich and Environs, Connecticut

The coastal section of Fairfield County, with its neatly preened towns inhabited by Fortune 500 CEOs and boldface names (Diana Ross has a home here, and the first President Bush was raised here), has long been called the Gold Coast. It's a land of massive mansions, exclusive yacht and country clubs, and elegant boutiques that overlooks calm Long Island Sound. Some have called Greenwich, on the border of New York State, a leafy extension of Manhattan's Upper East Side (it is 29 miles but worlds away). Just stroll through downtown, past the Aston Martin dealership and vaunted 120-year-old Betteridge Jewelers shop, and you sense the deep coffers enjoyed by this Old Money enclave.

West of downtown in the ritzy, largely residential Belle Haven district, you'll find the Homestead Inn–Thomas Henkelmann, an elegant 1799 farmhouse that was transformed into an Italianate Victorian inn in 1859. The place is filled with handsome antiques and art, sumptuous fabrics, and striking colors. Nine luxurious rooms are located in the Manor House (playwright William Inge lived here in 1953 while writing *Picnic*), with another eight rooms and suites in the Carriage House and a Cottage with an executive boardroom and bedroom nearby. Dining in the Homestead's celebrated restaurant, Thomas Henkelmann (named for the inn's German-born chef and owner), is a treat of the highest order. Beneath timber-beam ceilings and gilt chandeliers, diners enjoy French cuisine that seamlessly blends classic with contemporary: Dover sole is raised to new heights when served with truffles from Perigord, glazed baby carrots, and mushroom jus.

Nearby communities—such as Darien, New Canaan, and Westport (see p. 9)— showcase similarly imposing homes and fine shopping, but it's the small city of Norwalk, and especially historic South Norwalk (aka SoNo), that's enlivened the otherwise sedate Gold Coast in recent years. A vision of inner-city blight until an exciting revitalization in the 1980s and '90s turned it into a dynamic hub for food, shopping, nightlife, and culture,

SoNo is anchored by the stunning Maritime Aquarium at Norwalk, set inside a former 1860s ironworks factory. The state-of-the-art aquarium is devoted to the aquatic life of Long Island Sound, and a cavernous Maritime Hall offers boatbuilding workshops and houses exhibits on nautical history—there's also an IMAX theater.

Among SoNo's many cool restaurants, don't miss dinner at Match, an ultra-chic loft-like space with a postindustrial design and vibrant energy. Sit at the boisterous bar and sip craft cocktails before moving on to the dining room, where one of your choices might be PB&J halibut (served with mixed-nut corn, succotash, and concord grape jus).

WHERE: 35 miles northeast of New York City. *Visitor info:* Tel 800-663-1273 or 860-567-4506; visitwesternct.com. **HOMESTEAD INN–THOMAS HENKELMANN:** Tel 203-869-7500; homesteadinn.com. *Cost:* rooms from $350; dinner $80. **MARITIME AQUARIUM:** Norwalk. Tel 203-852-0700; maritimeaqua rium.org. **MATCH:** Norwalk. Tel 203-852-1088; matchsono.com. *Cost:* dinner $50. **BEST TIME:** early June for the Greenwich Concours d'Elegance, a 2-day festival of rare automobiles and motocycles (greenwichconcours.com).

There's No Place Like Home

THE MARK TWAIN HOUSE AND MUSEUM

Hartford, Connecticut

Literary fans come from around the world to visit the home of beloved author Samuel Clemens, aka Mark Twain, a pen name he derived from the term used by Mississippi River pilots to indicate a water depth of two fathoms.

"To us," Twain said, "our house . . . had a heart, and a soul, and eyes to see us with. . . . It was of us, and we were in its confidence, and lived in its grace and in the peace of its benediction."

Although more commonly associated with his hometown of Hannibal (see p. 449), as an adult the Missouri-born Twain always held this home in Hartford's Nook Farm neighborhood in a special light. The custom-designed High Victorian home was commissioned from well-known New York architect Edward Tuckerman Potter with input from Twain's wife, Olivia. Twain lived here with his family from 1874 to 1891, during which he penned some of his most acclaimed works, including *The Adventures of Tom Sawyer*, *The Adventures of Huckleberry Finn*, and *A Connecticut* *Yankee in King Arthur's Court*. The beautifully restored 25-room home features decorative work by Louis Comfort Tiffany and many of the family's original furnishings, including the carved wooden bed in which Twain died. Guided tours point out personal items, including the 3-ton Paige typesetter, an ill-fated invention in which Twain invested, leading to his bankruptcy. A striking contemporary museum stands adjacent to the house, further detailing the life and times of this master storyteller—a key feature is a small theater showing a 22-minute Ken Burns film biography.

Nearly across the street, the Harriet Beecher Stowe Center celebrates the legacy of the author of the greatest antislavery novel of all time, *Uncle Tom's Cabin*, considered to be the first international best seller. This compound is anchored by the brick Gothic Victorian "cottage" (though substantial, it is not nearly as grand as neighbor Twain's) where the author resided from 1873 until she died in 1896. Guided tours provide insights into Stowe's abolitionist politics and then-revolutionary social views.

WHERE: 115 miles northeast of New York City. Tel 860-247-0998; marktwainhouse.org. *When:* daily, Apr–Feb; closed Tues in Mar. **HARRIET BEECHER STOWE CENTER:** Tel 860-522-9258; harrietbeecherstowecenter.org. **BEST TIME:** Christmastime, when the Mark Twain House is decked out in holiday splendor.

The Mark Twain House contains many personal items, including the billiards table where the author spread out his manuscripts when editing.

America's Oldest Public Art Museum

THE WADSWORTH ATHENEUM

Hartford, Connecticut

The Wadsworth Atheneum opened in 1842 and has expanded a number of times since, but the Gothic Revival main building remains the architectural centerpiece of the nation's oldest continually operating art museum.

Hartford art patron Daniel Wadsworth founded the museum to share the wonders of art with the public—a novel concept at the time. The museum's permanent collection slowly grew to comprise some 50,000 works dating back a few thousand years. Be sure to view the unsurpassed collection of Hudson River School paintings, including some by Frederic Church, a Hartford native son and friend of Wadsworth. You can also view *Elizabeth Eggington*, the oldest dated American portrait (1664); a fine selection of Egyptian, Greek, and Roman bronzes; and some notable French and American Impressionist works, including some by Connecticut artists (see p. 6). It also holds a rich collection of early American furniture and decorative arts from the 1600s. Outside, note the enormous steel stabile

Stegosaurus (1973), by Alexander Calder, who spent much of his life in Connecticut.

Downtown Hartford has a few other noteworthy attractions. History buffs should seek out the Old State House, built in 1796, the nation's oldest still-standing statehouse. The famous *Amistad* trial, immortalized by Steven Spielberg's 1997 film, took place in this stunning building. Inside you can see an original Gilbert Stuart portrait of George Washington in the restored senate chamber. The state legislature met here until the early 1870s, when the new Connecticut State Capitol was constructed nearby in Bushnell Park. A leafy 50-acre oasis, it's one of the Northeast's most striking urban parks, with a number of sculptures and the still-working 1914 Bushnell Park Carousel. But the High

Victorian Gothic Connecticut State Capitol, one of the most distinctive such buildings in the country, is the park's most prominent feature. It was designed by Richard Upjohn and was completed in 1879 at a then-astonishing cost of $2.5 million.

At the end of your outing, enjoy a meal at Max Downtown, the centerpiece of the revered Max restaurant group (with several excellent eateries around the region). This swanky, clubby space is a favorite of the neighborhood's politicos and CEOs keen on the sophisticated regional American fare, such as prime aged ribeye with bacon marmalade.

WHERE: 115 miles northeast of New York City. *Visitor info:* Tel 860-787-9640; centerofct .com. **WADSWORTH ATHENEUM:** Tel 860-278-2670; thewadsworth.org. *When:* closed Mon–Tues. **OLD STATE HOUSE:** Tel 860-522-6766; cga.ct.gov/osh.org. *When:* Mon–Fri, Oct–July; Tues–Sat, Aug–Sept. **CONNECTICUT STATE CAPITOL:** Tel 860-240-0222; cga.ct.gov/capitol tours. *When:* Mon–Fri. **MAX DOWNTOWN:** Tel

The State Capitol is crowned by a gold-leaf dome.

860-522-2530; maxrestaurantgroup.com. *Cost:* dinner $45. **BEST TIMES:** early June for the Black-Eyed & Blues music festival in Bushnell Park; late June for Rose Weekend at Elizabeth Park's stunning rose gardens; mid-July for Greater Hartford Festival of Jazz.

Rural Sophistication Under the Elms

LITCHFIELD HILLS

Connecticut

The notion that the real New England is an endless drive from the urban chaos of New York City is dispelled upon approaching the Litchfield Hills, a bucolic swath of horse farms, verdant woodland, and sophisticated villages tucked into rolling hills. Unfolding beyond every bend is a classic Currier & Ives landscape of 18th- and 19th-century saltbox farmhouses, red barns, imposing clapboard mansions, stone walls, and quiet lakes such as Bantam, the largest in the state.

Dapper, neatly preserved Litchfield anchors the region, with its tidy, elm-shaded green, elegant storefronts, and refined restaurants. The once prosperous trading center played a valiant, behind-the-scenes role in the American Revolution. On the outskirts of town you'll find Connecticut's largest nature preserve, the 4,000-acre White Memorial Foundation, whose Conservation Center Museum contains extensive exhibits detailing the region's natural history. Some 35 miles of trails (including 6 miles of the Mattatuck Trail, which traverses the county before joining the Appalachian Trail in Cornwall, 13 miles northwest of here), are available for biking, horseback riding, hiking, and cross-country skiing.

In this naturally endowed corner of New England where little changes, the ultraluxurious Winvian Farm mini-resort indulges your fantasies with 18 highly eccentric cottages designed by 15 different architects, each with a story to tell. Beaver Lodge incorporates a real beaver lodge in the ceiling, Treehouse is set 35 feet above the ground, and Maritime is an ode to Connecticut's lighthouses. Set on 113 beaucolic acres, Winvian offers guided fly-fishing tours, a 40-foot pool, and luxurious treatments in a super-sophisticated 5,000-square-foot spa. Food for the restaurant comes from its own 3-acre organic garden.

About a half-hour drive north of Litchfield, in sylvan Norfolk, the Bavarian Tudor-style Manor House was built in 1898 by Charles Spofford, who designed London's subway system. He enlisted the assistance of his friend Louis Tiffany, who supplied 20 stained-glass windows for the parlor while elsewhere guest rooms come in many configurations, some with soaring pitched ceilings.

Litchfield's West Street Grill is king of the region's vaunted dining scene. Many foodies credit this unpretentious yet charming place for sparking the region's growth into a first-rate culinary destination. Since opening in 1990 in a popular location near the Litchfield Green, it has been the place to go when you want to linger for a couple of hours, savoring a bottle of wine from the well-chosen list. Menu highlights such as organic Scottish salmon served with parsnip fritters, saba-glazed acorn squash, and salmon caviar keep this place forever full.

WHERE: 35 miles west of Hartford. *Visitor info:* Tel 800-663-1273 or 860-567-4506; visitwesternct.com. **WHITE MEMORIAL:** Tel 860-567-0857; whitememorialcc.org. **WINVIAN FARM:** Morris. Tel 860-567-9600; winvian .com. *Cost:* from $499 (off-peak), from $799 (peak). **MANOR HOUSE:** Norfolk. Tel 866-542-5690 or 860-542-5690; manorhouse-norfolk .com. *Cost:* from $149, includes breakfast. **WEST STREET GRILL:** Litchfield. Tel 860-567-3885; weststreetgrill.com. *Cost:* dinner $55. **BEST TIMES:** June–Aug for chamber music in Norfolk; early Aug for Litchfield Jazz Festival (litchfieldjazzfest.com); Oct for glorious foliage.

America's Maritime Museum

MYSTIC SEAPORT & STONINGTON

Connecticut

Mystic is one of the Northeast's most visited spots, primarily because of Mystic Seaport—the Museum of America and the Sea. America's leading maritime museum, it houses the country's largest collection of historic boats and ships. Much of its 19-acre riverfront site encompasses a re-created coastal village complete with a schoolhouse, church, and dozens of homes, stores, and workshops that bring to life salty 19th-century maritime America. A number of fully rigged sailing ships docked here are open for visits, among them the *Charles W. Morgan* (1841), America's last surviving wooden whaling ship.

The Seaport's most ambitious exhibit, "Voyaging in the Wake of the Whalers," examines the history of the whaling industry in the country and world. The area's other major draw, the kid-popular Mystic Aquarium and Institute for Exploration, offers some 70 live exhibits of sea life, including more than 340 species, 5,000 specimens, and one of the world's largest beluga whale exhibits.

Take to the gentle nearby hills for sweeping harbor views, and follow privacy-seeking Lauren Bacall and Humphrey Bogart to the Inn at Mystic. The couple honeymooned here in a secluded cottage behind the stately 1904 Colonial Revival Haley mansion. Fifty-one rooms are located in the Main Building and East Wing, but romantics should hold out for the five guest rooms in the mansion.

Meander just 5 miles east to visit the little-known Borough of Stonington, the state's easternmost coastal community and one of New England's most endearing. First settled in 1649, this former whaling and ship-building center looks today much as it might have a century ago, its leafy streets lined with sea captains' homes and churches. Follow the smell of the sea down the main thoroughfare, Water Street, which ends at a small beach and an early 19th-century lighthouse. Stonington has a handful of low-key

The full-rigged ship Joseph Conrad *at Mystic Seaport was built in 1882.*

restaurants serving outstanding food, including the tiny, chef-owned Noah's, a homey spot known for "scratch" buttermilk pancakes at breakfast, homemade clam chowder at lunch, and char-grilled salmon with cucumber dill yogurt sauce at dinner.

At the very least, spend one idyllic night at the posh Inn at Stonington, overlooking the lovely harbor. For such a small town, this is worldly luxury; several of the 18 rooms have private decks overlooking the water. Twelve of the rooms are in a new building constructed in classic Greek Revival style. The rest are in the historic annex next door.

WHERE: 55 miles southeast of Hartford. *Visitor info:* Tel 860-536-8822; mystic.org. **MYSTIC SEAPORT:** Tel 888-973-2767 or 860-572-0711; mysticseaport.org. **MYSTIC AQUARIUM:** Tel 860-572-5955; mysticaquarium.org. **INN AT MYSTIC:** Tel 800-237-2415 or 860-536-9604; innatmystic.com. *Cost:* from $120 (off-peak), from $180 (peak). **NOAH'S:** Stonington. Tel 860-535-3925; noahsfinefood.com. *Cost:* dinner $35. **INN AT STONINGTON:** Tel 860-535-2000; theinnatstonington.com. *Cost:* from $180 (off-peak), from $230 (peak). **BEST TIMES:** June for Sea Music Festival; July for Antique and Classic Wooden Boat Rendezvous; mid-Oct for Chowder Days; the Christmas holidays for Lantern Light Tours.

A Panoply of Possibilities

NEW HAVEN DINING

Connecticut

Few small New England cities claim a more eclectic, polished, and creative culinary reputation than New Haven, home to Connecticut's greatest concentration of noteworthy eateries. What's more, this is a college city

(see next page), and many restaurants keep their price points geared toward indigent students and budget-minded professors.

You can appreciate the city's self-anointed

role as "Pizza Capital of the World" by visiting Little Italy, specifically Wooster Street, where a few acclaimed pizza joints stand cheek by jowl, the most famous being Frank Pepe's, which has been turning out incomparably delicious thin-crust pies since 1925. Purists insist on ordering Pepe's "white" pies, sans the usual red sauce. The one topped with freshly chopped clams is a revelation; add bacon to that and watch Pepe's regulars swoon. This is a no-frills dining room, short on character, and salad is the only other thing on the menu. Pepe's doesn't take reservations, and the line to get in here on weekends is a given; try to come on a weekday to avoid the legions of Pepe's *apasionati*.

Sally's Apizza is the city's pizza "newcomer," having opened in 1938 when Sal "Sally" Consiglio, a nephew of Pepe's, started his own place down the street. It also serves expertly prepared pies. Save a little room for dessert at Libby's Italian Pastry Shop, a revered source of gelato, Italian ice (15 or so flavors), and 12 varieties of Sicilian cannoli.

New Haven is also home to the restaurant that takes credit for having invented the hamburger. Louis' Lunch opened in 1895 in a tiny redbrick dining room, just steps from Yale's campus. The burgers are made fresh daily, cooked to order on the original 1898 cast-iron grills, and served on toast with your choice of cheese, tomato, and onion. Do not ask for ketchup. Do not ask for mustard. Neither is *ever* available, as the folks at Louis' Lunch claim that such condiments would only "corrupt" the "classic taste" of a perfectly grilled burger.

WHERE: 40 miles southwest of Hartford. *Visitor info:* Tel 800-332-STAY or 203-777-8550; newhavencvb.org. **FRANK PEPE'S:** Tel 203-865-5762; pepespizzeria.com. *Cost:* large white clam pie $25. **SALLY'S APIZZA:** Tel 203-624-5271. *Cost:* large pie $23. **LIBBY'S ITALIAN PASTRY SHOP:** Tel 203-772-0380; libbyscookies.com. **LOUIS' LUNCH:** Tel 203-562-5507; louislunch.com. *Cost:* burger $6. **BEST TIMES:** late Apr for Wooster Street's Cherry Blossom Festival (historicwoostersquare.org/cherryblossomfestival.html); late June for St. Andrew's Italian Feast celebration.

Louis' Lunch is thought to be the birthplace of the hamburger.

American Gothic

YALE UNIVERSITY

New Haven, Connecticut

The nation's third oldest university and the embodiment of preeminent Ivy prestige, Yale University and its host city have long been linked. Founded in nearby Saybrook in 1701, Yale moved to New Haven in 1716. Today Yale infuses the city with a vibrant, youthful buzz as well as vast cultural riches, from outstanding museums and theaters to regal Gothic architecture. New Haven's skyline is dominated by the university's 216-foot Harkness Tower, which soars high over Memorial Quadrangle. From its earliest years, the university graduated talented young minds that have gone on to accomplish great things, from lexicographer Noah Webster to inventor Eli

Whitney to various presidents including Bill Clinton (who, together with his wife, Hillary, attended the university's law school) and both Presidents George Bush.

Yale's campus makes for a fascinating architectural survey, and not just of the traditional collegiate Gothic variety. The Yale University Art Gallery is considered one of the finest architectural designs of Louis I. Kahn. Inside you'll find the renowned collections of Etruscan, Egyptian, and Greek art; the esteemed collection of Chinese and Japanese works; and Impressionist pieces by such

Most of Yale's older buildings were constructed in the Gothic style.

European masters as Cézanne, Van Gogh, and Picasso. Kahn is also responsible for the dashing building across the street, the Yale Center for British Art, in which you'll find the largest collection of English art outside Great Britain. Another Yale attraction of considerable note is the Beinecke Rare Book & Manuscript Library,

which is housed inside one of the campus's most avant-garde buildings, a minimalist geometric structure designed in 1963 by Gordon Bunshaft and sheathed in white marble panels. Highlights include the most comprehensive archive of playwright Eugene O'Neill (who summered in Connecticut) as well as an original Gutenberg Bible.

The southern side of campus borders one of New Haven's most dynamic neighborhoods, the Chapel District. You can wander along the tidy, tree-lined New Haven Green, which abuts campus and is home to three historic churches, and poke your head inside the dozens of hip cafés, coffeehouses, bookstores, and quaint shops in the area.

WHERE: 40 miles southwest of Hartford. Tel 203-432-2300; visitorcenter.yale.edu. **YALE ART GALLERY:** Tel 203-432-0600; art gallery.yale.edu. *When:* closed Mon. **YALE CENTER FOR BRITISH ART:** Tel 203-432-2800; britishart.yale.edu. *When:* closed Mon. **BEINECKE LIBRARY:** Tel 203-432-2977; beinecke.library.yale.edu. *When:* closed Sun. **BEST TIMES:** June for the International Festival of Arts & Ideas, featuring spoken word performances, theater, music, lectures, and tours (artidea.org); mid-Aug for New Haven Jazz Festival.

Tranquility, History, and Pastoral Good Looks

CONNECTICUT'S QUIET CORNER

Connecticut

Rarely does the congested Eastern Seaboard offer places of true peace and quiet, amid pastoral scenes of dairy farms and sleepy mill towns. Here in Connecticut's northeast corner is one such spot, "The Last Green Valley,"

a 35-town National Heritage Corridor created by Congress. Protected by the failure to build an interstate highway between Hartford and Providence, Rhode Island, the Quinebaug-Shetucket region is one of the last large

stretches of rural land in the largely metropolitan Boston-to-Washington corridor.

Route 169, designated by the Federal Highway Administration as one of America's Scenic Byways, meanders for 32 miles through the area, taking in the expansive Quinebaug and Shetucket rivers corridor, a well-preserved swath of tended farmland and protected parks and preserves. Follow it from the Massachusetts border to the village of Canterbury, and you'll pass more than 200 homes dating from the mid-19th century or before. One of the Quiet Corner's largest towns is Putnam, a former mill and manufacturing town that fell on hard times after WWII and languished until the 1980s, when it was reinvented as an important hub of antiques shopping.

The area's most luxurious lodging is found at the handsome Inn at Woodstock Hill in South Woodstock, whose rooms are housed in a renovated 1816 farmhouse. There are few more delightful ways to enjoy a meal than by having dinner at Brooklyn's Golden Lamb Buttery. The setting is a handsome red barn at the 1,000-acre Hillandale Farm, operated as an acclaimed restaurant by Bob and Virginia "Jimmie" Booth from 1963 to 2008, when granddaughter Katie took the reins. There's just one dinner seating at 7 P.M. on Friday and Saturday, and a prix-fixe meal of limited but reliably excellent choices—perhaps the perfectly prepared house specialty of roast duckling or chateaubriand with generous family-style sides of vegetables, followed by maple bread pudding. Dinner guests are also treated to live music and an old-fashioned hayride.

WHERE: Putnam is 50 miles east of Hartford. *Visitor info:* Tel 860-536-8822; mystic.org. **INN AT WOODSTOCK HILL:** South Woodstock. Tel 860-928-0528; woodstockhill .com. *Cost:* from $135 (off-peak), from $175 (peak). **GOLDEN LAMB BUTTERY:** Brooklyn. Tel 860-774-4423; thegoldenlamb.com. *Cost:* prix-fixe dinner $75. **BEST TIMES:** late Aug for Brooklyn Fair, the nation's oldest agricultural fair (brooklynfair.com); Labor Day weekend for Woodstock Fair (woodstockfair.com); Oct for Walktober walking weekends (thelast greenvalley.org).

A Corner of Country Splendor in the Nutmeg State

WASHINGTON & NEW PRESTON

Connecticut

Deep in the heart of verdant Litchfield County (see p. 14), tiny Washington has grown into a smart, sophisticated cultural crossroads, with some highly acclaimed restaurants, an inviting bookstore, galleries, and clothing and antiques shops. A diminutive 19th-century mill town of pretty clapboard Victorian buildings, neighboring New Preston contains shops selling antiques, decorative arts, and fine furniture. High-profile celebs with homes in the region enjoy their anonymity, ambling around the village or window-shopping within earshot of the East Aspetuck River's gushing waterfalls.

Drive southeast on Route 47 for about 9 miles to reach Woodbury, where dozens of shops selling all categories, periods, and styles of antiques have earned it the title of "Antiques Capital of Connecticut." But visitors are also drawn here by the reputation of the Good News Café, opened by Carole Peck, one of the first female graduates of the Culinary Institute of America in Hyde Park, New York (see p. 156). Peck changes her menu seasonally but has long featured a few standby favorites to please devoted regulars: The pecan-crusted oysters with cherry tomato and jicama salsa is second only to the unusual mac-and-cheese with lobster and Swiss chard, accentuated with white truffle oil and imported provolone.

Washington's best of show is the elegant Mayflower Grace, one of New England's most charming. The 30-room luxury hotel sits on 58 acres crisscrossed by trails, streams, gardens, and stands of rhododendron, its spacious interiors filled with English and French antiques; a 20,000-square-foot spa has further polished its image. Meals at the Mayflower are romantic and surprisingly unfussy. Expect the freshest and purest foods, such as Colorado rack of lamb, organic certified veal chop, and the season's tastiest vegetables. For dessert there are sweet dreams in four-poster featherbeds with Frette linens, and the promise of tomorrow's spa treatments, perhaps a restorative soak infused with wild seaweed and essential oils selected just for your constitution. Or head north out of Washington for a few miles to reach Lake Waramaug and its bucolic

The bucolic grounds of the Mayflower Grace are stunning in every season.

green hills, country cottages, and rambling farmsteads.

WHERE: 44 miles southwest of Hartford. **GOOD NEWS CAFE:** Woodbury. Tel 203-266-4663; good-news-cafe.com. *Cost:* dinner $50. **MAYFLOWER GRACE:** Washington. Tel 860-868-9466; gracehotels.com/mayflower. *Cost:* from $350; dinner $50. **BEST TIMES:** Sun from mid-Apr–Nov in nearby New Milford for the Elephant's Trunk Flea Market (etflea.com); late Sept–Oct for prime leaf-peeping; Dec for Annual Holiday Gift Fair at the Washington Art Association; Christmas Eve, when Woodbury's Main St. is lit with luminaria.

Rusticating Amid Nature's Grandeur

ACADIA NATIONAL PARK

Maine

Like other stretches of heaven on earth, much of the idyllic Maine coast has been bought up over the years by the well-to-do, who've fenced it off for their own private use. It's ironic, then, that in the case of Mount Desert Island, Americans owe a debt of gratitude to some rich folks who put the common good above their own interests, and handed this lovely island over to the public domain.

When French explorers began arriving in the early 17th century, they found the island inhabited by the Wabanaki Indians. Samuel Champlain, noting its barren, rocky summits, named it "Monts Desert." France and England vied for the island for the next 200 years;

somewhere along the line its name became a linguistic hybrid, written in English but pronounced with a French accent, making it sound like "dessert."

By the mid-to-late 19th century it began to gain fame for its beauty. Painters of the Hudson River School arrived, creating works that led their rich patrons to blaze a path to Mount Desert, to see the simple life for themselves. In time, the Rockefellers, Astors, Fords,

Vanderbilts, and their fellow "rusticators" founded a summer colony, building elegant estates they referred to as "cottages." Among the wealthy bunch was one George B. Dorr who, in 1901, began buying up land in the area, eventually turning over thousands of acres to the federal government. In 1929 the U.S. set aside much of that land as Acadia National Park. The park today totals 47,000 acres of craggy grandeur, covered with lush fir and spruce forests, dotted with lakes, and surrounded by great opportunities for offshore whale-watching.

The timeless serenity of the island is tested by the ever-increasing number of visitors—the 27-mile Park Loop Road, for instance, one of the most picturesque drives in America, attracts big crowds in summer. But avoiding traffic is easy

Acadia National Park contains more than 120 miles of historic hiking trails.

enough. In 1913, when John D. Rockefeller Jr. became unhappy with the arrival of noisy automobiles on the island, he began work on the 45-mile network of bridge-linked carriage roads that today offer some of the nation's loveliest car-free walking and bicycling, and become a splendid network of cross-country ski trails in winter. Hiking trails cross the island, offering great views and demanding only moderate effort. Most visitors, however, will need a car to watch the sunrise from Cadillac Mountain, a park tradition. At 1,530 feet the highest peak on the U.S. Atlantic seaboard, this is the spot where America catches its first rays of the morning sun.

Plan to arrive at Jordan Pond House on the Park Loop Road in time for late-afternoon tea and popovers on the restaurant's front lawn. Rusticate overnight at the Claremont Hotel and Cottages, sitting grandly on 6 shorefront acres since 1884. Grab a chair on the porch for poetry-inspiring views of the Somes Sound.

WHERE: 36 miles southeast of Bangor. Tel 207-288-3338; nps.gov/acad. *When:* Park Loop Rd. closed Dec–mid-Apr. **JORDAN POND HOUSE:** Tel 207-276-3316; acadiajordanpond house.com. *Cost:* lunch $20. **CLAREMONT HOTEL:** Tel 800-244-5036; theclaremonthotel .com. *Cost:* from $180 (off-peak), from $235 (peak). *When:* late May–mid-Oct. **BEST TIME:** July–Aug for the weather and whale-watching.

Charm, Chamber Music, and a Cozy Inn

BLUE HILL

Maine

Located right between the popular vacation destinations of Acadia National Park and Penobscot Bay, the tiny coastal village of Blue Hill is one of those "who knew?" places. Serene and charming, full of elm-shaded streets and

solid New England homes, it is also graced with one of America's best chamber music schools and one of the world's largest music libraries. Add in the winding roads,

picturesque farms, and coastal scenery of the surrounding Blue Hill Peninsula, and you have the kind of Maine destination people dream (but few know) about.

Five minutes from downtown Blue Hill, Kneisel Hall was founded in 1902 by Austrian violinist and concertmaster Franz Kneisel, and today maintains its position as one of the country's foremost chamber music schools. Each summer, it hosts a series of open rehearsals and concerts presenting works from Beethoven and Brahms to Ned Rorem and Henry Cowell. Elsewhere in town, the Bagaduce Music Lending Library began in 1983 as a teatime idea hatched by three Maine musicians and artists' managers with the goal of making sheet music available to the general public. The library expanded quickly with the help of generous donations, moving from its original two-car garage to the top floor of a storage barn. Today it's the largest lending library of sheet music in the world, with more than 250,000 titles and a million copies of printed music.

Near the heart of the village, just uphill from the bay and facing 950-foot Blue Hill Mountain, the Blue Hill Inn has welcomed visitors continuously since 1840. The 11-room Federal-style house (with two modern suites next door) offers a perfect mix of old-fashioned country ambience and high-end grace notes. Nineteenth-century antiques fill the cozy rooms and public areas, while old pumpkin pine floorboards creak reassuringly. Mornings begin with multicourse breakfasts; evenings include a daily innkeepers' reception in the main parlor.

WHERE: 137 miles northeast of Portland. **KNEISEL HALL:** Tel 207-374-2203; kneisel .org. *Cost:* concert tickets from $20. *When:* late June–Aug. **BAGADUCE MUSIC LENDING LIBRARY:** Tel 207-374-5454; bagaducemusic .org. *When:* closed Sat–Sun. **BLUE HILL INN:** Tel 800-826-7415 or 207-374-2844; bluehill inn.com. *Cost:* rooms from $155 (off-peak), from $195 (peak). *When:* main house May–Oct. **BEST TIMES:** summer for Kneisel concert series; 4th of July weekend for the Blue Hill Pops Festival, featuring everything from choral music to klezmer and Dixieland jazz.

Pursuit of Romance and Adventure

WOODENBOAT SCHOOL

Brooklin, Maine

It's a fantasy shared by wage slaves and cubicle inmates all over the world: to build one's own boat and sail away to romance and adventure. Maine's WoodenBoat School doesn't promise the latter, but it can sure get you started on boatbuilding. Founded in 1981 by the publishers of *WoodenBoat* magazine and situated on a gorgeous 64-acre coastal estate, the school offers expert instruction in boat design and construction, repair, seamanship, and woodworking. "Fundamentals of Boatbuilding" courses teach the craft from a global perspective, with students constructing difficult vessels on the theory that if they can build those, they can build anything. Many courses focus on specific types of boats, from sea kayaks and traditional wood-and-canvas canoes to ketches, skiffs, and dories; others teach basic seamanship, the mechanics of sailing, coastal navigation, joinery, ropework, and even bronze-casting your own marine hardware. With courses lasting one and two weeks, students have time to work, learn, explore Brooklin and other nearby towns, and take the school's rowing and sailing craft out onto some of the Northeast's best waters.

Days begin early, with American-style breakfast served in the dining hall, followed by classes from 8 A.M. to 5 P.M. After the evening meal, some students resume work on their boats, while others pick the brains of their instructors, visit the research library, go sailing, or just enjoy the cool summer evenings. Some return year after year, fueled by the same love of tradition and craft that animates the teaching staff. It's an admirable enterprise, a perfect antidote to our all-too-disposable culture. Maybe they do offer romance and adventure after all.

WHERE: 50 miles south of Bangor; 41 WoodenBoat Lane. Tel 207-359-4651; the woodenboatschool.com. *Cost:* 1-week courses from $750; room and board $490 per person, per week, doubles with shared baths. *When:* late May–Sept. **BEST TIME:** Sept for the annual WoodenBoat Sail-In, when the schooners of the Maine Windjammer fleet gather in the harbor for music and tours.

Skiing—or Golfing—in the Woods of Maine

SUGARLOAF

Carrabassett Valley, Maine

Though Sugarloaf is often called the best ski resort in the Northeast, it's not for everybody, which may be one of the reasons its aficionados are so dedicated to it. Credit the long drive (about four hours from Boston) and the bitterly cold winter winds that can whip through the mountain's higher reaches. But what are a few small inconveniences when balanced against such phenomenal skiing and small-town friendliness?

Opened for skiing in 1951, the resort came into its own in the 1970s with the construction of additional chairlifts and trailside condos. Today it's got a continuous one-mountain vertical drop of 2,820 feet (the longest of ski resorts in the East); the only lift-served, above-treeline skiing in the East; 163 trails and glades totaling

At 4,237 feet, Sugarloaf is the second highest peak in Maine.

more than 57 miles and accommodating everyone from kids to the most expert experts; two snowboarding half-pipes (one of them Olympic quality) and three world-class terrain parks; and an alpine village that's nicely glitz-free, keeping the focus on the snow. For the ultimate challenge, head to the Snowfields and take the very steep White Nitro run. The friendly, low-key atmosphere also makes Sugarloaf a great place to introduce kids to skiing, with a kids' program that offers lessons as well as non-ski activities for all ages.

Accommodations range from the Sugarloaf Mountain Hotel, a classic mountain hotel with 119 rooms and stupendous views, to more than 1,000 mountainside condos and townhouse apartments. Après ski, stop by the Shipyard Brewhaus, a ski-in/ski-out pub managed by Portland's Shipyard Brewing Company, Maine's largest microbrewery.

In summer, Sugarloaf transforms into a golf resort, home to an 18-hole Robert Trent Jones course that's consistently rated the best in Maine and one of the top 100 courses in the country. It could well be the finest wilderness mountain course in America, carved from pine and white birch forests and stretching to nearly 7,000 yards.

WHERE: 125 miles north of Portland. Tel 800-THE-LOAF or 207-237-2000; sugarloaf .com. *Cost:* lift tickets $86; greens fees from $60–$140, depending on availability of play.

When: mid-Nov–Apr for skiing; late May–mid-Oct for golf. **SUGARLOAF MOUNTAIN HOTEL:** Tel 800-THE-LOAF or 207-237-2000; sugarloaf.com. *Cost:* from $140 (off-peak), from $180 (peak). **BEST TIMES:** Jan for the smallest crowds; Mar for the heaviest snowfall; mid-Apr for Budweiser Reggae Festival.

A Leading Player in the Preppy Handbook

L. L. BEAN

Freeport, Maine

It all began with the boots. Back in 1911, Leon Leonwood Bean enlisted a local cobbler to stitch a leather upper to a waterproof rubber shoe. The next year he advertised his Maine Hunting Shoe, "designed by a hunter who has

tramped Maine woods for the past eighteen years." When most of the boots were returned to him with stitching problems, he issued full refunds and used the experience to perfect his product. It was a business model that over the next half century made his clothes the de facto uniform of New England: trustworthy, traditionally styled, and weatherproof as a duck.

The flagship store in Freeport is an institution. Opened in 1917, the walk-in business grew so large that in 1951 they took the locks off the front door, and have been open 24 hours a day, 365 days a year ever since. They have expanded and modernized along the way and now the place is as big as a small mall. It has its own zip code and greets over 3 million visitors every year. In addition to all the boots, sweaters, khakis, parkas, and rain gear you could ever

The Bean Boot stands 17 feet tall outside the L. L. Bean headquarters.

need, there's an outdoor department that stocks camping, boating, cycling, fishing, hunting, and winter sports gear; and introductory courses in kayaking, fly-casting, archery, clay shooting, snowshoeing, orienteering, and outdoor photography are offered anywhere from free to hundreds of dollars for private lessons. During the summer, Bean's outdoor concert series features a mix of jazz, rock, country, and whatever else comes along, with big names like Rosanne Cash highlighting the list. Come fall, Bean sponsors a hunting expo; a spring expo concentrates on fishing.

Be sure to plan some non-Bean time in Freeport, too: The town is home to scores of outlet stores. Respite can be found at the family-run Harraseeket Inn, just two blocks from Bean, complete with mahogany paneling, charming antiques, cozy fireplaces, and the award-winning Maine Harvest Dining Room.

WHERE: 17 miles north of Portland. Tel 800-441-5713; llbean.com. **HARRASEEKET INN:** Tel 800-342-6423 or 207-865-9377; harra seeketinn.com. *Cost:* from $140 (off-peak), from $235 (peak); dinner $40. **BEST TIMES:** summer weekends for local events; Oct weekends for foliage and great weather.

"Lighthouses are more helpful than churches."
—*Benjamin Franklin*

THE LIGHTHOUSE TRAIL

Maine

I f you had to pick one symbol to represent coastal Maine, it would have to be the lighthouse. Standing out on a cliff, or atop a storm-racked island, these beacons act as earthbound stars to sailors on the dark sea. More than 60 of them dot the state's shoreline, from Cape Neddick in the south to West Quoddy Head in the north, at the Canadian border; and many of them are accessible to the public.

Cape Neddick Light, aka the "Nubble Light," sits on a small, characteristically rocky Maine islet just 100 yards off the mainland. First lit in 1879, it's one of the most picturesque lighthouses in the country—so much so that the crew of the *Voyager II* space probe, launched in 1977 in the hope of finding extraterrestrial life, brought a picture of the Nubble with them, intending to use its image to represent all earthly lighthouses.

Farther north up the coast, the majestic Portland Head Light is Maine's oldest, dating back to 1791. Though the tower isn't open to the public, the grounds and outbuildings are: The former keeper's quarters houses a museum, while the Cliff Walk trail winds along the coast, offering spectacular views. Nearby, South Portland's conical "sparkplug"-style Spring Point Ledge Light sits at the end of a 950-foot stone breakwater that allows pedestrians and fishermen to walk out onto Casco Bay. At the foot of the jetty is the Portland Harbor Museum, with exhibits chronicling the history of the port.

South of Bath, 2.5 miles off the mouth of the Kennebec River, the Seguin Island Light is perched on an island that resembles a Scottish moor. Though the present tower dates to 1857, lighthouses have occupied the site since 1795. The Maine Maritime Museum in Bath offers boat departures that sail past the Seguin Light and various others.

About ten miles east of Boothbay, the Pemaquid Point Light is situated at the top of a dramatic granite ledge extending into the Gulf of Maine. Exceptionally well preserved, with an on-site art gallery and Fishermen's Museum, it's one of the most visited sites along the Maine coast and is featured on the Maine State Quarter. Visitors can climb the tower for incredible views, and if they're lucky they'll catch a distant glimpse of Monhegan Island, site of its own quaint lighthouse (see p. 27).

Seen as you head north toward Penobscot Bay, the Marshall Point Light guards the entrance to Port Clyde, a longtime artists' retreat where painter Andrew Wyeth held his first one-man show in 1937. The 31-foot lighthouse tower is extremely photogenic, with a long wood-plank walkway connecting to its Colonial-revival keeper's quarters, which dates from 1895 and now houses a museum.

In the town of Rockland, the Rockland Breakwater Light sits at the end of a nearly mile-long stone jetty. In town, the Maine Lighthouse Museum houses America's best collection of lighthouse memorabilia, including an extensive collection of Fresnel lenses, the last word when it comes to lighting the seas.

CAPE NEDDICK LIGHT: York. Tel 207-363-1040; nubblelight.org. **PORTLAND HEAD LIGHT:** Cape Elizabeth. Tel 207-799-2661; portlandheadlight.com. *When:* mid-Apr–mid-Dec. **SPRING POINT LEDGE LIGHT:** S. Portland.

Tel 207-699-2676; springpointlight.org. *When:* June–mid-Oct. **Seguin Island Light:** Tel

Portland Head Light partly inspired Henry Wadsworth Longfellow's famous poem "The Lighthouse."

207-443-4808; seguinislandlight.org. Boat tours from the Maine Maritime Museum, Bath. Tel 207-443-1316; mainemaritimemuseum .org. *Cost:* from $30. *When:* late June–late Oct. **Pemaquid Point Light:** New Harbor. Tel 207-677-2492; bristolparks.org/lighthouse.htm. *When:* early May–late Oct. **Marshall Point Light:** Port Clyde. Tel 207-372-6450; mar shallpoint.org. *When:* Sat–Sun in May; daily, June–mid-Oct. **Rockland Breakwater Light:** Rockland Harbor. Tel 207-542-7574; rocklandharborlights.org. *When:* Sat–Sun, late May–mid-Oct. **Maine Lighthouse Museum:** Rockland. Tel 207-594-3301; mainelight housemuseum.com. *When:* Mar–Dec. **Best time:** summer for weather.

George Bush Slept Here

THE KENNEBUNKS

Maine

The Kennebunks—Kennebunk, Kennebunkport, and Kennebunk Beach— are the quintessence of seaside Maine, brimming with magnificent architecture, beautiful lighthouses, rocky beaches, seaside hiking, bike routes, lobster rolls, and fine dining.

First settled in the early 17th century, the Kennebunks gained fame and wealth two centuries later as shipbuilding towns. That boom went bust after the Civil War, but its legacy—a profusion of grand Colonial- and Federal-style homes sitting amid a picture-perfect landscape—helped transform the Kennebunks into one of Maine's most popular resort areas. Over the following decades, vacationing notables included St. Louis businessman D. D. Walker, whose son George Herbert Walker later bought property in the area. George Herbert's grandson and great-grandson, the two President Bushes, still vacation here from time to time.

Kennebunkport's White Barn Inn & Spa is one of New England's finest, comprised of an

1820s gatehouse, carriage house, May's Cottage (where the inn's original owner once lived), and the main building, a classic autumn-gold clapboard with white trim. Twenty-six meticulously appointed European-style guest rooms are done up with four-poster, canopy, and sleigh beds, and modern amenities including Jacuzzis. A swimming pool offers an alternative to sandy Gooch's Beach, within walking distance but with water that's almost always too cold for swimming. A highlight of any stay is a meal in the inn's restaurant, considered one of the best dining north of Boston. Here, rustic and refined blend seamlessly in two lofty candlelit barns, while a more relaxed bistro offers a less-expensive alternative.

As a cozy, romantic alternative, the Federal-style Captain Lord Mansion has 16 guest rooms, each named for a ship built by its original owner. Gas fireplaces, Oriental rugs, and overstuffed furniture lend a period air. A rooftop cupola looks out over the vast lawn toward the Kennebunk River.

Despite their tony reputation, the Kennebunks aren't all about moneyed luxury. At the west end of the Kennebunkport Bridge, the Clam Shack is one of America's great seafood dives. Order your fried clams and lobster rolls through the walk-up window and roll up your sleeves.

WHERE: 20 miles south of Portland. **WHITE BARN INN:** Tel 207-967-2321; white barninn.com. *Cost:* from $250 (off-peak), from $410 (peak); dinner $109 for 4-course prix fixe. **CAPTAIN LORD MANSION:** Tel 207-967-3141; captainlord.com. *Cost:* from $179 (off-peak), from $349 (peak). **THE CLAM SHACK:** Tel 207-967-3321; theclamshack.net. *Cost:* $20 for lobster roll. *When:* May–Oct. **BEST TIMES:** spring–fall for idyllic weather; 1st weeks of Dec for Christmas Prelude festival (christmasprelude.com).

Where the Arts Meet the Atlantic

MONHEGAN ISLAND

Maine

Ten miles out to sea, tiny Monhegan Island is Maine in miniature, a 700-acre artist's rendering of everything that makes this stretch of coast called Down East great. On its eastern side, towering headland cliffs greet the pounding Atlantic, while from the western (village) side hikers can set out on 12 miles of wooded trails that crisscross the island. Only about 60 people live here year-round. There are no paved roads and few cars: Until 1984 there wasn't even electricity. What there is is peace and quiet—and artists, lots of artists.

First put on the map when Virginia governor John Smith visited in 1614, Monhegan didn't get any attention from the art world until 1858, when painter Aaron Draper Shattuck paid a visit. Over the years that followed, artists such as Edward Hopper, Robert Henri, and Jamie Wyeth arrived to take advantage of the island's incredible light and rugged landscapes. Thanks to a preservation movement led by Ted Edison in the early 1950s, two-thirds of Monhegan is maintained in its pristine, wild state. Visitors arrive by ferry, stepping off into a tidy coastal village, home to almost every bit of civilization on the island: its galleries, its lobstering fleet, its markets and restaurants, and its hotels. Nothing is more than a few minutes' walk from anything else, including some 20 artists' studios open to the public in summer.

Grab a trail map from anywhere in town and take off into the central forests. Head northeast, past the old ice pond toward Cathedral Woods, where tall stands of fir and spruce create a spiritual space Thoreau would have loved, its aisles carpeted with moss, ferns, and wildflowers. From here, head south along the coast to Burnt Head, whose 160-foot sea cliffs are among the highest in Maine, in summer filled with squawking seabirds. At lower points along the coast (especially at half-tide) you can see a profusion of harbor seals playing among the rocks. Ramble back to town by way of the Monhegan Island Light, which has provided a beacon for sailors since 1824. Next door, the keeper's cottage now houses the Monhegan Historical and Cultural Museum, with displays on all aspects of island life and Monhegan-related works by Rockwell Kent, Edward Hopper, and others.

Back in town, the turn-of-the-century Island Inn dominates from atop a bluff, literally a stone's throw from the harbor. Built between 1816 and 1910, it's Monhegan's largest and most comfortable hotel, with 32 rooms decorated in typical Maine style—antique furniture, painted wood floors, and cozy down bedding. Since there are no TVs or telephones to distract you, head to the Inn's wide porch for some real evening entertainment, watching the sun set over the water, with the Maine coast beyond. Now you know why all those artists came and stayed.

WHERE: 10 miles off the mid-Maine coast. **HOW:** Ferries run from Boothbay Harbor (Balmy Days Cruises, tel 800-298-2284 or 207-633-2284; balmydayscruises.com; June–Sept), Port Clyde (Monhegan Boat Line, tel 207-372-8848; monheganboat.com; year-round), and New Harbor (Hardy Boat Cruises, tel 800-278-3346 or 207-677-2026; hardyboat.com; May–Oct). **MONHEGAN MUSEUM:** Tel 207-596-7003; monheganmuseum.org. *When:* late June–Sept. **ISLAND INN:** Tel 207-596-0371; islandinnmonhegan.com. *Cost:* from $145 (off-peak), from $185 (peak). *When:* late May–mid-Oct. **BEST TIMES:** May and Sept for nice weather and the smallest crowds.

The Gateway to the North Woods

MOOSEHEAD LAKE

Maine

In 1853, Henry David Thoreau headed north from Boston on his second long trip into the Maine woods. Arriving at Moosehead, he wrote that it appeared "a suitably wild-looking sheet of water, sprinkled with small, low islands, which were covered with shaggy spruce and other wild wood." In the decades that followed, the 120-square-mile lake—Maine's largest—became a resort destination of the rich and famous, while at the same time the surrounding woods began to see the birth of a massive timber industry. It's a duality that persists to this day, with sportsmen, vacationers, and nature lovers pursuing their muses in wild areas wedged between clear-cuts.

At the lake's southern tip, unpretentious Greenville acts as a hub for both travelers and residents of the region's scattered villages. From here, visitors can head into the backwoods on wildlife safaris to see some of the thousands of moose that call the area home, or step into a canoe, kayak, or motorboat to explore the lake's 400 miles of incredible coastline and 80-plus islands. The historic steamer *Katahdin*, built in 1914 and serving over the years as ferry, cargo boat, and log-hauling towboat, also runs several different day cruises on the lake throughout the summer. The most interesting visit is Mount Kineo, the lake's most striking natural landmark. Located on a peninsula at Moosehead's midpoint, Kineo looks like a sleeping dinosaur, its eastern flank a sheer 700-foot cliff rising almost straight up from the water, its backbone a fringe of evergreens. Dock at the site of the former legendary Kineo House resort, which in its 19th-century heyday offered 300 rooms on the shore near the mountain's base. Hardly a stick of its majestic old buildings remains, but its storybook location is still stunning and provides a dock and two trails to the mountain's peak. A hike up is the most essential of all Moosehead experiences.

To rusticate in style, book yourself into the Lodge at Moosehead Lake, a 1917 Cape Cod residence-turned-country-inn located on a hill just outside Greenville, surrounded by woods, fields, and stunning lake views. Rooms are appointed with a mix of folksy lodge furnishings, modern lines, and unusual touches like the two beds that are suspended from the ceilings by antique logging chains. Meals in the dining room or on the outdoor deck offer incredible sunset views.

WHERE: 155 miles north of Portland.

Visitor info: Tel 207-695-2702; moosehead lake.org. **MOOSE SAFARIS:** Moose Country Safaris, tel 207-876-4907; moosecountry safaris.com. *Cost:* half-day safari $150 per couple. *When:* late Apr–Oct. **KATAHDIN CRUISES:** Tel 207-695-2716; katahdincruises .com. *Cost:* Mount Kineo cruise $38. *When:* late May–early Oct. **LODGE AT MOOSEHEAD LAKE:** Tel 800-825-6977 or 207-695-4400; lodgeatmooseheadlake.com. *Cost:* from $295 (off-peak), from $375 (peak). **BEST TIME:** late May–early Sept.

Where the Woods Are Lovely, Dark, and Deep

MOUNT KATAHDIN AND BAXTER STATE PARK

Maine

In his 1848 essay titled "Ktaadn," Henry David Thoreau wrote, "What is most striking in the Maine wilderness is the continuousness of the forest. . . . Except the few burnt lands, the narrow intervals on the rivers, the bare tops of the high mountains, and the lakes and streams, the forest is uninterrupted. It is even more grim and wild than you had anticipated." Eighty years later, it was that very quality of wildness—and the desire to preserve it—that inspired former Maine governor Percival P.

A bull moose crosses Sandy Stream Pond with Mount Katahdin looming in the background.

Baxter to begin buying up land in the North Woods and donating it to his state. In 1930, he bought the core of what would soon be known as Baxter State Park, a 209,644-acre wilderness that included Mount Katahdin, at 5,267 feet the state's highest peak. Unlike most parks, Baxter was to remain "forever wild," with human recreation regarded as secondary to the simple goal of just letting things be.

Almost nine decades later, it still is. Located amid millions of acres owned and managed by industrial and conservation companies, Baxter has no paved roads, no fancy picnic areas, and no campground bathhouses. Motorcycles, pets, radios, and cell phones are prohibited. Designed to be seen on foot, the park has 210 miles of trails ranging from easy boardwalks to rugged, boulder-strewn mountain paths, all maintained primarily by volunteers. All around, forests of spruce and fir are dotted with ponds and bogs and bisected by streams and waterfalls. Moose are not an uncommon sight during the summer months, grazing the edges of marshy ponds, while black bear are drawn to the park's abundant raspberry and blueberry patches. Plant life varies with the terrain, from alpine wildflowers to woodland ferns and wetland orchids.

The highlight of the park, of course, is Katahdin, "the greatest mountain" in the Penobscot language. A stark, mile-high, glacially scoured granite monolith, it's the most difficult climb in the Northeast, especially along the mile-long Knife Edge, a narrow spine that runs from Pamola Peak to Baxter Peak, with steep drop-offs of several hundred feet on either side. Less difficult routes include the Abol and Hunt trails, the latter the final stretch of the 2,175-mile Appalachian Trail (see p. 332). If you want to see Katahdin instead of climbing it, the 4-mile South Turner Trail offers wonderful views.

WHERE: 86 miles north of Bangor. Tel 207-723-5140; baxterstateparkauthority.com. Campsite reservations become available in mid-Jan for summer and after Nov 1 for winter and sell out fast. **BEST TIMES:** Aug and Sept for the best weather and the absence of black flies.

"'Tis a Gift to Be Simple"

SABBATHDAY LAKE SHAKER VILLAGE

New Gloucester, Maine

The United Society of Believers, commonly called Shakers after their habit of shaking ecstatically during worship, was founded in England in 1747 and brought to the States by Mother Ann Lee in 1774. Centered around the idea of giving oneself to God through an agrarian life of celibacy, pacifism, and communal living, and gaining fulfillment through work and building, the society grew to some 5,000 to 6,000 souls during the 19th century. The Shakers made an indelible mark on American life through their tradition of fine woodwork and their invention of several now-common tools and household items, including the wooden clothespin and the circular saw.

Founded in 1783, Sabbathday Lake was one of the smallest and most isolated of the Shaker villages. In less than a year it had attracted 200 believers, and by 1794 had begun construction of the wooden and brick buildings still in use today. It's the only active Shaker community in the United States, with just four members tending 1,800 acres of land.

Seventeen wooden buildings and the large brick Dwelling House are nestled among carefully tended gardens and fields. The community members are always busy and usually out of sight ("Hands to Work, Hearts to God," as Mother Ann used to say), but visitors can get a glimpse of their lifestyle by touring the community, taking in the displays and resources at its museum and library, or signing up for summer courses in herb gardening, woodcarving, and other crafts.

Sabbathday's museum, organized in 1931, contains 13,000 artifacts charting the history of Maine's Shaker culture, including examples of the wooden furniture that is the Shakers' most well-known cultural legacy; the Shakers believed in seeking the divine through functionality and a perfection of line.

The community's library, established in 1882, is a nationally known repository of Shaker history, with more than 3,000 books by and about the Shakers, plus thousands of photos, journals, scrapbooks, oral histories, and numerous recordings of Shaker hymns. Tours depart from the Museum Visitor Center and visit six of the community's buildings, including the 1794 Meetinghouse, still used for worship services; the Ministry's Shop; the 1816 Granary; and the Sister's Shop, where workers pack culinary herbs and herbal teas using methods the Shakers have employed for two centuries. They're available at a shop on the grounds, and—proof that the community isn't living entirely in the past—through their website. **Where:** 25 miles north of Portland. Tel 207-926-4597; maineshakers.com. *When:* Museum is open late May–mid-Oct. **Best times:** summer; Sun 10 A.M. services are open to the public; early Oct for Fall Harvest Festival; 1st Sat in Dec for the Shaker Christmas Fair.

Paddling in the Company of Moose, Loons, and Beaver

MAINE CANOE COUNTRY

Northern Maine

Way up in northern Maine, surrounded east, west, and north by Canada, the 92-mile Allagash Wilderness Waterway is the top canoeing destination in the northeastern United States, offering pristine lakes, amazing white water, towering forests, and a chance to commune with the soul of the great North Woods. Civilization is distant, effectively ending at the town of Greenville on Moosehead Lake (see p. 28), and other people are scarce—even in the relatively long May–October season, the area typically sees only about 10,000 paddlers.

The waterway was established in 1966 by Maine's state legislature, with the goal of conserving the Allagash's natural beauty and undeveloped character. Venture far by land and you'll eventually hit a logging road or clear-cut—evidence that this part of Maine is one vast tree farm, its 3.5 million acres primarily owned and managed by logging companies. Around the rivers and lakes, though, things remain as they've always been, the wet forest climate providing a perfect habitat for diverse plant and animal species, including moose, black bear, deer, beaver, bald eagles, loons, and Canada lynx.

Allagash canoe trips typically begin at Chamberlain Lake, west of Baxter State Park (see p. 29) and continue north to Allagash Village and the convergence of the Allagash and St. John rivers. The trip takes about a week, with more than half the route passing through a series of lakes, spiced by stretches of Class II white-water and milder rapids. Highlights along the route include gorgeous

The Allagash Wilderness Waterway is part of the National Wild and Scenic Rivers System.

views of Mount Katahdin from Chesuncook Lake and, at the northern end, the 35-foot tumble of Allagash Falls. Campsites are available along the route.

Northern Maine also offers prime canoeing on the St. John River and the Upper West Branch of the Penobscot. The St. John is a classic weeklong trip, with many Class I and II rapids and two stretches of Class III. The best time is in spring, soon after the ice has melted and the water is high. The Penobscot is a calmer passage with few rapids, none difficult.

Where: Chamberlain Lake is 130 miles north of Bangor, west of Baxter State Park. *Visitor info:* Tel 207-941-4014; maine.gov/doc/parks. **How:** Allagash Canoe Trips in Greenville (tel 207-280-1551; allagashcanoetrips.com) offers guided trips May–Oct; weeklong trips from $1,000 per person. *When:* May–Oct. **Best time:** Sept for solitude, lack of bugs, and moose mating season.

A Beautiful Place by the Sea

OGUNQUIT

Maine

Back in the day, Maine's native Abenaki Indians came to this spot on the southern coast, liked what they saw, and gave it a straightforward name: Ogunquit, "a beautiful place by the sea." What had caught their eye was Ogunquit Beach, a 3.5-mile stretch of pristine white sand that's generally regarded as New England's most beautiful. Nonnative vacationers discovered the stretch in 1888, and town residents, fearing it would be bought up and privatized, talked the state legislature into making it a public park in the 1920s. It was a wise and prescient move. Over the next century much of the 3,478-mile Maine coast did in fact fall into private hands, limiting public access, but you can still visit Ogunquit. In summer the village and its adjoining sands can be very busy. A little farther north is a stretch favored by Ogunquit's large contingent of gay vacationers.

For a scenic stroll, head south along Marginal Way, a paved, public footpath that hugs the coast for 1.25 miles from Beach Street to Perkins Cove, a small anchorage whose pedestrian drawbridge raises to allow sailboats through to the ocean. Once a vital part of the fishing economy, today the cove is rimmed with boutiques, restaurants, and art galleries, the latter a testament to Ogunquit's century-long history as an artists' haven. Just west of the cove, the Ogunquit Museum of American Art is the only museum in Maine devoted to American artists, with beautiful facilities situated on 3 landscaped acres looking toward the horizon. Opened in 1953 by

Called Marginal Way because it skirts the rocky cliffs and beaches of Ogunquit, the wooden footpath is popular for an afternoon or evening walk.

painter Henry Strater, the museum today holds a collection of more than 1,500 works, including paintings by Marsden Hartley, Reginald Marsh, Robert Henri, and Charles Demuth and sculpture by Carl Walters and Isabella Howland. Its galleries have an open feel, offering wonderful views of the coast.

Nearby, the Cliff House has been open as a resort since 1872, but those early visitors never conceived of some of the treatments available now at the on-site Cliff Spa—the Wild Maine Rose Body Wrap, for instance. Both the spa and the guest rooms look out over the sea from their perch atop Bald Head Cliff. For a postwrap meal, head to the Velveteen Habit, housed in an 18th-century farmhouse offering an innovative menu using regional ingredients and produce from its own gardens.

WHERE: 38 miles southwest of Portland. *Visitor info:* Tel 207-646-2939; ogunquit.org. **OGUNQUIT MUSEUM:** Tel 207-646-4909; ogunquitmuseum.org. *When:* May–Oct. **CLIFF HOUSE RESORT:** Tel 207-361-1000; cliffhouse maine.com. *Cost:* from $275 (off-peak), from $450 (peak). **THE VELVETEEN HABIT:** Tel 207-216-9884; thevelveteenhabit.com. *Cost:* dinner $40. *When:* late Apr–early Dec. **BEST TIME:** early morning for the smallest crowds on Marginal Way and the beach.

Picture Postcards of Maine Maritime Life

THE TOWNS OF PENOBSCOT BAY

Maine

I magine coastal Maine as a painting. The constituent elements: a dock where fishermen in yellow rain slickers are busy hauling lobster pots, buoys, and nets. In the background, weathered shingled houses and craggy coastline,

with maybe an intimation of dense green hills and forest behind. That's the idealized image people come north to see, and Penobscot Bay doesn't disappoint. Cutting a 40-by-25-mile gash in the center of the Maine coast, the bay is a scenic wonder, circled by some of the state's prettiest towns. In the south, the three towns of Rockland, Rockport, and Camden are the home of the bay's famous schooner fleet (see p. 36).

Camden is the archetypal coastal village, so charming that it was chosen in 1957 as the setting for the film *Peyton Place*. Many of its gorgeous old homes have been converted into B&Bs, while antiques and craft shops fill the old buildings along Main Street, and pleasure craft share space with fishing boats in the beautiful mountain-ringed harbor. Some of the best waterfront views are from Harbor Park, laid out between 1928 and 1931 by Frederick Law Olmsted, designer of New York's Central Park.

Farther north, in Searsport, the Penobscot Marine Museum is one of New England's finest small museums, housed in a dozen historic buildings. Its collection covers all aspects of Maine maritime life from the 19th century to the present, with displays of boats, tools, furniture, and art, from scrimshaw and figureheads to marine paintings by Thomas and James Buttersworth.

Around the curve of the bay, on the Blue Hill Peninsula, Castine is one of America's oldest communities, first settled in 1613. It's a small, serene place, full of beautiful Federalist, Georgian, and Victorian architecture, towering elm trees, and more than 100 historic sites, including Fort George, built by the British in 1779. For an overnight, try the

Pentagöet Inn & Restaurant, a turreted 1894 Queen Anne Victorian that's Castine's oldest original summer hotel and still a favorite choice. Or stay at the 19th-century Castine Inn. Just a block from the harbor, it boasts beautiful perennial gardens and fabulous breakfasts.

Castine is quiet and authentic, but the village of Deer Isle is even more so. Located just off the southern tip of the peninsula (accessible by bridge), it maintains an active fishing and lobstering fleet and serves as home to many artists and artisans, as well as the charming waterfront Pilgrim's Inn, built in 1793. The nearby Haystack Mountain School of Crafts offers one- or two-week residential workshops in clay, glass, blacksmithing,

weaving, woodworking, and other media, taught by internationally known instructors. The region is also famous for superb sea kayaking, especially along Merchant's Row, a string of islands and islets between the Deer Isle village of Stonington (known for great lobster) and Isle au Haut, a wild, rocky island whose southern half is part of Acadia National Park (see p. 20).

WHERE: Camden is about 86 miles northeast of Portland. *Visitor info:* Tel 207-596-0376; mainedreamvacation.com, mainesmidcoast.com, deerislemaine.com. **PENOBSCOT MARINE MUSEUM:** Searsport. Tel 207-548-2529; penobscotmarinemuseum.org. *When:* late May–mid-Oct. **PENTAGÖET INN:** Castine. Tel 800-845-1701 or 207-326-8616; pentagoet .com. *Cost:* from $110 (off-peak), from $160 (peak). *When:* May–Oct. **CASTINE INN:** Tel 207-326-4365; castineinn.com. *Cost:* from $120 (off-peak), from $150 (peak). *When:* May–Oct. **PILGRIM'S INN:** Deer Isle. Tel 888-778-7505 or 207-348-6615; pilgrimsinn.com. *Cost:* from $120 (off-peak), from $140 (peak). *When:* May–mid-Oct. **HAYSTACK MOUNTAIN SCHOOL:** Tel 207-348-2306; haystack-mtn.org. *When:* late May–early Sept. **SEA KAYAKING:** Old Quarry Ocean Adventures, Stonington; Tel 207-367-8977; oldquarry.com. *Cost:* half-day kayak trip $65 per person. *When:* late May–early Oct. **BEST TIMES:** summer; Oct for fall foliage.

Colorful exteriors and old-fashioned signs contribute to downtown Camden's timeless charm.

The Art of Maine

THE FARNSWORTH MUSEUM

Rockland, Maine

Lucy Copeland Farnsworth, daughter of wealthy 19th-century entrepreneur William Farnsworth, lived her whole life in her father's Rockland house, outliving her five siblings and leaving no children of her own. When she died in 1935 at age 97, her will stipulated that her $1.3 million estate would be used in part to fund an art gallery and library. That was the genesis of the Farnsworth, which over the following years has amassed a collection of works by artists such as Winslow Homer, Maurice

Prendergast, Eastman Johnson, and Andrew Wyeth, all intimately associated with Maine life and landscapes.

Beginning with the acquisition of five watercolors in 1944, the museum's relationship with Wyeth has been particularly fruitful, culminating in a 1996 agreement to create the Wyeth Center, dedicated to the works of Andrew; his son Jamie; and his father, N.C. Wyeth, who illustrated novels by Jules Verne, Robert Louis Stevenson, and James Fenimore Cooper. This high-profile association has allowed the Farnsworth to grow into one of the country's finest regional museums.

Today the heart of the museum is its collection, which documents Maine's cultural history from colonial times to the present, while newer galleries are dedicated to 20th-century works, including the nation's second largest collection of works by sculptor Louise Nevelson. Next door to the museum, Lucy Farnsworth's 1850s Greek Revival house is preserved much as she left it, outfitted with the family's furniture from the early 1870s. The Wyeth Center, with exhibitions, interpretive programs, and research facilities, is just

down the block in a 19th-century Methodist church building. About a half-hour's drive southwest, the Olson House completes the Farnsworth's holdings. It was depicted in over 300 works, including Andrew Wyeth's most famous painting, *Christina's World*, and is maintained in a rustic state, allowing visitors to, in effect, step into a Wyeth canvas.

WHERE: 80 miles northeast of Portland; 16 Museum St. Tel 207-596-6457; farnsworth museum.org. *When:* daily, June–Oct; closed Mon, Nov–Dec and Apr–May; closed Mon–Tues, Jan–Mar.

Turkey Pond, *by celebrated American painter Andrew Wyeth, was finished in 1944.*

Where Crustacean Is King

MAINE LOBSTER FESTIVAL

Rockland, Maine

Though the coastal Indians of Maine and eastern Canada knew about the pleasures of lobster (if not butter sauce) for hundreds or thousands of years, early European Americans were so disdainful of the spiny beast

that hardly anyone but prisoners and indentured servants ever took a taste. The upper class finally realized what they were missing in the late 19th century, and today Maine is a veritable lobster Valhalla, made famous by the sweet, succulent *Homarus americanus*, generally considered the finest crustacean in the sea.

Maine and lobster are all but synonymous and with good reason: The annual catch along the state's indented coastline generally exceeds well over 100 million pounds—80 percent of the national total. Rockland, on Penobscot Bay, is the capital of the lobster universe, hosting an annual Lobster Festival that since 1948 has offered five days full of live music, seafood-cooking and whoopie pie-eating contests, the coronation of a Maine Sea Goddess, and enough New England Americana (and *americanus*) to last through the winter.

Even if you're not in-state for the festivities, heavenly lobster dinners can be had almost any time of the year at the countless shacks, huts, pounds, and farms found scattered among Maine's coastal towns. Be sure to dine dockside, so you can enjoy the perfume of the salt air, the sound of the ocean, and the screech of gulls nose-diving for your french fries.

WHERE: 80 miles northeast of Portland. Tel 800-576-7512 or 207-596-0376; maine lobsterfestival.com. *When:* 5 days (Wed–Sun) in late July–early Aug.

Of Wind and Waves

SAILING THE MAINE WINDJAMMERS

Rockland, Camden, and Rockport, Maine

In the 19th century, Maine was to tall ships what Detroit is to cars, with thousands of vessels pouring from its shipyards and sailing to and from its harbors. Steam engines put an end to all that, replacing the old boats' quiet,

graceful sails with belching, roaring engines, and by the 1930s it seemed the few tall ships remaining were destined to fade into memory.

Enter Maine artist Frank Swift. In 1936, Swift founded Maine Windjammer Cruises and began offering pleasure cruises on a 65-foot schooner from 1886, confident that people would be glad to escape the bustle of modern life for a few days of relaxation and simple pleasures. On his first trip, he later

Windjammers were the grandest cargo sailing ships of their time.

recalled, "we had only three lady passengers from Boston," but demand over the next three decades not only allowed Swift to grow his fleet but also lured other captains into the business. Today Maine is home to the largest fleet of traditional wooden sailing vessels in the U.S., schooners and sloops that ply the waters between Bar Harbor and Boothbay. Most of them are historic vessels from the late 19th and early 20th centuries—many designated National Historic Landmarks—plus a few modern facsimiles. Most visible are the schooners of the Maine Windjammer Association, a loose consortium of nine owner-operated vessels specializing in three- to six-day sailing adventures among the islands of Penobscot Bay. It's a stunning place, full of craggy, pine-covered coastline, deliriously beautiful sunsets, and lighthouses that seem to come right out of Andrew Wyeth paintings.

By day, the Maine windjammers are all about sailing: Passengers help with the sails, take a turn at the wheel, scan the horizon for seals and porpoises, or just relax on the wooden decks. Often, two or more ships will meet up and take each other on in an informal race. In early evening, the captains steer into protected coves, running a skiff to shore to let passengers explore small fishing towns or uninhabited islands, sometimes anchoring at a quiet, rocky beach for a traditional lobster bake. Often, the evening will end with music, perhaps from the captain, or a passenger who has brought along their instrument. Everyone turns in early to their tiny cabins, which are usually furnished with little more than two simple wooden bunks piled with blankets. Some of the boats have running water; others have dry sinks with a barrel of water you can tap for washing. Restroom and shower facilities are shared. It's a rustic experience, but

that's the point. Before or after setting sail, stay at Captain Lindsey House Inn, an elegantly restored sea captain's home in the heart of Rockland's waterfront district.

WHERE: Cruises set sail from Rockland, Camden, and Rockport. Rockland is 80 miles northeast of Portland. Maine Windjammer Assoc. Tel 800-807-WIND; sailmainecoast .com. *Cost:* 3-night cruise from $585 per person, all-inclusive. *When:* mid-May–mid-Oct. **CAPTAIN LINDSEY HOUSE INN:** Rockland. Tel 207-596-7950; lindseyhouse.com. *Cost:* from $125 (off-peak), from $170 (peak). **BEST TIME:** late July–early Aug to tie in with Rockland's Maine Lobster Festival (see p. 35).

The Best Lobster Rolls Down East

RED'S EATS

Wiscasset, Maine

For some people, the lobster roll is a vacation destination in itself, the scenery of coastal Maine merely a pleasant backdrop. If you're one of those folks, you probably already know about Red's Eats, a tiny red-and-white shack sitting beneath a large Siberian elm at the corner of Route 1 and Water Street in Wiscasset, the self-proclaimed "Prettiest Village in Maine." Open since 1938 (and in its current location since 1954), Red's is almost universally recognized as serving the best lobster rolls on the Maine coast—therefore, by extension, the best anywhere. In season, a line of customers perpetually snakes out into the street. You order at the walk-up window and then chow down at one of the tables on the back deck, right next to the always snarled traffic on Route 1. As for the roll, imagine the flesh of a whole lobster (or more) crammed onto a toasted hot dog bun and served with melted butter and/or mayo on the side. There are also batter-fried clams, scallops and other seafood, burgers, and hot dogs with cheese, but save those for

your 10th or 12th visit, when you can afford to experiment.

WHERE: 45 miles northeast of Portland; 41 Water St. Tel 207-882-6128. *Cost:* lobster rolls $16. *When:* mid-Apr–mid-Oct. **BEST times:** late Apr and early May for smaller crowds.

A lobster roll at Red's Eats is among the highlights of any visit to Maine.

19th-Century Architecture in the Shadow of the State Capitol

BEACON HILL

Boston, Massachusetts

White-trimmed redbrick town houses, window boxes overflowing with flowers, gas lamps lighting uneven cobbled streets—that's Boston as you imagined it. It's certainly Beacon Hill. One of the city's oldest neighborhoods, "the Hill" is something of an architectural time capsule. Most of the graceful homes date to the first half of the 19th century, and their elegant Federal style makes this the archetypal New England residential area. It's also the natural habitat of the "Boston Brahmin." Oliver Wendell Holmes coined the term, borrowing the name of the highest Hindu caste to signify the well-educated, well-bred Protestant elite that dominated the city's politics and society well into the 20th century.

Find your way around the neighborhood on foot, following the steep streets up to the golden dome of Charles Bulfinch's 1797 Massachusetts State House. The south slope of the hill is Boston Common, and the "flat of the hill," between Charles Street and the Charles River, adjoins the Public Garden (see p. 46). Browse along Charles Street, where quirky gift shops share space with tasteful antiques stores. Stop at exquisite Louisburg Square, a tiny private park surrounded by some of the city's most exclusive and expensive real estate, including the stately home of John and Teresa Heinz Kerry.

Another way to see Beacon Hill is to follow the Black Heritage Trail, which links 14 historically significant sites, including a stop on the legendary Underground Railroad. At the end of the trail the Abiel Smith School (1834) and the African Meeting House (1806) make up the Museum of African American History, whose exhibits preserve the history of blacks in the city and state. The school was the first public school for black children; the meetinghouse is the oldest standing black church in the country.

Around the corner from the State House is XV Beacon, a state-of-the-art boutique hotel with just 63 rooms, each with a gas fireplace. The restaurant, a modern steakhouse named Mooo, is famous for its Beef Wellington and fine wine list. Another well-chosen wine list is a draw at nearby No. 9 Park, one of Boston's most renowned special-occasion restaurants. Chef-owner Barbara Lynch has won a James Beard Award for regionally inspired French and Italian dishes, with perfect ingredients and modern presentation. The dining room, a modern twist on a 1940s supper club that looks out on the Common, is one of many popular culinary experiences she oversees in Boston.

WHERE: bordered by Beacon, Bowdoin, and Cambridge streets and Storrow Drive. *Visitor info:* Tel 800-SEE-BOSTON or 617-536-4100;

Acorn Street, a narrow cobblestone lane, was built in the late 1820s.

bostonusa.com. **BOSTON AFRICAN AMERICAN NATIONAL HISTORIC SITE:** Tel 617-742-5415; nps.gov/boaf. **MUSEUM OF AFRICAN AMERICAN HISTORY:** Tel 617-725-0022; maah.org. *When:* closed Sun. **XV BEACON:** Tel 877-XV-BEACON or 617-670-1500; xvbeacon.com. *Cost:* from $395; dinner $70. **No. 9 PARK:** Tel 617-742-9991; no9park.com; barbaralynch.com. *Cost:* 3-course prix-fixe menu $76. **BEST TIMES:** Feb for Black History Month; late May for Hidden Gardens of Beacon Hill tour (beaconhillgarden club.org).

America's Biggest Birthday Gala

BOSTON HARBORFEST & BOSTON POPS FIREWORKS SPECTACULAR

Boston, Massachusetts

One of America's premier birthday bashes takes place in Boston. The city enjoys the Fourth of July far too much to confine its celebration to one day or one place: Boston Harborfest lasts five days, taking over downtown and the waterfront and attracting 3 million people. A separate event that feels like the climax of the festivities is the Boston Pops Fireworks Spectacular on the night of the Fourth, complete with church bells, cannon fire (during the finale of the *1812 Overture*), and a breathtaking display of fireworks set to music. The concert, which features at least one big-name guest vocalist, doesn't start until 8:30 P.M., but the party runs all day—spectators arrive on the Boston side of the Charles River at dawn to stake out a spot on the Esplanade in front of the Hatch Shell amphitheater, where the orchestra performs.

Earlier in the week, Harborfest's 200-plus events—concerts, cruises, tours, revolutionary reenactments, and more—entertain locals as well as visitors from all over the world. Children's Day features special activities for youngsters, and Chowderfest attracts crowds who vote on well-known (and not) local restaurants' entries in the competition for the title of best clam chowder (New England style, of course).

On July 3, the Pops rehearse the next night's program to a not-insignificant-size crowd. The orchestra has been an integral and

Fireworks burst into color over the city during Fourth of July celebrations.

much-loved part of Boston's music scene since they began in 1974, under the direction of the legendary Arthur Fiedler; today the engaging Keith Lockhart wields the baton. The official hotel of the Pops is the elegant Fairmont Copley Plaza, not far from the Esplanade. The gracious atmosphere and service suit the historic 1912 hotel, designed by the same architect as New York's opulent Plaza Hotel. The lobby is a Beaux-Arts masterpiece executed in mirrors, crystals, and gold accents. The Oak Long Bar + Kitchen off the lobby, has been restored to show off original ceilings and plasterwork within a more vibrant, modern space, and serves excellently prepared martinis. For the full Fourth of July experience, book the Boston Pops Suite, appointed with memorabilia and outfitted with CDs, and let the party continue.

The area around the Charles River is busy all year, but especially in the summer. The Hatch Shell shows family-friendly movies in a series called "Free Friday Flicks." The amphitheater is on the Esplanade, the Beacon Hill/Back Bay section of the 17-mile biking and walking loop that parallels the Charles River. To get out onto the river, you can take a Boston Duck Tour. The "Ducks" are amphibious vehicles that lumber around the city on wheels and then finish off with a plunge into the water, where the tour continues; the narrated 80-minute excursion is one of the city's best sightseeing experiences.

BOSTON HARBORFEST: Tel 800-SEE-BOSTON or 617-536-4100; bostonusa.com/harborfest. **BOSTON POPS FIREWORKS SPECTACULAR:** july4th.org. *When:* 1st week of July. **COPLEY PLAZA:** Tel 866-540-4417 or 617-267-5300; fairmont.com/copleyplaza. *Cost:* from $299. **FREE FRIDAY FLICKS:** Tel 617-787-7200; bostoncbslocal.com/flicks. *When:* mid-July–Aug. **BOSTON DUCK TOURS:** Tel 800-226-7442 or 617-267-3825; bostonducktours.com. *When:* late Mar–late Nov.

Spring Returns to New England on Foot

THE BOSTON MARATHON

Boston, Massachusetts

Spring arrives in Boston in various guises—a robin, a crocus, a legendary footrace. The Boston Marathon is the world's oldest annually contested marathon and one of the most prestigious. It's also the centerpiece of the city's celebration of Patriots' Day, the third Monday in April, a state holiday commemorating the start of the Revolutionary War. The tragic bombing of 2013 that killed five and injured many others has only increased the city's support for the race.

As thousands upon thousands of runners set out from suburban Hopkinton and make their way along the course, crowds pour into the streets to cheer them on. Half a million spectators line almost the entire route, raising spirits and bolstering resolve even on the toughest stretch, in the steep hills of Newton. (Paradoxically, the overall course loses so much elevation that an official world record can't be set in the Boston Marathon.)

The Boston Marathon dates to 1897, just a year after the first modern-day marathon (in the Athens Olympic Games). Eighteen men started, and the winner took nearly 3 hours to cover the 24.5-mile course. Today the race is the regulation 26.2 miles, and the runners are both male and female. Most of them start in four waves, with the elite men starting at 10 A.M. Professional competitors pursue cash prizes and international prestige, but the vast majority are amateurs motivated by the cachet of being able to say they "finished Boston." The 30,000 official runners qualify either by completing another marathon within a certain time or by joining a charity fund-raising program. Most of the field (98 percent, in fact) eventually winds up on Boylston Street in Boston's Back Bay, crossing the finish line in front of the Boston Public Library.

WHERE: starts in Hopkinton, 26.2 miles west of the finish line. *Race info:* Tel 617-236-1652; baa.org. *When:* Patriots' Day, 3rd Mon in Apr. **WHERE TO STAY:** Charlesmark Hotel (it's right on the finish line and rooms fill up a year in advance). Tel 617-247-1212; thecharlesmark.com. *Cost:* from $119 (off-peak), from $239 (peak). **BEST TIMES:** around noon in Kenmore Square, when the lead runners are passing by; near the finish line in late afternoon, when determined amateurs persevere.

Baseball's Preeminent Cathedral

FENWAY PARK

Boston, Massachusetts

Fenway Park is the oldest major league ballpark in America. When it opened in April 1912, William Howard Taft was president, the *Titanic* had just met its fate, and Babe Ruth wasn't yet in the minors. Boston is a baseball town, in large part because of the beloved park and World Series–winning team, the Red Sox. Part of the park's appeal is its quirky architecture. Left field is short (just 310 feet from home plate) but tall—"The Wall," which holds the hand-operated scoreboard, rises 37 feet. Famously known as the Green Monster, The Wall is painted green and topped with some of the most desirable seats in the park.

The most famous of the ballpark's 37,673 seats (one of the smallest in the majors) is seat 21 in deep right field, in row 37, section 42, the only red seat in a sea of blue. It marks the point, 502 feet from home plate, where Ted Williams deposited the longest home run ever hit in the park, on June 9, 1946.

Part of Fenway's appeal these days is the redemption the Red Sox earned by winning the World Series in 2004, for the first time since 1918, followed up by wins in 2007 and 2013. And a big part of it is the history that oozes from every brick and board. The gold standard of the Fenway experience is watching a late-season Red Sox–Yankees game with playoff implications as you devour a Fenway Frank, but even a lazy midsummer tilt with an uninspired visiting team and some soggy popcorn can be magical.

If you don't manage to see a game or take one of the year-round tours of the ballpark, you can always soak up the atmosphere at one of the area's many sports bars. The Cask 'n Flagon, across the street, is a traditional memorabilia-packed hangout. Right next to the park is Game On!, a high-tech sports-fan heaven, attracting a young crowd with its dozens of high-definition and plasma TVs, and a sound system designed to create the illusion that you're actually in the stands. It's nothing like the real thing, but it is close.

The first game at Fenway Park took place on April 9, 1912, between the Red Sox and Harvard College.

WHERE: Ticket office, 4 Yawkey Way. Tel 877-733-7699 (tickets) or 617-226-6666 (tour info); redsox.com. *Cost:* tickets $28–$500. *When:* regular-season games Apr–early Oct. **CASK 'N FLAGON:** Tel 617-536-4840; casknflagon.com. **GAME ON!:** Tel 617-351-7001; gameonboston.com. **BEST TIMES:** early–mid-Apr for Opening Day; any Yankees game; Oct for (fingers crossed) playoffs and World Series.

A Stroll Through a Young America's History

THE FREEDOM TRAIL

Boston, Massachusetts

One of America's great walking cities, Boston is best explored by following the 2.5-mile self-guided Freedom Trail that unfolds through its historic neighborhoods. Laid out in 1958, the trail connects 16 important sites, extending all the way across Boston Harbor to Charlestown. The signposted path is a line of red paint or redbrick (or both) that runs down the center of the sidewalk. It begins at Boston Common, the nation's oldest park (1640), and runs past Colonial and Revolutionary War–era landmarks such as churches, graveyards or "burying grounds," monuments, and houses of government, as well as the USS *Constitution*, better known as Old Ironsides, the oldest commissioned U.S. Navy warship (1797).

The Paul Revere House, constructed of wood around 1680 and purchased by the legendary silversmith (of "Midnight Ride" fame) in 1770, is the oldest building in downtown Boston. Still an active congregation, the Old North Church has stood in the North End since 1723 and makes a fascinating stop: This is the church where the "one if by land, two if by sea" lanterns were hung to warn people "the British are coming." Another famous house of worship is the Old South Meeting House, where disgruntled Bostonians gathered on a cold night in December 1773 and wound up throwing the so-called Boston Tea Party.

Also on the trail is Faneuil Hall (1742), Boston's original market building and once the colony's foremost meeting hall. Today it's the center of a five-building complex of shops, nightspots, and restaurants. Durgin-Park, a restaurant on the second floor of the North Market Building, boasts that your great-grandfather might have eaten there, which actually seems too modest—the restaurant opened in 1827. Known for its lively atmosphere and hearty New England food, its tried-and-true signature dishes are corn bread, Boston baked beans, and Indian pudding; the prime rib, turkey dinner, and Boston cream pie all need to be sampled, too.

Just across the street from the marketplace in the tiny, ancient area known as the Blackstone Block is Ye Olde Union Oyster House, opened in 1826 and the country's oldest restaurant in continuous service (Daniel Webster was a regular). Its famous raw bar is visible from the street, and you can see the shuckers opening oysters and clams so quickly that their hands are a blur. Regional classics like clam chowder, fresh Boston scrod, and homemade gingerbread are time-tested favorites here. The path to your table, across sloping wooden floors, may take you past Booth 18 upstairs, where John F. Kennedy used to dine in privacy.

WHERE: The trail begins at the Visitor Information Center on the Tremont St. side of Boston Common, but you can pick it up anywhere along the way. Tel 617-357-8300; thefreedomtrail.org. **Durgin-Park:** Tel 617-227-2038; durgin-park.com. *Cost:* dinner $40. **Ye Olde Union Oyster House:** Tel 617-227-2750; unionoysterhouse.com. *Cost:* dinner $45. **Best times:** May–Oct for pleasant walking weather; early July for Boston Harborfest; mid-Dec for Boston Tea Party reenactment.

A Woman's Palace Is Her Castle

Isabella Stewart Gardner Museum

Boston, Massachusetts

The plain facade of the 1901 mansion that houses one of Boston's low-profile gems gives no hint of the delights it conceals. Venture inside to marvel at the centerpiece of the interior, a dramatic four-story courtyard surrounded by elaborate balconies and archways, illuminated by a skylight, and filled with seasonal blooms from the museum's own greenhouse. The galleries that spread out from here hold an idiosyncratic assortment of European, Asian, and American art assembled to suit the museum's unconventional founder and namesake.

The Isabella Stewart Gardner Museum is the only private art collection in which the building, collection, and installations were created by one individual.

Designed in the style of a 15th-century Venetian palazzo, this building was the home of Isabella Gardner and was opened in 1903 as a museum while she still lived on the fourth floor. The permanent galleries remain exactly as she left them at her death in 1924, when she had already arranged for the collection to be held in public trust for the "education and enjoyment of the public forever." In 2012, the museum unveiled a new wing designed by Pritzker Prize–winning architect Renzo Piano that more than doubled the museum's space. It houses the museum's restaurant, Café G, studios, galleries, the intimate 300-seat Calderwood Hall, and a cozy living room for visitors to sit and relax.

In the 1890s, Gardner called on her friend Bernard Berenson, a prominent art historian, to help her assemble her collection. The museum opened to the public with more than 5,000 objects, including works by Giotto, Raphael, Rembrandt, and Botticelli. The Gardner is home to the only Pierro della Francesca fresco outside Italy and to Titian's *Europa*, one of the most important Italian paintings in the U.S. Another cherished holding is a John Singer Sargent portrait of

Gardner, who was called "the brightest, breeziest woman in Boston." Eccentric, too. She once took two lion cubs from a local zoo out in her coach, and after the 1912 World Series she appeared at Symphony Hall wearing a headband that read "Oh You Red Sox."

Today, almost a century later, the acoustically perfect Symphony Hall is home to the Boston Symphony Orchestra with a break built in for the Boston Pops' holiday concerts. The Pops' spring season ends with the nationally televised Fourth of July extravaganza on the Esplanade (see p. 39).

WHERE: 25 Evans Way. Tel 617-566-1401; gardnermuseum.org. *When:* closed Tues. **BOSTON SYMPHONY ORCHESTRA** and **BOSTON POPS:** Tel 888-266-1200 or 617-266-1200 (tickets), 617-266-1492 (info); bso.org. *Cost:* BSO tickets from $25; Pops tickets from $24. *When:* BSO Oct–early May; Pops Dec, May–July. **BEST TIMES:** Apr, when the museum's balconies drip with 20-foot nasturtium vines; Dec, when red and white poinsettias and holly bushes adorn the courtyard. The Calderwood Hall hosts the Sunday Concert Series, Sept–June.

Eight Millennia of Art and Artifacts

MUSEUM OF FINE ARTS

Boston, Massachusetts

Boston's Museum of Fine Arts is one of the nation's best, with collections that include some of the most beloved and recognizable works of art in the Western world. The galleries capture the history of human creativity, beginning with objects produced around 6000 B.C. and extending to the present day. Along the way they touch on works in various media from ancient Egypt, Greece, and Rome; Renaissance masterworks; American furnishings and decorative silver; and the Impressionists, including 37 Monets, one of the largest collections outside France. Images such as Degas dancers and Gilbert Stuart portraits feel familiar; Native American baskets and Chinese paintings lead visitors to think about art from unfamiliar perspectives.

The museum's best-known holdings include iconic American works such as John Singleton Copley's *Watson and the Shark*, Gilbert Stuart's *George Washington* and *Martha Washington*, and Childe Hassam's *Boston Common at Twilight*, and European masterpieces such as Renoir's *Dance at Bougival* and Gauguin's *Where Do We Come From? What Are We? Where Are We Going?*

The museum's eight curatorial areas range from textiles and fashion arts to art of Asia, Oceania, and Africa, including the finest collection of Japanese art outside Japan.

The MFA is home to so many pieces—more than 500,000 objects—that the sheer variety can be a bit overwhelming. Happily, the museum helps visitors find their way, scheduling tours (included in the admission price). However, there's a lot to be said for simply wandering around, trusting in serendipity to lead you to anything from a world-renowned bust of Homer (late first century B.C. or first century A.D.) to a 12th-century musical instrument.

The museum's design tells its own story. Murals by John Singer Sargent decorate the 1909 rotunda in the center of the building. The granite West Wing, an I. M. Pei design, called the Linda Family Wing for Contemporary Art, opened in 1981. A massive 2010 expansion opened the Art of the Americas Wing and a glass-enclosed courtyard designed by Foster and Partners, London, which designed the Great Court at the British Museum and the Sackler Galleries at the Royal Academy of Arts.

Where: 465 Huntington Ave. Tel 617-267-9300; mfa.org. **Best times:** Wed, voluntary contribution after 4 P.M.; First Fridays of each month from 6:00 to 9:30 P.M. for cocktails and live music.

A Taste of the Old Country in a Colonial Setting

BOSTON'S NORTH END

Boston, Massachusetts

One of the oldest parts of Boston, the North End is the city's best-known Italian neighborhood and one of the nation's most famous Italian American communities. After visiting the Paul Revere House and the Old North Church on the Freedom Trail (see p. 42), wander along the narrow streets, many of them lined with redbrick tenement buildings. For over a century, beginning in the mid-1800s during the Irish famines, this area teemed with recently arrived immigrants. One of the most famous North End natives was Rose Fitzgerald Kennedy, a granddaughter of Irish immigrants, daughter of Boston's Mayor John F. Fitzgerald, and mother of President John F. Kennedy. Her baptism (in 1890) and funeral (in 1995) both took place at St. Stephen's Church on Hanover Street. Across the street from St. Stephen's is Cyrus Dallin's equestrian statue of Paul Revere; every April on Patriots' Day, a reenactor dressed as Revere mounts a horse in front of the statue and begins his ride to Lexington and Concord (see p. 57).

Following the Irish to the North End were immigrants from Eastern Europe, Scandinavia, Portugal, and finally, around the turn of the 20th century, Italy. This is where you'll find some of Boston's best Italian restaurants, including the epitome of a neighborhood pizza place, Regina Pizzeria. Founded in 1926, this classic serves thin-crust pizza baked in a brick oven and, topped with mozzarella and house-made Italian sausage. Or just stop for a respite—an espresso or cappuccino and an Italian pastry or a scoop of gelato. Caffè Vittoria, the oldest Italian caffè in Boston, is another favorite with the locals, a bustling spot that attracts a lively mix of regulars and tourists.

You can also make the North End an evening of more formal dining without compromising its authenticity. An uncontested favorite is Mamma Maria, whose specialties are northern Italian cuisine and romance. The elegant town house is a popular place for marriage proposals, and the osso buco is worth its weight in diamond solitaires. If you prefer your jewelry plastic and your dough deep-fried, visit the North End in the summer. It's the season for feasts, otherwise known as street fairs; many of the generations-old social clubs that sponsor them bear the names of saints, and so do the festivals. The Fisherman's Feast, which dates to 1910, kicks off with the blessing of the fleet fishing waters and usually features a known entertainer (Frankie Avalon appeared in 2005) of Italian American heritage. Just don't overindulge in the sausage and peppers and sugar-dusted zeppoles—when the band strikes up traditional Italian tunes, you may find yourself dancing in the street. Everyone's Italian tonight. *Siamo tutti italiani!*

Regina Pizzeria: Tel 617-227-0765; regina pizzeria.com. *Cost:* dinner $20. **Caffè Vittoria:** Tel 617-227-7606; caffevittoria .com. *Cost:* $12. **Mamma Maria:** Tel 617-523-0077; mammamaria.com. *Cost:* dinner $60.

Best times: Patriots' Day (3rd Mon in Apr) for reenactments and commemorations; weekends in late July and Aug for feasts; mid-Aug for 4-day Fisherman's Feast (fishermansfeast .com).

Flowers, Trees, Swans, and Ducks in the Heart of the City

THE PUBLIC GARDEN

Boston, Massachusetts

Time seems to slow down in the Public Garden. Laid out in 1837, this was America's first public botanical garden. It abounds with flowerbeds and ornamental trees as well as fountains and famous birds. Find a shaded bench and take it all in, starting with the legendary Swan Boats propelled by college students working the pedals that make them go. The Swan Boats and one of the world's smallest suspension bridges dominate the lagoon at the center of the Public Garden, which encloses a delightfully miscellaneous statuary collection as well as four live swans. Near the corner of Beacon and Charles streets, *Make Way for Ducklings* is a string of tiny bronze waterfowl eternally following their mother toward the lagoon, as they did in Robert McCloskey's book of the same name. Near the exit onto Commonwealth Avenue, George Washington gazes down from the saddle of his landmark equestrian statue. And on that historical note, imagine this: The Public Garden sits on a landfill site that was once the "sea" (actually, a river) part of "One if by land, two if by sea."

Robert Paget designed the Swan Boats in the 1870s.

The Public Garden is also the front yard of two of the best hotels in all New England. The Taj Boston opened in 1927 and occupies a special niche befitting its age. Decorated in traditional style and outfitted with all the latest perks (call the front desk for the "Fireplace Butler"), it's the one truly legendary Boston hotel. Part of that legend is afternoon tea, a genteel and tasty old-school ritual, and part is the hotel's tony location on Newbury Street, known for the city's best shopping.

It has a worthy competitor in the Four Seasons, which combines over-the-top luxury with a gorgeous setting. The Public Garden is a constant presence; it's visible through huge windows from the lobby, restaurants, and swimming pool. The Bristol Restaurant offers house-aged steaks, a raw bar, seafood, and famous award-winning burgers. The genteel rivalry between the two hotels shows no signs of flagging, but the Taj Boston has an ace in the hole: Louis the trumpeter swan, the hero of E. B. White's delightful 1970 children's novel *The Trumpet of the Swan*, stayed there (when it was the Ritz Carlton) when he was working in the Public Garden lagoon.

WHERE: Back Bay. *Visitor info:* 617-635-4505; cityofboston.gov/parks. **SWAN BOATS:** Tel 617-522-1966; swanboats.com. *When:*

mid-Apr–mid-Sept. **TAJ BOSTON:** Tel 877-482-5267 or 617-536-5700; tajhotels.com/boston. *Cost:* from $395; afternoon tea $42. **THE FOUR SEASONS:** Tel 800-819-5053 or 617-338-4400; fourseasons.com/boston. *Cost:* from $425; dinner $50. **BEST TIMES:** early Apr–mid-Oct for flowers in bloom; look for tulips in Apr, roses in June.

A College Community on Boston's "Left Bank"

HARVARD SQUARE

Cambridge, Massachusetts

No visit to Boston is complete without a side trip to Cambridge, the lively and unabashedly intellectual city across the Charles River. Founded in 1630, it is home to two heavyweight seats of learning, the Massachusetts Institute of Technology and Harvard University.

Exuding gentility and timeless academia, Harvard University is the very heart of Cambridge. Life here revolves around Harvard Square and the tides of students, professors, and visitors who have flocked here from all over the world since Harvard was founded in 1636.

In a walk around Harvard Yard, the oldest part of the lovely campus, you'll see nearly three centuries' worth of architecture. The oldest building, Massachusetts Hall (1720), holds the university president's office and housing for first-year students. Sever Hall (1880) is a masterpiece by 19th-century American architect Henry Hobson Richardson. Nearby Widener Library (1913) bears the name of a Harvard graduate who died in the sinking of the *Titanic*. The Harvard Art Museums (HAM)—the Fogg, the Busch-Reisinger, and the Arthur M. Sackler—were brought together under one roof in 2014 in a Renzo Piano–designed building that is a work of art in itself. The Harvard Art Museums hold more than 250,000 objects; the depth and breadth of the collections (expect everything from 17th century Dutch to Kandinksy) make this complex one of the country's foremost university art museums and a place you'll want to spend your afternoon.

Harvard Square is anything but academic. It's a chic, upscale area with interesting boutiques, restaurants, and bistros. The posh Charles Hotel, a peaceful retreat steps away from the commotion of the square, is contemporary in style, with custom Shaker-inspired furnishings in the spacious accommodations, excellent restaurants, a jazz club, a fine spa, and a fitness center. A branch of the Legal Sea Foods restaurant chain faces the hotel courtyard. Internationally renowned for the quality and freshness of its fish, which the company processes in its own plant on the Boston waterfront, Legal Sea Foods originated in East Cambridge as a fish market in 1950; that location is long gone, but there are two always busy branches in Cambridge and eleven in Boston. Legal's fresh, chunky New England clam chowder is a must-sample, but so is the steamed or baked lobster (as big as you can afford), with a perfect rendition of Boston cream pie for dessert.

The student population long ago ensured a vibrant music scene in Cambridge. See who's performing at the Club Passim, one of the best folk and acoustic music venues around. A fixture of Harvard Square since it opened as a jazz venue named Club 47 in 1958, the subterranean coffeehouse is a friendly place with a no-frills, music-first atmosphere. The club has booked legendary musicians such as Joan Baez and Bonnie Raitt (both as teenagers), Tom Rush, Shawn Colvin, Nanci Griffith, Peter Wolf, and Bob Dylan, and that's just scratching the surface.

The Square is especially festive on warm weekends. Crowds pour in, growing even larger during frequent

Harvard Square, Cambridge's historic center-turned-commercial-district, enjoys a prime location on the St. Charles River.

street fairs (two of the biggest are Mayfair and Oktoberfest) and peaking in October for the Head of the Charles. The rowing regatta is the high point of the preppy social calendar, attracting more than 10,000 competitors to the river to race along the curving course as legions of supporters scream themselves hoarse in a state of near-frenzy.

WHERE: 4 miles northwest of Boston. *Visitor info:* Tel 800-862-5678 or 617-441-2884; cambridge.org. **HARVARD UNIVERSITY:** harvard.edu. **HARVARD ART MUSEUMS:** Fogg,

Busch-Reisinger, and Arthur M. Sackler Museums. Tel 617-495-9400; harvardart museums.org. **CHARLES HOTEL:** Tel 800-882-1818 or 617-864-1200; charleshotel.com. *Cost:* from $199 (off-peak), from $599 (peak). **LEGAL SEA FOODS:** Tel 617-491-9400; legal-seafoods.com. *Cost:* dinner $50. **CLUB PASSIM:** Tel 617-492-7679; passim.org. **BEST TIMES:** early May for Mayfair; early June when the Harvard campus is spruced up for graduation; early Oct for Oktoberfest; 3rd weekend in Oct for the Head of the Charles (hocr.org).

The North Shore's "Other Cape" Captivates

CAPE ANN

Massachusetts

Who hasn't heard of Cape Cod? But Massachusetts's "Other Cape," the small rocky coast of Cape Ann that juts out into the Atlantic just north of Boston, creates an equally dramatic shoreline that has

also inspired artists for generations. Cape Ann was a center of commercial fishing that began not long after the first group of European settlers declared Gloucester the best fishing

grounds in the New World upon their arrival in 1623. Descendants of Portuguese and Italian sailors who manned the early fleets are still in strong evidence today: The best-known celebration in a summer schedule full of weekend festivals is St. Peter's Fiesta, an enormous street fair that includes the blessing of the fleet.

Gloucester is still a seafaring town (as illustrated in Sebastian Junger's 1991 account of *The Perfect Storm;* the later movie version was filmed here), but the fishing industry has faded greatly. Whale-watching cruises have gained a growing popularity in its wake. Cape Ann's self-anointed role as "Whale-Watching Capital of the World" is due to the proximity of Stellwagen Bank, a shelf beneath the Atlantic running from Gloucester to Provincetown (see next page). Protected as a National Marine Sanctuary, it is a rich feeding ground for migrating finbacks, humpbacks, and other whales and marine life that happily dwell here between spring and fall. A half-day on the open sea on a Cape Ann Whale Watching cruise affords an unforgettable opportunity, with naturalists who narrate the voyage and pretty much guarantee multiple sightings.

Gloucester's gruff and ramshackle character takes a lyrical turn just outside town at Rocky Neck Art Colony, the nation's oldest continuously operating art colony. The tiny nearby town of Rockport, sitting at the tip of the peninsula, also has a vibrant artist community that has included Winslow Homer, Fitz Henry Lane and Childe Hassam; today the town overflows with gift shops and B&Bs but still retains its charm, especially if visited outside its summer peak. The lovely Emerson Inn by the Sea sits north of downtown's bustle right on the rocky coast, named for the famous philosopher and frequent guest. The gracious inn was built in 1846 and moved to this location in 1871, with a columned back veranda that overlooks a well-groomed lawn leading down to the sea.

For centuries nearby Essex supplied ships to Gloucester and countless other ports far and wide, a legacy proudly preserved in the small but impressive Essex Shipbuilding Museum. Model ships, tools, photographs, dioramas, and videos tell its story from 1668, when the

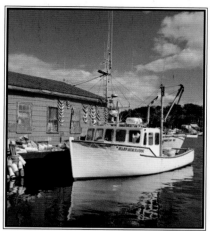

Once a prominent fishing town, Cape Ann maintains a nautical aesthetic.

first shipyard opened, to the mid-19th century, when as many as 15 manufacturers produced 50 or more vessels a year (more limited shipbuilding continuous today).

But there's still more. Cape Ann's far-reaching renown today is arguably as the hallowed birthplace of the fried clam. In 1916, Lawrence "Chubby" Woodman, of Woodman's restaurant in Essex, was the first to dunk a battered bivalve into sizzling oil, and the rest is history. Today, Woodman family members preside over the busy restaurant (they serve, on average, 2,000 people on a summer day) noted for clam chowder, steamed lobsters, lobster rolls, onion rings, and other sea-related delicacies as well as those peerless fried clams.

The red-and-white-striped eat-in/takeout Clam Box in nearby Ipswich opened in 1938 and has been packing them in ever since. A friendly rivalry pits their fried wonders against those of Woodman's. Sample a paper plate piled sky-high with their fried clams at an outdoor picnic table or inside dining room and decide for yourself.

If it happens to be that gorgeous month of October, you might consider a brief foray inland to the little town of Topsfield, whose classic country fair features lots and lots of retro carnival food and local entertainment.

Where: Gloucester is 36 miles northeast of Boston. *Cape Ann visitor info:* Tel 978-283-1601; capeannvacations.com. *Rockport visitor info:* Tel 978-283-1601; rockportusa.com. **Cape Ann Whale Watch:** Gloucester. Tel 978-283-5110; seethewhales.com. *When:* Apr–Oct. **Rocky Neck Art Colony:** Tel 978-515-7004; rockyneckartcolony.org. **Emerson Inn by the Sea:** Rockport. Tel 800-964-5550 or 978-546-6321; emersoninnbythesea.com. *Cost:* ocean-view from $169 (off-peak), from $259 (peak). **Essex Shipbuilding Museum:** Tel 978-768-7541; essexshipbuildingmuseum .org. *When:* open Wed–Sun, summer and fall; Sat–Sun, spring and winter. **Woodman's of Essex:** Tel 800-649-1773 or 978-768-2559; woodmans.com. *Cost:* dinner $20. **Clam Box:** Ipswich. Tel 978-356-9707; clamboxipswich .com. *Cost:* dinner $20. **Best times:** June for Rockport Chamber Music Festival (rockport music.org); late June for St. Peter's Fiesta in Gloucester; Labor Day weekend for Gloucester Schooner Festival; early Oct for Topsfield Fair (topsfieldfair.org); Dec for Christmas in Rockport celebration.

Anything Goes at the Tip of Cape Cod

PROVINCETOWN

Cape Cod, Massachusetts

Toward the tip of Cape Cod's northern end, the highway that crosses the rest of the peninsula dwindles to a two-lane road. Then Provincetown appears. A seaside town surrounded by gorgeous dunes and inviting beaches, the longtime fishing port and artists colony is one of the best-known gay communities in the world. The year-round population of just under 3,000 grows fifteenfold in the summer. Walking along Commercial Street is the best way to get the feel of this casual, welcoming place, equally popular for day-trippers and nighttime drag queens, seekers of tacky souvenirs and fine art, beach bums and party people.

Many year-round residents are Portuguese American (descendants of sailors and fishermen who immigrated in the years following the Civil War), and P-town has a lingering Iberian flavor. The Provincetown Portuguese Bakery specializes in traditional pastries and meat pies, and the first big event of the summer is the Portuguese Festival, with Portuguese flags draped everywhere—there's a lot of authentic food, music, dancing, and the blessing of the fishing fleet.

Few grade-school history classes stress that the *Mayflower* landed here first in 1620 before continuing across the bay to Plymouth (see p. 64) on the mainland; the Pilgrim Monument stands as a reminder atop High Pole Hill, visible from 40 miles away.

P-town is the closest port (6 miles away) to the Stellwagen Bank, an underwater plateau and rich fishing ground that's irresistible to migrating whales, with quasi-guaranteed sightings mid-April through October. Whale-watching cruises to see the magnificent mammals—finback, right, minke, and humpback—leave from MacMillan Wharf in the heart of downtown Provincetown.

Fine seafood restaurants have made Provincetown a popular dining destination. Patrons enjoy a water view at the Lobster Pot, whose creative menu includes Portuguese specialties such as cod crusted with linguiça sausage; bounteous *sopa do mar*, a mix of fish and shellfish poached in fish stock; and the signature Tim's clam chowder. The menu at Napi's draws inspiration from around the globe, featuring everything from bouillabaisse to Thai chicken and shrimp to savory Scallops Provençal. Built 30 years ago from salvaged materials, the funky restaurant overflows with local art and antiques and always promises an interesting crowd year-round.

There's no lack of variety in the accommodations department, either. The Land's End Inn is a 1904 shingle-style mansion famed for both its commanding location as well as its extravagant decor of plush fabrics, fine art, and elaborate antiques. Many of the individually decorated rooms have balconies, decks, or patios to enjoy P-town's famous sunsets. The best-known unit is the Bay Tower Room, which offers a 360-degree view from private wraparound wooden decks. Another special choice in town is the Crowne Pointe Historic Inn and Spa, a late 19th-century sea captain's house; guest rooms extend into three neighboring renovated carriage houses. Modern amenities blend with the elegant Victorian atmosphere, and many rooms have whirlpools and fireplaces. Its Shui Spa is P-town's best, with a wide range of options from deep-tissue massage or Gotu Kola firming wrap to a Reiki energy-balancing treatment.

The New Provincetown Players are the resident troupe at the venerable Provincetown Theater. When the artists began arriving in the early decades of the 20th century, so did playwrights and authors, whose ranks over time included such luminaries as Eugene O'Neill, Tennessee Williams, Norman Mailer, and E. E. Cummings. A busy cultural life is still one of P-town's biggest draws, with drama, dance, cabaret, concerts, and films that fill out the schedule at the theater.

Art's Dune Tours take visitors on excursions around Provincetown's

sandy surroundings, pointing out the battered "dune shacks" that for decades have served as retreats for the artists who came for the end-of-the-world atmosphere and special light; the shacks are now National Historic Landmarks.

WHERE: 115 miles southeast of Boston. *Visitor info:* Tel 508-487-3424; ptownchamber .com. **WHALE-WATCHING:** Dolphin Fleet of Provincetown, tel 800-826-9300 or 508-240-3636; whalewatch.com. *When:* mid-Apr–late Oct. **THE LOBSTER POT:** Tel 508-487-0842; ptownlobsterpot.com. *Cost:* dinner $40. **NAPI'S:** Tel 508-487-1145; napisrestaurant .com. *Cost:* dinner $40. **LAND'S END INN:** Tel 800-276-7088 or 508-487-0706; landsend inn.com. *Cost:* from $160 (off-peak), from $405 (peak). **CROWNE POINTE HISTORIC INN:** Tel 877-276-9631 or 508-487-6767; crowne pointe.com. **SHUI SPA:** Tel 508-487-3583; shuispa.org. *Cost:* from $109 (off-peak), from $239 (peak). **PROVINCETOWN THEATER:** Tel 800-791-7487 or 508-487-7487; province towntheater.org. *When:* year-round. **ART'S DUNE TOURS:** Tel 800-894-1951 or 508-487-1950; artsdunetours.org. *When:* Apr–mid-Nov. **BEST TIMES:** spring and fall for pleasant weather and relatively small crowds; mid-Apr–Oct for whale-watching; mid-June for Provincetown International Film Festival (ptownfilmfest.org); late June for Portuguese Festival; late Aug for Carnival Week, with Mardi Gras–style revelry.

The year-round population of Provincetown hovers around 3,000 people, but swells to more than 50,000 in the summer months.

Pristine and Wild, New England's Summer Playground

CAPE COD NATIONAL SEASHORE

Massachusetts

Cape Cod National Seashore is a 40-mile stretch of rolling dunes and gorgeous beaches. It lies on the Outer Cape, from popular Nauset Beach north to Provincetown (see p. 50). President John F. Kennedy, a longtime summer resident of Hyannisport, spearheaded legislation to create the Cape Cod National Seashore in 1961, well over a century after Henry David Thoreau (who wrote of "the bare and bended arm of Massachusetts") wandered the dunes, concluding at Highland Light in Truro that "a man can stand and put all America behind him."

Some 43,600 glorious acres unfold along the unruly Atlantic, where lighthouses overlook wide beaches, vast stretches of dune grass, walking trails, salt marshes, and kettle ponds, and where the play and quality of light have long drawn artists and writers. At some points, dunes soar 100 feet above the shore, and at low tide strings of sand bars stretch for miles. South of Chatham, the Monomoy National Wildlife Refuge extends 8 miles into the ocean and attracts 350-plus species of birds that use the Outer Cape as a flyway. Once a peninsula, the refuge now spreads over three distinct islands and is uninhabited except for its summer population of gray seals, which number around 16,000 on the Cape and islands. Back on terra firma, follow the two-lane Old King's Highway (modern-day Route 6A) from Orleans west to the Cape Cod Canal, which separates the peninsula from the mainland. Over its 34 miles, the road opens onto dramatic water views and passes a plethora of antiques shops, art galleries, potters' studios, and clam shacks.

The old sea captain's town of Chatham is one of the Cape's most desirable addresses. Shops, art galleries, and eateries line picture-perfect Main Street, a stretch of clapboard buildings, white picket fences, and flowering gardens and window boxes. Built in 1839, the dignified Captain's House Inn has romantic rooms with four-posters and fireplaces. You can walk to dinner at the Impudent Oyster, where the sophisticated menu (mainly seafood) and white-linen ambience are a welcome break from the ubiquitous clam shacks and sub shops. For the best dessert head to nearby Buffy's, where the ice cream is homemade daily and the plain old vanilla is heavenly.

Right on the Atlantic (and Pleasant Bay) is the Chatham Bars Inn, a 217-room establishment that offers guests the classic New England resort experience. Wicker rocking chairs line the porch overlooking the water. Many families return each summer for clam and lobster bakes under the stars.

WHERE: Chatham is 90 miles southeast of Boston. *Visitor info:* Tel 888-33-CAPE-COD or 508-362-3225; capecodchamber.org. **CAPE COD NATIONAL SEASHORE:** Tel 508-771-2144;

With a garden and a white picket fence, this clapboard house exemplifies Chatham's charm.

nps.gov/caco. **Monomoy National Wildlife Refuge:** Chatham. Tel 508-945-0594; fws.gov/refuge/monomoy. **Captain's House Inn:** Chatham. Tel 800-315-0728 or 508-945-0127; captainshouseinn.com. *Cost:* from $185 (off-peak), from $295 (peak). **Impudent Oyster:** Chatham. Tel 508-945-3545. *Cost:* dinner $55. **Buffy's:** Chatham. Tel 508-945-5990.

Chatham Bars Inn: Tel 800-527-4884 or 508-945-0096; chathambarsinn.com. *Cost:* from $199 (off-peak), from $599 (peak). **Best times:** spring and fall for smaller crowds; warmest water in mid- to late Aug; Sept for Harwich Cranberry Festival (harwichcranberry festival.org); traditional Thanksgiving and Christmas at Chatham Bars.

A Treasure Trove of Architecture in the City of Peace

Hancock Shaker Village

Hancock, Massachusetts

Hancock Shaker Village was the third of 19 major Shaker communities that flourished in the 1800s and extended from New England as far west as Indiana and Kentucky (see p. 407). The Shakers (so named for their trembling and whirling during worship) were a religious sect established in England in 1747. They lived communally, seeking to create heaven on earth, a goal they pursued by living simply, in a society that treated men and women as equals and practiced pacifism and celibacy. They added members through adult conversion and became one of the most successful separatist societies in America.

When the Hancock community was formally settled in 1783, its inhabitants called it the City of Peace—and so it seemed with some 3,000 acres of rich farmland, rolling meadows, lush woods, and 300 members at its peak in the 1840s. It gradually declined and by the 1960s concerned citizens stepped in to preserve the village, turning it into the largest restored Shaker community in the Northeast. Today it's a 750-acre living history museum consisting of 20 buildings that have gained Hancock a reputation as the best place in the East to experience and appreciate the Shaker architecture and aesthetic, an austere, unadorned style that is timeless in its appeal.

Inside many of the structures are displays that show off the members' tenet of worshiping God through handiwork: The village's collection of more than 22,000 objects of unparalleled craftsmanship includes baskets, boxes, furniture, clothing and textiles, and farm and kitchen equipment.

Hancock Shaker Village was primarily a farming community, and its best-known structures are the magnificent 1826 Round Stone Barn and the five-story Brick Dwelling from 1830 that housed nearly 100 community members, known as Brethren and Sisters. Among the other buildings on the property are the 1793 Meeting House and the Sisters' Dairy and Weave Loft, still furnished with butter churns, spinning wheels, and looms. The 1910 Barn holds the Discovery Room, where children can dress up like a Shaker, milk a (replica) cow, and make crafts to take home. In the Village Store parents can purchase some of the reproduced Shaker items so coveted by today's design enthusiasts.

Where: 153 miles west of Boston. Tel 413-443-0188; hancockshakervillage.org. *When:* self-guided tours Apr–Oct. **Best times:** Apr for Baby Animals; late Sept for Country Fair; Oct for Spirit Suppers.

A Gorgeous Setting for a Smorgasbord of Culture

BERKSHIRE SUMMER FESTIVALS

Lenox, Massachusetts

When warm weather sets in, performing artists from New York, Boston, and the rest of the world find their way to the Berkshires, where the life of the mind flourishes among the rolling, wooded hills of western Massachussetts. The Tanglewood Music Festival is the Berkshires' marquee event. The summer home of the Boston Symphony Orchestra, Tanglewood attracts top-flight artists from around the globe who perform works in a wide variety of genres. The lush 500-acre estate encompasses the Shed and Ozawa Hall with plenty of seating, but Tanglewood's calling card is a glamorous picnic dinner. Some music lovers spread out blankets and gourmet meals on The Lawn, dining by candlelight, sometimes with china, silver, and crystal. Others bring the kids and tuna sandwiches.

The internationally acclaimed Jacob's Pillow Dance Festival offers dance performances, lectures, demonstrations, films, and live music (always with dance). "The Pillow," founded by dance legend Ted Shawn, is famed for encouraging the dance world's rising stars. You can enjoy ballet one night and hip-hop, modern dance, or Spanish flamenco the next. Close to Lenox in the small town of Becket, the 220-acre property, a National Historic Landmark, is home to multiple performance spaces, a dance school, and carefully preserved wetlands that can be enjoyed on a self-guided tour of the grounds.

Shakespeare & Company's focus is—not surprisingly—on the Bard, but its three performance spaces also schedule contemporary works and revivals. The celebrated actor-training program gives the company an energy that makes it irresistible to established stars as well as talented unknowns. Literature is another art closely associated with the Berkshires. The Mount was the home of novelist Edith Wharton from 1902 to 1911. Wharton claimed to be "a better landscape gardener than novelist"—the judges who made her the first woman to win the Pulitzer Prize for fiction might disagree—and the Mount preserves her legacy.

The venerable Berkshire Theatre Group, created in 2010 by a merger between the Berkshire Theatre Festival in Stockbridge and The Colonial Theatre in Pittsfield, presents revivals of plays and musicals as well as original productions. Top-notch actors, directors, set designers, and playwrights make and build on their reputations on four stages. Across town in Stockbridge is the Norman Rockwell Museum, home to the world's largest collection of works by the beloved 20th-century American artist. The iconic *Four Freedoms* and numerous *Saturday Evening Post* covers are part of the 367 works from Rockwell's personal collection, bequeathed to the museum by Rockwell, who lived in Stockbridge for the last 25 years of his life.

Anchoring Stockbridge's Rockwell-perfect Main Street is the friendly Red Lion Inn, a landmark since the late 1700s. The inn offers a variety of accommodations, some with shared baths and some in village guesthouses near the main building. There's even a guest room in an 1899 firehouse down the block.

WHERE: Lenox is 130 miles west of Boston. *Visitor info:* Tel 413-743-4500; berkshires.org. **TANGLEWOOD:** Lenox. Tel 888-266-1200 or 617-266-1200; tanglewood .org. *Cost:* tickets from $15; lawn admission from $10. *When:* late June–early Sept. **JACOB'S PILLOW:** Becket. Tel 413-243-0745; jacobs pillow.org. *Cost:* from $25. *When:* mid-June–late Aug. **SHAKESPEARE & COMPANY:** Lenox. Tel 413-637-1199; shakespeare.org. *Cost:* tickets from $10. *When:* late May–Oct. **THE MOUNT:** Lenox. Tel 413-551-5111; edith wharton.org. *When:* closed for tours Nov–Apr. **BERKSHIRE THEATRE GROUP:** Stockbridge.

Tel 413-298-5576; berkshiretheatregroup.org. *Cost:* tickets from $35 for staged productions. **NORMAN ROCKWELL MUSEUM:** Stockbridge. Tel 413-298-4100; nrm.org. *When:* daily; studio closed Nov–Apr. **RED LION INN:** Stockbridge. Tel 413-298-5545; redlioninn .com. *Cost:* from $115 (off-peak), from $170 (peak). **BEST TIMES:** July–Aug for pleasant weather; mid-Sept–mid-Oct for foliage.

Living the High Life at a Gilded Age Estate

THE "INLAND NEWPORT"

Lenox and the Berkshires, Massachusetts

The Berkshires have long promised to nourish the mind, body, and spirit. Visitors flock to western Massachusetts in search of renewal at cultural venues, spas and retreats, and at the exquisite mansions that dot the landscape. Beginning in the mid-19th century, Gilded Age tycoons from New York and Boston turned their attention to Lenox and the vicinity, touching off a building boom of country estates with as many as 75 in the area by 1900. The resulting concentration of magnificent homes led the author and animal-rights activist Cleveland Amory to later dub the Lenox area "the Switzerland of America."

Thanks to the same false modesty once common to Newport, Rhode Island (see p. 83), the mammoth country houses were known as "cottages"; many of them survive, some as luxurious lodgings for visitors with gilded budgets. Sitting like a Scottish castle at the end of a regal drive on 100 acres of painstakingly tended grounds, Blantyre offers elaborately decorated guest rooms, rich with subtle floral fabrics and sumptuous draperies. The accommodations echo the formality of the rest of the property (it's preferred that men wear jackets and ties in the dining room). Tennis courts and croquet lawns join more modern amenities such as a small but lovely spa.

The other sumptuous sanctuary in town is Wheatleigh, an 1893 manse that aspires to be an Italian palazzo. Equally luxurious, but more sleek and modern where Blantyre is formal and ornate, the extensively restored hotel occupies a parklike setting on 22 acres originally designed by Frederick Law Olmsted, the landscape architect most famous for his design of New York City's Central Park. Contemporary art complements the antique and custom furnishings, creating a refined atmosphere in the tranquil guest rooms and dramatic public spaces. The inn overlooks a scenic lake, just part of the bucolic views enjoyed from the floor-to-ceiling windows in the dining room. Chef Jeffrey Thompson's cuisine is modern French with American, Spanish, and Italian touches, a celebrated combination of delicate flavors and local ingredients. The seven-course tasting menu changes frequently, but might include such delights as hot foie gras with golden raisins, turnip, and red sorrel.

Less baronial but no less comfortable lodgings can be found at the Old Inn on the Green in New Marlborough. Dating to around

1760 and over the years serving as a trading post, stagecoach stop, tavern, general store, and even a post office, it is done up in sophisticated country style with candlelit dining rooms and a summer terrace as the dramatic backdrop for owner-chef Peter Platt's seasonal New England cuisine.

WHERE: Lenox is 130 miles west of Boston. *Visitor info:* Tel 413-743-4500; berkshires.org. **BLANTYRE:** Tel 844-881-0104 or 413-637-3556; blantyre.com. *Cost:* from $315 (off-peak), from $475 (peak). **WHEATLEIGH:** Tel 413-637-0610; wheatleigh.com. *Cost:* from $715; 7-course dinner $175. **THE OLD INN ON THE GREEN:** New Marlborough. Tel 413-229-7924; oldinn.com. *Cost:* from $270; dinner $65. **BEST TIMES:** June–Aug for greatest variety of cultural offerings; late June–early Sept for Tanglewood Music Festival; mid-Sept–mid-Oct for foliage.

When the World Is Too Much with You

BLISS IN THE BERKSHIRES

Lenox, Massachusetts

Berkshire country grows lovelier with each season, passing from tranquil snow white to velvety green to raucous reds and golds. The lack of large cities nearby means relatively little light pollution; on a clear night, a canopy of stars brightens the ink-black sky. All this forms an inspiring backdrop for destinations that promise to renew the spirit and reinvigorate the body.

Cranwell Spa & Golf Resort is such a retreat, a luxurious Gilded-Age estate on 380 gorgeous acres. The property centers on a restored 1894 mansion, an architectural showpiece that evokes a Tudor-style English country house, rich with carved woodwork, wood paneling, and antique Oriental carpets. Cranwell has an excellent 35,000-square-foot spa, with 16 treatment rooms, indoor pool, an extensive fitness center as well as men and women's relaxation lounges complete with fireplaces. Stay in the comfy, modern Carriage House to reach the spa by glass-enclosed walkway. Golfers are equally pampered here: After a morning on the historic 18-hole championship course (with expert instruction available), a host of treatments await at the spa, many designed specifically for sore duffers.

Canyon Ranch in Lenox is the eastern outpost of the legendary Arizona spa (see p. 700). It offers the same total immersion health and wellness experience as befits Canyon Ranch's unrivaled international reputation. Its unique strength is the extensive, expert staff of doctors, life management therapists, nutritionists, exercise physiologists, and spiritual wellness providers to help you become healthier on every level. Its location sits on 120 acres with extensive outdoor excursions—hiking, biking, swimming, kayaking, tennis, skiing, and much more. Indoors, the 100,000-square-foot spa complex incorporates a gorgeous pool, tennis and squash courts, exercise and weight rooms, a jogging track, and numerous treatment rooms. The cuisine, which famously balances nutrition and flavor, is so appealing that "Lunch and Learn" with a chef is one of the most popular activities. Canyon Ranch schedules more than 40 fitness classes and expert lectures a day. It can be overwhelming, but you can meet with a program advisor to help create a schedule that best meets your goals. The whole idea is to bring what you learn back home.

Dramatically different, the Kripalu Center promises a focus on yoga, health, and personal growth. Partially housed in a former monastery and overlooking a lake from a hilltop that affords spectacular views of the 350-acre estate, Kripalu is the country's largest yoga education center. Guests wander the beautiful grounds, relax in a whirlpool or sauna, and experience an environment designed to be a nurturing retreat from the madding crowd. Suitably simple accommodations in the four-story redbrick building range from dorm rooms with bunk beds to private doubles. The

In addition to its resorts and retreats, Berkshire County is known for bucolic charm and rustic farmhouses.

friendships forged amid a delightful milieu of a fresh-air camp for adults with a higher mission are an inherent part of its specialness. Guests eat at long communal tables and chat at lunch and dinner but not at breakfast, which is a silent meal. The Kripalu R&R package is the most popular, with all the basics covered: room and board, yoga, meditation, and other activities. But it also offers workshops that focus on facing cancer, writing your life story, healing from loss, Ayurvedic cleansing, and countless other subjects.

WHERE: 130 miles west of Boston. *Visitor info:* Tel 413-743-4500; berkshires.org. **CRANWELL RESORT:** Tel 800-272-6935 or 413-637-1364; cranwell.com. *Cost:* from $195 (off-peak), from $375 (peak). **CANYON RANCH LENOX:** Tel 800-742-9000 or 413-637-4100; canyonranch.com/lenox. *Cost:* 2-night packages from $1,500 per person, includes meals and $150 service allowance per person. **KRIPALU CENTER:** Tel 866-200-5203 or 413-448-3152; kripalu.org. *Cost:* 2-night R&R Retreat from $400 per person (shared room, hallway bath) to $788 (private room, private bath), 2-night minimum, includes meals. **BEST TIMES:** June–Aug for cultural offerings in the area; July–Aug for weather, mid-Sept–mid-Oct for foliage.

Revolution, Literature, and Walden Pond

LEXINGTON AND CONCORD

Massachusetts

Reminders of the Revolutionary War abound throughout eastern Massachusetts, but nowhere more significantly than in Lexington and Concord. The first skirmish of the war took place just a couple of blocks from downtown Lexington on April 19, 1775. Tensions between the colonists and the British government had been building for many years, and the local militia would gather at Buckman Tavern to discuss the situation. Learning that British troops were on the march from Boston to seize arms, Paul Revere and his fellow riders rode into the countryside to sound the alarm. They roused the militia for miles around, and the

Lexington forces confronted the British on the Battle Green.

This affluent suburb of Boston looks nothing like a battlefield today, the historic site now a broad, peaceful lawn. Spend a moment at the visitor center, where a diorama illustrates the battle when the first shot was fired. If your visit coincides with the local tradition of waking before dawn on Patriots' Day, join the sleepy-eyed crowd to witness convincing battle reenactments followed by hearty community pancake breakfasts and a day full of family events.

The 1,000-acre Minute Man National Historical Park preserves sites and structures associated with the Revolution, most of them found along the 5-mile Battle Road Trail connecting Lexington and Concord. One of the trail's principal sites is Concord's North Bridge, where 400 colonists surprised the British regulars. A replica of the trestle bridge over the narrow Concord River is part of the park, which also preserves the Wayside, the only home writer Nathaniel Hawthorne ever owned, built in 1688 (it was also the childhood home of Louisa May Alcott).

The Wayside is but a glimpse of Concord's great literary legacy. The Orchard House, the adult home of Louisa May Alcott, who wrote *Little Women* here, and the prosperous-looking home of philosopher-poet Ralph Waldo Emerson, are, like Hawthorne's, open for tours (many of the town's literary and revolutionary artifacts have been gathered at the impressive Concord Museum across the way). In part because of Emerson's presence, Concord was a center of Transcendentalism, an early 19th-century philosophical movement that believed in the inherent goodness of people and nature. Under the shade of ancient trees in this writers' neighborhood is the late 19th-century Hawthorne Inn, a welcoming and romantic B&B with just seven guest rooms. Classic country decor of handmade quilts and antique four-poster beds mixes seamlessly with contemporary and traditional art, while everywhere a literary atmosphere prevails.

Watch the colonists and the British fight it out on Patriots' Day, the state holiday in April that commemorates the outbreak of the American Revolution.

Longfellow's Wayside Inn in nearby Sudbury is perhaps the area's most well-known destination for accommodations and dining. Licensed in 1716 and reputedly the oldest operating inn in the country, it was immortalized in Longfellow's *Tales of a Wayside Inn.* With just ten antiques-filled guest rooms decorated in comfortable country style, it once belonged to auto magnate Henry Ford, who amassed a number of historic structures on the leafy 130-acre property. The 1929 gristmill-cum-water-wheel still supplies flour used in the inn's baking, and Sunday Dinner in the Yankee style is a venerable local tradition at the restaurant. Linger afterward with a colonial-recipe rum concoction in the old bar.

Even with such tough competition, Concord native Henry David Thoreau is arguably the author most closely associated with the town, and lovely Walden Pond—a 102-foot deep glacial "kettle"—is the place most closely associated with the author. Thoreau lived on these sylvan shores from 1845 to 1847 in a one-room house he built on property owned by his friend Emerson. His objective? To escape a society in which "the mass of men lead lives of quiet desperation." He captured the experience in his 1854 essay *Walden,* inspiring the modern-day conservation movement while encouraging man's appreciation of solitude in untrammeled nature. The Walden Pond State Reservation preserves the site of the long-gone house (a replica stands nearby), surrounded by some 2,680 acres of largely undeveloped land where you can still find that moment of peace and quiet that changed Thoreau's life.

WHERE: Lexington is 14 miles northwest of Boston. *Visitor info:* Tel 978-457-6150; merrimackvalley.org or Tel 781-862-2480; lexingtonchamber.org. **BUCKMAN TAVERN:** Lexington. Tel 781-862-5598; lexingtonhistory.org. *When:* closed Nov–mid-Apr. **MINUTE MAN NATIONAL HISTORICAL PARK:** Tel 978-318-7825. *When:* North Bridge center daily, Apr–Oct; Tues–Sat, Nov–Mar; Minute Man center closed Nov–Apr. **CONCORD:** 20 miles northwest of Boston. *Visitor info:* Tel 978-369-3120; concordchamberofcommerce.org. **THE**

WAYSIDE: Tel 978-318-7863. *When:* closed Nov–Apr. **ORCHARD HOUSE:** Tel 978-369-4118; louisamayalcott.org. **RALPH WALDO EMERSON HOUSE:** Tel 978-369-2236. *When:* open Thurs–Sun, mid-Apr–Oct. **CONCORD MUSEUM:** Tel 978-369-9763; concordmuseum.org. **HAWTHORNE INN:** Tel 978-369-5610; concordmass.com. *Cost:* from $149 (off-peak), from $279 (peak). **LONGFELLOW'S WAYSIDE INN:** Tel 800-339-1776 or 978-443-1776; wayside.org. *Cost:* from $130; dinner $45. **WALDEN POND STATE RESERVATION:** Tel 978-369-3254; mass.gov. **BEST TIMES:** Patriots' Day (3rd Mon in Apr) for battle reenactments and commemorations; Sept–mid-Oct for foliage, especially lovely at Walden Pond.

Preserving the Legacy of the Industrial Revolution

LOWELL

Massachusetts

Founded in 1821 as the country's first planned industrial city, Lowell soon became the most prominent of the mill towns that fueled the economy of 19th-century New England. The mills shut down a long time ago,

but Lowell remains proud of its heritage. Established as an urban national park in 1978, the city features restored textile mills in the late–19th-century downtown, more than 5 miles of canals (whose harnessed power was the key to its success), and several museums that invite you to step back in time. Trolleys connect the national park's exhibits telling the story of the mills, the employees, and their struggle for better working conditions. Narrated boat tours on the canals and the Merrimack River make the educational experience a leisurely one.

The American Textile History Museum, housed in an enormous former machine shop and one of the largest textile museums in the world, covers "Spindle City's" heyday from the 1830s to '50s, and tells America's story through the art, history, and science of textiles. The

New England Quilt Museum displays textiles in high style, with permanent and rotating exhibits of antique and contemporary quilts.

The economic opportunity afforded by the mills made Lowell a true melting pot. In the early days, most "mill girls" came from New England. After the Civil War there was a large influx of workers from Canada and all over Europe. The beginning of the end came in the 1920s and '30s, when the industry fled south. The only Spinners in town these days are the minor league hockey and baseball teams that keep hometown pride high.

Native son Jack Kerouac has also helped secure a spot on the map for Lowell. The author of *On the Road* (1957) and patron saint of the Beat Generation is the focus of a birthday commemoration in March and a weekend-long event that includes performances of poetry and music in early October. Kerouac was the son of immigrants from Quebec who came to work at the mills, and Lowell remains a magnet for immigrants. Lowell is the second largest Southeast Asian community in America (they were relocated here in the 1980s). The summer's annual Lowell Southeast Asian Water Festival honors that heritage with boat races, parades, dancing, music, and food of a decidedly Asian bent.

In recent years, Lowell has become home to hundreds of artists and dozens of galleries. In July the city stages the Lowell Folk Festival, the largest free folk music festival in the U.S. Half a dozen stages are set up for every imaginable musical genre—from zydeco to klezmer and sacred music—performed by artists from as far away as Sweden and Vietnam. Booths sell ethnic food of every stripe, and it seems as if most of Boston has jumped on the half-hourly train to come and enjoy one of the state's liveliest festivals.

WHERE: 33 miles northwest of Boston. *Visitor info:* Tel 978-459-6150; merrimackvalley.org. **LOWELL NATIONAL HISTORICAL PARK:** Tel 978-970-5000; nps.gov/lowe. **AMERICAN TEXTILE HISTORY MUSEUM:** Tel 978-441-0400; athm.org. **NEW ENGLAND QUILT MUSEUM:** Tel 978-452-4207; nequiltmuseum.org. *When:* closed Mon, May–Oct; closed Sun–Tues, Nov–Apr. **BEST TIMES:** Mar for Kerouac's birthday and Oct for Lowell Celebrates Kerouac (lowellcelebrateskerouac.org); July for Folk Festival (lowellfolkfestival.org); Aug for Lowell Southeast Asian Water Festival (lowellwaterfestival.org).

New England Charm off the Coast of Cape Cod

MARTHA'S VINEYARD

Massachusetts

Christened in 1602 by British explorer Bartholomew Gosnold for his daughter, Martha's Vineyard is no longer covered in wild grapes. Today it's an island of beautiful beaches, woods, farmland, cranberry bogs, charming inns, and tourists, distinguished from its neighbor Nantucket by its proximity to the mainland and its Cape Cod–like variety of landscapes and communities.

The offbeat, fun village of Oak Bluffs, with hundreds of colorful Victorian cottages and a beloved 1876 carousel said to be the oldest working merry-go-round in the country, offers the most after-dark activity for the 20-something set; join in the carnival atmosphere, then stop in at Ben & Bill's to sample their ice cream flavors that range from "lobster" to "bubblegum." The ferry port of Vineyard Haven is known for the Black Dog Tavern, purveyor of the ubiquitous T-shirts (wait till you get home to wear yours), as well as tasty pub grub. The West Tisbury farmers market in and around the 1859 Grange Hall is alive with a wonderful selection of fresh produce. Also in West Tisbury is the Norman Rockwell–style Alley's General Store, the oldest retail business on the island (in business since 1858) and proud "Dealers in Almost Everything"—peek in just for the scenario.

Aquinnah (formerly known as, and often still called, Gay Head) is a perfect place to watch the sun set, perhaps while dining on a feast of lobster rolls or fried clams from Larsen's Fish Market or The Bite. One is a store, the other a traditional New England clam shack, and both are landmarks in the fishing village of Menemsha, not far from Aquinnah and its landmark lighthouse. Menemsha's Beach Plum Inn and Restaurant, situated on 7 secluded hilltop acres overlooking the historic harbor, has access to some of the island's best beaches. Blooming gardens surround rooms and cottages that bear the names (and colors) of its flowers. Its excellent water-view restaurant, with an emphasis on fresh seafood and farm-to-table, makes this the inn of choice for many return guests.

Seafood is just about every eatery's specialty on the island. Atria, a restaurant with a lively basement bar in handsome Edgartown (the largest of the Vineyard's villages), has a menu with dishes like "Cod Is Great, Cod Is Good" and "A Very Serious Steak." Gardens surround the 1890 sea captain's house; request a table on the porch or terrace to enjoy the full effect.

Old-fashioned and service-proud, the Charlotte Inn in Edgartown is the finest hostelry on the island. The 1864 main house is the center of a complex of four buildings with 17 guest rooms, 2 suites, and public areas awash with elaborate Edwardian furnishings and original art. Abundant gardens give the whole place the rarefied atmosphere of a country estate that is more England than New England.

WHERE: 7 miles offshore from Falmouth on Cape Cod. Ferries depart from Woods Hole year-round and seasonally from Hyannis & Falmouth on Cape Cod; New Bedford; Quonset Point, RI; Highlands, NJ; NYC; and Boston. *Visitor info:* Tel 800-505-4815 or 508-693-0085; mvy.com. **BEN & BILL'S:** Oak Bluffs. Tel 508-696-0008; benandbills.com. **BLACK DOG TAVERN:** Vineyard Haven. Tel 508-693-9223; theblackdog.com. *Cost:* dinner $55. **WEST**

Oak Bluffs is a vibrant village that appeals to both families and a younger crowd.

TISBURY FARMERS MARKET: thewesttisbury farmersmarket.com. *When:* Wed and Sat mornings, June–early Oct. **ALLEY'S GENERAL STORE:** West Tisbury. Tel 508-693-0088. mvpreservation.org/p.php/preservation/commu nity/alleys-general-store. **LARSEN'S FISH MARKET:** Menemsha. Tel 508-645-2680; larsensfishmarket.com. *When:* closed late Oct– Apr. **THE BITE:** Menemsha. Tel 508-645-9239. *When:* closed late Oct–Apr. **BEACH PLUM INN:** Menemsha. Tel 508-645-9454; beachpluminn .com. *Cost:* from $140 (off-peak), from $400 (peak); dinner $85. *When:* closed Nov–Apr. **ATRIA:** Edgartown. Tel 508-627-5850; atriamv .com. *Cost:* dinner $65. *When:* closed Dec–Mar. **THE CHARLOTTE INN:** Edgartown. Tel 508-627-4151; thecharlotteinn.com. *Cost:* from $325 (off-peak), from $395 (peak); dinner from $70. **BEST TIMES:** May–Oct for peak season; mid-June for A Taste of the Vineyard; July for the Edgartown Regatta.

A Remote World All Its Own

NANTUCKET

Massachusetts

The island's Wampanoag Indian name is thought to mean "faraway land," and Nantucket seems just that. It's only 30 miles off the coast of Cape Cod, but the 45-square-mile island floats in its own insular world of time and space. Some 11,000 year-round residents accommodate more than five times that many visitors each summer, yet the island manages to retain an unspoiled atmosphere. Here the descendant of the practical Yankee sea captain meets the cultured offspring of New England old money—and, increasingly, new money. They bond over their shared affection for the windswept island, with its abundant salt marshes and pristine beaches.

Stringent zoning laws help maintain the traditional New England appearance of the "Little Grey Lady of the Sea"—so named for the color of its cedar-shingled houses muted by exposure to the sea air. Movie-set–perfect Nantucket is one of the country's finest protected historic districts, with more than 800 Colonial, Georgian, Federal, and Greek Revival houses and Quaker sea captains' homes, constructed between 1686 and 1840.

Nantucket was the whaling capital of the world until the 1820s. The small Whaling Museum preserves Nantucket's eminence in the production of whale oil and candles, which were shipped all over the world. Displays include the skeleton of a 46-foot sperm whale, a whaleboat, a collection of 19th-century scrimshaw, and artifacts from the *Essex*, sunk by a sperm whale in 1820, inspiring the story recounted in *Moby-Dick*.

Heading the list of the island's finest hostelries is the Wauwinet, standing in romantic end-of-the-world isolation on a windswept spit of land between the ocean and Nantucket Bay. Cottages and manicured lawns surround the rambling 1875 main house, adjacent to 26 miles of shoreline protected as a wildlife sanctuary. The inn's restaurant, Topper's, is celebrated for its creative take on regional favorites (the smoked seafood chowder is a signature), enjoyed outdoors in warm weather or by a crackling fire when it's chilly, with an award-winning wine cellar to top the experience.

Under the same ownership, the White Elephant is right in town on the waterfront. Most of its 53 light, airy rooms and 11 guest cottages are decorated in chic country style

Nantucket was home to Herman Melville's fictional characters, Captain Ahab and First Mate Starbuck.

and face the water. Like its sister property, this island-chic inn emphasizes service, from the hotel operation to its well-known restaurant, Brant Point Grill. For a cozier, more intimate alternative, visit the 12-room Pineapple Inn, an 1838 whaling captain's home where the guestbook is full of raves about the baked goods at breakfast.

WHERE: 100 miles southeast of Boston. Year-round ferries from Hyannis; seasonal ferries from Harwich Port on Cape Cod. *Visitor info:* Tel 508-228-1700; nantucketchamber .org. **WHALING MUSEUM:** Tel 508-228-1894; nha.org. *When:* mid-Apr–mid-Oct. **THE WAUWINET:** Tel 800-426-8718 or 508-228-0145; wauwinet.com. *Cost:* from $195 (off-peak), from $675 (peak); 3-course prix-fixe dinner $85. *When:* closed Nov–Apr. **WHITE ELEPHANT HOTEL:** Tel 800-445-6574 or 508-228-2500; whiteelephanthotel.com. *Cost:* from $225 (off-peak), from $500 (peak); dinner $80. *When:* closed early Dec–mid-Apr. **PINEAPPLE INN:** Tel 508-257-4577; pineapple inn.com. *Cost:* from $110 (off-peak), from $250 (peak). *When:* closed Nov–mid-May (open for Christmas Stroll). **BEST TIMES:** May–June and Sept for smaller crowds; last weekend in Apr for Daffodil Festival; late May for the Figawi Race, the largest sailboat race on the East Coast; June for Nantucket Film Festival (nantucketfilmfestival.org); 1st weekend in Dec for Christmas Stroll.

Art Rejuvenates a Run-down Industrial Town

MASS MoCA

North Adams, Massachusetts

Τhe western Massachusetts community of North Adams was a typical former mill town that fell on hard times in the 20th century. But no other erstwhile manufacturing community has reinvented itself quite so creatively or stylishly. The engine of the transformation is a former industrial site converted into the largest contemporary-arts center in the country, MASS MoCA (the Massachusetts Museum of Contemporary Art). From the full-grown upside-down trees hanging outside the main entrance to the institution's commitment to nurturing and integrating the visual and performing arts, this is no ordinary museum.

The enormous galleries—one is the size of a football field—feature changing exhibitions in every imaginable medium, individually and in combination. The performing arts, including theater, music, dance, cabaret, and film, share the exhibit space and also have their own space within the complex. Emerging artists share the spotlight with works by famous artists. The list includes carved marble sculptures by Louise Bourgeois, a quarter-mile-long painting by Robert Rauschenberg, and a production and broadcast studio called "Radio Anderson" to complement Laurie Anderson's galleries of audio and video work.

Opened in 1999, the complex of 26 buildings, most of them built between 1872 and 1900 as textile mills, now holds a quarter-million square feet of gallery space, performance venues, studios, offices, and more. Specially commissioned pieces and touring exhibitions combine with a dynamic performance schedule to ensure that no two visits are ever the same.

In a delightful example of synergy, row houses once occupied by mill workers continue to accommodate people headed for the mill. Right across the street, the Porches Inn at MASS MoCA consists of six 1890s residences painstakingly restored and outfitted in sleek, colorful, contemporary style. The Victorian buildings blend high-tech features with offbeat flea-market touches like vintage decorative plates and lamps and paint-by-numbers pictures in the rooms and suites. Wooden floors and beadboard walls painted bright, warm colors create a homey feel; fine linens and Blu-Ray players boost the pampering quotient. The property's heated outdoor pool is open year-round, which means that autumn guests here can enjoy a dip as red and gold leaves drift down around them.

WHERE: 131 miles northwest of Boston; 87 Marshall St. Tel 413-662-2111; massmoca .org. *When:* daily, July–Aug; closed Tues, early Sept–June. **THE PORCHES INN:** Tel 413-664-0400; porches.com. *Cost:* from $149 (off-peak), from $199 (peak). **BEST TIMES:** July–Aug for the Berkshires' full range of cultural offerings; mid-Sept–mid-Oct for foliage.

MASS MoCA occupies the former headquarters of the Sprague Electric Company.

A Taste of History at America's Symbolic Doorstep

THANKSGIVING AT PLIMOTH PLANTATION

Plymouth, Massachusetts

At Plimoth Plantation, it's always 1624 for ye who enter here. The Pilgrim residents of the village are costumed interpreters working at the living museum, which re-creates New England's first successful European settlement as well as a Native village. History tells us that Thanksgiving dinner has its roots in a meal that approximately 50 Pilgrims shared with "some 90 men" from the native Wampanoag tribe in 1621, one year after the settlers had fled religious persecution in England. It included "wild fowl" (probably ducks and geese in addition to turkey), venison supplied by the Indians, corn, and fresh and dried fruits and vegetables. Every fall Plimoth Plantation re-creates harvest meals that are inspired by this but with concessions to please more modern palates.

The most popular choice, the bounteous America's Thanksgiving Dinner, features classic roast turkey and all the traditional New England trimmings: stuffing, mashed potatoes, butternut squash, creamed onions, cranberry relish, cider cake, gingerbread, and for dessert, Indian pudding, homemade pumpkin pie, and apple pie. Pilgrim role-players and Native interpreters are there to greet those who come from all over the country: Make your reservations early.

The Plimoth Plantation experience is not complete without a detour to the downtown waterfront to visit Plymouth Rock (now behind bars due to souvenir hunters) and *Mayflower II*, a full-scale, 106-foot-long replica that looks startlingly small. The rough voyage of the 102 Pilgrims (with their livestock, worldly goods, and a crew of about 30) took some 66 tempestuous days.

As important to New England history as the Pilgrims themselves is the area's role in the whaling trade. Whaling peaked in the mid-19th century, when the seaport of New Bedford—a 45-minute drive southwest of Plymouth—sent more sailors a-whaling than all other American ports combined. The galleries at the New Bedford Whaling Museum preserve a wide variety of artifacts, including scrimshaw, carved figureheads, marine paintings, navigation instruments, and harpoons, as well as the world's largest ship model, *Lagoda*, a half-scale whale ship built in 1916, and Kobo, the 66-foot skeleton of a juvenile blue whale.

WHERE: 43 miles southeast of Boston. Tel 800-262-9356 or 508-746-1622; plimoth.org. *Cost:* plantation admission $36; Thanksgiving Dinner $95 adults, includes museum admission. *When:* closed Mon after Thanksgiving to late Mar. **NEW BEDFORD WHALING MUSEUM:**

Plimoth Plantation was first built in 1947, with the English village added in 1959 and the Wampanoag Homestead in 1973.

Tel 508-997-0046; whalingmuseum.org. **Best times:** in Plymouth, Thanksgiving Day and the day after for America's Thanksgiving Dinner. In New Bedford, early Jan for marathon reading of *Moby-Dick* at Seaman's Bethel (chapel), across the street from the whaling museum.

Casting a Spell with Art and History

SALEM

Massachusetts

Salem has enough attractions and diversions for two cities—one obsessed with witches and Halloween, the other with history, art, and architecture. The city is best known for the infamous witch trials of 1692, a dark episode that saw innocent people imprisoned and executed after a local doctor made a diagnosis of "bewitchment" when two patients failed to improve. (Salem's name, ironically, is derived from the Hebrew word for peace.) A century later, the newly independent U.S. plunged into "the China trade," as the hugely lucrative commerce with Asia was known, and Salem became the richest city per capita in the country by 1790.

The Peabody Essex Museum captures both eras and much more. The oldest continuously operating museum in the country (since 1799), the Peabody Essex houses close to two million objects from around the world, including one of the best Asian art collections in North America. It also owns Yin Yu Tang, the only complete Qing Dynasty house outside China. Imported from Anhui province, the house is ornately decorated inside and out, and is well worth an in-depth visit.

The rambling House of the Seven Gables, the inspiration and setting for Salem native Nathaniel Hawthorne's novel of the same name, is a wooden waterfront mansion built in 1668 (and extensively restored in 1910) that was home to the author's cousin. A guided tour takes visitors up the secret staircase mentioned in the book and acquaints visitors with Hawthorne's life and work, the most famous of which is *The Scarlet Letter*.

The Salem Witch Museum tells the story of the notorious trials of 1692.

The Salem Witch Museum recounts the witch hysteria that originated in nearby Danvers with a couple of young girls with active imaginations during the long New England winter, and soon escalated into trials of adults accused of witchcraft on the flimsiest of pretexts. In the summer of 1692, a Salem court convicted 27 people, and 20 were put to death (19 of them hanged); countless others were thrown in gaol (jail) indefinitely. The museum puts this cautionary tale in context. Like most other Salem attractions, it keeps extended hours in October, when Salem throws a month-long party to celebrate Halloween.

Hang your hat at the historic Hawthorne Hotel, a 1925 building which is right across the street from the handsome Salem Common and is the classiest choice in town. Guests who check into any of the four guest rooms of the Morning Glory B&B can imagine life in 1808, the year this painstakingly restored home was built. It is within walking distance of everything, with a third-floor rooftop deck with ocean views for R&R at the end of the day.

Historically, Salem was home to the sea captains and wealthy merchants, while neighboring Marblehead, on the waterfront, was a fishing village and port. Today Marblehead, the self-appointed "Yachting Capital of America," is both a prosperous suburb and an antique seaport (and one of many locales that claim to be the birthplace of the American Navy). The tumble of narrow streets of historic Old Town is virtually an open-air museum of architecture; plaques on many houses give the name and occupation of the original owner and the date of construction, often predating the American Revolution. Many of them house artful shops, bakeries, quaint eateries, and specialty stores. The gracious Harbor Light Inn is a romantic choice of 21 rooms (and five off-site apartments suited for families) tastefully furnished in unfussy Federalist style, with the welcome surprise of a quiet garden patio and heated outdoor pool.

WHERE: 17 miles northeast of Boston. *Visitor info:* Tel 877-SALEM-MA or 978-744-3663; salem.org. **PEABODY ESSEX MUSEUM:** Tel 866-745-1876 or 978-745-9500; pem.org. **HOUSE OF THE SEVEN GABLES:** Tel 978-744-0991; 7gables.org. **SALEM WITCH MUSEUM:** Tel 978-744-1692; salemwitchmuseum.com. **HAWTHORNE HOTEL:** Tel 800-729-7829 or 978-744-4080; hawthornehotel.com. *Cost:* from $179 (off-peak), from $239 (peak). **MORNING GLORY B&B:** Tel 978-741-1703; morningglorybb.com. *Cost:* from $160 (off-peak), from $200 (peak). **HARBOR LIGHT INN:** Marblehead. Tel 781-631-2186; harborlight inn.com. *Cost:* from $149 (off-peak), from $199 (peak). **BEST TIMES:** late July for Marblehead Race Week; Oct for Halloween in Salem (hauntedhappenings.org), when the city pulls out all the stops.

Oldies but Goodies

BRIMFIELD AND STURBRIDGE

Massachusetts

The country's largest and best-known antiques market teems with more than 6,000 dealers and some 130,000 visitors, who come to forage through history's marketplace. Materializing in central Massachusetts three times a year and lasting less than a week, the Brimfield Outdoor Antiques Show occupies a 1-mile stretch of Route 20. More than 120 acres are blanketed in tents and thronging with sellers and buyers. Dealers come from all over the country, their choicest pieces in tow, to haggle with the decorators, designers, and merchants who descend in convoys of rental trucks and SUVs, ready for a major haul. They're not fooling around, either, and neither are the legions of amateurs who arrive before sunrise on opening day (Tuesday), loaded for bear.

Each of the show's 22 different fields keeps its own schedule, but dealers are open for business between dawn and dusk throughout the show's six days. By the weekend, latecomers to "the Brimfield fleas" can take advantage of slashed prices on items the sellers don't want to haul back home, so everybody wins. Bring cash or an ATM card, wear your most comfortable shoes, and remember this: Even if it rains, the show always goes on.

It's just 6 miles from here to nearby Sturbridge, where the main attraction is also a remarkable collection of antiques—and the buildings that house them. The largest living history museum in the Northeast, Old Sturbridge Village is a re-creation of a rural New England 1830s community, arranged on 200 pastoral acres. Its 40 period buildings—the earliest dating to 1704—were transported from all over New England beginning in the mid-1940s and reassembled and restored here. The community captures a transitional period in American history—the sawmill uses technology patented in 1830—in an interactive way that's especially appealing to children. Costumed guides bring alive everyday life that evolved around the small school, cider mill, tavern, store, and more, as well as homes furnished in period style, and a working farm and herb garden. The "residents" demonstrate their trades and crafts, from blacksmithing to cooking, and the village, open year-round, celebrates various holidays as well as the changing of seasons, while engaging visitors in the experience of sheep shearing and harvesting.

Authentically dressed performers re-create the 1830s in Old Sturbridge Village.

WHERE: Brimfield is 65 miles west of Boston. **BRIMFIELD OUTDOOR ANTIQUES SHOW:** Tel 413-283-2418; quaboag.com. *When:* 3 shows (Tues–Sun) yearly, early May, early July, early Sept. **OLD STURBRIDGE VILLAGE:** Tel 800-SEE-1830 or 508-347-3362; osv.org. *When:* daily, May–Nov. **WHERE TO STAY:** Freshly renovated Old Sturbridge Inn & Reeder Family Lodge offers 39 rooms on the grounds of OSV. Tel 774-304-1011; ovs.org/inn. *Cost:* from $110 (off-peak), from $150 (peak). **BEST TIMES:** Apr for Barnyard Babies; early July for Independence Day events; Dec for Christmas by Candlelight.

A Road Trip Filled with History and Culture

ALONG THE MOHAWK TRAIL

Williamstown and Deerfield, Massachusetts

Tucked into the rural corner shared by Massachusetts, Vermont, and New York, Williamstown rises to its self-appointed moniker of "The Village Beautiful," home to prestigious Williams College and a lively cultural scene that belies its isolated location. The picturesque town's signature event is the Williamstown Theatre Festival, where big names from Broadway and Hollywood as well as up-and-comers appear in revivals and contemporary works. Add to that workshops, talks, late-night cabaret, and other events, including free shows and children's activities, and you have a jam-packed schedule that includes some 200 performances each summer. Founded in 1954, the festival has launched the careers of such actors as

Christopher Reeve, Kate Hudson, and Gwyneth Paltrow.

Afternoons can be spent at the Clark Art Institute among its works by Renoir, Gauguin, Degas, and Toulouse-Lautrec as well as silver, porcelain, and furniture. The Williams College Museum of Art may pale by comparison, but it's a noteworthy museum with rich collections that span the history of art, from Egyptian times to the present, proudly highlighted with works by Picasso, Warhol, and Hopper.

Williamstown is the gateway to a plethora of outdoor activities. Follow the 8-mile drive almost to the top of 3,491-foot Mount Greylock, the state's highest peak and the anchor of Massachusetts' first state park. The 1896 House Inn & Country Lodgings sits in the mountain's shadow on a 17-acre estate dotted with Adirondack chairs, where guests can sit and take in the view of the lush countryside. The six B&B suites found in the renovated barn are lavishly decorated in the style of six distinct eras, such as the oft-requested Victorian suite. The Orchards Hotel, a contemporary hotel designed to evoke an English country estate, encloses a serene courtyard and gardens, over-looked by the interior rooms; units that face out have views of the mountains.

Williamstown is the western terminus of the Mohawk Trail (Route 2), which extends 63 miles east to the Connecticut River and the town of Millers Falls. Originally an ancient footpath worn by Native Americans, the trail was the main route connecting the British colonists in Boston and the Dutch in Albany. Covered with gravel in 1914, it's the only active motor road in the country that predates World War I and was one of the first scenic roads heralded to promote tourism. The narrow road twists and turns through gorgeous scenery and appealing towns such as North Adams (see p. 63), at other times encouraging motorists to take detours, such as the turnoff that leads to Shelburne Falls. Abuzz with creative energy thanks to a recent influx of crafts-people, galleries, shops, and eateries, this Victorian village is most known for its pedestrian Bridge of Flowers across the Deerfield River. The local women's club maintains the gardens on the bridge, keeping them festooned with plants that bloom from early spring through late fall.

Deerfield, settled in 1669 and perhaps best known as the target of a French and Indian raid in 1704, is a unique destination even in history-soaked Massachusetts. On the mile-long, tree-shaded main street are 12 houses dating from 1730 to 1872 and a contemporary building that comprise an engaging museum complex. Escaping the feel of a theme park, it preserves the town's architectural history as well as the history of American decorative arts—furniture, silver, glass, ceramics, and textiles.

Welcoming guests from its central location since it opened in 1884, the classic Deerfield Inn has a landmark front porch and the obligatory resident ghost. The decor includes an extensive collection of Colonial decorative arts. Beautiful countryside continues south of Deerfield, where the Connecticut River flows into the Pioneer Valley and an area called the Five Colleges for the mostly private institutions of higher learning clustered here: Amherst, Hampshire, Mount Holyoke, Smith, and UMass Amherst. Summers are quiet, but when school is back in session, the area is virtually buzzing with activity, both campus-related and otherwise.

WHERE: 136 miles northwest of Boston. *Williamstown visitor info:* Tel 413-458-9077; williamstownchamber.com. **MOHAWK TRAIL:** Tel 866-743-8127 or 413-743-8127; mohawk trail.com. **WILLIAMSTOWN THEATRE FESTIVAL:** Tel 413-597-3400; wtfestival.org. *When:* July–Aug. **THE CLARK:** Williamstown. Tel 413-458-2303; clarkart.edu. *When:* closed Mon. **WILLIAMS COLLEGE MUSEUM OF ART:** Williamstown. Tel 413-597-2429; wcma .williams.edu. *When:* closed Mon. **MOUNT GREYLOCK:** Lanesborough. Tel 413-499-4262; mass.gov/dcr/parks/mtgreylock. *When:* road open late May–Nov 1. **1896 HOUSE INN & COUNTRY LODGINGS:** Williamstown. Tel

888-999-1896 or 413-458-1896; 1896house
.com. *Cost:* from $84 (off-peak), from $94
(peak). **ORCHARDS HOTEL:** Williamstown. Tel
800-225-1517 or 413-458-9611; orchards
hotel.com. *Cost:* from $109 (off-peak), from
$279 (peak). **HISTORIC DEERFIELD:** Tel 413-
774-5581; historic-deerfield.org. **DEERFIELD**

INN: Deerfield. Tel 800-926-3865 or 413-
774-5587; deerfieldinn.com. *Cost:* from $149
(off-peak), from $261 (peak). **BEST TIMES:**
July–Aug for Williamstown Theatre Festival;
Mar, Sept, and late Nov for Old Deerfield Craft
Fairs (deerfield-craft.org); mid-Sept–mid-Oct
for foliage.

A Delicious Tradition Carries On

MAPLE COUNTRY

Bethlehem and Sugar Hill, New Hampshire

A sure sign of the coming of spring in New England is the ritual of turning
maple sap into syrup. The process, known as sugaring off, or maple
sugaring, involves tapping the tree trunks, collecting the sap, boiling
most of the water out, and (this part is optional)
devouring a stack of pancakes doused in the
thick amber syrup.

Head for The Rocks Estate, a nonprofit
conservation education center in Bethlehem,
to experience sugaring off firsthand. During
the New Hampshire Maple Experience Spring
Tour, visitors take a horse-drawn wagon around
the estate's 1,400 acres, learn to drill and tap a
maple, observe a working sugarhouse (it takes
40 gallons of sap to produce 1 gallon of syrup),
attend a chef demo about cooking with maple,
and finally, sample maple syrup and donuts.
Perfect conditions for good sap production
(cold nights and sunny days) dictate the timing
of the sugaring-off season. Since spring
weather also guarantees abundant mud, pack
boots that can get down and dirty.

Although it doesn't open until March,
Polly's Pancake Parlor in Sugar Hill reputedly
serves the best flapjacks in the country—that's
right, the country. Originally opened in 1938,
Polly's offers plain, whole wheat, cornmeal,
buckwheat, or oatmeal-buttermilk pancakes
that can be customized by adding walnuts,
blueberries, coconut, or chocolate chips—with
plenty of maple syrup to go on top. If you need

to lie down after all that, head to the Sugar Hill
Inn, a cozy 1789 farmhouse retreat with a generous porch and old, tilting pine floors, in
nearby Franconia. The current innkeepers
have created a delightful blend of a rustic hillside setting, top-notch dining, and relaxing spa
offerings. Dinner is served by candlelight and,
in winter, in front of the fireplace.

In December, Bethlehem honors its name
with a holiday festival and craft fair, and The
Rocks offers Christmas tree harvesting.
Families come from great distances to pick up
a tree and enjoy a wagon ride around the property, picture-perfect with its snow-covered
stone walls and old buildings hung with
wreaths.

WHERE: Sugar Hill is 150 miles northwest of Boston. *When:* Maple sugaring is generally 6 weeks in mid-Feb–Apr depending on
the location. *Maple Hotline:* Tel 603-225-
3757; nhmapleproducers.com. **THE ROCKS:**
Bethlehem. Tel 800-639-5373 or 603-444-
6228; therocks.org. **POLLY'S:** Sugar Hill. Tel
603-823-5575; pollyspancakeparlor.com. *Cost:*
breakfast $8. *When:* open March–Nov. **SUGAR
HILL INN:** Franconia. Tel 800-548-4748 or
603-823-5621; sugarhillinn.com. *Cost:* from

$170 (off-peak), from $220 (peak); dinner $68 for 3 courses prix fixe. **Best times:** mid-Feb–Apr for maple sugaring; Mar weekends for New Hampshire Maple Experience Spring Tour at The Rocks; late Nov–Dec for tree harvesting at The Rocks; early Dec for Christmas festival in Bethlehem (christmasin bethlehemnh.com).

Glimpses of a Lost World

CANTERBURY SHAKER VILLAGE

Canterbury, New Hampshire

For two centuries beginning in 1792, the Shakers made their own world in the wilderness of New Hampshire. A religious sect founded in England in 1747, the Shakers created a communal utopian society that espoused equality of the sexes and races, pacifism, and, above all, simple living. Perhaps best known for their furniture, baskets, and boxes, the Shakers were also known for hard work and ingenious inventions (like the clothespin).

The Canterbury community numbered as many as 300 in the 1850s. In 1969, the remaining sisters founded this fascinating 694-acre indoor/outdoor museum, and their spirit survives today. Considered one of the best preserved of the Shaker communities that dotted the East from Maine to Kentucky in the 19th century, the village, a National Historic Landmark, incorporates 25 restored original structures. You can tour the buildings and grounds, participate in agricultural and craft activities and demonstrations, and wander nature trails that are especially beautiful during foliage season. The museum features excellent shopping for organic produce and specialty food items as well as furniture and handicrafts. The village is connected to lovely countryside by way of the 12-mile Canterbury Shaker Village Byway, one of 20 designated scenic roadways in the state.

In 1923, Canterbury took in the last members of the sister community in Enfield, which had been established 50 miles away in 1793. That village is now the Enfield Shaker Museum, which centers on the Great Stone

A straw-broom maker at Shaker Village

Dwelling, a dramatic six-story granite structure built in 1841 where 20 simple rooms now welcome overnight guests. The self-guided walking tour takes in 10 of the 13 surviving buildings on the 21-acre property as well as the gardens, exhibits, and demonstrations of crafts on most Saturdays.

Where: 80 miles northwest of Boston. Tel 603-783-9511; shakers.org. *When:* open May–Oct and first two Sat in Dec. *Byway info:* nh.gov/dot/programs/scbp/tours/canterbury. htm. **Enfield Shaker Museum:** Tel 603-632-4346; shakermuseum.org. *Cost:* rooms from $110. **Best times:** at Canterbury, early May for the Heiter Parade; mid-Sept for Canterbury Artisan Festival; first two Sat in Dec for Christmas at Canterbury.

Roads Taken and Not Taken

THE ROBERT FROST TRAIL

Derry and Franconia, New Hampshire

More than five decades after his death, Robert Frost endures, not just in anthologies and textbooks but in our collective memory. No one who has seen the Kennedy inauguration will forget 88-year-old Frost reciting "The Gift Outright." A four-time Pulitzer Prize winner, Frost was the most popular American poet of the 20th century and was long considered the country's unofficial poet laureate.

As a New Hampshire resident, Frost was part of a rich literary tradition that encompasses such diverse talents as Nathaniel Hawthorne, E. E. Cummings, and Dr. Seuss. Drawing inspiration from his surroundings and giving voice to his sensitivity to the land, the seasons, and the details of everyday life, Frost came into his own as a poet during his time in the Granite State. "It's . . . restful just to think about New Hampshire," he wrote. Visiting his simple homes allows a glimpse of Frost as a young farmer in Derry, and as a newly successful author who treasured his property in Franconia.

The Robert Frost Farm in Derry is an 1885 farmhouse purchased by Frost's grandfather and was home to the poet and his family from 1900 to 1911. The farm had become an auto junkyard by the 1950s, and was bought by the state in 1965.

The renovated farmhouse, with simple furnishings chosen under the supervision of Frost's daughter Lesley, opened to the public in 1975.

The Frost family resided at the 19th-century home now known as the Frost Place, in Franconia, from 1915 to 1920 and summered there through 1938. Sixteen plaques mounted with Frost's poems dot the quarter-mile Poetry Nature Trail, perhaps the most famous being "Stopping by Woods on a Snowy Evening." Even at the height of summer, its hypnotic rhythm and the resonance of its final line ("And miles to go before I sleep") evoke the New Hampshire winter.

WHERE: Derry is 43 miles northwest of Boston. **ROBERT FROST FARM:** Tel 603-432-3091; robertfrostfarm.org. *When:* grounds open year-round; buildings closed early Oct–early May. **FROST PLACE:** Tel 603-823-5510; frostplace.org. *When:* closed mid-Oct–late May. **BEST TIMES:** Sun in July–Aug for the Literary Series at the Robert Frost Farm; early July for Robert Frost Day at Frost Place.

Luxury in the Heart of the Mountain Wilderness

THE GREAT NORTH WOODS

Dixville Notch and Whitefield, New Hampshire

Blankets of trees, picturesque lakes, and meandering streams envelope the northernmost part of New Hampshire—an area owned largely by lumber and paper companies. People are few and far between in these parts, though free-roaming moose are a common sight. As the name suggests, a cruise down the scenic 98-mile Moose Path Trail (Routes 16 and 26) offers excellent opportunities for wildlife sightings. (Use caution as you drive around moose country: A collision between a vehicle and one of the enormous animals can have dire consequences.) The trail runs from Gorham to Pittsburg, taking motorists through Dixville Notch into serene wilderness, where spots for camping, fishing, rafting, and hiking abound.

Nestled in an isolated mountain pass 16 miles south of the Canadian border is The Balsams, a magnificent, old-fashioned resort. The rambling hotel opened in 1886 and expanded over the years to include 11,000 acres, hundreds of guest rooms, and an astounding variety of recreational options. Donald Ross designed the challenging 18-hole Panorama golf course that spreads over Keazer Mountain, while 16 alpine runs and 59 miles of Nordic trails drew winter guests for skiing, snowboarding, and snowshoeing. The legendary resort was sold in 2011, shuttered, and at press time is undergoing a top-to-toe renovation. Stay tuned for a grand reopening in or around 2017.

Hidden in the small town of Whitefield is yet another landmark hotel, the recently renovated 19th-century Mountain View Grand Resort & Spa. It now features a luxurious top-floor spa with the same breathtaking views of the White Mountains that can be enjoyed from

Autumn is on brilliant display at Dixville Notch State Park.

its enormous front porch. Whitefield's other claim to fame is Grandma's Kitchen, a beloved old-timey diner that serves breakfast all day long—homemade pie is always an option.

WHERE: Dixville Notch is 215 miles north of Boston. *Visitor info:* Tel 603-271-2665; visitnh.org. **THE BALSAMS:** Tel 603-255-2500; thebalsamsresort.com. **MOUNTAIN VIEW GRAND:** Tel 855-837-2100; mountainviewgrand.com. *Cost:* from $189 (off-peak), from $279 (peak). **GRANDMA'S KITCHEN:** Tel 603-837-2525. *Cost:* breakfast $8. **BEST TIMES:** late Aug for the North Country Moose Festival in Colebrook and Pittsburg; mid-Sept–late Oct for foliage.

An Iconic College Town

HANOVER

New Hampshire

Imagine an Ivy League school: In your mind's eye, students stroll between stately brick buildings, crossing great lawns of emerald green grass, brilliant autumn leaves, or crystalline snow. That's Dartmouth College. Founded in 1769, the college—actually a university, with several prestigious graduate schools—has educated politicians such as Daniel Webster (class of 1801) and Nelson Rockefeller (a 1930 graduate), and such literary lights as Dr. Seuss (Theodor Geisel, class of 1925) and Robert Frost (see p. 71), who lasted less than a semester with the class of 1896. Dartmouth is the heart of Hanover, and it isn't just an intellectual center; it also dominates the area's cultural and recreational life.

The college's Hopkins Center for the Arts, known as "the Hop," presents performances of every description in a building designed by architect Wallace Harrison, and the Hood Museum of Art, which dates to 1772, is one of the nation's oldest and largest college museums with a collection of over 65,000 objects. For outdoor pursuits, the Dartmouth Outing Club maintains more than 70 miles of the Appalachian Trail, which runs right across the campus, and the best-known event on the college calendar is the world-famous Dartmouth Winter Carnival, an enormous festival (outdoors and in) that originated in 1911 as a weekend of ski races.

Hanover's Main Street is home to Lou's, a diner known since 1947 for bounteous breakfasts, homemade pies, and outstanding hamburgers. For less casual dining, visit the town's primo choice to hang your hat, the Hanover Inn. Originally built in 1769 as a private home, Hanover Inn has maintained traditions while getting major updates that extend to their restaurant Pine, whose menu relies on regional farms and purveyors. There's also a lovely terrace where you can enjoy a drink alfresco.

Nearby, the artists colony of Cornish (long the home of reclusive author J. D. Salinger) is where the famed 19th- and 20th-century sculptor Augustus Saint-Gaudens lived and worked. His property is now a lovely National Historic Site, where you can see over 100 of his artworks in the galleries and on the grounds.

WHERE: 125 miles northwest of Boston. *Visitor info:* Tel 603-643-3115; hanover chamber.org. **DARTMOUTH COLLEGE:** dart mouth.edu. **HOPKINS CENTER:** Tel 603-646-2422; hop.dartmouth.edu. **HOOD MUSEUM:** Tel 603-646-1110; hoodmuseum.dartmouth.edu. **LOU'S:** Tel 603-643-3321; lousrestaurant.net. *Cost:* breakfast $11. **HANOVER INN:** Tel 800-443-7024 or 603-643-4300; hanoverinn.com. *Cost:* from $199 (off-peak), from $299 (peak); dinner at Pine $60. **SAINT-GAUDENS NATIONAL HISTORIC SITE:** Cornish. Tel 603-675-2175; nps.gov/saga. *When:* exhibits closed (grounds open) Nov–late May. **BEST TIMES:** mid-Feb for Dartmouth Winter Carnival; late Sept–late Oct for gorgeous foliage.

An Honest-to-Goodness Winter Wonderland

JACKSON

New Hampshire

The mountain village of Jackson, with its lovely waterfall, swimming hole, and red covered bridge gained fame in the 19th century as a warm-weather destination, at a high enough elevation to provide relief from the summer heat of the urban Northeast, notably Boston. These days, the village is a year-round destination, renowned as home to one of the best cross-country skiing facilities in the country, the Jackson Ski Touring Foundation. The foundation maintains more than 90 miles of winding trails designed to accommodate all ability levels. The trail system connects to the downhill ski areas at Wildcat and Black Mountain, New Hampshire's oldest ski resort. In summer, a gondola takes visitors to Wildcat's summit, where there's a viewing platform and hiking trail. During foliage season, the citizens of Jackson get into the Halloween spirit, arranging scores of "Pumpkin People"—scarecrowlike dolls with pumpkin heads—in spots expected and not, all around town.

The foundation's trail system passes by and links a number of gorgeous lodgings. The Inn at Thorn Hill, designed by the legendary architect Stanford White in 1895 and rebuilt after a fire in 2002, is poised on a hill just outside the village. Guests enjoy elaborate and comfortable rooms (many with fireplaces) and a full-service spa, while the dining room, open to nonguests as well, draws high praise for its locally sourced seafood and award-winning wine list. The Wentworth is the descendant of a sprawling grand hotel that operated from 1869 to the mid-1980s. Saved from demolition and trimmed down to 61 rooms, it retains its Victorian atmosphere, with turrets and an awning-shaded porch replete with rocking chairs. The decor is suitably extravagant—some rooms have four-poster beds, Jacuzzis, and gas fireplaces—and the expansive grounds feature a scenic 18-hole golf course.

WHERE: 147 miles north of Boston. *Visitor info:* Tel 603-383-9356; jacksonnh.com. **JACKSON SKI TOURING FOUNDATION:** Tel 800-927-6697 or 603-383-9355; jacksonxc.org. *When:* mid-Nov–Mar. **WILDCAT MOUNTAIN:** Pinkham Notch. Tel 888-SKI-WILD or 603-466-3326; skiwildcat.com. *Cost:* lift tickets $75. *When:* late Nov–Apr. **BLACK MOUNTAIN SKI AREA:** Tel 800-698-4490 or 603-383-4490; blackmt.com. *Cost:* lift tickets from $55. *When:* mid-Dec–Mar. **INN AT THORN HILL:** Tel 800-289-8990 or 603-383-4242; innatthornhill.com. *Cost:* from $179; dinner $45. **WENTWORTH:** Tel 800-637-0013 or 603-383-9700; thewentworth.com. *Cost:* from $145 (off-peak), from $179 (peak). **BEST TIMES:** late Jan for New Hampshire Snow Sculpting Competition; Jan–Feb for best skiing conditions; early Mar for end-of-season parties at Wildcat Mountain and throughout the area; Oct for Pumpkin People events.

Summer Playgrounds and Golden Ponds

THE LAKES REGION

Lake Winnipesaukee and Environs, New Hampshire

The Lakes Region has the potential to be all things to all people. Rural villages, rustic summer colonies, elaborate "cottages," and family-friendly motels dot the shores of its 273 lakes and ponds, popular spots for swimming, boating, and fishing. At 72 square miles, Lake Winnipesaukee ("The Smile of the Great Spirit") is the largest lake in New Hampshire. Drive around it on the very scenic 97-mile Lakes Region Tour, or explore it by boat. A popular option is the 230-foot *Mount Washington*, which offers cruises from Weirs Beach that will take you by hidden coves and around the many islands that dot these shimmering waters en route to various lakeside towns.

With a local croquet club and distinguished lakeside homes, the elegant village of Wolfeboro on Winnipesaukee's eastern shore claims to be

America's oldest summer resort. Meredith is also a lovely town in a gorgeous spot between Lakes Winnipesaukee and Waukewan. Check into the historic Mill Falls at the Lake. Centered on a renovated textile mill and a former church, the waterside complex offers four inviting inns, lodges, cottages, a spa, and lots of interesting shops and small restaurants.

If Lake Winnipesaukee seems too bustling, consider quiet Squam Lake. (You might recognize it from the film *On Golden Pond*.) It's a Yankee summer colony with an exclusive air, and if you haven't inherited one of the homes on the privately owned lakefront, you can explore the lake by canoe, kayak, or a boat tour. Book a stay at one of the handful of lodgings with lake access. The Manor on Golden Pond, a lakefront property with an English-style manor house built in the early 20th century, offers romantic rooms and cottages with fireplaces and dramatic views. The "dressy casual" dining room is one of the best in the area, and, in wintertime, the manor's cozy nooks invite an afternoon of reading while sipping late-afternoon tea served on bone china.

The Lakes Region isn't all scenery and serenity—any popular summer destination promises a boardwalk, ice-cream parlors, and the chance to pick up a tattoo. Weirs Beach on the western shore of Winnipesaukee fills that role with a public beach, water slides, miniature golf, souvenir shops, and one of the largest video arcades in the country. Gentrified it's not, which is precisely what keeps many families returning for its fun, Coney Island appeal.

Lake Winnipesaukee has a total shoreline of about 288 miles, including islands.

The nearby city of Laconia is famous for its rowdy nine-day motorcycle rally that has its roots in a race that began in 1923. Today it draws hundreds of thousands of bikers and fans from all over the country.

WHERE: Wolfeboro is 103 miles north of Boston. *Visitor info:* Tel 800-605-2537 or 603-286-8008; lakesregion.org. **MOUNT WASHINGTON CRUISES:** Tel 888-843-6686 or 603-366-5531; cruisenh.com. *When:* late May–mid-Oct. **MILL FALLS AT THE LAKE:** Meredith. Tel 800-622-6455 or 603-279-7006; millfalls.com. *Cost:* from $150 (off-peak), from $199 (peak). **MANOR ON GOLDEN POND:** Holderness. Tel 800-545-2141 or 603-968-3348; manorongoldenpond.com. *Cost:* from $230 (off-peak), from $270 (peak). **BEST TIMES:** mid-June for Laconia Motorcycle Week (laconiamcweek.com); late July for Antique & Classic Boat Show in Meredith; late Sept–late Oct for foliage.

A Creative Presence Enhances an Old Mill Town

THE CURRIER MUSEUM

Manchester, New Hampshire

The industrial city of Manchester conceals an unexpected but delightful surprise: one of the best small art museums in New England. The Currier Museum of Art, named for its founders, New Hampshire governor

Moody Currier and his wife, Hannah, not only houses impressive American and European collections, but includes among its holdings an off-site Frank Lloyd Wright house.

The Currier's elegant main building, opened in 1929 and designed to resemble an Italian palazzo, houses a formidable collection that includes works by Degas, Hopper, Monet, O'Keeffe, Picasso, Rothko, and longtime New Hampshire resident Maxfield Parrish.

Founder Moody Currier hoped the museum would "elevate the quality of life in New Hampshire."

The museum's most distinctive holding is the 1950 Zimmerman House, one of five homes in New England designed by Frank Lloyd Wright and the only one open to visitors. The redbrick structure contains original furnishings (Wright designed everything from the couch to the tablecloth and the family mailbox, a miniature model of the house itself) as well as the owners' art collection.

The Currier is one of the institutions helping Manchester to shake off the "struggling industrial city" label. Water-powered mills operated here as long ago as the 18th century, and the city rose to prominence along with the textile industry in the 19th century. Incorporated in 1831, the Amoskeag Manufacturing Company founded Manchester and opened 64 mills, making it the largest cotton-milling business in the world. Job seekers came from Canada, Ireland, and countries all over Europe, creating cultural diversity that endures to this day.

During the 20th century, as mills across New England fell into disuse (Amoskeag closed in 1935), the cities whose economies depended on them met a similar fate. But today Manchester is on the rise again. Many of the brick mill buildings that line the banks of the Merrimack River have been renovated into office, laboratory, and restaurant spaces, and the city takes pride in its high-tech businesses and the ongoing development of the downtown area.

WHERE: 53 miles northwest of Boston. Tel 603-669-6144; currier.org. *Manchester visitor info:* Tel 603-666-6600; manchester-chamber.org. *When:* museum closed Tues; Zimmerman House closed Tues–Wed and early Jan–late Mar. Reservations required.

"The Quiet Corner" Brims with Currier & Ives Moments

THE MONADNOCK REGION

New Hampshire

Picturesque villages and dramatic physical features tied together by country roads make up New Hampshire's southwestern corner. The imposing 3,165-foot Mount Monadnock looms over it all, as America's most climbed mountain. Many of its 35 miles of trails lead to its summit, where a lack of vegetation—due to brush-clearing fires set in the 19th century—means dramatic views in every direction.

Gain access to the mountain through Monadnock State Park, just west of the lovely village of Jaffrey Center.

The memorable town of Walpole is the

home of L. A. Burdick Handmade Chocolates, whose tearoom serves delectable pastries and beverages. The Restaurant at Burdicks next door, known for its simple French cuisine, is reason enough to visit the town. The Bellows Walpole Inn is a picture-perfect Colonial inn built by one of the town's founders in 1752. It's comfortable rooms are decorated with refreshingly modern, soothing pastels and four-poster beds, while the Inn Pub serves "small plates" like grilled hanger steak with pico de gallo, lime sour cream, and tortillas. Leaving Walpole, head north toward Claremont on Route 12, part of the Connecticut River Scenic Byway: one of the most beautiful drives in New England.

One of the best known towns in the Monadnock region is Peterborough, home of the noted artists colony MacDowell since 1907. As a fellow at the multidisciplinary artists colony, playwright Thornton Wilder wrote *Our Town* here, basing Grover's Corners on Peterborough. The intellectual center of the region, the town is home to art galleries and the well-known Toadstool Bookshop. The shop serves as an informal community hangout, as does the character-filled Peterborough Diner, a classic throwback to the '40s, great for a grilled-cheese-with-ham or Yankee pot roast.

The most urban community in the region is Keene, a commercial center for the adjacent areas of Vermont and Massachusetts as well as the Monadnock region, but it's probably better known for repeatedly breaking its own world record for the most lit jack-o'-lanterns in one place—thanks to the efforts of the crowds at the annual Keene Pumpkin Festival. The current record of 30,581 was set in 2013.

WHERE: Peterborough is 73 miles northwest of Boston. *Visitor info:* Tel 603-924-7234; peterboroughchamber.com. **MONADNOCK STATE PARK:** Jaffrey. Tel 603-532-8862; nhstate parks.org. **L. A. BURDICK:** Walpole. Tel 603-756-2882 or 603-756-9058 (restaurant); burdickchocolate.com. *Cost:* lunch $25. **BELLOWS WALPOLE INN:** Tel 603-904-4022 (inn) or 603-756-3320 (restaurant); walpole inn.com. *Cost:* from $155 (off-peak), from $175 (peak); dinner $50. **BYWAY INFO:** fhwa .dot.gov/byways. **TOADSTOOL BOOKSHOP:** Peterborough. Tel 603-924-3543; toadbooks .com. **PETERBOROUGH DINER:** Tel 603-924-6202; peterboroughdiner.com. *Cost:* dinner $15. **BEST TIMES:** July–early Aug for Monadnock Music series at venues throughout the region (monadnockmusic.org); mid-Sept–mid-Oct for foliage; late Oct for Keene Pumpkin Festival.

The jack-o'-lanterns at the Keene Pumpkin Festival range from the classic spooky face to more creative designs.

Athletics and Aesthetics Meet at a Ski Mountain

LAKE SUNAPEE

Newbury, New Hampshire

I n a state that offers every conceivable outdoor distraction, the Lake Sunapee area is one of New Hampshire's prime playgrounds. Located an hour southwest of New Hampshire's Lakes Region (see p. 74), Sunapee boasts top-notch recreation opportunities year-round and is loved by boaters and boarders, skiers and swimmers. It is the centerpiece of Mount Sunapee State Park, a local favorite for fishing, sailing, canoeing, picnicking, biking, and hiking. Tour boats ply the 8-mile-long lake in the summer and fall, and in summer Mount Sunapee State Park Beach is a popular swimming destination.

The Mount Sunapee ski area has more than 1,500 vertical feet of terrain, and the panoramic view from the summit takes in the lake and the White Mountain's Presidential Range (see below). The Sunapee Express chairlift runs up the 2,743-foot peak in the warm weather months allowing visitors to enjoy the view year-round. Take in the vista then ride back down, or head down on foot.

Explore majestic Lake Sunapee by sailboat or canoe.

Below, the 25-mile Lake Sunapee Scenic and Cultural Byway is an alluring alternative to I-89. Beginning just outside Bradford on Route 103, the byway links up with Route 11 on the west shore of the crystalline lake, where you can see the state's only inland lighthouses.

For decades, the League of New Hampshire Craftsmen's Fair, the oldest in the country, has taken place in Newbury at the base of the mountain each August. For nine days, some 30,000 people come to shop for works by more than 350 master craftsmen. The juried fair is one of the largest and most prestigious in New England, and folks come to learn as well as shop. The schedule includes numerous demonstrations and workshops on everything from glassblowing to print-making.

WHERE: 98 miles northwest of Boston. *Visitor info:* Tel 877-526-6575 or 603-526-6575; lakesunapeenh.org. **PARK INFO:** Tel 603-763-5561; nhstateparks.org. **MOUNT SUNAPEE RESORT:** Tel 603-763-3500; mountsunapee .com. *Cost:* lift tickets from $69. *When:* late Nov–mid-Apr. **BYWAY INFO:** nh.gov/dot/programs/ scbp/tours/sunapee.htm. **CRAFTSMEN'S FAIR:** Newbury. Tel 603-224-3375; nhcrafts.org. *When:* 9 days beginning 1st Sat in Aug. **BEST TIMES:** Jan–Mar for best skiing conditions; mid-Sept–Oct for foliage.

The High Point of the Northeast

THE WHITE MOUNTAINS

North Conway and Environs, New Hampshire

The White Mountains inspire superlatives: tallest, coldest, windiest. Their crowning glory—Mount Washington, at 6,288 feet—is the highest in the Northeast and the views from the top are breathtaking: You can see

the Presidential Range of 13 mountains, nine of which are 4,000-footers. (In addition to the scenery, this spot can offer some of the most severe weather conditions in the world.)

Reach the summit by car on an 8-mile private road (the $28 admission includes a "This Car Climbed Mt. Washington" bumper sticker) or by train. In operation since 1869, the Mount

The Crawford Station was finished in 1874 in the valley between Mount Webster and Mount Willard.

Washington Cog Railway (the first such railway in the world) pushes train cars up the mountain at a steep grade. Another option, the Conway Scenic Railroad, operates beautiful restored vintage cars that run in a more horizontal fashion around the Mount Washington Valley and through the dramatic mountain gap, Crawford Notch.

The magnificent Omni Mount Washington Resort at Bretton Woods charms guests with its classic beauty redolent of another era. A sprawling white 1902 building with a cherry red roof anchors the 1,500-acre complex, which offers golf, tennis, and a stunning spa, but is probably best known for its downhill and cross-country skiing.

Hundreds of picturesque driving and hiking routes, including the Appalachian Trail (see p. 332), crisscross the White Mountains. The only interstate highway runs north-south, so driving east-west means using smaller state roads, such as the Kancamagus Highway ("the Kanc"). Part of the 100-mile White Mountains Trail, the 34.5-mile section of Route 112 that connects Lincoln and Conway has been designated a National Scenic Byway. The White Mountain National Forest, with

its waterfalls and backcountry lakes, surrounds the twists and turns of the Kanc, which climbs to 2,855 feet and offers numerous opportunities to pull off the road and take pictures.

The White Mountains also offer plenty of places for swimming and picnicking, among them Conway's Echo Lake State Park; its 700-foot Cathedral Ledge is accessible by road and hiking trail and allows gorgeous views of the Saco River Valley below.

WHERE: 137 miles north of Boston. *Visitor info:* Tel 800-346-3687 or 603-745-8720; visitwhitemountains.com. **MOUNT WASHINGTON AUTO ROAD:** Tel 603-466-3988; mountwashingtonautoroad.com. *When:* closed mid-Oct–mid-May. **COG RAILWAY:** Tel 800-922-8825 or 603-278-5404; thecog.com. *Cost:* $68. *When:* open late Apr–Nov. **CONWAY SCENIC RAILROAD:** Tel 800-232-5251 or 603-356-5251; conwayscenic.com. *When:* open mid-Apr–early Jan. **OMNI MOUNT WASHINGTON RESORT:** Tel 800-843-6664 or 603-278-1000; mtwashington.com. *Cost:* from $269. **BYWAY INFO:** fhwa.dot.gov/byways/states/NH. **WHITE MOUNTAIN NATIONAL FOREST:** Tel 603-536-6100; fs.usda.gov/whitemountain. **ECHO LAKE STATE PARK:** Tel 603-356-2672; nhstateparks.org/visit/state-parks/echo-lake-state-park.aspx. *When:* closed mid-Sept–late May. **BEST TIME:** mid-Sept–mid-Oct for foliage and for drive up Mount Washington.

The Omni Mount Washington Resort was designed by Joseph Stickney in the Spanish Renaissance style.

A Small Coastline with Big Attractions

PORTSMOUTH

New Hampshire

The can't-miss stop on New Hampshire's tiny seacoast is Portsmouth, on the Piscataqua River just inland from the Atlantic. A model New England harbor city, with a wealth of historic architecture, unique shops, cafés, and great restaurants, Portsmouth isn't just a tourist town—it's a working port with a busy naval shipyard just across the river in neighboring Maine.

Portsmouth boasts a number of celebrated dining establishments from the Black Trumpet, a family-owned bistro housed in an historic harborside brick building and a frontrunner in Portsmouth's food movement, to the funkier, more casual Blue Mermaid, a longtime favorite that satisfies the senses with Caribbean accents on the plate and in the dining room. Portsmouth's downtown area is home to one of New England's preeminent gourmet ice-cream purveyors, Annabelle's, whose 40 flavors include Chocolate Chip with Kahlúa and Cashew Caramel Cluster.

A good introduction to town is the Portsmouth Harbour Trail, a self-guided walking tour that takes in more than 70 points of interest, including 18th- and 19th-century buildings and the waterfront, where you'll find beautiful Prescott Park. The first English settlers arrived here in 1623 and named their community "Strawbery Banke," after the fruit that grew along the river. It became Portsmouth in 1653 and quickly grew into a prominent trading and shipbuilding center. To explore Portsmouth's history, head to the Strawbery Banke Museum, an extraordinary outdoor urban history museum encompassing more than 40 historic buildings, some with period furnishings (the oldest structure dates to 1695), as well as a series of restored and re-created gardens.

The best-known boat excursions take in Portsmouth Harbor's lighthouses and the Isles of Shoals, nine islands rich with historic associations. Local legend has it that Blackbeard buried treasure on one of them.

Just east of downtown, on New Castle Island at the mouth of the river, is the classic grand hotel, Wentworth by the Sea, a Marriott Hotel & Spa. A throwback to the era when the well-heeled moved their households to the seashore for the summer, this late 19th-century "wedding cake topper" building gained fame as the location of the 1905 Russo-Japanese War peace talks, but fell into near ruin in the 1980s. Now completely refurbished, the elegant resort offers sweeping water views from private balconies in most of its rooms, plus a swanky spa. During high season, the bistro Latitudes serves both traditional and inventive cuisine with an accent on the sea's bounty.

Boats dock at the waterfront of Portsmouth Harbor.

WHERE: 58 miles north of Boston. *Visitor info:* Tel 603-610-5510; portsmouthchamber .org. **BLACK TRUMPET:** Tel 603-431-0887; blacktrumpetbistro.com. *Cost:* $40. **BLUE MERMAID:** Tel 603-427-2583; bluemermaid .com. *Cost:* dinner $35. **ANNABELLE'S ICE CREAM:** Tel 603-436-3400; annabellesice cream.com. **STRAWBERY BANKE MUSEUM:** Tel 603-433-1100; strawberybanke.org. *When:*

daily, May–Oct. **ISLES OF SHOALS STEAMSHIP CO.:** Tel 800-441-4620 or 603-431-5500; islesofshoals.com. *When:* mid-Apr–Oct. **WENTWORTH BY THE SEA:** New Castle. Tel 866-384-0709 or 603-422-7322; wentworth .com. *Cost:* from $169 (off-peak), from $259 (peak). **BEST TIMES:** June–early Sept for Prescott Park Arts Festival (prescottpark.org); summer and fall for boat cruises.

Eleven Square Miles of Yankee Paradise

BLOCK ISLAND

Rhode Island

I n winter, Block Island is a cold, windswept place, home to only about 1,000 hearty souls who hunker down and enjoy the solitude—which disappears almost entirely in summer, when up to 20,000 tourists arrive each weekend.

But who can blame them for coming? This is, after all, a place the Nature Conservancy has named one of its "Last Great Places," an 11-square-mile gem that manages to contain 365 freshwater ponds, rolling green hills, and dramatic 230-foot bluffs that look as if they belong in Ireland.

Historic sites are conspicuously absent because Block Island has done a fair job of sidestepping history altogether. When Europeans first arrived in the early 17th century, it was inhabited by the Narragansett Indians, whose name for the island was Manisses, or "Island of the Little God." After the first English settlements were established in 1661, not much happened on the island for the next 200 years. Tourists began arriving in the 1850s (leading to a mini-boom in the construction of huge Victorian hotels) and continued through the years of Prohibition, when the island, like the rest of Rhode Island, was a hotbed of rum-running and speakeasies.

Today, despite the island's popularity with sophisticated New Englanders, it still manages to stay free of Martha's Vineyard–style social

The island is named after Dutch explorer Adriaen Block, who charted it in 1614.

fuss. Its residents—and its visitors—tend to be quiet, active, and protective of the natural beauty around them. Today, nearly half of the island is set aside as conserved open space, and 32 miles of hiking trails and gorgeous cliffside paths allow for motor-free sightseeing. The 3-mile Clay Head Trail skirts the island's northwest coast from Clay Head Bluffs to Settler's Rock, a stone memorial commemorating the first settlers from the Massachusetts Bay Colony. Situated on the Atlantic flyway, it's a favorite of bird-watchers during the fall migrations, when flocks representing more than 100 different species pass through. Down at the waterline, the island is ringed by some 17 miles of beach, while the Great Salt Pond on its western side serves as a protected harbor for hundreds of pleasure boats.

Dubbed the "Bermuda of the North" the island still boasts dignified, porch-fringed buildings that hark back to that quieter yesteryear. The Hotel Manisses is a big 1870s charmer that exudes traditional coziness and surprises with its delightful restaurant. The breakfast layout is legendary at the hotel's sister property, the nearby 1661 Inn. An intimate alternative is the 120-year-old Blue Dory Inn. Its 11 rooms are cozy and romantic, and the location, a few steps from the sea at the head of famous Crescent Beach, is perfect.

Where: 12 miles south of mainland Rhode Island. *Visitor info:* Tel 800-383-2474 or 401-466-2474; blockislandinfo.com. **How:** Ferries depart from Newport, Pt. Judith, and Fall River (Block Island Ferry, tel 866-783-7996 or 401-783-7996; blockislandferry.com); New London, CT (Block Island Express, tel 860-444-4624; goblockisland.com); and Montauk, NY (Viking Fleet, tel 631-668-5700; vikingfleet.com). *When:* All but the Pt. Judith car ferry are seasonal. **Hotel Manisses and 1661 Inn:** Tel 800-626-4773 or 401-466-2421; blockislandresorts.com. *Cost:* Manisses from $99 (off-peak), from $299 (peak); 1661 Inn from $275 (off-peak), from $550 (peak); dinner at Manisses $45. *When:* Hotel Manisses, May–mid-Oct; 1661 Inn, year-round. **Blue Dory:** Tel 800-992-7290 or 401-466-5891; blockislandinns.com. *Cost:* from $135 (off-peak), from $195 (peak). **Best times:** before or after the mid-June–early Sept peak period for fewer crowds; Aug for the nicest weather; Sept–Oct for bird-watching.

Jonnycakes for Everybody!

May Breakfasts

Rhode Island

I n England they dance around a pole and in Germany they light bonfires, but only in Rhode Island is the old pagan holiday of May Day celebrated with a good hearty breakfast. The tradition, now known as May Breakfasts, began in the village of Oak Lawn in 1867, dreamed up as a fund-raiser for the Old Quaker Meeting House. The event attracted more than 450 people and raised $155, and a bit of New England folk culture was born. Today close to 30 May Breakfasts are held each year around the state. Most are local events held in churches, firehouses, service clubs, community centers, and grange halls, serving variations on the traditional menu: eggs, bacon, ham, sausage, baked beans, home fries, muffins, maybe an oddity like french toast or quiche, plus a signature Rhode Island favorite known as a jonnycake—a hard cornmeal cake that was originally called a "journeycake" for its usefulness while traveling. Jonnycakes vary by locale: Some places make them thick and others thin; some serve them with syrup, while others use ketchup—a surprising amount of diversity, considering Rhode Island's small size.

The original Oak Lawn event, sponsored by the Oak Lawn Community Baptist Church, is still going strong after 150 years, with volunteer servers dressed in traditional Quaker garb. The menu is the same as it was for the very first breakfast: all-you-can-eat scrambled eggs, ham, corn bread, clam cakes, and homemade apple pie. Like most other May Breakfasts, it's cheap and casual—just show up, pay your $5 to $10, and start eatin'. A few variations on the traditional May Breakfast have popped up in recent years. At the Norman Bird Sanctuary in Middletown, for instance, the annual "Birds and Breakfast Sunday" gets you a guided bird walk to go with your vittles.

WHERE: various locations around Rhode Island. The *Providence Journal* publishes a list in late Apr. **OAK LAWN CHURCH:** Cranston. Tel 401-944-0864. **NORMAN BIRD SANCTUARY:** Middletown. Tel 401-846-2577; normanbird sanctuary.org. *Cost:* $30. *When:* generally the 1st weekend of the month, though some backslide into Apr and others slide into mid-May.

One Man's Cottage, Another Man's Castle

THE NEWPORT MANSIONS

Newport, Rhode Island

I n the 19th century, wealthy, socially prominent families like the Vanderbilts and Astors descended on Newport to escape the cities' stifling summer heat in their seaside "cottages." But their definition of "cottage" was one only an

aristocrat would understand. Built in the days before income taxes, antitrust laws, and other great levelers, each was grander than the next, with an aesthetic Louis XIV would have appreciated. Over time the profusion of these families turned Newport into America's regatta capital (see p. 88) and guaranteed a steady flow of "lifestyles of the rich and famous" tourism for decades to come. Today about 11 of the old "cottages" are open to the public, including The Breakers, a 70-room Italian

Renaissance–style palazzo built for Cornelius Vanderbilt II. Completely over-the-top in design and proportion, it has 23 bedrooms, a gilded 2,400-square-foot dining room lit by 12-foot chandeliers, and a great hall designed to resemble an open-air Italian courtyard, with a 45-foot sky blue ceiling. Begun in the fall of 1893 and completed in the summer of 1895, its construction took the work of some 2,000 workers and craftsmen, including a platoon of master artisans brought in from Europe.

Though none of the other Newport mansions is as grand as The Breakers, several come close. Marble House, built between 1888 and 1892 for Cornelius Vanderbilt's younger brother, William, was the precursor of all the other mansions, incorporating $7 million worth of marble into a design inspired by Marie Antoinette's Petit Trianon at Versailles. Rosecliff is another favorite, a 40-room manse built in 1902 by architect Stanford White after the Grand Trianon. The Elms, a stately home built for a Pennsylvania coal baron in 1901, was designed after the Château d'Asnières, a mid-18th-century home outside Paris.

The Marble House is one of the "cottages" owned by the Preservation Society, all located on 88 acres of gardens and parks.

Newport's 8 square miles are chockablock with other examples of impressive 18th- and early 19th-century architecture, including a collection of 81 houses acquired by the Newport Restoration Foundation, created by tobacco heiress Doris Duke in 1968. All are now owned and maintained by the foundation and marked with signs reading "NRF." Most are privately rented. Duke's own mansion, Rough Point, is open for tours. (For a taste of mansion living on your own, see below.)

Where: 39 miles south of Providence. *Visitor info:* Tel 800-326-6030 or 401-845-9123; discovernewport.org. **Preservation Society:** Tel 401-847-1000; newportmansions.org. *When:* The Breakers, Marble House, and The Elms are open daily; most others closed Jan–Mar. **Newport Restoration Foundation:** Tel 401-849-7300; newportrestoration.org. *When:* Rough Point tours mid-Apr–early Nov. **Best times:** summer into fall to coincide with Newport's various regattas; Dec when The Breakers, The Elms, and Marble House are decked out for Christmas and some historic inns and B&Bs open their doors for tours (christmasinnewport.org).

Rooms with a View

Cliff Walk and the High Life

Newport, Rhode Island

A bastion of American robber-baron aristocracy in the 19th century, Newport managed to maintain its Victorian elegance—as well as its mansions and yachts—through a turbulent 20th century, and is still looking fine. Cliff Walk, a 3.5-mile National Recreation Trail, hugs Newport's wild Atlantic shoreline, offering good views of many of its "cottages" (see previous entry) and even better views of its gorgeous coast.

A number of hotels and inns around town offer ample luxury, but if you've come looking for a stay right out of the Gilded Age, The Chanler at Cliff Walk is your best bet. Built in 1873 as the summer home of Congressman John Winthrop Chanler and his wife, Margaret Astor Ward, the house was the first mansion built along the Cliff Walk trail and is today the only hotel in town that overlooks the Atlantic. Originally named Cliff Lawn, the house went through several incarnations in its first 126 years—girls' school, apartment building for naval officers, historical museum, and hotel—but in 2000 it was purchased by Detroit businessman John Shufelt, who sank a fortune into a three-year renovation that restored its original beauty. Today visitors have their pick of 20 rooms, including 12 in the main French Empire mansion and another 8 with private entrances, including six villas with ocean or garden views. All are appointed with antiques representing different historical periods,

The Chanler at Cliff Walk is one of the few mansions of America's Gilded Age to be converted into a luxury hotel.

including Colonial, Greek Revival, and Tudor. In some cases, the furnishings are originals dating to the congressman's time. Seventeen of the guest rooms offer ocean views, including 12 that come with private decks. The hotel's restaurant, Spiced Pear, is overseen by well-regarded executive chef Thomas Duffy. While the dining room impresses with its subdued, perfectly balanced elegance (and the terrace with its fine views), Duffy's cuisine impresses with its delicacy, letting the flavors of fine seasonal ingredients speak for themselves.

About 5 miles to the west, the Castle Hill Inn offers a cozier, more secluded take on Newport living, its sprawling Victorian mansion sitting on a private 40-acre peninsula at the mouth of Narragansett Bay. The house was built in 1875 as a summer home for scientist and explorer Alexander Agassiz, and today visitors have a choice of 33 rooms and suites, including 7 in the main mansion and others in the nearby beach houses, beach cottages, and harbor houses, each with a semiprivate porch or deck and private beach access. Expect beautifully appointed rooms (especially the main inn's Turret Suite, a bi-level beauty with 360-degree views of the bay), gorgeous views from almost everywhere, and four woody, water-view dining rooms serving exceptional seafood dinners and a legendary brunch.

WHERE: 39 miles south of Providence. *Visitor info:* Tel 800-326-6030 or 401-845-9123; discovernewport.org. **CLIFF WALK:** cliffwalk.com. **THE CHANLER:** Tel 401-847-1300; thechanler.com. *Cost:* from $269 (off-peak), from $649 (peak); dinner at Spiced Pear $60. **CASTLE HILL INN:** Tel 888-466-1355 or 401-849-3800; castlehillinn.com. *Cost:* rooms from $399 (off-peak), from $899 (peak). **BEST TIMES:** June or July for the regattas; late July for the Newport Jazz Festival (newportjazzfest.org).

Playing in the Grass, Newport Style

INTERNATIONAL TENNIS HALL OF FAME

Newport, Rhode Island

Tennis in its modern form is a fairly young sport, having developed from handball in the 12th century into a sort of racquetball, and finally into an early version of its current self in 1874. Then things progressed quickly:

The first Wimbledon Championship was held in England in 1877 as a fund-raiser for the All England Croquet and Lawn Tennis Club. Four years later, the first U.S. National Lawn Tennis Championships—which later evolved into the U.S. Open—were played in Newport, at a sporting complex built just one year earlier and known as the Newport Casino. Designed by the great New York architectural firm of McKim, Mead & White, the Casino offered equestrian shows, lawn bowling, archery, tea parties, concerts, dances, and gentlemen's lodging—but it was tennis that ensured its lasting fame.

The Lawn Tennis Championships continued to be held at the Casino until 1915, when the honor was finally ceded to Forest Hills, New York. But though the championship games left, the Newport Casino is still there, its lavish, beautifully preserved complex, full of turrets and covered porches, retaining the magnificent aura of the Gilded Age. It is considered one of the world's finest examples of the Victorian shingle style. Now as then, though, it's the tennis—played on the original grass courts—that's paramount.

Today its own championship is the only Association of Tennis Professionals (ATP) event still played on grass courts in North America and it's the site of the International Tennis Hall of Fame. The newly renovated museum recounts the history of tennis, has interactive exhibits (including a Roger Federer hologram), and displays 1,900 objects from its collection of 25,000, including historic racquets and balls, period tennis clothing, trophies, photos, videos, memorabilia, and other artifacts, plus an extensive tennis library.

WHERE: 39 miles south of Providence; 194 Bellevue Ave. Tel 800-457-1144 or 401-849-3990; tennisfame.com. *Cost:* play on grass courts from $120 per hour for 2 players. *When:* museum daily; outdoor courts open late May–early Sept (indoor courts open year-round). **BEST TIMES:** summer for public grass court play; mid-July for the Hall of Fame Tennis Championships; late July–early Aug, when the Casino hosts the opening night of the Newport Jazz Festival (see below).

The Granddaddy of Them All

THE NEWPORT JAZZ FESTIVAL

Newport, Rhode Island

In the early 1950s, Elaine Lorillard, who found Newport "terribly boring in the summer," thought a jazz festival might liven things up. She brought her husband, tobacco heir Louis Lorillard, to a Boston jazz club called Storyville

to meet young club owner and pianist George Wein. Louis agreed to his wife's idea, and a year later, with Wein providing the organizational skills and the Lorillards providing a line of credit, the Newport Jazz Festival was born. That first year in 1954, Dizzy Gillespie, Billie Holiday, Ella Fitzgerald, Sarah Vaughan, and Dave Brubeck performed, among others. Miles Davis appeared the following year, turning in a performance that launched one of the most legendary periods of his career. Duke Ellington did the same in 1956, finishing his set with a medley that brought down the house and set hundreds of audience members dancing and leaping onto their chairs.

Newport changed the standard method of jazz presentation, giving jazzmen the opportunity to play before huge, appreciative crowds. In 1969 the festival began booking rock and R&B acts, but rowdy crowds in 1971 changed its character so much that Wein pulled the

Past performers have included Wynton Marsalis.

plug. For the next ten years he took his festival to New York City, Saratoga Springs, and Japan, but in 1981 returned it to Newport with a renewed focus on the music that had made it famous. Today it still attracts the biggest names in jazz each August—McCoy Tyner, Joe Lovano, Chick Corea, Carla Bley, Bill Frisell, and Wynton Marsalis among them.

Other festivals round out Newport's summer calendar. The Newport Folk Festival, another Wein brainchild, was first presented in 1959 and has seen many historic performances, including Bob Dylan's notorious "Dylan Goes Electric" set in 1965. Held over three days in late July, the Folk Festival attracts the likes of Nanci Griffith, Arlo Guthrie, Elvis Costello, Emmylou Harris, and Mavis Staples. The Newport Music Festival, which takes place over 17 days in July, presents more than 60 classical recitals and chamber music programs in Newport's spectacular 19th-century "cottages" (see p. 83), bringing those days of the Gilded Age back to life.

WHERE: 39 miles south of Providence. *Visitor info:* Tel 800-326-6030 or 401-845-9123; discovernewport.org. **NEWPORT JAZZ FESTIVAL:** Tel 401-848-5055; newportjazzfest .org. *Cost:* tickets from $45. *When:* late July–early Aug. **NEWPORT FOLK FESTIVAL:** 401-848-5055; newportfolk.org. *Cost:* tickets from $64. *When:* late July. **NEWPORT MUSIC FESTIVAL:** Tel 401-846-1133 or 401-849-0700 (box office); newportmusic.org. *When:* 17 days starting in mid-July. *Cost:* from $20.

Lighthouse Keepers Wanted: Apply Within

THE ROSE ISLAND LIGHTHOUSE

Newport, Rhode Island

For seekers of solitude, former literature majors, and other romantics, the idea of a lighthouse keeper's job may be a perennial dream. The trouble is, nobody's hiring: Since 1990, all lighthouses in the United States have been fully automated. But what if there was a spare, part-time lighthouse job available? That's sort of the situation at the Rose Island Lighthouse, a two-story, mansard-roofed cottage and light tower sitting atop the bastion of an 18th-century fort in Narragansett Bay, about a mile west of Newport. First lit in 1870, the light aided shipping for 101 years before it was decommissioned and replaced on navigational charts by the newly built Newport Bridge. For 13 years it was at the mercy of vandals and the elements, but in 1984 a group of locals stepped in, formed the Rose Island Lighthouse Foundation, and undertook eight years of intensive restoration. Today it's a beautiful sight, its interior restored to its 1912 appearance and its downstairs rooms functioning as a museum. Its light is also fully functional and listed on charts as a private aid to navigation—and that's where you come in.

Since its 1993 reopening, Rose Island Lighthouse has been maintained by private citizens who pay to volunteer for a week at a time, living in the modern second-floor keeper's quarters and attending to a variety of tasks, which vary depending on the level of keepership you've signed up for. Those in the "Keeper Vacation Week" program devote one to two hours a day to chores, responsibilities, and maintenance, and have the rest of their time free to relax, explore the 18-acre island (except from March to August, during bird nesting season when much of the island is off-limits), and enjoy the 360-degree views of Narragansett Bay. Participants in the "Full-Time Keeper Week" put in six to eight hours for five days, and though you don't have to man the light itself (it's automated), you do have to raise and lower the flag, manage the light's weather station, keep up its wind-powered electric system and rainwater-gathering system, greet visitors and overnighters, and collect money at the end of the day. (There's a bonus for full-timers, though—your stay is tax-deductible.) The keeper's quarters sleeps four (two in the bedroom, two on the living room sofa bed) and is outfitted with linens and cooking gear. Those who don't want to put in quite so much effort can overnight in one of the restored museum bedrooms downstairs, which operate on the same "no services" arrangement as the keeper's quarters: You do your own cooking, make your own bed, and have your room in order by 10 A.M., when the museum reopens.

WHERE: on Narragansett Bay, about a mile west of Newport. Tel 401-847-4242;

roseislandlighthouse.org. **HOW:** In summer, the Jamestown Ferry (tel 401-423-9900; jamestownnewportferry.com) has service to Rose Island from Jamestown or Newport. The rest of the year the foundation ferries in weekly keepers and overnight guests aboard its 32-foot lobster boat. *Cost:* overnight, in the first-floor Museum Room from $75 (off-peak), from $185 (peak); overnights as "relief keepers" on second floor from $1,284 per week (off-peak), from $2,100 (peak). **BEST TIMES:** Oct–Apr for seal-watching; July 4th for fireworks; before Memorial Day and after Labor Day to avoid day-trippers.

Messing About in Boats

THE SUMMER REGATTAS

Newport, Rhode Island

They don't call Newport the City by the Sea for nothing. Site of the U.S. Naval Academy during the Civil War and still home to the U.S. Naval War College, this small city on the western shore of Aquidneck Island is also

the spiritual and physical center of the U.S. sailing universe, long associated with the prestigious America's Cup race which was held here between 1930–1983. Begun in 1851, the cup was held by New York Yacht Club sailors (who maintain their summer base in Newport), from 1857 until 1983, when the

You can almost always find a race on Newport's waters during the warm weather months.

sloop *Australia II* overturned their winning streak, taking away both the cup and the contest. Despite the fact that U.S. boats won the cup again in three subsequent years, the race has never returned to Newport's waters—at least not yet.

In the meantime, Newport hosts more than 40 other races each summer and fall, some sailing entirely within local waters, others having their start or finish here. Held in early June, in odd-numbered years, the Annapolis-to-Newport race is one of the most historic on the East Coast, pitting crews against both the shallows and currents of Chesapeake Bay and the open waters of the Atlantic. At midmonth, the New York Yacht Club still holds its annual regatta here, the longest-running event of its kind in the United States. June also sees the start of the Newport-to-Bermuda race, one of the pinnacles of world ocean racing. Held in even-numbered years, it celebrated its 110th birthday in 2016.

All these events have a certain patina of wealth and prestige about them, but in mid-July the Newport Regatta adds a mighty breath of democracy to Newport's sailing scene. These races are open to anyone—professional or amateur—whose boat qualifies in one of its 16 design classes. In September the Newport International Boat Show brings in more than 600 sailboats and powerboats for one of the country's largest in-water shows, covering some 14 acres along America's Cup Avenue, while the Museum of Yachting's annual Classic Yacht Regatta offers racing for vintage yachts, modern classics, and "good old boats."

To learn something about how those classic craft remain seaworthy, drop by the International Yacht Restoration School (IYRS) on the harbor front, where you can watch students restore classic boats and view gallery exhibits and classic yachts afloat and ashore.

Among the school's ongoing long-term projects is the restoration of the grand Victorian yacht *Coronet*, built in 1885 for New York Yacht Club member Rufus T. Bush.

When it's time to eat, boat folks have long gravitated to the Black Pearl, right on the city's waterfront. A local institution since 1967, it's known for its signature clam chowder. Just a few blocks away, the handsome White Horse Tavern has been in business on and off since 1673; it has a welcoming ambience, with creaky wood floors, huge fireplaces, a classic menu wonderfully prepared, and a perfect wine list to match.

WHERE: 39 miles south of Providence. *Visitor info:* Tel 800-326-6030 or 401-845-9123; discovernewport.org. *Sailing info:* Tel 401-846-1983; sailnewport.org. **YACHT RESTORATION SCHOOL:** Tel 401-848-5777; iyrs.edu. **BLACK PEARL:** Tel 401-846-5264; blackpearlnewport.com. *Cost:* dinner $40. **WHITE HORSE:** Tel 401-849-3600; whitehorsenewport.com. *Cost:* dinner $50.

Fresh from the Oven

AL FORNO

Providence, Rhode Island

In 1980, George Germon and his future wife Johanne Killeen (both alumni of the Rhode Island School of Design) opened their first tiny restaurant on Providence's Steeple Street, serving breakfast and lunch, and naming it

Al Forno in honor of the huge oven that was initially their main piece of cooking equipment. A year after opening they installed a wood-fired grill that has since become their signature. As culinary pioneers, they expanded to dinner and, eventually, to a new two-story home along the Providence River. By 1994, they'd built a global reputation, with food critic Patricia Wells proclaiming Al Forno the world's number-one casual restaurant.

The starting point was Germon and Killeen's love of northern Italian cooking,

seasoned with the truth that Italian cuisine, at its core, is not a national cuisine at all but a collection of regional styles, all influenced by whatever fresh ingredients are available. At Al Forno, southern France makes its influence felt, along with dashes of Portugal, courtesy of Providence's long-established Portuguese community. Signature dishes include the famous grilled pizzas, with thin, oblong, faintly sweet crusts, topped with just the right amount of tomatoes, cheese, herbs, and other ingredients. Another staple, Dirty Steak, is cooked right on the wood embers, while Littleneck Clams Al Forno are steamed open in the oven in a spicy, pepper-flecked tomato broth. The presentation is more straightforward than artsy: food as food, rather than as architecture. The menu changes regularly to reflect the availability of seasonal ingredients.

Germon, a regional food icon, died in 2015 but Killeen is carrying the restaurant forward. For the optimal dining experience, the watchword is "early": Since the restaurant takes no reservations (except for parties of six or more), expect to wait a while in the always lively bar.

WHERE: 577 S. Main St. Tel 401-273-9760; alforno.com. *Cost:* dinner from $60. **BEST TIMES:** warm weather for dining on the

brick patio; cold weather, when the fireplaces are lit.

Al forno means "from the oven" in Italian.

An Unlikely Start to Art

RISD MUSEUM OF ART

Providence, Rhode Island

In 1876, the Rhode Island Women's Centennial Commission was formed to represent their state at that year's Philadelphia Exposition, the country's first world's fair. Like all early expositions, it was a mind-boggling display,

highlighting advances in science, industry, agriculture, horticulture, manufacturing, and the arts at a time when the pace of change was hot and heavy. Fired up by what she'd seen, commission member Helen Adelia Rowe Metcalf returned to Rhode Island with an idea: Why not use the $1,675 left over from the group's exhibit to found a school of art and design? Her idea took hold, and in 1877 the group incorporated the Rhode Island School of Design and a small but impressive museum. Today, after more than a century of bequests, acquisitions, and expansion, it ranks as one of the finest college art museums in the country.

Known locally as the RISD (pronounced Riz-dee) Museum, the collection stands out both for its breadth and for its democratic

approach to balancing the so-called ornamental and useful arts, the latter including textile design. In all, more than 90,000 works are displayed in 49 intimate galleries, running the gamut from ancient to modern and decorative to practical: Greek coins and vases, Egyptian burial objects, Etruscan bronzes, Paul Revere silver, Gilbert Stuart portraits, modern Danish coffee services, Calder mobiles, Cy Twombly oils, and video works by Bruce Nauman. Decorative arts from the 18th and 19th centuries and American fine arts and furniture are displayed in the galleries of Pendleton House, which opened in 1906 as the first American wing in any museum, anywhere.

WHERE: 224 Benefit St. Tel 401-454-6500; risdmuseum.org. *When:* closed Monday.

Darkness Visible

WATERFIRE

Providence, Rhode Island

Sometimes the simplest things can be the most moving—a tossed pebble that transforms a lake into kinetic sculpture, birdsong in an otherwise silent evening. That's the essence of *WaterFire*, Barnaby Evans's long-running art installation that traces a path of nighttime firelight along Providence's three downtown rivers. First erected in 1994 and now presented about 10–15 times annually, the work incorporates over 80 floating wood-fire braziers, illuminating two-thirds of a mile of downtown walkways and parks and using a simple, repeated device to provoke and frame the mind's associations, changing the way we look at our surroundings. On the one hand, the firelight calls to mind certain historical and nostalgic associations—Greek myth, warm fireplaces, and the city as it looked before electricity. On the other, the work's creation of an unnatural harmony between two opposing elements provides a psychic nudge that can widen our perceptions.

For the optimal experience, spend some time walking its full length (seeing it by boat is a recommended option) and keeping all your senses attuned. Watch the black-clad volunteers in the fire-tender boats keeping the braziers lit, like a silent Greek chorus. Listen to the music, which incorporates spiritually rich traditions from around the world. Breathe in the wood smoke, watch the shadows, and gaze into the faces of other people strolling around you who have been drawn out into the night to be part of this new kind of performance art.

WHERE: downtown, between Providence Place and the Crawford Street Bridge. Tel 401-273-1155; waterfire.org. *When:* 10–15 times between early May and early Nov, from sundown till past midnight. Partial lightings at Christmastime.

WaterFire *blazes on the Woonasquatucket, Moshassuck, and Providence rivers.*

Raising the Luxury Inn to an Art Form

TWIN FARMS

Barnard, Vermont

Secluded amid 300 stunning acres of woodlands and expansive meadows, this former Colonial-era farmhouse—a wedding gift from Nobel Prize–winning novelist Sinclair Lewis in 1928—is one of America's most luxurious and enchanting resort inns. A masterpiece by one of the nineties' most famous interior decorators, Jed Johnson, Twin Farms' magically exuberant design encompasses a $5 million art collection that includes paintings by Roy Lichtenstein and Milton Avery. All 20 accommodations (rooms, suites, and 10 secluded cottages) blend the impeccable with the magical—and with rates (up to $2,750 a night for

The Aviary, a 1,100-square-foot bilevel cottage with floor-to-ceiling windows, is a minimalist masterpiece.

the most expensive cottage) that might equal the GNP of some small countries.

Twin Farms gets its name from Sinclair Lewis, author of *Babbitt* (1922) and *Elmer Gantry* (1927). Lewis and his wife, journalist Dorothy Thompson, loved the property for its "sweeping lawns, run-down orchards and delicious air." When the two divorced in 1942 (amicably, it seems), they simply moved into separate farmhouses on the grounds, hence the name.

In the early 1970s, the Twigg-Smith family, owners of the Contemporary Museum in Honolulu, bought the main house as a vacation getaway, and when their time spent there began to dwindle, they created instead an exclusive and luxurious country estate. Dine on Maine lobster with truffled fava bean puree in spring; grilled Angus tenderloin over a bacon cheddar potato tart with braised wild morels in fall; and for dessert on a snowy night, chocolate caramel pannacotta with a white chocolate–sambuca profiterole. The service is clairvoyant, the meals endlessly inventive, and the 26,000-bottle wine cellar tantalizing in its breadth and depth.

WHERE: 8 miles north of Woodstock. Tel 802-234-9999; twinfarms.com. *Cost:* from $1,450, includes meals. **BEST TIME:** late Sept–early Oct for foliage.

A Rural State's Cosmopolitan City

BURLINGTON

Vermont

Known for its left-of-center politics, and famous for its battle to keep Wal-Mart away, Burlington is Vermont's biggest city, which is to say, not very big—just 42,000 people. Many are former students who never left this cosmopolitan college town, with its lively music and food scenes and splendid location on the shores of Lake Champlain, backed by the majestic Adirondacks to the west.

Burlington was first settled by independent-minded folks like Ethan Allen and his brother, Ira, of Green Mountain Boys fame. It rose to prominence as a major port after the opening of the Lake Champlain Canal in 1823 and by the late 1800s it had become a major timber port.

Lake Champlain provides an endless source of recreation and fun. Sailors, swimmers, rowers, and paddlers all find their favorite spots on its many calm bays and beaches. The Community Sailing Center offers rentals, lessons, and access to a fleet of sailboats, dinghies, and other craft. Or take the easy way out and climb aboard *The Northern Lights* for a 90-minute narrated cruise that relates tales of the lake's rich history, like its crucial role in the Revolutionary War. (The Champlain Islands, a picturesque archipelago that includes Isle LaMotte, are so far north they're easier to reach by car.)

Windsurfers prize the lake for its gusty location, while bikers follow the paved Burlington Bike Path, 12 pictorial miles of converted rail bed along the shoreline, which connects with the larger Champlain Bikeway, a 363-mile route that circumnavigates the lake.

Lake Champlain is also the scenic backdrop for the four-block pedestrian Church Street Marketplace, a vibrant mix of entertainment, restaurants, and shops that includes Ben & Jerry's, the uber-famous ice-cream company that got its start in Burlington in 1978. (The main factory in Waterbury, 27 miles from Burlington, is a point of pilgrimage for some.) Food fans also know not to miss Al's French Frys, a venerated burger-and-fries experience amid red booths and black-and-white tiles, in nearby South Burlington.

Some 23 idyllic miles from Burlington, Basin Harbor Club in Vergennes is a Vermont tradition begun in 1886, when Ardelia Beach opened the lakeside property. Still in the Beach family, the 700-acre resort has 43 rooms in three historic buildings, as well as 74 white clapboard summer cottages tucked along the shores. Attractions at this slow-paced, family-friendly establishment include golf and tennis, but more than anything else, all manner of sports on Champlain's inviting waters.

WHERE: 216 miles northwest of Boston. *Visitor info:* Tel 877-686-5253 or 802-863-3489; vermont.org. **COMMUNITY SAILING CENTER:** Tel 802-864-2499; communitysailingcenter.org. **LAKE CHAMPLAIN CRUISES:** Tel 802-864-9669; lakechamplaincruises.com. *When:* mid-June–mid-Oct. **LOCAL MOTION TRAILSIDE CENTER:** Tel 802-652-2453; localmotion.org. **CHURCH STREET MARKETPLACE:** Tel 802-863-1648; churchstmarketplace.com. **BEN & JERRY'S FACTORY TOUR:** North Waterbury. Tel 866-BJTOURS; benjerry.com. **AL'S FRENCH FRYS:** South Burlington. Tel 802-862-9203; alsfrenchfrys.com. *Cost:* quart of French Frys $5. **BASIN HARBOR CLUB:** Vergennes. Tel 802-475-2311 or 800-622-4000; basinharbor.com. *Cost:* from $230 (off-peak), from $290 (peak). **WHERE TO STAY:** The Essex Resort & Spa, with the well-known restaurant Junction and an 18-hole golf course. Tel 800-727-4295 or 802-878-1100; essexresortspa.com. *Cost:* from $139 (off-peak), from $349 (peak). **BEST TIMES:** June for Burlington Jazz Festival; July for Vermont Brewers Festival (vtbrewfest.com); summer for sailing, hiking, cycling; Sept–Oct for foliage and apples.

The Lake Champlain waterfront is the ideal spot for an evening stroll.

Cross-Country Thrills

THE CATAMOUNT TRAIL

From Harriman Station to North Troy, Vermont

A t 300 miles long, the Catamount Trail is the longest cross-country ski trail in the U.S., connecting wild terrain and finely groomed trails with many of Vermont's finest country inns located along its length. Named for the

eastern mountain lion, the Catamount Trail was conceived in 1984 by three geography students at the University of Vermont who researched the route for a thesis project, obtained access privileges from landowners, and skied every last mile of the route—the only one to run from one end of a state to the other. The route offers a tremendous range of experiences, from easy, well-groomed trails to breaking trail in two feet of newly fallen snow. (Snowshoers are allowed on its whole length

Some of the backcountry trails are old logging roads.

and snowmobilers on 70 miles of it.) In the remote backcountry, part of its magic is that you never know quite what conditions you'll find or who—if anyone—has been there before you.

Interconnecting with major Nordic ski centers at Okemo (see p. 99), Stowe (see p. 107), and Stratton (see p. 108), the Catamount Trail offers experienced skiers a chance to travel from inn to inn, spending the night in well-fed comfort before moving on. One stop is Blueberry Hill Inn in Goshen, a restored 1813 hostelry originally built by loggers and perched at the edge of the 22,000-acre Moosalamoo region of the Green Mountain National Forest. The 12-room inn has 45 miles of trails that feed into the Catamount from its doorstep, including one at an altitude of 3,000 feet. Tony Clark, who bought the inn in 1968, developed the Nordic Ski Center just across the road, making this a major destination for skiers of any skill level. To work out the kinks at the end of the day, try out the bracing real-deal Nordic experience: a plunge in the inn's pond before a race back to the heated sauna.

WHERE: from Readsboro (at the Massachusetts border, 180 miles south of Burlington), to North Troy (at the Canadian border). Tel 802-864-5794; catamounttrail .org. **BLUEBERRY HILL INN AND NORDIC SKI CENTER:** Goshen. Tel 802-247-6735; blue berryhillinn.com. *Cost:* from $175 (off-peak), from $269 (peak). *When:* open weekends only in Apr and Nov. **BEST TIMES:** Jan–Mar.

Where The Jungle Book *Was Born*

NAULAKHA

Dummerston, Vermont

One of Vermont's greatest surprises is the perfectly preserved home (right down to the golf clubs left behind) of Rudyard Kipling, the British author and poet who became a literary sensation by lifting his late-Victorian readers out of their tufted armchairs and dropping them into exotic, richly imagined landscapes. He is best known for *The Jungle Book*, which was inspired by his upbringing in India but was actually written in Vermont, where he lived between 1892 and 1896 with Caroline Balestier. Rudyard married Caroline at age 26 after his best friend, her brother Wolcott, died suddenly of typhoid fever.

Kipling's home, called Naulakha, a Hindu word literally meaning "900,000 rupees" but loosely translated as "jewel beyond price," was restored in the 1990s by Landmark Trust USA, which rescues historic properties in distress. Although not open for tours, it can be rented as an overnight literary getaway. Imagine playing on Kipling's own billiards table, or enjoying the same window-framed views he described as "lavish and wide."

The green-shingled farmhouse surrounded by 12 acres was named for a novel Kipling and Wolcott Balestier had written together. Gleaming with polished woods, it is simply but pleasantly furnished with Kipling's own wicker furniture, iron bedsteads, and Oriental rugs. "Three miles from anywhere and wonderfully self-contained," as Kipling wrote, the house—long and narrow and intended to resemble a ship—appears to be "riding on its hillside like a little boat on the flank of a far wave."

Both Jungle Books were written here as was *Captains Courageous*, but the family soon returned to England when Kipling's relationship with Caroline's other brother, a loud-mouthed drinker, went sour.

Kipling said that Naulakha brought him "sunshine and a mind at ease."

Kipling remarked of nearby Brattleboro, "the town has little to do," but things have picked up since then. Located 4 miles down the road, Brattleboro is Vermont's first permanent settlement, begun in 1724 as a fort to protect against Indian raids. Today it has a population of 12,000 and a college town air (without the college) that attracts alternative thinkers and political activists. Against a New England backdrop of white steepled churches and noble maples, its post-hippie capitalist vibe of art galleries, bookstores, and brewpubs promises a pleasant stay.

WHERE: 108 miles northwest of Boston. Tel 802-254-6868; landmarktrustusa.org. *Cost:* from $275 (off-peak), from $425 (peak), sleeps up to 8, minimum 3-night stay. *Visitor info:* Tel 877-254-4565 or 802-254-4565; brattleboro chamber.org. **BEST TIMES:** in Brattleboro, 1st weekend in June for the Strolling of the Heifers Festival (strollingoftheheifers.com); 1st weekend in Oct for Literary Festival (brattleboro literaryfestival.org).

A Cheese-making Village Spared the Ravages of Progress

GRAFTON

Vermont

A picture-perfect Vermont village credited with restarting the state's handcrafted cheese industry, Grafton is an architectural showcase of historically accurate buildings, including a 200-year-old tavern where you can still bed down, a famed cheese company that still makes Grafton Village cheddar, a well-stocked general store, and a working blacksmith shop. It is not a living museum peopled by staff in period costumes, but a real-life village with a population of 679, many of whom work in the town.

Originally founded in 1754, Grafton thrived in the early 1800s with farms, sawmills, gristmills, tanneries, woolen mills, a soapstone quarry, and a carriage and sleigh factory. It peaked in 1820 with a population of 1,482 people (and 10,000 sheep) but declined as New England's farmers moved west and the wool industry collapsed. Grafton survived as a stagecoach stopover between Boston and Montreal, but the advent of the automobile and interstate highway system left it a shell of its former self.

In 1963 Dean Mathey, an investment banker from Princeton, New Jersey, whose family used to summer in the area, created the Windham Foundation expressly to resuscitate Grafton. The foundation owns 25 buildings in the central village, including The Grafton Inn, a classic four-story white clapboard, black-shuttered inn, originally built in 1790, then lavishly restored and vastly improved in 1965. Today The Grafton Inn has 46 discreetly modernized rooms (11 in the main building and another 35 in nearby cottages and houses), each individually decorated with antiques to create its own particular charm. The Old Tavern restaurant is a major draw, with a nice selection of hard-to-find wines and local cuisine featuring fresh ingredients gathered from small local farms.

Grafton's cheese-making roots go back to 1892, when dairy farmers formed a cooperative so they could deliver surplus milk and receive cheese in return, preferred for its longer storage time. Today the Grafton Village Cheese Company makes one of the world's finest cheddars. You can sample it in the retail store, then watch it being made in the production facility close by. Drive to nearby Chester to catch the *Green Mountain Flyer*, a vintage seasonal sightseeing train that makes a 90-minute round-trip run to Rockingham, past vistas of covered bridges, bucolic small towns, and in autumn, an explosion of fall foliage.

The Grafton Inn is one of the oldest continuously operating hotels in the U.S.

But half the point of visiting Grafton is not having much to do and enjoying the lazy pace of yesteryear. Sit on the old inn's porch, amble on down to the swimming hole for a dip, watch the stars come out.

WHERE: 52 miles northeast of Bennington. *Visitor info:* graftonvermont.org. **THE GRAFTON INN:** Tel 800-843-1801 or 802-843-2231;

graftoninnvermont.com. *Cost:* from $129 (off-peak), from $219 (peak). *When:* closed Apr. **GRAFTON VILLAGE CHEESE COMPANY:** Tel 800-472-3866 or 802-246-2210; graftonvillage cheese.com. **GREEN MOUNTAIN FLYER:** Chester Depot. Tel 800-707-3530 or 802-463-3069; rails-vt.com. *When:* May–mid-Oct. **BEST TIMES:** Jan–Mar for snow sports; Sept–Oct for foliage.

Powder Paradise

JAY PEAK RESORT

Vermont

A scant 8 miles from the Canadian border in northern Vermont, Jay Peak is a remote wonderland loved by powderhounds. It has more natural snowfall than anywhere else in New England (some say the best east of Utah), and its numerous difficult trails make it an amusement park for serious skiers. Without any other sizable mountains to its west, Jay is perfectly positioned to capture the light, powdery snow that results from banks of cold air heading east off the Great Lakes. Just don't waste your time looking at weather forecasts—the "Jay Cloud" is a local phenomenon, stalling on the mountain and dumping snow when it may be clear and sunny 5 miles away.

Jay has the only aerial tram in Vermont—a 60-person ride in the sky that rewards you with more than a mile of descent—and 78 trails (80 percent of which are intermediate and advanced). It is also a haven for backcountry and extreme skiers—more than 1,200 acres of off-piste skiing have been added since 1987. Once described as the kind of remote skiing outpost that Vermont was famous for 30 years ago, the Jay area now features an ice arena, a beautifully sited championship golf course, and the 60,000-square-foot Pump House Indoor Water Park, making the resort a year-round destination. Three new hotels—the Tram Haus Lodge, The Stateside,

Expert skiers can venture into the resort's glades for backcountry skiing among the trees.

and the Hotel Jay—range in size from 57 to 176 accommodations catering to every budget.

The Grey Gables Mansion in nearby Richford is an elaborate Queen Anne Victorian B&B built by a wealthy lumber baron in 1890. The carved walnut and mahogany staircase leads to six tastefully decorated bedrooms with stained-glass windows.

WHERE: 70 miles northeast of Burlington. Tel 800-451-4449 or 802-988-2611; jaypeak resort.com. *Cost:* lift tickets from $79; on-site accommodations from $100. *When:* ski season, late Nov–Apr. **THE GREY GABLES MANSION:** Richford. Tel 800-299-2117 or 802-848-3625; greygablesmansion.com. *Cost:* $99. **BEST TIME:** Jan–Mar.

The King of the East Coast Mountains

KILLINGTON

Vermont

Unofficially dubbed "The Beast of the East," Killington isn't the classic and romantic Vermont ski destination (for that, you must head to Stowe; see p. 107), but it has plenty to brag about. Its vertical drop falls just shy of Aspen's, and its extensive system of 29 lifts (including two express gondolas) serves more terrain than anywhere else in the East.

Skiers who like Killington's big, brash aesthetic are drawn by 212 alpine ski runs across six mountains, ranging from long, narrow, old-fashioned trails to Outer Limits, one of the steepest and most challenging mogul trails in the country. Exhilarating double-black-diamond trails, ominously named Anarchy or Downdraft, explain some of Killington's appeal to thrill seekers.

For cozy accommodations that President Eisenhower once enjoyed, try the Mountain Top Inn on 350 acres surrounded by the Green Mountain National Forest. A popular summer resort since the 1940s and a Nordic skiing hot spot since the 1960s, it offers 30 guest rooms with stunning mountain views, and boating and horseback riding promise year-round returns.

If you prefer shopping and sightseeing, consider nearby Shrewsbury and the Crisanver House—a circa 1800s B&B on a backcountry road that was the major supply route linking Boston Harbor to Fort Ticonderoga, New York (see p. 159), during the Revolutionary War. Meticulously renovated by local artisans with the utmost respect for its original wide floor-boards, handhewn beams, and slate roof, Crisanver House has five guest rooms and three suites, all tastefully appointed with antiques in a country style, minus the swags and ruffles.

WHERE: 80 miles south of Burlington. Tel 800-621-6867 or 802-422-6201; killington.com. *Cost:* lift tickets from $94. *When:* ski season, Nov–May. **MOUNTAIN TOP INN:** Chittenden. Tel 800-445-2100 or 802-483-2311; mountaintopinn.com. *Cost:* from $200 (off-peak), from $245 (peak). **CRISANVER HOUSE:** Shrewsbury. Tel 800-492-8089 or 802-492-3589; crisanver.com. *Cost:* from $140 (off-peak), from $250 (peak). **BEST TIMES:** Jan–Mar for the best ski conditions; early Apr for the Bear Mountain Mogul Challenge; late Sept–early Oct for foliage.

Killington averages 250 inches of natural snow each winter and boasts 1,500 skiable acres.

A Family-Friendly Ski Destination

OKEMO MOUNTAIN RESORT

Ludlow, Vermont

In these days of big ski resorts owned by absentee mega-corporations, Okemo Mountain Resort (named for an Indian phrase that means "all come home") is one of the few family-owned mountains remaining in Vermont. Originally founded in 1955 by local businessmen, it was saved from bankruptcy in 1982 by Tim and Diane Mueller, who have since modernized it with up-to-date snowmaking, high-speed lifts, and the largest Super Pipe in the East, along with six terrain parks. It's one of the state's most family-friendly ski destinations—small enough for families to spread out without worrying about never finding each other again. Despite the steepest vertical drop in southern Vermont (2,200 feet), a third of its 121 slopes, trails, and glades are gentle enough for the novice skier.

When night falls, head to the former mill town of nearby Ludlow (population 2,449) and check into one of its first-rate B&Bs. The Governor's Inn is a richly appointed 1890 Victorian home that William Wallace Stickney built for his bride ten years before becoming governor of Vermont. The inn's delights include eight tastefully decorated guest rooms, three-course breakfasts, and afternoon tea—complete with sweets and tea sandwiches—served in the inn's charming dining room.

Four miles from town is the Inn at Water's Edge, a restored Victorian treasure offering 11 cozy rooms and a full English pub. This central part of the state also offers crafts of all kinds—glass, furniture, pewter, and woodwork, among others—so there is plenty to do on a rainy afternoon. Make a late winter/early spring trip to Green Mountain Sugar House, 4 miles north of Ludlow, to see maple sap turned into syrup and sample fudge and other sweet treats, calories be damned.

WHERE: 91 miles southeast of Burlington. Tel 800-78-OKEMO or 802-228-4041; okemo.com. *Cost:* rooms from $172; lift tickets from $86. *When:* ski season, Nov–Apr. **THE GOVERNOR'S INN:** Ludlow. Tel 800-GOVERNOR or 802-228-8830; thegovernorsinn.com. *Cost:* from $144 (off-peak), from $184 (peak). *When:* closed 3 weeks in mid-Apr and 3 weeks in mid-Nov. **INN AT WATER'S EDGE:** Plymouth. Tel 888-706-9736 or 802-228-8143; innatwatersedge.com. *Cost:* from $125. **BEST TIMES:** Jan–Mar for skiing; late Sept–Oct for foliage.

Okemo is one of the East's most family-friendly mountains; the Muellers designed it with their two young children in mind.

Where Ski Purists Let Loose

MAD RIVER VALLEY

Vermont

One of Vermont's best-kept secrets, Mad River Valley is a paradise of whitewashed church steeples, weathered sugarhouses, covered bridges, and traditional New England skiing you'll find nowhere else. While other resorts have succumbed to the siren call of heated gondola lifts, snowmaking, and ski-in/ski-out condominiums, the Mad River Glen ski area persists as a bastion of the classic downhill experience, so pure that it is restoring the last surviving diesel-powered single-chair lift (circa 1948) rather than replace it with something new (and less expensive). With narrow, winding trails (the motto here is "ski it if you can!"), natural snow, and no snowboarders, it is a time capsule of skiing as it was 30 years ago.

Mad River Glen's status as America's only cooperatively owned ski area is what makes its noncommercial stance possible. Those who ski this mountain (many of whom are shareholders) tend to be accomplished downhillers whose very expertise shapes the legendary bumps that provide thrilling runs down the mountain. With a vertical drop of 2,037 feet and 45 trails, nearly half of which are expert, Mad River Glen promises some of the most challenging skiing in the East. But it also has plenty of beginner and intermediate trails, and the relatively uncrowded slopes can be a friendly environment for first-time skiers.

Nearby Sugarbush Resort, dubbed "Mascara Mountain" in the 1960s because of the rich and famous party crowd it attracted, now offers ski-in/ski-out lodging, high-speed lifts, and energy-efficient snowmaking (snowboarders are welcome). While Sugarbush has some challenging, old-fashioned expert slopes à la Mad River Glen, its 111 highly varied trails across two peaks (including a horizontal lift that travels between them) offer more options for beginners and great intermediate cruising along the north slopes.

Located right along scenic Route 100 (see p. 104), the towns of Waitsfield and Warren form the bucolic heart of the Mad River Valley. Waitsfield boasts two surviving covered bridges, while Warren (pop. 1,872) is best known for luxurious outpost The Pitcher Inn, restored to its 1850s appearance after burning down in 1994. Eleven whimsically themed rooms, such as the Trout Room, the School Room, and the Ski Room (decorated with original trail maps), reflect the true character of this archetypal corner of Vermont. Superlative meals might start with foie gras and rhubarb-orange compote before moving on to Vermont-raised lamb, quail, or rabbit, accompanied by wines from a stellar selection. Be sure to visit the old-fashioned Warren Store to stock up on penny candy, turkey sandwiches, and gingersnap cookies.

WHERE: 40 miles southeast of Burlington. *Visitor info:* Tel 800-828-4748 or 802-496-3409; madrivervalley.com. *When:* ski season, Dec–Apr. **MAD RIVER GLEN:** Waitsfield. Tel 802-496-3551; madriverglen.com. *Cost:* lift tickets from $65. **SUGARBUSH:** Warren. Tel 800-537-8427 or 802-583-6300; sugarbush.com. *Cost:* lift tickets from $65. **THE PITCHER INN:** Warren. Tel 802-496-6350; pitcherinn.com. *Cost:* from $350; dinner $60. *When:* closed 2–3 weeks in Apr and Nov. **WARREN STORE:** Tel 802-496-3864; warrenstore.com. **BEST TIMES:** Jan–Mar for skiing; last Tues in Jan for "Roll Back the Clock" at Mad River Glen, including a $3.50 lift ticket (1948 prices); July 4th for the Warren parade.

An Archetypal New England Town

MANCHESTER

Vermont

Ringed by Vermont's Green Mountains, the maple-shaded streets of this appealing New England town have lured visitors since before Abe Lincoln's family started spending summers here. Manchester's impressive white mansions and marble sidewalks retain a peaceful historic feel (while the raft of high-end factory outlets in nearby Manchester Center offers a modern allure).

The village is centered around the Equinox Golf Resort & Spa, a white-columned Federal-style (and very blue-blooded) 1,300-acre property that has been a premier summer resort since 1769 and a favorite of U.S. presidents from Taft to Eisenhower. The Equinox's championship 18-hole golf course, designed by Walter Travis in 1926, updated in 1992 by Rees Jones, and now Troon-managed, is a classic with many hills and carefully sited hazards. The inn's upper-crust theme carries on with lessons in off-road driving and falconry. The family of famous fly-fisherman and fishing outfitter Charles Orvis (see next page) owned an inn on the property between 1853 and 1938, and their home, now the Charles Orvis Inn, is part of this lavishly restored, 195-room resort hotel. Stop by the state-of-the-art Equinox Spa, grab a book, or sunbathe on the outdoor patio within sight of Mount Equinox, the highest peak in the Taconic mountain range at 3,848 feet, practically in the hotel's backyard. (You can drive to the top of it via the nation's longest privately owned toll road, the 5-mile Skyline Drive, and on clear days be rewarded with vistas spanning five mountain ranges: the Green, the Whites, the Berkshires, the Taconics, and the Adirondacks.)

Another proud reminder of Manchester's distinguished pedigree is Hildene. Open for

Enjoy a horse-drawn carriage ride around the Equinox Resort.

tours, the lordly 24-room Georgian Revival mansion on 412 acres was built by Robert Todd Lincoln, who summered here from 1905 until his death in 1926. Presidential granddaughter (and Robert's daughter) Mary Lincoln Isham lived nearby in what is now the 1811 House, part of The Inns at Equinox (seasonal only). With four-poster canopied beds, fine Oriental rugs, and fireplaces, the 13 bedrooms in this cozy, comfortable inn are styled in the Federal period for which Manchester Village is known.

Up for Breakfast (named for its second-floor location) is a Manchester Center landmark famed for its buttermilk, buckwheat, and sourdough pancakes, glazed with pools of Vermont maple syrup (ask, and they'll pack in enough blueberries to stain your lips). Visit nearby Dorset, an exquisitely preserved town of just 2,000 residents who proudly maintain neat streets, lined with white clapboard homes. The sidewalks here are marble, not surprising considering the quarries at the edge of town. Said to be the oldest in the U.S., they provided the marble for landmarks such as the New York Public Library (see p. 186).

WHERE: 100 miles south of Burlington. *Visitor info:* Tel 802-362-6313; visitmanchester vt.com. **EQUINOX:** Tel 800-362-4747 or 802-362-4700; equinoxresort.com. *Cost:* from $229 (off-peak), from $299 (peak). **SKYLINE DRIVE:** equinoxmountain.com. *When:* open May–Oct. **HILDENE:** Tel 800-578-1788 or 802-362-1788; hildene.org. *When:* tours daily. **THE INNS AT EQUINOX:** Tel 877-854-7625 or 802-362-4700; equinoxresort.com. *Cost:* from $169 (off-peak), from $249 (peak). **UP FOR BREAKFAST:** Tel 802-362-4204. *Cost:* $8 for full stack of pancakes. **WHERE TO STAY:** Barrows House in Dorset, tel 802-867-4455; barrowshouse.com. *Cost:* from $165 (off-peak), from $275 (peak). **BEST TIMES:** May–mid-Sept for fishing; early June for Annual Manchester Antique & Classic Car Show at Dorr Field; 1st weekend in Oct for the Manchester Fall Art & Craft Festival.

Fly-Fishing Nirvana

THE ORVIS COMPANY

Manchester, Vermont

If *A River Runs Through It* didn't get you to grab a rod and reel, a visit to Manchester just might catch-and-release your inner angler. Local son Charles F. Orvis and his brother, Franklin, started out here as hoteliers in the mid-1800s, finding that the Battenkill and Mettawee rivers were a strong lure for tourists—and a fine way to sell their handcrafted rods and tackle. They built an empire that lives on in Manchester, the only place in America where you can see Orvis rods being built, study the history of fly-fishing, shop for gear, and take lessons on the hallowed Battenkill, famed for its rainbow and brook trout.

Privately owned by the Perkins family since 1965, Orvis is first and foremost a retailer, with a massive flagship store (complete with fieldstone fireplaces and trout pond) that offers a dizzying choice of fly-fishing tackle, water-fowling and hunting gear, boots, clothing, even travel accessories and home furnishings. If the displays of antique fishing gear catch your interest, follow the signs to the American Museum of Fly Fishing right behind the store, where you can peruse the world's largest collection of angling and angling-related objects. Right next to the museum is Orvis Rod Manufacturing and Warehouse (aka "The Rod Shop"), where you can step onto the production floor and see the entire process of rod production, from the raw materials coming in to the finished bamboo and graphite rods.

At some point you'll need to learn what to do next. While Orvis has other fly-fishing schools, the most popular location is right here in Manchester, which offers some of the best and prettiest angling in the world. A two-day class for adult novices covers gear and tackle, fly-casting techniques, knot-tying, stream entomology, proper fly selection, "reading" water, and how to play, land, and safely release fish. You'll log classroom time and work the casting ponds outside the store before the big payoff: field trips to the legendary Battenkill.

WHERE: 100 miles south of Burlington; 4180 Main St. Tel 888-235-9763; orvis.com. **AMERICAN MUSEUM OF FLY FISHING:** Tel 802-362-3300; amff.com. **ORVIS FLY FISHING SCHOOL:** Tel 866-531-6213 or 802-362-3750.

Cost: $489 for 2-day session. *When:* Apr–mid-Oct. **WHERE TO STAY:** The Inn at Manchester, tel 800-273-1793 or 802-362-1793; innatmanchester.com. *Cost:* from $165 (off-peak), from $235 (peak). **BEST TIME:** Mar–Oct for fishing.

Fall's Riotous Foliage, Unsurpassed

NORTHEAST KINGDOM

Vermont

In 1949, a former U.S. senator from Vermont, struck by the timeless beauty and isolation of his state's three most northeastern counties (Orleans, Essex, and Caledonia), dubbed them the Northeast Kingdom—and when fall's riotous palette of red, orange, yellow, and gold cloaks these hills, it could very well be the most beautiful place in America. Here, thickly forested hills of sugar maple, beech, and ash give way to sleepy hamlets, one-church villages, and gorgeous lakes—particularly the fjordlike Lake Willoughby, often compared to Switzerland's Lake Lucerne. The unofficial gateway to the region is St. Johnsbury ("St. Jay's"), where people often stop at the white-steepled Dog Chapel to leave notes and photos of pets they have lost. (A sign out front reads: "Welcome All Creeds All Breeds No Dogmas Allowed.")

The hill town of Peacham (population 732) is probably Vermont's most picturesque corner during foliage season, but keep driving until you get lost, through wide-open valleys of tidy farmlands where cows outnumber their proudly insular Yankee owners. Harsh winters and sheer isolation have kept development and tourism farther south, making these back roads and lanes a paradise for cyclists as well.

For the winter sports enthusiast, the high-country area of historic Craftsbury is home to the well-regarded nonprofit Craftsbury Nordic Ski Center, which features a 62-mile system of ski trails, including a stretch of the 300-mile Catamount Trail (see p. 94), the longest cross-country ski trail in the U.S. Summer is no less beautiful a season in these parts. Big Hosmer Pond offers rowing and paddling with miles of trails and dirt roads for biking, walking, and jogging.

In the peaceful time-forgotten village of Lower Waterford (whose population hovers around 50), the Rabbit Hill Inn has a tradition of hospitality dating to 1795. The Federal-style white-colonnaded inn sits on 15 unspoiled acres with a commanding view of the White Mountains to the south. Its 19 guest rooms are individually decorated (suites have gas fireplaces and two-person whirlpool baths), and dinner is an elegant affair of refined dishes like

Sip an iced tea on the porch of the Rabbit Hill Inn.

agnolotti of braised pheasant and ricotta, followed by herb-crusted Alaskan halibut. Breakfast is every bit as romantic, served by candlelight and as ample as it is scrumptious. Walk it all off on the 7 miles of meandering cross-country trails near the inn.

WHERE: St. Johnsbury is 75 miles east of Burlington. *Visitor info:* Tel 802-626-8511; info on New England's color scene at travelthe kingdom.com. **THE DOG CHAPEL:** St. Johnsbury.

Tel 800-449-2580 or 802-748-2700; dogmt .com. **CRAFTSBURY NORDIC SKI CENTER:** Tel 802-586-7767; craftsbury.com/skiing. *Cost:* $10. **RABBIT HILL INN:** Lower Waterford. Tel 800-762-8669 or 802-748-5168; rabbithill inn.com. *Cost:* from $170 (off-peak), from $240 (peak). **BEST TIMES:** late Sept–early Oct for peak foliage; late Sept for 1-week Northeast Kingdom Fall Foliage Festival (nekchamber .com) in various towns throughout the region.

A Scenic Road Through the Heart of Vermont

ROUTE 100

Vermont

Beginning at the Massachusetts border and continuing north for 200 scenic miles along the rugged spine of the Green Mountains, the winding two-lane Route 100 is one of the most beautiful drives in the country, connecting some nine major alpine ski resorts, including Stowe, Killington, and Mad River Glen (see pp. 107, 98, and 100).

In four hours of unhurried motoring, you can travel its full length, from Wilmington in the south to Newport in the Northeast Kingdom, gateway to Canada. But this might, in fact, defeat one of its main pleasures—that of stopping to explore its small wonders. Rolling up and then down through the peaks and valleys that define the state, Route 100 has plenty of waypoints to pull over, stretch, and take in the quiet rural isolation and gorgeous forests stretching as far as the eye can see. Enjoy what you don't see: large and gaudy road signage, banned by the state legislature back in 1963.

As it meanders from one river valley to the next, Route 100 also runs through a string of villages (one called Podunk begs for a visit) that are typical of this Yankee heartland. One of the most appealing is Weston (population 589), where the entire village is on the National Register of Historic Places. The town's biggest attraction is the Vermont Country Store, famous as "purveyors of the practical and hard-to-find," founded here in 1946 by Vrest Orton, whose proud family still owns the old-fashioned Yankee business. The store specializes in revived and much-missed products of yesteryear, like Evening in Paris cologne, Beeman's Clove Chewing Gum, and colored princess telephones, along with Vermont necessities like long underwear and woolen socks.

Weston's vital cultural scene includes small museums, art galleries, and the Weston Playhouse Theater, which features top-notch acting by the state's oldest theater company. Just steps from the green is the Inn at Weston, where 13 luxurious rooms (nine with fireplaces) are individually decorated with antiques, Persian rugs, and thoughtful touches like orchids.

Spiritual solace can be found just 3 miles from the village, at the Weston Priory, a Benedictine monastery built in 1953, where common prayer services are held in a large, barnlike structure. Several times a day the gentle echoing sound of the resident monks' blended voices drifts out across gardens, meadows, and into the shadowy woodlands, providing another glimpse of the profound beauty of Vermont.

WHERE: Route 100 runs from Wilmington in the south (20 miles east of Bennington) to Newport in the north (83 miles northeast of Burlington); weston-vermont.com. **VERMONT**

COUNTRY STORE: Weston. Tel 802-362-8460; vermontcountrystore.com. **WESTON PLAYHOUSE:** Tel 802-824-5288; westonplayhouse.org. *When:* late June–early Sept. **INN AT WESTON:** Tel 802-824-6789; innweston.com. *Cost:* from $185 (off-peak), from $235 (peak), includes breakfast. **WESTON PRIORY:** Tel 802-824-5409; westonpriory.org. **BEST TIMES:** Jan–Mar for skiing; late Sept–Oct for foliage.

An Invitation to a Vanderbilt Estate

SHELBURNE FARMS

Shelburne, Vermont

On a bluff overlooking 120-mile-long Lake Champlain and the Adirondacks beyond, the Inn at Shelburne Farms sits on 1,400 acres designed by the great landscape architect Frederick Law Olmsted, famous for his design of New York City's Central Park. Guests can feel like they're lord of the manor at the red-brick Queen Anne–style country mansion, built in 1887 by Lila Vanderbilt and her husband, William Seward Webb. Step into another era of oak paneling, fireplaces, turrets, towers, family portraits, and 24 guest rooms (and two tiny guest cottages), appointed with family-heirloom antiques—you might even sleep in William Henry Vanderbilt's enormous mahogany bed. The inn's candlelit restaurant, grand but cozy, offers a menu that might include roasted rack of New England lamb with apple-sorrel relish, complemented by organic produce direct from Shelburne Farms' garden. In addition to being a rural marvel (with a hands-on Children's Farmyard that's every kid's fantasy), Shelburne Farms produces an excellent cheddar cheese, compliments of the Brown Swiss cows grazing within sight.

It's just a 3-mile drive from the "Big House" to the 45-acre Shelburne Museum, which resembles a well-preserved village with 37 historic structures that hold the finest collection of Americana in the country. Dubbed "The Smithsonian of New England," the museum boasts some 100,000 artifacts, including cigar store Indians, pottery, pewter, glass dolls, quilts, eagles, folk art, even a carousel, representing the wide-ranging tastes of Electra Havermeyer Webb, who married James Watson Webb (son of William and Lila) in 1910 and spent a lifetime collecting.

Shelburne Farms has been designated a National Historic Landmark.

Culinary itineraries should include a tasting at Shelburne Vineyard (no relation to the farm), repeatedly awarded "Best in New England." And for a taste of Vermont's farm-to-table offerings, head to the small chef-owned Rustic Roots, where the region's freshest ingredients show up on the menu.

WHERE: 7 miles south of Burlington. **INN AT SHELBURNE FARMS:** Tel 802-985-8498; shelburnefarms.org. *Cost:* from $160 (off-peak), from $170 (peak). *When:* May–mid-Oct. **SHELBURNE MUSEUM:** Tel 802-985-3346; shelburnemuseum.org. *When:* mid-May–late Oct. **SHELBURNE VINEYARD:** Tel 802-985-8222; shelburnevineyard.com. **RUSTIC ROOTS:** Tel 802-985-9511; rusticrootsvt.com. *Cost:* breakfast $12. **BEST TIMES:** late May for Lilac Festival; mid-July for Vermont Cheesemakers Festival (vtcheesefest.com); 3rd weekend in Sept for the Harvest Festival at Shelburne.

Maple Mania and a Fiddler's Fest

VERMONT MAPLE FESTIVAL

St. Albans, Vermont

They say all Vermonters have a little maple in their blood, and there's no doubt they're mad for the stuff—maple is the official state flavor; the sugar maple is the state tree; and a sugarbush (a stand of maple trees) makes up the back of the state quarter. But maple mania reaches its absolute zenith at the annual Maple Festival in St. Albans, a quiet town of some 7,000 that each year is overrun with 20,000 people from all over America. Dig in to maple bread, maple candy, maple fudge, maple cookies, maple creemees (soft-serve ice cream in a cone), maple sugar cakes, maple doughnuts, maple mustard, maple lollipops, not to mention the light fluffy pancakes, maple sausages, and bottomless pitchers of pure maple syrup at the legendary pancake breakfast benefit at the City Elementary School. Enjoy the sell-out Fiddler's Variety Show (two hours of fancy fiddlin', singers, dancers, pickers, comedy, and clogging) on Saturday night; tours of a sugarhouse; and a fierce competition to name the best maple syrup maker in Vermont. That's high stakes—and high praise indeed—as Vermont is the largest producer of maple syrup in the country.

The festival always takes place after Mud Season, from late February down south through April farther north, when cold nights and warm days pump sap up into the trees. That's when trees are tapped, buckets are hung, and sugarhouses can be spotted by the rising steam plumes when the sap gets boiled down to varying shades of delicious.

WHERE: 31 miles north of Burlington. Tel 802-524-5800; vtmaplefestival.org. *When:* last weekend in Apr.

Vermont produces about 1.4 million gallons of maple syrup each year.

A Footpath Through the Wilderness

THE LONG TRAIL

Stamford to North Troy, Vermont

The oldest long-distance hiking trail in the U.S., the Long Trail is 273 miles (with 175 miles of side trails) of primitive footpath that unfolds from one end of Vermont to the other, running north/south along the crest of the Green Mountains from Canada to Massachusetts. Not only did it serve as the inspiration for Vermont's Catamount Trail (see p. 94), but also for the Appalachian Trail (see p. 332), which links the mountains from Maine to Georgia, sharing 100 miles with the Long Trail along the way. It is the raison d'etre and off-spring of the Green Mountain Club, founded in 1910 "to make the Vermont mountains play a larger part in the life of the people."

Scaling peaks like Mount Mansfield (at 4,393 feet, Vermont's tallest) and passing pristine ponds, alpine bogs, hardwood forests, and streams, the Long Trail took the club 20 years to build.

Most hikers start in the south and travel north, following the white blazes that guide the way. Some people collect segments of the Trail over many years, enjoying sights such as the 136-foot-long suspension bridge for hikers in Johnson spanning the Lamoille River. Trekkers range from day-trippers to intrepid backpackers who find rest in nearly 70 primitive huts along the way; those who have walked the entire trail earn the title "End-to-Ender."

The climate varies from peak to valley, so plan for temperature changes and expect wind and cold at higher elevations. The rugged northern trails get a lot of traffic, but in the gentler south you can do a two-day 19-mile loop that takes you to the Mount Glastenbury fire tower for one of the trail's wildest and most expansive views.

WHERE: from 185 miles south of Burlington to North Troy. *Green Mountain Club info:* Tel 802-244-7037; greenmountainclub.org. *When:* trails closed mid-Apr–Memorial Day weekend. **BEST TIMES:** June–July for more daylight; Aug–Sept for fewer bugs; mid-Sept–mid-Oct for foliage.

Where the Hills Are Alive

STOWE

Vermont

Stowe Mountain Resort was created in the 1930s—making it one of the oldest in the country—when, as part of the federal government's public works projects, trails were hand-cut on Vermont's highest peak, Mount Mansfield (4,393 feet), creating top-to-bottom, thrill-a-minute runs. Despite it's reputation for quaintness—an authentic 200-year-old town setting includes a white-steepled church and an old-fashioned grocery store—Stowe has recently reinvented itself as a resort to rival the nation's best, complete with 116 trails, over 485 skiable acres, and more mile-long lifts than any other eastern resort.

There's much here to keep beginners and intermediate skiers occupied, but Stowe's mythically steep Front Four trails on the face of Mount Mansfield are the highlights of the show, for expert skiers only. Stowe's warm-weather activities include the alpine slide and an exhilarating 2-mile zipline touted as the world's fastest—all meant to lure summertime visitors. The accommodation of choice, the 300-room Stowe Mountain Lodge, is the centerpiece of Stowe's renaissance and is the mountain's only ski-in/ski-out hotel. Stowe is also home to the country's first cross-country ski center, the 2,500-acre resort of the Trapp Family Lodge, created in 1950 by the Austrian family of *Sound of Music* fame who settled here in 1942 after fleeing the Nazis. The quality of Tyrolean coziness, old-world service, and the promise of Wiener schnitzel and spaetzle in the lodge's noted restaurant make this chalet-style lodge one of the loveliest around. Maria Von Trapp, who died here in 1987, left her legacy in the hands of her son, the ever-youthful Johannes.

The 68-room Topnotch Resort & Spa is a luxury retreat, with an excellent 35,000-square-foot spa on 120 acres that include some of the region's finest tennis facilities and hiking trails.

Families flock to Smugglers' Notch Resort, a self-contained slopeside resort village. The 1,000-acre "Smuggs" is famous for its family-friendly features like lots of easy and intermediate runs and day-long ski and snowboard camps for kids, along with waterslides, pools, and kid camps in summer, and a year-round zipline. When the snow melts, the Smuggler's Notch Scenic Drive lures sightseers with a route of vistas that begins in Stowe.

Among Vermont's plethora of intimate B&Bs, the nine-room tucked-in-the-woods Stone Hill Inn is Stowe's standout, with fireplaces in each room and an impressive breakfast menu served in a sunlit 40-window dining room.

WHERE: 36 miles east of Burlington. *Visitor info:* Tel 877-GOSTOWE or 802-253-7321; gostowe.com. *When:* ski season, Dec–Apr. **STOWE MOUNTAIN RESORT:** Tel 800-253-4849 or 802-253-3000; stowe.com. *Cost:* lift tickets from $92. **STOWE MOUNTAIN LODGE:** Tel 888-478-6938 or 802-760-4700; stowemountain lodge.com. *Cost:* from $199 (off-peak), from $349 (peak). **TRAPP FAMILY LODGE:** Tel 800-826-7000 or 802-253-8511; trappfamily.com. *Cost:* from $250 (off-peak), from $350 (peak). **TOPNOTCH:** Tel 800-451-8686 or 802-760-6330; topnotchresort.com. *Cost:* from $199 (off-peak), from $349 (peak). **SMUGGLERS' NOTCH:** Jeffersonville. Tel 800-419-4615; smuggs.com. *Cost:* from $175 (off-peak), from $456 (peak) for a studio (sleeps 4), includes lodging, lift tickets, ski lessons, and activities. **STONE HILL INN:** Tel 802-253-6282; stonehillinn.com. *Cost:* from $269 (off-peak), from $349 (peak). *When:* closed Apr and mid-Nov. **BEST TIMES:** Jan–Mar for winter sports; late Jan for the Stowe Winter Carnival; Feb for Stowe Derby.

Where Snowboarding Rules

STRATTON MOUNTAIN RESORT

Vermont

Stratton Mountain Resort in southern Vermont opened in 1961 and has since become the premier snowboarding destination in New England. Its snowboarding pedigree goes back to 1977, when Jake Burton Carpenter started one of the world's most successful snowboarding companies in Londonderry, a nearby speck of a town (Burton Boards has since moved to Burlington). Snowboarding wasn't invented here per se, but in 1983 Stratton became one of the first to allow snowboarders on the slopes. Today it encompasses 97 slopes and four terrain parks, including an expert park.

For the area's most comfortable rooms, visit the nearby Inn at Saw Mill Farm, a converted 18th-century former sawmill. First opened in 1969, it was purchased and refurbished in 2015. The previous well-known restaurant has been reincarnated as the immediately popular Nonna's, serving Italian cuisine. In winter the 21-room inn is the ideal spot from which to ski Mount Snow, a 3,586-foot mountain with a network of 135 trails and plenty of snowmaking capacity. It's also fun in summer, when it is known for great mountain biking.

Stratton is roughly midway between Manchester (see p. 101) and picture-perfect Newfane, whose village green and National Historic District are two of the most photographed spots in the state. Newfane is noted for its Greek Revival architecture, including the Four Columns Inn, built in 1832 by Pardon Kimball to re-create his Southern wife's childhood home. Nestled at the foot of a 150-acre private mountain with natural trails, Four Columns reopened in 2015 with new owners and 16 renovated rooms and suites, replete with luxury touches such as fireplaces and soaking tubs. The new restaurant, Artisan, prides itself on handmade pasta and local purveyors and farmers for the season's best. Stroll down a nearby country lane to Newfane's small shops stocked with all things Vermont; you'll find quilts, fudge, and maple candy galore.

WHERE: 115 miles south of Burlington. *When:* ski season, Thanksgiving–early Apr. **STRATTON MOUNTAIN RESORT:** Tel 800-STRATTON or 802-297-4000; stratton.com. *Cost:* lift tickets from $85. **INN AT SAW MILL FARM:** West Dover. Tel 802-464-8131; theinnatsawmillfarm.com. *Cost:* from $225 (off-peak), from $300 (peak). *When:* closed Apr–May. **MOUNT SNOW:** West Dover. Tel 800-245-SNOW or 802-464-8501; mountsnow .com. *Cost:* lift tickets from $90. **FOUR COLUMNS INN:** Newfane. Tel 802-365-7713; fourcolumnsvt.com. *Cost:* from $225. **BEST TIMES:** Jan–Mar for skiing and snow sports; VT Open for snowboarding in 2nd week of Mar at Stratton.

Vermont Village, Rockefeller-Style

WOODSTOCK

Vermont

Christmas-card-perfect, small, and cosmopolitan, Woodstock earned its place in ski history when adventuresome locals hooked a long loop of rope to a Model T Ford engine at the base of Gilbert's Hill in 1934, creating the first ski tow. While it still has some local skiing and is conveniently close to Killington and Okemo (see pp. 98–99), today Woodstock is more famous for being the "prettiest small town in America," according to the *Ladies'* *Home Journal.* The title is due in part to the vast fortunes and concerted efforts of Laurance Rockefeller (grandson of Standard Oil magnate John D. Rockefeller Sr.) and his wife, Mary Billings.

Woodstock beautifully showcases autumn colors.

The two married in 1934 and spent the next 60 years lavishing money and attention on the town, even burying the utility lines to maintain its pristine 19th-century feel. They donated 550 acres to create Vermont's only national park, significant for being the first scientifically managed forest, with a 19th-century mansion sitting at its edge. They were also the force behind the Billings Farm & Museum, known for its blue-ribbon Jersey cows.

In 1969 Laurance and Mary completely rebuilt the town's centerpiece, the genteel Woodstock Inn and Resort, on the village green. This 142-room Colonial Revival resort features top-drawer amenities like a 10,000 square-foot spa, a 41,000-square-foot Racquet and Fitness Club, and access to horseback riding and golf. The inn operates the Woodstock Ski Touring Center, with almost 40 miles of groomed cross-country trails, and the 24 downhill trails of the misleadingly named mountain, Suicide Six, which has a drop of just 650 vertical feet.

Woodstock was settled in 1765 by emigrants from southern New England who were attracted by its location on the Ottauquechee (AWT-ah-KWEE-chee) River. In the 19th century, the river powered woolen mills, one of which now houses the workshop of luxury glassware maker Simon Pearce. Find sustenance at the Simon Pearce Restaurant at the Mill, known for its cheddar soup and Irish soda bread.

The nearby Quechee Gorge State Park is a dramatic 165-foot-high, mile-long gorge carved some 13,000 years ago by glaciers, with stunning aerial views looking down from the 1911 trestle bridge. While tour buses frequently stop here, you can easily escape them by hitting the trails that wind past pretty waterfalls down to the bottom of the gorge.

For a final dose of Vermont history, visit Plymouth Notch, the birthplace and boyhood home of President Calvin Coolidge, and a quiet hill town that is nearly unchanged since the early 20th century. Considered one of the country's best preserved presidential sites, Coolidge's home remains exactly as it was the night in 1923 when he was sworn into office as the nation's 30th president; his father did the honors, right there in the parlor, upon receiving the news of President Warren G. Harding's untimely death. Nearby, the simple but imposing whitewashed Plymouth Artisan Cheese, established by the president's father in 1890, is once again making its tangy, rich cheeses.

WHERE: 19 miles east of Killington. *Visitor info:* Tel 802-457-3555. **MARSH-BILLINGS-ROCKEFELLER NATIONAL PARK:** Tel 802-457-3368; nps.gov/mabi. *When:* mansion tours late May–Oct. **BILLINGS FARM & MUSEUM:** Tel 802-457-2355; billingsfarm.org. *When:* May–Oct. **WOODSTOCK INN:** Tel 800-448-7900 or 802-457-1100; woodstockinn.com. *Cost:* from $199 (off-peak), from $450 (peak). **SIMON PEARCE RESTAURANT:** Tel 802-295-2711 (shop) or 802-295-1470 (restaurant); simonpearce.com. *Cost:* dinner $55. **QUECHEE GORGE:** Tel 802-295-2990; vtstateparks.com/htm/quechee.htm. *When:* mid-May–mid-Oct. **CALVIN COOLIDGE HOMESTEAD DISTRICT:** Plymouth Notch. Tel 802-672-3773; nps.gov/nr/travel/presidents/calvin-coolidge-homestead.html. *When:* late May–mid-Oct. **PLYMOUTH ARTISAN CHEESE:** Plymouth Notch. Tel 802-672-3650; plymouthartisancheese.com. **BEST TIMES:** Jan–Mar for skiing; May–Oct for hiking; mid-Sept–mid-Oct for foliage; mid-Dec for Woodstock's Wassail Weekend (wassailweekend.com).

MID-ATLANTIC

DELAWARE • MARYLAND •
NEW JERSEY • NEW YORK •
PENNSYLVANIA • VIRGINIA •
WASHINGTON, D.C. • WEST VIRGINIA

A Dutch Foothold, a Delaware First

LEWES

Delaware

The little coastal town of Lewes prides itself on firsts. It's "the first town in the first state," the original settlement in what would become, in December 1787, the first state to ratify the new U.S. Constitution.

Originally founded in 1631, Lewes (pronounced LOO-is) began as a Dutch whaling station; that first settlement was annihilated in a dispute with the Siconese Indians, and a refortified, permanent town was established in 1659. The earliest of the many well-preserved, cypress-shingled buildings in the town go back almost as far: The circa 1665 Ryves Holt House, a two-story former colonial inn, serving as Lewes Historical Society's visitor center, is the oldest house in Delaware. Other historic buildings include a circa 1700 early plank house in Swedish style, the handsome circa 1720 Hiram Burton House, and an 1884 Coast Guard life-saving station. The maritime museum occupies the 1765 Cannonball House, so named because it was hit in the April 1813 British bombardment of the town. One of the most striking structures is the Zwaanendael Museum, built in 1931 to commemorate Lewes's tricentennial and to house exhibits on the history of the area; the building is modeled after the *stadhuis* (city hall) of Hoorn, Holland, and features such distinctively Dutch design elements as a stepped gable, carved stonework, and decorated shutters.

Lewes is an ideal walking town (include the short walk on the Savannah Road bridge over the Lewes and Rehoboth Canal), and there's loads of great seafood, whether it's a casual lunch of grilled salmon on the porch at Striper Bites or at the perennial favorite, The Buttery, housed in a beautiful, garden-surrounded Victorian building. Just east of town is Cape Henlopen State Park—one of the nation's first public lands, a gift from William Penn in 1682. There you can see lighthouses (one dating to 1885) and WWII observation towers; watch for dolphins and whales or just stroll along the miles and miles of walking paths and ocean beaches to the sound of the waves and hovering gulls.

WHERE: 86 miles southeast of Wilmington. *Visitor info:* Tel 877-465-3937 or 302-645-8073; leweschamber.com. **RYVES HOLT HOUSE:** Tel 302-645-7670; historiclewes.org. *When:* daily, Apr–Dec; otherwise check website. **ZWAANENDAEL MUSEUM:** Tel 302-645-1148; history.delaware.gov, click Museums. *When:* closed Mon, Apr–Oct; closed Sun–Tues, Nov–Mar. **STRIPER BITES:** Tel 302-645-4657; striperbites.com. *Cost:* dinner $40. **THE BUTTERY:** Tel 302-645-7755; thebuttery restaurant.com. *Cost:* dinner $50. **BEST TIMES:** May–Sept for weather; 1st weekend in Oct for Boast the Coast and Coast Day festivals; 1st weekend in Dec for Christmas events, tour of historical homes, and parade.

The Zwaanendael Museum has a striking exterior modeled after 17th-century Dutch architecture.

A Colonial Gem on the Delaware

NEW CASTLE

Delaware

Like many places on the Eastern Seaboard, the Delaware River town of New Castle has plenty of old buildings to show for its long and rich history. Unlike the vast majority, however, New Castle is both an historic treasure and a functioning town of some 5,300 residents. An exemplary model of historic preservation, its handsome 135-acre historic district has survived intact into the 21st century. The town dates to 1651, when Peter Stuyvesant founded it as Fort Casimir; it changed hands for more than 20 years as the Dutch, Swedes, and British captured and recaptured it. The British prevailed, and the new landlord, William Penn, first set foot on American soil when he landed in New Castle in 1682. A plaque near the site commemorates the event, and a statue of Penn stands near the old Court House at the center of town.

You'll want to visit the Court House, completed in 1732, which served as the seat of Delaware's colonial and later state government until Dover became the capital in 1777.

The old New Castle Court House is one of the oldest surviving courthouses in America.

Be sure to peek at the old courtroom and the meeting room of the state assembly, where the Declaration of Independence was read. Pick up a brochure for the New Castle Heritage Trail to give you some guidance and background as you wander the brick sidewalks and cobblestone streets lined with centuries-old buildings. A main attraction is the Read House, the 22-room Federal-style home of a son of Declaration signer George Read (one of three signers from New Castle). Built in 1801 for the princely sum of $12,000 (about $2.5 million today), it features magnificent Palladian windows, rooms done up in a variety of period styles, and a Prohibition-era speakeasy, modeled after a German rathskeller, in the basement. The impressive formal gardens, begun in 1847, are the oldest in the state.

You can also get a taste of history—literally—at Jessop's Tavern, a cozy and fun pub in a circa 1724 building in the heart of the historic district. The menu aims at authenticity with "Dutch cheeses, English pub fare, Swedish sauces, and old American dishes," and it also offers a wide selection of Belgian beers.

WHERE: 7 miles south of Wilmington. *Visitor info:* Tel 302-322-9801; newcastlecity.delaware.gov. **NEW CASTLE COURT HOUSE:** Tel 302-323-4453. *When:* closed Mon. **READ HOUSE AND GARDEN:** Tel 302-322-8411; dehistory.org. *When:* closed Mon. **JESSOP'S TAVERN:** Tel 302-322-6111; jessops-tavern.com. *Cost:* dinner $38. **BEST TIME:** Many private homes and gardens are open to the public the 3rd Sat in May (dayinoldnewcastle.org).

All in the Family Fortune

THE DU PONT LEGACY

Wilmington, Delaware

No state is more closely associated with a single family than the small state of Delaware. Since shortly after Pierre Samuel du Pont de Nemours fled the aftermath of the French Revolution at the end of the 18th century to settle in the Brandywine Valley, the du Ponts have been prominent in Delaware's political and industrial landscape, and they've made many noteworthy contributions to the physical landscape as well. The first was the house and gunpowder factory established by Pierre's son Éleuthère Irénée in 1802 on a beautiful wooded riverbank outside Wilmington; it grew into a 235-acre complex, and all of it is preserved today as the Hagley Museum. Visitors can take in such details as a fully functional 1875 machine shop, or in a more contemporary exhibit, they can try on a space suit or sit behind the wheel of the DuPont NASCAR #24. High above the Brandywine River is the tastefully appointed 1803 Eleutherian Mills, the first du Pont home in America, which features memorabilia and, in the adjacent barn, antique autos from the DuPont Motors car factory. Workers' Hill offers a glimpse of employee life in the austere Gibbons House and Brandywine Manufacturers' Sunday School.

A century after E. I. du Pont built his house, his great-grandson Alfred Irénée du Pont built one for himself in the area: Nemours, a 47,000-square-foot Louis XVI–style mansion on 300 acres, named after the town Pierre represented in the French government. It's a gorgeous setting for unremitting extravagance. On exhibit are fine period furnishings; paintings dating back to the 15th century; and rare carpets, tapestries, and other examples of exquisite craftsmanship. Visitors can also have a look at his billiards room, bowling alley, and vintage Cadillacs, Buicks, and Rolls-Royces.

The du Pont family home for five generations is preserved as part of the Hagley Museum.

As at other du Pont properties, the formal gardens are superb.

Alfred's cousin Pierre, former chief of both the DuPont company and General Motors, is famed for his Longwood estate (see p. 211) across the state line in Pennsylvania. He also created what is referred to simply as "the hotel": the gilded Italianate Hotel du Pont, which opened in 1913 as grand lodging for visitors coming to Wilmington to do business with the corporation. A paean to European craftsmanship, this gracious Renaissance palazzo evokes the captains-of-industry era and the du Ponts' penchant for collecting.

HAGLEY MUSEUM: Tel 302-658-2400; hagley.org. *When:* daily. **NEMOURS:** Tel 800-651-6912 or 302-651-6913; nemoursmansion.org. *When:* closed Mon, May–Dec; closed Jan–Apr. **HOTEL DU PONT:** Tel 800-441-9019 or 302-594-3100; hoteldupont.com. *Cost:* from $229 (off-peak), from $439 (peak). **BEST TIME:** fall for spectacular foliage along the Brandywine.

The Riches of an American Country Estate

WINTERTHUR MUSEUM

Winterthur, Delaware

Winterthur, one of America's most renowned mansions, was first conceived in 1837 as the relatively modest 12-room residence of Evelina Gabrielle du Pont, daughter of DuPont company founder

E. I. du Pont (see previous page), and her husband, Jacques Antoine Bidermann, in the lush Brandywine Valley straddling Delaware's border with Pennsylvania. The place operated as a farm, but E.I.'s great-grandson Henry Francis du Pont, an obsessive collector and passionate horticulturist, had other plans for it: He transformed it into the world's premier museum of 17th- through 19th-century American antiques and decorative arts. Opened officially in 1951, the connoisseur's collection of more than 60,000

The extensive gardens feature snowdrops, yellow Adonis, Chinese witch hazel, winter jasmine, and lavender crocus.

objects (later acquisitions have brought the figure to about 90,000) ranges from exquisite furniture to fine porcelain to silver drinking vessels made by Paul Revere. Collections are arrayed in over 175 period rooms, most of which you can visit on tours led by knowledgeable guides. At Christmastime, expect to find several of the interiors lavishly decked out with historic holiday decorations—Yuletide at Winterthur is a beloved event.

The estate's garden, however, was H. F. du Pont's first love: He studied horticulture at Harvard well before he began to collect; he even selected the house's ever-changing textile arrangements and place settings according to what was in bloom outside. Today some 60 of the estate's 982 acres are given over to magnificent massings of native and exotic plants. The gardens are located close to the museum and are accessible via the garden tram, which supplies a running commentary. You can expect to find something in bloom almost year-round.

Not far away, on a former part of the estate, you can see where, if not exactly how, the other half lived. Montchanin Village used to be populated mostly by workers at the du Ponts' gunpowder mills; today it's a meticulously restored luxury inn. The old 1850s barn houses the reception and gathering area; nine old residences dating from 1799 to 1910 have been divvied up into 28 rooms and suites outfitted with antiques and marble bathrooms. The old blacksmith shop is now the inn's restaurant, Krazy Kat's, serving such delicacies as grilled elk medallions with rabbit sausage.

WHERE: 6 miles northwest of Wilmington. Tel 800-448-3883 or 302-888-4600; winterthur.org. *When:* closed Mon. **THE INN AT MONTCHANIN VILLAGE:** Montchanin. Tel 800-269-2473 or 302-888-2133; montchanin.com. *Cost:* from $192; dinner $35. **BEST TIMES:** Sun, 1st full weekend in May for the Winterthur Point-to-Point Steeplechase; mid-Nov–early Jan for Yuletide at Winterthur.

ANNAPOLIS

Maryland

Annapolis isn't just the capital of Maryland, it's also the self-appointed world headquarters of sailing, that breezy, brine-drenched activity that fills the upper Chesapeake Bay with sails on a daily basis.

Begun in 1649 as a Puritan settlement, today Annapolis is a handsome case study in preservation, with over 1,200 restored and preserved structures in its eminently walkable historic district.

Some of the capital's fame derives from its role as the home of the U.S. Naval Academy, established in 1845. Guided walking tours of the bucolic 338-acre campus along the Severn River start at "the Yard" and go on to the crypt of John Paul Jones—father of the American Navy—and Bancroft Hall, a 1906 Beaux-Arts–style building that's one of the largest dormitories in the world. The daily Noon Formation starts here, an assembling of midshipmen (Monday–Friday during the academic year) that is not to be missed.

And if all those boats in the harbor make you yearn to hit the water, head to the Annapolis Sailing School, the country's oldest and most prestigious. Classes range from the popular "Become a Sailor in One Weekend" to courses in coastal navigation.

Back on dry land, hit the town's high point with a visit to the William Paca House, a five-part Georgian mansion built in 1765 by a Revolutionary-era governor of Maryland. Its restored 2-acre pleasure garden unfolds in five terraces and is one of only two dozen formal English gardens in the U.S. To keep you in a Revolutionary mood, drop by for a tipple or good pub grub at the classic Middleton Tavern, where Benjamin Franklin and other luminaries gathered. But for dinner and the best views of the waterfront and the city skyline head to Carrol's Creek, serving some of the area's most memorable seafood. The circa 1770 Georgian and Greek Revival town house that's now the Annapolis Inn has just three exquisite suites, but with its tireless attention to detail (including a sumptuous breakfast), this supremely elegant historic inn is more like a miniature five star hotel.

WHERE: 32 miles south of Baltimore. *Visitor info:* Tel 888-302-2852 or 410-280-0445; visit annapolis.org. **U.S. NAVAL ACADEMY:** Tel 410-293-8687; usnabsd.com/for-visitors. **ANNAPOLIS SAILING SCHOOL:** Tel 410-267-7205; annapolis sailing.com. *Cost:* from $395 per person for 2-day basic sailing course. *When:* Apr–Oct. **WILLIAM PACA HOUSE:** Tel 410-267-7619; annapolis.org. **MIDDLETON TAVERN:** Tel: 410-263-3323; middletontavern.com. *Cost:* dinner $30. **CARROL'S CREEK:** Tel 410-263-8102; carrolscreek.com. *Cost:* dinner $45. **ANNAPOLIS INN:** Tel 410-295-5200; annapolisinn.com. *Cost:*

The city dock is the center of Annapolis, recalling its 17th-century days as a tobacco port.

from $260 (off-peak), from $320 (peak). **Best times:** 2nd weekend in Oct for Annapolis Sailboat Show; following weekend for U.S.

Powerboat Show (annapolisboatshows.com). During June Week, the Naval Academy's yearly pregraduation celebrations, the town is packed.

Windswept Beaches and Wild Ponies

ASSATEAGUE ISLAND

Maryland and Virginia

This long, skinny barrier island off the Maryland-Virginia border faces the restless Atlantic with 37 placid miles of sand backed by loblolly pine forests and salt marshes. Famous for its wild ponies, Assateague is home to a wide variety of wildlife, from sika deer (actually miniature elk from Asia) to migratory hawks that soar through in the fall. Two-thirds of the island is in Maryland, where a good portion of the 2.5 million annual visitors gain access. Assateague State Park offers 2 miles of gentle beaches and on the western side of the island; visitors use canoes and kayaks to explore salt marshes in Sinepuxent Bay. The rest of the Maryland section falls within the Assateague Island National Seashore, a wilder stretch of shoreline with backcountry campgrounds and a route for off-road vehicles (permits required) to the state line.

The southern third of the island consists of Virginia's Chincoteague National Wildlife Refuge (see p. 242), famous for the scruffy wild ponies that are its charming draw (technically, they're actually stunted horses and not true ponies, but try telling that to a ten-year-old). It's generally easier to see them on the Maryland side, where they tend to linger closer to the walking trails and roads and often roam the beaches in the evening. Most of the refuge is beach, accessible only by foot, and if you sign up for a tour with a park ranger you can see the ponies in a different light—sometimes up close and personal—during your walk through the wild.

Assateague can be crowded on summer weekends, especially given the Maryland end's proximity to Ocean City with its wash of high-rise hotels, amusement park rides, and 3-mile boardwalk: If this isn't your speed, consider a sojourn in the less commercialized town of Berlin, 10 miles inland, with a cluster of antiques shops and cafés and the town gem, the three-story Atlantic Hotel. The restored 1895 Victorian inn boasts the acclaimed Drummer's Café restaurant and 17 rooms that combine armloads of Old World charm with New World amenities.

Where: The Maryland entrance to Assateague Island is 106 miles southeast of Baltimore. **Assateague State Park:** Tel 410-641-2120; dnr2.maryland.gov. **Assateague Island National Seashore:** Tel 410-641-1441 (MD) or 757-336-6577 (VA); nps.gov/asis. **Chincoteague National Wildlife Refuge:** Tel 757-336-6122; fws.gov/refuge/chincoteague.

About 100 wild ponies wander freely on the island's Maryland side.

ATLANTIC HOTEL: Berlin. Tel 410-641-3589; atlantichotel.com. *Cost:* from $89 (off-peak), from $140 (peak); dinner $50. **BEST TIMES:** June and Sept for smaller crowds.

Quirky, Offbeat, and Wildly Fascinating

AMERICAN VISIONARY ART MUSEUM

Baltimore, Maryland

I f the word "museum" conjures up images of endless hallways lined with armless statues and ornately framed paintings of long-dead dowagers, does Baltimore have a treat for you. Sandwiched between Federal Hill and Baltimore Bay on the south side of the Inner Harbor (see p. 120), the American Visionary Art Museum (AVAM) ranks among the most interesting—and certainly most entertaining—art venues in the country.

By its own definition, the AVAM is dedicated to "art produced by self-taught individuals, usually without formal training, whose works arise from an innate personal vision." Often called "outsider art," this genre includes voodoo-inspired "shrines," mutated Barbie dolls, and 55-foot-high wind-powered "whirligig" sculptures. From naive to downright bizarre, the museum's 4,000-plus-piece permanent collection and continually changing exhibitions will challenge, tickle, surprise—and even stun—you with the creative potential of the human brain and hands.

These creations fill six galleries in the three-story main building, whose soaring hand-cast central stairway by David Hess is an attraction in itself. The Jim Rouse Visionary Center and the Tall Sculpture Barn hold larger pieces, including, at different times, a life-size chess set of metal angels and aliens and a car covered with 5,000 psychically bent spoons and forks. The adjacent sculpture plaza is home to a multicolored 55-foot creation by the mechanic, farmer, and artist Vollis Simpson, while the selection in the museum's gift shop is totally wacky and fun. Don't leave without a bit of recharging at the museum's third-floor Encantada restaurant. Its creative and delicious locally sourced and vegetarian-influenced menu has been packing them in since the day it opened.

Koday, *a mixed media piece by Pamela Smith, is part of AVAM's permanent collection.*

A whole slate of events challenges you to awaken your creative juices and design your own inventions during museum-sponsored workshops. The Visionary Pets Parade over the July 4th weekend offers awards for pet-owner resemblance and "animal least likely to succeed as a pet." The biggest happening is the annual Kinetic Sculpture Race in early May, during which human-powered works of art—from solo ships to 50-foot vehicles—are piloted by "kinetinauts" over land, water, and mud. It's part race, part moving art show, with prizes for originality, engineering, and finishing next-to-last.

AMERICAN VISIONARY ART MUSEUM: 800 Key Hwy. Tel 410-244-1900; avam.org. *When:* closed Mon. **ENCANTADA:** Tel 410-752-1000; encantadabaltimore.com. *Cost:* dinner $35.

Centuries of Masterworks

BALTIMORE MUSEUM OF ART

Baltimore, Maryland

The Baltimore Museum of Art's collection of Matisse paintings is the largest in the world. They are just part of the 95,000 objects in its permanent collection, making the museum—fresh from a renovation completed in 2015—the state's premier repository of art. The Cone Wing, named after Baltimore sisters Etta and Claribel Cone, is famous worldwide for its collection of late 19th- and early 20th-century European masters, including Matisse, Picasso, Renoir, Cézanne, Gauguin, and Van Gogh. One room is set up to echo the Baltimore apartments in which the sisters began their astonishing collections.

Other highlights include the West Wing, which focuses on post-1945 artists like Robert Rauschenberg, Andy Warhol, and Jasper Johns, and the Jacobs Wing, which houses paintings and sculptures by European artists from the 15th through the 19th centuries. Thirty-four modern sculptures by Alexander Calder, Henry Moore, Auguste Rodin, and others populate the 2.7-acre outdoor sculpture gardens. The culinary feather in the museum's cap is Gertrude's, where you can enjoy a view of the sculpture garden while dining. Chef, cookbook author, and Baltimore native John Shields named the restaurant after his grandmother, who taught him the joy of cooking as a child, and the menu concentrates on dishes made with local, often organic, ingredients.

Baltimore's treasures don't stop here. Begun by the father-and-son team of William and Henry Walters in the early 20th century, the Walters Art Museum has blossomed into one of Baltimore's finest historic art collections. It spans 50 centuries—one of the few museums in the world to cover such a vast range—in over 35,000 objects, from ancient sarcophagi and Japanese armor to Fabergé eggs and Tiffany jewelry. The Walters' Egyptian holdings are said to be among the country's best, as is its collection of French paintings.

BALTIMORE MUSEUM OF ART: Tel 443-573-1700; artbma.org. *When:* closed Mon–Tues. **GERTRUDE'S:** Tel 410-889-3399. *Cost:* dinner $40. **WALTERS ART MUSEUM:** Tel 410-547-9000; thewalters.org. *When:* closed Mon–Tues. **BEST TIME:** summer for music series in the BMA garden.

At the Seafaring Heart of Charm City

INNER HARBOR

Baltimore, Maryland

Reborn decades ago from a downtrodden industrial zone to become the city's gleaming tourism epicenter, Baltimore's Inner Harbor was a catalyst for the citywide renaissance of Charm City (where everyone still calls you "hon") and is now one of the liveliest destinations in the city. It's still a working harbor full of prows and sails and sparkling white dress uniforms. On the west side of the harbor, Harborplace is chock full of stores and restaurants and has a handy visitors center at its northern end. Architect I. M. Pei designed the octagonal Baltimore World Trade Center that dominates the harbor's skyline, but the real action is closer to ground level—or, more accurately, sea level.

A significant Civil War ship, the USS Constellation *has its home at the harbor.*

Start under the three glass "sails" on top of the Baltimore National Aquarium, where close to 20,000 animals live both above and below the waterline, from bottlenose dolphins and sharks to puffins and frogs. Australia: Wild Extremes showcases life Down Under and is the only one of its kind in America.

Four boats and a lighthouse make up the Historic Ships of Baltimore. The U.S. Coast Guard Cutter *Taney* and the submarine USS *Torsk* both saw action in WWII; the former survived the attack at Pearl Harbor and the latter sank the last enemy warship of the war.

The lightship *Chesapeake* and the Seven Foot Knoll Lighthouse, relocated from the mouth of the Patapsco River, both steered sailors safely into the mouth of the Chesapeake Bay. The USS *Constellation*, a three-masted sloop of war launched in 1854, is the last vessel from the Civil War still afloat.

Head 3 miles southeast of the Inner Harbor to star-shaped Fort McHenry, built to protect the harbor: it was shelled by the British on the night of September 13, 1814, with "rockets' red glare and bombs bursting in air," thus inspiring local son Francis Scott Key to write the poem that became the U.S. National Anthem and still makes America's heart swell. The fort was never attacked again.

For the best views of the Inner Harbor, head to the Top of the World observation level on the 27th floor of the Baltimore World Trade Center, or else make the short climb to the top of Federal Hill and bring a picnic lunch.

WHERE: innermost section of Baltimore Harbor, between Pratt and Light Sts. *Visitor info:* Tel 877-BALTIMORE or 410-659-7300; baltimore.org. **BALTIMORE NATIONAL AQUARIUM:** Tel 410-576-3800; aqua.org. **HISTORIC SHIPS OF BALTIMORE:** Tel 410-539-1797; historicships.org. **FORT MCHENRY:** Tel 410-962-4290; nps.gov/fomc. **BEST TIMES:** late Jan for the Baltimore Boat Show; late Mar–early Apr for Light City Baltimore, a festival of lights and ideas (lightcity.org).

The Catch of the Day

MARYLAND CRABS

Baltimore, Maryland

Seldom is a city more associated with a specific crustacean than Baltimore is with the *Callinectes sapidus*, or blue crab. More than 50 percent of the country's harvest of these spindly-legged side-crawlers is hauled in from

the Chesapeake Bay every year, and when they are in season, one of the best places in town

(some say on the Eastern Seaboard) to find them is at the acclaimed Woodberry Kitchen, where

Baltimore-born chef Spike Gjerde commonly features what he calls "Maryland's holy trinity of seafood: blue crab, oysters, and rockfish." Gjerde was one of the first to forge relationships with local crabbers and other suppliers to nurture a revival of Maryland's culinary traditions.

For a communal crab-eating experience, try L. P. Steamers in South Baltimore. It's nothing to look at, but the family-owned neighborhood treasure serves crab-dominated seafood year-round and will even teach befuddled out-of-towners how to use a wooden mallet and butter knife.

For another take on no-frills epicurean delights, head to Baltimore's venerable Lexington Market, which claims to be the world's largest continuously running market. Started in 1782, today it houses more than 100 vendors. Nonshoppers should come just for the sounds and smells.

Or head straight to Faidley's, the seafood shop and raw bar whose all-lump crab cake has been called the best in the Chesapeake and perhaps the planet. Faidley's still occupies its original location in the Lexington Market, where it was opened in 1886 by John W. Faidley Sr. It's an egalitarian, stand-and-eat kind of place where you'll share space at waist-high counters with cops, tourists, and smartly dressed business types. Faidley's also serves delicious fried oysters and fried haddock, but

If you can't visit the store in the Lexington Market, Faidley's will cater and next-day air ship its delectable crab cakes.

the crab cakes have always been the real draw. You go out on a limb when attempting to anoint Baltimore's best crab cake, but if any place can claim the title, it's this one. Grab a plastic fork and dig in—and cast your vote.

Woodberry Kitchen: Tel 410-464-8000; woodberrykitchen.com. *Cost:* dinner $55. **L. P. Steamers:** Tel 410-576-9294; locustpoint steamers.com. *Cost:* dinner $35. **Lexington Market:** lexingtonmarket.com. **Faidley's:** Tel 410-727-4898; faidleyscrabcakes.com. *Cost:* lunch $15 per crab cake. **Best times:** May–July for soft-shell crabs; Aug–Nov for hard-shell.

Ballpark Bliss and the Birthplace of the Bambino

Oriole Park at Camden Yards

Baltimore, Maryland

The Colts may have packed up for Indianapolis in 1984, but Baltimore's pro sports fans scored big eight years later with the completion of Camden Yards, what many consider the best place in the country to catch a ball game.

The former railroad center just four blocks from the Inner Harbor (see p. 120) was reborn as a retro-themed stadium with an arched brick

facade and natural grass turf, uniformed ushers to show you to your seat, and a walkway behind the outfield peppered by the occasional home run. The black-and-orange clad "O's" play 81 home games here from April through September—try to see one. The next best way to take it all in is on a guided tour, which lets you experience firsthand the team dugout, the excitement of the JumboTron control room, and the clubby atmosphere of the press and suite levels. The emphasis is on history, from the days of local son Babe Ruth to infielder Cal Ripken Jr.'s record-setting streak of 2,632 consecutive games that ended on September 19, 1998.

Hot dogs are the classic baseball snack of choice, and an extravagant rendition is worth checking out at Stuggys—try their Early Bird Dog, an Esskay hot dog topped with a fried egg, shredded cheese, and bacon. True "Birds" fans, however, know that the best sustenance in Camden Yards is at Boog's BBQ. John Wesley "Boog" Powell, all-star Orioles first baseman from 1961 through '74, traded a baseball cap for a chef's hat and now serves up the city's favorite pit beef during home games.

Although he made his mark on history with the New York Yankees, George Herman "Babe" Ruth is one of Baltimore's most famous sons (together with Edgar Allan Poe). He was born here on February 6, 1895, in a modest brick rowhouse just three blocks—one long fly ball—from Camden Yards. Two rooms in

his grandparents' house have been turned into a museum-cum-shrine to the baseball legend, filled with memorabilia, photographs, films, and taped radio broadcasts from his unparalleled major league career.

ORIOLE PARK AT CAMDEN YARDS: 333 W. Camden St. Tel 888-848-BIRD or 410-685-9800; theorioles.com. *When:* games Apr–Sept; tours Feb–Dec. **BABE RUTH'S BIRTHPLACE AND MUSEUM:** Tel 410-727-1539; baberuth museum.org. **BEST TIMES:** during Orioles home games, and on Babe Ruth's birthday (Feb 6), when the Babe Ruth Museum offers free admission, a champagne toast, and birthday cake.

Oriole Park at Camden Yards became the official home of the O's on April 6, 1992.

Timeless Corner of the Chesapeake Bay

CRISFIELD AND SMITH AND TANGIER ISLANDS

Maryland and Virginia

The Chesapeake Bay's mouth opens into Virginia's Hampton Roads, one of the biggest, best, and busiest natural ports in the world. Up at the Maryland end, though, things are decidedly quieter. The sleepy town of Crisfield sits

on a peninsula at the southern tip of Maryland's Eastern Shore and has long been called the "Crab Capital of the World." Things come

alive during crab season (March to November), when the docks are busy and seafood-packing houses along the waterfront do a brisk trade.

Together with nearby Smith and Tangier islands (the latter belongs to Virginia), the area is a time-warp kind of place where life revolves around the fruits of the bay, and boats seem as common as cars.

Set up base on terra firma and revel in the charm of the My Fair Lady B&B, housed in a Victorian-style home built in 1900 during the prosperous years of Crisfield's seafood boom. Guests in any of the five period-furnshed guest rooms can enjoy a good book on the wraparound terrace, or leave everyday life even farther behind by heading just a few miles into the bay from Crisfield, to Smith and Tangier islands. Each has been isolated for so long that residents still speak with the faint but distinctive broguelike lilt reminiscent of their

A dock leads to a colorful crab shanty on Smith Island.

forebears from Cornwall, England. Most visitors just take a ferry over for the day, but B&Bs and homestyle restaurants can be found on both islands and encourage visitors to linger and unwind. Tylerton, on Smith Island, has only 44 residents, and the owners of the very special three-room Inn of Silent Music are the only nonfishermen. Stay in their old-fashioned farmhouse surrounded on three sides by water, and you'll long remember the serenity, the breakfasts of German apple pancakes (and a locally sourced dinner upon request) on the screened-in porch, and that sinking feeling that comes with the thought of having to leave it all for the real world.

WHERE: Crisfield is 155 miles southeast of Baltimore by car. **MY FAIR LADY:** Tel 410-968-0352; myfairladybandb.com. *Cost:* from $150. **SMITH ISLAND CRUISES:** Tel 410-425-2771; smithislandcruises.com. *When:* May–Oct. **TANGIER RAPPAHANNOCK CRUISES:** Reedville, VA. Tel 804-453-2628; tangier cruise.com. *When:* May–Oct. **INN OF SILENT MUSIC:** Tylerton, Smith Island. Tel 410-425-3541; innofsilentmusic.com. *Cost:* from $115; dinner $30. *When:* mid-Apr–Oct. **BEST TIMES:** in Crisfield, 3rd Wed in July for the all-you-can-eat J. Millard Tawes Crab and Clam Bake, and Labor Day weekend for the National Hard Crab Derby.

The Youghiogheny and the Great Outdoors

GARRETT COUNTY

Maryland

The far western tip of Maryland packs more outdoors options into one single county (Garrett) than any other in the state. Grab your gear and start at the top with rafting on the Youghiogheny (YOCK-uh-ganey) River,

the hallowed birthplace of commercial rafting in the U.S. From Sang Run to Friendsville, the Upper Yough boasts a heart-pounding succession of 19 Class IV and V rapids in a 10-mile stretch, with rightfully intimidating names like Bastard, Lost and Found, and Meat Cleaver. You can breathe again when you hit the milder, but no less beautiful, Middle

The rough rapids of the Upper Youghiogheny promise a thrilling adventure.

Yough, running from Confluence to Ohiopyle, whose Class I and II rapids are perfect for beginners and families. The Lower Yough, from Ohiopyle to Bruner Run, is the busiest section of white water east of the Mississippi, with Class III and IV rapids that are challenging without becoming overwhelming.

More serene waters beckon at the 3,900-acre Deep Creek Lake, Maryland's largest freshwater lake, with 65 miles of shoreline to explore. Vacationers flock here in the summer and enjoy the chance to revel in the lake community's old-time charm. Boating, naturally, is the most popular activity at this time of year, and it's also the fastest and easiest way to get around: You can go shopping, to the movies, and even to church by boat. Hiking, camping, fishing, and mountain biking are excellent here as well. Seven state forests and parks also fill Garrett County, including Savage River State Forest, Maryland's largest, and Swallow Falls State Park, named for the state's highest free-falling waterfall.

Rockies veterans might laugh at Maryland's only ski hill, the 700-foot-high Wisp Resort, but it proudly offers 34 slopes, some supplying handsome views of nearby Deep Creek Lake. Collapse at the cozy Arts-and-Crafts Lake Pointe Inn on a private slip of Deep Creek Lake's shoreline. All of the comfy guest rooms have views either of the lake or of nearby Wisp Resort.

WHERE: 176 miles west of Baltimore. **RAFTING:** Precision Rafting (tel 800-477-3723 or 301-746-5290; precisionrafting.com) offers trips on the Upper Yough from $115 per person. *When:* Apr–Oct. **BOAT RENTALS:** Deep Creek Lake Boat Rentals in McHenry (tel 301-387-9130; deepcreeklakeboatrentals.com) rents power boats from $275 per day. *When:* Apr–mid-Oct. **WISP RESORT:** McHenry. Tel 301-859-3159; wispresort.com. *Cost:* lift tickets from $49. *When:* Dec–Mar. **LAKE POINTE INN:** McHenry. Tel 301-387-0111; deepcreekinns.com. *Cost:* from $212 (off-peak), from $262 (peak). **BEST TIMES:** Jan–Feb for best skiing; Apr–Oct for good rafting; mid-Oct for the 5-day Autumn Glory Festival in Oakland.

One State's Thoroughbred Passion

THE HORSE SCENE

Maryland

Maryland's zeal for all things equine dates back centuries. The first hunting hounds arrived from Europe in 1650, the Maryland Jockey Club was established in 1743, and the state sport—jousting—has also been a fixture here since colonial times, although the event itself has evolved from a bone-breaking collision of horsemen to a test of speed and honed skill.

Laced by white-painted fences along rolling green farms, northern Baltimore and Harford counties are unquestionably horse country. "Point-to-point" or steeplechase races start on weekends in April at private farms in the area. The next-to-last Saturday of the month is saved for the Grand National Steeplechase in Butler. The following Saturday is even bigger: the Maryland Hunt Cup at Worthington Farms, which holds the claim as the oldest steeplechase race in the country. After the English Grand National, it's considered one of the greatest in the world, and is widely thought to be among the most difficult. Advance tickets are key to attending the 4-mile, 22-fence race and the attendant tailgate parties, where everyone seems to know everyone else and the bonhomie belies the money invested in these equine athletes.

The Maryland Jockey Club runs the Pimlico Race Course in Baltimore, the state's oldest and most prestigious Thoroughbred track. It was here in 1938 that Seabiscuit made history by beating Triple Crown winner War Admiral. Thoroughbreds thunder down the 1-mile, 70-foot-wide track from spring through fall, but the season peaks early, in late May, during the much-heralded Preakness Stakes, the middle jewel in the Triple Crown, sandwiched between the behemoth Kentucky Derby (see p. 413) and the Belmont Stakes in New York. The race itself is a raucous mix of T-shirts and beer in the infield and fancy dress and all manner of millinery in the grandstand. Over 150,000 fans ensure that even the standing-room-only tickets are in high demand.

MARYLAND JOUSTING TOURNAMENT ASSOCIATION: marylandjousting.com. MARYLAND STEEPLECHASE ASSOCIATION: marylandsteeple chaseassociaton.com. PIMLICO RACE COURSE: Baltimore. Tel 410-542-9400; pimlico.com. *When:* races Thurs–Sun, May and June. PREAKNESS STAKES: Pimlico Race Course. Tel 877-206-8042 or 410-542-9400; preakness .com. *Cost:* from $30. *When:* 3rd Sat in May. BEST TIME: Preakness Week, mid-May before the Preakness Stakes, with concerts, fireworks, hot air balloons, and parties.

Haunting Civil War History

ANTIETAM BATTLEFIELD

Sharpsburg, Maryland

Flush from his victory a month earlier at the Battle of Second Manassas (see p. 249), Confederate General Robert E. Lee set his sights on the heart of the Union in September 1862. But any thoughts of a quick invasion came crashing down on September 17th at the Battle of Antietam in Sharpsburg—the single bloodiest day in American military history. Like most Civil War battlefields, the site of the carnage is a peaceful scene of rolling farmland today, minus the countless monuments so prominent at Gettysburg (see p. 209). A self-guided driving tour leads to many sites that have entered Civil War legend, including the Cornfield, Burnside Bridge, and Bloody Lane. The Maryland Monument is the only memorial in the world to pay homage to casualties on both sides of a battle; two Confederate regiments and eight Union regiments came from Maryland.

Civil War buffs can settle in at the handsome Jacob Rohrbach Inn, an 1830s Federal-style B&B that was used as a hospital after the fighting stopped. With just five rooms, it promises a personal experience highlighted by the smell of home-baked cookies wafting through the historic quarters on your return from sightseeing.

Or you can opt to stay at the hilltop Antietam Overlook Farm. The front porch views are just one of the 19th-century-style inn's many lures: It sits at the center of a 95-acre mountain ridge spread, with vistas that stretch to Pennsylvania, Virginia, and West Virginia. A very private getaway, it has six luxurious rooms and a grand fireplace to stave off the chill of an autumn evening.

Antietam National Battlefield was the birthplace of triage, the first example of organized emergency battlefield medicine; and dozens of local buildings in nearby Frederick were turned into makeshift hospitals, one of which is now the National Museum of Civil War Medicine, located within its 30-block historic

A line of cannons serves as a somber reminder of one of the Civil War's bloodiest battles.

district. The museum's displays and life-size wax figures explain the use of hospital trains and vividly describe the horrors of Civil War–era operating rooms. The city itself abounds in history: It's where Lincoln addressed a crowd after the battle, and Clara Barton, who would go on to found the American Red Cross, had her first battlefield nursing experience.

WHERE: 80 miles west of Baltimore. Tel 301-432-5124; nps.gov/anti. **JACOB ROHRBACH INN:** Sharpsburg. Tel 877-839-4242 or 301-432-5079; jacob-rohrbach-inn.com. *Cost:* from $175 (off-peak), from $225 (peak). **ANTIETAM OVERLOOK FARM:** Keedysville. Tel 800-878-4241 or 301-432-4200; antietam overlook.net. *Cost:* from $165. **MUSEUM OF CIVIL WAR MEDICINE:** Frederick. Tel 301-695-1864; civilwarmed.org. **BEST TIMES:** 1st Sat in July for Salute to Independence, when the Maryland Symphony Orchestra is accompanied by live cannon fire and followed by fireworks; Sept 17 for anniversary commemorations at the battlefield; 1st Sat evening in Dec, when the battlefield is illuminated by 23,000 candles, one for each casualty, placed by 1,400 volunteers.

Home of Maryland's First Settlers

HISTORIC ST. MARY'S

Maryland

The Pilgrims had already landed at Plymouth Rock (see p. 64) when 140 English settlers waded ashore onto this unassuming, marsh-edged peninsula between the Patuxent and Potomac rivers in 1634 and became Maryland's first colonists. St. Mary's City was the original center of the Maryland colony and served as its colonial capital for its first 60 years (before the position was given to Annapolis; see p. 117). Today St. Mary's is an outstanding 800-acre living history museum and archaeological park with costumed interpreters who demonstrate the skills of living in the 17th century, as archaeologists continue to unearth and reconstruct the original town site. The cruciform shape of the first statehouse now rises again over recreations of Smith's Ordinary (offering "dyett and drink"), a Native American settlement, and a reconstructed ship that brought the first settlers here from England, with costumed sailors aboard to answer your questions.

St. Mary's County grew rich on its fertile soil, and numerous manor houses built on tobacco fortunes still stand. Sotterley Plantation, a colonial port of entry from the early 18th century, was once allegedly lost in a dice game. Older than Monticello or Mount Vernon in neighboring Virginia (see pp. 239 and 250), the Georgian manor house that sits on a bluff overlooking the Patuxent River can be visited with guided tours from May through October. If you're looking for a hotel with a similar piece of history, you'll find it at St. Michael's Manor. Built around 1805, it sits near Long Neck Creek on land granted to Governor Leonard Calvert in 1637 and is now an inn. Four guest rooms are decorated with quilts and antiques, and a working vineyard fills 3 of the property's 10 acres.

At the very tip of the peninsula stands Point Lookout, where Confederate prisoners were held during the Civil War. Point Lookout is now a state park, and includes one of the county's three lighthouses. Across the Patuxent River in Calvert County is the town of Solomons, where the popular Calvert Marine Museum is worth a day trip: It holds the second-largest collection of fossils from the Miocene era after the Smithsonian.

WHERE: 97 miles south of Baltimore.

Interpreters in 17th-century settings tell the story of Maryland's early years.

HISTORIC ST. MARY'S CITY: Tel 800-762-1634 or 240-895-4990; hsmcdigshistory.org. *When:* varies; see website. **SOTTERLEY PLANTATION:** Hollywood. Tel 301-373-2280; sotterley.org. *When:* grounds daily; manor house tours Tues–Sun, May–Oct. **ST. MICHAEL'S MANOR:** Scotland. Tel 301-872-4025; st-michaels-manor .com. *Cost:* from $70. *When:* Mar–Oct. **POINT LOOKOUT STATE PARK:** Scotland. Tel 301-872-5688. dnr2.maryland.gov/publiclands. **CALVERT MARINE MUSEUM:** Solomons. Tel 410-326-2042; calvertmarinemuseum.com. **BEST TIMES:** Mar 25 (Maryland Day); mid-June for the St. Mary's Country Crab Festival; mid-Oct during the St. Mary's County Oyster Festival.

Historic Charm on the Chesapeake Bay

TALBOT COUNTY

Maryland

O n the Eastern Shore of the Chesapeake Bay, Talbot County is a region defined by water, with pristine wetlands and quiet coves promising a slower pace of life. Start your visit at Easton, the unofficial capital of

the region. Browse through well-stocked antiques stores and stroll the picturesque streets lined with gracious homes.

Oxford, one of the oldest towns in the state, is the perfect place for an afternoon amble past street-side gardens to the waterfront, and it's a chance to enjoy one of the best-preserved colonial settlements in the country. The

Robert Morris Inn, built in 1710 as a home for a shipping agent, today houses 16 rooms. Dine at the inn's excellent restaurant and enjoy the crab cakes that James Michener—who was a guest at the inn while writing *Chesapeake*—called "the best on the Eastern Shore."

A ferry links Oxford to the Victorian village of St. Michaels, a busy shipbuilding center in colonial times. Today, yachts pack the harbor on summer weekends while the 1879 Hooper Strait Lighthouse stands guard. At the outstanding Chesapeake Bay Maritime Museum at Navy Point, watch expert boatbuilders at work or aspiring students who learn traditional skills through an apprentice program. Everyone seems to wind up next door at the casual and fun (and forever busy) Crab Claw, whose hot spiced Maryland blue crabs are plucked from these waters and are best enjoyed outside with a view.

Secure your boat-lover's fantasy as a pampered guest at the Inn at Perry Cabin, an exclusive, romantic getaway in a proud 19th-century mansion right on the Miles River. Its 78 rooms and suites are simply but handsomely decorated, and the elegant restaurant offers water views.

Tilghman Island was first charted by Captain John Smith in the early 1600s. It is home to one of the largest working fleet of skipjacks on the bay. A

seagull is your morning wake-up call at the Lazy Jack Inn, an 1850s waterfront home with four sunny rooms and views over the harbor.

WHERE: Easton is 70 miles southeast of Baltimore. *Visitor info:* Tel 410-770-8000; tourtalbot.org. **ROBERT MORRIS INN:** Oxford. Tel 410-226-5111; robertmorrisinn.com. *Cost:* from $99 (off-peak), from $145 (peak); dinner $46. *When:* closed Mon–Tues. **MARITIME MUSEUM:** St. Michaels. Tel 410-745-2916; cbmm.org. **THE CRAB CLAW:** St. Michaels. Tel 410-745-2900; thecrabclaw.com. *Cost:* dinner $30. *When:* Mar–Nov. **INN AT PERRY CABIN:** St. Michaels. Tel 800-722-2949 or 410-745-2200; perrycabin.com. *Cost:* from $275 (off-peak), from $450 (peak); dinner $65. **LAZY JACK INN:** Tilghman Island. Tel 800-690-5080 or 410-886-2215; lazyjackinn.com. *Cost:* $165. **BEST TIMES:** Mar–Nov when all the local eateries feature blue crabs; late Oct for Tilghman Island Day.

Boats crowd the harbor of St. Michaels, a village with a long maritime history.

Bert Parks Slept Here

ATLANTIC CITY THEN AND NOW

New Jersey

The city by the sea was created in the 1850s as a seaside escape and has worn a lot of hats over the years: from the glamorous 1920s (which saw the birth of A.C.'s signature event, the Miss America Pageant) to the 1930s (when the value of Boardwalk property lent the city's street names to the board game Monopoly) through the swingin' postwar years (when Dean Martin and Jerry Lewis first teamed up at Skinny D'Amato's legendary 500 Club) and on past the gritty 1960s to the post-1977 renaissance, when casinos saved the city's life. Today A.C. is a pastiche of all those things, juxtaposing remnants of its golden era with a certain retro seediness that some may find tantalizingly attractive.

Begin with the Boardwalk, that legendary stretch that started in the late 1900s as a way to keep sand out of the tourists' shoes and grew into a 6-mile, 60-foot-wide cultural icon. In 1929 (just months before the stock market crashed), *The New York Times* called it "a magnificent proof of America's newly found wealth and leisure . . . an iridescent bubble on the surface of our fabulous prosperity." Today, with its tangle of restored carnivalesque facades and tacky gift shops, the Boardwalk can create an irresistible urge to wear seersucker, ride in an old-time human-powered rolling chair, and eat saltwater taffy.

Inland, on Arctic Avenue, the little blue-and-white White House Sub Shop opened in 1946, naming its specialty in honor of WWII submarine crews. Back along the Boardwalk, across from the Taj Mahal, the Steel Pier was once advertised as "The Showplace of a Nation," presenting marathon dance contests, big bands, and a horse and rider who would

jump from a platform into a tank of water 60 feet down. The original pier buildings burned in 1982, but today the pier's up and running again, fresh from a top-to-toe renovation with dozens of rides and attractions.

Modern Atlantic City is, of course, all around. Far from the Boardwalk, the billion-dollar Borgata resort and casino opened its doors in 2003, setting a new (and still unmatched) A.C. standard with its sleek styling, luxurious rooms, 160,000-square-foot gaming floor, huge spa, and top-drawer restaurants, including the Old Homestead (a branch of the famous New York steakhouse) and Fornelletto (an upscale Italian restaurant from chef Stephen Kalt). Recent restaurant additions up the ante: Stand in line to enjoy the kitchens of Bobby Flay and Wolfgang Puck. Two large theaters bring in top-name acts and prizefights. The more recent addition of the Water Club Hotel completes the Borgata expansion. Elsewhere in town, The Quarter (an adjunct of the Tropicana) and the Playground are entertainment complexes full of theaters, restaurants, music, comedy and dance clubs, and upscale shops.

The Miss America Pageant, that annual celebration of swimsuits and world peace that got its start here in 1921, was never really the same after it dropped longtime host Bert Parks in 1980. In 2004 the pageant itself was dropped by ABC-TV and temporarily moved to Las Vegas until it returned to A.C. in 2014.

WHERE: 62 miles southeast of Philadelphia. **WHITE HOUSE SUB SHOP:** Tel 609-345-1564; whitehousesubshop.net. **STEEL PIER:** Tel 866-386-6659 or 609-345-4893; steelpier.com. **BORGATA:** Tel 609-317-1000; theborgata.com. *Cost:* from $99; dinner at Fornelletto $66; dinner at Old Homestead $80. **THE QUARTER:** Tel 800-THE-TROP or 609-340-4000; tropicana.net/quarter. **THE PLAYGROUND:** Tel 609-345-3100; playgroundpierac.com. **BEST TIMES:** Thurs in July and Aug for free jazz concerts on Chicken Bone Beach (chickenbonebeach.org); Aug or early Sept for the Atlantic City Airshow (airshow.acchamber.com).

The Atlantic City Boardwalk offers lots of options for food and souvenir shopping.

A *Victorian-Era Time Capsule "Down the Shore"*

CAPE MAY

New Jersey

Cape May is the oldest seaside resort in the U.S., but its real claim to fame is its juxtaposition of Victorian country-town atmosphere and prime Jersey Shore location. In the mid-1800s it was a place for the elite to flee the summer heat, its salty air and cool breezes drawing vacationers such as Abraham Lincoln, P. T. Barnum, and Henry Ford. Scores of homes were built during this period, of which some 600 survived the great fire of 1879 and the century of development that followed.

Today Cape May is a rarity—the whole town has National Historic Landmark status, its 2.5-square-mile historic district lined with grand old dowagers whose gingerbread excess and wedding-cake colors now house shops, cafés, boutiques, galleries, and gaslit inns. Victorian froufrou abounds from the boardwalk to the backstreets, all best seen via a rented bicycle or one of the horse-drawn buggies that congregate around the Washington Street pedestrian mall.

The South Cape May Meadows Nature Preserve, run by the Nature Conservancy, is a top spot for viewing rare seabirds. More than 300 species of migrating birds pass through annually.

Midway between the beach and the mall, the Virginia Hotel first opened in 1879 and continues to offer a sublimely Victorian hotel experience, with outstanding service. While the building's exterior is maintained in pristine period detail, the 24 guest rooms are furnished in an updated classic style. The hotel's restaurant, the Ebbitt Room, is consistently ranked among the state's finest, serving regional American cuisine with international accents.

Nearby, the Mainstay Inn was among the town's first B&Bs, and remains one of its undisputed gems. A dignified Italianate manor dating to 1872, it offers 14-foot ceilings, 8-foot chandeliers, and airy rooms that mix museum-quality antiques with 21st-century amenities. A stone's throw away, the Chalfonte has been serving guests since 1876, and with its wraparound veranda and Victorian details is one of the most photographed buildings in town. Simply furnished rooms in the main hotel and two cottages have ceiling fans and louvered doors to stir up the sea breezes.

Charming Victorian homes are a common sight on a stroll through Cape May.

WHERE: 93 miles south of Philadelphia. *Visitor info:* Tel 609-884-5508; capemaycham ber.com. **SOUTH CAPE MAY MEADOWS:** Tel 908-879-7262; nature.org/newjersey. **VIRGINIA HOTEL:** Tel 800-732-4236 or 609-884-5700; virginiahotel.com. *Cost:* from $149 (off-peak), from $375 (peak); dinner $55. **MAINSTAY INN:** Tel 609-884-8690; mainstayinn.com. *Cost:* from $165 (off-peak), from $250 (peak). **CHALFONTE:** Tel 888-411-1998 or 609-884-8409; chalfonte .com. *Cost:* from $90. *When:* May–Oct. **BEST TIMES:** fall for migrating birds; late Apr–early May for Spring Festival and mid-Oct for Victorian Week, both offering tours of Victorian mansions not usually open to the public.

Dogs as Delicious as the Atmosphere

RUTT'S HUT

Clifton, New Jersey

Located in the heart of North Jersey's industrial *Sopranos* country, Rutt's looks like the kind of place your mother wouldn't approve of—long and low-slung, saturated with the aroma of fried food. While much of the world makes do with boiled hot dogs, fans of Rutt's know that for a truly sublime frankfurter, hot water can't hold a candle to hot oil. Yes, that's right: Rutt's has been deep-frying its hot dogs since 1928, producing dogs that look like they've been savaged by wolves—hence their name, "rippers"—shredded, crisped, and oily on the outside, soft and tender on the inside. Top 'em off with some of Rutt's legendary relish (made with pickles, carrots, and chopped cabbage), a splat of spicy brown mustard, or some chili and gravy fries for the full effect. Those with weak stomachs can order an "in and out dog" (dipped quickly in the fat) while those with cast-iron innards can order a "cremator," cooked till it's charred black. Head for the roadhouse-like taproom bar if you want to sit and wash 'em down with a beer. If not, lean on one of the stand-up counters near the long serving window and enjoy the view of I-21 and the parking lot.

WHERE: 417 River Rd. Tel 973-779-8615; ruttshut.com. *Cost:* $2.20.

A Garden State Park with a Grand Vision

DUKE FARMS

Hillsborough, New Jersey

Anyone who wonders where New Jersey got the name the "Garden State" has only to visit Duke Farms, a lavish 2,740-acre estate created by tobacco and hydropower magnate James Buchanan "Buck" Duke beginning in 1893. North Carolina–born Duke had first come north in the mid-1880s to open a branch factory for his family's cigarette empire, and soon began buying up land in central New Jersey to re-create the farm atmosphere of his childhood. Within a decade, though, Duke had a change of heart and hired landscape architect James Greenleaf (an employee of Frederick Law Olmsted, designer of New York's Central Park) to transform his property into a grand public park. By 1905, the estate encompassed a reservoir, five lakes, woodlands, fountains, arbors, and a series of carriage paths. Things took a more European turn over the following six years, as English landscape engineer Horatio Buckenham added more formal elements to the original vision. For nearly two decades, Duke's park was open to the public, but incidents of vandalism in 1915 caused him to seal up the gates.

Buck Duke died in 1925, passing his property to his 12-year-old daughter, Doris, who would later add to her father's legacy by creating a Japanese garden, an aviary for exotic birds, and a series of indoor display gardens, the latter open to the public beginning in 1964. It would be almost 40 more years, though, before the rest of the property (343 acres)—one of the largest private estates in New Jersey—would reopen to visitors with miles of walking and biking paths. The 67,000-square-foot manor was the main residence of Doris Duke until her death in 1993. It is no longer open to the public.

Today, guests can once again marvel at the estate's flora, as well as its 9 man-made lakes, 10 waterfalls, 35 fountains, 54 bridges, and 2.5 miles of walls constructed from locally quarried stone. Beginning in 1958, Doris Duke spent six years traveling the world, assembling ideas and specimens for her 11 themed gardens, all housed in gorgeous Victorian-style greenhouses constructed by renowned greenhouse builders Lord & Burnham.

WHERE: 45 miles southwest of New York City; 1112 Dukes Parkway West. Tel 908-722-3700; dukefarms.org. **BEST TIMES:** mid-Apr–Nov for outdoor garden blooms; Sept–May for indoor garden blooms.

Springsteen Country

THE JERSEY SHORE

New Jersey

The Jersey Shore is a state of mind. If you're from the Garden State, it's a continuum that stretches from childhood beach weekends through college-age road trips and then right on back to vacationing with your own kids.

The original reason people started going "down the shore" (and still one of the main reasons today) is simple: humidity. In summer, the New York/New Jersey metropolitan area turns into one giant steam room, sending residents hightailing it to the Jersey Shore's nearly 130 miles of beaches. Resorts and boardwalk entertainment districts boomed beginning in the late 19th century, and today the shore is a glorious mishmash, from hard-partying seaside bars, famous rock 'n' roll clubs, and neon-lit boardwalk Americana to family-oriented beaches, beautiful lighthouses, and a whole galaxy of motels, inns, and summer rental properties.

The boardwalk towns are the heart of it all. Down south, near the very tip of the shore, Wildwood boasts a 38-block boardwalk with huge amusement piers, waterparks, carnival and arcade games, souvenir shops, tattoo parlors, pizza and funnel-cake stands, tram cars, and everything else you'd want from a great American boardwalk—including Skee-Ball, the classic arcade game

Bicycles line a boardwalk that runs along a crowded beach.

that's a cross between bowling, bocce ball, and darts. On one side of the boardwalk, Wildwood's white sand beach is nearly half a mile wide in places, and packed with families throughout the summer months. On the other side, the town is full of beautifully preserved "Doo-Wop" architecture, a 1950s style that mixes space-age angularity with Caribbean and Hawaiian tiki motifs. With approximately 100 Doo-Wop motels, restaurants, and shops, Wildwood is the grand high mecca of the style.

Twenty-five miles to the north, Ocean City's boardwalk offers a calmer, more polite version of the same, with roller coasters, games, miniature golf, and the Spanish-style Ocean City Music Pier, which dates to 1928 and still offers everything from the Ocean City Pops to the Miss New Jersey Pageant—as good as pageantry got in the Garden State when Miss America left Atlantic City for Vegas from 2004–2014 (Miss America has since returned).

Considerably farther north, only about 90 minutes from New York City, Seaside Heights completes the trilogy of active boardwalks, advertising itself as "Your home for family fun since 1913!" Perched on a narrow barrier island between the Atlantic Ocean and Barnegat Bay, with only about four blocks from shore to shore, the town has a mile-long boardwalk that's brimming with rides, games of chance, cotton candy and sausage stands, and raw bars. At the Casino Pier, the wooden 1910 Dr. Floyd L. Moreland Carousel is one of America's great remaining carousels, with hand-carved animals, 2,000 lightbulbs, and a 1923 Wurlitzer Military Band Organ providing the irreplaceable sound track.

Another kind of sound track—arguably the unofficial anthem of New Jersey—got its start even farther north, in Asbury Park. A major seaside resort city from 1870 until WWII, Asbury had experienced such a palpable decline by the early 1970s that its mood influenced local boy Bruce Springsteen's songs of desperation and redemption, spawning the "Born to Run" New Jersey zeitgeist. You can still hear the Asbury Park sound at the Stone Pony, the legendary rock club where Springsteen has made scores of appearances since 1975.

WHERE: from Cape May in the south to Sandy Hook in the north. *Wildwoods visitor info:* Tel 800-992-9732; wildwoodsnj.com. *Ocean City visitor info:* Tel 800-BEACH-NJ or 609-399-1412; oceancityvacation.com. *Seaside Heights visitor info:* Tel 732-793-9100; seaside-heightsnj.org. **DOO WOP PRESERVATION LEAGUE:** Wildwood. Tel 609-729-4000; doowopusa.org. **STONE PONY:** Asbury Park. Tel 732-502-0600; stonepony online.com. **WHERE TO STAY:** The retro StarLux, Wildwood. Tel 609-522-7412; thestarlux.com. *Cost:* from $80 (off-peak), from $235 (peak). **BEST TIMES:** mid-Apr for Ocean City's comedy-themed Doo Dah Parade; late May for the giant Wildwoods International Kite Festival; mid-Oct for Wildwood's Fabulous' 50s & Beyond Weekend.

The Unknown Jersey Shore

SPRING LAKE

New Jersey

Spring Lake is only about 5 miles down the shore from Asbury Park (see above), but it might as well be on another planet. It has a beach, but it's a quiet, peaceful, litter-free beach, with room to spread out and laze. It's got a boardwalk too, but it's glitz-free, with nary a fast-food vendor or neon sign to be seen. Most folks are just out for a stroll or pedaling along on bicycles built for two, and maybe heading to Susan Murphy's or Hoffman's for an ice cream cone.

Founded in the late 19th century as a summer destination for New Yorkers and Philadelphians fleeing city humidity, Spring Lake developed into an upscale, quiet, mostly residential community. In town, the large, spring-fed namesake lake is stocked with ducks and surrounded by floral displays and walking paths, while nearby Third Avenue offers a shopping district full of boutiques and interesting gift shops. On tree-lined streets, well-kept homes boast wraparound porches, big windows, and turreted roofs so emblematic of late 19th-century resort style.

Though it's primarily a residential town, Spring Lake offers several wonderful inns and restaurants. Located right across the street from the boardwalk, the Breakers on the Ocean is a classic Victorian beachfront resort, with its boxy five-story architecture and long covered porch. Inside, 75 rooms have kept up with the 21st century, the most outfitted offering whirlpool baths and fireplaces. A few blocks south and a few doors inland, the Spring Lake Inn is an 1888 former carriage house that's now a B&B with a classic Victorian porch. Some of its

It's just a short walk to the beach from one of Spring Lake's charming inns.

16 guest rooms offer fireplaces, Jacuzzis, and ocean views. Back near the Breakers, the Grand Victorian hotel's restaurant, the Black Trumpet, is acclaimed for the cooking of chef co-owner Mark Mikolajczyk. Menus favor seafood and the freshest ingredients, prepared in an exacting style that shows off the chef's training as an intern for New York City's celebrated David Bouley.

WHERE: 63 miles south of New York City. *Visitor info:* Tel 732-449-0577; springlake.org. **THE BREAKERS ON THE OCEAN:** Tel 732-449-7700; breakershotel.com. *Cost:* from $100 (off-peak), from $220 (peak). **SPRING LAKE INN:** Tel 732-449-2010; springlakeinn.com. *Cost:* from $99 (off-peak), from $199 (peak). **BLACK TRUMPET:** Tel 732-449-4700; theblacktrumpet catering.com. *Cost:* dinner $45.

Hot Meals, Cool Décor, and a Waitress Named Jeannie

CLASSIC NORTH JOISEY DINERS

New Jersey

The diner is an archetypal New Jersey icon, keeping alive the tradition of greasy burgers, any-hour breakfasts, and home-baked pies. First appearing as horse-drawn lunch wagons that made the rounds of factories in the 1870s, diners eventually grew roots in working-class neighborhoods nationwide. In the early 20th century, companies started manufacturing them in prefabricated kits, and by the '30s, you could pick your diner out of a catalog, send a check, and get the whole thing delivered to you—stools, stoves, dishes, and all—in about three months.

Of the ten major diner manufacturers, six were based in New Jersey, making the state the unofficial classic diner capital of America. Ideally, a classic diner should be prefab; it should be long and narrow like a railroad dining car (after which they were originally patterned); it should have a counter with stools (with leatherette booths optional); it should serve comfort food, preferably 24 hours a day; and it should be old, with as much of its original decor intact as possible.

The industrial areas of northern New Jersey, beginning just west of lower Manhattan and Staten Island and spreading inland for about ten miles, are a diner lover's mecca. Start at the White Mana in Jersey City, which began life at the 1939 World's Fair and claims to be the original fast-food restaurant. It's round, with a circular counter and tile floor, and serves legendarily tasty mini-burgers. (A second White Manna—squarishly shaped and retaining the chain's original spelling—survives in Hackensack.) Not far from Mana and flanked by highways on all sides, the Bendix Diner dates from 1947 and is a regular stop for Jerseyites returning from Manhattan after a night out. A steel rectangle with a can't-miss neon sign, it's essentially unchanged since the day it opened. The same

can't be said for the nearby Tick Tock Diner, which is a 24-hour Northern Jersey classic—some years ago its original 1949 exterior was covered over with an ugly chrome. The huge menu remains, as does the clock on the roof, surrounded by the diner's insightful motto: "Eat Heavy."

To the south, in East Orange, the double-size Harris Diner represents the move into the 1950s. It wins plaudits for its original steel-and-chrome exterior, its food, its booths with their individual jukeboxes, and its old-school waitresses.

Back in Jersey City, the Miss America Diner is another '50s-era chrome-and-steel classic with a block-lettered neon sign on top and good, solid food within. For a last treat on your tour, head inland to the Summit Diner, built in 1938. It's got a railroad-car exterior, deco lettering, and a wood-paneled interior with booths on one side and a long counter on the other. It's easy to imagine some down-on-his-luck character straight out of a Frank Capra movie slouched here during the Depression, having donuts and coffee.

WHERE: northern New Jersey. *Cost:* under $10. **WHITE MANA:** Jersey City. Tel 201-963-1441. **WHITE MANNA:** Hackensack. Tel 201-342-0914. **BENDIX DINER:** Hasbrouck Heights. Tel 201-288-0143. **TICK TOCK DINER:** Clifton. Tel 973-777-0511. **HARRIS DINER:** East Orange. Tel 973-675-9703. **MISS AMERICA DINER:** Jersey City. Tel 201-333-5468. **SUMMIT DINER:** Summit. Tel 908-277-3256.

An Aristocratic College Town

PRINCETON

New Jersey

N ew Jersey's Princeton University and its namesake town have a similar feel—*in* but not *of* the Garden State—existing as part of the American aristocracy's great old-money diaspora, full of Colonial-era architecture,

leafy parks, and manicured gardens, all overlaid with the energy of a busy college town.

The place got its start in the late 17th century, when six Quaker families established a community near the King's Highway. By the 1730s it had become known as Prince Town, named in honor of Prince William III of Orange and Nassau, and in 1756 was selected as the new home of the College of New Jersey, North America's fourth institute of higher learning. As if that's not enough, the town was also site of a major battle of the Revolution; hosted the Continental Congress for five months in 1783 (during which time Britain finally recognized U.S. independence); was home to two U.S. presidents (Grover Cleveland and Woodrow Wilson); and was headquarters for Albert Einstein from 1932 to his death in 1955.

The campus itself is gorgeous, a veritable garden of learning. At the main Nassau Street entrance, the 1905 wrought-iron FitzRandolph gate was designed by the great New York architectural firm McKim, Mead & White. The college's first building, Nassau Hall, was constructed in 1756 as the largest academic building in the colonies, and today serves as the office of the university president. Other historic structures on campus include the Gothic University Chapel, completed in 1928 and still one of the largest university chapels in the world; Alexander Hall, a venue that's hosted speeches by William Jennings Bryan, Einstein, and Eleanor Roosevelt; and the mid-19th-century Prospect House, which served as Woodrow Wilson's home during his time as the university's 13th president

Near Prospect House, the Princeton University Art Museum, founded in 1882, holds a collection of more than 92,000 works

Princeton University was originally intended to train Presbyterian ministers.

ranging from Claude Monet and Willem de Kooning to extensive holdings of pre-Columbian and Asian art. Off campus, Nassau Street is the main strip, lined with boutiques, bookstores, and beautiful architecture.

Just to the north, Palmer Square offers high-end shops and restaurants and is home to the Nassau Inn, which has hosted everyone from George Washington to William Shatner in its 250-year history, first in its original Nassau Street home, then beginning in 1937 in its 203-room Colonial-style abode. Its Yankee Doodle Tap Room is named for the 13-foot Norman Rockwell mural hanging behind the bar.

WHERE: 50 miles southwest of New York City. *Visitor info:* Tel 609-924-1776; visit princeton.org. **ART MUSEUM:** Tel 609-258-3788; artmuseum.princeton.edu. **NASSAU INN:** Tel 800-862-7728 or 609-921-7500; nassauinn.com. *Cost:* from $239. **BEST TIME:** Sun for the Historical Society's guided walking tours (princetonhistory.org).

Counting Sheep Along the Delaware

THE WOOLVERTON INN

Stockton, New Jersey

Perched on a hill above the Delaware River, surrounded by its own 10 acres of apple and maple trees and another 300 of forest and farmland, the Woolverton is the very paragon of romantic historic inns. Built in 1792 by mill owner and Revolutionary War veteran John Prall Jr. (and owned by the Woolverton family from 1850), the former manor house was converted to an inn in 1981 and carefully renovated to an historical ideal. Today, its 18th-century atmosphere is so complete that you half expect to see gentlemen in waistcoats and three-cornered hats strolling the gardens or ladies in petticoats swishing about its 13 rooms.

In the main 1792 building you can choose from eight individually decorated rooms and suites, some with whirlpool tubs and working

On the Woolverton Inn's preserved farmland, you can feed the free-roaming sheep.

fireplaces. Around the grounds, the 1860s carriage house and barn contain five cottage accommodations for an even more luxurious experience, from the classic styling of the Garden and Audubon cottages to the high-beamed, lodgelike feel of the Hunterdon. Each has a private entrance, whirlpool tub for two, fireplace, king-size feather beds, and views of the sheep pasture, woodlands, or hillside.

Days begin with extravagant breakfasts, with specialties like apple cranberry turkey sausage, lemon ricotta pancakes, and thick maple-glazed bacon. From here you can repair to the long, gracious front porch with its rocking chairs and wicker love seats, or roam the grounds greeting the resident black-faced sheep. There are riverside biking trails nearby, and the lovely antiques-rich towns of Lambertville and New Hope, Pennsylvania, are only five minutes away, with scenic Bucks County, Pennsylvania, just beyond (see p. 215).

WHERE: 66 miles southwest of New York City; 6 Woolverton Rd. Tel 888-264-6648 or 609-397-0802; woolvertoninn.com. *Cost:* from $155 (off-peak), from $190 (peak). **BEST TIME:** Sept–Nov for fall colors and great weather.

At One with Nature, Courtesy of America's Foremost Outdoorsman

TOM BROWN JR.'S TRACKER SCHOOL

Waretown, New Jersey

In 1957, a small boy named Tom Brown met a young Indian boy who took him home to meet his 83-year-old grandfather, the Apache medicine man Stalking Wolf. It was a moment that changed Brown's life. For the next ten years he

stayed at Stalking Wolf's side, absorbing his vast knowledge of nature, survival, tracking, and Native American philosophy. When Brown was ready, he left New Jersey and followed his teacher's path, wandering from wilderness to

wilderness around the Americas, learning from the land and surviving without the aid of modern tools. When he returned to civilization in the mid-1970s, he put his tracking skills to work finding missing persons and fugitives;

wrote the first of 17 books (and counting); and opened a school to pass on Stalking Wolf's wisdom to new generations. To date, several thousand students have accepted the challenge.

Though Brown himself has trained U.S. special forces and law enforcement officers, this isn't one of those hard-core, gun-obsessed survivalist schools. In fact, it's exactly the opposite. At its core, Brown's school emphasizes living in a state of complete awareness, balanced and in harmony with nature. In all, the school offers more than 75 courses, from "The Standard" to intensive courses in nature observation, tracking, survival, scouting, natural healing, and philosophy. Days are long, typically beginning before 7:30 and going on until 10 or 11 P.M. Advanced classes are extremely hands-on, while the standard class balances long, detailed lectures with time practicing the skills you're learning: building shelters using natural materials, finding water, harvesting wild edible plants, making fire with a bow-drill, tracking and trapping, and tanning hides. No animals are harmed during any of the courses—because it's not necessary and would be disrespectful to the animals. That kind of spiritual connectedness is what Brown and his school foster, taking refugees from modern society and teaching them to see the world in an entirely different way.

WHERE: 88 miles south of New York City. Tel 609-242-0350; trackerschool.com. *Cost:* weeklong classes from $800. *When:* May–Dec at one of two camps near Waretown. (Jan–May at facilities near Fort Myers, FL, or Boulder Creek, CA.)

Top-Drawer Dining in the Garden State

THE RYLAND INN

Whitehouse Station, New Jersey

Though big cities like New York and San Francisco typically get all the foodie press, some of the nation's most enjoyable restaurants flourish quietly in their hinterlands—such as the hamlet of Whitehouse Station,

New Jersey, where the Ryland Inn inhabits a meticulously well-kept 1796 farmhouse and former stagecoach stop.

Chef Craig Polignono prepares farm-to-table dishes at the Ryland Inn.

Situated on 50 acres of hills and pastures that evoke old America, this award-winning gastro getaway closed in 2007 but reopened in 2012 under new ownership. The 3-acre organic garden and year-round hydroponic greenhouse continue to nurture the Ryland Inn's seasonal backyard-to-table philosophy: much of the salad greens, vegetables, herbs, and fruits are picked just hours before they appear on your plate. The inn's new chef, Jersey-born Craig Polignono, crafts an American cuisine that is hearty yet refined, perfectly suited to a venue that epitomizes country elegance.

WHERE: 45 miles west of New York City; 111 Old Highway 28. Tel 908-534-4011; rylandinnnj.com. *Cost:* dinner $70.

Extravagant Isolation, Forever Wild

THE ADIRONDACKS

New York

The largest state park in the continental U.S.—larger than Yosemite or the entire state of Massachusetts—the 6-million-acre Adirondack State Park is legally protected to remain "forever wild," a debt owed to the tireless efforts of 19th-century lawyer-turned-surveyor Verplanck Colvin.

The park isn't completely wild, but rather a patchwork of public and private lands covering 12,000 square miles in northeastern New York state. The mountains it's named after are among the world's oldest peaks, made of billion-year-old Precambrian rocks. An 1830s geologist, Ebenezer Emmons, gave them the moniker after an Algonquin tribe who hunted here. (Ironically, it was originally a slur by the Mohawk who dubbed the tribe *adirondack*, or "bark-eaters.")

A whiff of aristocratic cachet remains from when 19th-century masters of the universe with names like Whitney, Vanderbilt, and Rockefeller chose this roadless wilderness to build their "Great Camps," with armies of servants in tow. Surrounded by dense forests, mountains, and more than 2,500 lakes and ponds, the lakefront compounds blended luxury and rustic charm, using minimally worked logs, twisted branches, and decorative twigwork in what has become known as the Adirondack style.

Not many of these great camps have survived, and precious few operate as hotels. The most magnificent is The Point, a nine-building compound built in 1933 by William Avery Rockefeller on 8-mile-long Upper Saranac Lake. With its lavish guest rooms, the atmosphere of a house party prevails, with candlelit meals and an exceptional wine list. Forced into extravagant isolation happy campers spend idyllic days canoeing, fishing, or exploring the hiking trails that extend into the parkland.

The relatively more affordable Lake Placid Lodge on the western shore of the lake was destroyed by fire in 2005. The 1882 camp was reconstructed to resemble the original as closely as possible, with five suites. The 1920s-era lakeside cabins are perfect for two, with stone fireplaces and modern comforts like feather beds and huge soaking tubs.

The village of Lake Placid, site of the 1932 and 1980 Winter Olympics, maintains its role as "Winter Sports Capital of the World" and includes an Olympic Museum. International athletes still train at its world-class skating rinks, ski jumps, and a thrilling bobsled run. Whiteface Mountain, scene of the downhill competitions, has the steepest vertical drop in the East as well as a trail system popular with families and beginners.

Mirror Lake Inn, a 131-room white clapboard, green-shuttered resort with one of the best locations in the country, is set right on the Mirror Lake, and every room has a view. It feels like a Bavarian lodge, both formal and rustic, with a private lakefront beach to complement the region's compelling winter sports (including dogsled rides). Famous for its signature Adirondack flapjacks, the inn offers the sanctuary of a plush spa.

Lake Placid is reached by way of High Peaks Byway (Route 73), a 30-mile stretch that winds through the Adirondack Park's tallest mountains. The Adirondack Museum at Blue Mountain Lake displays countless works of art including Adirondack scenes and a collection of artifacts that bring to life a vanished world of logging camps, Victorian hotels, and hermit cabins.

WHERE: Lake Placid is 285 miles north of New York City. *Adirondack visitor info:* Tel 518-846-8016; visitadirondacks.com. *Lake Placid visitor info:* Tel 800-44-PLACID or 518-523-2445; lakeplacid.com. **THE POINT:** Saranac Lake. Tel 800-255-3530 or 518-891-5674; thepointsaranac.com. *Cost:* from $1,600, includes meals and drinks. **LAKE PLACID LODGE:** Lake Placid. Tel 877-523-2700 or 518-523-2700; lakeplacidlodge.com. *Cost:* rooms from $499 (off-peak), from $699 (peak); dinner $75. **OLYMPIC CENTER AND MUSEUM:** Lake Placid. Tel 518-523-1655; whitefacelakeplacid.com. **SUMMER STORM BOBSLED RIDE:** Lake Placid. Tel 518-523-4436. *When:* June–early Oct. **WHITEFACE MOUNTAIN:** Wilmington. Tel 518-946-2223; whiteface.com. *Cost:* lift tickets $92. *When:* ski season, late Nov–mid-Apr. **MIRROR LAKE INN:** Lake Placid. Tel 518-523-2544; mirror

Autumn hikes through the Adirondacks afford spectacular vistas of colorful foliage.

lakeinn.com. *Cost:* from $290 (off-peak), from $419 (peak). **THE ADIRONDACK MUSEUM:** Blue Mountain Lake. Tel 518-352-7311; adkmuseum.org. *When:* late May–early Oct. **BEST TIMES:** late June for Lake Placid Film Festival; July for Woodmen's Days in Tupper Lake; early Sept for the Rustic Fair (sale of handmade Adirondack furniture and art) at the Adirondack Museum.

A City's Most Famous Export

BUFFALO WINGS

Buffalo, New York

Anchor Bar near downtown Buffalo may seem like just another funky joint with a Harley-Davidson hanging from the ceiling, but the modest redbrick building is the hallowed site where "buffalo wings" were born back in 1964. Teressa Bellissimo was in the kitchen when her bartender son, Dominic, asked her to whip up something for a bunch of ravenous friends. Ever frugal, she took chicken wings destined for the stock pot, threw them in the deep fryer, flavored them with a "secret sauce," then served them with blue cheese dressing and celery on the side. The impromptu dish spread like wildfire, becoming a beloved snack of choice in sports bars and family restaurants throughout the country. There are even a few other Anchor Bar locations, including one in Las Vegas, but true-blue wing devotees make the pilgrimage to this unassuming birthplace to experience the genius first put forth over 50 years ago.

In 2002, Buffalo hosted the first National Buffalo Wing Festival. Over Labor Day more than 30 eateries from as far as London serve 130 styles of chicken wings to 70,000 people, vying for the longest lines and prizes. There is a Miss Buffalo Wing contest and a bobbing-for-wings competition that can get pretty messy as goggled participants nab as many wings as possible from a kiddie pool filled with blue cheese dressing.

Buffalo locals are equally passionate about a dish called beef on 'weck, created by piling rare roast beef onto a hard roll sprinkled with caraway seeds and coarse salt and dipped in beef juice, topped off with eye-watering horseradish. The unique appeal of this hearty sandwich is best experienced at Schwabl's, whose dining rooms haven't changed much since 1942, down to the oilcloth table covers and the waitresses in white uniforms and matching shoes.

Every year the much awaited Taste of Buffalo, the country's second largest food festival after Chicago's (see p. 493), gives 450,000 hungry folks the chance to see what else the city has to offer, from sponge

Anchor Bar is the birthplace of the buffalo wing, drawing wing enthusiasts from near and far.

candy caramel cannoli to beef on weck ravioli.

WHERE: 375 miles northwest of New York City. *Visitor info:* Tel 800-283-3256 or 716-852-0511; visitbuffaloniagara.com. **ANCHOR BAR:** Tel 716-886-8920; anchorbar.com. *Cost:* 10 wings, $14. **NATIONAL BUFFALO WING FESTIVAL:** Tel 716-565-4141; buffalowing.com. *When:* early Sept. **SCHWABL'S RESTAURANT:** West Seneca. Tel 716-675-2333; schwabls .com. *Cost:* beef on 'weck $10. **TASTE OF BUFFALO:** tasteofbuffalo.com. *When:* early July.

Prayer, Dogs, and Cheesecake

MONKS OF NEW SKETE

Cambridge, New York

A mountaintop retreat in the Taconic range of upstate New York just 10 hilly miles from the Vermont border, New Skete is a small religious community of Eastern Orthodox monks, nuns, and lay companions.

They are known primarily to the outside world for two curious pursuits at which they have been remarkably successful and nationally recognized: German shepherds and cheesecake.

A bright red compound centered around a rustic chapel topped with gold-leaf onion domes so brilliant that local pilots use them as a point of reference, the monastery is a very special place where visitors are welcome to spend time in the meditation gardens, hike the 500-acre property, or join the twice-daily services when the Orthodox liturgy is chanted in a transcendental four-part harmony.

The monks, who started the contemplative community in 1966, believe that man is meant to be happy in this life, not just the next. To achieve economic self-sufficiency they began breeding, training, and selling German shepherds and inadvertently became superstars in the world of dog training with their cult classics, *How to Be Your Dog's Best Friend* and *The Art of Raising a Puppy*, which have sold nearly a million copies and generated so much demand for their puppies that requests are difficult to fill.

New Skete, named for one of the first Christian monastic settlements (in the desert of Skete in northern Egypt), became a rarity in the world of monasteries when, in 1969, it welcomed a group of nuns, who settled on a hilltop a respectable 3 miles away. Today the Nuns of New Skete have equalled their fellow brothers with the success of their classic New York–style cheesecakes produced in a calorie-laced array of flavors that are prized by local restaurants and fans in all 50 states.

Hundreds of visitors converge on the monastery in June when the nearby crossroads of Cambridge has its annual Balloon Festival and the monks offer tours and demonstrations of dog training. On a Saturday in early August, retreatants arrive (almost all return visitors) for the Annual Pilgrimage—time spent discussing issues that may range from the rewards of monastic life to the origin and history of religious icons.

Throughout the years, guests are welcomed in modest but comfortable accommodations—men with the monks, women with the nuns, and couples with the lay companions (a third community of married couples). You can join them in their simple schedule of work, prayer, and study.

Where: 40 miles northeast of Albany. Tel 518-677-3928; newskete.org. *When:* closed Mon. *Cost:* suggested donation $80 per night, minimum of 2 nights, includes meals. **Nuns of New Skete:** Tel 518-677-3810; newskete .com. **Best times:** 1st Sat in June for Open House, and the Cambridge Valley Balloon Festival; early Aug for Pilgrimage.

Of Borscht and Buddha

THE CATSKILLS

New York

With a wild beauty that captured the imagination of great painters like Thomas Cole, the Catskills have been an on-again, off-again vacation destination for 200 years. In the 19th century, trains from New York City made it an easy way to escape the beastly summer heat, still a motivator for the ever-growing numbers of weekenders and second-home hunters looking for the last great deal.

In the 20th century, European immigrants found the Catskills' scenic beauty reminiscent of the old country. Sullivan County became the center of the summer Borscht Belt universe with primarily Jewish bungalow colonies, all-you-can-eat buffets, mambo nights, and expansive family resorts like Browns, the Concord, and Grossingers, where Mel Brooks and Sid Caesar got their starts. At the southern edge of the Catskill Park, Delaware County is still very much a farming community whose "cow country" authenticity is an irresistible lure for city sophisticates, while at the northernmost reaches of the park, Greene County holds some of the most dramatic peaks and the best skiing in winter.

But today it's the very heart of the Catskills in Ulster County that appeals most to urbanites looking for a Walden Pond escape, with beautiful mountain interiors of deep forests and hidden waterfalls. Woodstock, where Bob Dylan and The Band hung out in the '60s, is the Catskills' most famous town, best known for the 1969 rock concert held nearby. Woodstock has had a bohemian streak since the early 1900s, when artists, writers, and alternative thinkers settled here. Today its tie-dyed heritage is slowly giving way to the film-and-fashion crowd most evident during the Woodstock Film Festival, which benefits from celebrities who live in the area or New York City.

Today, Woodstock remains a haven for creative types with a small but burgeoning film scene.

Meanwhile, to the south, Bethel has gotten a high dose of style and culture with the new Bethel Woods Center for the Arts, a 4,400-seat summer pavilion with space on the lawn for 12,000 more. They come for the variety of artists and musical styles—big names like Bob Dylan and Neil Young play here. Bethel also has a hall dedicated to the 1969 Woodstock concert, telling its story and influence on American culture.

Spiritual seekers are drawn to the special energy of these mountains and have created numerous ashrams, yoga camps, and Buddhist retreats. Zen Mountain Monastery offers traditional Zen training where students rise at 4:30 A.M. to join Buddhist monks for morning meditation. During themed weekend retreats guests learn about everything from psychology to the arts. The nearby Menla Mountain Retreat (affiliated with the Tibet House in New York City) also holds retreats, led by the likes of Tibetan Buddhist Robert Thurman (father of Uma), and it has a lovely spa.

Those who bond with nature while hip-high in cold mountain springs will want to make a pilgrimage to the Beaverkill River, the birthplace of American dry-fly-fishing and one of the most famous trout streams in the U.S. It is the raison d'être for the Beaverkill Valley

Inn, a classic 19-room trout fishing lodge (with a mile of frontage on the Beaverkill). Anglers are only a quick cast away from the revered Wulff Fly Fishing School, founded by American fly-fishing icon Lee Wulff. Since his death, his wife Joan carries on with the school, where you can learn everything from trout fishing basics to advanced casting techniques.

For those who prefer their great outdoors with refined indoor comforts, the Emerson Resort and Spa offers a clean, sophisticated country look at the Inn, which is connected to the spa. Both it and the Lodge next door provide a perfect family holiday. Along with skiing, hiking, biking, and fishing, there's tubing—a nice, slow ride down the dancing Esopus Creek in a big fat inner tube.

WHERE: 100 miles northwest of New York City. *Catskills visitor info:* visitcatskills.com. *Ulster County visitor info:* Tel 800-342-5826 or 845-340-3566; ulstercountyalive.com. **WOODSTOCK FILM FESTIVAL:** Tel 845-679-4265; woodstockfilmfestival.com. *Cost:* from $10 for individual films; $750 for full pass, includes screenings, panels, and parties. *When:* 4 days in early Oct. **BETHEL WOODS CENTER:** Tel 866-781-2922; bethelwoodscenter.org. *Cost:* from $25 for lawn seats. **ZEN MOUNTAIN MONASTERY:** Mount Tremper. Tel 845-688-2228; zmm.mro.org. *Cost:* from $250 for a 2-night meditation retreat, includes meals. **MENLA MOUNTAIN RETREAT:** Tel 845-688-6897; menla.org. *Cost:* from $350 per person for 2 nights, includes meals (retreat programs additional). **BEAVERKILL VALLEY INN:** Lew Beach. Tel 845-439-4844; beaver killvalleyinn.com. *Cost:* from $180 (off-peak), from $220 (peak). **WULFF FLY FISHING SCHOOL:** Livingston Manor. Tel 800-328-3638 or 845-439-5020; wulffschool.com. *Cost:* $595 for a 2½ day course ($720 with meals). *When:* late Apr–June. **THE EMERSON RESORT AND SPA:** Tel 877-688-2828 or 845-688-2828; emersonresort.com. *Cost:* Lodge from $180. **BEST TIMES:** Apr–mid-Oct for trout fishing; Oct for Woodstock Film Festival; mid-Oct for peak foliage.

Inspiring Marriage of Intellect and Spirit

CHAUTAUQUA INSTITUTION

Chautauqua, New York

One of the few utopian-minded communities to survive to the present day, the Chautauqua Institution is a 750-acre lakeside Victorian village founded in 1874 by a Methodist bishop and an Akron industrialist who believed that everyone has a right to learn. Peculiarly American in character for its optimistic emphasis on self-improvement, Chautauqua Lake Sunday School Assembly (as it was called) started as a non-demoninational summer camp for Sunday School teachers and quickly broadened to include lectures by experts on academic topics, inspirational talks, and performances of the arts for anyone who attended. Immortalized in the 1970s cult classic *Zen and the Art of Motorcycle Maintenance* by Robert Pirsig, Chautauqua is more than just a place on the map, it is an imaginative ideal of arts and learning. President Ulysses S. Grant came here as a participant; future president Bill Clinton spoke here as governor of Arkansas; and Franklin D. Roosevelt delivered his historic "I hate war" speech here.

Today 100,000 people attend at least one event during the nine-week-long summer season. Each week has its own theme, tending toward weighty subjects such as money and power, moral leadership in action, and global climate change. Any given day might include lectures by experts, addresses by divinity professors, performances of Anton Chekov's *The Cherry Orchard* by the Chautauqua Theater Company, or a concert by well-known names such as Chris Botti and Joshua Bell in the historic Bratton Theater. The heart of Chautauqua programming is the resident symphony, ballet, and opera companies that perform on rotating nights in the 4,000-seat open-air amphitheater.

Visitors who start with an overnight visit find the blend of intellectual stimulation, spiritual growth, and natural beauty so refreshing they often return for longer visits.

The most comfortable place to stay is the Athenaeum Hotel, an elaborate 151-room Victorian grande dame built in 1881 and beloved by those who appreciate a shabby chic aesthetic. There are plenty of rocking chairs overlooking a sweep of lawn that unfolds down to the shores of Lake Chautauqua.

WHERE: 75 miles southwest of Buffalo. Tel 800-836-ARTS or 716-357-6200; ciweb.org. *Cost:* 1-day ticket $82; weekly pass including all events $466. *When:* late June–Aug. **ATHENAEUM HOTEL:** Tel 800-821-1881 or 716-357-4444; athenaeum-hotel.com. *Cost:* from $220. *When:* late June–Aug.

Baseball, Bel Canto, and Bucolic Charm

COOPERSTOWN

New York

Agracious, tree-lined village amid upstate New York's woodlands, Cooperstown sits proudly stuck in time on the southern tip of placid Otsego Lake, a hill-ringed lake so crystal clear it is the source of the town's drinking water. According to legend, it was here, in 1839, that Abner Doubleday laid out the dimensions of a diamond and originated the game of baseball. That myth has since been debunked, but it's why the National Baseball Hall of Fame and Museum opened its doors here in 1939, becoming a pilgrimage site for baseball lovers. Set in a modest three-story brick building on the town's four-block-long Main Street, the museum's collection runs the gamut from Joe DiMaggio's locker and Brooks Robinson's glove to Babe Ruth's "Called Shot" bat from the 1932 World Series—in all, some 40,000 objects.

An unusually handsome small town with a year-round population of 1,800, Cooperstown draws throngs of tourists each summer, but they're not all here for the baseball.

Every July and August since 1975, Cooperstown hosts the prestigious Glimmerglass Festival, which blends classic repertory with operatic rarities, modern musicals, and conversations with masters like Stephen Sondheim. An intimate, acoustically perfect 900-seat house has walls that open to views of surrounding farmland. Nineteenth-century novelist James Fenimore Cooper, son of the New Jersey transplant who founded Cooperstown in 1786, referred to Otsego Lake as "Glimmerglass," and thus the festival's name.

Artifacts from the younger Cooper's life can be found at the Fenimore Art Museum, a 1930s neo-Georgian mansion on Lake Otsego, along with exceptional collections of North American Indian art, American folk art, and works of Hudson River artists like Thomas Cole.

The Farmers' Museum across the street is one of the country's oldest rural life museums, made up of early 19th-century buildings— general store, doctor's office, printer—and a working farmstead that offers a rich portrait of the life of early rural Americans. Founded in 1943 by the Clark family, heirs to the Singer sewing machine fortune, the museum is staffed by skilled guides in costume, with real cows and sheep as extras.

Amid it all sits the Inn at Cooperstown, a fine example of Second Empire architecture from 1874. The aroma of fresh-baked muffins and breads heightens the atmosphere of this warm and friendly B&B. For the grandest accommodation in town, head to the expansive Federal-style Otesaga Resort Hotel, commissioned in 1909 by the

In 1939 the National Baseball Hall of Fame and Museum held its first induction ceremony.

Clark family. Much has been made of its 400 windows, unrivaled lakefront setting, and venerable 18-hole Leatherstocking Golf Course, designed by Devereaux Emmet more than a century ago. Short by today's standards (6,406 yards from the back tees), Leatherstocking provides plenty of challenge with its hills and its famed island tee on the 18th hole.

WHERE: 77 miles west of Albany. *Visitor info:* Tel 607-322-4046; thisiscooperstown .com. **BASEBALL HALL OF FAME:** Tel 888-HALL-OF-FAME or 607-547-7200; baseball hall.org. **GLIMMERGLASS FESTIVAL:** Tel 607-547-2255; glimmerglass.org. *Cost:* from $26. *When:* July–Aug. **FENIMORE ART MUSEUM:** Tel 888-547-1450 or 607-547-1400; fenimoreart

museum.org. *When:* daily, mid-May–mid-Oct; Tues–Sun, Apr–mid-May and mid-Oct–Dec. **FARMERS' MUSEUM:** Tel 888-547-1450 or 607-547-1450, farmersmuseum.org. *When:* closed Nov–Mar except for holiday events. **THE INN AT COOPERSTOWN:** Tel 607-547-5756; innatcooperstown.com. *Cost:* from $135 (off-peak), from $198 (peak), includes breakfast. **OTESAGA RESORT:** Tel 800-348-6222 or 607-547-9931; otesaga.com. *Cost:* from $329 (off-peak), from $399 (peak). *When:* mid-Apr–Nov. **BEST TIMES:** Memorial Day for the National Baseball Hall of Fame Game; 3rd weekend of July for Induction Weekend; mid-Dec for the Candlelit Evening at the Farmer's Museum.

A Mesmerizing Blend of Art, History, and Science

CORNING MUSEUM OF GLASS

Corning, New York

A priceless treasury in the heart of New York's scenic Finger Lakes region (see p. 149), the Corning Museum of Glass holds the world's most comprehensive collection of historic and art glass, showcasing 3,500 years of glassmaking history from around the globe. It is, quite literally, dazzling, and even if you don't think you have an interest in glass, you will by the time you leave. The best of its kind in the country, the Corning Museum of Glass is New York's third-largest tourist destination, after New York City and Niagara Falls.

The museum was founded by the Corning Glass Works in 1950; it's a nonprofit institution with a broader mission than just showcasing its own wares: it aims to preserve and expand the world's understanding of glass from an artistic, historic, and scientific perspective.

Tilting sheets of glass hung on delicate steel spider supports form the dramatic entrance to the sprawling museum set on 11 acres. Inside, the galleries follow glassmaking from

antiquity through the grand factories of Europe, then America (including a section on the history of glassmaking in Corning, where Steuben glass originated), and the American Studio Glass Movement in 1962, where for the first time individual artists could complete all stages of glassmaking themselves. Highlights include a 3,400-year-old glass portrait of an Egyptian pharaoh, an 11-foot-high Tiffany window from 1905, and a table-long glass boat cut by Baccarat in 1900.

Kids gravitate to the Glass Innovation Center, three pavilions that explore the fascinating nexus of glass and science through exhibits like a 200-inch telescope, a walk-on glass floor that illustrates the story of strengthened glass in the 20th century, and a tower made of casserole dishes telling about the lucky accident that made the famed oven-proof dishes possible.

A stunning 100,000-square-foot contemporary Art & Design wing opened in 2015, showcasing the breadth and depth of the creativity of American and international glass artists in the last 25 years. Glassblowing demonstrations go on all day as master glassworkers take gobs of hot molten glass and transform them into beautiful bowls and vases in a 500-seat Amphitheatre Hot Shop with 360-degree views.

To experience the thrill of glass-making yourself, don a pair of safety glasses at the Make Your Own Glass workshop and create glass flowers, paperweights, or Christmas ornaments. The Studio, one of the finest glassmaking schools in the world, also offers classes taught by master glassmakers and artists and ranging from one-day workshops for families to two-week intensives.

WHERE: 75 miles west of Binghamton; 1 Museum Way. Tel 800-732-6845 or 607-937-5371; cmog.org.

The museum's collection includes over 45,000 glass objects.

A Slow Float Through History

THE ERIE CANAL

New York

The magic of piloting your own canal boat on the Erie Canal means moving at a 19th-century pace—6 miles per hour, to be precise. Opened in 1825, the Erie Canal was a 363-mile engineering marvel with 83 locks connecting Buffalo, on Lake Erie, to Albany on the Hudson River. The brainchild of Govenor DeWitt Clinton, the canal was initially derided as "Clinton's Ditch," but once built, it spurred unprecedented economic development in both the Great Lakes region and New York City, and along its entire length.

The mules (immortalized in song—"I've got a mule, her name is Sal") that once pulled barges are gone, but the canal and 34 locks are still there, intersecting with three lateral canals—the Champlain, Oswego, and Cayuga-Seneca. Today, pleasure boats, tour boats, cruise ships, canoes, and kayaks ply their waters.

Mid-Lakes Navigation is a family-owned company that has been running cruises since the 1960s and began making its own European-style canal boats in the 1980s. Up to 42 people sightsee by boat during the day, eat onboard, and sleep on land at hotels.

But the most adventuresome way to experience the canal is to captain your own rented boat for a week, piloting it through locks where the water level is raised or lowered before you enter the next section of canal. Powered by a 50-hp diesel engine, canal boats float calmly past fields and woodlands and 19th-century towns with museums and shops to explore. The mirror-still waters reflect bridges and farmhouses, as herons fly overhead and kids wave from small-town landings.

You can hike and bike along most of the old towpaths where mules once hauled the barges. Whether by foot or by car, the Mohawk Towpath Scenic Byway follows both the Erie Canal and the Mohawk River from Schenectady to Waterford (north of Albany). **Canal Info:** Tel 800-422-6254 or 518-471-5014; canals.ny.gov. **Mid-Lakes Navigation:** Macedon Landing. Tel 800-545-4318 or 315-685-8500; midlakesnav.com. *Cost:* 1-day cruise, $115; charters from $1,625 for 3 nights. *When:* mid-May–mid-Oct for

When the Erie Canal was first completed, it had 83 locks, each 90 feet wide by 15 feet deep.

cruises and charters. **Mohawk Towpath Scenic Byway:** Tel 518-406-8610; mohawk towpath.org. **Best times:** June–July; Sept–Oct for foliage.

World-Class Wines and Small-Town Americana

Finger Lakes

New York

The Iroquois attributed these long, relatively narrow lakes to the Great Spirit, who laid his hands in blessing on this particularly beautiful area of upstate New York. Unless the Great Spirit had 11 fingers, though,

it's more likely that glacier activity carved them out eons ago. Most are deep—Cayuga and Seneca, the two largest, are 435 and 618 feet deep respectively and each about 37 miles long, framed by steeply sloping banks. The parallel lakes cover an area no more than 100 miles across in a bucolic region where farm stands still work on the honor system, and the sleepy Main Streets of 19th-century towns like Geneva, Skaneateles, and Hammondsport invite strolling and antique-hunting.

The American Women's Rights movement was born in Seneca Falls on July 19, 1848. Elizabeth Cady Stanton, a local mother of three, organized the first Women's Rights Convention (whose Declaration of Sentiments

declared that "all men and women are created equal"); today the town's Women's Rights National Historic Park includes Stanton's house. A whiff of the region's countercultural tendencies can be found in Ithaca, home to Ithaca College and Cornell University on Cayuga Lake. Boats crisscross the lakes, and you can jump aboard the boat that delivers mail on Skaneateles Lake, a three-hour long route that takes in all the scenery

With soil and topography that mimic the best of the German winegrowing districts, the Finger Lakes "boutique" vineyards—today numbering more than 200—are recognized as some of the country's best, especially for their rieslings and chardonnays. Three distinctive wine trails lead visitors to wineries and picnic areas with spectacular lake views. The trail around Keuka, considered by many to be the prettiest of the lakes, includes the pioneering Dr. Konstantin Frank's Vinifera Wine Cellars, outside Hammondsport, and nearby Pleasant Valley Wine Company, whose eight historic stone buildings and lavish visitor center add up to one of the best tours in the region. Taste with abandon on the Wine Tour Trolley of Seneca Lake, a seven-hour romp leaving from Geneva, with five stops where you can sample the wares, and then let the trolley's designated driver get you back to your lodgings.

The Finger Lakes area is New York's largest wine-producing region.

Seneca Lake is the location of Geneva on the Lake, a 1910 Italianate mansion transformed into an elegant inn. The beautiful expanse of parterre garden leads to the lakeside pool. At the northern tip of ice blue Skaneateles Lake, Mirbeau Inn and Spa is a Francophile's dream of mud wraps and massages, with an exceptional restaurant and lily ponds straight out of a Monet painting.

Along Cayuga Lake Scenic Byway, which rings the lake, lies Aurora, a postcard-perfect town of just 778 residents that has experienced a multimillion-dollar renaissance thanks to Pleasant Rowland, creator of the line of American Girl dolls. In partnership with local Wells College, her alma mater, Rowland purchased MacKenzie-Childs, which makes wildly fanciful majolica dinnerware and whimsical furniture on a nearby 75-acre former dairy farm (with a great store). An unusually fine 15-room Victorian farmhouse made over as a MacKenzie-Childs showcase is open for tours. Rowland also restored the Aurora Inn, a redbrick Federal-style inn that dates back to 1833. Standing center stage on Main Street, its ten luxurious guest rooms and suites are perfectly appointed, and its waterfront restaurant dishes up great American classics. Next door stands a sister property, the seven-room E. B. Morgan House.

WHERE: Skeneatales is 20 miles southwest of Syracuse. *Visitor info:* Tel 585-394-3915; visitfingerlakes.com. **WOMEN'S RIGHTS PARK:** Tel 315-568-2991; nps.gov/wori. **FINGER LAKES WINE COUNTRY:** Tel 800-813-2958 or 607-936-0706; fingerlakeswinecountry.com. **DR. FRANK'S WINE CELLARS:** Hammondsport. Tel 800-320-0735 or 607-868-4884; drfrank wines.com. **PLEASANT VALLEY WINE COMPANY:** Hammondsport. Tel 607-569-6111; pleasant valleywine.com. *When:* daily, Apr–Dec; Tues–Sat, Jan–Mar. **SENECA LAKE WINE TOUR TROLLEY:** Tel 315-521-0223; winetourtrolley .com. *Cost:* from $55. *When:* Sat, May–Nov. **GENEVA ON THE LAKE:** Geneva. Tel 800-343-6382 or 315-789-7190; genevaonthelake .com. *Cost:* from $265 (off-peak), from $399 (peak); dinner $70. **MIRBEAU INN AND SPA:** Skaneateles. Tel 877-647-2328 or 315-685-5006; mirbeau.com. *Cost:* from $245; dinner $60. **MACKENZIE-CHILDS:** Aurora. Tel 888-665-1999 or 315-364-6118; mackenzie-childs.com. **AURORA INN AND THE E. B. MORGAN HOUSE:** Tel 866-364-8808 or 315-364-8888; innsofaurora.com. *Cost:* from $195 (off-peak), from $275 (peak); dinner $50. **BEST TIMES:** mid-July for Finger Lakes Wine Festival in Watkins Glen (flwinefest.com); last weekend of July for Antique and Classic Boat Show in Skaneateles (skaneateles.com); early Aug for NASCAR in Watkins Glen (theglen.com).

Where "America the Beautiful" Began

HUDSON VALLEY

New York

I n 1609, Dutch explorer Henry Hudson sailed up the river that now bears his name, looking for passage to the Orient's riches. He didn't find it, but he did uncover one of the most scenic waterways in the world. Two hundred years later, Robert Fulton first launched the steamboat on its waters in 1807, and as the centuries rolled by, the Hudson exerted such a profound effect on American history, art, literature, and environmental policies that Bill Moyers dubbed it "America's First River."

It begins as a tiny brook spilling out of Lake Tear of the Clouds, 4,293 feet up in the Adirondack Mountains (see p. 140), flowing 315 miles down to New York City, but it's not until the Hudson meets the Mohawk River at Waterford just north of Albany that it becomes the mighty waterway that helped link New York City to the west via the Erie Canal (see p. 148), opening up the Great Lakes states to America's first westward expansion. This stretch between Waterford and Yonkers has been deemed such an important cultural and recreational resource that a 4-million-acre area with 90 significant sites on either side of the river has been designated a National Heritage Area by the federal government.

Known to Native Americans as the "two-way river" because salty ocean tides are felt as far north as Albany, the Hudson River was crucial during the Revolutionary War. A third of the war's battles were fought in New York State, many along the banks of the Hudson, and George Washington's most important stronghold at the river's narrowest point would become the U.S. Military Academy at West Point (see p. 205).

The Hudson Valley's majestic panoramas inspired Thomas Cole, Frederic Church, and other landscape painters who created the important 19th-century Hudson River School (see p. 153). It was home to such literary figures as Washington Irving, whose "Rip Van Winkle" and "Legend of Sleepy Hollow" are set here, and wealthy (sometimes fabulously so) families like the Vanderbilts, Livingstons, Roosevelts, and Rockefellers built palatial mansions (see p. 154), still beautifully furnished and on view. The Catskills' wild beauty has drawn visitors for 200 years, and Mohonk Mountain House (see p. 165), one of the country's few remaining great 19th-century retreats, still welcomes travelers from atop the Shawangunk Mountains.

The Valley, with its fertile bottomlands and rolling hills famous for their unparalleled sweet corn and apples, has a new food export today: The Culinary Institute of America (see p. 156) in Hyde Park is one of the world's finest training grounds for chefs. The Hudson Valley is also the site of a bold experiment in sustainable dining—a restaurant that farms its own food—that has made Blue Hill at Stone Barns (see p. 200) a point of pilgrimage for dedicated foodies.

Take a drive on back roads past manicured horse farms, dairy farms, pick-your-own orchards, and wineries, then stop for lunch and antiquing in 18th- and 19th-century riverside towns such as Nyack, Kingston, Hudson, Rhinebeck (see p. 201), and Saugerties, the latter with its 1869 lighthouse-cum-B&B. For a rural setting the Hudson Valley hosts an impressive wealth of art museums (see p. 153), including the standout Dia: Beacon. Cold

Spring is a particularly charming 19th-century village with antiques shops, cafés, and a waterfront that offers stunning river vistas of looming Storm King Mountain and the Hudson Highlands. These same views add to the magic of nearby Boscobel Restoration, an early 19th-century mansion with one of the nation's leading collections of Federal-era furniture; it is the setting for highly regarded outdoor productions of *The Tempest*, *A Midsummer Night's Dream*, and *Macbeth* during the annual Hudson Valley Shakespeare Festival.

For bedding down afterward, The Garrison is a 300-acre river view resort with just four stylish rooms, golf, and superlative dining in the Valley Restaurant. There, a team of chefs serves up seasonal American cuisine that is sourced in part from the 2-acre garden out back. A little farther north, jutting out as the only structure on the tiny uninhabited Pollepel Island, is one of the river's great curiosities and most romantic silhouettes, Bannerman Castle, now open for tours. Looking every bit the haunted ruins of a medieval fortress, it was in fact an arsenal warehouse built by Scottish immigrant Francis Bannerman for his military surplus business (his clients included Buffalo Bill and WWI regiments).

Cool Hudson Valley evenings lend a certain magic to summertime concerts and festivals in open-air venues like the new Bethel Woods Center for the Arts (see p. 144) and the 90-acre Caramoor estate in Katonah, famous for its first-class classical music and opera concerts. This 1930s Mediterranean-style mansion with priceless art and entire rooms imported from European palaces was a gift to the public from collectors and musicians Walter and Lucie Rosen, in memory of their son, who was killed in WWII.

Washington Irving, who traveled widely (his works include the famous *The Alhambra*, about the Moorish palace in the city of Grenada, Spain), ultimately preferred the verdant, rolling landscape where he made his final home (see p. 155). "The Hudson Valley is, in a manner, my first and last love," he wrote, "and after all my wanderings and seeming infidelities, I return to it with a heartfelt preference over all the other rivers in the world."

WHERE: 150-mile stretch of river, from Yonkers to Waterford. *Hudson Valley visitor info:* Tel 800-232-4782; travelhudsonvalley .com. **BOSCOBEL RESTORATION:** Garrison. Tel 845-265-3638; boscobel.org. *When:* closed Tues, Apr–Dec. **HUDSON VALLEY SHAKESPEARE FESTIVAL:** Garrison. Tel 845-265-9575; hvshakespeare.org. *Cost:* tickets from $30. *When:* June–early Sept. **THE GARRISON:** Tel 845-424-3604; thegarrison .com. *Cost:* from $109 (off-peak), from $250 (peak); dinner $60. **BANNERMAN CASTLE:** Tel 845-831-6346 (trust), 855-256-4007 or 845-256-4007 (tours); bannermancastle.org. *When:* Sat–Sun, May 1–Oct 31. *Cost:* $35. **CARAMOOR:** Katonah. Tel 914-232-5035 or 914-232-1252; caramoor.org. *Cost:* tickets from $10. *When:* Wed–Sun, early Mar–mid-Dec. **BEST TIMES:** summer for a variety of festivals and events; autumn for foliage.

Bannerman Castle sits on the 6.5 acre Pollepel Island, just off the east bank of the Hudson near Beacon.

The Ultimate Road Trip for Art Lovers

HUDSON VALLEY ART

New York

With its great wealth of historic homes, rolling farmland, and protected wilderness, the scenic Hudson Valley invites many different routes for exploration, and the quest for art may be one of the richest.

The natural beauty that inspired Thomas Cole, Frederic Church, and other landscape painters of the 19th-century Hudson River School—the first truly American art movement—remains surprisingly unsullied. Church would find the views of the river from Olana, his eccentric 1872 blufftop Moorish mansion, little changed and the interiors exactly as he left them, with all the original furnishings and his personal art collection intact. Stay for sunset to see why Church claimed that this was "the center of the world." The old-world master most definitely would not recognize nearby Hudson, whose once-gritty stretch of downtown is being transformed by high-style refugees from Manhattan into a neighborhood of tasteful boutiques, antiques stores, and restaurants with young chefs from the Culinary Institute of America in nearby Hyde Park (see p. 156).

Downriver, great works of the modern, postmodern, and contemporary eras are clustered at the mid-point of the Hudson Valley. The once scrappy east bank industrial town of Beacon is a rising star in the art world since the 2003 opening of Dia:Beacon, a branch of the New York City–based foundation. With nearly 300,000 square feet illuminated by countless skylights, this 1929 riverside Nabisco Factory is the perfect home for major (and often oversize) works from the 1960s to the present, including pieces by Donald Judd, Andy Warhol, Richard Serra, and Cy Twombly that challenge your sense of perception.

Across the river and just north of West Point (see p. 205), the Storm King Art Center is known for its harmonious yet startling interaction between sculpture and the surrounding landscape of fields, hills, and woodlands. You'll find more than 100 carefully sited sculptures from the post-1945 period, including monumental works by Alexander Calder, Louise Nevelson, and Isamu Noguchi, among its 500 bucolic acres.

More outstanding sculptures by Calder, Nevelson, and Noguchi, along with Henry Moore and Pablo Picasso, can be seen at Kykuit, the hilltop paradise in Westchester's Pocantico Hills that was home to four generations of the Rockefeller family. When former governor of New York Nelson A. Rockefeller moved here in 1963, he began a transformation of the grounds by installing his collection of 20th-century sculpture throughout the elaborately terraced Beaux-Art gardens, which still enchant visitors.

Modern magnate Roy R. Neuberger (who made his fortune in mutual funds) started the Neuberger Museum of Art at Purchase College in 1974 by donating 108 first-rate modern and contemporary works. The collection has since grown to more than 6,000 pieces, including a fine collection of Dada and Surrealist objects as well as African art.

Feel like a king by staying among all these treasures at Tarrytown's Castle Hotel & Spa, a turreted replica of a Norman castle built in 1894 by New York journalist and Anglophile General Howard Carroll. Its thick granite walls and hand-hewn oak beams (and a less royal annex) now hold a 31-room luxury inn and spa.

WHERE: from 18 miles (Yonkers) to 150 miles (Albany) north of New York City. **DIA:BEACON:** Tel 845-440-0100; diaart.org. *When:* Thurs–Mon, Apr–Dec; Fri–Mon, Jan–Mar. **OLANA:** outside Hudson. Tel 518-828-0135; olana.org. *When:* grounds, daily; house tours Tues–Sun, mid-May–Oct. **STORM KING ART CENTER:** New Windsor. Tel 845-534-3115; stormking.org. *When:* Apr–Nov. **KYKUIT:** Sleepy Hollow. Tel 914-366-6900; hudsonvalley.org. *When:* Guided tours Thur–Sun, May–Sept; closed Tues, Oct–mid-Nov. **NEUBERGER MUSEUM OF ART:** Purchase. Tel 914-251-6100; neuberger.org. *When:* closed

Founded in 1960, the Storm King Art Center showcases sculptures in a natural landscape.

Mon. **CASTLE HOTEL & SPA:** Tarrytown. Tel 914-631-1980; castlehotelandspa.com. *Cost:* from $199 (off-peak), from $249 (peak).

America's Châteaux

GREAT ESTATES
OF THE HUDSON VALLEY

New York

Perched atop the prettiest bluffs of the Hudson River's undulating, tree-covered right bank, with sweeping views of the majestic waters below, is America's most astounding collection of great estates, many built in the

19th century by the rich and powerful as high-status getaways. Others, like the Roosevelt family's Springwood in Hyde Park (see p. 157) and Clermont in Germantown, served as the permanent residences for the Hudson Valley's most prominent Old Money families. Fortunately, descendants took great pains to see that the estates survived, and the houses remain furnished much as they were, as though the families would be walking through the front door at any moment.

Among the area's pleasure palaces, none is more grand than the Beaux-Arts Vanderbilt Mansion in Hyde Park, built in 1895 by Frederick William Vanderbilt, heir to the great

shipping and railroad fortune. Some say the site was chosen for its proximity to the Roosevelts, though the Vanderbilts used the opulent 54-room limestone mansion for just a few months in spring and fall. For the rest of the year, a staff of 63 was left to care for the house and gardens, for which the estate is still known.

Lyndhurst is an imposing limestone Gothic Revival estate purchased in 1880 by "robber baron" Jay Gould, the fabulously wealthy railroad magnate and stock manipulator. Designed by the master of Gothic Revival, Andrew Jackson Downing, and built in 1838, the impressively grand home has a dining room that looks like a medieval banquet hall, along with

Gilded Age must-haves like Tiffany stained glass windows and faux-finish paneling.

Two of the region's greatest estates are also noteworthy for their art connections: the Rockefellers' 1913 country home, Kykuit (its name means "lookout" in Dutch and refers to its hilltop position), and Olana, the enchanting Moorish fantasy palace where Frederic Church made his home (see p. 153).

A quintessential representation of Hudson Valley old money is the Livingston family, whose prominence began in 1686 when Robert Livingston Sr. was granted a royal patent of 160,000 acres along the Hudson River, becoming the first Lord of Livingston Manor. His son (Robert Jr.) began construction of a brick Georgian-style home in 1740, and though Clermont has gone through many changes (including a complete rebuilding after being burned by the British in 1777), it remains a glimpse into nearly three centuries of wealth, impeccable taste, and political prominence.

Not far from Clermont, just outside Rhinebeck (see p. 201), is Montgomery Place, erected in 1804 by Janet Livingston Montgomery, in honor of her husband, Richard, the first general killed in the Revolutionary War. The open porch of this elegant Classical Revival mansion (with dramatic views of the river and the Catskills beyond) was the first "outdoor room" in America. Scenic trails wend through the 380-acre estate, which still grows apples, peaches, plums, table grapes, and black raspberries that can be purchased at the estate's farm stand on River Road.

Old and new money merge in Staatsburgh just north of Hyde Park at a 25-room Greek Revival house on 334 acres, inherited in 1894 by Ruth Livingston Mills, who was married to financier and philanthropist Ogden Mills. They expanded it into a 65-room Beaux-Arts extravaganza for entertaining friends in the fall, and its imported 17th- and 18th-century French interiors, gilded furniture, and Baccarat

crystal bathroom accessories are just as they were when their son donated the property to New York State in 1938.

While all the grandeur is fun to look at, it's easier to imagine the good life at Sunnyside, the fairytale confection of turrets and gingerbread that was the home of Washington Irving, author of "The Legend of Sleepy Hollow" and "Rip Van Winkle." Originally a two-room farmer's cottage, beginning in 1835 the home was fancifully expanded with Tudor-style clustered chimneys, Dutch stepped gables, Gothic windows, a small piazza, and, later, a Spanish-style tower. Outside the front door, the wisteria Irving himself planted continues to bloom each spring, while the trails he laid out on the 27-acre estate are still a perfect place for a stroll by the river.

The nearby Sleepy Hollow Cemetery, where Irving set his tale of Ichabod Crane and the Headless Horseman, is especially popular around Halloween. The Dutch began burying their dead in an adjacent plot as early as 1650, but this cemetery was founded in 1849, and today holds more than 45,000 earthly remains, including those of Irving himself and many of the wealthy empire (and great estate) builders, including Andrew Carnegie and William Rockefeller.

VANDERBILT MANSION: Hyde Park. Tel 845-229-5320; nps.gov/vama. **LYNDHURST:** Tarrytown. Tel 914-631-4481; lyndhurst.org. *When:* closed Jan–Apr and most of Nov. **CLERMONT:** Germantown. Tel 518-537-4240;

Italian-style terrace gardens surround the stately Vanderbilt Mansion.

friendsofclermont.org. **MONTGOMERY PLACE:** Annandale-on-Hudson. Tel 845-758-5461; hudsonvalley.org/montgomeryplace. *When:* open Thurs–Sun, May–Oct. **STAATSBURGH:** Tel 845-889-8851; millsmansion.org. *When:* open Thurs–Sun, Apr–Oct, and for special hours Thanksgiving–Dec; open Sat–Sun, Jan–Mar. **SUNNYSIDE:** Tel 914-366-6900;

hudsonvalley.org. *When:* closed Mon–Tues, Apr–Oct; closed Jan–Mar; open Sat–Sun, Nov–Dec. **SLEEPY HOLLOW CEMETERY:** Tel 914-631-0081; sleepyhollowcemetery.org. **BEST TIMES:** Apr–June for those estates with gardens; Oct for fall foliage; Dec when some estates, like Lyndhurst and the Vanderbilt mansion, are decorated for the holidays.

The Harvard of Cooking Schools

THE CULINARY INSTITUTE OF AMERICA

Hyde Park, New York

A turn-of-the-19th-century Jesuit seminary transformed into the world's finest training grounds for chefs, the Culinary Institute of America is where aspiring cooks dream of becoming the next celebrity chef

extraordinaire. Todd English (owner of the Olive Group in Boston) and Cat Cora (Food Network's "Iron Chef" and co-host of *Around The World In 80 Plates*) are a mere sampling of successful grads of "The Culinary," as it is called by insiders (or "the other CIA"). Branch campuses now exist in California (see p. 834), Texas, and Singapore.

While a degree from the Culinary doesn't assure superstardom, it prepares its students for the exacting rigors of the professional kitchen. Wearing the standard-issue uniform of black-and-white houndstooth trousers, neat white chef's jackets, and toques, thousands of students scurry between dozens of professional kitchens and bakeshops on the lavishly outfitted campus, learning everything from how to make a simple brown sauce to ice carving to the world of wine. Even admission to the two-year associate's degree requires that applicants first work six months in professional foodservice to prove they can stand the heat. Every year the Culinary in Hyde Park turns out 1,900 grads—1,400 with associate's and 500 with bachelor's degrees.

It all started back in 1946 in New Haven, Connecticut, when Frances Roth, a lawyer who loved food, wanted to help returning WWII vets become skilled cooks. She and benefactor Katharine Angell opened the New Haven Restaurant Institute, the country's first culinary college. It changed its name to the Culinary Institute of America in 1951 and in 1972 moved to its current home on the Hudson River.

Call ahead for a guided tour of the premises given by students, or just drop in for a visit to the campus bookstore, a foodie's paradise. If you want to get into the kitchen and roll up your sleeves, there are plenty of one- and two-day classes, including some for kids. Serious gastronomes from all over the country hone their cooking talents at two-to-five-day "boot camps," where they learn, among other things, that cooking large quantities of food with the clock ticking is hard, sweaty work.

The easiest path to enjoyment is to dine at one of the Culinary's four restaurants, each with a unique character and menu. Staffed entirely by students, they are a relative bargain. Apple Pie Bakery Café specializes in baked goods, while Ristorante Caterina de' Medici features traditional and contemporary Italian dishes. Something as simple as venison loin with grappa sauce and potato-turnip gratin can approach heaven.

American Bounty Restaurant helped pioneer the very idea of regional American cooking—and celebrates it still with dishes like braised Berkshire pork shank with leeks and wild mushrooms. Set in a sleek, clean, contemporary space, the Bocuse Restaurant updates classic French cuisine with modern techniques. Strip loin of beef with chanterelles and gruyère foam, anyone?

WHERE: 90 miles north of New York City; 1946 Campus Dr. Tel 845-451-1588 (tours) or 845-451-1588 (restaurant reservations); ciachef.edu. *Cost:* 1-day classes from $250, 5-day Boot Camp from $1,750. *When:* guided

Chef Sandy Dominguez instructs her students in one of the "boot camps" at the CIA.

tours Mon–Fri when school is in session. Reservations required. **APPLE PIE BAKERY CAFÉ:** *Cost:* $18 (lunch only). **RISTORANTE CATERINA DE' MEDICI:** *Cost:* $45. **AMERICAN BOUNTY RESTAURANT:** *Cost:* $50. **BOCUSE RESTAURANT:** *Cost:* 3-course prix-fixe menu from $45.

History with a View

FDR's SPRINGWOOD

Hyde Park, New York

Offering a surprisingly vivid and personal glimpse of how American aristocrats once lived, Springwood was the lifelong home of Franklin D. Roosevelt, considered to be the 20th century's greatest American

president for his ability to steer the nation through the Great Depression and WWII, and the only president elected to four terms of office (1933–1945). The Roosevelt home represents Hudson Valley old money: a large, unpretentious stucco and fieldstone house furnished with polished mahogany woodwork, tufted sofas, Oriental rugs, and ancestral oil paintings, along with intimate touches like the cabinet of stuffed birds that FDR collected as a boy.

Perched on a bluff that affords beautiful views of the Hudson River, the home and estate were purchased in 1867 by Franklin's

father, James, who enjoyed the life of an English squire, busying himself with his horses and cattle, hunting, fishing, and riding, and iceboating on the Hudson. He passed his love of the outdoors on to his only child with Sara Delano Roosevelt. A strong woman involved in her son's life, Sara inherited the property from her husband in 1900 (rare in those days) and ruled the roost until her death in 1941. She kept the lady-of-the-house's bedroom to herself, even after Franklin's marriage to his distant cousin Eleanor in 1905. During guided tours you see all just as they left it, down to the old-fashioned bedroom telephone that was a hotline to the White House, and FDR's wheelchair. (He was unable to stand alone or walk unaided, as a result of contracting polio at age 39.)

Today Springwood has 290 acres, with walking trails and America's first presidential library, which Roosevelt designed himself in Dutch Colonial style and actually used while he was president. By donating his papers to it, Roosevelt established the precedent for public ownership of presidential papers, which soon became federal law. Highlights include an excellent documentary film, report cards from Groton and Harvard (bearing few A's), and the desk FDR used during his four successive terms of office. The Rose Garden is the location of the Roosevelts' simple graves and the tiny tombstone of their beloved Scottish terrier, Fala.

Originally a furniture workshop that Eleanor started in 1926 to teach manufacturing skills to underemployed farmworkers, nearby Val-Kill Cottage became the exceedingly modest home Eleanor came to prefer, down to the Colonial reproduction furniture, knotty pine paneling, and dimestore tumblers. She moved here full-time upon her husband's death (FDR died in 1945 in Warm Springs, Georgia, at the Little White House).

As FDR neared the end in 1944, Springwood was the place he longed to be. "All that is within me cries out to go back to my home on the Hudson River," he said.

WHERE: 90 miles north of New York City; 4097 Albany Post Rd. Tel 845-229-5320; nps.gov/hofr. **ELEANOR ROOSEVELT HISTORIC SITE:** Val-Kill. Tel 845-229-9422; nps.gov/elro. *When:* daily, May–Oct; Thurs–Mon, Nov–Apr.

Queen of American Lakes and Gateway to the Adirondacks

LAKE GEORGE

New York

Part spectacular beauty, part wealthy summer retreat, and part '50s-style tourist trap, Lake George is a stunning 32-mile-long spring-fed lake situated at the southeastern edge of the mighty Adirondack State Park (see p. 140). The crowded village of Lake George is a paradise for eight-year-olds who can't get enough of attractions like the House of Frankenstein Wax Museum and miniature golf, and for adults who enjoy the carnival-like atmosphere and full-blown tourist-town diversions. That world falls quickly away once you get out on the mountain-ringed lake, with 200-plus islands studding its crystal clear waters. "Lake George is without comparison, the most beautiful water I ever saw," wrote Thomas Jefferson. A boat tour is a time-honored way to view the mountain wilderness and western shore's historic mansions. Lake George Steamboat Company's full lake tour on the *Mohican* is

the way to go; converted to diesel in 1947, this steamboat has been plying local waters since 1908.

In the mid-1800s, Lake George boomed during the grand era of lavish, regal hotels, all of which have vanished. Recapture a glimpse of that heyday with a stay at the Sagamore, a lofty 390-room complex on its own 72-acre island. What you see today is its 1930 incarnation, a grand white resort with deck chairs lined up at the edge of its manicured front lawn to take in the expansive water views. The main hotel has 137 luxurious rooms and suites; the rest are tucked away among the island's seven modern lodges and a historic converted carriage house.

Donald Ross designed the Sagamore's 18-hole golf course in 1928.

As part of a strategic water route connecting Canada with New York City, Lake George played a critical role in both the French and Indian War and the American Revolution. Fort Ticonderoga, a massive star-shaped fortress perched on the narrow strip of land that separates Lake George from Lake Champlain, was constructed by the French on one of the most fought-over spots in American history. The fort was "the key to the continent" for the 18th-century superpowers France, which controlled the St. Lawrence River valley, and England, which controlled the Hudson Valley, and it changed hands several times during the French and Indian War (1754–63). That the English were the ultimate victors is reflected in the lake's name, changed from Lac du St. Sacrement. In 1775, the underdog Americans had their first victory of the Revolutionary War here when Ethan Allen, Benedict Arnold (once a patriot), and the Green Mountain Boys of Vermont realized the fort made an easy target.

Today, Fort Ticonderoga offers a vivid sense of fort life with costumed staff firing muskets and a fife and drum corps performing daily in July and August. There's much to explore—a museum, a tailor's shop, restored barracks, and a 1920s-era King's Garden with costumed interpreters. It is at its liveliest during reenactments and living history events, when volunteers dressed as Eastern Woodland Indians and British, French, and colonial

Lake George was named after King George II of Great Britain.

soldiers relive moments during the French and Indian War or the American Revolution. The fort is also a major stop on the 234-mile National Scenic Byway called Lakes to Locks Passage that follows the interconnected waterway through six counties.

WHERE: 70 miles north of Albany. *Visitor info:* Tel 800-958-4748 or 518-761-6366; visit lakegeorge.com. **LAKE GEORGE STEAMBOAT COMPANY:** Tel 800-553-2628 or 518-668-5777; lakegeorgesteamboat.com. *When:* early May–Oct. **THE SAGAMORE:** Bolton Landing. Tel 866-384-1944 or 518-644-9400; the sagamore.com. *Cost:* from $129 (off-peak), from $349 (peak); greens fees $115 for guests. *When:* golf Apr–Oct, weekends only Nov–Mar. **FORT TICONDEROGA:** Tel 518-585-2821; fortticonderoga.org. *When:* early May–Oct. **LAKES TO LOCKS PASSAGE:** *Tours/maps:* Tel 518-597-9660; lakestolocks.org. *Byway:* fhwa.dot.gov/byways. **BEST TIMES:** 1st full week of June for the Americade Motorcycle Touring Rally (americade.com); mid-Sept for Adirondack Balloon Festival.

The Town That Talks to the Dead

LILY DALE

New York

Have unfinished business with a loved one who has passed on? Think this might not be your first time on earth? Consider a visit to Lily Dale, home to 50 registered mediums and the Rome of Spiritualism, a religion that combines reverence for "the God of your own understanding" with a belief we can all communicate with spirits of the dead. Set on 173 wooded acres hugging the shores of Lake Cassadaga, Lily Dale has been the epicenter of Spiritualism since 1879, when followers moved the home of Kate and Margaret Fox, the founders of modern Spiritualism, to this site.

The Fox sisters started talking to spirits in 1848 when they heard mysterious rappings, and instead of running in fear, they asked questions, developing a system whereby raps could signify "yes," "no," or indicate a letter of the alphabet. The spirit, they said, was a peddler who had been murdered and buried in their basement. (The peddler's body and his trunk—the trunk is now at the Lily Dale Museum—were discovered in the house's cellar wall in 1904.) The Fox sisters became famous, starting a movement that was prominent well into the 1920s, gaining followers among men of science including evolutionary biologist Alfred Russel Wallace and physician and author Sir Arthur Conan Doyle. The movement lost popularity in the twenties as investigators like Harry Houdini exposed the trickery of charlatans. Today's mediums go through a rigorous testing process by Lily Dale's board of directors.

Lily Dale is at its busiest over ten weeks in the summer, when more than 22,000 people converge for a schedule offering over 100 talks and workshops, which cover how to channel the voices of spirits, finding your own spirit guide, yoga, and meditation. Notable speakers include America's famous psychic and TV personality James Van Praagh. Mediums conduct free daily services at "Inspiration Stump," a massive tree stump considered an "energy vortex." A sizable crowd quietly gathers on benches and listens to messages that mediums relay from the spirit world. With so many earthbound loved ones in the audience, not all the spirits get through, so if you want to ask questions directly, you must arrange your own private reading—the heart of the Lily Dale experience. Both quirky and serene with a mystical vibe, parts of Lily Dale may appear a little worn, but its leafy woodland trails wending through a fairy village (fanciful dwellings for fairies constructed of wood, grass, and stone) can encourage skeptics to reconsider.

Given its reputation for hauntings, the centrally located Maplewood Hotel is considered the place to stay, but don't expect luxury from this affordable Victorian hostelry (there are no phones, television, or air-conditioning).

WHERE: Lily Dale is 53 miles southwest of Buffalo. Tel 716-595-8721; lilydaleassembly .com. *Cost:* admission to the grounds $15; private readings from $80. **MAPLEWOOD HOTEL:** Tel 716-595-8721. *Cost:* from $84. *When:* late June–early Sept. **BEST TIME:** late June–early Sept (most of the town closes off-season).

Oceanside Colonies Where the Elite Meet and Greet

THE HAMPTONS

Long Island, New York

During summer months, the seaside towns on eastern Long Island known as the Hamptons—Westhampton, East Quogue, Southampton, Bridgehampton, Sagaponack, Sag Harbor, East Hampton—are inundated with beautiful people, their Jaguars and BMWs clogging the narrow roads in a conga line connecting hot spots. It's not exactly "going to the country"—you'll run into as many Manhattanites at an East Hampton celebrity-sighting eatery or at Bridgehampton's 1920s-soda-fountain Candy Kitchen as you would on Madison Avenue. But along with polo fields, there are still potato fields, roadside farm stands (leave correct change in the can), and seafood shops owned by local farming and baymen families with 350 years of roots in these parts.

What lures the crowds are miles and miles of glorious beach where golden sand meets blue Atlantic. The only problem is parking anywhere near it. (Town-run beaches in East Hampton and Southampton have day parking, but get there by 9 A.M. or take your chances.) The well-to-do, of course, are delivered by their drivers; for everyone else there's pleasantly flat, easy riding by bicycle.

The towns of the Hamptons may seem to merge with one another but they differ greatly in character. Southampton is the grande dame of old money and sweeping estates, but today East Hampton is arguably the East End's most fashionable town and boasts beautiful Main Beach. Founded in 1648 and "discovered" by society as an escape resort in the late 1800s, East Hampton was later the favored destination of artists like Willem de Kooning and Jackson Pollock (and, more recently, Eric Fischl), who came for the big sky and golden light.

East Hampton is a peculiar mix of rustic charm and urban taste, year-rounders and vacationing celebs. For a fleeting glimpse of a serene and unspoiled corner of the Hamptons, spend an afternoon in Sagaponack where the region's last stretches of farmland are fragrant with flowers in August. There isn't much to do here except head toward beautiful Sagg Main Beach, but that's the point.

Creature comforts in the Hamptons are taken seriously, and restaurants have grown to be as fine as their New York City peers. You'll do less begging for a table off-season at East Hampton classics like Nick & Toni's, the star-sighting venue of choice. Health-conscious (and not) foodies have put the much more informal Babette's on the map, a vegetarian and vegan-friendly restaurant where everyone shows up sooner or later. Overnighters looking for the marriage of excellent food and perfect accommodations should book way in advance at The Maidstone, a 19th-century white clapboard inn with a quirky Scandinavian design that reflects its Swedish owner. It's on-site Living Room restaurant is a local staple. Just down the street sits the Baker House 1650, a glorious English manor house converted to a luxury inn with seven sumptuous rooms, and flowering gardens, a small pool, a newly restored Carriage House on the grounds, and the most coveted guest amenity of all—beach parking permits.

A few miles to the north is the former whaling port of Sag Harbor, the most un-Hampton of the Hamptons, happy in its classic New Englandness, down to its rocky shores and busy marina. In 1846, at the height of the town's whaling prosperity, the handsome eight-room redbrick American Hotel was built on the all-American Main Street now chockablock with interesting shops and restaurants. It offers some of the area's best dining—and drinking, with a 104-page wine list. For someplace that knows no pretensions, it's a short stroll to The Corner where moguls and minions order its famous burgers, complete with secret sauce.

For those with a passion for golf, the East End is the mother lode, though the best courses are private clubs, so you'll need to work your Rolodex to wangle an invitation. Shinnecock Hills, National Golf Links, the Maidstone Club, and Atlantic Golf Club are all in the Hamptons, all ranked among the nation's finest. For those without blue-blood or green-money connections, nearby Montauk Downs State Park features a highly-regarded Robert Trent Jones Sr. designed golf course, and Bethpage State Park 70 miles away includes the Black Course, host of the 2002 and 2009 U.S. Opens.

The grand finale of the Hamptons' social season is the prestigious Hampton Classic Horse Show, which takes place every year in Bridgehampton. Encompassing various divisions and categories that culminate with the Grand Prix jumping shows, the Hampton Classic draws the world's top jumper and hunter riders (many of them Olympic-team level) with lucrative prize money, while others are lured by the chance of a celebrity sighting and the social events that take place around the show. **WHERE:** 90 miles east of New York City. *Visitor info:* Tel 877-FUN-ON-LI or 631-951-3900; discoverlongisland.com. **CANDY KITCHEN:** Bridgehampton. Tel 631-537-9885. *Cost:* dinner $25. **NICK & TONI'S:** East Hampton. Tel 631-324-3550; nickandtonis.com. *Cost:* lunch $90. **BABETTE'S:** East Hampton. Tel 631-329-5377; babettesrestaurant.com. *Cost:* dinner $55. **THE MAIDSTONE INN:** East Hampton. Tel 631-324-5006; themaidstone .com. *Cost:* from $285 (off-peak), from $545 (peak). **BAKER HOUSE 1650:** East Hampton.

Tel 631-324-4081; bakerhouse1650.com. *Cost:* from $295 (off-peak), from $595 (peak). **THE AMERICAN HOTEL:** Sag Harbor. Tel 631-725-3535; theamericanhotel.com. *Cost:* from $195 (off-peak), from $325 (peak); dinner $75. **THE CORNER:** Sag Harbor. Tel 631-725-9760; cornerbarsagharbor.com. *Cost:* lunch $16. **MONTAUK DOWNS STATE PARK:** Montauk. Tel 631-668-5000; nystateparks.com/golf-courses/ 8/details/aspx. *Cost:* greens fees from $43 (NYS residents). **BETHPAGE STATE PARK:** Farmingdale. Tel 516-249-0700; nystateparks .com/golf-courses/11/details/aspx. *Cost:* greens fees from $38 (nys residents). **HAMPTON CLASSIC:** Bridgehampton. hamptonclassic.com. *Cost:* admission from $10. *When:* late Aug–early Sept. **BEST TIMES:** July–Aug for nicest weather; off-season, mid-Sept–late May; early Oct for Hampton's International Film Festival (hamptonsfilmfest.org).

Deep-Sea Fishing and Thalassotherapy

MONTAUK

Long Island, New York

At the very farthest reach of Long Island, the narrow spear of land that separates the Atlantic Ocean from Long Island Sound, lies Montauk, nominally part of the Hamptons (see p. 160) but in flavor light-years apart. The landscape changes from well-tended towns and farmland to windswept, barren terrain where the beach is wider, the surf is stronger, and you're never more than a mile from water.

Montauk is a prime destination for sport fishermen after deep-sea trophies like giant bluefin tuna and marlin. Its remote location at the tip of the island is what gives Montauk some of the best deep-sea fishing in the Northeast—25 miles out and you will be where the big fish lurk.

Just as long as vacationers have been coming here, the place to stay has been Gurney's Inn, a rambling beachfront resort where every room has wondrous views of the ocean. Its Seawater Spa offers European-style thalasso-therapy—the use of seawater and seaweed to remineralize and restore. Even its indoor pool is filled with heated saltwater.

The picturesque (and much photographed) red and white Montauk Point Lighthouse, commissioned by Congress in 1792, still warns boats away from its shores. The museum in the 1860 Keepers House details the lonely life of the lighthouse keeper, and you can climb the 110-foot tower to get the area's grandest view.

Montauk's Ditch Plains Beach is recognized as one of the best surfing beaches in America. Offshore rocks are the secret here, causing the waves to wrap around and result in pipelines that promise long, fast rides.

No surprise that seafood is the fare of choice in town, and no seafood house has a better pedigree than Gosman's Dock, a true Montauk institution that has evolved from a simple chowder stand into a complex of waterside shops and seafood restaurants (from the outdoor Clam Bar to the still-casual but more expensive Gosman's Dock Restaurant). Its always-busy seafood shop sells everything fresh off the boat, and the best potato salad and coleslaw in the Hamptons. Gosman's Dock

The Montauk Point Lighthouse was first lit in 1797.

Restaurant is famous for its Fisherman's Platter, piled high with deep-fried flounder filets, panko-breaded shrimp, clam strips, and fries.

Ten miles west of Montauk is Amagansett, staunchly un-Hamptons-like in character. Its Lobster Roll (affectionately known as "Lunch" because of the 1950s-era sign perched on the roof) began as a seafood shack with long lines for its clam chowder, steamers, and plump lobster rolls, but has expanded to include indoor and outdoor dining. Scrumptious deep-dish pies remind you of Long Island's farmland heritage, with thick lumpy fillings of seasonal fruit.

WHERE: 116 miles east of New York City. *Visitor info:* Tel 631-668-2428; montauk chamber.com. **MONTAUK FISHING CHARTERS:** Tel 631-668-1635; montaukfishingcharters .com. *Cost:* half-day inshore for up to 6 people, $550 with crew. *When:* late Apr–Dec. **GURNEY'S INN:** Tel 631-668-2345; gurneys montauk.com. *Cost:* from $200 (off-peak), from $450 (peak). **MONTAUK POINT LIGHTHOUSE MUSEUM:** Tel 888-MTK-POINT or 631-668-2546; montauklighthouse.com. *When:* daily, May–mid-Oct; Sat–Sun, Nov and mid-Mar–Apr. **GOSMAN'S DOCK RESTAURANT:** Tel 631-668-5330; gosmans.com. *Cost:* dinner $35. **LOBSTER ROLL:** Amagansett. Tel 631-267-3740; lobsterrollamagansett.com. *Cost:* lobster roll $30. **BEST TIMES:** May–Oct for fishing; last weekend of Sept for the Montauk Surf Classic at Ditch Plains (ny.surfesa); spring and fall for crowd-free moments.

The Deliciously Sleepy Sister to the Hamptons

NORTH FORK

Long Island, New York

With quiet bays, half-empty beaches, and small villages of white clapboard houses and steepled churches, the North Fork is the last bastion of old Long Island, a finger of land that sits just across the

Peconic Bay from the South Fork's glamorous Hamptons (see p. 160). While there are a few signs of looming trendiness (most notably the Frisky Oyster with its sophisticated menu in downtown Greenport), nightlife on the North Fork tends to mean camping under the stars. And though the farms that made Long Island duckling famous are mostly gone, the North Fork retains its agricultural heritage, with 3,000 acres of neatly tended vineyards—producing cabernet sauvignons and merlots that some in the wine world consider worthy competitors to California and France.

The quiet village of Cutchogue (one house dating back to 1650 stands testimony to its history) is the wine center of Long Island, with the more notable of the area's nearly 50 wineries located here: Bedell Cellars, Pellegrini Vineyards, Pugliese Vineyards, and Castello di Borghese, among others.

Cutchogue also lays claim to a great beach—as do Greenport, Jamesport, Mattituck, and Southold. Head out to Orient Beach State Park at the eastern end of the island, where footprint-free sand meets open water alongside a bird sanctuary. Nine miles of undeveloped waterfront is flanked by a thick maritime forest of blackjack oak and red cedar, making this a delight for hiking, biking, swimming, and picnicking.

The two-lane Route 25 connects most of the North Fork's dots, lined with farm stands that offer plump heirloom tomatoes and organic corn, or famous homemade pies at the always popular Briermere Farms in Riverhead. And if you really want to get the feel of the countryside, stop by Wickham's Fruit Farm outside Cutchogue, roll up your sleeves, and pick your own fruit—blueberries, peaches, apples—from whatever's in season.

Floating in the bay between the North Fork and the South Fork and reached only by ferry is Shelter Island, with quiet beaches and wooded hills. In addition to impressive homes and peaceful villages, Shelter Island boasts the 2,100-acre Mashomack Preserve, with miles of coastline, tidal creeks, fields, pine swamps, and

pathways leading through cool oak and beech forest and one of the East Coast's largest concentrations of nesting osprey.

For years, the Ram's Head Inn with its weathered shingle exterior and white trim offering views of Coecles Inlet was one of the only places to hang your hat. A small private beach, swimming and sailing, and a nice restaurant keep it a favorite choice. Hotelier Andre Balazs later opened the quietly chic Sunset Beach with a casual style of flip-flops and mojitos that is more Miami than Long Island. The 20 guest rooms all have private sun decks and views of the bay, while the restaurant offers alfresco dining on simple delicacies.

WHERE: 80 miles east of New York City. *Visitor info:* Tel 631-298-5757; northfork.org. **THE FRISKY OYSTER:** Greenport. Tel 631-477-4265; thefriskyoyster.com. *Cost:* dinner $70. **LONG ISLAND WINE COUNCIL:** Tel 631-722-2220; liwines.com. **BEDELL CELLARS:** Cutchogue. Tel 631-734-7537; bedellcellars .com. **PELLEGRINI VINEYARDS:** Cutchogue. Tel 631-734-4111; pellegrinivineyards.com. **PUGLIESE VINEYARDS:** Cutchogue. Tel 631-734-4057; pugliesevineyards.com. **CASTELLO DI BORGHESE:** Cutchogue. Tel 631-734-5111; castellodiborghese.com. *When:* Apr–Dec. **ORIENT BEACH STATE PARK:** Orient. Tel 631-323-2440; nysparks.com/parks/106/details.aspx. **BRIERMERE FARMS:** Riverhead.

Cedar Beach on the south side of the North Fork is one of many serene stretches of shoreline in the area.

Tel 631-722-3931. **WICKHAM'S FRUIT FARM:** Cutchogue. Tel 631-734-6441; wickhams fruitfarm.com. *When:* closed Sun, Apr–Dec. **MASHOMACK PRESERVE:** Shelter Island. Tel 631-749-1001; shelter-island.org/mashomack .html. *When:* closed Tues; weekends only in Jan. **RAM'S HEAD INN:** Shelter Island. Tel 631-749-0811; theramsheadinn.com. *Cost:*

from $150 with shared bath. **SUNSET BEACH:** Shelter Island. Tel 631-749-2001; sunset beachli.com. *Cost:* from $365 (off-peak), from $475 (peak). *When:* open May–Sept. **BEST TIMES:** June for Strawberry Festival in Mattituck (mattituckstrawberryfestival.org); Sept for the East End Greenport Maritime Festival in Greenport (eastendmaritimefestival.org).

A Victorian Grande Dame in the Wilderness

MOHONK MOUNTAIN HOUSE

New Paltz, New York

For more than one hundred years Mohonk Mountain House has looked much the same—a fairy-tale castle sitting on a pristine glacial lake at the top of the Shawangunk (pronounced by locals SHONG-gum) mountain ridge.

Often confused with the nearby Catskills (see p. 143), "the Gunks" have their own unique geologic makeup, with white quartz cliffs that offer the best rock climbing in the Northeast.

One of the country's few remaining great 19th-century mountain houses, Mohonk has been owned by the same family since Albert Smiley, a Quaker, made his original purchase of 280 acres and a ten-room inn in 1869. His brother Alfred soon joined him in creating a glorious lakeside hodgepodge of Victorian turrets, gables, and crenellated stone towers standing seven stories high, drawing such distinguished visitors as Theodore Roosevelt, Andrew Carnegie, and Arturo Toscanini. Today it stands at the center of a magnificent 40,000-acre wilderness made up of the Mountain House property, Monhonk preserve, and Minnewaska State Park. With 85 miles of trails from its doorstep, Mohonk is a hiker's paradise in summer and a cross-country skier's delight in winter; a steep 1-mile hike to Sky Top Tower rewards climbers with a breathtaking 360-degree view of the Hudson Valley and the Catskills.

Some of the 19th-century traditions remain: Meals served in the stunning dining

Mohonk Mountain House is one of the last wooden mountain resorts in the mid-Hudson Valley.

room are included in the price; there are no TVs in the rooms; and air-conditioning is a fairly recent innovation. Evening lectures and special themed programs draw guests interested in gardening, cooking, ballroom dancing, and almost everything else under the sun. The emphasis is still focused on slowing down, and the rocking chairs lining the great porch with its mesmerizing views of the lake are prized as are afternoon tea and homemade cookies.

The main house sits on the compact Lake Mohonk, less than a half-mile long and 534 feet wide. The lake makes up in beauty what it lacks in size, with undeveloped shores that are dotted with enormous boulders or "erratics," dropped in place when the glaciers melted 12,000 years ago. Rustic Adirondack-style gazebos are perched at all the best vantage points around the lake and throughout the expansive grounds.

Now there's another way to relax—a lavish adjacent 30,000-square-foot spa wing blends seamlessly with the Mountain House's 19th-century look, and though built for Mohonk's loyal clientele, who requested an indoor pool, it has attracted a whole new crowd that drives up from New York City to soothe body, mind, and spirit.

WHERE: 90 miles north of New York City; 1000 Mountain Rest Rd. Tel 855-764-6950; mohonk.com. *Cost:* from $646 for two, includes all meals. **BEST TIMES:** 1st half of Oct for peak foliage; winter for the open stone-and-wood skating pavilion with 39-foot fireplace.

An Urban Miracle and Manhattan's Backyard

CENTRAL PARK

New York, New York

Laid out between 1859 and 1873 on a design by the great landscape architects Frederick Law Olmsted and Calvert Vaux, Central Park is an urban miracle, an 843-acre oasis of green surrounded on all sides by high-rise buildings. Fields follow meadows, streams feed into lakes, and cool woods cover hillsides all the way from 59th Street to 110th, stretching more than half a mile wide from Fifth Avenue to Central Park West in the very heart of Manhattan. The site was chosen because its hilly terrain, rocky outcroppings, and swamps made it unappealing to developers, but the perfect raw material for a great garden to rival those of Europe. All told, 20,000 workers reshaped the landscape, planting 270,000 trees and shrubs. Lakes were created from swamps for boating, horse trails for riding, and various entertainments placed all around to give Gothamites their day in the sun and their evenings of fun.

The highlights are many. In the southeast quadrant sits the Central Park Zoo, where real grizzly bears, sea lions, reptiles, and other animals live in the shadow of the famed Delacorte Musical Clock, whose mechanical animals dance on the hour. To the west, the 1908 Central Park Carousel is one of the largest, with 57 hand-carved horses and chariots, and to the north is the Mall, a grand, 40-foot-wide promenade flanked by towering American elms, statuary, and a band shell. At the Mall's northern end, the Bethesda Terrace is probably the park's most recognizable space, its two stone staircases leading down to the great Bethesda Fountain and its Angel of Waters centerpiece and a 22-acre lake (you can rent rowboats at the Loeb Boathouse). It's also home to the popular

Though it's the most visited urban park in the country, Central Park offers many secluded and restorative spots.

Boathouse Restaurant, with contemporary American cuisine served indoors or (in season) on the lakeside deck, in view of the ducks, turtles, rowboats, and a real Venetian gondola.

North of here is the Ramble, a 36-acre maze of woods and winding paths, one of the many places in the park where you can really forget that the city is around you. Still farther north, Belvedere Castle is a Victorian folly set at the second-highest natural elevation in the park, providing a great view of the park. From here it's not far to the Great Lawn, venue of Simon and Garfunkel's Classic 1981 reunion show and appearances by world-famous names like the Dalai Lama.

Every season has its wonders. In summer, there are free performances by the New York Philharmonic on the Great Lawn; the Public Theater's "Shakespeare in the Park" series at the Delacorte Theater; or performances of popular and world music and dance at Summerstage, just behind the Mall. In fall, Central Park foliage is near New England's in quality, enhanced by the city's special light. In early November, the nearly 50,000 runners who complete the prestigious New York Marathon end up here, after traversing all five of the city's boroughs. In winter, you can go ice-skating at the Wollman Rink, and in spring, the 6-acre Conservatory Garden is a gem, a riot of blooms, from indigenous flowers to cultivated heirloom roses. Buds start peeping out in March, just when the gray winter seems like it will never end, and New Yorkers fall in love with Central Park all over again.

WHERE: between 59th and 110th Sts., and Fifth Ave. and Central Park West. Tel 212-310-6600; centralparknyc.org. **BOATHOUSE RESTAURANT:** Tel 212-517-2233; thecentralparkboathouse.com. *Cost:* dinner $60. *When:* Apr–Nov. **SYMPHONY:** centralparknyc.org. *When:* June–Sept. **SHAKESPEARE IN THE PARK:** Tel 212-539-8500; publictheater.org. *When:* June–Aug. **SUMMERSTAGE:** Tel 212-360-2756; summerstage.org. *When:* June–Aug. **BEST TIMES:** any warm weekend for musicians and lots of activity; late Sept–mid-Oct for foliage; after a snowfall for a magic winter moment.

A Miracle—and Not Just on 34th Street

CHRISTMAS IN NEW YORK

New York, New York

For all its hard-bitten reputation, New York is crazy for Christmas. It's a time when the city is at its most beautiful, strung with lights, bundled for winter, and brimming with the warmth of human kindness—as long as you steer clear of the last-minute Christmas shoppers on a mission.

At the heart of it all is Rockefeller Center. Built in the 1930s by John D. Rockefeller Jr., the complex of office buildings is a masterpiece of art deco architecture. The center looks its best at Christmas, when a towering light-strewn Norway spruce is displayed above the small but incredibly romantic ice-skating rink in the lower promenade plaza off Fifth Avenue between 49th and 50th streets. Take a spin, or grab a meal at the elegant Sea Grill right next door, its windows offering an eye-level skater view. On the other side of the rink, the Rock Center Café is a larger, brighter spot serving high-end comfort food. For a different perspective, the Top of the Rock observation deck offers stunning 360-degree city views from the 70th floor of 30 Rockefeller Center. In the evening, head to Radio City

Music Hall for the annual Christmas Spectacular, a grand stage show starring the legendary Rockettes, who have been high-kicking their way across this stage since 1932.

North and south of Rockefeller Center, mostly along Fifth Avenue, the city's high-end department stores mount elaborate holiday window displays that draw locals and tourists by the thousands. Start at Bloomingdale's and Barneys, then head down Fifth Avenue past Bergdorf Goodman, St. Patrick's Cathedral (not a retail stop, granted, but a vital Christmas stop nonetheless), Saks Fifth Avenue, Lord & Taylor, then cut west on 34th to see the extravagantly decorated windows at Macy's, billed as the world's largest store and the most historic of them all. Stop in and see Santa while you're there.

Head back uptown to Bryant Park, behind the New York Public Library (see p. 186),

Oversized Christmas ornaments are part of the annual holiday display at Rockefeller Center.

where an ice-skating rink and some 125 stalls selling gifts and crafts keep the air festive. Farther uptown, the Metropolitan Museum of Art (see p. 184) sets up a Christmas tree in its Medieval Sculpture Hall, surrounded by an exquisite baroque nativity crèche. At Lincoln Center's David Geffen Hall, the National Chorale performs its annual Messiah Sing-In, in which 2,700 audience members are invited to sing along with the choir. The Cathedral of St. John the Divine (see p. 178) hosts the annual winter solstice performance by the Paul Winter Consort, with a big dash of world flair that has always set the cathedral apart.

ROCKEFELLER CENTER: Tel 212-632-6868; rockefellercenter.com. *Skating info:* Tel 212-332-7654; therinkatrockcenter.com. *When:* tree-lighting ceremony, week after Thanksgiving; skating Oct–Apr. **SEA GRILL:** Tel 212-332-7610; patinagroup.com. *Cost:* dinner $75. **ROCK CENTER CAFÉ:** Tel 212-332-7620; patinagroup.com. *Cost:* dinner $50. **TOP OF THE ROCK:** Tel 212-698-2000; topoftherocknyc.com. **RADIO CITY CHRISTMAS SPECTACULAR:** Tel 212-247-4777; radiocity christmas.com. *Cost:* from $45. *When:* Nov–Dec. **BRYANT PARK:** bryantpark.org. *When:* skating rink late Oct–mid-Jan. **LINCOLN CENTER MESSIAH SING-IN:** David Geffen Hall. Tel 212-721-6500 or 212-333-5333; lincoln center.org. *When:* mid-Dec. **ST. JOHN THE DIVINE:** Tel 212-316-7540; stjohndivine.org.

Above It All and Backward in Time

THE CLOISTERS & WAVE HILL

New York, New York

Near the northernmost tip of Manhattan, atop a riverside cliff within beautiful, flower-decked Fort Tryon Park, sits a complex of buildings where modern New York life holds no place whatsoever. It's called the Cloisters—five medieval cloisters in a complex designed to resemble the period and show off fine examples of Europe's medieval art and architecture. Arched walkways surround gardens planted according to descriptions in medieval poetry. To the New Yorkers lounging on the grass, listening to the burble of fountains, it's the Manhattan equivalent of a silent retreat.

The museum had its start in the early years of the 20th century, when American sculptor George Grey Barnard brought a large collection of medieval sculptures and architectural artifacts from France and opened his original Cloisters in upper Manhattan. A decade later, using funds provided by John D. Rockefeller Jr., the collection was acquired by the Metropolitan Museum of Art, and in 1927 plans were laid to move it to its larger present location. It was the kind of grand public gesture still fashionable at the time: Not only did Rockefeller provide funds to convert nearly 67 acres into what is now Fort Tryon Park, but he also donated 700 acres of forest and cliff in New Jersey so the view across the Hudson would remain unsullied.

Visitors today get much the same experience they did when the museum opened in 1938, touring galleries laid out in a logical flow from the Romanesque Hall (12th century) through the early and late Gothic (13th–15th century), most radiating out from the Cuxa Cloister, with its original 12th-century elements from the Benedictine monastery of Saint-Michel-de-Cuxa in the Pyrenees. All told, the Cloisters is home to some 5,000 items, many from Barnard's original collection, some donated by Rockefeller (including the seven Hunt of the Unicorn tapestries that have become a symbol of the museum), and others acquired in the intervening decades—illuminated manuscripts, stained-glass windows, reliquary shrines, elaborate crucifixes and gold chalices, and sculptures depicting Christian saints.

Continue the sensation of disconnect by traveling another 3 miles north to the residential Riverdale section of the Bronx. This is where you'll find Wave Hill, a bucolic 28-acre cliffside garden and cultural center offering gorgeous views of the Hudson River and Rockefeller's Palisades cliffs. Originally a private estate, the property at one time or another was leased to the family of the young Theodore Roosevelt, to conductor Arturo Toscanini, and to Mark Twain, who wrote of its winter winds: "They sing their hoarse song through the big tree-tops with a splendid energy that thrills me and stirs me and uplifts me and makes me want to live always." Deeded to the city in 1960, Wave Hill continues to be a special oasis dedicated to fostering connection between people and nature. On weekday mornings and afternoons its pastoral gardens, greenhouses, and woodlands provide the setting for serene contemplation, while weekends offer concerts, lectures, exhibitions, and workshops.

THE CLOISTERS: Fort Tryon Park near 190th St. Tel 212-923-3700; metmuseum.org. **WAVE HILL:** West 249th St. and Independence Ave., the Bronx. Tel 718-549-3200; wavehill .org. *When:* closed Mon. **BEST TIMES:** May–Oct for the Cloisters' free garden tours; May–June for peak gardens and Oct for foliage at Wave Hill; Dec for medieval concerts at the Cloisters.

The Cloisters are dedicated to the art and architecture of medieval Europe.

A Playground for Millionaires

COLUMBUS CIRCLE

New York, New York

For all its centrality as the gateway to the beautiful Upper West Side, one of the city's finest residential neighborhoods, Columbus Circle was, until recently, a total mess, dominated by the nearly Stalinesque New York Coliseum convention center, the empty hull of the defunct Huntington Hartford Gallery (a nearly windowless white marble slab directly facing a great view of Central Park), and a skinny 44-story office tower, creaking like a ship in high winds and making workers on high floors queasy.

What a difference a few decades make. Today the Coliseum has been replaced by the dazzling 55-story Time Warner Center, the swaying tower has been shored up and transformed into Donald Trump's Trump International Hotel & Tower, and the Hartford Gallery got a major makeover and is now home to the Museum of Arts & Design. In the center of things, standing atop a 53-foot pedestal and column and surrounded by newly landscaped fountains, stands a Carrera marble statue of Christopher Columbus, erected in 1892 to mark the 400th anniversary of his voyage.

The Time Warner Center is the real star here, the lodestone that's transformed this onetime pass-through block into a serious center of white-glove living, indulgent dining, and high-culture entertainment. Built on a design by David Childs and Mustafa Kemal Abadan, the building takes the form of two parallelogram-shaped glass-and-steel towers rising from a common base whose facade follows the curve of Columbus Circle. Inside, it's a veritable city unto itself. At street level and just above are dozens of upscale shops; on the 12th floor is the home of Jazz at Lincoln Center (see p. 179), with artistic and managing director Wynton Marsalis at the helm.

Levels 3 and 4 offer half a dozen extraordinary restaurants and cafés. The 26-seat Masa gets the award for conspicuous consumption, its *omakase* dinner—five artfully composed appetizers followed by a sushi entrée of 15 to 20 exotic seafoods (some flown in from Japan)—going for a cool $450. Designed with a Zenlike sense of order and calm, the restaurant offers seating at small tables or at a Japanese cedar bar, where you can watch sushi god Masayoshi Takayama work his pricey magic. Next door, the less templelike Bar Masa brings costs back down to earth. At Per Se, Thomas Keller of Napa's French Laundry (see p. 863) has created a Gotham version of his vaunted flagship, with elegant contemporary decor and views over Central Park setting the stage for nine-course tasting menus. A cluster of other more moderately priced options—Bouchon Bakery and Café, Landmarc, and Parkview Lounge—fill out the roster.

The Upper West Side, Central Park, and the theater district are all steps from Columbus Circle.

The upper levels of the Time Warner Center are given over to offices, millionaires' condominiums, and the uber-luxurious Mandarin Oriental Hotel; its 198 rooms and 46 suites occupy floors 35 to 54 of the center's north tower. Feeling like a city in the clouds above the real city below, the hotel offers views of either the park, the Hudson River, or Midtown from every room, and is designed with a seamless blend of urban contemporary, Asian, and updated 1940s style—totally sophisticated, totally chic, and totally expensive. On the 35th floor, the hotel's exquisite 14,500-square-foot spa is a tranquil aerie whose indulgent menu of long "rituals," massages, and various body treatments adapted from traditions around the world knows few rivals.

Across Columbus Circle, in the Trump building, Jean Georges restaurant is the brainchild of Jean-Georges Vongerichten, one of America's most creative culinary forces, and is among the city's finest restaurants. From the simplest dish to the most complex, each masterpiece is a combination of obscure flavors, innovative pairings, and dazzling presentations of the kind that have captivated Vongerichten's devotees since he first debuted on the New York dining scene in 1986.

WHERE: intersection of Broadway and Central Park South (W. 59th St.); theshops atcolumbuscircle.com. **MASA:** Tel 212-823-9800; masanyc.com. *Cost:* prix-fixe dinner $450; Bar Masa $75. **PER SE:** Tel 212-823-9335; thomaskeller.com/per-se. *Cost:* 9-course chef's tasting menus $310. **BOUCHON BAKERY & CAFÉ, LANDMARC, AND PARKVIEW LOUNGE:** theshopsatcolumbuscircle.com. **MANDARIN ORIENTAL HOTEL:** Tel 866-801-8880 or 212-805-8800; mandarinoriental.com. *Cost:* from $695 (off-peak), from $895 (peak). **JEAN GEORGES:** Tel 212-299-3900; jean-georges.com. *Cost:* 3-course prix-fixe dinner $138.

Coming to America

CUNARD'S *QM2*

New York, New York

The Golden Age of the passenger liners ended when jets cut the transatlantic travel time from five days to just a few hours, but what travelers gained in convenience, they lost in pure élan: long, leisurely days at sea; white-glove service; elegant formal dinners; a real sense of onboard community; and the feeling of being truly away from it all, with thousands of miles between you and landfall.

Since the early 1970s, when point-to-point liners morphed into round-trip cruise ships, the great Cunard Line has been the only shipping company to continue offering regularly scheduled transatlantic service in season, transiting between home ports in New York and Southampton, England. And who better? Cunard, after all, was the line that started it all back in 1840, when Sir Samuel Cunard secured the first royal contract to carry mail by steamship between Britain and North America. A sequence of legendary vessels followed: *Mauritania, Lusitania, Aquitania, Berengaria, Queen Mary, Queen Elizabeth,* and finally, in 1969, *Queen Elizabeth 2,* the ship that kept up the transatlantic tradition for over three decades. Everyone assumed she was the last of the true ocean liners . . . but they were wrong.

In 1998, under the new ownership of American shipping giant Carnival Corporation, Cunard announced its intention to build a new liner, the largest ever, and to create "a new

Golden Age of sea travel for those who missed the first." Nearly six years and more than $800 million later, in 2004, that dream became a reality when Britain's Queen Elizabeth II christened the 2,620-passenger *Queen Mary 2*, a vessel built to sail the roughest of the North Atlantic's waters well into the 21st century. She's big, fast, and tough, with a knife-shaped prow, uncommonly thick hull plating, and incredibly powerful engines. Inside, she's a veritable love letter to the old ocean liner days, merging art deco themes with modern, safety-conscious materials. Standout rooms include the formal Queen's Room ballroom with its classic grandeur; the high-ceilinged Chart Room with its green glass deco maps and 1940s-style furnishings; and the forward-facing Commodore Club, its handsome leather chairs looking out over dramatic bow views. An extensive 2016 refurbishment added a wine room, boutique shops, the Carinthia Lounge, and new cabins and state rooms.

At meals, Cunard is the last passenger line still segregating guests by class. Those booking the top-level suites dine in the 206-seat Queen's Grill, while junior-suite passengers dine in the 180-seat Princess Grill and everyone else dines in the 1,351-passenger Britannia Restaurant. The two grills are the model of restrained good taste, while the Britannia is a dramatic, three-deck space designed to recall the magnificent first-class restaurant on the original *Queen Mary* (now permanently docked in California, see p. 817). *QM2* continues some other traditions long gone by the wayside on other vessels (such as offering onboard kennels for passengers' dogs and cats), but her archetypal nod to tradition is her singular schedule of transatlantic crossings, offered May through early December. The trip westbound, from Southampton to New York, offers an entrance to New York that is unrivaled, clearing the Verrazano Narrows Bridge by just 13 feet at the highest tide and entering New York Harbor with the Statue of Liberty and the downtown skyline up ahead.

Be sure to listen for the two 7-foot Tyfon steam whistles mounted way up on the classic black-and-red funnel. Their sound is evocative enough—a low bass "A" that literally shakes the rafters—but here's the bit of history that makes them sublime: One was borrowed permanently from the original *Queen Mary*. It's the same whistle that sounded when the ship entered New York Harbor in 1945, carrying 14,526 American servicemen home from WWII, celebrating victory. Welcome to New York.

CUNARD: Tel 800-7-CUNARD or 661-753-1000; cunard.com. *Cost:* 7-night transatlantic crossings from $1,199 (off-peak), from $1,499 (peak) per person (double occupancy). *When:* May–early Dec. **BEST TIME:** spring and summer for the calmest seas.

Where New York Was New Amsterdam

HISTORIC DOWNTOWN

New York, New York

This is the New York you remember from all those black-and-white 1930s movies: narrow streets, looming skyscrapers, businesspeople in suits, and cabbies with that quintessential New Yawk accent. Today the cabbies hail from all over the world, but the rest is pretty much the same—that is, as long as you bear in mind that the one constant in New York is change.

It was down at the southernmost tip of Manhattan Island that the Dutch colony of Nieuw Amsterdam was born in 1625. In 1626, the colony's governor, Peter Minuit, made his now-legendary $25 purchase of the island from the Indians near what is now the Bowling Green, a tiny triangular park at the very base of Broadway. Once a larger patch that served as a cattle market and parade ground, it was converted to a park for lawn bowling in 1733. Immediately south is the U.S. Customs House. Designed by Cass Gilbert and completed in 1907, it's one of the finest Beaux-Arts buildings in New York and is now home to the New York branch of the National Museum of the American Indian.

Just next door, in Battery Park, is Castle Clinton, which welcomed over 8 million arrivals as the city's official immigration facility between 1855 and 1890, when operations moved to Ellis Island. Built as a fort on the rocks at Manhattan's southernmost tip during the War of 1812, subsequent landfills later encompassed it. Part of The Battery, it's now a historic monument, a concert venue, and the jumping-off point for ferry service to the Statue of Liberty and Ellis Island (see p. 192). Around the park are a series of monuments to various casualties of war and history, among them Fritz Koenig's 25-foot bronze sculpture *The Sphere*, which stood in the plaza of the World Trade Center until the September 11 attacks. Rescued from the rubble, it was moved here in March 2002 to serve as a temporary memorial.

For an authentic piece of colonial history, head a few blocks east to the Fraunces Tavern. Built in 1719, this Georgian-style yellow brick house was the site where Washington gave his farewell address to the Continental Army, in 1783. You can tour the museum upstairs or enjoy a meal in its quaint restaurant downstairs. From here, walk north to legendary Wall Street. Named for an earthen wall erected by the Dutch in 1653 to ward off Indian attacks, it's been the center of commerce in the New World since the Dutch moved in. The New York Stock Exchange, the largest securities market in the world, sits at the center of the action at Broad and Wall, housed in a handsome 1903 neoclassical building. The city is expected to erect a historic marker to commemorate the slave market that operated in this area from 1711 to 1762. Across the street, a statue of George Washington marks the entrance to Federal Hall, where he was inaugurated as the country's first president in 1789. Federal Hall served as the first seat of U.S. government from 1789 to 1790—when New York was the capital of the newly formed U.S.—but it was demolished in 1812 to make room for the current structure, which served as New York's customs house from 1842 to 1862. It now serves as a museum and memorial to the first president and the nation's beginning.

Wall Street is also home to Trinity Church, at one time the tallest structure on the New York skyline at 284 feet (this is the third Trinity Church in this location; the first was built in 1697). Built in 1846 by Richard Upjohn, the Episcopal church is now dwarfed by practically everything around it, but still functions as a house of worship and as a peaceful refuge, its graveyard holding the remains of such notables as Alexander Hamilton and Robert Fulton. Five blocks north is St. Paul's Chapel, part of the Trinity Parish (see p. 195) since 1766.

Farther north on Broadway, you won't be able to miss the lovely 58-story Woolworth Building, which was the tallest building in the world when it was built in 1913. Designed by Cass Gilbert in the Neo-Gothic style, it resembles an extremely tall, narrow Notre Dame, full of lacy stone traceries, gargoyles, turrets, and spires. Just across the street is the south end of City Hall Park, a pretty public space surrounded by municipal government buildings, including the surprisingly small City Hall (not open to visitors). To the east, South Street Seaport encompasses the largest concentration of restored early 19th-century commercial buildings in the city, complete with historic cobblestone streets. Much of the area is taken up with mall-like shopping and dining establishments, but the South Street Seaport Museum is another matter, its galleries providing a view of the days when

Manhattan was ringed with the masts of sailing ships, bringing cargo from around the world. Outside, at its piers on the East River, the museum's collection of historic vessels sits permanently moored or at anchor.

WHERE: the southern tip of Manhattan island. *Visitor info:* Tel 212-484-1200; nycgo .com. **MUSEUM OF THE AMERICAN INDIAN:** Tel 212-514-3700; nmai.si.edu. **FRAUNCES TAVERN:** Tel 212-425-1778 (museum) or 212-968-1776

(restaurant); frauncestavernmuseum.org. or frauncestavern.com. *Cost:* dinner $60. **TRINITY CHURCH:** Tel 212-602-0800; trinitywallstreet .org. **SOUTH STREET SEAPORT MUSEUM:** Tel 212-748-8600; southstreetseaportmuseum.org. *When:* closed Mon, Apr–Dec; Fri–Mon, Jan– Mar. **BEST TIMES:** Wed and Thurs at 1 P.M. for free concerts at Trinity Church; Friday nights in July–Aug for Free Seaport Music Festival concerts (seaportmusicalfestival.com).

Beacon of Romance, Symbol of a City

THE EMPIRE STATE BUILDING

New York, New York

Soaring 1,454 feet into the New York sky, the Empire State Building is the most perfect, enduring symbol of the city, a Promethean achievement that rose during the Great Depression. It reigned as the tallest building in the world for over 40 years, but is now outsized by One World Trade Center, which replaced the Twin Towers in 2012 (see p.195). Though perhaps not the most beautiful of New York's skyscrapers (the Chrysler Building usually wins that title; see p. 186), it is undoubtedly its most iconic and beloved, its art deco peak lit up in the colors of the season, transforming it into a lighthouse that marks the metaphorical center of town.

The idea for the 102-story building was born in the mind of John J. Raskob, a former General Motors executive who wanted to compete with Walter Chrysler's new building up at 42nd and Lexington. The announcement of the building's construction came on August 29, 1929, just days after the stock market hit its then all-time peak, but by the time work on the foundation began in January 1930, the market had crashed. Whether because of the crash or in defiance of it, work went on. It officially opened in March 1931—only 13 months after construction began—and was a huge commercial flop.

Only 30 percent of its office space had been rented, and 56 of its 103 floors had no occupants whatsoever. In its first year, the building's owners made as much money from tickets sold to its observation decks as they did in rent, and it was derided as "The Empty State Building."

But in the long run, none of that mattered. Nor does the fact that an early plan to tie up dirigibles to the building's tower never materialized. The fact is that before it was even

The Empire State Building's name derived from the nickname for New York, The Empire State.

complete, the Empire State Building had become New Yorkers' proudest collective achievement, and an international icon too. In the 1933 film, King Kong scaled the building after escaping from his captors, battling biplanes before tragically falling to his death. In 1957, Cary Grant and Deborah Kerr made plans to meet on the observation deck and resolve their star-crossed love. In 1993's *Sleepless in Seattle*, Tom Hanks and Meg Ryan mimicked that *Affair to Remember* with their own sky-high rendezvous. And every year, 4 million visitors make their own elevator trip up to the observatories on the 86th and 102nd floors (the lower one the perennial favorite, the higher one glassed in and cramped) for a view that can stretch up to 80 miles in all directions.

WHERE: 350 5th Ave. Tel 212-736-3100; esbnyc.com. **BEST TIME:** Feb for the Empire State Building Run-Up, when more than 400 runners tackle the 1,576 steps leading to the 86th floor.

America's Original Bohemian Quarter

GREENWICH VILLAGE

New York, New York

In 1917, the artist and provocateur Marcel Duchamp, along with John Sloan and several cohorts, climbed to the top of the memorial arch in Washington Square Park, brandishing Chinese lanterns, cap pistols, and glasses of wine.

Poet Gertrude Dick declared Greenwich Village "a free and independent republic," and so it has remained, karmically if not politically.

The Village dates to the early 17th century, when the Dutch farmed the land. After the English took control of Manhattan in 1664, the area became known as Grin'wich, and in 1713 it was formally incorporated as an independent village—a northern suburb of New York, which was still concentrated down at the tip of the island (see p. 172). Increasing numbers of New Yorkers settled in the area, and the Village became so established that in 1811, when New York officials adopted a plan to segment all of Manhattan Island into a rigid street grid, they were forced to exempt the Village from the new rules—which is why today, even New York residents sometimes get lost trying to find their way through the Village's illogical tangle.

Fame settled on the Village gradually during the 20th century, when it became one of the capitals of American bohemianism. First came the artists such as Duchamp and Edward Hopper, writers Eugene O'Neill and Henry Miller, and all manner of radicals drawn by the area's low rents and tolerant sensibility. By the 1950s, the Village drew Beat Generation writers such as Allen Ginsberg, and in the '60s it was the center of America's folk music revival, its coffeehouses birthing the careers of Bob Dylan and countless others. At the end of the decade, the Village saw the birth of the American gay rights movement when police raided a gay bar called the Stonewall Inn—and the patrons fought back.

Though its most radical days may now be behind it, the Village still provides much-needed relief from New York's more business-like quarters, its maze of streets and alleys holding architectural gems, classic bars, off-Broadway theater, and vibrant street life. Washington Square Park is the epicenter of the area, its 10 acres surrounded by the myriad buildings of New York University. On the park's northern side, the Washington Arch was erected on a design by Stanford White between 1890 and 1892, commemorating George Washington's inauguration as president 100 years before. Behind it, lining the park, is a row of landmark Greek Revival mansions dating to the mid-19th century, when the park was one of New York's best addresses. Today, the park is still a hotbed of activity on most days, with performers clustered around its central fountain and Village residents taking their ease on benches, playing chess, and walking their dogs.

A hub of life in Greenwich Village, Washington Square Park is always abuzz with activity.

To the south, Macdougal Street and Bleecker Street still retain some of their boho 1960s flavor, lined with shops, classic low-rent restaurants like Mamoun's Falafel, and music clubs like Café Wha?. Near Mamoun's, tiny Minetta Street is an exemplar of the Village's screwy street pattern, snaking through to Sixth Avenue in a way you don't find uptown. Around the corner, on West 3rd Street, the Blue Note is the city's most upscale jazz club, attracting big-name performers. Farther west, on Seventh Avenue, the Village Vanguard is its most revered, a tiny, triangular basement venue that in its 80-plus years has seen performances by the likes of John Coltrane, Ornette Coleman, and Miles Davis. Farther west, the epicenter of the Village's gay community is Christopher Street and Sheridan Square at Seventh Avenue, site of the famous Stonewall Inn.

West of Seventh Avenue the Village turns into a gingerbread town full of narrow tree-lined streets, small cafés, pocket-size parks, and legendary bars like the White Horse

Tavern, where poet Dylan Thomas literally drank himself to death in 1953. Newer spots, such as the always-packed "gastropub" The Spotted Pig, became immediate legends.

Visit in late October and you'll get swept up in the annual Greenwich Village Halloween Parade, the country's biggest and arguably most entertaining Halloween celebration. It offers a kind of pass to the Village's historical mystique, allowing anyone who shows up—masqueraders and watchers alike—the illusion that they too are part of a great, free-spirited bohemian continuum.

South of the Village, the onetime manufacturing district (and later arts haven) known as SoHo is now a high-end retail district dominated by beautiful 19th-century cast-iron architecture, as exemplified by the Haughwout Store building at the corner of Broadway and Broome. East of Broadway from Houston to 14th, what's now known as the East Village was originally part of the Lower East Side (see p. 180) until renamed by realtors in the 1960s. It extends all the way to the East River, the grungy vibe from the 1970s–'80s punk scene having given way to a playground for NYU students. A smattering of Polish and Ukrainian restaurants from distant immigrant days still survive.

WHERE: The Village is bounded by Broadway on the east, the Hudson River on the west, Houston St. to the south, and 14th St. to the north. *Historical info:* gvshp.org. **MAMOUN'S:** Tel 212-674-8685; mamouns.com. *Cost:* lunch $9. **CAFÉ WHA?:** Tel 212-254-3706; cafe wha.com. **BLUE NOTE:** Tel 212-475-8592; bluenote.net. *Cost:* tickets from $30. **VILLAGE VANGUARD:** Tel 212-255-4037; villagevanguard .com. *Cost:* tickets from $30. **STONEWALL INN:** Tel 212-488-2705; stonewallinnnyc.com. **WHITE HORSE:** Tel 212-989-3956. **SPOTTED PIG:** Tel 212-620-0393; thespottedpig.com. *Cost:* dinner $50. **HOW:** Big Onion Walking Tours (tel 212-439-1090; bigonion.com) offers tours of the Village (as well as other neighborhoods). **BEST TIMES:** late June for the annual Gay Pride March (nycpride.org); Oct 31 for the Halloween Parade (halloween-nyc.com).

The Spiritual Home of Black America

HARLEM & UPPER MANHATTAN

New York, New York

For the first 200 years of its history, Harlem was a tiny agricultural village first settled by the Dutch in 1658, but in the 1880s, it began to grow rapidly, as elevated railroads reached farther north. Grand homes and apartment buildings began to rise, turning the area into a desirable alternative to the city's more congested downtown. In the early years of the 20th century over-development meant rents were low enough for immigrant families and later for African Americans who arrived in huge numbers from the South. By the 1920s, Harlem was home to such towering figures as W.E.B. DuBois, Zora Neale Hurston, Langston Hughes, and Duke Ellington, who forged what became known as the Harlem Renaissance, the first great flowering of black arts and letters in the U.S. By the late 1970s, overcrowding, neglect, poverty, drugs, and violence had degraded the neighborhood into a symbol of urban decay. But in the late 1990s, Harlem again turned a corner, with an explosion of new businesses and block after block of historic homes slowly restored to their earlier glory.

At the southern end is 125th Street, a vibrant retail corridor with national chains standing side by side with locally owned shops, restaurants, and offices—including those of former president Bill Clinton. Between Adam Clayton Powell and Frederick Douglass Boulevards is the landmark Apollo Theater, a 1913 "whites only" theater that opened to blacks in 1934. It debuted Amateur Night and Ella Fitzgerald, one of the first winners, led a parade of greats that's included Billie Holiday, James Brown, Ray Charles, Marvin Gaye, and Richard Pryor. Amateur Night is still held every Wednesday, along with a variety of headliner concerts.

To get a glimpse of where the Harlem Renaissance was born, head north to the historic neighborhood of Sugar Hill, once home to notables like Justice Thurgood Marshall and baseball great Willie Mays, and still full of dignified row houses. A little south, backing up to each other on 138th and 139th Streets between Seventh and Eighth Avenues, is a group of 1890s town houses, some designed by McKim, Mead & White. In the 1920s and '30s, when upwardly mobile black professionals began to move in, the streets became known as "Strivers Row."

On Sunday mornings, visitors are a common sight at many of Harlem's gospel church services, famous for their energetic music, passionate preaching, and spiritual lift. Best bets are the Abyssinian Baptist Church, led by the influential Reverend Calvin Butts and renowned for

The Apollo Theater, built in 1913–1914, remains a cultural icon at the heart of Harlem.

its choir, and Mother A.M.E. (African Methodist Episcopal) Zion, the state's oldest black church, founded in 1796, and with a history that connects it to the Underground Railroad.

Storied restaurants are also a big draw, including the family-run Sylvia's on Malcolm X Boulevard and West 126th. Since 1962, this Harlem institution has served up classic soul food like mouthwatering fried chicken and heavenly corn bread. Meanwhile, over on West 131st Street near the Hudson River, new restaurants like the biker-themed Dinosaur Bar-B-Que testify to Harlem's increasing gentrification.

South of 125th on the west side, the neighborhood of Morningside Heights encompasses Columbia University and its grand main campus, as well as the incredible Cathedral of St. John the Divine, the world's largest Gothic cathedral, with a nave as long as two football fields. Under continuous construction since 1892, it remains unfinished, with no completion date in sight. Along with lack of funds, the use of traditional Gothic building techniques accounts for the slow pace of construction, but it may also contribute to the cathedral's

powerful spirituality, which has made it a favorite of everyone from the resident Episcopal congregation to musicians such as New Age saxophonist Paul Winter, who performs winter solstice concerts here annually.

WHERE: Harlem starts around 125th St. on the west side and around 96th St. on the east. It extends north to 155th St., and east-west from the Harlem and East Rivers to the Hudson. **APOLLO THEATER:** Tel 212-531-5300; apollotheater.com. *Cost:* from $18. **ABYSSINIAN BAPTIST CHURCH:** Tel 212-862-7474; abyssinian.org. **MOTHER A.M.E. ZION CHURCH:** Tel 212-234-1545; amez.org. **SYLVIA'S:** Tel 212-996-0660; sylviasrestaurant .com. *Cost:* dinner $25. **DINOSAUR BAR-B-QUE:** Tel 212-694-1777; dinosaurbarbque .com. *Cost:* dinner $30. **ST. JOHN THE DIVINE:** Tel 212-316-7540; stjohndivine.org. **HOW:** Harlem Heritage Tours offers 2-hour walking tours covering a range of themes and topics. Tel 212-280-7888; harlemheritage.com. *Cost:* from $29. **BEST TIME:** late July–Aug for Harlem Week (harlemweek.com), a month-long cultural celebration that includes the Harlem Jazz & Music Festival.

Twin Beauties in Downtown's Meatpacking District

THE HIGH LINE AND THE WHITNEY

New York, New York

An abandoned train trestle has been transformed into the 1.5-mile long High Line, New York's beloved elevated park that has played a prominent role in the transformation of the once derelict Meatpacking District. Running

north from Gansevoort Street to West 34th Street, it is a long and narrow landscaped park that puts visitors in the midst of vintage brick buildings and sleek contemporary high-rises that arrived with the neighborhood's burgeoning regentrification.

Just steps from the banks of the Hudson, the High Line may be the city's finest stroll, with sweeping river views and incomparable people-watching (though you'll want to avoid the weekend crush). Take a seat at a bench or picnic table, and admire the landscaping—

many of the wild plantings are meant to recall the overgrown tracks of the trestle's recent past.

The Whitney Museum, relocated downtown to the High Line's southern cap in 2015 with

The High Line was inspired by a 3-mile elevated park in Paris called the Promenade Plantée.

much fanfare, embraces its new location with massive windows, 360-degree views, and expansive indoor and outdoor exhibition spaces that showcase one of the country's foremost collections of modern and contemporary American art. Designed by Renzo Piano, famed architect and designer of multiple museums around the world (including the Pompidou Center in Paris, one of his earliest projects), the Whitney's new steel-and-glass home sits like a cultural anchor at the base of the High Line.

THE HIGH LINE: Tel 212-206-9922; thehighline.org. **WHITNEY MUSEUM:** Tel 212-570-3600; whitney.org.

If You Can Make It Here, You Can Make It Anywhere

LINCOLN CENTER & CARNEGIE HALL

New York, New York

Located in the heart of the largely residential Upper West Side, 16-acre Lincoln Center is the largest arts complex in the world and the centerpiece of New York's performing arts scene, providing a sort of one-stop-shopping opportunity for high culture since 1962. The center's three main theaters—the Metropolitan Opera House, the David H. Koch Theater (home to the New York City Ballet), and David Geffen Hall (home to the New York Philharmonic) surround a large central plaza, inspired by Michelangelo's Piazza del Campidoglio in Rome, and a fountain designed by Philip Johnson. Look up to view *The Sources of Music* and *The Triumph of Music*, two enormous Marc Chagall murals hanging behind the Opera House's glass facade. Also off the main plaza are several smaller theaters and rehearsal spaces; Lincoln Center Theater, with smaller venues for stage plays and musicals; the Juilliard School, the country's foremost college for the performing arts; the School of American Ballet, established in 1934 by George Balanchine; the Film Society of Lincoln Center, with showings throughout the year; and Damrosch Park, a park and band shell for outdoor performances, where in summer, dance bands playing swing, salsa, and more perform in the plaza as part of the Midsummer Night Swing series. Five blocks down Broadway, the new Time Warner Center is the home of Jazz at Lincoln Center (see p. 170). It maintains the 1,233-seat Rose Theater as well as an intimate jazz club and the amphitheater-style Appel Room, where the stage backdrop is an enormous glass wall offering magnificent nighttime views across Columbus Circle and straight down Central Park South.

At 57th Street and Seventh Avenue, Carnegie Hall is without a doubt the most famous performance venue in the U.S., if not the world. Built in 1890–91 through the largesse of industrialist Andrew Carnegie, the hall quickly became one of the most important stages anywhere, and over the decades it has seen a who's who of the world's greatest musicians, including

Sergei Rachmaninoff, Leonard Bernstein, Maria Callas, Miles Davis, Isaac Stern, Mel Tormé, and Judy Garland. Behind the building's Italian Renaissance brick and terra-cotta facade are three halls: the main 2,804-seat auditorium, where remarkable acoustics have made it a favorite of performers and audiences for more than a century; the smaller Weill Recital Hall; and Zankel Hall, presenting classical, jazz, world, and pop music, plus family concerts and education programs.

The lower reaches of the Upper West Side hold several wonderful options for pre- and post-theater dining. The Lincoln Center crowd flock to Lincoln Ristorante at the heart of campus, or across the street to celebrity chef Daniel Boulud's Boulud Sud for Mediterranean fare. Nearby, Rosa Mexicano is famous for upscale Mexican cuisine including fresh guacamole and killer pomegranate margaritas.

Lincoln Center: Tel 212-875-5456; lincolncenter.org. *When:* The seasons generally run from Sept or Oct–May or June. **Carnegie Hall:** Tel 212-247-7800; carnegiehall.org. *When:* generally closed July–Aug. **Lincoln Ristorante:** Tel 212-359-6500; patinagroup.com. *Cost:* $50. **Boulud Sud:** Tel 212-595-1313; bouludsud.com. *Cost:* $55. **Rosa Mexicano:** Tel 212-977-7700; rosamexicano.com. *Cost:* dinner $40. **Best times:** at Lincoln Center, late June–early July for Midsummer Night Swing; July–Aug for the Lincoln Center Festival, with performances of music, dance, theater, and opera from around the world; late July–late Aug for Mostly Mozart; late Sept–early Oct for the New York Film Festival.

Never Pay Retail

THE LOWER EAST SIDE

New York, New York

Think of anything you know about the Jewish experience in the U.S. and it probably has its roots in the Lower East Side. Impelled by pogroms and lack of economic opportunity, 2.5 million Eastern European Jews (particularly Russian) came to the United States between 1880 and 1924, and nearly 85 percent of them came to New York City. At its peak in 1910, the tiny area—less than 2 miles north to south, and only a mile wide—was one of the most densely inhabited spots on earth, with more than half a million residents crammed into block after block of five- and six-story tenement houses. Inside, tiny apartments often served as homes to as many as ten family members and boarders, and doubled as piecework sewing factories during the day. Outside, the streets were crowded with pushcart vendors, while every business in sight was Jewish-owned. To an immigrant arriving from violently anti-Semitic Russia or Poland, it must have seemed like the safest place on earth, for all its crowding and hardships. It was the greatest concentration of Jewish life the world had seen in almost 2,000 years.

But things change, and after the Immigration Act of 1924 slowed eastern and southern European migration to a trickle, Jewish families began leaving the Lower East Side in search of greater space and more opportunity. Still the neighborhood remained home, a bit of the old country in this new country, even as Latin American and Chinese immigrants who succeeded the Jews were themselves displaced by gentrification. Today, hip bars, trendy boutiques, and restaurants occupy storefronts that were once bodegas, and before that, kosher delis. The Yiddish theaters that once dotted Second Avenue are gone, and the small synagogues that hang on throughout the area often have difficulty assembling a minyan, the minimum of ten adults required for communal prayer.

But still, some things remain. The Moorish-style Museum at Eldridge Street was the first synagogue in America built by Eastern European Jews, in 1887. In its heyday it drew thousands for worship, but as Jews left the area beginning in the 1930s, the synagogue fell into decay. In the late 1980s a 20-year restoration began, rescuing its vaulted 50-foot ceiling, remarkable stained-glass windows, and ornate wood and plasterwork.

Farther north, the Lower East Side Tenement Museum preserves an entire five-story tenement building as a time capsule of immigrant life, offering guided tours of apartments meticulously reconstructed to mirror the lives of actual residents like the Levines, Polish immigrants who operated a garment factory from their apartment here in the 1890s, and the Rogarshevskys, Lithuanian immigrants who lived in the building from 1910 to 1941. The museum also organizes neighborhood tours.

A handful of the neighborhood's old-time Jewish eateries have managed to weave themselves firmly into the fabric of contemporary New York life. Step inside the cavernous Katz's Delicatessen, in business since 1888, where timeless classics like thick-sliced pastrami sandwiches and blintzes are washed down with a nice cream soda. Every film buff knows this was where Meg Ryan had her fake orgasm in *When Harry Met Sally*.

Nearby, Russ & Daughters is a beloved fourth-generation food emporium opened by immigrant Joel Russ in 1920. Its gleaming white-and-stainless-steel interior is home to New York's best smoked fish, lox, and other Jewish favorites. You can sample it all at their new café a few blocks away. Down the street, Yonah Schimmel Knish Bakery is of the same vintage, its brick ovens turning out knishes—pockets of dough stuffed with delicious fillings—since 1910.

WHERE: bounded roughly by Houston St. to the north, the Bowery to the west, Catherine St. to the south, and the East River. **MUSEUM AT ELDRIDGE STREET:** Tel 212-219-0302; eldridgestreet.org. *When:* closed Sat. **TENEMENT MUSEUM:** Tel 877-975-3786 or 212-982-8420; tenement.org. **KATZ'S DELI:** Tel 800-4HOTDOG or 212-254-2246; katzdelicatessen.com. *Cost:* pastrami sandwich $20. **RUSS & DAUGHTERS:** Tel 800-RUSS-229 or 212-475-4880; russand daughters.com. **YONAH SCHIMMEL:** Tel 212-477-2858; knishery.com. *Cost:* knish $4. **BEST TIMES:** avoid Sat for crowds; the un-air-conditioned tenement museum can be very hot in summer.

Pilgrims, an Inflatable Mickey, and Santa

MACY'S THANKSGIVING DAY PARADE

New York, New York

The Macy's Thanksgiving Day Parade is as much a part of America's most beloved holiday as turkey, cranberry sauce, and football. Although an annual tradition since 1924, when it got its start in the midst of the radio age, the parade is a true child of TV, having reached generations nationwide since its first broadcast in 1946.

It all started as the Macy's Christmas Parade to boost sales. A group of mostly immigrant employees dressed up as Mother Goose favorites (to match store displays) for a march down Manhattan's West Side. They were accompanied by marching bands, clowns, fairy-tale floats, and animals borrowed from the Central Park Zoo—and Santa Claus tagged along to ring in the holiday season. In 1927, they changed the name and giant inflatable animals replaced the real ones, beginning a tradition that's become the centerpiece of the parade to this day. In the 1930s, popular cartoon and comics characters like Mickey Mouse, Pluto, and Superman made their first appearance. Following a hiatus during WWII, the parade returned in shortened form and has remained essentially the same ever since, with classic balloons like Uncle Sam, Freida the Dachshund, and Humpty Dumpty now replaced by contemporary creations like

The Macy's Thanksgiving Day Parade is a national tradition televised across the country.

Ronald McDonald and SpongeBob Square-Pants. Human participants range from TV, sports, and pop stars to Miss USA, the Radio City Rockettes, and marching bands from around the country, all led by a huge Tom Turkey float. Santa Claus rides the parade's last float, and his arrival at Herald Square signals the parade's terminus and the "official" beginning of the Christmas season.

For New York City kids and their parents, the experience begins the night before, when thousands turn up alongside the American Museum of Natural History (see p. 185) to watch as the balloons are inflated. The next morning, the families make their way to the route up to three hours early to get a good spot among the 3.5 million other parade goers.

The Thanksgiving Parade is only one of dozens of parades staged in New York each year, most of which are ethnic community events. The most famous of these is the St. Patrick's Day Parade on March 17, when 250,000 marchers, bagpipers, drummers, and marching bands parade up Fifth Avenue. The celebration dates back to 1762 and is billed as the largest civilian parade in the world. On Easter Sunday, Fifth Avenue from 49th to 57th Streets is cordoned off for the annual Easter Parade, which originated as a chance for New York gentry to show off their Easter finest. Things get considerably crazier at the annual Greenwich Village Halloween Parade (see p. 176), but that's another story.

THANKSGIVING PARADE: Tel 212-494-4495; social.macys.com/parade. **ST. PATRICK'S DAY PARADE:** Tel 718-231-4400; nycstpatricks.org.

Modern City, Modern Art

MoMA & More

New York, New York

New York is the city where Jackson Pollock and Willem de Kooning helped launch Abstract Expressionism. It's the city where Jean-Michel Basquiat transformed graffiti into high art, and where Christo and

Jeanne-Claude's *The Gates* transformed Central Park into a luminous 16-day saffron-colored dream. It's a place where modern matters.

Founded in 1929, the Museum of Modern Art (MoMA) is home to the world's largest and most inclusive collection of works from the late 19th century to the present, including 3,600 paintings and sculptures—among them Van Gogh's *The Starry Night*, Cézanne's *The Bather*, and Jackson Pollock's *One: Number 31, 1950*—plus 10,000 drawings, 28,000 works tracing the history of modern architecture and design (from appliances and tableware to cars and helicopters), 53,000 prints and illustrated books, 22,000 films, and more than 25,000 photographs, including work by Man Ray, Walker Evans, and Ansel Adams.

Housed from 1939 in an International-style building designed by Philip L. Goodwin and Edward Durell Stone, the museum underwent a total transformation in 2002 under the guidance of architect Yoshio Taniguchi, emerging two years later with double its exhibition capacity and a new look that emphasizes light and open space. Outside, the beloved Abby Aldrich Rockefeller Sculpture Garden was preserved in its original design, as conceived by architect Philip Johnson in 1953, while expanded with various vantage points from within the museum itself. Overlooking the garden, The Modern restaurant offers patrons the chance to linger over French-American cuisine at the elegant Dining Room or enjoy Alsation cuisine in the more casual Bar Room.

The Whitney Museum of American Art, once located at 75th and Madison, relocated to the meatpacking district in 2015 (see p. 178). The building left behind—a somber landmark designed by the Bauhaus-trained Hungarian architect Marcel Breuer—now serves as The Met Breuer, the modern and contemporary art-focused offshoot of the Metropolitan Museum of Art (see

next page). The other repository of modern art on the Upper East Side is the seashell-shaped Guggenheim (see next page).

Elsewhere in Manhattan and around New York's outer boroughs, modern art aficionados have a wealth of options. In Queens, P.S.1 operates as an affiliate of MoMA, presenting contemporary art in a former public school—thus the name. Nearby, the Noguchi Museum presents the works of Japanese-American Isamu Noguchi, including stone, metal, wood, and clay sculptures; models for public projects and gardens; and the artist's famous bamboo-and-paper lanterns, an icon of 1950s modern design. Across the street, right on the East River, the Socrates Sculpture Park offers artists the chance to create and exhibit large-scale sculptural works in a parklike neighborhood setting.

MoMA: 11 W. 53rd St. Tel 212-708-9400; moma.org. **THE MODERN:** Tel 212-333-1220; themodernnyc.com. *Cost:* 3-course prix-fixe dinner $112. **THE MET BREUER:** 945 Madison Ave. Tel 212-731-1675; metmuseum.org/visit/met-breuer. **P.S.1 CONTEMPORARY ART CENTER:** Long Island City, Queens. Tel 718-784-2084; momaps1.org. **NOGUCHI MUSEUM:** Long Island City, Queens. Tel 718-204-7088; noguchi.org. *When:* closed Mon–Tues. **SOCRATES SCULPTURE PARK:** Long Island City, Queens. Tel 718-956-1819; socratessculpturepark.org. **BEST TIME:** Sun evenings in July for MoMA's Summergarden concerts in the Sculpture Garden.

MoMA's sleek, glass facade reflects the neighboring buildings in Midtown Manhattan.

New York's Boulevard of Arts

MUSEUM MILE & BEYOND

New York, New York

O n Manhattan's tony Upper East Side, Fifth Avenue was once lined almost exclusively with millionaires' mansions, but now it's home to riches of another kind. Here, fronting Central Park between 82nd and 105th

Streets, lies one of the world's greatest concentrations of museums, with several others just a few blocks to the south and one directly across Central Park.

The Metropolitan Museum of Art is the linchpin of the lot. With a collection of more than 2 million works from around the world, from the Stone Age to the digital age, it ranks as one of the world's largest and finest repositories of art and culture. Founded in 1870, the museum has expanded to such a degree that its original Gothic Revival building is now completely surrounded by additions. Highlights include the Greek and Roman galleries; the Costume Institute; the collections of Byzantine and Chinese art; the collection of European paintings; the Arms and Armor collection; the musical instrument collection (with some 5,000 pieces from six continents and the Pacific Islands, dating from 300 B.C.);

and the Egyptian collection, with its mummies, sphinx, and the amazing Temple of Dendur, a complete 1st-century B.C. Egyptian temple presented as a gift of the Egyptian government to the people of the U.S.

The American Wing comprises one of the best American art collections in existence, with more than 17,000 paintings, sculptures, and decorative art objects, including more than a dozen period rooms that offer a window into American style and domestic life. The museum's Roof Garden Café and Martini Bar is a favorite summertime haunt for New Yorkers, with its great view of Central Park and rotating series of site-specific art installations. The Met Live Arts program includes classical music performances and "pop-up concerts" at different venues throughout the museum.

Walk uptown to the Solomon R. Guggenheim Museum, designed by Frank Lloyd Wright and completed in 1959. With a kind of spiraling seashell form, its top wider than its bottom, the structure reflects the architect's use of organic form. Begin at the top and walk slowly down through the circling uninterrupted gallery, viewing a collection that spans from the late 19th century to the present, including Mr. Guggenheim's original collection of nonobjective art; niece Peggy Guggenheim's collection of Surrealist and abstract works; and pieces from various other schools, including the Impressionists, Post-Impressionists, early Modernists, Minimalists, and Conceptualists.

A little farther uptown, the Museum of the City of New York is a must for Gotham

The Guggenheim Museum was architect Frank Lloyd Wright's last major work.

aficionados, with its collections of paintings, drawings, photographs, decorative arts, costumes, and clothing from the 17th century to the present, all tracing the city's history from a small Dutch colony to the capital of the world. The Theater Collection covers New York theater from the late 18th century to the present, with original set renderings, scripts, costumes, props, posters, and more. On the fifth floor, John D. Rockefeller's 19th-century bedroom and dressing room are preserved intact, moved here from his house at 4 West 55th Street.

At 91st Street, the Cooper-Hewitt Smithsonian Design Museum occupies the former mansion (built between 1899 and 1902) of another famous New York tycoon, Andrew Carnegie. It's the only museum in the U.S. devoted solely to historic and contemporary design, with more than 210,000 design objects spanning 30 centuries. One block north, the Jewish Museum celebrates 4,000 years of Jewish culture through fine art and folk art, Judaica, antiquities, and broadcast media—more than 30,000 pieces in all.

Other museums on Museum Mile include El Museo del Barrio, dedicated to preserving Puerto Rican and all Latin American art and culture; the National Academy Museum, with its collection of 19th- and 20th-century American art; and the special Neue Galerie New York, devoted to early 20th-century German and Austrian art and design.

And then there are the museums that aren't technically part of Museum Mile at all, but why quibble? Located a little south of the Mile on Fifth Avenue, the Frick Collection offers a collection of European masters housed in an 18th-century French-style mansion built in 1914 by steel and railroad magnate Henry Clay Frick. Highlights include works by Rembrandt, Vermeer, Titian, El Greco, and Goya. Much loved for its intimacy, the museum is particularly enchanting at Christmastime, when beautifully decorated.

Across Central Park from the Met, the American Museum of Natural History has a collection of more than 33 million objects,

At the Met's Temple of Dendur, visitors have the rare chance to explore a real ancient Egyptian structure.

from moon rocks to the Star of India (the world's largest gem-quality blue star sapphire at 563 carats). Don't miss the famous dinosaur halls, the Hall of Biodiversity, the classic dioramas of animal and village life, or the futuristic Rose Center for Earth and Space, a four-story glass sphere that holds the Hayden Planetarium, a large and powerful virtual reality simulator that sends visitors through the Milky Way and beyond.

METROPOLITAN MUSEUM OF ART: Tel 212-535-7710; metmuseum.org. **GUGGENHEIM MUSEUM:** Tel 212-423-3500; guggenheim.org. *When:* closed Thurs. **MUSEUM OF THE CITY OF NEW YORK:** Tel 212-534-1672; mcny.org. **COOPER-HEWITT MUSEUM:** Tel 212-849-8400; cooperhewitt.org. **JEWISH MUSEUM:** Tel 212-423-3200; jewishmuseum.org. *When:* closed Sat. **EL MUSEO DEL BARRIO:** Tel 212-831-7272; elmuseo.org. *When:* closed Mon. **NATIONAL ACADEMY OF DESIGN:** Tel 212-369-4880; nationalacademy.org. *When:* closed Mon–Tues. **NEUE GALERIE:** Tel 212-628-6200; neuegalerie.org. *When:* closed Tues–Wed. **FRICK COLLECTION:** Tel 212-288-0700; frick.org. *When:* closed Mon. **AMERICAN MUSEUM OF NATURAL HISTORY:** Tel 212-769-5100; amnh.org. **BEST TIME:** mid-June for the Museum Mile Festival, when Fifth Avenue is turned into a pedestrian mall full of art and music, and admission to all Museum Mile museums is free.

NEW YORK'S ARCHITECTURAL LANDMARKS

New York, New York

For every bulldozer-driving developer New York produces, it also yields a preservationist dedicated to retaining the best of what's gone before. That explains the city's streetscape, in which Gothic gargoyles and Greek-Revival columns vie with Georgian, early Federalist, art deco, Internationalist, and ultra-modern freeform styles, all overlapping and interweaving. It's a visual bonanza that seems inexhaustible.

Some of New York's architectural masterworks are described elsewhere in this section, but there are countless others that stir the soul, and are essential components of the organism we know as New York.

The skyscrapers are the most visible, having largely defined the image of New York throughout the 20th century. The first rose at that century's beginning, made possible by the near-simultaneous development of load-bearing steel frames and cast-iron, bird cage elevators (combined with Manhattan's super-strong bedrock). The 22-story Flatiron Building at the intersection of Fifth Avenue and 23rd Street was one of the earliest triumphs. Designed by Daniel H. Burnham and built in 1902, the building's distinct triangular shape is heavily ornamented with limestone and terra-cotta columns and sculptural elements, all topped off with a magnificent overhanging cornice. In midtown, the 77-story Chrysler Building is generally considered the city's most beautiful skyscraper and probably the finest example of the art deco tower anywhere. Designed by William Van Alen and constructed from 1928 to 1930 as the Chrysler Corporation's headquarters, the building is clad in white and dark gray brickwork for the majority of its floors, but the upper peaks explode with deco ornamentation: stylized American eagle gargoyles, sunburst-shaped rings, and a towering spire that points to the heavens, all made of stainless steel that gleams in the sunshine.

Just steps away, Grand Central Terminal dates to 1913. Its triumphant Greco-Roman Beaux-Arts exterior is adorned with statues of Hercules, Minerva, and Mercury; its huge main concourse is covered by a ceiling that mimics the sky (complete with constellations); its arched, tiled passageways are as graceful as the domes of a Moorish mosque; and its lofty windows illuminate its marble interior with the kind of light usually seen only in pictures. For a classic experience of the station, have lunch amid the hubbub of the Oyster Bar on the lower level. Since 1913, it has been serving fresh seafood daily, including its famous New England clam chowder and dozens of different kinds of oysters.

A few blocks west on Fifth Avenue is the regal main branch of the New York Public Library, which opened in 1911. Another magnificent Beaux-Arts structure, the building offers a heroic entrance up its wide marble stairs, past a pair of lion sculptures (named *Fortitude* and *Patience*) that have become symbols of the library system. Inside, the great Main Reading Room is nearly as long as a football field, with a heavily ornamented ceiling 52 feet above and 42 heavy oak tables below, with room for more than 600 readers.

Midtown's Beaux-Arts trio is completed by the 1913 General Post Office, designed by the great New York firm of McKim, Mead & White. Once a companion to the grand Penn Station across the way (destroyed in 1963 and replaced by Madison Square Garden), the building offers a grand facade with block-wide stairs and grand Corinthian columns, all crowned by the words "Neither snow nor rain nor heat nor gloom of night stays these couriers from the swift completion of their appointed rounds." At this writing, work has started for converting most of the building into Moynihan Station, providing access for Amtrak riders.

Although it is located in New York City, the United Nations Headquarters is considered "international" territory.

The 1940s and '50s saw the last bright flashes of New York architectural genius before a long dry spell that continued through the 1990s. At Park Avenue and East 53rd Street, Lever House was an Internationalist-style interloper amid very traditional neighbors when it rose in 1952 on a design by Gordon Bunshaft. Essentially two oblong steel-and-glass boxes—a 24-story tower set in beautiful geometric relation to a low horizontal base that seems to float on supporting stilts—it established the modern European model for nearly every office building that rose in the city for the next 50 years. Across the street, the 38-story Seagram Building extended that model higher, offering an unbroken curtain of bronze and dark glass set back 90 feet from the street and juxtaposed against a granite-paved plaza and reflecting pools. It was designed by Ludwig Mies van der Rohe, opening in 1958 with interiors by Philip Johnson.

On the East River, the United Nations Headquarters was built between 1948 and 1952 by a design team that included Wallace K. Harrison, Le Corbusier, and Oscar Niemeyer. The 18-acre site is dominated by the rectangular 39-story Secretariat Building and the low, slope-roofed General Assembly Building, where the troubles of the world are debated.

For a glimpse of New York's architectural future, head to the corner of Eighth Avenue and West 57th Street, where in 2006 the geometric 46-story Hearst Tower sprouted from the top of the original Hearst headquarters, a six-story art deco building from 1928. Designed by Sir Norman Foster as the city's first "green" skyscraper, it is a series of interlocking four-story stainless-steel triangles whose corners zigzag in and out as they rise.

For a deeper exploration of the design and history of New York's skyscrapers, head downtown and visit the Skyscraper Museum, a space dedicated to celebrating New York's signature buildings through a rotating series of exhibits and public programs.

GRAND CENTRAL: grandcentralterminal.com. *When:* docent-led tours daily at 12:30 P.M. **OYSTER BAR:** Tel 212-490-6650; oysterbarny.com. *Cost:* dinner $55. **NEW YORK PUBLIC LIBRARY:** Tel 917-275-6975; nypl.org. *When:* tours Mon–Sat. **UNITED NATIONS:** Tel 212-963-8687; visit.un.org. **SKYSCRAPER MUSEUM:** Tel 212-968-1961; skyscraper.org. **BEST TIME:** weekend in mid-Oct for Open House New York (ohny.org), when visitors can tour hundreds of significant architectural sites across the five boroughs.

Slice of Heaven

NEW YORK'S BEST PIZZA

New York, New York

The great New York pizza pie was invented by one Gennaro Lombardi, an immigrant grocer from Naples who began selling lunchtime "tomato pies" to workers around 1905, based on a classic Neapolitan recipe: fresh dough topped with real tomatoes, mozzarella, olive oil, a pinch of garlic, and maybe a smattering of sausage, all cooked in a super-hot coal-fired oven. The decades that followed saw pizza become steroidally supersized and often pre-fab, adding factory-made cheeses, alternative meats, all manner of vegetables, and even fruits. The quality varies wildly among the hundreds of pizzerias dotting the five boroughs, but luckily, there are some gems. Pizza connoisseurs have battled for decades over who serves the best pie in town, but the differences are largely a matter of territoriality.

Down in what remains of Little Italy, Lombardi's is still serving the pizza first created here over a century ago, just down the block from its original location. Inside, red-checked tablecloths and friendly service set the stage for beautiful pizza pies baked in a coal-fired oven, their smoky crusts blackened just slightly and daubed with warm blobs of fresh mozzarella, tomato sauce, and basil, plus toppings like homemade meatballs, double-cut pepperoni, and kalamata olives.

Way uptown in East Harlem, Pasquale "Patsy" Lancieri, who learned his craft at Lombardi's, opened his own place in 1933. It was a longtime favorite of Frank Sinatra, whose portrait now hangs on the restaurant's wall. As for the pizza, its sauce is slightly sweet, its crust is thin and perfectly baked—not too crisp, not too soft—and unlike at Lombardi's, its cheese is melted evenly across the pie. Because of its location, it's the least touristy of the great NYC pizzerias.

The original Patsy's also begat Grimaldi's (now a national chain) when Patsy Grimaldi, Lancieri's nephew, opened his own pizzeria in 1990 in Brooklyn, right in the shadow of the Brooklyn Bridge. The pizza here has a thin, smoky crust; pools of fresh, warm mozzarella; chunky yet delicate and savory tomato sauce; fresh basil; and prime-quality toppings like roasted red peppers and sausage. There are pizza connoisseurs who also swear by nearby Juliana's, which flourishes now in a former Grimaldi location.

Back in Manhattan, John's of Bleecker Street is another true classic of the genre. Fans come for the perfect crust—not too chewy, not too crusty—with full-spread mozzarella, fresh sauce, and generous toppings. The interior is woody and lived-in, with tables completely covered with carved initials and messages going back 1929, when it opened.

Along with the classic pie and its knock-offs, New York is awash with designer pies by

Lombardi's was the first pizzeria in the United States.

celebrity chefs. But why mess with the original?

LOMBARDI'S: Tel 212-941-7994; first pizza.com. *Cost:* large pies from $22.50. **PATSY'S:** Tel 212-534-9783; thepatsyspizza .com. *Cost:* large pies from $18. **GRIMALDI'S:** Brooklyn. Tel 718-858-4300; grimaldis-pizza .com. *Cost:* large pies from $16. **JULIANA'S:** Tel 718-596-6700; julianaspizza.com *Cost:* large pies from $19. **JOHN'S:** Tel 212-243-1680; johnsbrickovenpizza.com. *Cost:* large pies from $17.50.

Where the Elite Meet to Eat and Greet

NEW YORK'S RESTAURANT EMPIRES

New York, New York

The restaurant scene in New York is a contact sport, fueled by competition (most estimates put the total number of city restaurants, bars, and cafés at 24,000), high real estate prices, and a demanding and fickle population.

Restaurants open, burn like a supernova for a year, and then are gone. Celebrity chefs come to town like Caesar crossing the Rubicon, only to be knocked off their pedestal by the Next Big Thing. The restaurants here are the ones that have sticking power. Like the song says, if they can make it here . . .

Manhattan is home to a constellation of celebrity chefs. Connoisseurs know to head just off tony Park Avenue in Midtown, where Daniel Boulud's self-titled restaurant Daniel proves why fellow chefs and devoted patrons regard him as one of the country's most brilliant French-trained talents, trailblazing the future of haute cuisine. Refined fantasy describes both the restaurant's decor and its poetic menu, which features technically complicated, perfectly executed, and artistically presented dishes. You can revel in Boulud's inventive spirit less expensively at his neighborhoody Café Boulud, the French-American DB Bistro Moderne (justly famous for its sumptuous hamburger), Boulud Sud for the Lincoln Center crowd, and DBGB down on the Bowery.

In bustling Midtown West, French-born Eric Ripert, a permanent fixture among the

Chef Eric Ripert prepares artful plates in the kitchen of Le Bernardin.

city's lineup of star chefs, heads the kitchen at Le Bernardin, an elegant temple that first revolutionized seafood cooking in the 1980s. Whether lightly sauced, barely cooked, or simply raw, his ever-changing dishes surprise even the most jaded palates. Not far away, star chef Jean-Georges Vongerichten has an eponymous restaurant with a high "Wow!" factor (see p. 171).

At the helm of a well-oiled and impressively successful NYC empire (including the newly relocated Union Square Café, Maialino, the

Modern and others) is the amiable Danny Meyer, who wrote the manual on genuinely warm service, good value, and unfussy, Mediterranean-based comfort food. This sure-fire formula explains the popularity of his much-loved downtown venue, the elegantly handsome Gramercy Tavern, a modern reinterpretation of the classic tavern, serving tasting menus of refined American cuisine in the main dining room and à la carte dishes in the Tavern Room.

Farther south, is the stylishly comfortable Bouley, the lauded restaurant steered by world-ranked chef David Bouley. Although Gallic to the max, the owner-chef absorbs foreign influences and flavors and transforms them into inspired, extraordinary creations.

Among the flourishing scene of Italian restaurants, television personality Mario Batali—also known as Molto Mario—continues to strike gold with everything he touches. Together with his partner Joe Bastianich, Battali first opened Babbo, introducing New Yorkers to lamb's tongue and ravioli stuffed with beef cheek, among other previously unknown delicacies. Batali's Del Posto offers a similar menu served in a vast but posh space in the once-edgy but now gentrified Meatpacking District. After a decade of global expansion, Batali's latest venture is La Sirena, serving exceptional housemade pasta.

Down below Canal Street, in the restaurant-heavy TriBeCa neighborhood, Nobu remains one of the most famous and most copied sushi restaurants in the world, and deserves much of the credit for having initiated New Yorkers into the mysteries of raw fish. The master sushi chefs keep the spare dining room in thrall with fragrant, deftly prepared, and utterly fresh seafood. Next door is the aptly named Nobu Next Door, serving the same menu. Nobu brought its downtown popularity uptown with Fifty Seven, named after the street now known as a high-dining enclave.

DANIEL BOULUD RESTAURANTS: daniel boulud.com. **LE BERNARDIN:** Tel 212-554-1515; le-bernardin.com. *Cost:* tasting menus from $180. **DANNY MEYER RESTAURANTS:** ushgnyc.com. **BOULEY:** Tel 212-964-2525; davidbouley.com. *Cost:* 6-course tasting menu $185. **MARIO BATALI RESTAURANTS:** mario batali.com. **NOBU:** Tel 212-219-0500; nobu restaurants.com. *Cost:* dinner $75.

Puttin' on the Ritz

NEW YORK'S PREMIER HOTELS

New York, New York

There are hundreds of hotel choices in New York, from grand European-style palaces to boutique gems, budget boxes, and even a few B&Bs scattered here and there. Many have charm, grandeur, glamour, and style—but these are the best. Soaring 52 stories above some of the city's priciest real estate, the I. M. Pei–designed Four Seasons Hotel is the destination for the recognizable and those who follow in their Manolo footsteps. Since opening, it's raked in just about every accolade in the business. Inside, the cool, sleek three-story lobby projects an almost templelike sense of quietude, with 33-foot columns rising between the geometrically patterned marble floor and the backlit limestone ceiling. Terraced lobby lounges lead past registration to several restaurants and bars: The Garden for American regional cuisine, the TY lounge for cocktails and afternoon tea, and the TY Bar for martinis and light fare. The hotel offers 368 ultra-spacious, flawlessly decorated rooms and suites with 10-foot ceilings, huge marble bathrooms, and views out over the city.

A more classic New York experience can be had two blocks south at the St. Regis Hotel, a grand Beaux-Arts building constructed by John Jacob Astor IV in 1904 and still living up to that era's gilded grandeur. Uniformed doormen escort you into the white marble lobby, full of Louis XV furnishings, trompe l'oeil ceilings, Waterford crystal chandeliers, and gilded detailing. Upstairs, the 238 spacious rooms and suites are done in dreamy whites and creams, with marble baths, and the services of a 24-hour butler. Downstairs, the King Cole Bar and Salon is one of the world's greats, a small rectangle with leather chairs and a tiny bar where, in 1931, bartender Fernand Petiot perfected a drink he'd been working on: the Bloody Mary, or as it's still called here, the Red Snapper. On the wall, Maxfield Parrish's mural of Old King Cole gave the place its name.

Since 1907, the iconic Plaza Hotel has reigned over the tony corner of Central Park South and Fifth Avenue. Recent renovations have transformed it into a mixed-use luxury landmark, with 282 hotel rooms, many of them with Central Park views. Tea in the Palm Court and a drink in the clubby Oak Room remain perennial must-dos.

Midtown's newest five-star player is the stream-lined Park Hyatt, tucked into the first 25 stories of the 90-story One57 condo tower. Located on the newly-minted "Billionaires' Row" on West 57th St directly across from Carnegie Hall, Park Hyatt is the result of the collaborations between a veritable who's who of design, fashion, and architecture. Guests can enjoy classical music underwater in the 25th-floor swimming-pool-with-view (the longest of its kind in the city), get a spa treatment on a private high-floor terrace, then retire to any of the 210 rooms outfitted in rich

The King Cole Bar and Salon is the birthplace of the Bloody Mary.

browns and creams featuring custom furniture pieces.

For pure five-star swank on the city's West Side, it's hard to beat the Mandarin Oriental on the edge of Central Park in the Time Warner Center (see p. 170).

Of course, hanging your hat at these high-end, full-service grande dames is not the only option in town. New York has long been awash in small-scale, chic-boutiques such as The Inn at Irving Place, a little-known refuge of no pomp but great charm. Set just a few blocks from the genteel 19th-century enclave of Gramercy Park, the 12-room inn was created in the early 1990s by combining two adjacent brownstone town houses dating to 1834. Outside, it's identified only by its address. Inside, the atmosphere of the 19th century, with period furnishings, Persian rugs, fireplaces, and flowers, conveys old-style New York grace, dignity, and charm.

Four Seasons: Tel 800-819-5053 or 212-758-5700; fourseasons.com/newyork. *Cost:* from $895 (off-peak), from $995 (peak). **St. Regis:** Tel 877-787-3447 or 212-753-4500; stregisnewyork.com. *Cost:* from $695 (off-peak), from $995 (peak). **The Plaza:** Tel 212-759-3000; theplazany.com. *Cost:* from $625 (off-peak), from $1,050 (peak). **Park Hyatt:** Tel 646-774-1234; newyork.park.hyatt.com. *Cost:* from $795. **Inn at Irving Place:** Tel 800-685-1447 or 212-533-4600; innatirving .com. *Cost:* from $295 (off-peak), from $345 (peak). **Best times:** fall, when New York is at its peak of beauty; during Dec holidays (expect higher rates).

I Lift My Lamp Beside the Golden Door

THE STATUE OF LIBERTY & ELLIS ISLAND

New York, New York

People think of the Statue of Liberty as an all-American symbol, but she's not, really. Born and bred in France, she was intended to symbolize not one country but rather an abstract, revolutionary idea: liberty, for everyone,

everywhere. The idea for Lady Liberty, whose proper given name is *Liberty Enlightening the World*, was born in 1865, when Frenchman Edouard de Laboulaye, an important political thinker, proposed that France give America a monument honoring democracy. His friend, sculptor Frédéric-Auguste Bartholdi, was a great supporter of the project. Funds were raised from the common people: the French paid for the statue, Americans for the pedestal.

It wasn't until 1886 that the 151-foot-tall copper-clad statue finally took her place atop a 27,000-ton stone-and-concrete pedestal for a total height of 305 feet. Enclosed by the star-shaped walls of Fort Wood on Bedloe's Island

Lady Liberty's tablet reads (in Roman numerals) "July 4, 1776," the date of American Independence.

(now Liberty Island), the statue sits just over a mile from lower Manhattan. Lady Liberty's timing couldn't have been better: Beginning in 1892, the U.S. saw the largest wave of immigrants in its history. For many of the newcomers arriving at the port of New York, the Statue of Liberty became the first and most perfect glimpse of their new land.

Today, you can reach the island by tour boat from Battery Park (see p. 173), but only those who make advance reservations through Statue Cruises may visit the pedestal, climb the 162 steps to the crown, and visit the museum. (Most visitors arrive with grounds-only tickets and are sorely disappointed.) The pedestal's observation platform offers a view of the statue's interior framework, designed by Alexandre Gustave Eiffel (of Eiffel Tower fame). Liberty's torch has been off-limits since 1916 after it was damaged when German saboteurs blew up a munitions dump on nearby Black Tom Island. The torch was replaced during the 1980s and the original now sits in the lobby museum.

Slightly to the north, and accessible only by Statue Cruises, Ellis Island was the processing station for roughly 12 million immigrants between 1892 and 1954. A six-year renovation in the 1980s rescued Ellis Island from disuse, turning it into a moving memorial and interpretive center where an intricate computer database allows Americans to research their heritage and retrace their ancestors' arrival.

A good view of Lady Liberty and the Manhattan skyline can also be found on the Staten Island Ferry, which runs to and from New York's outermost borough—and it's free, too. For a longer ride, the Circle Line offers sightseeing around the harbor or all the way around Manhattan Island—it's a New York classic.

STATUE OF LIBERTY: nps.gov/stli. **STATUE CRUISES TO LIBERTY & ELLIS ISLAND:** Tel 877-523-9849 or 201-432-6321; statuecruises .com. **ELLIS ISLAND:** nps.gov/elis. **STATEN ISLAND FERRY:** siferry.com. **CIRCLE LINE TOURS:** Tel 212-563-3200; circleline42.com (grounds-only access to Statue of Liberty). **BEST TIME:** weekdays, when the lines can be shorter.

Crossroads of the World

TIMES SQUARE

New York, New York

Times Square is the most recognizable intersection in the world, a six-block stretch where Broadway and Seventh Avenue cross, creating a heady vortex of light and energy. Over the years it's been a stage for some of the most enduring images in American history, from Alfred Eisenstaedt's 1945 *Life* magazine photo of a sailor and nurse kissing to celebrate WWII's end to the annual New Year's Eve ball-drop. This is the place where Damon Runyon's guys and dolls earned their lettuce in the 1930s, and where peepshows and drug addicts forged New York's apocalyptic reputation in the 1970s. That all started to change in the early '90s, when the city invited Disney and a number of other business giants to collaborate in the area's revitalization, and today the place is once again the Great White Way, a family-entertainment and business district where the old movie palaces have been restored and the sidewalks are paved with tourists, TV crews, multinational retail locations, and some of the brightest and most visible advertisements on earth.

Though the business of New York is business, Times Square still does a brisk trade in musical theater. Today there are some 40 theaters between West 41st and West 53rd Streets, their marquees lit up with a mix of revivals, new contenders, modern classics like *Chicago*, and seemingly everlasting troupers like *Phantom of the Opera*. Ticket prices tend toward the stratospheric (with orchestra seats usually around $150 and sometimes higher), but if you wait in line you can get same-day half-price orchestra seats at the TKTS booth under the red steps on Duffy Square, the central traffic island at West 47th Street. Boards list available shows, but don't count on being able to score tickets for the newest hits.

Pre- or post-theater, area restaurants range from classics to themed tourist traps. On West 46th Street between 8th and 9th Avenues—a stretch known as Restaurant Row—Joe Allen

Times Square is widely considered the "crossroads of the world."

has been busy since 1965, serving diners drawn to its legendary hamburgers, butcher paper tablecloths, and exposed brick walls full of signed theater memorabilia. A few blocks east, Virgil's Real Barbecue is on the themey side with its two-story roadhouse interior and good ole boy knickknacks, but it has surprisingly delicious meat—Texas beef brisket, Carolina pulled pork, and Memphis pork ribs. If that's just not NYC enough for you, walk up to the Carnegie Deli, an only-in-New-York kosher deli whose air is redolent of pastrami and Henny Youngman jokes. Tables are set elbow to elbow, and the seasoned waiters like to chide wide-eyed tourists as part of their shtick, but when they tell you that you won't be hungry till next week after eating one of their mile-high sandwiches, they aren't kidding. The Algonquin Hotel on West 44th Street is where through the 1920s leading wits and tastemakers like writer Dorothy Parker, comedian Harpo Marx, and playwright George S. Kaufman met daily for lunch, creating the legend of the Algonquin Round Table. You can stop for a drink or eat in the restored Round Table Restaurant, which has a portrait of all the original Round Table regulars. Despite its reputation as a "tourist joint," the circa-1921 Sardi's still draws a steady crowd with its caricature-covered wall and the hopes of Broadway star sightings.

And then there's New Year's Eve, when Times Square is the world's party central. Crowds that sometimes reach 1 million brave the cold and amped-up security for star-studded performances and that moment when the ball drops, a ton of confetti is released, and fireworks are set off simultaneously in Times Square and Central Park. *The New York Times* got the tradition rolling here in 1904 when it held a fireworks display to celebrate the official opening of its new headquarters, introducing the ball that drops at midnight in 1907. *The Times* has since moved to larger digs nearby, and the ball has changed seven times. Today, a 12-foot Waterford crystal ball still drops from a post atop the old Times Tower, which these days serves entirely as a home for advertising signage—another tradition that started when the famous *Times* news "zipper" was unveiled in 1928, informing pedestrians of breaking news in suitably flashy style.

TIMES SQUARE: between 42nd and 48th Sts. along Broadway and 7th Ave. *Visitor info:* nycgo.com. **TKTS:** tdf.org/nyc/7/TKTS-overview. *Cost:* generally half the price of orchestra seats. **JOE ALLEN:** Tel 212-581-6464; joeallenrestaurant.com. *Cost:* dinner $45. **VIRGIL'S:** Tel 212-921-9494; virgilsbbq.com. *Cost:* dinner $45. **CARNEGIE DELI:** Tel 800-334-5606 or 212-757-2245; carnegiedeli.com. *Cost:* pastrami sandwiches from $20. **ALGONQUIN:** Tel 888-304-2047 or 212-840-6800; algonquinhotel.com. *Cost:* dinner $45. **SARDI'S:** Tel 212-221-8440; sardis.com. *Cost:* $60. **BEST TIME:** New Year's Eve, come early (newyearseve.com).

A Place of Memory and Dreams

THE ONCE AND FUTURE WORLD TRADE CENTER

New York, New York

It's difficult for first-time visitors to New York to understand just how tall the twin towers of the World Trade Center stood before they were felled on that terrible September morning in 2001. But "Ground Zero" has been transformed into a sprawling 16-acre mixed-use environment composed of five office towers, an eight-acre Memorial Plaza, and a half-million feet of shopping and dining. The World Trade Center has been reborn.

Of all the towers, the most significant symbolically is architect David Child's 1,776-foot One World Trade Center (initially called the Freedom Tower), a sustainable shining beacon for downtown and the tallest building in the Western Hemisphere. The 360-degree view from the floor-to-ceiling windows on the 102nd floor of One World Observatory is sure to get your heart pumping.

The 9/11 Memorial—*Reflecting Absence,* a design by architect Michael Arad, centers around two waterfall-fed pools 30 feet below-ground, in the footprints of the Twin Towers. Each is almost an acre in size, and the names of everyone who died in the 2001 and 1993 attacks are inscribed on bronze panels edging the pools. The adjacent 9/11 Memorial Museum is organized as a historical exhibition in three parts: the Day of 9/11, Before 9/11, and After 9/11. Photographs pay tribute to the nearly 3,000 victims, with touch screens available for visitors interested in learning more. Foundation Hall houses the surviving retaining wall of the original World Trade Center.

Just across the street from the WTC site, and so close it is hard to believe it survived undamaged, is St. Paul's Chapel, New York's only remaining pre-Revolutionary church. George Washington worshiped here after his inauguration as president in 1789, and following September 11 it became a 24-hour relief center for recovery workers. In the days and months after the attacks, the church's iron fence was festooned with missing-persons posters, notes, firemen's hats, banners, and other items dedicated to the 2,749 victims of the attack. The impromptu memorial has been archived, and today hundreds of the objects fill three sides of the church's interior. Around the corner, at the home of the New York Fire Department's Engine Co. and Ladder Co. 10,

One World Trade Center towers over the surrounding high-rises near the 9/11 memorial pools.

is the first large-scale 9/11 monument to be unveiled. The 56-foot street-level bronze bas-relief depicts the morning from the firefighter's perspective, with the burning towers and the NYFD's rescue efforts as the centerpiece—and the names of all 343 firefighters who died, including five from Company 10 and a volunteer firefighter. A few doors away, the 9/11 Tribute Center tells vivid stories of those who were there through films, personal objects, and images.

Where: the Financial District in southern Manhattan; wtc.com. **9/11 Memorial Museum:** Tel 212-266-5211; 911memorial .com. **FDNY Memorial Hall:** fdnytenhouse .com/fdnywall. **St. Paul's Chapel:** Tel 212-602-0800; trinitywallstreet.org/about/stpauls chapel. **9/11 Tribute Center:** Tel 212-393-9160; tributewtc.org. **Best time:** September 11 for annual memorial tributes, including a reading of victims' names and powerful banks of searchlights projected straight up into the sky from dusk till dawn, simulating the Twin Towers.

Urban Jungle and Garden of Eden

THE BRONX ZOO & NEW YORK BOTANICAL GARDEN

Bronx, New York

The 265-acre Bronx Zoo was opened in 1899 and has grown to be the world's largest urban zoo, its 4,000 animals representing both endangered species like gorillas, snow leopards, and mandrills and crowd favorites like penguins and sea lions. After early missteps, like exhibiting a Mbuti Pygmy in 1906, the zoo's mission evolved to be about protection and conservation rather than just exhibiting animals for our entertainment. The zoo's parent organization, the Wildlife Conservation Society, works worldwide to address new and ongoing threats to animals and their habitats.

At JungleWorld, a 37,000-square-foot recreation of an Asian rain forest, you can watch white-cheeked gibbons, ebony langurs, and Malayan tapirs going about their business in a landscape that includes a mangrove swamp and a plethora of Asian plants. The 6.5-acre Congo Gorilla Forest is home to 400 animals from 55 species, including red river hogs, African rock pythons, and two breeding troops of lowland gorillas (about 20 in all).

At the 3-acre Tiger Mountain exhibit, visitors can go nose-to-nose (through glass partitions) with beautiful Siberian tigers. Three times daily, trainers engage the enormous cats (they can grow up to 900 pounds) in training and play sessions designed to encourage their natural instincts and behaviors. The newest exhibit, Madagascar, features ring-tailed lemurs, crocodiles, and the mongoose—more than 150 animals from 30 species.

Just north of the zoo, the New York Botanical Garden is a 250-acre oasis of another sort, home to some 50 individual gardens and plant collections. Founded in 1891 after a visit by Columbia University botanist Nathaniel Lord Britton to London's Kew Gardens, the institution has grown into one of the world's great centers for plant conservation, research, and education. The landmark Enid A. Haupt Conservatory, erected between 1899 and 1902, is the largest Victorian glasshouse in America—New York's own Crystal Palace. Inside, you'll find towering palms, tropical rain forest and desert environments, plus seasonal displays including the annual Orchid Show and the Holiday Train Show, in which toy trains and trolleys wend their way past more than 150 miniature replicas of New York landmarks, all made from natural plant materials like twigs, bark, moss, and leaves.

The 2.5-acre Rock Garden is a dramatic sanctuary populated by tiny alpine flowers

The pools surrounding the Enid A. Haupt Conservatory are lush with aquatic plants in summer.

and woodland plants sprouting among stone outcroppings. Nearby, the Native Plant Garden offers native woodland wildflowers and shrubs under a canopy of tall trees. The surrounding 50-acre forest is the largest uncut expanse of the woodlands that once covered all New York City, and offers walking paths, abundant birdlife, and a seasonally changing palette of color. For kids there's the Ruth Rea Howell Family Garden, where they can learn how food is grown, and also the Everett Children's Adventure Garden, a playful space

where nature can be explored through microscopes and other hands-on activities.

Bronx Zoo: 2300 Southern Blvd. Tel 718-220-5100; bronxzoo.com. **Botanical Garden:** 2900 Southern Blvd. Tel 718-817-8700; nybg.org. *When:* Rock Garden and Family Garden closed Nov–Mar. **Best times:** at the Botanical Garden, late Feb–early Apr for the Orchid Show; late Apr–early May for the tulips and Mar–May for cherry trees; June for the height of Rose Garden; Dec for the holiday decorations and the Train Show.

The House That Ruth Built

YANKEE STADIUM

Bronx, New York

Love 'em or hate 'em, the New York Yankees have always been central to the great mythology that is American baseball—just as visiting Yankee Stadium is central to the ultimate New York experience. If you can score

tickets to a game, arrive when the gates open and go down to Monument Park (at center field) to see the plaques honoring Yankee greats like Babe Ruth, Lou Gehrig, Joe DiMaggio, Yogi Berra, and Mickey Mantle—and then buy a hot dog and an ice-cold beer and find your seats.

The team began back in 1903 (though they wouldn't be called the Yankees until ten years later), but it was in January 1920 that they acquired Babe Ruth from the Boston Red Sox, an event that turned the tide for the till-then unremarkable team. Their new Ruth-fueled popularity enabled them to move from the Polo Grounds, home of the New York Giants, to

The new Yankee Stadium is one block away from the original location, and incorporates many design elements from the old stadium.

a new stadium of their own in the Bronx. The three-deck stadium they constructed, already known as "The House That Ruth Built," was inaugurated on April 18, 1923, when 74,217 people showed up to watch the Yanks beat the Red Sox 4-1. The team went on to win its first

World Series that year, a feat it's achieved 26 more times since, and counting.

Except for the addition of lights in 1946, Yankee Stadium remained mostly unchanged until 1973–1975, when it was almost completely demolished and rebuilt, bigger and better. In 2006, the team broke ground on a brand-new four-level stadium just north of the 1923 field. While the new stadium's facade mimics the look of the original and its field retains the same dimensions, the rest is up-to-the-minute ballpark chic, making it an excellent place to catch a ball game.

WHERE: 161st St. and River Ave. Tel 718-293-4300; newyork.yankees.mlb.com. *Cost:* tickets from $17. *When:* Baseball season is Apr–Oct. **BEST TIME:** late June or early July for Old Timer's Day, with a friendly game between former Yankees preceding the real game; or any time the Red Sox are in town.

The Eighth Wonder of the 19th-Century World

THE BROOKLYN BRIDGE

New York, New York

O nce upon a time, the island of Manhattan and Brooklyn were two distinct cities, Manhattan a bustling commercial metropolis, Brooklyn a mostly rural place separated from its neighbor by the turbulent, mile-wide expanse of the East River. In 1855, John Roebling proposed a mighty suspension bridge whose roadway would soar 135 feet above the water, supported by steel cables anchored to two huge granite towers—a design that would leave boat traffic on the river unimpeded. Just before construction began in 1869, John Roebling's foot was crushed on site and he died of tetanus. He was succeeded by his son Washington, who was paralyzed by "the bends" while directing construction but continued to supervise work from his Brooklyn home while his wife, Emily, oversaw the engineers and builders on site. Work was finally completed in 1883, and the "Great East River Bridge" was officially opened by President Chester Arthur and New York Governor Grover Cleveland.

From the first, New Yorkers knew it was special. An editor for *Scientific American* called it "a marvel of beauty . . . [with] a character of its own far above the drudgeries and exactions of the lower business levels." And so it remains today. In a city where two centuries of architectural styles (and lack thereof) wage a continual war against greed and the elements, the Brooklyn Bridge continues to soar gracefully above it all, a dignified, well-dressed visitor from another time.

Walking the bridge is a beloved experience for many New Yorkers, including joggers, lovers, and commuting businessmen. Walk from the Brooklyn side toward Manhattan for the full effect, traversing the boardwalklike central promenade between the iconic spiderweb of the bridge's supporting steel cables. First, though, spend some time in Brooklyn Heights, a colonial-era village that remains one of New York's loveliest neighborhoods, with block after block of beautiful brownstone homes and even a few wood-frame houses—a rarity in this once very fire-prone city. The Brooklyn Heights Promenade, an overlook sitting on a rise above the East River and immortalized in films such as *Annie Hall* and *Moonstruck*, provides one of the city's grandest views, taking in the sweep of New York Harbor, the Statue of Liberty, the great lower Manhattan skyline, and the bridge in all its serene majesty.

Right beneath the bridge's Brooklyn tower, the River Café offers probably the best restaurant view in all New York. The cuisine is reliably good, but most people come for the candlelit tables, the Woody Allen–sound track piano music, and the cinematic views of Manhattan and the bridge lights shimmering off the East River. Just next door, at Fulton Ferry Landing, Bargemusic presents intimate chamber music concerts year-round aboard a 103-foot floating barge. A large picture window behind the performers lets onto a stunning Manhattan view. About 3 miles northeast, under the Williamsburg Bridge, Peter Luger is one of the country's finest steak houses, drawing happy carnivores to its tavernlike, old New York premises since 1887. Each perfect, butter-tender prime beef steak is hand-picked and dry-aged on-site, then prepared to perfection and served by amiable waiters who aren't half as gruff as the guidebooks claim.

WHERE: The bridge runs from Center St. in Manhattan to Adams St. in Brooklyn. **RIVER CAFÉ:** Brooklyn Heights. Tel 718-522-5200; rivercafe.com. *Cost:* 3-course prix-fixe dinner $120. **BARGEMUSIC:** Brooklyn Heights. Tel 718-624-4924; bargemusic.org. *Cost:* tickets from $35. **PETER LUGER:** Williamsburg. Tel 718-387-7400; peterluger.com. *Cost:* dinner

The Brooklyn Bridge stretches 5,989 feet across the East River.

$75. **BEST TIME:** July 4th for dinner at the River Café and a prime view of New York's annual fireworks, which are launched from barges on the East River.

A Tree Grows in Brooklyn

PROSPECT PARK & THE BROOKLYN BOTANIC GARDEN

Brooklyn, New York

Outsiders are constantly surprised to learn that there are many Brooklyns, from old and new immigrant neighborhoods to old- and new-money enclaves and sections that, more than almost anywhere else, reflect what all New York looked like more than a century ago.

The latter is what you'll find in and around Prospect Park, a grand 585-acre parkland designed and constructed over a 30-year period (1865 to 1895) by Frederick Law Olmsted and Calvert Vaux, the landscaping geniuses behind Manhattan's more famous Central Park (see p. 166). The pair considered Prospect Park their more successful New York creation. It's easy to see why: To Olmsted, a park was a place where a city's residents could feel immersed in tranquility, and that's just what Prospect Park offers, even on busy weekend days when it becomes a giant playground. Pass through any of its entrances and the city outside drops away, hidden by trees. Inside are treasures: the Long Meadow, whose one-mile expanse is the longest in any urban park in the world; the Ravine, a steep gorge that contains Brooklyn's only remaining stand of forest; the 60-acre, stream-fed Prospect Lake (catch-and-release fishing is allowed); the Boathouse, a 1905 Beaux-Arts structure that now houses an Audubon Nature Center and is surrounded by 2.5 miles of interpretive nature trails; and a classic 1912 carousel with wooden animals carved by Charles Carmel, one of the greatest carousel designers of the time. The highlights are balanced by thousands of grace notes designed to create the perfect urban escape: woodland springs and waterfalls, sandstone bridges and arches, music pavilions, playing fields, a small zoo, and even the Dog Beach, a corner of the small Upper Pool pond set aside for man's best friend.

The park's main entrance is the magnificent Grand Army Plaza at the park's northwest corner. Its great memorial arch, crowned by bronze statues of the winged goddess of victory and her attendants, was dedicated in 1892 as a tribute to Union soldiers and sailors of the Civil War. Just east of the plaza, the grand 1897 Beaux-Arts Brooklyn Museum is the borough's premier art museum, with a collection that stretches from ancient Egyptian sculpture to contemporary art. Behind the museum, filling a 52-acre triangle that skirts the edge of Prospect Park, the Brooklyn Botanic Garden is perhaps the most popular garden in New York. Dating to 1910, it displays more than 10,000 plants from around the world, laid out in numerous specialty gardens including the Japanese Hill and Pond Garden, the English-style Shakespeare Garden, and the Cherry Esplanade, where in spring more than 42 different cultivars of Japanese cherry trees offer one of the finest spots outside Japan for cherry blossoms viewing.

During your visit, be sure to set aside some time to walk the residential streets on the western slope of Prospect Park. Known as Park Slope, it's one of the best-preserved 19th-century residential neighborhoods in all New York, full of the three- and four-story brownstone row houses that remain the archetypal, idealized New York home today. For an entirely different Brooklyn experience, head north a mile from Grand Army Plaza along commercial Flatbush Avenue to Junior's Restaurant, known since 1950 as the home of the world's best cheesecake (with more than a dozen varieties to choose from). Wash it down with an egg cream, a classic Brooklyn blend of milk, chocolate syrup, and seltzer that's increasingly difficult to find (and, weirdly enough, contains neither egg nor cream).

PROSPECT PARK: Tel 718-965-8951; prospectpark.org. **BROOKLYN MUSEUM:** Tel 718-638-5000; brooklynmuseum.org. **BROOKLYN BOTANIC GARDEN:** 990 Washington Ave. Tel 718-623-7200; bbg.org. *When:* closed Mon-Tues. **JUNIOR'S:** Tel 718-852-5257; juniors cheesecake.com. *Cost:* cheesecake $6.95 per slice. **BEST TIME:** late Apr for Sakura Matsuri, the Brooklyn Botanic Garden's 2-day Cherry Blossom Festival (bbg.org/sakura).

A Lavish Paean to Local Food and Good Eating

STONE BARNS

Blue Hill at Pocantico Hills, New York

Blue Hill at Stone Barns is more than just a hot restaurant destination for gastronomes and luminaries like Michelle Obama and Hillary and Bill Clinton (they have a home in nearby Chappaqua). It's the most talked-about part of a not-for-profit experiment called the Stone Barns Center for Food and Agriculture, a sustainable farm aimed at educating the unknowing about locally raised food. It was founded by David Rockefeller, grandson of the oil magnate.

Fashioned out of unusually elegant Normanstyle stone barns built in the 1930s as part of the Rockefeller family's private farm, the center is an 80-acre organic farm and educational facility designed as a fitting memorial to David Rockefeller's wife, Peggy, a founder of the American Farmland Trust. Guests can stroll about, past flocks of chickens and turkeys, penned Berkshire pigs, gardens of heirloom tomatoes, and a vast state-of-the-art greenhouse.

The undeniable highlight of a visit here is mealtime at Blue Hill at Stone Barns, co-owned by chef Dan Barber and his brother, David. Barber made his name in New York City with the original Blue Hill, his Greenwich Village restaurant dedicated to local farmers. Decorated in earth tones, the airy restaurant is a converted dairy barn whose high, vaulted ceiling is crisscrossed by steel beams. The chefs are often seen in the fields picking,

weeding, even composting along side the farmers. As a result, the restaurant is not just lip service to seasonality, but a deep expression of the farm and integrity in food. When tomatoes are in season, you can sample an entire spectrum of them—marinated, as tartare, as confit, even as sorbet. Blue Hill celebrates the quality of the ingredients and doesn't dare mask them with fancy sauces or spices—it's all about the sheer intensity of flavor.

The Stone Barns Center is far more than just an eating experience. Shop the farmer's market, attend a workshop, take a tour, and then pick up a warm sandwich made from Hudson Valley cheeses and fresh sausages at the casual Blue Hill Café. The experience is designed to make you think more deeply about what you eat and where it comes from, an idea that might seem too highbrow if it wasn't so intensely pleasurable.

WHERE: 30 miles north of Manhattan; 630 Bedford Road. Tel 914-366-6200; stonebarnscenter.org. *When:* closed Mon–Tues. **BLUE HILL AT STONE BARNS:** Tel 914-366-9600; bluehillfarm.com. *Cost:* $75. **BEST TIMES:** June–Oct for weather; early Oct for Harvest Fest.

Manhattan's Perfect Weekend Getaway

RHINEBECK

New York

Astorybook village just inland of the Hudson River, Rhinebeck is a perfect weekend getaway for Manhattan's serenity-seeking crowd. One of its strongest draws is the Omega Institute, the nation's largest holistic learning center. Located just miles outside town, this 250-acre campus is a place where people can be exposed to new ideas by leading thinkers including Gloria Steinem, Pema Chödrön, and Deepak Chopra, or learn how to write songs, improve their relationships, and live more sustainably.

Just outside the village near the river, the glorious 1888 Queen Anne mansion called Wilderstein, with Tiffany windows and a dramatic five-story circular tower, was home to three generations of Suckleys (related to the prominent Livingstons and Beekmans, whose estate houses were in the Hudson Valley from the 17th century to the 19th). Its last resident, Miss Margaret Lynch Suckley (known as Daisy), gave Franklin Delano Roosevelt his famous Scottie, Fala, and lived here until she died at the age of 100 in 1991. The home provides a fascinating social history of the rise and gentle decline of one prominent Hudson Valley family.

The village of Rhinebeck is a treasure trove of Manhattan-worthy shops, restaurants, antiques stores, even a spa, all within a couple blocks of the Beekman Arms, a colonial-era inn that claims to be the oldest continuously running inn in America. It began catering to travelers in 1766 (George Washington slept there), and FDR concluded every one of his successful campaigns for governor and president from the white-pillared front porch. Just down the street, the Beekman Arms also runs the Delamater Inn, an 1844 masterpiece of the American Gothic movement designed by Andrew Jackson Downing.

The 107,000-square-foot Richard B. Fisher Center for the Performing Arts at Bard College houses two theaters and rehearsal studios for dance, theater, and music.

A few miles to the north, the stunningly beautiful Richard B. Fisher Center for the Performing Arts at Bard College is a modernist palace of undulating stainless steel panels that reflect the light and colors of the sky. Designed by famed architect Frank O. Gehry, the complex of performance spaces is at its liveliest during Bard SummerScape, eight weeks of opera, music, theater, film, dance and cabaret. One of its premier events, the long-standing Bard Music Festival, delves deeply into the work of a single great artist (Franz Schubert and Igor Stravinsky are among the recent subjects) each year by blending performances with panel discussions, talks, and films in order to better understand the composer's influences and times.

But it's not all highbrow entertainment in these parts. The Old Rhinebeck Aerodrome is as close to a 1920s airfield as you can get, with hangars, hand-painted signs, and a collection of more than 100 vintage and reproduction aircraft. At weekend airshows crowds thrill to old-fashioned barnstorming and mock WWI dogfights, and you can even go for a ride in a classic open cockpit biplane with the wind in your hair and the lush beauty of the Hudson Valley below you.

Nearby Millbrook is a wealthy insider's town, a polished enclave of rural estates and dignified horse farms where residents fox hunt and attend polo matches.

WHERE: 90 miles north of New York City. *Visitor info:* Tel 845-876-5904; rhinebeck chamber.com. **OMEGA INSTITUTE:** Tel 800-944-1001 or 845-266-4444; eomega.org. *When:* May–Oct. *Cost:* 2 nights from $348 for a small private room with shared hall bath, includes meals; programs extra. **WILDERSTEIN:** Tel 845-876-4818; wilderstein.org. *When:* Thurs–Sun, May–Oct. **BEEKMAN ARMS AND DELAMATER INN:** Tel 845-876-7077; beekman delamaterinn.com. *Cost:* large variety of rooms; call for rates. **FISHER CENTER:** Annandale-on-Hudson. Tel 845-758-7900; fishercenter.bard .edu. *Cost:* tickets from $25. *When:* July–Aug for Bard Summerscape; 2 weekends in Aug for the Bard Music Festival. **OLD RHINEBECK AERODROME:** Tel 845-752-3200; oldrhinebeck .org. *When:* museum, mid-June–Oct; weekend airshow, mid-June–mid-Oct; biplane rides, Sat–Sun, June–Oct. **BEST TIMES:** May–Oct for weather; Aug for the Bard Music Festival and the Dutchess County Fair.

A 19th-Century Queen of Spas

SARATOGA SPRINGS

New York

The name Saratoga Springs has long evoked a privileged life of horse racing, polo matches, fancy hats, and genteel garden parties. This oasis of Victorian elegance, known as the "Queen of Spas," was a summer playground for the moneyed, thanks to its naturally carbonated springs, which can still be visited.

The elegant Saratoga Race Course, America's oldest and loveliest sports venue, is the flower-decked town's main attraction. A who's who of thoroughbreds and jockeys has long made Saratoga's summer the nation's best racing season. Today's main course was built in 1864, and retains a lovely Victorian grandstand. Across from the track, the National Museum of Racing and Hall of Fame is home to a diverse collection of memorabilia that documents thoroughbred racing in America from the 18th century to the present.

Horses break from the gate at the Saratoga Race Course.

Saratoga Springs is also a cultural hotbed, especially during the summer, when the open-air Saratoga Performing Arts Center (SPAC) hosts the New York City Ballet, followed by the Philadelphia Orchestra. Big-name artists from opera to pop fill out the summer season. Spring and summer are the best times for strolling the inspiring Italian classical gardens at the famous artists colony of Yaddo, founded in 1900 by financier Spencer Trask and his wife Katrina, a poet. Yaddo is the gold standard to which all others aspire and getting a residency here (up to two months) is still a highly sought-after plum.

The landmark Adelphi Hotel, built in 1877, is undergoing a $40 million renovation at press time, transforming it into a culinary-focused luxury inn with two- and three-bedroom suites. It is scheduled to open in 2017. Saratoga Springs also has a wealth of unusually fine inns and B&Bs, foremost among them the Batcheller Mansion Inn, a splendid example of high Victorian Gothic architecture built in 1873. President Ulysses S. Grant was once a guest of the Batcheller, enjoying, no doubt, its fantastic blend of French Renaissance Revival, Italianate, and Egyptian architectural influences (the original owner had lived in Cairo).

About 10 miles east of town is the site of the Battle of Saratoga, the first significant military victory of the American Revolution. Replica British cannons and an interpretive trail at the Saratoga National Historical Park tell the story of how, in 1777, American forces met and defeated a major British army, leading France to recognize the independence of the U.S. and enter the war as a military ally of the struggling Americans.

WHERE: 185 miles north of New York City. *Visitor info:* Tel 855-424-6073 or 518-584-1531;

discoversaratoga.org. **SARATOGA RACE COURSE:** Tel 518-584-6200; nyra.com/saratoga. **MUSEUM OF RACING:** Tel 518-584-0400; racingmuseum .org. **SARATOGA PERFORMING ARTS CENTER:** Tel 518-584-9330; spac.org. *When:* June–Sept. *Cost:* lawn tickets from $15. **YADDO:** Tel 518-584-0746; yaddo.org. **ADELPHI HOTEL:**

theadelphihotel.com. **BATCHELLER MANSION INN:** Tel 800-616-7012 or 518-584-7012; batchellermansioninn.com. *Cost:* from $150 (off-peak), from $310 (racing season). **SARATOGA NATIONAL HISTORICAL PARK:** Tel 518-670-2985; nps.gov/sara. **BEST TIME:** late July–early Sept for racing season.

An American and Canadian Boater's Paradise

THOUSAND ISLANDS

New York

A glittering necklace of mansion-studded outposts that straddle the Canada-U.S. border along a 50-mile stretch of the St. Lawrence River, Thousand Islands (in fact there are 1,864, the majority belonging to Canada) is best known for the salad dressing created onboard the yacht of George Boldt, one of many wealthy New Yorkers who built lavish summer homes (called "cottages") here beginning in the 1870s.

Today, both powerboaters and sailors are drawn to the beauty of the islands, while fishermen are attracted by the water's bounty. Hire a local fishing guide and he can stop on one of the islands to whip up a shore dinner— the breaded pan-fried fish you just caught, with potatoes and corn on the cob (and there's

A monument to true love, Boldt Castle has 120 rooms, a tunnel system, Italian gardens, and a drawbridge.

dessert too: batter-dipped bread fried in butter and topped with maple syrup, cream, and brandy). The region also affords some of the best freshwater wreck diving, with crystal clear waters and dozens of wrecks, many dating to the War of 1812.

Thousand Islands' most wondrous relic (and most popular tourist stop) is Boldt Castle; its lavish construction was interrupted in 1904 with the death of the wife of hotelier George Boldt (he of the salad dressing fame). Unable to imagine the cavernous Rhineland-style palace without her, George ordered the workmen to drop their tools. Left to ruin until 1977, the castle and five other stone structures on 5-acre Heart Island have since been restored, complete with furnishings, and are now open for self-guided tours. In nearby Clayton, a charming village of 2,000 people, the Antique Boat Museum has the continent's largest and best collection of freshwater wooden vessels, with more than 100 on display, including a lavishly outfitted 1904 Gilded Age 110-foot houseboat. Sign up for a ride in a Hacker-Craft triple-cockpit runabout and imagine yourself a part of the Boldt entourage.

WHERE: Alexandria Bay is 340 miles northwest of New York City. *Visitor info:* Tel 800-847-5263 or 315-482-2520; visit1000 islands.com. **WHERE TO STAY:** Riveredge Resort, Alexandria Bay. Tel 800-ENJOY-US or 315-482-9917; riveredge.com. *Cost:* from $85 (off-peak), from $215 (peak). **BOLDT** **CASTLE:** Heart Island. Tel 800-8-ISLAND or 315-482-9724; boldtcastle.com. *When:* mid-May–mid-Oct. **THE ANTIQUE BOAT MUSEUM:** Clayton. Tel 315-686-4104; abm.org. *When:* early May–mid-Oct. **BEST TIME:** Aug for the Antique Boat Show and Antique Raceboat Regatta.

Spit, Polish, and Riverine Beauty

U.S. MILITARY ACADEMY

West Point, New York

Located on a high, rocky outcropping at a sharp bend where the Hudson River is at its narrowest (making it a strategic stronghold during the Revolutionary War), the U.S. Military Academy at West Point is America's oldest and best-known military service school, the very epitome of military tradition. Although occupied since 1778, West Point wasn't a military academy until 1802. Today, its highly competitive program trains some 4,400 male and female army cadets in the art of war. Illustrious graduates include Generals Ulysses S. Grant, Robert E. Lee, Douglas MacArthur, George Patton, and Dwight Eisenhower.

West Point's rich history, Gothic campus, magnificent river and mountain views, and fascinating military museum all make it well worth a visit. Though it used to be wide open for wandering, since 9/11 the only way to tour the campus (unless you are coming for public events such as concerts, sporting events, cadet reviews, and graduation) is on guided bus tours that leave from the Visitors Center, itself worthwhile to see for its exhibits on cadet life. Tour stops include the Cadet Chapel, lined with stained-glass windows; the Plain, a wide-open parade ground by the mess hall (at its best around 11:45 A.M., when the cadets step into lunchtime formation); and the cemetery, dating back to the American Revolution, where more than 7,000 graduates are buried. Modest tombstones mark the graves of Gen. George Armstrong Custer, who met his death at Little Big Horn (see p. 618); Lt. Edward H. White II, the first American to walk in space; and Gen. William Westmoreland, who commanded American military operations in Vietnam.

Military history buffs can spend hours perusing West Point Museum's collection of weaponry, from Stone Age axes to atomic bomb casings, with highlights like Hitler's pistol, and

The U.S. Military Academy campus sits on a 16,000-acre site on the west bank of the Hudson River.

Sitting Bull's death mask. On special occasions in the fall (especially before football games) and in April and May you can see the cadets marching to the military band during parades, a West Point tradition that instills discipline and order while fostering esprit de corps. During the summer, West Point's Concert Band gives outdoor concerts at the Trophy Point amphitheater, against the same views of the Hudson River that George Washington once used to track movements of the enemy.

Built in 1926 and directly on the banks of the Hudson River, the Thayer Hotel is the place to stay. Its imposing Gothic exterior blends seamlessly with the rest of the campus, while grand flourishes abound inside.

WHERE: 50 miles north of New York City. **VISITORS CENTER:** Pershing Center. Tel 845-938-2638; usma.edu. **THAYER HOTEL:** Tel 800-247-5047 or 845-446-4731; thethayer hotel.com. *Cost:* from $119 (off-peak), from $299 (peak). **BEST TIMES:** Apr–May for the parades; weekly Trophy Point concerts, every Sun from June–Aug; fall for foliage.

Bargain-Hunting in the "Antiques Capital of the World"

ADAMSTOWN'S ANTIQUES MILE

Adamstown, Pennsylvania

Adamstown, the self-proclaimed (but, say connoisseurs, accurately named) "Antiques Capital of the World," is where a mile and a half of Route 272 hosts more than 5,000 dealers on any given Sunday, with assorted co-op

and showcase shops open weekdays as well. Top vendors include the Stoudt's Black Angus Antiques Mall (with about 300 indoor and outdoor dealers) and Renninger's Antique & Collectors Market (with about 375 dealers indoors and another 300 outside in spring, summer, and fall). Arrive with an agenda or take a more unstructured approach—either way, get there early: Shoppers begin arriving around 5 A.M., "tailgating" for finds as the dealers unload their merchandise. Bring a flashlight!

For four solid days of uber-antiquing, go during one of Renninger's blowout weekends in April, June, or September. At their secondary market in nearby Kutztown (which holds a weekly Saturday market), more than 1,200 dealers from across the nation set up camp from Thursday through Saturday. The next day, the Adamstown market holds "Special Sundays" that often attract twice as many dealers as the regular weekly shows. For extreme shopping,

hit Kutztown on Thursday or Friday; decamp Saturday for Shupp's Grove (an old-timey mart near Antique Mile, with dealers' tables set up under the trees April through October); then be at Renninger's Adamstown and Black Angus bright and early Sunday.

WHERE: 65 miles northwest of Philadelphia. *Visitor info:* antiquescapital.com. **STOUDT'S BLACK ANGUS:** Tel 717-484-4386; stoudts .com/antiques. *When:* Sun, indoor market year-round; outdoor market spring–fall. **RENNINGER'S ADAMSTOWN:** Tel 717-336-2177; renningers .net. *When:* Sun, indoor market year-round; outdoor market spring–fall. **RENNINGER'S KUTZTOWN:** Tel 570-385-0104 or 610-683-6848; renningers.net. *When:* Sat. **SHUPP'S GROVE:** Tel 717-484-4115; shuppsgrove.com. *When:* Sat–Sun, mid-Apr–Oct. **BEST TIMES:** last full Thurs, Fri, and Sat in Apr, June, and Sept for Extravaganzas at Renninger's Kutztown; followed by Special Sundays at Renninger's Adamstown.

The Land of Falling Water

RICKETTS GLEN STATE PARK

Benton, Pennsylvania

Those enamored of waterfalls may think of Niagara, or Zambia and Zimbabwe's Victoria Falls. But for scenic beauty, ease of access, and the sheer number of its falls, Ricketts Glen should also come to mind: there's simply nothing like it. Within a single day, you can see 22 waterfalls, thundering like God's own water-garden amid some of Pennsylvania's most gorgeous scenery.

In the 19th century, all this beauty was the private reserve of Col. Robert Bruce Ricketts, a Civil War veteran whose heirs worked to have it declared a national park. When WWII interrupted, that idea was dropped in favor of turning it into a state park built around the gorgeous Glens Natural Area, whose creeks and falls flow amid one of the last old-growth forests in Pennsylvania. Additional purchases have brought the park to its present size of 13,050 acres.

The 7.2-mile Falls Trail takes you past 21 of the 22 falls, while the short Evergreen Trail, starting from the parking lot on the south side of Route 118, will take you to No. 22, the beautiful but little-visited Adams Falls. Pick up the Falls Trail on the north side of Route 118. The first three-quarters of a mile are fairly flat, then the trail ascends as you reach little Murray Reynolds Falls, its waters cascading in two streams around a rock outcrop. In rapid succession you'll reach Sheldon Reynolds and Harrison Wright Falls before coming to Waters Meet, the spot where streams flowing out of Glen Leigh to the east and Ganoga Glen to the west unite dramatically. From here the trail becomes a loop, curving west past ten more falls, including the park's highest, Ganoga, a "wedding cake" falls that cascades 94 feet down over multiple layers of rock. (The other main type of falls is the

Waterfall heaven—you can see more than 20 waterfalls over the course of an afternoon at Ricketts Glen.

"bridal veil," where water plunges over a high ledge into a pool below.) Just beyond is Cayuga, the park's smallest falls at only 11 feet. Soon the trail switches off to the east, passing through huge blocks of sandstone at Midway Crevasse before heading south again through Glen Leigh, with eight falls of its own. Terrain in both glens is rocky and can be slippery, so wear good boots and walk slowly—you'll want to take your time anyway. After all, it took nature millions of years of erosion, glacial action, and tectonic shifting to make Ricketts Glen what it is today.

WHERE: 141 miles northwest of Philadelphia. Tel 570-477-5675; dcnr.state.pa.us/stateparks/findapark/rickettsglen. **WHERE TO STAY:** Campsites and 20 cabins are available near Lake Jean, north of the trail loop. Campsite reservations, tel 888-PA-PARKS or 570-477-5675. **BEST TIMES:** early mornings for smallest crowds; late May–Sept for weather.

From Moravian Colony to Big Steel to Christmas City, U.S.A.

BETHLEHEM

Pennsylvania

Bethlehem and the neighboring Lehigh Valley towns of Allentown and Easton mark a significant notch on the Rust Belt, that swath of the Northeast and Midwest where, in the space of just 100 years, heavy industry came, saw, conquered—and was displaced by cheap foreign labor. But Bethlehem has always been about more than its namesake steel mill. Founded in 1741 by a group of Moravian missionaries—hardworking pacifists from Germany—the town jumped into the Industrial Revolution with both feet. In 1857, Bethlehem merchant Augustus Wolle and a group of investors established the Saucona Iron Company, which within four decades morphed into Bethlehem Steel. At its peak, the company was the second-largest steel producer in the world, its 1,800-acre plant employing more than 30,000 workers forging steel for skyscrapers, battleships, bridges, and the locks of the Panama Canal. Within a few decades, though, the company was experiencing hard times, and in 1995 it shut the Bethlehem plant permanently. It was a time of transition in the Lehigh Valley, but the development of alternative industries and a vibrant preservation movement have combined to make a region that thrives today.

Bethlehem is a mix of its three distinct eras, part 18th-century colonial museum, part 19th- and 20th-century industrial giant, and part 21st-century New Economy work-in-progress. Within the oldest section of town, off the north bank of the Lehigh River, lovely slate and brick sidewalks lead to 20-plus colonial-era buildings. The oldest, the Gemeinhaus, erected in 1741—and the largest 18th-century log building in the U.S.—is today the home of the Moravian Museum of Bethlehem. On Main Street, the Moravian Book Shop has been in continuous operation since 1745, making it the country's oldest. Nearby, the Colonial Industrial Quarter was America's first industrial park, with a tannery from 1761, a waterworks from 1762, a reconstructed smithy from 1750, and a mill from 1869. All are preserved beautifully, with period implements and machinery.

Bethlehem's peak season is—naturally—Christmas, when it celebrates not only the birth of Jesus, but its own birth, having been named on Christmas Eve 1741. Around town, the area's distinctive 19th-century industrial and residential architecture is festooned with lights—white lights in the northern half of town and multicolored lights in the southern half, in tribute to the district's diverse immigrant worker history. From Thanksgiving through Christmas, the annual five-weekend Christkindlmarkt offers crafts, plus German holiday music, storytelling, and a sampling of German and Austrian cuisine. Up on South Mountain, the 81-foot Star of Bethlehem has been shining down on the Lehigh Valley since 1937—the year Bethlehem designated itself "Christmas City, U.S.A."

Lodging options include the centrally located Historic Hotel Bethlehem, offering a classic city-hotel vibe, its 1920s ambience perfectly intact. Murals by George Gray chronicle Bethlehem's history from its founding to 1937, when they were painted. For more intimacy, the 22-room Sayre Mansion Inn, across the river in South Bethlehem, offers an upscale 22-room B&B experience in an elegant 1850s mansion.

WHERE: 70 miles north of Philadelphia. *Visitor info:* Tel 800-MEET-HERE or 610-882-9200; discoverlehighvalley.com. **MORAVIAN MUSEUM:** Tel 610-882-0450; historicbethlehem.org. *When:* Sat–Sun. **MORAVIAN BOOK SHOP:** Tel 888-661-2888 or 610-866-5481; moravianbookshop.com. **COLONIAL INDUSTRIAL QUARTER:** Tel 610-691-6055; historicbethlehem.org. **CHRISTKINDLMARKT:** Tel 610-332-3378; christmascity.org/christkindlmarkt. *When:* Fri–Sun, late Nov–Christmas. **HISTORIC HOTEL**

BETHLEHEM: Tel 800-607-2384 or 610-625-5000; hotelbethlehem.com. *Cost:* from $149 (off-peak), from $239 (peak). **SAYRE MANSION INN:** Tel 877-345-9019 or 610-882-2100; sayremansion.com. *Cost:* from $139. **BEST TIMES:** Dec for Christmas celebrations, including concerts by the Bach Choir of Bethlehem (bach.org) and walking tours; Aug for the 10-day Musikfest (musikfest.org); Sept for the 3-day Celtic Classic (celticfest.org), with Highland games, parades, and even a haggis-eating contest.

Honoring the Fallen

GETTYSBURG NATIONAL MILITARY PARK

Gettysburg, Pennsylvania

If there is a home for the soul of America, it is almost certainly on the battlefields of Gettysburg. Here, in July 1863, the Union and Confederate armies clashed in the bloodiest battle ever fought on American soil. In three days of fighting, an estimated 51,000 men were killed, wounded, captured, or went missing (nearly a third of all those who fought there); when all was said and done, the once unstoppable Confederate army was forced to retreat. Though the Civil War dragged on for nearly two more years, Gettysburg was the turning point. Never again would the South mount a major offensive into the North.

Four months after the battle, Abraham Lincoln read the brief words of his Gettysburg Address at the dedication of the battlefield's National Cemetery, where 3,555 soldiers were interred. Today the battlefield's 6,000-acre grounds are protected as a national park, with more than 1,400 statues, monuments, and cannons marking 26 miles of avenues that wend past the battlefield's most legendary sites, including Robert E. Lee's temporary headquarters, Cemetery Hill, and the field on which General George Pickett and 12,500 Southern infantrymen made their doomed charge against the Union lines, sustaining more than 6,500 casualties in 50 minutes.

The annual Gettysburg Civil War Battle Reenactment takes place during the week surrounding July Fourth. There are concerts, lectures and tours given by park rangers and

The Gettysburg National Military Park was established in 1895.

prominent Civil War scholars, living history encampments, even a Civil War–period wedding, but skirmishes reenacted near the park by volunteers dressed in Confederate gray and Union blue are the highlight. Take some quiet time to recall these words of Col. Joshua Lawrence Chamberlain, whose 20th Maine volunteers held the Union's left flank at Little Round Top, helping to turn the tide of the battle and the war. In 1889, at the dedication of the monument to his troops, he said, "In great deeds something abides. On great fields something stays. Forms change and pass; bodies disappear, but spirits linger, to consecrate ground for the vision-place of souls. . . . Generations that know us not and that we know not of, heart-drawn to see where and by whom great things were suffered and done for them, shall come to this deathless field to ponder and dream."

WHERE: 41 miles south of Harrisburg. Tel 717-334-1124; nps.gov/gett. *Visitor info:* Tel 800-337-5015 or 717-334-6274; destination gettysburg.com. **GETTYSBURG BATTLE REENACTMENT:** Tel 800-514-3849; gettysburg reenactment.com. **WHERE TO STAY:** Antrim 1844, the area's finest historic inn, Taneytown, MD, tel 410-756-6812; antrim1844.com. *Cost:* from $165. **BEST TIMES:** late May for the country's oldest Memorial Day commemoration; July 1–3 for the Civil War Battle Reenactment; mid-June–mid-Aug, park rangers offer daily free guided programs and tours of the battlefield and cemetery.

Chocolate City, U.S.A.

HERSHEY

Pennsylvania

B orn to a strict family in the area's sizable Mennonite community in 1857, Milton Hershey started young, apprenticing himself to a Lancaster candy maker at age 15. He developed an interest in chocolate at the 1893 Chicago World's Columbian Exposition, and within a few years had perfected the first American recipe for milk chocolate (until then a Swiss secret). In 1900, he began mass-producing the famous Hershey bar, earning himself the gratitude of chocoholics everywhere.

Faced with huge demand for his new product, Hershey purchased a large plot of land in his hometown of Derry Township, Pennsyslvania. There he began to build—but he didn't stop with a factory. Convinced that workers are more productive in a comfortable, stimulating environment, he constructed a model community. Over time the area, with its streetlights shaped like Hershey Kisses, has grown into a tourist destination.

If you're expecting a Willy Wonka experience, sorry: Hershey stopped its factory tours in 1973. Instead, visit Hershey's Chocolate World for your official introduction to the town's namesake and the chance to create your own candy bar. Then walk over to the Hershey Museum for displays on the history of the town and chocolate making. Nearby Hersheypark, with more than 70 rides and attractions, is one of the best amusement parks in the Northeast, yet retains its old-fashioned feel, exemplified by the all-wood 1919 carousel with its Wurlitzer band organ.

For more adult distractions, head to the family-friendly Hotel Hershey. Built in the early 1930s, the hotel features a Mediterranean design, complemented with formal gardens, fountains, 276 elegant guest rooms, and a circular dining room with views of the gardens from every table. Guests can mingle with Hershey characters who visit the lobby, play tennis, swim indoors or out, go cross-country skiing or tobogganing, ride horses, go hiking, or play golf at the Hershey Country Club. Now the golf capital of Pennsylvania, the club has three 18-hole courses (including the 7,061-yard, par-71 East Course and the 6,860-yard, par-73 West Course), and a 9-hole course for young golfers, designed by Maurice McCarthy. After a round, head for the Hershey Spa, where the treatments are sweet: Options include the whipped cocoa bath, chocolate fondue wrap, and chocolate sugar scrub. Not far from the hotel, the 23-acre Hershey Gardens boasts 3,500 roses, rare trees, themed gardens, an outdoor Butterfly House (home to over 300 North American butterflies), a children's garden, and seasonal displays.

WHERE: 95 miles west of Philadelphia. Tel 800-HERSHEY; hersheypa.com. **HERSHEYPARK:** *Cost:* $65. *When:* May–Sept, and some weekends in Apr and around Halloween and Christmas. **HOTEL HERSHEY:** Tel 844-330-1711 or 717-533-2171; thehotelhershey.com. *Cost:* from $259 (off-peak), from $399 (peak); greens fees from $65. **HERSHEY GARDENS:** *When:* late Mar–late Oct. **BEST TIMES:** Halloween and Christmas, when Hersheypark has seasonal lights, a 50-foot tree, and a Santa-in-residence.

A Glimpse of Aristocracy in the Valley

LONGWOOD GARDENS

Kennett Square, Pennsylvania

Longwood is one of the world's finest horticultural displays, with 20 outdoor gardens, 20 greenhouse gardens, four lakes, many acres of forest, and 9,000 different types of plants spread out over 1,050 acres. It all started in 1700, when Quaker farmer George Pierce bought 402 acres from William Penn's land commission. Nearly a century later, two of George's great-grandsons began collecting trees and exotic plants, creating an arboretum that grew into a pleasure garden open to the public. When a subsequent owner announced plans to cut down the trees for lumber, avid landscaper Pierre du Pont, of the DuPont chemicals empire, stepped in. Over the next 30 years he increased its landholdings, and added gardens and improvements as inspiration touched him.

Longwood's huge Conservatory includes an orchid room displaying the best of the garden's 3,200 different types of orchids and a courtyard filled with aquatic plants from all over the

The idyllic Italian Water Garden is one of nearly 30 themed outdoor gardens at Longwood.

world, including South American waterplatters whose leaves grow to more than 6 feet in diameter. Nearby, the Open Air Theatre is animated by 750 illuminated water jets, which create a water curtain in front of the stage on which hundreds of special events a year are held—from Broadway musicals and jazz concerts to flower shows and fireworks displays. In the West Gardens, the Chimes Tower houses a 62-bell carillon that plays a musical selection each hour on weekdays and every half-hour on weekends, plus special 45-minute concerts from spring through fall. At Christmastime, the gardens are transformed with 420,000 Christmas lights, thousands of poinsettias in the Conservatory, dancing fountain displays, and topiary reindeer.

Longwood is surrounded by the beautiful and historic Brandywine Valley, which stretches across the Delaware border to encompass the Winterthur Museum and garden, founded by Pierre's cousin Henry Francis du Pont (see p. 115). Just 4 miles east of Longwood is the Brandywine River Museum, known for its paintings by illustrator N. C. Wyeth and his celebrated descendants— Andrew, Henriette, Carolyn, and James. N. C. Wyeth's house and studio on nearby Rocky

Hill has been restored to the way it looked in 1945, when he died. Tours are available from the museum, as are visits to nearby Kuerner Farm, inspiration for approximately 1,000 of Andrew Wyeth's paintings. Farther east, Brandywine Battlefield Park was the site of the largest battle of the Revolutionary War; soon after Washington's army lost there, he led them through the hard winter at Valley Forge (see p. 232).

LONGWOOD GARDENS: 36 miles west of Philadelphia. Tel 800-737-5500 or 610-388-1000; longwoodgardens.org. **BRANDYWINE RIVER MUSEUM:** Chadds Ford. Tel 610-388-2700; brandywine.org/museum. *When:* museum daily; Wyeth House and Kuerner Farm tours daily, Apr–Nov. **BRANDYWINE BATTLEFIELD PARK:** Chadds Ford. Tel 610-459-3342; brandywinebattlefield.org. *When:* varies by month. **BEST TIMES:** Apr–May for profusions of tulips and flowering trees; several evenings weekly from late May–early Sept for half-hour illuminated fountain shows (as well as the spectacular Rose and Topiary Gardens); Sept–Oct for foliage.

Where the Plain People Live

PENNSYLVANIA DUTCH COUNTRY

Lancaster, Berks, and adjacent counties, Pennsylvania

"Humble yourselves in the sight of the Lord, and He shall lift you up" (James 4:10). That's the prescription that Pennsylvania's Amish and Mennonite communities have lived by since the 1720s, when they

settled here as part of William Penn's grand experiment in religious tolerance. Both groups had their beginnings in the European Anabaptist movement of the 16th century, which taught that baptism should occur at adulthood, and that those so baptized should live apart from the larger society.

Today, the counties of southeastern Pennsylvania are home to some 60,000 of the

"Plain People," including members of the strict Old Order Amish; the more liberal New Order Amish, Mennonites, and Brethren; and more than a dozen other Anabaptist splinter groups. The Old Order, some 25,000 strong, dresses as it has for centuries, with plain, colored aprons and bonnets for the women, and suspenders and broad-brimmed straw hats for the men. They get around by foot or in horse-drawn buggies. They educate their own and live mainly by farming, maintaining patchwork fields that look much as they did when their German and Swiss ancestors first arrived. It's an appealing image, one that inspired *Witness*, a hit movie of the 1980s, and draws tourists every summer.

The "English"—that means you, and all other outsiders—should respect the communities' privacy, but that doesn't mean you can't take a nice meander down the area's back roads. Area towns—with names like Paradise, Bird-in-Hand, and Intercourse—each have attractions, markets, and a slew of B&Bs to recommend them. Lancaster City features the Lancaster Mennonite Historical Society, the Phillips Museum of Art, and a Central Market that has been in operation since the 1730s. Stop in for crafts and locally grown produce, meats, cheeses, and homemade pretzels and shoofly pie. For an overnight, the Kings Cottage B&B does the trick, with eight classically elegant rooms in a 1913 Spanish-style mansion.

To the north, the town of Lititz was founded by Moravians in the late 1700s as a closed religious community, only opening to outsiders nearly 100 years later. Today its quaint Main Street boasts Colonial houses, antiques shops, and the Sturgis Pretzel House, the oldest commercial pretzel bakery in the U.S. Just outside town, the lakeside Swiss Woods B&B offers seven rooms done in modern country style, and can arrange for guests to have dinner in an Amish home.

The Ephrata Cloister was founded by Conrad Beissel and his followers, who, between 1735 and 1746, built homes, meetinghouses, bakeries, mills, and a printing office, all while practicing their own distinct blend of proto-mysticism, Anabaptism, and celibacy. Today, a dozen of the cloister's original buildings have been restored and are open for tours. Little more than a quarter-mile from the cloister, the Historic Smithton Inn has been welcoming guests since 1763, when it was

built as a stagecoach stop. About 12 miles east, Churchtown offers another great choice: the Inn at Twin Linden, with bucolic grounds and country-style guest rooms with whirlpool tubs and fireplaces.

Farther north, in Berks County, Kutztown hosts the country's oldest ongoing folklife festival every July. You can pick up a hex sign here—one of those colorful bits of folk art that is a trademark of Pennsylvania Dutch Country.

WHERE: Amish heartland is east of Lancaster, 60 miles west of Philadelphia. *Visitor info:* Tel 800-723-8824 or 717-299-0470; discoverlancaster.com. **CENTRAL MARKET:** Lancaster. Tel 717-735-6890; centralmarket lancaster.com. *When:* Tues, Fri, and Sat. **KINGS COTTAGE B&B:** Lancaster. Tel 717-397-1017; kingscottagebb.com. *Cost:* from $175. **SWISS WOODS B&B:** Lititz. Tel 800-594-8018 or 717-627-3358; swisswoods.com. *Cost:* from $175. **EPHRATA CLOISTER:** Ephrata. Tel 717-733-6600; ephratacloister.org. *When:* daily, Apr–Dec; closed Mon–Tues, Jan–Feb; **HISTORIC SMITHTON INN:** Ephrata. Tel 877-755-4590 or 717-733-6094; historicsmithtoninn.com. *Cost:* from $149 (off-peak), from $169 (peak). **INN AT TWIN LINDEN:** Narvon. Tel 866-445-7614 or 717-445-7619; innattwinlinden.com. *Cost:* from $150. **KUTZTOWN FOLK FESTIVAL:** Tel 888-674-6136; kutztownfestival.com. *When:* early July. **BEST TIME:** Dec 26–29 for lantern tours at the Ephrata Cloister.

Dedicated to their families and their farms, the "Plain People" enjoy a simple, peaceful lifestyle.

Location, Location . . . and Architect

FALLINGWATER

Mill Run, Pennsylvania

According to a 1991 poll of American Institute of Architects members, the most architecturally significant building in the U.S. is Fallingwater, the vacation home designed by Frank Lloyd Wright in 1935 for Pittsburgh department-store magnate Edgar Kaufmann and his wife, Liliane. Built above a small waterfall on the Bear Run stream, the house exemplifies Wright's concern with creating a perfect relationship between architecture and its environment. Like the rock ledges of the waterfall, the house's three floors descend in huge horizontal concrete slabs cantilevered into the hillside, while its walls are made from the same sandstone that forms the rocks in the stream below. Low ceilinged and austere, the house has Zen-like window frames that create the sensation that there is no separation of inside and out. Nearly as much floor space is devoted to outdoor terraces as to indoor rooms; from the living room a stone stairway descends to the stream below. A private residence until 1963, Fallingwater is now the only Wright house open to the public with all its original elements in place, including 169 pieces of furniture that Wright designed for the house, plus nearly 800 other furnishings, textiles, and artworks collected by the Kaufmanns.

Seven miles south, the mountains near Uniontown hold another Wright home, Kentuck Knob. Designed when the architect was 86, the hillside house mirrors the low profile and sandstone construction of its better-known cousin, but focuses on land rather than water. Outside, a sculpture garden displays more than three dozen works by artists such as Claes Oldenburg, Anthony Caro, and Ray Smith. It's just a 30-mile drive to Polymath Park, where Wright buffs can spend the night at Duncan House. Wright built the house in Illinois in 1957 (two years before his death), and in 2004 it was dismantled and reassembled here. It's available to rent by the night.

This is a lovely corner of the state. And you can enjoy all its attributes in Farmington, at the Nemacolin Woodlands Resort & Spa. Opened in 1987, the resort is best known for its two 18-hole championship golf courses (including the 7,526-yard, par-72 course Mystic Rock, designed by the legendary Pete Dye). Falling Rock Hotel can be found at Mystic Rock's 18th green, one of a handful of lodging choices scattered across the resort's bucolic 2,000-acre spread. The striking 42-room boutique hotel is a tribute to the architectural style of Frank Lloyd Wright. The resort also includes a roster of activities, such as an equestrian center, ten downhill ski slopes and trails, off-road driving, fly-fishing, clay shooting, and a small casino.

Following Wright's organic design principles, Fallingwater is in harmony with its natural surroundings.

The Woodlands Spa provides massages and other treatments, including the Water Path, a hydrotherapy using a pebble-filled pool and water of varying temperatures to promote circulation and well-being.

WHERE: 60 miles southeast of Pittsburgh. Tel 724-329-8501; fallingwater.org. *When:* closed Jan–Feb; daily except Wed, mid-Mar–Nov; weekends in Dec and early Mar. **KENTUCK KNOB:** Chalk Hill. Tel 724-329-1901; kentuckknob.com. **DUNCAN HOUSE:** Polymath Park. Tel 877-833-7829; franklloydwright overnight.net. *Cost:* entire house from $299, sleeps 6. **NEMACOLIN WOODLANDS RESORT:** Farmington. Tel 866-344-6957 or 724-329-8555; nemacolin.com. *Cost:* Falling Rock from $299 (off-peak), from $699 (peak). **BEST TIMES:** Fri and Sat in May–Aug for Fallingwater's special sunset tours, which include hors d'oeuvres served on the terrace.

Charm with a Capital "C"

NEW HOPE & BUCKS COUNTY

Pennsylvania

Located on the western bank of the Delaware River, New Hope has only four main streets crisscrossed by cobblestone alleys and fronted by historic buildings—some 150 of them on the National Register of Historical Places.

Originally owned by William Penn, the site became an important mill town and ferry point across the Delaware, but by the end of the 19th century, the town's economy began to shift from industry to aesthetics. Seduced by its gorgeous landscapes, painters moved to the area, and in the 1930s members of the New York literati, among them Dorothy Parker, Pearl S. Buck, and Oscar Hammerstein, followed. In 1938, a group that included playwright Moss Hart purchased the old New Hope Mills and converted it into the Bucks County Playhouse, which remains one of America's foremost regional theaters. As the decades passed, antiques stores, galleries, restaurants, B&Bs, and all the other accoutrements of a small arts town began to pop up, until New Hope achieved its current status as a weekend getaway spot that's getting a lot of love. Take in the scene, take in some history (the Parry Mansion, dating from 1784, is filled with period furnishings), or have a little touristy fun on a mule-drawn canal barge, complete with music and historic narration. After a short stroll along the towpath, cross the bridge to Lambertville, New Hope's New Jersey twin; a few miles to the south, both the Pennsylvania and New Jersey sides of the river have state parks commemorating George Washington's famous crossing of the Delaware on Christmas night 1776.

New Hope is known for its plethora of welcoming inns and charming B&Bs, perhaps best epitomized by the nine–guest room Pineapple Hill. The converted farmhouse is surrounded by 5 acres of well-tended grounds, which offer respite and shade, as well as a small pool. Across the river, the Lambertville House, with an equally fine reputation, was built as an inn and stagecoach stop in 1812. Of its 26 rooms, 21 have a gas fireplace, marble bath, and a mix of period antiques and reproductions.

Heading deeper into Bucks County, Route 202 is lined by antiques shops and seasonal flea markets. In Holicong, just beyond Peddlers Village (a collection of gift and crafts shops), the 1740 Inn at Barley Sheaf Farm, once owned by playwright George S. Kaufman, is today a luxurious inn, restaurant, and spa located on a peaceful 100 acres.

About 10 miles southwest of New Hope, Doylestown offers more Bucks County charm. In the early 20th century, all-around Renaissance man Henry Chapman Mercer constructed the Mercer Museum, a veritable castle that houses a collection of preindustrial American vehicles, folk art, furnishings, and implements, including upward of 40,000 tools representing 60-odd early American crafts and trades, plus Conestoga wagons and Native American implements dating back 10,000 years. Down the road, another Mercer enterprise, the Moravian Pottery and Tile Works, produced handcrafted tiles during the Arts and Crafts movement. It's still in operation today, and offers tours and an apprentice program. The Fonthill Museum, Mercer's third great Doylestown building, was his 44-room home, built from his own design and decorated with his handcrafted tile designs.

WHERE: 44 miles north of Philadelphia. *Bucks County visitor info:* Tel 800-836-BUCKS or 215-639-0300; visitbuckscounty .com. *Lambertville–New Hope visitor info:* Tel

Stroll down the streets of New Hope and visit some of its many restaurants and antiques shops.

609-397-0055; glnhcc.org. **BUCKS COUNTY PLAYHOUSE:** New Hope. Tel 215-862-2121; bcptheater.org. *When:* Apr–Dec. **PINEAPPLE HILL:** Tel 888-866-8404; pineapplehill.com. *Cost:* from $155. **LAMBERTVILLE HOUSE:** Tel 888-867-8859 or 609-397-4400; lambertville house.com. *Cost:* from $190 (off-peak), from $210 (peak). **INN AT BARLEY SHEAF FARM:** Holicong. Tel 215-794-5104; barleysheaf. com. *Cost:* from $250. **MERCER MUSEUM & FONTHILL CASTLE:** Doylestown. Tel 215-345-0210; mercermuseum.org. **MORAVIAN POTTERY:** Doylestown. Tel 215-348-6098; buckscounty .org/government/MoravianPotteryTileworks. **BEST TIME:** fall for scenic beauty.

A Passion for Sharing the Beauty of Art

THE BARNES FOUNDATION

Philadelphia, Pennsylvania

D r. Albert C. Barnes was an up-by-your-own-bootstraps type, born in 1908 in a working-class Philadelphia neighborhood. He left to study medicine and then founded a pharmaceutical company that made him very wealthy.

Like many new millionaires, he began collecting art. But unlike many, he remembered where he had come from. First, he hung some of the paintings he had acquired in his factory, inviting his employees to discuss the works. Then, he began offering them free educational seminars. Eventually, he came to share his passion with

the wider world through the establishment of the Barnes Foundation, which has become one of the world's premier private art collections.

Barnes's displays, which often grouped works from different cultures and periods in unorthodox juxtapositions, were intended to illustrate universal stylistic and thematic continuities. That's the way it was during Barnes's lifetime, and that's the way it remained when the foundation relocated in 2012 from the same 12-acre suburban Merion arboretum that Barnes purchased in the 1920s to downtown Philadelphia.

The foundation is home to more than 3,000 masterpieces, including one of the most important collections of French Impressionist and post-Impressionist paintings anywhere—with 181 works by Renoir, 67 by Cézanne, 59 by Matisse, and 46 by Picasso. Other major European artists include van Gogh, Degas, Corot, Seurat, Monet, Modigliani, Manet, Goya, and El Greco. True to Barnes's vision (and as stipulated in the foundation's governing documents), works by the masters are arranged cheek by jowl with African art and quirky items such as rustic door hinges, emphasizing shared form and/or content. The beautiful arboretum, which remains in Merion, is landscaped following a similar democratic aesthetic.

In late 2004, following a protracted, emotional struggle, the foundation received the legal go-ahead to move its gallery from out-of-the-way Merion to a new, modern facility in Center City Philadelphia. The move was cheered by some as a return to Albert Barnes's original populist notions, relocating his collection where it will be more accessible. Others feared that the unique Barnes experience would be lost forever. The new building, by architects Tod Williams and Billie Tsien, is just a stone's throw from the Philadelphia Museum of Art (see p. 224) and the other cultural institutions of Franklin Parkway, and its minimalist design was intended to focus attention on the foundation's quirky history. The founder's original intention and spirit flourishes in the new location.

WHERE: 2025 Benjamin Franklin Pkwy. Tel 215-278-7000; barnesfoundation.org. *When:* museum closed Tues; arboretum open Sat–Sun, May–early Sept.

The Gladiator Spirit Lives On

THE ARMY-NAVY GAME

Philadelphia, Pennsylvania

Held for the first time in 1890, the annual game between the military academies of West Point (see p. 205) and Annapolis (see p. 117) remains one of the signature rivalries in American sport. It may also be the last

big amateur game in football: Whereas players on most college teams are just warming up for the NFL, the majority of these players are in it for the love of the game—and their schools. Played in early December, this game is the last for most seniors, or "first classmen," who often graduate from school into their respective services—and sometimes into war. It's this sense of old-fashioned honor that makes the Army-Navy game what it is: an anachronism, but also a pageant, a tradition, a touchstone of American life, and a reminder

that sport doesn't have to be about money and stardom.

About two hours before the game, bands from each academy lead some 8,000 members of the Army Corps of Cadets and the Navy Brigade of Midshipmen onto the field, all marching in perfect cadence along with color guards carrying the flags of the nation, the schools, and the two services. As game time approaches, the stadium is saluted by fly-overs, while the academy bands play the national anthem. Then, it's game time! (The results show no historical trend: At this writing, the score stands at 49 wins for Army and 60 for Navy—plus 7 tied games. Navy has won the last 13 games.) Postgame, the school songs of the two academies are played and sung as the winning and losing teams salute the cadets from both schools in a show of solidarity, and the rivalry is forgotten—at least until tomorrow, when the countdown to next year begins.

Where: Philadelphia, roughly equidistant from the 2 schools, has hosted the majority of the Army-Navy games since 1890. The Philadelphia games are played at Lincoln Financial Field (lincolnfinancialfield.com). For information on the game and location, visit armynavygame.com. *Ticket info:* Most tickets are reserved for academy boosters and holders of season tickets, though some make their way to the general public through various ticket agents. Contact Army Sports (tel 877-TIX-ARMY; goarmywestpoint.com) or Navy Sports (tel 800-US4-NAVY; navysports .com). *When:* early Dec.

Founding Fathers, Founding Mothers

Franklin Court
& the Betsy Ross House

Philadelphia, Pennsylvania

In his day, Benjamin Franklin was arguably the most famous and recognized man in America. By age 23 he was owner and publisher of the *Pennsylvania Gazette*, at 26 he began publishing his *Poor Richard's Almanack*, at 31 he was postmaster of Philadelphia, and at 41 he founded Pennsylvania's first militia and began making notes on his experiments with electricity. By turns an inventor, soldier, firefighter, author, scientist, shopkeeper, cartoonist, antislavery agitator, and deist, he was, most famously, a patriot—serving as a delegate to the Continental Congress, signing the Declaration of Independence, negotiating peace with Great Britain, and acting as the new nation's first ambassador to France.

Franklin's Philadelphia home was razed in 1812, but Franklin Court, a collection of museums that illuminate the man's incredible life, now stands on the site. A full-size sculptural outline of a house now hovers above archaeological excavations of Franklin's foundation, wells, and privy. An underground museum displays many of his inventions (including the Franklin Stove and the swim fin) while nearby, the U.S. Postal Service Museum displays original copies of Franklin's *Pennyslvania Gazette* (the Post Office next door still stamps letters with his postmark).

When Franklin died at the age of 84, some 20,000 mourners witnessed his funeral procession before he was laid to rest in Christ Church Burial Ground, just around the corner from Franklin Court, where four other signers of the Declaration of Independence are also buried. The stone on his grave reads simply, "Benjamin and Deborah Franklin, 1790." Pennies typically dot the surface, reflecting the local tradition that tossing them there brings good luck.

Two blocks east, on Arch Street, is the Betsy Ross House. Born into a large Quaker family in 1752, Ross was trained as an upholsterer and by 1776 was running her own business when—as legend has it—George

Washington (whom Ross sat near in church), George Ross (Betsy's uncle), and Robert Morris of the Continental Congress came calling. They had a sketch with them—thirteen red and white stripes plus thirteen six-pointed stars in a blue inset. Ross suggested five-pointed stars, and after seeing her demonstrate how easy they would be to cut, the gentlemen agreed, and the Stars and Stripes was born. Today, you can see the house and workshop restored to how they looked in 1777.

Less than a block north, Elfreth's Alley is considered the oldest continuously inhabited street in the country, its oldest house dating to the 1720s. Originally inhabited by tradesmen and artisans, the 32 two-story homes are now some of the most coveted real estate in Philly. At number 126, the Elfreth's Alley Museum has displays on the street's history, with an 18th-century garden out back and restored bedroom and dressmaker's shop inside.

FRANKLIN COURT: 314-322 Market St. Tel 800-537-7676 or 215-965-2305; phlvisitor center.com/attraction/franklin-court. *When:* open daily. **BETSY ROSS HOUSE:** 239 Arch St. Tel 215-686-1252; betsyrosshouse.org. *When:* daily, Mar–Nov; Tues–Sun, Dec–Feb.

ELFRETH'S ALLEY MUSEUM: Tel 215-574-0560; elfrethsalley.org. *When:* closed Mon. **BEST TIMES:** Fete Day, 1st weekend in June, when homes on Elfreth's Alley open to visitors; 10 days around July 4th for the big celebration (visitphilly.com).

The Betsy Ross House was restored in 1937.

Go Fly a Kite

THE FRANKLIN INSTITUTE SCIENCE MUSEUM

Philadelphia, Pennsylvania

Founded in 1824 in honor of Benjamin Franklin, the Franklin Institute became one of the first hands-on science museums when its current home opened in 1934 and is now one of Philadelphia's most-visited attractions.

It'd be nice to think that's because the American people harbor a deep and abiding scientific curiosity, but it's more likely they come because this place is just plain fun. Attractions are divided among a dozen exhibition halls. At KidScience, children five to eight learn the foundations of light, water, earth, and air science by taking a storybook journey through the Island of the Elements, navigating mazes of mirrors and lasers, designing fountains and river channels, sounding foghorns, and learning the principles of sailing. Hovering above the Franklin Air Show, which is designed to simulate the environment of a busy air show, is an original 1911 Wright Model B Flyer. Space Command includes dozens of interactive exhibits, one of which lets you pinpoint your house from an orbital satellite. The Fels Planetarium explores the heavens using a state-of-the-art Digistar projection system. At the Train Factory, visitors get a hands-on introduction to railroad engineering, while at the Sportszone, they can test their skills at a variety of simulators (surfing,

An imposing marble statue of Benjamin Franklin greets visitors in the rotunda.

throwing a speedball, etc.), while learning about the physics and physiological aspects of sport. In another section, you can tour the inside of a giant human heart.

The institute's rotunda is home to the official Benjamin Franklin National Memorial, its centerpiece a 20-foot marble statue in a hall modeled after the Roman Pantheon. The Franklin Institute Science Museum offers an exhibit on the scientific side of Franklin's life, from meteorology and electricity to music, optics, and aquatics. A number of his inventions are on view, including bifocals, and the glass armonica, a musical instrument on which sound is produced by rubbing the edges of different-size glass bowls. And yes, there's a large key, a reminder of his most famous 1752 kite-flying experiment that proved lightning is an electrical current.

Outside, 25,000-square-foot First Union Science Park is full of sundials, hide-and-seek tunnels, mini-periscopes, and pendulums that create geometric patterns in the sand. On the other side of the park, located in the historic Memorial Hall, is the Please Touch Museum, the first museum in the country designed for kids seven and younger.

FRANKLIN INSTITUTE: 222 N. 20th St. Tel 215-448-1200; fi.edu. **PLEASE TOUCH MUSEUM:** Tel 215-581-3181; pleasetouch museum.org. **BEST TIME:** Mon at the Please Touch Museum, when there are no school groups.

The Birthplace of American Democracy

INDEPENDENCE NATIONAL HISTORICAL PARK

Philadelphia, Pennsylvania

The L-shaped swath around the old Pennsylvania State House—now known as Independence Hall—is the most important historic district of any American city. Created by an act of Congress in 1948, Independence

National Historical Park encompasses almost 55 acres, with some 20 buildings open to the public.

Built between 1732 and 1753, Independence Hall is not only where the Declaration of Independence was debated and approved, but also where the Articles of Confederation were adopted in 1781, and the Constitution finally enacted in 1787. Today, it's furnished with period pieces, including the chair used by George Washington when he presided over the Constitutional Convention. In the building's West Wing, the Great Essentials exhibit displays original copies of the Declaration, the Articles, and the Constitution, along with a silver inkstand used in their signing.

Next door, Congress Hall, which served as the home of the U.S. Congress from 1790 to 1800, has been restored to its late 18th-century look. Across Chestnut Street, the Liberty Bell Center was built in 2003 to house the most famous bell in the world. Probably cast to commemorate the 50th anniversary of William Penn's 1701 Charter of Privileges (which guaranteed religious freedom and expanded the voice of Pennsylvanians in their own government), the bell was inscribed with scripture from Leviticus 25:10: "Proclaim Liberty throughout all the land unto all the inhabitants thereof." Hung in the steeple of Independence Hall, the bell may or may not have been rung to announce a public reading of the Declaration of Independence on July 8, 1776, but there's no doubt about its importance to the antislavery movement, who adopted it as a symbol of freedom. Plagued by cracks from the beginning, it is believed that the bell was finally rendered unringable in 1846 after it was sounded in honor of the late George Washington's birthday.

Visitors wishing to explore U.S. history further have a wealth of options here. A block and a half east of Independence Hall, Carpenters Hall was the site of the first meeting of the Continental Congress in 1774. To the north, on Arch Street, the National Constitution Center offers more than a

Originally called the State House Bell, abolitionists renamed it the Liberty Bell when it became a symbol for their movement.

hundred interactive and multimedia exhibits, artifacts, photos, sculpture, text, and film. If you're afflicted with hunger or thirst during your visit, pop over to the City Tavern. A regular haunt of Jefferson, Adams, and Franklin, the original tavern burned to the ground in 1854 but was rebuilt in 1976. Today it offers an authentic 18th-century dining experience, right down to the pepperpot soup, braised rabbit, turkey potpie, and beers brewed from Washington's and Jefferson's own recipes.

WHERE: The Independence Visitor Center at 6th & Market Sts. acts as a gateway to the historic district. Tel 800-537-7676 or 215-925-6101; phlvisitorcenter.com/national-park. Timed tickets to Independence Hall are required Mar–Dec (tel 877-444-6777; recreation.gov). **HOW:** Context Walking Tours offers various 3-hour themed tours for small groups. Tel 800-691-6036; contexttravel.com. *Cost:* $85. **CITY TAVERN:** Tel 215-413-1443; citytavern.com. *Cost:* dinner $45. **BEST TIME:** 10-day July 4th celebration includes fireworks, exhibits, concerts, and activities around town (welcomeamerica.com).

"Give us whiskey, give us gin, open the door and let us in!"

THE MUMMERS PARADE

Philadelphia, Pennsylvania

The history of Philadelphia's Mummers Parade goes back to the 17th century, when Swedish immigrants made the rounds of their friends and neighbors after Christmas, banging on pots and pans to scare away devils, in a Christianization of the old Roman festival of Saturnalia. As the city grew, other immigrant traditions began spicing up the mix, and before long New Year's Day began to look like Halloween, with parties of costumed men going from door to door, shooting guns in the air, singing songs, and calling for cake and strong drink. In the late 19th century, the celebrations started to take on an organized character, and in 1901 they received the official imprimatur of the city that had banned such celebrations a century before.

The word "mummer" comes from the Old French *momer*—"to wear a mask"—which in Philly at this time of year describes anywhere from 10,000 to 15,000 people. Like the New Orleans krewes that prepare floats for Mardi Gras, Philadelphia's mummers clubs work all year to get ready for the big day, sewing costumes, arranging music, and preparing themes and props. Participants are grouped into five divisions. The Comics, decked out in ragtag costumes, continue the ancient traditions of clowning and lampoon—some say because they start imbibing around sunrise, but of course that could be just to keep warm. They're the first up Broad Street, strutting past nearly a million spectators en route to the judges' stands at City Hall. Behind them, the Fancy Clubs are just what you'd expect, dressed in elaborate costumes that match the themes of their floats. Following them are the most popular divisions, the String Bands, playing 19th-century music, and the Fancy Brigades, which make a detour off Broad Street and proceed instead to the

A Fancy Club mummer struts his stuff in the parade.

Philadelphia Convention Center for two indoor shows, at noon and 5 P.M. In all, the parade takes eight to ten hours to traverse its 2-mile route, ending with the awarding of cash prizes for the best in each division. (If you can't make the parade, you can get a taste of mummery at the Mummers Museum.)

If you're in town for the holidays, head to the old Wanamaker's on Market Street, a National Historic Landmark and now the home of Macy's. It is also home to the famous Christmas Light Show, an old-fashioned electrical extravaganza that's been a Philly tradition since 1956. It takes place in the building's Grand Court, a 150-foot atrium that's also home to the great Wanamaker Organ. Built for the 1904 World's Fair, today it has 28,677 pipes, making it the world's largest playable pipe organ, with a legendarily magnificent, celestial sound. Regular recitals coincide with the light show twice daily. **WHERE:** Broad St., between Oregon Ave. and Market St. (visitphilly.com/events/Philadelphia/the-mummers-parade). Best viewing is in the judges' stands at 15th and Market. Tickets for the judges' stands are available in the fall at the Independence Visitor Center (tel 215-965-7676; phlvisitorcenter.com). *When:*

Jan 1, starting at 9 A.M. **MUMMERS MUSEUM:** Tel 215-336-3050; mummersmuseum.com. *When:* free String Band concerts 8 P.M. on Thurs evenings May–Sept. **CHRISTMAS LIGHT SHOW/WANAMAKER ORGAN:** Tel 484-684-7250; wanamakerorgan.com. *When:* Christmas light shows from the Fri after Thanksgiving through Dec 31; organ recitals Mon–Sat year-round.

---

*"Bread feeds the body, indeed,
but flowers feed also the soul."—The Koran*

THE PHILADELPHIA FLOWER SHOW

Philadelphia, Pennsylvania

"**P**eople from a planet without flowers," wrote author Iris Murdoch, "would think we must be mad with joy the whole time to have such things about us." The Philadelphia Flower Show, which has been held nearly every year since 1829, is the country's oldest, largest, and most prestigious celebration of flowers, its bounty transforming 10 acres of Philadelphia Convention Center exhibition space into a fantasy garden of bursting buds and blooming trees. Sixty major exhibits are enough to make you gape in wonder —and inhale in delight—while 2,000 amateur exhibits in hundreds of competitive classes give the pros a run for their money. More than 200 judges and 260,000 enthusiasts attend the weeklong event, which is filled with competitions, seminars, how-to demonstrations (pruning, replanting, bonsai and topiary training, fertilizer debates), and a hard-to-resist marketplace, plus attractions, shopping, and dining in the Grand Hall. It would all certainly please city founder William Penn, who in 1681 envisioned a city in which every house had "ground on each side for gardens or orchards, or fields, that it may be a greene country towne, which will never be burnt and always wholesome."

The Philadelphia Flower Show has a different theme each year.

WHERE: Pennsylvania Convention Center, 12th and Arch Sts. Tel 215-988-8800; the flowershow.com. *When:* early Mar.

Temples of Culture in the City of Brotherly Love

PHILADELPHIA MUSEUM OF ART & THE RODIN MUSEUM

Philadelphia, Pennsylvania

S tanding like a Roman temple at the head of the broad, tree-lined Benjamin Franklin Parkway, the Philadelphia Museum of Art looks every bit the archetypal museum that it is. Built in the neoclassical style in 1928, it's the country's third-largest art museum and one of its best, with a permanent collection of more than 225,000 objects housed in more than 200 galleries. The museum is also noted for the 72 marble steps that lead up to it, immortalized in the *Rocky* movie franchise when Rocky Balboa uses the iconic staircase as part of his boxing fitness training. A statue of Rocky (aka Sylvester Stallone) stands near the base of the stairs and will reportedly be left untouched during the museum's upcoming renovation and expansion by master architect Frank Gehry, scheduled for completion in 2028, the museum's centennial.

The museum's American collection is considered one of the finest in existence, with galleries devoted to the colonial and federal periods, Amish and Shaker crafts, works by early Philadelphia silversmiths, and the foremost collection of paintings by 19th-century Philadelphia artist Thomas Eakins. European galleries include masterpieces such as van Gogh's *Sunflowers* and Cézanne's *Large Bathers*. East Asian art covers a vast period, from the third millennium B.C. to the present, with a fantastic collection of Oriental carpets, sculpture, and paintings, and an entire 1917 Japanese teahouse. Other architectural transplants include a pillared 16th-century Hindu temple, a Chinese palace hall, a 13th-century French cloister, and the stone entranceway from the 12th-century French abbey of Saint-Laurent. Modern and contemporary art includes works by Picasso, Dalí, Miró, Léger,

The Philadelphia Museum of Art's quasi–Greek-Revival style was designed by Horace Trumbauer, a prominent architect of the Gilded Age.

de Kooning, and Pollock, plus the world's largest collection of works by Marcel Duchamp, including the huge *The Bride Stripped Bare by Her Bachelors, Even* (*The Large Glass*), still sitting exactly where the artist placed it in 1954.

Four blocks east, the Rodin Museum was a gift to the city from Philadelphia-born movie mogul Jules Mastbaum, who spent three years amassing a collection of sculptor Auguste Rodin's work and then commissioned French architect Paul Philippe Cret and landscape Architect Jacques Gréber to design a Beaux-Arts building and formal garden to display it—all for "the enjoyment of my fellow citizens." The museum houses the largest collection of Rodin's work outside Paris. Highlights include a cast of *The Thinker* outside the museum's entrance and *The Gates of Hell*, a monumental 20-foot doorway decorated with scenes from Dante's *Divine Comedy*.

North of the two museums, along the Schuylkill River in Fairmount Park, is one of the country's most significant collections of 18th- and 19th-century historic homes. The Philadelphia Museum administers and offers tours of two homes: Mount Pleasant, built between 1762 and 1765, is celebrated as one of the most elegant surviving examples of 18th-century Georgian architecture in the United States, while Cedar Grove, dating from 1746, is noted for its exceptional collection of early American furniture. Also along the river,

Boathouse Row is a group of private Victorian boathouses built beginning in 1860 that, collectively, remain the heart of the nation's rowing community. Illuminated at night by 12,000 twinkling bulbs, it's one of Philadelphia's most postcard-perfect views.

PHILADELPHIA MUSEUM OF ART: 26th St. and Benjamin Franklin Pkwy. Tel 215-763-8100; philamuseum.org. *When:* closed Mon. **RODIN MUSEUM:** 22nd St. and Benjamin Franklin Pkwy. Tel 215-763-8100; rodin museum.org. *When:* closed Tues. **BEST TIME:** mid-Nov for the Philadelphia Museum Contemporary Craft Show at the Pennsylvania Convention Center (pmacraftshow.org).

The Good Life in the City of Brotherly Love

RITTENHOUSE SQUARE

Philadelphia, Pennsylvania

Philadelphia's most fashionable residential and shopping neighborhood is also one of the city's oldest. Rittenhouse Square is one of five parks carved out in the late 17th century by city-founder William Penn, serving first as a pasture for local livestock and then as a busy brickyard. By the mid-1800s, the streets flanking this 7-acre green space were lined with opulent Victorian mansions owned by the city's elite. Today, not much has changed except the skyline. Rittenhouse Square, now ringed by high-rise residencies and luxury apartments, is more popular than ever, a tree-filled oasis where people jog, walk their dogs, and linger over al fresco lunches. The square is also one of Philadelphia's major rendezvous points, with festivals and concerts, a year-round farmers market, and many of the city's top restaurants just steps away.

Just west of the square, Vernick Food & Drink is one of Philadelphia's top dining rooms, a charming two-story restaurant offering artful, inventive cooking that never strays too far from its hearty American roots. Chef-owner and Philadelphia-native Greg Vernick serves up a tempting selection of small plates, including broccoli and bacon jam on toast and warm parmesan custard with baby artichokes.

The more casual Pizzeria Vetri is always abuzz, offering thick, square-cut pizza-of-the-day slices and a life-changing *rotolo*, a crispy pinwheel of pizza dough filled with ricotta and house-made mortadella and topped with pistachio pesto. The ever-popular pizzeria is operated by the same family as Philadelphia's top Italian restaurant Vetri, a rustic 32-seat dining room a few blocks east of Rittenhouse Square serving some of the finest Italian cuisine west of Rome.

You'll also find the city's best accommodations here. The newly renovated Rittenhouse Hotel was built in 1989 on the site where painter Mary Cassatt's family mansion once stood. A modern facade belies the classic luxury found inside, with 116 spacious guest rooms and suites, formal afternoon tea service in the Mary Cassatt Tea Room, and exquisite multicourse fine dining in the coolly sophisticated Lacroix dining room. For a more intimate and historic experience, the Rittenhouse 1715 hotel is just off the square, a beautifully preserved series of brick-and-stone structures centered around a handsome, three-story 1903 carriage house.

WHERE: Walnut St. at S. 18th St. **VERNICK FOOD & DRINK:** Tel 267-639-6644; vernick philly.com. *Cost:* dinner $65. *When:* closed Mon.

PIZZERIA VETRI: Tel 215-763-3760; pizzeria vetri.com. *Cost:* large pizza from $22. **VETRI:** Tel 215-732-3478; vetriristorante.com. *Cost:* multi-course dinner $155. **RITTENHOUSE HOTEL:** Tel 800-635-1042 or 215-546-9000; rittenhouse hotel.com. *Cost:* from $399. **RITTENHOUSE 1715:** Tel 877-791-6500 or 215-546-6500; rittenhouse1715.com. *Cost:* from $229. **BEST TIMES:** Sat year-round for farmers market; 3rd Sat in May for Rittenhouse Row Spring Festival; early Dec for tree lighting ceremony.

Life, Liberty, and the Pursuit of Cholesterol

PHILLY FOOD

Philadelphia, Pennsylvania

N ew York has pastrami, Maine has lobster rolls, and Philly has the cheese steak—plus half a dozen other hometown street-food faves. Unless you're a gourmet snob, strictly vegetarian, or under doctor's orders, leaving Philly without sampling the goods would be like going to Napa and not sipping the wine.

Start with a cheese steak. Legend has it that back in 1930 South Philly hot dog vendor Pat Olivieri, tired of eating his own grub for lunch, tossed some shaved steak slices and onions onto his griddle, cooked 'em up, and piled it on a hot dog roll. A classic was born. In time, Italian bread replaced the bun, cheese entered the mix, and fans like Humphrey Bogart and Frank Sinatra pumped up the sandwich's cachet. Today, you can visit the eponymous restaurant Pat opened in the 1930s at the southern end of Philly's famed 9th Street Italian Market. It's still run by the Olivieri family, still open 24 hours, and still serving from a take-out window, with seating under a sheet-metal awning. Although American and provolone cheeses are available, the classic is "whiz, wit'," a steak smothered in gobs of molten Cheez Whiz . . . with onions.

Right across the street is Pat's nemesis since 1966, Geno's. Though bright compared to Pat's Depression-era authenticity, it offers essentially the same menu, fueling a friendly decades-long argument about whose is the best. Jim's Steaks (also known for their hoagies) is in the running, too. Decide for yourself: Try all three if your heart can bear it, then take a walk around the Italian Market's other stalls to work it all off.

Spread over a dozen South Philly blocks, the Italian Market is the oldest and largest working outdoor market in the country, dating from the early years of the 20th century, and one of the most recognizable: Sylvester Stallone ran through it in the training scenes in *Rocky*. You'll find Sarcone's Deli, home to another Philly culinary gem, the hoagie. Allegedly named after Philadelphia's Hog Island Shipyard (workers looking for cheap sandwiches were called "hoggies," which mutated into "hoagies"), it's a straightforward sandwich—a mountain of Italian meats, cheeses, vegetables, herbs, and oil—but Sarcone's secret is its bread, perfectly crisp outside and soft inside.

After leaving the Italian Market, head to the Reading Terminal Market, home to more than

80 merchants. Opened as part of the grand Reading Railroad terminal in 1892, it was actually a continuation of a market that had occupied the site since 1653. There's another couple of cheese steak joints here (Carmen's and Spataro's), as well as vendors selling scrapple, soft pretzels, and other Pennsylvania Dutch specialties. For dessert, sidle up to the marble counter of Bassett's, which has been serving its particularly creamy ice cream at the Reading Terminal since day one.

The sprawling Italian Market is the best spot in town to grab a hoagie.

PAT'S KING OF STEAKS: Tel 215-468-1546; patskingofsteaks.com. *Cost:* cheese steak from $10. **GENO'S:** Tel 215-389-0659; genosteaks.com. *Cost:* cheese steak from $10. **JIM'S STEAKS:** Tel 215-928-1911; jimssteaks.com. *Cost:* from $10. **ITALIAN MARKET:** phillyitalianmarket.com. **SARCONE'S DELI:** Tel 215-922-1717; sarconesdeli.com.

Cost: hoagies from $7.50. **READING TERMINAL MARKET:** Tel 215-922-2317; readingterminal market.org. **BASSETT'S ICE CREAM:** Tel 215-925-4315; bassettsicecream.com. *Cost:* cones from $4.75. **BEST TIME:** mid to late May weekend for the 9th Street Italian Market Festival (italianmarketfestival.com).

"It's just another job."—Andy Warhol, on being an artist

THE ANDY WARHOL MUSEUM

Pittsburgh, Pennsylvania

Pittsburgh native Andy Warhol had a peculiar relationship with almost everything—art and his hometown among them. The fragile, devoutly Catholic son of working-class Central European immigrants, a natural artist in a city more concerned with coal and steel, he took from his upbringing a work ethic that by age 27 made him the best-known, highest-paid fashion illustrator in New York.

"An artist," Warhol once said, "is someone who produces things that people don't need to have but that he—for some reason—thinks it would be a good idea to give them." And so, determined to make a name for himself as a serious artist, he began creating works that drew from commercial and pop-culture images, most famously his Campbell's Soup can portraits. Today, the influence of that work

is so pervasive in western art, fashion, and culture that it could arguably be said to have created its own mainstream.

Founded in 1994, seven years after the artist's premature death, the Andy Warhol Museum (one of the city's four Carnegie museums) is a celebration of the entirety of Warhol: the artist, the provocateur, the obsessive collector, the cultural icon. Its permanent collection includes more than 8,000 works, with some 500 of them on display at any one time. Highlights include creations from his student years at Pittsburgh's Carnegie Tech (now

Carnegie Mellon), commercial art and sketch-book drawings, Pop Art touchstones (including his Campbell's Soup cans and Brillo boxes), silk screens from all his major series, commissioned portraits, and early-'80s collaborations with artist Jean-Michel Basquiat. The collection also includes thousands of films and videotapes, as well as a huge archive of scrapbooks, publicity posters, audiotapes, books, and personal items, such as more than 30 of his distinctive silver-white wigs. Among the archive's most treasured pieces are 610 Warhol "Time Capsules": cardboard boxes into which he would toss ephemera—newspapers, fan letters, lunch checks, postcards, collectibles, and occasionally even food.

Mao, *Warhol's pop art portrait of Chairman Mao Zedong, hangs in the Andy Warhol Museum.*

When one was full it would be taped shut, dated, and put into storage. The contents of at least one Time Capsule—one of his most personal artistic statements—are always available for viewing.

In 1963, Warhol moved to a new studio in a former hat factory and dubbed it "The Factory," a name that he retained for his subsequent studios, and a comment on both his work ethic and the techniques he used. About a mile to the north of the Warhol Museum, the unrelated Mattress Factory is a "research and development lab" that commissions artists to create large-scale site-specific works while maintaining a permanent collection of sculptural and installation art. Over the years it's transformed several properties in its North Side neighborhood into exhibition galleries, artist residences, and an artist-created garden.

WHERE: 117 Sandusky St. Tel 412-237-8300; warhol.org. *When:* closed Mon. **MATTRESS FACTORY:** Tel 412-231-3169; mattress.org. *When:* closed Mon. **BEST TIMES:** Fri nights for "Good Fridays," with half-price admission to the museum, a cash bar, and events that may include film screenings or musical performances; daily for "The Factory," when visitors can create art using Warhol's preferred techniques, helped by artists and volunteers.

"Farewell, then, Age of Iron; all hail, King Steel."
—Andrew Carnegie

PITTSBURGH'S STEEL HERITAGE

Pittsburgh, Pennsylvania

For most people the word "Pittsburgh" is more likely to evoke smokestacks than a beautiful riverside city full of striking architecture and rich ethnic neighborhoods. But think again. To gain perspective, board the

Monongahela or Duquesne Inclines, the last of the late 19th-century funicular railways that once transported people, freight, and vehicles up and down the residential hills, and get a stunning view of Pittsburgh's downtown, known as the Golden Triangle. Look for any of the 15 major bridges crisscrossing the downtown area, or the more than 700 others within the city limits. Or to gain a vantage on the city's three main parts, go to Point State Park, where the Allegheny and Monongahela Rivers converge to form the Ohio: Downtown will be behind you, the South Side off to your left, and the North Shore (along with PNC Park, one of the coziest ballparks in the major leagues) across the water to your right.

The town's most famous resident, the Scottish immigrant Andrew Carnegie, opened his first steel mill here in 1875; by 1901 he had turned southwestern Pennsylvania into the steel-producing capital of America—and himself into the world's richest man. It was a process not without problems: In 1892, at his Homestead Works mill, locked-out union workers engaged in a 12-hour gun battle with hired guards from the Pinkerton Detective Agency. Though the workers won the battle, they lost the war: Within days, Pennsylvania governor Robert Emory Pattison ordered in 8,500 members of the state militia to break the strike.

Many of the city's neighborhoods retain a whiff of the character of the ethnic groups who provided labor for Carnegie's mills: German on the North Shore, eastern European on the South Side, and Italian in Bloomfield, just east of downtown. Near the last, the Strip District is a mile-long stretch that is now home to great food, nightlife, and shopping, not to mention Primanti Bros. sandwiches (see next page). On the North Shore, the tiny neighborhood of Allegheny West is known for its late 19th-century Victorian homes. In early December, the Allegheny West Civic Council offers a popular Christmas tour of several homes made up for the season.

Ironically, the seeds of Pittsburgh's post-industrial resurgence were planted by the robber barons who spent half a century choking the city with smoke. In 1895, Andrew Carnegie founded the Carnegie Museum of Art with the intention of displaying "the Old Masters of tomorrow." One of the country's first contemporary art museums, it fulfills its founder's promise with works by Winslow Homer, James McNeill Whistler, and other American greats, plus French Impressionist paintings, Asian and African art, and works in film and video. Every three to five years (the next is in 2018), the museum hosts the Carnegie International, presenting new art and artists from around the world. It is the oldest exhibition of contemporary international art held in North America. In the same building, the Carnegie Museum of Natural History is known for its dinosaur collection. On the city's North Shore, there's the Andy Warhol Museum (see p. 227) and the kid-friendly Carnegie Science Center, the latter boasting hundreds of interactive exhibits, an Omnimax theater, and the Buhl Planetarium. In downtown's residential East End, the Frick Pittsburgh is centered around the beautifully restored 19th-century home of Henry Clay Frick, the Carnegie chairman who called in the troops on the Homestead strikers.

To explore what remains of Pittsburgh's steel era, take one of the tours offered by the Rivers of Steel National Heritage Area, which include visits to what remains of the Homestead Works, including its 92-foot blast furnaces.

ALLEGHENY WEST VICTORIAN CHRISTMAS TOUR: Tel 412-444-8687; alleghenywest.info/tour. *When:* 2 days in early Dec. **CARNEGIE MUSEUMS OF ART AND NATURAL HISTORY:** Tel 412-622-3131; carnegiemuseums.org. *When:* closed Mon. **CARNEGIE SCIENCE CENTER:** Tel 412-237-3400; carnegiesciencecenter.org.

Take a ride on the Duquesne Incline and see the breathtaking view of Pittsburgh from Mount Washington.

FRICK PITTSBURGH: Tel 412-371-0600; thefrickpittsburgh.org. *When:* closed Mon. **RIVERS OF STEEL TOURS:** Tel 412-464-4020; riversofsteel.com. *When:* May–Sept. **BEST**

TIMES: early June for the 10-day Three Rivers Arts Festival (3riversartsfest.org); summer for steel tours; 2018 for the Carnegie International (cmoa.org/ci-history).

Pittsburgh's Best Sandwich

PRIMANTI BROS.

Pittsburgh, Pennsylvania

Imagine a sandwich 6 inches high, wedged between two slices of thick-cut Italian bread. Imagine a pile of grilled meat, a fried egg for extra protein, a nice slice of tomato, a mound of coleslaw, and, right there in the sandwich,

spilling out on every side, a huge fistful of hand-cut french fries. Underneath is a sheet of wax paper, to one side your beverage of choice, and all around is Iron City atmosphere.

That's what you can get at Primanti Bros., a Pittsburgh institution that's been serving its mountain-size sandwiches from the same neighborhood joint since 1933. That was the year (according to legend) that Lou, Dick, and Stanley Primanti opened up their hole-in-the-wall to serve meals to night-shift workers and truck drivers. Whether it's true that the brothers forgot to buy plates and forks in time for opening day or that they intentionally stuffed the side dishes into their sandwiches so workers and drivers could work with one hand and eat with the other is beside the point.

After the local produce industry started to dry up in the 1970s, the neighborhood, known as "the Strip," reinvented itself as a shopping and nightlife hub, its brick warehouses and offices transformed into ethnic and specialty foods stores, fashionable restaurants, boutiques, galleries, dance clubs, and loft apartments. But Primanti's is still here, still open round the clock, and bigger than ever, with branches around town, in the suburbs, and even in Ft. Lauderdale, Florida. You've got to go to the original, though, for the full experience. Grab a stool at the long counter, or one of the no-frills wooden tables, order a sandwich and a beer, and enjoy yourself. Forget about McDonald's; this is American food.

WHERE: 46 18th St. Tel 412-263-2142; primantibros.com. *Cost:* sandwiches from $6.

Hoisting a Few at America's Oldest Working Brewery

D. G. YUENGLING & SONS

Pottsville, Pennsylvania

Beer has a noble history. Some claim it's why man gave up his nomadic lifestyle; he had to stay put if he wanted to see his beer ferment. In the U.S., beer was an essential part of the colonial experience.

George Washington, Thomas Jefferson, and, of course, Samuel Adams brewed their own—and it was at Philadelphia's India Queen Tavern that the concept of the United States' federal government was born. By the mid-19th century, there were more than 4,000 breweries in the land, most producing brews for local consumption. Prohibition shut down most of them in 1919, but a few of the more clever brewers survived, some by producing nonalcoholic beer.

Such a one was D. G. Yuengling & Sons, started in 1829 by German immigrant David G. Yuengling. When Prohibition ended in 1933, the Yuenglings celebrated by sending a truckload of beer to President Roosevelt and settled back into their role as regional brewers. Even during the late 1970s, when there were fewer than 90 brewers in the U.S., as big national brands drove the smaller names out of business, Yuengling pressed on. Today, it is the fourth-largest brewer in the country, yet it remains a family-owned, dress-down operation that sticks to its Pottsville roots.

The original brewery, still churning out quality beer, offers one of the best brewery tours around. Located right in the middle of Pottsville, it's a 19th-century time warp, a big redbrick slab with steep, narrow stairs, wet floors, and tunnels underneath, where they used to store the beer. Tours begin at the beginning, with visitors peering into the brew kettles to see the as-yet-unfermented beer. Don't miss the stained-glass ceiling, installed in 1888. Other stops include a museum display; the bottling line; a peek into the brewmaster's office; the old racking room (aka the kegging room); and, best of all, a visit to the old storage caves, carved out in 1831 and maintaining a constant 42°F temperature year-round. The tour ends in the old-fashioned taproom bar, built in 1936 and hung with decades' worth of Yuengling memorabilia. Grab your free samples (beer for you, birch beer for the kids) and look around. You might see Dick Yuengling (the founder's great-grandson) or one of his daughters there, talking with visitors and keepin' it real.

WHERE: 41 miles northwest of Philadelphia; 5th and Mahantongo Sts. Tel 570-628-4890; yuengling.com. *When:* tours Mon–Sat year-round. **BEST TIME:** weekdays, since the brewhouse and bottling line aren't in production on weekends.

The World's Greatest Indoor Miniature Village

ROADSIDE AMERICA

Shartlesville, Pennsylvania

As you approach Shartlesville, a string of roadside signs promises "More Than You Expect," and that promise is fulfilled. Built by local resident Laurence Gieringer, Roadside America is a 6,000-square-foot scale model of an idyllic mid-20th-century American town. Every miniature structure, from the village barber shop to the cathedral with its 44 hand-painted windows, was lovingly crafted by Gieringer over the course of half a century, with wife, Dora, creating 10,000 trees and countless other tiny touches. Upon Gieringer's death in 1963, time in Roadside America essentially stopped, and was preserved unchanged by his daughters in time-capsule form.

The thing that elevates Roadside America above the merely charming is that it's as alive and moving as any real landscape, letting visitors play God to their own little Mayberry. Press a button and you might set one of the many trains or trolleys in motion, speeding the town's 4,000 tiny residents from place to place. Another button might set church bells to tolling, or lift a choir in song. Meanwhile, hidden motors pump water through fountains and waterfalls, set mills to grinding, and make planes and helicopters circle overhead. The level of detail is astounding, as is the historical scope: Scattered among the buildings and roads, unexpected touches like an Indian village, a coal mine, a Barnum & Bailey Circus rehearsal, a miniature Benjamin Franklin, and Gieringer's own father (the village harness

maker) reveal its creator's surrealist view of time and urban planning. The highlight comes every half hour as night descends on Gieringer's world, and the town's lights come on, as images of sunset, the American flag, and Christ himself are projected onto the walls, accompanied by Kate Smith singing "God Bless America." For a certain kind of visitor—and you know who you are—this is the kind of odd, yet curiously revelatory, experience that small-town travel is all about.

WHERE: 39 miles northeast of Hershey. Tel 610-488-6241; roadsideamericainc.com.

The Crucible of Our Nation

VALLEY FORGE

Pennsylvania

I n September 1777, British troops defeated George Washington's Continental Army at the Battle of Brandywine, near the Pennsylvania/Delaware border (see p. 212). Within two weeks, the British were in control of Philadelphia.

Washington counterattacked at Germantown, but was unable to take back the city. By December, with the British firmly entrenched and winter coming on, he moved his army to the winter camp he'd selected 20 miles northwest of Philadelphia, at a place called Valley Forge.

Everybody knows at least part of the story: how the 12,000 men of Washington's ragtag army, their feet bound in rags, their clothing and equipment in tatters, hunkered down through the long, terrible winter. As many as 2,000 of them died. Washington, holding his army together through sheer force of will, conceded that "unless some great and capital change suddenly takes place . . . this Army must inevitably . . . starve, dissolve, or disperse."

Change did come, though, from across the Atlantic. The first to arrive was Baron Friedrich von Steuben, a Prussian drillmaster

sent from Paris by Benjamin Franklin, who was negotiating an alliance with the French. Von Steuben immediately set about standardizing the army's training; within three months, he'd welded its diverse units into a unified fighting force. During this time, supplies finally began appearing, along with new troops. Morale was given yet another boost when word arrived that Franklin had succeeded in drawing France into the conflict, both parties pledging "not to lay down their arms, until the Independence of the United States shall have been formally or tacitly assured." A month later, in June, the American army marched from Valley Forge, entirely transformed. The war would drag on for another five years, but this was the turning point.

Today, you can honor those early patriots at Valley Forge National Historical Park, a 3,600-acre preserve of rolling hills, dogwood forest, and historical sites. Washington's headquarters has been restored and furnished, and is staffed by interpreters in period costume. On the edge of the Grand Parade Ground, replica log huts mark the camp's outer defensive line. Toward the encampment's center, Artillery Park displays period cannons. Memorials include the grand National Memorial Arch, dedicated in 1917 to the "patience and fidelity" of the soldiers who wintered there, as well as statues of von Steuben and General "Mad Anthony" Wayne, commander of the Pennsylvania troops.

The Dewees's House at Valley Forge National Historical Park was used for mealtime, courts-martial, and arms storage during the winter encampment.

WHERE: 20 miles west of Philadelphia. Tel 610-783-1077; nps.gov/vafo. **BEST TIMES:** Dec 19 for a reenactment of the army's arrival at Valley Forge; Sat closest to June 19 for a celebration and reenactment of the day Washington left Valley Forge.

Hotbed of Appalachian Arts and History

VIRGINIA HIGHLANDS FESTIVAL

Abingdon, Virginia

A bingdon, the oldest English-speaking settlement west of the Blue Ridge Mountains, is a mannerly little city justifiably proud of its rich history and arts heritage. The town was named for Martha Washington's English home of Abingdon Parish, and the surrounding county was named Washington for the general who would soon win the American colonies their independence. Today, the Abingdon Historic District is full of 18th- and 19th-century homes and commercial buildings that now house museums, specialty shops, and small hotels.

Every August the local population of about 8,000 swells during the Virginia Highlands Festival, a showcase for Appalachian music, visual arts, and literature that has few equals in the country. A 45,000-square-foot antiques market is just the start; there are also Civil War history reenactments, a local home and garden tour, craft displays, juried art and photography shows, and a quilt extravaganza. Nonstop concerts range from Celtic and bluegrass to rock and gospel, and for kids there are puppet shows, parades, and free pony rides.

In the center of Abingdon's historic downtown district, the redbrick Martha Washington Inn is one of Virginia's standout luxury hotels. Built in 1832, it passed through periods as a college and makeshift Civil War hospital before becoming a grand hotel in 1935 fit for the likes of Eleanor Roosevelt, Harry Truman, and Jimmy Carter. Occupying an entire block of West Main Street, its Southern hospitality starts with 63 guest rooms and continues to rocking chairs on the wide veranda, antique treasures filling the rooms and public areas, and a superb Sunday brunch.

Directly across from "the Martha," the venerable Barter Theatre occupies a former church built in 1829. The official State Theatre of Virginia got its start in 1933, when a local actor hit on the idea of accepting produce in exchange for theater seats to make his productions accessible to the masses. The gorgeous old place is now one of the longest-

Bagpipers celebrate Celtic music at the annual Highlands Festival event.

running professional repertory theaters in the country. Gregory Peck, Ernest Borgnine, and Kevin Spacey all have performed here, and productions range from musicals to Shakespeare, including many world premieres. At least one performance a year celebrates the Barter heritage by accepting donations to an area food bank in exchange for tickets. Right at the end of Main Street, the former railbed of the Virginia-Carolina Railroad is now the Virginia Creeper Trail, a 33-mile hiking, biking, and horseback trail that leads across 47 railroad trestle bridges to the North Carolina state line.

WHERE: 134 miles southwest of Roanoke. *Visitor info:* Tel 800-435-3440 or 276-676-2282; visitabingdonvirginia.com. **VIRGINIA HIGHLANDS FESTIVAL:** Tel 276-623-5266; vahighlandsfestival.org. *When:* 2 weeks in early Aug. **MARTHA WASHINGTON INN:** Tel 888-999-8078 or 276-628-3161; themartha.com. *Cost:* from $185. **BARTER THEATRE:** Tel 276-628-3991; bartertheatre.com. **BEST TIMES:** mid-June for Mountains of Music; late June for the Abingdon Garden Tour; mid-Sept for the Washington County Fair (washcofair.com).

Colonial-Era Port City on the Edge of D.C.

OLD TOWN ALEXANDRIA

Virginia

The historic heart of Alexandria, on the western bank of the Potomac River just south of Washington, D.C., is an interesting blend of clapboard houses and modern art, cobblestone streets and wireless Internet.

One of the oldest port cities in the country, Alexandria was named in 1748 and was a regular stomping ground over the years for such luminaries as George Washington, the Marquis de Lafayette, and Robert E. Lee, among many others. Over 4,000 historic buildings—including 250 from the 18th century—have been preserved and restored in

the riverside area known as Old Town. Together with a plethora of shops, parks, restaurants, and historic sites, this venerable ambience makes Alexandria (population 149,000) an understandably popular escape from the capital.

Thomas Jefferson, James Madison, and John Adams all quaffed a brew or two over talk of politics at Gadsby's Tavern. Now a museum to eating and drinking in colonial America, its rooms have been restored to their late 18th-century appearance, and its tavern still serves traditional meals and drink. You can explore the history of the pharmaceutical arts at the Stabler-Leadbeater Apothecary, now also a museum; it opened in 1792 and was in business for almost 150 years. President Washington attended services with his wife at Christ Church Episcopal. Established in 1773, it still holds regular services. Towering over town atop Shuter's Hill to the west is the neoclassical spire of the George Washington Masonic National Memorial, enclosing a 17-foot bronze statue of the first Worshipful Master of Alexandria Lodge No. 22. On the ninth floor, an observatory offers views of Old Town Alexandria, the Potomac, and Washington, D.C., in the near distance.

For a dose of the modern, head to the riverfront and the three-story Torpedo Factory Art Center, where paintings, ceramics, sculptures, and photographs have replaced the missiles and munitions made and stored here by the U.S. Navy from 1918 to 1945. Eighty-two artists' studios, seven galleries, and two workshops fill the three floors, giving you the opportunity to chat with the 165 resident artists before buying a one-of-a-kind piece. At night, check into the Kimpton Morrison House, an elegant 45-room Federal-style hotel with a quietly formal atmosphere and exemplary service befitting heads of state and weary travelers alike.

WHERE: 9 miles south of Washington, D.C. *Visitor info:* Tel 800-388-9119 or 703-746-3301; visitalexandriava.com. **GADSBY'S TAVERN:** Tel 703-548-1288; gadsbystavern restaurant.com. *Cost:* dinner $40. **STABLER-LEADBEATER APOTHECARY MUSEUM:** Tel 703-746-3852; alexandriava.gov/apothecary. **CHRIST CHURCH:** Tel 703-549-1450; historicchrist church.org. **GEORGE WASHINGTON MASONIC NATIONAL MEMORIAL:** Tel 703-683-2007; gwmemorial.org. **TORPEDO FACTORY ART CENTER:** Tel 703-838-4565; torpedofactory.org. **KIMPTON MORRISON HOUSE HOTEL:** Tel 866-834-6628 or 703-838-8000; morrisonhouse .com. *Cost:* from $179. **BEST TIME:** Feb for George Washington's birthday (washington birthday.net).

The True Cost of War

ARLINGTON NATIONAL CEMETERY

Virginia

A merica's most famous and affecting cemetery spellbinds visitors with rows upon rows of nearly identical white marble headstones covering rolling acres of grass, where the occasional crack of a rifle salute and the mournful notes of "Taps" are often all that punctuate the silence. Over 400,000 veterans from the U.S. armed forces, from the Revolutionary War to the war in Iraq, have been laid to rest in these 624 serene acres overlooking the Potomac, and more than 100 graveside services are still held every week—so many that the cemetery is projected to run out of space by 2025. It's beautiful and sobering, a resting place for American heroes and a reminder that history is measured one life at a time.

Originally, the property was owned by Robert E. Lee, who spent many happy years in the Greek Revival mansion called Arlington House—located on a hill with a sweeping view of the capital—before accepting a commission in the Confederate army when Virginia seceded from the Union. Federal forces crossed the Potomac and seized Arlington soon after, and in 1864 a Union general decided the best way to punish Lee would be to bury Union dead literally in his backyard. Some 16,000 Union soldiers were laid to rest here, and after the war the estate and 200 surrounding acres were set aside for a national cemetery.

In addition to Arlington House, filled with antiques and reproductions nearly to its 12-foot ceilings, the most visited destination at Arlington (and the most visited grave in

The Tomb of the Unknowns has been guarded continuously since July 2, 1937. Being chosen to serve as a sentinel at the tomb is one of the highest honors a soldier can receive.

America) is the grave site of President John Fitzgerald Kennedy. Adorned with an eternal flame and a low marble wall inscribed with quotations from his famous "Ask not" speech, it is located near the graves of his brother Robert F. Kennedy and wife, Jacqueline Kennedy Onassis. Past the massive white marble Memorial Amphitheater, the Tomb of the Unknowns holds the bodies of unidentified soldiers from WWI, WWII, and the Korean War, guarded by soldiers from the U.S. Third Infantry in a reverent display of 21 faultless steps and 21-second pauses, back and forth, over and over, symbolizing the 21-gun national salute, among the nation's greatest honors.

Dozens of other famous grave sites and memorials are dispersed throughout Arlington, from the Civil War Unknowns to the Space Shuttle Challenger Memorial. Just outside the northern boundary of the cemetery is the U.S. Marine Corps War Memorial, the largest cast bronze statue in the world, which re-creates Joe Rosenthal's famous image of U.S. Marines raising the flag over Iwo Jima during WWII.

WHERE: directly across Arlington Memorial Bridge from the Lincoln Memorial to the end of Memorial Ave. Tel 877-907-8585; arlington cemetery.org. **ARLINGTON HOUSE:** Tel 703-235-1530; nps.gov/arho. **BEST TIMES:** Memorial Day (late May) and Veterans Day (Nov 11) for public services at the Memorial Amphitheater.

Driving Virginia's Beauty Road

BLUE RIDGE PARKWAY

Virginia

The Blue Ridge Parkway is a 469-mile moving postcard that unfolds meadows, forests, and seemingly endless mountain views into one long masterpiece. It's one of America's most beautiful scenic routes, running

north from just outside the Great Smoky Mountains National Park (see p. 464) across the North Carolina border and through the

Blue Ridge Mountains, and connecting up with Shenandoah National Park's Skyline Drive (see p. 252) at Waynesboro. Virginia's 217-mile section, especially the 114 miles from Waynesboro to Roanoke, is the most delightful part, lined with national forests and mountaintop views that are nothing short of sublime.

Heading south from Shenandoah National Park, the Humpback Rocks Visitor Center offers a self-guided trail through a reconstructed 19th-century farmstead, and a steep 1-mile trail to the top of Humpback Rocks, with its stunning 360-degree view of the mountains. Shortly after it hits its lowest point (649 feet) crossing the James River, the Parkway climbs to its highest point in Virginia (3,950 feet), just before the Peaks of Otter at milepost 86. Here you'll find another visitors center and the year-round Peaks of Otter Lodge, overlooking Abbott Lake. Trails lead to a 1930s farm and the pinnacle of Sharp Top (3,875 feet). South of Roanoke is Mabry Mill, one of the most popular and most photographed stops on the Parkway. The early 20th-century mill still offers fresh-ground cornmeal and flour for sale. The Chateau Morrisette Winery has been making wine here since 1980, and their Our Dog Blue, a semisweet mix of riesling and Vidal, is one of the state's most popular wines. An inviting restaurant serves regional dishes such as bacon-wrapped trout and shrimp and grits, on the patio with sweeping views.

The Blue Ridge Mountains stretch from Georgia to Pennsylvania, with countless beautiful vistas along the way.

WHERE: runs from Waynesboro south to Great Smoky Mountains National Park, NC. Tel 828-298-0398; nps.gov/blri. *When:* road open year-round; most facilities other than Peaks of Otter closed Oct–May. **PEAKS OF OTTER LODGE:** Tel 866-387-9905 or 540-586-1081; peaksofotter.com. *Cost:* from $109 (off-peak), from $119 (peak). **CHATEAU MORRISETTE WINERY:** Tel 540-593-2865; thedogs.com. *Cost:* dinner $35. **BEST TIMES:** spring for blooming azaleas and rhododendrons; late July and Aug for Chateau Morrisette's Black Dog Music Festival concerts; fall for glorious foliage.

The Great Beyond

THE STEVEN F. UDVAR-HAZY CENTER

Chantilly, Virginia

From the day it opened in 1976, the Smithsonian's National Air and Space Museum on D.C.'s National Mall was already too small, able to display only 10 percent of its total collection (see p. 261). Luckily, the

Steven F. Udvar-Hazy Center opened in 2003, named for the Hungary-born businessman who donated $65 million to the project and big

enough to allow display of some of its biggest birds in open hangarlike settings.

The main Boeing Aviation Hangar, ten

stories high and three football fields long, houses countless aircraft, some on its main floor, others suspended from two hanging levels beside elevated overlooks. Highlights include a Concorde supersonic airliner; the *Enola Gay*, which dropped the atomic bomb on Hiroshima; and the only surviving Boeing 307 Stratoliner. There's also a collection of 45 aircraft engines and thousands of smaller artifacts such as uniforms, models, aerial cameras, and displays on famous aviators, including Charles Lindbergh and Amelia Earhart.

Off to one side, the 53,000-square-foot James S. McDonnell Space Hangar houses the museum's space collection, centered around the space shuttle *Discovery*, the longest serving orbiter, which flew 39 times from 1984 to 2011. Arrayed in three levels around *Discovery* are 113 other large spacecraft and rocketry artifacts, including a Spartan 201 satellite, a 69-foot Redstone rocket, sections of a Saturn V, a full-scale prototype of the Mars Pathfinder Lander, and the manned maneuvering unit used in the first-ever untethered space walk.

Elsewhere in the complex, SpaceWalk 2004 gives riders a simulated 3-D ride around the perimeter of the International Space Station, and an IMAX theater shows flight-related films throughout the day. For real flight action, take the elevator to the top of the 164-foot Donald D. Engen Observation Tower for air-traffic-controller views of planes landing and taking off at nearby Dulles International Airport.

WHERE: 25 miles west of Washington, D.C.; 14390 Air and Space Museum Pkwy. Tel 202-633-1000; airandspace.si.edu/visit/udvar-hazy-center. **BEST TIMES:** family days at the Udvar-Hazy Center, such as Space Day in early June, when visitors can meet and interact with an astronaut and NASA experts.

Jeffersonian Ideals in the Heart of the Virginia Wine Country

CHARLOTTESVILLE

Virginia

Along with penning the Declaration of Independence, Thomas Jefferson wished to be remembered in his epitaph as the father of the University of Virginia, whose development, building, and infancy occupied the last ten years of his life. Designed as a place where shared learning would infuse all of daily life (and now ranked as one of America's best public universities), the university occupies pride of place in Charlottesville, a town of some 44,000 that's one of the most enjoyable cities in the country. Here, lucky students attend classes in a UNESCO World Heritage Site that the American Institute of Architects has called the proudest achievement of American architecture.

Jefferson's beloved "academical village" was chartered in 1819 and opened as the country's first secular college in 1825, with 68 students and eight teachers. Then as now, the campus was centered on the long, grassy Lawn and its surrounding structures. At the head of the Lawn, Jefferson situated his distinctive Rotunda library, modeled after the Pantheon in Rome. Framing the Lawn, ten classical colonnaded Pavilions were designed to combine upstairs living quarters for professors and downstairs classrooms.

The outstanding Fralin Museum of Art at the University of Virginia, opened in 1935, sits amid the grand old fraternity houses on Rugby

Road, a block from the Rotunda. The permanent collection ranges from the 15th to 20th centuries with an emphasis on American works, especially those from 1775–1825, Jefferson's prime years. The 2-mile side trip to Jefferson's beloved Monticello is almost obligatory (see below).

Charlottesville sits at the center of the 1,500-acre Monticello Viticultural Area, one of Virginia's most important wine growing regions (Virginia is the fifth largest producer in the U.S. with 30 varieties of grapes grown here). Among the 40-some wineries, Barboursville

The Rotunda suffered a fire in 1895 and later an expansion, but was restored to Jefferson's original design in 1976.

Vineyards is the state's oldest and most scenic, anchored by the elegant 1804 Inn and acclaimed Palladio Restaurant. The Anglostyle Boar's Head Inn is a fine base, a 573-acre country resort with an 18-hole championship golf course and a top-rated tennis facility. Dine in the formal Old Mill Room, where the New American menu pairs well with some excellent wines from these very hills.

WHERE: 116 miles south of Washington, D.C. *Visitor info:* Tel 877-386-1103 or 434-293-6789; visitcharlottesville.org. **UNIVERSITY OF VIRGINIA:** Tel 434-924-0311; virginia.edu. **FRALIN MUSEUM OF ART:** Tel 434-924-3592;

virginia.edu/artmuseum. *When:* closed Mon. **BARBOURSVILLE VINEYARDS:** Tel 540-832-3824; bbvwine.com. *Cost:* suites at 1804 from $200; dinner at Palladio $80. **BOAR'S HEAD INN:** Tel 855-452-2295 or 434-296-2181; boarsheadinn.com. *Cost:* from $165 (off-peak), from $185 (peak). **BEST TIMES:** Apr for the local Dogwood Festival, Garden Week events, and the Steeplechase at Foxfield Races; Aug weekends for Barboursville Vineyards' annual "Shakespeare at the Ruins" festival; fall for the Virginia Film Festival (virginiafilmfestival.org) and Oct for Virginia Wine Month, when wineries across the state hold festivals.

In Pursuit of Life, Liberty, and Luxury

MONTICELLO

Charlottesville, Virginia

America's most famous historic home, Monticello was the dream house of Renaissance man Thomas Jefferson—visionary, principal author of the Declaration of Independence, founder of the University of Virginia, and America's third president. He designed the house over a 40-year period and said of it, "I am as happy nowhere else." Set on a hilltop overlooking Charlottesville and the 2,000 remaining acres of the Jefferson family's original 2,500-acre plantation, Monticello is one of America's outstanding architectural achievements, a gem that graces the back of the currency's nickel and serves as a kind of autobiography of the president who was known as a writer but chose not to pen the story of his life.

The three-story Palladian-style structure was entirely the product of Jefferson's own vision, begun in 1769 when he was just 26 and expanded and refined over four decades—especially after Jefferson's five-year stay in France as U.S. minister. The design that resulted was a blend of Italian and French styles, with elements that include the first dome on a residence in North America and an entrance hall filled with Indian artifacts, mastodon bones, and other relics from Lewis and Clark's expedition to the Pacific Ocean, a journey Jefferson himself had ordered. With a standard day pass, only the 11 first-floor rooms are open to the public; they look as if the owner had just stepped out for a stroll. With a Behind the Scenes day pass you can climb the narrow stairs for a guided tour of the upper floors. Touches of ingenuity and whimsy fill the place, from a handwriting copier and seven-day clock to an alcove bed that allowed Jefferson to rise in either of two rooms, depending on his mood.

After serving as president, Jefferson retired to Monticello, where he concentrated on the founding of the University of Virginia (see p. 238). He died here at age 83 on July 4, 1826, and is buried on the extensive grounds. These fields, orchards, and gardens reflect Jefferson's love of agriculture and landscape design. In 1807, he planted one of the earliest crops of European vinifera grapes in the New World, and today the Jefferson Vineyards offer tours and tastings daily. Stop by for lunch at the 1784 Michie Tavern, originally built as a stagecoach stop and today serving an all-you-can-eat colonial-style buffet.

End your day at Ash Lawn–Highland, the official residence of the fifth U.S. president, James Monroe, from 1799 to 1823. Overnighters can stay at the Clifton Inn, built in 1799 by Jefferson's son-in-law, and today offering 17 unique rooms and a well-regarded restaurant. For more opulence, head to Keswick Hall, a 1912 Italianate villa on a 600-acre spread that has been turned into an exclusive country resort. Accommodations are grand and guests are kept busy on the tennis courts and golf course (one of Arnold Palmer's favorites on the East Coast) and at the excellent restaurant, Fossett's.

WHERE: 4 miles southeast of Charlottesville. Tel 434-984-9800; monticello.org. **JEFFERSON VINEYARDS WINERY:** Tel 434-977-3042; jeffersonvineyards.com. **MICHIE TAVERN:** Tel 434-977-1234; michietavern.com. *Cost:* lunch buffet $18. **ASH LAWN–HIGHLAND:** Tel 434-293-8000; ashlawnhighland.org. **CLIFTON INN:** Tel 434-971-1800; cliftoninn.net. *Cost:* from $229 (off-peak), from $269 (peak); dinner $62. **KESWICK HALL:** Tel 888-778-2565 or 434-979-3440; keswick.com. *Cost:* from $279 (off-peak), from $449 (peak); dinner $58. **BEST TIME:** July 4th for the Monticello Independence Day Celebration and Naturalization Ceremony, when new U.S. citizens are sworn in.

A small brick pavilion marks the Thomas Jefferson vegetable garden at Monticello.

Real Old-Time Mountain Music

THE CROOKED ROAD MUSIC HERITAGE TRAIL

Virginia

I f your idea of "country music" includes smoke, lasers, and tight leather pants, then a visit to this rugged, slow-moving southwest corner of the state might just change your mind. You'll find one of the main taproots of American

music: traditional bluegrass and gospel songs passed down nearly unchanged through generations, still played in jam sessions in out-of-the-way venues along the corkscrewing back roads of the Appalachians. Once considered "hillbilly music," these songs and their players are now a recognized cultural treasure, and in southwestern Virginia a 333-mile driving route has been established, winding from one timeless musical venue, monument, or festival to another.

Opened in Clintwood in 2004, the Ralph Stanley Museum and Traditional Mountain Music Center celebrates the life and oeuvre of the local legend, bluegrass singer, and banjo picker whose work finally gained worldwide acclaim in the sound track to the 2000 film *O Brother, Where Art Thou?* and who performed with his band, The Clinch Mountain Boys, until his death in 2016.

In Hiltons, the renowned Carter Family, the royal family of country music, hosts performances at the Carter Family Fold, a covered, dirt-floored amphitheater with a capacity of about 1,000, that rings with the sounds of old-time harmonies and clog dancers every Saturday night. Alvin Pleasant Carter, the family patriarch, collected the haunting tunes he heard throughout Appalachia in the 1920s and went on to form the Carter Family with his wife, Sara, and sister-in-law Maybelle: Together they recorded over 300 classic songs between 1927 and 1942, including "Keep on

the Sunny Side." (Maybelle's daughter June went on to marry Johnny Cash.)

The Old Fiddler's Convention in Galax has grown from a small gathering in 1935 to a competitive event that draws thousands to the "World Capital of Old-Time Mountain Music." The tiny burg of Floyd hosts the weekly Friday Night Jamboree at the Floyd Country Store. Hardware cases are pushed aside and folding chairs set out, and at 7:30 P.M. the music and dancing start. The setting is almost too sincere for hardened city-dwellers to comprehend—smoking and alcoholic beverages are prohibited, and you won't hear a blue word all night.

WHERE: southwestern Virginia, near the North Carolina, Tennessee, and Kentucky borders. Tel 276-492-2409; thecrookedroad .org. **RALPH STANLEY MUSEUM:** Clintwood. Tel 276-926-8550; ralphstanleymuseum.com. *When:* closed Sun–Mon. **CARTER FAMILY FOLD:** Hiltons. Tel 276-386-6054; carterfamily fold.org. *When:* concerts Sat evenings. **OLD FIDDLER'S CONVENTION:** Galax. Tel 276-236-8541; oldfiddlersconvention.com. *When:* 6 days in early Aug. **FLOYD COUNTRY STORE:** Floyd. Tel 540-745-4563; floydcountrystore .com. *When:* Fri evenings. **BEST TIMES:** early Aug for the Galax Old Fiddler's Convention; 1st weekend in Aug for the annual Traditional Music Festival at the Carter Family Fold; Memorial Day weekend for Ralph Stanley's annual Hills of Home Festival (drralphstanley festival.com).

Wild Ponies in a Beautiful Land Across the Water

THE EASTERN SHORE & CHINCOTEAGUE

Virginia

Virginia's Eastern Shore, separated from mainland Virginia by the waters of Chesapeake Bay, forms the southern tip of the Delmarva Peninsula, the 180-mile spur of land that also holds all of Delaware, plus about a third of Maryland. This oft-forgotten corner of the state is a bit of a time warp consisting of rural farms, fishing towns, piney woods, and salt breezes. Roadside stands selling local produce and just-caught seafood run the length of U.S. 13, from the Chesapeake Bay Bridge-Tunnel at the southern end (connecting with Norfolk) to the Maryland border. The Atlantic side is some 50,000 acres comprising 14 barrier islands—most reachable only by boat—and is the largest stretch of unspoiled coastal wilderness in the country.

At the northern end of the shoreline on the island the Indians called Chincoteague (pronounced Shink-o-teeg, meaning "Beautiful Land Across the Water") is the Eastern Shore's largest community. It has achieved a measure of fame as the home of the wild horses—mistakenly called "ponies"—popularized in Marguerite Henry's 1947 children's book (and later movie) *Misty of Chincoteague*. They are thought to be the descendants of horses turned loose by 17th-century colonial settlers, stunted by centuries of drinking brackish water and eating salty marsh grass. The horses—some 300 strong—are separated into two herds, one occupying the southern end of neighboring Assateague Island (which is protected as Virginia's Chincoteague National Wildlife Refuge and is also an important birding destination) and the other occupying Assateague's northern half, in Maryland (see p. 118). During the yearly Pony Swim and Penning near the end of July, the Chincoteague Volunteer Fire Department herds the animals together to swim across the narrow channel from Assateague to Chincoteague. Then, in order to manage the herd's impact on the island ecology, some are auctioned off at the carnival grounds.

The town of Chincoteague blends touristy souvenir shops with the air of a fishing village—it's dotted with old-fashioned storefronts, hotels, and seafood restaurants, and there are active fishing and oystering fleets in its harbor. In early October—the beginning of oyster season—the popular Chincoteague Oyster Festival celebrates with a day of all-you-can-eat bivalves, plus lots of entertainment and contests. On Main Street, Miss Molly's Inn was the place Marguerite Henry boarded while writing *Misty of Chincoteague*. It's a cozy Victorian jewel with seven individually decorated rooms, five porches, and a large second-floor deck that's been looking out over the bay since 1894.

A wild horse grazes peacefully on Chincoteague.

WHERE: 170 miles southeast of Washington, D.C. *Eastern Shore visitor info:* Tel 757-331-1660; esvatourism.org. *Chincoteague visitor info:* Tel 757-336-6161; chincoteaguechamber.com. **MISS MOLLY'S INN:** Tel 800-221-5620 or 757-336-6686; missmollys-inn.com.

Cost: from $115 (off-peak), from $215 (peak). **BEST TIMES:** every Fri and Sat in July for the Fireman's Carnival; the last Wed–Thurs of July for the Pony Swim and Penning; early Oct for the Chincoteague Island Oyster Festival.

North America's Bloodiest Landscape

FREDERICKSBURG

Virginia

F redericksburg, the largest city between the former Confederate capital of Richmond and the Union capital of Washington, D.C., is best known for the terrible fighting that raged nearby during the four-year American Civil War,

when it changed hands no less than seven times. But Fredericksburg's history didn't start there. Founded in 1728, it was intimately associated with the most famous name in early American history, founding father George Washington.

Today, a 40-block National Historic District along the Rappahannock River preserves over 350 buildings from the 18th and 19th centuries, many of which are linked to George Washington's family. Here, you'll find the Mary Washington House, home of the president's mother for the last 17 years of her life. The legacy continues at the Hugh Mercer Apothecary Shop, where George was one of many patients who submitted to the Revolutionary-era surgeon's techniques, including leeches for bleeding and saffron to "quicken the brain." Washington himself lived from ages 6 to 19 at Ferry Farm across the river, before moving to Mount Vernon (see p. 250) in his early twenties. The farm is home to two of the more enduring myths of Washington's youth: throwing the silver dollar across the river and chopping down the cherry tree.

Between 1861 and 1865, some of the worst fighting of the Civil War took place within a day's ride of the city. Some 15,000 soldiers died and another 85,000 were wounded on the

four major battlefields that now make up the Fredericksburg and Spotsylvania National Military Park. A 15-mile driving tour connects the battlefields of Chancellorsville, the Wilderness, and Spotsylvania. During the Battle of Fredericksburg in December 1862, some 8,000 Union soldiers were mowed down by Lee's army during a futile assault on Marye's Heights, now the site of Fredericksburg National Cemetery. Witnessing the massacre prompted Robert E. Lee to say, "It is well that war is so terrible, or we should grow too fond of it."

WHERE: 53 miles south of Washington, D.C. *Visitor info:* Tel 800-678-4748 or 540-373-1776; visitfred.com. **MARY WASHINGTON HOUSE:** Tel 540-373-1569; washingtonheritagemuseums.org. **HUGH MERCER APOTHECARY:** Tel 540-373-3362; washingtonheritagemuseums.org. **FERRY FARM:** Tel 540-370-0732; kenmore.org. **FREDERICKSBURG AND SPOTSYLVANIA NATIONAL MILITARY PARK:** Tel 540-693-3200; nps.gov/frsp. **WHERE TO STAY:** The historic Kenmore Inn with pub and restaurant, tel 540-371-7622; kenmoreinn.com. *Cost:* from $130 (off-peak), from $155 (peak). **BEST TIME:** 4th of July weekend for the Heritage Festival with live music and food.

Jeffersonian Rejuvenation and Historic Hot Springs

THE HOMESTEAD

Hot Springs, Virginia

Follow in the footsteps of Thomas Jefferson for a sybaritic and therapeutic soak in mineral-rich 98°F waters—an experience akin to bathing in warm Perrier. The pools are part of Virginia's preeminent resort, The Omni Homestead, which was founded in 1766, and occupies 2,300 acres in the town of Hot Springs. Fresh from a $25 million renovation, the resort is renowned for a gorgeous setting, championship golf, and a host of other activities, in particular the natural hot springs that made it special in colonial days and continue to fill the hotel's magnificent indoor pool today (opened in 1904), as well as the twin Jefferson Pools, owned by the hotel and located 5 miles north in the town of Warm Springs. Used by native peoples for centuries, the springs began attracting Virginia's colonial elite in the early 1760s, their waters reputed to possess restorative powers. Thomas Jefferson came in 1818 to take the waters, spending three weeks and declaring the springs "of first merit." After a hot soak, visit the newly refurbished 34,000-square-foot Homestead Spa, which was one of the first European-style spas in the U.S. when it opened in 1892. Enjoy the kind of Swedish-style massage that's been offered here since its earliest days, or opt for an up-to-the-moment treatment like the exfoliating lemongrass body polish, followed by a rubdown with bergamot and wild lime oil in one of the 29 new treatment rooms.

The 483-room resort is centered around an impressive Georgian brick-and-limestone main building, its Great Hall distinguished by soaring columns, fireplaces, and comfy chairs. Rooms and suites have a relaxing but upscale air, and most offer views of the gorgeous Allegheny Mountains rising all around. Dinners are jacket-and-tie affairs, whether at the large, gracious formal dining room with its refined

Join the centuries-old tradition of "taking the waters" and enjoy a relaxing soak in the Homestead's indoor pool.

cuisine and piano music, or at the more intimate Jefferson's Restaurant & Bar, which offers regional American grilled meats, and views of the grounds. During the day, guests can choose from dozens of activities, from falconry, horseback riding, fishing the private 4-mile stocked stream to hiking and biking over 100 miles of trails. Winter activities include cross-country or downhill skiing and snowshoeing on a nine-trail mountain, the first in the South. Among the resort's three golf courses, the Cascades Course, designed by William S. Flynn in 1923 and site of seven USGA championships, is consistently ranked among the country's best. The resort's Old Course, completed in 1892, has the distinction of offering the oldest first tee in continuous use in the U.S.

WHERE: 96 miles west of Charlottesville; 7696 Sam Sneed Hwy. Tel 800-838-1766 or 540-839-1766; omnihotels.com. *Cost:* from $180 (off-peak), from $220 (peak). **BEST TIMES:** spring for flowers; fall for foliage.

Genteel Reminders of a Time Long Past

JAMES RIVER PLANTATIONS

Virginia

In the 17th and 18th centuries, the fertile banks of the lower James River below Richmond were the province of colonial and early American gentry, who built imposing Great Houses at the center of enormous tobacco plantations. It was a world of contrast, where the toil of thousands of slaves and servants supported a small landowning aristocracy who lived in great wealth and privilege. When slavery ended after the Civil War, that society collapsed, but many of the great houses have been restored and are now open to the public. You can see many along scenic Route 5 (aka the John Tyler Highway), which winds from Richmond through bucolic Charles City County to historic Williamsburg (see p. 255).

Shirley Plantation, Virginia's oldest, and the oldest family-owned business in North America (dating to 1638), is anchored by an early Georgian mansion built between 1723 and 1738. It survived Indian uprisings, the Revolutionary War, the Civil War, and the Great Depression. It's still owned by the Hill-Carter family (descendents of Robert E. Lee), and is chock-full of family portraits, silver, and antique furniture and woodwork. A unique square "flying" stairway—the only one in North America—ascends three stories without any visible means of support.

Berkeley Plantation, set on a beautifully landscaped hilltop just downriver, has seen as much history as any place in Virginia. It was the site of America's first Thanksgiving celebration, on December 4, 1619, when Capt. John Woodlief of the Berkeley Hundred colony instructed his people that the day of their arrival from sea should be "perpetually kept holy as a day of thanksgiving to the Almighty God." (The Plymouth Pilgrims' harvest feast, held in 1621, actually became the model for Americans' yearly Thanksgiving holiday; see p. 64.) The mansion at the Berkeley Plantation was built in 1726 by Benjamin Harrison IV, grandfather of William Henry Harrison, ninth president of the U.S. and great-great-grandfather of Benjamin Harrison, the nation's 23rd president. Today, the house is restored to its 18th-century appearance, with period antiques inside and five outstanding terraced gardens, planted before the Revolution.

Sherwood Forest is the only home owned by two U.S. presidents, William Henry Harrison and John Tyler; the latter took over both the presidency and the property when Harrison died after a month in office. The white clapboard building is the longest wood-framed house in the country, with scars in the woodwork that bear witness to Civil War fighting. Ask about the Gray Lady, whose ghostly rocking has been reported in the Gray Room for over 200 years.

SHIRLEY PLANTATION: Charles City is 26 miles east of Richmond. Tel 804-829-5121; shirleyplantation.com. **BERKELEY PLANTATION:** Charles City. Tel 888-466-6018 or 804-829-6018; berkeleyplantation.com. **SHERWOOD FOREST PLANTATION:** Charles City. Tel 804-829-5377; sherwoodforest.org. **BEST TIMES:** mid- to late Apr for Historic Garden Week (vagardenweek.org), when the gardens and grounds at Berkeley and other James River Plantations are at their peak; early Nov for Berkeley's First Thanksgiving Festival.

Where America Was Born—Twice

JAMESTOWN & YORKTOWN

Virginia

Before the Pilgrims landed in Plymouth, Massachusetts (see p. 64), a group of 104 English settlers led by Capt. John Smith sailed for the New World seeking gold and a water route to the Orient. They landed on May 14, 1607,

on Jamestown Island, where they established a fort and later a town. Poor planning, sickness, and understandably hostile Indian tribes nearly caused the colony to fail, but through luck and strong leadership, it managed to hang on until the English foothold in the New World was secure.

The settlement is preserved as Historic Jamestowne, a part of Colonial National Historical Park that displays foundations and artifacts uncovered during decades of ongoing study and excavation. Visitors can see the triangular footprint of the original fort (rediscovered only in 1996); a 1647 brick church tower that's the only surviving 17th-century structure at Jamestown; and a working reproduction of the original 1608 glassblowers' workshop. The visitor center's museum is worth a visit for its collection of 17th-century colonial artifacts.

Near the entrance to Historic Jamestowne is the state-managed Jamestown Settlement, a living history museum with expansive galleries

chronicling Jamestown's origins, the colony's first century, and the convergence of cultures in 17th-century Virginia. Interpreters in traditional dress explain native life in the Powhatan Indian village where Pocahontas was born, and the roar of matchlock muskets echoes from the re-created James Fort. In between are life-sized reproductions of the *Discovery, Godspeed,* and *Susan Constant,* the small sailing ships that transported the colonists across the Atlantic.

The 23-mile Colonial Parkway, a scenic, forest-lined driving/bicycling highway, connects Jamestown with the other two towns of Virginia's "Historic Triangle": Colonial Williamsburg (see p. 255) and Yorktown, 25 miles east. One of the Virginia colony's major ports in the 18th century, Yorktown gained its most lasting fame as the site of the last battle of the American Revolution, when on October 19, 1781, British General Cornwallis marched his men ("much in liquor," according to one witness) across Surrender Field and capitulated to George Washington, setting a new country off and running. The park museum holds Washington's field tents and a rifle stock broken by a British soldier in disgust. Across U.S. 17 from Yorktown, still a working village, sits the Yorktown Victory Center, where museum exhibits lead to a re-created Continental Army encampment and a modest reconstructed farm, typical of life in the late 18th century.

WHERE: Jamestown is 58 miles southeast of Richmond. **COLONIAL NATIONAL HISTORICAL PARK:** Tel 757-898-2410; nps.gov/colo. **JAMESTOWN-YORKTOWN FOUNDATION:** Tel 888-593-4682 or 757-253-4838; historyisfun.org.

Costumed interpreters demonstrate 17th-century military drills.

commemorating Washington's victory over Cornwallis with parades, costumed skirmishes, and military drills.

Equestrian Oasis Beyond the Beltway

HUNT COUNTRY

Leesburg, Virginia

It may be only a few dozen miles from D.C., but northern Virginia's Loudoun County is a world away in attitude. Known as Hunt Country ever since colonial lords first followed packs of braying hounds across the lush, rolling countryside, this area is still home to some of the country's wealthiest folks, many of whom carry on a strong equestrian tradition. The landscape is laced with long wooden fences, stone walls, and centuries-old dirt lanes leading to hidden ancestral homes. Antiques shops and tack stores fill the main streets of the villages.

Leesburg, with a population of almost 50,000, is Hunt Country's largest city. It served as an outfitting post during the French and Indian Wars of the 17th and 18th centuries and was named for Robert E. Lee's ancestors. Among the 18th- and 19th-century buildings in its downtown historic district is Lightfoot Restaurant, serving southern-accented New American food inside a circa-1888 Romanesque Revival bank. Nearby Waterford on the banks of Catoctin Creek is postcard-perfect. Most of the quiet village has been declared a National Historic Landmark. Middleburg—located halfway along the stagecoach route from Alexandria to Winchester—seems to have changed very little since it was founded in 1787. It's still a one-stoplight place—equal parts quaint and upscale—and home to the Red Fox Inn, the second-oldest tavern in the country. Begun as Mr. Chinn's Ordinary in 1728, it has hosted everyone from a young George Washington to JFK, who occasionally held press conferences here. The first-floor restaurant is a favorite of hunt folks for its dark, cozy atmosphere and signature dishes like peanut soup and Maryland crabcakes.

A meandering drive outside Middleburg leads you to the bucolic Goodstone Inn, an ultra-luxurious 265-acre country estate that was first established in 1768, and which supplied provisions to the Continental Army during the Revolutionary War. A working dairy and livestock farm for its entire history, the estate became an inn in 1998. It offers tastefully furnished rooms and suites in six restored buildings, including the former stables and a French-style farm cottage.

Where: 40 miles west of Washington, D.C. *Visitor info:* Tel 800-752-6118 or 703-771-2170; visitloudoun.org. **Lightfoot:** Tel 703-771-2233; lightfootrestaurant.com. *Cost:* lunch $25. **Red Fox Inn:** Middleburg. Tel 540-687-6301; redfox.com. *Cost:* rooms from $175; dinner $45. **Goodstone Inn:** Middleburg. Tel 877-219-4663 or 540-687-3333; goodstone.com. *Cost:* from $275 (off-peak), from $325 (peak); dinner $50. **Best times:** late May for the Hunt Country Stable Tour (trinityupperville.org/hunt-country-stable-tour); Oct for the Virginia Fall Races (vafall races.com) in Middleburg, Epicurience Virginia (epicvirginia.com), and the Waterford Fair (water fordvillage.org/waterford-fair.htm), Virginia's oldest juried crafts fair; early Sept for the Leesburg Food & Wine Festival.

Gracious Mountain City, Civil War Shrine

LEXINGTON

Virginia

ocated in the heart of the beautiful Shenandoah River valley (see p. 252), gracious Lexington is one of the best-preserved historic communities in Virginia, a charming college town, steeped in Civil War history.

Its downtown historic district takes visitors back to the 1800s, its streets lined with dignified homes and restored 19th-century commercial buildings.

Founded in 1777, the city was an educational hub almost from its beginning, home to the Virginia Military Institute, the first state military college in the country (in 1839) and often known as the "West Point of the South." Thomas "Stonewall" Jackson, who later gained fame as one of the Confederacy's most revered generals, taught here from 1851 until the beginning of the Civil War. The VMI Museum houses a collection of Jackson's personal belongings, including his favorite hat, items from his VMI classroom, and his taxidermied warhorse, Little Sorrel. Today, crew-cut cadets still drill on the huge central Parade Ground, surrounded by the academy's crenellated stone-and-brick buildings (look for review parades held here most Friday afternoons). Jackson

Lee Chapel was built during 1867–1868 at the request of Robert E. Lee.

lived in a brick building on East Washington Street, now the Stonewall Jackson House Museum, with displays that tell the story of his time here. A brilliant but quirky commander, he was accidentally killed by his own troops during the battle of Chancellorsville in May 1863 and is buried in a cemetery located at the south end of Main Street.

After the Civil War, Confederate general-in-chief Robert E. Lee accepted the presidency of Washington College, today known as Washington & Lee University. He served until his death in 1870, and is buried in a simple Romanesque chapel on the compact but beautiful grounds of the university.

One of the area's top tourist attractions, the 215-foot-tall limestone span of Natural Bridge is just south of Lexington. Called "The Bridge of God" by Indian tribes, it was once owned by Thomas Jefferson. You can hike down the trail to the stream-cut base of the 36,000-ton formation and look at a set of initials carved into the stone by a young surveyor named George Washington (yes, that George Washington).

WHERE: 190 miles southwest of Washington, D.C. *Visitor info:* Tel 540-463-3777; lexington virginia.com. **VIRGINIA MILITARY INSTITUTE:** Tel 540-464-7230; vmi.edu. **STONEWALL JACKSON HOUSE:** Tel 540-464-7704; stonewalljackson .org. **WASHINGTON & LEE UNIVERSITY:** Tel 540-458-8400; wlu.edu. **LEE CHAPEL AND MUSEUM:** Tel 540-458-8768; wlu.edu/lee-chapel-and-museum. **NATURAL BRIDGE:** Tel 800-533-1410 or 540-291-2121; naturalbridgeva.com. **BEST TIME:** fall for foliage.

Bookends of the Civil War

MANASSAS & APPOMATTOX

Virginia

The alpha and omega of America's greatest calamity, the towns of Manassas and Appomattox, located 149 miles apart in northern and central Virginia, respectively, saw the beginning and conclusion of the four-year Civil War that would tear the country apart and birth political, social, and racial fissures that are still playing out today. Through it all, Virginia was at the center, home to both the Confederate capital and some of the worst battles of the war.

In the summer of 1861, fighting broke out among gentle hills near the vital railroad junction of Manassas, just 32 miles west of Washington, D.C. Several days later, the First Battle of Bull Run, also called First Manassas, pitted 28,450 Union troops against 32,230 Confederates. The Union troops were forced to retreat, finding themselves entangled with the carriages of confused civilians on the roads back to the capital. The Civil War had begun in earnest. A little over a year later, Gen. Robert E. Lee and his 55,000 men defeated Gen. John Pope here at the Second Battle of Bull Run (Second Manassas), even though at one point the Confederate troops were reduced to throwing rocks.

Start your visit at the Henry Hill Visitor Center, named for 85-year-old Judith Henry, who refused to leave her home during the first battle despite having Rebel sharpshooters firing from her windows. The 1-mile loop trail of the First Manassas battlefield passes a statue of Gen. Thomas Jackson, who earned his everlasting nickname during the battle when Gen. Bernard Bee saw him refusing to give up the hill and remarked, "There stands Jackson, like a stone wall." A driving tour connects nine nearby sites of Second Manassas.

Despite Robert E. Lee's brilliant military tactics, the Confederate army proved no

Confederate Cavalry Lieutenant General Wade Hampton was among the many wounded at the Battle of First Manassas.

match for the Union's overwhelming advantages in manpower and manufacturing. Lee surrendered to Gen. Ulysses S. Grant on April 9, 1865, in the tiny town of Appomattox Court House. Today, the village of Appomattox Court House has been restored to its 1865 appearance, including a reconstruction of the McLean House where the actual surrender took place.

WHERE: Manassas is 32 miles southwest of Washington, D.C. **MANASSAS NATIONAL BATTLEFIELD PARK:** Tel 703-361-1339; nps.gov/mana. **APPOMATTOX COURT HOUSE NATIONAL HISTORICAL PARK:** Tel 434-352-8987; nps.gov/apco. **BEST TIMES:** summer months at Appomattox for living history presentations and ranger talks; late Aug for the annual 2-day commemoration and reenactment of the Second Manassas.

George Washington Slept Here

MOUNT VERNON

Virginia

George Washington may have a towering memorial to his name in the heart of Washington, D.C. (see p. 264), but off across the Potomac sits a more personal memorial raised by his own hand and reflecting his strong, virtuous, independent, and wholly American character. It is Mount Vernon, Washington's home, set on land originally granted to his great-grandfather in 1674. Washington inherited the estate in 1761 at the age of 29, and over the next four decades gradually expanded it to 8,000 acres, making it one of the finest plantations in Virginia. Like Thomas Jefferson and many other 18th-century gentlemen, Washington himself acted as architect and planner, creating a home for himself and Martha and forging an image of substance, probity, and prosperity that would propel him first into the ranks of colonial society and later into the history books. After commanding the Continental Army and serving as the country's first president, Washington was finally able to return home, spending two quiet years with Martha before dying in his bed on December 14, 1799, at age 67.

Today, as then, the main house at Mount Vernon sits on a hillside, enjoying such a dramatic view over the Potomac that Washington once remarked, "No estate in America is more pleasantly situated than this." The grand three-story mansion has 21 rooms, a two-story columned porch, and a cupola topped with a dove-shaped weathervane, symbolizing peace. Rooms are in their original bright shades of green and blue, and numerous original pieces, including a swivel chair Washington used during his presidency and a large globe that sat in his study, have been tracked down and returned to their rightful spots.

A variety of outbuildings occupies the grounds of the now-500-acre estate, including a kitchen, a stable, a smokehouse, a restored version of Washington's whiskey still, and the quarters that housed the 316 slaves Washington owned at his death. Since Mount Vernon is still a working farm, there are also a barnyard full of animals, thriving gardens, and a reconstructed 16-sided barn. The president's and Martha's tomb is also on the property, its markers stating simply "Washington" and "Martha, consort of Washington."

Getting to Mount Vernon can be half the fun. In addition to driving, you can bike there along the 18-mile Mount Vernon Trail from Memorial Bridge in Washington, D.C.

WHERE: 18 miles south of Washington, D.C. Tel 703-780-2000; mountvernon.org. **BEST TIMES:** Feb 22 for George Washington's birthday celebration and wreath-laying ceremony; July 4th for Independence Day celebrations; late Nov–Dec for period holiday decorations and traditions and tours by candlelight.

Under Washington's care, Mount Vernon grew into one of Virginia's most prominent plantations in the 18th century.

Grand Dame of the Confederacy

HISTORIC RICHMOND

Virginia

Here in the capital of the Commonwealth of Virginia, Civil War ghosts bump up against chic nightclubs, and some of the state's best restaurants inhabit century-old buildings near the rapids of the James River

downtown. During the war, Richmond served as capital of the Confederacy under Confederate President Jefferson Davis. That all ended in April 1865, when Ulysses S. Grant marched in and retreating Confederate troops burned much of the city. Afterward, Richmond began to rebuild with help from the tobacco and iron (and later banking) industries. Today, the city is a hub of the New South, balancing preservation of its long history with a modern vibrancy.

Any tour of historic Richmond should start at the White House and Museum of the Confederacy, home to the largest collection of Confederate artifacts in the world, including Stonewall Jackson's revolver and the sword Robert E. Lee wore to the surrender at Appomattox (see p. 249). In nearby Capitol Square stands the Virginia State Capitol, designed by Thomas Jefferson and begun in 1785. The Executive Mansion to one side is the oldest continually inhabited governor's residence in America, in use since 1813.

The city's Civil War history and more is detailed at the Richmond Battlefield National Park, whose main visitors center occupies the brick Tredegar Iron Works buildings on the northern bank of the James River. Three floors of displays include high-tech animated battle maps and Civil War artifacts.

For the full experience, reserve a room at the Jefferson Hotel, built as the finest hotel in the country in 1895 by Major Lewis Ginter, founder of the American Tobacco Company. The 36-step central staircase in the ornate rotunda lobby leads to a life-size statue of

Downtown Richmond today is a medley of historic buildings and modern high-rises.

Thomas Jefferson under a Tiffany stained-glass dome in the Palm Court, where live alligators once splashed in the pool. The hotel's formal Lemaire restaurant is one of the finest in the state (and one of four at the hotel), offering an excellent Sunday brunch and a dinner menu that mixes an occasional French technique with regional dishes such as chicken-fried oysters and Chesapeake Bay soft-shell crab.

WHERE: 129 miles south of Washington, D.C. *Visitor info:* Tel 804-783-7450; visit richmond.va.com. **WHITE HOUSE AND MUSEUM OF THE CONFEDERACY:** Tel 804-649-1861; moc.org. **STATE CAPITOL:** Tel 804-698-1788; virginiacapitol.gov. **RICHMOND BATTLEFIELD:** Tel 804-226-1981; nps.gov/rich. **JEFFERSON HOTEL:** Tel 888-918-1895 or 804-649-4750; jeffersonhotel.com. *Cost:* from $305; dinner $55. **BEST TIMES:** early Apr for the Virginia Horse Festival at Meadow Event Park (virginia horsefestival.com); late Sept for the 10-day State Fair of Virginia at Meadow Event Park.

Valley of the Daughter of the Stars

SHENANDOAH VALLEY

Virginia

The name "Shenandoah"—a native word many believe means "daughter of the stars"—has long been attached to the mountainous region in western Virginia; to the fertile, 200-mile-long valley west of it; and to the lazy river that flows between them to the Potomac. Although memories linger of some of the worst fighting of the Civil War, today the Shenandoah—all of it—is one of the state's most enchanting regions.

Shenandoah National Park, a nearly 300-square-mile patch between the Allegheny Mountains to the west and the Blue Ridge Mountains to the east, is one of the country's most popular parks. Herbert Hoover, riding horseback along the crest of the Blue Ridge, was said to have remarked, "These mountains are made for a road." That came to pass in 1939 with the completion of the 105-mile Skyline Drive, which offers views that Hoover called "the greatest in the world." It winds among some 60 rugged peaks, running alongside the Appalachian Trail (see p. 332) for about 100 miles and connecting up with the Blue Ridge Parkway (see p. 236) at the park's southern border; from there the parkway continues all the way to Great Smoky Mountains National Park, in North Carolina.

Most visitors are content with the endless views over hazy farmland from the roadway's 75 balcony-like scenic overlooks, but those who get off the pavement find over 500 miles of hiking trails. Like the hardwood forests of New England, the Blue Ridge Mountains are home to sycamores, hickories, oaks, and maples that in autumn put on a breathtaking display of color. Skyland Resort was founded in 1894 at the park's highest peak and still offers spectacular views and comfortably rustic accommodations, plus Shenandoah staples like fresh trout and country ham in its restaurant.

Of the valley's many limestone caves, the most impressive are the landmark Luray Caverns. They're one of the most-visited caves in the East, with nearly translucent stone drapery, a 170-ton fallen stalactite, and the 2,500-square-foot Dream Lake, which is less than 20 inches deep. The caverns' "stalacpipe organ," which uses electronically controlled rubber mallets striking natural stalactites to produce tones, covers 3.5 acres, earning it a listing in *Guinness World Records* as the world's largest musical instrument.

WHERE: The valley runs from Front Royal (70 miles west of Washington, D.C.) in the north to Roanoke in the south. **SHENANDOAH NATIONAL PARK:** Tel 540-999-3500; nps.gov/shen. **SKYLAND RESORT:** Tel 877-847-1919

White-tailed deer graze in the 199,017-acre Shenandoah National Park.

or 571-255-7761; goshenandoah.com/lodging/ skyland. *Cost:* from $105. *When:* late Mar–Nov. **LURAY CAVERNS:** Tel 540-743-6551; luray caverns.com. **BEST TIMES:** late spring for blooming wildflowers; mid-Oct for vibrant foliage; 2nd Sat in Oct for Front Royal's Festival of Leaves.

Presidential Birthplace and Shenandoah Shakespeare

STAUNTON

Virginia

Almost exactly in the middle of Virginia's Shenandoah Valley (see previous page), Staunton (STAN-ton) is an attractive town that managed to avoid much of the destruction other cities in the region suffered during the Civil War. As a result, the modest-size city with a population of 25,000 has no fewer than five National Historic Districts filled with mid- and late-19th-century architecture, arranged across a series of hills above a railroad-era downtown. Woodrow Wilson, who served as president from 1913 to 1921, was born here in 1856, and his boyhood home is one of the few original presidential birthplaces open to the public. At an adjacent mansion, the museum of the Wilson Presidential Library holds a collection of Wilson's personal effects, such as his battered briefcase and favorite 1919 Pierce-Arrow limousine.

Staunton is a lovely showcase of 19th-century architectural styles.

After a morning spent perusing presidential memorabilia, you might pause at the 16th-century London theater located in the center of town. Its existence is credited to a touring Virginia Shakespeare company that in 1999 embarked on an ambitious plan to re-create the two London theaters most closely associated with the Bard: the open-air Globe Theatre (still in the planning stages) and the enclosed 300-seat Blackfriars Playhouse, co-owned by Shakespeare in the early 17th century. It's all part of the American Shakespeare Center, one of the premier Shakespearean venues in the country, presenting the Bard's works as they were performed in old London: on an unadorned stage where the actors share the same light as the audience. The result is an intimate—and authentic—experience, brought to life by the internationally acclaimed resident troupe.

For a real treat, swing by Mrs. Rowe's Family Restaurant, serving heaping helpings of down-home cooking, from fresh-baked biscuits and spoon bread to fried chicken and fried country ham steak.

WHERE: 157 miles southwest of Washington, D.C. *Visitor info:* Tel 800-342-7982 or 540-332-3865; visitstaunton.com. **WILSON PRESIDENTIAL LIBRARY:** Tel 540-885-0897; woodrowwilson.org. **BLACKFRIARS PLAYHOUSE:** Tel 877-MUCH-ADO or 540-851-1733; americanshakespearecenter.com. *Cost:* tickets from $20. **MRS. ROWE'S:** Tel 540-886-1833; mrsrowes.net. *Cost:* lunch $15. **BEST TIME:** 10 days mid-Aug for the Staunton Music Festival (stauntonmusicfestival.org).

Gourmet Sanctuary in the Blue Ridge Foothills

THE INN AT LITTLE WASHINGTON

Washington, Virginia

Great oaks from tiny acorns grow—if you give them the right care. That's the lesson behind the Inn at Little Washington, which opened in 1978 in a converted garage, with a self-taught chef in the kitchen, and has since managed to garner universal acclaim as one of the best, most romantic restaurants and country inns in the world. The setting, of course, helped. Laid out in 1749 by a 17-year-old surveyor named George Washington (yes, that one), the town of Washington looks today much as it did more than a century and a half ago, with roughly the same population it had in 1795 (around 180). Located in the foothills of the Blue Ridge Mountains and in the middle of Virginia Hunt Country (see p. 247), it's a place of timeless, rustic charm, just over an hour drive from Washington—big Washington.

The inn itself was the inspiration of chef Patrick O'Connell and Reinhardt Lynch, who created every aspect of its operations, from the formally dressed greeter at the modest entrance

Chef Patrick O'Connell incorporates local ingredients in a creative and inspired menu.

to the sumptuous decor by London designer Joyce Evans. It's a fantasy atmosphere, a distillation of the world's great country-house traditions that draws a steady stream of D.C. types, celebrities, and world-traveled gourmands, for whom sky-high prices are either an irrelevance or an attraction.

O'Connell's sublime cuisine defies pigeon-holing, highlighting ingredients and recipes from the Virginia countryside, at times appearing regional or country and at others nouvelle or haute American. Dishes are presented simply and service is precise and expertly paced, though friendly and with a sense of humor. The decor of the dining room is a Venetian-inspired dream, with 30 intimate tables, striped silk wall coverings, antique wall sconces, and a jewel-toned Oriental rug created specifically for the room. Order from the 14,000-bottle wine list and prepare to be amazed.

Repair to any of the inn's 24 exquisite bedrooms and suites, where Victorian eclecticism mixes with touches of whimsy. Twelve rooms are within the inn itself, and ten others occupy historic buildings just steps away.

If there's no room at the inn, just a few blocks down Main Street the Middleton Inn is a beautifully appointed brick estate home built in 1850 by Middleton Miller, who designed and manufactured the Confederate uniform during the Civil War.

WHERE: 69 miles west of Washington, D.C.; Middle and Main Sts. Tel 540-675-3800; theinnatlittlewashington.com. *Cost:* from

$505 (off-peak), from $630 (peak); prix-fixe dinner from $178. **MIDDLETON INN:** Tel 800-816-8157 or 540-675-2020; middletoninn .com. *Cost:* from $325. **BEST TIMES:** late May

for the annual Hunt Country Stable Tour, when private horse farms in the Middleburg area open to the public for 2 days; Oct for foliage.

A Typical Day in the 18th Century

COLONIAL WILLIAMSBURG

Williamsburg, Virginia

Colonial Williamsburg meticulously re-creates the crucial period of 1750 to 1775, the end of the colonial era and the anxious eve of the Revolutionary War. The level of detail is astonishing, from the actors who portray Revolutionary-era statesmen, blacksmiths, wig makers, and slaves to the flocks of squawking ducks and grazing sheep. It's the country's largest and most popular living history museum and one of the world's finest.

The cultural and political capital of Virginia from 1699 to 1780, Williamsburg was home to government buildings and a lively social scene among the colonial aristocracy. Thomas Jefferson and George Washington both spent time here debating the merits of forming an independent country. In 1926, John D. Rockefeller Jr. initiated a top-to-bottom $68 million restoration in which 88 original buildings and 500 other structures were restored or rebuilt, along with 90 acres of gardens and public greens. Today, it's impossible to tell which of the buildings were restored and which were totally reconstructed on their original foundations.

Williamsburg is a treat for both adults and kids. Walking the cobbled streets of the Historic Area, you might find yourself having an impromptu discussion with "Thomas Jefferson," "Martha Washington," or one of the wide cast of townspeople going about their daily lives. You can attend the trial of a pig thief; watch a gunsmith craft a flintlock rifle; sign up for a candlelit tour of the city's haunted spots; or view a

Thomas Jefferson was the last resident to live in the Governor's Palace before the capital was relocated to Richmond in 1780.

performance by the town's parading fife-and-drum corps. Tour the Georgian-style Governor's Palace with its extensive topiary gardens and holly maze, the H-shaped Capitol, the Courthouse of 1770 with its pillories and stocks out front, and the George Wythe House, home to Thomas Jefferson in 1776, when he was a Virginia General Assembly delegate. Stop for a tipple at any of the four historic taverns offering colonial dishes in period settings.

Built in 19th-century Regency style and furnished with exquisite reproduction furniture, the august 1937 Williamsburg Inn was created as part of the town's restoration and has hosted notables from queens to presidents since its earliest days. Three stellar golf courses at the nearby Golden Horseshoe Golf Club include the Gold Course, one of Robert Trent Jones Sr.'s finest. The Williamsburg Foundation also offers guest rooms in 26 restored colonial homes as accommodations, each with its own unique history.

Nearby is family fun of another sort: Busch Gardens, home to some of the highest-rated roller coasters in the country and great animal viewing. You can visit the gray wolves and marvel at the size of the Anheuser-Busch Clydesdales, each of which stands at least 6 feet tall and weighs between 1,800 and 2,000 pounds. About 5 miles south of Williamsburg is the Williamsburg Winery, Virginia's first modern winery in the state. It helped to launch the area's now-flourishing wine industry, numbering some 230 vineyards.

Where: 150 miles south of Washington, D.C. Tel 888-965-7254 or 757-220-7645; colonialwilliamsburg.com. **Williamsburg Inn & Colonial Houses:** Tel 888-965-7254 or 757-220-7978; colonialwilliamsburg.com. *Cost:* inn from $409 (off-peak), from $499 (peak); houses from $199 (off-peak), from $219 (peak). **Busch Gardens Williamsburg:** Tel 800-343-7946; buschgardens.com. *Cost:* $77. *When:* daily late May–early Sept; weekends Apr–May, Sept–Oct. **Williamsburg Winery:** Tel 757-229-0999; williamsburg winery.com. **Best time:** Dec for Williamsburg's Christmas celebration.

Home of the Great Washington Dinner Party

Historic Georgetown

Washington, D.C.

Established on the shores of the Potomac in 1751, Georgetown flourished first as a port town and later as a depot for military supplies during the Revolution. It was incorporated into the newly created District of Columbia in 1791, and has been a center for D.C.'s social and diplomatic life since the early 19th century. This was where Jack and Jackie Kennedy lived, where late *Washington Post* publisher Katharine Graham held court, and where Bob Woodward and John Kerry have homes today.

Georgetown is full of shady, tree-lined side streets where the architecture follows the curve of national styles, from early Georgian through Federal and Classical Revival to the ornate structures of the mid-19th century. The neighborhood's oldest building—and in fact, the oldest in all the District—is the Old Stone House, built as a shop and residence for cabinetmaker Christopher Layman in 1765 and now sitting in the middle of Georgetown's busiest shopping and dining area. Step inside to catch a glimpse of colonial middle-class life.

To the north, Tudor Place was built in 1816 by George and Martha Washington's granddaughter, Martha Custis Peter. Using an $8,000 legacy from the father of our country, she commissioned architect William Thornton, who also designed the U.S. Capitol, to design the grand, neoclassical house. The rooms are furnished as they appeared during the occupancy of the last owners, from the early 1920s to 1983. Outdoors, the house's pillared, domed portico entrance overlooks one of the last intact urban estates from the Federal period.

Not far away, the 1801 Federal-style house known as Dumbarton Oaks was the spot where U.S., British, Soviet, and Chinese representatives met in 1944 to plan the United Nations. It's surrounded by 10 acres of formal gardens that incorporate elements of French, English, and Italian garden design. The house and collection amassed by Robert and Mildred Woods was given to Harvard University. Its collections of Byzantine and pre-Columbian art are on public display, and the gardens are also open to the public.

Sitting regally among this Georgetown enclave is the turreted, ivy-covered campus of Georgetown University, the oldest Jesuit university in the country and world-acclaimed for its law school and School of Foreign Service. Those students rushing off to class come from all corners of the world to follow in the footsteps of respected alumni such as Bill Clinton.

Get a taste of Georgetown history at Martin's Tavern, a dark, cozy restaurant/bar that opened in 1933 and has served every president from Harry S. Truman to George W. Bush.

Proudly kept-up brick townhouses are a hallmark of Georgetown architecture.

WHERE: Georgetown is bordered by R St. to the north, the Potomac River to the south, Rock Creek Park to the east, and Georgetown University to the west. **OLD STONE HOUSE:** Tel 202-895-6070; nps.gov/olst. **TUDOR PLACE:** Tel 202-965-0400; tudorplace.org. *When:* closed Mon; closed Jan. **DUMBARTON OAKS:** Tel 202-339-6401; doaks.org. *When:* closed Mon. **MARTIN'S TAVERN:** Tel 202-333-7370; martinstavern.com. *Cost:* dinner $40. **BEST TIMES:** spring for Dumbarton Oaks gardens; early Oct for the annual Taste of Georgetown Festival (tasteofgeorgetown.com).

Modernists in a Neoclassical Land

THE HIRSHHORN MUSEUM & THE PHILLIPS COLLECTION

Washington, D.C.

The National Mall is lined with museums, but you won't be able to miss the Hirshhorn: It's the one that looks like a cylindrical tank, standing out among its Victorian and neoclassical neighbors. The museum had its birth as the private passion of financier Joseph H. Hirshhorn, who began collecting art at the age of 18 (two engravings by Albrecht Dürer) and by the 1960s had accumulated holdings that spanned the breadth of modernism. In 1966, Hirshhorn donated 6,000 pieces to the

Smithsonian Institution, forming the basis of the museum that bears his name. Today the museum's collection has more than doubled, its circular galleries holding works by Francis Bacon, Alexander Calder, Alberto Giacometti, Barbara Kruger, Auguste Rodin, and hundreds of others. About 250 pieces are on display at any one time. Outside, its tree-shaded Sculpture Garden and Plaza displays roughly

Architect Gordon Bunshaft designed the Hirshhorn Museum.

60 large-scale works. Farther afield from the Mall, the small, personal Phillips Collection was the country's first modern art museum, opened by collector Duncan Phillips in a wing of his beautiful Dupont Circle home in 1921. Within ten years, his collection had grown to the point that his family moved out, allowing the entire house to be converted for public use. More than nine decades later the works are displayed in oak-paneled galleries both in the original Georgian-revival house and in an annex built in 1960. Another expansion, completed in 2006, added nearly 12,000 feet of gallery space. The museum is particularly known for its impressionist and Post-Impressionist paintings, including Renoir's monumental *Luncheon of the Boating Party.*

HIRSHHORN: Independence Ave. at 7th St. SW. Tel 202-633-1000; hirshhorn.si.edu. **PHILLIPS COLLECTION:** 1600 21st St. NW. Tel 202-387-2151; phillipscollection.org. *When:* closed Mon. **BEST TIME:** Sun in Oct–May for the Phillips's classical music series.

Lest We Forget

HOLOCAUST MUSEUM

Washington, D.C.

In Europe, between 1939 and 1945, government-sponsored racism and hatred were responsible for the murder of 6 million Jews, 1.9 million non-Jewish Poles, about 220,000 Roma and Sinti, nearly 200,000 disabled people,

and hundreds of thousands of homosexuals, political dissidents, members of minority religious groups, and prisoners of war. We must never forget. And we must never allow it to happen again.

That's the message of the U.S. Holocaust Memorial Museum, which opened in 1993 just south of the Washington Monument. Architect James Ingo Freed's design for the building recalls both the Jewish communities the Nazis destroyed and the ghettos and extermination

camps they built, using red brick, glass, and dark industrial steel to conjure an image of time and place. The museum's permanent exhibit takes up three floors, beginning with the early 1930s and continuing through the Nazi rise to power, the subsequent tyranny and genocide, and finally, the Holocaust aftermath. On arrival, visitors are given a small booklet describing the experiences of a single individual, and at different points in the tour you can learn their fate as the Nazi era unfolds.

In all, the memorial contains more than 18,000 artifacts and artworks, 70 video displays, and four theaters showing historical film footage and eyewitness testimony, including a narrated film chronicling Hitler's rise to power in 1933. Displays include items from a German medical facility that was converted into a center for killing disabled children; photos from the Jewish ghettos in Warsaw and Lodz, Poland; a casting of the infamous Arbeit Macht Frei ("Work Makes One Free") sign that hung above the gate of the Auschwitz I death camp; a reconstructed barracks from Auschwitz-Birkenau; and a pile of shoes taken from prisoners at Majdanek before they were gassed. A separate exhibition titled "Remember the Children, Daniel's Story," is a history of the Holocaust for children ages eight and older, told from a youngster's point of view. In addition to its museum, the memorial also holds a vast archive of documents, books, photographs, oral histories, and film footage. On the second floor, the hexagonal Hall of Remembrance is the official U.S. memorial to Holocaust victims, and invites you to stop for a moment and be alone with your thoughts.

WHERE: 100 Raoul Wallenberg Pl. SW. Tel 202-488-0400; ushmm.org. **BEST TIMES:** select days in Apr–Aug for free First Person talks by Holocaust survivors.

Top Secrets and Breaking News

THE INTERNATIONAL SPY MUSEUM & THE NEWSEUM

Washington, D.C.

With the Pentagon closed to visitors since September 11 and the headquarters of the CIA and FBI also off-limits to tours, where is a curious conspiracy theorist in D.C. to go? Luckily, there's the International Spy Museum. Open since 2002, the museum puts you into paranoia mode from the get-go, with an orientation to the motivations and tools of the spy game followed by an interactive display on the importance of keeping your cover. From here, you're led through spy school, learning the history and development of espionage, how spies are recruited and trained, and how they function in the 21st century. At every stage, you're surrounded by the largest collection of international espionage artifacts ever placed on public display, including miniature cameras, lipstick-tube pistols, cipher machines, counterfeit currency, an American diplomat's shoe secretly equipped with a transmitter in its heel, secret writing detection kits, photos of formerly secret documents, spy training films, and video interviews with former spies.

Just to the south, the Newseum's focus is history of journalism, celebrating both the

The Newseum's New Media Gallery charts the evolution of global media through videos and interactive displays.

news itself and American journalism's basis in the First Amendment.

The Newseum is dynamic, engaging, and interactive, allowing visitors to experience the stories of yesterday and today through the eyes of the media. The museum offers 1.5 miles of exhibits dealing with journalism's origins and historic and current practices, 15 news theaters and galleries that draw from a collection of more than 16,400 artifacts, and 35,000 print news items in the Historic Print News Collection. A 90-foot Big Screen Theater plays signature films related to changing exhibits, and interactive displays allow you and the kids to play reporter for a day.

SPY MUSEUM: 800 F St. NW. Tel 202-393-7798; spymuseum.org. **NEWSEUM:** Pennsylvania Ave. and 6th St. NW. Tel 888-NEWSEUM or 202-292-6100; newseum.org.

Memory, Reason, and Imagination

THE LIBRARY OF CONGRESS

Washington, D.C

This is the country's official library and the world's largest. Close to 38 million books are here—as well as 70 million manuscripts, 14 million photographs, 5.5 million maps, 3 million recordings, and millions of prints, drawings, and other items, filling more than 838 miles of shelves.

The library was established by an act of Congress in 1800, but its original collection of 964 books and nine maps went up in smoke when British soldiers burned the Capitol in 1814. Former president Thomas Jefferson offered his own comprehensive library of 6,487 books as a replacement, arranged under three main headings: Memory (history), Reason (philosophy, including law, science, and geography), and Imagination (fine arts, including architecture, music, literature, and sports). You can even see a recreation of Jefferson's library with the collection he sold for $23,950. That was the seed from which the current collection grew . . . and grew. Today, some 15,000 items arrive at the library every day, of which approximately 12,000 become part of the permanent collection.

The library is now housed in three main buildings, but visitors in search of history should concentrate on the Jefferson Building. It's absolutely astounding, with its grand marble Great Hall illuminated by stained-glass skylights in a 75-foot ceiling and its stunning Main Reading Room topped by an ornate 160-foot dome. Any adult with an ID can get a free "reader identification" pass to read books on the premises. The Main Reading Room is

The Library of Congress's main building, the Jefferson Building, opened in 1897.

your entrée to the collection, which is primarily kept in closed stacks. Library staff will collect what you need.

If you don't want to sit down and read, you can just drop in to peruse the architecture and the library's permanent and temporary exhibitions. Exploring the Early Americas uses rare maps, documents, paintings, prints, and artifacts to explore indigenous cultures, their dramatic encounters with European explorers and settlers, and the world-changing results. Exhibitions are rotated in and out of public viewing for preservation reasons, but you can also see them online (loc.gov/exhibits). Other displays include a Gutenberg Bible (one of three perfect copies on vellum); the Gershwin Room, with the composer's piano, music manuscripts, and other artifacts; and Bob Hope's memorabilia, including his 85,000-page Joke File.

WHERE: 1st St. SE, between Independence Ave. and E. Capitol St. Tel 202-707-8000 (general info) or 202-707-0919 (tour info); loc.gov. *When:* closed Sun; free guided tours daily. **BEST TIMES:** evenings at the Mary Pickford Theater in the Madison Building for showings of films from the museum's collection (check calendar).

The Final Frontier

THE NATIONAL AIR AND SPACE MUSEUM

Washington, D.C.

For those in thrall with the notion of flight, this is your place. Under one roof you'll find Charles Lindbergh's *Spirit of St. Louis*, Chuck Yeager's *Glamorous Glennis* Bell X-1, John Glenn's *Friendship 7* capsule, the Skylab space station, and some moon rocks collected by *Apollo 17.*

Orville and Wilbur Wright made history's first manned flight in 1903 (and yes, *The Wright Flyer* is on display here), but the Smithsonian's aeronautical collection actually predates that by 17 years, beginning with its 1876 acquisition of a group of Chinese kites. Today the museum's facility on the National Mall houses 2,230 artifacts, including aircraft, space vehicles, and smaller pieces, and is the most visited museum in the United States and an unrivaled hit with kids. The Steven F. Udvar-Hazy Center, a new sister facility in nearby Chantilly, Virginia (see p. 237), displays another 3,000 pieces of the full collection (there are 66,000 objects in all).

In addition to aircraft and spacecraft,

The National Air and Space Museum maintains the largest collection of aircraft and spacecraft in the world.

displays include engines and instruments, armaments, flight suits, robotic exploration, and pop-culture space artifacts, including one of the USS *Enterprise* models used in the original *Star Trek* TV series. Displays are arranged thematically, with separate galleries covering early flight, aviation milestones, jet aviation, rocketry, the space race, lunar exploration, and other topics. One gallery explains the principles of flight through 50-plus hands-on activities, while a flight simulator allows visitors to test-pilot dozens of different aircraft, including some that are in the museum's collection. Regularly scheduled shows at the 220-seat Albert Einstein Planetarium simulate the heavens on a 70-foot overhead dome, and an IMAX theater shows films specially prepared for the museum on a screen five stories high and seven wide.

WHERE: Independence Ave. between 4th and 7th Sts. Tel 202-633-2214; nasm.si.edu. **BEST TIMES:** Astronauts speak at the museum's lecture series throughout the year.

The Charters of American Freedom

THE NATIONAL ARCHIVES

Washington, D.C.

The U.S. has a government of the people, by the people, and for the people. If anybody tries to tell you otherwise, point them to the rotunda of the National Archives, where glass display cases allow everyone to view the original handwritten copies of the Declaration of Independence, the Constitution, and the Bill of Rights, just as the founding fathers drafted them.

The rotunda exhibit is the centerpiece of the National Archives Museum, with permanent and temporary exhibits. The newest permanent exhibit is Records of Rights, which explores how groups such as women, immigrants, and African-Americans sought to share in the same freedoms guaranteed to white men. The William G. McGowan Theater shows films exploring great issues of American history, as well as hosting public programs related to the National Archives, its holdings, and its mission.

Anyone with curiosity, patience, and time on their hands can go much deeper, and genealogists flock to search among the Archives' vast holdings of federal paperwork, including census records, immigration documents, ship manifests, maps, military records through WWI, homestead records, and the like. All you need to do is show ID, fill out a form, and start digging.

WHERE: 700 Constitution Ave. NW. Tel 866-272-6272; archives.gov. **BEST TIME:** July 4th for the annual public reading of the Declaration of Independence.

The National Archives documents our country's past.

Where Art and Politics Collide

THE NATIONAL GALLERY OF ART

Washington, D.C.

Founded in 1937, the National Gallery, one of America's greatest art museums, was a gift to the nation from former Secretary of the Treasury Andrew W. Mellon, who donated both the money for its construction and his personal art collection to act as its nucleus.

The gallery's original neoclassical West Building was designed by John Russell Pope, the architect responsible for the Jefferson Memorial and the National Archives. Today its collection of European and American painting and sculpture is one of the world's finest, spanning from the 13th and 18th centuries (respectively) through the early 20th. Highlights from the American collection include Gilbert Stuart's portraits of the first five presidents and works by James Whistler, John Singer Sargent, and Winslow Homer. The European collection features Dutch masters, French impressionists, and the only painting by Leonardo da Vinci in the Western Hemisphere. The I. M. Pei–designed East building next door houses the museum's contemporary art collection. Highlights here include works by Alexander Calder, Henri Matisse, Pablo Picasso, Joan Miró, Jackson Pollock, Mark Rothko, and Andy Goldsworthy. When D.C.'s oldest art museum, the Corcoran Gallery, was dismantled in 2014, the NGA

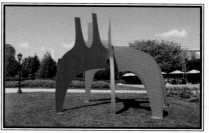

Stroll through the National Gallery of Art's Sculpture Garden to see Alexander Calder's abstract stabile Cheval Rouge *(Red Horse).*

acquired some 8,000 works from its stellar collection. Adjacent to the West Building, the gallery's 6.5-acre Sculpture Garden displays works of modern and contemporary sculpture.

WHERE: between 3rd and 9th Sts. at Constitution Ave. NW. Tel 202-737-4215; nga.gov. **BEST TIMES:** Fri evenings in summer for free "Jazz in the Garden" concerts; winter for ice-skating in the garden.

Shrines of Secular Democracy

THE NATIONAL MALL

Washington, D.C.

To the surprise of many visitors, the seat of American government is also a beautiful city, a celebration in marble and stone of the ideals on which democracy was founded. Though laid out roughly according to the original

1791 plan by French-born American military engineer Pierre Charles L'Enfant, the city has changed considerably over the years. Even its centerpiece National Mall—a majestic 2-mile greensward running west from the Capitol Building to the Lincoln Memorial, lined with some of the nation's most important monuments and civic and cultural institutions—didn't assume its current form until the early 20th century.

At its center, the Washington Monument was the Mall's first presidential memorial, completed in 1885. Thrusting skyward 555 feet, it offers visitors a spectacular 360-degree view from its peak. To the west, the neoclassical Lincoln Memorial is probably the most emotional of the Mall's presidential memorials. Designed by Henry Bacon to resemble a Greek temple, it has 36 Doric columns representing the 36 states in the Union at the time of Lincoln's death. Inside, Daniel Chester French's massive sculpture of the seated president gazes out. The powerful words of his Gettysburg Address and Second Inaugural Address are etched in two flanking chambers, and a mural depicts the unity of North and South. For the most profound experience, visit at night, after the crowds have thinned out.

South of the Washington Monument on the banks of the Tidal Basin, the Thomas Jefferson Memorial was designed in 1936 by John Russell Pope and modeled on the Pantheon in Rome. Inside, a 19-foot bronze statue of the third president stands surrounded by quotes from his work, including the Declaration of Independence. The Jefferson Memorial was planned and constructed

The Mall offers a different experience at night when the monuments are brightly illuminated.

during the presidency of Franklin Roosevelt, so it's apt that the next presidential memorial built on the Mall was to that great man himself. Dedicated in 1997, the Franklin Delano Roosevelt Memorial is composed of four outdoor rooms, one for each of his terms in office, with waterfalls, shade trees, statuary, and the president's words carved into walls of red South Dakota granite. Near the entrance, visitors are greeted by a statue of Roosevelt seated in his wheelchair, his beloved Scottish terrier, Fala, and First Lady Eleanor nearby.

The Mall's most moving memorial is to the men and women who fought and died in America's longest war. The Vietnam Veterans Memorial is a simple V-shaped wall of polished black granite set into the earth, inscribed with the names of more than 58,000 soldiers killed or MIA as a result of the war. Dedicated in 1982, the wall's unconventional design, by Maya Lin, was initially controversial but has since been recognized for its powerful evocation of the personal cost of war. Nearby, the Korean War Veterans Memorial consists of sculptures of 19 infantrymen and a 164-foot black granite wall with over 2,400 photographs of those who fought in the war. Located at the other end of the slender reflecting pool that stretches between the Lincoln and Washington memorials, the National World War II Memorial honors the 16 million Americans who served in that war. Its central plaza and fountain are surrounded by 56 granite pillars and a "Freedom Wall" with 4,048 sculpted gold stars commemorating the more than 400,000 Americans who died in the war.

The Mall is particularly beautiful when illuminated at night, and in early spring when thousands of Japanese cherry trees burst into bloom around the Tidal Basin.

NATIONAL MALL VISITOR INFO: Tel 202-426-6841; nps.gov/nama. **BEST TIMES:** late spring and fall for weather; late Mar–mid-Apr for Cherry Blossom Festival; 2 weeks in late June–early July for Smithsonian Folklife Festival (folklife.si.edu); July 4th for Fireworks on the Mall; Mon nights in July–Aug for "Screen on the Green" outdoor movie classics.

America's Attic

THE NATIONAL MUSEUM OF AMERICAN HISTORY

Washington, D.C.

The inventory housed within these hallowed walls of the Smithsonian is nothing less than mind-boggling: a selection of Groucho Marx's home movies; the Star-Spangled Banner, the flag that inspired the national anthem; the first John Deere tractor; one of the original Howdy Doody puppets; more than 30,000 pieces of American clothing from the 1700s through today; one of the first Teddy bears; the Woolworth's lunch counter from Greensboro, North Carolina, that was the site of the first civil rights sit-in; the Lone Ranger's mask; a crumpled piece of the World Trade Center's exterior sheathing; a group of Thomas Edison's earliest lightbulbs; the oral histories of 200 Southern farmers; a 1989 Game Boy; George Washington's surveying compass, camp chest, and tent; Superman comic books; Julia Child's home kitchen; B. F. Skinner's experimental nose cone for a pigeon-guided missile; a turn-of-the-century Washington, D.C., streetcar; Evel Knievel's Harley; the ruby slippers worn by Judy Garland in *The Wizard of Oz;* 50,000 sound recordings dating back to 1903; a classic green and gold steam locomotive; a 1926 Model T Ford; life jackets from the *Titanic;* the contents of a medieval apothecary and an 1890s drugstore; an original model of Eli Whitney's cotton gin; Albert Einstein's pipe; a compass from the Lewis and Clark expedition; original Jim Henson Kermit the Frog and Miss Piggy puppets; Muhammad Ali's boxing gloves and robe; Duke Ellington's sheet music; Custer's buckskin jacket; a display of presidential hair called "Locks of Hair from Distinguished Heads"; and some 150,000 other items, representing only a fraction of the 3 million in the museum's total collection . . . wear comfortable shoes.

WHERE: 14th St. and Constitution Ave. NW. Tel 202-633-1000; americanhistory .si.edu. **BEST TIMES:** free concerts, workshops, lectures, and other events every month.

Dinosaurs and Diamonds

THE NATIONAL MUSEUM OF NATURAL HISTORY

Washington, D.C.

To kids this is what good museums are all about: dinosaurs, bugs, moon rocks, mummies, and maybe a caveman or two to bring it all home. And that's exactly what you'll find at the Smithsonian's National Museum of

Natural History, the largest, most comprehensive natural history collection in the world.

On entering the rotunda, visitors are met by a giant stuffed African elephant, his trunk raised in greeting. The National Fossil Hall, immediately to the right, is closed for renovation until 2019 so it can better display its unrivaled collection of fossils and dinosaurs. Explore the ocean's past, present, and future in the 23,000-square-foot Sant Ocean Hall, with 674 marine specimens and models. The

The stuffed 12-ton, 14-foot-tall African bull elephant has fiberglass tusks because the original ivory ones were too heavy for it to support.

45-foot-long replica of a North Atlantic Right Whale is based on Phoenix, a whale tracked by scientists since her birth in 1987. The interactive Hall of Mammals examines mammalian evolution, and the displays on human evolution include three dioramas that show early human species in three different times and places including a Neanderthal burial.

One of the museum's big all-time drawing cards resides upstairs: the 45.52-carat Hope Diamond, donated by Harry Winston in 1958. There are 2,500 minerals and gems in the Janet Annenberg Hooker Hall of Geology, which uses a recreation of four mines and a large gallery devoted to earthquakes, volcanoes, and meteorites to add pizzazz to the earth sciences. Kids will get a kick from the O. Orkin Insect Zoo, home to tarantulas, centipedes, and other creepy crawlies. Outside the museum, the Butterfly Habitat Garden explores the natural relationship between plants and butterflies across four different habitats.

WHERE: 10th St. and Constitution Ave. NW. Tel 202-633-1000; mnh.si.edu. **BEST TIMES:** spring for early-season butterflies; fall, when the butterflies feed on nectar before migrating south.

The Legacy of America's First Peoples

THE NATIONAL MUSEUM OF THE AMERICAN INDIAN

Washington, D.C.

Opened in 2004, the Smithsonian's National Museum of the American Indian is the first national museum in the U.S. dedicated exclusively to Native Americans, and the first to present all exhibitions from a native point of view. The collection got its start when, in 1897, New York oil heir George Gustav Heye began collecting Native American art and artifacts while working in Arizona. Over the next 60 years he amassed a staggering 700,000 items, with the goal of possessing the most complete and encompassing collection possible. His collection first went on display in

Manhattan in 1922, and was incorporated into the Smithsonian system in 1989. Like many museums begun with a 19th-century mindset, Heye's collection was static, presenting Native American culture from a purely historical point of view. With the opening of the National Museum in D.C., however, all that changed, and the collection now shows America's first peoples as participants in a living culture, 12,000 years old and counting. Further, the museum preserves, studies, and exhibits the life, languages, literature, history, and arts of Native Americans of the Western Hemisphere.

The museum's Native sensibility permeates every aspect of its operation. Outside, the rough-textured Minnesota limestone building itself was designed to evoke wind-sculptured rock. Its five-story entrance faces east, in deference to Native traditions that find it desirable to face the rising sun. The 4.25-acre museum grounds consist of four indigenous local habitats: an upland hardwood forest, lowland freshwater wetlands, meadowlands, and a planting of corn, tobacco, and other Native crops. Around the grounds, 40 large Canadian boulders called the "Grandfather Rocks" serve as reminders of Native peoples' long relationship to the environment.

The museum's collection now consists of more than 825,000 items, only a fraction of which can be displayed. All the objects in the exhibits—including feathered headdresses, arrowheads, pottery, woven baskets, and pre-Columbian gold figures—are treated not as museum pieces but as living elements of Native traditions. In addition to historical displays, the museum also offers works by contemporary Native American artists, and its central rotunda, illuminated by prisms designed to catch the sun's rays, serves as a venue for demonstrations of Native arts and craftwork, including boatbuilding, while an outdoor theater invites visitors to enjoy Native dance, music, theater, and storytelling performances.

WHERE: 4th St. & Independence Ave. SW. Tel 202-633-1000; nmai.si.edu. **BEST TIMES:** July for the Living Earth Festival; early Dec for the Native Art Market.

The curvilinear National Museum of the American Indian building has a large space for contemporary Native performances.

Mei Xiang, Tian Tian, and Friends

THE NATIONAL ZOO

Washington, D.C.

President Nixon's 1972 goodwill trip to China normalized relations between the U.S. and China, but it also secured a pair of giant pandas, Ling-Ling and Hsing-Hsing, for the National Zoo. Presented by Chinese premier Chou En-lai as a gift to the American people, they were a smash, and over time the scientists at the National Zoo became leaders in giant panda biology and conservation.

Four decades later, Ling-Ling and Hsing-Hsing are no more, but the zoo's panda legacy lives on in Mei Xiang and Tian Tian, a pair sent in 2000 on loan from the China Wildlife Conservation Association. You can see them comfortably munching bamboo, playing with heavy-duty rubber barrels and other "panda toys" in their indoor/outdoor habitat, or just lolling luxuriously in the sun. Mei Xiang has given birth to three cubs, the most recent, Bei-Bei, born in 2015.

Of course, the National Zoo, part of the Smithsonian Institution, isn't just about pandas. More than 2,000 animals representing about 400 species live at the zoo's 163-acre D.C. facility, many of them endangered—the giant pandas themselves, as well as Asian elephants, western lowland gorillas, and Sumatran tigers. Now more than 125 years old, the zoo has opened the Asia Trail, which provides new, larger homes for the giant pandas, red pandas, sloth bears, and fishing cats, as well as clouded leopards and giant salamanders. Wander through the American Trail to encounter sea lions, beavers, and wolves, and visit Elephant Trails to witness a thriving multi-generational herd.

WHERE: 3001 Connecticut Ave. NW. Tel 202-673-4888; nationalzoo.si.edu.

Museums Fit for a Nation

THE SMITHSONIAN AND BEYOND

Washington, D.C.

In 1829, Scottish scientist James Smithson left his entire estate, more than $500,000 in U.S. currency, to the United States "to found at Washington, under the name of the Smithsonian Institution, an establishment for the increase and diffusion of knowledge among men." No one knows exactly why he did this—Smithson had never traveled to the U.S. and had no known correspondents here—but in 1846 Congress officially established Smithson's institution, which has since grown to encompass 19 museums and galleries, the National Zoo (see previous page), and nine research centers, making it the world's largest museum and research complex.

Some of the names are familiar—the National Air and Space Museum (see p. 261) and the National Museums of American History and Natural History (see p. 265)—while others don't have quite as much name recognition. Start your visit at the beginning, at the red sandstone building known as "The Castle." Located on the south side of the National Mall, it was the Smithsonian's original building and now functions as its visitor center. The Italian Renaissance–style building immediately west is the Freer Gallery of Art, which displays one of the world's finest

The red sandstone Smithsonian Institution Building ("The Castle") is the anchor for the National Mall.

collections of Asian art—more than 24,000 pieces encompassing the Far and Near East. Besides Asian art, the Freer houses a collection of 19th- and early 20th-century American art, including the world's largest gathering of works by James McNeill Whistler. The Freer is connected by an illuminated exhibition space with the underground Arthur M. Sackler Gallery, which continues its sister museum's Asian theme. Above ground, attention has been focused on the Smithsonian's latest addition, the national Museum of African American History and Culture.

Northeast of the Mall, the National Postal Museum would have made Ben Franklin proud, with displays showing the importance of the Postal Service in uniting the country and contributing to the free flow of ideas essential to a democracy. When you're done, make a detour across 1st Street to historic Union Station. The largest railroad station in the world when it opened in 1907, it's been meticulously restored and augmented by shopping and eating options.

Not all Washington's museums are part of the Smithsonian, of course. A few blocks northeast of the White House, the National Museum of Women in the Arts was established by art collectors Wilhelmina Cole Holladay and Wallace F. Holladay and has a collection of some 4,700 pieces, including works going back to the Renaissance and extending up to

the present, with pieces by Mary Cassatt, Frida Kahlo, Georgia O'Keeffe, Lee Krasner, and Louise Nevelson. In northwest Washington, the Hillwood Museum and Gardens overlook Rock Creek Park. Housed in the former home of Marjorie Merriweather Post, the cereal heiress and socialite, today the 40-room Georgian mansion brims with her huge collection of French and Imperial Russian decorative and fine arts, including icons and Fabergé eggs. The Russian collection is the largest of its kind outside Russia. Outdoors, 25 acres of natural woodlands and formal gardens flow around the house, including a French parterre, a Japanese-style garden, and a rose garden.

SMITHSONIAN INFORMATION CENTER: Tel 202-633-1000; si.edu/visit. **FREER & SACKLER GALLERIES:** Tel 202-633-4880; asia.si.edu. **NATIONAL MUSEUM OF AFRICAN AMERICAN HISTORY AND CULTTURE:** Tel 202-633-1000; nmaahc.si.edu. **NATIONAL POSTAL MUSEUM:** Tel 202-633-5555; postalmuseum.si.edu. **UNION STATION:** unionstationdc.com. **NATIONAL MUSEUM OF WOMEN IN THE ARTS:** Tel 202-783-5000; nmwa.org. **HILLWOOD MUSEUM AND GARDENS:** Tel 877-HILLWOOD or 202-686-5807; hillwoodmuseum.org. *When:* closed Mon; closed for 3 weeks in Jan. **BEST TIME:** 1st Sun of each month for the Museum of Women in the Arts Community Days, with performances and hands-on workshops.

Truth, Justice, and the American Way

THE U.S. SUPREME COURT

Washington, D.C.

If you've toured the Capitol (see next page) and the White House (see p. 272), you're almost duty-bound to drop in on the U.S. Supreme Court, the third pillar of America's federal government. Despite its equal stature with the

other two branches, the court didn't have its own home until 1935, a full 147 years after the Constitution was ratified, instead meeting

in several different areas within the Capitol building. It wasn't until 1929 that Chief Justice (and former president) William

Howard Taft was able to persuade Congress to give the court its own home. That building, designed by famed architect Cass Gilbert in a classical Corinthian style, stands today as a living testimony to the court's mission, which is etched right above its doors: providing "equal justice under law." The main entrance, facing the Capitol, is also decorated with sculptural depictions of justice and law. Enter through the huge bronze doors, each of which weighs 6.5 tons and is engraved with scenes showing the development of law through the centuries. Inside, the Great Hall corridor is lined with busts of all former chief justices. At the east end of the Hall, oak doors open into the Court Chamber, from whose raised bench the nine justices hear cases.

The Supreme Court moved into its own purpose-built home in 1935.

From the first Monday in October through late April, the court hears oral arguments in approximately 100 different cases, selected from about 8,000–10,000 petitions filed each term. Visitors can attend these sessions for a chance to hear how justice is mulled at the highest level. The court's ground floor houses various exhibits, and on days that the court isn't sitting, lectures about the court are held in the courtroom. To continue the Capitol Hill experience, visit The Monocle, which has been serving congresspersons, judges, and anyone else who drops in since 1960. In the casual pub, loose-tie staffers talk shop over beer. In the dining room, autographed politico photos look over your shoulder as you dine on steaks and seafood.

U.S. Supreme Court: 1 1st St. NE. Tel 202-479-3211; supremecourt.gov. *When:* open for visitors Mon–Fri. Court is in session half of each month Oct–Apr; call for schedule. **The Monocle:** Tel 202-546-4488; themonocle.com. *Cost:* dinner $60. **Best time:** late Mar–mid-Apr to coincide with the Cherry Blossom Festival.

The Pinnacle of Politics

THE UNITED STATES CAPITOL

Washington, D.C.

Located at the east end of the National Mall, the placement of the Capitol Building was conceived by city planner Pierre Charles L'Enfant, who noted that Jenkins Hill, which rose 89 feet above the level of the Potomac, was

"a pedestal waiting for a monument." Picking the location was easy, but building the home of Congress wasn't. George Washington laid the cornerstone in September 1793, but it wasn't until December 1863 that the building attained the form we recognize now. That was the month Thomas Crawford's 19-foot-tall statue of *Freedom* was placed atop the new cast-iron dome, a classic female figure standing 288 feet above the east front plaza. Philip Reid, the man who supervised the bronze casting of *Freedom*, was a slave, one of hundreds involved in the Capitol's construction.

Guided tours include the Rotunda, the enormous circular hall under the building's dome, where eight huge oil paintings depict signature events in American history, including Columbus's landing in the West Indies and the presentation of the Declaration of Independence. In the dome itself is Constantino Brumidi's 1865 fresco *The Apotheosis of Washington*, depicting the first president rising into the heavens, flanked by female figures representing Liberty and Victory. Below the Rotunda, the cryptically named Crypt (which has never served as a tomb) is sometimes used for exhibits and sculptural displays.

A new Capitol Visitor Center is located below ground to preserve the views of the Capitol and the historic landscaping designed by Frederick Law Olmsted, of New York's Central Park fame. The Capitol's south and north wings contain the House and Senate chambers, respectively, where visitor galleries are open to anyone who obtains a gallery pass in advance from the office of their senator or congressperson.

To complement your visit, drop in for lunch at the Old Ebbitt Grill, a classic Victorian-style saloon frequented by businesspeople and Secret Service agents. For dinner, get a reservation at Bistro Bis, Chef Jeffrey Buben's place adjacent to the Hotel George on the slope of Capitol Hill, with its French menu and comfortable bar. The table next to you might be full of Capitol Hill bigwigs.

The Capitol: 1st St. and Independence Ave. SW. Tel 202-226-8000; visitthecapitol.gov. *When:* Mon–Fri. **Old Ebbitt Grill:** Tel 202-347-4800; ebbitt.com. *Cost:* lunch $30. **Bistro Bis:** Tel 202-661-2700; bistrobis.com. *Cost:* dinner $50. **Best times:** June–Aug for free concerts by the Navy, Air Force, Marine, and Army bands; July 4th for the celebration on the National Mall, with a performance by the National Symphony Orchestra on the Capitol's west lawn; first week of Dec for tree-lighting on the West Lawn.

The United States Capitol building is an exemplar of the neoclassical style of architecture.

Art, American Style

Washington's Art Museums

Washington, D.C.

D.C. is the nation's capital, so it's only right that it have some museums dedicated chiefly to American art. After 145 years as one of D.C.'s most venerable museums, the Corcoran Gallery sadly closed its doors in 2014.

Within a year, it was decided that the more financially stable National Gallery of Art (see p. 263) would acquire close to half of its stellar collection. You can still visit the Corcoran's first (of two) homes, a landmark Second Empire–style building at 17th Street and Pennsylvania Avenue, that now houses the Renwick Gallery, the nation's premier collection of American craft objects and decorative arts from the 19th to the 21st century. The Renwick is a branch of the Smithsonian's American Art Museum, which shares space with the National Portrait Gallery in the historic 1836 Patent Office Building (called "the noblest of Washington buildings" by Walt Whitman). With a new free-form glass roof enclosing its monumental 28,000-square-foot courtyard, the American Art Museum exhibits what started as the first federal art collection, begun in 1829. More than 40,000 works from four centuries of American history are on display, making it the largest collection of American art in the world.

The National Portrait Gallery was established by Congress in 1962 to display portraits of

"men and women who have made significant contributions to the history, development, and culture of the people of the United States." It's the only U.S. museum dedicated solely to portraiture, with 18,600 works ranging from paintings and sculpture to photographs, drawings, and original artwork from more than 1,900 *Time* magazine covers. Highlights include political works—the iconic "Lansdowne" portrait of George Washington by Gilbert Stuart and Alexander Gardner's photographic portrait of Abraham Lincoln—and pop-culture items, such as Andy Warhol's silkscreen of Michael Jackson.

The National Building Museum opened in 1985 with a mission to celebrate American architecture and urban planning. It is housed in the former home of the U.S. Pension Bureau, whose Renaissance-style Great Hall is among Washington's most impressive spaces, nearly as long as a football field, with colossal Corinthian columns supporting its 159-foot ceiling and a 28-foot fountain. No wonder it's been used as the site of presidential inaugural balls since Grover Cleveland took office the year it opened.

RENWICK GALLERY: Tel 202-633-2850; americanart.si.edu/renwick. **AMERICAN ART MUSEUM:** Tel 202-633-7970; americanart.si .edu. **NATIONAL PORTRAIT GALLERY:** Tel 202-633-8300; npg.si.edu. **NATIONAL BUILDING MUSEUM:** Tel 202-272-2448; nbm.org. **BEST TIME:** mid-Apr for the prestigious Smithsonian Craft Show at the National Building Museum (smithsoniancraftshow.com).

The Renwick Gallery building was constructed in 1859.

"May none but honest and wise men ever rule under this roof."
—John Adams

THE WHITE HOUSE

Washington, D.C.

The grassy Ellipse, north of the Washington Monument, links the National Mall to the White House, one of the world's most famous and recognizable residences. George Washington himself chose the site of the executive mansion in 1791, but the house wasn't ready for occupancy until 1800, at which point second president John Adams moved in with his wife, Abigail. Since then every president has made the home his own, though a few incidents over the years have caused temporary relocation. In 1814 the British torched the place, completely gutting its interior. Harry Truman and family also had to move out in the 1940s when the structure was found to be unstable, leading to another complete renovation. But the exterior is still exactly as Irish-born architect James Hoban designed it in 1792. Called the President's Palace on early maps, the building was officially named The Executive Mansion in 1810 to avoid the hint of royalty. It was nicknamed "The White House" early on, owing to the lime-based whitewash applied to keep the stone walls from freezing. Paint eventually replaced the wash, and in 1901 Theodore Roosevelt made the nickname official.

Those lucky enough to join a tour (heightened security means limited access and advance arrangements through your congressperson) can see a number of historic areas of the mansion, including the State Dining Room (once Thomas Jefferson's office); the Blue Room, with furniture selected by James Monroe after the 1814 fire; and the East Room, where Lincoln, Kennedy, and five other presidents lay in state. (There are tours of the West Wing— the area where government business is done—but they are reserved for celebrities, business and political leaders, major donors, movers and shakers, and people who know someone who works at The White House.) To get some idea of what you can't see, stop at the White House Visitor Center, which offers films and displays on the house and its history.

If your invitation for a night in the Lincoln Bedroom hasn't come through, you can arrange a stay across Pennsylvania Avenue at the 1927 Italian Renaissance–style Hay-Adams Hotel, long a favorite of diplomats and visiting heads of state.

WHERE: 1600 Pennsylvania Ave. NW. Tel 202-456-7041 (tour info); whitehouse .gov/participate/tours-and-events. **HAY-ADAMS HOTEL:** Tel 800-853-6807 or 202-638-6600; hayadams.com. *Cost:* from $329 (off-peak), from $849 (peak). **BEST TIMES:** Apr for annual White House Spring Garden Tours, including the Rose Garden and the Jacqueline Kennedy Garden; Easter for the annual children's Easter Egg Roll; early Dec for the Pathway of Peace at the Ellipse in President's Park, including the National Christmas Tree Lighting.

The White House, built from Aquia sandstone that's painted white, is designed in the late Georgian style.

George Washington Bathed Here

BERKELEY SPRINGS

West Virginia

Tucked in a narrow valley of sandstone cliffs along the Cacapon River, Berkeley Springs is America's original spa town. It first came to the notice of George Washington in 1748 when he was just a sprout of 16, surveying the vast land holdings of Lord Thomas Fairfax, an Englishman who had moved to America to oversee his interests. Washington was taken with the warm mineral waters that surged from the base of Warm Springs Ridge and when the budding spa town grew, he returned many times, helping build its reputation as a fashionable destination for Virginia's social elite. Today the main attraction of this artists' town of 613 is the decidedly egalitarian Berkeley Springs State Park, a beautifully manicured, tree-shaded refuge that serves as the town center. In 1776, Lord Fairfax conveyed the springs and 50 acres to the Colony of Virginia for "suffering humanity," and it was originally developed as the town of "Bath." Visitors to the 4-acre park can still drink spring water directly from Lord Fairfax's public tap, wade in the colonial stone-lined pools, or ponder George Washington's bathtub, a replica of the way he bathed. The affordable 1930 public bathhouse offers two ways to take waters that come from the spring at a constant temperature of 74.3°F and are heated up to 102°F: Either walk into a private ceramic-tiled Roman bath or luxuriate in a whirlpool bathtub in a private room. Things have quieted down since America's first Methodist bishop, Francis Asbury, took the waters for his health and preached against the town's "overflowing tide of immorality." After the Revolution, there were card games and gambling, horse racing in the streets, and dancing at twice-weekly balls. Now it's all about wellness. Massage therapists outnumber lawyers three to one, and there are plenty of spas (along with acupuncturists, chiropractors, and homeopaths), just in case you, like our forefathers, are one of suffering humanity.

WHERE: 100 miles northwest of Washington, D.C. *Visitor info:* Tel 800-447-8797 or 304-258-9147; berkeleysprings.com. **BERKELEY SPRINGS STATE PARK:** Tel 304-258-2711; berkeleyspringssp.com. **BEST TIME:** Oct for the Apple Butter Festival.

Getting Steamed on Cheat Mountain

CASS SCENIC RAILROAD

Cass, West Virginia

In the early 1900s, more than 3,000 miles of track carried logging trains deep into the highlands of West Virginia, where steam-powered log skidders were used to carry timber down steep hills to waiting railcars. Overlogging spurred the creation of the Monongahela National Forest (see p. 280), and in 1961 the state of West Virginia purchased the logging town of Cass, deep in the heart of the forest. Here, the same generation of mighty steam-powered Shay locomotives that once hauled 1.2 billion board feet of timber off Cheat Mountain still ply the state's last 11 miles of logging track, only now they carry visitors toting cameras and coolers.

Departing from the former mill town of Cass, classic black locomotives leave plumes of steam as they push open-sided passenger cars up inclines of up to 11 percent (a 2 percent grade on conventional railroads is considered steep!). The huff of the stack, the clackety-clacks of the rails, and the scream of the whistle at the crossings all transport riders to another era as they travel to Whittaker Station, a restored logging camp from the 1940s. Folks who want to sleep on the mountain can rent a tidy pine-paneled caboose dating from the 1940s, equipped with a coal stove and bunks. It's hauled up by the steam engine, dropped off, then picked up again when you're ready to leave. Backcountry adventurers can haul their mountain bikes and packs up the mountain by train on Wednesdays, be dropped off in the wilderness, and arrange to be picked up on a later day.

Right in Cass, two-story company cottages that once housed loggers and their families have been transformed into guesthouses for 4 to 14 people, while the West Virginia Pulp & Paper Company Store has been reincarnated as a casual café/restaurant where you can pick up a sandwich to go. It's a good base from which to explore the 78-mile Greenbrier River Trail, a converted rail trail that goes all the way to the outskirts of Lewisburg (see p. 279) and is perfect for easy biking, hiking, horseback riding,

and cross-country skiing. The waters near Cass are rich with trout and smallmouth bass farther south, but most folks rent an inner tube for a gentle float downstream.

Where: 225 miles west of Washington, D.C. **Mountain Rail Adventures:** Tel 866-460-7265 or 304-636-9477; mountainrailwv .com. **Cass Scenic Railroad State Park:** Tel 800-CALL-WVA or 304-456-4300; cassrail road.com. *Cost:* rail excursions from $34; caboose trip/stay at Bald Knob $275 (up to 4 people) for 1st night, $190 for each additional night; cottages in Cass from $83 (off-peak), from $113 (peak). *When:* late Apr–Oct for train rides. **Greenbrier River Trail:** Tel 304-799-7416; greenbrierrailtrailstatepark.com. **Best time:** late Sept–Oct for fall colors.

An Intimate Performance for a Huge Audience

MOUNTAIN STAGE

Charleston, West Virginia

B efore most people had heard of them, performers like Lyle Lovett, Alison Krauss, and Norah Jones had already charmed *Mountain Stage* audiences. In production since 1983, the 2-hour live-performance radio show began as a showcase for state and regional traditional musicians, but over the years its host and artistic director Larry Groce developed a knack for spotting emerging star-quality talent in all musical genres, then showcasing it in a laid-back, performer-friendly setting. Today it's the longest-running live-performance public radio program in the country.

Out-of-towners and locals alike flock to the 460-seat state-of-the-art Culture Center Theater on the grounds of the State Capitol. The intimate setting and semi-unplugged style (performers use acoustic instruments, or at least turn down the volume) creates a connection between artist and audience that is rare in larger halls and bigger cities. Despite the down-home feeling, *Mountain Stage* reaches a vast audience, airing

Mountain Stage features seasoned legends and emerging artists in country, blues, folk, indie rock, and beyond.

on more than 150 stations across the U.S. via National Public Radio. After the show, performers and audience often mosey on over to the Empty Glass, considered possibly the best place for live music in West Virginia.

WHERE: Culture Center Theater. Tickets: mountainstage.org. *Cost:* from $20. *When:* 26 shows annually, usually on Sun afternoons. **THE EMPTY GLASS:** Tel 304-345-3914; emptyglass.com.

Old-Time Music in the Heart of Appalachia

THE VANDALIA GATHERING

Charleston, West Virginia

West Virginia is the only state that is fully contained within the mighty Appalachian Mountain range (see p. 372), giving it the hilly, winding topography that makes folks joke it would be bigger than Texas if it were pulled out flat. Those hills gave rise to old-time music—a 1920s term generally understood to mean rural folks playing fiddle, dulcimer, and other stringed instruments in an unschooled (though by no means artless) style passed down from generation to generation. Every year those same hills produce the finest fiddlers, flat-foot dancers, and tall-tale-tellers at the Vandalia Gathering, a three-day celebration of the time-honored traditions of West Virginia's mountain culture—music, dance, stories, crafts, and food galore.

"Vandalia" was the name envisioned for "the first West Virginia"—a 14th colony proposed by entrepreneurs and land speculators that nearly came into being in the 1770s, and it lives on when thousands of people descend on the grounds of the State Capitol for the family-friendly Memorial Day festival. The hottest hands at old-time fiddle, bluegrass banjo, mandolin, lap dulcimer, and flat-pick guitar compete for top honors on the big performance stages, and dancers from Irish, Scottish, and Appalachian folk traditions strut their stuff. The public is invited to square dance and flat foot dance, and it's standing room only at the competition for "Biggest Liar" (outrageous, minutes-long humorous stories that are told with utter

conviction). And of course there are traditional crafts, a quilt show, and plenty of food, including barbeque and homemade blackberry cobbler.

But the real magic of the Vandalia Gathering often takes place away from the performance stages. Throughout the days and long into the nights, clusters of musicians can be found under shade trees, on tailgates and porch steps, jamming out great sounds with long-lost friends or pickers they just met, and the city feels alive with traditions and music that are not just old-time but timeless.

WHERE: West Virginia State Capitol complex. Tel 304-558-0220; wvculture.org/vandalia. *When:* Memorial Day weekend (late May).

Square dancing at the Vandalia Gathering

World's Largest BASE Jumping Event

BRIDGE DAY FESTIVAL

Fayetteville, West Virginia

Every October, the New River Gorge Bridge attracts some 350 BASE jumpers who leap off the 876-foot-high bridge, making more flips and turns than is probably wise before deploying their single parachute, thrilling the 75,000-plus spectators who watch from the bridge or shores below. It's safe (usually), it's legal (but only on Bridge Day), and it lasts for just six glorious hours with a jump every 30 seconds.

"BASE" refers to the four things from which such jumpers like to leap—Buildings, Antennas, Spans, and Earth—and the New River Gorge is a perfect launching pad. The 3,030-foot-long bridge is the longest single-arch span in the Western Hemisphere and the second highest after Colorado's Royal Gorge Bridge. Completed in 1977, it didn't take long to catch the eye of BASE jumpers, with five taking the plunge at the first Bridge Day in 1980. Not just anyone can jump off the bridge, however. Registrants, who come from as far away as Russia and Australia, must have at least 100 prior skydives or BASE jumps under their belts.

It's wall-to-wall people at the festival, which also includes all manner of food, vendors, arts and crafts, and the music-packed Bridge Jam festival. Take advantage of some less extreme sports options while you're here—fishing (the New River is famous for its smallmouth bass), hiking, mountain biking, rock climbing, rafting through some of the best white-water rapids on the continent (see p. 281), or just strolling across the bridge.

WHERE: 58 miles southeast of Charleston. Tel 800-927-0263 or 304-465-5617; official bridgeday.com. **BRIDGE JAM:** thebridgejam .com. *When:* 3rd Sat in Oct.

Bridge Day is the world's largest extreme sports event.

Breathtaking Beauty and Bloody Ground

HARPERS FERRY

West Virginia

Thomas Jefferson saw the captivating shale bluffs and confluence of the Shenandoah and Potomac rivers at Harpers Ferry as "perhaps one of the most stupendous scenes in nature," but history remembers it best as the site of John Brown's ill-fated slave rebellion in 1859, a significant spark for the Civil War. Hoping to start a slave uprising, Brown and a band of 21 men tried to seize 100,000 rifles and pistols at the U.S. Armory and Arsenal. Instead, the small force was decimated within 36 hours and Brown was executed for treason six weeks later.

Today, Harpers Ferry's narrow streets are remarkably well preserved, with a history far more complex than a single event or individual. Not only did great men like George Washington, Robert E. Lee, and Abraham Lincoln pass this way, Harpers Ferry also witnessed the first industrial production of rifles using interchangeable parts; the first successful American railroad; the largest surrender of Federal troops during the Civil War (during which it changed hands eight times); and the education of former slaves in one of the nation's first integrated schools.

Try to book one of the three rooms at Jackson Rose, a 1795 redbrick B&B where West Point graduate and West Virginia native Colonel Thomas Jonathan Jackson (not yet the legend known as "Stonewall" for his cool-headed ability to hold a line under blistering fire) established his headquarters in April 1861. A four-poster bed and period decor appoints Jackson's second-floor room overlooking the rose garden and the "nice, green yard" he wrote of in letters to his wife. The

Appalachian Trail (see p. 332) runs right through Harpers Ferry, and the Appalachian Trail Conservancy is headquartered here, with photo albums produced by "thru-hikers" (individuals who intend to complete the entire trail in a single hiking season). Cool off during summer visits with an inner tube trip down the Potomac: Choose between peaceful flat water and white water.

A good base from which to explore both Harpers Ferry and Antietam (see p. 126) is nearby Shepherdstown, a small, tree-lined community that is West Virginia's oldest, first settled in the 1720s and perched on a bluff overlooking the Potomac River. The center of town is a pleasure to stroll, and a surprisingly authentic French meal can be found at charming Bistro 112. The menu is both classic and creative, all sourced by local purveyors. Near the historic downtown, the 73-room Bavarian Inn is a German-themed hotel centered around the 1930 Grey Stone Mansion, with stunning views of the river. With a master chef from Germany, the well-known dining room specializes in traditional Bavarian dishes like spaetzle (German noodles) and Wiener Schnitzel—not easy to find so well prepared this far from Munich.

WHERE: 64 miles west of Washington. *Visitor info:* Tel 304-535-6029; nps.gov/hafe. **JACKSON ROSE B&B:** Tel 304-535-1528; thejacksonrose.com. *Cost:* from $140 (off-peak), from $160 (peak). *When:* closed Jan–Feb. **APPALACHIAN TRAIL CONSERVANCY:** Tel 304-535-6331; appalachiantrail.org. **TUBING:** River Riders, tel 800-326-7238 or 304-535-2663; riverriders.com. *Cost:* from $28, includes tube and shuttle (May–Sept). **BISTRO 112:** Tel 304-876-8477; bistro112.com. *Cost:* dinner $35. **THE BAVARIAN INN:** Shepherdstown. Tel 304-876-2551; bavarianinnwv.com. *Cost:* rooms from $99 (off-peak), from $179 (peak); dinner $45. **BEST TIMES:** May and Oct for the weather; July 4th for living history demonstrations, free tours, and bugle corps performances; Thanksgiving–Dec 20 for old-time Christmas events (shepherdstown.info).

Robert Harper established the location of Harpers Ferry in 1751 at the confluence of two rivers.

The Charms of Carnegie Hall, Confederates, and Caves

LEWISBURG

West Virginia

A sk a passerby in Lewisburg how to get to Carnegie Hall, and you won't be told to "practice, practice, practice." Instead, you'll be directed to Church Street, where in 1902 philanthropist Andrew Carnegie donated the funds

for a white-columned classroom building for a women's college that was later transformed into a performing arts center in 1983, just one of many surprises in this historic community of cool, tree-canopied streets. One of the prettiest towns in the state, Lewisburg is a 236-acre National Register Historic District set amid the lush, rolling Greenbrier Valley, with good antiquing, live theater, and art galleries. All mighty impressive for a town of 3,800 folks, making it a favorite weekend getaway for people from Washington, D.C., and beyond.

Check in for a stay at the family-owned General Lewis Inn, a 1929 addition to a home constructed in 1834. Its 25 rooms are decorated with antique spool and canopy beds, chests of drawers, and old prints. The inn's restaurant is known for its fine country cooking—golden, crispy fried chicken and fresh caught local rainbow trout, but don't miss the freshly baked cornbread and cobblers, always served warm. Work off the calories hiking and biking on the 78-mile converted rail trail known as the Greenbrier River Trail; its scenic southern end starts near town.

Lewisburg annually attracts 180,000 people to the State Fair of West Virginia. With all the funnel cakes, carnival rides, and stage performances you can stand, it's a large ten-day fair with a healthy dose of agriculture—strong on livestock shows, draft-horse pulls, and competitions for the best garden vegetables, flowers, and baked goods—that's a lot of Americana.

Lewisburg is right on the historic Midland Trail, which leads to nearby White Sulphur

Lewisburg's Carnegie Hall is one of four buildings of the same name still in continuous use in the world.

Springs, home to the legendary Greenbrier Resort (see p. 285) and America's first organized golf club, the 9-hole Oakhurst Links. Recently purchased and operated by the Greenbrier, golf is played here with sand tees, hickory-shafted clubs, and gutta-percha balls (made of hard natural latex from Malaysia), just as it was when the course was laid out in 1884.

Set aside a day of one-stop shopping for handmade West Virginia arts and crafts some 50 miles west at Tamarack, whose striking fire-engine red roofline calls to mind the Statue of Liberty's crown. Half a million visitors a year come here to buy rigorously juried crafts—blown glass and wood carvings alongside sock monkeys and miniature outhouses. Resident artisans sit at work in glass-walled studios while live music, theater, dance, and storytelling invite you to linger.

WHERE: 80 miles northwest of Roanoke, VA. *Visitor info:* Tel 800-833-2068 or 304-645-1000; greenbrierwv.com. **CARNEGIE HALL:** Tel 304-645-7917; carnegiehallwv.com. **GENERAL LEWIS INN:** Lewisburg. Tel 304-645-2600; generallewisinn.com. *Cost:* rooms from $110; dinner $35. **GREENBRIER RIVER TRAIL:** greenbrierrivertrail.com. **STATE FAIR OF WEST**

VIRGINIA: Tel 304-645-1090; statefairofwv .com. *When:* 10 days in Aug. **OAKHURST LINKS:** White Sulphur Springs. Tel 304-536-1110; greenbrier.com/oakhurstlinks. *Cost:* greens fees $75. *When:* May–Oct. **TAMARACK:** Beckley. Tel 88-TAMARACK or 304-256-6843; tamarackwv.com. **BEST TIME:** Apr for Lewisburg Chocolate Festival.

A Million Untamed Allegheny Acres

"THE MON"

West Virginia

One of the East Coast's largest wilderness areas and best-kept secrets, the Monongahela National Forest is a 919,000-acre backcountry behemoth extended over ten counties in West Virginia, offering 1.3 million

backpackers, birders, berry pickers, mountain bikers, rock climbers, cross-country skiers, canoers, kayakers, and anglers more than enough Allegheny outback to explore without crossing each other's path.

Running roughly 130 miles along the crest of the Allegheny Mountains and protecting the watershed of the Monongahela River (thought to be a Delaware phrase that means "river of falling banks"), the "Mon" includes 800 miles of backwoods hiking trails, 23 camping

grounds, and eight federally designated wilderness areas—Otter Creek, Dolly Sods, Laurel Fork North, Laurel Fork South, Cranberry (see p. 282), Big Draft, Roaring Plains West, and Spice Run. The Spruce Knob–Seneca Rocks National Recreation Area encompasses some of the forest's most dramatic scenery. At 4,863 feet, Spruce Knob is the highest point in West Virginia, which you can reach via an easy half-mile hike past thickets of mountain laurel, rhododendron, and fire azaleas (all abloom in June and July) to commanding 360-degree views. Seneca Rocks, a magnificent formation of craggy Tuscarora quartzite rising nearly 900 feet above the North Fork River, is beloved by rock climbers for its challenging mapped routes (more than 375 of them), but less daring folks can hike a switchback trail to the top.

The mountain town of Elkins (population 7,200) is the Mon's largest gateway city and a destination in its own right thanks to the Augusta Heritage Center, where Appalachian folkways are kept alive through intensive week-long workshops on fiddling, quilt-making, clogging, tinsmithing, storytelling, rag-weaving, and accordion repair. The heart of the season

The white and gray quartzite Seneca Rocks are one of the best-known landmarks in West Virginia.

is five weeks in July and August with 300 different workshops offered, honoring not only the Appalachian region but also other music traditions including Irish, Cajun/Creole, blues, and swing, and culminating in the performance-packed, dance-filled Augusta Festival in Elkins City Park.

WHERE: along the crest of the Allegheny Mountains, on the eastern border of West Virginia. Tel 304-636-1800; fs.usda.gov/mnf.

Visitor info: Tel 800-458-7373 or 304-292-5081; tourmorgantown.com. **AUGUSTA HERITAGE CENTER:** Elkins. Tel 304-637-1209; augusta heritage.com. *Cost:* 5-day classes from $450, lodging and food extra. **WHERE TO STAY:** dormitory housing on campus. Or try the Graceland Inn, tel 800-624-3157 or 304-637-1600; gracelandinn.com. *Cost:* from $85. **BEST TIME:** Oct for October Old-Time Week and Old-Time Fiddler's Reunion.

From Black Gold to White Water

RAFTING THE NEW AND GAULEY RIVERS

West Virginia

In the 19th century, the New River Gorge region of south-central West Virginia produced the coal that fueled America's Industrial Revolution, the state's land honeycombed with mine shafts drilled down into the apparently limitless

seams. Today mining's share of the state economy has shrunken considerably, and the New River and nearby Gauley River have become instead two of the top white-water rafting destinations in the country, if not the world.

The New (which is among the world's oldest rivers) offers a range of rafting experiences along 53 scenic miles in West Virginia, curving between 1,000-foot forested slopes and passing abandoned mining towns. The 15-mile stretch of the upper river offers easy to moderate rapids that require little maneuvering skill, making it a favorite of families and beginners. (Opportunities for hiking, mountain biking, fishing, and rock climbing don't hurt, either.) The lower river, on the other hand, drops 250 feet in 16 miles, with big waves on more than two dozen rapids ranging from Class II to Class VI. This is the stretch some call the "Grand Canyon of the East," with its high walls and huge volume of water, especially in spring. Toward the end of the

run, rafters can see the enormous New River Gorge Bridge, at its wildest when hundreds of folks don parachutes and jump from it on Bridge Day (see p. 277).

North of the New, near Summersville, the Gauley River is one of the country's most challenging runs. In the 1960s, the U.S. Army Corps of Engineers built a 390-foot-tall, 2,280-foot-wide rock-fill dam in the river's upper reaches, creating West Virginia's largest lake. In summer, Summersville Lake is kept full to an elevation of 1,652 feet above sea level, maximizing opportunities for boating, fishing, water-skiing, and even scuba diving. In September and early October, the Corps must lower the lake to make room for the next spring's floods, turning the Gauley into a roaring beast with more than 60 steep Class IV and V rapids that have earned names like "Heaven Help You" and "Pure Screaming Hell." The Upper Gauley is the more difficult section, flowing through a narrow canyon with drops averaging 32 feet per mile. On the Lower Gauley, tough rapids are followed by calm pools, giving you a chance to catch your breath and soak in the beauty of the rough, wooded Appalachian terrain.

WHERE: 60 miles southeast of Charleston. *Visitor info:* Tel 800-927-0263 or 304-465-5617; newrivercvb.com. **HOW:** New & Gauley River Adventures, Lansing. Tel 800-759-7238 or 304-574-3008; gauley.com. *Cost:* 1-day New River rafting trips from $94, Lower Gauley trips from $140. *When:* Mar–Oct on the New River; Fri–Mon, early Sept–mid-Oct on the Gauley. **BEST TIMES:** Oct for foliage; 3rd weekend in Oct for Bridge Day (see p. 277).

Cruising the Crest of the Mountain State

HIGHLAND SCENIC HIGHWAY

Richwood to Edray, West Virginia

Built for the sheer pleasure of mountain driving, the Highland Scenic Highway spans 43 miles of unbroken forest in West Virginia's Allegheny Highlands, a quiet two-lane highway that transports you to the wild heart of the 919,000-acre Monongahela National Forest (see p. 280). Travelers will encounter not a single house, business, utility pole, billboard, or traffic signal along the 22-mile section of Route 150, modeled on Virginia's Skyline Drive (see p. 252). The original and most lauded portion of the Highland Scenic Highway, Route 150 offers a feast of panoramic vistas as it travels along the ridgetop. Over 60 percent of Route 150 is above 4,000 feet, with hardwood forests of maple and oak. There's no plowing in the winter, so when the snows arrive, so do snowmobilers and cross-country skiers—the road is all theirs.

Most people begin the drive just outside the lumber town of Richwood on Route 39/55, which leads to the U.S. Forest Service's educational Cranberry Mountain Nature Center. While not quite as dramatic, this initial stretch of road is nearly as pristine and has some of the area's most interesting stops. Walk the half-mile boardwalk that penetrates (and protects) the 750-acre Cranberry Glades Botanical Area, a series of primordial bogs usually found much farther north and in Canada.

In addition to well over 100 miles of hiking trails, prime trout waters are also easily accessible from several points along the way, including the North Fork of the Cherry River (which parallels the route for 15 miles after leaving Richwood) and the Williams River (which the highway crosses about 10 miles from its eastern end). If you've come for the glorious display of autumn foliage in late September, head to nearby Marlinton and the popular West Virginia Road Kill Cookoff. The half-serious wild-game cooking contest stipulates that all entries be made from animals commonly seen along the road—possum, raccoon, squirrel, deer, rabbit—though never scraped off it.

WHERE: begins on Rte. 39/55 outside Richwood (95 miles east of Charleston) and heads north on Rte. 150. *Visitor info:* Tel 800-336-7000, pocahontasvalleywv.com. **CRANBERRY MOUNTAIN NATURE CENTER:** Tel 304-653-4826. *When:* open mid-Apr–mid-Oct. **BEST TIMES:** late Sept–early Oct for fall colors; last Sat in Sept for the Autumn Harvest Festival/West Virginia Road Kill Cookoff in Marlinton (pccocwv.com/roadkill).

Where Quilts, Bees, and Apple Butter Meet

MOUNTAIN STATE ART AND CRAFT FAIR

Ripley, West Virginia

I t's not every day that you get the chance to see a man sporting a beard of swarming honeybees, hear Appalachian music performed as it was generations ago, and enjoy kettle-fresh apple butter smeared on just-baked bread.

That's why people flock to the Mountain State Art and Craft Fair: An Appalachian Experience, an institution since 1963 when it was first held to celebrate the birth of the state 100 years prior. (West Virginia was the only state to come into existence because of the Civil War, when it voted in 1863 to break away from Virginia and join the Union cause.)

Set on the 300-acre open-air campus of rustic buildings, barns, and lodgings that began in 1950 as a camp for the Future Farmers and Future Homemakers of America, the three-day Mountain State Fair attracts more than 100 of the very finest jewelers, basket weavers, saddle makers, blacksmiths, soap makers, and expert quilters demonstrating how they craft their quality wares. One specialty, West Virginia glassmaking, goes back some 200 years, a result of the state's abundant supplies of fine silica and clean-burning natural gas. When First Lady Jacqueline Kennedy wanted stemware for the White House, she chose West Virginia glass. The state is also known for its hardwoods, and woodworkers here turn out everything from small, intricate puzzle boxes to whimsical wood-sculpted carousel steeds. An almost nonstop program of old-time music provides a live sound track, and foods like barbecued chicken and homemade ice cream provide endless sustenance.

Aspiring crafters return to the Cedar Lakes Conference Center for year-round programs that include weaving chair bottoms out of hickory bark, hand-forging cutlery, or working under the careful tutelage of a master quilter. **WHERE:** Cedar Lakes Conference Center; 36 miles north of Charleston. Tel 800-CALL-WVA or 304-372-3247; msacf.com. *When:* 3rd weekend in Sept, Fri–Sun. **CRAFTS PROGRAM:** Tel 304-372-7860; cedarlakes.com. *Cost:* 4-day retreats in quilting, rug hooking, and other crafts, $700, includes lodging and meals.

A Thrilling Blend of Down-Home and Downhill

SNOWSHOE MOUNTAIN RESORT

Snowshoe, West Virginia

S outhern hospitality and skiing just don't seem to go together, but then West Virginia is the Mountain State and plenty of snow piles up on the Alleghenies in winter. Just ask Washington, D.C., snowhounds, who hightail it to

Snowshoe, a 4,848-foot monster mountain with a 1,500-foot vertical drop.

First developed in 1974, Snowshoe Mountain Resort is an "upside-down resort," with a nearly mile-high village at the top of the mountain instead of the base. Thanks to a quirk of West Virginia geology, you ski down into the hollow and then ride the lift back up. Now backed by megabucks from Intrawest, owners of Colorado's Steamboat (see p. 722), Canada's Tremblant ski resorts (see p. 1014), and Vermont's Stratton (see p. 108), Snowshoe Mountain has become a stellar property, with 57 trails and 14 lifts. Better skiers head to one of the original trails, Cupp Run, designed by Olympic gold medalist Jean-Claude Killy, and Shay's Revenge, as challenging as some black-diamond runs you'll encounter out west. Another surprise on the 11,000-acre tract of alpine wilderness is the backcountry log cabin you can reach via cross-country ski, snowshoe, or (most popular) a snowmobile trip of 2-plus miles. Stop in for lunch or dinner prepared by the hutmaster, or stay overnight and enjoy a cooked-to-order breakfast before hitting the slopes or trails.

Come summer, Snowshoe Mountain is one of the country's best places for downhill mountain biking—just sail down the single-track trails, downhill runs, and free-ride courses, then ride the lift back up again with your bike in tow. At the base of the mountain, golfers can enjoy their game with temperatures that rarely exceed 80°F at Raven Golf Club. With spectacular tees high above fairways and greens, it's regularly rated the best public course in West Virginia.

WHERE: 230 miles west of Washington, D.C. Tel 877-441-4386 or 304-572-1000; snowshoemtn.com. *Cost:* lift tickets from $75; lodgings from $84 (off-peak), from $100 (peak); dinner at Hut $245 for two. **BEST TIMES:** Jan–Mar for best snow; Feb for the West Virginia Open ski and snowboard freestyle competition; late Sept–early Oct for fall colors.

Giant Snowflakes and Cinderella on a 19th-Century Estate

OGLEBAY WINTER FESTIVAL OF LIGHTS

Wheeling, West Virginia

One of the largest and most splendid holiday light displays in the country, the Oglebay Winter Festival of Lights is a 6-mile driving show that benefits not just from the spectacular setting—a Gilded Age tycoon's

1,700-acre 19th-century ridgetop estate that is now the Oglebay Resort—but from a world-renowned landscape lighting expert. Every year a million people enjoy more than 80 giant displays (recently all converted to LED), like the 60-foot-tall candles and poinsettia wreath floating on a hillside, the 300-foot drive-through Rainbow Tunnel lined with 30 arches of multi-colored lights, and Cinderella's dazzling castle and pumpkin coach drawn by six prancing horses. The artistry comes from the Netherlands' Dick Bosch, who from 1985 until his death in 2005 set the style of extravagant displays combined with uplighting to create the perfect balance of light, shadow, and silhouette.

Oglebay Resort is owned by the city of Wheeling, a 1926 gift from Ohio-born Earl

W. Oglebay, one of West Virginia's most successful businessmen and philanthropists. Anchored by the 270-room Wilson Lodge and 54 charming cottages, Oglebay Resort is a family-friendly destination with skiing, snowboarding, and West Virginia's only zoo (30 acres of wildlife enclosures viewed from a 1.5-mile train ride). And it's a golfer's paradise, with four golf courses, including two championship courses designed by Arnold Palmer and Robert Trent Jones Sr. (Palmer devotees can try another acclaimed course 110 miles away at Stonewall Resort, a 196-room lodge in the Stonewall Jackson Lake State Park.)

The holiday lights don't stop with Oglebay: The town of some 28,000 residents really gets into the spirit by coming ablaze with lights itself. That includes holiday decorations at Coleman's Fish Market, located in an historic 1890s building and famous for its fish

Twinkling lights create an enchanting fairy-tale display.

sandwich—clusters of deep-fried fresh North Atlantic pollock between two pieces of soft white bread, the best snack in town. Downtown Wheeling is unusually handsome, embellished by the 19th-century fortunes made by outfitting pioneers after the Wheeling Suspension Bridge was built across the Ohio River in 1849.

In July, the big excitement in these parts is found across the bridge in Ohio, where the nearby Jamboree in the Hills takes place, a four-day outdoor festival featuring more than twenty country-and-western megawatt acts like Reba McIntyre, Carrie Underwood, and West Virginia's own Brad Paisley.

WHERE: 60 miles southwest of Pittsburgh, PA. *Visitor info:* Tel 800-828-3097 or 304-233-7709; wheelingcvb.com. **OGLEBAY RESORT:** Tel 800-624-6988 or 304-243-4000; oglebay-resort.com/festival. *Cost:* from $119 (off-peak), from $166 (peak); greens fees from $62. **STONEWALL RESORT:** Roanoke. Tel 888-278-8150 or 304-269-7400; stonewallresort.com. *Cost:* from $119; greens fees from $80. **COLEMAN'S FISH MARKET:** Wheeling. Tel 304-232-8510. *Cost:* fish sandwich $5. **JAMBOREE IN THE HILLS:** Tel 800-624-5456; jamboreeinthehills.com. *Cost:* 4-day pass, $210. *When:* 4 days in mid-July. **BEST TIMES:** late Mar–Apr for the annual display of 50,000 tulips, daffodils, and hyacinths; Nov–early Jan for Winter Festival of Lights.

Where Presidents Take the Waters

THE GREENBRIER

White Sulphur Springs, West Virginia

In 1778, Mrs. Amanda Anderson, who suffered from terrible rheumatism, went deep into the Allegheny Mountains in search of a natural spring that the Shawnee Indians believed had curative powers. There she drank her fill,

soaked lengthily in a tub made from a hollow tree, then waited for the cure to take effect.

Miraculously it did, and a health resort was born. In 1784, Virginia lawyer Michael Bowyer received the title to the valley land around the spring, and over the following years built a tavern and several log cabins to accommodate visitors. Around 1810 Bowyer's family began transforming the property into a proper resort, and in 1858 added a majestic, pillared hotel that became famous as "The Old White," attracting visitors like Davy Crockett, Daniel Webster, and numerous presidents—26 at last count.

Today the Greenbrier stands grandly amid 10,000 scenic acres, offering 710 rooms and promising over 50 activities. Golf is the leading attraction, with four 18-hole championship courses open to the public plus a respected golf academy. The Greenbrier Course, site of both the Ryder (1979) and Solheim (1994) Cups, was laid out in 1924 and redesigned by Jack Nicklaus in 1977. Elsewhere, the 40,000-square-foot spa continues the Greenbrier's 240-year tradition of aquatherapy, with sulphur soaks in the same healing waters that once cured Mrs. Anderson and more modern touches like executive health programs and cosmetic surgery. Gaming is a relatively new addition to the property with the

The Greenbrier offers horse-drawn carriage rides, and sleigh rides in winter.

arrival of a 103,000-square-foot casino, part of a $350 million investment by native West Virginian Jim Justice who purchased the resort in 2009. Activities like tennis on indoor and outdoor courts, horseback riding, fishing, mountain biking, and even falconry assure that non-golfers will hardly feel neglected.

A house-proud staff of 1,800 exemplifies the resort's characteristic elegance and decorum. Expect musicians at teatime in the spacious, marble-floored lobby and later at dinner, where a jacket-and-tie dress code prevails beneath sparkling crystal chandeliers. The decor, created by designer Dorothy Draper after WWII and reinterpreted by her protégé Carleton Varney, features a mix of stripes and flowers and an unconventionally bright color palette. Greenbrier's most unique feature is its underground fallout shelter. During the Eisenhower administration, the government excavated a huge complex beneath the property intended to house members of Congress in the event of nuclear war. The bunker was finally declassified after *The Washington Post* reported its existence in 1992, and is now open for tours.

The Greenbrier is a major stop on the Midland Trail (U.S. Route 60), a buffalo trail followed by Indians and pioneers. Offering beautiful vistas of wooded mountains and rolling farmland, it travels the entire length of the state.

Where: 120 miles southeast of Charleston; 300 W. Main St. Tel 855-453-4858; greenbrier.com. *Cost:* from $149 (off-peak), from $199 (peak); greens fees from $75 for guests. **Midland Trail Highway:** Tel 866-ROUTE-60 or 304-343-6001; midlandtrail.com. **Best time:** Oct for foliage.

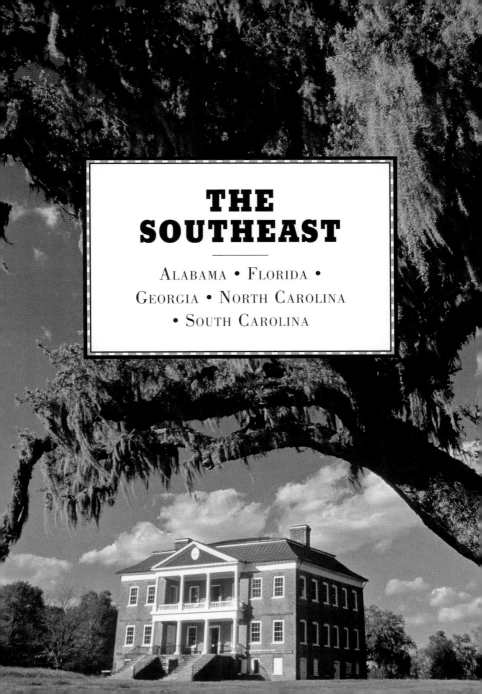

THE SOUTHEAST

Alabama • Florida •
Georgia • North Carolina
• South Carolina

THE

SOUTHEAST

Red, White, and BBQ'ed All Over

ALABAMA BARBECUE

Alabama

U nlike barbecue in some states, which can easily be pigeonholed (beef in Texas; pork in Tennessee), Alabama barbecue offers vast regional variety. Each has its own special spices, seasonings, and devoted following.

And it's all good. In northern Alabama, you're likely to find pork drenched in a peppery vinegar bath or chicken glazed with a mayonnaise base, while barbecuers to the south slather their meat in tomato-based sauces.

The best-known of Alabama's barbecue joints is Dreamland in Tuscaloosa (home to the football-crazed University of Alabama), which has been making heavenly pork ribs since 1958, when brick mason John "Big Daddy" Bishop Sr. opened his café. Big Daddy

Mr. John "Big Daddy" Bishop's legendary Dreamland ribs draw fans from near and far.

is gone, but Dreamland (with locations statewide) remains the lip-smacking ultimate for barbecue buffs, who swear by the meaty spareribs that have been salted and soaked in spicy vinegar sauce before being slowly grilled over hickory-wood flames.

A white barbecue sauce may sound like an oxymoron, but those who hail from the northwest corner of the state will beg to differ. Decatur claims to be the birthplace of barbecued chicken with a mayonnaise-based sauce. Big Bob Gibson Bar-B-Q, a fourth-generation eatery in business since 1952, is named for a railroad worker who loved entertaining in his backyard, where he hand-dug his own roasting pit. As legend has it, Gibson concocted the white sauce of vinegar and black pepper, adding mayonnaise to keep the chicken from drying out on the barbecue spit. At Miss Myra's Pit outside Birmingham, tomato-based barbecue sauce over pork and chicken is also on the menu, but white is the sauce of choice for those who know better.

Gibson isn't the only "Big Bob" in Alabama barbecue history. Bob Sykes Bar-B-Q in Bessemer (look for a cartoon pig on the roof) has been famous for its pork ribs since 1968. The family still carries on the late Bob's tradition of his two-fisted, pickle-topped "Big Bob" sandwich of succulent pulled pork—the tender meat pulled from the bone and chopped up. There's barbecued chicken, too, and plenty of great sides, such as baked beans and handmade onion rings.

Barbecue in the bayside city of Mobile can

only mean the Brick Pit, where you're invited to etch your signature on the popular restaurant's walls (or ceiling, if you can reach) while patiently waiting for tender pork ribs cooked for at least 12 hours, while pulled pork roasts for up to 30 hours, over pecan- and hickory-wood fires. Whether you choose the spicy or sweet sauce, don't forget to use that slice of white bread to mop up your plate.

DREAMLAND: Tuscaloosa. Tel 205-758-8135; dreamlandbbq.com. *Cost:* $20. **BIG BOB GIBSON BAR-B-Q:** Decatur. Tel 256-350-6969; bigbobgibson.com. *Cost:* $15. **MISS MYRA'S PIT:** Cahaba Heights. Tel 205-967-6004. *Cost:* $14. **BOB SYKES BAR-B-Q:** Bessemer. Tel 205-426-1400; bobsykes.com. *Cost:* $13. **BRICK PIT:** Mobile. Tel 251-343-0001; brickpit.com. *Cost:* $20.

An Eden Built by Coca-Cola

BELLINGRATH GARDENS

Theodore, Alabama

Bellingrath's sea of springtime azaleas, summer roses, or fields of fall chrysanthemums will awaken the inner gardener in even the most indifferent visitor. One of the top public gardens in the U.S., Bellingrath

Gardens is a lush 65-acre floral oasis near Alabama's Gulf Coast that has been delighting nature lovers for over eight decades. Here in the heart of the Camellia State, a trip in any season makes the importance of this world-class garden abundantly—and fragrantly—apparent.

Walter Bellingrath, owner of Mobile's first Coca-Cola bottling plant, bought the former fishing camp on the banks of the Fowl River in 1917. The overgrown property was pruned and cleared for a grand expanse of gardens, and opened to the public in 1932. In 1936 he built a lavish home on the grounds, for which his architect salvaged materials from 19th-century Mobile, including flagstone and slate walkways fashioned from the ballast of English ships that sailed here when cotton from the American South was king. Framed by oaks dripping with Spanish moss, the home has become a modern-day museum, filled with fine art, antiques, and the country's largest collection of Boehm porcelain.

Bellingrath's spectacular garden walkways and meadows are in a constant state of verdant evolution. Early spring brings fluffy

Pink azaleas bloom along the banks of Mirror Lake.

peonies, multicolored tulips, snapdragons, lilies, and flowering cabbage and kale. Slightly warmer spring temperatures beckon the hydrangeas, delphiniums, petunias, and ruffled azaleas in shades of purple, pink, and white. In fact, spring is the ultimate time to visit nearby Mobile, known as Azalea City. The hot early summers are perfect for roses, and with more than 50 varieties, Bellingrath has twice won the top honor as America's most outstanding rose garden. Exotic flamingo flowers and caladiums complete what feels like a living landscape painting. Fall means 60,000 chrysanthemums that overflow from flower beds and cascade from bridges and balconies. Even winter is a tourist season here, as the mansion and gardens are awash in poinsettias, tinsel, and some 3 million twinkling holiday lights during the well-known Magic Christmas in Lights festival.

WHERE: 15 miles southwest of Mobile; 12401 Bellingrath Rd., Theodore. Tel 800-247-8420 or 251-973-2217; bellingrath.org. **BEST TIMES:** Mar–Apr for azaleas; spring and summer for festivals; late Nov–Dec for Magic Christmas in Lights festival.

Gourmet Grits and Fried Green Tomatoes

THE HIGHLANDS BAR AND GRILL

Birmingham, Alabama

Frank Stitt's perennially popular Highlands Bar and Grill in Birmingham's historic Five Points South district is an upscale yet refreshingly unpretentious place whose cuisine has been described as a marriage of the American South and the South of France. Stitt, a country doctor's son born in the small northern Alabama farming town of Cullman (known for its sweet potatoes, a proud staple of his restaurant's menu today), fled the South after high school, attended Tufts University in Boston, trained with chefs in Provence, and landed in the San Francisco Bay Area, where he was influenced by, among others, the renowned Alice Waters of Chez Panisse (see p. 805). With its emphasis on organic produce and sustainable agriculture, Stitt's philosophy has been embraced by chefs and their followers throughout the South and beyond.

A warm, bistrolike atmosphere, exquisite service, and artfully presented dishes are hallmarks of Highlands Bar and Grill, which opened to immediate acclaim in 1982. (Highlands's sister restaurants include Bottega and Chez Fonfon, both also in Birmingham.) Any season's menu features bounty from Alabama's Gulf Coast, such as grilled snapper with ham hock and butternut squash or gulf swordfish with roasted artichoke, and meatier entrées might include pork tenderloin with persimmon relish. Starters are at once downhome and sublime: mixed seafood fry with satsuma aioli and fried chicken livers with black peppercorn biscuit and sorghum dressing. Don't miss the sweet potato and pecan tart with cinnamon anglaise, the cornmeal cake with dulce de leche ice cream and salted caramel, or the creamy banana pudding topped with meringue. Little wonder that Stitt is known in savvy food circles as the "Culinary King of Alabama."

Outside of Birmingham in the small town of Irondale, you can experience the equally tasty but simpler flip side of Alabama's gastronomic coin: The Irondale Café, an archetypal railroad-depot diner, whose Southern and soul food menu is a proud example of a "meat-and-three (side dishes)" cafeteria. At this one, made famous as the inspiration for Alabama author Fannie Flagg's novel *Fried Green Tomatoes at the Whistlestop Café* (and its 1991 movie adaptation), hungry patrons seated at red-and-white-checkered tables hunker down over comfort food chosen from the voluminous lunch buffet. There are chicken and dumplings, fried chicken, fried steak with brown gravy, and side dishes of macaroni and cheese, fried okra, collard greens, black-eyed peas, and, of course, fried green tomatoes—thick-sliced rounds dredged in cornmeal and fried to a golden brown. Leave

room for fresh peach cobbler or buttermilk pie. **WHERE:** 2011 11th Ave. S. Tel 205-939-1400; highlandsbarandgrill.com. *When:* closed Sun–Mon. *Cost:* dinner $60. **IRONDALE CAFÉ:** Tel 205-956-5258; irondalecafe.com. *When:* daily. *Cost:* lunch $12.

Birthplace of a Blues Legend

W. C. HANDY FESTIVAL

Florence, Alabama

"Where the Tennessee River, like a silver snake, winds her way through the clay hills of Alabama," wrote musician W. C. Handy, "sits high on these hills, my hometown, Florence."

Born in a log cabin on November 16, 1873, William Christopher ("W. C.") Handy is a seminal figure of American blues and jazz. The grandson of a minister, Handy was inspired early by church gospel music and the field hollers of black cotton pickers. A gifted trumpeter and bandleader, he left his home in northwestern Alabama to travel with an orchestra to Chicago and then St. Louis, Kentucky, and Missouri before winding up in Memphis. It was there that he penned the world's first blues songs on Beale Street (see p. 468), including "St. Louis Blues" in 1914. He also lived for a time in Henderson, Kentucky, and died in New York City in 1958, but he remains the pride of Florence, where an annual ten-day festival in late July celebrates the prolific composer and his music.

Among Florence's other tourist attractions are the Handy Home and Museum, the humble two-room rural cabin where Handy was born, and the Frank Lloyd Wright Rosenbaum House, a single-story house commissioned in 1939 by newlyweds Stanley and Mildred Rosenbaum. It's the only Wright-designed structure in the state and is open for tours.

In nearby Tuscumbia, in the music-rich area known as the Shoals, the Alabama Music

The annual W. C. Handy Festival features more than 250 events, including outdoor concerts with prominent blues and jazz musicians.

Hall of Fame Museum honors Handy and an impressive list of homegrown musical heroes, including Nat "King" Cole, Hank Williams, Sonny James, Tammy Wynette, Emmylou Harris, Lionel Richie, and country supergroup, Alabama. Tuscumbia is also Helen Keller's hometown. Be sure to see the play *The Miracle Worker*, which has been performed every summer since 1961 at the white clapboard house where Keller was born and lived.

For lunch, head over to Trowbridge's, a third-generation family-owned restaurant in

Florence that began as a creamery in 1918. Try the ham-and-biscuits, chili, olive-studded egg salad, or old-fashioned banana splits. Don't forget nearby Muscle Shoals, where legendary Sam Phillips, who founded Sun Records in Memphis, once worked as a DJ. It is best known as hallowed recording studio ground, where Percy Sledge's "When a Man Loves a Woman," the Rolling Stones's "Brown Sugar," Wilson Pickett's "Mustang Sally," and countless other hits were born.

WHERE: 100 miles northwest of Birmingham. *Visitor info:* Tel 888-FLO-TOUR or 256-740-4141; visitflorenceal.com. **W. C. HANDY FESTIVAL:** Tel 800-472-5837 or 256-

766-7642; wchandymusicfestival.org. *When:* late July. **W. C. HANDY HOME AND MUSEUM:** Tel 256-760-6434. **FRANK LLOYD WRIGHT ROSENBAUM HOUSE:** Tel 256-740-8899; wrightinalabama.com. **ALABAMA MUSIC HALL OF FAME:** Tuscumbia. Tel 800-239-AMHF or 256-381-4417; alamhof.org. *When:* Tues–Sat. **HELEN KELLER BIRTHPLACE AT IVY GREEN:** Tuscumbia. Tel 888-329-2124 or 256-383-4066; helenkellerbirthplace.org. *When: The Miracle Worker* Fri–Sat, June–mid-July. **TROWBRIDGE'S:** Florence. Tel 256-764-1503. *Cost:* lunch $8. **MUSCLE SHOALS SOUND STUDIOS:** Sheffield. Tel 256-783-2641; msmusicfoundationorg.

World's Biggest Flea Market

THE HIGHWAY 127 CORRIDOR SALE

Gadsden, Alabama, to Hudson, Michigan

"I drove, I stopped, I shopped till I dropped." That's the battle cry of the legions of bargain hunters who take part in the four-day extravaganza known as the Highway 127 Corridor Sale, proudly billed as the world's

largest yard sale. The sale was created in 1995 by officials at the Fentress County Chamber of Commerce in Jamestown, Tennessee, as a way to encourage travelers to detour off the monotonous highway to discover the natural beauty and slower pace of the less-traveled back roads of eastern Tennessee and Kentucky. The outdoor shopping-palooza, which begins each year on the Thursday prior to the first Saturday in August, has expanded over the years to span 690 miles and five states, from Noccalula Falls Park in Gadsden, Alabama, across the northwestern tip of Georgia and through Tennessee, all the way north to Covington, Kentucky, then up through Ohio, and finally just across the border 5 miles beyond Addison, Michigan.

Tens of thousands of cars, RVs, SUVs, and motorcycles idle through "America's most scenic shopping mall," where millions of items are hawked at side-by-side yard sales along the route, as some 3,500 weekend sellers—householders and professional vendors alike—display their wares on their front lawns, in parking lots, on flatbed trucks, and in rural fields. Whatever you're looking for, if you look hard enough, you'll find it.

You can start on the 93-mile Alabama portion of this scavenger hunt, which encompasses the beautiful Lookout Mountain Parkway. From Gadsden, the route follows Tabor Road to Alabama Highway 176, which becomes County Road 89 through Dogtown, Fort Payne, and DeSoto State Park to Alabama

Highway 117 in Mentone (see next page). From there, take Highway 117 into Georgia, and then follow the signs to Tennessee 27 and the U.S. Highway 127 Corridor for the remainder of the trip north. And make sure you empty out the trunk first.

WHERE: 690 miles, from Noccalula Falls Park in Gadsden (50 miles northeast of Birmingham) to outside Addison, MI. Tel 800-327-3945 or 931-879-9948; 127sale.com. *When:* The 4-day sale begins the Thurs before the 1st Sat in Aug.

The Great Beyond

U.S. SPACE & ROCKET CENTER

Huntsville, Alabama

The year was 1941, the advent of WWII, and the U.S. government had just chosen Huntsville as the site for one of its important munitions plants, Redstone Arsenal. The small town located in the Tennessee River Valley in northern Alabama would never be the same. In the years following the war, Uncle Sam converted Redstone to a missile research center, and Huntsville was well on its way to earning its nickname "Rocket City." Huntsville's population of about 16,000 swelled to over 50,000, as people were drawn to the promise of good jobs in a burgeoning space industry. A team of German rocket scientists, led by Wernher von Braun, created the first ballistic missile here, a feat that would eventually help American astronauts land on the moon.

The Pathfinder *is a 75-ton steel simulator initially built and used by NASA to practice the handling and moving of actual space shuttles.*

In 1960, just two years after the founding of the National Aeronautics and Space Administration (NASA), President Dwight D. Eisenhower dedicated the Marshall Space Flight Center at Redstone for the purpose of space exploration and research. (It is still used today by NASA to research, develop, and manage projects such as the International Space Station and the new Space Launch System.) But it was not until 1965 that the public could get a glimpse of it all, with the opening of the U.S. Space & Rocket Center. The museum houses one of the world's largest collections of spacecraft, including the 1972 *Apollo 16* command module and a massive,

awe-inspiring life-size replica of the space shuttle. (NASA's Space Center in Houston, Texas, has a similar space shuttle.)

Don't miss the gravity-defying effects of weightlessness in a centrifuge, or the far gentler IMAX screening of outer-space films shot on location by real astronauts. Let the kids test their game-playing skills at the Lunar Lander simulator before scrambling up the Mars Climbing Wall.

Another very popular component of the center is the camp program. The Space Camp, Robotics Camp, and Aviation Challenge Camp offer a fascinating roster of educational day and overnight space programs for children, adults, and families ranging from three to six days. In addition to classes and hands-on activities, such as navigational training in a cockpit simulator and rocket construction, overnight campers also have after-hours access to all the center has to offer.

The town of Huntsville, in the foothills of the southern Appalachian Mountains, is also worth exploring. Scout out the scenic downtown district of Twickenham, where wealthy cotton merchants and planters built one of the largest collections of antebellum homes in the southeastern U.S. long before anyone ever dreamed of the Space Age.

WHERE: 90 miles north of Birmingham; One Tranquility Base. Tel 800-63-SPACE or 256-837-3400; spacecamp.com. *Visitor info:* Tel 800-SPACE-4-U or 256-551-2230; huntsville.org.

Lofty Gateway to the Appalachian Mountains

MENTONE

Alabama

Perched atop Lookout Mountain in the northeastern corner of Alabama at a lofty elevation of 1,736 feet is Mentone, a diminutive village that's home to 400 lucky residents, and a leafy and secluded summer retreat for savvy regulars. Mentone's crisp air and mineral waters were famous for their restorative properties in the late 19th century. Today the area is better known for the numerous children's camps and rental cabins dotting the hillsides, but the countless B&Bs, shops, and cozy tearooms in town—and surrounding vistas of rocky canyons and pristine waterfalls—continue to lull guests into forgetting that

A 45-foot waterfall and dramatic gorge are among the highlights of Little River Canyon National Preserve.

traffic jams and strip malls ever existed. And getting there is a joy: The Lookout Mountain Parkway was named one of America's most scenic drives by *Reader's Digest*.

Blessed with their location in the foothills of the Appalachian Plateau, Mentone and surrounding DeKalb County offer hang gliding, rock climbing, spelunking, fishing, and horseback riding. Believe it or not, you can even ski in the winter months at the Cloudmont Ski and Golf Resort, the southernmost ski destination in America, where snow-making machines are put to work for slalomers and snowboarders alike.

When the 130-year-old Victorian-style Mentone Springs Hotel burned to the ground in 2014, Alabama lost its oldest wooden hotel and the town lost a beloved icon. A fine alternative is the Mentone Inn, not quite as old (it was built in 1927) and just across the street from where the older dowager once stood. It puts you within striking distance of bright and attractive Kamama, a café-cum-art gallery popular for lunch or dinner and the best Sunday brunch in town.

Pack a lunch for a day trip through the scenic Little River Canyon National Preserve. The rugged 14,000-acre park is home to a 700-foot gorge, one of the deepest east of the Mississippi. "The Grand Canyon of the East" is visible from the 23-mile drive that wends along the rim. Alabama river buffs would prefer to keep this gorge a secret, but the Class III–IV rapids that sluice down the gullet of Lookout Mountain are world-class challenges for advanced kayakers, while other stretches promise more placid runs.

WHERE: 35 miles south of Chattanooga, TN. *Visitor info:* Tel 888-805-4740 or 256-845-3957; discoverlookoutmountain.com. **CLOUDMONT SKI & GOLF RESORT:** Tel 256-634-4344; cloudmont.com. *Cost:* lift tickets from $20. *When:* mid-Dec–early Mar. **MENTONE INN:** Tel 256-634-4836; mentoneinn.com. *Cost:* $130. **CAFÉ KAMAMA:** Tel 256-634-3001; kamamamentone.com *Cost:* lunch $12. **LITTLE RIVER CANYON:** Fort Payne. Tel 256-845-9605; nps.gov/liri. **BEST TIMES:** mid-May for Mentone Rhododendron Festival; Aug for the Highway 127 Corridor Sale (see p. 293); 3rd weekend in Oct for the Fall Colorfest.

Magnolias, Bay Breezes, and White Beaches

MOBILE BAY'S EASTERN SHORE AND THE ALABAMA GULF COAST

Alabama

Flung along the eastern shore of Mobile Bay, the small picture-perfect communities of Fairhope, Point Clear, and Magnolia Springs—and the tiny fishing villages between them—form a scenic route southward to the beach resort of Gulf Shores and beyond to the Florida Panhandle. The area's nickname, the "Redneck Riviera," doesn't do justice to the sugar-white sand beaches and translucent turquoise waters of the Gulf of Mexico in southern Alabama.

Fairhope, founded in 1894, is a vibrant and artistic-minded community. City parks bloom with magnolias and roses, and downtown's tree-shaded brick streets are lined with cafés, galleries, and eclectic shops. A few miles south, Point Clear has Civil War–era roots but now thrives in the orbit of the posh Grand Hotel Marriott Resort, Golf Club & Spa. The "Queen of Southern Resorts" pampers guests with ten tennis courts, a marina busy with sailboats and charter yachts, a European-style spa, and the celebrated Lakewood Golf Club—with two 18-hole courses designed by Perry Maxwell in the 1940s—that is part of the Robert Trent Jones Golf Trail (see p. 299). The Dining Room offers lavish meals, Sunday brunch with live jazz, and waterfront views fading into Bay sunsets. Point Clear's other site of pilgrimage is the casual yet chic Wash House Restaurant, specializing in Southern coastal cuisine pulled from these very waters. Try the sesame-encrusted yellowfin tuna or seared shrimp with roasted poblano and cheese grits, and save room for Key lime bread pudding.

Heading south along the bay, you'll come to Magnolia Springs, scented with the creamy white blossoms that gave it its name. Moss-draped oaks rim the banks of the Magnolia River, which carves through this genteel, century-old town, the home and inspiration to Alabama authors Winston Groom (*Forrest Gump*) and Fannie Flagg (*Fried Green Tomatoes at the Whistlestop Café;* see p. 291). Settle in to savor the lazy pace of this town at the immaculately restored five-bedroom Magnolia Springs B&B, an 1897 Victorian inn filled with cozy furnishings and polished heart-pine floors.

Nine miles farther south at Gulf Shores, Alabama's four-day Annual National Shrimp Festival takes place in mid-October, drawing in crowds of some 250,000, who come to devour crustaceans that are fried, grilled, sautéed, and skewered by the boatload.

WHERE: Fairhope, Point Clear, Magnolia Springs, and Gulf Shores are between 12 and 35 miles southeast of Mobile. *Eastern Shore visitor info:* Tel 251-928-6387; eschamber.com. *Gulf Shores visitor info:* Tel 800-745-SAND or 251-968-7511; gulfshores.com. **GRAND HOTEL MARRIOTT:** Point Clear. Tel 800-544-9933 or 251-928-9201; marriottgrand.com. *Cost:* from $299. **WASH HOUSE:** Point Clear. Tel 251-928-4838; washhouserestaurant.com. *Cost:* dinner $45. **MAGNOLIA SPRINGS B&B:** Tel 800-965-7321 or 251-965-7321; magnoliasprings.com. *Cost:* from $199. **BEST TIMES:** Apr–May and Oct–Nov for best weather; mid-Oct for the shrimp festival in Gulf Shores (myshrimpfest.com).

Where History Was Made

CIVIL RIGHTS TRAIL

Montgomery, Selma, and Birmingham, Alabama

Alabama was at the violent forefront of the nation's civil rights movement in the late 1950s and '60s. Tourists today make pilgrimages to places such as Montgomery, Selma, and Birmingham, where bombings, riots, and peaceful protests galvanized the nation—and profoundly changed the world.

Begin your journey in the state capital of Montgomery, where the Rosa Parks Library and Museum recounts the courageous act of defiance by the Montgomery seamstress who, in 1955, refused to give up her seat on the city bus to a white man. Exhibits and interactive displays narrate her arrest and the watershed Montgomery Bus Boycott the following year that lasted for 381 days, eventually leading to the ban of segregation on all public transportation and intrastate buses. Outside the Civil Rights Memorial Center, also downtown, water flows over a black granite time line, which lists the names of those who were killed during the movement, ending with the date of April 4, 1968—the day Martin Luther King Jr. was shot and killed in Memphis (see p. 471).

Selma, on the banks of the Alabama River about an hour's drive west of Montgomery, was the site of one of the movement's pivotal moments. Here on the Edmund Pettus Bridge, on March 7, 1965, about 500 demonstrators marching to the state capital in Montgomery were beaten with clubs by state troopers and the sheriff's posse. Television news footage sparked rioting in dozens of U.S. cities and motivated others to join the cause. Two weeks later, thousands of supporters returned to the scene for the triumphant 54-mile, five-day trek from Selma to Montgomery. Later that year President Lyndon Johnson signed the 1965 Voting Rights Act, outlawing the literacy tests and poll taxes that denied some blacks the vote.

A single downtown intersection in Birmingham, Alabama's largest city, is home to the city's most important civil rights sites. The Birmingham Civil Rights Institute features emotionally charged displays, exhibits, and interactive media stations, relating to the human struggle—in the South and internationally—

for freedom. Across the street, Sixteenth Street Baptist Church provides a chilling look back at the 1963 Ku Klux Klan bombing that killed four girls preparing for a Sunday School program. Visitors may tour the sanctuary, watch a documentary film about the event, and walk through the basement of the fellowship hall that serves as a memorial. Across the street lies Kelly Ingram Park, which was a protest assembly point and the scene of vicious attacks during the first week of May 1963, when police unleashed guard dogs and water hoses on people who were protesting segregation. Statues, plaques, and an audio tour (available at the Civil Rights Institute) honor the demonstrators' bravery.

The Rosa Parks Library and Museum tells the story of the fateful 1955 bus ride and how Parks's act of resistance helped change history.

Civil Rights Trail: Tel 334-877-1983; alabama.travel. **Rosa Parks Library and Museum:** Montgomery. Tel 334-241-9576; troy.edu. *When:* closed Sun. **Civil Rights Memorial Center:** Tel 888-414-7752 or 334-956-8200; splcenter.org. *When:* closed Sun. **Selma to Montgomery March:** nps .org. **Birmingham Civil Rights Institute:** Tel 205-328-9696; bcri.org. *When:* closed Sun–Mon. **Sixteenth Street Church:** Tel 205-251-9811; nps.org. *When:* Tues–Fri 10 a.m.–3 p.m.; Sat by appointment. **Best times:** Apr–May and Oct–Nov to avoid summer's heat and humidity.

Folk and Outsider Art—and the "Mud Man"

Kentuck Festival of the Arts and Jimmy Lee Sudduth

Northport, Alabama

One of the best folk art festivals in the country, the Kentuck Festival of the Arts takes place in western Alabama, in what may seem like an out-of-the-way area. But the sleepy small towns and the region's landscape of pine and red clay dirt have inspired nationally renowned folk artists. Foremost among them is Jimmy Lee "Mud Man" Sudduth, whose paintings put the Kentuck Festival on the map of unconventional art.

Always dressed in his denim overalls, Sudduth (1910–2007) worked as a grist miller, lumberyard worker, and gardener. His compulsion to paint began in childhood, although he didn't hit his stride until the 1960s. Sudduth's simplistic, self-taught style—like that of other Southern so-called "outsider" or visionary artists, such as Clementine Hunter of Louisiana (see p. 423), and Howard Finster of Georgia (see p. 347)—was not as surprising as his medium. Sudduth preferred to make his own pigments by mashing together dirt, grass, leaves, berries, charcoal, coffee grounds, molasses, and even the juicy "pot likker" from boiled turnip greens that he applied to plywood boards with his fingers. While waiting for his childlike self-portraits, pictures of dogs (his beloved pooch Toto shows up frequently), landscapes, and imagined skyscrapers to dry, Sudduth would often entertain visitors or himself by playing the harmonica for hours. "Mud Man" first achieved widespread fame with a 1982 exhibition at the Corcoran Museum of Art in Washington, D.C. Sudduth's early mud pieces have become sought-after collectors' items.

Music enlivens the festival, where children's crafts activities are a big draw as well, with opportunities to make corn-husk dolls, throw a clay pot, and touch and experiment with the musical instruments in the Tuscaloosa Symphony Guild's "petting zoo."

Visit the Art Center, the Kentuck Festival's home base, housed in a two-story 1920 masonry building in Northport's historic downtown, on the banks of the Black Warrior River. It features the galleries and working studios of several Alabamian artists with shops selling fine arts and crafts. Folk art fans and arts-minded festival attendees will want to make the drive to nearby Fayette, Sudduth's birthplace, where his art (along with works by other Southern artists) is displayed year-round in the small Fayette Art Museum.

KENTUCK FESTIVAL OF THE ARTS: just outside Tuscaloosa, 60 miles southwest of Birmingham. *Visitor info:* Tel 205-349-3870; tuscco.com. *When:* 3rd weekend in Oct. **KENTUCK ART CENTER:** Northport. Tel 205-758-1257; kentuck.org. *When:* closed Sun–Mon. **FAYETTE ART MUSEUM:** Fayette. Tel 205-932-8727; fayetteartmuseum.vpweb.com. *When:* closed Sat–Sun.

World-Class Golf in the Heart of Dixie

ROBERT TRENT JONES GOLF TRAIL

Alabama

You may not think golf when you think Alabama, but the state's Robert Trent Jones Golf Trail features more than 460 holes at 11 different sites, in total over 100 miles of golfing bliss. What began as a pragmatic plan to help boost Alabama tourism and beef up the state pension fund's bottom line now lures travelers from all over the globe to this idyllic corner of Dixie.

In the late 1980s, Dr. David G. Bronner, CEO of Retirement Systems of Alabama, came up with the idea to develop a golf course system that would attract retirees and visitors. Renowned golf architect Robert Trent Jones Sr. was tapped for the ambitious state-funded effort, in what would become the largest construction project of its kind in American history.

The trail, which opened in 1992, is diverse in topography and difficulty. In addition to honing your skills at the sport, playing the Robert Trent Jones Trail also lets you enjoy the state's natural beauty. You can tee off in the hazy Appalachian foothills of its northernmost reaches, play through the enchanting cypress-rich swamps of the south, and wind up beachside, by the crystalline coast of the Gulf of Mexico. The trail ends at the elegant Grand Hotel Marriott in Point Clear (see p. 296), where you can sneak in some seaside R&R.

Scattered throughout the state, the trail sites—such as Highland Oaks in Dothan, Capitol Hill in Prattville, and Grand National in Auburn-Opelika—are all located with easy highway access, and no two are more than a 2½-hour drive apart. Flexibility is another attraction of the trail. All courses offer multiple tees, and most have a separate short course to vary the challenge. One of the newer courses, the 18-hole Ross Bridge that opened in Birmingham in 2005, stretches almost 8,200 yards from the back tees, making it the third-longest golf course in the world.

Golf Digest named the Short Course at Magnolia Grove in Mobile the best Par 3 course in the nation. *The New York Times* declared that the entire trail offers "some of the best public golf on Earth," while *The Wall Street Journal* said the trail may well be the biggest golf bargain in the country.

TRAIL INFO: Tel 800-949-4444 or 205-942-0444; rtjgolf.com. *Cost:* greens fees from $65. **WHERE TO STAY:** Marriott Shoals Hotel and Spa, Florence, tel 800-593-6450 or 256-246-3600; marriottshoals.com. *Cost:* from $149. **BEST TIMES:** Mar–May for good weather but busiest greens; fall is just as nice, but less crowded.

NASCAR Nirvana

TALLADEGA SUPERSPEEDWAY

Talladega, Alabama

For 75 million NASCAR fans, Talladega Superspeedway is *the* transcendent track, the mother lode of racing lore and legend. At this 143,000-capacity motorhead mecca, located on close to 3,000 acres just outside Birmingham, spectators have witnessed some of the fastest recorded NASCAR stock car racing speeds on a closed oval course.

NASCAR (the National Association for Stock Car Auto Racing), founded by Bill France Sr., held its first race in 1948 in Daytona Beach, Florida (see p. 305), still the organization's hallowed headquarters. France branched out to other states (North Carolina is the unofficial epicenter), in 1969 building the Alabama International Motor Speedway, which changed its name in 1989 to Talladega Superspeedway for the small town it's located just outside.

There's no better time to experience the thrill than during NASCAR's top competition, the Sprint Cup series, a grueling gauntlet of 36 races over ten months at various venues (Talladega hosts two). NASCAR tracks are all different, varying from about half a mile in length to Talladega's 2.66 miles (the longest). It was here that Bill Elliott achieved the fastest qualifying lap ever recorded, in 1987: 212.809 mph. Beginning the following year, NASCAR required cars to run with restrictor plates, which prohibit such excessive speeds, but the track is still known for its frequent accidents.

Despite the "Southern redneck" stereotype, NASCAR's intensely loyal fans have a broad demographic. Only about 37 percent of them live in the South, and 38 percent are women.

The International Motorsports Hall of Fame and Museum, on the grounds adjacent to Talladega, showcases over 140 mint-condition cars, trucks, and other racing vehicles going back to a 1919 Ford raced at Indy (see p. 507). Among the cars on display are Bill Elliott's 1985 Ford Thunderbird; Darrell Waltrip's favorite race car, "Bertha;" and Daytona 500 winners driven by Dale Jarrett, Richard Petty, and Bobby Allison. Although unrelated to NASCAR, the nearby Barber Vintage Motorsports Museum is a common side trip for motor buffs visiting the area. Founded by local businessman George Barber, who restored and raced Porsches in the 1960s and '70s, the non-profit museum traces the history of the motorcycle through a stunning array of more than 1,400 machines. The hands-down favorite? A replica of the Harley-Davidson from the classic 1969 film *Easy Rider*. Adjacent to the museum is the lovely Barber Motorsports Park, a winding 2.3-mile road course used for motorcycle and historic sports car races and home to schools and clubs such as the Porsche Driving Experience.

WHERE: 40 miles east of Birmingham. Tel 877-Go2-DEGA; talladegasuperspeedway.com. *When:* Apr–Oct. *Cost:* from $20. **INTERNATIONAL MOTORSPORTS HALL OF FAME:** Tel 256-362-5002; motorsportshalloffame.com. **BARBER VINTAGE MOTORSPORTS MUSEUM:** Birmingham. Tel 205-699-7275; barbermuseum.org. **BEST TIMES:** Apr or Oct, when Talladega hosts the NASCAR Nextel Cup Series.

Easy Livin' on the "Isle of Eight Flags"

AMELIA ISLAND

Florida

Floating off the northeastern tip of Florida and measuring just 13 miles by 4 miles, Amelia Island has always been a crossroads of culture. Over the course of 450 years it's been claimed by the French, the Spanish, the English, the Amelia "Patriots," the Republic of the Floridas, Mexico, the United States, and the Confederacy.

Why all the geopolitics? Geography. Amelia is blessed not only with the deepest natural harbor in the South, but with a location that made it perfect for ocean-based commerce and military ventures. Amelia did not develop as a major city like Miami thanks to oil tycoon Henry Flagler, who bypassed the town when he created the first rail line down Florida's east coast in the 1890s, opening the region to tourism. The result is a time warp of Victorian beauty while other Florida vacation spots became fun-in-the-sun theme parks.

At the island's northern end, Fernandina Beach is Amelia's only town, with a 50-block center listed in the National Register of Historic Places. In total, more than 450 of its buildings went up before 1927, including some of the nation's finest examples of Queen Anne, Victorian, and Italianate mansions, left over from the Goodyears, Pulitzers, and other wintering socialites. Cobbled Centre Street is

A horseback ride along the white sandy beach is one of many nature excursions on Amelia Island.

the island's most appealing stretch, lined with galleries, B&Bs, century-old restaurants, and the Palace Saloon, open since 1903 and thus the oldest original-location bar in Florida. It's one of the town's unofficial headquarters during the spring Shrimp Festival, when the island is flooded with visitors who show up for boatloads of seafood, music, and a parade.

Away from town, Amelia's landscape blends maritime forests, salt marshes, and gorgeous coastline; both the northern and southern ends of the island are preserved as state parks. Nature-oriented visitors can explore by bike via a network of trails, kayak or bird-watch in its marshes and rivers, or ride horseback along its 13 miles of white sand beaches and high dunes. In late spring and early summer, loggerhead turtles lay their eggs in the island's soft sand, while from December to March northern right whales are sometimes spotted along the coast.

One of Amelia's choicest, most pristine stretches of beach belongs to the Ritz-Carlton, Amelia Island, where guest rooms all enjoy enviable views and perfect sunrises. Frequently voted one of the finest resorts in the South, the Ritz-Carlton offers southern hospitality, tennis, golf at the adjacent Golf Club of Amelia Island's championship course, and exceptional dining in its acclaimed restaurant, Salt. A little to the south, its friendly rival, the huge Omni Amelia

Island Plantation, sits on 1,350 beachfront acres and offers an outstanding array of nature, recreational activities, and sports options. It includes three golf courses designed by Pete Dye, Tom Fazio, and Bobby Weed; 23 clay tennis courts; miles of bike trails and beaches; and its own nature center.

For an alternative to the big resort hotels, head to the Elizabeth Pointe Lodge, a Nantucket-shingle–style beachfront inn with the look and feel of the 1890s. Twenty rooms and two cottages are decorated in crisp, stylish beach decor, with hardwood floors, oversize marble bathtubs, and a strong maritime theme. Here, the emphasis is on pure relaxation, rocking-chair-on-the-porch, kite-flying-on-the-beach style.

WHERE: 30 miles northeast of Jacksonville. *Visitor info:* Tel 904-277-0717; ameliaisland .com. **THE RITZ-CARLTON:** Tel 800-241-3333 or 904-277-1100; ritzcarlton.com/ameliaisland. *Cost:* from $279 (off-peak), from $449 (peak); dinner at Salt $80. **OMNI AMELIA ISLAND PLANTATION:** Tel 888-444-OMNI or 904-261-6161; omniameliaislandplantation.com. *Cost:* from $249 (off-peak), from $329 (peak). **ELIZABETH POINTE LODGE:** Tel 904-277-4851; elizabethpointelodge.com. *Cost:* from $245 (off-peak), from $295 (peak). **BEST TIMES:** late Apr–early May for the Shrimp Festival (shrimpfestival.com); spring, fall, and winter for golf and tennis.

"We choose to go to the moon."—JFK, Sept. 12, 1962

KENNEDY SPACE CENTER

Cape Canaveral, Florida

Set amid 150,000 acres of marshland and mangrove swamp, Kennedy Space Center has been the headquarters of American rocketry and space exploration since the launch of the unmanned *Bumper 8* research rocket in July 1950. Eleven years later Alan Shepard lifted off from the Cape's Launch Pad LC-5 to become the first American in space, and in July 1969 *Apollo 11* blasted off from Pad 39A, carrying Neil Armstrong, Buzz Aldrin, and Michael Collins to the moon. Since the end of the Apollo missions in 1972 and the space shuttle missions in 2013 (all 135 space shuttle missions from 1981 to 2011 were launched here), the base has been home to the International Space Station programs, and to unmanned missions that have traveled to Mars and beyond. Visitors can tour portions of the facility, beginning at the Kennedy Space Center Visitor Complex, which houses a collection of NASA rockets, the actual Mercury Mission Control Room from the 1960s, two 3-D IMAX theaters showing films about space exploration, the U.S. Astronaut Hall of Fame, and numerous exhibits detailing 50 years of NASA projects. Various programs offer chances to meet astronauts and tour other sections of the facility. A bus drives visitors past launch pads for the former Apollo missions and space shuttles, with a stop at the Apollo/Saturn V Center, housing artifacts, photos, interactive exhibits, and a 363-foot Saturn V, the most powerful rocket ever launched by the U.S.

The Space Center continues to evolve and expand, and its most dazzling addition is the Space Shuttle Atlantis. The $100 million,

Unmanned research and supply rockets launch periodically at Kennedy Space Center.

90,000-square-foot attraction contains four multimedia and cinematic productions and more than 60 immersive, interactive experiences that invite guests to imagine how it feels to "be an astronaut." Guests come nose-to-nose with the actual space shuttle that flew in space 33 times and still bears the scars, scorch marks, and space dust of its last mission.

WHERE: 55 miles east of Orlando. Tel 866-737-5235; KennedySpaceCenter.com. **BEST TIME:** the launch of a rocket (see website for details).

Contacting the Other Side

CASSADAGA SPIRITUALIST CAMP

Cassadaga, Florida

The American school of Spiritualism, which stresses the eternal nature of the spirit and the ability of the dead to communicate with the living (and vice versa), dates back to 1848 when sisters Kate and Margaret Fox claimed to commune with spirits in their Hydesville, New York, home (see p. 160). That same year saw the birth of George P. Colby, who in 1875 followed a spirit guide to a patch of wilderness in central Florida.

That parcel formed the heart of the Cassadaga Spiritualist Camp, a community dedicated to living, working, and worshiping according to Spiritualist principles. Originally a collection of tents, the community eventually assumed the character of a small college campus, with wood-frame houses, a place of worship, and a cluster of other public buildings.

Utopian and other ideology-based communities weren't unusual in the 19th century, but Cassadaga stands out today as one of the rare survivors. Still occupying its original 57 acres, it's the oldest active religious community in the southeastern United States, with about 100 residents living on the property, of whom nearly 60 are certified mediums who offer readings and spiritual healing from their homes. A board at the information center and a page on the community's website list contact information for the mediums, some of whom are usually available on a walk-in basis. Each has his or her own style, but you won't find any

wearing satin turbans and bangle jewelry. This is serious business, not theater, and its practitioners are dedicated professionals.

WHERE: 25 miles southwest of Daytona Beach. Tel 386-228-3171; cassadaga.org. *Cost:* readings from $65. **WHERE TO STAY:** Cassadaga Hotel. Tel 386-228-2323; cassadagahotel.net. *Cost:* from $75. **BEST TIME:** Sun morning for the Adult Lyceum, featuring lectures about Spiritualism.

Rubenesque Mermaids on the Gulf Coast

SWIMMING WITH MANATEES

Crystal River, Florida

Their bodies look like battleship-gray zeppelins and they've got faces like sad-eyed hound dogs, so it must have been the manatees' plaintive, squealing voices that made old-time sailors think they were mermaids,

giving them the name *sirenia*. Sirens they are not, but manatees do have the good fortune to be completely adorable: gentle, endearingly playful, and amazingly graceful despite their 800–1,200-pound bulk.

Historically, contact with humans has been devastating for the manatees, which tend to swim just below the surface and so are frequently killed in collisions with boats. In 1981 former Florida governor Bob Graham and singer/songwriter Jimmy Buffett established the Save the Manatee Club, a nonprofit organization dedicated to research, advocacy, and protection efforts on behalf of manatees and their habitats. Manatee populations have increased over the past decade, but they're not out of danger yet.

The U.S. population of more than 6,000 West Indian manatees lives almost exclusively in the warm-water bays, estuaries, and rivers of Florida's eastern and western coasts, wintering particularly in Citrus County, the only place in the world where you can have a face-to-face manatee encounter. A number of outfitters in the small city of Crystal River equip

Manatees are slow-moving, curious animals, who spend half their day sleeping.

visitors with snorkeling gear and provide boat transportation to nearby Kings Bay, where a manatee gathering can range from five to a few hundred at any one time, depending on the temperature (the colder it is, the more they gravitate to these warm spring waters). Federal laws prohibit certain behavior: Snorkelers cannot pursue the animals, for instance, but must wait for the manatees to approach on their own. At press time the rules for viewing them in or on the water are in flux. Be sure to check ahead of your arrival.

WHERE: 85 miles northwest of Orlando (savethemanatee.org). **HOW:** Crystal Lodge Dive Center. Tel 352-795-6798; manatee-central .com. *Cost:* $25 for 2.5-hour guided tour, gear extra. **BEST TIMES:** Nov–Feb when temperatures are below the 40s at night; morning, before the manatees go out to feed.

The Home of Speed

THE DAYTONA INTERNATIONAL SPEEDWAY

Daytona Beach, Florida

NASCAR racing is said to be the most popular spectator sport in the U.S. It all started in 1935, when Daytona Beach mechanic Bill France Sr. entered a race for street-legal family sedans on the beach. Two years later, when nobody else wanted to promote a follow-up, he took the reins. In 1947, when racing resumed after the war, France organized the National Association for Stock Car Auto Racing (NASCAR), then opened the Daytona International Speedway in 1959 on a 447-acre property at the southern end of the beach. The first Daytona 500 ran in February of that year, with a field of 59 cars, a purse of $67,760, and more than 41,000 spectators watching the 200-lap, 500-mile race. Today it's the biggest auto race in America, marking the official start of the NASCAR season with 100,000-plus fans in the stands, another 9 million on TV, and a total purse of almost $20 million. The two-week period before the big event, known as Speedweeks, attracts thousands for half a dozen races (including Daytona 500 qualifying rounds) and race-related events.

The big race aside, Daytona has become a mecca for nearly all aspects of motorsports, hosting eight different race weekends annually. In early March, motorcycle enthusiasts gather for Bike Week, a ten-day festival of road racing, supercross, dirt track racing, road rallies, demo rides, auctions, exhibitions, and bike shows, all leading up to the Daytona 200, the most important two-wheeled race in the U.S. and held annually since 1937. In late December, go-kart enthusiasts flood in for Daytona Kartweek.

You can take behind-the-scenes tours, but for the ultimate thrill, the Richard Petty Driving Experience lets guests slip behind the wheel or ride as a passenger on the Daytona International track.

WHERE: 60 miles north of Orlando. Tel 800-PIT-SHOP; daytonainternationalspeedway.com. *When:* Speedweeks starts in early Feb and

The speedway is known as the "World Center of Racing" because it has the most diverse schedule of racing found anywhere.

culminates with the Daytona 500. Bike Week happens in early Mar (officialbikeweek .com). *Richard Petty Driving Experience:* Tel

800-237-3889; drivepetty.com. *Cost:* from $135 (ride), from $399 (drive). **BEST TIME:** late Feb for the Daytona 500.

The River of Grass

EVERGLADES NATIONAL PARK

Florida

Covering 1.5 million acres and spanning the southern tip of the Florida peninsula, Everglades National Park is just a slice of the great wetland—called Pahayokee ("river of grass") by the Seminole Indians—that once

stretched from Lake Okeechobee to Florida Bay, 120 miles long and 50 miles wide. Once a broad, slow-moving sheet of water one foot deep, it's a complex and fragile ecosystem whose wading bird population was once so vast, wrote John James Audubon, that they blacked out the light from the sun when they flew to their evening roost. Today the region is still home to thousands of animal, bird, and plant species, tangled mangrove thickets, and shallow, labyrinthine channels, but its integrity is hanging by a thread following decades of disastrous South Florida water projects, which have effectively diverted the steady flow the Everglades needs to survive, and sugar cane farming in the northern Everglades, which pollutes with fertilizers and pesticides.

Luckily, environmentalists have made their voices heard, and today government, big agriculture, and conservation groups alike are working to implement the Comprehensive Everglades Restoration Plan (CERP), a 20-year effort that would help restore the region's ecological balance. Visitors can explore the peripheral marshland—beginning almost in Miami's backyard—via wooden walkways and bicycle trails, but to really explore the mystery of the Everglades you'll want a kayak or canoe, and ideally a knowledgeable and sensitive guide. All around, the beautiful, constantly shifting light across the

Even at 2,410 square miles, the Everglades National Park represents less than 20 percent of the region's original wetland.

landscape is unlike anything else, underscoring the region's endangered fragility. Despite the drop in the avian population since the 19th century, bird-watching can still be outstanding, especially when the winter's migratory guests are included in the count of more than 350 documented species. Flora fanciers have more than a thousand species to study beyond the native sawgrass prairie, and if you look hard enough you may spot some of the swamp's animal residents: alligators, turtles, manatees, and, if you're exceedingly lucky, one of the rare Florida panthers who call the park home.

WHERE: about 40 miles southwest of Miami; main park entrance and visitors center just south of Homestead and Florida City. Tel

305-242-7700; nps.gov/ever. **How:** Everglades Adventures offers canoe and kayak rentals with and without guides departing from Ivey House B&B, Everglades City. Tel 877-567-0679 or 239-695-3299; everglidesadventures.com. *Cost:* from $35 a day for canoe rental; from $89 per person for 3-hour guided kayak trip. Down

South Airboat Tours offers guided departures from Everglades City. Tel 239-331-6613; down southairboattours.com. *Cost:* from $100 per person per hour. *When:* park, year-round; outfitters operate Nov–Apr. **Best times:** Dec–Apr, when the climate is comfortable, the bugs minimal, and the wildlife—especially birds—abundant.

Where Hemingway Still Looms Large

KEY WEST

Florida Keys

Key West is the farthest-flung and most populated town on the Florida Keys, a string of 1,700 low-lying islands (about 30 of them inhabited) stretching from mainland Florida southwest into the Gulf of Mexico.

Famously billed as the southernmost point in the continental U.S., and reached by the 42-mile Overseas Highway, the town is tropical not only in its physical locale, but in its attitude, which combines elements of Cuban, West Indian, Bahamian, and American culture into a relaxed, flip-flop, Margaritaville lifestyle. Ernest Hemingway put Key West on the map, settling here with his second wife Pauline in 1928, and today the population is a mix of deeply tanned locals (known as "Conchs"), writers, artists, retirees, and a large gay community, all living in quaint white-framed cottages or restored Bahamian-influenced pastel Victorians.

In high season, the island's population swells with thousands of cruise ship passengers and gaggles of weekend bikers, all of them heading to mile-long Duval Street, with its string of legendary bars. Papa Hemingway himself used to drink at a rough-and-tumble place on Greene Street called Sloppy Joe's, now known as Captain Tony's Saloon. A newer Sloppy Joe's, on Duval Street, draws in hordes of tourists who act like they've never been in a bar before—and maybe they haven't. Scores of pictures of winners

of the annual Hemingway Look-Alike Contest line the walls—the highlight of the island's annual Hemingway Days celebration, which also includes an arm wrestling championship and a running of the bulls where Papa look-alikes are chased by rolling wooden *toros*.

Visitors interested in the real deal can tour the house and studio where Hemingway wrote "The Snows of Kilimanjaro" and *To Have and Have Not*. Many of his possessions are on display, presided over by some 50 polydactyl (many-toed) cats, about the same number that Hemingway kept on the property between 1931 and 1939. President Harry Truman was another

Cayo Hueso, meaning "bone islet," was the original Spanish name for the island of Key West.

Key West devotee, spending vacations at the so-called Little White House. It has been restored to look just as he left it, with a perfect late 1940s decor and numerous Truman relics.

Mallory Square pier is the place to be at sundown, when the daily sunset-watching ritual (and ephemeral green streak) is augmented by a cast of jugglers, fire-eaters, and buskers. At the end of the day, return to your room at the Gardens Hotel, named for the passion of former owner Peggy Mills, who considered gardening an art form. If not for the meandering footpaths of centuries-old bricks, one could get lost in the small otherworldly courtyard, lush with bougainvillea, orchids, and ferns blooming beneath a canopy of hardwoods and palms. The restored two-story West Indian plantation-style main building (dating to 1870) and two similarly styled new buildings hide behind thick walls in the heart of Key West's historic Old Town district.

For an excursion, hop a boat for the 70-mile trip to the Dry Tortugas, seven small, undeveloped islands that represent the *real* end of the Keys chain. Bird-watching is the big draw, with nearly 300 species stopping for a rest during the annual migration, but there's also historic Fort Jefferson, a monumental six-sided 19th-century citadel that seems to rise right out of the aquamarine ocean.

WHERE: 165 miles southwest of Miami. *Visitor info:* Tel 800-FLA-KEYS or 305-296-1552; fla-keys.com. **CAPTAIN TONY'S:** Tel 305-294-1838; capttonyssaloon.com. **SLOPPY JOE'S:** Tel 305-294-5717; sloppyjoes.com. **HEMINGWAY HOME:** Tel 305-294-1136; hemingwayhome.com. **LITTLE WHITE HOUSE:** Tel 305-294-9911; trumanlittlewhitehouse.com. **GARDENS HOTEL:** Tel 800-526-2664 or 305-294-2661; gardenshotel.com. *Cost:* from $195 (off-peak), from $375 (peak). **DRY TORTUGAS:** Tel 305-242-7700; nps.gov/drto. **BEST TIMES:** mid-Mar–mid-May for peak bird-watching in the Dry Tortugas; July for Hemingway Days; late Oct for Fantasy Fest (fantasyfest.com), 10 days of Halloween fun; New Year's Eve, for family-friendly events.

Sportfishing Mecca

THE UPPER AND MIDDLE KEYS

Florida Keys

On June 1, 1912, fishing guide Charlie Thompson set out from Miami, sailed past Pigeon Key, and hooked what seemed to be a sea monster. Thirty-nine hours, five harpoons, and 151 bullets later, he hauled in a 45-foot, 30,000-pound whale shark, which he towed back to Miami. A local entrepreneur mounted it on a flatbed train car, and began touring the country—and the legend of the Keys as a fishing paradise was born.

Today, the town of Islamorada stretches across four different islands in a region known as the sportfishing capital of the world, a jumping-off point for charters heading into the Atlantic for sailfish, tuna, and mahi mahi, and into the waters of Florida Bay for tarpon and bonefish. The atmosphere is pure Keys, one step down on the party scale from Key West (see previous page) but still active. Divers can explore the coral reef, fishermen can head out on charter or party boats, and those who just want to get a gander at a sea monster or two can head to the pier at Robbie's, the island's best-known outfitter, where a school of more than 100 huge tarpon show up every day to be fed by visitors.

About 31 miles southwest, in Marathon, the respected Dolphin Research Center offers guests the opportunity to interact with its resident family of more than 25 Atlantic bottlenose dolphins and four sea lions, many of whom were born at the facility and live in its natural saltwater lagoon. Programs range from a brief "Meet the Dolphin" encounter (where you "shake hands" from the dock) to a daylong "Ultimate Trainer for a Day" program, which includes swimming with the dolphins and learning to use hand cues to request specific actions and behaviors.

In Islamorada, stay overnight at the 214-room Cheeca Lodge, a mid-Keys mainstay since 1946, nestled on 27 beautifully landscaped acres beside 1,200 feet of palm-fringed beach. All rooms have small balconies and a casual Florida feel, and the 5,700-square-foot spa includes an adults-only pool area with cabanas and butler service. For a whole other overnight experience, you can go deep and bond with the fish at Jules' Undersea Lodge, about 20 miles northeast in Key Largo. Built as an underwater research lab in the 1970s, it's now a one-of-a-kind two-bedroom hotel lying 30 feet deep in a protected lagoon. You enter by diving 21 feet down and popping up through a pool in the lodge's floor. Large, round 42-inch windows provide a fish-eye view, and overnight rates include unlimited scuba tanks. At dinnertime a call to the surface can summon a meal, delivered in a waterproof container.

The inhabitants of the Dolphin Research Center greet visitors with open flippers.

WHERE: Islamorada is 80 miles southwest of Miami. *Visitor info:* Tel 800-FLA-KEYS or 305-296-1552; fla-keys.com. **ROBBIE'S:** Islamorada. Tel 877-664-8498 or 305-664-8070; robbies.com. **DOLPHIN RESEARCH CENTER:** Grassy Key. Tel 305-289-1121; dolphins.org. *Cost:* Meet the Dolphin program $25; Ultimate Trainer for a Day $695. **CHEECA LODGE:** Islamorada. Tel 844-993-9713 or 305-664-4651; cheeca.com. *Cost:* from $179. **JULES' UNDERSEA LODGE:** Key Largo. Tel 305-451-2353; jul.com. *Cost:* $800 per person, double occupancy, includes hot pizza dinner and unlimited diving tanks. **BEST TIMES:** May–June for the fishing; Dec–May for weather.

The South Seas in South Florida

LITTLE PALM ISLAND RESORT AND SPA

Little Torch Key, Florida Keys

A tiny 5-acre dot in the lower Florida Keys, Little Palm Island was once a fishing camp for President Harry Truman and other dignitaries. In 1988 it realized its paradise potential, opening as a private resort for the rich, the famous, and anyone else with a platinum credit card and a Gauguin dream.

The theme is South Pacific meets Florida Keys, with the former's languid aesthetic and the latter's spectacular sunsets. After arriving via a sleek 1930s-style motor launch from neighboring Little Torch Key (seaplane is also an option), guests are immersed in exotic perfection, lolling around in rope hammocks, sunbathing on the sandy white beaches, strolling the crushed-seashell paths, or surrendering to an Indonesian treatment or over-the-water massage at one of SpaTerre's outdoor massage pavilions. Socializing isn't key here; privacy is. In all, there are just 28 thatched-roof guest bungalows and two larger grand suites, shaded by rustling palm trees and outfitted with

Little Palm Island is an exclusive tropical paradise reached by seaplane or boat.

whirlpool baths, Indonesian and Polynesian furnishings, and private verandas overlooking the ocean. Grand suites offer sunset views, slate floors, and redwood hot tubs on private decks. Though TVs and telephones have been banished in the interest of quiet, there is wi-fi to keep you quietly connected.

If you can rouse yourself from your luxury stupor, you might take out one of the island's kayaks or windsurfing boards, meditate in the Zen garden, swim in the freshwater pool, or watch for one of the island's tiny Key deer, which come out to graze at sunset and after dawn. The hotel will also arrange off-island trips to Key West (see p. 307) or nearby Looe Key National Marine Sanctuary, where divers can explore the only living coral reef in North America. Dinner showcases modern tropical cuisine, which mixes classic French preparations with Floridian, Cuban, and other pan-Latin flavors. If the candlelit dining room doesn't float your boat, you can eat at a table down on the sandy beach, with the water lapping at your toes.

WHERE: 140 miles southwest of Miami. Tel 800-343-8567 or 305-872-2524; littlepalmisland.com. *Cost:* from $1,000, meals extra. **BEST TIMES:** Jan–May for weather; June–Oct for fishing.

The Fountains of Youth

FLORIDA'S NATURAL SPRINGS

Florida

In 1512 Spanish explorer Juan Ponce de León learned from the Caribbean Indians of a land to the north called Bimini, where flowed a natural spring so miraculously pure that anyone who bathed in it would instantly become

young again. Full of enthusiasm, Ponce de León mounted an expedition and, along the way, discovered Florida.

That's the legend. In fact, Ponce de León was actually searching for gold, land, and slaves, but the fountain story has a glimmer of truth to it.

Florida does contain one of the world's largest systems of natural springs—more than 900 known springs, including some of the largest and deepest on earth. The springs are fed by an enormous underground aquifer insulated by layers of clay, sand, and limestone, and bubble up at a constant 69° to 73°F. Some are more crowded than others, some more developed, but in general all are great for swimming, tubing, snorkeling, and even diving, and most are surrounded by thick subtropical Florida vegetation.

In Apopka, 7,000-acre Wekiwa Springs State Park is located at the headwaters of the Wekiva River, only 20 minutes northwest of Orlando but 1,000 miles away in spirit. The Wekiwa spring ("bubbling water" in Creek) offers swimming and snorkeling, while the river it feeds is popular for canoeing, kayaking, and paddleboarding below a lush canopy of trees. Nearby, Kelly Park's Rock Springs Run flows from a cavern at the base of a limestone bluff, forming a fast, choppy stream that's extremely popular for tubing.

To the north, west of Orange City, Blue Spring State Park is home to the largest spring along the St. Johns River, and is popular with swimmers and scuba divers. It is also the winter home to a growing population of West Indian manatees. You can't swim with the friendly beasts, but you can take guided boat tours on the river and observe the manatees from a boardwalk.

Northwest of Gainesville, the Ichetucknee River is fed by nine named springs along its first 3.5 miles, protected as Ichetucknee Springs State Park. The northernmost headwater spring,

known as the Head Spring, is a beautiful blue pool full of small fish and is the jumping-off point for a great tubing run, passing through a landscape rich with white-tailed deer and other wildlife.

Below Tallahassee, at the cusp of the Panhandle, Wakulla Springs is one of the world's largest and deepest. Discharging up to 260 million gallons a day, its bowl covers 4 acres and is edged by a hardwood forest and a vast system of caverns where diving expeditions have discovered the bones of several Ice Age animals over the years. Swimming is allowed at the spring itself, and glass-bottom boat tours explore the spring and the Wakulla River.

WHERE: 500 springs are located between Jacksonville west to the Panhandle and south to Tampa and Orlando; floridasprings.org. **WEKIWA:** Apopka. Tel 407-884-2009; florida stateparks.org/park/Wekiwa-Springs. **ROCK SPRINGS RUN:** Apopka. Tel 407-254-1902; floridastateparks.org. **BLUE SPRING:** Orange City. Tel 386-775-3663; floridastateparks.org/ park/bluespring. **ICHETUCKNEE:** Fort White. Tel 386-497-4690; floridastateparks.org/park/ Ichetucknee-Springs. **WAKULLA:** Wakulla Springs. Tel 850-561-7276; floridastateparks .org/park/Wakulla-Springs. **BEST TIMES:** spring and fall for smaller crowds; Nov–Mar at Blue Spring for manatee viewing.

The Heart and Soul of Little Havana

CALLE OCHO

Miami, Florida

C ubans have been living in downtown Miami since the early 20th century, but it wasn't until the Cuban Revolution of 1959, when this neighborhood became the principal entry point for refugees (500,000 between 1959

and 1980), that the Cuban community assumed a central place in Miami's social, political, and cultural life. By the late 1970s the neighborhood bound by Southwest 8th

Street ("Calle Ocho") west of I-95 had been transformed into Little Havana. At its peak in 1980, it was 85 percent Cuban; today it is also home to many refugees from Nicaragua,

Honduras, and other Central American countries. The neighborhood is brimming with Cuban coffee shops, restaurants (the venerable institution called Versailles is a casual spot where locals gather for plates piled high with traditional island food), markets, theaters, music and clothing stores, and small cigar lounges. At the small, shaded Maximo Gomez (aka Domino) Park, Cuban men gather daily to play the traditional game, while nearby Cuban Memorial Boulevard holds monuments to Cuban political prisoners, journalists, and those who died at the Bay of Pigs.

On the last Friday evening each month, the nonprofit group Viernes Culturales ("Cultural Fridays") holds a street fair featuring *musica cubana*, dancing, food, and more than 100 artists displaying their creations. It's a great party, but for a real celebration show up in mid-March for the annual Calle Ocho Festival, the finale of the ten-day Carnaval Miami. Running

for 20 blocks along Calle Ocho, it's the biggest celebration of Latin music and dance in the United States, with more than 30 stages and pavilions where some of the best merengue, salsa, and pop musicians perform. With a million people attending, give yourself over to the crowd and join a massive 100,000-strong conga line like the one that set the world's record in 1988. Hungry or not, sample Cuban tamales, Mexican tacos, Colombian arepas, barbecue, and a sea of other specialties. Cuban coffee may be Little Havana's favorite beverage most of the year, but at this fiesta, *cerveza* (beer) is the drink of choice.

WHERE: Little Havana stretches along SW 8th St. from about 12th to 27th Aves. **VERSAILLES:** Tel 305-444-0240. *Cost:* dinner $20. **CULTURAL FRIDAYS:** Tel 305-643-5500; viernesculturales.org. **CALLE OCHO FESTIVAL:** Tel 305-644-8888; carnavalmiami.com. *When:* 2nd Sun in Mar.

Big. Spectacular. Orange.

THE ORANGE BOWL

Miami, Florida

In 1932 the national mood was poor, and the economic climate hurting. In Pasadena, California, the Rose Bowl (see p. 839) was such a popular distraction that the city had to enlarge its stadium twice in five years. Back in

Miami, city officials saw the Rose Bowl's popularity, looked at their empty hotels and beaches, and hatched a copycat plan.

Initially called the Palm Festival, the first game pitted powerhouse Manhattan College against the University of Miami on New Year's Day. Miami won, and the rest is history. In 1935 the game changed its name to the Orange Bowl, and in 1937 it was broadcast on national radio for the first time, then direct from its new home at Orange Bowl Stadium in 1938. Since then it has grown into one of the country's most colorful annual spectacles, with the weeks

before the game filled with events and a huge pregame tailgate party called Fan Fest that draws some 20,000 partyers. Halftime shows are among the most extreme in the biz, with top-name singers. So many fans show up each year that in 1996 the game had to move from its longtime home to the 65,326-seat Dolphins Stadium (now the Sun-Life Stadium).

Along with the Fiesta, Sugar, Rose, Cotton, and Peach Bowls, the game is part of the College Football Playoff system. Two semifinal games rotate among these six major bowls, leading to a National Championship in a city with a stadium that can hold at least 65,000 people. Under the old system, the Orange Bowl hosted 20 national championships, the last in 2013.

WHERE: 2269 Dan Marino Blvd. Tel 305-341-4701; game.orangebowl.org. *When:* on or around New Year's Day. *Cost:* tickets from $95.

Reliving the Renaissance in Gilded Age Florida

VIZCAYA MUSEUM AND GARDENS

Miami, Florida

Built between 1914 and 1922, Vizcaya was the extravagant wintertime retreat of Chicago industrialist James Deering, who wintered there until his death in 1925. More than a thousand European and Caribbean artisans and laborers were employed in the 14-year construction of the Italian Renaissance–style estate, sometimes called the "Hearst Castle of the East." By design, the house and gardens were created to appear as if they had stood for centuries and been occupied by many generations—an irony considering that Deering's retreat went unoccupied after his death in 1925. Opened as a museum in the mid-1950s, Vizcaya is a marvel, only a mile from downtown Miami but an age away in temperament. In the house itself, 34 of its 54 rooms are open to the public, displaying the wealth of furniture, paintings, sculpture, tapestries, wall panels and ceilings, and decorative arts brought from Europe by Deering and his cadre of designers. Outside, the 10 acres of gardens evoke an old Mediterranean grandeur with their stone fountains, grottoes, statuary, and plant life, and are a favorite place for Miami wedding photos. The garden's waterfront teahouse, with its little footbridge, is a traditional proposal spot.

WHERE: 3251 S. Miami Ave., Miami. Tel 305-250-9133; vizcaya.org. **BEST TIME:** Oct–May for the most pleasant weather.

A Gatsby-Era Landmark Reborn for Our Times

THE BILTMORE HOTEL

Coral Gables, Florida

The Miami suburb of Coral Gables was built during the Florida land boom of the 1920s by developer George Merrick, who filled the area with Mediterranean-style homes, golf courses, country clubs, and banyan trees.

In 1924, at the height of the boom, Merrick persuaded hotel magnate John McEntee Bowman to build "a great hotel" in Coral Gables, which "would serve as a center of sports and fashion." One year and $10 million later, the Biltmore opened as one of the greatest resort hotels, a playground for visiting royalty, Hollywood starlets, and assorted elite.

Big bands played and synchronized swimmers performed in the largest hotel pool in the continental U.S. Future Olympian and Tarzan actor Johnny Weissmuller taught swimming and, in his spare time, broke world records in the pool—while sundry extras wrestled alligators, sashayed in bathing suits, and leapt from the 85-foot dive platform. Those were the days, but they came to an end with the dawn of WWII, when the Biltmore was converted into a hospital for the Army Air Force and later the Veterans Administration. Following the army's withdrawal in 1968, the Biltmore sank into 15 years of disuse.

Today, following a $55 million, 4-year refurbishment in the 1980s and more investments since, the Biltmore is once again a world-class hotel. A National Historic Landmark, with 275 rooms and suites, a rolling 18-hole golf course, and a 300-foot copper-clad tower whose Everglades Suite is the best in the house, the hotel has hosted luminaries like Bill Clinton, Calvin Coolidge, and Lauren Bacall over the years. Throughout the hotel, Italian marble floors, hand-painted ceilings, open-air courtyards, and cool fountains evoke the era of the hotel's birth, while the lobby with its vaulted 45-foot ceiling is the setting for weekday afternoon tea. At the Palme d'Or restaurant, 60 patrons dine on exquisite French cuisine within view of that famous 700,000-gallon pool, and on Sundays the hotel's Fontana Restaurant is home to a lavish champagne brunch. Repair to the Biltmore Spa whose treatment rooms have picture windows overlooking the golf course, Coral Gables, and beyond.

WHERE: 14 miles southwest of Miami Beach; 1200 Anastasia Ave. Tel 855-311-6903; biltmorehotel.com. *Cost:* from $229 (off-peak), from $459 (peak); 4-course tasting menu at Palme d'Or $95, Sun champagne brunch $85. **BEST TIME:** Sun for historic tours (dadeheritagetrust.org).

A New Icon Earns the World's Attention

PÉREZ ART MUSEUM MIAMI

Miami, Florida

A relatively recent addition to the city's cultural landscape, the Pérez Art Museum Miami, known locally as PAMM, opened in 2013 to much fanfare as the city's first world-class museum. Its status was solidified by the future-forward design of Pritzker-prize winning Herzog & de Meuron, the Swiss architecture firm who also turned a London power plant into the Tate Modern. PAMM's three-story structure, built at an angle directly on Biscayne Bay, cost $131 million. It houses a collection of modern and contemporary artworks from the 20th and 21st centuries that reflect the cosmopolitan makeup of Miami as a cross-cultural hub, with an emphasis on temporary exhibitions.

The museum began in 1984 as the Center for the Fine Arts and was later rechristened as Miami Art Museum (MAM). City officials expressed a desire to create something more deserving of national and international attention, a dream made possible with the help of a $40 million donation by real-estate developer and art lover Jorge Pérez (who also contributed his private art collection). Hanging gardens made up of over 770 species and suspended from a slatted roof and indoor/outdoor spaces evoke a sun-filled South Florida aesthetic that is enjoyed by both local school groups and streams of visibly impressed foreign visitors. The Miami vibe continues at the museum's immediately popular Verde restaurant and bar that promises a beautiful and delicious locally-inspired menu. Drink highlights include handcrafted specialty cocktails and a frosted glass of the signature Bayfront Sangria.

WHERE: 1103 Biscayne Blvd. Tel 305-375–3000; pamm.org. *When:* closed Wed. *Cost:* dinner at Verde $35. **BEST TIME:** during Art Basel Miami.

The International Art Market Does Miami

ART BASEL MIAMI BEACH

Miami Beach, Florida

I t began in the Swiss town of Basel, where since 1970 art collectors and connoisseurs have gathered each June for the prestigious Art Basel fair. In 2002 the fair's management held its first U.S. sister fair in Miami Beach,

and within three years the event had become the hottest annual art event in the country, eclipsing longtime standouts like New York's Armory Show and Art Chicago. Blame Miami itself, maybe. Already feeling confident as one of the new stars of international favor, the city took to the fair.

Art Basel Miami Beach represents the apotheosis of the art scene arguably created by Andy Warhol in the 1970s and '80s: a mixture of fine art, fashion, film, music, nightlife, and ostentatious wealth. Nearly every major

Art Basel Miami Beach features 20th- and 21st-century artworks by over 1,500 artists.

contemporary gallery in the world competes for the limited number of exhibitors' spaces at the Miami Beach Convention Center, with the winners trucking in untold millions in art. Works by modernist and contemporary masters such as Matisse, Picasso, Francis Bacon, and David Hockney have been displayed and sold in various years, but the real focus is on the new, with prices ranging from a few thousand dollars into the multimillions.

Aside from the main show, other events include hot-ticket receptions and panel discussions; crossover events featuring music, film, and design; video and music installations at some of Miami's most happening hotels; and exhibit space where less established galleries showcase the work of emerging artists. Meanwhile, around town, various events compete for the attention of the 70,000-plus curators, collectors, celebrities, critics, hangers-on, and honest workaday art lovers who show up from every corner of the globe. Miami's museums stage special exhibits, buildings by renowned architects offer tours, private collectors open their homes for invitation-only parties and exhibitions, and the unaffiliated New Art Dealers Alliance stages its own fair nearby. The great part, of course, is that you don't have to be an art collector to enjoy Art Basel and its attendant circus.

WHERE: Miami Beach Convention Center and other venues. Tel 305-674-1292; artbasel .com. *Cost:* day tickets $47; 3-day pass $100. *When:* 3 days in early Dec. **NEW ART DEALERS ALLIANCE FAIR:** newartdealers.org. *When:* 3 days in early Dec.

A South Beach Institution

JOE'S STONE CRAB

Miami Beach, Florida

In 1913, Hungarian-born Joe Weiss came to Miami Beach from New York hoping the sea air would cure his asthma. He and his wife, Jennie, started the original Joe's Restaurant selling fish sandwiches and fries. In 1921 a visiting ichthyologist, having observed that the waters around Miami Beach were literally crawling with stone crabs, brought Joe a bagful, hoping to find out if they were edible. And so an institution was born. Today in an expanded location, Joe's is still in the Weiss family, and many of the employees have been around from 10 to more than 40 years. On the menu is the stone crab: a delicacy of sweet meat found only in southwestern Florida, the Keys, and along the Gulf of Mexico, especially coveted because of its limited-season availability (mid-October to mid-May). Every day, crabbing boats head offshore, loading up and then shucking furiously to satisfy the daily demand for a ton of claws in the 450-seat indoor/outdoor restaurant. They come in four sizes, medium to jumbo, the standard order an imposing mound served with mustard sauce or melted butter, cottage-fried potatoes (or "skinny sweets"), coleslaw, and creamed spinach. Save room for Key lime pie; it's the real thing. Joe's crabs aren't cheap—Damon Runyon quipped that they were sold by the carat—and the no-reservations policy means long waits for a table. But it's all part of the experience, along with the formally dressed waiters and the lingering allure of nearly a century of Miami players, including Al Capone, Frank Sinatra, and Howard Cosell.

WHERE: 11 Washington Ave. Tel 305-673-0365; joesstonecrab.com. *Cost:* from $50 for large claws. *When:* open daily during stone crab season, mid-Oct–mid-May; open Wed–Sun, mid-May–early Aug; closed mid-Aug–mid-Oct. **BEST TIME:** Lines tend to be shortest 5 P.M.–6:30 P.M.

Behind the Velvet Rope

MIAMI'S STYLISH HOTELS

Miami Beach, Florida

Hipness is such an ephemeral, ever-changing thing, but Miami Beach locked itself in as one of America's few permanent hip zones back in the '40s, and has never looked back. And no matter where the epicenter of cool is at the moment, some hotels just keep appearing on the radar.

The Tides, a quietly elegant deco queen dating from 1936, has hosted the likes of Jennifer Lopez, Jimmy Fallon, and Harrison Ford. They enjoyed some of the best views of Ocean Drive from their oversize seaward-facing rooms, looking toward the expansive beach and its tanned denizens. Downstairs the small but excellent lobby-level restaurant remains a popular scene-and-cuisine experience.

The very essence of hipness, in the '50s and for all time, was surely Frank, Sammy, and Dean, the Rat Pack of fact and fable. When they convened in Miami, it was at the Fontainebleau, the archetypal Miami Beach resort, with its sweeping 1954 design by architect Morris Lapidus. Hollywood has also paid a few calls to this legendary property, using it as a setting for the James Bond classic *Goldfinger*, Al Pacino's remake of *Scarface*, and Jerry Lewis's *The Bellboy*. Today you can stay in the classic Lapidus building or in a new hotel tower.

The all-white tropical Delano hotel has been a South Beach trailblazer since its 1995 top-to-toe overhaul by designer Philippe Stark and famed hotelier and then-owner Ian Schrager. The nexus of star power soon shifted to the nearby Shore Club, before landing squarely on the palm-shaded grounds of the Miami Beach Edition, Schrager's unlikely yet immediately popular collaboration with Marriott in 2014 that transformed a 1955 landmark hotel into a modern luxury destination while maintaining an Old-Havana vibe.

There is no lack of additions that keep the neighborhood abuzz with of-the-moment appeal, such as the ideally situated 1 Hotel South Beach, the 2014 arrival from Barry Sternlicht, the hospitality impresario who founded the W Hotels in New York in 1998. The 400-plus Zen-like rooms are some of the largest in town, as is the rooftop pool-with-a-view, just one of four the luxury hotel offers.

Philippe Stark made a triumphant return to the area as the designer of the SLS Hotel South Beach, a 140-room beachfront property housed in an art deco building. The design is surreal, whimsical, and quintessentially South Beach.

THE TIDES: Tel 305-604-5070; thetides southbeach.com. *Cost:* from $295 (off-peak), from $450 (peak). **THE FONTAINEBLEAU:** Tel 800-548-8886 or 305-538-2000; fontaine bleau.com. *Cost:* from $220 (off-peak), from $440 (peak). **THE DELANO:** Tel 800-606-6090 or 305-672-2000; delano-hotel.com. *Cost:* from $325 (off-peak), from $450 (peak). **THE SHORE CLUB:** Tel 800-606-6090 or 305-695-3100; shoreclub.com. *Cost:* from $349. **MIAMI BEACH EDITION:** Tel 786-257-4500; edition hotels.com. *Cost:* from $399 (off-peak), from $599 (peak). **1 HOTEL SOUTH BEACH:** Tel 305-604-1000; 1hotels.com. *Cost:* from $330 (off-peak), from $575 (peak). **SLS HOTEL:** Tel 305-674-1701; slshotels.com. *Cost:* from $290 (off-peak), from $550 (peak). **BEST TIMES:** Jan–Apr for the weather; 1st week in Dec for the Art Basel Miami Beach festival (artbasel.com).

The Philippe Stark–designed Delano Hotel was a trailblazer for Miami's hotel scene.

Art Deco on the American Riviera

SOUTH BEACH

Miami Beach, Florida

Some places and times just go together, and South Beach enjoys being one of those places, embodying the cultural mash-up of fashion, celebrity, design, hip beach culture, and wealth that defines American fabulousness.

The city's location as a kind of center point between Europe, New York, L.A., and South America has no doubt contributed to its current ascendancy, but credit must also go to Miami's architectural forefathers, who between the late '20s and early '40s built a backdrop as beautiful as today's bronzed and buffed denizens.

South Beach's Architectural District—aka the art deco district—crowds into a mere one square mile some 800 pastel-colored buildings in the art deco, streamline moderne, and Mediterranean revival styles—altogether, the largest concentration of 1920s and '30s resort architecture in the U.S. Tours are available from the Miami Design Preservation League (MDPL) but there's every chance you'll get distracted from the architecture—all painted in the district's trademark teals, lavenders, pinks, and peaches—by the alarmingly good-looking parade of people on the beach and off. Open 24 hours a day, the News Café on Ocean Drive was one of the early fixtures of the South Beach renaissance and is still one of the best people-watching spots in town.

Ocean Drive's (if not South Beach's) most inviting hotel is the Betsy, an elegant three-story boutique hotel built in 1942 in a breezy nouveau-Colonial style by L. Murray Dixon, one of the architects responsible for many of the neighborhood's art deco buildings. South Beach is now home to world-class modern architecture, as well, with the 2011 arrival of Frank Gehry's New World Center, home to the New World Symphony led by artistic director Michael Tilson Thomas. For an après-concert dinner, stroll over to beachside Lincoln Road and stop by the half-retro, still trendy Nexxt Café, where a mix of models and out-of-towners fill the indoor/outdoor tables and pour over the 100-item menu.

WHERE: roughly bounded by the Atlantic Ocean, 6th St., Alton Rd., Dade Blvd., and 23rd St. **MDPL:** Tel 305-672-2014; mdpl.org. **NEWS CAFÉ:** Tel 305-538-6397; newscafe.com. *Cost:* dinner $35. **THE BETSY:** Tel 866-792-3879 or 305-531-6100; thebetsyhotel.com. *Cost:* from $275 (off-peak), from $575 (peak).

One of the many preserved art deco buildings along Ocean Drive in South Beach

NEW WORLD SYMPHONY: Tel 800-597-3331 or 305-673-3331; nws.edu. **NEXXT CAFÉ:** Tel 305-532-6643. *Cost:* dinner $35. **BEST TIME:** weekend in mid-Jan for annual Art Deco Weekend (artdecoweekend.com), with films, lectures, music, and street vendors.

The Birth of Modernity, One Piece at a Time

THE WOLFSONIAN

Miami Beach, Florida

S ome people collect stamps. Others collect rare books. Miami millionaire Mitchell Wolfson Jr. collects the modern era from the 1850s to the 1950s, or at least the material things that are its signifiers. Born in 1939, Wolfson began his 180,000-piece collection with illustrated books. From there he progressed to industrial and commercial design, advertisements, decorative arts, paintings and books, furniture and glasswork, and ephemera like toys, matchbook covers, pamphlets, and ashtrays. His collecting stems from a desire "to fathom human behavior and the motivation behind it in each object."

In 1987, Wolfson purchased a landmark Mediterranean-revival warehouse in Miami Beach's historic art deco district to store and exhibit the collection. The museum opened in 1995, and Wolfson donated it to the state of Florida in 1997. Now under the auspices of Florida International University, the museum's collection looks at objects as both agents and expressions of change. It includes pieces from the Arts and Crafts movement; Dutch and Italian art nouveau; American industrial design; and materials relating to the World's Fairs, zeppelins, and ocean liners. There's also a corner given over to the country's largest collection of international political propaganda.

WHERE: 1001 Washington Ave. Tel 305-531-1001; wolfsonian.org. *When:* closed Wed. **BEST TIME:** early Dec to coincide with the Art Basel Miami Beach fair (see p. 315).

Florida's Antiquing Capital

MOUNT DORA

Florida

I n a stretch of land so flat that a 184-foot elevation is enough to deem a place "Mount" sits Florida's Mount Dora, a town which has managed to hang on to its charming, historic, and authentic character despite being less than an hour's drive from Orlando, the happiest—but most artificial—place on earth. If theme park overstimulation sets in, escape to Mount Dora for a real-life respite.

Founded in 1880, Mount Dora has an unspoiled Old Florida air, a great old inn, a gorgeous location on the shores of 4,500-acre Lake Dora, and more than a dozen major festivals throughout the year (including antiques and crafts fairs, an arts and music festival, a bicycle festival, and the oldest sailing regatta in the state) help round out the picture. In the downtown historic district, the streets are lined with tall oaks and buildings that are never more than three stories high.

Antiquing has long been popular here and is focused around Renninger's Twin Markets, a 117-acre complex where hundreds of dealers set up for its Flea Market every weekend. On the third weekend of every month (except November, January, and February, when the huge Extravaganza happens), the monthly Antiques Fair brings in an additional 100 dealers who set up outdoors on the tree-shaded grounds. As at Renninger's markets in Pennsylvania (see p. 206), the very best time to visit is during the thrice-yearly Antique Extravaganzas, when more than 1,500 dealers take over the town.

For a stay in Mount Dora, no place offers as much local history as the 87-room Lakeside Inn, opened in 1883, and the last remaining Victorian-era hotel in central Florida. The original inn, with its wide veranda porch, now houses the lobby and reception area, a dining room, and a tavern with nightly entertainment. The newer sections, built beginning in 1929, match the old, with gables, balconies, and Victorian detailing. Inside, rooms are dollhouse pretty. Outside, oak trees dot the rolling grounds down to the shores of Lake Dora, one of more than 1,000 named lakes here in Florida's Lake County.

WHERE: 30 miles northwest of Orlando. *Visitor info:* Tel 352-383-2165; mountdora.com. **RENNINGER'S:** Tel 352-383-8393; renningers .net. *When:* Fri–Sun. **LAKESIDE INN:** Tel 800-556-5016 or 352-383-4101; lakeside-inn.com. *Cost:* from $129. **BEST TIMES:** 3rd weekend in Jan, Feb, and Nov for Renninger's Antique Extravaganzas; Oct for The Crafts Festival; Dec for the annual Christmas celebration, when the town is strung with more than 2 million lights.

Palm Beach Lite

NAPLES

Florida

L ike many other south Florida towns, Naples was born in the minds of real estate speculators. First settled in the 1860s, one promoter described its beauty as "surpassing the bay in Naples, Italy," thus giving the town

its name. In 1887, a group of wealthy Kentuckians led by Walter N. Haldeman, owner of the *Louisville Courier-Journal*, bought up 8,700 beachfront acres, drew up a town plan, built a 600-foot pier, and started selling lots. This was, as time proved, a good plan: What went for $125 in 1900 now hovers around $10 million in a city where gentrification means billionaires are forcing out yesterday's millionaires.

But that doesn't mean the place puts on airs. Instead, its mostly new-money, baby-boomer citizens seem to exist in a sort of permanent dress-down Friday, relaxing with their investment advisers in a sidewalk café as they banter about the equities market and grandkids. Within the central "Old Naples" part of town, building restrictions have kept things low and peaceful, with grand homes and pastel commercial buildings nestled among banyan, palm, and flowering poinciana trees. Ritzy Third and Fifth Avenues are the shopping and dining district, while from the old pier—a beloved icon that's been rebuilt several times in its 100-year history—you can admire the mansions of Millionaires' Row, which back up to the town's beautiful, pristine beach. For a touch of Naples history, stop in at Palm Cottage, built for Walter Haldeman in 1895 and now a local museum.

Where there's wealth, there's golf, and in Naples (or Florida, for that matter) visitors can do no better than to settle in at The Ritz-Carlton Golf Resort Naples, a grand Mediterranean-style property where rooms and suites all overlook the vaunted 36-hole Tiburón golf course, designed by golf legend Greg Norman. Only a few minutes away, the 14-story sister property The Ritz-Carlton, Naples is regularly named one of Florida's and the country's best, its interior decorated with the impeccable Ritz finery and its views out over the Gulf of Mexico. Three miles of beaches are just outside; inside, the templelike spa is among Florida's best, its 51,000 square feet given over to sun-filled conservatories, pools, steam rooms, saunas, an outdoor mineral pool, and general over-the-top sumptuousness. Reciprocal use of amenities means guests can luxuriate in the best of both worlds.

WHERE: 107 miles west of Fort Lauderdale. *Visitor info:* Tel 800-688-3600. **PALM COTTAGE:** Tel 239-261-8164; napleshistoricalsociety.org. **RITZ-CARLTON GOLF RESORT NAPLES:** Tel 800-241-3333 or 239-593-2000; ritzcarlton .com/naplesgolf. *Cost:* from $239 (off-peak), from $499 (peak); greens fees from $85. **RITZ-CARLTON, NAPLES:** Tel 800-241-3333 or 239-598-3300; ritzcarlton.com/naples. *Cost:* from $419 (off-peak), from $799 (peak). **BEST TIMES:** sundown at the pier; Jan for the 3-day Naples Winter Wine Festival (napleswinefestival.com); Dec–May for weather.

Upscale development has slowly spread along the idyllic Gulf shore of Naples.

In the Shadow of Disney

UNIVERSAL ORLANDO RESORT AND SEAWORLD

Orlando, Florida

Who would have thought back in the '60s, when Walt Disney bought up 42 square miles of Orlando on which to build his resort, that it wouldn't be enough to keep the competition away? In 1973, SeaWorld took a shot at the burgeoning Orlando market by opening a park just east of Disney's massive property (see next page), and 17 years later, Universal Studios bought up its own chunk of land to the north. While neither can rival Disney's acreage, both have managed to carve out their own hugely popular niches—Universal as the home of the adrenaline rush and SeaWorld as the home of killer whales.

Created in consultation with director Steven Spielberg, the Universal Studios park grew out of the actual Hollywood film and television studio (famous for blockbusters like *E.T.*, *Jurassic Park*, and *Harry Potter*) with the idea of letting fans "ride the movies." Today Universal Orlando has more than 25 rides and attractions based on its films and TV programs, many created in collaboration with the shows' directors. The newer the ride, the faster the thrills. Revenge of the Mummy, based on the Brendan Fraser films, is a perennial favorite, whipping guests through faux Egyptian crypts, while the newer additions include Diagon Alley (2014), part of the fully immersive Wizarding World of Harry Potter, and Race Through New York starring Jimmy Fallon (2017), a fun and exciting ride from deep subway tunnels to the highest skyscrapers. Actors portraying Universal movie characters roam around at random, and movie and TV filming is occasionally done at sound stages around the property.

Even bigger thrills are to be found at Universal's second themed park, Islands of Adventure, generally acknowledged as the best Orlando park for adrenaline junkies. Covering 110 acres, it's divided up into eight islands whose themes include Dr. Seuss, classic cartoons (Popeye, Dudley Do-Right), *Jurassic Park* (featuring animatronic dinosaurs), and Marvel comics (its Amazing Adventures of

Spider-Man 3-D ride is one of Orlando's most, well, amazing). The Hogsmeade Village section of the Wizarding World of Harry Potter was the first of the two Harry Potter–themed attractions to open. You can travel between Hogsmeade and Diagon Alley on the Hogwarts Express.

Things are a lot quieter down at SeaWorld, a 200-acre paean to entertainment and the animal kingdom. The main draws are still Shamu the Killer Whale and his family (avoid the first 14 rows if you want to stay dry), but the park also includes up-close animal encounters, a water park you share with dolphins, and several roller coasters including a water-coaster through Atlantis and a family ride that reveals Antarctica through the eyes of a penguin. Various animal-interaction programs let you learn more about the animals and their care, even allowing you to spend a day helping the staff care for dolphins, whales, sea lions, and walruses.

UNIVERSAL ORLANDO & ISLANDS OF ADVENTURE: Tel 407-363-8000; universalorlando.com. *Cost:* 1-day/1-park ticket $102 adults, $97 kids. **SEAWORLD:** Tel 407-363-8000; seaworldparks.com. *Cost:* $99 (age 3 and up). **BEST TIME:** smallest crowds Jan–Apr.

America's Most Popular Resort

WALT DISNEY WORLD

Orlando, Florida

The brainchild of entertainment giant and genius animator Walt Disney is an ever-expanding universe of make-believe and escapism, celebrating magic, technology, nature, and, of course, Mickey Mouse. Walt Disney World is *the* ultimate theme park and the most popular tourist attraction on the planet. In the 45 years since it opened its doors in 1971, the 30,000-acre former cow pasture has grown to encompass four distinct parks and an assortment of other entertainments.

The original park is the Disneyland-ish Magic Kingdom, with the iconic Cinderella's Castle at its center and six themed "lands" radiating outward, full of classic rides and entertainment like Pirates of the Caribbean, the Hall of Presidents, Country Bear Jamboree, and the beloved It's a Small World. The old and the new collide in Tomorrowland, which features the '70s-era Space Mountain and the 21st-century Buzz Lightyear's Space Ranger Spin.

Epcot, the Experimental Prototype Community of Tomorrow, isn't *exactly* what Walt had in mind when he conceived of a residential community that would also be a laboratory, continually trying out new theories and technologies to improve urban life. Finally opened in 1982, almost 16 years after Walt's death, it's a mix of science-oriented films, rides, and exhibitions with 11 countries and their cultures represented in pavilions around a 40-acre lagoon. Thrill rides include the Mission: Space astronaut adventure and Test Track, which mimics the stress tests new cars are put through.

Disney's Hollywood Studios is, appropriately enough, the most theatrical of the Disney parks, in a big-budget Hollywood sense: all fast editing, big explosions, and pricey special effects (plus a few movie-themed shows starring the Muppets, the Little Mermaid, and the cast of *Toy Story*). The Force is strong with new Star Wars experiences, including an epic tour of the galaxy aboard Starspeeder 1000, which features a flight simulator, digital 3-D video, Audio-Animatronics characters, and in-cockpit special effects and music. Things are a lot different over at Disney's newest park, the 400-plus acre Animal Kingdom, where real jungle creatures and landscapes create an African safari experience not unlike that of a trip to Botswana. In addition to the theme parks, Disney also operates two themed water parks: Typhoon Lagoon and Blizzard Beach. Of the 36 hotels scattered all around the Disney property and near the Magic Kingdom, the Grand Floridian Resort & Spa may be the nicest, decorated in a Victorian style imbued with a relaxed romantic air. Not far away, across the Seven Seas Lagoon, the Wilderness Lodge is more family style, with a huge swimming area and the feel of a national park lodge. To the south, near Epcot, Disney's

A spectacular fireworks display lights up the sky over Cinderella's castle at the heart of the Magic Kingdom.

Beach Club Resort is designed after the grand New England "cottages" of the 1860s. Nearby, the Boardwalk Inn re-creates the Atlantic City Boardwalk scene of the 1930s, while Disney's Old Key West Resort shoots for a laid-back vibe and scores with a quiet, homey feel. The game-lodge-style Animal Kingdom Lodge is pretty far from anything except its namesake, but its savanna-view rooms let you watch giraffes grazing in the treetops and feel as if you're in the Serengeti. Value options are available at considerably less.

Where: 20 miles southwest of Orlando. Tel 407-939-5277; disneyworld.disney.go.com. *Cost:* 1-day/1-park tickets from $105 (10 and up). Value hotels from $85 per night. **Best times:** Mar–May for Epcot's International Flower and Garden Festival; Sep–Nov for Epcot's International Food and Wine Festival; Oct for the Magic Kingdom's Not-So-Scary Halloween Party; from mid-Nov for the Unforgettable Christmas Celebration.

PALM BEACH

Florida

For a peek into the life of the landed gentry, look no farther than Palm Beach, a 16-mile barrier-island enclave about 70 miles—but a world of difference—north of Miami. Established as the winter home of America's uber-rich in the 1890s, Palm Beach has remained ever since the essence of insular, upper-crust prestige.

Start your anthropological journey with a trip down the amusingly named Worth Avenue, home to more than 200 boutiques, galleries, and restaurants. This was the stretch along which Lilly Pulitzer, skylarking rich girl and newlywed, opened her little juice stand in 1959. The cute, bright-patterned sleeveless dress she designed became such a hit that she exchanged juice for the clothing business full-time. Today you can shop up a storm at Worth Avenue shops like Bulgari, Chanel, Gucci, Hermés, and Tourneau, then drop in to an old-line bistro like Ta-boo for lunch. The Bloody Mary was allegedly invented here one day to soothe heiress Barbara Hutton's hangover (though a competing legend has it invented at the St. Regis hotel in New York; see p. 191). Open since 1941, the place has the air of an updated Victorian palm garden, with excellent service and great people-watching.

Next, head out for a bike ride on the 5.5-mile Lake Trail, which winds along the Lake Worth section of the Intracoastal Waterway. On one side, fleets of yachts bob on the water with the mainland West Palm Beach skyline in the distance. On the other, you pass the pristinely manicured grounds of the sumptuous mega-mansions. On the Atlantic side of the island, Ocean Boulevard is home to another agglomeration of estates, including Mar-a-Lago, the former home of heiress Marjorie Merriweather Post, now reincarnated as a country club owned by Donald Trump.

"The Season" in Palm Beach unofficially runs from Thanksgiving through Easter, when the most parties, charity balls, and high-profile events take place. On the mainland, the social set gathers for the January start of polo season at International Polo Club Palm Beach in Wellington, its 3,000 box seats filled with stars, heirs, minor royalty, and lookers-on, dressed in their blue blazers and finery. Nearby, the Palm Beach Polo Golf and Country Club's Winter Equestrian Festival (late January through March) is the nation's largest equestrian show-jumping competition. And with 160 golf courses in the area—more per capita than anywhere else in the U.S.—Palm Beach proudly wears the title of Florida's Golf Capital.

Your day in the sun ideally concludes with a stay at either The Breakers Palm Beach (see next page) or the Brazilian Court Hotel. The latter first opened its doors in 1926, welcoming the likes of Greta Garbo, Cary Grant, and a host of tastemakers to its old-world Spanish-style suites and private courtyards. Rooms are elegant, and service is impeccable. For dinner it's French-American cuisine at the hotel's Café Boulud, outpost of New York celebrity chef and restaurateur Daniel Boulud.

WHERE: 70 miles north of Miami. *Visitor info:* Tel 800-554-7256; palmbeachfl.com. **TA-BOO:** Tel 561-835-3500; taboorestaurant.com. *Cost:* lunch $30. **INTERNATIONAL POLO CLUB:** Tel 561-204-5687; internationalpoloclub.com. *When:* peak polo tournament play Sun, late

Jan–Apr. **Palm Beach Polo Golf and Country Club:** Tel 561-798-7405; palm beachpolo.com. **Brazilian Court:** Tel 561-655-7740; thebraziliancourt.com. *Cost:* from $209 (off-peak), from $629 (peak); dinner at Café Boulud $68. **Best times:** Nov–May for weather; Jan–Mar for the peak of "the Season" and the top social events.

America's Own Villa Medici

The Breakers

Palm Beach, Florida

Henry Morrison Flagler, who'd made his fortune as John D. Rockefeller's partner in Standard Oil, first visited Florida in 1878 and immediately recognized its resort potential, as well as the impediment to fulfilling that potential—a lack of transportation. In the mid-1880s, Flagler began buying up railroads, standardizing their gauges to create an uninterrupted line of tracks down Florida's east coast, and then developing towns and resorts along the route—including The Breakers at Palm Beach. Originally built in 1896 and constructed entirely of wood, The Breakers burned to the ground in 1925. From its ashes rose one of the grandest resorts ever envisioned in North America and maybe the world. Designed by the architectural firm Schultze & Weaver (later designers of New York's Waldorf-Astoria hotel) on the model of Rome's 16th-century Villa Medici, the new seven-story hotel was immediately hailed as a masterpiece—from its 200-foot marble lobby to its terraced patios to its half-mile private beach.

Today, with a minimum of $25 million invested each year in ongoing enhancements, the 538-room, 140-acre resort continues to set its own standard; its vaulted ceilings, Venetian chandeliers, 15th-century Flemish tapestries, and a friendly, snap-to staff of 2,000 combine with a cool Floridian palette of light greens and blues to create the ultimate warm-weather resort. Exquisitely manicured, fountain-splashed grounds are shaded by more than 3,000 regal palms and include two 18-hole championship golf courses and ten Har-Tru tennis courts. Meandering pathways lead down to the private beach, the breezy location of the hotel's Mediterranean-style Beach Club, a newly transformed luxury spa, and a 6,000-square-foot indoor/outdoor fitness facility. The glamorous HMF restaurant is designed as a modern ode to the Palm Beach cocktail party of the '50s and '60s.

Just west of the hotel grounds, Whitehall, Henry Flagler's private estate, is open to the public as the Flagler Museum. Called "more wonderful than any palace in Europe" when it was built in 1902, the 75-room mansion is a veritable summation of the Gilded Age aesthetic, with a grand entrance hall made from seven different kinds of marble and a Louis XV–style Grand Ballroom.

The Breakers offers the full resort experience, with luxury accommodations, pools, a spa, and a half-mile stretch of private beach.

WHERE: 70 miles north of Miami; 1 South County Rd. Tel 888-273-2537 or 561-655-6611; thebreakers.com. *Cost:* from $349 (off-peak), from $649 (peak); dinner at HMF $50.

FLAGLER MUSEUM: Tel 561-655-2833; flagler museum.us. *When:* closed Mon. **BEST TIMES:** weekends for Sunday brunch, a Palm Beach tradition; late Nov–Mar for peak winter scene.

A Beachcomber's Paradise

SANIBEL AND CAPTIVA ISLANDS

Florida

Down on Florida's southern Gulf coast, Old Florida lives on. Of the more than 100 sunny, carefree coastal islands, the best-known of them are Sanibel and Captiva, connected to the mainland by a 3-mile causeway

and with a reputation for palm-stenciled sunsets, unparalleled tarpon fishing, and some of the country's most romantic beaches and best seashell-hunting. This may be the only warm-weather vacation spot where tourists pray for a storm, since a good northwest wind can fill the white sand beaches with shells. On any given day, a visitor can expect to find 50 or more different varieties, most in one piece thanks to the gentle coastal slopes and lack of offshore reefs. Fanatical collectors wake before dawn and patrol the beaches with flashlights, scrunched over in what some call the "Sanibel Stoop" or the "Captiva Crouch." To see the rarest of shells, visit Sanibel's Bailey-Matthews Shell Museum, the only natural history museum of its kind in the U.S. devoted solely to the mollusk, with a collection of over 750,000 specimens.

Take a break from all that shell-stooping, and visit Sanibel's J. N. "Ding" Darling National Wildlife Refuge, a cool preserve of over 6,400 acres of mangrove estuary, cordgrass marshes, and West Indian hardwood hammock. Famous for its bird-watching, the refuge provides habitat to some 245 species, including bald eagles, wood storks, and flamingos. Footpaths, bicycle trails, and kayak and canoe routes crisscross the area, or you can visit by car along the 4-mile Wildlife Drive.

If you're not feeling detached enough from the mainland and its everyday demands, visit Captiva and Sanibel's three most interesting neighbor islands, located in Pine Island Sound, all of them car-free and accessible only by boat. Cayo Costa State Park is an uninhabited barefoot Eden with deserted beaches whose shelling is arguably the best around. Cabbage Key, a 100-acre, down-home, real-life Margaritaville, is said to have inspired Jimmy Buffett's song "Cheeseburger in Paradise," and offers some of that old Florida R&R at the historic Cabbage Key Inn. Useppa Island is a privately owned club that welcomes overnighters (as well as day-trippers who come for excellent seafood

Browse Sanibel Island's shops for exquisite seashells like coquinas, scallops, whelks, and sand dollars.

lunches) at its genteel Collier Inn, where Teddy Roosevelt used to vacation with his tarpon-fishing friends. Today Boca Grande, on nearby Gasparilla Island, hosts an annual big-purse tarpon tournament.

WHERE: 135 miles south of Tampa. *Visitor info:* Tel 800-237-6444 or 239-338-3500; fortmyers-sanibel.com. **SHELL MUSEUM:** Sanibel. Tel 888-679-6450 or 239-395-2233;

shellmuseum.org. **"DING" DARLING REFUGE:** Sanibel. Tel 239-472-1100; fws.gov/refuge/jn_ding_darling. **CABBAGE KEY INN:** Tel 239-283-2278; cabbagekey.com. *Cost:* from $100. **COLLIER INN:** Useppa Island. Tel 239-283-1061; useppa.com. *Cost:* from $150; lunch $35. **BEST TIMES:** May–mid-July for tarpon season; May–Nov for peak shelling; Nov–May for weather and bird-watching.

A Glimpse of Imperial Spain on the Florida Coast

ST. AUGUSTINE

Florida

The year is 1565 and the place is *La Florida*, "The Land of Flowers." Juan Ponce de León had claimed it for Spain in 1513, and the conquistadors were busy destroying a settlement of French Huguenots and establishing

St. Augustine, the first permanent settlement on the North American continent (beating Jamestown by 42 years). The Spanish held Florida until 1763, regained it after the American Revolution, then in 1821, just a decade before railroads began ushering in the modern age, finally ceded it to the young U.S. It was a long run—long enough that St. Augustine retains a Spanish feel to this day, its historic district mirroring the boundaries of the old colonial city, with horse-drawn carriages and reenactors enlivening the picture.

The Historic District includes some 60 buildings dating from the 16th through the 19th century. Around Plaza de la Constitución, once the colony's central meeting ground, you can see the Government House museum, built between 1706 and 1713 and once the Spanish governor's mansion; Trinity Episcopal Church, dating from 1825; and the Cathedral of St. Augustine, which incorporates the 1797 parish church and is one of the oldest Catholic churches in the U.S. East of the Plaza, the Spanish Renaissance Revival–style Hotel Ponce de León was one of three St. Augustine

Cannons were fired from the Castillo de San Marcos' corner bastions.

resorts built or owned by railroad and resort king Henry Flagler. Today it's the centerpiece of Flagler College, a small liberal arts school. Across the street, Flagler's similarly styled Alcazar Hotel is now home to the Lightner Museum and its collection of American Gilded Age treasures, including costumes, furnishings, musical instruments, and Tiffany glass. More historic spots can be found lining pedestrian-only St. George Street, including the

Colonial Quarter, a two-acre attraction where you can experience three centuries of colonial life with living history demonstrations by costumed interpreters and historic activities for kids.

Near the Quarter, the imposing Castillo de San Marcos was built to protect Spanish territory and shipping routes and remains the only extant 17th-century fort in the country. Though attacked repeatedly, it was never taken by force, and served its military duties for over two centuries. Today the double drawbridge entrance leads to beautifully preserved battlements, prison cells, a chapel, and other chambers, some with museum displays. The limestone "coquina" walls, composed of tiny shell fragments and sand bound with calcite, survived cannon balls and hurricanes.

By the time the Castillo was decommissioned, Florida was in its Gilded Age heyday as America's resort capital—an era you can relive by booking a room at the Casa Monica Hotel, a member of Marriott's Autograph Collection and the only one of Henry Flagler's Augustine trio that still serves its original purpose. Built in 1888, it's a romantic Moorish Revival-style castle plunked down in modern Florida, its 138 rooms done up with wrought-iron beds, mahogany tables, and Iberian-style armoires.

WHERE: 105 miles northeast of Orlando. *Visitor info:* Tel 800-653-2489 or 904-829-1711; floridashistoriccoast.com. **LIGHTNER MUSEUM:** Tel 904-824-2874; lightnermuseum.org. **COLONIAL QUARTER:** Tel 904-342-2857; colonialquarter.com. **CASTILLO DE SAN MARCOS:** Tel 904-829-6506; nps.gov/casa. **CASA MONICA:** Tel 888-213-8903 or 904-827-1888; casamonica.com. *Cost:* from $179 (off-peak), from $259 (peak). **BEST TIME:** late Nov–Jan for Nights of Light, when 3 million holiday lights glow throughout the historic district.

A Surreal Collection

THE DALÍ MUSEUM

St. Petersburg, Florida

Born and educated in Spain, resident of Paris and New York, the surrealist painter Salvador Dalí probably appreciated the bizarre fact that the most comprehensive collection of his work anywhere resides in St. Petersburg, Florida. In 1942, Ohio businessman A. Reynolds Morse and his wife, Eleanor, began collecting the artist's work, soon becoming part of Dalí's inner circle, and in 1971 opening a Dalí museum in Cleveland, Ohio. Visitor demand eventually mandated a move to larger quarters, so in 1982, after an exhaustive search, the collection found its way to downtown St. Petersburg, a site then reminiscent of Cadaques, Dalí's boyhood home on the Spanish coast.

Today the museum's collection encompasses works from every major period of Dalí's long career, spanning the years 1917 through 1976 and including 96 oil paintings; 45 watercolors and gouaches, 107 drawings, 400 photographs, 1,900 prints and book illustrations, and 276 objets d'art including holograms, jewels, and surrealist objects. Standout paintings include *Still Life—Fast Moving* (1952–54), an update of the classic Dutch still life, with its characteristic elements—a knife, a fruit dish, wine—floating above the table, symbolizing the atom bomb's effect on human perceptions of normalcy. *Daddy Longlegs of the Evening—Hope!*, the first painting in the original Morse collection, is characteristic of the artist's 1929–1940 surrealist period, with its melting plane, violin, and human figure.

Dalí's works often display a deep symbolic complexity in their exploration of psychological, scientific, historical, and religious themes, so take a free, public docent-led tour to get beyond the surface.

Where: 24 miles southwest of Tampa; One Dali Blvd. Tel 727-823-3767; thedali.org.

The Boys of Summer

Baseball Spring Training

Tampa, Florida

S pring training is an American ritual of low-key exhibition games that almost, *almost* brings the sport back to its small-town roots for a few precious weeks each year in March till opening day on April 1. On the East Coast,

Florida is the locus of the action, a tradition that goes back to 1914, when the St. Louis Browns wintered in St. Petersburg. Today, 15 teams train and compete here, making up what's known as the Grapefruit League.

By some estimates, the Phillies have the most fan-friendly stadium in the area, the 8,500-seat Bright House Field in Clearwater. The Yankees, though, are the biggest marquee team, and their stadium, George M. Steinbrenner Field, is the largest in the Grapefruit League, with seating for 11,026 fans and field dimensions identical to those at the team's Bronx home. Fans can tour a miniature Monument Park with plaques commemorating dozens of Yankees legends, or crowd above the dugout before the first pitch to try for autographs. Those who want to live the experience can sign up for Yankees Fantasy Camp, a weeklong immersion into the world of Yankee baseball, with daily instruction and coaching from former players and current coaches, your own Yankee uniform, a locker in the clubhouse, and a dream game against the pros. Batter up!

George M. Steinbrenner Field: 1 Steinbrenner Dr. Tel 813-875-7753; steinbrennerfield.com. *Price:* from $16. *When:* spring training games throughout Mar. **Yankees Fantasy Camp:** Tel 800-368-CAMP or 813-875-7753; yankees.com. *Cost:* $4,950 per person (minimum age 30) for 6 nights, includes a hotel room, meals, and transportation. *When:* Jan and Nov.

Images of Gone With the Wind

The Antebellum Trail

Georgia

"A ntebellum" means "existing before the war." In this part of the world, that's pre-1861, as the war in question is the War Between the States, the War of Northern Aggression, the War of the Rebellion, or the

Home to eight governors, headquarters of General Sherman, and part of Georgia College & State University, the Old Governor's Mansion was designated a National Historic Landmark in 1973.

Civil War, depending on whom you ask. The Union general who ultimately secured control of Georgia, William T. Sherman, practiced a harsh scorched-earth policy, burning communities during his vigorous campaign across the state. As a result, most of Georgia's great antebellum buildings are long gone. But luckily a number of notable exceptions survived, and the state's Antebellum Trail—running through the heart of Lake Country—traces a string of towns east of Atlanta containing a remarkable concentration of houses that still evoke the romantic imagery of the *Gone With the Wind* era.

The route begins in Athens (see p. 333) and runs south for about 100 miles to Macon (see p. 345), passing through such history-rich towns as Watkinsville, Madison (see next page), Eatonton, Milledgeville, Gray, and Old Clinton. Called "the prettiest small town in America," Madison makes a great base for exploring, and many of its fine buildings were spared by Sherman—thanks to his favorable connection to a local anti-secessionist, then-U.S. Senator Joshua Hill. Most of the grand mansions here remain in private hands, but you can stroll about admiring their stunning, well-preserved exteriors, or enjoy the countless antiques stores (see next page), using the architecturally elegant Madison Oaks Inn & Gardens as your base.

Eatonton is most famous as the birthplace of *Uncle Remus Tales* novelist Joel Chandler Harris and contemporary writer Alice Walker, author of *The Color Purple*. From here, head south to "Georgia's antebellum capital," Milledgeville, which served as the state's legislative capital from 1804 to 1868 and is an especially worthy destination for history and architecture buffs. General Sherman briefly used the Old Governor's Mansion as his headquarters during the war, and the majestic 1839 Greek Revival is now one of the region's top historic attractions. Another Milledgeville claim to fame is the home of Flannery O'Connor, the late novelist and short-story writer (*Wise Blood, A Good Man Is Hard to Find*) perhaps most identified with the Southern Gothic genre. Visit her farmhouse, Andalusia, where she lived and raised some 100 peafowl until her death in 1964 at the age of 39. Then immerse yourself in history at the Grand Antebellum Inn, with just six guest rooms fitted out with period pieces.

Macon marks the official end of the trail, but it's worth continuing to Warner Robins, an excellent antiquing destination.

WHERE: Madison is 60 miles east of Atlanta. *Trail info:* antebellumtrail.org. *Madison visitor info:* Tel 800-709-7406 or 706-342-4454; madisonga.org. *Milledgeville visitor info:* Tel 800-653-1804 or 478-452-4687; visit milledgeville.org. **OLD GOVERNOR'S MANSION:** Milledgeville. Tel 478-445-4545; gcsu.edu/mansion. *When:* closed Mon. **ANDALUSIA:** Tel 478-454-4029; andalusiafarm.org. *When:* closed Mon–Wed. **MADISON OAKS INN:** Madison. Tel 706-343-9990; madisonoaksinn.com. *Cost:* from $195. **ANTEBELLUM INN:** Milledgeville. Tel 478-453-3993; antebelluminn.com. *Cost:* from $149. **BEST TIMES:** mid-Apr for Milledgeville's Tour of Homes; late Apr–early May for Madison's Spring Tour of Homes; Dec for holiday-themed home tours in Madison and Christmas at the Mansion in Milledgeville.

A Historic Heartland Full of Finds

AN ANTIQUES TRAIL AND OTHER TREASURES

Georgia

F ew of the South's many—and there are *many*—great spots for antiquing can compare with the clutch of towns east of Atlanta along Interstate 20, connecting the dots of Conyers, Covington, Social Circle, Madison, and Greensboro. Conyers is the first stop along the trail, with a number of browsing-worthy antiques shops in its historic Olde Town neighborhood, but Covington is brimming with antebellum and Victorian homes you may recognize from movies like *Sweet Home Alabama* and the made-for-TV movie *Coat of Many Colors*, and worth a longer linger.

Social Circle is a frozen-in-time 1830s mill town that takes its name from the well in the middle of town where folks used to swap news. Abundant with great shops, it is justly famous for one of the best traditional Southern eateries anywhere, the Blue Willow Inn, a Greek Revival mansion where guests take second and even third helpings from a constantly replenished buffet line (most ample on weekends) featuring the signature fried chicken, country-cured ham, fried green tomatoes, and a host of desserts that usually includes warm fruit cobbler. The Blue Willow was a favorite of the late, legendary Georgia humorist Lewis Grizzard long before the Food Network named it one of the Top 5 "Bodacious Buffets" in America.

In Rutledge, known for handmade furniture and folk art, stop for a root-beer float or home-made pralines at the Caboose, a bright-red vintage railcar converted into a restaurant.

Madison, the area's hub, is also the most prominent town on the famed Antebellum Trail (see p. 329). You'll find most of the 100-plus antiques shops in the city's historic district of well-kept, tree-shaded brick sidewalks built around the post office square. From here, it's a 20-mile detour to reach Greensboro and the acclaimed Lake Oconee resort area, which has become well known for its cluster of outstanding golf courses. Greensboro was founded in 1803, and today has more than a half-dozen antiques shops, an antiques mall, and environs rich with excellent fishing, camping, and boating.

One of the South's most opulent contemporary resorts, the Ritz-Carlton Lodge Reynolds Plantation has 99 beautifully laid-out holes of golf as a main attraction, but also offers kayaking, canoeing, fishing, biking, and a slew of sybaritic services in its 26,000-square-foot spa. On staff, a "BBQ butler" helps guests create their own memorable cookouts.

WHERE: beginning about 25 miles east of Atlanta. *Visitor info:* Tel 800-266-9377 or 770-929-4270; treasuresalongi20.org. **BLUE WILLOW INN:** Social Circle. Tel 800-552-8813 or 770-464-2131; bluewillowinn.com. *Cost:* $20. **THE CABOOSE:** Rutledge. Tel 706-557-9021; thecabooseinrutledge.com. *Cost:* lunch $10. **RITZ-CARLTON LODGE REYNOLDS PLANTATION:** Greensboro. Tel 800-241-3333 or 706-467-0600; ritzcarlton.com. *Cost:* rooms from $289. **BEST TIMES:** early Mar for Madison Antique Show and Sale; early Feb and early Dec for Madison Tour of Homes; last weekend in Sept for Lake Oconee BBQ and Blues Festival.

A 2,185-Mile Walk in the Country

THE APPALACHIAN TRAIL

Georgia to Maine

Born in Stamford, Connecticut, in 1879, Benton MacKeye was a naturalist, an early employee of the U.S. Forest Service, and a man who thought big. In 1921, fearing that the pace of urban-industrial life along the eastern

seaboard was taxing people's sanity, he proposed a trail that would run from the highest point in New England to the highest point in the South, with wilderness camps along the way.

The camps never got built, but the Appalachian Trail did, its last link blazed in 1937. Today between 2 and 3 million people hike a portion of the trail every year, while 800 or so "through-hikers" now complete the entire 2,185-mile journey from Georgia's Springer Mountain to Maine's Mount Katahdin (see p. 29)—a trek of about 5 million steps, passing through 14 states, 8 national forests, and 6 national parks.

Most through-hikers travel north, leaving Springer Mountain in March or early April and finishing on Mount Katahdin in September. The first leg of rugged wilderness hiking runs through the Chattahoochee National Forest in the southern Appalachians near Dahlonega (see p. 340). The AT then threads the border between Tennessee and North Carolina, with

more than 70 miles within Great Smoky Mountains National Park (see p. 464). A full quarter of the trail (544 miles) runs through Virginia including 107 miles through Virginia's Shenandoah National Park (see p. 252), known for its gorgeous scenery and an excellent option for people who want to do only part of the trail. West Virginia's section is only 4 miles long, but ironically, the state's Harpers Ferry (see p. 277) is the home of Appalachian Trail Conservancy headquarters. In Maryland, the trail runs for 41 miles across the Potomac River and along the C&O Canal.

Once you cross into Pennsylvania you're about halfway done, heading along easy trails in the Michaux State Forest and the Cumberland Valley and then crossing the Susquehanna River and beginning a hard, rocky route northeast along the eastern rim of the Alleghenies. At the Delaware Water Gap the trail enters New Jersey, passing through High Point State Park and on clear days letting onto views of the Manhattan skyline at spots. The New York section includes popular Harriman–Bear Mountain State Park, which was the first portion of the trail completed, in 1923. From here it's all New England, with a short 51-mile passage through Connecticut's scenic Taconic Range and Housatonic River Valley. In western Massachusetts the AT runs through the beautiful Berkshire Mountains and into Vermont, where it approaches tree line at Killington (see p. 98) and Stratton (see p. 108). In New Hampshire, the highlight is the ruggedly gorgeous White Mountains (see p. 78), a strenuous section that attracts more day-hikers and

In 1968, the Appalachian Trail was designated by Congress as a National Scenic Trail.

backpackers than any other part of the trail. In Maine, things just get harder, with the 281-mile homestretch considered the most difficult along the entire route, with treacherous footing, unpredictable weather, and many boggy sections. The state's southernmost section includes a mile-long scramble among the huge boulders, crevices, and caves of Mahoosuc Notch, after which it's a straight shot north along the famous "Hundred Miles," an isolated section of mountains, lakes, and forest between Monson and the peak of Katahdin—and the end of the road.

WHERE: 2,185 miles from Georgia to Maine. Tel 304-535-6331; appalachiantrail .org. **HOW:** designated campsites and back-country shelters along the AT, all marked in the official guidebooks and maps. *When:* Mar–Sept (northbound) or June–Dec (southbound). **BEST TIMES:** mid-May in Damascus, VA, for Appalachian Trail Days (traildays.us). For shorter hikes, high points include June and July in the southern Appalachians for flowering shrubs, and late Sept–Oct in VT, NH, and MA for fall foliage.

Rockin' and Noshin' in a College Town

ATHENS AND ATHFEST

Georgia

People choose to live in the "Classic City" of Athens for many reasons: The University of Georgia (UGA) fosters an open-minded population, as does the edgy arts, theater, and revered alternative-music scene that has spawned such vaunted music acts as the B-52s, R.E.M. (lead singer Michael Stipe has a home here), and the Drive-By Truckers. And every June, Athens celebrates its music heritage with AthFest, a five-day live-music and arts festival that lines up over 100 performances by dozens of talented music acts.

In a setting beside the Oconee River, Athens—one of the few Georgia communities spared by Gen. William T. Sherman during his infamous Civil War "March to the Sea"—contains numerous antebellum homes found within 15 national historic districts and is the beginning of Georgia's popular Antebellum Trail (see p. 329). America's first state-chartered university (incorporated in 1785), UGA abuts the gallery-laden downtown. Nearby, the State Botanical Gardens of Georgia is the ideal place to be alone with your thoughts, where a glass conservatory with tropical plants complements thousands of colorful outdoor plantings, and 5 miles of marked

Two outdoor stages—one electric, one acoustic—provide free live music during AthFest.

nature trails lead you through 313 acres of fascinating flora.

Among Athens's memorable dining options, The Grit, a favorite of R.E.M.'s Stipe, serves up famously delicious vegetarian/vegan food loved by all, such as tofu Reuben sandwiches, black bean chili, falafels, and a wonderful array of homemade desserts. But the toast of the town is the 5 & 10 (in a former five-and-dime store), helmed by talented self-taught chef Hugh Acheson. Book at least a couple of days ahead for the chance to taste the re-imagined Southern specialties, such as crispy panko-crusted catfish with grits, tomato chutney, and a subtle vermouth emulsion.

WHERE: 70 miles east of Atlanta. *Visitor info:* Tel 800-653-0603 or 706-357-4430; visit athensga.com. **ATHFEST:** Tel 706-548-1973;

athfest.com. *When:* late June. **BOTANICAL GARDENS:** Tel 706-542-1244; uga.edu/bot garden. *When:* grounds daily; visitor center and conservatory closed Sun. **THE GRIT:** Tel 706-543-6592; thegrit.com. *Cost:* dinner $15. **5 & 10:** Tel 706-546-7300; fiveandten.com. *Cost:* dinner $45. **WHERE TO STAY:** The Graduate Athens, tel 706-549-7020; graduate athens.com. *Cost:* from $89 (off-peak), from $159 (peak). **BEST TIMES:** June for AthFest; Feb for Taste of Athens; Sept–May for Athens' music and performing arts scene.

Big-City Food with Down-Home Spirit

ATLANTA'S GREAT NEIGHBORHOOD RESTAURANTS

Atlanta, Georgia

A tlanta has grown steadily since the 1980s into one of America's world-class cities, and its dining scene has kept pace. In just about every neighborhood of this ever-expanding metropolis you can find an

impressive number of special restaurants with strong local followings, imaginative chefs, and stylish digs. Here's a condensed culinary tour of "Hotlanta," with three venues in every price range.

The longevity of Mary Mac's Tea Room speaks volumes about its popularity among all strata of Atlantans, from ladies who lunch to powerful CEOs to urban hipsters to Jimmy Carter, who has long been a fan. Mary McKinney opened this no-nonsense diner ("tea room" lent an air of propriety) in 1945, and although it's changed hands a couple of times, it holds forth as a local institution serving traditional chicken and dumplings, fried shrimp and oyster combos, cheese grits, fried okra, barbecued ribs, chunky peach cobbler, and banana pudding. In 2011, Georgia's House of Representatives recognized Mary Mac's as Atlanta's Dining Room.

Another down-home joint with a more contemporary take on Southern cooking, the Flying Biscuit Cafe has six locales in Atlanta.

Delicious breakfast platters are served all day at the colorful Flying Biscuit Cafe.

The original—which has the most personality—is in a gentrified, mostly residential neighborhood in East Atlanta called Candler Park. Among the breakfast-all-day treats, consider orange-scented french toast topped with raspberry sauce and honey-crème anglaise, or the savory Meggxican wrap with eggs, cheddar, onions, and serrano chiles wrapped in a flour tortilla. But how to find room for the restaurant's signature feathery biscuits and apple butter? (Each location averages 5,000 biscuits a week.)

Just north of Atlanta, a gorgeously landscaped garden on the Chattahoochee River is the delightful setting for Canoe. Helmed by executive chef Matthew Basford, Canoe is all about exceptional contemporary Southern cuisine—try the slow-roasted Carolina rabbit with Swiss chard and parsnip or the grilled duck breast with masala-spiced kabocha squash. Save room for dessert—there's Dutch apple pie with ice cream and sweet potato crème brûlée with buttered pecans.

Mary Mac's Tea Room: Tel 404-876-1800; marymacs.com. *Cost:* dinner $25. **Flying Biscuit Cafe:** Tel 404-687-8888; flyingbiscuit.com. *Cost:* dinner $18. **Canoe:** Tel 770-432-2663; canoeatl.com. *Cost:* dinner $50.

An Underwater Eden and Olympic-Size Family Fun

THE GEORGIA AQUARIUM AND DOWNTOWN DRAWS

Atlanta, Georgia

Rarely has the opening of an aquarium elicited such excitement and intrigue as the new one in Atlanta did in 2006. The $250 million gift of Bernard Marcus to the city where the company he co-founded, Home Depot, began, it is the country's largest aquarium. Located in downtown Atlanta, traditionally the domain of office workers, not tourists, it is a 13-acre state-of-the-art facility with a staggering 10 million gallons of both fresh and salt water that contains more than 100,000 different animals, representing over 500 of the planet's marine species.

The aquarium is divided into several marine-life areas. One of the most popular, perhaps owing to its appearance in sultry Georgia, is the Cold Water Quest, a habitat for creatures that thrive in the world's icier seas. Here you'll see beluga whales, southern sea otters, African penguins, a giant Pacific octopus, and Japanese spider crabs. The Ocean Voyager is another crowd pleaser, where stingrays, whale sharks (the largest species of fish in the world), and groupers swim gracefully through a 100-foot-long saltwater tunnel.

Next to the aquarium, visit the World of Coca-Cola, an exuberant (if unabashedly commercial) tribute to the world's most popular soft drink. Then wander the 21-acre Centennial Olympic Park, the focal point for the 1996 Summer Olympics, and walk to the CNN Center (the Cable News Network's studio headquarters), where a behind-the-scenes tour is a uniquely Atlanta experience.

If all this walking and gawking has you feeling hungry, make the short drive to the world's largest drive-in, the Varsity, open for business since 1928. There's seating for 800 people who consume some 2 miles of hot dogs and 300 gallons of chili every day.

Servers traditionally bark "What'll ya have?" to customers, who respond with orders for cheeseburgers (topped with pimento cheese), crisp onion rings, and hulking chili cheese dogs—with a gigantic cup full of Coca-Cola, the local drink of choice.

GEORGIA AQUARIUM: 225 Baker St. NW. Tel 404-581-4000; georgiaaquarium.org. **WORLD OF COCA-COLA:** Tel 404-676-5151; worldof coca-cola.com. **CNN:** Tel 877-4CNNTOUR or 404-827-2300; cnn.com/tour. *Cost:* $16. **THE VARSITY:** Tel 404-881-1706; thevarsity.com. *Cost:* $7. **BEST TIME:** Holiday in Lights display in Centennial Olympic Park mid-Nov–early Jan.

The Georgia Aquarium affords visitors the opportunity to observe jellyfish and countless other marine animals up close.

The Heart of the Arts

MIDTOWN ATLANTA

Atlanta, Georgia

Downtown may be Atlanta's commercial center, but just to the north, Midtown claims the lion's share of the city's major cultural attractions— from museums to performance halls—amid a bevy of eye-catching

architecture, great hotels and inns, hip shops and restaurants, gay and straight bars and coffeehouses, offbeat art galleries, and parkland. If Atlanta looks like a poster child for urban renewal, much of it is due to the Richard Meier-designed High Museum of Art's spectacular expansion in 2005 that saw the design of three new buildings by architect Renzo Piano. Now one of the South's great cultural institutions, the High contains a superb permanent assemblage of some 15,000 works, including work by self-taught Southern artists such as folk preacher Howard Finster (see p. 347) and African American sculptor Ulysses Davis.

Literary and film buffs have long made it a point to visit the Margaret Mitchell House and Museum, the former home of the woman who wrote *Gone With the Wind.* Mitchell herself referred to the Tudor revival brick house, then divided into apartments, as "The Dump," but

it's looking far more dapper today, following a major renovation after a pair of devastating fires in the mid-1990s. Walk through the very room in which she penned her Pulitzer Prize–winning novel and view a number of enlightening exhibits. The film (none of which was filmed in Georgia) made its world premiere in Atlanta in 1939, with Mitchell in attendance.

The crown jewel of Piedmont Park, a 185-acre dogwood-dappled plot of greenery that forms the entire eastern border of Midtown, is the Atlanta Botanical Garden, a 30-acre spread anchored by a conservatory and orchid center.

Midtown is chock-full of great restaurants, including Einstein's, a cheery, bustling community melting pot set inside a turn-of-the-20th-century cottage. Try for a seat on the lushly landscaped patio, and enjoy a kitchen that turns out deliciously eclectic American fare, from crab cakes and fried green tomatoes to stellar burgers. During the popular weekend brunch, opt for the classic shrimp and grits and one of the restaurant's signature Bloody Marys.

Hotels dominate Midtown's skyline, but the cream of the crop is the Four Seasons Atlanta, an elegant contemporary tower that occupies 19 stories of a 50-story skyscraper. The most sought-after rooms, all of which are spacious and tastefully done in soothing tan, gold, and gray color schemes, have large picture windows and terraces with great views of downtown or the park.

WHERE: bordered loosely by 14th St. NE, Piedmont Park, Monroe Dr., and Spring St. NW. *Visitor info:* Tel 800-ATLANTA or 404-521-6600; atlanta.net. **HIGH MUSEUM OF ART:** Tel 404-733-4444; high.org. *When:* closed Mon. **MARGARET MITCHELL HOUSE:** Tel 404-249-7015; atlantahistorycenter.com. **ATLANTA BOTANICAL GARDEN:** Tel 404-876-5859; atlantabg.org. *When:* closed Mon. **EINSTEIN'S:**

Tel 404-876-7925; einsteinsatlanta.com. *Cost:* dinner $25. **FOUR SEASONS:** Tel 800-819-5053 or 404-881-9898; fourseasons.com/atlanta. *Cost:* from $299. **BEST TIMES:** early Apr for the Atlanta Dogwood Festival; late May for the Jazz Festival; mid-Oct for the Pride Festival.

Margaret Mitchell lived in Apartment #1 from 1925 until 1932, looking out the leaded glass window while writing her masterpiece, Gone With the Wind.

The Roots of the Civil Rights Movement

SWEET AUBURN AND MARTIN LUTHER KING JR. HISTORIC DISTRICT

Atlanta, Georgia

The roughly mile-and-a-half stretch of downtown Atlanta's Auburn Avenue known as Sweet Auburn is the birthplace of Rev. Martin Luther King Jr. and where the city's vibrant African American community came into its

own during the 1890s. During the years of enforced racial segregation in the early 20th century, Auburn Avenue was so prosperous that local civic leader John Wesley Dobbs declared it the "richest Negro street in the World," and the nickname Sweet Auburn stuck. The neighborhood fell into decline following WWII and slid into an especially bad state by the 1970s, the victim of

depopulation, crime, and the construction of Interstate 75/85, which crudely split the district in two. It earned its National Historic Landmark designation in 1976 and the Historic District Development Corporation (HDDC) soon formed to reverse its fortunes. Since then, residents have started moving back into the neighborhood, and a number of businesses are following.

Today many of Sweet Auburn's most significant buildings are open for tours. Start off at the African American Panoramic Experience (APEX), an engaging, highly interactive museum with a re-creation of the Yates & Milton Drug Store, opened in 1923 as one of the city's first prominent black-owned businesses.

At the Martin Luther King Jr. National Historic Site, park rangers lead tours of the King Birth Home as well as the Ebenezer Baptist Church Museum, where three generations of the King family preached—it continues to serve a large congregation today. Another important site is the Martin Luther King Jr. Center for Nonviolent Social Change, which his widow, the late Coretta Scott King, established to help spread her husband's

teachings. Freedom Plaza, across the street, is the site of King's white-marble tomb inscribed with his words "Free at last. Free at last. Thank God Almighty I'm Free at last." His wife was interred here following her death in January 2006.

WHERE: stretching roughly from Courtland St. to Randolph St. *Visitor info:* sweetauburn.com. **APEX:** Tel 404-523-APEX; apexmuseum.org. *When:* closed Mon. **MARTIN LUTHER KING JR. NATIONAL HISTORIC SITE:** Tel 404-331-5190; nps.gov/malu. **THE KING CENTER:** Tel 404-526-8900; thekingcenter.org. **BEST TIMES:** Feb for Black History Month at the Martin Luther King Jr. National Historic Site; 3 days in early May for the Sweet Auburn Springfest; Oct for the Sweet Auburn Music Fest.

Golf's Most Time-Honored Event

AUGUSTA AND THE MASTERS GOLF TOURNAMENT

Georgia

Attending a practice round at the legendary Masters Tournament may not sound like much to nongolfers, but it's a dream come true for fans of the sport. The Masters, the first of men's professional golf's four annual major tournaments—and considered by many the most prestigious in the world—has delivered some of golf's finest moments since it began in 1934 (such as Arnold Palmer's 43rd Masters appearance in 2004). Only the best of the best vie for the symbolic Green Jacket of questionable sartorial merit. Would-be visitors hoping to sneak a peek at the course should be forewarned: No part of it is visible from the streets, and the Augusta National Golf Club is guarded as tightly as Fort Knox. So, unless you've been invited by a member, don't even try.

The lone exception is Masters Week each April, when you might be able to score a ticket to one of the practice rounds, which allows you to soak up some of the preliminary buzz and walk the hallowed grounds. Tickets or "badges" to the actual Masters Tournament are nearly impossible to obtain, as they're sold to the same people year after year on a legacy basis. Tickets to the practice rounds on Monday, Tuesday, and Wednesday are distributed in an annual lottery drawing.

Although you may never get a chance to play at Augusta, the area does have several notable courses open to the public, including historic Forest Hills Golf Course, an old-school sentimental favorite designed in 1926 by Donald Ross and reworked twice since then. A snazzier, newer course is Jones Creek

Golf Club, in Evan, Georgia. Expect elevated greens fees during Masters week.

WHERE: 125 miles northwest of Savannah. *Visitor info:* Tel 800-726-0243 or 706-724-4067; augustaga.org. **THE MASTERS TOURNAMENT:** Tel 706-667-6700; masters.org. For practice-round ticket applications, log onto the website and follow the online registration process. *Cost:* from

$65. *When:* 1st week in Apr. **FOREST HILLS GOLF COURSE:** Tel 706-733-0001; theforest hillsgolfcourse.com. *Cost:* greens fees from $27. **JONES CREEK GOLF CLUB:** Tel 706-860-4228; jonescreekgolfclub.com. *Cost:* greens fees from $47. **WHERE TO STAY:** Partridge Inn, tel 706-737-8888; curiocollection3hilton.com. *Cost:* from $129.

Aristocracy in the Wilds

CUMBERLAND ISLAND

Georgia

It's the largest, southernmost, and most pristine of Georgia's many delightful coastal islands (see p. 342) and possibly the most enchanting. Occupied at various times by Guale Indians, Spanish missionaries, and British militia,

the 17-mile-long island drew its most famous residents in the 1880s, when Andrew Carnegie's steel-baron brother and partner Thomas came here and built several opulent summer cottages, as did a handful of other wealthy northerners. Some of these homes still stand—one as Cumberland Island's only accommodation, the courtly plantation-style Greyfield Inn. But mostly Cumberland Island is blessedly devoid of development, free of cars, and without residents—at least the human kind. You'll see sea turtles, armadillos, wild horses, and more than 300 species of birds amid the island's 36,415 acres, much of which consist of marshland and tidal creeks.

The park service established Cumberland Island National Seashore here in 1972 and has administered most of the island, which can only be reached by ferry, ever since.

Guests at Greyfield Inn, a white-columned 1900 plantation inn, escape modern-day distractions of TVs, phones, and cars and instead enjoy the delicious sensation of being very, very far from civilization, nestled deep in the canopied woodlands of live oaks, pine, and magnolia trees. The handsomely furnished mansion with

16 rooms and suites is still run by Carnegie's great-great-grandchildren, and contains many of the family's original antiques and mementos from their gilded past. Its under-the-radar profile was blown forever when, in 1996, the late John F. Kennedy Jr. and Carolyn Bessette secretly married and honeymooned here, taking over the island with family and friends.

To experience Cumberland on a somewhat tighter budget, take the ferry to the island and walk extensive nature trails and miles of pristine beaches. Back on the mainland, enjoy wonderfully historic and charming accommodations in

Originally built in 1900 for Thomas Carnegie's daughter, Margaret, Greyfield was converted into an inn in 1962 and is still run today by the Carnegie descendants.

St. Marys at the Spencer House Inn, a rambling 1872 Victorian house that will send you off with a picnic lunch for your day on Cumberland.

Nearby lies one of the largest preserved freshwater wetlands in the U.S., Okefenokee National Wildlife Refuge, a 628-square-mile refuge (the Creek Indians called it "the land of trembling earth") teeming with alligators, hawks, black bears, and great blue herons. Enter the vast swampland via the Suwannee Canal, a man-made offshoot of the eponymous river (as in "Way down upon the Swanee River," the famed lyric of Stephen Foster). Take a guided boat tour through the swamp, or rent a kayak or motorboat to explore it on your own.

WHERE: 345 miles southeast of Atlanta. *Visitor info:* Tel 866-868-2199 or 912-882-4000; stmaryswelcome.com. **CUMBERLAND ISLAND NATIONAL SEASHORE:** Tel 877-860-6787 or 912-882-4336; nps.gov/cuis. **GREYFIELD INN:** Tel 866-401-8581 or 904-261-6408; greyfieldinn.com. *Cost:* from $425 (off-peak), from $475 (peak), includes meals, round-trip ferry transportation, and activities. **SPENCER HOUSE INN:** St. Marys (mainland). Tel 888-840-1872 or 912-882-1872; spencerhouseinn.com. *Cost:* from $135. **OKEFENOKEE NATIONAL WILDLIFE REFUGE:** Tel 912-496-7836; fws.gov/okefenokee. **BEST TIMES:** spring and fall for balmy weather and fewer crowds.

Head of the Appalachian Trail in the Chattahoochee Forest

DAHLONEGA

Georgia

Here in the foothills of the Blue Ridge Mountains, once the home of the Cherokee Indians, Dahlonega was America's first gold-rush town. Miners and mountaineers flocked here in search of gold, discovered in 1828, and mined until as recently as the 1920s. Dahlonega (derived from the Cherokee word meaning "precious yellow") beat California's gold rush by 20 years and soon welcomed a branch of the U.S. mint, which stamped gold coins here from 1838 until the Civil War. The boom went bust and Dahlonega has gradually become known as the gateway to northern Georgia's majestic Chattahoochee National Forest—the town lies just a few miles east of the southern terminus of the 2,185-mile Georgia-to-Maine Appalachian Trail (see p. 332).

The town's handsome square has shops selling a mix of Appalachian crafts, distinctive art, and handcrafted gold jewelry (and other gold-related items—such as scales and pans—attesting to Dahlonega's past). The former Lumpkin County Courthouse dates to 1836, when the gold rush was in full swing, and now houses an intriguing Gold Museum.

The head of the Appalachian Trail may be the region's greatest outdoor claim to fame, but you can also drive to 729-foot-high Amicalola Falls, the highest cascade in the Southeast. Or

The Lumpkin County Courthouse, now the home of the Dahlonega Gold Museum, was built during the nascent days of the town's gold rush.

enjoy hiking trails, cool swimming holes, and roaring rivers ideal for rafting and kayaking in the 750,000-acre Chattahoochee National Forest.

Satisfy your mountain-man hunger by diving into a bountiful meal of delicious country food at the Smith House, in business since 1922 and using family recipes twice as old. Probably no dish earns more kudos than their crispy fried chicken, but this casual all-you-can-eat restaurant also serves family-style platters heaped with sweet baked country ham, collard greens, fresh corn muffins, and fried okra. There's never room for banana fritters and warm peach cobbler, but that doesn't stop anyone. For those who are too full to move, the Smith House puts up guests in their main house and a cozy carriage house.

The sustenance at Dahlonega Spa Resort is just as abundant, albeit of the spiritual kind. This intimate 22-room getaway, anchored by a farmhouse-style main building, offers unsurpassed views of the mountainous countryside beyond. The day revolves around yoga, hiking the 72-acre grounds, and appreciating that Dahlonega's wealth is no longer measured in gold.

WHERE: 65 miles northeast of Atlanta. *Visitor info:* Tel 800-231-5543 or 706-864-3711; dahlonega.org. **DAHLONEGA GOLD MUSEUM HISTORIC SITE:** Tel 706-864-2257; gastateparks.org/dahlonegagoldmuseum. **SMITH HOUSE:** Tel 800-852-9577 or 706-867-7000; smithhouse.com. *Cost:* from $99; lunch $15. **DAHLONEGA SPA RETREAT:** Tel 866-345-4900 or 706-865-7442; dahlonegasparesort.com. *Cost:* from $127 (off-peak), from $162 (peak). **BEST TIMES:** late Apr for Bear on the Square Festival with live bluegrass bands and Gold Panning Championships; mid-May for the Mountain Flower Art Festival; mid-Oct for Gold Rush Days.

A Civil War Memorial in the TAG Corner

CHICKAMAUGA AND CHATTANOOGA NATIONAL MILITARY PARK

Fort Oglethorpe, Georgia, and Chattanooga, Tennessee

The Battle of Chickamauga was the first major battle of the Civil War on Georgia soil and the only one that resulted in a Confederate victory; it also ranks among the bloodiest, with nearly 35,000 casualties. The battle commenced September 19, 1863, when 66,000 Confederates defeated 58,000 Union soldiers just south of Chattanooga, Tennessee, at Georgia's Chickamauga Creek. Union troops were forced back to Chattanooga, but they soon received reinforcements. Two months later, at the Battle of Chattanooga, Union forces soundly defeated the Confederates and advanced into Georgia and nearby Alabama. The following spring, General William T. Sherman launched his famous march from Chattanooga to Atlanta and on to the sea.

The park—consisting of two main battle sites, one in Georgia and one in Tennessee—covers more than 8,000 acres. Established relatively soon after the war, in 1890, as the nation's first military park, and today its largest, it is commonly ranked together with those in Gettysburg (see p. 209) and Vicksburg (see p. 445) as the nation's most important. After a visit to the Chickamauga Battlefield

The Florida Monument, on the Chickamauga Battlefield, commemorates the Confederate soldiers from the Sunshine State who perished here.

Visitor Center, follow a 7-mile self-guided automobile tour through the park, where you'll find monuments, tablets, original cannons mounted atop iron display carriages, artillery-shell pyramids, and other markers telling the story of these pivotal Civil War battles. With over 80 miles of trails, exploring the park's natural beauty is popular with bicyclists, hikers, and horseback riders.

On the Tennessee side, the Lookout Mountain Battlefield Visitor Center sits high above Chattanooga (see p. 462), affording magnificent vistas of the TAG corner, where Tennessee, Alabama, and Georgia meet.

WHERE: 115 miles northwest of Atlanta. Chickamauga Battlefield Visitor Center: Tel 706-866-9241; nps.gov/chch. Lookout Mountain Battlefield Visitor Center: Tel 423-821-7786. **BEST TIMES:** summer for interpretive programs; spring and fall for cool weather and fewer crowds.

History, Aristocrats, and Splendid Isolation

THE GOLDEN ISLES

Georgia

The rice and cotton plantations that made these four islands famous disappeared after the Civil War, and America's 19th-century aristocrats, fleeing snowy northern winters, started to vacation on Georgia's stunning

barrier islands. Floating off the state's 150-mile long coast, St. Simons Island, Little St. Simons Island (see next page), Jekyll Island, and Sea Island came to be known as the Golden Isles, as much for their special light as their privileged lifestyle. Astors, Rockefellers, Vanderbilts, Goodyears, and Pulitzers all had homes on these jewels in the Atlantic, separated from the mainland by rich marshes. These days, the Golden Isles are considerably more egalitarian, with careful planning and a strong conservation ethic contributing to the islands' unhurried pace and unspoiled appearance.

It was back in 1886, during America's Gilded Age, that 9-mile-long Jekyll Island first began earning a reputation as a ritzy wintertime version of Newport. Today, the state-owned island, two-thirds of which is protected from development, offers 20 miles of paved bike paths past 11 designated landmark homes (modestly called "cottages"), along the beach-hugging boardwalk, and through the cool maritime forests of live oak and pine. The turreted Queen Anne–style Jekyll Island Club Hotel, which served as the island's social hub until around WWII, is the rambling anchor of the 240-acre historic district and retains the aura of a Victorian millionaire's club.

On the 9-mile-long Sea Island, the quiet good taste of the legendary Cloister at Sea Island resort has hosted presidents, celebrities, and pedigreed families for generations. Some have come for the golf—the three challenging and scenic courses rank among the best in the Southeast—and some for romance: About 36,000 guests (and counting) have honeymooned here. Designed in classic Spanish-Mission style, the resort is surrounded by

Modern guests at the Jekyll Island Club Hotel enjoy the Gilded Age ambience that once drew some of America's wealthiest families.

palmetto palms and live oaks dripping with Spanish moss and boasts a lavish 65,000-square-foot spa where Victorian soaking tubs are the preferred form of hydrotherapy. Horseback riding, beachcombing, and sunning fill idyllic days on the resort's 5-mile swath of pinkish-white sandy beach.

More accessible and affordable than the other Golden Isles, St. Simons Island is no less beautiful, with reedy salt marshes and courtly live oak trees. Since 1872, the 104-foot-tall St. Simons Lighthouse has stood guard over the island, whose main village contains a clutch of specialty boutiques, antiques shops, and seafood restaurants.

WHERE: 80 miles south of Savannah. *Visitor info:* Tel 800-933-2627 or 912-265-0620; goldenisles.com. **JEKYLL ISLAND CLUB HOTEL:** Tel 855-787-3857 or 912-635-2600; jekyllclub.com. *Cost:* from $189. **THE CLOISTER:** Sea Island. Tel 800-SEA-ISLAND or 912-638-3611; seaisland.com. *Cost:* from $293 (off-peak), from $700 (peak); greens fees from $175 (off-peak), from $210 (peak). **BEST TIMES:** fall and spring for best weather; Aug for Jekyll Island's Beach Music Festival; Dec for Jekyll Island's Holiday Island festival.

Saintly Seclusion

LITTLE ST. SIMONS ISLAND

Georgia

It's the least-visited of the Golden Isles (see previous page), and for that very reason, Little St. Simons Island is perhaps the most special to visit. You'll need to take a ferry to reach this 10,000-acre oasis, which pencil magnate

Philip Berolzheimer purchased in 1908 with plans to harvest its cedar trees. He was so taken by the island, he reconsidered and preserved the beautiful woodlands, to create a family getaway. To this day, his descendants own the island and carry out his mission of conservation. There is just one public accommodation

here, the Lodge, opened in 1979. With a maximum of 33 guests at any given time, it's easy to imagine that you have the entire island all to yourself.

On this sandy, wooded sliver of paradise, you're left largely to your own devices. Wander all you want—by yourself or with the Lodge's naturalist—taking in the unspoiled beauty of the cool moss-draped forests, meandering waterways, 20 miles of winding trails, and 7 miles of shell-strewn beaches. Transportation options are many: walking, horseback riding, biking, canoeing, kayaking, motorboating. What you won't find, happily, are cars.

Little St. Simons is heaven for fly-fishing, surf-casting, and loggerhead-sea-turtle-tracking. Bird-watching is also a popular activity here; in fact, the island sits along the Atlantic Migratory Flyway and has been designated by the Audubon Society as an Important Bird Area, with more than 300 species in all, from orange-billed American oystercatchers to red-tailed hawks.

Accommodations at the Lodge are more rustic summer camp than posh summer resort. Among the handful of buildings are the 1917 Hunting Lodge, with a brick fireplace and antique pine bough and wicker furniture, and the dramatic Helen House, a 1928 structure built with oyster-shell masonry. The food is fresh, unfussy, delicious: think pecan-crusted pork loin with port wine and pear sauce served with Southern sweet potato soufflé.

A limited number of day-trippers can savor a glimpse of the Little St. Simons experience. Rates include ferry transportation from neighboring St. Simons Island (see p. 342), a guided nature tour, lunch at the lodge, and a full afternoon to laze on the beach where the only footprints other than your own may be those of an errant turtle.

Where: 90 miles south of Savannah. *Visitor info:* Tel 800-933-2627 or 912-265-0620; goldenisles.com. **The Lodge:** Tel 888-733-5774 or 912-638-7472; littlestsimonsisland .com. *Cost:* from $450 (off-peak), from $650 (peak), includes meals, transportation, and activities. Day visitors, from $75. **Best times:** spring and fall for weather.

A scenic kayak trip is one of the many ways to experience the beauty of Little St. Simons.

Bavarian Outpost on the Edge of the Chattahoochee

Helen

Georgia

On the edge of the pine-shaded, rugged Chattahoochee National Forest is a village right out of the Bavarian Alps, complete with dozens of gingerbread-style shops, beer gardens, and German restaurants. This region was once a thriving hub of Cherokee Indian life, then part of North Georgia's brief gold-mining boom of the 1820s and '30s, and finally a lumber stronghold in the early 20th century in its days as a major sawmill operation. Once the area's timber supply was exhausted, Helen devolved into a virtual ghost town—until local business owners hatched a plan to reinvent the community in the image of a Bavarian village. Cobblestone lanes were installed, and buildings were decked with gingerbread trim and painted with murals depicting German scenes. And so Alpine Helen, named long ago after the daughter of a lumber company manager, was reborn in 1969.

Not surprisingly, the apex of Helen's year is the hugely popular six-week Oktoberfest from late September into early November. More than 100,000 German-for-the-day visitors—some dressed up in authentic lederhosen and Bavarian costumes to attend this festival—enjoy a jam-packed schedule of nonstop German oompah bands, polkas, waltzes, beer tents, and the smell of grilling bratwurst.

Helen is one of the leading gateways to 750,000-acre Chattahoochee National Forest, filled with parks and hiking trails beneath a canopy of hardwoods and evergreens. It's also the start of the 41-mile Russell-Brasstown Scenic Byway, which loops through the forest passes near the summit of Brasstown Bald, at 4,783 feet the highest point in Georgia (and worth the steep trek for sweeping views of South Carolina, North Carolina, Tennessee, and Georgia). The Wild and Scenic Chattooga River cuts through the forest, offering some of the best white-water rafting in the country, while the far gentler Chattahoochee River is ideal for tubing.

The upscale-rustic Lodge at Smithgall Woods, an idyllic mountain retreat operated by the Georgia State Parks department in a 5,600-acre conservation area, is best known for its serene environs and premier trout fishing.

Further out, the circa 1870s Glen-Ella Springs Inn is a rare and fully restored example of one of the traditional inns that once dotted the mountains of northern Georgia. The 16 rooms, filled with handsome antiques and locally handcrafted furnishings, range from relatively simple units to spacious suites. Glen-Ella's restaurant has long earned kudos for its creative regional American cuisine, such as just-caught rainbow trout topped with pecans and a lemon caper sauce, followed by rich, house-made apple bread pudding with cinnamon ice cream.

WHERE: 90 miles northeast of Atlanta. *Visitor info:* Tel 800-858-8027 or 706-878-2181; helenga.org. **RUSSELL-BRASSTOWN BYWAY:** byways.org. **HOW:** Cool River Tubing, tel 800-896-4595 or 706-878-2665; coolriver tubing.com. *Cost:* from $5 per person. *When:* late May–early Sept. **LODGE AT SMITHGALL WOODS:** Tel 800-864-7275 or 706-878-3087; gastateparks.org. *Cost:* from $165, includes meals. **GLEN-ELLA SPRINGS INN:** Clarksville. Tel 888-455-8786 or 706-754-7295; glenella. com. *Cost:* rooms from $160; dinner $45. **BEST TIMES:** 3rd week in Apr for Spring Volksmarch, a series of hikes through the surrounding countryside; early June for the Helen to the Atlantic Hot Air Balloon Race and Festival; 6 weeks from mid-Sept–early Nov for Oktoberfest.

Tutti-Frutti and Pink Everything

MACON AND THE CHERRY BLOSSOM FESTIVAL

Georgia

Every spring America's attention turns to the 3,000 trees that ring Washington, D.C.'s Tidal Basin for its much-awaited Cherry Blossom Festival (see p. 265). But consider this: Macon has more than three

Yoshino cherry trees for every resident—that's more than 300,000 trees—which makes our nation's capital pale in comparison. Georgia may be the "Peachtree State," but Macon is the "Cherry Blossom Capital of the World." And each March, when the trees bloom with cotton-candy-colored flowers, Macon puts on the refined—and wacky—International Cherry Blossom Festival, the biggest party in the South. Thousands of enthusiasts head to town for this ten-day celebration that includes concerts, a parade, a hot-air balloon festival, historic-house tours, a soap box derby, fireworks, lots of food trucks, and much more. The moment for all things pink crescendos at Pink in the Park, when the city's Central City Park is decked in pink decorations, and hosts the Pink Pancake Breakfast.

More distinctly Southern in a way that Atlanta—where everybody seems to hail from somewhere else—is not, Macon is worth visiting year-round. A city full of grand white-pillared antebellum homes (only Savannah's architecture is as striking) built during the cotton boom, Macon is also a good place to learn a great deal about Georgia history, from its role in the Civil War to its deep-rooted music heritage.

The cherry blossoms transform one of the many verdant squares for which the city is known.

Macon has a long history of musical talent, from Otis Redding to Little Richard. The iconic Allman Brothers Band has long been associated with Macon, and The Big House is a surprisingly interesting museum housed in a three-story home where members of The Allman Brothers—along with their families, friends, and roadies—lived, worked, and played from 1970–1973.

Members of the Allman Brothers Band are among the legions of fans of the soulful home cookin' of one Mama Louise, proprietress of Macon's H&H Restaurant. She's been serving up big portions of straightforward Southern fare since 1959, making bacon, eggs, and grits for breakfast like no one else can. The "dinner" menu, which is actually served from lunchtime typically features super-crispy fried chicken, juicy barbecue ribs, macaroni and cheese, and warm peach cobbler for dessert. New owners took over in 2014, but Mama Louise still spends a lot of time here.

Macon's most distinctive accommodation is the regal 1842 Inn, an antebellum Greek Revival mansion with ten welcoming rooms in the main house and another nine across the garden courtyard in the 1900 Victorian Cottage. It is just a block away from the city's premier museum, the Hay House, a beautiful 24-room mansion and fascinating showcase of life in the years leading up to the Civil War.

Where: 80 miles southeast of Atlanta. *Visitor info:* Tel 800-768-3401 or 478-743-3401; maconga.org. **Cherry Blossom Festival:** Tel 478-330-7050; cherryblossom.com. *Cost:* $12 for the Street Festival Party. *When:* 10 days in Mar. **The Big House:** Tel 478-741-5551; thebighousemuseum.com. **H&H Restaurant:** Tel 478-742-9810; mamalouise.com. *Cost:* lunch $20. **1842 Inn:** Tel 877-452-6599 or 478-741-1842; 1842inn.com. *Cost:* from $189. **Hay House:** Tel 478-742-8155; hayhouse macon.org. **Best times:** early May for Macon's Gardens, Mansions, & Moonlight home tours (georgiatrust.org) and the Georgia State Fair (georgiastatefair.org).

A *Personal Wonderland of Vision and Whimsy*

HOWARD FINSTER'S PARADISE GARDENS

Summerville, Georgia

F ew self-taught artists have so captured the fancy of both critics and everyday fans as Howard Finster, the visionary folk painter who lived in a small town in Georgia's Appalachian foothills (one collector called him the Andy Warhol of the South). Born in Alabama in 1916, Finster followed his spiritual calling as a preacher for the better part of three decades before deciding he could better spread the word of the Lord by using his unique artistic talents.

In 1961, Finster began to develop Paradise Gardens, an elaborate landscape of fanciful turreted structures threaded by concrete paths embedded with colorful bits of tile and glass, the perfect setting to post quotes from the Bible and folksy philosophies. A few years after starting the gardens, Finster began creating his now-famous folk drawings, paintings, and sculptures—and began to attract worldwide acclaim. His inimitable folk works hang in such lauded museums as the Smithsonian Institution and Atlanta's High Museum (see p. 336). All told, he completed nearly 47,000 works of art, plus handmade wooden clocks, doll furniture, and picture frames.

Two themes emerge during a stroll through the gardens, which were restored in the early 2000s: Finster's deep devotion to the Lord, and an uncanny ability to transform junk and abandoned objects into works of beauty. Both of these themes are embodied in the centerpiece of the gardens, the stunning five-story Folk Art Church. Howard Finster, who passed away in 2001 at age 84, took everyday "garbage" throwaways and transformed them into creations of beauty and inspiration, answering an inner voice.

WHERE: 50 miles south of Chattanooga, TN; 200 North Lewis St. Tel 706-808-0800; paradisegardenfoundation.org. *When:* open Thurs–Sun. **BEST TIME:** Mar–Oct when the gardens are in full bloom.

An *Eden of Birds and Butterflies*

CALLAWAY GARDENS

Pine Mountain, Georgia

I n 1952 Cason J. Callaway developed an idyllic resort amid the cotton country of western Georgia, aiming to create a preserve where humans could connect with nature. And so was born Callaway Gardens at Pine Mountain, today Georgia's own botanical paradise, a full-scale, nature preserve and blooming garden landscape comprising some 6,000 acres of flower beds, azaleas, rhododendrons, and a panoply of trees.

Callaway has the added draw of two highly respected golf courses, ten lighted tennis courts, a 10-mile paved trail for biking, and six hiking trails through cool woodlands. A mile-long sandy beach encircles 65-acre Robin Lake, and you can also fish for large-mouth bass, bluegills, and bream in Creek Lake. Or lose yourself inside the Cecil B. Day Butterfly Center, a glass conservatory filled with lush tropical plants and more than 1,000 freely fluttering butterflies, from swallowtails to paper kites—some as large as small birds.

The Lodge and Spa, owned by Marriott, promises the nicest Callaway Gardens experience, with a friendly, unfussy air, and everything from classic, affordable rooms to cushy suites. For Southern-style breakfast of fluffy biscuits and gravy served all day long, head to the resort's Country Kitchen, a mile away at the top of Pine Mountain. Keep driving to Warm Springs, the curative corner of Georgia that Franklin Delano Roosevelt put on the map during his frequent visits.

More gardens await 140 miles north in Adairsville, in the lush foothills of the Blue Ridge Mountains. Barnsley Gardens Resort is an intimate, upscale retreat with the air of a 19th-century English village. The resort, which opened in 1991, was the brainchild of German Prince Hubertus Fugger, who developed it around a restored 1842 estate (the original English owner's daughter was said to be the inspiration for Scarlett in *Gone With the Wind*) that had sat dormant since 1942. The ruins of the original manor house overlook 3,300 acres, including spectacular 19th-century gardens brimming with 200 varieties of roses. Golf widows can opt for pampering in the spa, while spouses test the par-72, rolling 7,350-yard golf course by Jim Fazio. Everything about Barnsley has garnered top-drawer accolades, including the Woodlands Grill, ranked among the state's best steak houses.

WHERE: 70 miles southwest of Atlanta. Tel 800-892-2793 or 706-663-2281; callaway gardens.com. *Cost:* from $99. **LODGE AND SPA:** Tel 888-236-2427 or 706-489-3300; callawaylodgeandspa.com. *Cost:* from $149 (off-peak), from $269 (peak); breakfast at Country Kitchen $15. **BARNSLEY GARDENS:** Adairsville. Tel 877-773-2447 or 770-773-7480; barnsleyresort.com. *Cost:* from $259; dinner at Woodlands Grill $50. **BEST TIMES:** spring and fall for gardens and golf. At Callaway, Jan for the Southern Gardening Symposium, early Sept for the Sky High Hot Air Balloon Festival, and mid-Nov–Dec for the Fantasy in Lights holiday festival.

Dining Highs in Georgia's Lowcountry

SAVANNAH'S BEST EATERIES

Savannah, Georgia

From temples of haute cuisine to down-home country restaurants, this hub of Georgia's lowcountry celebrates its food with inimitable gusto and panache. Housed in an elegant turn-of-the-century beaux arts mansion on the periphery of the Historic District, Elizabeth's on 37th (aka "Miz Terry's place") has been Savannah's most famous restaurant since Michael and Elizabeth Terry opened it in 1981. Executive chef Kelly Yambor thrills loyalists with classic lowcountry recipes and local ingredients interpreted by a young and affable staff led by co-owners, brothers Greg and Gary Butch. For dessert don't miss the Savannah cream cake.

There's no sign outside Mrs. Wilkes Dining Room, but that doesn't stop the lines forming every morning at 10:30. When the lunch bell rings at 11:00, the hungry crowd shuffles inside to fill large communal tables-for-ten, which soon disappear under the brimming family-style platters and bowls of fried chicken and corn bread dressing, okra gumbo, sweet potato soufflé, and the lowcountry specialty, Savannah red rice. Mrs. Wilkes opened the place in 1943 and died in 2002. Today it's run by two generations of her comfort-food-savvy family, serving old-time traditional favorites that are as unpretentious as the restaurant's homey setting.

Not all Savannah's most treasured food finds have been around for generations, nor are they all helmed by Southerners. A Yank from outside Philadelphia, Chris Nason is the chef-owner of Sapphire Grill, a city mainstay that continues to dazzle the palates of Savannahans with dishes like garlic-seared magret duck breast and sweet potato hash. Exposed brick walls and polished wood floors lend warmth to the sleek, softly lit dining room.

Finally, for some quality Southern comfort food, try The Lady & Sons restaurant from the Food Network's show, *Paula's Home Cooking.* Chef Paula Deen began her career modestly, with a bag-lunch delivery service in 1989. Today this icon of honest good Southern cookin' draws loyal fans to her enormous restaurant (which she operates with her sons Jamie and Bobby) in a former hardware store. What's all the fuss about? Some of the best crab cakes in town (no reason Maryland should get all the attention), plus heavenly chicken potpie, crab stew, shrimp-and-grits, and old-fashioned pecan pie with lots of whipped cream. You can eat at the buffet or order à la carte.

ELIZABETH'S ON 37TH: Tel 912-236-5547; elizabethon37th.net. *Cost:* dinner $60. **MRS. WILKES DINING ROOM:** Tel 912-232-5997; mrswilkes.com. *Cost:* lunch $20. **SAPPHIRE GRILL:** Tel 912-443-9962; sapphiregrill.com. *Cost:* dinner $55. **THE LADY & SONS:** Tel 912-233-2600; ladyandsons.com. *Cost:* dinner $35.

Georgia's Jewel

SAVANNAH'S HISTORIC DISTRICT

Savannah, Georgia

An urban masterpiece, Savannah is America's best walking city, a living museum that is the largest National Historical Landmark District: 2.5 square miles hold more than 2,300 significant Colonial and Victorian homes and buildings, most of them lovingly restored. Savannah stands out for its leafy 1-acre squares that punctuate the district—21 (out of an original 24) of them remain. America's first planned city, Savannah was laid out in 1733 on a perfect grid by its founder, British General James Oglethorpe.

"White gold" (King Cotton) subsequently filled the port city's coffers with real gold, and handsome mansions prospered, those that survived the centuries eventually coming under the protection of the Historic Savannah Foundation, born in 1955. Some historians believe it was at President Lincoln's request that Savannah's fabled architecture was spared burning during General William Tecumseh Sherman's scorched-earth military campaign in 1864.

There are various ways to take in the district—horse-drawn carriage, trolley, bus, or bicycle—and many companies offer tours of the area. Some focus on sites mentioned in John Berendt's 1994 best-selling book (and the film that followed), *Midnight in the Garden of Good and Evil,* which chronicled the eccentric lives of some of the city's most colorful residents a decade earlier. "The Book," as locals still call it, brought a certain scandalous but good-natured notoriety to Savannah and continues to play a big part in boosting tourism.

Many of Savannah's historic homes have been meticulously renovated and restored.

Many of the city's most prominent historic buildings now house inns and B&Bs (see below), fine restaurants, and shops that may allow you a glimpse inside. Still others offer even greater access as museums. The lordly Davenport House Museum, headquarters of the Historic Savannah Foundation, dates to 1820 and is one of the finest Federal-style city homes in the nation, filled with fine furnishings from the period.

British architect William Jay, who introduced the Regency style to America, designed many of the city's most notable buildings. Among his best is the Owens-Thomas House and Museum, which deservedly earns more oohs and aahs than any other structure in the district. Overlooking stunning Oglethorpe Square, the 1819 mansion is most famed as the place that hosted Revolutionary War hero the Marquis de Lafayette in 1825, and today it contains a magnificent exhibit of decorative arts, many collected by the Owens family, who lived in the house from 1830 to 1951.

The nearby Telfair Mansion and Art Museum is another of William Jay's finest works and the South's oldest public art museum, containing 4,500 works from the U.S., Europe, and Asia, most dating from the 18th century to the present. The sculpture collection contains a work that will be familiar to those who own a copy of "The Book": Sylvia Shaw Judson's 1936 sculpture *Bird Girl* appears on its cover.

WHERE: 250 miles southeast of Atlanta. *Visitor info:* Tel 877-SAVANNAH or 912-944-0455; savannahvisit.com. **DAVENPORT HOUSE:** Tel 912-236-8097; davenporthouse museum.org. **OWENS-THOMAS HOUSE:** Tel 912-790-8800; telfair.org. **TELFAIR MUSEUM:** Tel 912-790-8800; telfair.org. **BEST TIMES:** 4 days in late Mar for Savannah Tour of Homes and Gardens (savannahtourofhomes.org); late Apr for spring tour of historic gardens.

The Essence of Southern Gentility

SAVANNAH'S ROMANTIC INNS

Savannah, Georgia

To fully appreciate Savannah's seductive charms, stay in one of the dozens of inns or B&Bs that have opened in some of the city's most impressive historic homes. Competition is stiff, but most agree that the genteel

Gastonian is a front-runner. Encompassing two Italianate town houses and a carriage house dating from 1868, it has been magnificently restored using authentic Savannah colors and Scalamandré wallpaper of original patterns. Nearly all of the 17 guest rooms have working fireplaces, and most have chandeliers and lavish baths. It's a challenge to walk off the Gastonian's legendary Southern breakfast, which might include melon soup and lemon cheese pancakes with strawberry glaze.

The Ballastone Inn has come a long way since its days as a boardinghouse and brothel. Built in 1838, this mansion in the heart of the Historic District is now considered one of the South's most distinguished small hotels, its 16 rooms decked with fine antiques and period reproductions. Guests arrive to rooms made up with high-count cotton sheets subtly scented with lavender, and there's a house-proud staff on hand round the clock.

The 1892 Kehoe House, a handsome red-brick Renaissance Revival mansion overlooking Columbia Square, one of the city's most picturesque, has also earned a spot as one of the city's top hostelries. The 13 guest rooms are named after noted past Savannahans, such as John Wesley, Johnny Mercer, and Juliette Gordon Low (who founded the Girl Scouts), and have original gleaming hardwood floors, plush linens, and understatedly luxurious furnishings.

One of Savannah's newer arrivals is the Mansion on Forsyth Park, which was renovated and reopened in 2005. Partially fashioned out of a regal mansion built in 1888 in the Victorian Romanesque style, this full-service hotel contains 125 spacious rooms, a spa, and a fine restaurant, 700 Drayton, where you might dine on such inventive American fare as braised pork shank with cheddar grits. Score a room overlooking leafy Forsyth Park, where you'll want to join the locals for a morning constitutional.

THE GASTONIAN: Tel 800-322-6603 or 912-232-2869; gastonian.com. *Cost:* from $171. BALLASTONE INN: Tel 800-822-4553 or 912-236-1484; ballastone.com. *Cost:* from $249. KEHOE HOUSE: Tel 800-820-1020 or 912-232-1020, kehoehouse.com. *Cost:* from $174. MANSION ON FORSYTH PARK: Tel 888-213-3671 or 912-238-5158; mansionon forsythpark.com. *Cost:* from $199. BEST TIME: late Mar for the Savannah Music Festival (savannahmusicfestival.org).

Sky-High Family Fun

STONE MOUNTAIN

Georgia

If you fly into Atlanta from the north, you can't miss the bare, lichen- and moss-draped face of elliptical Stone Mountain, rising some 825 feet above the Piedmont Plateau, with a base circumference of about 5 miles. In 1825,

settlers built a stagecoach terminus at its western base, kicking off its enduring run as a popular resort. These days it's one of the South's premier family destinations, with attractions like the Summit Skyride, a Swiss cable car that whisks visitors to the mountain's peak for a view of Atlanta's skyline. It passes right by the Confederate Memorial Carving, the world's largest bas-relief sculpture, depicting Jefferson Davis, Robert E. Lee, and Stonewall Jackson riding their horses over some 3 acres of mountain. The Stone Mountain

Scenic Railroad, a vintage 1940s locomotive, offers narrated excursions.

And that's just the tip of the iceberg at this 3,200-acre park, which also features an antebellum plantation and farmyard; a re-created 1870s town; a 4-D theatre; a barn packed with kids' activities; hiking trails; fishing; two hotels; two golf courses; and the world's largest laser light show, a 45-minute extravaganza culminating with a fireworks finale (mid-April to October).

Homemade sustenance can be found in the unassuming but fun and welcoming Sweet Potato Café. All the Southern standbys are offered, along with a few surprises like grilled salmon and meatloaf. If you've spent the day hiking, you'll be very happy here.

WHERE: 16 miles east of Atlanta. Tel 800-401-2407; stone mountainpark.com. *Cost:* 1-day all-attractions pass $28. **SWEET POTATO CAFÉ:** Tel 770-559-9030; thesweetpotatocafe.net. *Cost:* $20. **BEST TIMES:** early Sept for Yellow Daisy Festival; mid-Oct for the Stone Mountain Highland Games & Scottish Festival; Oct for the Pumpkin Festivals.

The Scarlett O'Hara Riverboat was built at the Stone Mountain Park in 1976.

Antebellum Grandeur in Magnolia Country

PLANTATION COUNTRY

Thomasville, Georgia

For a true taste of Georgia's rich plantation heritage, head for Thomas County, in the scenic southern region of the state. The heart of the area is the gracious town of Thomasville, a city of 18,000 that flourished during the Civil War as a railroad hub for moving troops and supplies. Following the war, more than a few industrialists from Chicago, New York, and Philadelphia began to spend winters here and built lavish estates, many of which still stand today. Glimpse some of the 70 Greek Revival, neoclassical, Georgian Revival, and classic plantation-style homes simply by driving along Thomasville's main roads.

One of Thomasville's most spectacular grande dames, Pebble Hill Plantation, established in the 1820s, is also the only one open to the public as a museum. The Hanna family from Ohio purchased the plantation following the Civil War, and the last occupant, Elisabeth "Pansy" Ireland Poe, stipulated that this Tara-style 3,000-acre plantation be opened to the public upon her death (she passed away in 1978). A tour of the magnificent 40-room main house, designed in 1850 and largely rebuilt following a fire in 1934, reveals the many collections of 19th-century furniture, porcelain, glasswork, silver, and art amassed by Miss Pansy during her extraordinary life. Overnight guests can now stay in two of the many restored small buildings on the grounds.

The area's lodging of choice is the 1884 Paxton House, an ornate Victorian Gothic home known for its priceless collection of porcelain and china. It's just blocks from the tree-lined streets of the town center, which offer antiques shops, quaint stores, and down-home cafés.

WHERE: 40 miles northeast of Tallahassee, FL. *Visitor info:* Tel 866-577-3600 or 229-228-7977; thomasvillega.com. **PEBBLE HILL:** Tel 229-226-2344; pebblehill.com. *When:* closed Mon. *Cost:* rooms from $250. **1884 PAXTON HOUSE INN:** Tel 229-226-5197; thepaxton1884.com. *Cost:*

The original house at Pebble Hill, built by Thomas Jefferson Johnson, was replaced in 1850 and anchored the family's 3,000-acre plantation.

from $245. **BEST TIMES:** late Feb for the Thomasville Antiques Show & Sale; Apr for the Annual Pinewoods Bird Festival at Pebble Hill Plantation and the Annual Rose Show downtown; Dec for Victorian Christmas.

Sun, Sand, and Seafood

TYBEE ISLAND

Georgia

A popular seaside resort since the late 1800s, easygoing Tybee Island has all of nearby Savannah's quirky joie de vivre without any of the formality. It's a low-key, slightly honky-tonk antidote to more elegant (and developed)

coastal destinations up and down the shoreline, such as Hilton Head (see p. 377) and the Golden Isles (see p. 342). The 2.5-mile-long, mile-wide barrier island takes its name from the Euchee Indian word for "salt," though you'll be more inclined to think "sand" these days. The beaches here are a huge draw, great for catching rays, watching migrating birds, or sighting an occasional bottlenose dolphin. Take in the pleasant local scene by strolling out on the island's long wooden pier, or for the most dramatic views, head to Tybee Island Light Station and Tybee Museum, site of the

state's oldest and tallest lighthouse.

The island has a slew of laid-back, funky eateries, including The Crab Shack on the waterfront, an unabashedly quirky restaurant with a slogan that boasts: "Where the elite eat in their bare feet!" Indeed, you'll see plenty of fancy wheels pulled up in front of this kitschy former fish camp with a tin roof, a habitat of about 80 live alligators, and loads of personality. The menu's pretty simple: crabs are the draw. We're talking not only local blue crabs but also Dungeness, stone, snow, and Jonah crabs. But you can also order shrimp, oysters,

The Tybee Island Light Station

clams, mussels, and a few non-seafood dishes like barbecued ribs.

The Breakfast Club earned national acclaim when John F. Kennedy Jr. hired chef Jodee Sadowsky to cater his wedding down the coast on Cumberland Island (see p. 339). This happy little place decked with Chicago Cubs memorabilia (from the chef's hometown) serves up splendid morning fare, including homemade breakfast sausage, custom omelettes, cinnamon raisin French toast, shrimp and grits, and pecan waffles. No wonder Savannahans think nothing of driving in just for breakfast.

WHERE: 17 miles east of Savannah. *Visitor info:* Tel 800-868-2322 or 912-786-5444; tybeeisland.com. **TYBEE ISLAND LIGHT STATION & TYBEE MUSEUM:** Tel 912-786-5801; tybeelighthouse.org. *When:* closed Tues. **THE CRAB SHACK:** Tel 912-786-9857; thecrabshack.com. *Cost:* dinner $25. **THE BREAKFAST CLUB:** Tel 912-786-5984, the breakfastclubtybee.com. *Cost:* breakfast $10. **BEST TIMES:** spring and fall.

Hog Wild

BIG PIG JIG & GEORGIA BARBECUE

Vienna, Georgia

The first weekend in October is *not* a good time to be a hog in the southern Georgia town of Vienna (vie-ANN-uh, unless you're an outsider). That's when some 25,000 barbecue fanciers descend upon the Dooly County seat for the Big Pig Jig, aka the Georgia Barbecue Cooking Championship, which draws more than 120 teams of grillin' experts from all throughout the Southeast to compete for the pig-stigious title of Georgia Grand Champion. Concerts, a parade, and even a Miss Jiggy Piggy Pageant fill out the weekend.

Just about every state in the South has its own style of barbecue, and Georgia is no exception, although the recipes here can vary greatly according to region. In the north, you'll find North Carolina–style vinegar sauces; to the south and east, you'll taste the mustard-sauce influences of South Carolina; and to the west, you'll typically encounter the thick and spicy tomato-based sauces popular in nearby Alabama. But wherever you eat barbecue in Georgia, you're gonna find pork, slow-cooked in a pit (never on a grill or in a smoker) fired up with oak and hickory (and sometimes apple and pecan wood).

Georgia barbecue meat usually comes with baked beans and coleslaw, but the side dish that's most loved is Brunswick stew, invented in the coastal town of the same name, the jumping-off point for the Golden Isles. The tomato- and corn-based stew contains a whole slew of vegetables along with some combination of chicken, pork, and beef—these days anyway. If you want to go old-school and eat Brunswick stew the way it was originally intended, make sure its ingredients count squirrel or rabbit.

Appropriately, one of the state's best

purveyors of barbecue and Brunswick stew can be found in Brunswick at the endearingly shabby Gary Lee's Market, a roadside family-run market and eatery since 1968. The crowd by the front door gathers for the chunky Brunswick stew, tender brisket, and meaty and juicy ribs that are smoked over pecan and oak.

WHERE: 55 miles south of Macon. **BIG PIG JIG:** Tel 229-268-8275; bigpigjig.com. *Cost:* $8. *When:* 1st weekend in Nov. **GARY LEE'S MARKET:** Brunswick. Tel 912-265-1925. *Cost:* $12.

Green Without Envy

ASHEVILLE

North Carolina

A s soon as roads could bring them, health-conscious travelers began flocking to this mountain retreat for its curative sulphur springs and crisp mountain air. These days Asheville stands out as a haven for progressive

and creative spirits: artists and craftsmen, New Agers, musicians, innovative chefs, retirees, environmentalists. It's also a terrific base for outdoors enthusiasts, with outstanding hiking, white-water rafting, and golfing.

This sophisticated city of 83,000 blends a laid-back country vibe with urbane cultural attractions and striking architecture. In addition to the hallowed Biltmore Estate (see next page) and the Arts and Crafts–inspired Grove Park Inn (see p. 357), downtown boasts one of the greatest concentrations of art deco architecture in the Southeast, approximately some 170 buildings.

Following on the heels of George Washington Vanderbilt II (who completed the Biltmore in 1895) came such Roaring '20s movers and shakers as Henry Ford, Thomas Edison, F. Scott Fitzgerald and his wife, Zelda. Native son Thomas Wolfe's semiautobiographical novel *Look Homeward, Angel* was set in his mother's boardinghouse and offered a thinly veiled glimpse into the somewhat scandalous lives of Ashevillians. The book was banned from the local library and Wolfe was persona non grata for years. Learn about the author at his boyhood home, the Thomas Wolfe Memorial, where a visitors center displays many of his personal belongings.

Downtown Asheville's key cultural draw, Pack Place, contains the Asheville Art Museum, the YMI Cultural Center (which celebrates the city's African American

Asheville is ideally situated in the Blue Ridge Mountains; hiking and scenic driving opportunities abound just outside the city.

community), and the much-acclaimed Diana Wortham Theatre. Follow the 1.7-mile self-guided Urban Trail to see over 30 sculptures that tell the story of Asheville's history, and browse art galleries, shops, and offbeat coffeehouses, including the one at Malaprops, a beloved and free-spirited independent bookshop. And don't miss the Grove Arcade; one of the country's first indoor marketplaces, it contains dozens of specialty food shops, eclectic restaurants, and fine crafts galleries.

An elegant three-course breakfast begins your day at the 1889 White Gate Inn & Cottage, a romantic B&B named for the year it was built. Meticulous attention to detail is evident in the award-winning gardens and every one of the 11 guest rooms and suites spread out across the main house, bungalow, and cottage. The accommodations, all named after poets and authors, are a perfect blend of craftsmanship and sumptuous style.

WHERE: 130 miles northwest of Charlotte. **WOLFE MEMORIAL:** Tel 828-253-8304; wolfe memorial.com. *When:* closed Sun–Mon. **MALAPROPS:** Tel 828-254-6734; malaprops .com. **GROVE ARCADE:** Tel 828-252-7799; grovearcade.com. **1889 WHITE GATE INN & COTTAGE:** Tel 800-485-3045 or 828-253-2553; whitegate.net. *Cost:* from $200 (off-peak), from $275 (peak). **BEST TIMES:** spring for weather, rafting, and golfing; late July for Bele Chere festival (belecherefestival.com); early Aug for Mountain Dance & Folk Festival (folkheritage.org); last week of Oct for foliage.

America's Grandest Estate

THE BILTMORE

Asheville, North Carolina

"Strange, colossal, heartbreaking . . . in effect, like a gorgeous practical joke," said Henry James upon visiting George Vanderbilt II's new palace in the Blue Ridge Mountains. Designed by Richard Morris Hunt, who also conceived the family's similarly grandiose Breakers mansion (see p. 83) in Newport, Rhode Island, the Biltmore was completed in 1895 after a five-year construction. It took 1,000 laborers to lay the 11 million bricks for this "weekend getaway," which has hosted Edith Wharton, Henry Ford, and Woodrow Wilson. Believed to be the largest private home ever built in America, the Biltmore contains 35 bedrooms, 43 bathrooms, and 65 fireplaces. The Vanderbilts' vast shipping and railroad empire financed the home's extravagances, many of them—telephones, hot and cold running water, elevators, and refrigeration—unheard of at the turn of the century.

You can see the estate—still owned by the Vanderbilts and decorated as it was when George II lived in it—on a variety of tours, including a memorable behind-the-scenes look that ventures into the Biltmore's sub-basement. All told, the public can explore about 60 rooms, including a bowling alley and an 11,000-volume library. On view are over 1,700 works of art, including masterpieces by Renoir, Whistler, and Sargent. You can also tour the Biltmore Estate Winery. Once the grazing land for family cattle, the vineyards now produce over a dozen well-respected wines.

Arguably as breathtaking as the house are the Biltmore's 8,000 acres of gardens, meadows, and woodland, designed by Frederick Law Olmsted, of Central Park fame. Each spring, the Festival of Flowers showcases the magnificent daffodils, azaleas, roses, dogwoods, and more than 75,000 tulips. Christmastime features evening candlelight tours with songs by local choirs, the aroma of crackling fires, dozens of glimmering candlelit trees, and 10,000 feet of evergreen swags.

Pretend you're a Vanderbilt by spending the night at the Inn on Biltmore Estate, where many of the rooms have balconies overlooking the surrounding wilderness. You can take in the estate's lush panorama while sipping sparkling wine on the inn's veranda, or savor a full meal of regional food served on Vanderbilt china in the Dining Room.

The 175,000-square-foot, French Renaissance–inspired Biltmore House is a magnificent portrait of America's Gilded Age.

Four miles north in Asheville's Montford Historic District, a more intimate experience can be had at the Black Walnut Bed and Breakfast Inn, designed in 1899 by the Biltmore's supervising architect, Richard Sharp-Smith. Many of the eight graciously appointed guest rooms feature sleigh beds and keep wood-burning fireplaces. A delightful high tea is served each afternoon before the parlor's pine-mantel fireplace.

WHERE: 1 Approach Rd. Tel 800-411-3812 or 828-225-1333; biltmore.com. *Cost:* guided tours from $17. **INN ON BILTMORE ESTATE:** Tel 800-441-3812 or 828-225-1600. *Cost:* from $160 (off-peak), from $417 (peak). **BLACK WALNUT INN:** Tel 800-381-3878; blackwalnut.com. *Cost:* from $225 (off-peak), from $260 (peak). **BEST TIMES:** Apr for Spring Festival of Flowers; May–Sept for winery weekends; some weekends in July for Summer Evening Concerts. Nov–Dec for Christmas celebrations.

A Showcase of Arts and Crafts

THE GROVE PARK INN

Asheville, North Carolina

E. W. Grove envisioned "a big home . . . with all the old-fashioned qualities of genuineness with no Sham." A search for a chronic bronchitis cure brought Grove, a pharmaceuticals magnate, to Asheville in 1897, and in

1912 work began on his shrine to the Arts and Crafts movement. A year later the Omni Grove Park Inn—inspired by the rough-hewn lodges of the country's national parks and built of

massive granite boulders with a red-clay-tile roof—stood on the side of Sunset Mountain. Politicians and celebrities arrived in droves, from Franklin D. Roosevelt to F. Scott Fitzgerald.

At an elevation over 3,000 feet, the Grove Park affords spectacular views of Asheville and the Blue Ridge Mountains. The 510-room inn completed a massive renovation in 2004, which saw the restoration of the short but tight Donald Ross–designed golf course, the expansion of its top-ranked tennis facilities, and the addition of a magnificent spa. It offers such treatments as the Mountain Honey Wrap and the Blue Ridge Symphony Massage. Vue 1913 is a hotel restaurant you shouldn't miss—order the grilled lamb loin with mint pistou and roasted shallot-garlic croquettes.

Despite its proportions (the lobby is 120 feet long), a sense of stylish coziness prevails. The Grove Park contains the world's largest collection of Arts and Crafts furniture, with names like Stickley and Morris adorning virtually every chair and lighting fixture. Each of the 124 original guest rooms contains solid oak pieces with hand-hammered copper

Garden views abound at the Grove Park Inn.

drawer pulls designed by Roycroft, while newer wings are furnished with a seamless mix of originals and reproductions.

Appropriately, the resort hosts the highly respected Arts & Crafts Conference, a three-day affair that draws hundreds of collectors, dealers, teachers, and craftspersons each year. The Grove Park has helped transform Asheville into a leading crafts and design hub. Each fall, you can further explore this legacy at the Craft Fair of the Southern Highlands, a juried festival held at the U.S. Cellular Center, featuring dozens of potters, blacksmiths, furniture makers, glassblowers, jewelers, and basket makers. Fifty miles up the picturesque Blue Ridge Parkway is the Penland School of Crafts, which was established in 1929 to revive traditional craftsmanship in the wake of increased industrialization and mass production. Although the teaching studios aren't open to the public, you can tour the campus.

WHERE: 290 Macon Ave. Tel 828-252-2711; omnihotels.com. *Cost:* from $159 (off-peak), from $199 (peak); dinner at Vue 1913 $50. **CRAFT FAIR OF THE SOUTHERN HIGHLANDS:** Tel 828-298-7928; southernhighlandguild.org. *When:* 4 days in July and Oct. **PENLAND SCHOOL OF CRAFTS:** Tel 828-765-2359; penland.org. *When:* tours Tues and Thurs, early Mar–mid-Dec. **BEST TIMES:** Feb for the Arts & Crafts Fair Conference at the hotel; spring for weather and golfing; Oct for foliage.

Appalachia Croons from Flat Rock to Boone

MUSIC IN THE MOUNTAINS

Blue Ridge Mountains, North Carolina

The vertiginous Blue Ridge Mountains lure visitors for all kinds of reasons: challenging and scenic hiking, good skiing, renowned arts and crafts shopping, down-home country cooking, and rustic but elegant B&Bs and lodges. The majestic Blue Ridge Parkway cuts right through the mountains, on its way from Asheville up into the mountains of Virginia (see p. 252). But as much for their great scenery and down-to-earth friendliness, North Carolina's Blue Ridge Mountains are notable for their rich music tradition, evident in a variety of summertime concerts, festivals, and museum exhibits.

Near tiny Linville, Grandfather Mountain is, at 5,964 feet, one of the highest peaks in the state. In July, it hosts the world's largest Highland Games and Gathering of Scottish Clans, during which a torchlight ceremony summons lads clad in kilts for four days of bagpipes, tree-trunk tossing, and Gaelic sing-alongs. In

Stop at the Blue Ridge Parkway's milepost 413.1 to see the 3,969-foot-high Looking Glass Rock.

June, you can attend the annual Singing on the Mountain concert here, when voices of the faithful resonate from base to peak at the region's oldest ongoing gospel convention. About 20 miles north, the mountain town of Boone, known as one of the coolest locales in the South, has summer highs that rarely exceed 80°F. Throughout July, the university presents an Appalachian Summer Festival, featuring diverse music, dance, theater, and visual arts talents, from The Beach Boys to the Duke Ellington Orchestra.

Just 8 miles south of Boone is the gusty town of Blowing Rock, a low-keyed village that earned its name for a dramatic 4,000-foot rock precipice above the John Rivers Gorge with fierce swirling updrafts. For a prime view of the gorge and Grandfather Mountain, grab a table by a window or on the deck at Canyons Historic Restaurant. The food is good, the view is spectacular, and the popular Sunday brunch offers live jazz. Around the corner in Valle Crucis, the Mast General Store dates to 1883, back in the days when it supplied everything from horseshoes to lard. The nearby Mast Farm Inn, a handsomely updated 1880s farmhouse with seven rooms and eight

ultra-romantic cottages and cabins, promises memorable meals in its popular restaurant.

Forty miles east is Wilkesboro, where MerleFest is held each spring. What began as a benefit concert for the late Merle Watson, the renowned guitarist and son of Doc Watson, has grown into a four-day mecca for Americana music.

WHERE: Linville is 65 miles northeast of Asheville. **BLUE RIDGE PARKWAY:** blueridge parkway.org. **GRANDFATHER MOUNTAIN:** Tel 828-733-4337; grandfather.com. **SCOTTISH HIGHLAND GAMES:** Tel 828-733-1333; gmhg .org. *Cost:* $75 for 4-day ticket. *When:* 2nd full weekend in July. **APPALACHIAN SUMMER FESTIVAL:** Tel 800-841-2787 or 828-262-4046; appsummer.com. *When:* June–Aug. **CANYONS HISTORIC RESTAURANT:** Tel 828-295-7661; canyonsbr.com. *Cost:* $35. **MAST GENERAL STORE:** Valle Crucis. Tel 866-367-6278 or 828-963-6511; mastgeneralstore .com. **THE MAST FARM INN:** Valle Crucis. Tel 828-963-5857; mastfarminn.com. *Cost:* from $100 (off-peak), from $209 (peak); dinner $50. **MERLEFEST:** Wilkesboro. Tel 800-343-7857 or 336-838-6267; merlefest.org. *When:* 4 days in late Apr. *Cost:* 1-day pass from $40.

Let Them Eat Crab Cakes

THE CAPE FEAR COAST

North Carolina

Sailors once feared its treacherous shipwrecking shoals, but these days the ominous-sounding Cape Fear is an easygoing, picturesque beach region in southeastern North Carolina, which also takes in the charming seaside city of Wilmington (see p. 373).

The tony enclave of Wrightsville Beach, a small island joined to the mainland by a drawbridge, is loved for its flip-flop atmosphere, attractive architecture, and fantastic fishing. Get your seafood fix at the Oceanic Restaurant. Housed in a tri-level beach house on the ocean, with its own wooden pier, it serves up super-fresh platters of oysters, fish-and-chips, shrimp tacos, and unbelievably meaty crab cakes.

Tool on down the coast on U.S. 421 to Pleasure Island, preferably spending some time in Carolina Beach and bustling Kure (pronounced "curry") Beach, home to Fort Fisher State Historic Site, which comprises an important Civil War battlefield at Fort Fisher, the last fort to fall to the Union army, and a museum. Near Fort Fisher, be sure to visit the impressive North Carolina Aquarium.

From Fort Fisher, catch the ferry across the Cape Fear River to quiet Southport, a richly historic town rife with galleries, boutiques, and a great marina. Southport is also home to a favorite seafood dive, the Yacht Basin Provision Company. Grab a beverage from the cooler and order from the bounty of the sea: conch fritters, the best fresh steamed shrimp, and lumpy crab cakes on paper plates. Founded in 1792, Southport is the official Fourth of July capital of North Carolina, with a four-day celebration including sand castle contests and fireworks.

Lying 2 miles and a 20-minute ferry ride off the coast of Southport is car-free Bald Head Island, the northernmost semitropical environment on the East Coast. Although it is popular with day-trippers and sailors who drop anchor, you can make a weekend of it by checking into Marsh Harbour Inn, which offers an alfresco breakfast and your own golf cart (the principal means of transportation here).

WHERE: Wilmington is 113 miles southeast of Raleigh. *Visitor info:* Tel 877-406-2356 or 910-341-4030; wilmingtonandbeaches.com. **OCEANIC RESTAURANT:** Wrightsville Beach. Tel 910-256-5551; oceanicrestaurant.com. *Cost:* dinner $25. **NORTH CAROLINA AQUARIUM:** Kure Beach. Tel 800-832-3474 or 910-772-0542; ncaquariums.com. **YACHT BASIN PROVISION COMPANY:** Southport. Tel 910-457-0654. *When:* closed Dec–Mar. *Cost:* lunch $15. **4TH OF JULY CELEBRATION:** Southport. Tel 800-457-6964 or 910-457-5578; nc4thofjuly.com. *When:* July 1–4. **MARSH HARBOUR INN:** Tel 800-680-8322 or 910-454-0451; marshharbourinn.com. **BEST TIME:** 3rd weekend in Oct for the North Carolina Oyster Festival in Ocean Island Beach (nc oysterfestival.com).

The marshes surrounding Bald Head Island offer a unique environment for fishing.

Crook's, Books, and Basketball

CHAPEL HILL

North Carolina

The nation's oldest public university, the University of North Carolina (UNC) was founded in Chapel Hill in 1789. The university struggled financially early on, even closing for several years following the Civil War.

Finally, in 1881 the North Carolina state assembly appropriated money to fund the school, and the next half-century or so saw the construction of many of the campus's gracious, ivy-draped buildings.

Anchoring one corner of the Research Triangle (the other two corners being the cities of Raleigh and Durham), Chapel Hill has an intellectual, liberal vibe—leading disgruntled conservatives to call it "The People's Republic of Chapel Hill." Visitors explore the city's charming downtown shopping district, museums, and verdant 700-acre North Carolina Botanical Garden; laced with nature trails and supervised by the university, it's one of the most beautiful in the Southeast.

On campus, visit the Morehead Planetarium and Science Center, where astronauts once trained, and the Ackland Art Museum, whose 17,000-piece collection includes exceptional Asian and African works. And be sure to get a glimpse of UNC alum Michael Jordan's #23 basketball jersey, hanging in the Memorabilia Room at the Smith Center, where Tar Heels games are played.

Owned by the university, the grand 1924 Colonial-style Carolina Inn has hosted discerning guests for generations. High tea is served each afternoon, and "Fridays on the Front Porch" begin every weekend with live bluegrass music overlooking the tree-shaded north lawn. The inn's acclaimed Crossroads Chapel Hill restaurant is its heart, where a dignified and genteel ambience sets the scene for regionally sourced contemporary fare.

Downtown Chapel Hill contains a delightful clutch of boutiques and bookstores, coffeehouses and cafés, many of them lining Franklin Street, the main drag. The beloved Mama Dip's serves up true soul food. Mildred Cotton Council, a self-trained cook, opened the restaurant in 1976 and has earned praise for her "dump cooking" method ("cooking by feel and taste," as she explains in the introduction of her *Mama Dip's Kitchen* cookbook). Tuck into brown-gravy-slathered fried pork chops and eggs with sweet-potato biscuits at breakfast or crispy fried chicken with corn bread and string beans for lunch or dinner.

Crook's Corner is another much-loved institution where country meets cool in a former bait shop, a refreshingly informal but handsome space hung with local art. Bypass the longtime signature shrimp and cheesy grits for something more innovative and leave room for the hot fudge pecan brownie.

WHERE: 32 miles northwest of Raleigh. *Visitor info:* Tel 888-968-2060 or 919-254-4320; visitchapelhill.org. **UNC:** Tel 919-962-1630; unc.edu. **THE CAROLINA INN:** Tel 800-962-8519 or 919-933-2001; carolinainn .com. *Cost:* from $140 (off-peak), from $285 (peak); dinner at Crossroads Chapel Hill $45. **MAMA DIP'S:** Tel 919-942-5837; mamadips .com. *Cost:* dinner $20. **CROOK'S CORNER:** Tel 919-929-7643; crookscorner.com. *Cost:* dinner $30. **BEST TIMES:** Mar for NCAA basketball playoffs; spring to see Chapel Hill's dogwood and crape myrtle in full bloom.

Where Academia and Culture Flourish

DUKE UNIVERSITY

Durham, North Carolina

Out of Civil War ashes, Washington Duke developed an empire. During America's bloodiest war, soldiers developed an insatiable taste for smoking the brightleaf variety of tobacco, and Duke, already a successful cigarette producer, capitalized on the demand by working with inventor James Bonsack to automate the cigarette-making process. By 1890, Duke and his son, Buck, had founded Durham's American Tobacco Company.

The Dukes accumulated great riches, and in 1924 they made a $40 million endowment to Duke University (formerly called Trinity), which has since grown into one of the nation's finest educational institutions. Much of Durham's cultural activity centers on this idyllic 1,000-acre campus of neatly manicured lawns, ancient trees, and courtly Gothic Revival architecture. Be sure to visit the Nasher Museum of Art, opened in fall 2005 with a dramatic design by architect Rafael Viñoly. It contains 13,000 works, from ancient Greek vases to paintings by Andrew Wyeth, Joan Miró, and Andy Warhol. Adjacent to the museum are the Sarah P. Duke Gardens, some 55 acres of seasonal flower beds, stone terraces, a fish pool, and a rose garden. The Washington Duke Inn & Golf Club abuts the campus with its own 300-acre expanse, including a Robert Trent Jones Sr. 18-hole golf course and a three-mile running trail through Duke Forest.

Also be sure to see the Duke Chapel, a Gothic masterpiece whose 210-foot tower soars high over campus; there is no lovelier sound than its 50-bell carillon. The building's 77 stained-glass windows depict between 800 and 900 figures, and its four organs (especially the 5,033-pipe Flentrop) are among the finest anywhere and attract world-renowned organists who hold recitals here.

Where there is a vibrant cultural scene, food is never far behind, and Durham earns kudos for its superb culinary options (see next page). Food-lovers shouldn't pass up a chance to visit the original Foster's Market, a casual country-store/café that is the brainchild of Sara Foster, a former chef for Martha Stewart. Try the locally blended coffee, or Foster's Nutty Shake—vanilla ice cream, espresso, and hazelnut syrup.

WHERE: 25 miles northwest of Raleigh. Tel 919-684-8111; duke.edu. **NASHER MUSEUM:** Tel 919-684-5135; nasher.duke.edu. *When:* closed Mon. **WASHINGTON DUKE INN & GOLF CLUB:** Tel 800-443-3853 or 919-490-0999; washingtondukeinn.com. *Cost:* from $140 (off-peak), from $230 (peak). Greens fees from $45 (off-peak), from $85 (peak). **FOSTER'S MARKET:** Tel 919-489-3944; fostersmarket.com. *Cost:* lunch $12. **BEST TIMES:** 6 weeks in June and July for the highly acclaimed American Dance Festival (americandancefestival.org); fall and spring for cooler weather; winter for a basketball game, especially against longtime rival UNC.

Completed in 1935, the Duke Chapel was designed by African American architect Julian Abele.

Culinary Royalty of the South

POOLE'S DINER

Raleigh, North Carolina

Poole's Diner opened as a pie shop in 1945, but in the 1950s the menu expanded to include diner staples and quickly became one of downtown Raleigh's early hotspots, with lines wrapping around the corner. Self-taught chef-restaurateur Ashley Christensen took over in 2007 when she was just 30 years old and developed a menu of seasonal and fresh ingredients that both paid homage to the diner's roots (mac 'n' cheese is still a favorite of loyal patrons) and introduced more creative choices to offset the tried and true.

Poole's remains a perennial Raleigh favorite and was key to Christensen winning the 2014 James Beard Award for Best Chef: Southeast, though Poole's is only one part of a growing restaurant empire. In 2011 she opened Beasley's Chicken + Honey (fried chicken and Southern sides), Chuck's (gourmet burgers and homemade shakes), Fox Liquor Bar (craft cocktails), and café/restaurant Joule (pronounced "jewel")—all immediately popular, helping to resuscitate an area of downtown that was once desolate and sleepy.

Christensen's most recent can't-miss venture is Death & Taxes, opened in 2015 in an elegant, early 20th-century three-story structure on Salisbury Street. The restaurant's name is a nod to the history of the building, which was once the location of a funeral home and later a bank (the craft cocktails are themed, as well, with names like "Widow's Delight" and "Dearly Beloved"). The menu is inspired by the open kitchen's massive wood-burning grill—oysters, whole fish (from Carolina waters), "foraged and fought for" mushrooms, and dry-aged steak (a porterhouse or a bone-in Kansas City strip is as good as anything you'll find in a NYC steak house).

All of Christensen's restaurants guarantee fresh, creative cuisine while securing Raleigh's newfound role on the Southeast's culinary map.

WHERE: 426 S McDowell St., Raleigh. Tel 919-832-4477; ac-restaurants.com. *Cost:* $30.

Get Your Pig On

NORTH CAROLINA BBQ

Lexington, North Carolina

With a barbecue joint per thousand citizens, Lexington has been rightly dubbed the swine, slaw, and hush puppy capital of the world. Founded in 1962, Lexington Barbecue #1 ("Honey Monk's" to locals) is the open-pit, hickory-smoke daddy of 'em all. Even during a slow week, this humble joint serves up six tons of pork shoulder. Don't get any ideas about copying their recipe for success—owner Wayne Monk makes his smokehouse sauce each Sunday, hidden from onlookers, and locks his recipe inside a safe-deposit box.

The restaurant's first barbecue stand opened in 1919, and the cooks have been employing the same methods ever since: 3 hours on the face, 3 hours on the back, then 3 hours on the face again—by the time the pork emerges from the pit, it's tender enough to pull by hand. But some fans of this beloved treat scoff at Lexington's supposed lock on barbecue. At best, this small city (also home to the prestigious Bob Timberlake furniture factory) can safely claim to be North Carolina's focal point for western-style barbecue, which uses only the pork shoulders and a vinegar sauce and slaw that's tinged red and sweet from a dash of ketchup.

About 160 miles east, in Goldsboro, Wilber's Barbecue epitomizes *eastern-style* North Carolina barbecue, where the entire pig is smoked and served up with white or yellow slaw and nary a hint of ketchup. During a typical weekend at Wilber's, 25 pigs are rendered fork-tender for the hungry masses.

In the devoutly partisan world of Carolina pig-smokin', seemingly academic distinctions in meat and method make all the difference in the world. It's not impossible to find barbecue devotees enamored of both the eastern and western disciplines, but most diehards fiercely prefer one over the other. Decide which you prefer at the Barbecue Festival, held each October in Lexington right about the time the leaves on the town's oak and dogwood trees turn the color of ketchup-infused barbecue sauce. This gut-busting one-day party draws as many as 100,000 loyal BBQ'ers for country music, arts and crafts sales, rides, and some highly competitive cook-offs.

WHERE: 36 miles southwest of Greensboro. **LEXINGTON BARBECUE #1:** Tel 336-249-9814; lexbbq.com. *Cost:* $10. **WILBER'S BARBECUE:** Goldsboro. Tel 919-778-5218; wilbersbarbecue.com. *Cost:* $12. **LEXINGTON BARBECUE FESTIVAL:** Tel 336-956-1880; barbecuefestival.com. *When:* Sat in late Oct.

The Lexington Barbecue Festival began in 1984 and is one of the largest street festivals in North Carolina.

Gorgeous Gorges

NANTAHALA NATIONAL FOREST

North Carolina

N antahala Gorge, a profound crevasse that's 1,800 feet at its deepest and 100 yards wide at its narrowest, has been inspiring awe in onlookers for centuries. The word *nantahala* comes from the Cherokee for "land of the

noonday sun": Only when the sun is directly overhead can rays reach the floor, where eons of river flow have carved out the gorge. Nantahala National Forest, which at 530,000 acres covers an area more than half the size of Rhode Island, extends south of Great Smoky Mountains National Park, west to the Tennessee border, south to the Georgia border, and east to where it meets with the Pisgah National Forest (see p. 369).

A rafting and boating nirvana, the Nantahala River offers 8 miles of superlative white-water rapids, and the respected Nantahala Outdoor Center, in Bryson City, provides instruction and tours to get you onto this or any of the other seven rivers that charge through this dense forest (also home to the 811-foot Whitewater Falls, the highest cataract east of the Rockies). Other rivers that rafters love to fear include the Nolichucky or "Noli") and the Chattooga, whose rapids starred in the darkly frightening film *Deliverance.*

Stay dry by driving the ravishing 43-mile Nantahala Byway, which skirts the gorge for some 20 miles. Take a detour up Highway 129 to reach Joyce Kilmer Memorial Forest, home to one of the last stands of old-growth hardwood forest in the East. Or follow in the footsteps of 18th-century naturalist and artist William Bartram on the Bartram Trail, which stretches for 115 miles from northeast Georgia up the crest of the Blue Ridge Mountains, joining the Appalachian Trail (see p. 332) before descending to Nantahala Gorge and climbing the summit of Cheoah Bald.

Nestled between Nantahala and the Great Smoky Mountains National Park, the 56,000-acre Cherokee Indian Reservation is home to

Nantahala National Forest is the largest of North Carolina's four national forests.

the superb Museum of the Cherokee Indian, with interactive exhibits and tribal artifacts. A memorable way to learn about the Cherokees is to attend a summer production of *Unto These Hills,* which depicts the tribe's story from the first encounters with Europeans in 1540 to the tragic Trail of Tears forced exodus to Oklahoma 300 years later (see p. 649).

Forest info: Tel 828-257-4200; fs.usda .gov. **Nantahala Outdoor Center:** Bryson City. Tel 828-785-4835; noc.com. **Nantahala Byway:** go-north-carolina.com. **Bartram Trail:** ncbartramtrail.org. **Museum of the Cherokee Indian:** Cherokee. Tel 828-497-3481; cherokeemuseum.org. *Unto These Hills:* Cherokee. Tel 866-554-4557; visit cherokeenc.com. *When:* Mon–Sat, June–Aug. **Best time:** spring brings raging white water and blooming mountainsides.

World's Longest Stretch of Barrier Islands

THE OUTER BANKS

North Carolina

S ome of the most unusual and beautiful beaches on America's Atlantic coast are in North Carolina's Outer Banks, a string of skinny barrier islands that stretches 130 miles from the Virginia border to the southernmost point at

Cape Lookout and Beaufort. With more than 600 shipwrecks here (and hence notoriety as "Graveyard of the Atlantic"), the Outer Banks evokes an illustrious seafaring past, but is also a great sporting playground. Fine fishing awaits anglers on charter boats, atop numerous piers and bridges, and off miles of ocean and sound shores. There may be pockets of unwelcome sprawl, and it can get maddeningly over-crowded in summer, but most of the Outer Banks has been preserved by the National Park Service and looks blissfully unfettered.

The northern Outer Banks consists largely of seasonal beach towns, such as Kitty Hawk and Kill Devil Hills, where the Wright Brothers pioneered airplane flight. The winds that aided the brothers' quest today draw serious wind-surfers. In nearby Duck, the inviting Sanderling Resort adjoins 2,600-acre Pine Island Audubon Sanctuary. Explore miles of lonely windblown beach, or sign up for a tour offered by the eco-sensitive inn. The guest accommodations are beautifully decorated, and its spa offers such invigorating treatments as sea-stone massage and brown sugar scrub. The most popular of the inn's four bars and restaurants, housed in a restored 1899 U.S. Lifesaving Station and decked out in nautical artifacts, serves New South treats like lump crab cakes with mint yogurt sauce and grilled jumbo shrimp with pimento grits.

The midportion of the Outer Banks is domi-nated by bustling Nags Head (one of the Outer Banks' largest and oldest communities) and Jockey's Ridge State Park, home to towering sand dunes and a tree-lined boardwalk.

Continue south to Cape Hatteras National Seashore, a 70-mile stretch comprising Bodie, Hatteras, and Ocracoke islands. Check out the country's tallest brick lighthouse, the candy-striped Cape Hatteras Lighthouse, one of five such structures throughout the Outer Banks. Huff and puff your way up 257 steps for an amazing view of the area. Hatteras has terrific sailboarding conditions, while laid-back Ocracoke Island offers beautiful beaches. It's also a great community for fishing and

bicycling around the harbor or for an informal lunch of lumpy Hatteras-style clam chowder.

The southern end of the region is known as the Crystal Coast and encompasses Cape Lookout National Seashore, where wild horses have roamed Shackleford Banks for centuries. It extends west through a number of family-oriented beach villages, such as Atlantic Beach and Emerald Isle. Skip just inland to the town of Beaufort (pronounced bo-fort) to visit the North Carolina Maritime Museum, where you'll find relics from Blackbeard's 18th-century flag-ship, the *Queen Anne's Revenge*, which sits nearby on the ocean floor.

Beaufort, founded in 1713, has some 100 buildings more than a century old. When you're hungry, visit the Beaufort Grocery Company, a charming white-clapboard storefront for a casual lunch of homemade gumbo or a *gougère* (cheese puff) stuffed with shrimp or chicken salad; the atmosphere grows more sophisti-cated by evening.

WHERE: 225 miles east of Durham. *Visitor info:* Tel 877-629-4386 or 252-473-2138; outerbanks.org. **THE SANDERLING:** Duck. Tel 855-412-7866; sanderling-resort.com. *Cost:* from $129 (off-peak), from $250 (peak); dinner $65. **MARITIME MUSEUM:** Beaufort. Tel 252-728-7317; ncmaritime.org. **BEAUFORT GROCERY COMPANY:** Tel 252-728-3899; beaufortgrocery .com. *Cost:* dinner $48. **BEST TIMES:** Mar–Apr and Sept–Oct for weather, though beware of fall hurricanes; mid-July for the original Wright Kite Festival at Kill Devil Hills.

Join the native "Bankers" and relax on the Outer Banks' inviting beachfronts.

ROANOKE ISLAND

Outer Banks, North Carolina

More than 30 years before the *Mayflower* dropped anchor in Massachusetts, a group of more than 100 British immigrants, led by Sir Walter Raleigh, established a settlement on Roanoke Island, in North Carolina's fabled Outer Banks (see p. 365). Part of the fun in visiting Roanoke Island and its main town of Manteo is investigating the strange legacy of that early settlement, which not only failed but disappeared. Three years after Raleigh and his cohorts settled here, some members of the group were sent back to England for supplies. When they returned, the colony was gone, having left just two enigmatic clues: the words "croatoan" and "cro," carved on a post and a tree, respectively. The colonists, perhaps, had set out for Croatoan Island (now called Hatteras Island), near Cape Hatteras (see previous page)—but what became of them remains a mystery.

You can learn about as much as is known by attending a performance of the famous play *The Lost Colony*, which the Roanoke Island Historical Association has been producing since 1937 at the historic Waterside Theatre. A huge and talented ensemble cast (alumni include actors Andy Griffith and Chris Elliott) tell the story of the brave inhabitants, including infant Virginia Dare, said to be the first British child born in the New World.

The theater is adjacent to 513-acre Fort Raleigh National Historic Site, with exhibits that shed further light upon the Lost Colony. The best reason to tour the site, however, is for a chance to amble through the stunning Elizabethan Gardens, a botanical memorial to the Lost Colony. Stroll the Rhododendron Walk or visit the antiques-filled Gatehouse, which is patterned after a 16th-century orangery.

Just across from the downtown Manteo waterfront and sitting on its own 25-acre island is Roanoke Island Festival Park. Here you can board and tour a re-creation of the Lost Colony's three-masted ship, *Elizabeth II*, or chat with colony reenactors at the Settlement Site living-history area.

The once rather ordinary downtown of Manteo, which faces the water, has happily come into its own in recent years, as a number of fine shops have opened, from booksellers to antiques emporia, joined by a handful of excellent restaurants. One of the nicest places on the island to unpack your bag is the aptly named Tranquil House Inn. A small, light-filled hotel overlooking the waterfront, built in 1974 with weathered cypress and beveled- and stained-glass windows, it looks like it's always been here. There are 25 rooms with simple, elegant furnishings, including four-poster beds, and either town or water views. Plan for dinner at the inn's acclaimed, nautical-themed 1587 Restaurant, known for nice water views and such inventive fare as duck breast with dried cherry slaw and red curry and ginger mussels.

WHERE: 213 miles east of Durham. *Visitor info:* Tel 877-629-4386 or 252-473-2138; roanokeisland.net. **WATERSIDE THEATRE:** Manteo. Tel 252-473-2127; thelostcolony.org. *When:* Mon–Sat, late May–mid-Aug. **FORT RALEIGH HISTORIC SITE:** Tel 252-473-2111 (park) or 252-473-3234 (gardens); nps.gov/fora (park) or elizabethangardens.org (gardens). **FESTIVAL PARK:** Tel 252-475-1500; roanokeisland.com. **TRANQUIL HOUSE INN AND 1587 RESTAURANT:** Tel 800-458-7069 or 252-473-1404 (inn); 252-473-1587 (restaurant); tranquilhouseinn.com. *Cost:* from $109 (off-peak), from $219 (peak); dinner $55. **Best time:** summer to catch a performance of *The Lost Colony* and enjoy the flowering Elizabethan Gardens.

Pins, Pines, and Needles

PINEHURST

North Carolina

I f bunkers, birdies, and divots send your pulse racing, catch a cart to Pinehurst, the world's second largest golf resort (with eight courses) and the informal nickname for an entire region of stellar driving and putting. America's answer

to St. Andrews, Scotland, this legendary golfer's haven is home to an astonishing 43 courses (that's 165 miles of fairway, folks!), many along the scenic and curving Midland Road, the so-called Fifth Avenue of Golf. Pinehurst has plenty of golf open to everyone, and *Golf Magazine* regularly names three of the Pinehurst-area facilities among the nation's "Top 100 You Can Play."

In 1895, James Walker Tufts purchased 5,000 acres for $1 apiece in the remote, rolling sandhills of North Carolina, and brought the architectural firm of Frederick Law Olmsted to lay out a health-oriented winter retreat. When a local farmer complained that guests were hitting little white balls into his cows, Tufts built a 9-hole course and hired Scotsman Donald Ross as his golf pro. Ross went on to design a number of championship courses, including his masterpiece, the No. 2 Course, which hosted the 2014, 2005, and 1999 U.S. Opens.

Away from the links, Pinehurst Resort keeps guests entertained with a plethora of top-drawer distractions—an awesome spa, tennis courts, croquet lawns, swimming pools, and a lake for kayaking and fishing. The resort is in the midst of the historic 1900s Village of Pinehurst, with its brick sidewalks and original spires. Superlative accommodations can be found to suit many tastes. For all-out

pampering, you can't beat the 82-room Holly Inn; its 1895 Grille serves such flawless fare as grilled chipotle jumbo shrimp with chive grits. About 5 miles east of Pinehurst, Pine Needles Lodge & Golf Club sits among hundreds of acres of rolling hills and offers a smaller and less formal setting. An intimate and more afford-

Fred Couples is just one of many pro golfers to have played the No. 2 Course at Pinehurst.

able option in the heart of the Village of Pinehurst is the Pine Crest Inn & Restaurant. Owned for 27 years by Donald Ross, it contains pleasant, no-frills rooms that'll save you money better spent on golfing. Dinner in this 1913 B&B's esteemed restaurant should not be missed. Afterward, while away an evening in Mr. B's Lounge, the convivial piano bar, where duffers swap stories over burgers and bourbon.

Where: Pinehurst is 70 miles southwest of Raleigh; 1 Carolina Vista Dr. Tel 855-235-8507 or 910-235-8507; pinehurst.com. *Cost:* Donald Ross package from $567 per person, double occupancy, includes room, 2 meals, and 1 round of golf per day. **Holly Inn:** rooms from $145;

dinner $50. **Pine Needles:** Southern Pines. Tel 910-692-7111; pineneedles-midpines.com. *Cost:* The Ultimate package from $310 per person (off-peak), from $445 per person (peak), double occupancy, includes room, meals, and 2 rounds of golf per day. **Pine Crest Inn:** Tel 800-371-2545 or 910-295-6121; pinecrest innpinehurst.com. *Cost:* from $75 per person, double occupancy, includes breakfast and dinner. **Best times:** mid-Mar–mid-May for weather and spring blooms; Sept–mid-Nov for similarly balmy climes and fewer crowds.

White Water, Waterfalls, Fall Foliage

Pisgah National Forest

North Carolina

Named for the biblical mountain from which Moses saw the Promised Land after wandering in the wilderness for 40 years, Pisgah (PIZZ-guh) National Forest is a modern-day kingdom come for urban-weary travelers.

Straddling the Blue Ridge Parkway, this half-million-acre forest comprises four districts in western North Carolina, where the state juts into Tennessee and abuts Georgia.

Enter the forest in the county of Transylvania ("across the woods") and traverse the forest's leafy miles by car, mountain bike, or even on foot. But with thousands of scenic trails begging for boot treads, including a good chunk of the Appalachian Trail (see p. 332), this is an ideal place to launch hard-core camping or day-hiking expeditions. Admire Mount Pisgah and Mount Mitchell—the latter the highest peak east of the Mississippi, at 6,684 feet—or visit the slightly shorter but more famous Cold Mountain, inspiration for Charles Frazier's Civil War–era novel set in this area.

Kayakers, canoeists, and rafters regularly head to the Nolichucky River Gorge, the deepest canyon in the East, while fishing fanatics mine the region's trout-rich streams. Of Pisgah Forest's famed 250 or so waterfalls, highlights include 60-foot-high Looking Glass Falls and the only slightly shorter Moore's Cove Falls.

Naturalists and shutterbugs will have a field day in these virgin forest reserves,

Pisgah was the first National Forest to be established in the United States.

blooming with rhododendrons and fragrant balsams, mountain laurel, flame azalea, and dogwoods. Pisgah lies at the heart of America's forest conservation movement, a legacy shared at the Cradle of Forestry, the nation's earliest forestry school, near Brevard. This historic site, on land originally purchased by George W. Vanderbilt II as the intended site for his Biltmore Estate (see p. 356), now contains a Discovery Center with hands-on exhibits.

Mountain bikers take to one of the most revered single-tracks on the East Coast, as well as some 200 miles of tortuous trails snaking up the forest's many mountainsides. Then there's Max Patch Bald, a treeless swath atop Max Patch Mountain, where you can catch a stunning 360-degree view of the Smoky Mountains. This isolated promontory is nature's planetarium—a popular yet private spot for camping under the constellations where you'll feel like king of the mountain.

WHERE: 35 miles south of Asheville. Visitor Center is near Brevard. Tel 828-257-4200; pisgahnationalforest.info. **CRADLE OF FORESTRY:** Tel 828-877-3130; cradleof forestry.com. *When:* mid-Apr–Nov. **WHERE TO STAY:** Pisgah Inn. Tel 828-235-8228; pisgah inn.com. *Cost:* from $150. *When:* late Mar–Oct. **BEST TIMES:** Apr–May for white-water rafting; Oct–Nov for foliage.

High Tea with the Belties

FEARRINGTON HOUSE INN

Pittsboro, North Carolina

I
t began in 1786 when William Cole laid claim to 60 acres of land, which he used to build a successful dairy farm. Nearly 200 years later, Cole's great-great-grandson, Jesse Fearrington, sold the family farm, and it has since been developed into one of the South's most inviting country retreats, a picturesque village whose centerpiece is the Fearrington House Restaurant and Country Inn. Just 8 miles south of charming Chapel Hill (see p. 361), the Fearrington is the perfect spot for a peaceful respite.

Today the farm's original barn and silo are surrounded by newly built white-clapboard structures, all within walking distance of the village's stretch of boutiques, bookshops, antiques stores, and eateries. The inn has 32 handsome guest rooms and suites, half opening onto a romantic courtyard and half overlooking a 17-acre garden. All are appointed with a mix of antiques, fine reproductions, and original artwork that create an air that's unfailingly luxurious yet happily unfussy. Marble vanities, heated towel racks, and robes and slippers come with every room, and an impressive slate of in-room spa treatments is available, from aromatherapy to therapeutic foot massage.

This is as much a food destination as a place to spend the night. The farm's old homestead houses the inn's acclaimed Fearrington House Restaurant, which serves exquisite three- and four-course prix-fixe dinners as well as a regularly changing tasting menu that strictly follows the region's four seasons. The restaurant also holds several popular cooking-class weekends throughout the year.

Perhaps the most memorable tradition at the Fearrington is afternoon high tea in the lounge. While Belted Galloways, the

Surrounded by cow-dotted pastures and trellised English gardens, the Fearrington House Inn is an idyllic rural retreat.

distinctive brown-and-white cows that are the village's pampered mascots, graze on emerald green pastures outside, you feast on an embarrassment of finger sandwiches and dozens of different delicate pastries.

WHERE: 8 miles south of Chapel Hill;

2000 Fearrington Village. Tel 919-542-2121; fearrington.com. *Cost:* from $325; 3-course prix-fixe dinner $95. **BEST TIMES:** during cooking-school retreats held at Fearrington House (check website for schedule); spring for garden blooms; fall for brilliant foliage.

Pottery Capital of the World

SEAGROVE

North Carolina

"Blunge," "fettle," and "sgraffito" look like words a Scrabble champion ought to know, but here in Randolph County, they're common terms from the potter's glossary. More than 90 potteries within a 25-mile radius make tiny Seagrove one of the world's great pottery centers. Nearly smack-dab in the center of the state, some 30 miles from the furniture-making stronghold of High Point, you'll find small-town charm, country-style cooking, and the rich clay deposits first utilized by Native Americans.

Some of today's potters can trace their kin's kiln to the area's English and German immigrants who made functional earthenware. Today Southern potters no longer "throw" pots, they "turn" them; wheels are called "lathes" (pronounced "lays"), and pots aren't "fired" but "burned." Potteries line Highway 705 (aka "Pottery Highway"), their sheer density providing an unparalleled opportunity to glimpse a thousand years of Carolina pottery-making culture. You can learn a great deal about the area's heritage at downtown Seagrove's North Carolina Pottery Center, which displays local works and can also supply maps pinpointing area potteries.

Visitors are welcome to step inside working potters' studios and learn about this time-honored craft. Amidst bucolic scenery, learn the differences between gas-fired and pit-fired, raku and salt-glaze—and hear stories about the generations-old turning and glazing techniques behind eccentric "face jugs" once used as grave markers and then, legend goes, as ugly deterrents to keep the kids out of grandpa's moonshine. The handmade wares range from affordable cups and saucers to abstract, contemporary treasures that command huge ransoms and sometimes find their way into renowned museum collections.

As you explore the region's winding back roads and visit potteries with names like Turn & Burn, Whynot, and Jugtown, bring along a bottle of wine and a basket of cheese and baguettes—many galleries have picnic tables on their pine-shaded grounds. Don't miss tenth-generation turner Ben Owen III or—50 miles east in Pittsboro—the British-born Mark Hewitt, whose spring, summer, and pre-Christmas kiln openings inspire pottery hounds to camp out overnight for first dibs on one of his 2,000 massive stoneware pots, vases, and grave markers.

WHERE: 41 miles south of Greensboro. *When:* potteries around town generally closed Sun–Mon. **NORTH CAROLINA POTTERY CENTER:** Tel 336-873-8430; ncpotterycenter.org. *When:* closed Sun–Mon. **BEST TIME:** weekend before Thanksgiving for annual Seagrove Pottery Festival.

When You Need an Altitude Adjustment

HIGH-COUNTRY RAMBLE

Waynesville, Highlands, and Cashiers, North Carolina

In the far western reaches of North Carolina is the Appalachian mountain range, where Southerners from sultry climes flock to soak up the clear, cool mountain weather. There's not much in the way of formal attractions and diversions, and therein lies its beauty. You might take in the spectacular high-country scenery, hike the deep cool forests, motor along a winding two-lane highway, or raft the roaring rivers. Summer festivals fill mountain towns with the sound of music at every turn.

Begin a tour of this high-country terrain in Waynesville. Check in to the Swag (named for a dip between two mountains), a charming 14-room country inn comprising five historic buildings, including hand-hewn Appalachian cabins and an 18th-century former church that now serves as a guest lounge. The rooms are the exemplar of country chic, with such traditional features as handmade country quilts and Early American antiques. A roaring stone fireplace, folk art, and a player piano complement the million-dollar views from this cushy 250-acre retreat atop the Cataloochee Divide. In the backyard you'll find none other than Great Smoky Mountains National Park (see p. 464) and the inn's own footpath to take you there.

From here it's a rocking and rolling 40-mile ride southwest down U.S. 23, and then 20 miles on dramatically beautiful U.S. 64 to the dapper summer resort community of Highlands. The road climbs past mesmerizing waterfalls, including the 250-foot-high Cullasaja River Gorge and Falls. At an elevation of over 4,000 feet, Highlands is green with lichens and moss and boasts an archetypal Main Street lined for several blocks with diverting boutiques and inviting cafés. The population swells from 3,200 to over 18,000 in summer, when it can be challenging to book a room at the historic Highlands Inn. At the snazzier Old Edwards Inn & Spa, turn yourself over for a Sweet Mountain Meadow Metamorphosis body treatment, before dining in the inn's well-known Madison's Restaurant. It's a heady experience (maybe it's the altitude) just to peruse the menu with specialties such as slow-roasted duck breast with roasted sweet potatoes and fig chutney.

Continue east for 10 miles along tortuous U.S. 64 to Cashiers (pronounced CASH-ers), an unpretentious town with only a solitary traffic light. Little changes here beside the seasons, and the High Hampton Inn is no exception. Built as a hunting lodge before the Civil War, this 1,400-acre getaway is enveloped by tall hemlocks and white pines. You're not going to find TVs, phones, or even clocks in the rooms, and rates include three hearty square meals a day, served buffet-style. Free from 21st-century distractions, you'll have plenty of time to swim the lake, golf, swing croquet mallets, or rock away a few hours on the porch.

WHERE: Waynesville is 30 miles west of Asheville. **THE SWAG:** Waynesville. Tel 800-789-7672; theswag.com. *Cost:* from $495 (peak), includes meals. *When:* late Apr–Nov. **HIGHLANDS INN:** Tel 828-526-9380; highlandsinn-nc.com. *When:* open Apr–Nov. *Cost:* from $139 (off-peak), from $189 (peak). **OLD EDWARDS INN:** Highlands. Tel 866-526-8008; oldedwardsinn.com. *Cost:* from $199 (off-peak), from $295 (peak); dinner $55. **HIGH**

Hampton Inn: Cashiers. Tel 828-743-0263; highhamptoninn.com. *Cost:* from $275 (off-peak), from $315 (peak), includes meals.

Best times: May for spring flowers; summer months are crowded but the cool evenings are a joy; Oct for foliage.

Hollywood East Meets Old-World South

WILMINGTON

North Carolina

The cosmopolitan hub of North Carolina's idyllic Cape Fear Coast (see p. 360), Wilmington wears that same stamp of the good life often applied to other small-but-dynamic cities, such as Asheville (see p. 355) and Chapel Hill (see p. 361). Here you'll find a walkable downtown with a handsome river-front, a beautiful 230-block historic district, and a friendly and well-cultured community. Dominating the southern Outer Banks' string of sea-loving communities (see p. 365), Wilmington actually lies 30 miles inland from the ocean. It is also the northernmost East Coast city with palm trees—even in January, temperatures rarely fall below freezing, and spring arrives early in a blaze of blossoms.

Since its 1739 founding, emphasis has been placed on the importance of Wilmington as a shipping center. But these days Wilmington is known more as a film and TV hub, earning it the nickname "Hollywood East." More than 400 movies and TV shows, including *Dawson's Creek*, *Iron Man 3*, *Weekend at Bernie's*, and *Crimes of the Heart*, have been filmed in the area since it was first "discovered" by Dino De Laurentiis in the 1980s. Locals may not want the world to know, but Wilmington actually bears a close resemblance to such tourist-driven Southern belles as Charleston and Savannah, with a fraction of the crowds and much lower costs.

Start your visit by taking either a stroll down the vibrant Riverwalk or a riverboat cruise on the busy Cape Fear River. Then explore funky, artsy downtown, with its art galleries, antiques shops, coffee bars, after-hours

Stroll the Riverwalk, have lunch at a café, and watch the boats go by on the Cape Fear River.

lounges, and a mix of both avant-garde and sophisticated boutiques. One of Wilmington's cultural highlights is the Cameron Art Museum, which focuses on American art (there's a vast collection of Mary Cassatt prints and etchings) with an emphasis on North Carolina artists.

There are plenty of urbane restaurants to choose from, several of them by the lushly landscaped pedestrian way fringing the river. For the ultimate Wilmington dining experience, book a table at Catch. Helmed by Keith Rhodes, a native son of Wilmington and widely considered the city's best chef, the Catch menu showcases the best the local waters offer (Rhodes is a stickler for wild caught and sustainably raised seafood). Try the day's fresh catch, accompanied by NC Sweet Potato Salad and Conch Fritters.

There's also no shortage of historic B&Bs in town. Built as a private home in 1905 by a local family of great wealth, the Graystone Inn invites the guests of its nine spacious rooms and suites to enjoy a similar lifestyle of yore. Start with a decadent breakfast that revolves around the inn's famous Key Lime Stuffed French Toast, and then walk it off on a self-guided tour of the city—everything is just steps away.

WHERE: 113 miles southeast of Raleigh. *Visitor info:* Tel 877-406-2356; wilmingtonand beaches.com. **CAMERON MUSEUM:** Tel 910-395-5999; cameronartmuseum.com. *When:* closed Mon. **CATCH:** Tel 910-799-3847; catchwilm ington.com. *Cost:* $40. **GRAYSTONE INN:** Tel 800-763-4773 or 910-763-2000; graystoneinn .com. *Cost:* from $160. **BEST TIMES:** early Apr for the Azalea Festival (ncazaleafestival.org); 4 days in late Sept–early Oct for Riverfest; Halloween for haunted house tours; Dec for Old Wilmington by Candlelight.

Moravian Yesteryear Resurrected

OLD SALEM

Winston-Salem, North Carolina

Both a living history museum in the vein of Virginia's Colonial Williamsburg (see p. 255) and a dynamic working neighborhood, Old Salem is brought to life by costumed interpreters who introduce visitors to the daily life of the Moravians, persecuted Protestants who settled here in 1766 after fleeing what is now the Czech Republic.

Among the 100-plus restored buildings in Old Salem, you'll find St. Philips African Moravian Church (est. 1861), the state's longest-standing African American church. The neighborhood also contains one of America's oldest women's colleges (est. 1772), Salem Academy and College, testimony to the Moravians' progressive belief that women deserved educations on par with those available to men. Make it a priority to visit the Museum of Early Southern Decorative Arts (MESDA), a trove of period rooms and galleries showcasing regional furniture, paintings, and ceramics produced throughout the early mid-South. The Old Salem Single Brothers' Gardens, an immense plot of nine gardens set upon three terraces containing crops and flora grown in Salem two centuries ago, makes a perfect afternoon in April and May, when it is vibrantly abloom.

Stop for a snack of paper-thin tea cookies and sugar cakes, baked in a wood-fired oven, at Winkler Bakery, which dates to 1800. And follow the smell of Moravian gingerbread into the 1816 Tavern in Old Salem, with its simple

The Denke House is one of many charmingly restored buildings found in Old Salem.

varnished wooden tables, wide-plank floors, and a menu of German and Southern favorites (don't miss the chicken pie) that are prepared with innovative accents and delivered by servers dressed in 19th-century costume. On sunny days, you can dine alfresco on the patio.

To make a weekend of it, book a room at the redbrick Augustus T. Zevely Inn, the only lodging in the historic district and the former home of a local physician. It's straight out of the mid-19th century, albeit with modern concessions. On winter evenings, cozy up to the parlor fireplace with a complimentary snifter of brandy. Enjoy coffee and Moravian baked specialties the following morning in the breakfast room fashioned out of Dr. Zevely's old office.

WHERE: Visitor Center at 900 Old Salem Rd. Tel 888-653-7253 or 336-721-7300; oldsalem.org. *When:* closed Mon. **TAVERN IN OLD SALEM:** Tel 336-722-1277; taverninoldsalem.com. *Cost:* dinner $25. **ZEVELY INN:** Tel 800-928-9299 or 336-748-9299; winston-salem-inn.com. *Cost:* from $110. **BEST TIMES:** springtime for the gardens; Christmastime for a vintage holiday experience.

Legacy of a Founding Family

THE REYNOLDA MILE

Winston-Salem, North Carolina

The name Reynolds is to Winston-Salem what the name Ford is to Detroit. A trip to this city founded by persecuted Moravians is not complete without a visit to the home of the family that, in 1874, established R. J. Reynolds, the nation's second-largest tobacco company (after Philip Morris).

The Reynolds family rose from humble beginnings to attain fabulous wealth. The grand 1917 home of tobacco barons Katharine Smith Reynolds and Richard Joshua Reynolds is now the Reynolda House Museum of American Art. It regally anchors the city's fabled Reynolda Mile, a seminal stretch of imposing homes and cultural institutions in northwest Winston-Salem. The rambling 64-room house contains furnishings original to the family, such as priceless table linens, silver serving pieces, opulent chandeliers, and an organ with 2,566 pipes that's draped by Flemish tapestries.

And then there's the phenomenal art collection, with more than 130 pieces including works by Thomas Eakins, Frederick Church, Jasper Johns, and Georgia O'Keeffe. The collection spans the mid-1700s to the 1980s and also contains a display of Lady Reynolds's early- to mid-1900s wardrobe. Don't leave the grounds without a visit to her exquisite private gardens.

The Reynolda Mile also encompasses Reynolda Village, where Reynolds's servants and employees lived, and which is now a neighborhood of specialty shops and restaurants patterned after a quaint English country village.

Other highlights include the 129-acre Reynolda Gardens, which abound with rolling woodlands, greenhouses, and formal gardens designed by noted landscape architect Thomas Sears. SECCA, the Southeastern Center for Contemporary Art, occupies the former home of textile mogul and undergarment tycoon James G. Hanes, and displays works by some of 20th-century America's most talented artists and crafts makers.

WHERE: 1-mile stretch between Wake Forest Dr. & Coliseum Dr. **REYNOLDA HOUSE:** Tel 888-663-1149; reynoldahouse.org. *When:* closed Mon.

Steeplechases and Polo Matches

SOUTH CAROLINA'S THOROUGHBRED COUNTRY

Aiken, South Carolina

Established in the 1830s as a railroad hub, the small, charming western South Carolina city of Aiken is the Southeast's premier equestrian community. In the late 19th century, wealthy northerners began building stately "cottages" in Aiken, turning the pine-scented village with balmy winters and gently rolling hills into a prime cold-months resort. Astors, Vanderbilts, Mellons, and Whitneys flocked here from the North to partake of the society balls and crisp country air, followed by the horse set, who appreciated the area's soft clay soil and open countryside. Take a drive or walk through the town's three Winter Colony Historic Districts, exploring the miles and miles of both paved and unpaved roads and bridle paths. Riders can also enjoy the 2,100-acre Hitchcock Woods, considered to be the largest urban forest in the nation.

The horse scene here is professional and highly competitive. Numerous races and events draw top equestrian enthusiasts throughout the year, particularly during March for the renowned Aiken "Triple Crown": the Aiken Trials, the prestigious Aiken Spring Steeplechase, and the Pacers and Polo Competition, which pulls in some of the world's top players. The last weekend of March or first weekend in April, the annual Aiken Horse Show—now over 100 years old—takes place at Hitchcock Woods, providing still more horse-related pomp and circumstance. October brings the much-awaited Fall Steeplechase. Throughout both spring and fall you can also enjoy a Sunday afternoon of polo, played here since 1882—longer than anywhere else in the nation.

To catch up on the local gossip among jockeys, horse owners, regular Joes, and society types, visit the Track Kitchen, a down-home breakfast joint close to Aiken's track, where you'll find tasty unpretentious fare. Aiken's very special accommodation is the Willcox, a regal 1898 inn that hosted Franklin D. Roosevelt and has become one of the state's most luxurious small hotels. The white-pillared beauty containing 22 lavishly appointed rooms with fireplaces and antiques from the late 19th and early 20th centuries is the unofficial headquarters of the horse set during any of Aiken's annual events. Stop by for a drink in the lobby bar or stay for dinner in the inn's well-known restaurant.

WHERE: 130 miles northwest of Charleston. *Visitor info:* Tel 888-245-3672 or 803-293-7846; visitaikensc.com. **AIKEN TRIPLE CROWN:** Tel 803-648-4631 (Aiken Trials), 803-648-9641 (Steeplechase), 803-641-3630 (Pacers and Polo); aikentrials.com, aikensteeplechase .com, pacersports.com. *When:* mid- to late Mar. **AIKEN HORSE SHOW:** Tel 803-642-0528; aikenhorseshow.org. *When:* late Mar–early Apr. **TRACK KITCHEN:** Tel 803-641-9628. *Cost:* breakfast $12. **THE WILLCOX:** Tel 877-648-2200 or 803-648-1898; thewillcox.com. *Cost:* from $189; dinner $40. **BEST TIMES:** mid-Mar–Apr for the top horse activities (when gardens are in full bloom); mid- to late Oct for the Western Carolina State Fair; late Oct for the Fall Steeplechase.

Where the Old Times Aren't Forgotten

BEAUFORT & THE LOWCOUNTRY

South Carolina

The honeycombed coastline south of Charleston stretches for 200 miles, dissolving into peninsulas, channels, and subtropical "sea islands" that make up South Carolina's lowcountry. Kiawah (see p. 386) and neighboring Seabrook are well-heeled island resorts, while the pristine 5,000-acre Hunting Island State Park, once a private hunting resort, is now blessedly protected as a nature reserve, rife with loggerhead turtles, alligators, herons, and oystercatchers.

The small waterfront town of Beaufort (a kind of Charleston in miniature) is the gateway to the Sea Islands and the most practical and popular base for exploring the area. Known for its many antebellum houses, Beaufort (pronounced BYEW-fert) was once a prosperous shipping center and has enjoyed a renaissance owing to its popularity with Hollywood filmmakers (*The Big Chill*, *Forrest Gump*, and *Prince of Tides* were shot here). Quite a few celebs have parked their bags at the alluring Rhett House Inn. A short walk from the restored waterfront and the town's main drag (lined with antiques stores, art galleries, and innovative restaurants), the white-columned 1820s inn epitomizes Southern hospitality. Guests can use complimentary bicycles to pedal around the backstreets, with their mammoth magnolias and gnarled oaks and graveyards commemorating the Confederate dead.

St. Helena Island promises an intriguing history lesson at the Penn Center, established in 1862 as the first school in the South for freed slaves, and the nerve center of the area's Gullah community. The descendants of Angolan Mende, Kisi, Malinke, and Bantu slaves have managed to preserve their West African culture thanks to the area's isolation. The Penn Center anchors a historic grassy district with 19 buildings related to Gullah heritage, as well as a nature trail and a modest but informative museum.

Test the simple cuisine at St. Helena's no-frills Gullah Grub restaurant, filled with documents and artifacts tracing the area's culture. There's no better venue for rice and shrimp, catfish chowder, barbecue ribs, and seafood or okra gumbo. Sample more down-home eating at the roadside Shrimp Shack, where the delicious shrimp burgers and fresh seafood come from the docks across the road.

Hilton Head Island, just 40 miles and a universe away, is one of the most popular (and developed) resort areas on the eastern seaboard. It's a veritable playground with more than 20 championship golf courses and more than 300 tennis courts—of which 18 courses and 145 courts are open to the public.

WHERE: 70 miles south of Charleston. *Visitor info:* Tel 800-638-3525 or 843-525-8500; beaufortsc.org. **RHETT HOUSE INN:** Tel 888-480-9530 or 843-524-9030; rhetthouse inn.com. *Cost:* from $179 (off-peak), from $219 (peak). **PENN CENTER:** St. Helena. Tel 843-838-2432; penncenter.com. *When:* closed Sun. **GULLAH GRUB RESTAURANT:** St. Helena. Tel 843-838-3841; gullahgrubs.com. *Cost:* dinner $20. **SHRIMP SHACK:** St. Helena. Tel 843-838-2962. *Cost:* dinner $12. **BEST TIMES:** Apr–June and mid-Sept–Jan for weather; May for Beaufort's Gullah Festival; early July for the 10-day Beaufort Water Festival; 2nd weekend in Oct for the Shrimp Festival; 2nd weekend in Nov for Penn Center Heritage Days.

Nothing Could Be Finer

THE HEART OF CHARLESTON

Charleston, South Carolina

A t the time of the American Revolution, Charleston stood as one of the young nation's largest, wealthiest, and most dynamic communities, a city some called Little London. Plenty of cities have since surpassed Charleston in population, but this sultry and gracious metropolis at the confluence of the Cooper and Ashley rivers remains unparalleled in charm. Its downtown historic district contains one of the nation's largest collections of Colonial architecture, not to mention a fair share of distinctive Victorian beauties, all handsomely preserved. Charleston also seduces visitors with its antiques shops, amiable residents, and a plethora of sophisticated restaurants and cafés. More recently, the city's growing arts scene has transformed Charleston into a cultural gem.

The British laid much of Charleston to waste during the Revolution, and just one century later the city became the symbol of Southern resistance when the first shots of the Civil War were fired at Union-occupied Fort Sumter, which fell to Confederate forces. The stalwart fort still stands guard over Charleston Harbor and can be visited by ferry. Back on the mainland, the park service's Fort Sumter Visitor Education Center uses interactive exhibits to shed further light on the role the fort and the city played in the Civil War.

Take a crash course on the city's heritage at the Charleston Museum, the South's oldest (founded in 1773), in the upper part of the Historic District. The museum's extensive collection of cultural and historic artifacts trace the city's infamous legacy as a major slave-trade center, its development as a rice-shipping powerhouse (rice was king in this part of the antebellum South), and its eventual growth into a winter playground for wealthy industrialists. The museum also operates two meticulously preserved house museums, the 1803 Joseph Manigault House and the 1772 Heyward-Washington House, both of which are filled with priceless antiques that illustrate the life of the city's affluent residents during the city's Golden Age.

WHERE: 110 miles northeast of Savannah. *Visitor info:* Tel 800-774-0006 or 843-779-2881; charlestoncvb.com. **FORT SUMTER:** Tel 843-883-3123; nps.gov/fosu. **CHARLESTON MUSEUM:** Tel 843-722-2996; charlestonmuseum .org. **BEST TIMES:** mid- to late Mar for the peak blooming season; Mar–June and Sept–Dec for weather.

The first shot of the Civil War was fired at Fort Sumter, designed to house 135 guns and 650 men.

A Southern Belle Opens Its Heart

HISTORIC HOMES AND GARDENS OF CHARLESTON

Charleston, South Carolina

Imagine being admitted to Charleston's grandest homes, getting a peek inside to admire their intricately carved woodwork and museum-quality antiques, and being able to stroll through handsomely laid-out gardens that are otherwise off-limits to the public. You can do all this by taking one of the seasonal home tours that have become a prime draw to this belle of Southern cities. Choose between spring, when the Historic Charleston Foundation hosts its annual fundraiser, the Festival of Houses and Gardens, and fall, when the Preservation Society of Charleston hosts the similar Fall Tours of Homes and Gardens. The majority of these homes are open to the public only during these tours, offering visitors a new dimension of Southern hospitality.

Begun in 1947 by the Historic Charleston Foundation, the Festival of Houses and Gardens is one of the nation's most famous home tours, when more than 150 magnificent private houses and walled gardens open their doors to visitors. The festival kicks off with the prestigious Charleston International Antiques Show, an opportunity to browse for pieces similar to the furnishings you'll covet in the homes you tour. In addition to the house tours, several other excursions are offered during the festival. Glorious Gardens Tours explore both private and public landscaped gardens throughout the city, with guides discussing plantings, design, and history (spring's riot of blooms and fragrances make this the optimal time for viewing). The indefatigable can also begin their day with the informative two-hour walking tour through the shaded streets of Charleston's Historic District, offered each morning except Sunday during the festival.

The meticulously groomed gardens are as impressive as the grand homes they surround.

Established in 1920 with the mission of maintaining the city's distinctive and important architectural legacy, the Preservation Society of Charleston has been instrumental in saving and preserving houses and heightening public awareness about the significance of this historically unique city. The society has been hosting the Fall Tours of Homes since 1976, and like the Festival of Houses and Gardens, the event has grown dramatically in attendance. Tours are held on 21 evenings over four long weekends and cover a different neighborhood each day. On one evening, for example, guests may stroll through several fine Colonial homes along Rutledge Avenue, while the following evening may find them visiting the eclectic 19th-century houses of Vanderhorst Street.

For a historic overnight in a home-turned-inn, stay at the splendid Two Meeting Street Inn, the city's oldest continuously operating accommodation, having opened more than 50 years ago. With an impressive Queen Anne facade, the 1892 building that houses the romantic inn is even more resplendent indoors, with oak-paneled walls, stained-glass windows by Louis Tiffany, and nine guest rooms decorated with American and English Victorian antiques. Ask for the turreted Spell Room, the original master suite, which offers access to the curvaceous second-floor veranda. Breakfast in the courtyard is truly magical, amid the magnolias and azalea bushes, shaded by Japanese cherry trees and centuries-old oaks.

Visitor info: Tel 800-774-0006 or 843-779-2881; charlestoncvb.com. **Festival of Houses and Gardens:** Historic Charleston Foundation. Tel 843-722-3405; historic charleston.org. *Cost:* tour tickets $50. *When:* 4 weeks, beginning mid-Mar. **Fall Tours:** Preservation Society of Charleston. Tel 800-519-3849 or 843-722-4630; thefalltours.org. *Cost:* tour tickets $50. *When:* 4 consecutive long weekends beginning in late Sept. **Two Meeting Street Inn:** Tel 888-723-7322 or 843-723-7322; twomeetingstreet.com. *Cost:* from $215 (off-peak), from $259 (peak).

Mouthwatering Dining from the Old South and the New

Lowcountry Cuisine

Charleston, South Carolina

Taken by the spell of Charleston? Wait till you taste the food: This is the home of lowcountry cuisine, from South Carolina's coastal plain. A harmonious marriage of French, Spanish, African, and Caribbean influences took root here over the somewhat tumultuous centuries, drawing upon traditional ingredients like shrimp, oysters, crab, rice, grits, okra, fried greens, and tomatoes. As with other regional cuisines with staying power, lowcountry food has enjoyed a creative contemporary spin in recent years. At many of

Hominy Grill offers authentic Southern cooking for breakfast, lunch, dinner, and even brunch.

Charleston's top restaurants, you'll find a mix of tried-and-true classic recipes alongside more innovative dishes, like cashew-crusted grouper, or lobster-and-corn chowder.

Among the city's most hallowed culinary institutions are the Peninsula Grill (see p. 383) and Charleston Grill (see p. 384) and the slightly more casual but still highly refined, Magnolia's, housed in the city's original 1739 customs house. It is immensely popular with locals who come for the heavenly shrimp-and-sausage-grits or a lowcountry-inspired bouillabaisse that's packed with fresh fish and shellfish, andouille sausage, corn, and okra. For some of the city's most creative and stylish lowcountry fare, two trail-blazing favorites remain as popular with Charlestonians as out-of-towners. Zealous chef Sean Brock has secured Husk as one of the South's most beloved culinary destinations thanks to his love of all things heirloom, organic, and local. Also showcasing the distinct food traditions of the lowcountry is FIG (Food Is Good), where award-winning chef Mike Lata creates an ever-changing menu dictated by the seasons and his creative whims.

You can't really appreciate the high style of the New South until you've experienced the homey excellence of the no-frills Old South. For that, head to Hominy Grill, a beloved neighborhood restaurant with daily chalkboard specials and slow-spinning ceiling fans. Devotees adore the hearty breakfasts of buttermilk pancakes and biscuits with sausage gravy, but there's also delicious lunch and dinner, such as shrimp bog, similar to jambalaya, with andouille sausage and Carolina gold rice (leave room for the excellent sweet potato layer cake). Or join the legions of soul food fans at Jestine's Kitchen for corn bread with honey butter, crispy fried chicken, oyster po'boys, and the unforgettable chocolate-cola cake.

Since 1946, family-run Bowen's Island (on its own 13-acre island) is a down-home must, serving some of the best roasted oysters and fresh shrimp around. Rebuilt after a fire in 2006 destroyed much of the property, this beloved Charleston institution is still going strong with its famously casual and laid-back atmosphere. Try the "big ol' seafood platter" or enjoy shovelfuls of just-roasted oysters straight from Bowen's Island's own beds, best accompanied by ice-cold beer and inspiring views of the sea just outside.

Magnolia's: Tel 843-577-7771; magno liascharleston.com. *Cost:* dinner $50. **Husk:** Tel 843-577-2500; huskrestaurant.com. *Cost:* $65. **FIG:** Tel 843-805-5900; eatatfig.com. *Cost:* $60. **Hominy Grill:** Tel 843-937-0930; hominygrill.com. *Cost:* dinner $30. **Jestine's Kitchen:** Tel 843-722-7224; jestineskitchen .com. *Cost:* dinner $21. **Bowen's Island:** Tel 843-795-2757. *Cost:* dinner $15. **Best times:** late Jan–early Feb for the Lowcountry Oyster Festival; late Sept–early Oct for the MOJA Arts Festival (mojafestival.com); late Sept for the Taste of Charleston festival.

Eloquent Testimony to America's Heritage

Plantations of the Ashley River

Charleston, South Carolina

The fertile land along the Ashley River was once covered by rice farms that launched the vast fortunes of local planters, from the 17th through 19th centuries. Several of these dramatic plantations are connected by the 11-mile stretch of Highway 61 known as the Ashley River Road National Scenic Byway. Leave Charleston behind and pay homage to a time when rice was king and the easy lowcountry living for some came at a terrible cost for others.

Drayton Hall is one of the oldest and finest examples of Georgian-Palladian architecture in the U.S., having been proudly maintained for seven generations. The nation's oldest plantation house museum open to the public, Drayton was never modernized—there is no running water, electric lighting, or central heating—and remains much as it was when John Drayton built it in the mid-18th century. Known for its enlightening historical and architectural tour (there are no furnishings) and a contemplative walk through the 630-acre property, it illustrates the lives of slaves, workers, and Drayton family members who lived and toiled here from the 18th through the early 20th centuries. Each December, a capella concerts of African American spirituals in the candlelit Great Hall offer a moving opportunity to hear music similar to that which was sung in the fields and "praise houses" in the lowcountry.

One of the great showpieces of the South, and considered by the late travel writer Charles Kuralt as his "greatest Charleston pleasure," Magnolia Plantation is renowned for its spectacular 30-acre gardens. Welcoming visitors since just after the Civil War, these are the oldest public gardens in America, with breathtaking displays of azaleas and camellias that date to the plantation's late-1600s origins. Magnolia Plantation was established by the same wealthy family of Drayton Hall, and 15 generations of the Drayton family have lived here to this day. A 45-minute "Nature Train" tour allows a look at restored slave cabins, a Native American ceremonial mound, and alligators splashing around in a cypress swamp.

Middleton Place is named for its original owner, Henry Middleton, president of the first Continental Congress. The baronial estate was first built in 1705, with expansive grounds that contain 65 acres of one of America's oldest and most stunning gardens landscaped after the grand classic style, the vogue in Europe at that time. The current house is a 1755 guest wing that became the primary residence when the plantation house was destroyed during the Civil War. Today it contains a priceless trove of museum-quality furniture, family portraits, and paintings. Touring the original Plantation Stableyards and Eliza's House (a preserved slave dwelling) provides an insightful account of the hardships and contributions of the slaves who built and sustained the country's plantations. Middleton Place's acclaimed restaurant serves first-rate lowcountry cuisine.

Adjacent to the plantation and secluded among tall pines and massive live oaks, the contemporary Inn at Middleton Place offers a

striking minimalist contrast to Ashley Road's historic plantation homes. The 55 airy rooms with floor-to-ceiling windows occupy four postmodern buildings with wood floors, plantation shutters, and understated, handcrafted wood furniture.

East of Charleston, Boone Hall Plantation is approached via the regal half-mile Avenue of the Oaks, a corridor of live oaks that date from 1743. The plantation house is actually a 1930s replica of the original. Scenes from the 2004 film *The Notebook* were shot on the 738-acre grounds of this beautiful estate. Boone Hall is the popular venue for both the annual Taste of Charleston festival in late September, when dozens of local eateries dish up their finest fare, and the Lowcountry Oyster Festival in January.

A red footbridge crosses a pond in the lush gardens of Magnolia Plantation.

WHERE: within 15 miles of downtown Charleston. **ASHLEY RIVER ROAD:** byways.org. **DRAYTON HALL:** Tel 843-769-2600; drayton hall.org. **MAGNOLIA PLANTATION:** Tel 800-367-3517 or 843-571-1266; magnoliaplantation .com. **MIDDLETON PLACE:** Tel 800-782-3608 or 843-556-6020; middletonplace.org. *Cost:* dinner $50. **INN AT MIDDLETON PLACE:** Tel 800-543-4774 or 843-556-0500; theinnatmiddleton place.com. *Cost:* from $165 (off-peak), from $225 (peak). **BOONE HALL PLANTATION:** Mount Pleasant. Tel 843-884-4371; boonehall plantation.com. **BEST TIMES:** Drayton Hall hosts oyster-roast picnics during the Annual Festival of Houses and Gardens in mid-Mar–mid-Apr. Plantation gardens are most colorful from early Mar–early Oct; in Dec the plantations are decorated for Christmas.

A Southern City's Architectural Jewels

THE ROMANTIC INNS OF CHARLESTON

Charleston, South Carolina

Charleston is undeniably one of America's most elegant cities, perfectly suited for strolling the leafy backstreets and enjoying the hidden stories they reveal. But check into any of its highly romantic hostelries, where over-the-top sumptuousness is the rule, and you may very well never leave your room. The alluring roster of possibilities includes Charleston Place (see next page), and Two Meeting Street Inn (see p. 379), but few hotels enjoy a more enviable location than the Planters Inn, a quiet 62-room oasis beside the bustling City Market, where artisans sell arts and crafts and horse-drawn carriage tours gather. The property was neglected for decades before a painstaking restoration in the mid-'90s and the construction of a lavish neighboring wing. Rooms are smartly furnished with high-quality colonial antiques and convincing reproductions; in many, working fireplaces amp up the romance factor. The stunning inn's highly regarded Peninsula Grill is one of the city's great temples of New South cuisine, serving coastal favorites with a discrete twist.

For a chance to relive Charleston's heyday as a winter playground for America's wealthiest industrialists, stay at the spectacular Wentworth Mansion, a Second Empire wedding cake that dates to 1886. A lavish top-to-toe renovation in the mid-'90s resuscitated its old glory, complete with Tiffany stained-glass windows, hand-carved marble fireplaces, and a soaring rooftop cupola. The Wentworth has 21 spacious rooms and suites, most with gas fireplaces, all overseen by a young, house-proud staff. One of Charleston's most respected eating destinations is Circa 1886, located in the carriage house just behind the inn, where chef Marc Collins creates artful lowcountry dishes, such as tender buttermilk chicken with wild rice pilaf.

The Wentworth's nearby sister property, the 19-room John Rutledge House Inn, reveals an entirely different period of Charleston: its prosperous colonial years. Built by one of the 55 signers of the U.S. Constitution, the house hosted George Washington. Although it was built in 1763, the house's Italianate exterior (complete with lavish ironwork) and quite a few of its interior details were added during the mid-19th century. The rooms in the grand original residence, with their 13-foot ceilings and elaborate plaster moldings, are the most opulent, while those in two adjoining carriage houses offer more privacy and no less character.

VISITOR INFO: Tel 800-774-0006 or 843-853-8000; charlestoncvb.com. **PLANTERS INN:** Tel 800-845-7082 or 843-722-2345; plantersinn.com. *Cost:* from $260 (off-peak), from $300 (peak); dinner at Peninsula Grill $70. **WENTWORTH MANSION:** Tel 888-466-1886 or 843-853-1886; wentworthmansion.com. *Cost:* from $310 (off-peak), from $440 (peak); dinner at Circa 1886 $55. **JOHN RUTLEDGE HOUSE INN:** Tel 800-476-9741 or 843-723-7999; johnrutledgehouseinn.com. *Cost:* from $169 (off-peak), from $219 (peak). **BEST TIMES:** spring and fall for weather and city events; Dec when the inns are decked out beautifully for the holidays.

An Eclectic All-Purpose Arts Explosion

SPOLETO FESTIVAL USA

Charleston, South Carolina

Few events in America are more closely associated with their respective cities than Spoleto is with Charleston. This 17-day festival has become the most important arts showcase in the South, with more than 150 performances of opera, dance, theater, and music—from symphonic to choral to jazz. It originated in 1977 as the American counterpart to the Festival of Two Worlds in Spoleto, Italy, begun by the late Italian-born American composer Gian Carlo Menotti in 1958. He also established Spoleto USA and in a particularly apt city: Charleston was the first American city to stage opera, in 1735. Menotti withdrew years ago, but his efforts helped spawn a full revitalization of this already culturally rich city. The growing popularity of Spoleto inspired the concurrent Piccolo Spoleto, which captures the irreverent spirit of the famed Edinburgh Fringe Festival and brings hundreds of additional musical and theatrical performances (mostly free or inexpensive) by artists of the Southeast region.

The main Spoleto Festival, however, is hardly stuffy. It draws youthful, cutting-edge performers from all over the world and cultivates an air of vitality and creativity. Past performers include Mikhail Baryshnikov, Renée Fleming, humorist David Sedaris, violinist Joshua Bell, and the Emerson String Quartet. The excitement peaks with the Festival Finale symphonic concert under a panoply of stars and brilliant fireworks at the 18th-century riverside Middleton Place plantation (see p. 382), 15 miles northeast of Charleston. It's a long-standing custom for concertgoers to bring lavish preconcert picnic dinners (local celebrity judges wander from blanket to blanket awarding prizes), and many arrive early to enjoy America's first landscaped gardens.

The elegant Charleston Place is the favored roost, right in the heart of the city's historic district. Festival performers and goers help fill this grand 440-room hotel, with its sumptuous lobby, glittering Venetian chandelier, and sweeping staircases. Rooms are predictably cushy, and the full-service spa is the perfect venue for a warm-stone massage between performances. The hotel's refined, clubby restaurant, the Charleston Grill, serves sophisticated lowcountry fare, the specialty of master chef Michelle Weaver, to the nightly sounds of a jazz trio.

WHERE: various venues in downtown Charleston. Tel 843-579-3100; spoletousa.org. *Cost:* tickets from $20; Festival Finale $35. *When:* 17 days in late May–early June. **CHARLESTON PLACE:** Tel 888-635-2350 or 843-722-4900; charlestonplace.com. *Cost:* from $265; dinner $72. **BEST TIMES:** 2nd and 3rd weekends, when tickets and hotel accommodations are more easily available.

The Spoleto Festival USA features all kinds of performing arts from opera to modern dance.

The Town That Rice Built

GEORGETOWN

South Carolina

South Carolina's third-oldest city differs from many other historic Southern coastal communities not by what it has, but by what it doesn't have: swarms of tourists. With a handsome riverside downtown rife with Colonial and Victorian buildings, and a handful of easygoing but sophisticated B&Bs, antiques shops, and unpretentious seafood restaurants, Georgetown is an underrated gem. Twelve miles from the Atlantic, it offers the perfect antidote to crowded Myrtle Beach (40 miles north) and pricier Charleston (60 miles south). The town developed as a prominent rice producer, an industry fed by five lazy rivers that are now known for kayaking, canoeing, and bird-watching.

Locals here are proud of Georgetown's low-key, lowcountry vibe. Zoning laws keep out miniature-golf centers and buildings taller than three stories, and careful preservation of more than 50 antebellum structures sustains a flavor of yesteryear and a hint of the town's rice planters' aristocratic lifestyle. Downtown's Harborwalk overlooks the Sampit River, where tall ships once loaded up with local goods—"Carolina Gold" (a rice variety prized in Europe whose seeds came from Madagascar), indigo (used for blue dye), cotton, and timber—en route to Europe. The Rice Museum occupies the town's Old Market Building and Kaminski Hardware Building, where displays tell the story of the region's former rice-derived riches. During the 18th and 19th centuries the region produced nearly half the total U.S. rice crop.

With Charleston just an hour's drive away, a daytrip here is easy and fun—and delicious, if you stop at the Atlantic House, a perennial lunch-only favorite, or at Townhouse, the dinner venue of choice. Don't miss the chance to spend the night at the 18th-century Mansfield Plantation on a 900-acre spread that was once one of the largest rice plantations in the states.

WHERE: 60 miles north of Charleston. *Visitor info:* Tel 800-777-7705 or 843-546-8436; georgetownchamber.com. **RICE MUSEUM:** Tel 843-546-7423; ricemuseum.org. **ATLANTIC HOUSE:** Tel 843-520-6918; atlantichouserestaurant.com. *Cost:* lunch $15. **TOWNHOUSE:** Tel 843-527-2021. *Cost:* $30. **MANSFIELD PLANTATION:** Tel 866-717-1776; mansfieldplantation.com. *Cost:* from $150. **BEST TIME:** Treasures of the Wooden Boat Show in late Oct.

Downtown's Harborwalk is an ideal place to spend a laid-back afternoon and catch a fresh fish lunch.

Links in the Lowcountry

KIAWAH ISLAND

South Carolina

The Charleston area's pine- and palmetto-strewn barrier islands have long helped protect the historic city from the full brunt of hurricanes, but sports enthusiasts appreciate them for their scenic, challenging golf courses.

Kiawah Island, in particular, is one of the most talked-about golfing resorts in North America, one enhanced by the stunning Sanctuary hotel at its core.

The land was the domain of Kiawah Indians when Europeans began populating the region during the mid-17th century. Fast-forward to the 1970s, when eco-minded developers purchased the then–nearly deserted, 10,000-acre island, and designed the handsome yet restrained residential community that has become an exemplar for coastal resort planning. It's not unusual to see wild deer darting among the sea oats and myrtle trees or to glimpse an osprey or a bald eagle.

Kiawah Island Golf Resort manages more than 550 villas, condos, and private homes on the island, but the Sanctuary is the jewel in its crown. Designed with an eye toward local history, this contemporary four-story property recalls Greek Revival plantation architecture, with vintage building materials (wrought iron and hammered copper, wide-plank floors, and weathered brick) and regal gardens. More than 160 transplanted live oaks complete a scenario that oozes *Gone With the Wind*, while the spa's list of replenishing treatments includes a thermal infusing facial using all-natural products and an island stone massage. Of the 255 rooms and suites, even the smallest are spacious; most have French doors opening onto balconies with vistas of the esteemed Jack Nicklaus–designed Turtle Point golf course and the frothy Atlantic beyond. Golfers can choose among five different top-ranked courses at Kiawah Island resort—a tough choice. The famed Ocean Course invariably lands atop the heap. Designed by Pete Dye, it has hosted the Ryder Cup and World Cup and has humbled the world's greatest golfers. Its sister course Osprey Point, a Tom Fazio layout, runs a close second.

But Kiawah Island Resort is much more than a golfing retreat. Its sterling tennis facilities—including 24 Har-Tru and hard courts—are highly acclaimed. Ten miles of uninterrupted beachfront are ideal for early morning walks, while bikers and hikers can get happily lost on some 30 miles of paved forest trails. With this much pristine coastline, kayaking, canoeing, and boating tours and rentals are at the ready, and angling enthusiasts can alternate time on the golf course with casting a line or two for

Nestled between wide expanses of ocean and forest, the Sanctuary embodies the serenity of Kiawah Island.

flounder, tarpon, or other game fish. Dining and cocktail options are many, but the special-occasion destination is the Ocean Room at the Sanctuary, a romantic venue with ocean views and stellar New American fare.

WHERE: 21 miles southwest of Charleston. **KIAWAH ISLAND GOLF RESORT:** Tel 800-576-1570 or 843-768-2121; kiawahresort.com. *Cost:* from $240 (off-peak), from $545 (peak); greens fees at Ocean Course from $255; dinner at Ocean Room $75. **BEST TIMES:** popular year-round, but spring and fall enjoy the best combination of verdant greenery and moderate climes.

Golf and Seafood Amid the Dunes and Marshlands

PAWLEYS ISLAND

South Carolina

O ver many decades, the Palmetto State's coast has developed into a golfer's paradise. In some areas, the transformation from wild ocean dunes and untouched wetlands has been jarring. But the tiny, low-key resort community of Pawleys Island on the south end of the Grand Strand—and connected to the mainland by two bridges—with just 103 permanent residents, has retained its unspoiled air. Amid the island's lovely salt marshes and beaches, ten golf courses look as though they were laid down by Mother Nature.

The Jack Nicklaus–designed 18-hole course and first-rate golf school distinguish Pawleys Plantation Golf and Country Club among the area's many resorts. Meandering creeks and estuaries and reedy marshes come into play along many fairways. One hundred and eighty stylish one- to four-bedroom villas and town houses with fully equipped kitchens, hot tubs, and pretty patios lure guests into dreaming they could easily retire here. You can play tennis or do laps in the pool, or explore Pawleys Island's other golf offerings, namely the Caledonia Golf & Fish Club, which consistently ranks among the top public courses in the nation. The meandering, pine-studded course has been laid out over a former rice plantation beside the Waccamaw River, and the clubhouse is an exact replica of an 18th-century planter's house, reminiscent of a lifestyle long gone.

If golf isn't your thing, Pawleys Island is also a great location for bird-watching.

But beyond the world of beach resorts and golf clubs, there is plenty to be enjoyed for those in search of a barefoot walk back in time. The charming, old-style Sea View Inn, right on the ocean, prides itself on the absence of TV and A.C., and offers three delicious home-cooked meals to the guests of its 20 simple rooms. The much-loved beachfront Pelican Inn is a friendly eight-room contender, also proudly keeping the island's "shabby chic" aesthetic alive.

It's only a 10-mile drive northeast of Pawleys Island to the picturesque fishing village of Murrells Inlet, justly considered South Carolina's best destination for seafood. Close your eyes and pick from the town's dozens of great restaurants for that only-in-South-Carolina evening.

WHERE: 70 miles northeast of Charleston. *Visitor info:* Tel 800-777-7705 or 843-546-8436; georgetownchamber.com. **PAWLEYS PLANTATION:** Tel 877-648-4007 or 843-237-6000; pawleysplantation.com. *Cost:* from $75 (off-peak), from $130 (peak); greens fees from $62. **CALEDONIA GOLF & FISH CLUB:** Tel 800-483-6800 or 843-237-3675; fishclub.com/caledonia. *Cost:* greens fees from $90. **SEA VIEW INN:** Tel 843-237-4235; seaviewinn.com. *Cost:* from $225, all inclusive. **PELICAN INN:** Tel 843-325-7522; pawleyspelican.com. *Cost:* $250, all inclusive. **BEST TIMES:** late Sept for Atalaya Arts & Crafts Festival at nearby Huntington Beach State Park; early Oct for the 2-week Pawleys Island Festival of Music & Art (pawleysmusic.com); Dec for holiday lights during Nights of a Thousand Candles.

MISSISSIPPI VALLEY

ARKANSAS • KENTUCKY •
LOUISIANA • MISSISSIPPI •
MISSOURI • TENNESSEE

MISSISSIPPI
VALLEY

Pristine and Free-Flowing

BUFFALO NATIONAL RIVER

Arkansas

The Buffalo is that great rarity: 150 miles of pure, wild water with not a dam in sight. Snaking past towering limestone bluffs, it is one of the nation's prettiest places for canoeing and a stellar example of why Arkansas, with its mountains, rivers, and abundant wildlife, is called "The Natural State."

Sufficiently scenic to be singled out for protection as America's first national river back in 1972, the emerald green Buffalo starts as a trickle in the Ozarks and flows eastward before merging with the White River (see p. 396). A 95,000-acre national park stretches for 135 miles on both sides, protecting a magnificent mix of oak and hickory forests, open fields, and box canyons—a wild landscape that supports mink, beaver, bobcat, even elk and black bear.

The best way to see the Buffalo is by canoe—whether on half-day trips or leisurely ten-day explorations that take you camping down the length of the river. You can bring your own canoe or rent one from outfitters who set you in the river at any one of 20 access points and have your car waiting for you wherever you pull out. To navigate the scenic upper Buffalo, featuring the 500-foot Big Bluff, you can rent a canoe or rubber raft at the Buffalo Outdoor Center in Ponca; the center also offers log cabins and a mile-long zip-line canopy tour that lasts two to three hours. Azalea Falls Lodge offers two rental homes as well as elegant rooms in the Beauty Lodge B&B.

Along the river there's a stretch for every skill level, from the Class I and II white-water rapids of the upper Buffalo in early spring to the easy family jaunts of the middle and lower Buffalo, which can be floated year-round. The parkland on either side of the Buffalo invites other forms of exploration, especially hiking.

The Rimrock Cove Ranch offers guided horseback rides and even hayrides on trails that wind through woods and meadows up to the top of the bluffs for panoramic scenes that have changed precious little over the centuries.

WHERE: Tyler Bend visitors center near St. Joe is 110 miles northwest of Little Rock. Tel 870-439-2502; nps.gov/buff. **BUFFALO OUTDOOR CENTER:** Ponca. Tel 800-221-5514 or 870-861-5514; buffaloriver.com. *Cost:* $62 per canoe per day; cabins from $129; zip-line canopy tour $89. **AZALEA FALLS LODGE:** Kingston. Tel 870-420-3941; azaleafalls.com. *Cost:* from $135 for the B&B. **RIMROCK COVE RANCH:** Ponca. Tel 870-553-2556; rimrockcoveranch.com. *Cost:* $35 per person per hour for horseback rides. **BEST TIMES:** spring and early summer for float trips.

The 150-mile Buffalo National River passes through a lush and scenic national park.

Victorian Village in the Mountains

EUREKA SPRINGS

Arkansas

L iterally built into the side of the Ozarks, the tiny village of Eureka Springs is a charming collection of Victorian architecture and higgledy-piggledy streets snaking past cliff-clinging homes, confounding new visitors. Folks easily fall in love with this place, so appealingly antithetical to modern urban planning. It is the only city in the country whose entire downtown area is on the National Register of Historic Places—and there's not a traffic light to be found.

With a population that hovers around 2,000, Eureka Springs is tucked away in the remote and lush northwest corner of Arkansas. Surrounded by miles of lakes and rivers and packed with small shops, galleries, B&Bs, and hotels, Eureka Springs' Victorian charm is remarkably intact. Founded as a health resort in 1879, Eureka benefited from at least 63 reputedly curative springs, used for both drinking and bathing at a time when society was mad for water cures. Health-seekers immediately began arriving by stagecoach, but the resort town's success was assured with the arrival of the railroad in 1882 and the wilderness was transformed into a flourishing resort spa.

A French Gothic "Grand Old Lady of the Ozarks" from the town's heyday, the 1886 Crescent Hotel & Spa (a sister property to the younger 1905 Basin Park Hotel) is so famous for ghosts that it conducts daily tours of spectral sightings. Thrill-seekers always request room 218, where guests have heard the cries of a falling man. Scared yet? Calm down at the hotel's modern New Moon Spa or with a historic bath experience at the Palace Hotel and Bath House, around since 1901. Most people go for "The Works"—a mineral bath in a 7-foot long claw-foot tub followed by a eucalyptus steam treatment and 30-minute massage.

Since 1979, Bubba's has been serving up gigantic pork shoulder sandwiches and tender baby back ribs; true pork junkies come to do battle with the Bubba Link, a lightly spiced, hickory-smoked sausage smothered with thick chili and gobs of cheddar cheese on ciabatta bread.

Eureka Springs was rediscovered by hippies in the 1970s and ever since has been a haven for artists, with more than 30 galleries. An independent Ozark spirit permeates the town, at its best during the May Festival of the Arts. Locals turn out in droves for the White Street Walk, when artists open up their studios and homes to anyone who cares to visit, while outside there's dancing in the moonlit streets. Music lovers arrive in town for the Eureka Springs Blues Festival and the Ozark Folk Festival, both promising to keep various clubs and bars around town full with the sound of music.

The No. 1 tourist draw for the area is the outdoor drama called the *Great Passion Play*, a 2-hour reenactment of Christ's final days. Nearby is a monumental sculpture known as Christ of the Ozarks—an all-white, 67-foot-high figure with arms starkly outstretched, suggesting a cross. Dedicated in 1966, it is the work of Emmet Sullivan, who had his training in the field of oversized sculpture while working at Mount Rushmore (see p. 657).

WHERE: 182 miles northwest of Little Rock. *Visitor info:* Tel 479-253-7333; eurekasprings.org. **CRESCENT HOTEL:** Tel 877-342-9766 or 479-253-9766; crescent-hotel.com. *Cost:* from $150 (off-peak), from $200 (peak).

PALACE HOTEL AND BATH HOUSE: Tel 866-946-0572 or 479-253-7474; palacehotelbath house.com. *Cost:* rooms from $129 (off-peak), from $189 (peak); $80 for "The Works". **BUBBA'S:** Tel 479-253-7706; bubbasbarbecue eurekasprings.com. *Cost:* Bubba Link $9. *GREAT*

PASSION PLAY: Tel 800-882-7529 or 479-253-9200; greatpassionplay.com. *Cost:* $27. *When:* May–Oct. **BEST TIMES:** May for the Festival of the Arts; Father's Day weekend for Eureka Springs Blues Festival; 2nd weekend in Oct for Ozark Folk Festival.

Where the King Biscuit Show Began

KING BISCUIT BLUES FESTIVAL

Helena, Arkansas

If you want to hear authentic Delta blues, just show up in October for the King Biscuit Blues Festival. With a tradition of cotton-growing and sharecropping in the deep alluvial soils of the Delta, eastern Arkansas is closer culturally to Mississippi than to the mountainous western part of the state. And nowhere is that clearer than in the small river-port town of Helena (population 11,500) on the banks of the Mississippi.

Delta blues, characterized by a spare style and passionate vocals, might have remained in the fields and juke joints were it not for *King Biscuit Time*, a radio show broadcast out of Helena since 1941. Sponsored by King Biscuit flour, it originally featured local talent —guitarist Robert Lockwood Jr., harmonica

The three-day King Biscuit Blues Festival draws the country's best Delta blues musicians to the stage.

player Sonny Boy Williamson, and (starting in 1951) host Sonny "Sunshine" Payne—and was such a huge success that it made Helena a center for the blues. *King Biscuit Time* is still a daily show produced out of the Delta Cultural Center, a museum that preserves the cultural heritage of the Arkansas Delta, a 27-county region covering the eastern third of the state.

In 1986, the King Biscuit Blues Festival began as a one-day event held on the back of a flatbed truck, and over the years it's become one of the best-known blues festivals in the country. (From 2005 to 2011 it was briefly called the Arkansas Blues & Heritage Festival, but with a legal glitch now cleared up it has returned to its original name.) Today's Delta blues legend Bobby Rush continues showing up for the three-day festival, featuring 60 artists including headliners like Taj Mahal and Jimmie Vaughan.

And the flavor is unchanged. Music runs on several stages down by the levee and spills out into the streets of downtown, where blues musicians unfold a chair, open up their guitar cases, and play their hearts out. You couldn't ask for a nicer setting: Helena sits on an unusually pretty site at the tip of Crowley's Ridge, a long, low hill formed when the Mississippi shifted course millions of years ago.

Here's the rub: finding a place to lay your head (the whole town has only 350 hotel rooms). The best B&B in town is the Edwardian Inn, a 1904 Colonial Revival home with quarter-sawn oak paneling, staircases, and ceilings. Music lovers from England, the Netherlands, and Germany pay their deposits well over a year in advance (though you can try the waiting list). Most folks are willing to travel from towns just over the border in Mississippi like Clarksdale (see p. 435), Batesville, Tunica—or east from Little Rock, over two hours away, or southwest from Memphis (see p. 468). It's worth the drive.

WHERE: 120 miles east of Little Rock. Tel 870-572-5223; kingbiscuitfestival.com. *When:* 3 days in early Oct. *Cost:* $50 for 3 days' access to main stage; 4 other stages are free. **DELTA CULTURAL CENTER:** Tel 800-358-0972 or 870-338-4350; deltaculturalcenter.com. *When:* closed Sun–Mon. **EDWARDIAN INN:** Tel 870-338-9155; edwardianinn.com. *Cost:* $540 for 3-day minimum during festival; from $95 otherwise.

America's First Spa

HOT SPRINGS

Arkansas

The word "spa" comes from the Latin phrase *sanus per aquam*, or "health through water." And with its dozens of hot springs, healing thermal waters protected within an urban national park, this is America's very first spa in the purest sense. A destination for the wealthy and others in search of cures since the 19th century, Hot Springs was considered such a precious resource that it was named a federal reservation in 1832. It still has the grandest collection of bathhouses in America—eight European-style spas called Bathhouse Row, built in the early 20th century with such grand amenities as stained-glass windows and billiards rooms. With magnificent magnolias in front of the bathhouses and a sweeping, brick-lined Grand Promenade behind, the elegant spas evoke a leisurely time when people flocked here to take a three-week, 21-bath cure.

An imposing neoclassical structure with massive columns and blue-and-white-striped awnings, the Buckstaff Bathhouse has been in continuous operation since 1912 and still offers the elaborate bathing ritual of bygone days. It begins with a 20-minute whirlpool bath and proceeds through various mysterious-sounding but delicious-feeling treatments, including hot packs, sitz baths, steam cabinets, and needle showers, best enjoyed when followed by a Swedish massage.

Therapeutic baths fell out of favor in the U.S. in the 1960s, and most of the bathhouses stand empty in various stages of preservation. The newly renovated Quapaw Baths & Spa, built in 1922, reopened in 2007. The grandest one of all, Fordyce Bathhouse, has been reincarnated as a visitors center for Hot Springs National Park, which boasts 26 miles of hiking trails that lead up Hot Springs Mountain. From here the town's hot springs emanate at the mighty warm temperature of 143°F before being regulated for public use. Hike through dense oak forest to the Hot Springs Mountain Tower and a panoramic view of both the heavily wooded city and the nearby Ouachita Mountains.

Artists began flocking to Hot Springs in the 1990s, making it a hot spot for galleries as well as arts festivals. The subject of the documentary *The Sound of Dreams*, the Hot Springs Music Festival celebrates classical music through symphony and song as 125 apprentices are mentored by 30 masters. The Documentary Film Festival is the year's other highlight, proving so successful that a year-round institute now enjoys a permanent home in the ultra-cool 1950s-era Malco Theater.

Plan to arrive or depart by means of the Arkansas Scenic 7 Byway (you can pick it up 30 miles from here), 160 miles up over hills and down into valleys, offering a mesmerizing show of great natural beauty.

WHERE: 50 miles southwest of Little Rock. *Park info:* Tel 800-772-2489 or 501-620-6715; nps.gov/hosp. *Hot Springs visitor info:* Tel 800-543-2284 or 501-321-2277; hotsprings .org. **BUCKSTAFF BATHHOUSE:** Tel

501-623-2308; buckstaffbaths.com. *Cost:* $71 for Traditional Bathing Package with massage. *When:* closed Sun. **ARKANSAS BYWAY:** byways.org. **BEST TIMES:** early June for Music Festival; 3rd week of Oct for Documentary Film Festival.

The eight historic spas along Bathhouse Row hark back to the early 20th century, the heyday of theraputic treatments.

The Hottest Thing Going

MCCLARD'S BAR-B-Q

Hot Springs, Arkansas

Barbecue brings out fiery passions in otherwise cool-headed people, and nowhere is this more evident than in Arkansas. While grown men resort to fisticuffs when discussing who serves the best barbecue in the country,

President Bill Clinton, weatherman Willard Scott, and the band Aerosmith have all weighed in on the side of McClard's Bar-B-Q, whose crusty-on-the-outside, pink-on-the-inside ribs have been wowing customers since 1928. (When Clinton was in office and passing through, McClard's would run a special order out to *Air Force One*.) Located within Hot Springs National Park (see previous entry), McClard's Bar-B-Q got its start when motel owners Alex and Gladys McClard had a customer who couldn't pay his $10 bill. He

offered his secret recipe for the world's greatest barbecue sauce in lieu of cash, and a deal was struck.

In 1942, McClard's moved into a white-washed stucco building with neon signs, and it's been the scene of mealtime pandemonium ever since as barbecue lovers line up at two different entryways. The blowout dish to order here is Ribs and Fry, a hefty slab of ribs requiring only a gentle pull to separate the sweet meat from the bone, completely buried under a mountain of hand-cut, perfectly golden french fries. The secret here is an old-fashioned hickory pit—no gas starters and nothing electric.

The spotlight may be on the ribs, but no one passes on a side of McClard's barbecued beans, which capture the authentic Ozarks spirit with their hot, sweet, tangy flavor.

McClard's Bar-B-Q serves more than 7,000 pounds of meat, 3,000 pounds of fries, and 250 gallons of beans each week.

Another place to go in search of Arkansas barbecue is Craig's, an unrepentantly dumpy shack in DeValls Bluff (population 589), where the smoky ribs and piles of chopped pork are brushed with a thick, spicy sauce made with Laurence Craig's own secret ingredient—a healthy dose of meat drippings from the hams that are cooked in the pit he built in the 1940s. Mr. Craig has since passed, but it's still in the family, who closely follow his time-honored traditions. Here, the standout side dish is coleslaw snapping with crispness and spiked with apple and green pepper.

Where: 505 Albert Pike. Tel 501-623-9665; mcclards.com. *Cost:* Ribs and Fry $15. **Craig's:** DeValls Bluff. Tel 870-998-2616. *Cost:* rib dinner $9.

The World's Largest Brown Trout

THE WHITE RIVER

Lakeview, Arkansas

Y ou don't have to be an expert angler to bag your limit in the cold, clear waters of the White River, renowned for the best trout fishing in America. All up and down the lush, green river, rainbow trout practically jump into

your boat, courtesy of state and federal hatcheries that stock it with 1.2 million farm-raised rainbows every year. The wily brown trout stands apart: wise to the ways of fisherfolk, it is the trophy that expert anglers seek. Get out on the river early, when the heavy fog turns orange with the sunrise, and you might snag a 5- or 6-pound brown trout—you might even give the 40-pound, 4-ounce record some competition. The trout grow to gargantuan sizes here because conditions are ideal—a constant water temperature near 50°F year-round and an ample food source.

Wild cutthroat and brook trout are also found in these waters, though they're elusive. The White River is one of the rare places where it's possible to bag the Grand Slam of trout: brown, rainbow, cutthroat, and brook. It was not always like this. The White River used to be a warm-water river with bream, catfish, and smallmouth bass, but the building of Bull Shoals Dam in 1951 made the water too cold for the native fish. To make up for it, the federal government agreed to stock trout.

The dam is also what makes conditions so challenging for anglers in search of the brown trout. The waters rise and drop unpredictably in a single day, depending on how many of the dam's generators are open, and finding the best fishing in shifting conditions requires extensive knowledge of the area. You're better off using professional guides, no matter what your angling expertise.

Some of the best guides can be found at Gaston's White River Resort, 78 cottages perched on 2 miles of riverfront with a landing strip for private planes. The cottages are decorated with wood paneling and colonial furniture, and some offer fireplaces and redwood decks. The restaurant has a "you catch 'em, we cook 'em" policy, but serves plenty of trout dishes for those who didn't make it out onto the river. You can sign up for fly-fishing classes, too.

WHERE: 150 miles north of Little Rock. **GASTON'S WHITE RIVER RESORT:** Tel 870-431-5202; gastons.com. *Cost:* cottages from $105 without kitchen, from $162 with kitchen. **BEST TIMES:** Jan–Mar for the best brown trout fishing; Mar–Nov for most comfortable weather.

Arkansas's Most Famous Son

WILLIAM J. CLINTON PRESIDENTIAL CENTER

Little Rock, Arkansas

Our 42nd president has always been a bit larger than life, so it's no surprise that the William J. Clinton Presidential Library Complex is one of the largest and most popular of all the presidential libraries in the U.S. (it attracts 300,000 visitors per year).

Literally perched over the Arkansas River, the Clinton Presidential Center is a modern architectural masterwork that evokes, by some accounts, both a $165 million double-wide and a Star Wars battle cruiser hovering in flight. (You might be more inclined to agree with the intended symbolism: a bridge to the 21st century.) Highlights of the museum include a life-size replica of the Oval Office, the armored Cadillac limousine used for the second Clinton inauguration, and the sunglasses he wore while playing sax on *The Arsenio Hall Show*. For students of history, there's a 100-foot-long time line of the Clinton presidency (1993 to 2001), from successes to scandals.

Set in 30-acre Clinton Park on the eastern fringe of downtown Little Rock, the center is no mere repository of papers and memorabilia, but an embodiment of President Clinton's philosophy of what can be accomplished through good government. On the formerly contaminated site of abandoned warehouses, the center was itself constructed with the latest "green" building materials and techniques. And it has helped spark a renaissance in downtown Little Rock, where a $20 million trolley system links the center to hotels and the bustling River Market District, a restored food hall filled with shops and restaurants on the banks of the Arkansas River. Things really rev up here during the annual RiverFest, a three-day music extravaganza with 100 acts on five stages.

Other stops on the Clinton trail include the Governor's Mansion and the Old State House Museum, an 1836 Greek Revival structure where Clinton launched both of his presidential bids and which now serves as a museum of Arkansas history. It's an easy 50-mile drive to Hot Springs (see p. 394) to pass by three important Clinton touchstones: the house he lived in from age 7; Park Place Baptist Church, which he attended through high school; and the former Hot Springs High School, where he played tenor saxophone in the band (and in a jazz trio called The Three Kings), which now houses artists as the Clinton Cultural Campus.

At the 1992 Democratic National Convention, Clinton ended his acceptance speech by saying, "I still believe in a place called Hope." Tucked away in the southwest corner of the state, about 110 miles from Little Rock, the town of Hope is where Clinton had two boyhood homes and attended kindergarten and first grade. The President William Jefferson Clinton Birthplace Home has been restored to look as it did from 1946 to 1950, when he lived there with his grandparents while his mother studied to be a nurse in New Orleans. But Hope is also home to the biggest watermelons in Arkansas (how does 268 pounds sound?) and has been holding a watermelon festival since 1925. These days it's a food fest with good clean fun like watermelon throwing, seed-spitting, and melon-eating contests, along with gospel singing and a dog show to boot. The watermelon is used in the city's logo: "A Slice of the Good Life."

WHERE: 1200 President Clinton Ave. Tel 501-374-4242; clintonlibrary.gov. **RIVER MARKET:** Tel 501-375-2552; rivermarket.info. **GOVERNOR'S MANSION:** Tel 501-324-9805; arkansasgovernorsmansion.com. **OLD STATE HOUSE:** Tel 501-324-9685; oldstatehouse.com. **CLINTON BIRTHPLACE:** Hope. Tel 870-777-4455; nps.gov/wicl/index.htm. **BEST TIMES:** late May for RiverFest Arts and Music Festival; mid-Aug for 4-day Hope Watermelon Festival.

The William J. Clinton Library and Museum features 2 million photographs, 78 million pages of official records, 20 million e-mail messages, and over 100,000 gifts from Clinton's presidency.

Where Old-Time Music Got a New Start

ARKANSAS FOLK FESTIVAL

Mountain View, Arkansas

Just when the dogwoods and redbuds burst into bloom, the town square of Mountain View (population 2,862) comes alive with the sound of music—traditional folk tunes with a faint echo of Scotland and Ireland. Someone announces, "It's jig time!" and children kick up their heels in a timeless reel imported from across the Pond. During the three-day festival in April, a big stage sits in front of the old stone courthouse for better-known fiddlers and pickers, but groups spring up all over town—on the front porch of a music store, over by the library, in lawn chairs in the square.

Known as the "Folk Music Capital of the World," Mountain View has hosted this festival since 1963, when Grand Ole Opry star and local boy Jimmy Driftwood (whose monster hit was "Battle of New Orleans") came back home to put on a show with local amateur musicians—"timber cutters, farmers, housewives, and all plain people of the hills," as he said. To everyone's surprise, 4,000 people showed up, and within a few years 100,000 (mostly hippies and hill folk) were descending on the town during festival weekend. Things have quieted down since then to about 30,000 people, and now the biggest festival in town is the October Beanfest, when one ton of pinto beans are cooked in antique iron pots set up around the courthouse; at noon everyone feasts on beans and corn bread. Beanfest also holds the Great Arkansas Championship Outhouse Race in which teams from Arkansas and states as far as Louisiana and Missouri push outhouses built on wheels in a bid for the coveted gold toilet seat trophy.

The Arkansas Folk Festival and the October Beanfest bookend the season at Ozark Folk Center State Park just a few miles up the road, the only park in America devoted to the preservation of Southern mountain folkways and music. (It opens the same weekend as the Folk Festival, when the public is admitted for free.) A living museum of traditional mountain skills such as furniture making and quilting, Ozark Folk Center has both a Crafts Village and a 1,000-seat Music Auditorium; you can see a dulcimer being constructed during the day and then hear live traditional Ozark folk music using similar instruments that evening. Anything after 1941 (when Ernest Tubb launched honky-tonk music with "Walking the Floor Over You") is strictly off-limits to these mostly local musicians.

Take a break with a trip to Blanchard Springs Caverns, an underground world of crystalline formations—sparkling flowstone, towering columns, and delicate soda straws. Choose your adventure: the Dripstone Trail (the easiest and prettiest), the Discovery Trail (best for learning how caves are formed), or the Wild Cave Tour (scrambling in sections that have no stairways or lights).

WHERE: 105 miles north of Little Rock. *Visitor info:* Tel 888-679-2859 or 870-269-8068; yourplaceinthemountains.com. **OZARK FOLK CENTER STATE PARK:** Tel 870-269-3851; ozarkfolkcenter.com. *When:* Wed–Sat, mid-Apr–Sept; closed Mon, Oct; closed Nov–mid-Apr. *Cost:* $45 for 1-day family pass to Crafts Village and music. **BLANCHARD SPRINGS CAVERNS:** Tel 888-757-2246 or 870-757-2211; blanchardsprings.org. *When:* closed Mon–Tues, Nov–Mar. *Cost:* $10 for Dripstone Trail; $75 for Wild Cave Tour. **BEST TIMES:** 3rd weekend in Apr for Folk Festival; last full weekend in Oct for Beanfest; spring for the dogwoods; fall for foliage; Dec for Caroling in the Caverns.

In Search of All That Glitters

THE CRATER OF DIAMONDS

Murfreesboro, Arkansas

I t's no guaranteed get-rich-quick scheme, but a few people *have* gotten lucky at the Crater of Diamonds, the only place in the world where the public can search for diamonds where they naturally occur—and keep them. Fabulous finds include the Strawn-Wagner Diamond, the most perfect diamond ever certified by the American Gem Society and on permanent display at the visitors center. Unearthed in 1990 by local resident Shirley Strawn, the 1.09-carat diamond (3.03 in the rough) was valued at $37,000 when it was cut. Incredible discoveries are still being made, including a 6.19-carat diamond found in 2014.

Diamonds (and 40 other rocks, minerals, and semiprecious stones like jasper, amethyst, and garnet) can be found in this 37-acre plowed field because of movements in the earth's plates. About 100 million years ago, instability in the earth's mantle allowed a plume of hot magma to escape, creating a volcanic vent that brought diamonds to the surface. It is the world's eighth-largest diamond-bearing deposit in surface area.

Geologists noticed the peridotite soil in the 19th century, but not until 1906 were the first diamonds found by John Huddleston, a local farmer. The site was mined in the early years, but proved more valuable as a tourist attraction starting in 1952. Since Arkansas purchased the land in 1972 to develop it as a state park, more than 30,000 diamonds have been found here, and more than 75,000 since 1906.

There are three ways to look for diamonds. After a good hard rain, just walking back and forth and keeping your eye peeled can work. Serious rock hounds dig deep trenches and follow a painstaking process called sluicing. But most rookie visitors just dig around in the first 6 inches of soil (you can bring your own trowels and screens or rent them at the visitors center) and pray for beginner's luck. It helps to know what you're looking for: a smooth polished stone, translucent but not necessarily clear, with a metallic luster and a slightly oily feel. The Diamond Discovery Center offers digging tips and free rock identification, and will weigh and certify your diamonds. An average of two diamonds a day are found (you generally will hear lots of whooping when that happens).

The largest diamond ever found in America came out of the Crater of Diamonds, a monster white diamond called "Uncle Sam," found in 1924: It was 40.23 carats (12.42 carats after being cut). The 15.33-carat "Star of Arkansas" wasn't bad pickins either. Although most of the diamonds unearthed here are about the size of a paper match head—so small they would not be cut—that shouldn't stop you from dreaming.

WHERE: 110 miles southwest of Little Rock; 209 State Park Rd. Tel 870-285-3113; craterofdiamondsstatepark.com.

At the Crater of Diamonds, visitors can mine for treasure—and keep any gems they find.

Just Don't Call the Winner a Quack

WORLD'S CHAMPIONSHIP DUCK CALLING CONTEST

Stuttgart, Arkansas

Every Thanksgiving duck hunters converge on the small town of Stuttgart for the World's Championship Duck Calling Contest, first held in 1936 and now the world's largest competition of its kind. A major stop on the

Mississippi Flyway, a superhighway for mallards and other waterfowl, Stuttgart calls itself the Rice and Duck Capital of the World. No coincidence, since ducks are attracted to the rice fields of Arkansas County, the biggest rice producer in the state (Arkansas in turn is responsible for 48 percent of the country's rice production, thanks to the rich "gumbo soil" of the Delta that holds water while the hardpan underneath keeps it from draining away). Located near the convergence of three major rivers (the White, Arkansas, and Mississippi), Stuttgart is also at the heart of marshy open fields that create ideal conditions for duck hunters.

There's no better time to visit than during the World's Championship Duck Calling Contest, now part of a weeklong celebration called Wings Over the Prairie Festival. It kicks off with the crowning of the Queen Mallard, usually a blonde, blue-eyed descendant of the German immigrants who founded Stuttgart in 1878 and arguably the only beauty pageant winner ever to officiate, for at least some of her reign, in head-to-toe camouflage. And while folks love the Duck Gumbo Cook-off, the social Sportsman's Party, and the opportunity to buy rare duck calls in the Collectibles Tent, it's the afternoon Duck Calling Contest that really gets the juices flowing. Competing in the contest are 73 callers from 39 states, as well as Canada and New Zealand, who have won sanctioned state or regional contests (the championship is limited to 55 teams and the waiting list to compete is long). Inspired by a stage decorated like a duck blind, they strut their stuff with hail calls (calling the ducks to them), feeding calls (the sounds ducks make when they're eating), mating calls (otherwise known as the lonesome duck), and comeback calls (to lure startled ducks to return). So exaggerated in style that a real duck would do a double-take, competition-style calls are designed to demonstrate both range (volume and pitch) and control (no squawking, which can easily happen with acrylic duck calls).

Over 30,000 people attend the World's Championship Duck Calling Contest each year to hear calls played by virtuosos.

Whether you hunt in the timber or open water, whether your calling style is loud and aggressive or soft and quiet, or whether your budget allows for $15 or $155, Rich-N-Tone Duck Calls has the perfect purchase for you. When you're done shopping, head to the Museum of the Arkansas Grand Prairie, where you can learn the story of 150 years of settlement, agriculture, and waterfowling.

The only place where duck is not the name of the game is the Sportsman's Drive-in, a café that no longer offers drive-in service but welcomes hunters with the best, juiciest burgers in town. Caveat: The double cheeseburger special has 22 ounces of meat, so don't expect to have room for pie.

WHERE: 55 miles east of Little Rock. *Visitor info:* Tel 870-673-1602; stuttgart arkansas.org. *When:* Thanksgiving weekend; Wings Over the Prairie Festival starts Sat before Thanksgiving. **RICH-N-TONE DUCK CALLS:** Tel 888-768-2255 or 870-673-4274; rntcalls.com. *Cost:* calls from $43. *When:* closed Sat–Sun. **MUSEUM OF THE ARKANSAS GRAND PRAIRIE:** Tel 870-673-7001; grand prairiemuseum.org. *When:* closed Sun–Mon. **SPORTSMAN'S DRIVE-IN:** Tel 870-673-7462. *Cost:* double cheeseburger $11. *When:* closed Sun.

Abolitionists and Artisans

BEREA

Kentucky

In central Kentucky, where the foothills of the Appalachian Mountains meet rolling bluegrass horse farms, lies bucolic Berea, an idyllic Appalachian arts and crafts center. Hundreds of potters, painters, furniture makers, weavers, and other artisans whose works are coveted throughout the country for their high quality are among this quiet town's population of 15,000. Perfect for strolling, Berea's quaint town square includes more than 50 artists' galleries, studios, and crafts shops selling everything from hand-stitched quilts and cornhusk flowers to folk-art paintings, woodcarvings, and handblown glass.

Across the street, Berea College is a tree-shaded, 140-acre campus that originated when wealthy landowner Cassius M. Clay (yes, the late Kentucky-born boxer Muhammad Ali was a namesake) gave this land to the Rev. John Fee in 1853. Along with abolitionist missionaries, Fee formed a village, church, and school dedicated to educating people of all races.

From its origins as a one-room schoolhouse in 1855, Berea College later became the South's first interracial and coeducational institution of higher education. Today private, nondenominational, and consistently rated among America's leading liberal arts colleges, Berea admits only low-income students with high academic abilities and provides them full scholarships. Since 1893, the Berea College Student Crafts program has been teaching traditional handicrafts, which are sold through the Log House Craft Gallery (and online) to support the tuition-free college.

Students are required to offset their room and board by working part-time for the college. Those who don't opt for the craft program can choose to work at the handsome Boone Tavern Hotel and Restaurant (named for pioneer Daniel Boone), a gracious 1909 landmark that offers comfortable rooms, the hearty Kentucky classics spoonbread and chess pie, and updated dishes like filet mignon with blue cheese grits.

Outside of town with easy interstate access, the 25,000-square-foot Kentucky Artisan Center at Berea sells Kentucky-made crafts including jewelry, pottery, baskets, dulcimers, and furniture from more than 750 artists and artisans. Or take a back-roads driving tour to Tater Knob Pottery and Farm, where hand-thrown hunks of clay are spun into coffee mugs and casserole dishes, bowls, and birdbaths.

WHERE: 40 miles south of Lexington. *Visitor info:* Tel 800-598-5263 or 859-986-2540; berea.com. **LOG HOUSE CRAFT GALLERY:** Tel 859-985-3225; berea.edu/studentcrafts. **BOONE TAVERN HOTEL AND RESTAURANT:** Tel 800-366-9358 or 859-985-3700; boonetavernhotel.com. *Cost:* from $138; dinner $50. **KENTUCKY ARTISAN CENTER:** Tel

A craftsman creates handmade dulcimers in his workshop in Berea.

859-985-5448; kentuckyartisancenter.ky.gov.
Tater Knob Pottery: Tel 859-986-2167;
taterknob.com. **Best times:** early July for

the Berea Craft Festival and the Festival
of Learnshops; Oct for the Kentucky Guild of
Artists and Craftsmen Fairs.

America's Great Homegrown Spirit

THE BOURBON TRAIL

Kentucky

Rich, amber-colored bourbon, a kind of whiskey distilled almost exclusively in Kentucky distilleries and declared "America's native spirit" by Congress, is the intoxicating product of native corn and local limestone-rich springs. About 95 percent of the world's bourbon comes from Kentucky, each brand claiming its own unique taste, defined mostly by the charred new American white oak barrels where it is aged a minimum of two years. A whiskey renaissance that began in the 1980s has garnered bourbon newfound attention and respect, with exclusive small-batch premium bourbons helping to elevate the drink's image; usually stronger than the normal 90 proof, they're generally aged six to eight years.

Bardstown is the de facto capital of Bourbon Country, with its cluster of seven distilleries open for guided tours. Heaven Hill Distilleries' modern Bourbon Heritage Center features educational exhibits, an introductory film, gift shop, and barrel-shaped tasting room for designated nondrivers. Jim Beam is just 12 miles west and Maker's Mark, a national historic landmark and the nation's oldest working distillery (1805), is 17 miles south. World-famous Wild Turkey and Four Roses are 40 miles east of Bardstown near Lawrenceburg, and in nearby Woodford County is Labrot & Graham, dating back to 1812; its elixir has been praised by everyone from Mark Twain to Walt Whitman.

Bourbon buffs should not miss the annual Kentucky Bourbon Festival, a five-day event with live music, dancing, historic tours, tastings, great food (including many bourbon-flavored specialties), and lots of Kentucky

hospitality. Also worthy is the Oscar Getz Museum of Whiskey, whose rare artifacts (antique bottles, a moonshine still, and even Abe Lincoln's liquor license) trace American whiskey production from pre-colonial to post-Prohibition years.

Founded in 1780, Bardstown offers a number of nonalcoholic diversions. My Old

A Maker's Mark employee draws a sample from a whiskey barrel.

Kentucky Home State Park includes a golf course and the imposing Federal Hill, the 1812 plantation (open for tours) that inspired American songwriter Stephen Foster's folk tune "My Old Kentucky Home." My Old Kentucky Dinner Train offers guests gourmet food in elegant 1940s-era railcars while traveling through Kentucky's beautiful countryside. Across the street from Federal Hill, the family-owned Kurtz Restaurant has dished out comfort food since 1937. Specialties are skillet-fried chicken, Kentucky country ham, and biscuit-and-bourbon bread pudding. Drop in for a drink at the atmospheric Old Talbott Tavern (1779), the oldest western stagecoach stop in America.

Spend the night in nearby Springfield, at the 1851 Maple Hill Manor, an antebellum B&B offering seven cozy guest rooms. Alpacas and llamas roam in the farm's fields, and abundant breakfasts feature fresh fruit from the orchards in season.

WHERE: Bardstown is 40 miles southeast of Louisville. *Visitor info:* Tel 800-638-4877 or 502-348-4877; visitbardstown.com. **HEAVEN HILL:** Tel 502-337-1000; bourbonheritage center.com. **KENTUCKY BOURBON FESTIVAL:** Tel 800-638-4877; kybourbonfestival.com. *When:* 2nd week in Sept. **OSCAR GETZ MUSEUM:** Tel 502-348-2999; whiskeymuseum.com. **MY OLD KENTUCKY HOME:** Tel 800-323-7803 or 502-348-3502; parks.ky.gov/parks/recreationparks/old-ky-home. **MY OLD KENTUCKY DINNER TRAIN:** Tel 866-801-3463 or 502-348-7300; kydinnertrain.com. *Cost:* dinner $85. **KURTZ RESTAURANT:** Tel 502-348-8964; bardstown parkview.com/dining. *Cost:* dinner $25. *When:* closed Jan–Feb. **THE OLD TALBOTT TAVERN:** Tel 800-482-8376 or 502-348-3494; talbotts .com. *Cost:* dinner $35. **MAPLE HILL MANOR:** Springfield. Tel 800-886-7546 or 859-336-3075; maplehillmanor.com. *Cost:* from $159. **BEST TIME:** Sept–Oct, especially during the Bourbon Festival.

A Byway to Butcher Hollow and Beyond

COUNTRY MUSIC HIGHWAY

Kentucky

Fire up a Ricky Skaggs tune and your car's engine and hit this winding ribbon of mountain road for a one-of-a-kind Kentucky adventure. Highway 23, the "Country Music Highway," winds 144 miles along the state's craggy eastern backbone, from Greenup County in the north to Letcher County in the south. Besides visual splendor, this National Scenic Byway provides a primer on many musical legends who have emerged from these ancient Appalachian hills and hollows. Highway markers signal the hometowns of country stars Skaggs, Patty Loveless, The Judds, Billy Ray Cyrus, Crystal Gayle, Hylo Brown, Gary Stewart, Rebecca Lynn Howard, Dwight Yoakam, and many more.

Allow two days for a leisurely exploration of the road, which connects the towns of Greenup and Whitesburg. Along the midway point near Paintsville lies legendary Butcher Hollow, where a dusty gravel road leads to the humble wood framed house where the Queen of Country Music, America's beloved "Coal Miner's Daughter" Loretta Lynn, was born on April 14, 1932. Today, her brother Herman Webb still gives occasional tours of the family home. Nearby in Staffordsville sits the Mountain Homeplace, an 1850s working farm with a blacksmith barn, church, school, and gift shop where quilts, painted gourds, and handmade dolls are sold. TV's John Boy Walton himself (actor Richard Thomas, a native of these parts) narrates a film about the early Appalachian settlers, who first arrived in the late 1700s and early 1800s.

In Prestonsburg, visit the Mountain Arts Center (MAC), a performance hall that's home to the Kentucky Opry, a musical variety show modeled after the one in Nashville, TN (see p. 473).

WHERE: runs from Greenup (121 miles northeast of Lexington) south to Whitesburg. *Visitor info:* Tel 877-868-7735 or 606-677-6095; tourseky.com, countrymusichighway.com, byways.org. **BUTCHER HOLLOW:** Van Lear. Tel 606-789-3397. **MOUNTAIN HOMEPLACE:** Staffordsville. Tel 606-297-1850; visitpaints villeky.com/homeplace. *When:* closed Nov–Mar. **MOUNTAIN ARTS CENTER:** Prestonsburg. Tel 606-866-2623; macarts.com.

An Unchanged Corner of the Appalachians

CUMBERLAND GAP & DANIEL BOONE COUNTRY

Kentucky

Springtime is sublime in Cumberland Gap National Historical Park. The winding, 4-mile drive to Pinnacle Overlook is awash in wildflowers— colorful columbine, bloodroot, and trillium. No less glorious are the second and third weeks of October, when the hazy mountainsides are ablaze in scarlet and gold foliage. And then there are all the months in between.

Cumberland Gap, at 24,000 acres, is one of the largest national historic parks in America, part of an expanse of land in southeastern Kentucky near the Virginia and Tennessee borders, loosely known as Daniel Boone country. Before the Pennsylvania-born frontiersman Boone came upon Cumberland Gap in 1769, English settlers had no way to cross the formidable Appalachian Mountains. He returned in 1775, accompanied by a band of axe-wielding men, to blaze the rugged Wilderness Trail, which followed an old Indian path and opened Kentucky and beyond to westward expansion. By 1810, almost 300,000 settlers had streamed through the passageway.

Along with 85 miles of hiking trails, the park's seasonal highlights include Pinnacle Overlook, a dramatic vista reached via the

At 68 feet high and 125 feet wide, Cumberland Falls is known as the Niagara of the South.

4-mile Skyland Road. A visit to Hensley Settlement, on a plateau on Brush Mountain, evokes life on a rustic Appalachian settlement dating from 1903 to 1951. Park rangers lead visitors through the cabins, barns, granary, springhouse, and blacksmith shop and explain life's daily challenges.

Stretching north of Cumberland Gap is the vast Daniel Boone National Forest, a 21-county area that includes 708,000 acres of federal land used for recreation, wildlife, fishing, and timber. Encompassing rugged terrain, three lakes, and a lush landscape of oaks, pines, and hemlocks, the forest attracts hikers, campers, boaters, and rock climbers. The Red River Gorge Scenic Byway is a 46-mile paved road that begins in Stanton and loops through a scenic landscape of natural sandstone arches, caves, cliffs, and the Red River itself.

West of the Gap, the Cumberland River and its tributaries spill into the Big South Fork National River and Recreation Area, encompassing 125,000 acres of gorges, mountains, and valleys extending from Kentucky through Tennessee. White-water rafting, hiking, fishing, and biking pull in adventure seekers. A more sedentary but no less spectacular option is a ride (originating in small-town Stearns) on the Big South Fork Scenic Railway, which traverses mountain streams and passes through places like the Blue Heron Mining Community, where the skeletal remains of an early 1900s mine, company store, and church stand eerily silent.

CUMBERLAND GAP: Park visitor center is 130 miles south of Lexington in Middlesboro. Tel 606-248-2817; nps.gov/cuga. *Visitor info:* Tel 877-868-7735 or 606-677-6099; tourseky .com. **DANIEL BOONE FOREST:** Winchester. Tel 859-745-3100; fs.usda.gov/dbnf. **RED RIVER GORGE BYWAY:** Tel 606-663-8100; byways.org. **BIG SOUTH FORK RECREATION AREA:** Stearns. Tel 423-569-9778; nps.gov/ biso. **BIG SOUTH FORK RAILWAY:** Tel 800-462-5664 or 606-376-5330; bsfsry.com. *When:* closed Jan–Mar. **BEST TIMES:** Apr for wildflowers; Oct for foliage.

Kentucky's Oldest Frontier Town

HARRODSBURG & THE BEAUMONT INN

Kentucky

Named for Colonel James Harrod, who founded this first permanent English-speaking settlement west of the Allegheny Mountains in 1774, quaint Harrodsburg bears the dual distinction of being the state's oldest town as well as the home of Kentucky's oldest family-owned-and-operated inn, the renowned Beaumont.

This unique past comes alive at Old Fort Harrod State Park, where log structures replicate the frontier village's 1774 fort. Costumed interpreters demonstrate woodworking, basket making, and blacksmithing, as billy goats bleat from straw-lined pens. A picnic area lies beneath the gnarled boughs of an Osage orange tree dating back to the late 1800s, and a hilltop pioneer cemetery contains 18th-century headstones. The 1813 Greek Revival Mansion Museum boasts an unexpectedly rich trove of Kentucky weaponry and Civil War exhibits related to two Kentucky-born opponents: President Abraham Lincoln and Jefferson Davis, president of the Confederacy. Opposite the museum is the Lincoln Marriage Temple, a steepled brick building that enshrines the one-room cabin where Abe Lincoln's parents (Thomas Lincoln and Nancy Hanks) were married on June 12, 1806.

Among Harrodsburg's 50-some historical sites is the stately three-story Greek Revival Beaumont Inn. In the Dedman family since

1919; this charming plantation-style property rests on a tree-shaded hill within walking distance of downtown. Originally the site of the boyhood log home of John M. Harlan, Chief Justice of the U.S. Supreme Court, the Main Inn was built as a ladies' finishing school in 1845. Virginian Thomas Smith, a Civil War colonel under Stonewall Jackson, renamed it Beaumont, French for "beautiful mount."

It remains an apt description for the grand property, with its columned front porch lined with rocking chairs and its double parlor appointed with Empire and Victorian furniture. Other treasures include a grand piano dating back to 1893 and a carved wooden chair used by President Franklin D. Roosevelt when he visited in 1934. Overnight guests may choose to stay in the inn's cozy antiques-furnished rooms, larger rooms in the 1935 Goddard Hall, or in Greystone House, a 1931 limestone mansion whose suites feature fireplaces and whirlpools.

Hospitality at the Beaumont Inn's restaurant is available to everyone who stops by. The house specialty is Kentucky country ham—hickory-smoked and cured on site—served with biscuits and corn pudding, and best followed by General Robert E. Lee orange lemon cake. The inn's pub-like Old Owl Tavern is a former carriage house whose crackling stone fireplace invites you to stop awhile and nurse a local bourbon.

WHERE: 32 miles southwest of Lexington. *Visitor info:* Tel 800-355-9192 or 859-734-2364; harrodsburgky.com. **OLD FORT HARROD STATE PARK:** Tel 859-734-3314; parks .ky.gov/parks/recreationparks/Fort-Harrod. **BEAUMONT INN:** Tel 800-352-3992 or 859-734-3381; beaumontinn.com. *Cost:* from $123 (off-peak), from $138 (peak); dinner $35. *When:* inn closed Jan–Feb. **BEST TIMES:** May and Oct for the best weather, flea markets, and festivals.

An Extraordinary Society, Preserved

SHAKER VILLAGE OF PLEASANT HILL

Harrodsburg, Kentucky

Shaker Village of Pleasant Hill's plank-and-stone fences lace together 3,000 lush acres that contain 34 fully restored 19th-century buildings. The communal religious sect known as the Shakers lived, worked, and worshipped in these family dwellings, a Meeting House, and farm buildings throughout much of the 1800s. Overnight stays help guests understand something of the inspiration the early residents found in this pastoral parcel of central Kentucky.

Immigrants from England who moved to upstate New York and New England beginning in 1774, the Shakers were peaceful, celibate men and women who believed in equal rights for all races and both sexes. The United Society of Believers in Christ's Second Appearing acquired the name Shakers because of the ecstatic dancing and singing during their worship services. By 1823, there were almost 500 Shakers living at Pleasant Hill, which flourished for many years until its numbers began to dwindle in the late 1800s; it closed in 1910.

A visit to "Shakertown," as it's known to locals, is a retreat into a slower, more reflective way of life, where simplicity and peacefulness extol the Shaker ideal of an environment that was heaven on earth. The largest and most completely restored Shaker community in the country, the site offers guided tours of the distinctive 19th-century brick and stone Shaker buildings, while costumed interpreters and craftspeople demonstrate such Shaker skills as broom making, woodworking, and weaving. Shop for quality Shaker reproduction furniture, cookbooks, pottery, and textiles; take a ride along the Kentucky River aboard the *Dixie Belle* paddle wheeler; or wander the farm's 40 miles of nature trails.

The Pleasant Hill Shakers owned nearly 4,500 acres and built 260 structures, including large, stone family dwellings.

The austerely beautiful Trustees' Table is a first-rate restaurant, where diners can expect such traditional Kentucky favorites as country ham and fried chicken along with such Shaker specialties as tart lemon pie. Take the twin spiral staircase to the second floor to find the spare but comfortably furnished guest rooms with thick cotton bedspreads, rocking chairs, and handmade rugs accenting the hardwood floors. Venture out to find the 12 other historic buildings throughout Shaker Village where you can enjoy a contemplative overnight stay, imagining a life free of modern-day demands.

WHERE: 25 miles southwest of Lexington; 3501 Lexington Rd. Tel 800-734-5611 or 859-734-5411; shakervillageky.org. **INN AT PLEASANT HILL:** *Cost:* from $100; dinner $35. **BEST TIME:** early Aug for the Pleasant Hill Craft Fair.

America's Largest Inland Peninsula and "Quilt City, U.S.A."

LAND BETWEEN THE LAKES & PADUCAH

Kentucky

The largest inland peninsula in the U.S., the Land Between the Lakes National Recreation Area (LBL) is a vast, unspoiled treasure of 170,000 wooded acres and 300 miles of undeveloped shoreline. LBL runs from Grand Rivers, Kentucky, in the north, to just beyond the Tennessee border in the south. A scenic 45-mile, two-lane paved road known as The Trace bisects LBL. This corner of western Kentucky boasts four rivers—the Cumberland, Ohio, Tennessee, and Mississippi—and the largest man-made lake in the eastern U.S., Kentucky Lake (184 miles long) and the connected Lake Barkley (134 miles long). With 30 boat ramps and six beaches, the area is popular with families for boating, fishing, and swimming galore.

Wildlife abounds at LBL. Bison and elk roam freely on a 700-acre restored prairie, and white-tailed deer and wild turkeys are among the more than 50 mammals and 240 bird species that call the preserve home. Bald eagles were successfully introduced to the area in the 1980s, and LBL offers viewing tours in January and February. Educational interpretive programs take place at the Woodlands Nature Station, where owls, coyotes, and red wolves can be spotted.

Hiking and mountain biking trails are abundant here, and Kentucky Lake's Turkey Bay is the nation's first federally designated area for all-terrain vehicles, offering 100 miles of wooded trails. In addition to back-country camping, LBL has nearly 1,000 developed campsites in four campgrounds. At Wranglers Riding Stables, an equestrian campground with 100 miles of horse trails, LBL visitors are permitted to camp with their own horses. If you've left your mount at home, guided horseback rides are also available.

Founded in 1827 by William Clark of Lewis and Clark fame, nearby Paducah is known as "Quilt City, U.S.A." The town sits at the confluence of the Ohio and Tennessee rivers and is distinctive for its late 19th-century architecture and the National Quilt Museum. Each April, the American Quilter's Society holds a QuiltWeek in Paducah with contests and vendors. You may not be able to buy the works of art displayed, but you can sign up for classes and workshops in an attempt to make some yourself.

LAND BETWEEN THE LAKES: from 200 miles southwest of Louisville to 90 miles northwest of Nashville, TN. *Visitor info:* Tel 800-525-7077 or 270-924-2000; landbetween thelakes.us. **WRANGLERS RIDING STABLES:** Tel 270-924-2211; wranglersridingstables .yolasite.com. **PADUCAH:** *Visitor info:* Tel 800-723-8224 or 270-443-8784; paducah .travel.com. **NATIONAL QUILT MUSEUM:** Paducah. Tel 270-442-8856; quiltmuseum .org. **BEST TIMES:** in Paducah, Apr for QuiltWeek (quiltweek.com); winter for eagle watching at LBL.

Horse Heaven

BLUEGRASS COUNTRY

Lexington, Kentucky

C entral Kentucky's bluegrass country is one of America's most genteel and elegant landscapes, spread over 15 counties and 4,000 square miles of Tara-style manor houses and classic oak plank fences. It is also

The many horse breeding and training farms in Lexington have produced numerous Derby and Triple Crown racers.

the undisputed international center of Thoroughbred horse breeding. Horses live better here than most humans do, in cupola-topped barns and handsome stables with hand-forged gates, stained-glass windows, and impeccable housekeeping.

Two of America's most scenic byways, the Old Frankfort Pike and the Paris Pike, meander through the region under canopies of century-old trees and past more than 450 farms, their jade fields dotted with mares and foals. Many of the grandest farms are home to past Derby winners (four-legged gold mines now employed as fabulously well-paid studs). Most of these farms are closed to the public.

North of Lexington, the 1,200-acre Kentucky Horse Park is a horse-lover's dream. Its extensive International Museum of the Horse examines the role of horses throughout history (with a special Arabian horse gallery), while the American Saddlebred Museum highlights the importance of this breed in American culture. As an equine competition venue, the park hosts scores of annual events, including the Rolex Kentucky Three Day Event (held in late April), showcasing Olympic hopefuls vying for the U.S. Equestrian Team.

Although Louisville's Churchill Downs may be the site of the storied Kentucky Derby (see p. 413), the Keeneland Race Course in Lexington is the South's most beautiful track, with its elegant limestone grandstands and tree-shaded setting near some of the region's most impressive horse farms. Show up in time to watch workout sessions from 6 A.M. to 10 A.M., and follow up with breakfast and gossip at the Track Kitchen, a Keeneland tradition.

WHERE: 75 miles east of Louisville. *Visitor info:* Tel 800-845-3959 or 859-233-7299; visitlex.com. **KENTUCKY HORSE PARK:** Tel 800-678-8813 or 859-233-4303; kyhorsepark .com. **KEENELAND RACE COURSE:** Tel 800-456-3412 or 859-254-3412; keeneland.com. *When:* 3 weeks of racing in both Apr and Oct; auctions and special events at other times. **BEST TIMES:** Apr and Oct for Thoroughbred racing; June for the Kentucky Horse Park's unique Egyptian Arabian horse show (pyramidsociety.org) and for its annual Festival of the Bluegrass weekend; Sept, Nov, and Jan for horse sales at Keeneland (open to the public).

A Local Son's Old Kentucky Homes

THE LINCOLN TRAIL

Kentucky

"Ihope to have God on my side, but I must have Kentucky," President Abraham Lincoln reportedly said at the outset of the Civil War. Lincoln was born February 12, 1809, in Kentucky, where he lived until the age

of seven. Although his hardworking frontier family moved to Indiana (and later Illinois; see p. 500) in search of work, Kentucky remained a cherished place for Lincoln throughout his life and career as lawyer, politician, and the nation's 16th president during the Civil War. Kentucky was a border state that began the war as a "neutral," but joined the Union when the Confederates invaded in 1861.

In LaRue County, about 55 miles south of Louisville, the Abraham Lincoln Birthplace National Historic Site has a grand neoclassical memorial building housing an early 19th-century log cabin representing the one in which Lincoln was born. Young Abe lived here with his family on this 348-acre farm, known as Sinking Spring, until he was about 2½ years old. A national park since 1914, the grassy, wooded park includes hiking trails and picnic areas. A focal point, reminiscent of the Lincoln Memorial in Washington, D.C. (see p. 264), is the imposing memorial, set on a knoll reached by 56 steps—one for each year of his life. (President Theodore Roosevelt laid the cornerstone in 1909 to commemorate Lincoln's 100th birthday.)

In nearby Hodgenville, look for the elegant bronze sculpture of a seated Lincoln dominating the town square. Behind it, the endearing Lincoln Museum provides a rather old-fashioned visual immersion experience in all things Abe, through the lifelike wax figures and dioramas depicting 12 scenes from Lincoln's life, including his Kentucky boyhood, drafting the Emancipation Proclamation, and his assassination at a Washington, D.C., theater on April 14, 1865. Upstairs, historic newspaper clippings, campaign materials, and Civil War memorabilia are on display.

Many other sites associated with Lincoln dot the Kentucky landscape. Just outside Springfield, the Lincoln Homestead State Park contains yet another log-cabin replica, this one of the simple home in which Thomas Lincoln, Abe's father, was raised. Lincoln's mother, Nancy Hanks, lived in a two-story log cabin called The Berry Home, and the original was moved here from a nearby location. The park also has leafy picnic areas and an 18-hole golf course.

The city of Lexington is the site of the Mary Todd Lincoln House, a brick Georgian home and former inn that was purchased in 1832 by the family of 13-year-old Mary Todd, who became Abraham Lincoln's wife years later. The first house museum in America honoring a First Lady, the home's 14 rooms showcase period antiques, portraits, and family heirlooms. On guided tours, docents retell lively stories of when Abraham and Mary Lincoln stayed here, including their three-week visit in 1847, after he was first elected to the U.S. Congress.

WHERE: Hodgenville is 55 miles south of Louisville. **ABRAHAM LINCOLN BIRTHPLACE:** Hodgenville. Tel 270-358-3137; nps.gov/abli. **LINCOLN MUSEUM:** Hodgenville. Tel 270-358-3163; lincolnmuseum-ky.org. **LINCOLN HOMESTEAD STATE PARK:** Springfield. Tel 859-336-7461; parks.ky.gov/parks/recreationparks/lincoln-homestead. *When:* May–Oct. **MARY TODD LINCOLN HOUSE:** Lexington. Tel 859-233-9999; mtlhouse.org. *When:* mid-Mar–Nov.

A re-creation of the log cabin where Lincoln grew up is housed in a stately neoclassical memorial structure.

Finger-Lickin' Fun

THE LAND OF COLONEL SANDERS

London, Kentucky

Pardon the pun, but more than 250,000 visitors each year flock to the World Chicken Festival, held in late September in downtown London, in the heart of southeastern Kentucky's Daniel Boone National Forest

(see p. 405). The four-day fowl fest includes parades, carnival rides, and such silliness as rooster-crowing and chicken-wing–eating contests. Car shows, kids' activities, and live entertainment on four stages abound at this unique free event. Colonel Harland Sanders is recognized across the world as the goateed Southern gentleman in the white suit who first perfected the still-secret "finger-lickin' good" recipe of 11 herbs and spices, and who first franchised the product we know today as Kentucky Fried Chicken. The festival's greasy good fun all comes down to fried chicken, as 7,000 pieces of chicken are fried in the world's largest skillet—a 700-pound pan that measures more than 10 feet wide.

Fifteen miles south in Corbin, Colonel Sanders's original restaurant has been restored on one side, to look much as it did in 1940 with vintage cookware, mixers, and appliances. On the other side, photographs and a life-size statue of the kindly colonel are on display within a modern-day KFC. Sitting inside among the antiques and memorabilia,

customers can order up buckets of Original Recipe or Extra Crispy chicken along with the requisite mashed potatoes, gravy, and coleslaw. Some things never change.

Today, Louisville-based Yum! Brands Inc., which includes KFC as well as Pizza Hut and Taco Bell, is the world's largest restaurant company. KFC alone is the world's top fast-food chicken chain, with more than 14,200 outlets in 115 countries. Colonel Sanders died in 1980, but it's estimated that over a billion pieces of his famous chicken are served every year in the U.S. alone. A Kentucky picnic wouldn't be complete without the Colonel.

WHERE: 76 miles south of Lexington. **WORLD CHICKEN FESTIVAL:** Tel 800-348-0095 or 606-878-6900; chickenfestival.com. *When:* 4 days in late Sept. **HARLAND SANDERS CAFÉ AND MUSEUM:** Corbin. Tel 606-528-2163.

Pulitzer Prize Winners Premiere Here

THE HUMANA FESTIVAL OF NEW AMERICAN PLAYS

Louisville, Kentucky

66 The festival, year after year, has been a broad, unpredictable, noisy colloquium on the nature of dramatic art," wrote Pulitzer Prize–winning playwright Tony Kushner (*Angels in America*). He was referring to the

Humana Festival of New American Plays, which galvanizes audiences, actors, critics, and playwrights alike each March at Actors Theatre of Louisville. The praise has been universal since its inception. "The Humana Festival has evolved into the Kentucky Derby of the American Theater," hailed the *Los Angeles Times*, while *Time* magazine proclaimed: "The Humana Festival is the center of the theater world."

Founded in 1964, Actors Theatre of Louisville is an internationally renowned, Tony

Award–winning professional theater that annually produces more than 350 performances, from the classical to the contemporary, in its multilevel facility on downtown's historic Main Street. Praised for the overall excellence of its programming and performances—as well as for its nurturing relationship with new and established playwrights—Actors Theatre also produces an annual National Ten-Minute Play Contest.

But its crowning achievement is the prestigious Humana Festival of New American Plays, which began in 1976 and has been underwritten since 1979 by the Humana Foundation, the philanthropic arm of the Louisville-based health care company Humana Inc. Among the more than 450 plays by 370 playwrights that have been produced here over the past four decades are the select few that went from relative obscurity to universal acclaim: modern-day American masterworks and Pulitzer Prize winners Beth Henley's *Crimes of the Heart*, D. L.

Coburn's *The Gin Game*, and Donald Margulies's *Dinner with Friends*, as well as works by Pulitzer finalists, including Tony Kushner, Marsha Norman, and Regina Taylor.

WHERE: Actors Theatre of Louisville; 316 W. Main St. Tel 800-428-5849 or 502-584-1205; actorstheatre.org. *Cost:* tickets from $25. *When:* end of Feb–mid-Apr (regular season is Sept–Feb).

Run for the Roses

KENTUCKY DERBY

Louisville, Kentucky

"This Kentucky Derby, whatever it is—a race, an emotion, a turbulence, an explosion—is one of the most beautiful and violent and satisfying things I have ever experienced," wrote novelist John Steinbeck.

Billed with little exaggeration as "the greatest two minutes in sports," the Kentucky Derby is the oldest continuously held sporting event in America and one of the most prestigious races in the world. Although horse racing in Kentucky goes back to 1789, Louisville's Churchill Downs didn't officially open as the home of the Derby until almost 100 years

About 1.25 miles in length and 2 minutes in duration, the Kentucky Derby is the first race in the Triple Crown series.

later. By tradition, up to 20 three-year-old Thoroughbreds vie to be the winning horse draped with a blanket of red roses and rewarded with the lion's share of the $2 million purse, split among the top five finishers.

The two-week Kentucky Derby Festival that precedes the race is the nicest time of year in the Bluegrass State, when the dogwoods are in magnificent bloom. Thunder Over Louisville, the largest annual fireworks display in the country, kicks things off as spectators flood the banks of the Ohio River, where the extravaganza takes center stage. Other festivities (most of them free) include hot-air balloons, a marathon, the Pegasus Parade, and The Great Steamboat Race that pits the hometown *Belle of Louisville* (toting party-loving passengers and Derby dignitaries) against the *Belle of Cincinnati*.

During "Dawn at the Downs," beginning the Saturday before the Derby and continuing through Thursday of Derby Week, visitors enjoy a Kentucky-style buffet breakfast while watching celebrity equines train. Finally, Oaks Day, held the day before Derby, is when crowds pack the paddocks, grandstands, and infield to watch the three-year-old fillies race.

If you happen to miss Derby season, relive the excitement of past races at the Kentucky Derby Museum, where the inspiring careers of the Derby's many champions are documented.

For lodging during these events, well-heeled Derby veterans have checked into the Seelbach Hotel since its 1905 opening. Its comfortable grandeur so impressed hotel guest F. Scott Fitzgerald that he used it as a model for various scenes in *The Great Gatsby*. The hotel's opulent fine-dining restaurant, the Oakroom, once had a private poker room that hosted the likes of Al Capone.

WHERE: Churchill Downs; 700 Central Ave. Tel 502-636-4400; churchilldowns.com. *Cost:* nonseated general admission tickets sold the day of the race, $60; seated tickets in the bleachers from $340. Reserved tickets go on sale at kentuckyderby.com/tickets in early Nov. *When:* 1st Sat in May. **KENTUCKY DERBY FESTIVAL:** Tel 800-928-3378 or 502-584-6383; kdf.org. **KENTUCKY DERBY MUSEUM:** Tel 502-637-1111; derbymuseum.org. **SEELBACH HOTEL:** Tel 800-333-3399 or 502-585-3200; seelbachhilton .com. *Cost:* from $269; Derby weekend prices upon request; dinner in Oakroom $80. **BEST TIMES:** late Apr–early May for Derby events; late Apr–early July for racing; Nov for Fall Meet.

Home of the Hot Brown—and Much More

LOUISVILLE CUISINE

Louisville, Kentucky

Louisville Slugger baseball bats, boxing legend Muhammad Ali, bourbon-infused mint juleps, and the Kentucky Derby are all synonymous with this grand old city on the Ohio River. But another aspect of its growing reputation is its dynamic restaurant scene. Inarguably the city's signature treat, the simple but delicious Kentucky Hot Brown was invented at the Seelbach Hotel (see above) in 1926 when some patrons, after having danced until the wee hours, craved something more interesting than ham and eggs. Thus was born the open-faced roasted turkey breast sandwich, covered with creamy Mornay sauce and pecorino cheese, baked golden brown, and topped with bacon. The hotel's fancy English Grill still proudly serves the best in town.

A few years later in 1933, Jack Fry's opened as a sportsman's hangout. Today, this Louisville landmark still promises a delightful fine-dining experience that attracts the city's old-school horse set.

At the forefront of the city's contemporary food movement is renowned chef Kathy Cary, whose Lilly's Bistro (and the more casual La Peche next door) has remained a perennial favorite, a showcase of farm-to-table dining, and an early influence on the local scene since it opened in 1988. Cary paved the way for newer arrivals such as the contemporary yet rustic 610 Magnolia, and Proof on Main in the trendy 21c Museum Hotel. Locals and visitors alike linger at Proof's always popular bar, stocked with more than 75 Kentucky bourbons.

Meanwhile, the nostalgic Homemade Ice Cream and Pie Kitchen is a bakery and ice-cream parlor that churns out a mind-boggling array of homemade ice creams, cookies, and decadent cakes and pies (the gooey Dutch apple-caramel defies description). Yet Louisville's most famous pie of all is Derby-Pie—a chocolate nut pie best enjoyed with whipped cream or a spoonful of Kentucky bourbon. After originating more than 50 years ago at a local inn, the recipe's name was patented in 1968 by Kern's Kitchen Inc., a family-owned business that still bakes and distributes Derby-Pie (a registered trademark) at restaurants and supermarkets throughout Kentucky and beyond.

THE ENGLISH GRILL: Tel 502-583-1234; brownhotel.com. *Cost:* dinner $45; Hot Brown $22. **JACK FRY'S:** Tel 502-452-9244; jack frys.com. *Cost:* $60. **LILLY'S BISTRO:** Tel 502-451-0447; lillyslapeche.com. *Cost:* prix-fixe lunch $19. **610 MAGNOLIA:** Tel 502-636-0783; 610magnolia.com. *Cost:* $75 4-course prix fixe. **PROOF ON MAIN:** Tel 502-217-6360; proofonmain.com. *Cost:* $45. **HOMEMADE ICE CREAM AND PIE KITCHEN:** Tel 502-459-8184; piekitchen.com. *Cost:* pie à la mode $6.50.

World's Biggest Baseball Bat

LOUISVILLE SLUGGER MUSEUM AND FACTORY

Louisville, Kentucky

You can't miss this place: It's the redbrick compound downtown with the giant bat leaning against the building. The world's biggest, the carbon-steel replica of Babe Ruth's own 1920s-era bat stands 120 feet tall by 6.5 feet wide—and weighs 34 tons. Inside the museum, families can view exhibits on the history of America's national pastime and revel at the signed bats of Ruth, Ty Cobb, Mickey Mantle, Joe DiMaggio, Ken Griffey Jr., and countless others. Though its current location, which houses the museum, working factory, and corporate headquarters, opened in 1996, the company dates back to 1884, when it produced its first bat for Pete "The Louisville Slugger" Browning of the old Louisville Eclipse baseball team, giving the company its name. Today, more than 300,000 visitors per year watch as wood from maple, white ash, and birch trees is crafted into bats (the factory produces more than 2,000 a day). Free mini-bat souvenirs are given to each guest who tours, though you might not resist the urge to order your own full-size bat, personalized with your name or actual signature.

To catch some live baseball action, the Louisville Bats, a Triple A affiliate of the Cincinnati Reds, play each season at Louisville

The 120-foot-tall bat leaning against the Louisville Slugger Museum is a replica of Babe Ruth's bat.

Slugger Field. The retro stadium opened downtown near the banks of the Ohio River in 2000, but it feels like it's been there forever. In addition to all the familiar concessions (popcorn, peanuts, and hot dogs), the family-friendly venue with a playground and kids' carousel houses two sit-down restaurants.

Muhammad Ali, the other famous Louisville slugger, gets his due downtown at the $80 million Muhammad Ali Center. Although the colorful, interactive "visitor experience" (it's not a traditional museum) celebrates the life and achievements of one of the greatest boxers of all time with photographs, artifacts, murals, videos, and other multimedia exhibits, the center's true focus is on empowering visitors to achieve their personal bests. In the ring,

The Greatest's mantra was "Float like a butterfly, sting like a bee." But the Ali Center's motto is "Be Great. Do great things," and teaches Ali's six core principles, including dedication—"devoting all of one's energy, effort, and abilities to a task."

LOUISVILLE SLUGGER MUSEUM: 800 W. Main St. Tel 877-775-8443; sluggermuseum .org. **LOUISVILLE BATS AND SLUGGER FIELD:** Tel 855-228-8497 or 502-212-2287; batsbaseball.com. *When:* Apr–early Sept. **MUHAMMAD ALI CENTER:** Tel 502-584-9254; alicenter.org.

Turn-of-the-Century Splendor

OLD LOUISVILLE

Louisville, Kentucky

A few blocks south of the Ohio River and downtown lies Old Louisville, a neighborhood of elegant homes, mansions, and churches from the late 1800s and early 1900s. It is the third largest historic preservation district in the U.S. (48 square blocks), with some 1,400 structures lining wide boulevards and narrow side streets. Sidewalks shaded by towering trees provide the perfect opportunity for a constitutional through the Dickensian cityscape of various architectural styles—Victorian is predominant (the largest contiguous collection in the U.S.). You'll also find plenty of arts and crafts, Romanesque, and Italianate, with some Beaux-Arts and Queen Anne as well. Many of the carefully restored multistory homes feature such decorative elements as turrets, stained-glass windows, and tidy yards rimmed with black wrought-iron fences. Consider spending the night at the DuPont Mansion, an elegant and painstakingly restored seven-room B&B.

At the southern edge of this neighborhood, on the campus of the University of Louisville, is the Speed Art Museum, founded by Hattie Bishop Speed as a memorial to her husband, James Breckinridge Speed, a prominent Louisville businessman and philanthropist. His father (also named James) was the U.S. attorney general under Presidents Abraham Lincoln and Andrew Johnson. Opened in 1927—and with a total renovation and expansion scheduled for completion in 2016—Kentucky's largest and oldest museum focuses on Western art from antiquity to the present day, with paintings by Rembrandt, Rubens, Monet, Picasso, and more contemporary artists.

There is art and architecture aplenty, but Old Louisville's charms also extend to browsing the area's boutiques and eateries. One of the finest restaurant choices is 610 Magnolia (see p. 414), as well as Buck's, a Southern charmer tucked in the historic Mayflower Hotel and beloved for its classical menu and its wealth of bourbons.

The loveliest time to visit Old Louisville is in spring, when the azaleas, redbuds, and dogwoods are in bloom. But summertime means the Kentucky Shakespeare Festival, staged at the outdoor amphitheater in Central Park and free of charge. Autumn is desirable for its vivid foliage, and during the first full weekend in October, more than 750 artists from throughout the Americas showcase their fine art and craftsmanship at the closely juried St. James Court Art Show. Held rain or shine in the grassy, gas-lit courtyards of St. James and Belgravia Courts, the free festival attracts 300,000 visitors each year.

Visitor info: Tel 502-635-5244; oldlouisville.org. **DuPont Mansion B&B:** Tel 502-638-0045; dupontmansion.com. *Cost:* from $130. **The Speed Art Museum:** Tel 502-634-2700; speedmuseum.org. **Buck's:** Tel 502-637-5284; buckslou.com. *Cost:* $50. **Kentucky Shakespeare Festival:** Tel 502-574-9900; kyshakes.org. *When:* early Aug. **St. James Court Art Show:** Tel 502-635-1842; stjamescourtartshow.com. *When:* 1st full weekend in Oct. **Best time:** Apr, when azaleas are in bloom.

Ancient Caves and a Modern Classic

Mammoth Cave & National Corvette Museum

Kentucky

Prehistoric man roamed the world's longest, most extensive cave system 2,000 to 4,000 years ago, leaving behind woven sandals, gourd containers, and cane torches. Established as a national park in July 1941, Mammoth Cave continues to draw serious spelunkers and the merely curious, all looking for a little subterranean adventure.

Would-be explorers can enjoy short, easy walks past dramatic stalactites and stalagmites or take on strenuous 6-hour tours that require climbing and crawling through dark, damp, and muddy rock formations, while equipped with headlights, hard hats, and knee pads. Aside from its 400 miles of mapped underground passageways (geologists think there may be another 600 miles yet uncharted), the 350-million-year-old natural wonder offers other pleasures. Aboveground, dense hardwoods lure nature lovers, bird-watchers, and hikers to explore more than 85 miles of trails. Wildflowers abound spring through fall, and anglers have a field day in the fish-rich waters of the Nolin and Green rivers. Together they run 30 miles through the park, and are open for boating, canoeing, fishing, and flood plain camping.

When you're ready to hit the open road, head back along I-65 toward Bowling Green. Be on the lookout for the 11-story conical yellow building with a red spike. It's part of the National Corvette Museum, the only nonprofit

Displaying everything from the oldest models to the latest and greatest, the National Corvette Museum is a mecca for America's sports car enthusiasts.

museum devoted to a particular car—in this case, America's best-loved sports car. Auto enthusiasts can rev their adrenaline with a brief film about Corvettes and view more than 60 cars, including one of the 300 built the year it was first introduced (1953), the one-millionth model (1993), and various experimental proto-types. Life-size dioramas lead visitors past a 1950s Main Street barbershop, a '60s gas sta-tion, and a stretch of Route 66 in Arizona. Naturally, mint-condition Corvettes are the centerpieces of each vignette. The General Motors assembly plant—a quarter-mile from the museum and the only place the Corvette is manufactured—is also open to the public.

MAMMOTH CAVE NATIONAL PARK: 89 miles south of Louisville. Tel 270-758-2180; nps.gov/maca. **NATIONAL CORVETTE MUSEUM:** Bowling Green. Tel 800-538-3883 or 270-781-7973; corvettemuseum.com. **BEST TIMES:** mid-Mar–Apr for spring flowers; summer for cave tours; fall for foliage.

Bluegrass, Burgoo, and Barbecue

OWENSBORO & HENDERSON

Kentucky

A 19th-century riverside trading post where bourbon, coal, and tobacco were bought and sold, Owensboro lies in the western half of Kentucky on the Ohio River bordering Indiana. Bill Monroe, the father of bluegrass

music, was born in 1911 in nearby Rosine, and his presence is felt in the innovative Inter-national Bluegrass Museum at downtown's RiverPark Center. In interactive exhibits, the evolution of mountain music plays out in old photographs, weathered fiddles and mandolins, and vintage recordings of such gems as Monroe's seminal "Blue Moon of Kentucky," the Stanley Brothers' sorrowful "Angel Band," and the frenzied "Foggy Mountain Breakdown," by Lester Flatt and Earl Scruggs.

As renowned as it is for bluegrass, Owensboro is also famed for its barbecue. Mutton is the star here, slowly cooked over hickory logs and basted in a vinegar sauce. Moonlite Bar-B-Q Inn is the definitive place to feast on the city's signature dish as well as that other regional specialty, burgoo, a thick, hearty mutton-based stew in a spicy tomato base. But Moonlite's fearsome buffet offers much, much more than just burgoo or mutton: Its brisket and various barbecued meats include equally deli-cious chicken, ribs, and pulled pork. Burgoo is

also a staple at Old Hickory Bar-B-Que, with a pedigree that dates to 1918.

May is the best time to visit Owensboro, when the downtown area overlooking the Ohio River lures thousands of hungry visitors to its annual International Bar-B-Q Festival for samples of slow-cooked chicken, pork, beef, and mutton. Music and barbecue go hand in hand here, alongside lots of kids' activities, arts and crafts, and a car show.

About 30 miles west of Owensboro, also overlooking the Ohio River, is the small town of Henderson, where the great naturalist and art-ist John J. Audubon lived and studied birds from 1810 to 1819. John James Audubon State Park includes a museum that interprets his life through his art and memorabilia, in the context of world events. Henderson's other famous for-mer resident, W. C. Handy (who lived here for about a decade), is the inspiration behind the free and hugely popular W. C. Handy Blues & Barbecue Festival, held each June.

OWENSBORO: 106 miles southwest of

Louisville. *Visitor info:* Tel 800-489-1131 or 270-926-1100; visitowensboro.com. **INTERNATIONAL BLUEGRASS MUSEUM:** Tel 888-692-2656 or 270-926-7891; bluegrass museum.org. **MOONLITE BAR-B-Q INN:** Tel 270-684-8143; moonlite.com. *Cost:* buffet dinner $15. **OLD HICKORY BAR-B-QUE:** Tel 270-926-9000. *Cost:* lunch $12. **HENDERSON:**

Visitor info: Tel 800-648-3128 or 270-826-3128; hendersonky.org. **JOHN JAMES AUDUBON STATE PARK:** parks.ky.gov/parks/recreation parks/john-james. **W. C. HANDY FESTIVAL:** Tel 800-648-3128 or 270-826-3128; handy blues.org. *When:* 1 week in mid-June. **BEST TIME:** 2nd weekend in May for the International Bar-B-Q Festival (bbqfest.com).

Art and Fine Food in the Piney Woods

NEW ORLEANS' NORTHSHORE

Covington and environs, Louisiana

If you cross mammoth Lake Pontchartrain from New Orleans, you'll reach the Northshore, where several bustling communities offer an appealing blend of big-city sophistication and small-town charm. The St. Tammany Parish towns of Covington, Slidell, and Mandeville boast groves of pine trees and nature preserves, and downtowns dotted with independent shops and restaurants. The 31-mile Tammany Trace bike path laces through the region, providing cyclists, joggers, and walkers easy access to the area's verdant scenery.

The Northshore isn't about museums or formal attractions; it's more a place to hide away in a B&B, dine on exceptional local cooking, browse farmers markets, or tour galleries. Covington has the area's most engaging downtown as well as the most charming B&B, Annadele's Plantation, where cypress and magnolias shade lawns overlooking the Bogue Falaya River. The four guest rooms are large and lovely, but it is the restaurant that makes Annadele's so special. Its signature dish is just-caught Gulf fish topped with sautéed shrimp and jumbo crabmeat.

From Covington, it's a short drive through pastoral horse country to Bush, home of the small but prestigious Pontchartrain Vineyards. Visitors are welcome to help out with the harvest, sample award-winning vintages in the old world–inspired tasting room, or attend a Jazz'n the Vines concert (held bimonthly March through October). Southwest of Covington is tiny Madisonville, located on the banks of the Tchefuncte River and filled with appealing cottages and houseboats.

Another great little low-key town, Abita Springs is best known for brewing the beer that bears its name (the factory is open for tours), as well as one of the more unusual attractions in the South, the wacky Abita Mystery House (aka the UCM museum). Local

The Tammany Trace meanders through loblolly pines, live oaks, and magnolias from Slidell to Covington.

folk artist John Preble dreamed up and operates this quirky, touch-friendly repository of strange sights, which include a stuffed 24-foot-long "bassigator" named Buford (a bizarre work combining the looks of an alligator and a bass), the House of Shards (an oddity painstakingly put together from recycled machinery, license plates, bottle parts, and other shiny debris), and—as the brochure proclaims—pure junk. **WHERE:** 40 miles northeast of New Orleans. *Visitor info:* Tel 800-634-9443 or

985-892-0520; neworleansnorthshore.com. **ANNADELE'S PLANTATION:** Covington. Tel 985-809-7669; annadeles.com. *Cost:* from $175; dinner $50. **PONTCHARTRAIN VINEYARDS:** Folsom. Tel 985-892-9742; pontchartrain vineyards.com. *When:* Wed–Sun; Jazz concerts twice monthly, Mar–Oct. **ABITA MYSTERY HOUSE:** Abita Springs. Tel 985-892-2624; ucmmuseum.com. **BEST TIMES:** early Oct for the Madisonville Wooden Boat Festival (wood enboatfest.org); 2nd weekend in Nov for the juried Covington Three Rivers Art Festival.

Where Cajun and Zydeco Music Rule

EUNICE

Louisiana

T he friendly, largely agricultural community of Eunice is Louisiana's hub and incubator of Cajun and zydeco music. Its infectious rhythms pour out of laid-back, top-notch venues around the region and at various festivals

throughout the year. Cajun and zydeco music share some similarities, and both trace their lineage to this part of the world. Cajun music originated with the Acadian settlers who peopled southwestern Louisiana during the late 18th century (see next page), and is almost always sung in French. Zydeco was begun by African American sharecroppers, slaves, and farmers of the area during the mid-19th century. Each form had considerable influence on the other, and some of the same instruments are used in both (especially the mainstay accordion), but Cajun music bears a closer resemblance to French and other European folk music, while zydeco is closer to blues, Afro-Caribbean music, and R&B.

One of the best places to learn about the music and the heritage of the Cajuns is the Prairie Acadian Cultural Center (part of the Jean Lafitte National Historical Park and Preserve), in downtown Eunice. This handsome museum hosts Cajun and zydeco

concerts in its theater, offers Cajun cooking demonstrations, and has programs and exhibits on local music, crafts, and on farming.

Saturday evening in Eunice means one thing: the family-oriented variety show, *Rendezvous des Cajuns,* best described as the Cajun version of the *Grand Ole Opry.* It's broadcast live on local radio from the handsome Liberty Center for the Performing Arts, a 1920s former vaudeville theater. Today's *Rendezvous* features zydeco and Cajun bands, with locals dancing just beneath the raised stage and the host's animated patter of jokes, recipes, and storytelling in a mix of Cajun and English.

Just outside Eunice at the Savoy Music Center, Saturday morning jam sessions have been drawing musicians well-known and unknown for decades. The music store's owner, Mark Savoy, handcrafts Cajun accordions, and every weekend he and his cronies show how they're meant to be played. Not far away in tiny Mamou, a live music radio program on Saturday mornings packs them in at Fred's Lounge. The place always fills up with folks enjoying beer for breakfast and some of the best live foot-stomping Cajun music in Louisiana.

WHERE: 42 miles northwest of Lafayette. *Visitor info:* Tel 877-948-8004 or 337-457-2565; cajuntravel.com. **PRAIRIE ACADIAN CULTURAL CENTER:** Tel 337-457-8499; nps.gov/jela. *When:* closed Sun–Mon. **LIBERTY CENTER FOR THE PERFORMING ARTS:** Tel 337-457-7389; eunice-la.com. *When:* Rendezvous, Sat evenings. **SAVOY MUSIC CENTER:** Tel 337-457-9563; savoymusiccenter.com. *When:* Sat. **FRED'S LOUNGE:** Mamou. Tel 337-468-5411. *When:* Sat morning. **BEST TIMES:** late Mar for the World Championship Crawfish Étouffée

At the Savoy Music Center, everyone is welcome to join the Saturday morning jam session.

Cook-Off; early Sept for the Southwest Louisiana Zydeco Festival (zydeco.org) in nearby Plaisance; late Oct for the Eunice Folklife Festival.

The Epicenter of Cajun Heritage

ACADIAN CULTURAL CENTER & VERMILIONVILLE

Lafayette, Louisiana

The bustling city of Lafayette is ground zero for exploring southwestern Louisiana's French-speaking and history-rich Cajun Country. It buzzes with restaurants of all kinds, galleries, live-music haunts, excellent museums, and great festivals, and is a must-see for anyone with an interest in Cajun culture.

The place to begin is the informative Acadian Cultural Center, a component of Jean Lafitte National Historic Park and Preserve. Styled like a traditional Cajun cottage, the building contains exhibits on Cajun music, folklore, food, language, and history, and shows a moving 35-minute film, *The Cajun Way: Echoes of Acadia*, about the forced removal of the French Acadian people from eastern Canada in the mid-18th century. By the turn of the 19th century, nearly 4,000 displaced Acadians (the origin of the word "Cajuns") settled in southwestern Louisiana's wetlands and prairies.

Spend a day exploring Vermilionville, a wonderful living-history museum spread across 23 acres. The re-created Cajun village sits along Bayou Vermilion and contains a convincing mix of reproduction 18th- and 19th-century buildings and actual historic structures. Docents in period attire demonstrate aspects of daily Cajun life, such as weaving, spinning, boatbuilding, and blacksmithing. Enjoy an authentic Cajun lunch in the village's La Cuisine de Maman restaurant, accompanied by live Cajun music.

One of Lafayette's most lauded restaurants, Café Vermilionville (no relation to the museum), occupies a charming, newly renovated, two-story Creole house. In a rustic but elegant high-ceilinged dining room, owner Ken Veron blends traditional Cajun and Creole ingredients with modern sensibilities. Start with the crawfish beignets with mustard aioli and fried pickles and proceed to sweet Louisiana Gulf fish of the day—topped with jumbo lump crabmeat in a light dill beure

Vermilionville's traditional Cajun cooking demonstrations are second only to its restaurant's authentic Cajun lunches.

blanc. To hear terrific Cajun, zydeco, and swamp pop music, head to the Blue Moon Saloon, a homey back-porch bar popular with locals. The beer is cold, the music hot, and the atmosphere laid back.

WHERE: 135 miles west of New Orleans. *Visitor info:* Tel 800-346-1958 or 337-232-3737; lafayettetravel.com. **ACADIAN CULTURAL CENTER:** Tel 337-232-0789; nps.gov/jela. **VERMILIONVILLE:** Tel 866-99-BAYOU or 337-233-4077; vermilionville.org. *When:* closed Mon. **CAFÉ VERMILIONVILLE:** Tel 337-237-0100; cafev.com. *Cost:* dinner $50. **BLUE MOON SALOON:** Tel 877-766-BLUE or 337-234-2422; bluemoonpresents.com. *When:* Wed–Sun. **BEST TIMES:** 5 days in late Apr for Festival International de Louisiane (festivalinternational .com); late May–early June for the 11-day Cajun Heartland State Fair; mid-Oct for the Festivals Acadiens et Creoles, celebrating the region's Cajun and Creole heritage.

Meat Pies and Steel Magnolias

NATCHITOCHES

Louisiana

Louisiana's earliest permanent European settlement is not New Orleans but rather the jewel-like town of Natchitoches (pronounced NACK-ih-tish)—the name comes from the region's original inhabitants, the Natchitoches Indians. Established in 1714 by the French as a trading post on the Red River, this charming town has a genteel European air especially distinct in its fine 33-block National Historic District overlooking Cane River Lake. Its enclave of mostly late 18th- and 19th-century buildings is sometimes compared to the French Quarter in New Orleans.

Home to Northwestern State University, Natchitoches was something of a sleepy backwater until Hollywood arrived to film *Steel Magnolias* in 1989. Adapted from a play by native son Robert Harling III (who based the

main characters upon the women in his family), the film transformed the town. Streetcars and horse-drawn carriages give tours pointing out the various buildings and businesses featured in the movie. Many of the town's historic Queen Anne and Victorian homes (and the occasional Creole cottage) operate as B&Bs or restaurants, but for the best peek inside them, take a guided tour during either the Fall Pilgrimage or the Christmas holiday, when a choice few are open to the public. Topping the B&B list is the romantic Judge Porter House. Built in 1912, the grand Queen Anne–influenced building stands out for its two-story gallery porch and tall windows overlooking a small, colorful garden and pool. The multicourse breakfast by candlelight is an opulent affair—a specialty are the puff pastries filled with fresh berries and topped with raspberry sauce.

The town's great culinary claim is a meat pie, popular in these parts since the late 1700s. For more than 40 years, the best have been served at Lasyone's Meat Pie Kitchen. One delicious half-moon pastry, consisting of ground beef and pork with onions and parsley, Worcestershire sauce, and Cajun spices, is a meal unto itself. Don't forget to sample the Cane River cream pie, not unlike Boston cream pie, but Natchitoches style.

Make time to visit Melrose Plantation, 15 miles south of town. Built between 1796 and 1833 by the descendants of a freed slave, it was eventually sold to Mrs. Cammie Garrett Henry and her husband in 1899. After her husband's death in 1918, Mrs. Henry began a tradition of welcoming artists and writers: William Faulkner, Erskine Caldwell, and Alexander Woollcott found their muse here. Her cook was no exception; inspired by paintings left behind by visiting artists, she began illustrating her own impressions of plantation life. That artist was Clementine Hunter, one of

The historic district of Natchitoches overlooks the Cane River Lake.

the South's finest and most prolific primitive folk artists, who lived at Melrose from the age of 16 until she died in 1988 at 101.

WHERE: 75 miles southeast of Shreveport. *Visitor info:* Tel 800-259-1714 or 318-352-8072; natchitoches.com. **JUDGE PORTER HOUSE:** Tel 800-441-8343 or 318-352-9206; judgeporterhouse.com. *Cost:* from $135. **LASYONE'S:** Tel 318-352-3353; lasyones.com. *Cost:* lunch $15. **MELROSE PLANTATION:** Tel 318-379-0055; melroseplantation.org. **BEST TIMES:** mid-Sept for the Meat Pie Festival (meatpiefestival.com); mid-Oct for the Fall Pilgrimage (natchitoches.com); mid-Nov–early Dec for the Christmas Festival (holidaytrailoflights.com); late winter for Mardi Gras.

The Spanish Jewel of Acadiana

NEW IBERIA

Louisiana

A cadiana, or Cajun Country, extends from the Texas border to just west of New Orleans. The small city of New Iberia offers some of the area's top attractions—fine old homes, appealing boutiques, Cajun restaurants,

and a pretty downtown. Spanish immigrants from the Iberian Peninsula city of Málaga settled here in 1779—hence its name. The town developed as a farming hub and soon attracted displaced Cajun arrivals. Today New Iberia retains a culture and personality decidedly more Cajun than Spanish. Downtown New Iberia revolves around the town's historic jewel, Shadows-on-the-Teche (named for its location directly on Bayou Teche), a regal white-columned, brick plantation house built in 1834 by sugarcane planter David Weeks. An intimate plantation museum, it displays an impressive collection of documents and memorabilia illustrating the Weeks family story.

Among the more unusual geographical features of Acadiana are its salt domes, called "islands" in these parts. The most famous is Avery Island, which has been owned by the McIlhenny family since long before the Civil War and is still mined for salt. Edward McIlhenny developed America's favorite hot sauce, Tabasco, here first selling it in 1868; the factory offers an amusing tour, and the adjacent Tabasco Country Store stocks every imaginable kind of Tabasco memorabilia. A visit to the Jungle Gardens and Bird City, the McIlhenny family's lush 170-acre wildlife and wetlands nature preserve, allows you to wander dense forests and gardens (and view the world's largest collection of camellias) and get an up-close look at deer, turtles, raccoons, and alligators. Each spring 20,000 egrets and herons raise their young in the preserve.

Take a short walk up the town's lovely Main Street to enjoy lunch at Victor's Cafeteria. This no-frills spot features prominently in the popular crime novels by local author James Lee Burke, whose protagonist Detective Dave Robicheaux routinely dines here. Expect simple Cajun and Creole fare and lots of it, such as fried shrimp or red beans and sausage. Have

The Shadows-on-the-Teche features a Louisiana Colonial floorplan, with exterior staircases and no interior hallways.

dinner at Clementine's, named for the primitive painter Clementine Hunter (see p. 423) and decorated with local artwork. You'll enjoy such dishes as shrimp remoulade and crispy catfish with crab étouffé, along with friendly service and live music on most weekends.

WHERE: 20 miles southeast of Lafayette. *Visitor info:* Tel 888-9-IBERIA or 337-365-1540; iberiatravel.com. **SHADOWS-ON-THE-TECHE:** Tel 337-369-6446; shadowsontheteche.org. **MCILHENNY TABASCO CO., JUNGLE GARDENS AND BIRD CITY:** Tel 337-369-6243; junglegardens.org. **VICTOR'S CAFETERIA:** Tel 337-369-9924. *Cost:* lunch $10. **CLEMENTINE'S:** Tel 337-560-1007; clementinedowntown.com. *Cost:* dinner $30. **BEST TIMES:** early Apr for Cajun Hot Sauce Festival; Dec for Christmas on the Bayou festivities.

A Gumbo of Pleasures in America's Most Un-American City

THE FRENCH QUARTER

New Orleans, Louisiana

It's a fascinating, sultry melting pot of French, Spanish, Italian, Caribbean, African, and Southern styles that magically blends decadence and elegance, conservatism and debauchery, extroversion and sleepiness, gentility and tawdriness. It's hard to imagine a more impulsive or seductive city (this is where Rhett Butler brought Scarlett O'Hara for their honeymoon). Much changed superficially and profoundly when one of the nation's fiercest storms ever, Hurricane Katrina, damaged the levees, which led to widespread flooding in 2005. But the city showed formidable resilience. The French Quarter was only marginally damaged and the majority of the sites that made the Big Easy a perennially favorite tourist destination were soon back and going strong.

Many of these myriad pleasures are packed within the lively grid of streets that make up the Vieux Carré (aka the French Quarter), which received little flooding and relatively minor storm damage. It is the city's most touristy area, yet also its heart. The French laid out the Quarter's 78 square blocks of narrow streets in the 1720s, and the Spanish—who ruled the Louisiana Territory during the mid- to late 18th century—further developed it. Indeed, despite its name, the neighborhood looks architecturally more Spanish than French. Gloriously faded landmark buildings with wrought-iron balconies contain quirky, sometimes swanky, stores selling museum-quality antiques, alongside others hawking alligator T-shirts and voodoo paraphernalia.

The French Quarter's Royal Street boasts elegant antiques shops and art galleries.

Wherever you stroll, you risk sensory overload from the musicians, mimes, and tap dancers (who use bottle caps on their shoes). Jackson Square is the epicenter of activity—you can take it all in from the alfresco 24-hour Café du Monde, famous for its beignets (deep-fried fritters dusted in powdered sugar) and chicory-charged café au lait. Decatur Street offers souvenir stands, offbeat boutiques, and charming restaurants. Royal and Chartres Streets are your best bets for upscale shopping, holding the majority of the top antiques emporia and art galleries. And notorious Bourbon Street is lined with boisterous music clubs and restaurants of varying quality—it's a nightly parade of revelry that some visitors adore and others abhor. Pop into the tacky but fun Pat O'Brien's, and be sure to order their signature "Hurricane," the renowned—and potent—fruity rum cocktail.

WHERE: bounded by the Mississippi River and Rampart St., and Canal St. and Esplanade Ave. *Visitor info:* Tel 800-203-2144 or 504-636-1051; frenchquarter.com. **CAFÉ DU MONDE:** Tel 800-772-2927 or 504-587-0833; cafedumonde .com. *Cost:* beignets and café for two, $8. **PAT O'BRIEN'S:** Tel 504-525-4823; patobriens .com. **BEST TIMES:** Jan–Feb for Mardi Gras; Mar–May and Oct–Nov for weather; early Apr for the 4-day French Quarter Festival. Christmas is magical and often overlooked.

The Essence of New Orleans High Society

THE GARDEN DISTRICT

New Orleans, Louisiana

The epicenter of New Orleans high society and its richest architectural heritage, the Garden District covers what once was a number of plantations in the 1700s. Over time it was split into smaller parcels, and in the 19th

century wealthy Anglo residents (as opposed to the French-speaking Creoles a couple of miles downriver in the French Quarter; see p. 424), whose wealth came from the city's busy shipping trade, built massive mansions. Many of these stunning displays of Greek Revival, Second

Empire, and Italianate influence still stand.

The Garden District is one of the loveliest neighborhoods in all the South for a stroll. Tour companies give narrated rambles along the character-rich streets, describing its many illustrious residents, including Sandra Bullock, John Goodman, and Archie Manning. Until 2005, novelist Anne Rice of vampire fame lived in the Brevard House, a stunning Greek Revival–Italianate.

New Orleans has long been famous for its burial grounds, or "cities of the dead." Their raised graves (a high water table didn't allow for digging) were marked by elaborate headstones and a maze of mausoleums. Visit the Garden District's Lafayette Cemetery No. 1 with a tour guide from Save Our Cemeteries, a nonprofit organization working to preserve New Orleans's

This handsome Greek Revival–style mansion sits in the heart of the Garden District.

31 historic cemeteries. (They also give colorful tours of St. Louis Cemetery No. 1, on the edge of the French Quarter, whose most visited tomb is that of Marie Laveau, Voodoo Queen of New Orleans.)

Just across the street from Lafayette Cemetery, a frothy blue-and-white Victorian mansion houses Commander's Palace, a hallowed temple of gastronomy. Its daring mix of rich, old-school Creole cuisine and more innovative fare ensures a devoted following. Whether you're in the Garden Room or in the shade of the open courtyard's massive oak, order the signature turtle soup with dry sherry, the crispy, pecan-crusted Gulf fish, and the famous bread pudding soufflé wading in whiskey cream sauce. In the city where jazz was born, the Jazz Brunch is a weekend tradition cherished by New Orleanians and tourists alike.

The south end of the Garden District is edged by the city's most popular shopping thoroughfare, Magazine Street, where you'll find superb antiques shops, plus a riot of funky clothiers, offbeat coffeehouses, upscale bistros, down-home po'boy shops, and delightful Creole and West Indies–inspired cottages.

Visitor info: Tel 800-672-6124 or 504-566-5003; neworleansonline.com. **Historic New Orleans Tours:** Tel 504-947-2120; tourneworleans.com. **Save Our Cemeteries:** Tel 504-525-3377; saveourcemeteries.org. **Commander's Palace:** Tel 504-899-8221; commanderspalace.com. *Cost:* dinner $55. **Best times:** Mar–May and Oct–Nov, when temperatures are a bit cooler, but gardens are in bloom.

"Laissez les Bons Temps Roulez"

Mardi Gras

New Orleans, Louisiana

M ardi Gras would be heaven without the multitudes of half-lit partygoers, but it also wouldn't be Mardi Gras. Those who subscribe to the old saw that hell is other people, should stay far, far away. Celebrated by those of the "laissez les bons temps roulez" mentality, Mardi Gras is America's biggest, liveliest, and most show-stopping party. Just six months after Hurricane Katrina struck the city, Mardi Gras 2006 drew smaller crowds than in previous years, but its success still provided a raucous, heartfelt confirmation that New Orleans will always be one of America's most loved tourist destinations. Mardi Gras is the Big Easy's unrivaled party, and the world is invited.

Months before the late-winter festival, intense preparations begin with the creation of elaborate two- and three-story floats and costumes to match, crescendoing to a funky marching-band beat during the 12-day lead-up to Mardi Gras itself. (Mardi Gras, which means "Fat Tuesday" or Shrove Tuesday, is the day before Ash Wednesday; it generally falls in February and ushers in the 40 days of the somber Catholic period of Lent that leads up to Easter.)

This is New Orleans's exuberant feast before the famine, a dizzy intertwining of its centuries-old Caribbean and European cultural roots, as much a commercial show to reap tourism dollars as a revered local tradition. Arrive early to stake out a spot along the parade routes of St. Charles Avenue and Canal Street, amid a sea of carnivalistas chanting "Throw me something, mister!" demanding the plastic doubloons and cups, trinkets, and coveted necklaces that are tossed by float-borne revelers. During the height of Mardi Gras season, New Orleans is covered with more than 3 million plastic cups, another

An exquisitely dressed fantasy prince marches in one of the many Mardi Gras parades.

3 million strands of beads, and more than 20 million doubloons. Of the many parades that begin in earnest two weeks prior to Fat Tuesday, the biggest and best, featuring the famous floats, take place day and night beginning the previous Thursday. King cakes, tasty confections iced in the colors of Mardi Gras, fill bakery windows throughout the city, and restaurants and music clubs are open into the wee hours.

VISITOR INFO: mardigras.com. *When:* The season begins Jan 6 and ends on a Tues, usually in Feb, depending on the changing Easter calendar.

The Lifeblood of the Big Easy

NEW ORLEANS'S MUSIC SCENE

New Orleans, Louisiana

The music we know as jazz was born in late 19th-century New Orleans, derived from a confluence of European harmonies and African rhythms. It was honed by musicians like cornetist Buddy Bolden, drummer Papa

Jack Laine, and pianist Jelly Roll Morton—who performed in the high-class bordellos of the legendary Storyville district—and given a new and clear voice in the 1920s and '30s by locally born Louis "Satchmo" Armstrong. Though the city's importance as a musical center faded during the subsequent big band, bebop, and postbop eras, by the late 1980s local trumpeter Wynton Marsalis and his family had succeeded in repopularizing the traditional New Orleans sound by nurturing their own particular strain of modern jazz.

The Big Easy's annual Jazz and Heritage Festival (aka "Jazz Fest") is one of America's great music parties. For ten days in late April and early May, hundreds of musicians perform on ten stages to an audience whose recent numbers approached 500,000. They offer not just jazz but Cajun, Latin, zydeco, R&B, rock, gospel, and African-Caribbean music—with exuberant brass bands marching tirelessly through it all. Today's jazz and soul luminaries (including such New Orleans natives as Harry Connick Jr. and the Neville Brothers) wouldn't miss this shindig, which in recent years has also drawn Tony Bennett, Lady Gaga, John Legend, Paul Simon, and Bruce Springsteen. Hundreds of artisans sell their wares, and the best of Louisiana's culinary heritage (from shrimp po'boys to alligator piquante) shares the spotlight at over 100 stalls. Sweet tooths should save room for sweet potato pone, Key lime pie, and white chocolate bread pudding.

If you're not here at Fest time (and even if you are), visit the dark and spartan Preservation Hall, beloved by purists, showcasing classic New Orleans jazz. With a worn wooden floor, no food or drinks, and only a few wooden benches for seating, the place is a diamond in brown-paper-bag clothing, a world-famous institution since it opened in 1961.

The musical pilgrimage continues at the legendary Tipitina's, an uptown club where jazz, Cajun, country, and R&B keep the dance floor full in what once was a gambling hall and whorehouse. The club helped launch the sterling careers of such legends as Dr. John and Allen Toussaint. Snug Harbor, an intimate storefront jazz bistro in the hip Faubourg Marigny (a short walk from the French Quarter), is the best place to find contemporary jazz and R&B, with random appearances by big names like Ellis Marsalis and Charmaine Neville. You'll find lively zydeco, Cajun, R&B, and jazz at Mid-City Bowling Lanes, aka Rock 'n' Bowl. And then there are those days when it seems that the solitary sax player in front of the cathedral in Jackson Square is the best thing you've heard all week—and it's free.

VISITOR INFO: Tel 800-672-6124 or 504-566-5003; neworleansonline.com. **JAZZ AND HERITAGE FESTIVAL:** Tel 800-488-5252 or 504-410-4100; nojazzfest.com. *Cost:* $70 at the gate. *When:* late Apr–early May. **PRESERVATION HALL:** Tel 504-522-2841; preservationhall .com. **TIPITINA'S:** Tel 504-895-8477; tipitinas .com. **SNUG HARBOR:** Tel 504-949-0696; snugjazz.com. **MID-CITY BOWLING LANES:** Tel 504-861-1700; rockandbowl.com.

In "jazz funerals," a New Orleans tradition, musicians parade to and from the cemetery while mourners and onlookers follow.

THE NEW ORLEANS RESTAURANT SCENE

New Orleans, Louisiana

In the Crescent City, a place where food is religion, the funkiest neighborhood joint is as beloved as the grandest or most traditional restaurant. New Orleans has always been a place where people take food seriously, ranking among America's best gastro cities, like New York, Chicago, Las Vegas, and San Francisco.

In the French Quarter, dining at Galatoire's has been a New Orleans tradition since 1905, even though its egalitarian no-reservations policy (for the main dining room downstairs) means that celebrities, tourists, and locals alike sometimes must line up along Bourbon Street, men in jackets (at dinner and all day Sunday) to conform to the restaurant's dress code. Its timeless decor of brass fixtures, gleaming mirrors, polished wood, and a dozen ceiling fans has changed little over the years. Tuxedoed waiters bear appetizers of shrimp rémoulade or oysters Rockefeller, and such classic entrées as lamb chops béarnaise, pan-seared duck with confit, and shrimp Marguery. The food is surpassed only by the floor show, which peaks at Friday lunchtime: Everyone is drinking, table-hopping, and recounting loud stories; the chatter crescendos, corks pop, "Happy Birthday" is sung at least once. Even newcomers get into the spirit of camaraderie. The Galatoire empire expanded in 2013 with the addition of Galatoire's 33 Bar & Steak next door.

When the urge strikes for a nonwhite-linen locale, nothing will satisfy better than Acme Oyster House. In addition to its award-winning fresh and salty raw oysters and 12 types of po'boy, there is also jambalaya, red beans and rice, and seafood étouffée. Or try Central Grocery, an old-fashioned Italian deli with counter seating and shelves of delicious imported foods, from oils and vinegars to gnocchi and pine nuts. Its claim to fame is having perfected (some say invented) one of the city's classic sandwiches, the muffuletta: sesame-seed Italian bread slathered with tangy olive salad spread and packed with Italian cold cuts and provolone cheese. Chase it down with a bottle of Barq's root beer.

A few blocks downriver from the French Quarter, in the hip, bohemian Faubourg Marigny neighborhood, you'll find some of the best soul-Creole food around at Praline (pronounced PRAW-leen) Connection, housed in a dapper storefront with black-and-white tile floors. There are fried chicken livers with sweet hot-pepper jelly, and sides of fried okra, candied yams, red beans and rice, and fried alligator sausage. Honor the eatery's name with an order of the fluffy cheesecake, dripping with gooey praline sauce.

The weathered and funky Napoleon House has been a fixture since it opened in 1914. It serves its muffuletta sandwich hot, as well as heavenly meatball sandwiches and jambalaya with chicken, shrimp, and sausage. A few other favorite contenders: Emeril's is the Lagasse flagship and a longtime favorite; Cochon, showcasing downhome Cajun cooking; the high-altar, tradition-bound Antoine's; the contemporary, globe-hopping fare of locally renowned chef Susan Spicer at Bayona. The working-class po'boy haven of Mother's, in the Central Business District, demands at least one visit. Try their Ferdi po'boy with roast beef, baked ham, and gravy, and ask for extra "debris" (the roast-beef carvings that have fallen into the gravy).

GALATOIRE'S: Tel 504-525-2021; galatoires .com. *Cost:* dinner $45. **ACME OYSTER HOUSE:** Tel 504-522-5973; acmeoyster.com. *Cost:* dinner $15. **CENTRAL GROCERY:** Tel 504-523-1620. *Cost:* lunch $10. **PRALINE CONNECTION:** Tel 504-943-3934; pralineconnection.com. *Cost:* dinner $25. **NAPOLEON HOUSE:** Tel 504-524-9752; napoleonhouse.com. *Cost:* dinner $20. **EMERIL'S:** Tel 504-528-9393; emerils restaurants.com. *Cost:* dinner $60. **COCHON:** Tel 504-588-2123; cochonrestaurants.com. *Cost:* $45. **ANTOINE'S:** Tel 504-581-4422; antoines.com. *Cost:* dinner $55. **BAYONA:** Tel 504-525-4455; bayona.com. *Cost:* dinner $50. **MOTHER'S:** Tel 504-523-9656; mothers restaurant.net. *Cost:* lunch $15.

Mother's serves breakfast all day, but the big draw is the po'boy.

Sweet Dreams in Splendid Surroundings

NEW ORLEANS'S ROMANTIC HOTELS

New Orleans, Louisiana

O f the Big Easy's charming and historic hotels, arguably the most beautiful choice is the genteel Soniat House in the central French Quarter. Comprised of three 19th-century Creole town houses, the hotel was built

by a prosperous plantation owner and today houses an eclectic mélange of choice period pieces and modern-day comforts. It's 31 attractive rooms offer four-poster beds, toile de Jouy bedspreads and goosedown pillows, and thoughtfully chosen French and English antiques (similar pieces are for sale at the on-premises antiques shop run by the hotel's owner). Many rooms overlook the romantic fountain in the interior courtyard, where guests breakfast on just-out-of-the-oven buttermilk biscuits with homemade strawberry preserves.

The Hotel Maison de Ville offers equal charm and is also secluded from the touristy quarter's hubbub. The elegant 18th-century main house was once the home of the man who created New Orleans's now-legendary Sazerac cocktail. Guest rooms can also be found in the carriage house and former bachelor quarters, boasting a green landscaped courtyard and a small pool. Just a few blocks from the French Quarter in offbeat Faubourg Marigny, the supremely characterful Elysian Fields Inn occupies a handsomely restored 1860s Greek

Revival house. Nine guest rooms have high ceilings, Egyptian cotton bedding, and floors done in rich South American mahogany, all overseen by attentive and amiable innkeepers.

For a big-hotel experience and a high dose of history, it's hard to beat the lavish (and recently renovated) 1886 Hotel Monteleone, the 573-room grande dame in the heart of the French Quarter. Such notable literati as Ernest Hemingway, Tennessee Williams, and William Faulkner encamped in this 17-floor beauty crowned by a distinctive red neon sign. The hotel overlooks the French Quarter's most elegant thoroughfare, Royal Street, lined with fine antiques shops and art galleries. Enjoy a Detox Day wrap in the hotel's Spa Aria; then, rejuvenated, sip their signature Vieux Carré cocktail in the famed Carousel Bar and Lounge, with its elaborate circus-themed decor.

For sheer opulence and seamless white-glove service, the swank Windsor Court Hotel is tops, as famous for its multimillion-dollar collection of European art (including originals by Van Dyck, Reynolds, and Gainsborough) as for its palatial accommodations (more than 80 percent of the 316 rooms are suites). Conveniently located in the Central Business District, the hotel is steps from the French Quarter and the arty Warehouse District. Its restaurant, the Grill Room, is one of the top dining venues in town and serves sophisticated interpretations of local favorites.

Soniat House: Tel 800-544-8808 or 504-522-0570; soniathouse.com. *Cost:* from $240. **Hotel Maison de Ville:** Tel 504-324-4888; maisondeville.com. *Cost:* from $199. **Elysian Fields Inn:** Tel 866-948-9420 or 504-948-9420; elysianfieldsinn.com. *Cost:* from $129. **Hotel Monteleone:** Tel 866-338-4684 or 504-523-3341; hotelmonteleone.com. *Cost:* from $179. **Windsor Court Hotel:** Tel 800-928-7898 or 504-523-6000; windsorcourt hotel.com. *Cost:* from $199; dinner $55.

Stately Homes of the Old South

PLANTATION COUNTRY

Louisiana

The customs, architecture, and traditions of the Old South come to life in the myriad homes along the banks of the Mississippi, in Louisiana's Plantation Country. Antebellum-dressed guides recount tales of Confederate

spies, yellow fever, love stories, and Civil War tragedies, and give an intimate glimpse of plantations that grew rich on indigo, cotton, rice, tobacco, and sugarcane. The 100-mile serpentine segment of the Great River Road between New Orleans and Baton Rouge is home to numerous plantations, mostly in rural towns that haven't changed much in the past century.

Make sure to visit two of the area's gems: Oak Alley and Laura, in the small town of Vacherie. Few homes are more often photographed than Oak Alley, whose imposing facade is bracketed by a magnificent quarter-mile-long "allée" of 28 moss-draped, centuries-old live oak trees. Oak Alley mansion is surrounded by some 25 acres dotted with crape myrtle trees, azaleas, and flower gardens.

Just down the River Road from Oak Alley is Laura, a Creole plantation, whose multicolored and rather modest facade distinguishes it from the white-columned Greek Revival mansions built by the Anglo American planters. Based on the extensive memoirs left by the four generations of Creole women who presided over the plantation, the tours focus more on the family who occupied it than the house itself, and reveal an honest, sometimes disturbing, always illuminating look into the inner workings of the plantation. The slave cabins are particularly interesting as the setting for the West African folktales of Br'er Rabbit. Another must-see is the 250-acre Whitney Plantation, 35 miles west of New Orleans. The 18th-century indigo, sugar, and cotton operation (scenes from *Django Unchained* were filmed here) is a mix of

Iconic Oak Alley Plantation has been featured in many films, including Gone with the Wind *(1939) and* Cat on a Hot Tin Roof *(1958).*

original and restored structures that opened to the public in late 2014 following an $8 million investment from a local real estate mogul. It offers a unique experience as a museum dedicated exclusively to telling the story of slavery.

The area's best lodging can be found at the lovely Madewood Plantation in Napoleonville. The 21-room Greek Revival beauty, built in 1846, can be visited by tour, but the treat here is to unpack your bag and stay the night. The rooms are decorated according to the period, and the rates include an elegant candlelit four-course dinner at a long oak dining table, coffee and brandy afterward in the drawing room, and a full plantation breakfast the next morning.

WHERE: Vacherie is about 50 miles west of New Orleans. *Visitor info:* Tel 225-562-2266; stjamesla.com. **OAK ALLEY:** Vacherie. Tel 800-44-ALLEY or 225-265-2151; oakalleyplantation.com. **LAURA:** Vacherie. Tel 888-799-7690 or 225-265-7690; lauraplantation.com. **WHITNEY PLANTATION:** Wallace. Tel 225-265-3300; whitneyplantation.com. **MADEWOOD:** Napoleonville. Tel 985-369-7151; madewood.com. *Cost:* rooms from $229, includes dinner. **BEST TIMES:** 3rd weekend in Oct for the Br'er Rabbit Folk Festival at Laura Plantation; Dec for the Christmas Bonfire parties when towns along the river construct massive bonfires.

Deep in the Bayou

HONEY ISLAND SWAMP TOURS

Slidell, Louisiana

Louisiana is associated with its swamps more than any other state in the South. The southern half of the state has been virtually carved out of wetlands and reclaimed from nature. Although storms like 2005's hurricanes Katrina and Rita have pummeled southern Louisiana since time immemorial and man has changed—and in many respects damaged—the region's wetlands through various flood-control and development projects, Louisiana's swamps remain almost unbelievably resilient and are home to countless animals and plants that thrive only here.

To get a true sense of the state, sign up for a boat swamp tour and venture deep into the heart of one of its primeval wetland wildernesses. One of the most interesting tours explores the fascinating Honey Island Swamp, departing from the town of Slidell, on New Orleans' Northshore (see p. 419). Naturalists accompany the motorized flat-bottomed boats that quietly penetrate the swamp, all the while recounting wetlands folklore, including tales of a mythical swamp creature called Wookie, as well as helping visitors arrive at a thorough understanding of how the wetlands have shaped the history of southern Louisiana.

With nearly 70,000 acres of lost-in-time wilderness, Honey Island Swamp is the second largest in Louisiana, after Atchafalaya, and is fed by the Pearl River. This is a tranquil, unspoiled place full of tupelo, cypress, and river birch trees. Tours travel 7 or 8 miles into the swamp's almost impenetrable backwaters, where you're apt to see alligators (from spring through fall), grey herons, kingfishers, ancient snapping turtles, and furry nutria

(members of the beaver family). A visit here will awaken your inner Audubon.

WHERE: 32 miles northeast of New Orleans. **HONEY ISLAND SWAMP TOURS:** Tel 985-641-1769; honeyislandswamp.com. *Cost:* $23 for half-day tour. **BEST TIMES:** Apr–May and Sept–Nov, when wildlife is more abundant.

Honey Island Swamp is one of the least altered river swamps in the U.S.

Magnolias and Mansions

ST. FRANCISVILLE

Louisiana

The state's second-oldest incorporated town (after Natchitoches; see p. 422), St. Francisville (population 1,700) maintains a quiet dignity and old-fashioned character. A monastery dedicated to St. Francis was established

in 1785 atop a bluff above the port, and the town of St. Francisville followed in 1809. It prospered during the 19th century, as ships' captains and industrialists built cotton plantations and grand homes, a good number of which have survived.

Chockablock with antiques shops, restaurants, and handsome inns, the St. Francisville Historic District preserves many of the finest homes and churches and is a lovely place for a stroll. You'll pass buildings of virtually every architectural style on streets lined with

magnolias and other flowering trees. East of downtown is St. Francisville's most prominent attraction, Rosedown Plantation. Daniel Turnbull, one of the wealthiest men in America at the time, built this immense cotton plantation and filled the 1835 neoclassical manor house at its center with museum-quality antiques from Europe and the U.S. There are excellent tours of the restored house and the 18 remaining acres of ornamental gardens.

Also on the outskirts of town, the Audubon State Historic Site is the anchor of a lush

100-acre park graced by the West Indies–influenced Oakley House, built circa 1806. The famed nature painter, John J. Audubon lived here in 1821 and created all or part of at least 32 of his beloved bird paintings. The park's 6-mile trail is, as you might expect, excellent for bird-watching in the spring and fall. Each spring, during the Audubon Pilgrimage, antebellum-costumed guides lead tours of various plantations, private homes, gardens, and churches.

A taste of that antebellum lifestyle can be yours during an overnight stay at the circa 1796 Myrtles Plantation, said to be one of the

The 17-room Oakley House, former home of John J. Audubon, is shaded by ancient oak and crape myrtle trees.

most haunted homes in the nation. The daily guided tours provide a great sense of the house and its past, but the Mystery Tours offered on weekend evenings are particularly fun, recounting stories of the spirits who are said to live here. Accommodations include six rooms in the main house, some with private verandas and massive four-poster beds. You can dine in the Carriage House restaurant on the grounds, known for Cajun-style seafood dishes as well as more standard fare. Try the Louisiana Étouffée over a bed of rice.

WHERE: 31 miles north of Baton Rouge. *Visitor info:* Tel 800-789-4221 or 225-635-4224; stfrancisville.us. **ROSEDOWN PLANTATION:** Tel 888-376-1867 or 225-635-3332; nps.gov/nr/travel/louisiana/ros.htm. **AUDUBON STATE HISTORIC SITE:** Jackson. Tel 888-677-2838 or 225-635-3739; lastateparks.com. **MYRTLES PLANTATION:** Tel 800-809-0565 or 225-635-6278; myrtlesplantation.com. *Cost:* from $175; dinner at Carriage House $35. **BEST TIMES:** mid-Mar for the Audubon Pilgrimage (westfeliciana historicalsociety.org). In mid-Apr and every Sun in Oct, the notorious Angola prison (25 miles north of St. Francisville), America's largest maximum security prison, holds the famous Angola Prison Rodeo (angolarodeo.com).

The Birthplace of Cajun Culture

ST. MARTINVILLE & BREAUX BRIDGE

Louisiana

The Cajuns (a corruption of "Acadians") are the Louisiana descendants of French settlers who had emigrated to Canada's Maritime provinces in the 17th and 18th centuries. When the British expelled them from Canada,

a small group fled to southwestern Louisiana in 1765, establishing the now historic community of St. Martinville on the banks of Bayou Teche. Its commercial center revolves around dramatic

Church Square, dominated by one of the oldest Catholic churches in the South, St. Martin de Tours, whose congregation dates back to 1765. The town grew rapidly during its first century and was, by the 1850s, one of Louisiana's largest cities, nicknamed "Petit Paris" for its upscale hotels and theater scene. Although other Cajun towns have surpassed it in growth and prominence, St. Martinville proudly retains its appealing character and ardently celebrates a rich Cajun heritage.

Many visitors come to admire the famed Evangeline Oak, overlooking Bayou Teche and supposedly the site where the betrothed lovers immortalized in Longfellow's 1847 poem *Evangeline* were reunited following their tragic separation during the expulsion from Canada. The St. Martinville Cultural Heritage Center, composed of an African American Museum and a Museum of the Acadian Memorial, contains well-presented exhibits tracing the heritage of these two groups.

Thirteen miles to the north is the culturally rich community in nearby Breaux Bridge, its small, bustling downtown hopping with

Two St. Martinville locals entertain passersby with an accordian and a triangle.

boutiques and pleasant restaurants. Check into Maison des Amis, an 1860 Caribbean-Creole cottage with four guest rooms overlooking Bayou Teche. Breakfast is offered around the corner at the first-rate Café des Amis, a down-home-elegant storefront serving up some mighty fine (and creative) Cajun fare. Breaux Bridge is called the Crawfish Capital of the world, so be sure to order the corn bread smothered with crawfish étouffée. Saturday mornings Café des Amis presents the not-to-be-missed Zydeco Breakfast, with live music and dancing to go with your eggs and boudin sausage or traditional *couche couche*, Cajun cornmeal cereal with syrup and sugar.

On the edge of downtown is the loud and raucous dance hall Mulate's, also much ballyhooed as the world's most famous Cajun restaurant, where the house specialty is catfish Mulate's (piled high with crawfish étouffée). Live bands draw crowds onto the well-worn dance floor every night of the week. It's touristy, but this is one of those places where more is merrier.

WHERE: St. Martinville is 16 miles southeast of Lafayette. *Visitor info:* Tel 888-565-5939 or 337-442-1597; cajuncountry.org. **ST. MARTINVILLE CULTURAL CENTER:** Tel 337-394-2258; acadianmemorial.org. **MAISON DES AMIS:** Breaux Bridge. Tel 337-507-3399; maisondesamis.com. *Cost:* from $120. **CAFÉ DES AMIS:** Breaux Bridge. Tel 337-332-5273; cafedesamis.com. *Cost:* breakfast $12. **MULATE'S:** Breaux Bridge. Tel 504-522-1492; mulates.com. *Cost:* dinner $45. **BEST TIMES:** early May for Breaux Bridge's Crawfish Festival; late Nov for its Cajun Christmas Bayou Parade.

Mythical Crossroads in the Mississippi Delta

THE BLUES HIGHWAY

Clarksdale, Mississippi

Highway 61 is the storied two-lane road that carried poor rural musicians and sharecroppers out of the dusty Mississippi cotton fields in the 1930s and '40s. This "Blues Highway" led them north toward Memphis and

St. Louis, where audiences first clamored for the raw, emotional singing and guitar playing that emerged from the Jim Crow South.

The cradle of the American blues movement, Clarksdale is an eerily compelling place—a flat, gritty town of 17,292 that lies at the famed intersection of Highways 61 and 49—the crossroads, legend claims, where aspiring blues musician Robert Johnson sold his soul to the devil in exchange for the prodigious guitar-playing skills he acquired seemingly overnight. Johnson, a traveling man, lived only for music, whiskey, and women, and sang of a "Hellhound on My Trail." Only 27 when he was allegedly poisoned in 1938 at the Three Forks juke joint in Greenwood (see p. 438) by a jealous husband, Johnson has influenced generations of blues and rock artists around the world.

Clarksdale has also produced such musical greats as Jackie ("Rocket 88") Brenston, Sam Cooke, Ike Turner, and Muddy Waters. Join the stream of music lovers from all over the world who peregrinate to the Delta Blues Museum, located in a 1918 train depot at the edge of town. Here you can see, among countless displays, the actual wood cabin where Waters grew up as a sharecropper in the 1920s, as well as vintage guitars, photographs, and other artifacts.

Other must-see sites include Cat Head Delta Blues and Folk Art, where you can browse bookshelves and record bins for obscure gems and one-of-a-kind art. The Ground Zero Blues Club, a cotton warehouse reconstructed as a juke joint and within spitting distance of the Delta Blues Museum, serves plate lunches by day and smoldering live blues by night. It is co-owned by Oscar-winning actor Morgan Freeman (a native Mississippian).

Generally, though, eating options in town are more down-home, like the dishes at Abe's Barbecue, serving "Swine Dining"—sliced or chopped pork barbecue sandwiches that have been something of a legend since 1924; Hicks' Variety Foods, known for spicy cornhusk-wrapped tamales as well as fried catfish; and

With its rough-around-the-edges ambience and regular "Jam Camps," the Shack Up Inn promises a unique lodging experience.

Ramon's, a real-deal dive with whiskey-bottle table lamps, where the soul-food specialty is spaghetti with tomato sauce and deep-fried chicken livers.

Sure, a few chain motels line the outskirts of town, but why stay there when you can flop in a once dilapidated sharecropper's quarters at the Shack Up Inn? Located on Hopson Plantation, the former farming enterprise is now home to an isolated rural "B 'n' B"—bed and beer. A row of shacks (now with indoor plumbing and air-conditioning) are a big draw for blues tourists who embrace the funky rusticity of the place, especially during "Jam Camps" featuring professional musicians. Another atmospheric option is the old Riverside Hotel, a no-frills ranch house whose overnighters have included Ike Turner and the late blues fan John F. Kennedy Jr. A locally owned boardinghouse/budget hotel since 1944, the Riverside is notorious as the former hospital for blacks where pioneering blues singer Bessie Smith died in 1937, following a car crash on Highway 61. Many of the blues greats stay here regularly, and during music festivals it is booked solid.

For sultry summer weather and live music that's both lowdown and uplifting, make a point to be in Clarksdale the second weekend in August for the Sunflower River Blues and Gospel Festival, held downtown. In mid-

October, when the cotton is high, visit the literary Mississippi Delta Tennessee Williams Festival. Williams, renowned for such masterpieces as *The Glass Menagerie* and *A Streetcar Named Desire*, grew up in Clarksdale.

WHERE: 75 miles south of Memphis, TN. *Visitor info:* Tel 800-626-3764 or 662-627-6149; visitthedelta.com. **DELTA BLUES MUSEUM:** Tel 662-627-6820; deltabluesmuseum.org. *When:* closed Sun. **CAT HEAD DELTA BLUES AND FOLK ART:** Tel 662-624-5992; cathead.biz. *When:* closed Sun. **GROUND ZERO BLUES CLUB:** Tel 662-621-9009; ground zerobluesclub.com. *When:* closed Sun. **ABE'S BARBECUE:** Tel 662-624-9947; abesbbq.com. *Cost:* lunch $7. **HICKS' VARIETY FOODS:** Tel 662-624-9887. *Cost:* 6 tamales for $6. **RAMON'S:** Tel 662-624-9230. *Cost:* dinner $15. **SHACK UP INN:** Tel 662-624-8329; shackupinn.com. *Cost:* from $65. **RIVERSIDE HOTEL:** Tel 662-624-9163; cathead.biz/riverside.html. *Cost:* from $65. **BEST TIMES:** Apr for the Juke Joint Festival; early June for Delta Jubilee; Aug for Sunflower River Blues and Gospel Festival (sunflowerfest.org); mid-Oct for the Mississippi Delta Tennessee Williams Festival.

Cool Blues and Hot Tamales in the Mississippi Delta

GREENVILLE

Mississippi

Despite its claim as the state's largest city on the Mississippi River (and highest, perched on a bluff), the old cotton town of Greenville (population 33,000) is a languid place, where massive trees shade centuries-old cemeteries, and antebellum plantations and graceful lakes brighten the flat landscape.

The topographical exceptions are the flat-topped ceremonial mounds found just outside town, evidence of a thriving pre-Columbian civilization. The Winterville Indian Mounds, a National Historic Landmark, include 12 mounds arranged around a 43-acre plaza. Most were built between A.D. 1200–1350.

Of course, the Greenville area is better known for its blues singers. Their rich legacy, past and present, can be explored at the Highway 61 Blues Museum nearby in the old railroad town of Leland. The Old Temple Theater houses photos and signed memorabilia belonging to B.B. King, Little Milton, and many others. But Leland's star attraction for blues lovers is inarguably the new and highly informative B.B. King Museum and Delta Interpretive Center.

For the ultimate musical journey, blues aficionados come for Greenville's annual Mississippi Delta Blues & Heritage Festival. The laid-back outdoor concerts and jam sessions that began in 1977 in a cotton field draw enthusiasts the third weekend in September. A more recent arrival is the Mighty Mississippi Music Festival when three generations of Delta Blues artists and nationally known names fill two stages in Warfield Point Park. The B.B. King Homecoming Festival, staged by his hometown of Indianola, carries on since King's passing in 2015. If you've missed the area's festivals, you can hear great live music most nights at one of the Delta's finest venues, the informal Walnut Street Blues Bar.

Greenville's greatest culinary attraction is the world-famous original Doe's Eat Place, a grocery-store-turned-steakhouse ironically best known for its hot tamales—and a loyal clientele of fans including the likes of President Bill Clinton and the late, great Elvis Presley. The tamales caught on when the little diner first opened in 1941 (the weathered white storefront with a faded neon Pepsi sign hasn't changed much since then) and have become a curious culinary staple throughout the Delta and much of Mississippi. If you're looking for a place to hang your hat, check out The Thompson House, a Colonial Revival mansion on the banks of Deer Creek in nearby Leland.

WHERE: 150 miles south of Memphis, TN. *Visitor info:* Tel 800-467-3582 or 662-334-2711; visitgreenville.org. **WINTERVILLE INDIAN MOUNDS:** Winterville. Tel 662-334-4684; nps.gov/nr/travel/mounds/win.htm. **HIGHWAY 61 BLUES MUSEUM:** Leland. Tel 866-285-7646 or 662-686-7646; highway61blues.com.

MISSISSIPPI DELTA BLUES & HERITAGE FESTIVAL: deltablues.org. *Cost:* $50. *When:* 3rd Sat in Sept. **MIGHTY MISSISSIPPI MUSIC FESTIVAL:** mightymsmusic.com. *When:* 1st weekend in Oct. **B.B. KING MUSEUM:** Indianola. Tel 662-887-9539; bbkingmuseum .org. **WALNUT STREET BLUES BAR:** Tel 662-378-2254. **DOE'S:** Tel 662-334-3315; doeseat place.com. *Cost:* 6 tamales, $10. *When:* closed Sun. **THE THOMPSON HOUSE:** Leland. Tel 662-820-7829; thompsonhousebb.com. *Cost:* from $125. **BEST TIMES:** Memorial Day weekend for B.B. King Homecoming Festival; mid-Oct for Delta Hot Tamale Festival (hottamalefest .com).

Dixie's Contemporary Hub

GREENWOOD

Mississippi

From a one-time Cotton Capital of the World to a contemporary hub with a forward momentum and trailblazing energy not common in these parts, Greenwood owes its modern-day vibe to the presence of the Viking Range

Corporation. In 1990, company founder Fred Carl moved production of the line to his hometown along the banks of the Yazoo River. The intervening years have seen the Viking empire expand quite literally, renovating buildings around town for its operation.

World-famous for its ultrapremium appliances such as refrigerators, range tops, and ovens, Viking is better known locally for its chic enclave encompassing several historic structures, such as the 1912 Greenwood Opera House and the luxury boutique Alluvian Hotel, with 45 rooms and six suites. Across the street is a 7,000-square-foot spa and the first-rate Viking Cooking School. Its year round roster of classes helps students perfect Cajun, Creole and Delta specialties like pecan-crusted catfish and sweet potato soufflé.

In addition to its history as the one-time Cotton Capital of the World, the town is also famous for its association with blues pioneer Robert Johnson (see p. 436), who died at a juke joint outside Greenwood in 1938. To this day no one is certain where he is buried.

Greenwood surprisingly is also known as a dining destination. Giardina's, located on the ground floor of the Alluvian, is the new reincarnation of the eponymous eatery founded by a Sicilian family who've been feeding hungry Deltans since the 1940s. A longtime friendly rivalry can be found at Lusco's, one of the Delta's better-known restaurants, where fresh seafood and serious steaks dominate the menu. Born as a grocery store opened by Italian immigrants in 1933, fourth- and fifth-generation owners still serve Italian fare and broiled shrimp in a nostalgic atmosphere with private dining alcoves separated by curtains that once hid the moonshine.

The menu is a long and irresistible one at the Crystal Grill, another longtime family-owned spot. Regulars know to save room for dessert, namely the signature homemade coconut and chocolate cream pies, piled high with clouds of homemade meringue.

WHERE: 130 miles south of Memphis, TN. *Visitor info:* Tel 662-453-9197; greenwoodms.org.

THE ALLUVIAN: Tel 866-600-5201 or 662-453-2114; thealluvian.com. *Cost:* from $195. **VIKING COOKING SCHOOL:** Tel 662-451-6750; vikingcookingschool.com. *Cost:* classes from $89. **GIARDINA'S:** Tel 662-455-4227; giardinas .com. *Cost:* dinner $35. **LUSCO'S:** Tel 662-453-5365; luscos.net. *Cost:* dinner $35. **CRYSTAL GRILL:** Tel 662-453-6530; crystal grillms.com. *Cost:* dinner $20. **BEST TIMES:** July for cotton blooms; Oct for weather.

Old-Time Beauty and Offbeat Elvis

HOLLY SPRINGS

Mississippi

Less visited and commercial than the area's better-known destinations of Memphis (see p. 468), the blues mecca of Clarksdale (see p. 435), or the literary enclave of Oxford (see p. 444), Holly Springs offers unexpected

charms and, in its own way, perhaps a more authentic introduction to Southern small-town life. It is one of Mississippi's most architecturally and historically significant rural communities.

Union General Ulysses S. Grant and his family spent the last months of 1862 in Holly Springs, regrouping after his victory in Shiloh (see p. 444). Because it was on the rail line, the town was occupied by Union soldiers and much fought over, with 63 distinct raids during the war. Nonetheless, the town of about 7,550 residents retains some 175 buildings on the National Historic Register, including 63 ante-bellum homes. Since most are private residences, the best time to visit is April, when the much-heralded Holly Springs Pilgrimage House & Heritage Tour jump-starts the town. Local residents dress up in period costume and lead tours of the properties, including a handful of slave quarters, reminiscent of the area's early cotton plantations. Carriage rides, proper afternoon teas, and organ recitals in historic churches also take the town back in time.

Holly Springs' old-fashioned air lingers year-round. To experience it, pick up a self-guided tour brochure at the local tourism bureau, housed in the town's first brick building (1832), and enjoy a leisurely amble. A variety of historic sites includes Walter Place, the 1859 Gothic and Greek Revival mansion where Grant and his family stayed, and Montrose, a Greek Revival mansion built in 1858 and now operated by the Holly Springs Garden Club as a house museum and arboretum. Overlooking

Walter Place, once the residence of Ulysses S. Grant, was carefully restored in the 1970s and remains one of the most expensive houses in Mississippi.

the town square is First Presbyterian Church (1860), a Romanesque Revival structure that still bears a lead bullet from the Civil War embedded in its heart-pine floor. Religion was temporarily displaced during the war when Grant used this church, and others, as stables for his Union horses.

Rust College was founded in 1866 by Methodist missionaries from the North for the education of freed slaves and stands on the site where slave auctions took place and Grant's troops encamped during the Civil War. Classical music lovers will especially appreciate the Leontyne Price Library, named for the world-renowned opera star who hails from Mississippi.

A much-loved local institution, Phillips Grocery is a dilapidated 1882 saloon-turned-grocery store next to the railroad tracks that has been serving memorable hamburgers and cheeseburgers since 1948. The half-pound Super Deluxe Hamburger is a thing of beauty, whose secret ingredient was once rumored to be peanut butter (not true, say the owners, who admit to locking the door when making the guarded mix). Only the fried peach pie is as good.

WHERE: 52 miles southeast of Memphis, TN. *Visitor info:* Tel 888-687-4765 or 662-252-2515; visithollysprings.com. **RUST COLLEGE:** Tel 662-252-8000; rustcollege.edu. **PHILLIPS GROCERY:** Tel 662-252-4671. *Cost:* hamburger $5. **BEST TIMES:** Apr for the Holly Springs Pilgrimage Home and Heritage Tour (holly springspilgrimage.com); Apr–June for weather and blooming gardens; Sept for Hummingbird Migration and Nature Celebration; Dec for Christmas in Holly Springs (homes open).

The Inspiration and Refuge of a Literary Icon

EUDORA WELTY HOUSE

Jackson, Mississippi

A massive oak tree shades the front yard of the 1925 Tudor-style home where Pulitzer Prize–winning author Eudora Welty spent an idyllic childhood and most of her adult life, and which is considered one of the most intact literary homes in America. Graceful and grand, the tree might be seen as a metaphor for Welty, known for her genteel nature, hospitality, and humility, despite her stature as one of the great American writers of the 20th century.

In 1936, the 27-year-old Welty published her first short story, "Death of a Traveling Salesman," and today she is regarded as a master of the form. Her early novels include *Delta Wedding* (1946) and *The Ponder Heart* (1954). The winner of many awards, she received her Pulitzer for fiction in 1973 for *The Optimist's Daughter*. All her success—and her abiding affection for her Mississippi home—made her the pride of Jackson until the day she died in 2001 at the age of 92.

Welty left her home, books, and letters to the Mississippi Department of Archives and History, and it is now open for visits. She was 16 and ready to start college when her family moved here. She transferred to the University of Wisconsin and then to Columbia University in New York. Unable to find a job at the height of the Depression, she returned to Jackson in 1931, shortly before her father died. She lived in the family house with her mother, Chestina.

Original furnishings fill the two-story dwelling. The living room was the site of Welty's Christmas morning eggnog-filled open-house celebrations (whiskey was a key ingredient). Other glimpses of Welty's literary life include a bedroom turned into an office, and the dining room table where she often

The Eudora Welty House has remained just as it was in 1986, when the writer bequeathed her home to the state as a living trust.

spread out her manuscripts in progress, cutting out a single sentence or a paragraph and repositioning it with straight pins.

Welty and her mother were both avid gardeners, and tended lovingly to the plants and flowers in the home's leafy backyard. The trellised gardens designed by Chestina have been carefully restored to how they appeared from 1925–1945. Various garden rooms are filled with camellias, roses, and bulbs, and evoke the gentler time and place so prevalent in Welty's written works.

Where: 1119 Pinehurst St. Tel 601-353-7762; mdah.state.ms.us/welty. *When:* tours offered Tues–Fri; visitor center open Mon–Fri. **Best times:** Apr for dogwood and roses; Dec–Mar for camellias.

The Sweet Potato Queens Go Irish

Mal's St. Paddy's Parade

Jackson, Mississippi

The annual Mal's St. Paddy's Parade and postparade street party, held downtown on the Saturday after St. Patrick's Day, was started in 1983—on a lark—by Jackson entrepreneur Malcolm "Mal" White, as a way to replicate a bit of the Mardi Gras–style madness he sorely missed from the years he lived in New Orleans. The event has grown tremendously since, with 50 floats and 75,000 people, and an after-parade party with live music at Hal & Mal's, a restaurant and brewery owned by Mal and his brother.

But there are plenty of other eating options in town. Skip the traditional Irish fare of corned beef and cabbage and go for local favorites: Order hand-cut fries seasoned with lemon pepper and a 14-ounce cheeseburger—voted the best in town—at Stamps Superburgers. Or check out the Big Apple Inn, where the specialties are hot tamales, "smokes" (smoked sausage) sandwiches, and (for those who think they've had it all) pig's ear

sandwiches. Homemade soul food such as pork-seasoned greens and meat loaf are standouts at Bully's Restaurant—and don't even think about passing on the banana pudding or peach cobbler for dessert. Finally, fill up on barbecue at Sweet Daddy's Smokehouse, located at an Exxon gas station on Interstate 55 North. Ribs, chicken, pork chops, and turkey legs are slow-cooked throughout the day and are available at 10 A.M., 1 P.M., and 4 P.M. When they're gone, they're gone.

Once a highlight of the St. Paddy's Parade, the sassy, middle-aged Southern belles—the self-crowned so-called Sweet Potato Queens™ (SPQ)—now have their own: the Zippity Doo Dah Parade, benefitting the local Blair E. Batson Hospital for Children since 2011.

Dressed in glitzy gowns and flame-red wigs, these wantonly brazen women pose on frilly golf cart floats while waving and tossing sweet potatoes to the cheering crowds and the thousands of wannabe queens who follow them.

WHERE: Parade begins on State Street, then snakes around town. malsstpaddysparade.com. *When:* Sat following Mar 17th. *Visitor info:* Tel 800-354-7695 or 601-960-1891; visitjackson .com. **HAL & MALS':** Tel 601-948-0888; halandmals.com. **STAMPS SUPERBURGERS:** Tel 601-352-4555. *Cost:* lunch $10. **BIG APPLE INN:** Tel 601-354-9371. *Cost:* lunch $5. **BULLYS:** Tel 601-362-0484. *Cost:* lunch $9. **SWEET DADDY'S SMOKEHOUSE:** Tel 601-366-6933. *Cost:* whole slab of ribs $15. **ZIPPITY DOO DAH PARADE:** zddparade.com. *When:* 4th Sat in Mar.

Antebellum Life in the Old South

NATCHEZ

Mississippi

Once a bustling port and the wealthiest pre–Civil War city in America per capita, Natchez is a living museum of antebellum architecture and charm. The city's wealth came from cotton, as Natchez was in the center of the richest cotton producing lands in the world. That wealth funded the construction of many very beautiful homes. More than 1,000 historic treasures remain intact, some still inhabited and lovingly preserved by the original owners' descendants, who make up this quiet but welcoming city on the banks of the Mississippi.

Begun in 1932, the Natchez Spring Pilgrimage is an annual highlight, when azaleas, magnolias, and annuals create the perfect setting for the two-dozen private homes (many with significant gardens) that open to the public. The Historic Natchez Tableaux (formerly the Confederate Pageant) is also held during this time. Hundreds of costumed volunteers re-create vignettes of the Old South, exploring issues of slavery and the defeat and destruction that followed the war.

Ten historic homes remain open to visitors year-round, with a few of them functioning as unique inns and B&Bs. One of the most luxurious is Monmouth Historic Inn, the former 1818 Greek Revival residence of the Mississippi governor John Anthony Quitman. Ask for his room, which contains his four-poster bed and a dresser where he stashed his many wigs, and opens onto views of the famous 26-acre garden. Most guest rooms are found in seven restored cottages on the manicured grounds while the acclaimed 1818 Restaurant is in the Main House. Another grand Greek Revival "temple" is Dunleith, built in 1856 and enveloped by 40 grassy acres. The plantation home has 22 rooms and suites, including some in a refashioned 1790s dairy barn, but

The gardens surrounding Monmouth Historic Inn were designed by a skilled local horticulturist.

the largest and most lavish are in the Main House. The Castle Restaurant is housed in a converted carriage house, but be sure to stop by Fat Mama's Tamales for one of your meals and try the signature Gringo Pie—tamales smothered with chili, cheese, onions, and jalapeños, and best washed down with a "Knock-You-Naked" margarita.

The setting grows almost surreal when you follow Highway 61 south to Mammy's Cupboard, an unabashedly politically incorrect 1940 building in the shape of a black "mammy" figure. Enter the door in her "hoop-skirt" to enjoy sandwiches on house-made bread and prized meringue pies.

WHERE: 115 miles southwest of Jackson.

Visitor info: Tel 800-647-6724 or 601-446-6345; visitnatchez.org. **NATCHEZ PILGRIMAGE TOURS:** Tel 800-647-6742 or 601-446-6631; natchezpilgrimage.com. *When:* Spring Pilgrimage, 5 weekends and 4 weeks in early Mar–early Apr; Fall Pilgrimage, 2 weeks in late Sept–early Oct. **MONMOUTH:** Tel 800-828-4531 or 601-442-5852; monmouthhistoricinn .com. *Cost:* from $195. **DUNLEITH:** Tel 800-433-2445 or 601-446-8500; dunleith.com. *Cost:* from $165 (off-peak), $225 (peak). **FAT MAMA'S TAMALES:** Tel 601-442-4548; fatmamas tamales.com. *Cost:* dinner $12. **MAMMY'S CUPBOARD:** Tel 601-445-8957. *Cost:* lunch $7. **BEST TIME:** The Historic Natchez Tableaux during Spring Pilgrimage (Mar–Apr).

An Ancient Trail Delivers History and Elvis

THE NATCHEZ TRACE

Mississippi

Stretching from Natchez (see previous entry) on the banks of the mighty Mississippi River to the green hills surrounding Tennessee's state capital of Nashville, the Natchez Trace Parkway is one of America's best driving and biking destinations. "The Trace" is a natural travel corridor once used by buffalo and the Natchez, Choctaw, and Chickasaw tribes who hunted them, as well as early explorers from Spain, France, and England. Today it unwinds through 444 miles of kudzu-draped lowlands, seasonal wildflowers, cypress and pine groves, and gently rolling woodlands. A National Scenic Byway maintained by the National Park Service, the two-lane parkway offers campsites, leafy picnic spots, plantation ruins, charming small towns, and off-the-beaten-path discoveries. Refreshingly free of billboards and commercial development, the Trace is a pleasant and unhurried (50 mph) way to catch a glimpse of the Old South, from Natchez to Jackson to Tupelo (traveling southwest to northeast), then heading north through a snippet of northwestern Alabama into southern Tennessee.

The Trace Visitor Center is located near the byway's midway point in Tupelo, best known as the birthplace of Elvis Aaron Presley. Tupelo's most-visited tourist attraction is the two-room house where the King entered this earthly realm on January 8, 1935. Each year, Elvis fans travel from all parts of the world to tour the wooden shotgun house built by his dad, Vernon, to visit Elvis's childhood church, and to wander the grounds of the 15-acre Elvis Presley Park. The first weekend in June marks the Elvis Presley Festival: A Hometown Tribute to the King of Rock 'n' Roll.

An easy and interesting detour from the Trace, north of Tupelo, is the town of Corinth. By virtue of its strategic location at the junction of the Memphis & Charleston and Mobile & Ohio railroads, more than 300,000 Union and Confederate soldiers occupied the town and surroundings between 1861 and 1865. When Confederate troops made a preemptive strike north of Corinth on April 6–7, 1862, the result was the bloody Battle of Shiloh. Shiloh National Military Park in south-central Tennessee commemorates this battle, but stop here first, at the Corinth Civil War Interpretive Center, to understand the town's significant role in the war.

WHERE: 444 miles, from Natchez, north through the tip of Alabama, to Nashville, TN. Tel 800-305-7417 or 662-680-4025; nps.gov/natr or scenictrace.com. **ELVIS PRESLEY BIRTHPLACE & MUSEUM:** Tupelo. Tel 662-841-1245; elvispresleybirthplace.com. **CORINTH CIVIL WAR INTERPRETIVE CENTER:** Corinth. Tel 662-287-9273; nps.gov/shil. **BEST TIMES:** spring and fall for driving the Trace; Apr 6–7 for anniversary events for Civil War battles of Shiloh and Corinth; 1st weekend in June for Tupelo's Elvis Presley Festival (tupeloelvisfestival.com).

Faulkner Country

OXFORD

Mississippi

A pretty and prosperous little town about an hour's drive from Memphis, Oxford is home to literary great William Faulkner, and one of America's most beautiful campuses, the University of Mississippi, better known as "Ole Miss." Rowan Oak is the name of the graceful antebellum mansion Faulkner purchased in 1930 for $6,000. The Pulitzer and Nobel Prize–winning author of such classics as *The Sound and the Fury, As I Lay Dying,* and *Light in August* spruced up the Greek Revival mansion and lived there until his death in 1962. Walk down the brick walkway, lined by towering cedar trees, to enter the private world where the pipe-smoking, mustachioed "Mr. Bill" lived and worked. His sparse study holds a cot, his manual Underwood typewriter—and a whiskey bottle within easy reach. Scrawled on the white wall is the outline for his novel *The Fable.*

The literary life of the town now centers on Square Books—widely regarded as one of the best independent bookstores in the country. Its finest amenity is a second-story open air porch overlooking "the Square" where you can enjoy a fresh-brewed coffee. Down the street are Square Books, Jr., and a bargain annex, Off Square Books.

Oxford's all-American town square offers a slice of Southern life rarely seen today, with quaint shops and eateries. The palpable sense that this is the prototypical Southern college town is never more ubiquitous than during home football games at Ole Miss—late August to late November—when marathon tailgating and good-natured mayhem abounds.

Oxford boasts a fair number of food destinations that lure day-trippers from nearby Memphis and gastronomes from farther afield. One of the state's best eateries is John Currence's City Grocery, where fresh, inventive Southern cuisine consistently draws rave reviews and hungry crowds. The second-floor bar with a balcony overlooking the Square is the best place in town to enjoy happy hour. Currence's popularity has spawned the nearby Bouré—also in the Square—boasting an "upscale/downhome fare" with a decidedly Creole flair. The Square's more down-home Ajax Diner specializes in plate lunches with two sides and jalapeño corn bread. On the outskirts of town is the one-of-a-kind Taylor Grocery and Restaurant, an old-time former grocery store that habitués swear serves the most sublime cornmeal-crusted catfish in all the South.

And where to park your luggage? Treat yourself to the Graduate Oxford—big, clean, modern, and fun.

WHERE: 85 miles southeast of Memphis, TN. *Visitor info:* Tel 662-232-2367; visit oxfordms.com. **ROWAN OAK:** Tel 662-234-3284; rowanoak.com. *When:* open daily, June–July, closed Mon, Aug–May. **SQUARE BOOKS:** Tel 800-648-4001 or 662-236-2262; square books.com. **CITY GROCERY:** Tel 662-232-8080; citygroceryonline.com. *Cost:* dinner $40. **BOURÉ:** Tel 662-234-1968; citygroceryonline .com/boure. *Cost:* $40. **AJAX DINER:** Tel 662-232-8880; ajaxdiner.net. *Cost:* dinner $35. **TAYLOR GROCERY AND RESTAURANT:** Taylor. Tel 662-236-1716; taylorgrocery.com. *Cost:* dinner $30. **GRADUATE OXFORD:** Tel 662-234-3031; graduateoxford.com. *Cost:* from $149. **BEST TIMES:** late Apr for the Double Decker Arts Festival (doubledeckerfestival.com); July for the Faulkner and Yoknapatawpha Conference at the U. of Mississippi (olemiss.edu).

Gibraltar of the Confederacy

VICKSBURG NATIONAL MILITARY PARK

Vicksburg, Mississippi

❝ See what a lot of land these fellows hold, of which Vicksburg is the key. The war can never be brought to a close until that key is in our pocket.❞ Those words of President Abraham Lincoln rang true on July 4, 1863,

when Vicksburg, located at a strategic bend of the Mississippi River, surrendered to Union troops following a fierce 47-day siege. Ulysses S. Grant had been trying to take the "Gibraltar of the Confederacy" since the summer of 1862. Considered one of the most brilliant— and decisive—military campaigns of the Civil War (1861–65), it ended with the Confederacy effectively divided by the river. Modern-day Vicksburg is a sleepy town perched on a 200-foot bluff along Highway 61 and a portion of the Great River Road (see p. 448), which follows the Mississippi from Minnesota to the Gulf of Mexico.

Take a 16-mile self-guided drive to immerse yourself in the somber heritage of Vicksburg National Military Park, among the most stirring of the nation's battlefield memorials. Cannons, trenches, and over 1,350 historical markers and monuments honoring the soldiers who fought and died here dot the vast expanses of meadows and wooded knolls that make up the 1,728-acre

Forty-seven steps lead up to the striking Illinois Memorial—one for each day of the siege.

battleground and park. At milepost 1.8 along the trail, the white marble Illinois State Memorial is modeled after the Roman Pantheon. Its grand staircase has 47 steps, one for each day of the Siege of Vicksburg.

Beyond the tranquil fields and wooded hills of the cemetery, Vicksburg offers pleasurable pastimes that evoke the genteel Southern charm of the Magnolia State. Dating to antebellum times, the Bazsinsky House B&B was home to four generations of the same Jewish family until the early 21st century. Totally restored to accommodate modern amenities, its historic charm remains elegantly intact.

Steamboat memorabilia adorns the lofty redbrick Belle of the Bends, a stunning redbrick Victorian mansion built in 1876. A painstaking renovation has transformed it into one of the state's loveliest B&Bs, named after one of the old steamboats that plied the waters of the Mississippi. The blufftop Corners Mansion and Inn, built in 1873, offers the perfect vantage point for sweeping views and sunsets over the Mississippi and Yazoo rivers.

If you're looking for old-fashioned Southern cooking, you'll find it at Walnut Hills. Fried chicken, homemade biscuits and gravy, fried green tomatoes, and corn bread are served family style, in big bowls placed on lazy Susans.

In addition to antiques stores, coffee shops, and quaint brick-paved streets, downtown Vicksburg features the Biedenharn Coca-Cola Museum, a factory-turned-shrine where, in 1894, the popular fountain drink was first bottled (Vicksburg also lays claim to having concocted the first mint julep). And don't miss the imposing Old Court House Museum perched on the town's highest hilltop, a beautiful neoclassical structure of stone porticos and Ionic columns built in 1858 by highly-skilled slave artisans. A museum since 1948, the landmark building houses exhibits about the Battle of Vicksburg, Southern culture, and Mississippi history.

About 30 miles south of Vicksburg lies Port Gibson, a magnolia-shaded town Ulysses S. Grant declared "too beautiful to burn" when passing through in 1863. Historic churches from the mid-1800s and wide, leafy avenues are among its quiet pleasures.

WHERE: 44 miles west of Jackson. Tel 601-636-0583; nps.gov/vick. *Vicksburg visitor info:* Tel 800-221-3536 or 601-636-9421; visit vicksburg.com. *Port Gibson visitor info:* Tel 601-437-4351; portgibsononthemississippi.com. **BAZSINSKY HOUSE:** Tel 601-634-8404; bazsinskyhouse.com. *Cost:* from $114. **BELLE OF THE BENDS:** Tel 800-844-2308 or 601-634-0737; belleofthebends.com. *Cost:* from $139. **THE CORNERS MANSION AND INN:** Tel 800-444-7421 or 601-636-7421; thecorners.com. *Cost:* from $125. **WALNUT HILLS:** Tel 601-638-4910; walnuthillsms.com. *Cost:* dinner $25. **BIEDENHARN COCA-COLA MUSEUM:** Tel 601-638-6514; biedenharncoca-colamuseum.com. **OLD COURT HOUSE MUSEUM:** Tel 601-636-0741; oldcourthouse.org. **BEST TIMES:** Apr and Oct for weather; June–1st week of Aug for living history programs at Vicksburg National Military Park; Mar–Apr and Oct for the Pilgrimage & Tour of Homes.

The Bible Belt Goes Vegas

BRANSON

Missouri

A viva-Las-Vegas for good clean fun, Branson is a little bitty Ozarks town of 11,000 that attracts 8 million people every year to 100 glitzy shows in more than 50 theaters on its own neon-studded "Strip." But with headliner acts like Johnny Mathis and Yakov Smirnoff, the wildest Branson gets is when the buffalo come thundering onstage to open Dolly Parton's Dixie Stampede Dinner Attraction.

That's just fine with the families and seniors who have been coming to southwestern Missouri for multiple-generation entertainment since 1959. That's when four brothers who called themselves The Baldknobbers started playing country tunes and goofing around in a converted roller-skating rink on State Highway 76, or the Strip. The Baldknobbers Jamboree is Branson's longest-running show, but the entertainment options exploded in the 1980s and '90s. Big-name country entertainers burned out from too many grueling tours discovered that if they bought or built theaters in this beautiful setting, carved out of the ancient, wooded Ozark Mountains, their audiences would come to them. These days you can hear just about every style of music—rock 'n' roll, jazz, Cajun, gospel, big band, you name it. And when you get tired of music, there are comedians, magicians, dancers, and "tribute artists" who bring beloved icons such as Red Skelton back to life. Even the theme park, Silver Dollar City, a recreation of an 1880s mining town that once stood here, is as wholesome as it gets.

To explore the countryside, hop on the Branson Scenic Railway for a 40-mile ride through the cool and otherwise inaccessible Ozark foothills and river valley. The vintage train leaves from a 1905 depot in Branson (head for the Vista-Dome panoramic cars for the best seats).

You can also escape the hullabaloo of the Strip at Big Cedar Lodge—a luxury getaway styled after the grand wilderness architecture of the Adirondacks—that sits atop a ridge near Table Rock Lake. It's many attractions include Top of the Rock, nine holes designed by Jack Nicklaus and the first-ever par-3 course to be included in a PGA Tour-sanctioned event, and Buffalo Ridge Springs, a challenging par-71 championship course designed by revered golf course architect Tom Fazio where duffers play year-round, thanks to

The Baldknobbers Jamboree Show started in 1959 and is still going strong.

mild winters. Branson's other draw is the nearby 10,000-acre Dogwood Canyon Nature Park, a veritable wonderland for hiking, biking, horseback riding, and—for the less active—wildlife tram or private jeep or Segway tours. Anglers can head for its trout-rich waters or sign up for a two-day session at Orvis Fly Fishing School. Both Big Cedar Lodge and Dogwood Canyon are affiliated with the sporting goods retail giant Bass Pro Shops, whose worshipped flagship store in nearby Springfield offers eight football fields' worth of fishing, hunting, and sporting goods.

Branson really picks up in April when the flowers start to bloom. Things can get traffic-jammed in summer (slip down a pretty back road to avoid the Strip), and conga lines of motor coaches are common in October (the Ozarks deliver resplendent leaf peeping), November, and December. Branson may very well be at its loveliest during the holiday season, when every square inch of town is decked out for the award-winning Branson Area Festival of Lights.

WHERE: 45 miles south of Springfield. *Visitor info:* Tel 417-334-4084; explorebranson .com. **DOLLY PARTON'S DIXIE STAMPEDE:** Tel 800-520-5544 or 417-336-3000; dixiestampede .com. *When:* closed Jan–Feb. *Cost:* $45, includes dinner. **BALDKNOBBERS JAMBOREE:** Tel 800-998-8908 or 417-334-4528; baldknob bers.com. *When:* closed Jan–Feb. *Cost:* $39. **Silver Dollar City:** Tel 800-952-6626 or 417-336-7100; silverdollarcity.com. *When:* closed Jan–Feb. *Cost:* $60. **Branson Scenic Railway:** Tel 800-287-2462 or 417-334-6110; bransontrain.com. *When:* closed Jan–Feb. *Cost:* $27. **Big Cedar Lodge:** Ridgedale. Tel 800-225-6343 or 417-335-2777; bigcedar.com. *Cost:* from $129 (off-peak), from $229 (peak). **Dogwood Canyon Nature Park:** Lampe. Tel

417-779-5983; dogwoodcanyon.org. *Cost:* $15. Orvis Fly Fishing School, $489 for 2 days, lodging extra. **Top of the Rock and Buffalo Ridge Springs Golf Course:** Hollister. Tel 800-225-6343 or 417-339-5430; topoftherock. com. *Cost:* greens fees from $80. **Best times:** Apr for flowers; summer for swimming, fishing, and boating; Nov–Dec for Ozark Mountain Christmas and the Branson Area Festival of Lights.

3,000 Miles of Scenery and History

THE GREAT RIVER ROAD

Missouri

Few rivers have captured America's imagination like the Mississippi, which begins as a relative trickle from a glacial lake in northwestern Minnesota, gathering strength as it is joined by the Ohio, Illinois, Missouri, and Arkansas rivers in its southward flow toward the Gulf of Mexico. Its enduring spell is due in part to Hannibal native Samuel Clemens (see next page), who under the pen name Mark Twain wrote about 19th-century river life at its apex. "The Mississippi is in all ways remarkable," he wrote.

Discover the mighty Mississippi by motoring leisurely along the Great River Road (GRR), over 3,000 miles of scenery, culture, and history that follow both sides of the river through ten states—Minnesota, Wisconsin, Iowa, Illinois, Missouri, Kentucky, Tennessee, Arkansas, Mississippi, and Louisiana. Created in 1938 as a connected network of federal, state, and local routes, the sprawling GRR is the nation's oldest, longest—and arguably the most varied—scenic byway. There are stunning views and tacky strip malls, historic towns on the rebound and abandoned industrial sites, the excitement of big cities and the quiet respite of wildlife refuges. At times the road literally runs out, and it's over to the nearest interstate for an unromantic interlude.

But anyone who takes the time to travel the GRR will come away with a deeper and wider understanding of the Mississippi River Valley, so intensely different as it travels from north to south. Two multimillion-dollar museums that offer a broad look at the big river are the National Mississippi River Museum and Aquarium in Dubuque, Iowa (see p. 518), which examines the river from beginning to end, and the Mississippi River Museum at Mud Island in Memphis, Tennessee, which focuses on the lower Mississippi, including its rich musical heritage. But there are other museums, forts, and national monuments, each telling a compelling story, from the American Indian "Mound Builder" cultures a thousand years ago (see p. 517) to the comeback of the American bald eagle in places like Red Wing, Minnesota (see p. 555). The Great River Road, like the mighty Mississippi itself and the nation whose history it helped shape, is vast, rich, and complex.

Great River Road visitor info: Tel 763-212-2560; experiencemississippiriver.com.

Mark Twain's Mississippi Muse

HANNIBAL

Missouri

One of America's greatest literary figures, Samuel Clemens wrote so powerfully about life on the Mississippi that his hometown of Hannibal (population 17,883) is still considered the seminal river town. Sitting between two big hills, this star-stop along the Great River Road (see previous page) is one big and utterly charming love letter to Mark Twain—his name is on half the signs in town, and his characters' names are on the other half.

Clemens took his pen name "Mark Twain" from his early career as a steamboat pilot. If shallow water measured 2 fathoms (12 feet)—deep enough to navigate—the crewmen bellowed "mark twain." Twain introduced some of American literature's most unforgettable characters—Huckleberry Finn, Becky Thatcher, and Jim—in *The Adventures of Tom Sawyer* (1876), but it was *The Adventures of Huckleberry Finn* (1885) that earned his place among the literary greats.

Ground zero for Twain lovers is the Mark Twain Boyhood Home & Museum, which includes seven historic buildings near the river that have been faithfully preserved. Tour the tidy, two-story white clapboard house where the family lived in the 1840s; the home of Laura Hawkins, who was the model for Becky Thatcher; the office where his father, J.M. Clemens, practiced law; and the fetchingly old-fashioned Grant's Drug Store, also known as the Pilaster House, where the family lived for nine months after J.M. went bankrupt in 1846.

In an attractive downtown building, the Mark Twain Museum & Gallery has a standout collection of 15 original oil paintings by Norman Rockwell, who was commissioned in the 1930s to illustrate special editions of *Tom Sawyer* and *Huckleberry Finn*. Literature buffs enjoy Twain's writing desk and original manuscripts, while kids can act out scenes of the book in interactive exhibits.

Twain fans won't want to miss the hour-long tour of the Mark Twain Cave, now well lit with paved walkways, written about so vividly in *Tom Sawyer*.

Mark Twain mania reaches its height over July 4th weekend when 100,000 people turn out for National Tom Sawyer Days, a special time marked by a small-town parade, fireworks, fence-painting contests, and the crowning of the town's new Tom Sawyer and Becky Thatcher, a competition among local 7th graders since the 1950s.

Though he lived out his final years in Hartford, Connecticut (see p. 12), Clemens often returned to

Mark Twain's boyhood home on Hill Street has been open to the public since 1912.

Hannibal to stay with old friends at the handsome Garth Woodside Mansion, now one of the loveliest B&Bs in the country, an 1871 Second Empire home built on 36 hilltop acres just outside Hannibal. It's filled with museum-quality Victorian furniture like the 1869 Steinway square grand piano, and charming touches like nightshirts laid out in each of the eight lavishly decorated bedrooms, including the one where Clemens slept.

WHERE: 115 miles northwest of St. Louis. *Visitor info:* Tel TOM-AND-HUCK or 573-221-2477; visithannibal.com. **MARK TWAIN BOYHOOD HOME & MUSEUM:** Tel 573-221-9010; marktwainmuseum.org. **MARK TWAIN CAVE:** 573-221-1656; marktwaincave.com. **GARTH WOODSIDE MANSION:** Tel 888-427-8409 or 573-221-2789; garthmansion.com. *Cost:* from $185. **BEST TIME:** July 4th weekend for National Tom Sawyer Days.

Rhineland in Miniature

MISSOURI WINE COUNTRY

Hermann, Missouri

A long the banks of the Missouri River west of St. Louis is a romantic remnant from Missouri's wave of German immigration in the mid-19th century—a miniature Rhineland where vineyards gently blanket every hillside. The most historically important of the many small, immaculate towns is Hermann (population 2,400), a bastion of German culture since 1837. That was the year a group of Germans from Philadelphia bought land with the hopes of creating a colony that would be "German in every particular." Today Hermann retains its delightfully Old World character, with original 19th-century architecture, interesting shops, and gnarled grapevines.

When the first settlers arrived, they found steep terrain unsuitable for farming, but they noted the abundance of wild vines and set about making wine. By 1900, one out of every twelve bottles of wine sold in America came from Missouri, nearly all of it from Hermann's 66 wineries. The most important was Stone Hill Winery, the second-largest winery in the country by the early 1900s, but Prohibition destroyed Hermann's wine industry overnight.

Stone Hill Winery came out of hibernation in 1965, sparking a renaissance that boasts seven wineries here in Hermann and many more just across the river along a stretch known as the Weinstrasse, or Wine Road, including the towns of Dutzow and Augusta.

Stone Hill offers tours, tastings, and a view of the town's tree-covered hills and church

St. George Church's mid-19th-century steeple towers over the quaint town of Hermann.

steeples that is worth the drive even for the teetotaling. Its Vintage Restaurant, fashioned from former horse stables, serves up German specialties like schnitzel and sausages, considered some of the best in town by a populace almost entirely of German descent. Little wonder that Hermann is at its busiest during Oktoberfest, four weekends of oompah bands, bratwurst on the grill, and swarms of parties. Come spring, Maifest offers German national dress, dancing, music, and, of course, rivers of wine. Most visitors stay in B&Bs (there are close to 100 in the vicinity), and one of the most centrally located is housed in the late 19th-century Begamann Building, the well-known Wine Valley Inn.

WHERE: 80 miles west of St. Louis. *Visitor info:* Tel 800-932-8687 or 573-486-2744; visithermann.com. **STONE HILL WINERY:** Tel 573-486-2221; stonehillwinery.com. *Cost:* dinner at Vintage Restaurant $30. **WINE VALLEY INN:** Tel 573-486-0706; wine-valley-inn.com. *Cost:* from $115 (off-peak), from $198 (peak). **BEST TIMES:** 3rd weekend in May for Maifest, and 1st 4 weekends in Oct for Oktoberfest.

Where the Buck Stops and the Trails Start

INDEPENDENCE

Missouri

I n his early years, America's 33rd president, Harry S. Truman, lived in Independence with in-laws who regarded him as an inferior match for their beloved Bess. Such is the sort of intimate glimpse into Truman's life that you'll glean from a visit to the white 14-room Victorian home where he and Bess lived upon their marriage in 1919 (it took him nine years to convince her) and to which they returned in 1952 after his eight years in the White House. "I have had all of Washington I want," he said at the time. "I prefer my life in Missouri." Everything in the house is just as they left it, down to the 1950s kitchen with the patched linoleum floor and Truman's signature flat-brimmed hat and cane hanging behind the front door, ready for his morning walk.

The very first presidential library to be built (in what is now a suburb of sprawling Kansas City), the Truman Presidential Library & Museum tells of the unlikely rise of Truman, who was born into a modest family, never went to college, and went into politics only because his clothing store failed, launching a political career distinguished by integrity and hard work. The famous "The Buck Stops Here" sign still sits on the desk in a replica of Truman's Oval Office. Built in 1957, the library was recently updated with interactive "decision theaters" that put into visitors' hands life-and-death decisions that Truman faced, such as whether to use atomic weapons during WWII or to send troops to fight in Korea. Truman died in 1972; he and Bess are buried in the library courtyard.

Independence is also known as the "Queen City of the Trails" because three of the great routes that led pioneers west from the 1820s to the 1850s—the Santa Fe, California, and Oregon—began right around here, when western Missouri was the edge of civilization. The only museum in the country dedicated to all three trails, the National Frontier Trails Museum shows the massive preparations that were made before people set off across the vast prairie grasslands.

Every Labor Day weekend 300,000 visitors swarm to the city to celebrate SantaCaliGon Day, a four-day street festival named for the three mid-19th-century superhighways. Men dress up as trappers, and women in long calico dresses tend big pots of kettle corn. Modern-day folks listen to top country music acts, watch root-beer-chugging contests, and cruise displays of crafts in nine huge tents on historic Independence Square.

Independence is not just about all things trails or Truman; the Mormon Independence

The original "The Buck Stops Here" sign, displayed in the full-scale replica of Truman's Oval Office, reads "I'm from Missouri" on the back.

Visitors Center regularly rivals the Truman Library as the most visited site. Mormons came to town in 1831 led by founder Joseph Smith, but were ultimately driven out. The majority continued on to Salt Lake City (see p. 799), but some stayed in the region and eventually returned to Independence. Another showpiece is the magnificent 31-room Vaile Mansion, one of the finest examples of Second Empire Victorian architecture in the country. The opulently decorated mansion has such marvels of the day as toilets that flushed, Carrara marble fireplaces, and something oenophiles can only dream of—a 48,000-gallon wine cellar.

WHERE: 10 miles east of downtown Kansas City. *Visitor info:* Tel 800-748-7323 or 816-325-7890; visitindependence.com. **HARRY S. TRUMAN NATIONAL HISTORIC SITE:** Tel 816-254-9929; nps.gov/hstr. **HARRY S. TRUMAN LIBRARY & MUSEUM:** Tel 800-833-1225 or 816-268-8200; trumanlibrary.org. **NATIONAL FRONTIER TRAILS MUSEUM:** Tel 816-325-7575; frontiertrailscenter.com. **MORMON INDEPENDENCE VISITORS CENTER:** Tel 816-836-3466; lds.org/locationstovisit/independence-visitors-center. **VAILE MANSION:** Tel 816-325-7430; vailemansion.org. *When:* closed Nov and Jan–Mar. **BEST TIME:** early Sept for SantaCaliGon Days Festival.

Where Jazz Got Its Swing

18TH & VINE

Kansas City, Missouri

Jazz was born in New Orleans (see p. 427), but it grew up in Kansas City, Missouri. Around 18th & Vine in the 1930s, to be precise, and it still swings there at local clubs that have been packing in jazz lovers for decades. It's the city where Count Basie hit it big, and the place where saxophone genius (and K.C. native) Charlie Parker, trumpeter Dizzy Gillespie, and drummer Max Roach met up after hours and developed the improvisational style that evolved into the virtuosity of bebop, which endures to this day.

The city's rich jazz legacy dates to the Prohibition era, when the local political boss Tom Pendergast turned a blind eye to the liquor flowing freely in Kansas City despite the federal ban. Musicians who had been driven out of work in other cities flocked here, and by the 1930s more than 60 smoke-filled clubs had sprung up around 18th & Vine, the heart of a vibrant segregated black neighborhood.

That storied musical history lives on at the ultra-snazzy American Jazz Museum, the only museum in the country dedicated exclusively to what some call "America's classical music." The Blue Room, a 1930s-era nightclub (minus the smoke), is museum exhibit by day, jazz club by night. The centerpiece of a $26.5 million redevelopment project to revive the whole neighborhood, the museum also features over a hundred historic recordings and memorabilia like Ella Fitzgerald's pink evening gown, Louis Armstrong's trumpet, and Charlie Parker's famous acrylic sax. Under the same roof, the Negro Leagues Baseball Museum chronicles the great players of the Kansas City Monarchs and tells the story of segregated baseball. Across the street, the 1912 Gem Theatre has a gleaming, newly restored neon sign and glass-tiled facade with a brand-new 500-seat interior that sells out during the annual "Jammin' at The Gem" jazz masters' concert series.

Jazz disciples will want to make the pilgrimage to the Mutual Musicians Foundation, a former union hall where Parker and Gillespie reputedly met. There's little pretense but plenty of atmosphere as musicians filter in when it opens, sometime around 12:30 or 1 A.M. on weekend nights, to jam with whoever shows up and entertain fans often till dawn.

In the heart of old downtown, the good times still roll at the Phoenix Piano Bar, in a handsome corner brick building (reputedly a former brothel). The swankiest digs are found at The Majestic Restaurant, complete with a mural of local jazz greats and a menu that includes

juicy porterhouse steaks. Housed in a modest 1911 building that was a former saloon and bordello, it is another reminder that K.C. and sin have long been acquainted.

Instead of boozy nights and cigarettes, enjoy a wholesome barbecue contest while national and local jazz, blues, and R&B artists heat things up onstage at Kansas City's 18th and Vine Jazz and Blues Festival, an annual affair held in October right behind the American Jazz Museum complex. Kansas City's best barbecue talents work their magic for 3,000 people, who come for the irresistible combination of good food and music, linked in this town like nowhere else.

American Jazz Museum: Tel 816-474-8463; americanjazzmuseum.org. *When:* closed Mon. **The Blue Room:** Tel 816-474-6262; americanjazzmuseum.org. *When:* closed for music Tues, Wed, Sun. **Negro Leagues Baseball Museum:** Tel 888-221-6526 or 816-221-1920; nlbm.com. *When:* closed Mon. **The Gem:** Tel 816-474-6262. *Cost:* call for ticket prices to individual events. **Mutual Musicians Foundation:** Tel 816-471-5212; mutualmusiciansfoundation.org. *When:* Fri–Sat. **Phoenix Piano Bar:** Tel 816-221-5299; thephoenixkc.com. *Cost:* dinner $35. *When:* closed Sun. **The Majestic Restaurant:** Tel 816-221-1888; majestickc.com. *Cost:* dinner $60. **Best time:** Oct for Kansas City's 18th & Vine Jazz and Blues Festival.

Near the American Jazz Museum, a 17-foot-high bronze sculpture of sax man Charlie Parker dominates the plaza bearing his name.

Cow Town's World-Class Collections

NELSON-ATKINS MUSEUM OF ART

Kansas City, Missouri

The Nelson-Atkins is the unlikely and unplanned collaboration between two wealthy patrons—one a newspaper magnate who bequeathed a fortune to buy an art collection, the other a parsimonious schoolteacher. The result is one of the country's finest art museums, housing an astonishingly rich collection of 35,000 works, including one of the finest collections of Chinese art in the world and a 22-acre outdoor sculpture garden with the country's largest collection of abstract bronzes by the English sculptor Henry Moore.

It all came about because newspaper magnate William Rockhill Nelson moved to Kansas City in 1880 and, finding the cow town "incredibly commonplace and ugly," willed that his substantial fortune go to purchase works of art for the public enjoyment after his wife and daughter died. Mary Atkins then astonished the town by leaving $300,000 to build an art museum, an amount that had grown to $700,000 by the time the $12 million Nelson fortune became available. The bequests were combined in 1927, and in 1933 a grandiose neoclassical structure was finally opened. Its imposing presence is now playfully set off by the four gigantic sculptures by Claes Oldenburg and Coosje van Bruggen called *Shuttlecocks*, which lighten the museum's somber mood.

The strength of the museum's Asian holdings is owed to Laurence Sickman, a Harvard-educated connoisseur who bought ancient Buddhas and paintings directly from the exiled Puyi, the famed last emperor of China. Art critics respectfully call the Chinese galleries one of the most impressive single curatorial achievements in museum history. Other collections include great works by Caravaggio, Rembrandt, Titian, and Van Gogh, and countless works by Missouri native Thomas Hart Benton, who painted common folk and everyday farm scenes.

To display more of its collection, the museum commissioned architect Steven Holl to create a new wing, The Block Building, running 840 feet long and mostly underground. But five stunning glass structures, called lenses, erupt from the landscape alongside the original grande dame of a building. Confirming Kansas City's reputation as the "City of Fountains" (there are more than 200), the moodily elegant reflecting pool at the entry plaza is a work of art by Walter De Maria.

WHERE: 4525 Oak St. Tel 816-751-1278; nelson-atkins.org.

A four-part outdoor steel sculpture of 18-foot badminton shuttlecocks offers a whimsical welcome to the unique Nelson-Atkins Museum of Art.

K.C.'s Culinary Masterpieces

KANSAS CITY CUISINE

Missouri

B arbecue is the official dish of Kansas City, an ongoing passion and obsession that commonly erupts into white-hot arguments about where to savor the best. And there are plenty of candidates—at least 100 joints

serve up brisket, baby back ribs, and burnt ends (aka "brownies," the crispy, coveted scraps of beef brisket). K.C. (yes, even the locals call it that) prides itself on its anything-goes attitude (pork, beef, mutton, sausage, and chicken) and this includes the variety of sauce ingredients as well (tomatoes, vinegar, sugar, honey, molasses, mustard, garlic). Taste alone reigns supreme.

Barbecue and K.C. have gone together since 1908, when a Tennessean pitmaster named Henry Perry started selling smoked meats (including standards of the day—possum, woodchuck, and raccoon) to workers in the garment district. He passed on his secrets to apprentices who helped launch the two best-known names in Kansas City barbecue, Arthur Bryant and George Gates.

Arthur Bryant's Barbecue catapulted to fame in 1974 when native son and food writer for *The New Yorker* Calvin Trillin declared that it was not only the best barbecue in town but the best restaurant in *the world*. With beige formica counters, red vinyl seating, and a certain greasy patina, there's no decor to speak of—never was. "Give-'em-Hell" Harry Truman dined here, perhaps ordering the signature half-pound of ultra-slow-cooked brisket slapped on plain old white bread, with a hot, gritty, paprika-packed barbecue sauce and the best skin-on french fries in America, cooked in fresh lard.

George Gates founded his empire starting in 1946 in the segregated black neighborhood around 18th & Vine (see p. 452). That location

Arthur Bryant's has long been a much-loved institution for locals and food pilgrims alike.

is closed, but there are six others serving up a sweeter style of barbecue under the name Gates Bar-B-Q (George's son Ollie now runs the show).

In truth, you just can't get bad barbecue in K.C., and sampling its many different joints is something just short of heaven. B.B.'s Lawnside Bar-B-Q is an unremarkable road-house dishing out killer rib tips (the burnt ends of spareribs) and smoked sausage, along with live blues music. Once a downtown hole-in-the-wall, Danny Edward's and its smoky brisket proved so popular that it relocated to a more spacious but still soulful location on Southwest Boulevard. And people travel all the way to the southern suburb of Belton for Snead's famous log sandwich—a savory blend of smoked beef, pork, and ham chopped up together and stuffed into a long loaf of bread.

For a full-tilt barbecue experience, come during the American Royal World Series of Barbecue, which ranks up there with the Memphis Barbecue Contest in May (see p. 471), the Olympics of the barbecue world. Roughly 500 teams from all over the U.S. set up camp at Arrowhead Stadium and fire up their meats, with each tent emitting an aroma more tantalizing than the last.

Of course, K.C. does have a taste for the other good things in life—great steak, for instance, a fundamental since Kansas City had stockyards stretching to the horizon. Those are gone, but Hereford House, opened in 1957, still serves sirloins, strips, filets, T-bones, rib eyes, and pound-plus cowboy cuts.

And last but never least, Stroud's is the place that pays homage to four-star pan-fried chicken, very possibly the best on earth—crispy golden on the outside and impeccably moist within, served with superb mashed potatoes, cream gravy, and cinnamon rolls that aren't too sweet.

ARTHUR BRYANT'S BARBECUE: Tel 816-231-1123; arthurbryantsbbq.com. *Cost:* lunch $12. **GATES BAR-B-Q:** Tel 816-531-7522; gatesbbq.com. *Cost:* dinner $15. **B.B.'s LAWNSIDE BAR-B-Q:** Tel 816-822-7427; bbslawnsidebbq.com. *Cost:* lunch $15. **DANNY EDWARD'S BOULEVARD BBQ:** Tel 816-283-0880; dannyedwardsblvdbbq.com. *Cost:* full slab rib dinner $20. **SNEAD'S:** Belton. Tel 816-331-7979; sneadsbbq.com. *Cost:* log sandwich $8. **AMERICAN ROYAL WORLD SERIES OF BARBECUE:** Tel 816-221-9800; americanroyal.com. *When:* 1st weekend in Oct. **HEREFORD HOUSE:** Tel 816-584-9000; herefordhouse.com. *Cost:* dinner $45. **STROUD'S:** Tel 816-454-9600; stroudsrestaurant.com. *Cost:* dinner $25.

An Abandoned Train Track Finds New Life

ST. CHARLES & THE KATY TRAIL

Missouri

Originally a fur-trading post established in 1769, St. Charles has seen its fair share of travelers. In 1804 it was Lewis and Clark's last point of contact with the "civilized" world before they sailed up the Missouri River into the vast unknown interior of the continent. Later the small river town grew prosperous from pioneers passing through on their way west on the Santa Fe, California, and Oregon trails (see p. 451). But these days the town is equipping travelers to explore yet another trail, the white crushed gravel paths and pretty scenery of the Katy Trail, a 240-mile-long converted rail bed named for the old Missouri-Kansas-Texas line, the M-K-T, or "Katy." Bicyclists, hikers, and birders come from near and far to experience the country's longest, skinniest state park.

Mostly flat and easy riding, the Katy is unusually enchanting, especially in the wine country that unfolds between St. Charles and Hermann (see p. 450). Abundant B&Bs and restaurants in the tiny hamlets along the route mean you don't have to take much more than a knapsack and credit card (though camping is an option).

St. Charles warrants a good walkabout before setting off. The riverfront downtown dates to the 1820s, when St. Charles was Missouri's first state capital. Today it's a jostling blend of small shops (including plenty of bike rental places), restaurants, grand mansions, and museums, all an easy day trip from nearby St. Louis. The Lewis & Clark Boat House and Nature Center has three replicas of the Corps of Discovery keelboat.

The famously peripatetic frontiersman Daniel Boone lived out his final years in this area, moving here in 1799 because Kentucky was "too crowded." Upon his wife Rebecca's death in 1813, Boone settled at an impressive four-story limestone Georgian home belonging to his youngest son, Nathan, and his wife and 14 children. Boone lived in the home until his death in 1820. Located in Defiance on the Katy Trail west of St. Charles, the Boone Home is full of surprises, including a ballroom on the top floor, and the revelation that Boone preferred tall, black felt hats—he considered coonskin caps unkempt and uncivilized.

The Boone family made a good living by blazing an old Indian trail that led to a salt lick 100 miles away. Known as Boone's Lick Trail, it became a major road for pioneers heading west and today is the namesake of an historic B&B in St. Charles, Boone's Lick Trail Inn. This 1840s Federal-style auberge has guest rooms filled with antiques, and a deliciously indulgent breakfast of cheese-stuffed french toast with strawberry sauce.

WHERE: 25 miles northwest of St. Louis. *Visitor info:* Tel 800-366-2427 or 636-946-7776; historicstcharles.com. **KATY TRAIL:** 240 miles beginning at St. Charles riverfront and ending in Clinton. Tel 800-334-6946 or 573-449-7402; katytrailstatepark.com. **LEWIS & CLARK BOAT HOUSE:** Tel 636-947-3199; lewisandclark.net. **BOONE HOME:** Defiance. Tel 636-798-2005; lindenwood.edu/boone. **BOONE'S LICK TRAIL INN:** St. Charles. Tel 888-940-0002 or 636-947-7000; booneslick .com. *Cost:* from $130. **BEST TIMES:** spring and fall for weather; Nov–Dec for Christmas Traditions.

Home of the Pony Express

ST. JOSEPH

Missouri

S aint Joe (as the natives call it) was once the westernmost edge of civilization, the last stop before pioneers crossed the Missouri River into Indian territory, and the beginning of the American West's most glorious business failure:

the Pony Express. It lasted a mere 18 months, but the daring of riders trading off mounts and mailbags between St. Joseph and Sacramento, California, lives on in America's imagination.

Housed in the original Pike's Peak Stables where the first rider hightailed it out on April 3, 1860, St. Joe's Pony Express National Museum explains that the overland mail service began here because it was where the telegraph lines ended. Lightning-fast riders galloped away, switching horses at relay stations every 10 to 15 miles, handing off a 20-pound pouch to a fresh rider after 75–100 miles. Even at exorbitant rates—$5 per half-ounce in 1860 dollars!—the Pony Express couldn't cover its costs (especially once the telegraph lines were completed) and went bankrupt.

Its headquarters were at an ultra-fancy four-story hotel built in 1858 that has since been converted into the Patee House Museum. It has preserved many old storefronts in an exhibit called the Streets of Old St. Joe, including the dentist's office owned by the father of legendary CBS news anchor Walter Cronkite. (Another hometown hero is the jazz saxophonist Coleman Hawkins, whose legacy is celebrated in a jazz festival in June.) Right next to the Patee is the small white house where outlaw Jesse James made the mistake of taking in former gang member Robert Ford, who gunned James down in 1882 for reward

The famed Pony Express statue rides on at St. Joe's City Hall Park.

money and a pardon. The bullet hole is still in the wall.

Of St. Joseph's many worthy museums, certainly the oddest is the Glore Psychiatric Museum, which tells the story of how mental illness has been viewed and treated over the last seven millennia—"cures" that included a restraint cage for bloodletting, a human-sized gerbil wheel, and whirling cages to drive out evil spirits. On a less neurotic note, amble around downtown to admire St. Joe's goodly stock of Gothic, Victorian, and Romanesque homes.

WHERE: 50 miles north of Kansas City. *Visitor info:* Tel 800-785-0360 or 816-233-6688; stjomo.com. **PONY EXPRESS NATIONAL MUSEUM:** Tel 816-279-5059; ponyexpress.org. **PATEE HOUSE & JESSE JAMES HOME:** Tel 816-232-8206; ponyexpressjessejames.com. **GLORE MUSEUM:** Tel 800-530-8866 or 816-364-1209; stjosephmuseum.org. **BEST TIMES:** June and Sept for the Coleman Hawkins music festivals.

The Colossus of Beers

ANHEUSER-BUSCH

St. Louis, Missouri

Anheuser-Busch, the world's largest brewing company, got its start in St. Louis back in 1860 and still maintains its vast 140-acre world headquarters here. In the 1840s a great wave of German immigrants to

the area opened a flood of new breweries (and planted vineyards just west of here; see p. 450). A soap manufacturer named Eberhard Anheuser bought the failing Bavarian Brewery in 1860, but his most fortuitous move proved to be the marriage of his daughter Lily to the ambitious Adolphus Busch. Busch pioneered the use of refrigerated railcars and set up a network of icehouses to make Budweiser the first beer widely available across the U.S. The Busch family is still a major stockholder,

and August Busch III and IV serve in top management.

The St. Louis property is the largest of Anheuser-Busch's 12 U.S. breweries. The tour cuts to the chase and starts with a visit to the Clydesdales, America's most famous and cosseted horses, who live in enviable grandeur amid polished wood and stained glass in the late 19th-century Circular Stables. Today Anheuser-Busch maintains three traveling eight-horse "hitches" to be trotted out for parades and special events, and they are a magnificent spectacle. Every day, each of these high-octane creatures consumes 50 pounds of hay, 25 quarts of mixed feed, 30 gallons of water, and endless adulation from those experiencing them up close.

Follow brick paved streets, past gargoyles hanging from the cornices of buildings, to the historic Brew House, where you learn how Budweiser is made. The vintage Bevo Packaging Plant, with its decorative trim and 19th-century wrought iron, is mesmerizing with its high-speed bottling and canning lines. At the end of the tour is the Hospitality Room, everyone's favorite, where samples of Budweiser and other A-B brands await.

If you can't get enough of the Clydesdales, visit Grant's Farm, a 281-acre exotic animal park, petting zoo, and Bavarian-style farm built in 1914 by August Busch Sr. Eighty acres of the land originally belonged to Ulysses S. Grant, who built a log cabin (it's still here) in 1855, calling it Hardscrabble Farm, but lived there for only a few months. Today kids ride the tram past grazing buffalo,

zebras, and red deer that roam freely, but it's hard to beat the fresh crop of young Clydesdales in training to become part of a hitch team. Everyone eventually winds up at the courtyard Bauernhof for a bratwurst and a cold beer—Budweiser, of course.

WHERE: 12th & Lynch Streets. Tel 800-342-5283 or 314-577-2626; budweisertours .com. **GRANT'S FARM:** Tel 314-843-1700; grantsfarm.com. *When:* closed Nov–Mar.

Anheuser-Busch's iconic Clydesdales are a highlight of the brewery tour.

A Giant Work of Art That Beckons Your Inner Child

CITY MUSEUM

St. Louis, Missouri

The first thing you see is a big yellow school bus that appears to be driving off the building's roof into thin air. Housed in a former shoe factory in downtown St. Louis, City Museum is the quirkiest museum in America,

a giant piece of installation art that requires even the most jaded grown-up to experience it as freshly as a four-year-old.

The museum is the wildly eccentric work of sculptor and founder Bob Cassilly, who opened it as a museum-in-progress in 1997. Twenty welders, masons, sculptors, and painters worked full-time to re-assemble architectural relics salvaged from local buildings slated for

destruction and other "leftovers" into a delightful and disorienting collection of pits, tanks, slides, tubes, tunnels, chutes, caves, ponds, and mazes. There are nearly 100 installations with names like "Slinky Climber" (a huge stainless-steel coil that was part of a cooling tank used by Anheuser-Busch), "Bottle Wall" (made with 70,000 bottles from local Vess Soda Company's discontinued bottle line), and "Shoelace Factory" (a collection of working shoelace machines where you can pick your thread-color combinations and walk away with a pair made to order).

This continually changing work of art has outgrown three floors of the old factory and has spilled over onto the parking lot and up the side of the ten-story building to the roof. The museum includes a one-ring circus, its own railroad, an aquarium, several restaurants, two jet planes, a skate park, a dance floor, an architectural museum, and a fire engine. Word has spread, and annual visits surpass the one-million mark. Kids may dive right into the Enchanted Caves and Big Tube Slide, but it is interesting to note that Cassilly actually created the museum for adults (hence the midnight closing time on Fridays and Saturdays).

Regardless of age, a post-museum visit to Ted Drewes Frozen Custard, a St. Louis tradition since 1929, is de rigueur. This rich, velvety concoction packed with milkfat, sugar, eggs, and honey comes in one flavor—vanilla—but then there's the fun part of adding whatever you want: fruit, nuts, chocolate, caramel, M&M's. Everyone's favorite is the concrete ("crete" for short), a milkshake so thick that it's handed out through the window upside down, with spoon and straw firmly planted. It's so good that one of the two simple white stands on St. Louis's south side stays open even in the bitterly cold winters, when you can buy a Christmas tree along with your "crete."

WHERE: 750 N. 16th St. Tel 314-231-2489; citymuseum.org. **TED DREWES FROZEN CUSTARD:** Tel 314-481-2652; teddrewes.com. *When:* closed Jan.

Rich Legacy of the 1904 World's Fair

FOREST PARK

St. Louis, Missouri

The grandest, giddiest fair the world has ever known was held to celebrate the centennial of the Louisiana Purchase, President Thomas Jefferson's historic land acquisition, and attracted 20 million people in just seven months. The 1904 World's Fair popularized such American culinary institutions as the hamburger, the hot dog, ice-cream cones, peanut butter, and a "health drink" called Dr. Pepper. It also showcased Buster Brown Shoes and scientific wonders like X-ray machines, and thrilled crowds with a 2,160-seat Ferris wheel.

Most of the fair's 900 structures and fantastic "palaces" were made of wood and inexpensive building materials that could easily be demolished. But the Palace of Fine Arts, an august blend of classical and Renaissance architecture designed by Cass Gilbert, was meant to become a permanent home for art. Today it houses the St. Louis Art Museum, the crown jewel of the sprawling 1,370-acre Forest Park that dwarfs New York City's Central Park by 500 acres. Sitting atop Art Hill, the museum houses a comprehensive collection of 33,000 works, a testament to the fortunes that made St. Louis the country's fourth-largest city at the time of the fair.

While its galleries and marble corridors house first-rate collections of Asian and Western painting and sculpture, the St. Louis Art Museum is best known for its pre-Columbian and Oceanic art and its superlative 20th-century German collection, including the world's largest collection of Expressionist Max Beckman paintings.

Forest Park itself dates back to 1876, when it was a tract of forest well outside the city limits (hence the name), but the flourishing city grew to eventually envelop it. Today it's an inviting expanse, the city's green soul, a

Once a dense swath of woods, Forest Park today is a 1,370-acre public space with a number of attractions.

few miles west of downtown. Another fair-era highlight of the park is the Flight Cage, one of the world's largest walk-through aviaries. It became the nucleus of the 93-acre St. Louis Zoo, and has been transformed into a cypress swamp habitat with 16 species of birds that thrive along the Mississippi River. Forest Park also includes lakes, a boathouse, two golf courses, a skating rink, and the Missouri History Museum. Visit the museum's permanent exhibit on the World's Fair that embodies its sights, sounds, and splendor.

St. Louis Art Museum: Tel 314-721-0072; slam.org. **St. Louis Zoo:** Tel 800-966-8877 or 314-781-0900; stlzoo.org. **Missouri History Museum:** Tel 314-746-4599; mohistory.org. **Best times:** late May–mid-June for Shakespeare Festival of St. Louis (sfstl.com); mid-Sept for Great Forest Park Balloon Race (greatforestparkballoonrace.org).

Where the West Began

St. Louis Arch

St. Louis, Missouri

More than twice as tall as the Statue of Liberty, the Gateway Arch is the world's grandest contemporary monument—a shining sliver of silver in the morning, a shimmering white arc by day, and a glowing pink ribbon

in the evening light. Soaring 630 feet above the Mississippi River, the gigantic stainless steel arch is Missouri's best-known landmark. It commemorates one of the most important events in American history, the Louisiana Purchase of 1803, when President Thomas Jefferson doubled the size of the young U.S. by paying France $15 million for 530 million acres stretching from New Orleans to Montana—about three cents an acre. He immediately dispatched fellow Virginians Meriwether Lewis and William Clark to examine the goods. Lewis spent five months making preparations in St. Louis (then still a French

outpost) while Clark trained their Corps of Discovery before meeting up at St. Charles (see p. 456) and sailing up the Missouri into uncharted territory. Things were never the same in America—or St. Louis, which flourished as a major stopover for people heading to Santa Fe, California, and Oregon, making it truly the "Gateway to the West."

A perfect inverted catenary curve (the shape a free-hanging chain takes when held by two ends), the hollow Gateway Arch was considered an engineering marvel when it was unveiled in 1965. Designed by the architect Eero Saarinen, the Arch is a part of the Jefferson National Expansion Memorial. Subterranean exhibits focus on colonial St. Louis, Thomas Jefferson's vision, the St. Louis waterfront and more, but there's no denying that the biggest attraction here is the "Journey to the Top," a tram ride up either leg of the Arch to an enclosed observation platform. Sweeping views can reach as far as 30 miles on a clear day.

Just below, you can see the Old Courthouse where in 1847, a black man named Dred Scott and his wife, Harriet, sued for, and were granted, their freedom, helping to spark the Civil War. Today, it's a museum that charts the history of St. Louis. Get a taste of the glory days by boarding one of the Gateway Arch Riverboats, replicas of 19th-century steamboats, which depart frequently from the levee at the base of the Arch.

An easy walk from the arch, the National Blues Museum tells the history of blues music through a mix of interactive exhibits, immersive experiences, and an art gallery. Don't miss a live music performance in the museum's nightclub setting, which also boasts a full bar.

Nearby is the Missouri Botanical Garden, a 79-acre phantasmagoria that is one of America's oldest and most important botanical gardens and a world leader in plant science and conservation. The garden is at its best during the Whitaker Music Festival in June and July,

when people spread out blankets and settle in with picnic baskets for the best local jazz, blues, bluegrass, pop, and rock 'n' roll, a bit of excitement in this otherwise peaceful haven.

WHERE: Tel 877-982-1410 or 314-982-1410; gatewayarch.com. **GATEWAY ARCH RIVERBOAT CRUISES:** Tel 877-982-1410 or 314-982-1410; gatewayarch.com. **NATIONAL BLUES MUSEUM:** Tel 314-925-0016; nationalbluesmuseum.org. **MISSOURI BOTANICAL GARDEN:** Tel 314-577-5100; missouribotanicalgarden.org. **BEST TIMES:** spring for early blooms; June–July for Whitaker Music Festival; late Aug/early Sept for Japanese Festival, all in the Botanical Garden.

On a windy day, perceptive visitors to the top of the Arch can actually feel the structure sway slightly.

Soaring Views and Moon Pies

CHATTANOOGA & ROCK CITY

Tennessee and Georgia

Barn roofs and billboards scream for miles, "See Rock City!" It's actually in Georgia but lies on the outskirts of Chattanooga, Tennessee's fourth-largest city. From atop the soaring bluff of Lookout Mountain, Rock City promises spectacular views of seven states: Alabama, Georgia, Kentucky, North Carolina, South Carolina, Tennessee, and Virginia. Visitors can drive to the mountaintop before

walking the less-than-a-mile-long Enchanted Trail. Ancient rock formations and dense woodlands envelop such natural wonders as a 90-foot waterfall and hundreds of native plants, including mosses, ferns, wildflowers, and rhododendrons. Natural outcroppings and peculiar rock formations boast names like Needle's Eye and Fat Man's Squeeze. Most dramatic of all (but not for the vertigo-inclined) is the Swing-a-Long Bridge, a 180-foot-long suspension bridge that sways above the Chattanooga Valley far below.

In Chattanooga, grab a Moon Pie—a chocolate-and-marshmallow graham cracker snack invented at a bakery here in the early 1900s—and take a look around. Perched on the Tennessee River, Chattanooga has a vibrant, redeveloped downtown waterfront whose shops, restaurants, and attractions have made it a family-vacation favorite. The biggest lure is its state-of-the-art Tennessee Aquarium (the world's largest freshwater aquarium), where visitors can follow a raindrop from its fall to earth in the Appalachian Mountains to its eventual splash into the Gulf of Mexico, meeting some 12,000 resident fish, birds, mammals, reptiles, amphibians, and crustaceans along the way.

A pedestrian bridge connects downtown with the Bluff View Art District, a charming riverside neighborhood made for strolling, with an outdoor sculpture garden, cafés, galleries, B&Bs, and the Hunter Museum of American Art. The stunning glass-and-steel structure offers spectacular views and houses collections ranging from Hudson River School and American Impressionist paintings to contemporary studio glass and 20th-century sculpture.

The Hunter Museum of American Art is part of the Bluff View Art District overlooking the Tennessee River.

Chattanooga and the nearby Cumberland Plateau also draw outdoor adventure-seekers, who come for the rock climbing, bungee jumping, kayaking, and white-water rafting. Civil War history is also part of the city's past, with the Chickamauga and Chattanooga National Military Park (see p. 341), the nation's first and largest, straddling the Georgia–Tennessee border near Rock City.

WHERE: 116 miles southwest of Knoxville. *Visitor info:* Tel 800-322-3344 or 423-756-8687; chattanoogafun.com. **ROCK CITY:** Lookout Mountain, GA. Tel 800-854-0675 or 706-820-2531; seerockcity.com. **TENNESSEE AQUARIUM:** Tel 800-262-0695 or 423-265-0698; tnaqua.org. **HUNTER MUSEUM:** Tel 423-267-0968; huntermuseum.org. **WHERE TO STAY:** The StoneFort Inn, tel 855-734-7829 or 423-267-7866; stonefortinn.com. *Cost:* from $155. **BEST TIME:** mid-Nov–Dec for the Enchanted Garden of Lights at Rock City.

Civil War History in a Preserved Corner of the South

FRANKLIN

Tennessee

I t's as if a gentler time and place were captured and preserved in picturesque Franklin, nestled in the rolling landscape south of Nashville. Centered on a statue of an unnamed Civil War soldier, the charming town square is a focal point of the immaculate 200-year-old historic district, where slender church steeples rise among the treetops and Main Street is lined with brick sidewalks. Scores of antiques shops, art galleries, and cafés beckon visitors to linger. The family-owned Puckett's Grocery and Restaurant offers a lot under one roof—breakfast, lunch, and dinner to stay or to go and live entertainment by some mighty talented performers.

Things weren't always so serene and idyllic here in Williamson County. Among the wealthiest areas of Tennessee before the Civil War, the destruction of its plantation system was a blow from which its economy did not recover for

The Carnton Plantation, site of the 1864 Battle of Franklin, is open to visitors.

more than a century. Visitors can tour the hillside Carnton Plantation, where, on November 30, 1864, Gen. John B. Hood and more than 20,000 Confederate soldiers attacked a well-fortified Union position. The Battle of Franklin lasted only five hours, but it was one of the war's bloodiest, claiming 10,000 casualties and the lives of six Confederate generals. In the battle's aftermath, Carnton's owners turned their house into a field hospital. Two years later, they gave over 2 acres to be used as a Confederate cemetery. Within view of the plantation grounds, it's a graceful patch of field in which black wrought-iron gates and shade trees envelop the limestone markers of 1,481 Confederate soldiers. Today, it's the largest privately owned military cemetery in the country.

WHERE: 20 miles south of Nashville. *Visitor info:* Tel 615-591-8514; visitfranklin .com. **PUCKETT'S:** Tel 615-794-5527; pucketts gro.com/franklin. *Cost:* lunch $10. **CARNTON PLANTATION:** Tel 615-794-0903; boft.org. **WHERE TO STAY:** Blue Moon Farm B&B, tel 800-493-4518 or 615-497-4518; bluemoon farmbb.com. *Cost:* cottage from $350. **BEST TIMES:** late Apr for the Main Street Festival; Nov 30 for the Battle of Franklin Annual Illumination.

Cloaked in Blue Haze

THE GREAT SMOKY MOUNTAINS

Tennessee and North Carolina

Stretching across 800 square miles of the Southern Appalachians and straddling the Tennessee and North Carolina border, Great Smoky Mountains National Park is the most popular national park in the country,

drawing more than twice as many visitors as any of the system's other parks—even the Grand Canyon runs a distant second. Within its bounds, 16 peaks rise higher than 5,000 feet. Visual drama abounds, but equally astounding is the diversity of the park's plant and animal

life. The Smokies boast 100 species of native trees; over 1,500 flowering plants, which blanket the mountains and meadows from early spring to late autumn; some 4,000 kinds of nonflowering plants; 200 varieties of birds; and more than 66 species of mammals (1,500 black bears live here), 67 native fish species, and other wildlife. It's this vast diversity that caused the United Nations to designate the park as an International Biosphere Reserve.

Among the world's oldest mountains (formed 200 to 300 million years ago), the Smokies are named for the bluish haze that often shrouds them, caused by humidity and water vapor emitted by the dense forests that cover 95 percent of the park (30 percent of which is old growth). The 150 hiking trails range from short-and-easy walks to a rugged 72-mile stretch of the Appalachian Trail (see p. 332). About 550 of the park's 850 miles of marked trails allow visitors to explore the way the early mountain settlers did: by horse. Stables in the park rent horses for guided rides, or you can bring your own. Or strike out by car along the Newfound Gap Road, which stretches 32 scenic miles from the Sugarlands Visitor Center outside Gatlinburg to the Oconaluftee Visitor Center outside Cherokee, North Carolina. Laid out in the 1930s, the road's views encompass 6,593-foot Mount LeConte; Clingmans Dome, the park's highest summit at 6,643 feet; and Newfound Gap Overlook at the road's highest point (5,046 feet). Cades Cove Loop winds for 11 miles through the valley of the same name, a 19th-century settlement that includes log homes, churches, and a working grist mill.

Lodging options abound in towns bordering the park. If you want to stay within the Smokies, LeConte Lodge is for only the hardiest souls. Guests must hike four or five hours to Mount LeConte's summit; the three rustic lodges and cabins accommodate about 60 guests per night. Bed linens, kerosene lamps, and meals are provided; there is no electricity or running water (except for a privy with flush toilets), but the air is pristine and the views are spectacular. For more upscale rusticity, consider the posh, 26-acre Lodge at Buckberry Creek, an Adirondack-style inn outside Gatlinburg.

WHERE: Tennessee's main park entrance is the Sugarlands Visitor Center, 4 miles south of Gatlinburg. Tel 865-436-1291. *Park info:* Tel 865-436-1200; nps.gov/grsm. **LECONTE LODGE:** Tel 865-429-5704; lecontelodge.com. *Cost:* $136 per adult, includes dinner and breakfast. *When:* closed mid-Nov–mid-Mar. **LODGE AT BUCKBERRY CREEK:** Tel 866-305-6343; buckberrylodge.com. *Cost:* from $180 (off-peak), from $265 (peak). **BEST TIMES:** Apr–May for spring flowers; Oct for foliage; mid-Mar–late Nov for horseback riding.

The Great Smoky Mountains' Grotto Falls

"If history were taught in the form of stories,
it would never be forgotten."—*Rudyard Kipling*

NATIONAL STORYTELLING FESTIVAL

Jonesborough, Tennessee

The most acclaimed storytelling festival in the U.S. takes place the first full weekend in October each year in historic Jonesborough, tucked back in a corner of the Appalachian Mountains. In 1973, inspired by hearing country comedian Jerry Clower tell a story about Mississippi raccoon hunting on the *Grand Ole Opry* broadcast, a local high school journalism teacher decided to found a story-telling festival in his part of northeastern Tennessee. About 60 people showed up at the first festival to hear a handful of people tell stories from the back of a hay wagon. Since then the event has grown in scope and stature, attracting more than 10,000 annual visitors from throughout the country and abroad. They come to relish the humor and heartache of tall tales and ancient myths, to revel in the unique phrasings and dialects of each storyteller, and to learn more about a craft that people have been practicing since the first caveman version of "once upon a time."

It all takes place in circus tents set up in downtown Jonesborough, a restored frontier town with a population of just 5,174 (founded in 1799, it's Tennessee's oldest town). During festival weekend the classic, small-town Main Street—lined with brick sidewalks, quaint shops, and churches—is closed to vehicles, food is sold from outdoor booths, and stories are spun around every corner. After-dark goosebumps are delivered along with ghost stories, while adults can opt for midnight cabaret performances.

WHERE: 98 miles northwest of Knoxville; 116 W. Main St. Tel 800-952-8392 or 423-753-2171; storytellingcenter.net. *Visitor info:* Tel 866-401-4223 or 423-753-1010; historic jonesborough.com. *Cost:* 3-day pass $165. *When:* 1st full weekend in Oct.

The King's Castle on the Hill

GRACELAND

Memphis, Tennessee

Elvis Presley's Graceland Mansion, where he lived from 1957 till the day he died 20 years later, is hokey and something of a hoot, but it is also intriguing, entertaining, and at times very moving. Visitors have heard about the crystal chandeliers, peacock blue curtains, and the legendary "Jungle Room," with its waterfall wall, shag-carpet ceiling, and

Elvis Presley's living room features stained-glass peacock windows and a baby grand piano.

fake-fur upholstery. But irreverence soon fades: Graceland goes far beyond simple kitsch.

It has something to do with the fans who travel thousands of miles to see the King's last resting place in the Meditation Garden, surrounded by the graves of his mother, father, and paternal grandmother, Minnie Mae. It also has something to do with the greatness of Elvis himself, a poor boy from Mississippi who took the music of the Black South and the White South and ran them through a set of vocal cords that could get young girls, old women, and God himself all jittery. From the day he moved in with his mama and daddy in fulfillment of a boyhood promise to buy them the biggest house in town, Graceland was Elvis's escape and refuge, a place where he could kick back in an atmosphere that to him said "home." Graceland became an instant mecca for fans and today ranks as one of the nation's most visited homes, with more than 600,000 visitors per year. In the frozen-in-time Graceland mansion, the living room, music room, dining room, kitchen, TV room, pool room, Jungle Room, and a bedroom are open for visitors. Elsewhere within the 14-acre complex are Elvis's office; a racquetball building; and a trophy hall lined with gold and platinum records, stage costumes, guitars, jewelry, and mementos. Across the street is Elvis's collection of motorcycles and cars, including his famous 1955 pink Cadillac Fleetwood, and his two private jets. About 100

miles southeast of Memphis, true pilgrims can also visit Elvis's birthplace (see p. 443), a simple two-room house in Tupelo, Mississippi, where the King was born on January 8, 1935.

WHERE: 3734 Elvis Presley Blvd. Tel 800-238-2000 or 901-332-3322; graceland.com. *Cost:* from $36. *When:* closed Tues, Dec–Feb. **WHERE TO STAY:** The Heartbreak Hotel, tel 877-777-0606 or 901-332-1000; graceland .com/visit/heartbreakhotel.aspx. *Cost:* rooms from $115; themed suites from $555. **BEST TIMES:** 1st week of Jan for Elvis's birthday celebration; Aug 8–16 for Elvis Week, which culminates in a candlelight vigil at the grave site on Aug 16, the anniversary of Elvis's death.

The Blues Had a Baby and They Named It Rock 'n' Roll

MEMPHIS'S MUSIC MUSEUMS

Memphis, Tennessee

Hailed as home of the blues and birthplace of rock 'n' roll, Memphis welcomes music enthusiasts from around the globe. They come to walk in the footsteps of Elvis Presley (see previous entry), and to see the haunts of revered blues legends including Furry Lewis (a Memphis native), John Lee Hooker, B.B. King, and countless others. With its laid-back funk and unmistakable mojo, modern-day Memphis is the Holy Grail of American popular music, with three mesmerizing museums that pay homage to the city's legacy.

Stax Museum of American Soul Music, the newest and best of the tune-filled triumvirate, stands south of downtown on hallowed ground at the site of the razed Stax recording studio, where from 1960 to 1975, talent such as Otis Redding, Albert King, Booker T. and the MG's, and the Staple Singers cut a flood of chart-topping records. The museum is chock-full of multimedia displays, interactive listening stations, and galleries that reverberate with performance videos and continuous soundtracks of infectious Stax hits, including "(Sittin' on) The Dock of the Bay," "Hold On (I'm Coming)," and "I'll Take You There." Along with albums and autographed concert posters, there are filmed interviews with artists and displays crammed with vintage guitars, recording equipment, flashy threads, and—for pure bling appeal—the gold-trimmed Cadillac once owned by Oscar-winning singer-songwriter Isaac Hayes.

Broader in scope is the Memphis Rock 'n' Soul Museum, where film footage, photographs, and field recordings enliven thoughtful displays created in partnership with the venerable Smithsonian Institution. Audio tours guide visitors through galleries tracing rock and soul's origins back to gospel, blues, and country music in turn-of-the-century America and beyond our shores to Africa. Memphis's emergence as a cultural crossroads is explored via hundreds of well-known and obscure artists, among them hometown heroes such as Elvis, Al Green, and Earth, Wind & Fire.

Anyone looking for a deeper understanding of Elvis's early career will find it at Sun Studio, a two-story brick building where, in the mid-1950s, owner Sam Phillips pioneered the raw, electrifying sounds of country bluesman Howlin' Wolf and rockabilly sensations Jerry Lee Lewis and Carl Perkins, as well as Johnny Cash, Roy Orbison, and Elvis himself. It was here that the King recorded his first hit in 1954, "That's All Right (Mama)," which heralded the dawn of rock 'n' roll. Mercilessly devoid of upscale refurbishment and polish, the battered

little studio still looks just as it did half a century ago. With his clunky metal microphone still front and center, it looks as if Elvis never left the building. Knowledgeable guides narrate tours of the studio daily. By night, Sun's still in demand as a revered recording venue by acts ranging from Beck to U2.

The music scene continues to expand with two new arrivals: The Blues Hall of Fame (blues.org) and the Memphis Music Hall of Fame (memphismusichalloffame.com).

Stax Museum: Tel 888-942-7685 or 901-946-2535; staxmuseum.com. **Memphis Rock 'n' Soul Museum:** Tel 901-205-2533; memphisrocknsoul.org. **Sun Studio:** Tel 800-441-6249 or 901-521-0664; sunstudio.com. **Best time:** mid-Aug for Elvis Week.

From Dawn 'til Dusk

THE MEMPHIS MUSIC SCENE

Memphis, Tennessee

So, you've been to the gates of Graceland (see p. 466), and dutifully made the pilgrimage to the city's major rock and soul museums (see previous entry). But now you're ready to cut loose the ghosts of Memphis past and experience

The original B.B. King's Blues Club is one of many spots that keep Beale Street hopping around the clock.

some sizzling live rock 'n' roll or low-down, greasy blues. Look around, and listen: It's everywhere, from the booze-soaked bars of Beale Street to the sanctified pews of the Rev. Al Green's Full Gospel Tabernacle.

Downtown, Beale Street throbs with blues and rock bands every afternoon—and all night long. Beale's best bets are B.B. King's Blues Club, named for the beloved guitarist who got his start in Memphis, and the Rum Boogie Café, which has a killer house band and stellar guitar collection. Free music happens at Handy Park, where a statue honors W. C. Handy, the turn-of-the-century bandleader whose 1912 recording "Memphis Blues" launched 12-bar blues into popular culture. Handy's historic home, a wooden shotgun house furnished with early 1900s furniture, instruments, and sheet music, has been preserved as a museum here on the fabled street widely regarded as the birthplace of the blues.

Nearby, Automatic Slim's Tonga Club is a chic cocktail spot and site of occasional live music. Along Main Street, the Center for Southern Folklore, a cultural and heritage center with archived audio and video tapes and a folklore store lures nationally known singer-songwriters of all musical genres on Friday and Saturday nights.

Elsewhere around town, cutting-edge hipsters and garage rock bands can be heard at the Hi-Tone Café, while laid-back blues and beer sold by the quart draw dancing-room-only crowds to Wild Bill's, a no-frills juke joint opening at 10 P.M. on the outskirts of downtown. Redemption for such revelry awaits a stone's throw from Graceland, where most Sunday

mornings the Grammy Award–winning soul singer and ordained reverend Al Green preaches and leads a hand-clapping, sing-out-to-Jesus service from the pulpit at his Full Gospel Tabernacle.

B.B. KING'S BLUES CLUB: Tel 901-524-5464; bbkings.com/memphis. **RUM BOOGIE CAFÉ:** Tel 901-528-0150; rumboogie.com. **W. C. HANDY HOME:** Tel 901-522-1556; wc handymemphis.org. **AUTOMATIC SLIM'S TONGA CLUB:** Tel 901-525-7948; automaticsmemphis .com. **CENTER FOR SOUTHERN FOLKLORE:** Tel 901-525-3655; southernfolklore.com. **HI-TONE CAFÉ:** Tel 901-490-0335; hitonememphis.com. **WILD BILL'S:** Tel 901-207-3975. **FULL GOSPEL TABERNACLE:** 787 Hale Road, 11 A.M. Sunday service. **BEST TIMES:** 1st weekend in May for the Beale Street Music Festival, part of Memphis in May (memphisinmay.org); Sept/Labor Day for the Memphis Music and Heritage Festival.

Take Me to the River

BEALE STREET MUSIC FESTIVAL

Memphis, Tennessee

For pure star power and atmosphere, the Beale Street Music Festival— which kicks off the annual month long, citywide international cultural extravaganza known as Memphis in May—rivals the New Orleans Jazz and

Heritage Festival (see p. 428) as one of the best outdoor musical events in the U.S. For three days and nights, hundreds of musicians perform on open-air stages and in a sun-sheltering tent along the grassy expanse of Tom Lee Park, on the banks of the mighty Mississippi River. Against orange sunsets, barges glide lazily along the wide river, and the graceful M-shaped bridge that connects downtown Memphis with rural Arkansas to the west sparkles with decorative lights. The 25-acre park takes on a carnival-like setting as vendors hawk everything from beer, barbecue, and funnel cakes to tie-dyed T-shirts and Memphis souvenirs.

Opening night always draws huge crowds.

Music blares at every turn: rock, reggae, and rap; country, Cajun, and classical; and, of course, gospel and blues. Eclectic past performers have included such artists as Lenny Kravitz, Hall and Oates, The Flaming Lips, Ed Sheeran, and The Smashing Pumpkins. Naturally, Memphis musicians are always crowd favorites. In recent years, headliners included an embarrassingly rich array of hometown heroes, including Jerry Lee Lewis, B.B. King (before his death in 2015), Star & Micey, and Blind Mississippi Morris.

While overall the Memphis in May Festival is family friendly, it's mostly young-adult to middle-aged fans who travel from all over the country to attend the rowdy festival, and to party until the wee hours in the clubs along Beale Street (see p. 468), just a few blocks away.

WHERE: Tom Lee Park, at Beale St. and Riverside Dr. **MEMPHIS IN MAY:** Tel 901-525-4611; memphisinmay.org. *When:* 1st weekend in May for Beale Street Music Festival; entire month of May for Memphis in May Festival.

It's All About the Pork

MEMPHIS BARBECUE

Memphis, Tennessee

Among the various barbecue capitals in America, Memphis is a standout. Unlike in Texas, which is all about beef (see p. 755), BBQ in Memphis means pork, and it comes in two versions: pulled pork shoulder and ribs served either "wet" (with sauce) or "dry" (with a rub of spices and herbs instead).

More than a hundred barbecue joints clog Memphis, some so famous that they've expanded to other cities, while others have retained their quiet, local vibe. In business since 1948 and claiming to serve 10,000 meals on busy days, the Rendezvous lies in a busy cellar down an alley near the grand Peabody Hotel, known for the trained ducks that waddle through its lobby twice daily to the music of John Philip Sousa. For the full Rendezvous experience, order the dry charcoal-broiled ribs, red beans and coleslaw, and a pitcher of beer. The other big Memphis name for dry ribs is Corky's Bar-B-Q, with multiple locations, a string of franchises across the country, and a long list of favorite dishes headed by its succulent sandwiches.

On the funkier, more down-home side of things is Payne's, housed in a simple cinderblock building and offering one of the most legendary chopped pork sandwiches in town, served on a bun with pickly sweet slaw and hot sauce. At another great casual joint, the paper-plate-style Cozy Corner, specialties are BBQ Cornish game hens, sliced pork sandwiches with sauce and coleslaw, and

The annual World Championship Barbecue Cooking Contest is a Memphis institution.

surprisingly tasty BBQ baloney sandwiches. Central BBQ, with three locations in town, has developed a following for meaty ribs (both dry and wet) and homemade potato chips. At the beloved Jim Neely's Interstate Bar-B-Que, wet ribs are slathered with a thick, sweet-and-tangy basting sauce—the same sauce that also flavors the curiously delicious house specialty, barbecued spaghetti. This town even figured out how to barbecue pizza: Coletta's Italian Restaurant, open since 1923, is this category's self-proclaimed winner.

For all-around barbecue nirvana, show up at the cutthroat World Championship Barbecue Cooking Contest, part of the city's annual Memphis in May bash (see p. 469). More than 200 teams from around the world congregate to grill on the waterfront, using their own secret recipes.

RENDEZVOUS: Tel 901-523-2746; hogsfly .com. *Cost:* ribs $19. **CORKY'S:** Tel 901-685-9744; corkysmemphis.com. *Cost:* large ribs $20. **PAYNE'S:** Tel 901-272-1523. *Cost:* sandwich $5. **COZY CORNER:** Tel 901-527-9158; cozycornerbbq.com. *Cost:* large ribs $20. **CENTRAL BBQ:** Tel 901-272-9377; cbqmemphis.com. *Cost:* large ribs $21. **INTERSTATE BAR-B-QUE:** Tel 901-775-2304; interstatebarbecue.com. *Cost:* BBQ spaghetti dinner $8. **COLETTA'S:** Tel 901-948-7652; colettas.net. *Cost:* large BBQ pizza $23. **BARBECUE COOKING CONTEST:** Tel 901-525-4611; memphisinmay.org. *When:* 3 days in mid-May.

"Our lives begin to end the day we become silent about things that matter."—MLK

NATIONAL CIVIL RIGHTS MUSEUM

Memphis, Tennessee

On the evening of April 4, 1968, 39-year-old Dr. Martin Luther King Jr. stepped from his room onto the balcony of the Lorraine Motel in downtown Memphis, and was fatally shot. That moment, a watershed in American history, is preserved as the focal point of the National Civil Rights Museum, opened in the old Lorraine building in 1991. While the highlight is the museum's time-capsule look at the unchanged room where Rev. King was staying the day he was killed, the exhibits take in a wider scope, documenting the dark history of hatred and racial discrimination in our nation from the beginning of slavery in 1619 through the Civil War era to the present, along with the heroic struggle for freedom. Interactive multimedia exhibitions chronicle the exploitation of slaves on Southern cotton plantations and the postwar Jim Crow laws that denied equal rights to black citizens. Riveting archival video footage and period

The Lorraine Motel reopened in 1991 as the National Civil Rights Museum, with the nation's first comprehensive exhibit chronicling America's civil rights movement.

artifacts detail the brutal lynchings, church and bus bombings, and riots that erupted throughout the Deep South and beyond in the 1960s. Also chronicled are the enlightened efforts of others, such as the Freedom Riders, to help blacks rise above poverty and oppression through peaceful protests and the U.S. judicial system. A recent museum expansion includes the Legacy Building, the Main Street rooming house from which James Earl Ray is believed to have fired the gun that took King's life. Other displays trace the hunt for Ray in the days following King's murder, and lay out in exhaustive detail the conspiracy theories about how and why the powerful civil rights leader was targeted.

In the spirit of King's legacy, each fall the museum's Freedom Awards honor distinguished individuals who have fought for justice, peace, and human rights. Among past honorees are Nelson Mandela, Mikhail Gorbachev, Colin Powell, Bill Clinton, Bono, and Oprah Winfrey. A series of lectures and special programs are planned each year in conjunction with the awards ceremonies, with some of these star-studded events free and open to the public.

WHERE: 450 Mulberry St. Tel 901-521-9699; civilrightsmuseum.org. *When:* closed Tues. **BEST TIMES:** Jan for the national Martin Luther King holiday; Oct for the Freedom Awards activities.

Queen of the Antebellum Trail

BELLE MEADE

Nashville, Tennessee

From the French meaning "beautiful meadow," Belle Meade is the best preserved of Tennessee's plantations and at one time was a world-renowned horse-breeding farm, from which many of the best-known

An elegant carriage at Belle Meade speaks to the plantation's horse-breeding history.

racehorses of the 20th century could trace their bloodlines, including Seabiscuit in the 1930s and Secretariat in the 1970s. John Harding, a prosperous Virginia farmer who bought the land near the northern tip of the Natchez Trace (see p. 443) in 1807, originally built Belle Meade as a two-story redbrick, Federal-style farmhouse in 1820. Its current Greek Revival grandeur is the result of an architectural upgrade that occurred in 1853, after the plantation had become widely known for producing the region's finest horses. Today, costumed docents lead visitors through the elegant mansion, which is now filled with furniture and art returned by descendents of the family. Guests may also roam the carriage house, smokehouse, and creamery that dot the tree-shaded grounds, a tranquil site for outdoor concerts and picnics. **WHERE:** 8 miles from central Nashville; 5025 Harding Rd. Tel 800-270-3991 or

615-356-0501; bellemeadeplantation.com. May–Aug to see horses on the grounds; Nov–Dec for A Century of Christmas: 1853–1953.

The Home of Country Music

THE GRAND OLE OPRY

Nashville, Tennessee

Nashville has been known as "Music City, U.S.A." for the better part of a century, since the Grand Ole Opry began broadcasting its weekend radio show in 1925, then called *The WSM Barn Dance*. The world's longest-running radio show, it was broadcast between 1943 and 1974 from downtown's Ryman Auditorium, revered as the "Mother Church of Country Music." Built as the Union Gospel Tabernacle in 1892, the Ryman has since hosted U.S. presidents and performers like Enrico Caruso, but it's country legends like Hank Williams and Patsy Cline who embody the spirit of the place. Each weekend from 1943 to 1974, the rising stars of so-called "hillbilly" music performed to standing-room-only crowds and Nashville became synonymous with country music: The Ryman was its home.

When the Grand Ole Opry moved to a new performing arts center in the suburbs in 1974, the Ryman fell into disrepair until preservationists restored it to its acoustically perfect splendor. Today the Ryman is a choice concert hall favored by musicians of all genres and is open for self-guided and guided backstage tours that shed light on its rich heritage. Visitors can even stand center stage—for just an *American Idol* moment—and dream.

Meanwhile, the modern Grand Ole Opry dominates the entertainment district of Nashville known as Music Valley, and on Friday and

Saturday nights country stars still perform in family-friendly live radio and TV shows. The Opry returns to the Ryman's hallowed walls a few times each year, giving audiences a glimpse into the heyday when country music first swept the nation.

Downtown, around a bend of the Cumberland River, the Country Music Hall of Fame and Museum is an impressive repository of more than 2 million artifacts, from Elvis's 1960 "solid gold" Cadillac to Minnie Pearl's straw hat. From the museum, you can book a bus tour to the nearby Historic RCA Studio B on Music Row, where Elvis, Chet Atkins, Roy Orbison, and others cut hit records.

On any given weekend, Opry audiences can hear some of the best talent in the country, bluegrass, and gospel music worlds.

For live music and honky-tonk ambience, the Bluebird Café showcases new talent. On Lower Broadway, lovable dives include Robert's Western World Bar and Tootsie's Orchid Lounge. Nearby, big-name acts play B.B. King's Blues Club, which is just a few doors down from the Wildhorse Saloon, a popular club that perfected the line-dancing craze and is family-friendly until 10 P.M. on Fridays and Saturdays.

RYMAN: Tel 615-889-3060; ryman.com. GRAND OLE OPRY: Tel 800-733-6779 or 615-871-OPRY; opry.com. *Cost:* tickets from $42. *When:* Tues, Fri–Sat; additional shows in summer. COUNTRY MUSIC HALL OF FAME: Tel 800-852-6437 or 615-416-2001; countrymusic halloffame.com. BLUEBIRD CAFÉ: Tel 615-383-1461; bluebirdcafe.com. TOOTSIE'S ORCHID LOUNGE: Tel 615-726-0463; tootsies.net. ROBERT'S WESTERN WORLD: Tel 615-244-9552; robertswesternworld.com. B.B. KING'S BLUES CLUB: Tel 615-256-2727; bbkings.com. WILDHORSE SALOON: Tel 615-902-8200; wild horsesaloon.com. BEST TIMES: June for the 4-day Country Music Association Music Festival (cmaworld.com); Thurs in June–July for Bluegrass Nights at the Ryman; Oct for the annual Grand Ole Opry Birthday Bash.

A Presidential Estate and the State's Best Hotel

THE HERMITAGE

Nashville, Tennessee

Andrew Jackson, seventh president of the United States, may have been a native of the Carolinas, governor of Florida, and a war hero in the Battle of New Orleans, but from 1804 until his death in 1845 he made his official home here in Tennessee, at an estate known as The Hermitage. Situated on 1,120 wooded acres east of Nashville, the august Greek Revival home has been restored to its appearance in 1837, the year Jackson retired

Visitors enjoy a horse-drawn carriage ride through the grounds of The Hermitage.

after his second term, and is almost entirely furnished with the family's original possessions and personal items such as books and swords. The tombs of Jackson and his wife, Rachel, are on the grounds, along with her gardens and various outbuildings, which include a smokehouse and several log cabins. The third most visited presidential home in the U.S., The Hermitage hosts more than 250,000 visitors a year, with costumed interpreters offering tours.

Downtown Nashville's landmark Hermitage Hotel was named for Andrew Jackson's estate, but that's as far as the connection goes. Built in 1910, the imposing Beaux-Arts hotel has been a city landmark for decades, a ritzy place to see and be seen. The lobby makes a lasting impression with its gleaming marble floors, welcoming fireplace, and brilliant stained-glass skylight. All the beef at the Capitol Grille, a gourmet rathskellar-style restaurant in the lower level of the hotel, comes from its own herd of 150 Red Poll cattle, and vegetables are harvested from the hotel's own gardens.

THE HERMITAGE: 14 miles east of downtown Nashville; 4580 Rachel's Ln. Tel 615-889-2941; thehermitage.com. THE HERMITAGE HOTEL: Tel 888-888-9414 or 615-244-3121, 615-345-7116 (Capitol Grille); thehermitagehotel.com. *Cost:* from $299; dinner $60. BEST TIMES: spring and fall for weather; mid-May for peak blooms at the nearby Cheekwood Botanical Garden (cheekwood.org).

Praise the Lord and Pass the Potatoes

NASHVILLE FOOD

Nashville, Tennessee

Music City's restaurant scene is unexpectedly sophisticated and diverse, with everything from elegant French bistros and upscale steakhouses to ethnic eateries serving sushi and paella. But nothing will ever substitute for the beloved "meat and three" tradition—a meat entrée served with three well-seasoned sides, most always served with corn bread or biscuits.

Swett's, a soul food landmark dating back to 1954, is an old-school cafeteria whose steam tables brim with country-fried steak and gravy, breaded catfish, slow-roasted pork, buttered corn and okra, bubbly macaroni and cheese, sweet potato pudding, and warm peach cobbler. Downtown, mixed in with the honky-tonks of Lower Broadway, is Jack's Bar-B-Que, a nondescript hole-in-the-wall where some of the city's best smoked Tennessee pork shoulder is served on sandwiches or platters.

For old-fashioned comfort food, served family-style in a genteel 19th-century farmhouse cluttered with charming antiques, come hungry to Monell's, located in the historic Germantown neighborhood. Diners are seated at long tables and told to pass to the left, as waitresses bring out endless bowls of piping hot, skillet-fried chicken, pot roast, corn pudding, green beans, mashed potatoes, and biscuits with homemade peach preserves. Even among strangers, conversation flows easily over such good food and gracious hospitality.

For breakfast, drive along Highway 100 on the outskirts of town to find the Loveless Café, a Nashville institution since 1954. Long favored by country music stars, local folks, and foodies in quest of a Southern fix, the cramped old house packs in crowds who endure hour-long waits to enjoy the signature slow-cured country ham, fried in cast-iron skillets, and the ham drippings that are

Breakfast is served all day long at the Loveless Café.

blended with coffee to make red-eye gravy—best when ladled over buttermilk biscuits. Among the café's other rib-sticking options are pancakes with molasses and peach and blackberry preserves by the bowlful.

Sweet tooths can look forward to the Elliston Place Soda Shop, a nostalgic 1950s diner near Vanderbilt University, with red-and-white decor and small jukeboxes on each table. Come just for a malt or milk shake that's thick and rich, or go for broke with a burger, a baloney sandwich, or a meat-and-three.

SWETT's: Tel 615-329-4418; swettsrestaurant.com. *Cost:* lunch $10. **JACK'S BAR-B-**QUE: Tel 615-254-5715; jacksbarbque.com. *Cost:* lunch $8. **MONELL'S:** Tel 615-248-4747; montellstn.com. *Cost:* dinner $18. **LOVELESS CAFÉ:** Tel 615-646-9700; lovelesscafe.com. *Cost:* breakfast $10. **ELLISTON PLACE SODA SHOP:** Tel 615-327-1090; ellistonplace sodashop.com. *Cost:* lunch $8.

Mountain Village of Yesteryear

MUSEUM OF APPALACHIA

Norris, Tennessee

John Rice Irwin, a former Anderson County school superintendent whose ancestors settled in eastern Tennessee in the 1700s, collected stories from his grandparents . . . but he didn't stop there. As the old mountain folk died or moved away, he also began collecting discarded farm implements and household items—hand-carved wooden dolls, corn-husk brooms, and even banjos made from bedpans and ham tins. In 1969, those treasures became the core of the Museum of Appalachia, the largest and most unique entity of its kind anywhere, with some 250,000 artifacts displayed in two large exhibit halls and throughout a re-created homestead in the Appalachian foothills of northeastern Tennessee.

Resembling a mountain village in the mid-1800s, the homestead encompasses 15 tranquil acres dotted with historic log cabins and other furnished structures, such as a loom house, grist mill, and the Tater Valley Schoolhouse, along with sloping barns and rickety corncribs and outhouses. Most of the buildings were moved here from throughout the area to create this scene of pastoral, bygone rural life, and to show the resilience and ingenuity of people who had to make almost everything they needed. Hens, sheep, cows, and horses graze the green grasses. Stroll the grounds, and admire the simplicity of a split-rail fence or the graceful arc of tree-branch-trellised gardens, bursting with sunflowers and cornstalks and bordered by dried-gourd birdhouses.

In October, the aromas of wood smoke and sorghum molasses mingle with mountain music and the clang of blacksmithing at the Museum of Appalachia's Tennessee Fall Homecoming, celebrating the self-reliant lifestyle of early mountain pioneers. Country food is cooked in iron

Farm animals roam across the museum's 15 acres, adding to the sense of rural life.

kettles as farmers demonstrate skills such as sheepherding, log sawing, and tilling the rich, brown earth with horses and plows. Artisans carve dulcimers, split shingles, churn butter, or weave baskets from hickory bark or white oak, and there is a daily hymn sing in the hillside chapel in the woods. For anyone with an appreciation of American heritage, this is bliss. **Where:** 21 miles northwest of Knoxville. Tel 865-494-7680; museumofappalachia.org. *Cost:* $18 per adult, $42 families. **Best time:** 2nd weekend in Oct for Tennessee Fall Homecoming.

Down-Home Family Fun

Dollywood

Pigeon Forge, Tennessee

Dolly Parton, America's buxom blonde with the voice of a songbird and a laugh as big as the hills, is a native of Sevierville, a small town deep in the Smoky Mountains. Since she opened her eponymous "family adventure (don't-call-it-an-amusement) park" in 1986, Dollywood has largely outgrown its mostly corny image to become Tennessee's most-visited attraction with 2.5 million visitors annually.

The park is perched on 150 acres on the outskirts of Pigeon Forge, an endless commercial strip of putt-putt courses and go-kart rides in the shadow of the Great Smoky Mountains National Park (see p. 464). Natural beauty is still within view, whether from the top of a 60-foot Ferris wheel or from the hairpin turns of a thundering wooden roller coaster. Old-time music, plucked from the strings of dulcimers, banjos, and fiddles, provides a twangy soundtrack for the country fair atmosphere, and Dolly's appreciation for all things Appalachian is also reflected in the park's folksy arts and crafts shops, where wood carving, glassblowing, and quilting are demonstrated. A steam train chugs through leafy hills and over bridges, past more than 30 rides and attractions, including musical shows and a quaint replica of Dolly's mountain homestead.

Hundreds of top-notch entertainers from around the world converge on the park for six

After the thrill rides, catch your breath with a performance at Dollywood's Dreamsong Theater.

weeks each spring for the Festival of Nations. Other events showcase Southern gospel music and special children's activities, and during Smoky Mountain Christmas, Dollywood is strung with miles of Christmas lights. **Where:** 28 miles southeast of Knoxville. Tel 800-365-5996 or 865-428-9488; dollywood.com. *Cost:* adults $62, children $49. *When:* closed Jan–mid-Mar. **Best times:** Apr, when Dolly kicks off the season opening and Festival of Nations; May, when Dolly returns for Homecoming; Nov–Dec for the Smoky Mountain Christmas.

Equestrian Nirvana

TENNESSEE WALKING HORSE NATIONAL CELEBRATION

Shelbyville, Tennessee

In 1886, a foal named Black Allan was born to the Morgan mare Maggie Marshall, his sire a Hambletonian trotter named Allendorf. Black Allan, aka Allan F-1, became the foundation sire of the whole Tennessee Walking Horse breed, a great pleasure, show, and trail-riding horse and the first and only breed to bear the name of its home state. Fifty-some years after Black Allan's birth, local man Henry Davis had the idea of creating an annual festival to celebrate his home county's most famous asset, and in 1939 the Tennessee Walking Horse National Celebration was born. Today, Shelbyville's population of 21,000 swells to more than a quarter of a million over the course of the family-friendly event, which kicks off in late August with a barbecue cook-out. Over the next 11 days, some 2,000 horses from throughout the country compete in over 180 classes. Magnificent stallions and geldings prance and preen as judges eye their overall performance and noble signature gait. Colorful banners and bunting festoon the 30,000-seat outdoor arena, where box seats are handed down from generation to generation.

The festival has the air of an old-fashioned county fair, replete with a carnival, a stable-decorating contest, the naming of the World Grand Champion Tennessee Walking Horse, and plenty of leisurely interaction between the gentle steeds and their breeders and fans. The 105-acre festival grounds include outdoor practice areas with bleacher seating, food concessions, and 50 barns. In addition to the outdoor arena, which is illuminated at night and flanked by large video screens, a 4,200-seat indoor arena is used for various equestrian events throughout the year.

About 10 miles east of Shelbyville, the Tennessee Walking Horse National Museum is located in historic Wartrace, the cradle of the Tennessee Walking horse. This modest museum displays photos, trophies, saddles, horseshoes, and other memorabilia from the celebration, whose past winners sport names such as Main Power and Out on Parole.

WHERE: 60 miles southeast of Nashville. Tel 931-684-5915; twhnc.com. *When:* 11 days in late Aug–early Sept. *Cost:* from $7 per night. **WALKING HORSE MUSEUM:** tennessee walkinghorsenationalmuseum.org.

Tennessee Walking Horses compete to be one of the Celebration's 20 World Champions.

Moonshine and Magnolias

TENNESSEE WHISKEY TRAIL

Tennessee

W. C. Fields advised people to "Always carry a flagon of whiskey in case of snakebite . . . and furthermore always carry a small snake"— sage words when traveling the crooked back roads of south-central Tennessee en route to two historic distilleries that make Tennessee's finest sipping whiskey. Like Kentucky bourbon (see p. 403), Tennessee whiskey begins as a blend of corn, rye, barley, yeast, and water that is cooked to form a porridgelike mixture known as sour mash. What sets Tennessee whiskey apart, though, is a process in which the clear, newly distilled spirit slowly drips through layers of sugar maple charcoal before aging. This filters out impurities, producing a softer, drier flavor.

About 80 miles south of Nashville, the George Dickel Distillery can be found within the secluded hills beyond small-town Tullahoma. Dickel, a Nashville merchant who started his distillery in 1870, discovered that "whisky" (Dickel's preferred spelling) made in the cooler winter months tasted the smoothest. Today, the modest distillery that bears his name makes 80-proof George Dickel No. 8 and 90-proof No. 12 year-round. It's chilled before being poured into charcoal mellowing vats and aged in new American white oak barrels whose interiors are charred to caramelize the wood sugars and to help flavor the whiskey as it ages. The county is still "dry," but the local government now allows for tastings at the distillery.

Established in 1866, the Jack Daniel's Distillery in nearby Lynchburg has a much bigger name, and the operation to go with it. Tour buses crowd the gravel parking lot of the visitor center, furnished with antique moonshine-making equipment and whiskey-related artifacts. Tour guides lead visitors through the magnolia-landscaped grounds past a statue of the young Jack Daniel, who was just 13 when a local lay preacher (and moonshiner) took him in and taught him the trade. Guests get an under-the-lid whiff of the potent sour mash fermenting in large tubs and see the whiskey drip through the sugar-maple slats before being barreled and bottled for shipment around the world. In late October, the distillery hosts the Jack Daniel's World Championship Invitational Barbecue Festival. About 70 teams—at least one per state—compete, and 25,000 BBQ buffs show up to sample the smoked meats, enjoy clog-dance performances, and take part in games like the ladies' rolling-pin toss.

Nearby on the historic Lynchburg town square, Miss Mary Bobo's Boarding House and Restaurant has been feeding hungry customers since 1908. The dinner bell is still rung before guests are seated at large tables and served a family-style meal that might include skillet-fried chicken, mashed potatoes and gravy, creamed peas, fried okra, and spiced apples—flavored with a bit of the local product.

GEORGE DICKEL DISTILLERY: Tullahoma. Tel 931-857-4110; dickel.com. *When:* closed Sun. **JACK DANIEL'S DISTILLERY:** Lynchburg. Tel 931-759-6357; jackdaniels.com. **MISS MARY BOBO'S:** Lynchburg. Tel 931-759-7394; *Cost:* lunch $16. *When:* closed Sun. **BEST TIME:** late Oct for the Barbecue Festival.

A River Runs Through It

BLACKBERRY FARM

Walland, Tennessee

Only 4 miles from Great Smoky Mountains National Park (see p. 464), Blackberry Farm is one of the most highly regarded small hotels in America, mixing a bucolic setting with effortless sophistication and impeccable service. Sixty-eight rooms are spread among 6 houses and 16 cottages on the 9,200-acre property. The main house's wide veranda lined with rocking chairs offers extraordinary mountain views.

Horseback riding, biking, and hiking are all available on the grounds or in the national park next door, but Blackberry Farm is best

Blackberry Farm's large pond is stocked with largemouth bass, catfish, and bream for a tranquil day of fishing.

known for fly-fishing, with two ponds and a stream onsite, more than 700 miles of fishable trout streams in the neighboring park, and the well-known Clinch River a day trip away, just north of Knoxville. The first lodge in the eastern U.S. to be endorsed by the outfitter Orvis Company, Blackberry Farm has first-rate instructors to help hone your talents.

At the end of the day, relax in the Blackberry's newly built Wellhouse Spa. The evening's highlight is chef Cassidee Dabney's "Foothills Cuisine," a delicious combination of haute cuisine and Southern country traditions. This could very well be the best dining in Tennessee, just one reason for Blackberry Farm's reputation as a "Ritz-Carlton in the woods."

WHERE: 27 miles south of Knoxville; 1471 W. Millers Cove Rd. Tel 800-648-2348 or 865-380-2260; blackberryfarm.com. *Cost:* from $845 (off-peak), from $1,095 (peak), includes meals. **BEST TIMES:** Apr–June and late Aug–early Nov for the best fishing; Oct–Nov for a frenzy of colored foliage.

THE MIDWEST

Illinois • Indiana • Iowa
• Michigan • Minnesota •
Ohio • Wisconsin

Masterworks on Lake Michigan

THE ART INSTITUTE OF CHICAGO

Chicago, Illinois

For most of its history, Chicago has trailed New York City in key rankings in America—hence its nickname "Second City"—but its cultural offerings today put it in the top tier of cities anywhere. At the top of the list are the Chicago Symphony and Lyric Opera; top theaters such as the Steppenwolf, Second City, and Goodman; public art including sculptures by Pablo Picasso and Joan Miró in and around Daley Plaza; and the Art Institute of Chicago, the crowning glory of the city's lakefront. Opened in 1893, the Art Institute houses one of the world's greatest art collections, more than 300,000 works spanning nearly five millennia, in a handsome Beaux-Arts structure built for the 1892–93 World's Columbian Exposition.

The Art Institute is known worldwide for its collection of Impressionist and Post-Impressionist paintings, the world's most extensive outside of Paris's Musée d'Orsay. Among the more than 30 Monets are a half dozen from the *Haystacks* series occupying nearly an entire wall; there are also important works by Cézanne, Renoir, van Gogh, Gauguin, Toulouse-Lautrec, and Seurat (his pointillist masterpiece *A Sunday on La Grande Jatte*). Gustave Caillebotte's *Paris Street, Rainy Day* takes center stage at the top of the staircase leading to the second level. The American collection is renowned—it includes the iconic *American Gothic* by Grant Wood (see p. 515) and Edward Hopper's somber portrait of urban loneliness, *Nighthawks*—as is the pioneering collection of photography.

The building itself is a Chicago landmark and its broad front steps, a favorite meeting place, are flanked by two large bronze lions, which get dressed up for holidays and other special occasions. And in the best Chicago

The bronze lions that guard the Art Institute of Chicago's western entrance are sometimes dressed up for events and holidays.

tradition, the Art Institute has further raised its profile with cutting-edge architecture in its 2009 addition, making it the second largest museum in the country after the Metropolitan Museum of Art in New York (see p. 184). With a typically light-filled and gravity-defying design by Renzo Piano, the new Modern Wing houses exhibits of modern and contemporary art such as the Edlis Neeson Collection, a major private contemporary art collection that was donated to the Art Institute in 2015—42 iconic works by Andy Warhol, Jasper Johns, and other immediately recognizable names. The Modern Wing also features a roof-top terrace for views of the Second City that are second to none.

WHERE: 111 S. Michigan Ave. Tel 312-443-3600; artic.edu.

Better Than Bangkok

ARUN'S

Chicago, Illinois

The higher strata of Chicago's more than 7,000 restaurants constitute a part of the city more Paris than prairie, populated by a galaxy of stellar chefs. Among the very best is Arun Sampanthavivat, who showcases Thai food as

creative haute cuisine at his restaurant, Arun's, which first opened in 1985 in a nondescript storefront building on the city's northwest side.

Born and raised on a rubber plantation in Thailand, Sampanthavivat spent many years bouncing from Hamburg to Tokyo to Chicago in pursuit of one advanced academic degree after another. While studying at the University of Chicago, he was offered a partnership in a new Thai restaurant even though he had no restaurant experience. His partners eventually dropped out, but Sampanthavivat forged ahead, and within months he had a loyal customer base and his first review, glowing praise from the *Chicago Tribune*.

Today Sampanthavivat is considered by colleagues, critics, and patrons alike to be both genius and artist for his elegant and sensitive take on his native cuisine's blend of flavors. The waitstaff inquires about your preferences and adventurousness, spice tolerances, and any dietary restrictions, and the kitchen takes it from there. The presentation is exquisite, the ingredients are super fresh, the balance of flavors intricate, from shrimp soup, flower-shaped seafood dumplings, and roast duck salad on Thai basil to tenderloin in red curry and peanut sauce and sticky rice with green papaya.

WHERE: 4156 N. Kedzie Ave. Tel 773-539-1909; arunsthai.com. *Cost:* prix-fixe dinner $85.

Top of the Food Chain

CHICAGO'S CELEBRITY CHEFS

Chicago, Illinois

When you visit Chicago, be sure to bring your appetite. With its rich immigrant history and omnipresent love of food and drink, Chicago boasts one of the most distinctive—and distinguished—gastro scenes

in the U.S., with its own constellation of star chefs and splendid restaurants.

Of Alinea, Chicago's multistarred, multi-award-winning bastion of cutting-edge dining, food reviewer Ruth Reichl wrote, "This is food as performance, food as surprise, food as

you've never seen it before." Led by Chef Grant Achatz and cofounder Nick Kokonas, Alinea is celebrated for its always-evolving tasting menu of 18–22 eye-popping mini courses that are simultaneously whimsical, highly technical, and delicious, such as lobster ice cream with poppy-seed foam, and edible helium-filled balloons entirely made of apples.

Achatz and Kokonas have extended their dining empire into Chicago's fast-gentrifying Meatpacking District just west of The Loop. At Next, the menu is thematic, inspired by a particular place, time, or concept that changes every few months (think Paris 1906, or Childhood). Adjacent is Aviary, a redefined cocktail bar with multicourse cocktail tasting menus and food to match. Roister opened next door in 2016, the Alinea team's more casual, midpriced option, with a huge wood-fired hearth and an open kitchen in the middle of the dining room. Note that for Alinea group restaurants, reservations (which are transferable but not refundable) are treated like tickets to sports or arts events: You pay for the meal in advance and pricing is dynamic (reservation prices rise with demand).

Spiaggia is Chicago's most revered Italian restaurant, presenting a dining experience that blends equal parts tradition and invention into exquisite modern Italian cooking. With chef-partner Tony Mantuano once again at the helm, the restaurant draws a steady stream of celebrities and regular folks to the soaring dining room overlooking Lake Michigan. Next door, Cafe Spiaggia offers a more rustic (and affordable) take on Italian comfort foods, with a wine list featuring bottles all made by female winemakers.

Rick and Deann Bayless helped introduce regional Mexican cuisine to the U.S. through their cookbooks, TV shows, and wildly popular Chicago restaurants. With flavors that practically jump off the plate, their cooking is creative yet rooted in centuries-old traditions. With several locations in the River North neighborhood, Frontera Grill is casual with a lively bar scene, while Topolobampo ("Topolo" to regulars, including the Obamas) takes Mexican cooking upscale.

Alinea: Tel 312-867-0110; alinearestaurant .com. *Cost:* multicourse dinner $210. *When:* open Wed–Sun. **Next:** Tel 312-226-0858; nextrestaurant.com. *Cost:* multicourse dinner $95. *When:* open Wed–Sun. **Aviary:** Tel 312-226-0868; theaviary.com. *Cost:* multicourse tasting menu $135. **Roister:** roisterrestaurant .com. *Cost:* dinner from $50. **Spiaggia and Cafe Spiaggia:** Tel 312-280-2750; spiaggia restaurant.com. *Cost:* dinner at Spiaggia $90; dinner at Cafe Spiaggia $60. **Frontera Grill and "Topolo":** Tel 312-661-1434; rickbay less.com. *Cost:* dinner at Frontera Grill $50; 5-course dinner at "Topolo" $90. *When:* both closed Sun–Mon.

A Vast Open-Air Museum

Chicago's Architecture

Chicago, Illinois

After the Great Chicago Fire of 1871 reduced a huge swath of the city to cinders, architects seized the opportunity to create one of the world's great centers of innovative buildings by literally reaching for the heavens.

Individually, their names are legendary in American architecture: William Le Baron Jenney, Louis Sullivan, Daniel Burnham, John Wellborn Root, William Holabird, and Martin Roche; together, they created the commercial style later known as the Chicago School. One of its hallmarks was the use of a new technology, steel-frame construction, which enabled designers to push buildings to unprecedented heights and gave birth to a new form: the skyscraper.

The first high-rise anywhere was Jenney's ten-story Home Insurance Building, built in 1884–85. It was demolished in 1931, but others of its era still stand, such as the Rookery and the Fisher Building. The Monadnock Building precisely marks a turning point in architectural history: The northern half, designed and built by Burnham & Root in 1889–91, features load-bearing masonry walls, while the southern half, designed and built by Holabird & Roche in 1891–93, uses a steel frame.

Louis Sullivan, who thought buildings should reflect America's democratic identity, joined the German-born engineering genius Dankmar Adler in a historic partnership; one of their many masterpieces is the Auditorium Theater, dedicated in 1889 and now part of Roosevelt University. The late 1800s also saw the arrival in Chicago of a young Frank Lloyd Wright, who worked for Adler and Sullivan and would conceive the Prairie School of design (see p. 496). In the mid-20th century, Ludwig Mies van der Rohe made his mark on the city with minimalist structures of steel and glass, of which his Lake Shore Drive apartments and the Federal Plaza are prime examples.

All this makes for a magnificent open-air museum of a city. You can wander about on your own or let the Chicago Architecture Foundation enlighten you. The foundation conducts a variety of walking tours, and in good weather they offer tours by boat down the Chicago River. The foundation is housed in Daniel Burnham's noteworthy Santa Fe Building, opened in 1904 and originally home to Burnham's own offices.

Within walking distance of the Santa Fe, three hotels are also venerable Chicago institutions: the Palmer House Hilton, with its grand lobby; the Hilton Chicago, built in 1927 and touted then as the world's largest hotel; and the Hotel Burnham, a classic dating from 1895. Dining at each hotel is memorable as well. The Palmer House Lockwood Restaurant serves seasonally influenced menus specializing in dry-aged steaks; the Hilton Chicago's 720 South Bar and Grill serves interesting dishes all day long; and the Burnham's Atwood (named for a codesigner of the building, Charles Atwood) serves up hearty dishes like potato stout soup, pumpkin gnocchi, and bacon-wrapped meat loaf.

For a bird's-eye view of Chicago, visit the observation decks of two of the tallest skyscrapers in America, the Willis Tower (formerly the Sears Tower) and the John Hancock Center (see p. 489). And as you contemplate the architectural riches that surround you, recall Daniel Burnham's dictum: "Make no little plans. They have no magic to stir men's blood."

CHICAGO ARCHITECTURE FOUNDATION: Tel 312-922-3432; architecture.org. *When:* walking tours daily; cruises Apr–mid-Nov. **PALMER HOUSE:** Tel 312-726-7500; palmerhouse.hilton .com. *Cost:* from $189; dinner at Lockwood Restaurant $60. **HILTON CHICAGO:** Tel 312-922-4400; hiltonchicagohotel.com. *Cost:* from $189; dinner at 720 South Bar and Grill $60. **HOTEL BURNHAM:** Tel 312-782-1111; burnhamhotel .com. *Cost:* from $139; dinner at Atwood Café $45. **BEST TIME:** Oct for Open House Chicago.

There's Something Funny Going On Here

CHICAGO'S COMEDY SCENE

Chicago, Illinois

Just as it's hard to imagine American architecture without the profound influence of Chicago's cityscape, one can't conceive of American (and Canadian) comedy without the city's great talents. Jack Benny, standup and sitcom pioneer, was born in Chicago; Bob Newhart, from the nearby suburb of Oak Park, cultivated his deadpan shtick here. But Chicago's greatest claim to comedy fame is as the birthplace of modern improvisational theater, and the most influential of its practitioners have been the members of the Second City, a troupe from the Near North Side that helped define the style of sketch comedy broadly popularized by NBC's long-running late-night hit *Saturday Night Live*. Founded in 1959, the company grew out of a University of Chicago undergraduate group that included Alan Alda, Elaine May, and Mike Nichols. The students took the name Second City as a self-deprecating gesture, referring to a series of derisive essays about Chicago by A. J. Liebling that appeared under that title in *The New Yorker* a decade before. Among its alumni are some of the most recognized names in television and movie comedy: Alan Arkin and Joan Rivers in the early years; John Belushi, Bill Murray, Gilda Radner, and Dan Aykroyd in the '70s; and Steve Carrell, Amy Poehler, and Tina Fey since then. (The young David Mamet was a busboy at the club.) Second

City's Toronto troupe—whose alums include John Candy, Martin Short, and Mike Myers—was the first offshoot, followed by Hollywood.

Shows in the intimate 290-seat Mainstage theater and the 180-seat Second City e.t.c. present edgy, satirical humor in semi-improvised scenes combined with scripted bits. Touring troupes take shows on the road, and a training center offers classes and workshops. Many Second City alumni—including Chris Farley, Stephen Colbert, and Tim Meadows—have also passed through iO (formerly ImprovOlympic), where the players spin out long-form improvisations like comedic free jazz. In *The Harold*, iO's signature piece, an idea suggested by the audience grows through a succession of scenes and games into (ideally) a complex set of interwoven themes, narratives, and characters; another favorite show is the improvised one-act musical *The Deltones*, performed every Saturday night. You'll never see the same show twice.

THE SECOND CITY: Tel 312-337-3992; secondcity.com. *Cost:* from $17. **iO:** Tel 312-929-2401; ioimprov.com/chicago. *Cost:* from $5.

Pie in the Sky

CHICAGO-STYLE PIZZA

Chicago, Illinois

Ask ten Chicagoans who makes their favorite pizza, and you'll get as many different answers. With an estimated 2,000-plus pizzerias around, they take pride in their pie here; from small, family-owned neighborhood joints to popular downtown draws to suburban chains, pizza is to Chicago what strudel is to Vienna. The dominant style is deep-dish, a pizza-meets-casserole well over an inch thick that is generally what people mean by Chicago-style. Who deserves the credit remains a mystery (it might have been bartender Rudy Malnati Sr.). What is certain is

that Texan Ike Sewell and Italian-born restaurateur Rick Riccardo opened Pizzeria Uno in a Victorian brownstone in the River North section of Chicago in 1943. Their pizza with a thicker crust and loads of cheese and tomato topping became so popular that, 12 years later, they opened Pizzeria Due in another Victorian a block away. Both have the same

1940s-vintage walnut veneers and black-and-white-tiled floors, and both are still immensely popular. You can count on a long wait before sitting down, and another long (and perhaps vino-rosso-fueled) wait while your pie's being made. The menu has expanded to include salads, sandwiches, and pasta—just as the restaurants have grown into a Boston-based

Pizzeria Uno's signature pizza, Numero Uno, is piled high with sausage, pepperoni, onions, peppers, and mushrooms.

international chain, Uno Pizzeria & Grill, with 82 locations—but the pizza is still the big draw and still mighty good.

Also in River North are Lou Malnati's and Gino's East, both of which trace their lineage to Pizzeria Uno; Malnati used to work there (he was Rudy Sr.'s son), as did Alice Redmond, an original Uno chef, who was hired to devise the recipe at Gino's East. Other joints with major followings include Pizano's (opened by Rudy Malnati Jr. in 1991), Giordano's, and the Exchequer Pub; some make all three types of Chicago pizza (stuffed, thin crust, or deep-dish), some just one. If you want to know which is best, gather a few locals, put the question to them—and stand back.

Pizzeria Uno: Tel 312-321-1000; unos .com. **Pizzeria Due:** Tel 312-943-2400. *Cost:* large pizza $26 at Uno or Due. **Lou Malnati's:** Tel 847-673-0800; loumalnatis.com. *Cost:* large pizza $22. **Gino's East:** Tel 312-266-3337; ginoseast.com. *Cost:* large pizza $28.

An Awe-Inspiring Stretch of Luxe and Bustle

THE MAGNIFICENT MILE

Chicago, Illinois

If there's one place where you can be both out of the loop and in the middle of all the action, it's the 13-block stretch of North Michigan Avenue known as the Magnificent Mile. It lies outside the Loop, Chicago's central downtown

area, but its flagship retail establishments and posh hotels represent an essential image of the city's dynamism and bustling commerce. The southern end, at the Michigan Avenue Bridge over the Chicago River, is anchored by The Wrigley Building, erected in the 1920s as headquarters of the Wrigley Chewing Gum Company; its white terra-cotta finish sparkles in the sun by day and glows by night, thanks to powerful lighting near the bridge. The 1925 neo-Gothic Tribune Tower, headquarters of the *Chicago Tribune*, was the winning entry in

an international competition staged for the paper's 75th anniversary in 1922; embedded in the exterior walls are stones from such notable sites as the Taj Mahal, the Parthenon, and the Great Wall of China.

Farther north stands the famous Water Tower, built in 1869 to conceal a huge pressure-equalizing standpipe. This 154-foot limestone structure and its companion Pumping Station across the street survived the Great Fire of 1871 and became symbols of Chicago's determination to rebuild. The tower now houses the City Gallery, featuring Chicago-themed images by local photographers and artists, while the Pumping Station (which still pumps water) is home to the Lookingglass Theatre. Both structures stand in the shadow of a newer icon, the John Hancock Center. "Big John" is the city's fourth tallest skyscraper, a towering black obelisk crisscrossed by external steel braces. You can see as far as 80 miles from 360 Chicago, its 94th-floor observatory, whose newest addition "Tilt" extends out 30 degrees over the Magnificent Mile, 1,000 feet below.

The Chicago Water Tower was completed just before the Great Fire.

Anchoring the north end of the Mag Mile since 1920 is the lavish Drake Hotel, Chicago's white-glove landmark with a bevy of top-drawer amenities. Diners can loosen their ties in the hotel's informal Cape Cod, a classic seafood restaurant since 1933 with a killer New England clam chowder and the initials of Joe DiMaggio and Marilyn Monroe carved into the wooden bar. The area's younger but already legendary restaurants include Tru, which offers cutting-edge French cuisine, and the ultra-refined Spiaggia (see p. 485), one of the most revered Italian restaurants in the country.

And let's talk shopping. With high-end, high-profile stores everywhere you look, the street is a retail paradise. You can knock yourself out at Nieman Marcus, Bloomingdale's, Saks Fifth Avenue, and dozens of other such upscale emporiums. The Water Tower Place mall is attached to the Ritz-Carlton, one of the city's most luxurious addresses.

WHERE: N. Michigan Ave. between Wacker Dr. and Oak St. **360 CHICAGO OBSERVATORY:** 360chicago.com. **DRAKE HOTEL:** Tel 800-55-DRAKE or 312-787-2200; thedrakehotel.com. *Cost:* from $179; dinner at Cape Cod $65. **RITZ-CARLTON:** Tel 800-621-6906 or 312-266-1000; ritzcarlton.com. *Cost:* from $350. **BEST TIME:** mid-Nov–early Mar when the Mag Mile celebrates the holidays with more than a million lights.

A New Ornament for Chicago's Front Lawn

MILLENNIUM PARK

Chicago, Illinois

G rant Park, otherwise known as Chicago's front lawn, has been one of America's greatest civic spaces for over a century, and it's still a work in progress. Since its establishment in 1844, it's been enhanced by additions such as the Art Institute of Chicago (see p. 483) and the beloved Buckingham Fountain. Extending beyond is the Museum Campus (see next page) and Millennium Park, a sweeping redevelopment of a railyard at the north end. Spearheaded by Mayor Richard M. Daley, the hugely ambitious 24.5-acre Millennium Park was plagued by delays and costly overexpenditures, but what a beauty it turned out to be. An estimated 300,000 people turned up for the inaugural festivities in 2004, and the park has remained wildly popular since.

Its centerpiece is the Jay Pritzker Pavilion, a stunning band shell named in memory of the philanthropist and Hyatt Hotels cofounder who, with his wife, Cindy, established architecture's most prestigious prize in 1979. Honors for the pavilion design went to 1989 Pritzker Prize–winner Frank Gehry, and its exterior bears his signature billowing sheets of stainless steel. A steel trellis, which holds a state-of-the-art speaker system, extends over 4,000 fixed seats and the Great Lawn (with space for 7,000), distributing indoor-quality sound to the farthest reaches of the audience. The resident Grant Park Orchestra gives free summertime concerts, just as it has done in the park since the 1930s, and the adjacent Harris Theater provides indoor music and dance programs.

Two of Millennium Park's top attractions are major additions to Chicago's collection of public art. Anish Kapoor's 110-ton 33-by-66-foot *Cloud*

Walk through the Cloud Gate's 12-foot-high arch, which provides access to the sculpture's carved-out interior chamber.

Gate dominates AT&T Plaza, offering funhouse-mirror reflections of sky, skyline, and spectators in its highly polished steel surface. (Chicagoans call it by the more tangibly descriptive nickname the "Bean.") South of the plaza is the *Crown Fountain* by Spanish artist Jaume Plensa, which features two 50-foot glass block towers on either side of a very shallow reflecting pool. LED screens behind the glass blocks display faces of Chicago citizens from a broad social spectrum, with water literally spouting from the mouths of the video images.

At the northwest corner of the park is the Millennium Monument, a replica of the semicircular colonnade, or peristyle, that sat on this same spot from 1917 to 1953. At the opposite corner is the Lurie Garden, a lush urban retreat with shrubs, grasses, flowering plants, a canal, and walkways. The 5-acre garden is meant to reflect the city's natural and cultural history, and the 15-foot "shoulder" hedge evokes Carl Sandburg's famous description of Chicago as the "City of Big Shoulders."

Where: Welcome Center, 201 E. Randolph St. Tel 312-742-2963; millenniumpark.org. **Best times:** early June for the Gospel Music Festival; June–Aug for the Grant Park Music Festival; Nov–Mar for free ice-skating at the McCormick Tribune Plaza.

Popular Institutions Uniting Earth, Sea, and Space

MUSEUM CAMPUS

Chicago, Illinois

The 57-acre Museum Campus, one of Chicago's newest lakefront attractions, unites three of the city's oldest institutions. Located at the southern edge of Grant Park, it opened in 1998 after the city rerouted the northbound

lanes of heavily trafficked Lake Shore Drive and replaced the asphalt with terraced gardens and broad walkways connecting the Shedd Aquarium, the Adler Planetarium, and the Field Museum.

Opened in 1930 thanks to the munificence of John G. Shedd, the stock clerk who became president of Marshall Field and Co., the Shedd is one of the oldest aquariums in the world and is the second largest indoor aquarium in the

U.S. after the one in Atlanta (see p. 335). The extensive facility is home to 32,000 animals—over a million, the staff will tell you, if you count all those tiny coral polyps. They come in a dizzying variety, with sharks and rays, frogfish and parrotfish, and an octogenarian Australian lungfish named "Granddad," the oldest fish in any aquarium anywhere and on display since 1933. Among the more recent additions are the Abbott Oceanarium, with its belugas, sea otters, and other mammals, and the Wild Reef's 26 interconnected habitats, including a diver's-eye view of more than 20 sharks through 12-foot-high curved windows.

At the end of a long jetty east of the aquarium, Adler Planetarium offers explorations of the heavens in the state-of-the-art virtual-reality Grainger Sky Theater. Built in 1930 as the first modern planetarium in the Western Hemisphere by Max Adler, another philanthropist who made his fortune in retail, it is also home to one of the world's finest collections of scientific instruments, rare books, and maps. At certain times of the year the Adler gives the public the chance to view planets and lunar eclipses through telescopes set up on the grounds.

Established in 1893, the Field Museum was funded by Marshall Field, founder of Chicago's legendary department store. The museum's encyclopedic collection covers subjects as wide-ranging as evolution, ancient Egyptian

funerary customs, and Plains Indian life, but the most famous of its holdings is Sue, the world's biggest and best-preserved *Tyrannosaurus rex.*

Recharge with a leisurely lake cruise in summer (cruises board near the aquarium) or a Bears game during football season (Soldier Field is just to the south). It won't be long before the projected 2020 completion of the Lucas Museum of Narrative Arts, endowed and built by film creator and director George Lucas. It will be the most recent addition to the waterfront.

SHEDD AQUARIUM: Tel 312-939-2438; sheddaquarium.org. **ADLER PLANETARIUM:** Tel 312-922-7827; adlerplanetarium.org. **FIELD MUSEUM:** Tel 312-922-9410; fieldmuseum.org.

Field Museum's Tyrannosaurus rex *measures 42 feet from snout to tail.*

Outdoor Showcases of America's Music

MUSIC IN THE PARK

Chicago, Illinois

Chicago played a critical role in the development of three great American musical forms—blues, jazz, and gospel—and today the city devotes individual festivals to each in Grant Park, the great 319-acre civic space

that the Illinois Supreme Court ruled in 1909 was to remain "forever open, clear and free of any . . . obstructions." The ruling speaks to the

spirit of these festivals—they're open to all, with free admission, and they celebrate the free spirit of Chicago's musical greats.

As the music most indelibly associated with the city, the blues take pride of place in Chicago. Born in the Mississippi Delta, blues music came to Chicago with the great migration of African Americans from the South in the 1920s and '30s. On the hard streets of the South Side, it was electrified and expanded by the likes of Muddy Waters, the father of Chicago blues, and Howlin' Wolf. In June, the Chicago Blues Festival, the nation's biggest, draws 500,000 fans from around the world to hear dozens of top acts on five stages in Grant Park. Everyone who's anyone has played here, including Buddy Guy, Ray Charles, Bonnie Raitt, the late Bo Diddley, B. B. King, and Koko Taylor. Grant Park does an about-face in July with Lollapalooza, a festival which celebrated its 25th anniversary in 2016 and highlights alternative rock, punk rock, heavy metal, pop, hip-hop, and electronic dance music.

The city also claims a major role in the history of jazz. Jazz artists like Joe "King" Oliver and his protegé Louis Armstrong flocked to Chicago from New Orleans, establishing it as the new jazz capital. In the 1970s, three separate organizations established festivals—memorials to Duke Ellington and John Coltrane, plus an event staged by the Jazz Institute of Chicago—that eventually coalesced under the umbrella of the Chicago Jazz Festival held in nearby Millenium Park (see p. 489). Miles Davis, Ella Fitzgerald, and Sarah Vaughan are just a few of the musical luminaries who have been headliners. In the 1920s and '30s, blues, jazz, and the negro spiritual joined hands in church and helped beget gospel. It was in the Pilgrim Baptist Church (a magnificent Adler & Sullivan building tragically lost to fire in 2006) that Thomas Dorsey, with his choir and musicians, gave birth to that soulful expression of religious faith today found in all its glory at the Gospel Music Festival, originally held in Grant Park but now also taking place in Millennium Park.

Cassandra Wilson performs at the 33rd annual Jazz Festival.

The success of these events spawned other festivals, such as the World Music Festival Chicago and the Windy City LakeShake Country Music Festival. Of course, you don't need festivals to hear great music in the city. Jazz lovers gravitate to the Jazz Showcase and the Green Mill, while the top spots for blues include Buddy Guy's Legends, Blue Chicago, House of Blues Chicago, B.L.U.E.S. Bar, Rosa's Lounge, and Kingston Mines.

WHERE: Grant and Millennium Parks. *Visitor info:* Tel 312-744-3316; cityofchicago .org. *When:* early June for Chicago Gospel Music Festival; mid-June for Chicago Blues Festival and Windy Cindy LakeShake Country Music Festival; late July for Lollapalooza; early Sept for Chicago Jazz Festival; mid-Sept for World Music Festival Chicago.

Get Your Red Hots Here!

SUPERDAWG

Chicago, Illinois

Chicago's finest restaurants rank among the best in the world (see p. 484), but if you want to get folks in this working-class city fired up about food, just bring up the subject of hot dogs, or "red hots," as they were once commonly known. Most everyone agrees on the recipe—boiled or steamed all-beef frank on a poppy-seed bun, with kosher dill pickle, mustard, chopped onion, relish, hot peppers, a green tomato wedge, and a dash of celery salt—but what you're not likely to get consensus on is where to find the city's top dog.

The original Fluky's, the place where the Chicago-style red hot is said to have been born as the five-cent "Depression sandwich" in 1929, is no more, but now several contenders vie for Chicagoans' loyalty. Byron's buries its plump dogs under nine toppings; Gold Coast Dogs serves them steamed or grilled (a "Char Dog"), with a side of the best cheese fries in town; the Wiener's Circle offers late-night red hots with attitude; and Portillo's has tasty dogs as well as burgers, salads, and pastas for the, well, dog-tired.

But for a complete experience, there's nothing quite like Superdawg, opened in 1948 by Maurie and Flaurie Berman. The magnificently retro exterior includes two 12-foot hot dog statues with blinking eyes on the roof above the door; the "male," wearing a leopard-skin Tarzan getup meant to symbolize Superdawg's superstrength, flexes his biceps while his skirt-clad companion winks at him adoringly. Superdawg is one of the last of the classic drive-ins: You place your order through "Order Matic" speakers and have your tray delivered by a carhop who attaches it to the side of your car with a smile. The food comes in a box that reads, "Your Superdawg lounges inside contentedly cushioned . . . in Superfries and comfortably attired in mustard, relish, onion, pickle, hot peppers." An ultrathick milkshake—so thick, they say, that they put straws in it just to prove they won't work—tops off the meal.

The uninitiated should bear one thing in mind: Ketchup is taboo. "I see more and more desecrations of the Chicago hot dog," Maurie Berman once said. "Yes, we provide ketchup, but we have the customer defile it himself."

WHERE: 6363 N. Milwaukee Ave. Tel 773-763-0660; superdawg.com. *Cost:* lunch $6.

The Super Bowl of Cookouts: Come Prepared to Chow Down

TASTE OF CHICAGO

Chicago, Illinois

C hicago is serious about food. The city is deservedly famous and not just a little bit fanatical about its own versions of pizza (see p. 487) and hot dogs (see above), as well as its Italian beef sandwiches, ribs, and Polish sausage.

It's the home of Eli's cheesecake, the birthplace of Twinkies, and the place where Wonder Bread was launched as an archetypal national brand. For decades beginning in 1883, the near North Side was the site of a meat market run by a Bavarian immigrant named Oscar Mayer, and it was in a Chicago suburb that the first McDonald's franchise opened in 1955. This prodigious appetite for legendary food of various shapes and flavors is center stage during Taste of Chicago, one of the world's largest and most fun food festivals.

"The Taste" began in 1980 as a one-day Fourth of July celebration when a scattering of vendors spread out along three blocks of Michigan Avenue. Hugely popular from the start, the cookout to end all cookouts moved, appropriately, to the city's front yard, Grant Park. It's now a five-day affair with more than three dozen restaurants, as well as food trucks, featuring a wide range of ethnic and traditional cuisine, and judging from the crowds—totaling a million people—attendance is mandatory. Everything is laid out through the heart of the park, and a pavilion by the Buckingham Fountain offers cooking demonstrations throughout each day of the festival. There's also plenty of live music (this is a city

Taste of Chicago's smorgasbord takes over Grant Park for five days each summer.

whose other love is music). The biggest crowds turn up for the concert by the Grant Park Orchestra, culminating in a performance of Tchaikovsky's 1812 Overture.

One mainstay at the Taste is the Billy Goat Tavern and Grill. Most famous as the inspiration for a *Saturday Night Live* sketch ("Cheezborger! Cheezborger! No fries, cheeps!"), the Goat is also part of sports history. When his pet goat was ejected from Wrigley Field during the 1945 World Series, tavern founder Billy Sianis declared that the Cubs would never win the championship as long as the goat wasn't allowed in the stadium. The "Curse of the Billy Goat" may be just superstition, but the formerly mighty Cubs haven't made it to the Series since.

Where: Columbus Dr. between Balbo and Monroe. Tel 312-744-3315; tasteofchicago .org. *Cost:* $9 for 12 food tickets. *When:* 5 days in late June–early July. **Billy Goat Tavern:** Tel 312-222-1525; billygoattavern.com. *Cost:* lunch $8.

This Diamond Is Forever

Wrigley Field

Chicago, Illinois

When it opened on April 23, 1914, Weeghman Park was a typical stadium of its time, with seating angled close to the field and no upper decks or skyboxes. Today it's called Wrigley Field, and there's no other

place quite like it in baseball. Charles Weeghman built it for his Chicago Whales, a club in the short-lived Federal League; when the upstart league disbanded after the 1915 season, he joined a group of investors to buy the National League Cubs and move them to his stadium—and thus began nearly a century of hardball history (and heartbreak) on Chicago's North Side. Chewing gum magnate William Wrigley gained full ownership of the team in 1921, and the ballpark was renamed Wrigley

Field in 1926. It's the second oldest park in the majors, after Boston's Fenway Park (see p. 41), and the only one remaining from the Federal League.

Upper deck and skybox seating have been added over the years to increase its seating capacity from the original 14,000 to over 41,000, but Wrigley retains the intimacy that earned it the name the "Friendly Confines." In 1937, the center field wall was rebuilt in brick-fronted concrete with Boston ivy planted in front of it, creating one of the park's most distinctive features; a hit lost in the dense leaves is an automatic ground-rule double. The 27-by-75-foot manual scoreboard, one of the last two of its kind (along with Fenway's), was installed the same year—no batted ball has hit it yet—and postgame, a "W" or "L" flag still flies above it to announce the result to train commuters.

Wrigley had the first permanent concession stand in baseball (1914), the first organ (1941), and the first cell phone system between dugout and bullpen (2006). It was where fans were first allowed to keep foul balls hit into the stands, and where they first threw visiting teams' home-run balls back onto the field (a tradition that is strictly enforced by a jeering crowd). It was the last major league park to install lights for night games (its first game under lights, in 1988, was rained out in the fourth inning). It was reportedly where, in game 3 of the 1932 World Series, Babe Ruth pointed to a spot in the center field bleachers just before sending a home run right there; and where legendary announcer Harry Caray led the crowd in a boisterous rendition of "Take Me Out to the Ball Game" during the seventh-inning stretch. It was also where the Bears, Chicago's football team, played for 49 years and won eight league championships before Soldier Field became their home. What

Wrigley has never seen is a World Series victory by the Cubs, who won back-to-back titles in 1907 and 1908, but their fans' contagious this-is-our-year hopefulness is a key part of the Wrigley experience.

In Wrigleyville, the neighborhood around the park, you'll find souvenir hawkers, street musicians, and loads of nightlife including, of course, sports bars; at perennial favorites such as the Cubby Bear Lounge, there's an ongoing party, win or lose.

Where: 1060 W. Addison St. Tel 773-404-CUBS; cubs.com. *Cost:* tickets from $19. *When:* Apr–Oct. **Cubby Bear Lounge:** Tel 773-327-1662; cubbybear.com. **Best times:** early Apr for opening day; June–Sept for weather.

Wrigley Field's classic sign, a throwback to the 1930s, looms over West Addison Street.

A Great Orchestra's Summer Camp

RAVINIA FESTIVAL

Highland Park, Illinois

When Ravinia Park opened in 1904 as a 36-acre amusement park 25 miles north of Chicago, the idea was to attract riders to the fledgling Chicago & Milwaukee Electric Railroad. The railroad soon went bankrupt, but Ravinia became a resounding success. Today it's the site of North America's oldest outdoor music festival, one of the biggest in the world, attracting some 600,000 listeners to as many as 150 events every summer.

The first piece performed at Ravinia was "Bill Bailey, Won't You Please Come Home," played on a steam calliope, but fancier fare soon arrived in the form of the New York Symphony (now the Philharmonic), conducted by Walter Damrosch, in 1905. Classical music has been at the core of Ravinia's performance schedule ever since: Music lovers climbed the trees to see George Gershwin play *Rhapsody in Blue* in 1936, the same year that the renowned Chicago Symphony Orchestra adopted Ravinia as its summer residence, and they remain the centerpiece of the music festival today. Early highlights were many. From 1964 to 1968, Seiji Ozawa served as the first music director of the Ravinia Festival, and in 1969 as the festival's principal conductor.

Though classical music still rules here, the Ravinia Festival has grown to embrace jazz, dance, musical theater, and even rock, as Mahler mingles with Steve Miller, Beethoven with the Bob Dylan, and the Emerson String Quartet with Emmylou Harris. Even Tony Bennett and Lady Gaga have been a recent draw.

A 3,400-seat open-air pavilion is surrounded by trees and open grassy areas, allowing you to spread out, relax, and picnic to your heart's content while a state-of-the-art sound system delivers the music. There are also indoor concerts in two spaces: the 450-seat Bennett-Gordon Hall and the 850-seat Prairie-style Martin Theater, the only building left from the original 1904 park and beautifully restored.

Enjoy the wonderful drive to Ravinia by following Sheridan Road from the Far North Side of Chicago; it winds through some of the city's most affluent suburbs, with spectacular homes, spacious grounds, and scenic views of Lake Michigan. Or you can hop on Metra's Union Pacific North Line, successor to the ill-fated—yet inadvertently successful—Chicago & Milwaukee Electric Railroad.

Where: 25 miles north of Chicago; 200 Ravinia Park Road, Highland Park. Tel 847-266-5100; ravinia.org. *Cost:* from $10. **Best time:** July–Aug for Chicago Symphony Orchestra.

Design Laboratory of the Prairie Style

FRANK LLOYD WRIGHT HOME AND STUDIO

Oak Park, Illinois

The unabashedly ambitious Frank Lloyd Wright once declared, "I intend to be the greatest architect of all time." Whether he achieved his goal is debatable, but his transformative influence is not. And it all started in the Chicago suburb of Oak Park. In 1889, the self-taught wunderkind was just 22, newly married, and newly employed by the esteemed partnership of Dankmar Adler and Louis Sullivan, leaders of the Chicago School of Architecture (see p. 485), when he designed and built a house in which to raise his family. He made numerous changes to the original Shingle style structure as his ideas (and family) developed, including a barrel-vaulted playroom designed to nurture and inspire his six children.

The studio wing that he added to the property in 1898 incorporates raw-textured materials, octagons repeated through rooms and fixtures, and a balcony with a chain suspension rather than the typical beams. Wright designed roughly a fourth of his output in this studio, espousing an organic, craftsmanly sensibility, anticipating the linearity and openness of modernism, and taking cues from the local landscape in horizontal lines, all of which became the timeless hallmarks of the Prairie style.

The best-known example of Wright's use of this style is the Robie House, built in 1910 on the University of Chicago campus, featuring a low-pitched roof, strong exterior horizontal lines, art leaded glass, and furnishings designed by the architect. But there are abundant examples of his early work in Oak Park, such as the Nathan Moore House, an English Tudor hybrid from 1895, and the Edwin Cheney House (1903), significant both architecturally and biographically (Wright fell in love with Mrs. Cheney and slipped away to Europe with her in 1909). Wright's only public building in town is the 1908 Unity Temple, a Cubist shrine in poured concrete that he called his little jewel box. If your travels take you to Springfield (see p. 500), you can also visit the 1904 Dana-Thomas house, a stunning 12,600-square-foot Prairie-style mansion.

In 1911, Wright returned to his native Wisconsin to create his home and studio at Taliesin (see p. 586); the name means "shining brow" in Welsh. Also on the FLW pilgrimage is Taliesin West, his winter home in Arizona (see p. 695), where he would live, work, and study from 1937 until his death in 1959.

WRIGHT HOME & STUDIO: 11 miles west of downtown Chicago; 951 Chicago Ave. Tel

A young Frank Lloyd Wright borrowed $5,000 from his employer, Louis Sullivan, to build his home and studio.

312-994-4000; flwright.org. **DANA-THOMAS HOUSE:** Springfield. Tel 217-782-6776; dana-thomas.org. *When:* closed Mon–Tues. **How:** The Frank Lloyd Wright Trust manages five properties, including the Home & Studio, Robie House, and Unity Temple, and arranges all tours. Tel 312-994-4000; flwright.org. *Cost:* from $17. The Chicago Architecture Foundation offers various bus tours to Wright sites in Oak Park. Tel 312-922-3432; architecture.org. *Cost:* from $15. **BEST TIME:** The Wright Plus Housewalk offers access to a number of privately owned Frank Lloyd Wright houses the 3rd Sat in May (flwright.org).

Civil War Pride and 19th-Century Charm in the Heartland

GALENA

Illinois

Galena has twice escaped inexorable forces. The first time was during the last ice age when, as part of the Midwest's "Driftless Area," it was bypassed by the glaciers that elsewhere crushed and scoured the land;

as a result, the local topography is atypically rugged for the region (the 1,235-foot Charles Mound, the highest natural point in the state, is 11 miles away). The second time was during the century following the Civil War, when the formerly prosperous city suffered a decline

and slept on picturesque bluffs above the Mississippi River, as urban development left other cities scrambled and sprawling.

Galena was rediscovered as a historic gem in the 1960s and carefully restored; now its National Register Historic District protects

85 percent of Galena's buildings, most from the 19th century.

The city took its name, in no-nonsense fashion, from the area's mineral resource, galena (otherwise known as lead sulfide). By the 1850s, the burgeoning mining and shipping industries had created great wealth here, paying for handsome architecture throughout the town. A main attraction is the Italianate house that grateful citizens gave to Ulysses S. Grant after he returned victorious from the Civil War. (Grant first came to Galena in 1860 to work in his father's leather-goods store, housed in an 1838 building currently occupied by a gourmet Italian restaurant called Fried Green Tomatoes.) Another landmark structure is the 1855 DeSoto House Hotel, the oldest operating hotel in the state. Abraham Lincoln spoke from its balcony, and Grant used the place as headquarters for his successful 1868 presidential campaign. There are three restaurants in the hotel, including the much-lauded Generals' Restaurant, named in honor of the nine Civil War generals who hailed from Galena.

The city is also home to several resorts. The best is the 6,800-acre Eagle Ridge Resort with 63 holes of golf. The General course is one of the country's top public layouts. Lake Galena anchors the Eagle Ridge expanse with 7 miles of shoreline and a charming marina. Total relaxation is offered at the Stonedrift Spa, and 23 miles of hiking and biking trails are worth exploring. For a scenic drive, follow the Stagecoach Trail, 38 miles that wind from Galena to Lena, portions of which overlap the old stagecoach routes from Chicago to Dubuque, Iowa.

WHERE: 164 miles west of Chicago. *Visitor info:* Tel 877-464-2536 or 815-777-3557; galena.org. **ULYSSES S. GRANT HOME:** Tel 815-777-3310; granthome.com. *When:* closed Mon–Tues. **FRIED GREEN TOMATOES:** Tel 815-777-3938; friedgreen.com. *Cost:* dinner $40. **DESOTO HOUSE HOTEL:** Tel 800-343-6562 or 815-777-0090; desotohouse.com. *Cost:* from $130; dinner at Generals' $45. **EAGLE RIDGE RESORT AND SPA:** Tel 800-892-2269 or 815-777-5000; eagleridge.com. *Cost:* from $159 (off-peak), from $209 (peak). **BEST TIMES:** 4th weekend in Sept for tours of 4 restored private homes (galenahistory.org); early Oct for the Galena Country Fair (galenacountryfair.com); weekend before Thanksgiving in Nov for the Nouveau Wine Weekend (nouveauweekend.com).

The Beautiful Place

NAUVOO

Illinois

When the Latter-day Saints fled hostility in Missouri in the wake of the 1838 Mormon War, thousands reestablished their community by a bend of the Mississippi River in Illinois. A largely abandoned settlement there, Commerce, had never flourished (much of the site was a malarial swamp, and land values crashed in the post-depression years), but Mormon leader Joseph Smith saw potential in the desolate location. He called it Nauvoo, "beautiful," from Hebrew, owing to the early Mormons' close kinship with the House of Israel. The settlers drained the swamp and set to building; within five years, Nauvoo was one of the largest cities in the country, with a population topping 10,000. On a bluff high above the city, they built a huge limestone temple in Greek Revival style.

But conflict again erupted between the Mormons and their neighbors, and internal struggles arose among Smith's followers. Smith was killed by an angry mob in 1844, the state legislature repealed the city's charter, and in 1846 most of the Mormons, led by Brigham Young, fled westward and eventually settled in Utah (see p. 799). Destroyed by arsonists and a tornado, virtually no trace of the temple was left by 1850. Meanwhile, French utopian Étienne Cabet and his followers, the Icarians, established a small commune in Nauvoo, but that too was short-lived; it lasted only from 1849 to 1856. German immigrants soon followed.

Today, as many as 30 sites in Nauvoo have been richly restored to their mid-1800s appearance, earning the town the nickname "Williamsburg of the Midwest." Tour the historic district by horse carriage or on foot, passing beautiful brick homes surrounded by white picket fences; follow the scent of baking gingerbread to the Scovil Bakery, with an oven dating from the 1840s, or visit the Webb Brothers Blacksmith Shop. The Mormon Church reacquired the temple site and, in 2002, dedicated a new temple whose exterior is an exact replica of the original. Every year, hundreds of thousands of Mormons make pilgrimages here to visit the Joseph Smith Historic Center and pay their respects at his grave.

French Icarian settlers are responsible for planting the first grape vines here and today their descendants still run, among others, Baxter's Vineyards, Illinois's oldest winery.

The lovingly maintained Hotel Nauvoo provides more history: Built as a residence in 1841 by Latter-day Saint J. J. Brendt and finished by German immigrant Adam Swartz, it has served as a hotel since 1885 and has been run by the Kraus family for three generations. A fine example of Prairie Mormon architecture, the two-story building has a charming upper veranda and cupola and eight historically decorated guest rooms. Its five dining rooms are always filled with those drawn by accounts of the bountiful buffet stocked with Southern fried chicken, catfish, homemade breads, and wild rice dressing.

WHERE: 262 miles southwest of Chicago. *Visitor info:* Tel 217-453-6648; beautifulnauvoo .com. **JOSEPH SMITH HISTORIC CENTER:** Tel 217-453-2246; historicnauvoo.net. **BAXTER'S VINEYARDS:** Tel 217-453-2528; nauvoowinery .com. **HOTEL NAUVOO:** Tel 217-453-2211; hotel nauvoo.com. *Cost:* from $85; lunch $17. **BEST TIMES:** July for the Nauvoo Pageant about early Nauvoo; early Sept for the Nauvoo Grape Festival (nauvoograpefestival.com).

Trails Old and New Between the Ohio and Mississippi

SHAWNEE NATIONAL FOREST

Illinois

To anyone who pictures the Midwest as a monotonous expanse of cornfields, the 280,000-acre Shawnee National Forest will come as a big surprise. Named for an American Indian tribe who once lived here ("Shawnee" means "southern people" in the Algonquian tongue), it encompasses a vast stretch of hills and dense forest in southernmost Illinois between the Ohio and Mississippi Rivers. One of the most ecologically rich environments anywhere, it is where North and South and East and West overlap in a display of unique rock formations and unusual natural diversity.

Hundreds of thousands of years ago, the area lay at the southern margin of a vast ice sheet; glacial runoff packed with ice and stone carved out features of interest such as the 200-foot-deep Little Grand Canyon.

Cutting through it all is a 160-mile hiking path called the River-to-River trail, which runs from Battery Rock on the Ohio River to Devil's Backbone Park in Grand Tower on the Mississippi. (The trail is part of the American Discovery Trail, which runs around 6,800 miles across 15 states from California to Delaware.) Among its high points—literally—is the Garden of the Gods, one of seven wilderness areas in the Shawnee Forest. With spectacular rock formations some 320 million years old and awe-inspiring panoramas, it provides some of the Midwest's best hiking. Another route through small towns and great natural scenery, between Harrisburg and Karnak, is the 45-mile Tunnel Hill Trail that follows a former railroad track.

The sandstone formations in the Garden of the Gods invite exploration.

There are opportunities for nearly every kind of outdoor recreation, including horseback riding, fishing, and rock climbing.

If you'd rather take in the view from behind your windshield, drive the 180-mile Ohio River Scenic Byway from New Haven to Cairo. Following the river along the Illinois-Kentucky border and through small towns that seem to have changed very little in nearly 200 years, the byway runs to the southern tip of Illinois, where it connects with the Great River Road (see p. 448). Drive north 160 miles to the area across the state border from St. Louis, Missouri, and you can take in a fascinating part of early American Indian history, the Cahokia Mounds at Collinsville, once the largest prehistoric city north of Mexico. As many as 20,000 people lived here in A.D. 1150, when they built the largest man-made earthen mound in the Americas, rising over 90 feet in two terraces. A view from the top offers a marvelous look at the surrounding countryside and even the St. Louis Arch (see p. 461) in the distance.

WHERE: 151 miles southeast of St. Louis, MO. Tel 618-253-7114; fs.usda.gov/shawnee. **RIVER-TO-RIVER TRAIL:** rivertorivertrail.com. **AMERICAN DISCOVERY TRAIL:** discoverytrail .org. **OHIO RIVER SCENIC BYWAY:** fhwa.dot .gov. **CAHOKIA MOUNDS:** Collinsville. Tel 618-346-5160; cahokiamounds.org. **BEST TIME:** spring–fall (hikers will find Aug the least pleasant).

Land of Lincoln

LINCOLN HISTORIC SITES

Springfield, Illinois

The Lincoln Trail is the unofficially designated thousand-mile string of sites along Abraham Lincoln's route from his Kentucky birthplace (see p. 410) through Indiana and on into Illinois, where he ended up in Springfield.

The 28-year-old politician and newly minted lawyer moved here in 1837, the same year the

central Illinois town became the state capital, and stayed until February 1861, when he left for Washington, D.C., to become the nation's 16th president.

The most recent Springfield attraction is the Abraham Lincoln Presidential Library and Museum (see below), but the city is home to several other Lincoln sites, most within easy walking distance of each other. The Old State Capitol is where Lincoln urged opposition to the expansion of slavery in 1858, declaring that "a house divided against itself cannot stand"; seven years later, he lay in state here, the first American president to be assassinated. Across the street are the Lincoln-Herndon Law Offices, which he shared with his partner, William Herndon.

Nearby is a favorite attraction, the Lincoln Home, where Lincoln and his wife, Mary Todd, raised their children. It was the only home he ever owned. A mid-19th-century atmosphere is maintained around the place: The street is covered in gravel, lit by gas lamps, and lined with wooden sidewalks. Two blocks away is the Great Western Railway's Lincoln Depot, where the president-elect boarded the train to Washington. "I now leave, not knowing when, or whether ever, I may return," he said in farewell. He did return, of course, to his final resting place, the Lincoln Tomb in Springfield's Oak Ridge Cemetery. An imposing granite structure with a 117-foot obelisk, the softly lit burial chamber holds the bodies of Lincoln, his wife, and three of their four sons.

Twenty miles northwest of the city is New Salem, where the young Lincoln broadened his education and received his introduction to law

The Greek Revival–style Old State Capitol is a reconstruction of Illinois's fifth statehouse, the first to be located in Springfield.

and politics in 1831. With its 23 rustic buildings, folks in period dress, and active farming techniques from Lincoln's time, New Salem gets you as close as possible to frontier life in the 1830s. Also in the area are three of central Illinois's circuit of courtrooms where Lincoln practiced law. Both the Mount Pulaski and Metamora courthouses have been restored to their original appearance; the Postville Courthouse in Lincoln is a replica, the original having been purchased by Henry Ford and moved to Greenfield Village in Dearborn, Michigan (see p. 526), in 1929.

OLD STATE CAPITOL: Tel 217-785-7960; illinois.gov. *When:* open Wed–Sun. **LINCOLN-HERNDON LAW OFFICES:** illinois-history.gov. **LINCOLN HOME:** Tel 217-492-4241; nps.gov/liho. **LINCOLN DEPOT:** Tel 217-544-8695; lincolndepot.org. **LINCOLN TOMB:** Tel 217-782-2717; lincolntomb.org. **NEW SALEM:** Tel 217-632-4000; lincolnsnewsalem.com. **BEST TIME:** Tues evenings in summer, Civil War Reenactors perform a flag retreat ceremony at the Tomb.

A Shrine to Honest Abe: A Man for the Ages

LINCOLN PRESIDENTIAL LIBRARY

Springfield, Illinois

When Lincoln left Springfield for Washington on February 11, 1861, a civil war was fast approaching and his qualifications as a national leader were still to be tested. Nearly a century and a half later, the

Abraham Lincoln Presidential Library and Museum was established in his honor, the first such facility dedicated to Lincoln and the largest repository of Lincoln artifacts anywhere. Opened in 2005, the complex aims not merely to house the papers and personal effects of the 16th president, but also to give visitors an experience of the self-taught man and his tumultuous times; as much a respectful theme park as a museum, it is a successful blend of scholarship and showmanship.

The exterior of the complex, designed in a sort of stripped-down Prairie style, features clean lines and broad eaves. Once inside the airy central plaza, visitors set out on "exhibit journeys" populated by mannequins of Lincoln, his family, and other figures. They begin with Lincoln's youth in the Indiana wilderness, where his family moved after meager early years in Kentucky, then move on to his career

Statues of the Lincoln Family (left to right): William "Willie" Wallace Lincoln, Robert Todd Lincoln, Mary Todd Lincoln, Abraham Lincoln, and Edward "Eddie" Baker Lincoln.

as attorney and politician in Springfield, his troubled presidency, and his assassination at Ford's Theatre on the evening of April 14, 1865.

Exhibits come to life with evocative sound, from whispered insults of detractors to music from Lincoln's era. "Ghosts of the Library" summons holographic imagery, Disney-like special effects, and a live actor to bring history to life. In the Union Theatre, "Lincoln's Eyes" shows the president from the perspective of an artist commissioned to paint his portrait, with digital projection screens and even a vibrating floor and fake cannon smoke to simulate the effects of an artillery barrage.

The Treasures Gallery offers a more old-fashioned museum experience, with intimate artifacts from the life of Lincoln and his Kentucky-born wife, Mary Todd, that rotate in and out of the collection. Two standouts you can hope to glimpse are a copy of the Emancipation Proclamation, signed by Lincoln on January 1, 1863, and a draft of the Gettysburg Address written in his own hand. In the museum are reproductions of several significant places; once you've seen a reproduction of Representatives Hall in the Old Capitol, you can head out the door to visit the real thing just a short walk away (see p. 501).

WHERE: 112 N. 6th St. Tel 217-558-8844; illinois.gov/alplm. *When:* museum daily; library closed Sat–Sun. **BEST TIME:** Lincoln birthday celebrations on Feb 12.

A Rare Gem in the Midwest

STARVED ROCK STATE PARK

Illinois

From Chicago it's just 100 miles to rural LaSalle County and a natural area of rich history remarkable for its geologic beauty in an otherwise uninteresting terrain. Starved Rock is a 125-foot-high sandstone butte laid down 425 million years ago; at the end of the last Ice Age, starting 15,000 years ago, glacial meltwater cut 18 canyons in it, which today feature dramatic moss-covered walls and an abundance of waterfalls. The seasonal falls are most impressive in spring, and those in French, LaSalle, and St. Louis canyons tend to promise the most show.

People have lived in this region for 10,000 years, including the Archaic, Woodland, Hopewell, and Mississippian Cultures, and the group of more recent tribes known as the Illiniwek (from which Illinois got its name). The name Starved Rock comes from a grim legend: In the 1760s, a group of Ottawa and their allies are said to have trapped a band of Inoka on the butte until they starved to death.

People flock here today for recreation, and lots of it. To enjoy the park's 2,800 acres, strike out on any of the 13 miles of well-marked trails through heavily wooded areas, or take to the river, popular with boaters and fishermen. The park is also a major year-round birding spot, with more than 225 species ranging from cedar waxwings to red-tailed hawks. In winter, the avian stars are American bald eagles; Starved Rock gives a bird's-eye view of the majestic raptors feeding on nearby Plum Island. The best time to see them is during Eagle Watch Weekend at the end of January, although they can be spotted from December to March when the waters of their homes in Canada and other northern states freeze over.

Within the park is the Starved Rock Lodge, a 1930s-era stone, timber, and shingle complex featuring a massive fireplace in its Great Room and both rustic lodge rooms and individual cabins. B&B travelers can opt for the Brightwood Inn on 14 acres near neighboring Matthiessen State Park. Built in 1996 to resemble an old farmhouse, it offers Jacuzzi suites, hot tubs, and private balconies.

Starved Rock is Illinois's most popular state park, but you'll feel as if you have this sylvan wilderness all to yourself.

WHERE: 100 miles southwest of Chicago. Tel 815-667-4726; dnr.illinois.gov. **STARVED ROCK LODGE:** Tel 800-868-7625 or 815-667-4211; starvedrocklodge.com. *Cost:* from $110. **BRIGHTWOOD INN:** Oglesby. Tel 815-667-4600; brightwoodinn.com. *Cost:* from $115. **BEST TIMES:** Jan–Feb for eagle-watching; late Jan for the Eagle Watch Weekend; Sept–Oct for foliage.

Tonti Canyon is just one of many serene spots where you can see waterfalls at Starved Rock State Park.

Oldest Continuous Outdoor Bluegrass Festival in the U.S.A.

BILL MONROE BLUEGRASS FESTIVAL

Bean Blossom, Indiana

Bean Blossom old-timers recall the early days of bluegrass jam sessions here, when down-home audiences fanned out on grassy meadows or in shady groves on the creek bank to listen to musicians cut loose on the strings of their mandolins, guitars, and fiddles. In October 1951, Kentucky native Bill Monroe traveled to the area to play a concert at the old Bluegrass Jamboree Barn, which had been staging concerts since 1940, and liked the venue so much that he bought the 50-acre property. A member of the Grand Ole Opry in Nashville (see p. 473), he occasionally hired other big-name acts—stars such as Ernest Tubb, Grandpa Jones, and Roy Acuff—to join him onstage.

In 1967, Monroe launched the annual outdoor bluegrass festival (the longest continuously running event of its kind in the U.S.). Increasingly large crowds came to hear Monroe's high-mountain tenor voice and his legendary Blue Grass Boys. Monroe enjoyed getting to know the fans and took breaks from the music to give children horse-drawn wagon rides throughout the grounds. He often recounted the local tale of how Bean Blossom (formerly known as Georgetown) got its name: A wagon hauling a load of beans broke down over a creek bed, and the next spring the creek was abloom with beanstalks.

Today, the Bill Monroe Bluegrass Festival may very well be the mecca of bluegrass, yet it retains much of the simple charm of yesteryear. Concertgoers arrive by foot, motorcycle, RV, and SUV to pitch lawn chairs in the meadow in front of the stage where Monroe presided as the Father of Bluegrass Music. The much-loved mandolin-playing Monroe is gone now (he died in 1996), but the stars still turn out for this epic ode to the style he perfected over the course of a long and distinguished career. The festival draws headliners like Ralph Stanley, Marty Stuart, Cherryholmes, J. D. Crowe and the New South—even bluegrass acts from as far away as Japan.

WHERE: 50 miles southwest of Indianapolis; Bill Monroe Memorial Music Park. Tel 800-414-4677 or 812-988-6422; billmonroemusicpark.com. *Cost:* 1-day gate admission $35. *When:* 8 days in June, ending on Father's Day.

Small-Town Marvel of Contemporary Architecture

COLUMBUS

Indiana

"It is said that architecture is frozen music," wrote Lady Bird Johnson, "but seldom in history has a group of devoted artists produced such a symphony in stone as presents itself to the eye in Columbus." The former First Lady echoed the praise of architecture lovers around the world when singling out the 20th-century wonders of Columbus, a small city in rural southern Indiana.

Surrounded by farmers and cornfields, Columbus's repository of contemporary architecture comprises more than 60 buildings created by a host of world-renowned architects, including seven designed by Pritzker Prize winners. Gothic, Romanesque, and Queen Anne dominated downtown until 1942, when Finnish architect Eliel Saarinen arrived with a more progressive vision and built the boldly modern First Christian Church, with its boxy dimensions and slender 166-foot bell tower. An equally contemporary Irwin Union Bank was designed in 1954 by his son Eero, who later designed the landmark St. Louis Arch (see p. 461).

The momentum had begun. In 1957, local industrialist J. Irwin Miller offered to pay the fees for A-list architects to work with the community in creating a showcase of modern architecture. The results have been astounding; Harry Weese, Robert Venturi (who created the fire station in 1966), Richard Meier, and their peers joined the parade.

Today this mostly middle-class city of 44,000 people is proud of highlights such as the Cleo Rodgers Memorial Library, designed by I. M. Pei in 1969. On the tree-shaded plaza in front of the library (and across from the First Christian Church) is the monumental stone *Large Arch* by Henry Moore. Nearby, Gunnar Birkerts's design for St. Peter's Lutheran Church showcases a circular sanctuary with a skylight and stunning copper spire that can be seen for blocks. Swiss artist Jean Tinguely's *Chaos I,* a 30-foot, 7-ton kinetic sculpture made of junk machinery, is the centerpiece of a downtown shopping mall and indoor playground park known as the Commons, originally built in 1973 by Cesar Pelli.

In a survey several years ago, the American Institute of Architects ranked Columbus sixth in America for architectural innovation and design (just behind urban heavyweights Chicago, New York City, San Francisco, Boston, and Washington, D.C.). See for yourself by taking a guided two-hour architecture tour, which departs from the Columbus Area

The dynamic, modern design of First Christian Church inspired a wave of innovative architecture in Columbus.

Visitors Center. (While you're there, look up: You'll be dazzled by Dale Chihuly's *Yellow Neon Chandelier,* made with 900 pieces of delicate handblown glass.)

WHERE: 46 miles south of Indianapolis. *Visitor info:* Tel 800-468-6564 or 812-378-2622; columbus.in.us. **BEST TIMES:** summer; 2nd weekend of Sept for the Columbus Scottish Festival; 2nd weekend of Oct for Ethnic Expo.

Ketchup-Based Sauce as Art

WOLF'S BAR-B-Q

Evansville, Indiana

There are vinegar-doused meats in Memphis, Tennessee (see p. 470); mustardy sauces in South Carolina (see p. 380); hot and spicy marinades in Kansas City (see p. 455); and the sweet, ketchup-based goodness of . . .

Evansville, Indiana. If that doesn't grab you, just wait. At the local Wolf's Bar-B-Q, your taste buds are in for an even bigger shock.

Founded in 1925, the third-generation family restaurant is a landmark in Evansville

—Indiana's third-largest city—and known throughout the state's southwestern region, near Illinois and Kentucky (whose barbecue capital is Owensboro, just across the border from here; see p. 418). Wolf's platters of pit beef, pork, or chicken come with substantial squares of brown, rye-like bread—suitable for use as a barbecue mop—and sides such as their famed homemade potato salad. Each week they sell more than 6,000 pounds of it, plus 6,000 pounds of pork, 400 to 500 pounds of beef, and 1,500 chicken halves—and even then it's barely enough to keep everyone happy.

Graze the buffet line or order from the vast menus at this cavernous, if nondescript, dining room. A separate entrance is busy at all hours of the day and night with take-out orders.

When you have a little downtime between meals, Evansville is at its best during the summer, when visitors and locals flock to the Ohio River waterfront for special events and outdoor activities. In late June, the three-day Evansville ShrinersFest features an air show that has included the U.S. Navy's Blue Angels,

hydroplane racing, a sock hop, parade, blue-grass and other live music, and fireworks along the downtown riverfront. Barbecue makes an important appearance here, as well as at the food-driven West Side Nut Club Fall Festival held every October on Franklin Street, said to be one of the largest street festivals in the U.S. The main attraction of the century-old festival is the food, with unusual offerings such as deep-fried hog jowls and cricket suckers. The barbecue booth, as you might expect, seems to do the most business.

WHERE: 123 miles west of Louisville, KY; 6000 1st Ave. Tel 812-424-8891; wolfsbarbq .com. *Cost:* dinner $20. *Evansville visitor info:* Tel 800-433-3025; visitevansville.com. **BEST TIMES:** late June for Evansville ShrinersFest; 1st full week of Oct for the West Side Nut Club Fall Festival (nutclub.org).

The Hoosier State's Little-Known Corner

INDIANA DUNES NATIONAL LAKESHORE

Indiana

"The dunes are to the Midwest what the Grand Canyon is to Arizona," the poet Carl Sandburg once wrote. "They constitute a signature of time and eternity." Here in Indiana, they rise along a 25-mile stretch of shoreline on Lake Michigan, and 15 of these miles are protected within the boundaries of national and state parks.

Families come to bask on the golden quartz-sand beaches that fringe the deep blue expanse of water. Sailboats bob in the distance; graceful white gulls soar high overhead; and if you listen carefully as you walk along the beach, you might hear the musical, tuning-fork-like hum created by the friction of super-fine wet sand underfoot.

Indiana's unexpected sand dunes and beaches are a unique ecosystem for plants and

wildlife. In fact, the 15,000-acre coastal area that dates back 12,000 to 14,000 years to the last glacial melt is widely regarded as the "birthplace of ecology" (the dunes themselves are only 1,500 years old). Starting in 1896, botanist Henry C. Cowles did landmark research here, and other scientists and envi-ronmentalists followed, all proclaiming the uniqueness of this living botanical laboratory and the need to preserve it for future genera-tions. Today, environmental education and research remain a focus of the Indiana Dunes National Lakeshore's mission and outreach.

This is a magical place, bursting with more than 1,400 different plant species, including 90 that are threatened or endangered. Ranking fourth among the 380 national parks in terms of

The Indiana Dunes National Lakeshore is a gorgeous anomaly in this landlocked state.

biodiversity, the landscape runs the gamut from sand dunes, swamps, and tallgrass prairies to deciduous forests, trout-filled streams, and areas with such diverse vegetation as orchids and prickly-pear cactus. Bird-watching is another prime pursuit, as more than 350 species of migratory birds have been spotted here.

Some of the sand dunes rise as high as 190 feet, including Mount Tom, where on a clear day you can see the Chicago skyline to the west.

Located within the Lakeshore area is the 2,200-acre Indiana Dunes State Park, with 45 miles of multiple-use trails for hiking, bicycling, horseback riding, and cross-country skiing when the dunes and the surrounding area are covered with snow.

WHERE: 47 miles southeast of Chicago, IL. Tel 800-283-8687 or 219-926-2255; indiana dunes.com. **BEST TIMES:** spring and fall for bird migration; summer for beach weather.

World's Largest Spectator Sporting Event

INDIANAPOLIS 500

Indianapolis, Indiana

Fervor for NASCAR racing may have overshadowed the long-running Indianapolis 500 in recent years, but you'd never know it from the spectacle of more than 250,000 fans flooding into the Indiana capital Memorial Day weekend. (For the vehicularly challenged, the fundamental difference between the two schools of racing is that NASCAR vehicles are fully enclosed passenger cars, while Indy cars have no roofs, open wheels, rear engines, and four times the horsepower of the average passenger car.)

What is still billed as the largest single-day sporting event in the world takes place at the Indianapolis Motor Speedway, a 2.5-mile oval track, essentially unchanged since it was built in 1909. The first 500-mile race followed two years later in 1911; the winning speed averaged around 74 miles per hour and the purse was $27,500.

On race day, autograph hounds, photographers, and celebrities create a circuslike atmosphere as VIPs mingle around the track and grounds. Be on the lookout for legends with last names like Andretti and Unser—or even for David Letterman, a hometown hero and racing enthusiast who co-owns an Indy team. One of the biggest stars in the last decade was the young brunette named Danica Patrick. Only the fourth woman ever to race in the Indy 500, she placed third in 2009 before retiring from Indy in 2011.

From the grandstands, the Indy 500 can seem like a deafening marathon blur as the 33 cars scream past at speeds over 200 miles per hour. Behind the steering wheels, the heavily protected drivers experience G-forces comparable to those of astronauts blasting off from the launch pad. Pit stops, pile-ups, and rare fiery crashes aside, the only lull in the roar comes under yellow caution flags, requiring drivers to slow down. Tension mounts leading up to the final, 200th lap, as drivers surge toward the finish line and that famous black-and-white checkered flag. The winning purse was more than $13 million in 2015, split among all 33 drivers and crews. The winner, who traditionally chugs cold milk in Victory Lane, gets a big chunk of that ($2.5 million in 2015).

If you can't make it to Indy on race day, you can whet your need for speed with a trip through the Indianapolis Motor Speedway Hall of Fame Museum on the track grounds. Browse the showroom, which displays about 75 cars, including such automotive treasures as a 1927 Duesenberg and a 1957 Corvette, as well as the cars driven by four-time champion A. J. Foyt. For some, a highlight of the

museum experience is a bus ride around the oval track. It's not as fast as an Indy car, which can travel the length of a football field in one second, but it will have to do.

WHERE: 5 miles northwest of downtown Indianapolis; 4790 W. 16th St. Tel 800-822-INDY or 317-492-8500; indianapolis motorspeedway.com. *Cost:* from $40. *When:* Sun of Memorial Day weekend (late May). **HALL OF FAME MUSEUM:** Tel 317-492-6784; indianapolismotorspeedway.com/at-the-track/museum. **BEST TIME:** May for events and festivities leading up to race day.

Cars burn about 1.3 gallons of fuel per lap at the Indianapolis Motor Speedway.

America's Model 19th-Century Main Street

MADISON

Indiana

The meandering Charles Kuralt sang high praises of Madison, an American "princess of the rivers" founded in 1809 and named for then-president James Madison. This sleepy town of 12,000 on the Ohio River in southeastern Indiana holds more 19th-century architectural beauties per block than any other place in the state—or most parts of the country. Its entire downtown area (approximately 1,500 residential, commercial, and industrial structures across 133 blocks) is listed on the National Register of Historic Places—a rare and intact mix of Georgian, Federal, Regency, Greek Revival, Gothic Revival, and Italianate buildings.

Of the many landmarks favored with views of the river, the most visited is the Lanier

Mansion (1844), the Greek Revival home of a railroad magnate and banker. You can also visit a building from the former Eleutherian College (1848), the nation's first to admit students regardless of race or gender and a staunch opponent of slavery. Take one of several self-guided walking tours and learn of the town's role in the Underground Railroad, admire some of the most elegant wrought-iron work north of New Orleans (much of the railings and fences in the Big Easy were produced here), and don't miss the grand fountain on Broadway.

The town's handsome Main Street is a particular point of pride, shaded by 200-year-old trees and lined with ornate 19th-century storefronts with appealing boutiques and cafés. A noticeable absence of fast-food joints and franchises evokes a sense of nostalgia, especially if you visit the local institution Hinkle's, the town's "greasy spoon" known for its unbeatable hamburgers, french fries, and milkshakes—favored by Frank Sinatra when he was on location here in 1958 to film *Some Came Running*.

Madison has an array of historic B&Bs, but just outside town you can check into the Clifty Inn, within Clifty Falls State Park. Since 1924 it has offered views of the river and downtown Madison from its blufftop perch, gracious service, home-style dining, and a welcoming swimming pool. Clifty Falls is Madison's backyard, 1,300 beautiful acres of natural landscapes, with four waterfalls that plunge between 60 and 83 feet and more than 12 miles of hiking trails.

Downtown Madison is not just about architecture and history. September brings the Chelsea Jubilee—drawing visitors to its live music, swine rodeo, cornhole tournament, and dozens of arts and crafts booths—and the Chautauqua Festival, a juried fine arts and crafts show. A select number of historic and private homes are decked out and open for tours during the Nights Before Christmas Candlelight Tour of Homes, but the biggest splash in town is the Madison Regatta boat race on the Ohio River, held the Fourth of July weekend.

WHERE: 90 miles southeast of Indianapolis. *Visitor info:* Tel 800-559-2956 or 812-265-2956; visitmadison.org. **LANIER MANSION:** Tel 812-265-3526; indianamuseum.org. **ELEUTHERIAN COLLEGE:** Tel 812-866-7291; nps.gov/nr/travel/underground/in3.htm. *When:* by appointment only. **HINKLE'S:** Tel 888-514-3919 or 812-265-3919; hinkleburger.com. *Cost:* lunch $5. **CLIFTY FALLS STATE PARK:** in.gov/dnr. **CLIFTY FALLS INN:** Tel 877-LODGES1 or 812-273-5720; in.gov/dnr. *Cost:* from $92. **BEST TIMES:** July 4th weekend for the Madison Regatta (madisonregatta.com); early Sept for Chelsea Jubilee and late Sept for Chautauqua Festival (madisonchautauqua.com); late Nov–early Dec for Christmas Candlelight Tour of Homes (nightsbeforechristmas.com).

Storybook Splendor in Brown County

NASHVILLE AND STORY

Indiana

Wooded hills, log cabins, and pastoral back roads contribute to Brown County's exquisite scenery, notably in Brown County State Park (Indiana's largest) and the quaint towns of Nashville, Bean Blossom (see p. 503), Story, and Gnaw Bone. Trademarked as the "Art Colony of the Midwest," Nashville has both a bohemian and an old-fashioned air. More than 300 galleries and shops sell everything from dulcimers and jewelry to garden ornaments and leather goods. Nashville's population of about 1,100 balloons to more than 10 times that on any given fall weekend, when droves of tourists converge here to browse against the backdrop of brilliant foliage. Restaurants, B&Bs, and inns abound—among them, the Nashville House Restaurant, serving crisp fried chicken, mashed potatoes, and homemade fried biscuits with apple butter since 1859. Right in the heart of town is the Shaker-inspired Artists Colony Inn, a cozy retreat with a stone fireplace and a restaurant popular for its homemade comfort food.

About 10 miles southwest of Nashville is the T. C. Steele State Historic Site, the former home and studio of Theodore Clement Steele, a well-respected American Impressionist landscape painter who is credited with nurturing the Nashville area as a magnet for artists. His paintings and the 211 acres that inspired them are open to tourists year-round.

The Story Inn, in the neighboring hamlet of the same name consists of a dilapidated former gas station and general store. It's surrounded by a cluster of 19th-century clapboard cottages with tin roofs, all set on the edge of the vast Hoosier National Forest. The town flourished in the timber trade until the Depression, and when

the U.S. Army Corps of Engineers created nearby Lake Monroe in 1960, what remained of Story was flooded and cut off, essentially preserving its simplicity and charm for decades. Today, incredibly, only three residents remain, including the couple who own the inn. Guests stay in the main inn and in several rustic cottages—some with porch swings and hot tubs, but don't expect phones or TVs. A fresh, all-natural gourmet menu and an extensive range of wines are served at the inn's well-known turn-of-the-century restaurant in what used to be a general store.

WHERE: Nashville is 44 miles south of Indianapolis. *Visitor info:* Tel 800-753-3255 or 812-988-7303; browncounty.com. **BROWN COUNTY STATE PARK:** Tel 812-988-6406; state .in.us/dnr. **NASHVILLE HOUSE RESTAURANT:** Tel 877-FRIED BISCUITS or 812-988-4554. *Cost:* dinner $22. **ARTISTS COLONY INN:** Tel 800-737-0255 or 812-988-0600; artistscolony inn.com. *Cost:* from $102 (off-peak), from $165 (peak). **T. C. STEELE SITE:** Tel 812-988-2785; tcsteele.org. **STORY INN:** Tel 800-881-1183 or 812-988-2273; storyinn.com. *Cost:* from $99 (off-peak), from $159 (peak); dinner $50. **BEST TIMES:** spring for flowering trees; Oct for foliage, but expect crowds that clog the narrow roads; winter for Christmas shopping.

19th-Century Utopia

NEW HARMONY

Indiana

Located on the banks of the Wabash River near the southwest tip of Indiana, New Harmony exemplifies the peaceful nature and simplicity implied in its name. This perfectly preserved microcosm of 19th-century architecture

was founded in 1814 by German Pietist George Rapp, who traveled here from Pennsylvania with his followers to await the Final Judgment. Their society stressed Christian perfection through orderly, productive lives, and the new

residents of the self-sufficient settlement soon built more than 180 log, wood-frame, and brick structures. After 10 years, however, Rapp became discouraged with the effort and declared that God wanted him to return with his followers to Pennsylvania. In 1825, Robert Dale Owen, a wealthy Welsh industrialist and social theorist, bought the entire town in order to establish America's first utopian community—one built on free education, strong intellectual and scientific curiosity, and the abolition of social classes.

The legacies of both these communities remain. The Harmonist Labyrinth is a small grotto enclosed by hedges grown in a concentric, circular design. Harmonists considered it a symbol of the difficult paths in life that must be encountered before reaching ultimate harmony and perfection. Another example in town, the Cathedral Labyrinth, is a rose-granite maze patterned after the famous Chartres Labyrinth in France and dedicated in 1998.

Designed by Philip Johnson and built in 1960, the nondenominational sanctuary known as the Roofless Church was commissioned by Jane Blaffer Owen to convey her belief that "only one roof, the sky, could embrace all worshiping humanity." A bronze sculpture by the famed Cubist Jacques Lipchitz sits under a sweeping domed canopy, and gates of his design lead to a garden and sculpture courtyard.

Guided tours of New Harmony—a compact, easily walkable community of fewer than 800 people—meander past log cabins and historic structures like the 1830 Owen House. They begin at the Atheneum/Visitors Center, named for Athena, the Greek goddess of wisdom and the arts. The angular white building, designed by internationally known architect Richard Meier in the late 1970s, houses a rooftop observatory, a theater, and educational exhibits about New Harmony's history.

Amenities such as free Wi-Fi, premium linens, and pillow-top mattresses at the New Harmony Inn might surprise you, but a sense of Harmonist simplicity still pervades its 90 Shaker-inspired rooms. The inn includes three 19th-century guesthouses, a heated pool, small day spa, and a popular restaurant.

WHERE: 180 miles southwest of Indianapolis. *Visitor info:* Tel 800-231-2168 or 812-682-4488; newharmony.org. *When:* no tours Jan–mid-Mar. **NEW HARMONY INN:** Tel 800-782-8605 or 812-682-4491; newharmony inn.com. *Cost:* $89 (off-peak), $129 (peak). **BEST TIMES:** 3rd weekend in Apr for Heritage Artisan Days; 3rd weekend in Sept for German Kunstfest honoring the original founders.

Covered Bridge Capital of the World

PARKE COUNTY

Indiana

Iowa can boast about its bridges of Madison County (see p. 522), but the lesser-known Parke County in west-central Indiana still proudly maintains its unofficial role as the covered bridge capital of the world. As many as

12,000 of the roofed wooden structures were built in the U.S. by 1885; nearly 90 percent of them are now gone. Thirty-two remain here, listed on the National Register of Historic Places (22 others were lost to natural disaster or arson, or dismantled before the days of preservationism).

Although covered bridges such as Bridgeton—which, with its companion mill and waterfall, is perhaps the most photographed bridge in the entire Midwest—are admired today as idealized reminders of bygone times, they were quite practical in the late 1800s and early 1900s. They provided shelter from the elements and comfort to horses skittish about crossing rushing water. They often served as outdoor settings for picnics, parties, and even wedding receptions. Most romantically, they were especially convenient for courting couples back in the days of horses and buggies—the nickname "kissing bridges" was born from the rare bit of privacy they offered.

The town of Rockville's courthouse square serves as headquarters for the Covered Bridge Festival in October. Small towns throughout the county each stage their own arts and crafts activities and entertainment. Take a color-coded bus or self-guided driving tour for an overview, and then pick your favorite area and explore it in detail. The oldest, Crooks Bridge (c. 1856), and the newest, Nevins Bridge (c. 1920), span Little Raccoon Creek. The shortest, Phillips Bridge (43 feet), crosses Big Pond Creek. At Sugar Creek, the West Union Bridge is the longest, measuring 315 feet.

On the last weekend in February and the first weekend in March, the county celebrates a time-honored tradition with the Parke County Maple Fair. Maple trees are tapped, and syrup is made at "sugar camps" throughout the county. Hearty winter breakfasts of pancakes and sausage add to the festive atmosphere.

WHERE: Rockville is 57 miles west of Indianapolis. *Visitor info:* Tel 765-569-5226; coveredbridges.com. **BEST TIMES:** late Feb–early Mar for the Parke County Maple Fair; 10 days beginning the 2nd Fri in Oct for the Covered Bridge Festival.

The 245-foot-long Bridgeton covered bridge was built in 1868.

Shopping the Simple Life

SHIPSHEWANA

Indiana

Horse-drawn buggies start arriving before daybreak at the weekly Antique and Miscellaneous Auction in Shipshewana, a time-locked town in the very heart of one of America's largest Amish and Mennonite communities.

Most of the town's 677 citizens are descendants of the 16th-century European Anabaptists, who began making the journey to the U.S. in 1727 in search of religious freedom. Today there are more than 241,000 Amish in the U.S.

The auction and market draw dealers and bargain hunters from as far away as California and New York, but it's the Amish farmers, whose religion restricts their use of modern machines, who flock here to find crockware, kitchenware,

and hand-powered tools—even old wringer washing machines. Since its inception in 1922, the auction has grown in size and now fills the Auction Barn, where 11 rings of auctioneers sell both valuable antiques and odd collectibles.

Shipshewana, named for an Indian chief who lived here until his people were relocated to Kansas in the early 19th century, is surrounded by the farm region of Elkhart and LaGrange counties, home to 20,000 Amish. The bucolic beauty of this area can be experienced with a slow meander along the 90-mile Heritage Trail, beginning and ending in the town of Elkhart. Audio CD commentaries on the trail (available at the Elkhart visitors center, or you can download the audio tour at amish country.com) lead motorists down narrow country lanes, behind unhurried clip-clopping black buggies, and past pristinely kept orchards and farms.

Amish Acres in Nappanee (south of Shipshewana) features tours of a restored Amish farm and homestead made up of 20 structures from the 19th century. You can view much of it on tractor-drawn wagon rides, enjoy musical theater in the Round Barn Theater, or watch demonstrations of traditional crafts like quilt making and cider pressing. The highlight here is the Thresher's Dinner served family style in the barn: farm-size platters of roast chicken, roast turkey, baked ham, or beef, plus mashed potatoes, homemade bread, and fresh-grown vegetables. Desserts include the must-sample molasses-based shoofly pie.

Amish country is awash in chain hotels and B&Bs. The Songbird Ridge B&B is newly constructed, spacious, and surrounded by farmland that is home to goats, sheep, and

The influence of the "Plain People" gives Shipshewana a unique old-fashioned atmosphere.

miniature horses. Wicker rockers beckon from the front porch, where you can watch the buggies of Amish neighbors pass by.

Where: 173 miles northeast of Indianapolis. *Visitor info:* Tel 800-262-8161; amishcountry.org. **Antique and Miscellaneous Auction:** tradingplaceamerica.com. *When:* every Tues and Wed, May–Sept. **Amish Acres:** Nappanee. Tel 800-800-4942 or 574-773-4188; amishacres.com. *Cost:* dinner $20. *When:* closed Jan–Mar. **Songbird Ridge:** Tel 260-768-7874; songbird ridge.com. *Cost:* $98. *When:* closed Dec–Mar. **Best times:** early July for the Elkhart County 4-H Fair (4hfair.org); early Aug for Arts & Crafts Festival at Amish Acres.

From the Heart of the Corn Belt

Yoder Popcorn Shoppe

Topeka, Indiana

If popcorn has a world headquarters, this could be it. Tucked amid the barn-studded back roads and horse-plowed fields of northern Indiana's thriving Amish country (see previous entry), the unassuming little store called Yoder

Popcorn Shoppe sells "popcorn the way you remember it." It all began in 1936 when local farmer Rufus Yoder planted his first popcorn crop. The Yoders (a very common name in these parts) still operate the company that now sells more than 250 million pounds of popcorn every year through their shop as well as several distributors in various states. The 1,700 acres surrounding the shop and as far as you can see is where the Yoder family grows white and yellow corn, with more coming from farms within a 100-mile radius.

While munching on free samples (scooped straight from the popper into red-and-white paper sacks), browse the quaint shop's trove of packaged kernels, with names like red, sunburst, and the trademarked hull-less Tiny Tender and Lady Finger. Yoder's specializes in unpopped corn sold by the sack, jar, or gift basket. In addition, they stock an assortment of salts and oils, as well as old-fashioned popcorn poppers and new-fangled kettles.

Plan a visit to Amish country in early September if you want to take in the Valparaiso Popcorn Festival. The nation's second oldest popcorn parade is a highlight of the one-day event, held since 1979 in honor of hometown hero Orville Redenbacher, who died in 1995. The bow-tied Farm Bureau agent developed a new corn hybrid that produced plump, fluffy popping corn, and in 1969 launched a commercial popcorn empire that still reigns supreme.

WHERE: 150 miles north of Indianapolis; 7680 W. 200 S. Tel 800-892-2170 or 260-768-4051; yoderpopcorn.com. **VALPARAISO POPCORN FESTIVAL:** Tel 219-464-8332; popcornfest.org. *When:* the Sat after Labor Day (early Sept).

Old-World Living in a Modern Age

AMANA COLONIES

Amana, Iowa

Iowa's rich immigrant heritage is alive and well in the group of seven villages called the Amana Colonies. The villages are filled not with costumed reenactors but with the German founders' descendants (some 1,600), who still

weave blankets, make fine hardwood furniture by hand, and attend Sunday services where men sit on one side and women on the other. Unlike the Amish (to which the Amana Colonies have no connection), the people of Amana Colonies long ago embraced such modern inventions as electricity and the automobile, and actively welcome tourists while sharing their time-honored ways.

Laid out on orderly Old World lines, each village has one main street for shops, with sprawling farm buildings on the outskirts; large, perfectly manicured 19th-century residences are shaded with grape trellises. A 17-mile drive through a pretty landscape of mixed farmland, pasture, and forest takes you through all seven colonies, founded by the Community of True Inspiration, a German religious society that

came to the U.S. to escape persecution. Between 1855 and 1862, its members bought 26,000 acres of prime farmland in Iowa and built seven villages—Homestead, Amana, Middle Amana, High Amana, West Amana, South Amana, and East Amana—all no farther apart than an hour's drive by oxcart. When demand for their hand-crafted woolens and other goods shrank during the Great Depression, they were forced to set aside communal life, an event known as the "Great Change."

You'll see (and smell) right away that food is a big draw here—not just fresh-baked streusel cakes and crusty breads, smoked sausages, and dark, sweet blackberry wines, but traditional German fare like wiener schnitzel served family-style with bowls of sauerkraut and fried potatoes. The Ox Yoke Inn in Amana, the first and largest of the villages, is a longtime favorite. Amana is also home to the Amana Heritage Museum, which offers an overview of the Colonies' history.

As you might expect of a place long noted for its handicrafts, good shopping is plentiful. Quilts, furniture, clocks, ironwork, baskets, pottery, handmade knives, and woolens are especially prized. (Amana manufactured the first upright freezer for the home in 1947; Whirlpool now owns the brand and still has a plant here.) Plenty of local microbrewed beer flows during Oktoberfest, the largest of Amana's many festivals.

The Amana Heritage Museum comprises three original 19th-century buildings.

The biggest and oldest of the plentiful B&Bs here is Die Heimat, an 1854 inn that was originally a stagecoach stop in Homestead. All the rooms are decorated in the simple Amana style—walnut and cherry furniture, hand-sewn quilts, and calming pastel walls that soothe the weary tourist today.

WHERE: 20 miles southwest of Cedar Rapids. *Visitor info:* Tel 800-579-2294 or 319-622-7622; amanacolonies.com. **OX YOKE INN:** Tel 800-233-3441 or 319-622-3441; ox yokeinn.com. *Cost:* lunch $16. **AMANA HERITAGE MUSEUM:** Tel 319-622-3567; amanaheritage .org. **DIE HEIMAT COUNTRY INN:** Homestead. Tel 319-622-3937; dieheimat.com. *Cost:* from $80. **BEST TIMES:** 1st weekend of May for Maifest; 1st weekend of Oct for Oktoberfest; 1st weekend of Dec for Prelude to Christmas.

The Artist Behind American Gothic

ON GRANT WOOD'S TRAIL

Cedar Rapids, Iowa

American Gothic, by Iowan artist Grant Wood, depicts a stereotypical Midwestern farmer and his dour-faced daughter, and it is arguably the nation's most famous—and most parodied—painting. Wood is now

recognized as the first of the Regionalists, a group of American artists who favored rural realism over the abstract styles developing in the early 1900s. The Art Institute of Chicago (see p. 483) bought *American Gothic* for $300 after it won third place in its 1930 juried exhibition. This enigmatic work and others painted at the peak of his career were created in a Cedar Rapids studio that's open to the public.

The son of modest farmers, Wood moved with his family to Cedar Rapids at the age of 10. In 1924 his longtime patrons, John B. Turner and his son David Turner, owners of a funeral home in Cedar Rapids, offered him the top floor of their 19th-century carriage house as a studio, rent-free. Dubbing it "5 Turner Alley," Wood finished the interior himself, aiming for a European peasant look, with exposed wooden beams, roughly textured walls, and built-in niches for flowers or art.

The Cedar Rapids Museum of Art, which owns the studio today, has added a visitors center with original artifacts like his majolica ceramics and steamer trunks, and re-created his front door with the built-in spinning pointers that indicated whether Wood was "In," "Out of Town," "Taking a Bath," or "Having a Party." The museum, just four blocks away, has the world's largest collection of his work—more than 200 pieces. Highlights include the landscape *Young Corn* (1931) and *Woman with Plants* (1929), a portrait of his mother.

Stone City was once a thriving limestone quarry town where Wood founded a summer art colony in 1932–33 that included the Green Mansion, where dorms and studios were located, the Ice House (used as a bar), and the colorfully painted ice wagons that served as the colony's male student housing (Wood stayed in one, too). The nearby town of Anamosa, Wood's birthplace and final resting place, is the beginning of the Grant Wood Scenic Byway, 68 miles

of back roads that wind through the rolling hills, past the rounded hay bales and church spires that inspired Wood's art, and end in the Mississippi River town of Bellevue. Farther south on the river is Iowa's biggest surprise, the Figge Art Museum, a stunningly modern 114,000-square-foot museum designed by British architect David Chipperfield. The luminous glass structure thrills architectural critics and infuses new life into the old river city of Davenport. The museum houses the Grant Wood Gallery, featuring the artist's only oil self-portrait, and the rich collection of objects and papers left by his sister, including his wire-rimmed glasses, scrapbooks, and correspondence that can also be viewed online.

Grant Wood Studio: 810 Second Ave. SE. *When:* open Sat–Sun. **Cedar Rapids Museum:** Tel 319-366-7503, crma.org. *When:* closed Mon. **Stone City:** Tel 319-462-2438; stonecity foundation.org. **Figge Art Museum:** Davenport. Tel 563-326-7804. *When:* closed Mon.

America's Most Famous Ag-stravaganza

Iowa State Fair

Des Moines, Iowa

Immortalized by the 1932 Phil Stong novel *State Fair* that inspired Rodgers and Hammerstein's Broadway musical and three motion pictures, the Iowa State Fair is a true American classic. For 11 days in August, more than a million

people enjoy all the signatures of the modern state fair: stomach-churning rides on the midway, sugar-dusted funnel cakes and deep-fried Oreos, and big-name talent like Carrie Underwood and Def Leppard. But the Iowa State Fair, which started in 1854 as a way to bring far-flung country folks together to promote the latest methods of agriculture and raising livestock, has managed to stay close to its rural roots. It is one of the world's largest livestock exhibitions—after all, it was Iowa that invented 4-H, the educational organization for rural youth.

There's still hog- (and husband-) calling, cow-chip throwing, wood-chopping contests, and of course, the Butter Cow, sculpted from 600 pounds of Iowa butter (much of it recycled and reused for up to ten years). For 22,000 people, the fair is the place to strut their stuff, competing in everything from cattle to needlepoint to vegetables. (There are nearly 900 food categories alone.) The competition includes the freakish—in 2010, a pumpkin weighed in at 1,323 pounds (bigger than most steers)—and the delicious: The pie department is an old-time favorite, with butterscotch, strawberry, pumpkin, apple, and countless other subdivisions. A blue ribbon is the ultimate prize—and a whopping 15,000 of them are awarded every year.

Just about everyone comes to fatten up on foods you can find only once a year—more than 70 kinds served on sticks. The trend started with the 1950s corn dog, a dough-dipped deep-fried hot dog on a stick, and has since spread to pork chops (Iowa raises 50 million hogs per year; that's 17 for every human denizen), dill pickles, hot bologna—even chocolate-covered cheesecake and deep-fried Twinkies. Local favorites include caveman-size turkey drumsticks, Carl's two-handful sandwiches called Gizmos, and fresh strawberry ice cream from Bauder Pharmacy, an establishment opened by the first lady pharmacist in Iowa in 1916.

The Iowa State Fair draws competitors of all ages.

WHERE: E. 30th and E. University Ave. Tel 800-545-FAIR or 515-262-3111; iowa statefair.org. *When:* 11 days in mid-Aug.

Earth Art: Ancient Burial Sites

THE EFFIGY MOUNDS

Iowa

Over 1,500 years ago, Indians from the eastern woodlands came upon a craggy limestone bluff overlooking the Mississippi River and, basketful by basketful of dirt, began sculpting a procession of 10 bears across the

landscape. While the grass-covered mounds are only a few feet tall, they are quite large and best perceived from above. Stretching close to a quarter-mile across, "The Marching Bears" is the largest and finest group of animal-shaped mounds (known as effigy mounds) in the country, one reason this site was declared a national monument in 1949.

"Mound Builders" is a general name given to the many ancient Indian cultures that, over a period of thousands of years, built mounds in a variety of shapes and sizes for different purposes. This culture stretched over a vast area, from the Great Lakes to the Gulf of Mexico, from the Mississippi River Valley to the Appalachians, but the mounds are most

common in Iowa and Ohio. Built between A.D. 600 and 1200, there were as many as 10,000 mounds in northeastern Iowa alone in the early 20th century, but fewer than 1,000 mounds and only 65 effigies survive, lost mostly to agriculture, road-building, and other development at a time when they weren't valued or understood.

The 2,526-acre Effigy Mounds National Monument contains 206 mounds, 175 of them in geometric shapes like cones or rectangles and 31 shaped like animals, primarily bears and birds. Many of the conical mounds here are burial sites, and it is illegal to disturb them, even for archaeological purposes. A deeply spiritual place, this pilgrimage site for

Indian descendants is best experienced in a meditative walk on the 14 miles of pathways. "The Marching Bears" can be seen only after a steep climb to the top of the bluff, and as you walk alongside them you can use your imagination to conjure their full scope and meaning (some archaeologists speculate they defined territorial boundaries). Stop at the visitors center to see the aerial shots that illustrate the forms and beauty of this ancient earth art.

The monument's 200-plus preserved mounds represent nearly 1,500 years of mound building along the Upper Mississippi River.

Located in the rugged country of northeastern Iowa, the Effigy Mounds are a stop on the Great River Road (see p. 448), a 3,000-mile network of federal, state, and county roads that parallels the Mississippi River on both sides from Minnesota to the Gulf of Mexico. While Iowa brings to mind corn more readily than paddleboats, it in fact has a significant river culture that can be explored at Dubuque's National Mississippi River Museum and Aquarium.

Four large aquariums represent four distinct marine habitats along the Mississippi, including the Gulf of Mexico. Meet beavers, otters, and alligators in the many animal exhibits. Outside in the boatyards, you can tour the national landmark *William M. Black* Steam Dredge Boat. A stroll through wetlands over boarded walkways reveals a timeless scene along the Mississippi, where turtles sun on logs and delicate herons haunt the shores.

WHERE: 65 miles northwest of Dubuque. Tel 563-873-3491; nps.gov/efmo. **NATIONAL MISSISSIPPI RIVER MUSEUM AND AQUARIUM:** Dubuque. Tel 800-226-3369 or 563-557-9545; rivermuseum.com.

Ancient Healing from India

THE RAJ

Fairfield, Iowa

An unexpected gem set among 100 acres of rolling Iowa meadows, the Raj is one of the few places outside India where you can experience a complete Ayurvedic cleansing, called *panchakarma*. This is not simply an

Ayurvedic massage, but rather a full, multiday process that is said to clear the body of toxins and restore its balance using treatments like Abhyanga, the mind-bendingly delicious application of warm herbalized oil by two massage therapists working as one. Let Western doctors scoff, but some sufferers of disorders like fibromyalgia and depression say they experience dramatic improvement after a stay at the Raj.

The Raj is here because Maharishi Mahesh Yogi—the Indian guru who introduced Transcendental Meditation to the Beatles and to America in the 1960s—and his followers bought Parsons University in the small town of Fairfield (populaton 9,500) in 1974. It is now reincarnated as the Maharishi University of Management, where those earning degrees counteract the stress of academia by practicing daily meditation. The Maharishi passed away in 2008, but his presence is still felt in the Maharishi Vedic City, made up of 150 homes, an observatory, an organic garden and dairy, and of course the Raj, which opened in 1993.

Days at the spa are highly structured: organic vegetarian meals; 2 to 3 hours of treatments; a gentle yoga class; and after-dinner lectures; plus lots of time for resting in between. The last treatment of the day is the optional *basti* (or enema, to the uninitiated). It's just one more weapon in the war on toxins like pesticides and PCBs, which the Raj claims it can reduce by 50 percent in one six-night stay.

The cleansing process begins before you arrive, as you're asked to avoid not just Cheetos but cold water, chocolate, and a host of other enjoyable things. Once there, an Ayurvedic practitioner assesses your current mind/body balance and recommends treatments. They vary, but can be as strenuous as relaxing in an herbal steam chamber (*swedana*) or having an attendant pour a stream of warm oil on your "third-eye" to pacify the mind (*shirodhara*). For beauty, your skin is cleansed with mud collected from remote regions of India, then nourished with organic milk from a local dairy, where the cows listen to ancient Vedic melodies.

WHERE: 110 miles southeast of Des Moines; 1734 Jasmine Ave. Tel 800-248-9050 or 641-472-9580; theraj.com. *Cost:* from $2,200 per person for a 4-night *panchakarma* package, includes meals and most treatments; overnight room $180.

A Rare Landform of Subtle Beauty

THE LOESS HILLS

Iowa

Rising from the floodplain of the Missouri River along Iowa's western border, the Loess Hills (pronounced like "bus") are an intriguing geological formation exceeded in size and scale only by a similar formation in China.

The region is populated by rare species, such as the ornate box turtle and prairie moonwort fern, which make their homes along this 200-mile border that resembles rumpled and steeply ridged velvet and reaches 200 feet high in some places. Unfolding from just north of Sioux City down into Missouri, this unusual stretch of hill country acts as a corridor for 19 species of raptors such as bald eagles, ospreys, and red-tailed hawks following its ridgelines on their annual migrations.

The Loess Hills were formed primarily between 10,000 and 14,000 years ago, when active glaciers covered a large portion of the northern United States. In summer, when the glaciers receded, water and sediment poured down the Missouri River, leaving mudflats behind. Strong winds blew the finer soil eastward in huge clouds of dust, which over the millennia became tall bluffs anchored by prairie. The Loess Hills provide a refuge for 49 rare plant and animal species in Iowa's largest tracts of never-tilled tallgrass prairie. This nearly extinct ecosystem can still be seen in its pristine form at the Nature Conservancy's Broken Kettle Grasslands in the northern swath of the hill country, 3,000 acres that are home to 175 bison and aflutter with rare prairie butterflies.

Those with wheels can follow the curves of the Loess Hills National Scenic Byway from Akron down to Hamburg. Appreciate its quiet beauty all on your own, or arrange for a paid guide from the Loess Hills Hospitality Association in Moorhead to jump in your backseat and point out subtleties along the way. The wide earth terraces, for example, are called "cat steps" and are the result of natural slippage in the superfine soil. The Lewis and Clark Trail and California Trail passed through this area;

In Loess Hills, some of the bluffs rise as high as 200 feet.

and the dugouts carved into the side of the hills were made by Mormons on their way to Utah in the 1840s. The guides also know the best places for a hike through this mostly privately owned land. Several trails wind their way through the 341-acre Preparation Canyon State Park, which offers some of the most dramatic views of the hills, then hook up to 38 miles of hiking trails through 11,600 acres of Loess Hills State Forest.

WHERE: stretching 200 miles from Sioux City to St. Joseph, MO. **BROKEN KETTLE GRASSLANDS:** Tel 712-568-2596; nature.org. **BYWAY INFO:** fhwa.dot.gov/byways/byways. **LOESS HILLS HOSPITALITY ASSOCIATION:** Moorhead. Tel 800-886-5441 or 712-886-5441; loesshillstours.com. *When:* closed Sat–Sun. **LOESS HILLS STATE FOREST AND PREPARATION CANYON STATE PARK:** Tel 712-456-2924; iowadnr.gov/Places-to-Go. **BEST TIMES:** late spring and fall for weather.

A 300-Year Walk Through Time

LIVING HISTORY FARMS

Urbandale, Iowa

An afternoon at Iowa's Living History Farms is like a semester back at school, but immensely more enjoyable. Learn firsthand the story of how Iowans transformed lush tallgrass prairie into tilled farmland that produces more corn, hogs, chickens, and eggs than any other state in America. This rich chapter in agricultural history is told across these 500 acres, not through glass exhibits and rusty farm tools, but through costumed interpreters who bring alive three working farms from 1700, 1850, and 1900 that look, feel, and smell like the real McCoy, replete with the crops and animals they raised. An 1875 frontier town called Walnut Hill includes a general store and a blacksmith shop.

The "300-year walk" through the three farms begins at a 1700 Ioway Indian village with both summer and winter homes and small patches of squash, beans, and corn that women farm with wooden and bone tools. Farther along, farmers at the 30-acre 1850 Pioneer Farm represent a time when the deep roots of the prairie were first being broken up by oxen pulling iron plows. Farmers relied on multipurpose heritage breeds like the Shorthorn cow, which were good for milk, meat, and plowing, and on subsistence farming, growing corn, wheat, and potatoes, mostly for their own use. By 1900, farmers had the draft horses and modern machinery necessary to work much faster and raise commodity corn (still Iowa's main crop, along with hogs), earning them enough money to build pretty white farmhouses. There are horse-drawn corn planters, cultivators, mowers, and hay racks on view out in the field, precursors to the latest farm gadgetry you'll see at today's Iowa State Fair (see p. 516).

Farms relied on small towns like Walnut Hill, the museum's 1875 community that demonstrates the need for craftsmen like broom makers and cabinet makers before the railroad brought inexpensive mass-produced goods from factories in the East. The small town's big draws were Mrs. Elliott's Millinery, Greteman Brothers' General Store, and the Church of the Land.

Production growth, technological advances, and the rise of big agribusiness have decimated Iowa's small farming towns. The grounds' modern Henry A. Wallace Exhibit Center explains the changes in the last 100 years, featuring interactive displays on changes in livestock, farming technologies, and even food preparation.

There are even some tracts of reconstructed tallgrass prairie, which, before it was plowed under, was so tall men on horseback could literally tie grass over their mount's neck. Once frightening to settlers because of the sweeping fires that tore across the land, the prairie that used to cover 80 percent of Iowa is nearly extinct now—less than one-tenth of 1 percent of Iowa's native prairies remain.

For a more authentic experience of tall grass prairie, make a visit to Neal Smith National Wildlife Refuge (20 miles east of Des Moines) where 5,600 acres of tall grass prairie, oak savanna, and sedge meadows are restored.

WHERE: 8 miles northwest of downtown Des Moines; 2600 111th St. Tel 515-278-5286; lhf.org. **NEAL SMITH NATIONAL WILDLIFE REFUGE:** Tel 515-994-3400; fws.gov/refuge/neal_smith. *When:* May–late Oct. **BEST TIME:** early Aug for Grain Threshing Reenactment.

A woman in period dress peddles her wares.

A Bucolic Backwater That Invites Lingering

THE VILLAGES OF VAN BUREN

Iowa

The villages scattered across southeastern Iowa's Van Buren County are famous for what they don't have—a single stoplight, four lane road, or fast-food franchise. These former industrial towns were some of Iowa's earliest settlements and in their heyday produced pottery, woolens, and flour in mills powered by the Des Moines River. Today the dozen-or-so villages of Van Buren County—each with its own character and pride of place—have converted their historic brick buildings into charming inns, B&Bs, restaurants, and gift shops.

With just 7,400 residents in the whole county, Van Buren is a place that enjoys a slower pace—do a little antiquing here, buy some fudge there. In Bonaparte (population 426), the 1879 gristmill is now a steak house called Bonaparte Retreat Restaurant, known for its juicy rib eyes and huge Windsor chops served with crusty pan-fried bread. The

Historic Bonaparte Pottery, dating to 1866, is now a private residence whose owner allows archaeologists to conduct an ongoing "dig" to learn more about Iowa's industrial past (tours can be arranged). Local ladies bake up a storm for September's A Taste of Chocolate, a veritable orgy of homemade candies, pumpkin chocolate muffins, and even chocolate bread with chocolate butter.

In nearby Bentonsport, travelers can bed down at the Mason House Inn, the oldest "steamboat hotel" in continuous service along the river and offering a 1952 railroad caboose option for an unusual yet comfortable stay. Nineteenth-century antiques decorate the rooms, though most attention goes first to the ample cookie jars in every room, stocked with buttery homemade cookies. For flat-out shopping charm, it's hard to beat the Dutchmen's Store a few miles west in Cantril; it supplies the locals, including folks from the Amish community who first settled in this corner of Iowa in the 1840s, with groceries and goods for life in the slow lane. There are clothes, clocks, toys, kitchenware, thousands of bolts of calico fabrics, and a kaleidoscopic array of candies that takes up a whole wall.

It is worth the drive to the sleepy town of Milton just to sample the goods at the well-known Milton Creamery, owned and run by a local Mennonite family. Their delicious cheeses are made with milk supplied by neighboring Amish farmers and have won awards and national recognition. The cheeses can be found in some of Chicago's better specialty stores.

WHERE: 115 miles south of Cedar Rapids. *Visitor info:* Tel 800-868-7822 or 319-293-7111; villagesofvanburen.com. **BONAPARTE RETREAT:** Tel 800-359-2590 or 319-592-3339. *Cost:* dinner $32. **HISTORIC BONAPARTE POTTERY:** Tel 800-592-3620 or 319-592-3620; bonapartepottery.com. *When:* call for tours. **MASON HOUSE INN:** Bentonsport. Tel 800-592-3133 or 319-592-3133; masonhouseinn.com. *Cost:* from $74. **DUTCHMEN'S STORE:** Cantril. Tel 319-397-2322. *When:* closed Sun. **MILTON CREAMERY:** Tel 641-656-4094; miltoncreamery.com. **BEST TIMES:** mid-Sept for A Taste of Chocolate; early Oct for Scenic Drive Festival, with arts, antiques, flea markets, and a car show.

Movie Magic in the Heartland

THE BRIDGES OF MADISON COUNTY

Winterset, Iowa

One hot, dusty summer, photographer Robert Kincaid turns onto Francesca Johnson's farm lane in Madison County to ask directions to the local covered bridges. Within four days the two have fallen deeply in love.

Robert asks Francesca to run away with him, but she has a duty to her family. It can never be.

Published in 1992, *The Bridges of Madison County* by Robert James Waller, who himself fell in love with the area as a freelance photographer, sold 50 million copies worldwide and even toppled the mighty *Gone with the Wind.* But it took the 1995 film adaptation, shot on location, to turn Madison County into a place of pilgrimage for romantics, who still come from as far away as Sweden and New Zealand to visit the covered bridges that Kincaid shot among a rolling terrain of fertile farmland and wooded hills.

Covered bridges may be romantic now, but they were built for practical reasons—to provide a moment's refuge during inclement weather while protecting the large, expensive floor timbers. Local farmers did the work to pay their property taxes, and the bridges were usually named for the nearest family—Roseman, Holliwell, or Imes. Madison County remains an agricultural community, its countryside one of open stretches and cattle farms, and visitors can follow its curving back roads for a meander from bridge to bridge.

Madison County originally had 20 bridges, but floods and arson have taken their toll. There are just five originals left, all built between 1870 and 1884, and a sixth reconstructed after arsonists burned it in 2002. (The bridges are now protected with cameras, motion sensors, and flame detectors.) "Francesca's House," originally open to the public, was nearly destroyed by arson in 2003 and has been closed ever since.

Thirty thousand people show up at the Covered Bridge Festival, which has been going on in the county seat of Winterset since 1970. The streets of downtown are closed off, and along with a parade, there's plenty of food, music, classic cars, entertainment, and a mad swirl of bus tours running off to see the bridges. Winterset is also the birthplace of John Wayne, and the tiny white four-room house where he started life as Marion Robert Morrison has been restored to look as it did when he was born in

Built in 1883, Roseman Covered Bridge was renovated in 1992. It is one of the most famous in this area.

1907. A new museum next door has more room for memorabilia like the eye patch worn in *True Grit*, the hat worn in *Lobo*, and a theater for screening John Wayne films. As a child, Marion never went anywhere without his Airedale terrier, Little Duke. It was not long before he became known as Big Duke.

WHERE: 37 miles southwest of Des Moines. *Visitor info:* Tel 800-298-6119 or 515-462-1185; madisoncounty.com. **JOHN WAYNE BIRTHPLACE & MUSEUM:** Tel 877-462-1044 or 515-462-1044; johnwaynebirthplace.museum. **BEST TIMES:** spring and fall for weather; 2nd weekend of Oct for Covered Bridge Festival (mccoveredbridgefestival.com).

A Hip College Town

ANN ARBOR STREET ART FAIR

Ann Arbor, Michigan

Take a smart and sophisticated university community, add a thousand talented artists from around the nation, set their works among a backdrop of pedestrian malls, Gothic academic buildings, and leafy campus quadrangles, and you've got the Ann Arbor Street Art Fair, considered the finest (and certainly one of the largest) art shows in the nation for several years running.

Actually, the Ann Arbor Street Art Fair is the first of four simultaneous award-winning art fairs that now take over Ann Arbor in July, sprawling across nearly every street and sidewalk and virtually shutting down the city. Together, they draw more than 1,100 national artists and more than a half-million art lovers perusing everything from fused glass to photography. The original show established in 1960 (now called "Ann Arbor Street Art Fair, the Original") is a carefully juried affair that sprawls across the campus of the University of Michigan. A powerhouse academic institution with a breezy indie spirit, the University of Michigan campus offers up its own artistic beauty, with classic vignettes of gargoyle-studded buildings and ivy-covered walls and a visit-worthy Museum of Art.

The enormous university (with over 40,000 students) tends to draw the spotlight from Ann Arbor itself, a beguiling city of 117,000. Even more than a quintessentially cool college town, it has become the hub of regional research and the suburb of choice for Detroit intellects and anyone with a bit of a bohemian soul. Wander Main Street, a pretty, pedestrian-friendly streetscape bright with renovated historic buildings, sidewalk cafés, an interesting mix of shops, and nightspots like the Ark, hosting all manner of quality musical acts. A few blocks north in Kerrytown, Zingerman's Deli enjoys a longtime devout following among foodies from around the country, thanks to unusual ethnic offerings (Greek *hondroelia* olives, Indian *corgi* coffee) and homemade smoked whitefish salad. The thousands of pounds of their signature corned beef cooked on the premises weekly seems barely to keep the masses satiated.

WHERE: 40 miles west of Detroit. *Visitor info:* Tel 800-888-9487 or 734-995-7281; visit annarbor.org. **STREET ART FAIR:** Tel 734-994-5260; artfair.org. **UNIVERSITY OF MICHIGAN:** Tel 734-764-1817; umich.edu. **UM MUSEUM OF ART:** Tel 734-763-0395; umma.umich.edu. **THE ARK:** Tel 734-761-1451; theark.org. **ZINGERMAN'S:** Tel 734-663-3354; zingermans deli.com. *Cost:* lunch $15. **BEST TIMES:** Mar for the Ann Arbor Film Festival (aafilmfest.org); mid- to late July for the Street Art Fair.

The Horror of Slavery, the Joy of Emancipation

THE CHARLES H. WRIGHT MUSEUM

Detroit, Michigan

In a city that boasts of great museums, the Charles H. Wright Museum of African American History is a standout, chronicling the poignant struggles and successes of the black community. The museum's flagship exhibit,

With its 100-foot diameter, the museum's impressive glass dome is two feet wider than the State Capitol's.

"And Still We Rise," takes visitors on an odyssey that begins in Africa 3.5 million years ago and culminates in modern-day Detroit. With cleverly designed dioramas, interactive exhibits, and twisting walkways, visitors are transported through life in an African bush village, passage on a slave ship, the unfolding of emancipation in America, the streets of Detroit during a blossoming era of African American independence, and much more. The stories stand heart-wrenching and horrifying at one turn, then sing of inspiration and admiration at the next.

The quality here is in the details. The conditions of the slave ship—complete with sound effects of suffering captives—are harrowing and lifelike. A look at the mid-20th century suggests how the auto industry helped create America's first black middle class. The museum does not sensationalize—nor does it shy away from—controversial topics. It discusses the rise in racial tensions in the 1960s and subsequent 1967 race riots in Detroit—which left 14 square miles of buildings destroyed—without placing blame.

Dr. Charles H. Wright, a Detroit physician, established the city's first International Afro-American Museum in 1965 with the help of a handful of local citizens. It slowly evolved into the current museum, a world-class facility in the heart of Detroit's Cultural Center. Along with its exhibits, the museum includes a research library; a 317-seat theater that hosts a variety of live performances; and an excellent museum store.

With the safe haven of Canada just across the Detroit River, Detroit played a key role in the Underground Railroad, the escape route slaves followed to the "free soil" northern states and the new life Canada promised. Several historical markers and sites downtown document this rich abolitionist history. Ironically, the route "north to freedom" was actually south of here: Because of an odd quirk in geography, Detroit is the only sizable city in the continental United States from which you can go south into Canada.

WHERE: 315 E. Warren. Tel 313-494-5800; thewright.org. **BEST TIME:** Feb for celebrations of Black History Month.

Motor City's Wealth of Artistic Masterpieces

DETROIT INSTITUTE OF THE ARTS

Detroit, Michigan

Detroit can thank the wealth generated largely by the auto industry for the collections at the Detroit Institute of the Arts, one of the nation's greatest art museums. The DIA has been the centerpiece of Woodward Avenue's Cultural Center since 1927. The imposing Italian Renaissance–style building is a masterpiece in its own right, and its labyrinth of more than 100 galleries houses an almost encyclopedic inventory.

Virtually every artistic period and genre is represented here, from ancient Mesopotamian stone sculptures to contemporary art. The museum's greatest strengths are Dutch-Flemish and French Impressionist paintings, German Expressionist art, medieval armor, and Egyptian art and artifacts.

Even those with little exposure to art may recognize some of the famous pieces on display: Rodin's *The Thinker* (one of eight bronze casts in the U.S.) and Vincent van Gogh's *Self*

Rodin's famous sculpture The Thinker *stands guard at the Detroit Institute of the Arts.*

Portrait. Not to be missed—in fact, hard to miss—are the *Detroit Industry* frescoes by Diego Rivera, the great Mexican muralist. Considered some of his most impressive and successful works, these complex murals occupy all four soaring walls of the museum's main hall (now called Rivera Court), and represent a thought-provoking visual essay on the evolution and influence of Detroit's industrial and labor movement of the 1930s. City leaders were outraged by Rivera's damning criticism of capitalism; ironically, it was a visionary

Edsel Ford who both commissioned the work and then saved it from being whitewashed.

DIA completed a $158 million renovation and expansion in 2007, part of a new vitality energizing the Cultural Center and down Woodward Avenue to the river, home to the new Comerica Park baseball stadium, renovated theaters, and a buffed-up waterfront.

WHERE: 5200 Woodward Ave. Tel 313-833-7900; dia.org. **BEST TIME:** Fri nights for Friday Night Live! with live music, artist demonstrations, and lectures.

The Monumental Legacy of the Motor City

DETROIT'S AUTO MUSEUMS

Detroit, Michigan

It's hard to imagine an industry that shaped a culture as much as the auto industry shaped America's in the 20th century. It eliminated streetcars and created suburbs. It introduced the assembly line and the hourly wage.

It spawned a transient nation of road trips, motels, drive-ins, and family summer vacations.

It all had its roots in Detroit, where Henry Ford, John and Horace Dodge, Walter Chrysler, Ransom Olds, and other inventive minds tinkered with the horseless carriage in the late 1800s and early 1900s, creating one

A 1956 Continental Mark II is one of the many cars on display at the Walter P. Chrysler Museum.

of the most powerful industries in the world (see p. 528). The global headquarters of the "Big Three"—Ford, Chrysler, and General Motors—remain in metropolitan Detroit, inextricably linking the city and its automotive legacy. The Motor City is where the latest, greatest designs are unveiled every January at the North American International Auto Show; it's where more than 40,000 classic and special-interest cars show up for the annual Woodward Dream Cruise in mid-August (the largest automotive event in the world, attracting over a million car enthusiasts); and it's where an array of fascinating museums and tours chronicle the origins and rise of it all.

The star has long been the Henry Ford Museum and Greenfield Village, part of a vast complex known collectively as "The Henry Ford" in Ford's hometown (and now Detroit suburb) of Dearborn. The 93-acre Greenfield Village features an amalgamation of some of America's most significant historic buildings—including

Thomas Edison's laboratory and the cycle shop where the Wright Brothers invented the airplane—both of which were moved here and painstakingly rebuilt. Inside an enormous 12-acre exhibit hall, the museum once dubbed "Ford's Attic" includes everything from one of the largest steam locomotives ever built to the Rosa Park's bus, an exhaustive car collection that traces the automobile's evolution, and limousines of 20th-century presidents.

The Henry Ford is also the departure point for a tour of the Ford Rouge Factory (named for the adjacent River), Detroit's only public tour of a vehicle-manufacturing plant. The original 1.5-mile-long Rouge plant is an icon of the Industrial Age: Built in 1917, it employed a staggering 100,000 workers and was considered "the first wonder of the industrialized world," where raw materials came in by freighter at one end and finished automobiles came out the other. Recent additions to the vast complex mean you'll begin with a virtual-reality theater experience before watching F-150 trucks being assembled along a quiet and spotless factory floor.

Also in Dearborn, the Automotive Hall of Fame is the Cooperstown of the auto industry, paying homage to the people who affected and advanced the industry. Here too are the anecdotes: When Henry Ford couldn't make a $5,000 payment to the Dodge brothers' machine shop, he instead paid them in Ford Company stock—profits from which the brothers later used to start their own car company.

Suburban Auburn Hills is home to Chrysler Group headquarters and the Walter P. Chrysler Museum. A railroad mechanic, Chrysler got his start in the auto industry when he became smitten at an auto show with a $5,000 Locomobile. He had it shipped home, where he immediately took it apart and reassembled it. Along with a gleaming collection of DeSotos, Hudsons, and muscle cars, this museum does a good job of explaining the evolution of auto engineering and design with a variety of hands-on displays about aerodynamics and other advancements. A time line illustrates the endless string of start-ups and mergers that track the worldwide auto industry, with Motor City at the helm.

THE HENRY FORD: Dearborn. Tel 313-982-6001; thehenryford.org. **AUTOMOTIVE HALL OF FAME:** Dearborn. Tel 313-240-4000; automotive halloffame.org. **WALTER P. CHRYSLER MUSEUM:** Auburn Hills. Tel 248-944-0439; wpchrysler museum.org. *When:* closed Mon. **BEST TIMES:** Jan for the North American International Auto Show (naias.com); mid-Aug for the Woodward Dream Cruise (woodwarddreamcruise.com); Dec for Holiday Nights at Greenfield Village.

Where Homegrown Talents Turned the World on Its Ear

MOTOWN MUSEUM

Detroit, Michigan

When it comes to creating and nurturing musical legacies, few American cities have proved as fertile as Detroit. The birthplace of Aretha Franklin and Madonna, rockers Bob Seger, Ted Nugent, and Kid Rock, Detroit is also where you'll find both the International Gospel Music Hall of Fame and 8 Mile, the road dividing the city and the more affluent suburbs that the rapper Eminem put on the map. A never-ending stream of talent pulses in its blues bars and jazz clubs, but the Motor City music scene will always be most identified with two modest row houses in downtown

Detroit that now contain the Motown Museum. It was here that Berry Gordy Jr. founded a record company and virtually created a new genre of music. In the early 1960s, the "Motown Sound" reverberated across America, shaping Western music for decades to come.

From 1959 to 1968 (when Motown Records moved to larger quarters nearby), Gordy and his fledgling record company ignited the careers of one talented singer after another: Smokey Robinson and the Miracles, Gladys Knight and the Pips, Stevie Wonder, the Jackson 5, Marvin Gaye, Diana Ross and the Supremes, and so many more. Most of them were local talent; it was Gordy, a shrewd manager, strict disciplinarian, and astute businessman, who channeled their talents into his well-orchestrated, star-making machine known as "Hitsville, U.S.A."

The Motown Museum is really two museums in one. The west house focuses on memorabilia: photos, press clippings, gold records, and album covers, along with artifacts like the original sequined glove Michael Jackson wore for his famous "moonwalk" and the 32-pound beaded dresses worn by the Supremes.

A passageway connects to the east house, permitting visitors to step into a time warp. Upstairs is Gordy's apartment, complete with 1960s furnishings. Downstairs is the Motown headquarters, looking as if Smokey Robinson walked through there yesterday. The reception area, telephone switchboard, tape library,

and control room are all original, down to the 35-cent cigarette machine. Guides tell behind-the-scenes stories and point out fun details: The control room's floor is worn through in spots from the endless tapping of feet to the music.

Also original is Studio A, nothing more than a renovated garage where all those Motown hits began. Guides explain how artists were invited to meetings here, where new recordings were played and Gordy asked his routine question: "If you were down to your last dollar, would you buy a sandwich or this record?" If they hesitated, Gordy figured the record was worth releasing.

Motown Records eventually moved to Los Angeles in 1972. But its glory days are perfectly preserved here, where it all began.

Motown Museum: 2648 W. Grand Blvd. Tel 313-875-2264; motownmuseum.org. **Best times:** Aug for the Ribs and R&B Music Festival (ribsrnbjazzfest.com); early Sept for International Jazz Festival.

The Motown Museum is housed in two adjacent row houses in downtown Detroit.

The Unfathomable Wealth of the Captains of Industry

Automakers' Mansions

Detroit and environs, Michigan

One of the best ways to grasp the remarkable wealth, power, and affluence created by the auto industry (see p. 526) is to catch a glimpse of the royalty-like lifestyles of the early 20th-century auto barons. A trio of their estates, architectural and artistic marvels all, are open to visitors for an intimate look at how the other half lived.

John Dodge died of influenza at age 56 in 1920 before he could enjoy the vast riches that the auto company he and his brother founded would yield, but his widow, Matilda, made out quite nicely. She was the wealthiest woman in the nation when she remarried a successful lumberman and decided to create a country estate like those she had seen in Europe. The result was Meadow Brook Hall, a lavish 88,000-square-foot Tudor Revival castle on a rolling farm estate 15 miles north of Detroit. Matilda Dodge Wilson celebrated American craftsmanship in every room, from Tiffany art glass and Stickley furniture, to 39 individually designed fireplaces, even custom doorknobs for each of the 110 rooms. Completed in 1929, it cost an unthinkable $4 million. In 1957, the Wilsons donated the 1,500-acre estate and $2 million to found Oakland University on the site.

Edsel Ford (Henry Ford's only son) and his wife, Eleanor, chose to highlight British artisans and architecture in their Cotswold-style mansion along Lake St. Clair, 9 miles northeast of Detroit. Designed in 1929 by noted local architect Albert Kahn, the home has interior paneling and furniture imported from old English manors; Cotswold roofers were brought in to split and lay the imported stone shingles. Evident throughout is the Fords' love of art, though copies stand in for the originals now hanging in the Detroit Institute of the Arts (see p. 525). Much of this rich estate remains as it was when the Fords lived here, down to the framed photos of family and friends like Charles Lindbergh.

Surprisingly, the least ostentatious home belonged to Henry Ford himself. Fair Lane, the 1914 estate of Henry and his wife, Clara, is remarkable for how well it reflects the inventive, detail-oriented mind of its owner. It is filled with technical innovations, including the powerhouse, designed with mentor Thomas Edison, which made the estate completely self-sufficient for heating, lighting, and refrigeration. The 72-acre grounds, designed by Jens Jensen, are one of the nation's finest examples of natural landscape art, with waterfalls added to the Rouge River, and plantings so precise that the setting sun is perfectly framed at summer solstice.

Meadow Brook Hall: Rochester. Tel 248-364-6200; meadowbrookhall.org. **Edsel & Eleanor Ford House:** Grosse Point Shores. Tel 313-884-4222; fordhouse.org. *When:* closed Mon. **Fair Lane:** Dearborn. Tel 313-884-4222; henryfordestate.org. *When:* closed Mon. **Best time:** June–Sept for gardens at Fair Lane.

A Tragic Chapter in World History

Holocaust Memorial Center

Farmington Hills, Michigan

This excellent museum in the western Detroit suburbs goes well beyond the textbook recitation of facts; it provides a thought-provoking look at the events leading to the torture and extermination of more than 6 million Jews by Adolf Hitler's Nazi regime between 1931 and 1945. The Zekelman Family Holocaust Memorial Center deftly explains not just what happened, but how and why such atrocities could happen, too. The center begins with a circular exhibit room featuring a detailed time line that tracks the history of the Jewish people in parallel with major events in world history. An adjacent room offers insights into Jewish family and community life, religion, and cultural traditions. From there, visitors quietly descend into an ominous tunnel that tells the story of WWII, the rise of the Nazis, and the beginnings of their campaign to annihilate the entire Jewish population of Europe. Subsequent rooms delve further into the downward spiral of the Holocaust—deportation, confinement to ghettos, slave labor, and finally, the death camps—which expanded throughout Europe as Germany invaded country after country. All told, these deaths would account for two-thirds of European Jewry and one-third of world Jewry. Of them, 1.5 million were children.

The chronology culminates in the "Abyss," a walkway surrounded by deeply disturbing photographs and film footage of the death camps as they were discovered by Soviet and Allied troops in the mid-1940s. (Nothing is spared here; the display is not appropriate for small children.) Many of these images were shot under the orders of General Dwight Eisenhower. He insisted that they appear in the news, with the hope that such crimes against humanity would never happen again.

WHERE: 28123 Orchard Lake Rd. Tel 248-553-2400; holocaustcenter.org. *When:* closed Fri afternoon–Sat.

An Angler's Bonanza of Blue-Ribbon Trout Streams

MICHIGAN'S GOLDEN TRIANGLE

Michigan

A web of rivers flow clear and cold through a swath of the Lower Peninsula in northern Michigan, comprising a "golden triangle" of blue-ribbon trout streams. The exact boundaries of the triangle may be open to interpretation (roughly delineated by the cities of Boyne City, Grayling, and Manistee, with Traverse City as its hub) but the rivers are storied among anglers: the Manistee, the Au Sable, the Boardman, the Betsie, the Jordan. Together, these and lesser-known streams make this corner of the state a premier fly-fishing destination for anglers of brown, rainbow, and brook trout.

Flowing east out of Grayling, the famed Au Sable runs over a pea-gravel bottom, coiling through the tall pines of eastern Crawford County. How strong is the fishing culture here? Trout Unlimited, the conservation organization dedicated to protecting trout fisheries and their watersheds, was founded along the banks of the Au Sable in 1959. Grayling is the hub for fishing activity, a town named for an indigenous game fish (which, ironically, died out in

The Au Sable River Festival in July is a competitive canoeist's paradise.

the 1930s because of rising water temperatures from logging along the river's banks).

The Boardman, considered a secret jewel by locals, twists gently through Grand Traverse County before melting into the West Arm of Grand Traverse Bay.

Ernest Hemingway knew a thing or two about fishing, and he favored streams like the Jordan, which flows north through Antrim and Charlevoix counties, Papa's childhood vacation home. Framed by weeping willows and grassy banks, it's considered to have some of the purest and coldest spring-fed water of any Lower Peninsula river, the perfect habitat for brown trout.

In contrast to the Jordan, the Manistee flows wide and lazy on its run to Lake Michigan. With its heavily wooded banks, a drift boat is the best way to work this river, renowned for enormous lake-run brown trout.

Canoeing—with or without fly rods in hand—is also a popular way to navigate many northwestern Michigan rivers and some areas (especially the Au Sable near Grayling) can get downright raucous with river traffic on summer weekends. But with hundreds of river miles, it's still pretty easy to avoid the crowds and find your own private moment somewhere in Michigan's golden triangle.

WHERE: Grayling is 200 miles northwest of Detroit. *Visitor info:* Tel 800-937-8837 or 989-348-4945; grayling-mi.com. **BEST TIMES:** late May–early July for dry-fly trout fishing. Anglers may want to avoid the last weekend in July, which is ultra-busy with canoeists for the Au Sable River Festival.

A Captivating Blend of Culture and Horticulture

FREDERIK MEIJER GARDENS

Grand Rapids, Michigan

Undulating hills, green meadows, wooded alcoves, mirrorlike ponds, and meandering pathways provide an exceptional natural stage for art at this 30-acre sculpture park, the anchor of a superb and superbly comprehensive 158-acre botanical center. The largest collection of outdoor sculpture in the Midwest, it includes more than 120 pieces, including works by such noted artists as Auguste Rodin, Louise Bourgeois, and Henry Moore. The settings greatly enhance the beauty: The land becomes a backdrop—even an integral part—of each piece. *The American Horse*, the 24-foot-high Nina Akuma bronze inspired by a series of Leonardo da Vinci sketches, exudes even greater grandeur against the starkness of a grassy knoll.

The wow factor is high throughout this Edenesque complex. The Lena Meijer Conservatory, five stories of striking glass architecture, houses orchids, bromeliads,

Iron Tree *by Ai Weiwei is one of over 100 outdoor sculptures at Frederik Meijer Gardens.*

cacti, and other succulents. Its much-awaited annual "Butterflies are Blooming" exhibit lets loose 6,000 tropical butterflies to flutter amid the 15,000-square-foot indoor tropical forest. The Children's Garden is one of the nation's largest, where kids can play in a treehouse village and learn about Michigan rocks and minerals in the Quarry. The Michigan Farm Garden re-creates a 1930 farmstead replete with vintage barn and farmhouse, and heirloom vegetable crops. A 1,900-person outdoor amphitheater hosts an ambitious summer concert series, with national acts that have included artists such as Harry Connick Jr., Bonnie Raitt, and Tony Bennett.

The complex is named in honor of businessman Frederik Meijer (cofounder with his father of a grocery/retail chain) and his wife, who collected sculpture and liked the idea of sharing it with the public. They donated 125 acres, their entire sculpture collection, and considerable financial resources to developing this regional treasure. It opened in 1995 and has been expanding since.

WHERE: 149 miles west of Detroit; 1000 E. Beltline Ave. Tel 888-957-1580 or 616-957-1580; meijergardens.org. **BEST TIMES:** Mar–Apr for the butterfly exhibit; 1st full weekend in June for Grand Rapids Festival of the Arts (festivalgr.org) and blooming gardens; mid-June–mid-Sept for Meijer's summer concert series.

A Little Bit of Europe on the Shore of Lake Michigan

THE DUTCH COMMUNITY OF HOLLAND

Holland, Michigan

In the melting pot of the U.S., this western Michigan town was long an anomaly—after its founding by Dutch religious separatists in the 1840s, it remained more than 90 percent Dutch for over a century. Its ethnic makeup has diversified in recent decades, but residents of this tidy community of 35,000 still know it's the Dutch touch that is its biggest draw.

Holland rolls out the *welkommen* mat with a variety of Dutch attractions, but none can top the spectacle of endless fields of blooming tulips bobbing in the breeze come late April. The city has designated 6 miles of signed "tulip lanes" that lead visitors down tulip-lined streets and past brimming tulip beds around town. The best view of blooms is at Veldheer Tulip Gardens, the nationally known bulb producer. Don't miss the drive-by view of its 30 acres of tulips, where more than 5 million bulbs in a rainbow of colors burst forth each spring. Adjacent to the gardens, the DeKlomp Wooden Shoe and Delft Factory remains the only working delftware factory in the U.S. Visitors can watch craftspeople carefully hand-paint the delicate blue-and-white patterns on earthenware using true delft glaze, and carve out authentic *klompen* (wooden shoes) on well-worn Dutch machinery.

The city's treasure is De Zwaan ("the swan"), built in 1761 and the last authentic windmill the Dutch government allowed to leave the Netherlands. It presides over Windmill Island municipal park, which is also home to other reconstructed Dutch structures, such as the 14th-century Posthouse and a Dutch carousel.

Dutch Village re-creates an entire 19th-century Dutch scenario, complete with canals, brick buildings with tile roofs, a farmhouse, and flowering gardens. The atmosphere is kept lively with music, craft demonstrations, and regular performances by high-kicking *klompen* dancers.

The Dutch factor gets cranked into high gear during Holland's Tulip Time Festival, a 10-day extravaganza often touted as the "Best Small Town Festival in America." Holland goes all out for the event, with countless costumed Dutch dancers, food (think smoked wurstel and spiced windmill cookies), three parades (one alone has dozens of marching bands), and townsfolk wearing meticulously researched costumes passed from generation to proud generation.

Where: 172 miles west of Detroit. *Visitor info:* Tel 616-394-0000; holland.org. **Veldheer Tulip Gardens and DeKlomp Factory:** Tel 616-399-1900; veldheer.com. **Dutch Village:** Tel 866-880-8439 or 616-396-1475; dutch village.com. **Best times:** late Apr–May when

De Zwaan is a 256-year-old working Dutch windmill.

acres of tulips are in bloom; early May for the Tulip Time Festival (tuliptime.com).

Splendid Island Wilderness Afloat in Lake Superior

Isle Royale National Park

Michigan

Bordered only by the vast waters of Lake Superior, Isle Royale (pronounced ROY-al) National Park is a model of what we imagine a national park to be: wild, rugged, roadless, and isolated from anything that resembles the

developed world. The park occupies an entire 45-by-6-mile island along with a surrounding archipelago of over 450 smaller islands and outcroppings. Rock Harbor and Windigo, two harbor areas that receive park guests by ferry, seaplane, and private boat, are the only dots of development that impinge on this watery wilderness. The rest of the 850-square-mile park is wild backcountry, home to wildlife and precious little else.

Isolation is a large part of Isle Royale's appeal and uniqueness. It serves as a living laboratory for scientists, who study the predator/ prey relationship of wolves and moose, for example, uncompromised by the effects of outside intruders. Isle Royale's isolation also contributes to its light visitation; more visitors pass through Yosemite's gates in an average summer day than visit Isle Royale in an entire year.

The majority of visitors arrive by ferry from Michigan's Upper Peninsula to Rock Harbor on the island's southeast shore. The Rock Harbor Lodge near the ferry dock provides the island's only lodging. It's a simple affair, but its basic motel-style rooms sidle right up against the rocky shoreline with glorious views of nearby islands and the open waters of Lake Superior. It's a fine base for noncampers who want to enjoy a taste of the park. You can set out on several day hikes and sign up for boat trips to attractions like a restored fishing camp, a lighthouse, and an old copper mine—and still enjoy a hot shower at the end of the day.

With 165 miles of foot trails threading across the island and linking a network of

Isle Royale National Park is a sanctuary for an abundant moose population.

36 campgrounds, Isle Royale is a backpacker's dream. The 42-mile Greenstone Trail traverses the island across its high basalt backbone, intersecting most of the park's other trails. Paddlers can portage canoes inland to explore dozens of interior lakes, where fishing and moose sightings are unmatched. Experienced sea kayakers can tackle the ragged Superior shoreline, a maze of rocky islands and secluded coves. No matter how you explore it, this unique national park offers a quintessential Great Lakes wilderness experience.

WHERE: 185 miles north of Green Bay, WI. Tel 906-482-0984; nps.gov/isro. *When:* mid-Apr–Oct. **How:** Several ferries and seaplane services run to Isle Royale (nps.gov/isro). **ROCK HARBOR LODGE:** Tel 906-337-4993 (May–Sept), 866-644-2003 (Oct–Apr); rockharborlodge.com. *Cost:* from $235 (off-peak), from $255 (peak). *When:* late May–mid-Sept. **BEST TIME:** late June–mid-Sept.

America's Forgotten Mineral Rush

KEWEENAW COPPER MINING HERITAGE

Keweenaw Peninsula, Michigan

Most North Americans are familiar with the California Gold Rush of 1849. But history books largely overlook the copper rush that occurred at the same time, when vast deposits of copper—a mineral highly coveted

in the 19th century—were discovered in the remote wilds of Michigan's Keweenaw (pronounced KEY-win-aw) Peninsula. The Keweenaw National Historical Park, established in 1992, now tells the tale, encompassing heritage sites that range from an opulent opera house to a mine tour that carries you deep under the earth.

Raking off the back of Michigan's Upper Peninsula, the 80-mile-long Keweenaw had always been an untamed place, a land of deep

piney woods and rocky Lake Superior beaches. But that changed in 1840 when the copper rush began almost overnight, first with prospectors straggling through the wilderness, then with extensive mining enterprises. By the time the most accessible copper was played out, King Copper had generated $9.6 billion—ten times more than the California Gold Rush.

The national park sites are scattered throughout the Keweenaw, with most of them concentrated in the cities of Houghton,

Houghton and Hancock are connected by the Portage Lake Lift Bridge, the heaviest aerial lift bridge in the world.

Hancock, and Calumet. In Hancock, the mammoth shaft house of the Quincy Mine is a monument to one of the largest, most lucrative copper mines in the world, in operation until 1967. A terrific tour takes you through the world's largest steam hoist (used to haul miners nearly 10,000 feet underground) and 2,400 feet into the mine, where you get a feel for what it was like to work in this oppressive environment. Many Finns came to work in the mines, and their influence is still felt in the area today, down to its street signs and foods. At the Suomi Home Bakery, try

the *pannukakku,* a Finnish pancake, or *nisu,* a yeast bread spiced with cardamom. Most bakeries also sell the ubiquitous Cornish pasty (PASS-tee), a potpie-type crust filled with beef, potatoes, onions, and rutabagas.

The largest mine was based in Red Jacket, now Calumet, a boomtown that roared with 50 steam hoists and 11,000 immigrant laborers. In this now-sleepy village, national park funds are helping restore the vestiges of the luxuries the copper rush created: a rococo opera house that attracted first-run celebrities like Douglas Fairbanks Jr. and Houdini, and the 1908 Laurium Manor Inn & B&B, two Victorian mansions now welcoming overnight guests to 18 rooms adorned with silver-leaf ceilings and period antiques.

WHERE: Houghton and Hancock are about 550 miles northwest of Detroit. *Visitor info:* Tel 800-338-7982 or 906-337-4579; keweenaw .info. **KEWEENAW NATIONAL PARK:** Calumet. Tel 906-337-3168; nps.gov/kewe. **LAURIUM MANOR INN:** Laurium. Tel 906-337-2549; laurium.info. *Cost:* from $99. **BEST TIMES:** Late June for Calumet's Pasty Fest; July–Sept for weather; early Oct for foliage.

Enormous Dunes, Endless Beaches, and Vineyards

LEELANAU PENINSULA

Michigan

I f eastern Michigan is considered Michigan's "Thumb," then the Leelanau Peninsula in the northwest could be its pinkie, a narrow digit of land wagging up between Grand Traverse Bay (see p. 544) and the open waters of Lake

Michigan. The 28-mile-long peninsula is a delight of waterfront villages, gentle farmsteads, sandy beaches, lighthouses, vineyards, and nearly 100 miles of Lake Michigan shoreline rimmed with some of the tallest freshwater dunes in the world.

Glaciers and millennia of wind and water created the Sleeping Bear Dunes, grand hills of

golden sand that rise directly from the lake nearly 500 feet into the sky. Sleeping Bear Dunes National Lakeshore (named for an Ojibwa legend) stretches along 65 miles of shoreline, protecting thousands of acres of stark dunescape, along with forest, beaches, and the North and South Manitou islands 17 miles offshore. The 7.4-mile Pierce Stocking Scenic

Drive and a variety of hiking trails spiral out into the dunes, leading to the shore and panoramic Lake Michigan overlooks. North of the national park, M-22 traces the peninsula's scalloped shoreline, linking together waterfront towns like Leland, where a jumble of 19th-century fish shanties have been preserved along the harbor. One commercial fishery, Carlson's, remains in business, with snub-nosed boats tied up along the mouth of the Carp River, and a small shop that sells fresh and smoked trout and whitefish. Most of the other buildings now house gift shops and galleries; the fishnets drying in the sun are solely for the benefit of photo-snapping visitors. At Cove Bar, try a Chubby Mary, a Bloody Mary with a smoked chub (a local fish) replacing the traditional celery stalk. Inland, the Leelanau eases into a mellow patchwork of pastures, orchards, and vineyards. The Leelanau Peninsula Wine Trail links together a growing number of Leelanau wineries—24 at last count—which regularly produce award-winning vintages, especially riesling, chardonnay, and pinot gris. Stop in for tastings at boutique vintners like L. Mawby Vineyards, known for its sparkling wines, and Black Star Farms, with a reputation for pinot gris and dessert wines that have been served at White House dinners. The Black Star Farms complex includes a grandiose tasting room, artisanal creamery, a championship

Along the Leelanau Peninsula, there are plenty of perfect spots for taking a refreshing dip in Lake Michigan.

equestrian facility, and an elegant inn and fine restaurant nestled between vineyards and horse pastures.

WHERE: 250 miles northwest of Detroit. *Visitor info:* Tel 231-994-2202; leelanau chamber.com. **SLEEPING BEAR DUNES:** Empire. Tel 231-326-4700; nps.gov/slbe. **LEELANAU PENINSULA WINE TRAIL:** Tel 231-642-5550; lpwines.com. **L. MAWBY VINEYARDS:** Suttons Bay. Tel 231-271-3522; lmawby.com. **INN AT BLACK STAR FARMS:** Suttons Bay. Tel 231-944-1270; blackstarfarms.com. *Cost:* from $275 (off-peak), from $330 (peak). **BEST TIMES:** June for Leland Wine & Food Festival; Oct for the wine harvest.

A Lakeside Resort Era Spanning the Centuries

LITTLE TRAVERSE BAY

Michigan

The cool northern air and beautiful teal waters of this Lake Michigan bay lured city residents north from Chicago and Detroit as soon as the railroad completed a line to the town of Petoskey in 1873, and by the turn of the

20th century, Petoskey's downtown was filled with fine shops, wealthy patrons, and more than a dozen grand hotels overlooking the bay.

Though much has changed, much has also remained the same along Little Traverse Bay. The towns that curve along the bay—from Bay

Harbor to Petoskey to Harbor Springs—are still exclusive enclaves, with upscale shops, restaurants, and deluxe resorts that appeal especially to golfers and boaters.

Over time, most of the big old Victorian hotels that once defined Petoskey (current population 5,700) were lost to fire. Thankfully, the 1899 Stafford's Perry Hotel survives with all its character and grace, along with a turn-of-the-century downtown known as the Gaslight District. Elegant boutiques (the kind of retailers that list their locations as something like "New York–Petoskey–Palm Springs") alternate with venerable throwbacks like Symons General Store, where you can buy penny candy and bulk pickles.

East of Petoskey, Bay View boasts more than 400 well-preserved Victorian homes, resplendent with gingerbread trim and gumball colors. At the bay's north end, tony Harbor Springs may be the quintessential summer resort town. Old Money gathered here early, lining its clear, spring-fed harbor—the deepest in the Great Lakes—with million-dollar yachts and its shores with crisp white mansions on emerald lawns. Downtown is marked by white church steeples and overflowing flower boxes.

In a state with one of the nation's highest rates of public golf courses per capita, the Little Traverse Bay region is quickly becoming one of Michigan's preeminent golf regions. At the south end of Little Traverse Bay, Bay Harbor is a glittering resort community anchored by the Inn at Bay Harbor—its architecture reminiscent of the grand old Victorian hotels—and flanked by four Arthur Hills–designed golf nines: Crooked Tree, the Links, the Quarry, and the Preserve, boasting more waterfront holes than Pebble Beach.

Boyne Highlands draws golfers far and wide for its four courses, including the Heather, a highly regarded Robert Trent Jones Sr. design, and its state-of-the-art golf academy. The area's best golf accommodations are found at Boyne's nearby sister resort, Boyne Mountain, which completed its Mountain Grand Lodge, home to luxe lodgings, the 19,000-square-foot Spa at Boyne Mountain, an indoor water park, and yes, more golf.

WHERE: Petoskey is 260 miles northwest of Detroit. *Visitor info:* Tel 800-845-2828 or 231-348-2755; petoskeyarea.com. **STAFFORD'S PERRY HOTEL:** Tel 800-737-1899 or 231-347-4000; staffords.com. *Cost:* from $119. **THE INN AT BAY HARBOR:** Tel 855-688-7023 or 231-439-4000; innatbayharbor.com. *Cost:* from $173 (off-peak), from $269 (peak). **BAY HARBOR GOLF CLUB:** Tel 231-439-4085; bayharborgolf.com. *Cost:* greens fees from $132. **BOYNE HIGHLANDS GOLF:** Tel 844-624-5297 or 231-549-6000; boyne.com. *Cost:* greens fees from $65. **MOUNTAIN GRAND LODGE & SPA:** Boyne Falls. Tel 866-858-3672 or 231-549-6000; mountaingrandlodge.com. *Cost:* from $157 (off-peak), from $193 (peak). **BEST TIMES:** mid-June for the Bay Harbor In-Water Boat Show; late July for the Little Traverse Bay Regatta in Harbor Springs; Sept for the Harbor Springs Cycling Classic.

A Victorian Fairy Tale Alive in the Great Lakes

MACKINAC ISLAND

Michigan

Mackinac Island boasts a rich history—as American Indian summering grounds, as the center of the North American fur-trading business, and as a colonial fortress—but it's the gilded Victorian era the island preserves like a living postcard. Horse-drawn carriages clip-clop down vehicle-free streets. Pedestrians stroll and bicyclists pedal past Main Street shops and cafés. Million-dollar Victorian "cottages" climb up hillsides, and storybook resorts like the world-famous Grand Hotel gaze out over sparkling lake views. It can seem a bit touristy at first blush, but there's no denying that Mackinac (pronounced MAK-i-naw) is also irrepressibly charming, especially if you venture away from downtown's snarl of fudge and trinket shops, linger awhile, and succumb to the relaxed island vibe as if a vacationing mogul of yesteryear.

Mackinac Island lies in the Straits of Mackinac, where Lakes Michigan and Huron meet, and where the immense Lower and Upper Peninsulas of Michigan are linked by the man-made tether of the Mackinac Bridge. (One of the world's longest suspension bridges, the 5-mile-long bridge is a marvel in its own right.) The clean lake air began drawing wealthy urbanites in the late 19th century by steamship and railroad. As the island's popularity grew, farsighted locals banned the automobile almost as quickly as it arrived, and today more than 500 horses are stabled on the island all summer to pull carriages and make service deliveries.

All ferries arrive downtown, where you'll be greeted by a bustling Main Street filled with shops selling ultra-rich, ultra-delicious fudge, the island's specialty (and hence the reason locals refer to tourists as "fudgies"). There are dozens of flavors to choose from—try the turtle, cranberry, or maple syrup. Walk off those calories on a hike up to Fort Mackinac, a military outpost built by the British in 1780 to ward off upstart American colonists. It's a fun place to wander around, with restored quarters, costumed guides, cannon salutes, and glorious views of downtown, the marina, and a broad sweep of Lake Huron. Seventy-eight percent of the 2,200-acre island is protected as state park, much of it woodlands sprinkled with wildflowers and limestone outcroppings. A flat 8-mile bicycle path encircles the island, hugging the shoreline and leading to interesting natural and historical sites at a pace those Victorian visitors would appreciate.

But Mackinac's most famous landmark is inarguably the opulent Grand Hotel with its much-photographed 660-foot-long front porch, impeccable grounds covered with blooming flowers, and a time-weathered ambience marked by afternoon activities like bocce ball and high tea. Built in 1887 (when rates were $3 a night for Midwestern tycoons) on its hilltop perch and regally setting the island's gracious turn-of-the-century tone ever since, the white Greek Revival palace is believed to be the largest summer resort hotel in the world. Movie fans will recognize it as the backdrop for the 1980 cult classic *Somewhere in Time*. The Chippewa Hotel Waterfront has its own set of devotees. A lovely Victorian landmark overlooking the marina, its Pink Pony Bar & Grill is a favorite watering hole among sailors, made famous as the "finish line" of the annual 333-mile Chicago–Mackinac Yacht Race ("the Mac") that turns the island on its ear every July.

WHERE: 280 miles north of Detroit in the Straits of Mackinac. *Visitor info:* Tel 800-454-5227 or 906-847-3783; mackinacisland.org. **HOW:** Several passenger ferries operate May–Oct from St. Ignace and Mackinaw City (mackinacisland.org). **GRAND HOTEL:** Tel 800-33-GRAND or 906-847-3331; grandhotel.com.

On virtually car-free Mackinac Island, the clip-clop of horses' hooves is a familiar sound.

Cost: from $608 (off-peak), from $772 (peak), includes meals. *When:* May–Oct. **CHIPPEWA HOTEL WATERFRONT:** Tel 906-847-3341; chippewahotel.com. *Cost:* from $109 (off-peak), from $189 (peak). *When:* May–Oct. **BEST TIMES:** late Apr–early May for Grand Opening Weekend; mid-June for the 10-day Lilac Festival; mid-July for the Chicago–Mackinac Yacht Race (cycracetomackinac.com); early Sept for the Bridge Walk; Oct for the Big Band Dance Extravaganza Weekend (at Grand Hotel).

Michigan's Would-Be Capital

MARSHALL

Michigan

When the Michigan legislature named Lansing its new state capital in 1847, no community was more surprised and disappointed than Marshall, which lost by one vote. Michigan's original state constitution called for the state capital to relocate from Detroit to this community in the south central part of the state, an important stagecoach and then railroad stop. Marshall was so sure of its destiny, it even built a governor's mansion and set aside an area known as Capitol Hill in anticipation.

Today, Marshall (population 7,500) is instead home to one of America's largest historic districts. More than 850 buildings provide a picture book of mid-19th-century architecture, block after tree-lined block of 1840s and 1850s Greek and Gothic Revival homes. Marshall's preservation ethic began in the 1920s, when savvy mayor Harold Brooks first recognized the town's architectural treasure trove and led a crusade to maintain it. One of the highlights—open to the public—is the Honolulu House Museum, built in 1860 by Judge Abner Pratt upon his return from a stint as consul to the Sandwich (now Hawaiian) Islands in the 1850s. He made every attempt to re-create his Polynesian paradise in his new home, with its pagoda-shaped tower, wide veranda, and decorative pineapple trim in teak and ebony. Pratt died of pneumonia shortly after its completion—an illness some attributed to his habit of wearing tropical

The Honolulu House is a blend of Gothic Revival architecture and heavy Polynesian influences.

clothing during Michigan winters. Another can't-miss is the nearby The Way Inn, a handsome late-19th-century home painted in six different colors and offering just three guest rooms decorated with period pieces.

The National House Inn is Michigan's oldest continuously operating inn. Built in 1835 as a stagecoach stop, this B&B still exudes warmth with polished plank floors and a massive beam-and-brick open-hearth fireplace. Pick up a walking tour map and wander along shady streets like Mansion, Prospect, Kalamazoo, and Hanover, lined with lovingly preserved homes. An eagerly awaited annual historic home tour the weekend after Labor Day affords you a rare glimpse inside, too.

Owned and operated by the Schuler family for three generations, Schuler's is a much-loved Michigan institution that's been serving classics like Bar-Scheeze (a spicy cheese spread), Swiss onion soup, and nut-crusted walleye since 1909. Tradition, not trendiness, after all, has always been the trump card in Marshall.

WHERE: 100 miles west of Detroit. *Visitor info:* Tel 269-781-5163; marshallmi.org. **HONOLULU HOUSE MUSEUM:** Tel 269-781-8544. *When:* May–Oct. **THE WAY INN:** Tel 269-420-1806; thewayinnmarshall.com. *Cost:* $120. **NATIONAL HOUSE INN:** Tel 269-781-7374; nationalhouseinn.com. *Cost:* from $110. **SCHULER'S:** Tel 269-781-0600; schulersres taurant.com. *Cost:* dinner $35. **BEST TIME:** early Sept for the Historic Home Tour.

Spectacular Sandstone Cliffs Rising from Lake Superior's Shore

PICTURED ROCKS

Munising to Grand Marais, Michigan

The Upper Peninsula's Pictured Rocks National Lakeshore showcases a stunning stretch of coastline along the forested southern shore of Lake Superior, a natural marvel of sculpted sandstone cliffs, rocky coves, and 300-foot high banks of sand. One road traverses the 40-mile-long park, leading to trailheads, waterfalls, Lake Superior overlooks, lighthouses, and other historic sites. Get your first view at Miners Castle overlook, where eons of wind and waves have transformed the cliffs into turrets and arches like dissolving sand castles. Near the park's east end, the Log Slide Overlook

Pictured Rocks National Lakeshore is covered with both hardwood and conifer forests.

is where loggers once jettisoned fresh-cut lumber 300 feet down into the lake. Today, you can enjoy the panorama, with the immense Grand Sable banks and dunes to the east and the 1874 Au Sable lighthouse 3 miles west.

Lace up your hiking boots and explore over 100 miles of trails. At Chapel Basin, footpaths loop past 60-foot Chapel Falls, then skim along the edge of precipitous sandstone cliffs several stories above Lake Michigan, like beaches in the sky.

To experience the park's most impressive panoramas, though, you need to get out on the water. The pretty little waterfront town of Munising, located on the park's west end, is the source for park information and a variety of boat excursions. Oldest and most popular is Pictured Rocks Cruises; its three-hour sightseeing trips sidle right up to the sculpted sandstone formations. Go in the late afternoon, when the sinking sun casts the multicolored cliffs in their most dramatic light.

Even more intimate is a sea kayak excursion. Paddling up to the rust-colored cliff face looming several stories above is like rafting up alongside an ore carrier.

WHERE: Munising is 400 miles northwest of Detroit. Tel 906-387-3700; nps.gov/piro. *Munising visitor info:* Tel 906-387-2138; munising.org. **PICTURED ROCKS CRUISES:** Tel 906-387-2379; picturedrocks.com. *Cost:* $37. *When:* mid-May–mid-Oct. **KAYAKING:** Northern Waters Kayaking, Munising. Tel 906-387-2323; northernwaters.com. *Cost:* from $125 for guided day trips. **BEST TIMES:** July–early Sept for weather.

The Art Coast of Michigan

SAUGATUCK

Michigan

Ever since the Art Institute of Chicago began sponsoring a summer camp in Saugatuck in 1910, this Victorian resort town has embraced its reputation as an arts colony and never let go. It's home to a thriving community of artists, art galleries (more per capita than any other small town in the Midwest), and events like the annual Saugatuck Gallery Stroll in October with artists in residence, special exhibitions, and artists' receptions in some 20 galleries. The Art Institute's Ox-Bow School of Art still runs its prestigious summer program here, hosting demonstrations and changing exhibitions on its beautiful 110-acre campus.

Saugatuck has a genteel quality, a grande dame among resort towns along the southeast Lake Michigan shore. Tucked into wooded sand dunes near the mouth of the Kalamazoo River, lovely Victorian mansions recall Saugatuck's heyday as a busy lumber port. Enjoy a stroll on the boardwalk along the harbor or listen to band concerts in the park. An impressive variety of restaurants and fine inns are always busy, and none more lovely than the Wickwood Inn, once the home of an early Saugatuck mayor and now owned by Julee Rosso Miller, coauthor of the seminal *The Silver Palate* cookbook series. Guests enjoy a firsthand taste of Rosso's Sips & Small Plates evenings and inventive, always-changing farm-to-table breakfasts.

A boardwalk in Saugatuck is a lovely place for an afternoon stroll along the shores of Lake Michigan.

Even when summer crowds seem to inundate downtown Saugatuck, there are plenty of places to escape and explore. Step aboard the frilly gingerbread Chain Ferry for the short shuttle across the Kalamazoo River to Mount Bald Head, a high dune perfect for sunset-watching, and Oval Beach, a lovely arc of sugary sand on Lake Michigan. Three miles north of town, Saugatuck Dunes State Park preserves over 2 miles of pristine beach and undulating dunes, some more than 200 feet high.

WHERE: 170 miles west of Detroit. *Visitor info:* Tel 269-857-1701; saugatuck.com. **OX-BOW SCHOOL OF ART:** Tel 800-318-3019 or 269-857-5811; ox-bow.org. *When:* 1- and 2-week courses offered in summer. **WICKWOOD INN:** Tel 800-385-1174 or 269-857-1465; wickwoodinn.com. *Cost:* from $189 (off-peak), from $339 (peak). **BEST TIMES:** July for the Venetian Festival; fall for smaller crowds and Indian summer weather; 2nd week of Oct for 2-day Gallery Stroll; Nov–Dec for holiday lights.

The Busiest Waterway in the World

SOO LOCKS

Sault Ste. Marie, Michigan

There's a 21-foot elevation difference between Lake Superior and Lake Huron, a geographical fact responsible for Sault Ste. Marie's place in history as the oldest city in Michigan. It's where the Ojibwa settled to fish the productive rapids, and where the French established a busy fur-trading post, and it's also why the Soo Locks were built—the first one completed in 1855—to finally tame those rapids and open Lake Superior's vast mineral riches to shipping.

In Sault Ste. Marie (often called "The Soo," shorthand for its French pronunciation), you can get an up-close look at the fascinating system of locks that now accommodates 1,000-foot-long freighters as they haul iron ore, limestone, and other commodities to the industrial cities clustered along the southern shores of the lower Great Lakes. The volume freight transported across Lake Superior and through the Soo Locks makes it one of the busiest lock systems in the world.

The U.S. Army Corps of Engineers manages the locks, along with two large outdoor viewing platforms right in the heart of downtown Sault Ste. Marie, where you can peer down on the ships as they slip into the locks with seemingly inches to spare. The visitors center has working models that explain the operation of the locks, as well as remote cameras and a public address system that keep visitors informed of approaching ship traffic. After viewing the locks, you can "lock through" yourself on a Soo Locks Boat Tour, which travels along the U.S. and Canadian shores and through two sets of locks. The tour boat deck gives a new perspective as the water rushes into the lock chamber and the boat begins its slow but steady rise. During busy shipping times, you might even be locking through with freighter traffic, dwarfed by their enormous steel hulls.

WHERE: 339 miles north of Detroit, Locks Park. Tel 906-253-9290; lre.usace.army.mil. *When:* mid-May–Oct. *Visitor info:* Tel 800-647-2858 or 906-632-3366; saultstemarie .com. **BOAT TOURS:** Tel 800-432-6301 or 906-632-6301; soolocks.com. *When:* May–mid-Oct. **BEST TIME:** late June for the annual Ojibwa Powwow and Summer Gathering.

A tour boat passes through the Soo Locks and into Lake Superior.

A Most Superior Southeastern Shore

SHIPWRECK COAST

Michigan

M uch of Michigan's Lake Superior shore has wild yet serene beauty— it's a timeless place where you're as likely to see a deer or bear wandering along a sandy beach as you are another human. But the waters offshore are quite a different story. For over a century, Lake Superior has been a busy waterway, where timber once was hauled on wooden schooners and steamships, and now bulk commodities like iron ore are loaded on 1,000-foot freighters. Dozens of lighthouses were built to guide them, but they're no match for 350-mile-long Lake Superior, the largest and fiercest of the Great Lakes. Especially along its southeastern shore and off the north shore of Michigan's Upper Peninsula, where prevailing northwest storms unleash their full fury, hundreds of shipwrecks litter its deep, dark bottom like skeletons.

Michigan protects its unusual wealth of sunken relics with 14 underwater preserves, marked for divers and regulated to prevent looting. At the Alger Underwater Preserve near Munising, nondivers can get a fascinating underwater look at century-old ships abandoned at the bottom of Munising Bay. Glass-bottom boats with large viewing wells glide right over the hulls and decks of wooden schooners, well preserved by Superior's clean and frigid water. Just a few feet under the glass, they silently slide into view like haunting historic paintings.

Canadian Gordon Lightfoot sang about the 29-man crew of the *Edmund Fitzgerald*, the freighter that sank in 1975 at the lake's east end off Whitefish Point: "The searchers all say they'd have made Whitefish Bay if they put 15 more miles behind her." The remote, windswept point is a fitting location for the Great Lakes Shipwreck Museum, which memorializes the dozens of vessels that failed to round it and reach the safety of the bay. The complex of renovated maritime buildings (some original, some relocated to the site) includes the museum—which displays the *Fitzgerald's* bronze bell—an 1861 light keeper's quarters, a fog signal building, a boathouse, theater, and a small inn housed in the 1923 Coast Guard crew quarters.

Of the handful of light keepers' homes in the Upper Peninsula that have been converted into B&Bs, the cliff-top, 14-room Big Bay Point Lighthouse B&B is perhaps the nicest. Several other Michigan lights are open to the public for visits, such as the Point Iroquois Light Station east of Whitefish Point where you can tour through the light keeper's home, then get a taste of his job by climbing the spiral stairway up the tower.

WHERE: Whitefish Point is 410 miles northwest of Detroit. *Visitor info:* Tel 800-562-7134 or 906-774-5480; uptravel.com. **GLASS BOTTOM SHIPWRECK TOUR:** Munising. Tel 906-387-4477; shipwrecktours.com. *When:* late May–Oct. **SHIPWRECK MUSEUM AND INN:** Paradise. Tel 888-492-3747 or 906-492-3747; shipwreckmuseum.com. *When:* May–Oct. *Cost:* from $125 (off-peak), from $150 (peak). **LIGHTHOUSE B&B:** Big Bay. Tel 906-345-9957; bigbaylighthouse.com. *Cost:* from $127. **BEST TIMES:** Apr for peak bird migration at Whitefish Point; July–Sept for weather.

Water, Water, Everywhere

TRAVERSE CITY & GRAND TRAVERSE BAY

Michigan

It's not tourism hyperbole to suggest that the waters of Lake Michigan's Grand Traverse Bay are as striking as the Caribbean. Cleaving into the ragged northwestern shore of the Lower Peninsula, this crystalline, sand-bottomed bay wows visitors with its shimmering, shifting bands of teal and turquoise.

The state of Michigan, hemmed in by four of the five Great Lakes—Michigan, Superior, Huron, and Erie (only Ontario is missing)—claims more than 3,200 miles of Great Lakes shoreline, which is more coast than the entire Atlantic seaboard. Thirty-mile-long Grand Traverse Bay is one of its most beautiful stretches, with resorts of every stripe and a wealth of water sports, "designer" golf, wineries, woods, and beautiful beaches.

Traverse City (population 15,000) anchors the region. It's a lively town meant for strolling on waterfront paths that string together marinas, parks, beaches, and other attractive public spaces. A block inland, Front and the surrounding downtown streets are filled with great shopping and dining at trendy spots and longtime institutions. Order fresh-from-the-lake perch at Sleder's Tavern and fresh-from-the-oven cherry pie at Grand Traverse Pie Co.

Not surprisingly, water activities take center stage here. Sailboats, fishing boats, and even a twin-masted tall ship ply the bay's West Arm. The shallower East Arm—on the other side of the Old Mission Peninsula that divides the bay—is lined with resorts.

Golf lures visitors with the same magnetic attraction as the water. The region parlays picturesque rolling terrain, plenty of water views, and an ideal summertime climate into an exceptional collection of more than 30 top-notch courses, including the famously humbling The Bear at the Grand Traverse Resort & Spa, designed by Jack Nicklaus. A surprising amount of agricultural land graces the area too, much of it given over to cherries and grapes. Drive out on the high ridgeline of the Old Mission Peninsula, and you'll be delighted by the sweeping water vistas and maze of orchards. The peninsula is responsible for three-quarters of the world's tart cherry crop, and the ubiquitous fruit appears in pancakes, ice cream, muffins, and pies—lots of pies.

Grapes thrive in the same climate, and today there are over 20 vineyards on the peninsula. The 65-acre estate of the Chateau Chantal is as idyllic a setting for its prizewinning wines as for its old-world B&B accommodations with lovely water views of both arms of Grand Traverse Bay.

Southwest of Traverse City, the renowned Interlochen Center for the Arts operates under a tall canopy of pines. Its gifted students give frequent concerts in the band shell next to Green Lake, which also hosts big-name national musical acts and theatrical performances from June through August—from ABBA to the Detroit Symphony Orchestra.

WHERE: 240 miles northwest of Detroit. *Visitor info:* Tel 800-872-8377 or 231-947-1120; traversecity.com. **GRAND TRAVERSE RESORT & SPA:** Acme. Tel 800-236-1577 or 231-534-6000; grandtraverseresort.com. *Cost:* rooms from $104 (off-peak), from $207 (peak);

greens fees from $45 (off-peak), from $65 (peak). **CHATEAU CHANTAL:** Tel 800-969-4009 or 231-223-4110; chateauchantal.com. *Cost:* from $169 (off-peak), from $195 (peak). **INTERLOCHEN CENTER FOR THE ARTS:** Interlochen. Tel 231-276-7200; interlochen.org.

BEST TIMES: mid-May for the Blessing of the Blossoms; June–Aug for Interlochen music performances; July for the National Cherry Festival (cherryfestival.org); Aug for Friday Nite Live, the music-filled block party on Front St.

A Paean to Consumer Consumption

MALL OF AMERICA

Bloomington, Minnesota

What wonders abound in this suburban shopping mall large enough to hold 32 Boeing 747s? For starters, you can plunge through the treetops on a roller coaster, take a virtual-reality submarine ride, get a degree, and even get married. Mall of America's (MOA) 500-plus stores, it turns out, simply provide the framework for a crazy compendium of attractions at this 5.6-million-square-foot monolith, the largest shopping mall in the U.S. (the West Edmonton Mall in Alberta, Canada, still gets top billing as the largest mall in North America) and Minnesota's No. 1 attraction. This four-story mega-mall lures more than 40 million visitors each year, a staggering statistic that tops the combined populations of North and South Dakota, Iowa, and Canada.

Mall of America opened in 1992 on the site of the old Metropolitan Stadium—where the Minnesota Twins and Vikings played. The Nickelodeon Universe occupies 7 acres in the center of the mall, comprising the world's first spinning roller coaster, a 74-foot-high Ferris wheel, and enough other adventures to make it the largest indoor theme park in the nation. Below the amusement park, a moving walkway transports visitors through Sea Life Minnesota Aquarium, its 1.2 million gallons home to sharks, sea turtles, piranhas, and the largest jellyfish exhibit in the world. Elsewhere you'll find a four-story LEGO Imagination Center, fighter jet flight simulators, a dinosaur

With more than 25 rides and attractions, the Park at MOA promises plenty of fun for the whole family.

museum, the Chapel of Love, bars and night-clubs in an entertainment district with live music on weekends, more than 50 restaurants from fast food to fancy, the National American University campus, and the Minnesota Children's Museum.

Oh, and the stores. Ironically, shopping may be the least interesting aspect of the MOA. Its 4.3 miles of storefronts feature many of the same names you'd find in a typical suburban shopping mall, just lots more of them. Remember to pace yourself—if you spent just ten minutes in each MOA store, it would take 86 hours to experience them all and you want to save some time for the attractions.

WHERE: 9 miles south of downtown Minneapolis. Tel 952-883-8800; mallofamerica.com. **BEST TIMES:** Nov and Dec, when Christmas shopping amid the decorations can actually be fun.

Where Minnesotans Go for R&R

BRAINERD LAKES

Brainerd, Minnesota

In a state that markets itself as the "Land of 10,000 Lakes," Brainerd well may be the centerpiece, both literally and otherwise. Located in the geographic center of Minnesota, the Brainerd Lakes area encompasses some 500 lakes (465 of them within 30 miles of Brainerd), not to mention the Mississippi River, several streams, an impressive array of challenging golf courses, and an inspiring network of more than 850 miles of hiking and biking trails. This appealing combination makes the region a classic Minnesota vacation area, whether tastes run to catching a trophy muskie or relaxing at a glamorous resort. In fact, so many Midwesterners spend "a week at the lake" here that Brainerd Lakes generates a healthy percentage of Minnesota's resort revenue.

Catch a sunset on the banks of one of the region's 465 lakes.

Several large century-old resorts still flourish, kept up to date with amenities like designer golf and full-service spas. You'll find a well-known pair on Gull Lake near Nisswa: Grand View Lodge and Madden's on Gull Lake each welcome guests with classic log cabins that exemplify north woods rustic elegance, flanked by championship courses challenging enough to test even scratch golfers. In all, the Brainerd Lakes area features 20 golf courses, all located within a 45-minute drive of each other.

Area lakes are renowned for walleye, largemouth bass, northern pike, and pan fish. Natural waterways link many of the lakes together in "chains," allowing boaters to travel among several without backtracking. Come winter, ice fishers are part of the culture here, either found sitting on an upturned bucket next to a hole cut in the ice or ensconced in an elaborate shanty decked out with propane heaters and electrical generators. Show up in January and join 10,000 other anglers for the Jaycees Ice Fishing Extravaganza on Gull Lake. On nearby Mille Lacs Lake, a temporary city called Frostbite Flats is erected each winter, with more than 5,000 shanties linked by plowed roads and shuttle service from area resorts.

BRAINERD: 135 miles northwest of Minneapolis. *Visitor info:* Tel 800-450-2838 or 218-829-2838; explorebrainerdlakes.com. **GRAND VIEW LODGE:** Nisswa. Tel 866-801-2951 or 218-963-2234; grandviewlodge.com. *Cost:* cabins from $128 without meals (off-peak), from $304 with breakfast, dinner, and golf (peak). **MADDEN'S:** Brainerd. Tel 800-642-5363 or 218-829-2811; maddens .com. *Cost:* from $164 (off-peak), from $270 (peak). **BEST TIMES:** Jan for the Jaycees Ice Fishing Extravaganza; mid-Apr for opening weekends at golf resorts; Sept for sunny days and few crowds.

Picture-Perfect Shoreline Along Superior's Big Blue

THE NORTH SHORE

Duluth to Grand Portage, Minnesota

Minnesotans understandably rate the land along Lake Superior's northwestern shore among its most precious real estate. This 150-mile stretch of rocky coastline is home to sweet waterfront villages and ten of Minnesota's finest state parks. Highway 61 links it all together, hugging the lakeshore and creating one of the nation's most acclaimed scenic drives. Though the area is busy with visitors and resorts, it remains untamed, sandwiched between the rugged Sawtooth Mountains of the Superior National Forest (see p. 550) and the wide, wild horizon of the world's largest freshwater lake.

Duluth is the southern gateway in the region, a busy shipping port of some 86,000 people that offers an array of charms for visitors—a parade of Great Lakes freighters passing beneath its iconic lift bridge, the handsomely refurbished waterfront, and several blocks of well-preserved 19th-century buildings along Superior Street, the downtown's main drag.

Travel north on Highway 61, though, and you quickly leave behind Duluth's small-city charms for the commanding scenery of Lake Superior. Twenty miles away, grab your camera to visit Split Rock Lighthouse, sitting atop a dramatic 170-foot bluff rising out of the lake.

Near Split Rock, the road begins skipping over one river after another, as they tumble from the Sawtooth Mountains over waterfalls and basalt ledges into Lake Superior. Many of the falls and river mouths are protected as state parks—including Gooseberry, Temperance, Waysides, Tettegouche, and Caribou Falls—offering plenty of hiking trails, overlooks, and access to Lake Superior beaches.

Northeast of Temperance, a trio of towns that have been dubbed the "Norwegian Riviera"—Tofte, Lutsen, and Grand Marais—are home to some of the region's best accommodations, including the Bluefin Bay Resort that mirrors a modern Norwegian fishing village, and the Lutsen Resort, a former 1885 Swedish homestead that still welcomes with Scandinavian charm, from its original lodge rooms to its newer villas, town houses, and cabins. Northeast of Grand Marais, Naniboujou Lodge looks at once perfectly north woodsy and oddly out of place. Built in the 1920s as an exclusive rustic retreat attracting the likes of Babe Ruth and Jack Dempsey, it has eye-popping orange, red, and blue interiors inspired by the Cree Indians, yet vaguely reflective of the era's art deco tastes. It's a captivating slice of history and a peaceful sanctuary on the Superior shore.

Completed in 1910, the 54-foot Split Rock Lighthouse offers sweeping views of Lake Superior below.

Grand Marais, with a year-round population of just 1,400, is the archetypal lakeside town, where sailboats rock gently in the harbor and unpretentious galleries and cafés sidle up alongside outfitters eager to help you organize a wilderness backpacking or paddling adventure. Grand Portage lies another 36 miles northeast, where Grand Portage National Monument commemorates an important rendezvous spot for French Canadian fur traders, with a reconstructed stockade and

displays of the voyageur's life. For fur traders it marked the beginning or end of a long journey. Today, Grand Portage marks the end of Minnesota's beloved North Shore. Get out your passport: The Ontario border and points north wait at the outskirts of town.

THE NORTH SHORE: 150 miles of Lake Superior shoreline. *Visitor info:* Tel 888-874-4866 or 651-296-5029; exploreminnesota.com. **BLUEFIN BAY RESORT:** Tofte. Tel 800-258-3346 or 218-663-7296; bluefinbay.com. *Cost:* from $119 (off-peak), from $185 (peak). **LUTSEN RESORT:** Lutsen. Tel 800-258-8736 or 218-206-8157; lutsenresort.com. *Cost:* from $79 (off-peak), from $119 (peak). **NANIBOUJOU LODGE:** Grand Marais. Tel 218-387-2688; naniboujou.com. *Cost:* from $100. *When:* mid-May–mid-Oct. **GRAND PORTAGE NATIONAL MONUMENT:** Grand Portage. Tel 218-475-0123; nps.gov/grpo. *When:* mid-May–mid-Oct. **BEST TIMES:** mid-July for Grand Marais Art Festival; early Aug for Fisherman's Picnic in Grand Marais; mid-Aug for Rendezvous Days and Powwow in Grand Portage and for Duluth's Bayfront Blues Festival (bayfrontblues.com).

An Immense Paddling Paradise Along the Canadian Border

BOUNDARY WATERS CANOE AREA WILDERNESS

Ely, Minnesota

More than 1,000 lakes—ranging from 10 to 10,000 acres each—are scattered throughout the piney woods along the Minnesota/Ontario border. On the Minnesota side lie 1 million protected acres of land known

as the Boundary Waters Canoe Area Wilderness, the largest U.S. wilderness preserve east of the Rockies. Ontario's Quetico Provincial Park encompasses another contiguous 1.2 million acres. It's an almost incomprehensibly vast lake country wilderness, with more than 1,200 miles of mapped canoe routes and not a single road. Free of cars, largely free of motorboats—even mostly free of planes in the airspace above—the BWCAW is truly a place that feels untouched by time.

For canoers, the Boundary Waters are an irresistible draw. You can paddle and portage (carry the canoe overland to the next lake) for days, weeks, even months, camping on the shores of a different lake every night, pulling fresh walleye or northern pike from its crystal clear waters for dinner. (The region's range of fish also includes smallmouth bass and lake trout.) The labyrinth of waterways was long used by the Ojibwa, then later by the French, Dutch, and British fur traders of the 17th century.

Boundary Waters is a pristine canoer's paradise.

Paddlers and anglers make the Boundary Waters the most heavily used wilderness area in the nation. Nevertheless, a strict permit system and the vastness of the area quickly disperses the humanity that sometimes bottlenecks at the designated entry points; once you dissolve into the wilderness, you'll more likely be among moose, loons—and the occasional wolf—than humans.

The wilds of northern Minnesota are the only places in the contiguous U.S. where the eastern timber wolf was not exterminated in the 1930s; today, more than 2,500 wolves still roam the woods here. Learn more at the International Wolf Center in Ely (pronounced EE-lee), filled with exhibits about wolf behavior and a variety of naturalist-run programs. Its highlight is the "ambassador pack" of four wolves (all born in captivity) that live in a 1.25-acre enclosure next to the center and can often be seen from large viewing windows.

Ely (population 3,500) is home base for outfitters ready to provide anything from basic gear rental to fully equipped week-long canoeing excursions into the backcountry. Come winter, Ely becomes dogsledding central. At Wintergreen Lodge, renowned polar explorer Paul Schurke offers lodge-to-lodge or camping dogsled trips across frozen Boundary Waters lakes and woods.

After several nights in the backcountry, treat yourself to a stay at the Burntside Lodge. Handsome log cabins, solidly built by expert local craftsmen, nestle in the woods at this early 20th-century lakefront resort. The Burntside is especially sought out for its excellent kitchen and wine list, an unexpected delight in this remote outpost.

WHERE: 100 miles northwest of Duluth. Tel 218-626-4300; bwca.com. *Ely visitor info:* Tel 800-777-7281 or 218-365-6123; ely.org. **How:** Williams & Hall Wilderness Guides & Outfitters, Ely. Tel 800-322-5837 or 218-365-5837; williamsandhall.com. *Cost:* from $118 per person for all-inclusive canoe/camping package. *When:* May–Sept. **INTERNATIONAL WOLF CENTER:** Ely. Tel 218-365-4695; wolf.org. **WINTERGREEN LODGE:** Ely. Tel 877-753-3386 or 218-365-6022; dogsledding.com. *Cost:* from $900 per person, 4-night lodge-to-lodge dogsledding package, all-inclusive. **BURNTSIDE LODGE:** Ely. Tel 218-365-3894; burntside.com. *Cost:* cabins from $165 (off-peak), from $215 (peak). *When:* mid-May–Sept. **BEST TIMES:** July–Aug for warmest weather; Sept for fall colors and fewer bugs.

A Legendary Backwoods Route to the Boundary Waters

THE GUNFLINT TRAIL & THE SUPERIOR NATIONAL FOREST

Grand Marais, Minnesota

The Superior National Forest in northeastern Minnesota is an outdoor person's dream, preserving a 150-mile-wide swath of glacial lakes, roiling rivers, and backcountry trails spiraling over the rounded Sawtooth Mountains. Better yet, it links two of Minnesota's natural jewels: Lake Superior's rocky North Shore to the east (see p. 547) and the renowned Boundary Waters Canoe Area Wilderness to the west (see p. 548). From mountain biking to birding to backpacking, there are few outdoor pursuits you *can't* enjoy here. And in the long winter months, it becomes nothing less than a wonderland.

From the North Shore between Tofte and Grand Marais, four well-marked and well-maintained roads delve into the forest: the Sawbill, Caribou, Gunflint, and Arrowhead Trails, former Indian footpaths offering easy access to endless lakes and trailheads. Best known is the Gunflint (aka County Road 12), which winds through the woods for 57 scenic miles from Grand Marais to the edge of the Boundary Waters at Saganaga Lake.

Among the many resorts that dot the well-traveled (and paved) Gunflint Trail for much of its length, the Gunflint Lodge was one of the first. Founded in the 1920s by local wilderness icon Justine Kerfoot and her mother, the year-round lodge artfully balances rustic charm and great-woods luxury, and is still proudly run by the Kerfoot family. Cottages, cabins, and lake homes hide among pines and birches overlooking Gunflint Lake along the Canadian border. Meals feature local fresh game and fish, along with locally harvested wild rice and maple syrup tapped in the area. The lodge's guides can outfit you for fishing, paddling, and camping trips, or lead excursions deep into the Boundary Waters wilderness.

Twenty-seven miles up the Gunflint Trail, the Bearskin Lodge provides yet another sublime year-round wilderness outpost, a scattering of cabins and townhomes tucked among the dense birches and pines on quiet Bearskin Lake. Paddle and portage from here and you can spend all summer without retracing your route. One of the nation's great footpaths, the 310-mile Superior Hiking Trail traverses Superior National Forest. It largely parallels Lake Superior, rising from lake level more than 1,000 feet to a high ridgeline. Shoulder a backpack for a classic multi-day adventure, sign on for a lodge-to-lodge hiking vacation, or simply set out for a stellar day of walking. One great segment: From the Gunflint Trail, hike west to Pincushion Mountain and along the rim of

The Gunflint Trail winds deep into vast forests of pine, birch, and aspen.

Minnesota's deepest canyon, where the Devil Track River slaloms through a gorge far below.

WHERE: Gunflint Trail begins in Grand Marais, 115 miles northeast of Duluth. **SUPERIOR NATIONAL FOREST:** Tel 218-626-4300. Ranger stations on Hwy. 61 in Tofte and Grand Marais. **GUNFLINT LODGE:** Tel 800-328-3325 or 218-388-2296; gunflint.com. *Cost:* from $129 (off-peak), from $249 (peak). **BEARSKIN LODGE:** Tel 800-338-4170 or 218-388-2292; bearskin.com. *Cost:* from $165 (off-peak), from $281 (peak). **SUPERIOR HIKING TRAIL:** Two Harbors. Tel 218-834-2700; shta.org. **HOW:** for lodge-to-lodge hiking arrangements, Boundary Country Trekking, Grand Marais: Tel 800-322-8327 or 218-388-4487; boundarycountry.com. *Cost:* from $445 per person for 3 nights. **BEST TIMES:** early June for Boreal Birding Days and Northern Landscapes Festival; Sept for fewer bugs.

The Wild Water Highway of the Fur Traders

VOYAGEURS NATIONAL PARK

International Falls, Minnesota

Stretching more than 50 miles along the Canadian border west of the Boundary Waters Canoe Area Wilderness (see p. 548), Voyageurs National Park remains almost as wild as it was three centuries ago, when French Canadian fur traders transported beaver pelts and other goods along this labyrinth of glacier-carved, island-studded lakes. Four enormous lakes—Rainy, Kabetogama, Namakan, and Sand Point—account for almost half the park's 218,000 acres, linked together by dozens of smaller lakes and waterways that would still look familiar to those grizzly old trappers. It is a completely water-based park, the only national park without a single road.

Roughly in the middle lies the 26-mile-long Kabetogama Peninsula, the park's largest landmass, home to beaver, black bear, moose, and the shy timber wolf. Hike the peninsula's 9-mile Cruiser Lake trail and you might be lucky enough to spot the rare paw print while immersing yourself in dense boreal forest.

Unlike the Boundary Waters, Voyageurs is open to motorized recreation, which means you'll hear the occasional hum of motorboats in summer and of snowmobiles when the lakes freeze over. To fully enjoy the park's natural richness, take advantage of the ranger-guided boat excursions, organized by the National Park Service. Offerings include wildlife cruises, canoe trips, and visits to the Kettle Falls Hotel, a 1910 historic landmark surrounded by wilderness and accessible only by boat or floatplane.

Thanks to a major renovation in 1988, the 20-room hotel and long screened porch now look much as they did when Kettle Falls was the rowdy center for gambling, boot-legging, and "fancy ladies." Spend a night or two, or boat over for a simple lunch (wild rice soup is a specialty): Boat shuttle service is available.

Voyageurs National Park is a mosaic of water and land.

Be sure to visit the bar, known for its off-kilter wooden floor and working nickelodeon that remain untouched by time.

Voyageurs has long been renowned for its fishing; these are considered some of the finest waters in the nation for walleye (Minnesota's state fish), smallmouth bass, and northern pike. Several resorts on the park's perimeter, like Sandy Point Lodge on Lake Kabetogama, offer boats with or without guide service. Houseboating is also exceptionally popular. Choose among several local charter companies and set out for any of the various houseboat campsites (complete with mooring buoys and a fire ring) found on many of the park's 1,200 islands.

Sea kayaks are a wonderful way to explore the park's smaller, protected waterways. Slip through narrow channels, accompanied only by the quiet dip of a paddle, the calling of a distant loon, and perhaps a bald eagle eyeing you from the treetops.

WHERE: 300 miles north of Minneapolis. Tel 218-283-6600; nps.gov/voya. **KETTLE FALLS HOTEL:** Tel 218-240-1724 (summer), 218-875-2070 (off-season); kettlefallshotel .com. *When:* May–mid-Oct. *Cost:* from $80. **SANDY POINT LODGE:** Ray. Tel 218-875-2615; sandypointlodge.com. *Cost:* from $105 (off-peak), from $200 (peak). **HOUSEBOATS:** Voyagaire Houseboats, Crane Lake. Tel 800-882-6287 or 218-993-2266; voyagaire.com. **KAYAKING:** Voyageurs Outfitters, International Falls. Tel 218-244-6506; voyageursoutfitters .com. *Cost:* kayak rental $30 per day. **BEST TIMES:** mid-May–Sept for prime walleye fishing; early June for peak bird migration; Sept–Oct for foliage.

An Urban Meander Through Verdant Parks and Parkways

GRAND ROUNDS NATIONAL SCENIC BYWAY

Minneapolis, Minnesota

Leave it to the outdoorsy city of Minneapolis to carve out a scenic urban drive like the Grand Rounds National Scenic Byway. A byway of this caliber and ambition typically runs through rural regions, but here some

Green space lines the Mississippi River and offers excellent skyline views.

50 miles of tree-lined parkways wander in a connect-the-dots loop around Minneapolis, linking many of the city's lakes, rivers, parks, and natural areas. Covering the whole route takes about three leisurely hours by car, and many visitors enjoy doing part of it by bike or on foot. True to the metro area's recreational ethic, a separate path parallels the road in many stretches for cyclists, runners, strollers, and—this being the heart of hockey country—in-line skaters.

The Grand Rounds is divided into seven distinct districts and includes more than 50 interpretive sites, from ancient Native American to bird sanctuaries. Together, the sites and routes help illustrate the natural heritage and human history of Minneapolis.

The Chain of Lakes district showcases one of Minneapolis's most endearing areas, where several interconnected lakes draw cyclists, skaters, and sailors in the shadow of the Minneapolis skyline. Parkways in the Mississippi River district skirt the river on both banks, offering dramatic vistas of the river gorge and the high bluffs that frame it.

Routes in the Downtown Riverfront district wend alongside city cafés, old flour mills, and working barges squeezing through locks as they haul grain and other commodities downriver. The Grand Rounds reveals an eclectic cross section of Minneapolis—urban and parklike, at work and at play—a diversity that is the essence of this unique city's appeal.

GRAND ROUNDS NATIONAL SCENIC BYWAY: Tel 612-230-6400; minneapolisparks.org. **BEST TIMES:** May for birding and spring flowers; Sept for fall colors along the Mississippi River.

Where Local Institutions Still Make Headlines and Waves

THE GUTHRIE THEATER & WALKER ART CENTER

Minneapolis, Minnesota

In a city already known for a lively arts scene, Minneapolis never stops showing the love. Year after year, the city continues its generous per capita support of civic culture, with several of its venerable theaters and art museums having undergone large expansions over the last few years.

Mention Minneapolis theater and the first name that springs to mind is the renowned Guthrie Theater. Acclaimed British theatrical director Sir Tyrone Guthrie founded the classical repertory company in 1963 in response to what he and others viewed as the commercialization of Broadway. The Tony Award–winning theater is a hallmark of the regional theater movement and enjoys a nationwide reputation for artistic excellence.

In 2006, the Guthrie made a major and controversial move from its original home next to the Walker Art Center to a $125 million, 285,000-square-foot complex across town on the banks of the Mississippi River. Designed by Jean Nouvel, celebrity architect of futuristic hotels, museums, and train stations around the world, the new Guthrie features the same

Spoonbridge and Cherry is one of the most important works in the sculpture garden at the Walker Art Center.

vibrant imagination, with a striking metal and glass exterior that evokes the silos and mills found along the Mississippi's working waterfront.

Another local art treasure is the Minneapolis Sculpture Garden, a 19-acre urban oasis, sidled up against the Walker Art Center and linked by a footbridge to lovely Loring Park. More than 40 modern-art sculptures fill the garden, including Coosje van Bruggen's whimsical *Spoonbridge and Cherry*, a 50-foot spoon topped with a water-fountain cherry that has become a Minneapolis icon. Other works include Frank Gehry's stunning *Standing Glass Fish*, along with pieces by notable sculptors from Henry Moore to Claes Oldenburg to Jenny Holzer. At press time, the garden is undergoing an intensive renovation that is scheduled for completion in summer 2017.

Next door, the Walker Art Center gleams with a 130,000-square-foot, $74 million addition completed in 2005 by the Swiss firm Herzog & de Meuron. This showstopper features a mesh skin of perforated aluminum panels rising from the street in a chunky, angular shape. The addition nearby doubles the exhibit space and allows for more of the permanent collections to be shown. The Walker, often considered the best contemporary art museum between the coasts, also boasts the McGuire Theater, home to contemporary music, theater, and dance.

GUTHRIE THEATER: Tel 612-377-2224; guthrietheater.org. **WALKER ART CENTER AND MINNEAPOLIS SCULPTURE GARDEN:** Tel 612-375-7600; walkerart.org.

Birthplace of Minnesota

ST. CROIX RIVER VALLEY

Pine, Chisago, and Washington Counties, Minnesota

I t's just 20 miles but a century away from modern Minneapolis to the bucolic river towns of the St. Croix River valley. Here steamboats and the mansions of lumber barons still look perfectly at home, and time seems to roll along at the easygoing pace of the river. Logs had already replaced furs as the St. Croix's lucrative cargo when the town of Stillwater was established in 1843. By 1850, the wealthy port town was the second largest city (after St. Paul) in Minnesota Territory, with 600 residents and grand Greek Revival and Italianate homes built by Scandinavian craftsmen. Today, Stillwater's population of 18,600 still embraces its river town heritage, and so do many Twin Cities visitors, who have made it a popular weekend getaway. An 1867 Italianate county courthouse—the state's oldest—presides over a turn-of-the-century Main Street lined with restaurants, galleries, and antiques shops. An abundance of 19th-century buildings now serve as museums and historic lodgings, while The Aurora Staples Inn, built in 1892 as the home of a wealthy merchant, offers atmospheric accommodations. Twelve miles south is the farming town of Afton, and the charming Afton House Inn, which has served as a hotel since 1867.

North of Stillwater, Highway 95 slaloms with the bends of the St. Croix as it wends through striking sandstone bluffs. The state's first Swedish immigrants settled in Scandia (the ancient name for Scandinavia), where the Gammelgarden Museum now preserves several early settlement buildings and each June residents celebrate Midsommar Dag (Midsummer's Day) with an arts and crafts festival and traditional foods.

Taylors Falls may be the region's prettiest town, with white clapboard homes perched on the bluffs over the deepening river valley and paddle wheelers churning past 100-foot sandstone cliffs. Highway 95 continues upriver to the St. Croix's wilder upper reaches; at the aptly named Wild River State Park, hiking trails weave along forested banks and swift-running waters.

STILLWATER: 20 miles east of Minneapolis/St. Paul. *Stillwater visitor info:* Tel 651-351-1717; discoverstillwater.com. *Taylors Falls visitor info:* Tel 715-843-3580; fallschamber .org. **AURORA STAPLES INN:** Tel 800-580-3092 or 651-351-1187; aurorastaplesinn.com. *Cost:*

from $159. **AFTON HOUSE:** Afton. Tel 651-436-8883; aftonhouseinn.com. *Cost:* from $110. **GAMMELGARDEN MUSEUM:** Scandia. Tel 651-433-5053. *When:* late Apr–mid-Dec. **TAYLORS FALLS SCENIC BOAT TOURS:** Tel 651-465-6315; wildmountain.com. *When:* early May–mid-Oct. **BEST TIMES:** May for the Rivertown Art Fair in Stillwater; mid-June for Midsommar Dag in Scandia; late Sept for foliage.

Wooded Bluffs and Winsome River Towns

RED WING & RIVER BLUFFS

Red Wing to Winona, Minnesota

Just southeast of the Twin Cities, the Mississippi takes on its signature grandeur, rolling strong and smooth between high bluffs of sandstone, from Red Wing to Winona. Some of Minnesota's oldest communities lie along its banks. These timeless river towns, which came into their own during the steamboating era, are linked by U.S. Highway 61, the northernmost segment of the 2,069-mile Great River Road (see p. 448) that shadows the Mississippi all the way to New Orleans.

Red Wing was surely one of the communities Mark Twain had in mind when he talked of stalwart Minnesota river towns built "with the air of intending to stay." Red Wing has indeed stayed, with a current population of some 16,000 residents. Handsome redbrick buildings line up for blocks, as clean and sturdy as they were in the 19th century, when the town prospered from shipping grain and milling flour. Tourism ranks as a key industry nowadays, and the proud buffed-up downtown and lovely location on a placid bend in the river delights visitors. The Red Wing Shoe Company, one of the town's oldest and largest employers, was the force behind much of the restoration, including the 1875 St. James Hotel (the city's finest lodging, with rooms named after riverboats). Pick up a historic walking tour brochure

at the visitor center—housed in a neat 1904 railroad depot—for other historic gems, including the grandiose Sheldon Theatre.

Downstream from Red Wing, the Mississippi yawns wide across the valley, its natural flow choked by silt deposited at the mouth of Wisconsin's Chippewa River. The resulting 22-mile-long bulge is known as Lake Pepin, where many sources believe waterskiing was invented. It most certainly was the

There are more than 100 sites on the National Historic Register in downtown Winona.

childhood playground of author Laura Ingalls Wilder, who drew from much of her pioneer life for her Little House books. Fans can visit a reconstructed cabin at her birth site across the river, near Alma, Wisconsin, or continue farther to DeSmet, South Dakota, the much-visited setting of five of her books (see p. 655).

A steamboat captain founded Winona, which quickly became a vital port, buzzing with sawmills fed by the surrounding forests and crowded with riverboats. The lumber industry helped it grow quickly, and by 1900 Winona had more millionaires per capita than almost any other place in the U.S. This wealth left its mark with a downtown of "Steamboat Gothic" architecture and lavish stained-glass windows, like the Tiffany Studios glass that glows in the 1916 Egyptian Revival Winona National Bank. At Levee Park, the Julius C. Wilkie Steamboat Center houses steamboat exhibits in a full-size replica steamboat. Stop by the Minnesota Marine Art Museum to view oil paintings, from late 18th-century British and American masters, depicting the twilight days of the great sailing ships.

RED WING: 50 miles southeast of Minneapolis. *Visitor info:* Tel 651-385-5934; redwing.org. *Winona visitor info:* Tel 800-657-4972 or 507-452-0735; visitwinona.com. **ST. JAMES HOTEL:** Red Wing. Tel 800-252-1875 or 651-388-2846; st-james-hotel.com. *Cost:* from $119 (off-peak), from $163 (peak). **MINNESOTA MARINE ART MUSEUM:** Winona. Tel 507-474-6626; mmam.org. **BEST TIMES:** mid-June for Steamboat Days, Winona; mid-Oct for fall colors and the Fall Festival of the Arts in Red Wing's historic district; Dec–Mar for eagle viewing.

Radio Show from a Midwestern Mark Twain

PRAIRIE HOME COMPANION

St. Paul, Minnesota

"It's been a quiet week in Lake Wobegon, my hometown up there on the edge of the prairie . . ." So began each endearing essay on small-town Minnesota life in this fictional town, a tale spun weekly by Garrison Keillor on the nationally syndicated public radio program *A Prairie Home Companion.* Minnesota native Keillor crafted a career as a Midwestern Mark Twain, making wry and witty observations about rural life on the radio show he began writing and performing in 1974.

Keillor retired in 2016, but with some adaptation, the show continues with musician and storyteller Chris Thile at the helm. The two-hour variety show—a mix of humorous essays, skits, and now with more emphasis on musical performances—is performed each Saturday afternoon in front of a live audience at St. Paul's Fitzgerald Theater. (Keillor played a role in renovating the ornate 1910 Schubert Theater and led efforts to rename it in honor of St. Paul's own F. Scott Fitzgerald.) The show is broadcast nationally on

New host Chris Thile sings with vocalist Sarah Jarosz on A Prairie Home Companion.

hundreds of public radio stations throughout the U.S., as well as on satellite radio, but it maintains a homespun feel.

WHERE: Fitzgerald Theater, 10 E. Exchange St. Tel 651-290-1200; fitzgeraldtheater.public radio.org. Ticket info, prairiehome.org.

The Coolest Celebration on Earth!

WINTER CARNIVAL

St. Paul, Minnesota

Get out your warmest long underwear, your insulated boots, maybe even that neoprene face mask. Minnesotans celebrate winter with an enthusiasm that would make most go numb, so it's only natural that

the capital city of St. Paul should host the oldest and most comprehensive winter celebration in the nation. The ten-day festival beginning in late January features ice carving, snow sculpting, snow sliding, ice-skating, hockey, dogsledding, sleigh riding, and a bounty of other frigid festivities at venues throughout downtown.

The winter extravaganza began in 1885, when a New York reporter proclaimed that St. Paul was "another Siberia, unfit for human habitation." St. Paul civic leaders responded with the carnival the following year to prove the locals' love of winter and a spirit unhindered by single-digit (and sometimes subzero) temperatures. It's been featured yearly ever since, making it one of America's longest-running civic events. Most famous on the roster are the "ice palaces" built from blocks of lake ice; the 1992 ice palace, the largest to date, stood 15 stories high and used 20,000 ice blocks. It topped the first one ever built in 1886, an astounding 14 stories high—the highest structure in St. Paul at the time. Because of the enormous expense of the undertaking, the palaces aren't erected every year, but they remain the very icon of the festival.

The annual carnival casts a spotlight on St. Paul, the oft-overshadowed Twin Cities sibling. In contrast with the steely skyline and stylish sophistication of neighboring Minneapolis, St. Paul is more sedate and stately,

A full moon presides over a colorful ice palace at St. Paul's Winter Carnival.

characterized by quiet neighborhoods, tree-lined boulevards, and a historic downtown punctuated with landmarks like the domed State Capitol and the immense Cathedral of St. Paul.

St. Paul's role as capital of the Minnesota Territory and its prominence as a wealthy 19th-century railroad hub is still in evidence along Summit Avenue, west of downtown, where blocks of opulent Victorian mansions stretch for more than 4 miles. A few of these Gilded Age relics are open for tours, including the 36,000-square-foot home of tycoon James J. Hill, builder of the Great Northern Railroad, and the 20-room English Tudor–style Governor's Residence.

Perhaps St. Paul's wealth provided some of the inspiration for *The Great Gatsby*. F. Scott

Fitzgerald grew up around the corner from Summit Avenue, a street he once described as "a mausoleum of American architectural monstrosities." Though his childhood home remains a private residence, the native son is honored by the Fitzgerald Theater, a renovated 1910 vaudeville palace and home of the weekly public radio program *A Prairie Home Companion* (see p. 556).

WHERE: Como Park, Rice Park, and other venues throughout downtown. Tel 651-223-4700; wintercarnival.com. *Visitor info:* Tel 800-627-6101 or 651-265-4900; visitsaintpaul.com. *When:* late Jan–early Feb.

Pigskin Pantheon

PRO FOOTBALL HALL OF FAME

Canton, Ohio

Built in 1963, the original complex of the Pro Football Hall of Fame echoes the modernist church architecture of the period, especially in its gleaming, football-shaped spire. This may not be a coincidence: Football is the nation's No. 1 spectator sport, and its most ardent fans approach professional games with the same fervor they bring to that other sacred Sunday ritual. The Hall of Fame is their cathedral, featuring relics from pro football's first century and, in the sanctum sanctorum, some 300 inductees immortalized in busts and displays. Even those who don't profess the football faith will recognize such figures as San Francisco 49ers quarterback Joe Montana, who was a household name in the 1980s (and the only player to win three Super Bowl MVP awards), or New York Giants halfback Frank Gifford from three decades earlier. A 7-foot bronze statue of Jim Thorpe occupies a central position at the entrance to the hall. Grandson of the famed warrior Chief Black Hawk, Thorpe grew up in Indian Territory in Oklahoma and was both a collegiate and pro football star—one of several sports he triumphed at as one of the most versatile athletes of all time. Inside the vast complex of galleries, fans can explore the history not just of the game, but also of the Super Bowl (first played in 1967), the NFL's 32 teams, and the various other leagues—especially the 1960s' American Football League—that have challenged the NFL's dominance over the years. Interactive displays invite visitors to test their trivia knowledge and their play-calling acumen, and three theaters—including the state-of-the-art Cinemascope-equipped Gameday Stadium—offer gridiron excitement in film and video.

Once a year, Canton becomes the epicenter of the pro football world when nearly 700,000 visitors gather for the Hall of Fame Festival, a ten-day pigskin extravaganza of parades, races, ribs, music, a hot-air balloon competition, a fashion show—and football, lots of football. The festival culminates in "Football's Greatest Weekend" in early August, when a new group of five or so greats is formally enshrined, and two teams selected by the league play the AFC-NFC Hall of Fame Game, the first preseason exhibition at Tom Benson Hall of Fame Stadium (across the street from the hall), where a crowd of screaming, cheering, hooting fans vocalize the nation's passion for its most beloved sport.

WHERE: 60 miles south of Cleveland; 2121 George Halas Dr. NW. Tel 330-456-8207; profootballhof.com. **BEST TIME:** late July–early Aug for the Hall of Fame Festival.

A Culinary Melting Pot

CINCINNATI CHILI

Cincinnati, Ohio

D on't mention this in Texas, but Cincinnati is widely regarded as the chili capital of the nation. Who knew? To the uninitiated, the city's version of the dish is one of the more peculiar gastronomic specialties to come out of the American melting pot: It's made of finely ground beef cooked with spices such as cinnamon and nutmeg, served over spaghetti with onions, kidney beans, Wisconsin cheese, and sometimes oyster crackers. Credit for the improbable dish goes to Athanas "Tom" Kiradjieff, a Macedonian Greek immigrant who arrived in Cincinnati in 1922 after a couple of years selling hot dogs in New York. With his brother John, he opened up a stand that sold "Coney Islands" or coneys—a nod to the dogs' New York origins—with a beef sauce seasoned Balkan-style. Likely taking a cue from pastitsio, the Greek pasta casserole, the Kiradjieffs began serving the sauce on spaghetti as well, and a food fad was born. Today chili is ubiquitous around Cincinnati, and its devotees order it two-way (chili and spaghetti), three-way (add grated cheese), four-way (add onions), or five-way, aka "the works" (add kidney beans).

Most of the chili parlors that dot the landscape of Greater Cincinnati are chain restaurants—the top two are Skyline and Gold Star—but legions of gastronomes swear by the stand-alone Camp Washington Chili. The funky, much-loved original restaurant was torn down in 2000, but a '50s-retro-styled new one sprang up just yards away, and patrons flocked back without missing a beat. Johnny Johnson, the Greek immigrant who started working at Camp Washington Chili in 1951 and bought it in the '70s, still runs the place with his wife, Antigone, making 60 gallons of Cincinnati's signature sauce and serving it over spaghetti and coneys 24 hours a day for those with 4 A.M. cravings.

Ethnicity and food have long played a role in the city's mosaic of history and culture. Cincinnati celebrates one of the main ingredients of its own vibrant melting pot—a rich German heritage—every September at Oktoberfest-Zinzinnati, the largest Oktoberfest in the U.S. Modeled after Munich's famous fair, Cincinnati's version also features lots of music, lederhosen, and copious beer and food. Half a million visitors consume over 80,000 bratwurst, 3,600 pounds of sauerkraut, and 700 pounds of Limburger cheese, to give just a small sampling of the menu; then they burn off the calories dancing to "The Chicken Dance," a popular German heritage tune from the 1970s. When 48,000 people participated in 1994, *Guinness World Records* anointed it the World's Largest Chicken Dance.

CAMP WASHINGTON CHILI: Tel 513-541-0061; campwashingtonchili.com. *Cost:* $6.30 for a five-way. *When:* Closed Sun. **OKTOBERFEST-ZINZINNATI:** oktoberfestzinzinnati.com. *When:* 3rd full weekend in Sept.

Camp Washington Chili's Johnny Johnson is committed to a lifetime of doing what he loves best.

CINCINNATI FLOWER SHOW & CINCINNATI MAY FESTIVAL

Cincinnati, Ohio

Winston Churchill reportedly called it America's most beautiful inland city, and in spring it's hard to argue: Cincinnati celebrates the season appropriately, in bloom and in song. In late April, the city hosts the Cincinnati Flower Show, the only exhibition of its kind on the continent endorsed by Britain's Royal Horticultural Society, the plantsman's Vatican. Produced by the Cincinnati Horticultural Society on the banks of the Ohio River at Yeatman's Cove Park—a new venue since the event was relaunched in 2015—it's fashion week for the horticulture set: Breeders unveil new specimens and the air is abuzz with talk of the latest trends and new colors.

Visions of Eden in miniature are everywhere in dozens of theme gardens, including single-genus displays devoted to specific plants such as hostas and geraniums. A show-within-a-show gives amateur gardeners an opportunity to strut their stuff, and other exhibits feature exquisite floral arrangements, table settings, and plants in interior design. The six-day schedule is jam-packed, with an opening gala, luncheons, lectures, and the "Spring Fling," a huge to-do for Cincinnati party people.

The city welcomes visitors again a month later, to the Cincinnati May Festival, the oldest continuously held choral festival in the Western Hemisphere. Established in 1873, the festival grew out of Cincinnati's Saengerfests, gatherings of German singing societies from around the region. Historic Music Hall, one of the country's oldest and largest concert venues, was built to house the event five years later. The May Festival Chorus was founded in 1873, and the illustrious Cincinnati Symphony Orchestra became part of the festival not long after its formation in 1895.

The Cincinnati Flower Show is a burst of color, with blooming plants from top-notch horticulturalists.

Premieres have long been a staple—including Gustav Mahler's *Symphony No. 3* and Benjamin Britten's *Gloriana*—and today the May Festival has few peers when it comes to presenting large-scale choral and orchestral works featuring world-class performers and soloists. The two consecutive weekends of concerts at Music Hall attract music lovers from all over the world.

CINCINNATI FLOWER SHOW: 705 East Pete Rose Way. Tel 866-568-5189 or 513-677-2799; cincinnatihorticulturalsociety.com. *Cost:* $20. *When:* 6 days in late Apr. **CINCINNATI MAY FESTIVAL:** Music Hall, 1241 Elm St. Tel 513-621-1919; mayfestival.com. *Cost:* single concert $15. *When:* 5 days over the last 2 weekends in May. **WHERE TO STAY:** Cincinnatian Hotel, tel 800-942-9000 or 513-381-3000; cincinnatian hotel.com. *Cost:* from $159 (off-peak), from $229 (peak).

Museum in the Promised Land

NATIONAL UNDERGROUND RAILROAD FREEDOM CENTER

Cincinnati, Ohio

The Roebling Suspension Bridge over the narrow Ohio River, built in 1867 as a handsome prelude to Roebling's Brooklyn Bridge, spans the two states of Kentucky and Ohio that used to represent two worlds, slave and free.

Today it points north directly at the National Underground Railroad Freedom Center, which opened just steps away in 2004 to commemorate the slaves—as many as 100,000—who fled north across the river to safety in the decades leading up to the American Civil War, and the network of abolitionists, former slaves, and others who helped them. The location is powerfully symbolic: The Ohio was likened to the River Jordan in those days, and Cincinnati, with a large African American population in the abolitionist state of Ohio, was one of the most important cities in the Promised Land.

Designed by the late Indianapolis architect Walter Blackburn, the grandson of slaves, the Freedom Center is a bold, technologically advanced work of architecture. The museum's most imposing and haunting artifact is a two-story slave trader's pen, built in 1830, that used to stand on a farm in Kentucky where men, women, and children would be held in shackles for days or even months at a time before auctions. Also on display are such items as wanted posters, abolitionists' diaries, and a replica of the wooden crate that Henry "Box" Brown, a burly 200-pound escaped slave, used to mail himself from Virginia to freedom in Pennsylvania. Another gallery tells the stories of central figures in the Underground Railroad, and an inspirational film, *Brothers of the Borderland*, plays in one of two theaters. There are tributes to Harriet Tubman, an escaped slave herself and "underground railroad conductor," who would return to the South 19 times to help more than 300 others escape.

Part of the center's mission is to promote the same kind of awareness and activism that animated the antislavery forces before the Civil War. To that end it also includes interactive exhibits on contemporary themes. Finally, there is a Family Search Center with names of more than 480,000 freed slaves, allowing visitors to trace their roots and hopefully understand better from where and from whom they come.

WHERE: 50 East Freedom Way. Tel 877-648-4838 or 513-333-7500; freedomcenter.org. *When:* closed Sun–Mon.

The National Underground Railroad Freedom Center displays large-scale quilts by artist Aminah Brenda-Lynn Robinson that depict important moments in African American history.

High Culture and Horticulture in an Oasis of Learning

CLEVELAND MUSEUM OF ART & THE BOTANICAL GARDEN

Cleveland, Ohio

A short drive east of downtown Cleveland, University Circle is one of the brainiest, artsiest, most culturally connected of all university districts: The square mile surrounding prestigious Case Western Reserve University and the adjacent Wade Park is home to dozens of world-class institutions including schools, museums, a hospital, and performing arts venues. At the heart of University Circle's refined setting is a true gem, the Cleveland Museum of Art. After an eight-year, $350-million-dollar renovation and expansion that was completed in 2013, it is one of the country's top-drawer repositories of art and culture.

What began with the modest first acquisition of an embroidered lace collar in 1914 has grown into a renowned collection of nearly 45,000 pieces, remarkable for it uncommon depth and breadth. On the front steps is a large cast of Rodin's *The Thinker*, damaged by a pipe bomb in 1970 and left unrestored. Inside the vast Beaux-Arts building are scores of galleries featuring 6,000 years of art from around the world, including especially fine Asian and pre-Columbian collections; Egyptian pieces acquired by Howard Carter, an agent for the museum who later went on to discover King Tut's tomb in 1922; and a medieval Armor Court bristling with all manner of weapons, a particular favorite of young visitors. Among the European and American works are objects from the famous collection of medieval German relics known as the Guelph Treasure; decorative arts by the likes of Louis Comfort Tiffany; and masterpieces from such revered painters as Nicolas Poussin (*The Holy Family on the Steps*) and Joseph Mallord William Turner (*Burning of the Houses of Parliament*).

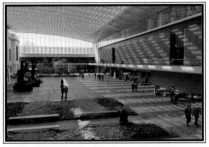

The Cleveland Museum of Art boasts a beautiful new atrium designed by Rafael Viñoly.

Across the street from this temple of man-made art is the 10-acre Cleveland Botanical Garden, which, in 2003, opened its spectacular 18,000-square-foot Glasshouse, where you can experience two captivating and wildly different environments. One, devoted to the otherworldly spiny desert of Madagascar, features North America's largest collection of baobabs, along with myriad wondrous, endangered plants indigenous to the remote, ecologically rich island of Madagascar; the other, a re-creation of a Costa Rican cloud forest, has more than 50 species of butterflies sharing the air with colorful birds, and a 25-foot-high canopy walk that offers lofty views of the lush greenery below. Gardens in many styles cover 10 acres outside the Glasshouse, including one of the nation's finest public herb gardens, with more than 3,500 plants representing some 300 species, and the hands-on Hershey Children's Garden, which offers such kid-friendly trappings as a giant tree house and dwarf forests. The gardens' integration-in-progress with the Holden Arboretum (see p. 566) in nearby Kirtland will form the 13th largest public garden in the U.S. **CLEVELAND MUSEUM OF ART:** 11150 East Blvd. Tel 216-421-7350; clevelandart.org. *When:* closed Mon. **CLEVELAND BOTANICAL GARDEN:** 11030 East Blvd. Tel 888-853-7091 or 216-721-1600; cbgarden.org. *When:* closed Mon. **BEST TIMES:** Feb–May for blooms and Orchid Mania; Christmastime for decorations at the Botanical Garden.

Alive with the Sound of Music

ROCK AND ROLL HALL OF FAME AND MUSEUM

Cleveland, Ohio

I. M. Pei admitted to knowing little about the music in question when he was chosen to design Cleveland's Rock and Roll Hall of Fame on the shores of Lake Erie. After a bit of remedial listening he set out to create a building that would embody rock's brash dynamism, and came up with a seven-story set of architectural power chords incorporating several of his signature elements: cantilevered spaces, angular masses clad in stark white tile, and a vast, pyramidlike glass atrium. Dedicated in 1995, it is the ideal home for the living heritage of rock and a bold showcase for a music genre that continues to impact our global culture.

Exhibits and interactive hands-on displays, many with sound and thought-provoking videos

The museum's drum-shaped tower houses an exhibit showcasing the Hall of Fame's inductees.

and films, pay tribute to the music and the people behind it: performers, songwriters, disc jockeys, producers, and others. The permanent collection contains more than 20,000 artifacts in dizzying variety—thousands of instruments and stage costumes from the likes of Jimi Hendrix and Iggy Pop, naturally, but also loads of quirky items, such as Jim Morrison's Cub Scout uniform and Elvis Presley's draft card. Janis Joplin's 1965 Porsche and ZZ Top's 1934 Ford coupe, the Eliminator, are on display, as are handwritten lyrics by Hank Williams and John Lennon and school report cards for John Lennon, the Everly Brothers, and legendary drummer Keith Moon of The Who ("shows promise in music").

Cleveland is hardly the hub of the music industry, and indeed the hall's highest-profile event, the annual induction ceremony, usually takes place in New York. But it's rich in rock history: It was in Cleveland that radio disc jockey Alan Freed, who is credited with coining the term "rock and roll," broke racial boundaries with his broadcasts and put on the country's first rock concert, the original Moondog Coronation Ball in 1952. By the time the Hall of Fame opened in 1995, it had become a catalyst for the renewal of a downtown that had been a famous example of urban decline. It symbolizes not just the energy of rock and roll, but the energy of the new Cleveland as well. Ohio claims a "Hall of Fame Corridor," and this is its northern cap: The National Inventors' Hall of Fame can be found in Akron and the hugely popular Pro Football Hall of Fame in Canton (see p. 558).

Where: 1100 Rock and Roll Blvd. Tel 216-781-ROCK; rockhall.com.

Geologic Drama in the Wild Midwest

HOCKING HILLS

Ohio

B etween Columbus and the Ohio River to the southeast lies a set of scenic wonders little known outside this part of the Midwest. Hocking Hills comprises several state parks and reserves where spectacular rock formations are cloaked in dense forest that goes Technicolor in autumn. Cliffs, gorges, and caves were created here as glaciers and running water scoured sandstone laid down in an ancient river delta over 330 million years ago, creating a natural magnet for those today in search of a chance to hike, canoe, rock-climb, and rappel, even catch a ride on the Hocking Valley Scenic Railroad.

Several of the area's most dramatic formations are gathered in the Hocking Hills State Park, at the center of the region. At the southern end of the park is the horseshoe-shaped Ash Cave, a huge rock shelter 700 feet long and 100 feet deep that is Ohio's largest recess cave, with evidence of prehistoric inhabitants; a tributary of Queer Creek pours

A bridge crosses over the upper falls by Old Man's Cave.

over the cave rim 90 feet from the floor. Old Man's Cave to the north, named after a hermit who supposedly lived in it two centuries ago (and is buried on the site), is a smaller version but perhaps the park's most frequented site, with seven different hiking routes from easy to intermediate leading to it through undisturbed woods and ravines. At the northern end of the park is Rock House, a 200-foot tunnel along a sandstone cliff face with enormous window-like openings carved out over time by water erosion. Among the highlights outside the park is the natural bridge at Rockbridge State Nature Preserve, a stunning span of more than 100 feet that stands 50 feet above the bottom of a gorge. Everywhere, hiking and horse trails meander through the hills, including a stretch of the Buckeye Trail, a 1,435-mile circuit trail that loops all around the state.

For a window into the life of the pioneers who settled here in the foothills of the Appalachians, Robbins Crossing, a village of early 19th-century log cabins complete with antique tools and furnishings, features interpreters in period garb who demonstrate such activities as blacksmithing, cooking, herb gardening, and lace making. Stay at the Inn & Spa at Cedar Falls, a 75-acre spread romantically nestled into a forest setting surrounded on three sides by the state park. In addition to a nine room lodge, there are five historic renovated cabins, newer cottages, a spa, and an atmospheric restaurant housed in an 1840s log cabin.

WHERE: Park headquarters are in Logan, 50 miles southeast of Columbus. Tel 800-HOCKING; hockinghills.com. **HOCKING VALLEY**

SCENIC RAILROAD: Nelsonville. Tel 740-753-9531; hvsry.org. *When:* Sat–Sun, late May–Oct. **ROBBINS CROSSING:** Nelsonville. Tel 877-462-5464 or 740-753-6344; hocking.edu/attractions/robbinscrossing. *When:* Sat–Sun, late May–Oct. **INN & SPA AT CEDAR FALLS:** Logan. Tel 800-653-2557 or 740-385-7489; innatcedar falls.com. *Cost:* from $169. **BEST TIMES:** fall for foliage; mid-Jan for Winter Hike.

Out of Place, Out of Time

OHIO'S AMISH COUNTRY

Holmes County, Ohio

Ohio's rural eastern region around Holmes County is home to the world's greatest concentration of Amish settlements. Often misunderstood and romanticized for their culture of peace and simplicity, the Amish are the most conservative of the Anabaptists who fled persecution in Europe and established flourishing farm communities in North America, beginning in the early 18th century. Following the biblical admonition to "Come out from among them and be ye separate," they avoid the ways of outsiders—whom they call the "English"—including, in varying degrees from group to group, modern technology (although the odd cell phone is not a complete rarity). Ohio's Amish country is a rolling pastoral landscape of family farms, one-room schoolhouses (each never more than a 3-mile walk for any student), plain dress, and black horse-drawn buggies.

The heart of eastern Ohio's 36,000-strong Amish community is the township of Berlin (accent on the first syllable), where the Amish & Mennonite Heritage Center introduces visitors to the sect's religious and historical background. The main attraction is *Behalt* ("To Remember"), a 10-by-265-foot cyclorama that depicts the course of Amish and Mennonite history, from grisly scenes of martyrdom to bucolic barn-raisings. Not far from town is Yoder's Amish Home, which offers buggy rides and guided tours of two 19th-century farmhouses, an Amish one-room schoolhouse, and a huge barn full of various animals sure to delight kids. A few miles north, in Kidron, the weekly livestock auction has been drawing English and Amish alike since 1923. After the excitement, drop by Lehman's, the famous general store that is a sort of Amish one-stop-shopping with a buggies-only section in the parking lot, and shelves inside stocked with high-quality, old-fashioned tools, toys, and nonelectric appliances (think butter churns, gas refrigerators, and oil lamps).

Travelers can follow the 160-mile Amish Country Scenic Byway, a series of 25 east-west and north-south routes through the center of the mostly agricultural county, or just head out on their own. In small towns with names like Charm and Mount Hope, crafts stores, antiques shops, farmers markets, and flea markets abound and plenty of restaurants beckon with hearty, often German-influenced fare.

On the eastern edge of Amish country, and on one of the obscure back roads of American history, is another picturesque village founded by religious separatists: Germans escaping

Lutheran persecution founded Zoar in 1817, taking the name from the place where Lot took refuge after fleeing Sodom. After a period of prosperity, the commune disbanded in 1898, and today Zoar's population is just 169, most of the residents direct descendants of those first settlers. Many of the fine historic buildings have been preserved as Historic Zoar Village, where visitors can take guided tours and costumed interpreters give crafts and cooking demonstrations.

WHERE: Berlin is 73 miles south of Cleveland. *Visitor info:* Tel 877-643-8824 or 330-674-3975; visitamishcountry.com. **AMISH & MENNONITE HERITAGE CENTER:** Berlin. Tel 877-858-4634 or 330-893-3192; behalt.com. *When:* closed Sun. **YODER'S AMISH HOME:** Millersburg. Tel 330-893-2541; yodersamish home.com. *When:* closed Sun, late Apr–Oct. **LEHMAN'S:** Kidron. Tel 800-438-5346 or 330-828-8828; lehmans.com. *When:* closed Sun. **WHERE TO STAY:** The 90-room Inn at Honey Run, Millersburg. Tel 800-468-6639

A typical scene in Ohio's Amish country: A man drives his horse and plow in Holmes County.

or 330-674-0011; innathoneyrun.com. *Cost:* from $149 (off-peak), from $179 (peak). **AMISH COUNTRY SCENIC BYWAY:** byways.org. **HISTORIC ZOAR VILLAGE:** Tel 800-262-6195 or 330-874-3011; historiczoarvillage.com. *When:* stores closed Jan–Feb; open Fri–Sun, Mar; Wed–Sun, Apr–Dec. **BEST TIMES:** spring for baby animals at Yoder's; fall for harvest; weekly livestock auction Thurs in Kidron.

The Hardy Eden of the Western Reserve

HOLDEN ARBORETUM

Kirtland, Ohio

In 1912, mining executive Albert Fairchild Holden, a scion of Cleveland society, had intended to bestow some of his vast fortune on Harvard University's esteemed Arnold Arboretum, but his sister, Roberta Holden Bole, argued that the Cleveland area should have an arboretum of its own. Holden agreed, and when he died in 1913, he left a trust to provide for the establishment of an arboretum in memory of his daughter Elizabeth, who had died at age 12. From its original site—100 acres in Kirtland Township donated by Bole and her husband in 1931—Holden Arboretum has grown to 3,600 acres in the stretch of northeastern Ohio known as the Western Reserve. In 2014, it initiated a period of integration with the nearby Cleveland

Botanical Garden (see p. 562), and as the arboretum celebrated its 85th birthday in 2016, it was lushly evident that this massive Eden had taken root and is flourishing in its prime.

The arboretum specializes in woody plants hardy enough to thrive in the climatic extremes of northern Ohio, not far from the Lake Erie shore, interestingly mixed with an abundance of specimens from similar climes in China, Korea, and other far-flung places—a vast collection of more than 19,000 plants. Among Holden's trees are magnolias, conifers, maples, and nut trees, and yes, there are even a few Ohio buckeyes (a cousin of the horse chestnut) scattered about. The arboretum is not made up of trees alone: A blanket of blooms, season by season, includes more than 260 lilac bushes and a nearly equal number of showy viburnum shrubs, 280 crabapple trees, 800 perennials, 10,000 spring bulbs, and the famed rhododendron garden: more than 1,200 specimens spread beneath a canopy of mature maple, oak, and beech trees, with azaleas, witch hazels, mountain laurels, heaths, and heathers thrown in for good measure. There is a wildflower garden; a garden created to attract butterflies and hummingbirds; and even a hedge collection, with 27 specimens that may awaken your inner Edward Scissorhands.

Trails wind all over the place, and the arboretum offers guided hikes through Stebbins Gulch and Little Mountain, two unique natural sites on the arboretum grounds designated as National Natural Landmarks by the National Park Service. The many classes and tours extend even into the cold days of late winter. Visitors can trudge through the snow in the arboretum's Bicknell sugarbush (sugar maple forest) to see a local Amish family (eastern Ohio has the world's largest Amish community; see p. 565), contracted by the arboretum, tapping trees and making maple syrup in a timeless vignette.

WHERE: 28 miles northeast of Cleveland; 9500 Sperry Rd. Tel 440-946-4400; holden arb.org. *When:* daily. **BEST TIMES:** early Mar for the Sugarbush Trail; Apr–May for blooming magnolias, azaleas, lilacs, and rhododendrons; summer months for the butterfly garden and a cool escape; Oct for spectacular foliage along the Leaf Trail.

A Charming Riverboat Town and a Covered Bridge Byway

MARIETTA

Ohio

Settlers made a first foothold at the confluence of the Ohio and Muskingum rivers in 1788, when "Northwest Territory" meant not the remote Canadian arctic but a vast area west of Pennsylvania stretching to the Mississippi.

In recognition of France's assistance in the recent Revolutionary War, they called the new rivertown Marietta, after the French queen Marie Antoinette. The town fared better than she did: The introduction of steamboats in 1811, and the local discovery of oil 50 years later, fueled a century-long boom, and today the small and once affluent Marietta is a handsome, leafy riverside town of Victorian homes that wears its history proudly.

Its oldest attractions go back over 2,000 years—earth mounds constructed by a culture known as the Adena that may date to as far back as 500 B.C. The most prominent is the 30-foot Conus Mound at Mound Cemetery downtown, where many of the city's founders occupy graves nearby. On the site of the town's first settlement is the Campus Martius Museum, which incorporates Ohio's oldest residence, the house of General Rufus Putnam, friend of George Washington and leader of the first group of 48 settlers from New England.

A three-minute stroll to the Ohio River Museum will enlighten visitors about the Golden Age of Steamboats through models and artifacts and a chance to board the 1918 *W. P. Snyder Jr.*, the nation's only remaining stern-wheeled steam towboat, moored just outside. Much of the downtown is on the National Historic Register, including the distinctive triangular Lafayette Hotel, one of the country's most atmospheric riverboat-era hotels still operating. Built in 1918 on the site of a former hotel, the Lafayette offers smallish Victorian-style guest rooms (most with river views), but its charm quotient is high, particularly in the convivial Riverview Lounge. It also houses the city's best-known restaurant, the Gun Room, where a collection of 16 antique long rifles adorns the walls.

Marietta is the jumping-off point for the Covered Bridge Scenic Byway, which meanders through 50 miles of pine-and-hardwood-covered hills along the Little Muskingum River in Wayne National Forest. The bridges that provide the main attraction were covered to protect their valuable deck timbers from the elements, and also provided a moment's relief for horse-and-buggy travelers in foul weather, and for locals to meet and, maybe, court and spark, hence the endearing term "kissing bridges." Ohio is second in the nation in the number of covered bridges still standing (150); the three along this scenic byway were first built between 1871 and 1887 (though one was washed away and rebuilt several times since then). Enjoy the grace and slow pace of this lovely stretch of the Ohio River Valley, dotted with 19th-century barns with Mail Pouch Tobacco ads painted across their sides and old oil rigs that still cough up the odd barrel.

WHERE: 124 miles southeast of Columbus. *Visitor info:* Tel 800-288-2577 or 740-373-5178; mariettaohio.org. **CAMPUS MARTIUS MUSEUM:** Tel 800-860-0145 or 740-373-3750; campusmartiusmuseum.org *When:* closed Sun. **OHIO RIVER MUSEUM:** Tel 800-860-0145 or 740-373-3750; campusmartiusmuseum.org. *When:* Mon, Wed–Sun, Apr–Labor Day; Sat–Sun, Sept–Oct. **LAFAYETTE HOTEL:** Tel 800-331-9336 or 740-373-5522; lafayettehotel.com. *Cost:* from $65; dinner in the Gun Room $30. **COVERED BRIDGE SCENIC BYWAY:** byways.org. **BEST TIMES:** mid-Mar for the River City Blues Festival; mid-Sept for Ohio River Sternwheel Festival; Oct for foliage.

Ohio Archipelago

LAKE ERIE ISLANDS

Northern Ohio

A n archipelago in Ohio? Yes, indeed. The Erie Islands are a little archipelago stretching north from the Marblehead Peninsula across the placid waters of Lake Erie, the warmest and most southern of the Great Lakes. Each of the four larger islands on the U.S. side of the border entices with its own character and distinctive attractions.

The charming lakeshore town of Port Clinton (known as the Walleye Capital of the World) is a favorite jumping-off point for the islands, and you can also catch ferries from the mainland towns of Catawba Island, Marblehead, and Sandusky. Some ferries will take your car, but bicycles and golf carts are the favored forms of travel once you arrive on these small islands.

South Bass is the island nearest to the mainland, and its village of Put-in-Bay is the islands' closest thing to a tourist hot spot; a party-hearty culture in the bars around the marina erupts at the height of summer. The town is the home of historic Heineman's Winery, a focal point of the area's recently resurgent wine industry. American varieties such as Catawba have been successful histori-cally, and frozen-harvested ice wines are emerging as Ohio's viticultural claim to fame.

The town also boasts the most massive Doric column in the world, the 352-foot Perry's Victory and International Peace Memorial, which commemorates the Battle of Lake Erie in the War of 1812 and the postwar friendship that endures between America and the British. An observation deck at the top provides a sweeping panorama of the lake and surrounding islands.

With an off-season population just above 300, quiet Kelleys Island to the east is the largest of the American Lake Erie islands and the only island in the U.S. to be designated in the National Register of Historic Places. It offers intriguing views of the distant past at Inscription Rock, a slab featuring Native American petroglyphs 400 to 800 years old, and at Kelleys Island State Park, where a retreating glacier scoured an awesome 400-foot-long chute in the limestone bedrock, creating one of the world's deepest and oldest glacial grooves. The pace of daily life is slow and quiet on Middle Bass and North Bass islands; the state of Ohio purchased most of the latter in 2003 and is in the process of restoring its natural habitat for low-impact recreation. Natural features are a strong draw

all over the islands, attracting birders and fishermen along with sailors and kayakers.

For less serene pursuits, you needn't go any farther than Cedar Point, a sprawling lakefront amusement park renowned as the Roller-Coaster Capital of the World. Located on the mainland on a peninsula north of Sandusky, it thrills riders on 18 coasters, including the wooden 1964 Blue Streak. The brand-new Valravn is the world's tallest, fastest, and longest dive coaster.

WHERE: in Lake Erie, 70 miles west of Cleveland. **HEINEMAN'S WINERY:** Put-in-Bay, South Bass. Tel 419-285-2811; heinemans winery.com. *When:* Apr–late Oct. **PERRY'S VICTORY AND INTERNATIONAL PEACE MEMORIAL:** Put-in-Bay, South Bass. Tel 419-285-2184; nps .gov/pevi. *When:* daily, mid-May–Oct. **KELLEYS ISLAND STATE PARK:** Tel 419-746-2546; parks .ohiodnr.gov/kelleysisland. *When:* Apr–Oct. **CEDAR POINT AMUSEMENT PARK:** Sandusky. Tel 419-627-2350; cedarpoint.com. *When:* daily, May–Sept; Fri–Sun, Sept–Oct. **BEST TIMES:** spring and fall for birding and fishing; 3rd weekend in July for Kelleys Island Island Fest.

Enigmatic Snake in the Grass

SERPENT MOUND

Peebles, Ohio

The Ohio River Valley was a focal point of the mound-building cultures of prehistoric North America, and even though untold numbers of the area's earthworks were lost to the plow or to development, many impressive

examples remain across central and southern Ohio. The best-known and most intriguing of all is Serpent Mound, the largest effigy earthwork in the world, believed to have been constructed around 1070 and preserved today above Brush Creek near the small farm town of Peebles.

Like its bearish counterparts at Effigy Mounds National Monument in Iowa (see p.

517), Serpent Mound is a representation of an animal significant to the ancient people who made it, in this case a stylized snake 20 feet wide and 1 to 5 feet high, writhing sinuously a quarter-mile long. At its front is a mysterious large oval, perhaps the eye or head itself, or possibly something—an egg? the sun?—that the snake is about to devour with open jaws. The mound's meaning and origins remain a

The Serpent Mound is believed by some to link back to the Cherokee legend of the Uktena, a large supernatural serpent.

mystery, though unlike many earthworks of the Midwest, it is not believed to be a burial mound, and it almost certainly had an astronomical purpose: The eastward curves of the body point to sunrise locations at solstices and equinoxes, and the head to sunset on the summer solstice. It is impossible to say whether it was also meant as a work of art, but it is as elegant and striking as Robert Smithson's far more contemporary *Spiral Jetty* in Great Salt Lake, Utah (see p. 798).

The nearby Serpent Mound Museum features exhibits on the various mysteries of the earthwork, the process of its construction (the form laid out in rocks and clay, then dirt piled on top basketful by basketful), and the geology of the area. There's also a pathway around the mound, and a three-story observation tower gives visitors the best view as well as a moment for solitary contemplation.

WHERE: 75 miles south of Columbus; 3850 State Rte. 73. Tel 800-752-2757; arcofappalachia.org/serpent-mound. *When:* park closed Mon; check website for museum schedule.

From Dayton to the Wild Blue Yonder

NATIONAL MUSEUM OF THE U.S. AIR FORCE

Wright-Patterson Air Force Base, Ohio

Working in their bicycle shop in Dayton, Wilbur and Orville Wright astonished—and changed—the world with the invention of a powered, heavier-than-air machine capable of controlled, sustained flight.

It's safe to say the Wright brothers would themselves be astonished if they could travel a century forward to the military facility that bears their name, Wright-Patterson Air Force Base, to see what became of their plane.

It's here you'll find the National Museum of the U.S. Air Force, a vast complex of connected hangars and the world's oldest and largest military aviation museum. It is also one of Ohio's top tourist attractions, welcoming millions of wide-eyed children and their parents in tow. The awe-inspiring display of aerial technology and might includes more than 360 aircraft and missiles. Visitors wander past graceful early fliers such as a 1911 Bleriot monoplane; chunky Boeing fighters from the 1930s; "Bockscar," the B-29 that bombed Nagasaki; and a breathtaking array of Cold War and contemporary designs. Thousands of other artifacts—squadron patches; a trombone owned by Maj. Glenn Miller, leader of the American Band of the Allied Expeditionary Force; a chunk of the Pentagon from the 9/11 attack—sit alongside, illuminating the long and fascinating history of the USAF.

The museum's main complex also includes a towering Missile Gallery, a flight simulator that mimics the experience of flying in a fighter jet, and a ride for up to 12 people through outer space and other virtual realities. A separate hangar houses presidential planes, among them the modified Boeing 707 known as SAM 26000, the first *Air Force One*, and the plane that flew JFK to and from Dallas that fateful November of 1963. The Research and Development Hangar displays mind-bending experimental aircraft such as the bladelike Lockheed

Martin–Boeing DarkStar. A cursory tour can easily take a day, and the technological complexity and historic impact of the exhibits may leave your mind feeling as though it's taken a test flight with Chuck Yeager.

You can return to a simpler age of aviation by following in the Wrights' footsteps at the Dayton Aviation Heritage National Historical Park, composed of six sites around Dayton. The bike shop where they built their first Flyer has been relocated to the Henry Ford Museum in Dearborn, Michigan (see p. 526), but the previous location is maintained as a museum, as is the Huffman Prairie Flying Field where they tested their designs in 1904–05.

WHERE: 10 miles northeast of Dayton; 1100 Spaatz St. Tel 937-255-3286; national museum.af.mil. **AVIATION HERITAGE PARK:** Tel 937-225-7705; nps.gov/daav.

Double Your Pleasure and Double Your Fun

TWINS DAYS

Twinsburg, Ohio

In 1819, New Englanders Moses and Aaron Wilcox arrived in Millsville, Ohio, to sell parcels of land on behalf of the Connecticut Land Company. The identical twins offered a deal to the residents of the small settlement,

which had been established just two years earlier: We'll give you six acres of land for a public square and $20 toward a school, if you change the name of the town to Twinsburg.

Jump ahead a century and a half to 1976. City officials planned to mark the nation's Bicentennial with a commemoration of the Wilcox brothers, who had stayed lifelong business partners, married sisters, died within a few hours of each other of the same disease, and were buried in the same grave in Twinsburg's Locust Grove Cemetery. Organizers extended an open invitation to all twins; 37 sets of twins participated, and twice that number came two years later. Today Twins

Days is the biggest festival of its kind, drawing over 2,000 sets of twins and triplets—and in some years, even quadruplets and quintuplets—to this city of nearly 19,000. Ranging in age from merely weeks old to over 90 years old, they (and in some cases their parents) come from as far away as Australia, Nigeria, and Japan for three days of socializing and entertainment. The full schedule includes most- and least-alike competitions in several age brackets, a 5K footrace, a twins talent show, the "Double Take Parade," and even the occasional double wedding. Little surprise that there is talk of establishing a Twins Hall of Fame and Museum.

Twins Days is mostly for multiples and their families and friends. But almost since the beginning, the festival has also attracted researchers, especially geneticists, interested in the mysteries of multiples' shared traits; parents toting their toddlers commiserate and exchange tales; and then there's the throng of spectators with no better reason to come than just to join in the fun.

WHERE: 20 miles southeast of Cleveland. Most of the festival is held at Glenn Chamberlain Park, 10270 Ravenna Rd. Tel 330-425-3652; twinsdays.org. *When:* 1st full weekend in Aug.

Dressed in all kinds of creative costumes, siblings strut their stuff during the Twins Days parade.

Under the Big Top in Baraboo

CIRCUS WORLD MUSEUM

Baraboo, Wisconsin

In 1884, five enterprising brothers named Ringling turned their back on the family farm, founded a circus, and took their show on the road. Eventually, they grew big enough to buy out even Barnum & Bailey, and brought the headquarters of the "Greatest Show on Earth" home to this quiet dairy-farming community in south-central Wisconsin. Baraboo served as the base for the Ringling Bros. Circus until 1918, when the troupe moved on to warmer digs in Florida. Today the original site celebrates the Ringling legacy—and more than two dozen other circuses that had their origins here—at the Circus World Museum, operated by the Wisconsin State Historical Society. Throughout the summer, a bona fide three-ring circus springs to life in all its frenzied glory under the museum's Big Top, with clowns, elephants, aerialists, tigers, jugglers, magic shows, steam calliopes, and a master of ceremonies presiding over it all in his booming baritone. It's a spectacle that delights older folks with its authenticity and young kids with its audience participation and pure sensory overload.

Circus shows are just one piece of this 64-acre complex, however. The museum itself is home to a grand collection of memorabilia, including more than 200 circus parade wagons and vehicles—easily the largest and most extensive collection anywhere in the world. Visitors can watch skilled workers repair, restore, and repaint the vintage wagons at the museum's Chappie Fox Wagon Restoration Center. Behind the scenes, the museum's Parkinson Library and Research Center is the world's foremost archive of circus history, preserving artifacts such as circus business records, handbills, rare photographs, and posters, all available for circus enthusiasts and scholars.

WHERE: 41 miles northwest of Madison; 550 Water St. Tel 866-693-1500 or 608-356-8341; circusworldbaraboo.com. **BEST TIMES:** mid-Mar–Oct for daily live performances under the Big Top.

Sanctuary in North America's Largest Lake

THE APOSTLE ISLANDS

Bayfield, Wisconsin

Strewn across 450 square miles of Lake Superior's pristine waters, the 22 Apostle Islands present a striking tableau: tiny jewels on an immense inland sea, the largest freshwater body in the world. With the exception of Madeline, the largest of the Apostles, all of the islands are undeveloped and uninhabited, a showcase for craggy shorelines, remnant old-growth hemlocks and hardwoods, and sculpted sandstone cliffs and caves. From tiny 3-acre Gull Island to 10,000-acre Stockton, the islands are protected as the Apostle Islands National Lakeshore, along with 12 miles of mainland Wisconsin shoreline on the adjacent Bayfield Peninsula. Natural beauty and outdoor recreation take center stage here, with more than 50 miles of trails crisscrossing the islands, and native populations of black bears, bald eagles, and more than 200 species of migratory birds. This watery playground is best explored by boat, and opportunities abound. The Apostle Islands Cruise Service offers a variety of narrated cruises that sail past rich russet sandstone formations, lighthouses, and other historic sites, sometimes dropping off passengers to explore for a few hours. Captained sailboat charters are another option. Guests and the wind determine the day's itinerary, which often revolves around beachcombing, hiking, and swimming in sun-warmed bays. The national lakeshore is home to nine historic lighthouses—more than any other national park—some of which are staffed in summer months for tours and interpretation.

Kayaks have become a popular way to explore the archipelago, perfect for open-water passages between islands and for ducking in and out of the sea caves that pock the sandstone shoreline. Loaded with food and camping gear, kayaks are the ticket to seeing the Apostles' island backcountry. Those with plenty of experience can tackle Superior's vast waters alone, but even beginners can paddle safely with a reputable outfitter.

With sweeping island views and a yacht-filled marina, the gateway village of Bayfield (population 530) makes a perfect "base camp" to explore the national lakeshore and arrange island excursions. Start at the handsome National Park visitors center, built in the 19th century with sandstone quarried from Basswood, Hermit, and Stockton islands. Bayfield also offers appealing entertainment like the acclaimed Big Top Chautauqua, featuring music and maritime-themed theater inside a huge tent. The Old Rittenhouse Inn pampers guests in a lovingly restored Queen Anne, and serves some of the best meals in town. Local favorite Maggie's, and its upscale cousin, Wild Rice, offer more great dining, with fresh whitefish and other local catch on the menu.

WHERE: 90 miles northeast of Duluth, MN. *Park info:* Tel 715-779-3397; nps.gov/apis. *Bayfield visitor info:* Tel 715-779-3335; bayfield.org. **APOSTLE ISLANDS CRUISE SERVICE:** Bayfield. Tel 800-323-7619 or 715-779-3925; apostleisland.com. *Cost:* tours from $40. *When:* mid-May–mid-Oct. **KAYAKING:** Living Adventure offers guided sea kayaking trips. Tel 866-779-9503 or 715-779-9503; livingadventure.com. *Cost:* half-day trips from $59. *When:* June–mid-Sept. **BIG TOP CHAUTAUQUA:** Tel 888-244-8368 or 715-373-5552; bigtop.org.

When: June–Sept. **OLD RITTENHOUSE INN:** Tel 800-779-2129 or 715-779-5111; rittenhouse inn.com. *Cost:* from $150; prix-fixe dinner $59. **BEST TIMES:** July–Aug for warm weather and calm waters; Sept for the annual lighthouse celebration and clear, warm days; Feb–early Mar for hiking to the ice-coated caves that form along the Bayfield Peninsula.

Elegant Escape Deep in the North Woods

CANOE BAY

Chetek, Wisconsin

The spring-fed lakes, deep pine forests, and clean air of northwestern Wisconsin's Indianhead Region have long been a getaway for everyone from industrial-era tycoons to U.S. presidents—Calvin Coolidge, for one, who so enjoyed his fishing trips on the Brule River during the 1920s that the Wisconsin lodge he frequented was renamed "the Summer White House." Near Chetek, the 300-acre Canoe Bay resort brings alive that era of contemplative, back-to-nature luxury for couples seeking solitude. With no children, telephones, or motorboats to pierce the serenity, Canoe Bay frequently makes the various magazine lists of "most romantic" getaways.

Couples at Canoe Bay enjoy an array of civilized indulgences: breakfast in bed, in-room massage, and innovative dining in a lakeside restaurant with an ever-changing menu and an extensive wine list. Twenty-seven elegant lakeside rooms and cottages each feature a stone fireplace, double whirlpool, and wilderness views. Recalling the genius of Wisconsin native Frank Lloyd Wright, buildings here blend beautifully with their natural surroundings. In fact, Wright's protégé and collaborator on New York City's Guggenheim Museum (see p. 184), John Rattenbury, designed two of the resort's exquisite stand-alone lodgings, the Rattenbury Cottage and Edgewood, a spacious and airy showpiece of stone, wood, and glass.

Guests can hike to three private lakes via 4 miles of scenic trails that wend through Canoe Bay's 300 forested acres, and the resort provides canoes and kayaks for gliding across the crystal-clear waters of Lake Wahdoon. Largemouth bass and panfish provide catch-and-release fishing opportunities, and swimmers can enjoy warm, sand-bottom waters on summer afternoons. The lakes are especially lovely in early morning and evening, when loons often float across the placid waters. Come winter, Canoe Bay rents snowshoes for traipsing around the snow-blanketed property, and Nordic skiers can enjoy 20 miles of

No motorized boats allowed—only canoes, kayaks, and rowboats on Canoe Bay's crystal clear, glacier-created Lake Wahdoon.

groomed trails on a county trail network nearby. A dancing fire and a big globe of pinot await you at the end of the day.

WHERE: 120 miles east of Minneapolis, MN; W16065 Hogsback Road. Tel 715-924-4594; canoebay.com. *Cost:* from $350. **BEST TIMES:** June–Aug for water sports; 1st half of Oct for peak foliage.

The Cape Cod of the Midwest

DOOR COUNTY

Wisconsin

D oor County occupies most of the 75-mile long Door Peninsula, which thrusts like a sword from Wisconsin's northeast corner into Lake Michigan. To the west lie the sheltered waters of Green Bay; to the east, the vast blue expanse of the open lake; and in between are Door County's 300-plus miles of ragged, rocky shoreline, dotted with 11 lighthouses, busy marinas, and quiet beaches. No matter where you wander, you're always less than 10 miles from water's edge. Drive the two-lane highways that connect the whitewashed waterfront towns: Egg Harbor, Fish Creek, Ephraim, and Sister Bay entice visitors with endless shops, galleries, restaurants, and streets made for strolling. Inland, cherry and apple orchards crosshatch the rural landscape, along with antiques shops, summer stock theater, and other surprises.

The bustling town of Fish Creek is the epicenter of the county's busy "bayside" and one of the upper Midwest's earliest resort communities. Tucked at the end of Main Street, the White Gull Inn has drawn vacationers for more than a century. The carefully tended white clapboard inn is still a lovely place to stay, and serves some of the finest meals in town, its menu often boasting whitefish and lake trout pulled from local waters. Be sure to make reservations at the White Gull or at Pelletier's, another area restaurant, for a fish boil—Door County's traditional fisherman's dish of whitefish, onions, and red potatoes boiled in an enormous pot over an open fire. Don't miss the drama when cooks splash

You are never far from water or beautifully rugged shoreline in bucolic Door Country.

kerosene over the flame, creating a fireball that boils over the kettle and removes fishy oils. Top it off with a piece of cherry pie made from fruit harvested from local orchards. In Sister Bay, Al Johnson's showcases the region's Scandinavian fare. Along with the Swedish pancakes and lingonberries, the restaurant is famous for its traditional sod roof, where a resident herd of goats graze.

Explore Door County's natural wonders at Peninsula State Park, a 3,776-acre limestone headland that juts out into the bay between Fish Creek and Ephraim. Nearby, volunteers give tours of the Eagle Bluff lighthouse, a buttery brick tower built in 1868.

You'll find greater solitude when you venture to Door County's "lake side" or its northern reaches, where low-key resorts lie hidden along sand beaches and rocky bays. You won't reach the end of the county until you've hopped a ferry across the Portes des Mortes Passage ("Death's Door") to Washington Island, then another to Rock Island State Park. Here, ringed by a horizon of water and woods, you can fully appreciate the landscape that has been luring vacationers for decades.

WHERE: Sturgeon Bay, gateway to the Door Peninsula, is 154 miles north of Milwaukee. *Visitor info:* Tel 800-527-3529 or 920-743-4456; doorcounty.com. **WHITE GULL INN:** Fish Creek. Tel 888-364-9542 or 920-868-3517; whitegullinn.com. *Cost:* from $176 (off-peak), from $300 (peak); fish boil $20. **PELLETIER'S:** Fish Creek. Tel 920-868-3313. *Cost:* fish boil $20. **AL JOHNSON'S:** Sister Bay. Tel 920-854-2626. *Cost:* dinner $18. **PENINSULA STATE PARK:** Fish Creek. Tel 920-868-3258. **BEST TIMES:** June for Ephraim's Scandinavian Fyr Bal Festival; July–Aug for warm weather; Oct for brilliant foliage.

The Country's Largest and Most Prestigious Cross-Country Ski Race

AMERICAN BIRKEBEINER

Hayward, Wisconsin

Each February, some 11,000 fit, Lycra-clad folks descend upon the Wisconsin northwoods to participate in the American Birkebeiner, a cross-country ski race that weaves 31.7 miles (51 kilometers) along a hilly, heavily wooded trail from the Telemark Resort near Cable to the finish line on Main Street in downtown Hayward. Since its inception in 1973, when only 35 people participated, the race has grown into the largest cross-country ski marathon in the nation.

For some, it's serious business. The Birkebeiner is part of the Worldloppet, a circuit of 20 Nordic ski races held on four continents. Named after a historic Norwegian ski event, the Birkebeiner is the only Worldloppet event held in North America, and attracts a top cadre of professional racers from roughly 20 countries. While pros may complete the course in about two hours, legions of weekend warriors soldier on for up to eight hours or more. Amateurs can compete in the full race—after all, sturdy Scandinavian stock runs thick in the upper Midwest—or can sign up for 23- or 12-kilometer options.

You don't even have to click into skis to join in on the party. More than 20,000 spectators line many portions of the route, and it seems all of Hayward is there cheering at the finish line. Equipment expos and demos, junior elite sprints, family fun races, and other events round out the weekend. Head to The Fireside for a celebratory dinner in a traditional Northwoods setting. Everyone seems to order the signature dish—dry-rubbed, smoked, and sauced baby back ribs.

The rest of the winter, most of the Birkie Trail is open to the public, groomed for both classical and skate skiing. Five miles of lighted loop trails near the County Highway OO trailhead are especially lovely for nighttime skiing.

WHERE: 150 miles northeast of Minneapolis, MN. Tel 715-634-5025; birkie .com. *Hayward visitor info:* Tel 800-724-2992 or 715-634-4801; haywardlakes.com. *Cost:* fee to participate from $125; Birkie Trail Pass $10 daily, $50 annually. **The Fireside:** Tel 715-634-2710; firesidehayward.com. *Cost:* $50. **Best time:** Jan–early Feb for most reliable snow coverage.

From Company Town to Luxe Golf Resort

The American Club

Kohler, Wisconsin

S ure, it sounds odd to build an exclusive resort around a plumbing factory, but that's exactly what happened in the village of Kohler, a name known for its fashionable, high-end plumbing fixtures. In 1918, company president (and later governor of Wisconsin) Walter J. Kohler built an impressive, block-long red-brick Tudor building directly opposite his factory, as a dormitory for his immigrant work-force, believing "a worker deserves not only wages, but roses as well." Today, one of Kohler's favorite quotes is etched in stained glass, radiating from the soaring windows of the handsome Wisconsin Room restaurant, once the workers' dining hall: "Life without labor is guilt; labor without art is brutality."

In the 1980s, the workers' dormitory was turned into a high-end inn, and the property was eventually expanded to encompass 240 rooms, five restaurants, handcrafted woodwork, and (not surprisingly) lavish bathrooms. The hotel's Immigrant Restaurant offers upscale dining and artisanal cheeses in its adjacent Winery Bar, while the more casual Horse and Plow reflects the region's German immigrant heritage, with its beer and cheese soup and grilled Sheboygan sausage sampler.

Golf is the primary—but far from the only—draw of the American Club. Four magnificent championship courses frame the resort, each designed by famed course architect Pete Dye and laden with praise by golf critics across the country. Blackwolf Run's two 18-hole courses (The River and The Meadow Valleys) take advantage of the region's naturally undulating glacier-scoured terrain. Dye proclaimed upon their opening that "there could not be a better natural setting for golf." He next created Whistling Straits in 1999, which required a bit more work: Some 7,000 truckloads of sand and dirt were brought in to create the rumpled landscape along a flat bluff above Lake Michigan that now evokes the windswept, rough-hewn courses of Scotland and Ireland, complete with grazing sheep. Whistling Straits hosted the 2004, 2010, and 2015 PGA Championships (a rare honor for a relatively new course).

Golfers at the American Club enjoy extraordinary views of Lake Michigan.

The Kohler attention to detail is evident throughout this tidy property, which at every turn feels as perfect and photogenic as a movie set. At the 500-acre River Wildlife nature preserve, guests can hike more than 18 miles of trails, ride horseback, hunt pheasant, entice trout and salmon from rivers, streams, and Lake Michigan, and dine on country gourmet at the rough-hewn log cabin River Wildlife Lodge restaurant. At the Forbes Five-Star Kohler Waters Spa, guests can choose from more than 50 treatments, many showcasing Kohler's plumbing marvels, such as the RiverBath, featuring a waterfall and river currents. For a nuts-and-bolts look at Kohler's namesake business, visit the Kohler Design Center, where the "Great Wall of China" fills one end of the showroom with a vast display of plumbing fixtures.

WHERE: 60 miles north of Milwaukee; 419 Highland Dr. Tel 800-344-2838 or 920-457-8000; americanclubresort.com. *Cost:* from $200 (off-peak), from $385 (peak); greens fees from $161. **KOHLER WATERS SPA:** Tel 920-457-7777; americanclubresort.com. *Cost:* RiverBath treatment $122. **BEST TIMES:** Oct for the Kohler Food and Wine Experience; Feb for In Celebration of Chocolate.

Newport of the Midwest

LAKE GENEVA

Wisconsin

The genteel town of Lake Geneva may be in southern Wisconsin, but with its location just 10 miles north of the state line, Chicago-area residents have long laid claim to this popular vacation area. Geneva Lake, a deep, spring-fed beauty some 21 miles in circumference, sits right on the town's doorstep, while three other smaller lakes add to the region's resortlike feel, luring legions of boaters, golfers, and multiple-generation vacationers.

The railroad first carried Chicago's elite north to the cool waters and woods of Lake Geneva in the mid-19th century, where they built elaborate summer homes along the lakeshore. But it was the Great Chicago Fire of 1871 that established Lake Geneva as "Newport of the West" or "Hamptons of the Midwest." Having lost their homes and businesses, leading industrialists with names like Wrigley, Maytag, and Montgomery Ward sought refuge here, building even more palatial estates and commuting back and forth to Chicago just 80 miles away.

You can enjoy a casual view of the mansions and their vast emerald lawns on foot thanks to a 26-mile Shore Path that wends along the lakeshore, traversing parks and estates. Long-standing tradition rather than law keeps this former Indian footpath open to the public, so be sure to respect the generosity of owners and stay on the path itself when out for a stroll. The greatest concentration of mansions lies along the north shore, so Lake Geneva's Library Park is a good starting point.

Lake Geneva Cruise Lines offers a cruise past the mansions, which provides informative narration about estates like Green Gables (the original getaway for the chewing-gum Wrigleys) and Stone Manor, the largest on the lake. Or sign on for the company's U.S. Mailboat Tour, one of the last such marine postal services in the country.

Along with all its elaborate private homes, the Lake Geneva area has some indulgent lodging for its guests as well. With the distinction of being the only hotel property directly on the lakeshore, the Geneva Inn resembles a grand English country house. Its grand lake views are enjoyed from guest rooms with private balconies, as well as the popular restaurant with bar and patio. A different kind of experience can be had in the elegant rooms at the Frank Lloyd Wright-inspired Grand Geneva Resort and Spa, located on a self-contained 1,300-acre complex with its own airstrip, a spa, tennis courts, ski hill, water park, and two award-winning golf courses, the Brute and the Highlands.

WHERE: 83 miles northwest of Chicago, IL. *Visitor info:* Tel 800-345-1020 or 262-248-4416; visitlakegeneva.com. **LAKE GENEVA CRUISE LINE:** Tel 800-558-5911 or 262-248-6206; cruiselakegeneva.com. *Cost:* tours $25–35. **THE GENEVA INN:** Tel 800-441-5881 or 262-248-5680; genevainn.com. *Cost:* from $169. **GRAND GENEVA RESORT:** Tel 800-558-3417 or 262-248-8811; grandgeneva.com. *Cost:* from $186 (off-peak), from $279 (peak). **BEST TIMES:** 1st weekend in Feb for Winterfest and the National Snow Sculpting Competition; Aug for Venetian Festival on the waterfront.

Where Politics and Produce Mix

THE DANE COUNTY FARMERS' MARKET

Madison, Wisconsin

Every Saturday morning from April to early November, over 150 farmers and other vendors from throughout south-central Wisconsin line the Capitol Square, all part of the Dane County Farmers' Market, widely considered to be the largest producer-only farmers' market in the country. The fabulous sun-dappled setting—a four-block green that skirts the Wisconsin State Capitol—certainly contributes to its popularity, but quality and authenticity are key: Only Wisconsin vendors are permitted, selling locally grown produce and meats, artisanal cheeses, and homemade baked goods. Not only is the market a fine place to shop for groceries (the products of some 300 purveyors and suppliers are for sale), it's a microcosm of free-spirited Madison—a happy melee of Birkenstocks, baby strollers, coffee carts, street performers, nonprofit organizations with petitions, and politicians vying for handshakes.

Join the throng circling the Capitol counterclockwise (always counterclockwise) sifting through piles of sweet corn, sampling aged cheddar, and loading down their backpacks and bike baskets (the city's much-used bike trail system is one of the most extensive in the country) with everything from homemade pesto to fruit preserves. Different displays of produce appear as the growing season evolves, and many vendors offer organic and unusual heirloom varieties. Food products like jam, jerky, farm-raised trout, and, of course, endless varieties of cheese are available spring through fall. The market is the place to sample a local favorite, a bag of surprisingly delicious fresh cheese curds—"guaranteed to squeak!" as one vendor promises passersby.

Chef Tony Miller is a fixture at the market, scanning the stalls for ingredients that later show up on the evening's menu at L'Etoile, the award-winning farm-to-table restaurant on Capitol Square. L'Etoile was founded in

1976 by Odessa Piper, an early proponent of "regionally reliant cooking" and sustainable farming, concepts still reflected in L'Etoile's impeccable dishes. Celebrating its 40th anniversary in 2016, L'Etoile has maintained its commitment to locally grown, organic produce, and to the nearby farmers' market. It remains a seminal influence on the city's food scene.

Where: Wisconsin Capitol Square. Tel 608-455-1999; dcfm.org. *When:* Sat, mid-Apr–early Nov; smaller market on Martin Luther King Jr. Blvd. Wed, mid-Apr–mid-Nov. **L'Etoile Restaurant:** Tel 608-251-0500; letoile-restaurant.com. *Cost:* dinner $65; 7-course tasting menu $125. **Best time:** depends on what crop you're after, but Wisconsin sweet corn in Aug is hard to beat.

A Moving Masterpiece on Lake Michigan

MILWAUKEE ART MUSEUM

Milwaukee, Wisconsin

Experiencing the works of art at the Milwaukee Art Museum begins long before you walk through the doors. As you approach via a pedestrian bridge, you see the 90-foot-high glass-walled reception hall capped by a stunning white cone composed of 72 steel fins that unfurl into wings stretching more than 200 feet from tip to tip. Situated on the shores of Lake Michigan in downtown Milwaukee, the enormous moving sculpture looks like a gull taking flight.

Renowned Spanish architect Santiago Calatrava designed the museum's Quadracci Pavilion and its unique roof, and the project complements existing museum buildings designed by noted architects Eero Saarinen (1957) and David Kahler (1975). The Quadracci was the first building in the United States designed by Calatrava, whose résumé includes the Olympic Stadium in Athens and the new PATH transportation hub at New York's World Trade Center (see p. 194).

The buzz over the addition, along with a $34 million renovation of the two older buildings in 2015, has brought renewed attention to the museum and its diverse collections, which include everything from a 16th-century Flemish tapestry to modern and contemporary art by Warhol, Miró, Kandinsky, Picasso, and others. Among its most notable permanent collections are one of the world's premier collections of 20th-century Haitian art and 25 works by Wisconsin native Georgia O'Keeffe, in the largest dedicated O'Keeffe gallery outside Santa Fe, New Mexico (see p. 750).

Where: 700 N. Art Museum Dr. Tel 414-224-3200; mam.org. **Best times:** The wings open when the museum opens, close when it closes, and flap open and closed each day at noon, weather permitting.

The Milwaukee Art Museum's movable brise soleil *(sun-shading structure) opens up during the day, and folds over the tall, arched structure at night or during bad weather.*

Waterfront Celebrations of Music and Culture

MILWAUKEE FESTIVALS

Milwaukee, Wisconsin

For much of the summer, Milwaukee's Lake Michigan lakefront is alive with music and the wafting aromas of ethnic cooking. It all began in 1968 with Summerfest, an 11-day celebration of music and food that gets bigger and better every year. Yesterday's tents have been replaced by 11 permanent stages, including the 23,000-seat open-air Marcus Amphitheater. One of the largest music festivals in the world, Summerfest welcomes everything from country to hip-hop, from up-and-coming garage bands to some of the biggest names in show business. Booths run by more than 45 area restaurants give everyone their fill of local specialties, too: Milwaukee classics include a sauerbraten sandwich from Mader's or frozen custard from Culver's. Local breweries are major sponsors of Summerfest, and beer tents abound throughout the 75-acre waterfront grounds. Other activities include a comedy cabaret, sports demonstrations, an arts and crafts market, a kids' activity tent, and more.

Before and after Summerfest's early summer run, the Henry W. Maier Festival Park (named for the mayor who started Summerfest) thrums with the energy of six weekend festivals that reflect Milwaukee's melting pot heritage, each with its own music, food, dance, crafts, traditions, and pride. You can sample pierogi at Polish Fest (mid-June), twirl to a tarantella at Festa Italiana, savor sauerbraten at German Fest (both in late July), enjoy a mariachi band at Mexican Fiesta (late August), and more.

WHERE: Henry W. Maier Festival Park. Tel 414-273-2680; summerfest.com (other festival info is also on the Summerfest website). *Cost:* Summerfest from $10, Marcus Amphitheater shows extra; prices vary for other festivals. *When:* Summerfest is 11 days in late June–early July. **BEST TIME:** opening night of Summerfest for the Big Bang fireworks show.

Brew City, U.S.A.

MILWAUKEE'S BEER HERITAGE

Milwaukee, Wisconsin

A hardworking populace of German immigrants is responsible for Milwaukee's sudsy heritage. In the mid-1800s, the city was home to dozens of breweries, iconic names like Blatz, Schlitz, Pabst, and Miller among them. By 1900, Milwaukee was producing a third of the nation's beer. Today, although competition and industry consolidation have lessened Milwaukee's dominance (only Miller Brewing Co. remains headquartered here), beer and the brewing heritage still remain a linchpin of the city. The city's pro baseball team, after all, is called the Milwaukee Brewers . . . and they play at Miller Park.

Miller's Milwaukee operations still sit on the original land purchased by Frederick Miller in 1855. Tours blend historical stops with modern demonstrations of the beer-making process; highlights include the Miller Caves—used to store and ferment beer before mechanical refrigeration—and a look at its modern brewhouse, high-speed packaging line, and shipping center. Tours conclude with free samples at Miller's Bavarian-style tasting room and outdoor beer garden.

Wisconsin's first microbrewery, the Sprecher Brewing Company, provides another look at suds in action, with tours and tastings of more than a dozen beers and its much-loved

Miller's vintage "Girl in the Moon" icon hangs in the brewery's storage caves.

root beer. Along with traditional tours, the locally owned, highly acclaimed Lakefront Brewery, along the Milwaukee River near downtown, ups the oompah factor with a Friday Night Fish Fry complete with polka band. This is about as Milwaukee as it gets. On summer Sundays, the *Brew City Queen* tour boat lets guests make a day of touring and tasting, with a three-hour cruise along the Milwaukee River and stops at two microbreweries, the Lakefront Brewery and Milwaukee Ale House.

For a glimpse at the wealth generated by Milwaukee's beer barons, visit the Pabst Mansion downtown. The Flemish Renaissance mansion was built in 1890–93 by Captain Frederick Pabst. It's a study in opulence—20,000 square feet, 37 rooms, 14 fireplaces, Milwaukee's first central heating and electricity, and intricate woodwork, including carved panels that once adorned Bavarian castles.

MILLER BREWING CO.: Tel 800-944-5483 or 414-931-2337; millercoors.com. **SPRECHER BREWING CO.:** Tel 414-964-2739; sprecher brewery.com. *When:* Fri–Sat. **LAKEFRONT BREWERY:** Tel 414-372-8800; lakefrontbrew ery.com. **BREW CITY QUEEN:** Tel 414-283-9999; riverwalkboats.com. *Cost:* from $23. *When:* Sun. **PABST MANSION:** Tel 414-931-0808; pabstmansion.com. *When:* guided tours mid-Jan–mid-Nov. **BEST TIME:** Fri for the Friday Night Fish Fry, when beer-battered perch and cod is served up at restaurants and taverns throughout the region.

The Heart of America's Dairyland

CHEESE COUNTRY

Monroe to Mineral Point, Wisconsin

In the 1800s, the lush rolling hills and river valleys of south-central Wisconsin were an irresistible lure for thousands of Swiss, German, and Scandinavian dairy farmers eager for fertile farmlands that reminded them of home.

Today this postcard-perfect rural area is the heart of Wisconsin's dairyland, producing most of the state's annual 2.8 billion pounds of cheese and taking home top titles in the World Championships, often beating out contenders from Switzerland and The Netherlands.

The region's Swiss culture shines most prominently in New Glarus (population 2,179), where a smattering of local elders still speak their native Swiss-German dialect and white-and-brown chalet-like architecture dominates the downtown. Shops sell everything from cuckoo clocks to Swiss pastries, while Swiss pioneer life is chronicled at the Swiss Historical Village Museum at the west end of town, where occasional demonstrations of cheesemaking can be seen. Another local draw is the New Glarus Brewing Co., creators of internationally award-winning beers like Spotted Cow and Totally Naked.

Nearby Monroe is known as the Cheese Capital of the U.S. Nearly 20 farmer-owned operations still churn out cheese in the area—predominantly varieties of Swiss, but also Havarti, Gouda, and even Limburger, the latter produced at the Chalet Cheese Cooperative, reportedly the nation's only remaining Limburger maker.

Several area factories offer tours by appointment, including the Chalet Cheese Cooperative. Also pay a visit to the National Historic Cheesemaking Center in Monroe, to understand the history and craft of it all. Downtown, you'll find several cheese shops on the old town square, lined with Victorian architecture and anchored by the red Romanesque Green County Courthouse. Stop at Baum-gartner's Cheese Store & Tavern for a sandwich popular in Monroe and maybe only in Monroe: Limburger cheese with onion and mustard on rye bread.

In the mid-19th century, Cornish miners were flowing into Mineral Point (38 miles northwest of Monroe) to dig the vast ore deposits hidden under the region's hills. Now a thriving artist community, the town still boasts some of the state's oldest and best preserved historic homes. Visit the limestone Cornish cottages along Shake Rag Alley, named for the old Cornish tradition of housewives shaking dishcloths to summon their husbands home from the mines, that are now occupied by antiques shops and art galleries. Farther down Shake Rag, the state historical society operates tours of Pendarvis, a well-preserved and oft-photographed collection of Cornish buildings.

At the end of Commerce Street lies the trailhead for the Cheese Country Trail, a 47-mile off-road route that winds along the Pecatonica River in brief stretches and through rolling dairy farm country to Monroe. It's open to hikers, bikers, horses, and ATVs, and largely follows a rail line that once hauled thousands of tons of lead.

WHERE: 100–150 miles west of Milwaukee. **SWISS HISTORICAL VILLAGE:** New Glarus. Tel 608-527-2317; swisshistoricalvillage.com. *When:* May–mid-Oct. **NEW GLARUS BREWING CO.:** Tel 608-527-5850; newglarusbrewing .com. **CHALET CHEESE COOPERATIVE:** Monroe. Tel 608-325-4343. *When:* closed Sat–Sun. **NATIONAL HISTORIC CHEESEMAKING CENTER:** Monroe. Tel 608-325-4636. *When:* May–Oct. **BAUMGARTNER'S:** Monroe. Tel 608-325-6157. **PENDARVIS:** Mineral Point. Tel 608-987-2122; wisconsinhistory.org. *When:* mid-May–Oct. **BEST TIMES:** in New Glarus, early Aug for the Volksfest (Swiss Independence Day) and early Sept for the Wilhelm Tell Festival (wilhelmtell .org). In Monroe, mid-Sept in even-numbered years for Cheese Days (cheesedays.com).

Discover how Wisconsin became a hub of cheese production at the National Historic Cheesemaking Center in Monroe.

Rural Beauty Tucked in Wrinkled River Valleys

THE DRIFTLESS AREA

Ontario, Wisconsin

The vast ice sheets that scoured flat much of the Midwest bypassed a pocket of southwestern Wisconsin east of La Crosse and north of the Wisconsin River. Free of glacial sediment (called "drift"), the landscape here is furrowed into serpentine valleys, crooked rivers, and craggy bluffs of sandstone and limestone. The result is a snapshot of rural America long gone in most places—a pastoral patchwork of tiny farmsteads, lazy canoeing rivers, bucolic Amish communities, grazing Holsteins, and thin roads that twist and turn with the topography.

The Kickapoo River perhaps best characterizes the Driftless Area's geology. Dubbed "the crookedest river in the nation," it may be one of the oldest river systems in the world. A crazy corkscrew that winds for 125 miles to cover a 65-mile distance between the communities of Wilton and Wauzeka, it is a delight for paddlers—clear, spring-fed, lethargic (except during spring rains), and lovely as it hugs sandstone cliffs and loops under a canopy of hemlock and pine. You can rent canoes and arrange shuttles in the tiny town of Ontario.

Nearly any road in this region could qualify as a scenic drive. From Ontario, for example, you can follow southbound Highway 131 for miles as it passes through pretty rural towns like Gays Mills, where acres of apple orchards hug the hillsides. Or watch for brown signs indicating a "Rustic Road," a series of scenic drives that are also perfect for biking (this is considered one of the top biking destinations in the U.S.). A few miles south of Ontario, Dutch Hollow Road is one such route, following high ridgelines and curving past Amish farms.

Ample state lands also make it easy to explore the area on foot, bike, or horseback. Near Ontario, 3,600-acre Wildcat Mountain State Park crowns a limestone escarpment, with hiking trails up to the 1,220-foot summit of Mount Pisgah. Nearby, the 8,569-acre Kickapoo Valley Reserve is especially popular with equestrians, who have more than 30 miles of meandering trails at their disposal.

WHERE: Ontario is 75 miles northwest of Madison. Tel 608-326-6658; driftlesswisconsin.com. **WILDCAT MOUNTAIN:** Tel 608-337-4775; dnr.wi.gov. **KICKAPOO VALLEY RESERVE:** Tel 608-625-2960; kvr.state.wi.us. **BEST TIMES:** July–Aug for paddling weather; late Sept for foliage.

The World's Largest Aviation Celebration

EAA AIRVENTURE

Oshkosh, Wisconsin

All the sky's a stage at the Experimental Aircraft Association's AirVenture, an annual weeklong event in which thousands of pilots from all over the world gather to showcase their historic, high-tech, and experimental aircraft. It's equal parts air show, trade show, educational workshop, and reunion, and its lure for aviation buffs is undeniable. The annual event, which began in 1953 with fewer than 150 attendees, now draws more than 500,000 from 70 countries. More than 10,000 aircraft wing in for the show, temporarily transforming little Wittman Regional Airport into the busiest airport in the world. Spectators may be treated to supersonic military jets,

Air show spectators watch the P-51 Mustang, a WWII fighter, cruise by on the runway.

precision aerobatic teams, homebuilt airplanes, vintage bombers, and delicate ultralights all in the same day.

As many as 200 aircraft participate in daily 30- and 60-minute air shows, which feature vintage WWII warbirds, wingwalkers, and other specialty acts. There's also plenty to see at the adjacent EAA AirVenture Museum, which is open all year and includes dozens of aircraft, exhibits on the pioneers of flight, and a "KidVenture" area with interactive rocket- and plane-building projects.

The EAA also sponsors "fantasy flight camps," where licensed pilots can fly vintage biplanes and early passenger transport craft like a 1929 Ford Tri-Motor "Tin Goose."

WHERE: 90 miles northwest of Milwaukee; 3000 Poberezny Rd. Tel 888-322-4636 or 920-426-4800; eaa.org. *Cost:* $47 per day. *When:* last week of July. **AIRVENTURE MUSEUM:** Tel 920-426-4818; eaa.org. **BEST TIMES:** Sat for extended warbird shows; opening day for arrivals of unusual aircraft.

Birds and Barges Along America's Greatest River

THE UPPER MISSISSIPPI BLUFFS

Prairie du Chien to Prescott, Wisconsin

In 1938, Franklin Roosevelt established a scenic byway running the length of the Mississippi River. Called the Great River Road, its course through Wisconsin slaloms between the Mississippi and its towering bluffs from the

mouth of the St. Croix River near Prescott to below Prairie du Chien and the mouth of the Wisconsin River. The 250-mile route (primarily along Wis. 35 and part of the greater 2,069-mile-long Great River Road; see p. 448) provides glimpses of everything from sleepy river towns and busy barge traffic to braided backwaters, wildlife preserves, and birds, birds, birds. The Mississippi Flyway ranks as one of the world's great migratory bird routes: More than 40 percent of the nation's waterfowl

and shorebirds pass through the Upper Mississippi River Valley each year, including tens of thousands of tundra swans. Eagles, ospreys, and other raptors winter here, often fishing in the open waters below the dams.

Tucked among high sandstone bluffs, Trempealeau, with a population of just over 1,500, could be a movie set for a slightly dilapidated and charming old river town. The Historic Trempealeau Hotel was built in 1871 as the centerpiece of town and remains such, with no-frills rooms, a reliably good restaurant, the busy "Saloon" bar with creaking wood floors, live music on most weekends, and a long porch overlooking the river. The restaurant serves local specialties like blackened catfish, baked walleye, and a famous meatloaf or vegetarian walnut burger.

The nearby 6,446-acre Trempealeau National Wildlife Refuge features a 4.5-mile wildlife drive and an observation deck overlooking the river bluffs and marsh—a good place to spot bald eagles. At nearby Lock and Dam Number 6, an observation platform lets visitors watch barges loaded with grain, coal, and other raw materials as they head for ports downriver.

The largest community in the region, La Crosse (population 52,240) was once singled out by Mark Twain as a "choice town." In Prairie du Chien, descendents of Wisconsin's first millionaire, fur trader Hercules Dousman, built the opulent Victorian mansion Villa Louis which is open for tours. Nearby, Wyalusing State Park crowns a 500-foot limestone bluff, offering an eagle's-eye view of the confluence of the Wisconsin and Mississippi Rivers. French explorers Jacques Marquette and Louis Jolliet stood at this very spot in 1673—where they first spotted the Upper Mississippi.

WHERE: The Wisconsin Great River Road starts at Prescott (about 22 miles east of St. Paul, MN) and runs to Kieler (about 8 miles north of Dubuque, IA); wigreatriverroad.org. **HISTORIC TREMPEALEAU HOTEL:** Tel 608-534-6898; trempealeauhotel.com. *Cost:* rooms from $55; dinner $30. **TREMPEALEAU WILDLIFE REFUGE:** Tel 608-539-2311; fws.gov/refuge/trempealeau. **BEST TIMES:** Mar–May and Oct for bird migration. In La Crosse, July 4th weekend for Riverfest (riverfestlacrosse.com) and early Oct for Oktoberfest (oktoberfestusa.com).

The Bucolic Home of Frank Lloyd Wright

TALIESIN

Spring Green, Wisconsin

Renowned architect and Wisconsin native Frank Lloyd Wright left an incredible legacy, from several notable houses (including his own first home and studio) in Oak Park outside of Chicago (see p. 496) to New York's Guggenheim Museum (see p. 184). But in Spring Green you can visit Wright's own rambling 37,000-square-foot home in his signature Prairie School style and his original architecture school, an estate he tucked among the rolling hills of his childhood.

Wright espoused the importance of designing in harmony with the surroundings and using local materials. Taliesin is the embodiment of Wright's tenets, its wings of limestone, wood, and glass meandering along the contours of the landscape. The name "Taliesin" means for "shining brow," a nod to his Welsh ancestry, and reflects the home's location along the "brow" of the hillside—enveloping, rather than overpowering, the site.

Wright lived at Taliesin for 48 years, from 1911 until his death at 91 in 1949. He also trained his apprentices here. He established Taliesin West in Arizona in the mid-1930s (see p. 695) and would spend winters there in his latter years, but many leading architects and Wright aficionados consider the Spring Green property his finest work.

Taliesin Preservation offers immensely popular tours of the 600-acre complex, which includes several Wright buildings, providing an intimate look at the home's dramatic history (including murder and arson) as well as the distinctive architectural style. Guides point out the architect's meticulous attention to detail and also indulge visitors with a few anecdotes of his legendary caustic and controlling personality. He banned Holstein cows from Taliesin in favor of coffee-and-cream Guernsey and Brown Swiss, for instance, because he felt the Holsteins' black-and-white hides didn't blend well with the pastures.

WHERE: 40 miles west of Madison. Tel 877-588-7900 or 608-588-7090; taliesinpreservation .org. *When:* daily, May–Oct, Fri–Sun in Apr and Nov. **BEST TIME:** May for the Tour du Taliesin, a bike ride of 38 or 100 miles.

Exploring his philosophy of "organic architecture," Frank Lloyd Wright mixed sienna into the stucco walls to evoke the Wisconsin River's golden-hued sandbars.

The Wilds of the Great Lake Country

WISCONSIN'S NORTH WOODS

Wisconsin

In Wisconsin, "Up North" is local parlance for escape: Escape to quiet wilderness beauty in the northern tier of the state, where farm and field segue into thick forests of pine, spruce, and fir, peppered with thousands of lakes. In parts of Wisconsin's lake country —especially in the Northern Highland–American Legion State Forest—the concentration of lakes is so intense that water makes up 40 percent of the surface area. With 15,047 lakes statewide, Wisconsin boasts a greater concentration of lakes than almost anywhere in the world, creating a recreational playground that has drawn generations of vacationers for fishing, boating, hunting, hiking, paddling, mountain biking, and other pursuits. Visitors come in winter too, for skiing, snowmobiling, ice fishing, and quiet moments.

Northwestern Wisconsin's pristine rivers are also a recreational paradise. The 98-mile Namekagon is part of the St. Croix National Scenic Riverway, and is popular for multiday canoe trips. A bit farther north, the Brule courses between old-growth red and white pines. Known as the "River of Presidents," it has attracted five—including Teddy Roosevelt—to fish its famous trout waters. Other rivers were dammed decades ago to form immense man-made lakes: Waterways like the Chippewa Flowage and the Turtle-Flambeau Flowage are prime fishing destinations, with healthy populations of bass, walleye, northern pike, and the state's most famous fighting fish, the muskellunge or "musky."

There are several early 20th-century Adirondack-style log lodges in the area, including the rustic waterfront Spider Lake Lodge, near Hayward and the vast Chequamegon National Forest; and Stout's Island Lodge, blissfully stranded on an island in Red Cedar Lake near Birchwood.

WHERE: Hayward is 349 miles northwest of

Milwaukee. **SPIDER LAKE LODGE:** Hayward. Tel 800-653-9472 or 715-462-3793; spiderlakelodge.com. *Cost:* from $169. **STOUT'S ISLAND LODGE:** Birchwood. Tel 715-354-3646; stoutsislandlodge.net. *Cost:* from $153. *When:* late May–Oct. **BEST TIME:** Sept for the Chequamegon Fat Tire Festival mountain bike race (cheqfattire.com).

Aquatic Adventures Abound

WISCONSIN DELLS

Wisconsin

Wisconsin Dells gets its name from the stretches of river valley chiseled through 100-foot-high honey-hued bluffs, but that's not what draws millions to this south-central Wisconsin tourist mecca. They come for the water parks: "The Dells" boasts the largest single water park, the largest indoor water park, and largest number and variety of water parks anywhere in the nation—more than 20 at last count.

And the water parks are merely the aquatic anchor of a full-fledged family vacation destination with an exhausting array of kid-pleasing attractions: amusement parks, go-kart tracks, boat tours, water-ski shows, ziplining, haunted houses . . . It's made this small city the state's No. 1 tourist destination.

It all began with the natural attraction of those sandstone bluffs. Visitors were stopping in the Dells in the mid-1850s to tour serpentine side canyons and towering escarpments by rowboat. Riverboats, amphibious "ducks," water-ski shows, and the rest all eventually joined in, too. The Ducks—immense WWII landing craft—are still a hugely popular attraction, trundling along downtown streets and then plowing right into the Wisconsin River for a tour of its rock formations. Traditional boat tours, too, offer views of the Dells' fern-draped canyons and pillars of stone.

Anyone with kids will find it hard to deny the simple pleasures of the water parks. Noah's Ark is America's largest, an eye-popping 70-acre array of 51 waterslides, two wave pools, two artificial rivers, and rides like "Flash Flood." Resorts in the area have built their own versions. The result is nearly two dozen indoor water parks, including the Kalahari Resort's 125,000-square-foot creation that includes a 570-foot-long roller coaster, and Great Wolf Lodge, with its 12-level tree house and water jungle gym (available to overnight resort guests only).

The elegant Sundara Inn & Spa is an organic-style inn hidden away in the pines on 26 acres. Services at the well-known spa include a "purifying ritual" that includes aroma steam and rainfall showers. Turns out, there are water attractions in the Wisconsin Dells for adults, too.

WHERE: 120 miles northwest of Milwaukee. **NOAH'S ARK:** Tel 608-254-6351; noahsarkwaterpark.com. *Cost:* $35. *When:* late May–early Sept. **KALAHARI RESORT:** Tel 877-253-5466 or 608-254-5466; kalahariresort.com. *Cost:* water park passes $34. **GREAT WOLF LODGE:** Tel 800-559-9653 or 608-253-2222; greatwolf.com/wisconsindells. *Cost:* water park passes $34; rooms from $350. **SUNDARA INN & SPA:** Tel 888-735-8181 or 608-253-9200; sundaraspa.com. *Cost:* from $199 (off-peak), from $299 (peak); spa treatments from $110. **BEST TIME:** July–Aug for outdoor waterpark fun.

GREAT PLAINS

IDAHO • KANSAS • MONTANA •
NEBRASKA • NORTH DAKOTA •
OKLAHOMA• SOUTH DAKOTA •
WYOMING

GREAT PLAINS

A Towering Pioneer Landmark

CITY OF ROCKS

Almo, Idaho

"A dismantled, rock-built city of the Stone Age" was one pioneer's description of the concentration of granite crags and promontories jutting up from the sagebrush scrublands of southern Idaho. At 2.5 billion years old, these ancient rocks were shaped by the elements rather than cavemen, but the name stuck. The 22-square-mile City of Rocks National Reserve is an impossible-to-miss landmark. The curious structures continue to excite the imagination, conjuring cities, steeples, castles, and dozens of symbolic shapes in the fractured stone. The Elephant Head, the Kaiser's Helmet, and the King's Throne are just a few of the scores of fancifully named formations in the park; the highest points are the Twin Sisters, two spires measuring 500 and 600 feet high.

The City of Rocks became an important milestone for pioneer emigrants along the California Trail, which left the Snake River Basin and the Oregon Trail to cut south to northern California. Traffic reached a frenzy in 1852, when some 52,000 people passed the formations on their way to the California goldfields. On Camp Rock, Register Rock, and many others, the names and initials of pioneer travelers are still visible, written in axle grease.

The dramatic range of elevations within the City of Rocks provides habitat for an unusual variety of flora and fauna—over 450 plant species have been recorded here. Raptors such as golden eagles, vultures, and falcons haunt the rocky heights, while mule deer graze the grasslands and bobcats and mountain lions make their homes in stony recesses. Rock climbing has become world-renowned at the park, with more than 600 designated routes of varying difficulty, but most visitors opt for hiking and camping, less strenuous ways to enjoy the majesty of this city from rocks.

WHERE: 85 miles southeast of Twin Falls. Tel 208-824-5901; nps.gov/ciro. **BEST TIME:** Wildflowers peak in May–June.

Eerie and Haunting: A Lunarscape on Earth

CRATERS OF THE MOON

Arco, Idaho

"The strangest 75 square miles on the North American continent" is how one traveler judged the Craters of the Moon National Monument and Preserve, a showcase of volcanic features and considered the largest lava field of its type in the contiguous U.S. But don't expect to find a typical volcano cone. The extensive lava flows at Craters of the Moon, which cover around 60,000 acres of the 750,000-acre preserve, are the result of a fissure in the earth's crust, which is exceptionally thin in this section of the Snake River Plain. When conditions have allowed, the molten magma, a mere 35 miles below the surface, has flowed up through underground faults, ultimately oozing out from enormous fissures called rifts.

The monument's Great Rift Zone began erupting about 15,000 years ago and ceased only 2,000 years ago (the Craters of the Moon rifts are considered volcanically dormant—for the moment). The resulting formations, which include lava tubes, bombs, cinder and spatter cones, and various types of lava flows, seem barren and inhospitable, but in fact they shelter a wide variety of plant and animal life, from cactus to pine trees, mule deer to marmots. In May and June, wildflowers put on a dynamic and colorful display.

This is not to say that life in the Craters of the Moon is easy. As little as 1 inch of rain may fall in summer, and moisture drains away quickly through the porous rock. The fractured lava formations can be very sharp, shredding the soles of shoes. Intense summer heat bakes the black lava, generating surface temperatures of 170°F. NASA astronauts learned the basics of volcanic geology here in 1969 while preparing for the Apollo lunar landings.

A 7-mile loop road explores the monument, leading to trailheads over the lava formations. The most striking features are the cinder cones

Some of the basalt lava deposits at Craters of the Moon are over 10,000 feet deep.

that rise above the generally flat flows—and serve as lookout points over the volcanic landscape. A hiking trail leads to a series of tree molds, where molten lava engulfed a forest and hardened around tree trunks it then incinerated. Bring a flashlight to explore the Indian Tunnel lava tube, at 800 feet, the longest in the monument. When winter conditions permit, the loop road is groomed for cross-country skiing, offering a unique juxtaposition of stark white-and-black landscapes and a solitude and silence that is inspiring.

WHERE: 84 miles west of Idaho Falls. Tel 208-527-1335; nps.gov/crmo. *When:* visitors center, daily; loop road closed seasonally, usually open mid-Apr–mid-Nov. **BEST TIMES:** Jan–Feb for cross-country skiing; May–June for wildflowers and weather.

A Bastion of Culture and Heritage

SAN INAZIO DE LOYOLA BASQUE FESTIVAL

Boise, Idaho

The arid rangeland of southwestern Idaho and the adjacent corners of Oregon and Nevada bear little resemblance to Euskal Herria, the European Basque homeland, a small territory that straddles the French-Spanish border along the western Pyrenees. Yet it was this rural and isolated ranch country that saw the immigration of thousands of Basques from the 1890s to the 1970s, who were drawn here initially to work as herders and laborers on the region's huge cattle and sheep operations. Boise became the hub for this growing and dynamic community—the largest in North America, now numbering around 15,000— with Basque-owned hotels, boardinghouses, groceries, and restaurants centering on Grove Street on the edge of downtown. In the old days, everyone in this thriving enclave spoke Euskera, the Basque language, and a hungry and lonely herder just in from the mountains wouldn't need to look far for a steaming dish of Basque lamb stew, or a chance to dance the traditional *jota* into the wee hours.

Boise celebrates its heritage during the San Inazio de Loyola Festival, honoring the patron saint of the Basques. The festival, held the last weekend in July, takes over a block of Grove Street, with the sound of music (usually heavy on the *trikitixa*, a button accordion dear to the Basque heart) and the tantalizing scent of grilling meats filling the air. Colorfully costumed dancers circle and swing to age-old melodies, and brawny athletes compete at traditional Basque contests (including rock dragging and exhibitions of *pala*, or handball).

And then there's the food—sandwiches of *solomo* (grilled marinated pork loin) and chorizo sausage, spicy with pimientos and onions, all washed down with glasses of *kalimotxo*—a mix of red wine and Coca-Cola that's a Basque specialty (and surprisingly refreshing). Every five years, in place of the normal San Inazio de Loyola festival, the community celebrates *Jaialdi* (meaning "Big Festival"), which extends the events to five days and welcomes visitors from around the world—in 2005, the president of the Basque Autonomous Community in Spain came to Boise for the festivities.

Even outside festival season, Grove Street remains a Basque stronghold. The Basque Museum and Cultural Center features exhibits on European and Idaho history. Across the street is the Basque Market, with artisanal cheeses, olive oil, wines, and other Basque food specialties, plus a selection of home-cooked food. Join the appreciative crowds at Bar Gernika, a pub and restaurant with excellent chorizo sandwiches, chunky lamb stew, and an admirable selection of Spanish wines.

But for the mother lode of traditional cooking, drive a dozen miles west of Boise to Meridian, where Epi's Basque Restaurant, a cozy family-oriented spot in a remodeled home, serves fantastic northern Spanish country-style cooking that many consider to be the best Basque cooking outside Europe.

San Inazio de Loyola Festival: basquecenter.com. *When:* last weekend in July. **Basque Museum:** Tel 208-343-2671; basquemuseum.com. *When:* closed Sun–Mon. **Basque Market:** Tel 208-433-1208; thebasquemarket.com. *When:* closed Sun. **Bar Gernika:** Tel 208-344-2175; bargernika.com. *Cost:* dinner $20. **Epi's Basque Restaurant:** Meridian. Tel 208-884-0142; episbasquerestaurant.com. *Cost:* dinner $30. *When:* closed Sun–Mon.

North America's Deepest River Gorge

Hells Canyon

Idaho and Oregon

On its long campaign across southern Idaho, the Snake River bisects a seemingly endless expanse of flat rangeland, with much of its water diverted for irrigation. Then, toward the Oregon border, as mountains edge in to constrict the valley, the Snake River gets down to business trenching its mighty Hells Canyon, the deepest river gorge in North America. Between Hells Canyon Dam and Lewiston, the Snake drops 1,300 feet in just 70 miles, within canyon walls that tower an average of 6,500 feet above. At its deepest point, the gorge walls rise nearly 8,000 feet, deep enough to hold 47 Niagara Falls stacked atop each other (and consider this: The Grand Canyon is at most 6,000 vertical feet deep from rim to river). For a distance of 106 miles, no bridge crosses the river, and few paved roads even come near the canyon.

These remote hinterlands are part of the 652,488-acre Hells Canyon Recreation Area, which straddles a 71-mile portion of the Snake River (the river canyon itself is preserved in the 216,981-acre Hells Canyon Wilderness Area). Most of the terrain is made up of precipitous rock walls and steep, slotlike side valleys, which means that just about the only way to experience this epic frontier is on foot, horseback, or—most excitingly—by boat. Outfitters

Hells Canyon is a popular destination for world-class white-water rafting.

arrange Snake River float trips on rafts, dories, or kayaks, providing high adventure as the waters blast through dozens of Class II to IV rapids in the most popular part of the canyon, the two- to three-day passage between Hells Canyon Dam and Pittsburgh Landing. For travelers with less time, turbine-powered jet-boat tours are also available—a less idyllic but equally exciting way to see the canyon in as little as a day. Jet boats depart from below Hells Canyon Dam and also from Lewiston, far to the north (downstream) of Hells Canyon.

Although it takes a bit of time—and in some cases, strong nerves—it's possible to explore parts of Hells Canyon by vehicle. For a bird's-eye view of Hells Canyon, the vista from Hat Point, reached on back roads from Imnaha, Oregon, is hard to top.

On the Idaho side, a number of gravel roads lead west from Riggins up to the Seven Devils Mountains, an area of rugged peaks and lake basins on the edge of the Snake River Canyon. Backcountry explorers recommend seeking out Heaven's Gate Lookout, reached by lengthy Forest Service roads from south of Riggins. At 8,430 feet, it's one of the highest viewpoints in the Hells Canyon area, with absolutely stunning views across one of the world's most uncompromising landscapes.

WHERE: on the northern border between Oregon and Idaho. **HELLS CANYON RECREATION AREA:** Joseph, OR. Tel 541-426-5546; fs.usda .gov/wallowa-whitman. **BEST TIMES:** May for wildflowers and good hiking weather; peak season for float trips is late May–mid-Sept.

Where the Great Outdoors Meets the Great Indoors

HENRY'S FORK LODGE

Island Park, Idaho

Idaho is one of America's most revered fishing destinations, with 2,000 lakes, 16,000 miles of streams, and 39 species of game fish. Angling for rainbow, brook, brown, and cutthroat trout in the high country of the Henry's

Fork of the Snake River—part of the greater Yellowstone ecosystem—is especially remarkable because of the concentration and variety of excellent waters within a relatively small area. The best fishing lodge in the area, Henry's Fork Lodge, is just minutes from the state park Railroad Ranch's renowned waters, and it's an easy drive to fishing spots in nearby Yellowstone National Park (see p. 676) and an honor roll of great fly-fishing rivers such as the Madison, Gallatin, and South Fork of the Snake. There's awesome diversity of both fish and their hideouts in these beautiful mountain valleys near the crest of the continent.

To characterize Henry's Fork Lodge as a fishing lodge is a bit like calling Rhode Island's coastal mansions summer cottages. Of course there's fantastic fishing here—the Henry's Fork of the Snake River is one of the most storied trout streams in North America—but the modern, architecturally striking buildings and sophisticated service here are light-years away from a typical rough-and-ready fishing camp. Designed by San Francisco–area architect Joseph Esherick (himself an avid fly-fisherman), the log-built lodge and guest cottages have been nominated for a national architectural award.

The lodge sits on an overlook above a secluded stretch of the Henry's Fork with the peaks of Yellowstone National Park and the Grand Tetons dominating the horizon. Guest rooms are wood-paneled (most with fireplaces of local volcanic stone), with hand-hewn log beds, down comforters, and Wi-Fi. Guests and nonguests with reservations head to the dining room for a wonderful low-key but refined dinner from a kitchen lauded as one of the region's finest.

Those less captivated by the world-class fly-fishing can hike, swim, boat, and stay busy destressing. Just two miles away is Harriman State Park, 11,000 acres that were owned by Union Pacific Railroad investors from 1902 to 1977. Now deeded to the state of Idaho, the ranch serves as a wildlife preserve, with hiking, biking, and horseback trails—and exemplary fishing—on the Henry's Fork, which winds through the property. During the summer there are regular tours of the historic ranch buildings.

As the Henry's Fork River leaves its high valley, about 25 miles south of the lodge, it drops through a series of steep waterfalls. The most thrilling of these falls is rainbow-misted Upper Mesa Falls, with a drop of 114 feet, best appreciated from footpaths that lead to cliff-edged viewpoints. Two miles farther downstream is Lower Mesa Falls, which drops 65 feet in a series of constricted cascades.

Where: 81 miles northwest of Idaho Falls. **Henry's Fork Lodge:** Tel 208-558-7953; henrysforklodge.com. *Cost:* from $540 per person, double occupancy, includes meals; dinner for nonguests $50. *When:* mid-May–mid-Oct. **Harriman State Park:** Tel 208-558-7368; parksandrecreation.idaho.gov. **Best times:** June–mid-July for dry-fly-fishing and warm weather; Sept for fewer crowds, wildlife viewing, beautiful early fall weather, and hungry spawning fish.

A Pine-Forest-Enshrouded Gem

LAKE COEUR D'ALENE

Idaho

I daho's Panhandle, wedged between British Columbia, Washington, and Montana, is an enclave of dense forests, mighty rivers, and over 60 deep glacial lakes. The town of Coeur d'Alene, named for the American Indian tribe that has lived along the Panhandle's waterways for millennia, sits at the head of the bewitchingly azure lake of the same name (which translates to "heart like an awl," French trappers' assessment of the natives' perceived trading shrewdness). Snaking through a glacier-dug channel between low, green-covered mountains, the lake offers fishing (there's plenty of Chinook salmon and trout), windsurfing, steamboat rides, water-skiing—essentially, if you can do it in the water, you can do it here.

Lake Coeur d'Alene has 109 miles of shoreline with several beaches.

It's not all about life on the water, however; the city serves as the honeymoon capital of the Northwest. Landlubbers will find meandering bike trails and groomed hiking paths, including one through pine-scented forests up to Tubbs Hill and a great vantage point of the lake, most of whose 128-mile shoreline has been blessedly protected from development. The Lake Coeur d'Alene Scenic Byway, which follows the eastern shoreline, offers a succession of windshield-wide lake views and is just one of many lovely back roads in the area. Even the I-90 freeway, which runs east to the historic silver-mining center of Wallace (see p. 606), is picturesque. Keep an eye out for birds, since the area is also home to the nation's largest population of ospreys as well as bald eagles.

Fine dining isn't just for the birds in Coeur d'Alene. Surrounded by water, Cedars Floating Restaurant is moored at the point where the lake pours into the Spokane River, with 180-degree views of the water and encircling slopes. Check the chalkboard for the day's fresh catch—you'll never go wrong with perennial favorites like cedar-plank–grilled salmon. East of Coeur d'Alene, tucked into a steep-sided bay, is the Wolf Lodge Inn, a timeworn roadhouse that serves up the area's best steaks amid antlers, faded Charlie Russell prints, and knotty pine walls. Bypass the appetizer and step up to "The Rancher," a 32-ounce combination of rib eye and sirloin. Curious diners who order the special "swinging steaks" may be surprised when crisp-fried calf testicles served with lemon wedges and cocktail sauce arrive.

The Coeur d'Alene Resort, sitting center stage on 6 beachfront acres, has done more to put Coeur d'Alene on the tourism map than anything since the glaciers melted. The hotel offers just about every lake-related diversion imaginable, as well as a newly redesigned 6,803-yard golf course with the reputation as one of the top resort courses in the U.S. Its most famous hole is the 14th, with the world's first movable, floating green. Golfers are ferried to the island, which is placed 100 to 175 yards from the shore (the island is moved to one of seven different locations each day), to complete their play. Daytime and dinner cruises explore the lake's steely waters. End your day at the new state-of-the-art resort spa and choose among its selection of Northwest-themed treatments and hydrotherapies. Then top it all off at Beverly's, the resort's 7th-floor restaurant. It is one of Idaho's best—a bastion of innovative Northwest cuisine that's complemented by million-dollar lake views and a million-dollar wine cellar (literally!) to match.

WHERE: 33 miles east of Spokane, WA. *Visitor info:* Tel 877-782-9232 or 208-664-3194; coeurdalene.org. **LAKE COEUR D'ALENE SCENIC BYWAY:** fhwa.dot.gov/byways. **CEDARS FLOATING RESTAURANT:** Tel 208-664-2922; cedarsfloatingrestaurant.com. *Cost:* dinner $50. **WOLF LODGE INN:** Tel 208-664-6665; wolflodgecda.com. *Cost:* dinner $50. **COEUR D'ALENE RESORT:** Tel 855-999-7998 or 208-209-5031; cdaresort.com. *Cost:* rooms from $149 (off-peak), from $329 (peak); dinner at Beverly's $50. **BEST TIMES:** July–Sept for warm and sunny weather; late Nov–early Jan for the Holiday Light Show, featuring 3 million lights in 250 different displays.

A Long-Dormant Wine Industry Now Thriving

IDAHO WINE

Caldwell and Boise, Idaho

Surprising to many, Idaho is emerging as a major winemaking region, with new vineyards sprouting up across the state in recent years and praise flowing in from wine aficionados. Idaho's winemaking history goes back to the 1860s, when viniferous grapes were first planted in the Clearwater River canyons near Lewiston. This area proved to be agreeable for wine grape production, sharing many characteristics with the Walla Walla Valley American Viticultural Area (AVA) in neighboring Oregon and Washington (see p. 903). By the 1870s, French and German immigrants had established a number of vineyards on the steep canyon walls. Idaho wines would go on to win gold medals at wine exhibitions from Portland to Buffalo.

In 1916, Prohibition spelled doom for Idaho's small but flourishing wine industry, and the state's pioneering role as a Pacific Northwest winemaker became a footnote of history until the 1970s, when wine grapes were again planted in the state, this time in southern Idaho's scenic Snake River Valley. Most vineyards can be found in the 82,000-square-mile Snake River Valley AVA, established in 2007 and stretching from Twin Falls in the east to the Snake River drainages of eastern Oregon.

To truly experience Idaho wine country, drive half an hour west of Boise to Caldwell's Sunnyslope Wine Trail, where nine of Idaho's most acclaimed wineries are clustered along steep, rocky cliffs overlooking the Snake River. From the octagonal, hillside tasting room at Ste. Chapelle, enjoy views of distant arid hills while sampling world-class riesling and chardonnay, then stop by Hat Ranch Winery for more unusual red wine varietals such as malbec and cabernet franc. At Koenig

Distillery and Winery, the winemakers' Austrian roots show up in the quality of its European-style wines and in the distillation of eau-de-vie liqueurs such as grappa and a gold-medal–winning pear brandy.

To pair Idaho's finest wines with cutting-edge cuisine, reserve a table at Boise's State and Lemp, which serves sophisticated locally sourced and seasonal dishes in a long, skinny dining room with a communal ambiance. Consider staying at downtown Boise's Modern Hotel, popular for its cool midcentury swank. This onetime traditional motor court has been totally transformed into an island of hip sophistication and also promises some of the city's best casual dining at its trendy bar and restaurant.

WHERE: Caldwell's Sunnyslope Wine Trail begins 26 miles west of Boise; sunnyslope winetrail.com. **STE. CHAPELLE:** Tel 208-453-7840; stechapelle.com. *When:* closed Sun Nov–Apr. **HAT RANCH WINERY:** Tel 208-994-6416; hatranchwinery.com. *When:* open Fri–Sun. **KOENIG DISTILLERY AND WINERY:** Tel 208-455-8386; koenigdistilleryandwinery.com. *When:* open Wed–Sun. **STATE AND LEMP:** Tel 208-429-6735; stateandlemp.com. *When:* open Wed–Sat. *Cost:* 5–6 course prix-fixe menu $75. **HOTEL MODERN:** Tel 866-780-6012 or 208-424-8244; themodernhotel.com. *Cost:* from $109; dinner $35. **BEST TIMES:** 1st Thurs in May for the Modern Art Festival at Hotel Modern (themodernhotel.com); late Aug for the Sunnyslope Wine Festival (sunnyslopewinetrail.com).

NORTHWEST PASSAGE SCENIC BYWAY

Idaho

Only one road—U.S. Highway 12—crosses north-central Idaho, and there's a reason for that. This is some of the coarsest terrain in the U.S., a vast wilderness of twisting canyons, raging rivers, and skyscraping mountain ranges that has long defied the efforts of highway engineers. Even Lewis and Clark turned back when faced with the Salmon River's mighty canyon, often referred to as the "River of No Return" (see next page). The explorers instead opted for the next river system north—the Lochsa and Clearwater—to make their east-west traverse of Idaho. Today's 202-mile Northwest Passage Scenic Byway (U.S. Highway 12) follows the Corps of Discovery's route along the Lochsa and Clearwater rivers, one of the most dramatic and ruggedly beautiful river valleys in the Rockies.

The Northwest Passage Scenic Byway passes through northern Idaho's rugged and beautiful terrain.

Highway 12 mounts the Continental Divide (and Montana border) at 5,233-foot Lolo Pass and then drops into the narrow, winding canyon of the Lochsa River, which charges down its precipitous channel, twisting and turning, jammed with house-size boulders. At the crossroads of Lowell, the Lochsa joins the Selway River to form the Middle Fork of the Clearwater River, and at Kooskia, it joins the main stem of the Clearwater River.

This 101-mile section of Highway 12 from Lolo Pass to Kooskia was completed only in 1962, since the formidable river canyons made road construction difficult and expensive. Beyond a couple of tiny settlements, evidence of humanity is limited along the route, making this prime territory for recreation. Hanging footbridges cross the Lochsa River, linking to long-distance hiking trails. The surging currents of the Lochsa and Selway are popular with white-water rafters and kayakers—in fact the Selway is considered one of the wildest rivers in the lower 48, flowing for 60 miles through untrammeled wilderness and dropping through 45 named rapids, many rated Class III and IV.

At Kooskia, the Northwest Passage Scenic Byway crosses into the 770,000-acre Nez Perce Indian Reservation. The history and culture of the Nez Perce tribe are celebrated in the Nez Perce National Historical Park, a series of 38 sites spread across four states. (The tribal name translates from French as "pierced nose," though the tribe refers to itself more simply as Nimiipuu, or "the People.") The park's visitor center and museum is located at Spalding, and represents the entire spectrum of the tribe's history. It pays particular attention to the Nez Perce War of 1877, which resulted when around 800 men, women, and children, with about twice that number of horses, were forced to flee eastward, crossing Idaho and then

Montana on their way to the Canadian prairies, where they hoped to continue their traditional lifestyle. After ten weeks and several battles with the U.S. Army, including the Battle of the Big Hole (see p. 630), the Nez Perce finally surrendered to U.S. forces after the Battle of the Bear Paw in north-central Montana. They were just 40 miles from sanctuary in Canada.

WHERE: north-central Idaho between Lolo Pass (45 miles southwest of Missoula, MT) and Lewiston (102 miles northeast of Walla Walla, WA); fhwa.dot.gov/byways. **HOW:** for info on rafting the Lochsa and Selway rivers, contact the Clearwater National Forest, tel 208-476-4541; fs.usda.gov/nezperceclearwater. **NEZ PERCE PARK:** Spalding. Tel 208-843-7009; nps.gov/nepe. **BEST TIME:** Apr for the Dogwood Festival in Lewiston (lcsc.edu/ce/dogwood).

Exploring Backcountry Wilderness by Car

SALMON RIVER SCENIC BYWAY

Idaho

Idaho's midsection is a mountainous and impossibly remote terrain, much of it contained in the 2.36-million-acre Frank Church River of No Return Wilderness, a contorted piece of real estate drained by the far-reaching branches of the Salmon River. This isn't country that easily yields its wonders to the casual visitor—with much of this land accessible only by hiking, floating, horseback riding, or driving long distances along marginal roads, experiencing it requires time and planning. To purists it may seem like cheating, but the 162-mile Salmon River Scenic Byway traces a picturesque route along the river's upper reaches, providing drivers a foretaste of the virgin landscapes beyond.

After leaving the Sawtooth Mountains near Stanley (see p. 603), the Salmon flows in every direction but up as it unwinds out of its tightly knotted central Idaho headwaters. From Challis

The Salmon River flows for 425 miles through central Idaho.

to Salmon, the region's recreational hub near the Montana border, large cattle ranches and irrigated meadows flank the river, and the steep mountains that rise on each side are mostly barren. Lewis and Clark passed through Salmon—in fact, Sacajawea, the Lemhi Shoshone woman who accompanied the Corps, was born and raised nearby. The Sacajawea Interpretive and Education Center just east of Salmon examines her life and role in the expedition, as well as traditional Shoshone culture.

Although float trips are available on just about every stretch of the upper Salmon, the real action begins at the village of North Fork, where the river pivots to thunder westward down the wild canyon, giving it its nickname, the River of No Return. A paved, then gravel, road follows the Salmon for 10 miles to the wilderness boundary, as it plunges into its canyon. Five- to six-day 75-mile float trips through Class III and IV rapids that attract river enthusiasts from all parts launch from sites along this stretch.

Get in touch with your inner adventurer—and the beauty of Idaho's pristine back country—at the Mackay Bar Outfitters & Guest

Ranch, east of Riggins and nestled within the Frank Church Wilderness. Buck and Joni Dewey passionately oversee this remote private setting on the shores of the Main Salmon River, and there are a variety of options to fill your days with as much, or as little, as you prefer. Jet boating is a highlight, but there is also swimming, horseback riding, and days spent fishing for steelhead trout (as well as rainbow, cutthroat, and Dolly Vardin), all capped off by topnotch home-cooked dinners (expect fresh salmon from the aptly named river just feet away). There are just three rooms in the main house and three freestanding cabins.

WHERE: runs between Stanley, on Hwy. 75, and Lost Trail Pass, on Hwy. 93; visitidaho .org/scenic-byways. *Visitor info:* Tel 800-727-2540 or 208-756-2100. **SACAJAWEA CENTER:** Salmon. Tel 208-756-1188; sacajaweacenter .org. *When:* daily, Memorial Day weekend– Labor Day; grounds year-round. **MACKAY BAR OUTFITTERS & GUEST RANCH:** Tel 208-965-8355; mackaybarranch.com. *Cost:* from $180 per person, double occupancy, includes lodging, breakfast, dinner, and some ranch activities. **BEST TIMES:** May–Sept for weather; mid-Aug for Sacajawea Heritage Days in Salmon (sacajaweacenter.org).

America's Greatest White Water

MIDDLE FORK OF THE SALMON RIVER

Idaho

Idaho has 3,100 white-water miles—more rushing water than any other state in the continental U.S.—and the very best for a rafting adventure is the Middle Fork of the Salmon River, considered by many in-the-know rafters as one of the top white-water rivers in the world.

The Middle Fork carves a mighty canyon through central Idaho's 2.36-million-acre Frank Church River of No Return Wilderness, the largest federally protected forest wilderness in the lower 48. The river drops some 3,000 feet in 100 miles, churning through 100 deep-rolling Class III and IV rapids. It carries you through spectacular forest and rocky gorges (should you have a moment to acknowledge your surroundings), and past sandy beaches for overnight camping and natural hot springs for soaking paddle-weary bones (one spring, called the Sunflower, spills over a rock to form a riverside hot shower). Sightings of bears, river otters, Rocky Mountain bighorn sheep, elk, and large birds of prey are common, and rafters can also sneak in some superb fishing—Idaho's acclaimed crystal clear waters are rich with rainbow, cutthroat, and Dolly Varden trout. Watch the canyon walls for vivid rock art, inscribed by the ancient Tukudeka people, who once claimed these wild canyons as their homeland.

To experience this unique and thrilling countryside, you must float—no motor craft allowed—on a four- to six-day camping expedition into the heart of the wilderness. Few Middle Fork outfitters are as experienced as Rocky Mountain River Tours, operated by Jared & Roni Hopkinson. Campfire dinners are Roni's domain, featuring favorite recipes from *The Outdoor Dutch Oven Cookbook* by Sheila Mills, a co-founder of the company, served under a brilliant canopy of stars.

Consider some post–white-water R&R in an

isolated, more-than-mile-high valley at the edge of the wilderness where you'll find the Diamond D Ranch, which has hosted families since 1952. The Diamond D offers get-away-from-it-all weeklong vacations with horseback riding and hiking to high wildflower-spangled meadows, alpine lakes, natural hot springs, and sharp mountain ridges, where the deeply trenched

The Middle Fork is the destination of choice for those seeking a top-notch white-water rafting experience.

valleys of central Idaho appear to go on forever. Cutthroat and rainbow trout—the wily quarry of patient fly-fishers—abound in quick-flowing streams and mirror-calm lakes. The striking scenery of Diamond D Ranch contrasts beautifully with the easy comforts of the ranch's modern log cabins, suites, and lodge rooms.

WHERE: The put-in for Middle Fork Salmon River rafting trips is 43 miles north of Stanley and 130 miles northeast of Boise. **ROCKY MOUNTAIN RIVER TOURS:** Tel 208-345-2400; rafttrips.com. *Cost:* from $1,095 per person for 4-day, all-inclusive trips, includes pickup in Stanley. *When:* June–Sept. **DIAMOND D RANCH:** Tel 800-222-1269 (winter) or 208-861-9206 (summer); diamondd ranch-idaho.com. *Cost:* from $1,350 per person per week, double occupancy, includes lodging, meals, and ranch activities. *When:* June–Sept. **BEST TIMES:** July–Aug for good weather and great rapids; Sept for calm, fun rapids and best fly-fishing.

Unexpected Pleasures in the Panhandle

SANDPOINT & THE SCHWEITZER SKI AREA

Idaho

Tucked away up in Idaho's panhandle, surrounded by the Selkirk and Cabinet mountains, Sandpoint (population 7,577) is an unexpected delight. The downtown comes right up to the edge of 43-mile-long Lake Pend Oreille

(pond-duh-RAY), which is so vast and so deep that during WWII the U.S. Navy established a training base here and used the lake as a stand-in for the ocean. Thanks to the quietness of the water—which reaches depths of 1,150 feet—the navy still maintains a lakeside submarine acoustic testing base.

Downtown Sandpoint is filled with lively restaurants, coffee shops, and boutiques. Walk to the lakefront, where you can admire the

pleasure boats docked at the marina, or go for a swim at City Beach. Rent a canoe, or take an afternoon cruise. If it's land-based activity you want, most of the southern half of the lake is surrounded by national forest, with good hiking and mountain biking.

Sandpoint still has a small-town feel, without the resort overlays of nearby Coeur d'Alene, with its larger and more upscale crowds (see p. 595). But that doesn't mean facilities at Sandpoint are secondary—just lower key. Stay at the lakeside Edgewater Resort, where the views are splendid and it's an easy walk to downtown. If you get the urge to explore the farther reaches of Lake Pend Oreille, head around the north end of the lake to the tiny town of Hope and enjoy a salmon dinner and a sunset from the outdoor seating at the aptly named Floating Restaurant.

When snow starts falling, Sandpoint changes gears and transforms itself into an après-ski mountain town. Nearby Schweitzer Mountain Resort is as uncrowded a ski area as you'd ever hope to find. The 2,900 skiable acres (50 percent beginning and intermediate) are spread across two large bowls and include 92 generally wide and well-groomed trails, plus an assortment of ungroomed chutes. It's worth a ride up the lift just for the slopeside view of Lake Pend Oreille.

WHERE: 80 miles northeast of Spokane, WA. *Visitor info:* Tel 800-800-2106 or 208-263-2161; visitsandpoint.info. **LAKE PEND OREILLE CRUISES:** Tel 888-726-3764 or 208-255-5253. *When:* May–Oct. **EDGEWATER RESORT:** Tel 800-635-2534 or 208-263-3194. *Cost:* from $129 (off-peak), from $239 (peak). **FLOATING RESTAURANT:** Hope. Tel 208-264-5311; hopefloatingrestaurant.com. *Cost:* dinner $40. *When:* Apr–Oct. **SCHWEITZER MOUNTAIN RESORT:** Tel 208-263-9555; schweitzer.com. *Cost:* lift tickets $73. *When:* early Dec–early Apr. **WHERE TO STAY:** Selkirk Lodge. Tel 877-487-4643; schweitzer.com. *Cost:* from $168 (off-peak), from $307 (peak). **BEST TIMES:** Feb for skiing; Aug for lake recreation; the 1st 2 weeks in Aug for the Festival at Sandpoint, a summer concert series (festivalatsandpoint.com).

Enraptured in the Realm of Raptors

SNAKE RIVER BIRDS OF PREY CONSERVATION AREA

Idaho

Apart from scrubby vegetation and a welcomed coating of green in the spring, the high desert landscape of the Snake River Birds of Prey National Conservation Area (NCA) in southwestern Idaho looks like a relatively lifeless place—until you train your eyes on the sky. Thanks to a unique ecosystem that stretches along 81 miles of the Snake River, the 485,000-acre NCA hosts the densest concentration of nesting birds of prey in North America. Deep, finely textured soils cover the surrounding plateau, making it an ideal habitat for large populations of burrowing mammals such as Paiute ground squirrels, kangaroo rats, and pocket gophers. The abundant critters eat shrubs and grasses, and are in turn eaten by keen-eyed avian hunters who pass through on their migration or nest in the cliffs that rise as high as 600 feet above the river.

Birders enraptured by raptors can beef up their life lists here. More than 700 nesting pairs represent 16 different species, nine diurnal (including American kestrels, golden eagles, northern harriers, and prairie falcons) plus seven types of owl, from the northern saw-whet to the long-eared to the great horned. Among the overwintering and migratory visitors are peregrine falcons, gyrfalcons, sharp-shinned hawks, and bald eagles. Birdlife on the NCA extends beyond raptors: The nearly

150 other species inhabiting the area include egrets and avocets, trumpeters, teals, terns, tanagers, and towhees. Visitors should bear in mind that facilities are few and far between, and Boise is your best bet for accommodations if you're not planning on camping.

The Birds of Prey National Conservation Area is centered around a long stretch of the Snake River.

If you don't have the time or patience for backcountry birding but you'd still like to get a glimpse of some of these elusive creatures, head to the World Center for Birds of Prey on the outskirts of Boise. A research and captive breeding facility operated by the Peregrine Fund, which works to conserve birds of prey worldwide, the center offers educational exhibits on raptor ecology and conservation; a kid-friendly display on bird basics; and an art gallery. The main attractions, however, are the birds themselves: In live stage presentations and from the viewing hall, visitors can behold such magnificent living specimens as the powerful harpy eagle, the massive Eurasian eagle-owl, and the endangered Aplomado falcon and California condor.

WHERE: northern boundary of the NCA is 20 miles south of Boise. Tel 208-384-3300; blm.gov. **WORLD CENTER FOR BIRDS OF PREY:** Boise. Tel 208-362-8687; peregrinefund.org. *When:* closed Mon. **BEST TIME:** mid-Mar–June for raptor viewing during nesting season.

A Mountain Paradise for Outdoor Adventure

THE SAWTOOTH NATIONAL RECREATION AREA

Stanley, Idaho

The old ranching community of Stanley, at the headwaters of the Salmon River, sits in the midst of some of the most glorious scenery in North America. The incredibly rugged and aptly named Sawtooth Mountains form a sudden wall of pink granite behind miles of lush meadows and spring-fed lakes. These stunning reflecting pools are ringed by campgrounds, small family resorts, and fishing lodges—just the beginning of the four-season recreation options that make the 750,000-acre Sawtooth National Recreation Area one of the most beloved outdoor destinations in the West.

The Sawtooths are just one range of mountains in the recreation area. There are more than 300 high mountain lakes here, many reached by the area's 700 miles of hiking trails. A popular overnight backpack trip is along the Toxaway Lake Loop, an 18-mile trail that leads past a series of pristine mountain lakes and culminates at Toxaway Lake, a mile-long body of water framed by jutting peaks. At Redfish Lake, the views are equally stunning, and the facilities a lot more comfortable. Just 6 miles south of Stanley and easily reached by vehicle, Redfish

Lake has lovely lakeside campgrounds, boat launches, and the venerable and woodsy Redfish Lake Lodge, a fixture for recreation-oriented family vacations since 1926. Choose from log cabins, condos, motel-style rooms, or guest rooms in the historic lodge, then hike trails through the lodgepole and Ponderosa pine forests, rent a kayak, or take a guided boat tour of the lake encircled by the beauty of the Sawtooths.

Another enticing area destination is the 900-acre Idaho Rocky Mountain Ranch, established in 1930 by a New York appliance tycoon who built it as a by-invitation-only hunting lodge. The ranch started accepting paying guests only

The dramatic peaks of the Sawtooth Mountains rise above the forest.

in the 1970s, and today reservations for its vintage cabins and lodge guest rooms are some of Idaho's most sought after. The centerpiece of the ranch is the 8,000-square-foot chinked log lodge, listed on the National Register of Historic Places, a beautifully atmospheric vestige of the 1930s. When it comes to organized activities, the ranch is laid-back, allowing guests to find their own pace and do as little or as much as they wish, whether that's trail riding or simply relaxing in the pool. The ranch is serious about its food, however; most meals are served fireside in the lodge, often serenaded by local musicians for a nice blend of Western luxury.

WHERE: Stanley is 132 miles northeast of Boise. Tel 208-774-3000; fs.usda.gov/sawtooth. *When:* late May–Aug. **REDFISH LAKE LODGE:** Tel 208-774-3536; redfishlake.com. *Cost:* from $84. *When:* late May–early Oct. **IDAHO ROCKY MOUNTAIN RANCH:** Tel 208-774-3544; idaho rocky.com. *Cost:* from $240 per person, double occupancy, includes breakfast, dinner, and use of ranch facilities. *When:* mid-June–mid-Sept. **BEST TIMES:** July–Sept for weather, wildflowers, and snow-free hiking trails; 4th weekend in Aug for the Sawtooth Salmon Festival.

Skiing in Classic Style

SUN VALLEY AND KETCHUM

Idaho

Sun Valley is an American classic. The country's original ski destination, created in 1936 by statesman Averell Harriman, it is still considered one of the finest ski resorts on the continent. Harriman was chairman of the board of Union Pacific Railroad in the 1930s, when he created the resort and its centerpiece, the luxurious Sun Valley Lodge, as a way to fill his trains during the quieter winter months. With the area's Sawtooth Mountains substituting when the Alps seemed just too far to go for the weekend, the resort, from its infancy, attracted a celebrity crowd. At the opening, some 300 guests, including Claudette Colbert, David Selznick, and Joan Bennett, strapped on skis to be photographed by the era's paparazzi.

The 80 percent sunshine rate and superb skiing remain the same, though much else has changed. Today's boldfaced names arrive by private jet, and speedy lifts and high-tech snowmaking equipment have picked up where the world's first alpine chairlift left off (price back then: 25 cents). Bald Mountain (Baldy), the resort's main ski slope, boasts a 3,400-foot vertical drop; of its 65 runs, 42 percent are an intermediate's dream. Cross-country skiers find a lot to like in the Sun Valley and neighboring Ketchum as well. The resort has its own Nordic and Snowshoe Center with about 25 miles of groomed trails, but located just north of (and higher than) Ketchum is the Galena Lodge, a county-operated cross-country ski center with 35 miles of trails, a full restaurant, a ski shop, and 17 miles of snowshoe trails. Summertime devotees find the entire area just as popular a playground, when the slopes become mountain bike runs.

One of the luminaries of the après-ski scene is the Sun Valley Resort's Duchin Lounge, where the ambience and live music is simultaneously relaxed, elegant, and just plain fun, and a limited menu of tasty bar food is on offer.

The action continues just down the road in the old mining town of Ketchum, first put on the map when Ernest Hemingway set up camp here in 1939. A recent influx of serious money, which has improved the shopping and dining options, might not have sat well with Papa, but his spirit is still present, in more ways than one:

Skiers descending Bald Mountain (aka Baldy) can see Ketchum in the distance.

He was buried here in 1961 after his death by suicide. His memory lingers on at the classy Pioneer Saloon, still the place for 32-ounce prime rib and Idaho's best potatoes.

WHERE: 150 miles east of Boise. **SUN VALLEY RESORT:** Tel 800-786-8259 or 208-622-4111; sunvalley.com. *Cost:* rooms from $284; lift tickets $60 (off-peak), $81 (peak). *When:* Ski season is late Nov–Apr. **GALENA LODGE:** Ketchum. Tel 208-726-4010; galenalodge.com. **PIONEER SALOON:** Ketchum. Tel 208-726-3139; pioneersaloon.com. *Cost:* dinner $40. **BEST TIMES:** Feb–Mar for skiing; late July–mid-Aug for free concerts by Sun Valley Symphony (svsummersymphony.org).

A High-Elevation, High-Spirited Lake and Resort

PAYETTE LAKE

McCall, Idaho

High in a basin between the Seven Devils and Salmon Mountain ranges in west-central Idaho, Payette Lake is 5,330 acres of radiantly blue glacial water edged by deep pine and fir forests. Here, at an elevation of 5,000 feet amid craggy Rocky Mountain peaks, the horizons seem broader, the crowds smaller, and the activities less packaged than at other Idaho lake resorts.

The former mill-town of McCall (population 3,000) sits on Payette Lake's southern shores, a lively, friendly town that's fronted by marinas, al fresco bars and restaurants, and, June through September, vivid floral displays. Getting out onto the 8-mile-long lake is summer's main activity, made simple by outfitters with boat and kayak rentals, guided tour-boat cruises, and the sandy beaches at 1,000-acre Ponderosa State Park. Wildlife from the park occasionally strolls onto the greens at the adjacent 27-hole McCall Golf Club, where deer, beavers, foxes, elk, and moose present photogenic course hazards. Summer visitors to Payette Lake also need to be on alert for other, more imaginative forms of wildlife: The lake is rumored to be home to a monster, a kind of American Loch Ness named Sharlie.

McCall receives over 300 inches of snow in winter and within a half hour drive from town are three fine ski resorts with a combined 2,600 skiable acres and vertical drops ranging from 1,800 to 2,800 feet. Nordic skiers can explore over 60 kilometers of groomed cross-country trails, and snowmobilers have access to 20,000 acres of deep-snow backcountry.

The highpoint of the year is McCall's Winter Carnival, ten days of rowdy, snow-focused revelry that draws over 60,000 people annually. The festival centers on snow and ice sculpture competitions, but packs in all sorts of other activities, including dogsled races, an ice-fishing derby, fireworks displays over frozen Payette Lake, and a raucous Mardi Gras parade followed by a polar plunge into icy lake waters.

The renovated Shore Lodge lives up to its name, fronting the lake at a point where the Payette River gathers its waters and begins its journey south. The lodge's huge log beams and rock fireplaces instill a feeling of warmth and comfort, and most of the 77 spacious rooms and suites offer dramatic lake and river views. At the lodge's The Narrows restaurant, refined dining meets the woodsy Northwest with such memorable dishes as grilled elk chops with smoked wild mushrooms and huckleberry compote. For a more casual meal, the Salmon River Brewery is a friendly brewpub with hand-crafted ales, hearty dishes, and an atmospheric location in McCall's historic train depot.

WHERE: Payette Lake is 100 miles north of Boise. Tel 800-260-5130 or 208-634-7631; mccallchamber.org. **MCCALL LAKE CRUISES:** Tel 208-634-5253; mccalllakecruises.com. *Cost:* 90-minute cruise $25. **PONDEROSA STATE PARK:** Tel 208-634-2164; parksandrecreation.idaho.gov. **MCCALL GOLF COURSE:** Tel 208-634-7200; mccallgolfclub.com. *Cost:* 18 holes from $27. *When:* late May–mid-Oct. **SHORE LODGE:** Tel 800-657-6464 or 208-634-2244; shorelodge.com. *Cost:* from $229 (off-peak), from $339 (peak); dinner at The Narrows $75. **SALMON RIVER BREWERY:** Tel 208-634-4772; salmonriverbrewery.com. *Cost:* $22. **BEST TIMES:** 10 days in late Jan–early Feb for McCall Winter Carnival (mccallchamber.org/winter-carnival); mid-July for the Summer Music Festival (thesummermusicfestival.com).

The Historic Town That Never Went Bust

WALLACE & THE SILVER VALLEY

Idaho

The upper reaches of the South Fork Coeur d'Alene River contain some of the richest silver and lead veins in the world. Since the 1880s the surrounding valley has been the scene of intensive industrial mining, and for many years the valley ranked first in the world for annual production of silver—even today, the silver mines are some of the country's most productive.

Wallace, which has long been the hub of the Silver Valley, is today one of the best preserved late-19th-century mining towns in the Northwest. But there's more to Wallace (population 781) than the estimated 1 billion ounces of silver it has produced. Located in a narrow, wooded valley just below the Lookout Pass in Idaho's eastern panhandle, Wallace is one of the very few towns listed in its entirety on the National Historic Register, with whole blocks that have remained intact for a century or longer. It's a lively place that makes the most of its colorful history. Of particular interest are the Wallace District Mining Museum, with vintage mining tools and a history of mining techniques, and the Oasis Bordello Museum, which tells a bawdier tale of mining town life. For a real experience of Wallace's underground, ride the open-air trolley from downtown to the Sierra Silver Mine, where retired miners lead tours deep into a mine.

A favorite watering hole is the 1313 Club Historic Saloon and Grill. An old-fashioned bar hung with big-game heads and antlers, it draws a lively, youthful crowd and serves up the town's best burger and fries, hands down.

Silver Mountain Ski and Summer Resort, just west of Wallace at Kellogg, has excellent powder snow—more than 300 inches of it annually—and wide-open, challenging terrain. Even if you're not a skier, you can ride the resort's gondola—the world's longest single-stage people carrier—which lifts winter skiers and summer hikers, bikers, and sightseers up 3.1 miles and 4,000 breathtaking vertical feet.

For bicyclists, the Route of the Hiawatha Rail Trail is an exceptionally exhilarating ride—15 miles of rail tunnels and trestles at the crest of the mountains between Idaho and Montana. The fun begins just past 4,710-foot Lookout Pass on the Montana side, where the trail enters Taft Tunnel, cut through solid rock, and emerges 8,771 feet later on the Idaho side. The trail then corkscrews down the mountain, winding through another nine tunnels and over seven trestles before reaching its end at Pearson (20 miles southeast of Wallace).

WHERE: 49 miles east of Coeur d'Alene. *Visitor info:* Tel 208-753-7151; wallaceidaho chamber.com. **MINING MUSEUM:** Tel 208-556-1592; wallaceminingmuseum.org. *When:* daily, May–Sept; closed Sat–Sun, Oct–Apr. **OASIS BORDELLO MUSEUM:** Tel 208-753-0801. *When:* May–Oct. **SIERRA SILVER MINE TOUR:** Tel 208-752-5151; silverminetour.org. *When:* May–Oct. **1313 CLUB HISTORIC SALOON AND GRILL:** Tel 208-752-9391. *Cost:* dinner $15. **SILVER MOUNTAIN RESORT:** Kellogg. Tel 866-344-2675 or 208-783-1111; silvermt.com. *Cost:* lift tickets $53. *When:* Dec–Mar. **ROUTE OF THE HIAWATHA TRAIL:** ridethehiawatha.com. Bike rentals are available from Lookout Pass Ski and Recreation Area, tel 208-744-1301; skilook out.com. *When:* May–mid-Oct. **BEST TIMES:** Jan–Mar for skiing; May–Sept for sunny weather; 3rd weekend in Aug for the Huckleberry Heritage Festival (wallaceidaho chamber.com).

A Top Competition Transforms a Small Town

NATIONAL OLDTIME FIDDLERS' CONTEST AND FESTIVAL

Weiser, Idaho

The sound of the fiddle has graced the fertile Weiser valley in far western Idaho since the 1860s, when pioneers on Oregon Trail wagon trains stopped here to rest and recharge before attempting the challenging

Snake River ferry crossing and the rugged mountains of eastern Oregon that lay ahead. As the town of Weiser (WEEZ-er) prospered from farming and orcharding, the love of the fiddle seemed to grow with it. Fiddling contests were held in Weiser as early as 1914, and the present National Oldtime Fiddlers' Contest—one of the most prestigious fiddling events in the world, and according to organizers, the largest in the U.S.—was inaugurated in 1953.

Held the third week of June, the fiddlers' contest transforms Weiser—normally a quiet agricultural town of approximately 5,300 folks with a core of beautiful late-Victorian storefronts and homes—into a kind of fiddle-focused Mardi Gras. First, there's the official competition, involving some 350 contestants from around the U.S. Then, on Saturday, the final competition comes down to a playoff among the Grand Champion Division finalists and the top five players in each of eight age categories, with the winners—whose playing is judged by danceability, old-time style, rhythm, and tone.

The excitement of the competition extends beyond the auditorium doors and brings a real carnival atmosphere to the whole town. Enthusiastic music lovers descend on these parts to partake of the festivities, and a good-natured, all-American sense of fun pervades the community. The fine fiddle playing is not restricted to the official contest venue.

Weiser's city park becomes Bluegrass Village and is the hub for a full slate of concerts—some scheduled, many impromptu—that start early and go late into the night. The high school football field, which is converted to a campground for the event, is another great spot for music: Spontaneous jam sessions spring up among the attendees, many of whom are themselves bluegrass players who have come from across the country to listen, play, and learn. Over the course of the week, Bluegrass Village also hosts an arts and crafts fair, farmers market, food booths, kids events, and good-natured competition. The festival atmosphere climaxes on the weekend, with a parade, rodeo, barbecue, and one final "battle of the bands," a fitting end to a homespun festival of traditional American music.

WHERE: 72 miles northwest of Boise. Tel 208-414-0255; fiddlecontest.org. *Cost:* tickets $5–$16. *When:* 3rd week of June.

Mushrooms, Munchkins, Russian Spacemen, and President Ike

ATOMIC OZ
ON THE KANSAS PRAIRIE

Kansas

For being so verifiably "heartland," Kansas is also an odd place, much of it so flat and featureless that early settlers were said to sometimes go insane from a kind of apeirophobia—the fear of infinity. Kansas is the center of the country (literally: the geographical center of the contiguous U.S. is in the town of Lebanon), and today it's part of the country's breadbasket (No. 2 in U.S. wheat production—following North Dakota—and scything more than 321 million bushels annually). It was the childhood home of Dwight D. Eisenhower, and in 1899 forever secured its place on the map when it served as the stand-in for all of American home life in L. Frank Baum's *The Wonderful Wizard of Oz*.

During the Cold War, Kansas began to take on an additional identity as home to scores of huge, impregnable underground nuclear-missile silos, positioned out among the wheat and sunflower fields. In 1958, a story in the *Topeka Capital* bore the headline "Missile Base Is Viewed with Joy." Within a few years, Kansas was the nation's No. 1 launching pad for intercontinental ballistic missiles. Today, with the Cold War behind us, those silos have been decommissioned, with many sold off to individuals and businesses. As many as a dozen have been turned into underground homes and, one, in the town of Holton, has been transformed into the local high school, Jackson Heights.

As if to demonstrate how far we've come in our relationship with the former Soviet bloc, the Kansas Cosmosphere and Space Center in Hutchinson tells the story of the U.S.–Russian space race through a collection of artifacts second only to the National Air and Space Museum in D.C. (see p. 261). It's got the *Apollo 13* command module ("Houston, we have a problem"), a Soviet Vostok capsule and Soyuz descent module, a U.S. SR-71 spy plane, and many displays on the human story of space.

About 60 miles north, in Abilene, the Eisenhower Center tells the story of our 34th president, who governed from 1953–61 during the first phase of the Cold War and the space race. It includes a museum with more than 30,000 square feet of exhibition space, the presidential library, Ike's boyhood home, which is decorated just as it was in 1946, and his grave.

Click your heels twice and transport yourself 50 miles northeast and you'll come to Wamego, home of the Oz Museum and its 2,000-item collection of Oz memorabilia, including Baum's early books and props from the classic 1939 film.

WHERE: Hutchinson is 50 miles northwest of Wichita. **COSMOSPHERE AND SPACE CENTER:** Hutchinson. Tel 800-397-0330 or 620-662-2305; cosmo.org. **EISENHOWER CENTER:** Abilene. Tel 877-RING-IKE or 785-263-6700; eisenhower.archives.gov. **OZ MUSEUM:** Wamego. Tel 866-458-TOTO or 785-458-8686; ozmuseum.com. *When:* open daily.

From Ashes to Art

LAWRENCE

Kansas

The U.S. Civil War "officially" started in 1861, when Southern troops fired on Fort Sumter in Charleston, South Carolina (see p. 378), but any Kansan can tell you that those shots were preceded by a decade of murderous battle here in "Bleeding Kansas." In 1854, a group of Free Staters from Massachusetts founded the town of Lawrence in an effort to increase the abolitionist vote. On August 21, 1863, 400 pro-slavery guerrillas rode into Lawrence, murdered more than 180 unarmed men and boys in their homes, and then burned the town to the ground. It stands as one of the great atrocities of the war.

Lawrence survived, though, and over time became the most progressive city in otherwise conservative Kansas. Lawrence also boasts one of the Midwest's best arts and music scenes, a beautiful setting among rolling hills (anomalous for Kansas), a vibrant downtown core full of historic architecture, and a college-town vibe courtesy of the University of Kansas and the Haskell Indian Nations University, the country's oldest intertribal university. In town, the Lawrence Arts Center is the hub for local arts, with two galleries putting on about 25 exhibitions yearly.

The Downtown Lawrence Outdoor Sculpture Exhibition displays works by nationally recognized artists (rotated annually) which share space with antiques shops, boutiques, and cafés. More than 30 galleries scattered around the area can be explored either ad hoc or as part of an organized gallery walk. Two blocks east of downtown, the Old West Lawrence neighborhood was once home to Lawrence's wealthiest families. Today, its profusion of ornate homes, representing

The University of Kansas sits on Mount Oread, the highest point in Lawrence.

17 different architectural styles, has earned it a listing in the National Register of Historic Places.

For a completely different experience, book a room at the Circle S Ranch & Country Inn, 14 miles to the north. Originally homesteaded in the 1860s, it's now a romantic B&B in the guise of a sixth-generation Kansas ranch, with 12 country-style rooms complemented by niceties like a hot tub housed in a former grain silo and purposefully lacking Wi-Fi or phones. Across its 600 acres you can find small herds of bison and longhorn, Hereford, and Angus cattle, as well as stone fences, cattle trails, fields of tallgrass prairie, and an 1870s schoolhouse.

WHERE: 40 miles west of Kansas City. *Visitor info:* Tel 888-LAW-KANS; visitlawrence.com. **LAWRENCE ARTS CENTER:** Tel 785-843-2787; lawrenceartscenter.org. **OUTDOOR SCULPTURE EXHIBITION:** lawrenceks.org. **CIRCLE S RANCH:** Tel 785-843-4124; circlesranch.com. *Cost:* from $150. **BEST TIMES:** late Oct for the Lawrence ArtWalk (lawrenceartwalk.org); the last Fri of the month for Final Friday art walks.

Monuments to a Vanished Sea

THE NIOBRARA CHALK

Kansas

About 80 or 90 million years ago, Kansas was part of a vast inland sea stretching from the Gulf of Mexico to Alaska, cutting the continent in two. While dinosaurs roamed its shores, sea monsters such as the

Xiphactinus audax, a fish with razor-sharp teeth and a body that could grow up to 18 feet long, swam beneath. Infinitely smaller but no less important in the grand scheme of things, untold numbers of tiny algae were busy photosynthesizing for food and regularly shucking off pieces of their protective calcium coating. This rained down to the sea floor and eventually produced a soft sedimentary layer hundreds of feet thick,

which is now known as the Niobrara Chalk. Nineteenth-century fossil hunters found a wealth of remains preserved in the sediment, and to this day dedicated visitors can easily find evidence of the long-gone sea here in northwestern Kansas, from oyster shells and fossilized fish vertebrae to sharks' teeth.

Even more visible than fossils, though, is the chalk itself. Glaciers, rains, and river flow sculpted the land, carving the Niobrara (as well as the more common regional sandstone and limestone deposits) into spires, hoodoos, and other dramatic formations. Set against the vast Kansas landscape, the stark whiteness of these monuments is almost otherworldly, simultaneously bringing to mind Moorish castles, Roman aqueducts, and giant dino-

The striking Niobrara Chalk formations had their beginnings 80 million years ago.

saur bones. In western Gove County, 15 miles from any town, the Monument Rocks (aka the Chalk Pyramids) were a landmark for the early pioneers. Located on private, undeveloped rangeland but open to the public, they stretch out in two elongated rows, their tops reaching 70 feet toward the endless sky. A fissure in one outcropping, known as the Keyhole, is among the most photographed sites in this part of Kansas. About 7 miles west, the Keystone Gallery is a museum of local Kansas fossils, an art gallery, and a gift shop.

Fifty miles to the east, Castle Rock rivals the Monument Rocks as the Niobrara's most famous outcrop. Standing alone and

convincingly castlelike on a wide plain, it's a living example of how fragile these ancient marvels are: In 2001, the castle's tallest spire collapsed after a storm. The relative softness of the chalk also makes it susceptible to human damage, so remember: Look, don't climb.

WHERE: Gove, Logan, and Scott counties, in northwestern KS. **MONUMENT ROCKS:** 18 miles north of Scott City, off U.S. 83. **KEYSTONE GALLERY:** Scott City; Tel 620-872-2762; keystonegallery.com. *When:* Apr–Oct. **BEST TIME:** early morning, since the chalk can be 10 degrees hotter than anything else once the sun warms it.

For Amber Waves of Grain

TALLGRASS PRAIRIE PRESERVE

Strong City, Kansas

Once there was tallgrass prairie as far as the eye could see, flowing like a green ocean from Ohio to the Rocky Mountains and from Texas up into Canada, covering some 266,000 square miles. That was the prairie of the

buffalo, the Indian, and our pioneer ancestors who, as they moved west, never imagined that their settling and plowing and building could possibly put a dent in its vastness. But it did. Today less than 4 percent of the tallgrass

prairie remains, just isolated pockets preserved in an effort to retain their richness for future generations. One such is Tallgrass Prairie National Preserve, a 10,894-acre former cattle ranch, designed to educate visitors about the prairie ecosystem, Kansas's ranching heritage, and the pre-settlement landscape.

Visitors can tour the preserve's historic buildings and grounds, which on many summer weekends are staffed by living-history interpreters building rock walls, working in the garden, churning butter, and performing other tasks of ranch and farm life between the 1880s and 1930s. The schoolhouse feels completely authentic with its period desks, schoolbooks, and blackboards. Nature trails allow you to explore creekside woodlands, tallgrass prairie (hiking from the park headquarters to the schoolhouse and back), and a section of

The Tallgrass Prairie Preserve is one of the last remaining sections of prairie in Kansas.

lowland prairie that's been restored after decades as farm- and ranchland.

From late April through October, daily bus tours take visitors deeper into the prairie, with explanation of its geology, Indian and Western history, and biological diversity. The area is home to 40 to 60 different kinds of grasses, and 300 species of herbs and flowers, not to mention coyote, jackrabbits, white-tailed deer, wild turkeys, red-tailed hawks, golden eagles, and more. Those wanting an even closer view can hike the preserve's backcountry trails.

The Tallgrass Prairie Preserve is located midway on the Flint Hills National Scenic Byway, which stretches along 47 miles of Highway 177 from Cassoday in the south to Council Grove in the north.

WHERE: 85 miles northeast of Wichita. Tel 620-273-8494; nps.gov/tapr. *When:* tours and backcountry trails May–Oct. **FLINT HILLS SCENIC BYWAY:** travelks.com/ksbyways. **WHERE TO STAY:** Cottage House Hotel, Council Grove. Tel 620-767-6828; cottagehousehotel.com. *Cost:* from $110. **BEST TIMES:** spring for spectacular green grass and for wildflowers; fall for autumn colors and the highest grass growth.

A Road to the Top of the World

BEARTOOTH SCENIC BYWAY

Montana

Called America's most beautiful road by no less a traveler than the late Charles Kuralt, the Beartooth Highway has viewpoints every bit as spectacular as those in neighboring Yellowstone National Park (see p. 676).

With 20 peaks reaching over 12,000 feet in elevation—including Montana's greatest, Granite Peak, at 12,799 feet—the Beartooth Mountains offer some of the highest and most rugged landscapes in the country. The byway also passes through a series of ecosystems, from lush pine forests to alpine tundra in the

space of just a few miles. The mostly two-lane highway climbs in looping switchbacks from the handsome small-town tourist mecca of Red Lodge over the massive uplift of the Beartooth Plateau to tiny Cooke City, at Montana's northeast entrance to Yellowstone. Plan to spend most of the day making this

68-mile drive: You'll want to pull off at every scenic viewpoint to study the rugged peaks with glacier-carved cirques spilling down into U-shaped valleys.

The byway crests at 10,974 feet at the aptly named "Top of the World," a photo opportunity with few rivals. From here to Cooke City are wonderful alpine meadows that, once the snow has melted (this can be as late as July), are filled with wildflowers, icy trickles of water, glistening lakes, and a number of inviting trailheads. Be sure to take the short spur road up to the Clay Butte Lookout for magnificent views.

This uber-scenic highway is bracketed by two appealing towns. At 7,608 feet, Cooke City is remote, retaining a bit of a wild edge from its mining-camp roots, while at the base of the byway, Red Lodge, a former coal-mining center, offers lovely mountain surroundings, excellent restaurants, and spring skiing at nearby Red Lodge Mountain. Both the city's history and its newfound status as a center for Rocky Mountain chic are represented by the Pollard Hotel. Built in 1893, it was the only brick building in the city, and it quickly became Red Lodge's hub. Restored in the 1990s, today it offers old-fashioned Western atmosphere—the pine-paneled lobby and dining room fairly breathe turn-of-the-20th-century elegance—fused with modern comfort and convenience.

Get a feel for this country, and for how people live here today, at the 12,000-acre Lazy E-L Ranch, a working livestock operation 20 miles west of Red Lodge. The Mackays, who have owned and operated the ranch for four

The Beartooth Mountains represent the largest contiguous land area above 10,000 feet in the U.S.

generations, open it up to small groups only: A family or group of eight can reserve the ranch to themselves for a week. Guests have the option of joining the ranch crew on horseback as they move cattle and perform ranch chores; exploring the glorious landscapes by fishing trout-rich creeks, hiking, or mountain biking; or simply kicking back and enjoying the comforts of their historic log cabin and the dramatic mountain scenery of this mighty beautiful corner of Montana.

WHERE: between Red Lodge and Cooke City in southern MT. fhwa.dot.gov/byways. *When:* closed mid-Oct–late May. **POLLARD HOTEL:** Red Lodge. Tel 406-446-0001; the pollard.com. *Cost:* from $110 (off-peak), from $155 (peak); dinner $40. **LAZY E-L RANCH:** Tel 406-328-6858; lazyel.com. *Cost:* from $2,176 per person per week, includes meals and activities. *When:* mid-May–Sept. **BEST TIME:** mid-June for the Red Lodge Music Festival (rlmf.org).

Montana's Prime Lakefront

FLATHEAD LAKE

Bigfork, Montana

For generations, Montanans have made the annual trip to Flathead Lake for idyllic summer holidays—swimming, boating, and fishing on the largest natural freshwater lake west of the Mississippi. Ringed by mountains, with plenty of state parks, campgrounds, and summer cabins to make this a perfect family vacation spot, Flathead Lake is 28 miles long, up to 15 miles wide, and more than 350 feet deep. It is so large that it never seems busy—and large enough to support the rumored existence of a Loch Ness–style creature, the Flathead Monster.

If you neglected to bring your own boat, the 150-passenger *The Shadow* tour boat offers trips onto the lake from near Polson, along the way passing 2,160-acre Wild Horse Island, the lake's largest, which is home to bighorn sheep, bald eagles, bears, deer, and—yes—wild horses.

The resort town of Bigfork, at the lake's northeast corner, is a beautiful bayside community alive with art galleries, fine restaurants, and high-end boutiques. Bigfork offers a certain arty sophistication. This is most palpable when the professional Bigfork Summer Playhouse opens for a four-production season of comedies and musicals.

Flathead Lake comprises more than 190 square miles.

Just south of Bigfork—and an easy 35-mile drive from Glacier National Park (see p. 620)—is one of Montana's most beloved (especially by families) dude ranches, Averill's Flathead Lake Lodge. With its waterfront location and 2,000 acres of woodlands, the lodge offers a mix of horseback riding, fishing, sailing, and other water sports—all served up with plenty of Western hospitality in a truly beautiful setting. The main lodge and cottages tucked into the forest were built in 1932 as a boys camp but then abandoned until a locally born fellow named Les Averill acquired the vacant property in 1945, then built his dream. Still owned and operated by the Averill family, Flathead Lake Lodge offers such a breadth of activities that one week's stay won't even begin to exhaust the roster of possibilities and helps explain the guest return rate of over 50 percent.

Where: 82 miles north of Missoula. ***The Shadow:*** Polson. Tel 800-882-6363 or 406-883-3636; kwataqnuk.com. *When:* mid-June–early Sept. **Bigfork Summer Playhouse:** Tel 406-837-4886; bigforksummerplayhouse .com. *Cost:* tickets from $26. *When:* mid-May–early Sept. **Averill's Flathead Lake Lodge:** Tel 406-837-4391; flatheadlakelodge .com. *Cost:* $3,808 per person per week, double occupancy, includes meals and all on-site activities. *When:* mid-June–early Sept. **Best times:** June–Sept for weather; late July for cherry season; 1st weekend in Aug for the Bigfork Festival of the Arts (bigforkfestivalof thearts.com).

Mountain Bliss Without the Crowds

Big Sky

Montana

When it comes to Big Sky, Montana's premier ski and resort destination, "big" is the operative word. At the head of a beautiful mountain valley an hour north of Yellowstone National Park (see p. 676), Big Sky came

Despite the popularity of Big Sky, its trails never feel crowded.

into being back in 1973 as the dream of Chet Huntley, the late NBC newscaster and a Montana native. The ski resort, which reaches across four mountains, including the pyramid-like crest of 11,166-foot Lone Peak, certainly qualifies as "The Biggest Skiing in America."

One hallmark of skiing at Big Sky is the breadth and variety of terrain. Its 5,532 spectacularly skiable acres, with (almost) uniformly excellent conditions and vaulting Rockies views, have an average of only two skiers per acre—meaning lift lines are practically unheard of. Much of the annual 400-inch snowfall is the bone-dry talc that local skiers reverently call "cold smoke," and while there's extreme white-knuckle skiing for sure (the aerial tram to the Matterhorn-like Lone Peak summit offers skiers a 4,350-foot vertical drop and some of the steepest chutes in the world), a good 25 percent of the resort's 300-plus trails are perfect for the intermediate skier.

In 2004, Moonlight Basin, on Lone Peak's north and west face, became the first new destination ski resort to open in the U.S. in over 20 years and in 2013 came under the same ownership as Big Sky. Today, Big Sky and Moonlight Basin have interconnecting ski trails accessed with a joint lift ticket.

The 90-room Lodge at Big Sky enjoys a perfect location at the base of Lone Peak, replete with outdoor hot tubs, a heated indoor pool, and free shuttle service to all the ski lifts. If you're more into cross-country than downhill skiing, visit the Lone Mountain Ranch. An elegant four-season lodge, it has 45 miles of exceptional cross-country ski trails. (It's also an Orvis-endorsed fly-fishing resort in the summer months.) Lone Mountain is special for its seclusion, yet its top-drawer amenities, like its acclaimed restaurant and easy shuttles to the Big Sky area, mean zero inconvenience. Guests stay in charming cabins hidden amid the forest. The ranch's snowy horse-drawn sleigh ride through the woods to a lantern-lit cabin offers an unforgettable old-time evening with great food and a spirited sing-along.

WHERE: 45 miles south of Bozeman. **BIG SKY RESORT:** Tel 800-548-4486 or 406-995-5900; bigskyresort.com. *Cost:* lift tickets from $106. *When:* Ski season is late Nov–Apr. **LODGE AT BIG SKY:** Tel 406-995-7858; lodgeatbigsky.com. *Cost:* from $110 (off-peak), from $150 (peak). **LONE MOUNTAIN RANCH:** Tel 800-514-4644 or 406-995-4644; lonemountainranch.com. *Cost:* from $2,300 per person per week, all-inclusive; dinner $85 for nonguests. *When:* mid-June–mid-Sept; mid-Dec–Mar. **BEST TIMES:** Jan–Feb for cross-country; Jan–Mar for downhill skiing; June–July for fly-fishing. Sat nights in winter, when fireworks illuminate the rocky face of Lone Peak.

In addition to skiing, the Big Sky Mountain Village includes lodges, cabins, and restaurants for the full resort experience.

Ancient Life in a Youthful City

MUSEUM OF THE ROCKIES

Bozeman, Montana

W ith a population of 37,000, Bozeman vacillates between being a small town and a jewel of Western sophistication. The downtown's historic redbrick storefronts are filled with galleries, fine restaurants, and a slew of hip hangouts that can't quite decide if they are coffee shops, bakeries, or wine bars. The city's youthful energy is explained in part by the presence of Montana State University's 15,000 students and by Bozeman's stunning, big-as-all-outdoors location in the forested Gallatin Valley surrounded by the peaks of the Bridger and Gallatin ranges—all reasons that Bozeman is commonly considered one of the country's "Most liveable places." The town has long drawn legions of tanned, fit adventurers who enjoy hiking, mountain biking, and fishing right out the backdoor.

The Museum of the Rockies, located on the university campus, is known worldwide for its vast collection of dinosaur fossils, most of which were excavated by the museum's own expeditions to Montana fossil beds and are now displayed in the Siebel Dinosaur Complex, designed by world-renowned paleontologist and adviser to the *Jurassic Park* films, Dr. Jack Horner. (Montana may never be considered the epicenter of modern life, but about 65 to 70 million years ago, during the late Cretaceous period, it was a happening place.) Almost as popular as the dinosaurs are the museum's planetarium, an excellent exhibit on the native peoples of the northern Rockies and Plains, plus displays on Montana's pioneer exploration and settlement, including an 11-acre Living History Farm that re-creates a rustic prairie homestead from the early 1900s.

The glory of the Bozeman area is scarcely confined to prehistoric life. West of Bozeman, the Gallatin River flows out of its mountain canyon to its appointment with the Madison and Jefferson rivers at Three Forks, forming the Missouri River. These rivers provoke near-religious fervor in fly-fishers—casting into these broad, fast-moving rivers for blue-ribbon wild rainbow and large brown trout is the life dream of many anglers.

The owners of the Howlers Inn B&B will suggest the area's best fly-fishing, white-water rafting, and horseback riding opportunities (you are also just one hour by car from Yellowstone National Park's northern entrance). But the real reason to stay here is the inn's role as Wolf Sanctuary, housing rescued and captive-bred wolves that cannot be released into the wild. Just be prepared to hear their nighttime howls as you drift off to sleep.

If you want to stay right in town, opt instead for the six-room Voss Inn, housed in a painstakingly restored Victorian home.

The Museum of the Rockies possesses the largest Tyrannosaurus rex skull ever discovered.

It's just three blocks from Main Street, but the period-furnished inn will transport you back to 1883.

WHERE: 95 miles southeast of Helena; 600 W. Kagy Blvd. Tel 406-994-2251; museum oftherockies.org. *Visitor info:* Tel 406-994-2682; bozemancvb.com. **HOWLERS INN B&B:** Tel 888-HOWLERS or 406-587-5229; howlersinn.com. *Cost:* from $125 (off-peak), from $145 (peak). **THE VOSS INN:** Tel 406-587-0982; bozeman-vossinn.com *Cost:* from $130 (off-peak), from $150 (peak). **BEST TIMES:** June for fishing; June–Sept for weather; 1st weekend in Aug for the Sweet Pea Festival (sweetpeafestival.org); 1st Sun in Dec for the Christmas Stroll.

Wilderness and Western Hospitality

THE BOB MARSHALL WILDERNESS & CHEFF GUEST RANCH

Charlo, Montana

The Rocky Mountain Front, a towering wall of rock that spans over 200 miles in northern Montana, forms the Rockies' eastern face. Formed by the same geologic forces that created Glacier National Park (see p. 620),

the Rocky Mountain Front hoists up directly from rangeland, providing an abrupt and dramatic transition from the flat prairies of the east to the rugged mountains rising sharply in the west. Here and there, narrow river-carved canyons slice through the Front, providing entry points to backcountry hiking and fishing in the Bob Marshall Wilderness, a million-acre preserve of deep forest, alpine lakes, and mighty river valleys. "The Bob," as the area is known, is named after an early 20th-century forester and conservation pioneer, and has more than 1,000 miles of trails, offering fit and well-prepared backpackers or trail riders access to one of the most completely preserved mountain ecosystems in the world. Many backpackers make the five-to-seven-day trek across it to view the Chinese Wall, a narrow 1,000-foot-high fin of rock that for 22 miles crowns the Continental Divide.

In this spectacular setting, some of the state's best-loved and most venerable guest ranches have operated for decades, providing memorable horseback and fishing holidays.

The Cheff family, one of the oldest and most respected outfitting families in Montana, founded the Cheff Guest Ranch & Outfitters in 1933 based on a love and respect for the surrounding mountain wilderness. Today, guests can choose to take part in the daily routine of the working ranch, where cattle and horses are raised on 15,000 stunning acres, or try horseback riding, canoeing, and fishing on the ranch's vast expanse and at nearby Flathead

The rising sun illuminates the Chinese Wall and Cliff Pass.

Lake (see p. 613), the largest freshwater lake in the western United States. Glacier National Park (see p. 620) is a scenic two-hour drive away, but even the most ambitious guests find themselves with plenty of activities and adventures to keep them busy around the ranch.

All-inclusive 6–8 day pack trips are a specialty of the Cheff family, whether into the untouched natural beauty of the Bob Marshall Wilderness or the nearby Mission Mountain Wilderness. World-class fishing trips of 3–8 days for trout, bass, bullhead, and perch can also be arranged. Along the way, you're likely to spot some of the wildlife that call this magnificent region home, including mountain goats, deer, elk, and badgers. You might even see a bald eagle soar overhead.

WHERE: Charlo is 55 miles north of Missoula. **BOB MARSHALL WILDERNESS:** Tel 406-466-5341; fs.usda.gov/attmain/flathead. **CHEFF GUEST RANCH:** Charlo. Tel 406-644-2557; cheffguestranch.com. *Cost:* $320 all inclusive (cabins available); 7-day pack trip $2,520, all inclusive. *When:* June–Nov. **BEST TIMES:** June–Sept for weather. There's a small-town parade in Charlo and a cookout along Main Street every 4th of July.

A Fateful Meeting of Divergent Cultures: Custer's Last Stand

LITTLE BIGHORN BATTLEFIELD

Crow Agency, Montana

On the hills above the Little Bighorn River in southeastern Montana, one of the most epochal clashes of American history took place, the Battle of the Little Bighorn. This is one of the West's most haunted landscapes:

On these slopes the U.S. Army's Seventh Cavalry, led by General George A. Custer, met the forces of the Lakota Sioux and Cheyenne warriors in battle on June 25, 1876.

The lives and cultures that collided at this battlefield are complex, fascinating, and filled with enigma. Ohio-born Custer graduated last in his class at West Point, at 23 became the youngest general in the Union Army's history, and, though court-martialed for being absent without leave after the Civil War, found himself a commanding officer at the Dakota frontier's Fort Abraham Lincoln when the orders came to force the nomadic Sioux and Cheyenne back onto their Great Sioux Reservation. A growing number of them—perhaps as many as 7,000—had left the reservation in the early summer of 1876 and migrated into Wyoming and Montana territory to live their old way of life.

The Grant administration sent three military columns to campaign against them. Custer and the Seventh Cavalry discovered the Indian encampment along the Little Bighorn, and without waiting for the other units, he divided his 647 men into thirds and took the offensive against one of the largest Indian forces ever gathered, up to 2,000 warriors. In the ensuing battle, 263 men from the Seventh Cavalry were killed, including Custer and his brother, and at least 60 Indian warriors died as well.

What actually happened during the short but decisive battle—most of the fighting was over in three hours on June 25 (although another 350 cavalrymen were held under siege for another day and a half)—is far from certain, and the monument's excellent visitors center provides compelling exhibits and background. Just up the hill from the visitors center is Last

Stand Hill Monument, where the last of the Seventh Cavalry died. Grave markers stand where the bodies of soldiers were found (Custer himself is buried at West Point; see p. 205). To look down the grassy hillside at the markers, some standing alone, others huddled together, many clumped around the swale where Custer's own body was found, is to vividly experience the full horror of the battle. In 2003, the National Park Service unveiled the Little Bighorn Battlefield Indian Memorial, dedicated to Indian perspectives on the conflict and consisting, in part, of bronze statues of "Spirit Warriors" representing the warriors and Native women involved in the battle.

The Little Bighorn Battlefield National Monument is located on the Crow Indian Reservation: At 2.2 million acres of rolling prairie and rugged foothills, it is Montana's largest reservation.

In late August, thousands of tribe members and visitors rendezvous to celebrate the Crow Fair, one of the largest American Indian gatherings, with dance contests, a daily parade, an all-Indian rodeo, and wild horse racing. This temporary encampment is known as the "Tepee Capital of the World," and you'll probably never see this many tepees in one place anywhere else.

WHERE: 18 miles east of Hardin. Tel 406-638-2621; nps.gov/libi. **CROW FAIR:** Tel 406-638-3896. *When:* 3rd weekend in Aug. **BEST TIME:** the week of June 25 for Big Horn Days in Hardin with a period-costume Grand Ball, carnival, rodeo, and Custer's Last Stand Reenactment (littlebighornreenactment.com).

The Custer National Cemetery is a reminder of the horror of the battle.

Ranch Romance in the Bitterroot Valley

TRIPLE CREEK RANCH

Darby, Montana

Tucked into the southern end of the scenic Bitterroot Valley, at the foot of 10,157-foot Trapper Peak, Triple Creek may be called a ranch but it's really a luxury hideaway bordered on three sides by national forest, where seclusion, beauty, and comfort are served up in Western-size portions. A menu brimming with outdoor adventures meets its match with the more refined pleasures of fine wine and a remarkable cuisine best described as France-meets-the-Northern-Rockies. Triple Creek shows off "The Last Best Place" state at its breathtaking finest.

The ranch's 24 hand-hewn log cabins and luxury homes are scattered amid 600 unspoiled acres of towering ponderosa pines, rushing streams, and meadows, all backed up to several million acres of wilderness in the Bitterroot Mountains. Much emphasis is placed on its fine stable of 40 horses at the ready, but you'll also find a pool, fitness center, tennis courts, and putting green. The three-story central lodge is tiered with balconies and houses the vaulted, wood-beamed dining room and a rooftop lounge and library.

As befitting a member of the exclusive Relais & Châteaux network, Triple Creek offers an exceptionally friendly though ever discreet staff that delivers true luxury: With more staff than guests, Triple Creek has honed sophisticated pampering into an art form.

Summer brings mountain biking, hiking, and trail riding, while winter months promise 300 inches of snowfall and short lift lines at the nearby Lost Trail Powder Mountain ski area. But there will be days when you want to just stay put and enjoy a hot buttered rum—a ranch specialty, concocted with a touch of ice cream—in front of a crackling fire.

WHERE: 75 miles south of Missoula's airport. Tel 800-654-2943 or 406-821-4600; triplecreekranch.com. *Cost:* from $950 per couple, includes meals and most on-ranch activities. *When:* closed Feb–mid-Apr and early Dec. **BEST TIMES:** late July for Darby's Strawberry Festival; early Sept for the Ravalli County Fair.

Ice-Sculpted Majesty: The American Alps

GLACIER NATIONAL PARK

Montana

The epic mountain scenery of Glacier National Park can stir the spirit in mystical ways. The Blackfeet Indians find its beauty so awesome that they believe the area to be sacred ground, and John Muir considered Glacier National Park "the best care-killing scenery on the continent." Often called the "Crown of the Continent" for its staggeringly rugged skyline, Glacier and its Canadian sister Waterton Lakes National Park (see p. 1035) together make up the world's first International Peace Park.

St. Mary Lake, the park's second largest, reflects Glacier's magnificent peaks.

"If it isn't God's backyard," quipped comedian Robin Williams, "He certainly lives nearby."

Glacier Park's awe-inspiring landscape was crafted by the movement of massive glaciers, trenching out valleys, many of which filled with lakes, and carving horns and cirques along mountain peaks. The distinctive finlike ridges that divide major watersheds look like upside-down boats, keels pointed skyward. The park's dramatic terrain is prime hiking and trekking territory, with more than 700 miles of maintained trails that pass through vibrant wildflower meadows and along multicolored rocky cliffs and slopes filled with the torchlike flowers of bear grass. As one of the most intact ecosystems anywhere in the temperate zone, it offers good opportunities for glimpsing wildlife, with a list that will keep any visitor busy— moose, bighorn sheep, elk, mountain lions, lynx, martens, fishers, wolverines, plus black and grizzly bears (with a population of around 300, the park is said to have the largest concentration of grizzlies in the contiguous U.S.).

The park also boasts one of the world's most spectacular mountain drives, the 50-mile-long Going-to-the-Sun Road. The 3-hour route roughly bisects the 1-million-acre wilderness (with another million in adjacent tracts), climbing from lake basins to the summit of the Continental Divide at 6,646-foot Logan Pass (the highlight of the trip, with fragile alpine meadows unfolding below sharp-toothed crags), passing as many as a thousand seasonal waterfalls among dense evergreen forests along the way.

There are currently 25 named glaciers within the park, down from about 150 in the mid-1800s. At this rate, experts believe the park's namesake glaciers will all but disappear by 2030.

The Great Northern Railway built massive log-and-stone lodges here in the early 1900s to lure the first vacationers and, of these, the Swiss-style Many Glacier Hotel is perhaps the most beautifully sited and popular. Sitting regal and isolated amid alpine grandeur on the banks of Swiftcurrent Lake, it is brimming with tradition. About 65 miles to the west, the charming Lake McDonald Lodge sits alongside its namesake lake. It has a rugged air that permeates its movie-set lobby decorated with trophy heads and a vast walk-in fireplace bordered by images resembling cave art, rumored to have been drawn by Charlie Russell (see below).

Avid hikers will consider Glacier's stone-built backcountry chalets the park's top lodging choices. Granite Park Chalet, a mountain shelter with lodging and kitchen facilities, is reached after a 7-mile hike, while Sperry Chalet, also only reached by foot, is midway between Logan Pass and Lake McDonald Lodge. More accessible and just outside the park's southern boundary is the beloved Izaak Walton Inn. Built in 1939 as a residence for rail workers, the three-story alpine-style lodge is now famed for its cozy Old World atmosphere, its excellent fishing, and cross-country skiing in the winter months.

WHERE: The park's west entrance is West Glacier, 30 miles northeast of Kalispell. Tel 406-888-7800; nps.gov/glac. *When:* year-round, but much of Going-to-the-Sun Rd. is open only mid-June–mid-Oct. **MANY GLACIER HOTEL/LAKE MCDONALD LODGE:** Tel 855-733-4522 or 303-265-7010; glaciernational parklodges.com. *Cost:* from $165 (Many Glacier), from $178 (Lake McDonald). *When:* late May–late Sept. **GRANITE PARK CHALET:.** Tel 888-345-2649; graniteparkchalet.com. *Cost:* $100 per person. *When:* July–early Sept. **SPERRY CHALET:** Tel 888-345-2649 or 406-387-5555; sperrychalet.com. *Cost:* $205 per person, includes meals. **IZAAK WALTON INN:** Essex. Tel 406-888-5700; izaakwaltoninn.com. *Cost:* from $129 (off-peak), from $159 (peak); dinner $45. **BEST TIMES:** Jan–Mar for cross-country skiing; July–Aug for wildflowers; Sept for fewer crowds.

Portraits of Old West Montana

C. M. RUSSELL MUSEUM

Great Falls, Montana

Charles Marion Russell was the archetypal Montana painter—an unschooled artist of remarkable gifts and exquisite visual sense who captured the spirit of the Old West. Along with Frederic Remington, his contemporary,

Charlie Russell is considered the West's finest and most famous painter—having lived the life of a cowhand for many years, he knew the area from the inside out. A native of St. Louis,

Missouri, Russell came west during the 1880s, when the "open range" of Central Montana's Judith Basin supported both vast cattle empires and the fading remnants of traditional Plains Indian culture. Russell began by sketching in bars and around campfires, and the lives of the Indians and cowboys that he encountered daily became his subject matter. He later moved to Great Falls, where he built a home and a log-cabin art studio.

Today, the largest Russell collection, which counts over 2,000 artworks, personal objects, and artifacts, can be found in the recently expanded C. M. Russell Museum, one of the finest Western art museums in the U.S. In addition to Russell's own paintings and sculpture, the works of other Western artists are displayed.

Named for falls in the Missouri River, Great Falls also figures prominently in Lewis and Clark lore. The Corps of Discovery, which, at the request of President Thomas Jefferson, traveled across the West in 1804–06 on an epic journey of discovery (see p. 643), reached here in June 1805 and spent a hellacious month portaging their boats around the five cliff-lined falls of the Missouri River. The 25,000-square-foot Lewis & Clark National Historic Trail Interpretive Center is perched on the cliffs overlooking the Missouri's Great Falls, and provides an excellent overview of

the expedition. As you look at the two-story diorama of Corps members, marvel that these men—dressed in just moccasins and buckskins, and living on rations—had the strength to carry and pull boats for 18 miles, filled with a total of about a ton of gear.

WHERE: 78 miles north of Helena; 400 13th St. N. Tel 406-727-8787; cmrussell.org. *When:* daily, mid-May–Oct; Tues–Sun, Nov–mid-May. **LEWIS & CLARK INTERPRETIVE CENTER:** Tel 406-727-8733. *When:* daily, Memorial Day–Sept; Tues–Sun, Oct–late May. **BEST TIME:** last weekend in June for the Lewis and Clark Festival, with a living history encampment and guided tours to out-of-the-way Lewis and Clark destinations (lewisandclarkfoundation.org).

Many consider Charlie Russell to be the greatest painter of the Old West.

A Gold Camp Turned Capital

LAST CHANCE GULCH

Helena, Montana

66 J ust one last chance before we leave." Those are the reported words of a Georgia-born prospector, one of four ex-Confederate soldiers panning for gold in 1864 on Prickly Pear Creek, on the eastern flank of the Continental

Divide. That "last chance" panning was a very rich one—the prospectors found gold in a narrow ravine that became known as Last Chance

Gulch, and the gold rush was on. As mining gave way to commerce, the narrow, winding gulch grew into the main commercial street of

Helena, Montana's capital city. Most of the miners' shacks from the gold rush days were soon replaced with grand structures of brick and stone, monuments to Helena's immense wealth—in the late 1880s, it had the most millionaires per capita in the nation.

Last Chance Gulch, now a three-block pedestrian mall, still preserves an impressive inventory of imposing Victorian commercial and business buildings, despite the effects of a 1935 earthquake. The Montana Club was the state's most prestigious private club: Designed by Cass Gilbert, the architect of the U.S. Supreme Court Building, the club was open only to millionaires. On the other end of the social scale, Reeder's Alley is a winding series of one-room brick shanties built in the 1870s to house the mining camp's many bachelors.

South of Last Chance Gulch stand two of Helena's most magnificent structures, the Cathedral of St. Helena, modeled after Cologne Cathedral with twin spires reaching 230 feet, and the newly renovated Montana State Capitol, a grandly neoclassical monument with a 100-foot cupola of pure Montana copper. Across from the capitol, the Montana Historical Society is the state's premier museum, featuring both historical exhibits and fine art—the collection of Charlie Russell paintings (see p. 621) is possibly its biggest draw.

Blending Helena's rich history and architecture with modern comfort, the Sanders B&B is an impressive mansion built at great

The Cathedral of St. Helena has anchored the town since the early 1900s.

cost in 1875 by Montana's first U.S. senator. This National Registry–listed property is amazingly well preserved and filled with lovely and elegant furnishings, many original to the home. Though a great deal of care is taken to maintain period authenticity, all seven guest rooms have modern appointments, and the owners provide a gracious and friendly welcome as big as, well, Montana.

WHERE: 81 miles southwest of Great Falls. *Visitor info:* Tel 406-442-4120; helenamt.com. **STATE CAPITOL:** Tel 406-444-4789; visit-the-capitol.mt.gov. **MONTANA HISTORICAL SOCIETY:** Tel 406-444-2694; mhs.mt.gov. *When:* closed Sun. **SANDERS B&B:** Tel 406-442-3309; sandersbb.com. *Cost:* from $130. **BEST TIMES:** June–Sept for weather; last weekend in July for the Last Chance Stampede and Fair (helenafairgrounds.com); Oct–late Dec for Eagle Watch at Canyon Ferry State Park.

Celebrating Sled-Dog History and Long-Distance Mushing

RACE TO THE SKY

Helena, Montana

The world's most famous dogsled race may be Alaska's Iditarod (see p. 909), but a number of races in the Lower 48 offer plenty of excitement and far easier access. Montana's 350-mile Race to the Sky is set in the high country southwest of Helena (with one leg of the race crossing the Continental Divide) and in the scenic Seeley-Swan Valley—the most mountainous course in long-distance mushing. The trail is a challenge for both mushers and dog teams as it climbs four times up and over 6,000-foot mountain passes and hugs a trail that borders three nationally designated wilderness areas.

The race, typically attracting up to 35 teams and some 500 sled dogs from across the U.S. and Canada, commemorates a largely forgotten chapter of local WWII history. Montana's Camp Rimini, a Civilian Conservation Corps (CCC) camp built during the Depression years, was converted for military use in 1942 under the Dogs for Defense Program. The Camp Rimini War Dog Reception and Training Center began by training sled and pack dogs to support a planned special service force invasion of Norway, which at the time was occupied by Nazi Germany. At its peak, Camp Rimini housed and trained about 800 sled dogs and 100 pack dogs,

with about 125 soldiers and dog trainers also in residence. In June 1943 the Norway invasion was scuttled, and the soldiers and dogs at Camp Rimini focused their attention on search-and-rescue efforts. During the war, the Camp Rimini dogsled teams worked in various arctic areas and helped rescue approximately 150 air crash survivors, 300 casualties, and many millions of dollars' worth of equipment.

Though Helena is headquarters for the race (with prerace festivities that begin with the Cool Dog Ball and Microbrew Review, Meet the Mushers, and an auction of dogsled rides), Camp Rimini remains the spiritual home of the Race to the Sky, and when snow conditions permit, the race starts here. The race ends in Lincoln three to five days later, where dogs and mushers all receive a rollicking welcome, followed by dinner, awards, and celebration for human and canines alike.

WHERE: 50 miles south of Lincoln. **RACE TO THE SKY:** Tel 406-881-3647; racetothesky .org. *When:* 3 to 5 days in early–mid-Feb.

The Rhythms on the Range

MONTANA COWBOY POETRY GATHERING

Lewistown, Montana

I t may well be the wide open spaces and the loneliness of life on the range that bring out the poet in a ranch hand. With one of the lowest population densities in the U.S. (Garfield County has just 0.27 people per square mile),

Montana offers plenty of solitude and open space to would-be bards.

Western poets, musicians, and artists from the U.S. and Canada gather every summer in the handsome central Montana city of Lewistown for the Montana Cowboy Poetry Gathering. This is one of the nation's largest events dedicated to cowboy verse and visual history of Montana and the West. Up to 120

cowboys—and cowgirls—recite their poems to over 2,000 fans who range from academic folklorists to cowboy wannabes to grizzled ranchers who have spent their lives on the range. The poetry gathering is part of a larger three-day cultural event that includes musical performances, a Western art and cowboy gear show and sale, Western dances, and even a cowboy church service.

The fertile, well-watered rangeland in this part of central Montana is some of the state's most bucolic and productive—open range cattle operations spread across the valleys here in the 1880s. Cowboy artist Charlie Russell (see p. 621) rode the land hereabouts, and the region's distinctive mountains and buttes form the background for many of his paintings. You can explore this landscape aboard the Charlie Russell Chew Choo dinner train on early-20th-century vintage railcars that travel through farm and ranch land while serving a pretty good prime rib supper.

WHERE: 108 miles north of Billings. Tel 406-538-4575; montanacowboypoetrygathering .com. *Cost:* 3-day pass to readings $10; music and poetry concerts Fri and Sat evenings from $20. *When:* 3 days in mid-Aug. **CHARLIE RUSSELL CHEW CHOO:** Tel 406-535-5436; montanadinnertrain.com. *Cost:* $100, includes dinner and round-trip train excursion. *When:* most Sat from mid-June–Oct; holiday runs in Dec. **WHERE TO STAY:** The Yogo Inn (where most events take place), tel 800-860-9646 or 406-535-8721; yogoinn.com. *Cost:* from $89. **BEST TIMES:** June–Sept for weather; mid-Sept when the Chokecherry Festival takes over Lewistown's Main Street (lewistownchokecherry.com).

An Authentic Celebration of the Wild West

MILES CITY BUCKING HORSE SALE

Miles City, Montana

For one weekend in May every year, the population of Miles City—about 8,500 people—doubles during an event some call "the cowboy Mardi Gras." The Miles City Bucking Horse Sale is one of Montana's top celebrations of the Wild West lifestyle, a three-day event that's part rodeo, part auction, part social gathering—and one of the most unpredictable cowboy-meets-wild-horse spectacles anywhere. Capping the bronc riding and lively auctions is a street dance in downtown Miles City, where live bands line the streets and bars throw open their doors to thousands of Stetson-wearing folks.

The Bucking Horse Sale shares its beginnings with Miles City itself. After the 1876 defeat of General G. A. Custer's Seventh Cavalry at the Battle of the Little Bighorn (see p. 618), the army built Fort Keogh at the convergence of the Tongue and Yellowstone rivers. As a cavalry remount station, Fort Keogh, and the little market town of Miles City that grew up beside it, were both very active centers for

Commanding high prices, these untrained horses often show up in rodeos all over the world.

horse trading. In 1914, Miles City held the first dedicated sale of bucking horses for rodeo stock, and the event soon proved as popular for spectators as for bucking horse buyers and sellers. Each year, the sale brings together rodeo stock contractors and around 250 untrained (or "unbroke") horses at the Eastern Montana Fairgrounds. Cowboys mount the previously unridden horses and buck them out of the chute in an event that looks a lot like rodeo bronc riding—except, since this isn't strictly a rodeo, the riders are rarely professional. What ensues is unpredictable—when untrained horses meet untrained riders, anything can happen. The weekend also features a parade, horse racing, bull riding, wild horse races, art shows, and barbecues: Miles City rolls out the red carpet for cowboys and tenderfeet alike.

Miles City has also long been known as the "Cow Capital of the West," owing to its location at the center of southeastern Montana's vast and fertile prairies. The area's rich history is on display at the Range Riders Museum, one of Montana's best regional museums. Next door is the Custer County Art and Heritage Center—newly renamed the Waterworks Art Museum—a gem of a regional gallery for Western art housed in the water holding tanks of the city's former 1910 waterworks building.

WHERE: 150 miles east of Billings. Tel 406-874-2825; buckinghorsesale.com. *When:* 3rd weekend in May. **RANGE RIDERS MUSEUM:** Tel 406-232-6146; rangeridersmuseum.com. *When:* Apr–Oct. **WATERWORKS ART MUSEUM:** Tel 406-234-0635; wtrworks.org. *When:* closed Mon.

The Written Word Rules in the Garden City

MONTANA BOOK FESTIVAL

Missoula, Montana

Missoula is bookish. For starters, this handsome and historic city is home to the University of Montana, noted for its Master of Fine Arts creative writing program (established in 1920, it is the nation's second oldest), which pumps out around 25 newly minted authors each year. The city has for years also held a curious allure to writers in general—a modern-day vision quest site for anyone with a novel struggling to be born.

Both established and novice writers come here to pound out manuscripts while partaking of Missoula's potent cultural brew: a near-irresistible blend of great fly-fishing, intellectual vigor, and unrepentant drinking in classic old bars where alcohol and yarns flow freely. At various times over the decades, writers as different as A. B. Guthrie Jr., Raymond Carver, Richard Hugo, James Lee Burke, Ian Frazier, James Welch, and Annie Dillard have parked their typewriters in Missoula.

The Montana Book Festival is an utterly appropriate celebration of Missoula's curious spot in the literary firmament. This three-day mid-September event focuses on readings by a

The Montana Book Festival draws old and young readers alike.

broad selection of authors, including local writers just beginning to find their audience as well as nationally recognized authors. In addition, the festival's more than 100 sessions feature lectures and panel discussions with more than 150 writers, and exhibits, performances, and seminars. The festival attracts an audience of about 5,000 literary mavens to various venues around downtown Missoula.

The city's wealth of bars and pubs is legendary, and no trip to Missoula is complete without dropping by the Missoula Club, Charlie B's, or the Oxford—in their own way, landmarks of Missoula's peculiar literary history.

The city is at the confluence of five western Montana river valleys, and this sense of being at the center of things is key to its usually charming, sometimes exasperating self-focus. Missoula is undeniably the cultural hub for the state, with excellent music, theater, and repertory cinema. On Saturdays from May to October, a large farmers market takes over the north end of downtown. Missoula is Montana's Garden City, as fertile and temperate as these things get in Montana.

Where: 115 miles northwest of Helena. montanabookfestival.org. *When:* 2nd week of Sept. *Visitor info:* Tel 406-543-6623; missoula chamber.com. **Missoula Club:** Tel 406-728-3740. **Charlie B's:** Tel 406-549-3589. **The Oxford:** Tel 406-549-0117. **Best times:** June–Sept for weather; mid-April for the International Wildlife Film Festival (wildlife films.org).

Hot Water in Paradise

Chico Hot Springs

Pray, Montana

You'll hear a lot about the Hollywood celebrities who come to soak in the hot-springs pool or hang out at the bar at Chico Hot Springs Resort & Spa, but Chico's best attribute is the way it embodies Western

egalitarianism. Just about anybody with any sort of travel budget can enjoy this historic lodge in the heart of Montana's aptly named Paradise Valley, where the Yellowstone River flows north out of Yellowstone National Park (see p. 676), flanked by the spiky Absaroka and the more rounded Gallatin mountain ranges. Yellowstone's famed thermal activity doesn't stop at the park boundary, some 30 miles to the south, and at Chico there's enough mineral-rich hot water coursing out of the ground to fill an enormous outdoor 96°F swimming pool and heat an adjacent smaller pool to 103°F. Day guests are welcome.

Most of the modestly priced rooms in the century-old Main Lodge are quite small and with shared baths, but more upscale options

The open-air mineral hot springs pools are relaxing and therapeutic for the whole family.

are available. Choose among rooms in the lodge's new wing or rent a cottage a little farther from the action. Be sure to schedule at least one dinner in Chico's well-known Dining Room, where the food—"Montana with a flair"—is excellent and the mood relaxed. Leave your cowboy hat on or take it off—anything goes here.

Most guests are content to loll at the pool all day long, with perhaps some time out for a massage at the lodge's day spa; the resort also offers trail rides through its mountain-fringed 150-acre property. But get out and discover why Paradise Valley got its name—it's an ideal place for a hike or a bike ride, and the trout-rich Yellowstone River is a prime fishing destination in a state that has many.

The nearest town, Livingston, is just north on the Yellowstone River. It started out as a division point in the 1880s for the North Pacific Railroad but is now known as an arts town, famous for its galleries and restaurants, in lovely late-Victorian redbrick storefronts. One of the best restaurants in this part of Montana, Livingston Bar & Grille, was owned by the famed landscape artist and lithographer Russell Chatham. The refined space is decorated with some of Chatham's serene paintings and prints of the local area, and its imaginative entrées such as pan-seared diver scallops with butternut risotto have replaced the hamburger of yesteryear.

WHERE: 50 miles southeast of Bozeman; 163 Chico Rd. Tel 406-333-4933; chico hotsprings.com. *Cost:* rooms from $60; dinner $55. **CHATHAM'S LIVINGSTON BAR & GRILLE:** Livingston. Tel 406-222-7909. *Cost:* dinner $50. **BEST TIMES:** the weekend closest to July 4th, for the Roundup Rodeo in Livingston, with an accompanying arts fair in downtown's Depot Square; early fall for weather.

Less Pretension, More Snow

WHITEFISH MOUNTAIN RESORT

Whitefish, Montana

D on't expect Vail-type amenities or attitudes at Whitefish Mountain Resort (called Big Mountain Resort until 2007), an undiscovered gem of a ski resort in northwestern Montana. Even the neighboring town of Whitefish,

which is (by Montana standards) an upscale boomtown, is pretty relaxed, especially during the winter. Two indicators of the rugged, slightly iconoclastic spirit of Whitefish Mountain are the popularity of telemark skiing and the easygoing attitude toward skiing outside the resort's official boundaries.

Not that the resort boundaries are likely to cramp your style: With over 3,000 acres draping out and down from the

A spectacular sunset casts a pink glow over the snowy peak of Whitefish Mountain.

mountain's 6,817-foot summit, there's plenty of territory for everyone. On a sunny day, hop off the gondola at the top of Whitefish Mountain and take in the peaks of Glacier National Park (see p. 620), the Canadian Rockies, and the entire Flathead Valley.

Whitefish Mountain's summer activities are no less alluring. Along with great mountain biking and hiking (stop and pick huckleberries in the late summer), the resort's Walk in the Treetops allows you to stroll along a boardwalk erected in the tree canopy up to 70 feet above the forest floor.

Although a flurry of condos has sprung up at the resort base, consider staying down the hill in Whitefish, at the inviting Grouse Mountain Lodge. The massive resort, a showcase of cedar, stone, and glass, offers sumptuous guest rooms and easy right-out-the-back-door access to some of Montana's top recreation: Glide along a 15-kilometer network of groomed cross-country ski trails or, in summer, take to the tees at two 18-hole golf courses. Cap off a day at Whitefish Mountain with a meal at the lodge's Logan's Bar & Grill, with thick steaks, grilled game, freshly caught trout, and other hearty mountain-man specialties expertly done.

WHERE: 129 miles north of Missoula. Tel 877-754-3474 or 406-862-2900; skiwhitefish .com. *Cost:* lift tickets $73. *When:* Dec–mid-Apr. **GROUSE MOUNTAIN LODGE:** Tel 800-321-8822 or 406-862-3000; grousemountainlodge .com. *Cost:* from $125 (winter), from $240 (summer); dinner $50. **BEST TIMES:** Jan–Mar for best skiing; 1st weekend in Feb for the Winter Carnival; June for Stumptown Days; Sept–Oct for fall foliage, fewer crowds, and generally sunny weather.

Big Sky, Big Fish, Big History

BIG HOLE COUNTRY & THE COMPLETE FLY FISHER

Wise River, Montana

A place called "big hole" was hardly an insult to men such as Jim Bridger and Jedediah Smith, who were among the first frontiersmen to explore and label the northern Rocky Mountains. The term was simply frontier-speak for a wide, deep valley. Montana's Big Hole Country, in the state's southwest corner, is one of its most beautiful valleys— a 6,000-foot-elevation prairie basin flanked by snowcapped peaks and drained by pristine streams and rivers, cherished by both anglers and rafters. Old-time cattle ranches dot the range, and meadows are filled with loose, unbaled haystacks, hence the Big Hole's epithet, the "Valley of 10,000 Haystacks." Automated agriculture has been slow to arrive in this remote valley, adding to its easygoing charm.

For fly-fishers, the focus here is the Big Hole River, one of the top blue-ribbon trout streams in a state blessed with superlative fishing. Montana lakes and streams are home to brown, rainbow, brook, bull, and cutthroat trout, plus trout cousins Arctic grayling and landlocked kokanee salmon. Add to all this the near-mystic sense that Montana is the spiritual home of fly-fishing, a sentiment perfectly captured in the first line of Norman Maclean's classic Montana novel, *A River Runs Through It:* "In our family, there was no clear line between religion and fly fishing."

The Big Hole's most famous lodge is the Complete Fly Fisher. Its location on the Big Hole River and proximity to other fabled streams guarantees lots of float and wading opportunities for excellent fishing, and its small size (12 guests is the limit) fosters camaraderie and personalized service. Even novices can pull in the big ones, with the help of the lodge's skilled long-time instructors. Dining in the lovely glass-paneled riverside restaurant is taken as seriously as fishing, and is far more sophisticated than you'd expect in this wilderness.

Despite the lulling sense of timeless serenity, the Big Hole Valley has had its moment of tragedy when, in 1877, it witnessed a historic clash of cultures. About 800 Nez Perce Indians, fleeing forced relocation from

The Big Hole River is an angler's paradise.

their Oregon homeland, trekked across Idaho (see p. 598) and Montana in a desperate attempt to evade the U.S. Army and escape into Canada. While camped in the Big Hole on August 9, the Nez Perce were ambushed by the Seventh Infantry. But the Nez Perce warriors fought back, successfully besieging the army until the rest of the tribe could escape eastward. The Big Hole National Battlefield, now protected by the National Park Service, has a visitors center and an extensive series of self-guided hiking trails that link the battle sites. The battlefield is part of the Nez Perce National Historic Trail, a 1,200-mile trail that follows the route of the Nez Perce from their homeland in Oregon to the Bear Paw Mountains in north-central Montana, where the army ultimately apprehended the natives, sending the survivors to reservations across the West.

WHERE: 40 miles south of Butte. **COMPLETE FLY FISHER:** Tel 406-832-3175; completeflyfisher.com. *Cost:* 5 days guided angling $4,500 per person, includes meals, lodging, and equipment. *When:* mid-May–mid-Oct. **BIG HOLE NATIONAL BATTLEFIELD:** Tel 406-689-3155; nps.gov/biho. **BEST TIMES:** May and Sept–Oct for productive angling; June–Aug for weather; mid-June for the salmon fly hatch and very active fly-fishing; the weekend closest to Aug 9 when the Big Hole battle is commemorated.

Immersed in the Animal Kingdom

HENRY DOORLY ZOO & AQUARIUM

Omaha, Nebraska

S ure, everyone has heard of the Bronx Zoo and the San Diego Zoo. But the Henry Doorly Zoo & Aquarium in Omaha often outranks them as America's favorite, securing an international reputation with "total immersion" exhibits that are considered among the best in the world. Attracting more than 1.5 million visitors a year, the 140-acre Henry Doorly Zoo (named for a benefactor back in the 1960s) has a secret weapon: Omaha's great wealth. The city ranks among the nation's largest cities in per capita billionaires (Warren Buffet was born in Omaha and heads one of five Fortune 500 companies that have their headquarters here) and the community gives generously to keep its animals (and kids) happy.

Perhaps Gorilla Valley best illustrates the zoo's vision and budget. Instead of passively gazing at caged (and mighty bored) gorillas, visitors stroll through a glass tunnel that discreetly winds through 2 acres of outdoor habitat lush with trees, wild grasses, and cool streams. There's plenty of room for nearly 20 lowland gorillas, along with screeching monkeys that swing through the trees, red river hogs, and birds.

In Kingdoms of the Night, the world's best and largest nocturnal exhibit, blind fish and alligators swim in the "bottomless pool" of the man-made wet cave, while a thousand fruit bats hang like laundry in the 70-foot-high Bat Cave. Directly above this underground world is the Desert Dome, where three different deserts have been re-created inside a 13-story-high biosphere. Pumas and peccaries roam

the sands beneath the biggest geodesic dome on the planet.

Other highlights include the Lied Jungle exhibit, where you walk on rope bridges past steep waterfalls through Asian, African, and South American geographic zones. And an aquarium with an underwater tunnel lets you stand in awe beneath sharks and stingrays, as if on the ocean floor. Nearby, an enormous aviary is home to 500 exotic species of birds that fly freely around you.

WHERE: 3701 S. 10th St. Tel 402-733-8401; omahazoo.com.

You can get up close and personal with the residents in Gorilla Valley, one of the zoo's highlights.

The Perfect Marriage of Corn and Beef

OMAHA STEAKS

Omaha, Nebraska

Walk into the headquarters of Omaha Steaks, selling beef every bit as good as what you'll tuck into at the best steak houses of America, and you'll understand why Nebraska has two nicknames. Officially it's called the Cornhusker State, celebrating the state's No. 1 grain crop, but many still understandably prefer the "Beef State," which dates back to the '50s. Nebraska slaughters 6.7 million head of cattle a year, more than any other state, and is synonymous with all-American premium, grain-fed beef so tasty and tender, it's an icon: Think Omaha Steaks.

Omaha and beef have gone together since the 1880s, when it was an important meat-processing center attracting thousands of immigrants from southern and central Europe. In 1917, a father-and-son team from Latvia, J. J. and B. A. Simon, founded a custom-cut butcher shop called Table Supply Meat Company (the name was already on the building when they

632 of GREAT PLAINS

moved in), selling to hotels and, in the 1940s, the Union Pacific Railroad. In the late 1950s, with the invention of Styrofoam, their mail-order business exploded. It became Omaha Steaks in 1966, and the rest is carnivore history.

Today, the fifth-generation family business sells most of their world-coveted steaks to 3 million direct-mail shoppers, almost all of whom are return customers. There's no plant tour (USDA inspectors don't allow it), but you can go home with the company's most popular item—four 6-ounce filet mignon steaks packaged to go—from the company's flagship store, one of more than 65 retail shops in 27 states. Prices are princely, but so is the product.

Another Omaha icon just as beloved to locals is Johnny's Café. It's been around since 1922, when Polish immigrant Frank J. Kawa bought a 10-seat saloon at the same location. With giant red letters that beckon beef-lovers, this third-generation family business specializes in top-quality midwestern grain-fed beef that it ages and hand-cuts right on the premises. It's all served in a retro-modern dining room, with red carpeting, black bar stools, and buffalo heads. Save room for the Ice Cream Turtle Pie, a frozen block of chocolate and vanilla ice cream layered with chocolate fudge, caramel, and pecans that will satiate most any post-prandial cravings.

WHERE: 4400 S. 96th St. Tel 402-593-4223 or 800-960-8400 (mail-order); omahasteaks .com. **JOHNNY'S CAFÉ:** Tel 402-731-4774; johnnyscafe.com. *Cost:* 1-lb T-bone $24.

Land of Unexpected Riches

THE PANHANDLE

Nebraska

The windswept emptiness of the plains gives way to a more rugged landscape in Nebraska's Panhandle, part of the great superhighway for gold-seekers, emigrants, and Mormons traveling the Platte River Valley from the 1840s to 1860s. The Great Western Migration was the largest voluntary human relocation in recorded history. Some 400,000 people passed through Nebraska, often on foot, while traveling nearly 2,000 miles to California and Oregon. By far the most-remarked-upon landmark in their diaries was Chimney Rock, a 120-foot sandstone spire atop a 200-foot mound, which seemingly came out of nowhere after miles and miles of the vast prairie. "Towering to the heavens," as one pioneer put it. (The Indians were less rhapsodic, calling it "elk penis.")

Cutting north on Highway 385 you'll come across a man-made (and decidedly more modern) landmark that is just as striking: 39 trashed automobiles from the 1950s and '60s painted gray and arranged in the exact size, shape, and conformation of Stonehenge, the 4,000-year-old site in England believed by some to be a solar and lunar calendar. Carhenge was built by Jim Reinders, a local engineer, and it allegedly "works," meaning it marks the solstices and equinoxes.

The Agate Fossil Beds National Monument near the Wyoming border interprets the 20-million-year-old fossils from the great mammals that perished in the Agate watering hole. This land was part of "Captain" James H. Cook's Agate Springs Ranch in the late 19th century, and his unusually enlightened attitude toward Indians made it a gathering place for Chief Red Cloud and other Oglala Lakota (Sioux). In return he received gifts such as Chief Red Cloud's porcupine-quilled antelope ceremonial shirt and Chief Crazy Horse's whetstone, all part of a small but exquisite 200-piece collection on display.

Nebraska is at its roughest in the northwestern corner of the state, sending a siren call to mountain bikers, hikers, and horseback riders. The Pine Ridge Trail cuts a ragged 100-mile arc through the Pine Ridge Ranger District and Oglala National Grasslands, running along rimrock ridges with vast panoramic outlooks. Bison roam Fort Robinson State Park, an active military post from 1874 to 1948 and the place where Crazy Horse, leader of one of the last bands of non-reservation Indians, was killed when he resisted arrest. Large groups who don't mind sleeping on cots can stay in 1909 barracks; or, for more comfortable stays, individual cabins where officers were once housed are an option.

CHIMNEY ROCK: Bayard. Tel 308-586-2581; nps.gov/nr/travel/scotts_bluff/chimney_rock.html. **CARHENGE:** Alliance. Tel 308-762-3569; carhenge.com. **AGATE FOSSIL BEDS:** Harrison.

Some of the automobiles at Carhenge are held upright in pits 5 feet deep, trunk end down, supporting other cars welded horizontally on top.

Tel 308-436-9760; nps.gov/agfo. **PINE RIDGE TRAIL:** Chadron. Tel 308-432-0300. **FORT ROBINSON PARK:** Crawford. Tel 308-665-2900; outdoornebraska.ne.gov. *Cost:* rooms from $65. *When:* lodging available mid-Apr–mid-Nov. **BEST TIME:** spring–fall.

One of Nature's Great Spectacles

THE ANNUAL CRANE MIGRATION

Platte River Valley, Nebraska

In the same way they have for thousands of years, a blizzard of sandhill cranes descends on a 40-mile stretch of the Platte River between late February and early April to rest and refuel while migrating north to their summer breeding grounds. It's the world's largest gathering of sandhill cranes—at least 500,000—along with some 10 million mallards, northern pintails, snow geese, and other water fowl. Fifty thousand bird lovers from as far as Tasmania and Tokyo come to experience the bugling calls and quasi-comical long-legged mating dances (both the male and female dance for each other) of these tall, imposing cranes with distinctive red foreheads.

The sandhill cranes are drawn to the Platte River because its shallow, braided channels keep predators like coyotes at bay while the migrating birds regain their strength and sleep safely at night. In the mornings they explode out of the river like fireworks, wheeling in the sky before settling in nearby wetlands and farm fields to feed and rest, while the yearlings court mates that will become life partners. At dusk they return to the river, landing like giant weightless moths, each with a wingspan of 5 to 6 feet. Sandhill cranes are the most abundant crane species, representing 80 percent of the world's crane population, and this critical sliver of habitat is essential to their survival.

Although there are viewing platforms and a walking bridge for free public viewings along the river, the best way to see them is on guided tours offered by The Crane Trust Nature & Visitor Center near Grand Island and the Iain Nicolson Audubon Center at Rowe Sanctuary near Gibbon. Led by experts, these tours take you into outdoor blinds right on the river, where you can observe the birds without disturbing them. There are two tours: one at 5 A.M. before the birds awake, and another at 5 P.M. before they roost for the evening.

Fowl aren't the only emigrants to make use of the Platte River. Although pioneers quipped it was "too thick to drink, but too thin to plow," as many as 500,000 travelers between 1840 and the 1860s found its combination of water, hard riverbanks, and nearly flat terrain made a natural "highway" for travel along the Oregon Trail, California Trail, and Mormon Trail, along with the Pony Express, the overland stage route, and the transcontinental railroad. The Great Platte River Road Archway Monument brings the experience to life with narrated dioramas, moving lights, and thunder—kitschy but fascinating exhibits that

show how our predecessors piled all their belongings into wagons and handcarts and walked across the country following that most powerful of instincts—hope.

Where: 100 miles west of Lincoln. **The Crane Trust Nature & Visitor Center:** Grand Island. Tel 308-382-1820; cranetrust .org. *Cost:* tours from $15. *When:* late Feb–early Apr. **Iain Nicolson Audubon Center:** Gibbon. Tel 308-468-5282; rowe.audubon .org. *When:* daily, late Feb–early Apr; closed Sat off-season. *Cost:* tours $25. **Great Platte River Road Archway Monument:** Kearney. Tel 877-511-2724 or 308-237-1000; archway .org. **Best times:** late Feb–early Apr for crane migrations, 5 A.M.–8 A.M. and 5 P.M.–7 P.M.

Half a million cranes descend on the Platte River Valley in early spring.

Where the Prairie Whispers

THE SANDHILLS OF NEBRASKA

Nebraska

This mesmerizing sweep of unspoiled, rolling prairie in north-central Nebraska escaped the plow for one reason only—the soil was too sandy to grow crops like corn. The Sandhills are the largest set of stabilized sand

dunes in the Western Hemisphere, ranchland still blanketed with Indian grass and bluestem that stretches across 20,000 square miles— one-quarter of the state. Achingly beautiful in its own quiet way, it is one of the least familiar of our country's geological curiosities. During long periods of drought in the past 10,000 years, sand dunes advanced over riverbeds and valleys, creating lakes and wetlands when the rains returned. The largest of these dunes are 400 feet tall and 20 miles long, creating an undulating topography unique in North America.

The best way to understand their full grandeur is to drive the Sandhills Journey Scenic Byway, a 272-mile trip that the late Charles Kuralt called one of the nation's most beautiful drives. It runs along Highway 2, starting in crane country's Grand Island (see previous page) and cutting northwesterly through mile after mile of rolling grassy dunes and endless sky. You can drive for long stretches without seeing another car—that's how empty it is.

With its lakes, marshes, and tall grasses, the 72,000-acre Valentine National Wildlife Refuge is a major stop for migrating songbirds and 150,000 ducks. Nearly 290 species of birds have been spotted here, including herons, terns, pelicans, and long-billed curlews. And when the prairie is carpeted with wildflowers in the spring, prairie chickens and sharp-tailed grouse gather to perform their elaborate, foot-stamping courtship displays, said to have inspired local tribal dances.

"Anyone can sit back at the seashore and be inspired, because it shouts at you," said Father Val Peters, a longtime director of Girls and Boys Town in Omaha. "But the prairie only whispers. You must listen closely and not miss the message."

WHERE: from North Platte in the south (228 miles west of Lincoln) to Valentine in the north and as far west as Alliance. **SANDHILLS JOURNEY SCENIC BYWAY:** Tel 308-546-0636; sandhills journey.com. **VALENTINE WILDLIFE REFUGE:** Tel 402-376-3789; fws.gov/valentine. **BEST TIMES:** May, Sept, and Oct for migrations; Apr for prairie chicken courtship.

A Town Devoted to an Author

LITERARY PILGRIMAGE TO CATHER COUNTRY

Red Cloud, Nebraska

One of the most famous novelists of the early 20th century, Willa Cather wrote of the richness and hardships of prairie life in the 1880s, a time still exemplified by her hometown and muse, Red Cloud. Surrounded by a grand sweep of plains and prairie farms, Red Cloud (named for the Oglala Sioux chief) is said to be immortalized in more books than any other small town in literature. Though she called it by other names—Black Hawk was one—it's easy to see through the thinly veiled guises of the sites she wrote about with such familiarity and love. "The United States knows Nebraska because of Willa Cather's books," wrote Sinclair Lewis.

Cather was born in Virginia in 1873, but her family moved here to Webster County when she was nine. After 18 months on the prairie they moved into Red Cloud, where they lived for six years before Cather left for college in Lincoln. Her life in Nebraska inspired her best work, including *My Ántonia* (1918), about an urban Czech family's tragic collision with farming in the New World. In fact, six of her dozen novels (including the

Pulitzer Prize–winning *One of Ours*) are set in Red Cloud and Webster County and celebrate the men and women who settled on the Great Plains at the end of the 19th century. The citizens of Red Cloud began to preserve and restore the most important Cather landmarks back in the 1950s, not long after her death in 1947 (she is buried in New Hampshire). Today it is the largest collection of historical sites dedicated to a single author in the U.S.

The Cather Foundation gives guided tours of seven historic buildings, starting with the 1885 Opera House, where Cather appeared in a student production of *Beauty and the Beast* and gave her high school commencement address. The high point of the tour is her childhood home, complete with original Cather furnishings.

Other stops include the St. Juliana Falconieri Catholic Church, where Antonia's baby was baptized, and the Farmers' and Merchants' Bank, now a museum that houses artifacts such as the Turkish doll described in *O Pioneers!*

When Cather left for New York City, her parents purchased a grand Queen Anne home. The Cather Foundation runs it as the Cather Second Home, a host-free B&B with six cozy guest rooms. Request the room that Willa's parents kept for her when she came to visit.

The Cather Foundation can arrange 60-mile Country Tours, with stops that include the Pavelka farmstead, the setting for the title character's home in *My Antonia*.

WHERE: 149 miles southwest of Lincoln. **CATHER FOUNDATION:** Tel 866-731-7304 or 402-746-2653; willacather.org. *When:* closed Sun, Oct–Mar; country tours by special arrangement. *Cost:* tours $15; country tours $50. **CATHER SECOND HOME B&B:** Tel 402-746-2653; willacather.org. *Cost:* from $75. **BEST TIME:** 1st weekend in June for the Willa Cather Spring Conference.

A Unique Convergence of Six Ecosystems

THE NIOBRARA RIVER

Valentine, Nebraska

For a 76-mile stretch between Valentine and Highway 137, the Niobrara is designated a National Scenic River; six distinct ecosystems meet here, offering up some of the country's best canoeing amid the beauty of America's heartland. The Niobrara is at its most dramatic at this ecological crossroads, with the steepest canyons, the tallest cliffs, and lots of pretty waterfalls.

The Ogallala Aquifer, one of the world's largest sources of underground water, runs right up against bedrock here, carving out a highly unusual plains landscape over the millennia. The ponderosa pine, paper birch, and quaking aspen of the Rocky Mountains meet the oak and box elder of eastern forests. There are unusual northern boreal plants, as well as three prairie ecosystems—eastern tall grass, western short grass, and the mixed grass prairie of the Sandhills (see p. 634). You won't find a combination like this anywhere else.

Fed by abundant springs, the Niobrara is a cool, clear river that flows at 2 or 3 miles per hour—fast enough for rafters to have plenty of fun without tipping into the brink. On Saturdays in the summer it turns into a party river as the young people of Lincoln and Omaha escape the heat by floating the Niobrara on oversize inner tubes with six-packs of beer.

You can camp at Smith Falls State Park, with a 63-foot waterfall Nebraska is proud to call its highest. If you're not the camping kind, Heartland Elk Guest Ranch has comfy 800- to 2,000-square-foot cabins that are the perfect place to regain your land legs.

Any trip on the Niobrara starts in Valentine. With its population of 2,820, it's the teeming megalopolis of sparsely populated Cherry County. Named for a popular Nebraska congressman from the 1880s, Valentine now makes the most of its name (getting hitched in town on February 14 is quite the thing) and invites people to send valentines in an outer envelope to Postmaster, P.O. Box 9998, Valentine, NE 69201, so they can be postmarked from Valentine.

Valentine is a cow town at heart, though, proclaimed loud and clear at the annual Heart City Bull Bash every February. Sixty pens of prize bull flesh take over Main Street, and breeders and buyers brave the chilly weather to make deals while everyone else enjoys food and family fun indoors. In October, cowboys show

their sensitive side at the Annual Nebraska Cowboy Poetry Gathering & Old West Days.

Just north of Valentine is the Rosebud Reservation, a million-acre home to 28,000 members of the Sicangu Lakota tribe, across the state line in South Dakota. It has *wacipis* (or powwows) that the public is invited to attend, as well as hunting, fishing, and—for the real risk-takers—gambling.

WHERE: 130 miles south of Pierre, SD. *River info:* Tel 402-376-1901; nps.gov/niob. *Valentine visitors info:* Tel 800-658-4024 or 402-376-2969; visitvalentine.org. **SMITH FALLS STATE PARK:** Tel 402-376-1306; outdoornebraska.ne .gov. **HEARTLAND ELK GUEST RANCH:** Sparks. Tel 402-376-2553; heartlandelk.com. *Cost:* cabins from $165. **ROSEBUD RESERVATION:** Tel 605-747-2381; rosebudsiouxtribe-nsn.gov. **BEST TIMES:** 1st Sat before Valentine's Day for the Heart City Bull Bash; May–Sept for floating the Niobrara; summer for Rosebud Reservation powwows; early Oct for Old West Days.

Building Your Life List in the Prairie Potholes

BIRDING DRIVES DAKOTA

North Dakota

North Dakota is one of the nation's great birding destinations, if one of its least visited. Dedicated birders can count more than 300 reasons to visit the state: sandhill cranes, Nelson's sharp-tail sparrows, American white

pelicans, chestnut collared longspurs, marbled godwits, upland sandpipers, and Wilson's phalaropes among them. Because of the distances between the best sites, an organization called Birding Drives Dakota has worked with professional biologists, ornithologists, and some of the state's 63 national wildlife refuges (NWRs) to create six "birding drives."

All are located in the central portion of the state, in and around Kidder, Stutsman, and Foster counties. With a total human population of only about 3,000—about two per

You can see the greater prairie-chicken and many other species along the six birding drives.

square mile—Kidder County is the essence of rural prairie land, with four NWRs. Long Lake NWR is a breeding and migratory stopover for more than 250,000 shorebirds. Thousands of sandhill cranes also stage here each spring and fall, and the endangered whooping crane can be seen occasionally as well. Visitors who come for Jamestown's Potholes & Prairie Birding Festival in early June might be treated to the intricate courtship dances of Clark's and western grebes, in addition to a diverse menu of prairie sparrows. The 4,385-acre Chase Lake NWR in Stutsman County is known as a nesting spot for gulls, cormorants, and the largest colony of white pelicans in North America.

If you need a break from the binoculars, check out some of the area's unique sculptures, such as the *World's Largest Sandhill Crane;* at 38 feet tall, it towers over the prairie outside of Steele. In Jamestown, the *World's Largest Concrete Buffalo* weighs 60 tons and stands 26 feet tall and 46 feet long. And "Salem Sue," the *World's Largest Holstein Cow,* stands atop a hill at I-94's exit 127. Farther west, along the Enchanted Highway, between Gladstone and Regent, local artists have erected the biggest collection of large metal animal sculptures in the world: giant pheasants, deer, and grasshoppers.

WHERE: Steele is 40 miles east of Bismarck. Tel 888-921-2473 or 701-952-5871; birdingdrives.com. **LONG LAKE:** Moffit. Tel 701-387-4397; fws.gov/refuge/long_lake. **CHASE LAKE:** Woodworth. Tel 701-752-4218; fws.gov/refuge/chase_lake. **BEST TIMES:** early June for the 3-day Potholes & Prairie Birding Festival in Jamestown (birdingdrives.com); Apr–May and Oct–mid-Nov, when both migratory birds and native species can be seen.

Celebrating the Culture of America's First Peoples

THE UNITED TRIBES INTERNATIONAL POWWOW

Bismarck, North Dakota

The term "powwow" originated in the Narragansett Algonquin language, where it meant a healing ceremony attended by medicine men. It was first spread across the continent by white Americans who thought it meant any large gathering or council, and was later adopted by the country's diverse Native tribes. The first modern powwows, in which Native Americans come together to celebrate their heritage in music, dance, prayer, and celebration, were organized in the 1920s, but the movement didn't gain full momentum until the Native American cultural renaissance of the late 1960s and early '70s. Today, more than 300 powwows are held annually, nationwide.

In North Dakota, which is home to more than a dozen powwows each summer, the United Tribes International Powwow is the heavyweight champ. Held annually since 1969, it typically attracts 1,000 dancers and drum groups from many tribes, as well as performers demonstrating the indigenous music and dance of other cultures—such as Andean, Hawaiian, Aztec, and Atka Alaskan—for more than 20,000 visitors.

Native Americans of all ages compete in 22 dance categories, including Traditional, Buckskin, Straight Dance, and Chicken Dance.

The competitors' regalia, made from both traditional and modern materials, attract as much attention as their moves, and are tailored to each dance. For example, participants in grass dances wear yards of trailing ribbon or yarn, symbolizing prairie grass, and the clothing of jingle dancers is covered with small metal cones that make music as they move. Traditional dancers incorporate feathers and beadwork into their costumes, with their dances mimicking the movements of animals or acting out the hunt. Fancy dress features neon-colored feathers, beads, and other elements that accentuate this energetic dance, which has its origins in the preparation for battle.

No celebration is complete without food, and powwows are no different: Elk burgers, roast buffalo, Indian tacos, and fry bread always make an appearance. Vendors representing dozens of cultures from across the country offer handmade arts and crafts for sale.

WHERE: United Tribes Technical College, 3315 University Dr. Tel 701-255-3285; unitedtribespowwow.com. *When:* early Sept.

Pax, Pace, Salaam, Shalom, Shanti

INTERNATIONAL PEACE GARDEN

Dunseith, North Dakota

It all started in the mind of Canadian horticulturist Henry J. Moore, who, in 1928 envisioned a grand garden straddling the U.S.-Canadian border, dedicated to the two nations' long and peaceful coexistence. Moore's plan was approved, and the site he chose was dedicated three years later, on July 14, 1932. There, amid low, undulating hills bounded by the American prairie and Canada's Manitoba Forest Preserve, the Peace Garden has grown steadily over the decades. Many of its roads, bridges, and shelters were built in the 1930s by the New Deal–era Civilian Conservation Corps, and its formal garden, reflecting pools, rock walls, and flagstone terraces were completed in the 1950s—the gap in construction caused, ironically enough, by WWII.

Today the Peace Garden boasts 2,339 acres of gardens, forest, manicured landscapes, fountains, walking paths, and several monuments and memorials. Typically the first week in June, 150,000 flowers are planted and are best viewed in full bloom from mid-July through August. The Floral Clock works; its arms revolve around a 14-foot hillside planted with 2,000 to 3,000 flowers in a new design each year. At the Peace Chapel, there's a

Stroll down the International Peace Garden's terraced walkway amid a colorful blanket of 150,000 flowers.

memorial list of all who died in the terrorist attacks of September 11, 2001, while nearby several girders salvaged from the wreckage at the World Trade Center form a stark memorial cairn.

WHERE: 200 miles northeast of Bismarck; Rural Rte. 1. Tel 701-263-4390 in the U.S., 204-534-2510 in Canada; peacegarden.com. *When:* daily year-round, but interpretive center and some other facilities only open June–Sept. **BEST TIME:** mid-July–Aug, for flowers and when summer programming features music, art, and dance performances.

All You Can Eat—at 20 Below Zero

THE FARGO KIWANIS PANCAKE KARNIVAL

Fargo, North Dakota

A yearly institution since 1958, the Fargo Kiwanis Pancake Karnival is a triple treat. It's your best opportunity to meet thousands of Fargoans, enjoy a super-hearty breakfast, and contribute to local youth groups, organizations, and community projects all at the same time.

It takes place in February in the Fargodome. On the menu every year: all-you-can-eat buttermilk and/or buckwheat pancakes, sausages, coffee, milk, orange juice, and all the usual accompaniments. Crowds begin lining up early: With an average attendance of more than 10,000 and only about 800 seats, the wait can stretch to 45 minutes.

Inside, the operation is run with a friendly but military precision, with 250 volunteers doing duty as infantry (ticket sellers, batter mixers, pancake flippers, sausage pit workers, juice servers, coffee makers, and table servers) or top brass (pancake grill sergeant, shift colonel, and line supply major). Out on the floor, politicians, news anchors, athletes, and other public figures act as floor captains, adding a touch of local celebrity. In an average year, 60 indefatigable flippers make more than 30,000 pancakes.

You're probably not going to go to Fargo in February *just* to eat pancakes, so take a tour of downtown while you're there. After breakfast, head to the Plains Art Museum, the region's largest fine arts center. Housed in a former International Harvester warehouse built in 1904, it showcases a 4,000-piece permanent collection—a mix of regional, Native American, and folk art. End your day with a movie at the amazing art deco Fargo Theatre, built in 1926. On most Friday nights, there's live intermission music played on its classic Wurlitzer pipe organ, which rises majestically from the orchestra pit via hydraulic lift.

WHERE: Fargo Civic Center, 207 4th St. N; fargo.kiwanisone.org. *When:* late Feb–early March. **PLAINS ART MUSEUM:** Tel 701-551-6100; plainsart.org. *When:* closed Mon. **FARGO THEATRE:** Tel 701-239-8385; fargotheatre.org.

Pancakes are serious business in Fargo, but these volunteers are having a good time.

A Sea of Grass

LITTLE MISSOURI NATIONAL GRASSLAND

North Dakota

The great prairie grasslands once covered North America like a whispering blanket a million square miles wide, home to bison, elk, and dozens of Native American tribes. So it was for thousands of years, but in 1862 the Homestead Act granted heads of households the right to claim tracts of government-owned land as their own, provided they settled it, cultivated it, and stayed for at least five years. Almost 6 million settlers headed west, intent on transforming the prairie into farmland. What they didn't know was that the grass, sometimes growing as high as 8 feet, was what protected the fertile topsoil from the prairie winds. Once the dry winds began to blow, they took the soil with them, leading to the Dust Bowl years of the 1930s. By then, the great buffalo herds that had sustained Plains Indians were gone, victims of a planned campaign of extermination. The sea of grass, which had seemed limitless and eternal to Indians and explorers alike, was almost completely gone.

Fortunately, beginning in 1933, the federal government began buying and restoring damaged prairie lands, and in 1960 Secretary of Agriculture Ezra Taft Benson established a system of national grasslands. There are now almost 4 million acres of intermingled public and private lands in 20 states. The largest and most ecologically diverse—the million-acre Little Missouri National Grassland—is located in western North Dakota.

The Little Missouri Grassland surrounds the Theodore Roosevelt National Park (see next page), encompassing rolling mixed-grass prairie, stark canyons and buttes, and stands of forest. Antelope, deer, coyotes, bighorn sheep, and buffalo make their home here,

Little Missouri National Grassland's scenic bike routes afford spectacular views of North Dakota country.

along with myriad birds and grazing cattle. Visitors come to hike, camp, and explore the Medora Ranger District, which includes the national park's South Unit. More adventurous souls hike, ride horseback, or mountain-bike along the 97-mile Maah Daah Hey Trail, which connects the South Unit with the North and is one of the longest continuous single-track mountain bike rides in the country, and one of the best. In the Mandan Indian language, *maah daah hey* means "a venerable place," entirely appropriate to the Badlands and the prairie landscape. The route winds from Sully Creek State Park (south of Medora) to the edge of the national park's North Unit, at elevations of 2,000 to 2,700 feet.

WHERE: from Watford City in the north almost to the South Dakota border. *Forest Service:* Medora Ranger District (south), tel 701-227-7800; McKenzie Ranger District (north), tel 701-842-8500; fs.usda.gov. **MAAH DAAH HEY TRAIL:** mdhta.com. **HOW:** Dakota Cyclery in Medora (tel 888-321-1218 or 701-623-4808) offers drop-off/pick-up shuttles at the trailheads and will transport your gear to spots along the trail. *Cost:* shuttle from $150.

When: mid-Mar–mid-Nov. The ride takes about 5 days. **BEST TIMES:** May and June can be wet, but they're also the most beautiful, with cool temperatures and spring flowers. Sept offers cool nights, lovely fall colors, and daytime temperatures in the high 60s to mid 70s.

The Badlands That Inspired a President

THEODORE ROOSEVELT NATIONAL PARK

North Dakota

Teddy Roosevelt first arrived in North Dakota at age 24, with the simple aim of seeing the prairie and shooting a bison. He did both, but the latter might well be the last destructive act the future president perpetrated in

the North Dakota Badlands, a place he grew to love and respect, and which he credited with fostering his belief in conservation. (For information on South Dakota's Badlands National Park, see p. 652.)

Formed by millions of years of sedimentation, volcanic activity, and erosion, and with weather that can range from 100°F summer heat to heavy blizzards even in late spring and early fall, the landscape is not what most people think of as "pretty." The Sioux called this area *mako shika*, or the "bad lands," a name that stuck in English as well. In the 1860s, U.S. General Alfred Sully described it as "hell with the fires burned out," and Roosevelt himself noted its "desolate, grim beauty," with some areas "so fantastically broken in form and so bizarre in color as to seem hardly properly to belong to this earth." In 1947, Congress set aside a national park in Roosevelt's honor, incorporating his own ranchlands, in order to offer all Americans a glimpse of what so inspired America's first environmentalist president: rugged, surreal beauty, abundant wildlife, and opportunities to live the outdoor life.

Light dances across the face of the Badlands in Theodore Roosevelt National Park's Painted Canyon.

The 70,000-acre park is divided into three widely separated sections, all located within the bounds of the Little Missouri National Grassland (see previous page). The South Unit, near Medora, is the "baddest" of the bunch with the famous Painted Canyon. The canyon is wide and shallow, with wind- and water-sculpted formations that glow in a kaleidoscope of colors.

A 36-mile scenic drive circumnavigates the South Unit's central section, with many astounding views and opportunities to see wildlife—bison, prairie dogs, mule deer, white-tailed deer, elk, wild horses, and coyotes.

Hikers can explore about 100 miles of trails, including the 10-mile Petrified Forest Trail.

Thirty-five miles north of Medora, Elkhorn Ranch was the location of Roosevelt's second ranch and principal home in the Badlands, though today only the foundations of the house remain. It's reached via a 20-mile dirt road (inquire at the visitor center about road conditions before attempting the drive).

The park's much less visited North Unit is 70 miles north of Medora. A 14-mile road takes you to the Oxbow Overlook, which lets onto a great view of the Little Missouri River. You can also get to it via the 18-mile Achenbach Trail, which takes you up clay buttes dotted with sagebrush and through river bottomland (you have to ford the river several times).

If you're visiting in summer, spend a night in old-timey Medora and head for the Pitchfork Steak Fondue, an outdoor, cowboy-style steak-and-potatoes dinner cooked on a pitchfork, with a sunset view of the surrounding landscape. Afterward, enjoy the Medora Musical, with Western music, dancing, yodeling, and the beautiful Badlands all around.

WHERE: The South Unit is 130 miles west of Bismarck. Tel 701-623-4466. **PITCHFORK STEAK FONDUE & MEDORA MUSICAL:** Medora. Tel 800-MEDORA-1 or 701-623-4444; medora .com. *Cost:* $29 for 14-oz rib eye; musical tickets from $35. *When:* June–early Sept. **WHERE TO STAY:** in Medora, the Rough Riders Hotel, tel 800-633-6721 or 701-623-4444; medora.com. *Cost:* from $99 (off-peak), from $199 (peak); dinner at Theodore's dining room $55. **BEST TIMES:** sunrise and sunset at the Painted Canyon; early Dec for Medora's Old-Fashioned Cowboy Christmas (medorand.com).

Where America Took Its First Steps West

FORT MANDAN & THE LEWIS AND CLARK TRAIL

Washburn, North Dakota

In mid-October 1804, Meriwether Lewis and William Clark crossed into the North Dakota Territory on the first leg of their great expedition, directed by Thomas Jefferson to find "the most direct and practical water communication across the continent." Traveling up the Missouri River, they arrived at the Mandan Indian villages of Mitutanka and Nuptadi, which were major trade centers for numerous Native tribes and European traders. Here they spent the winter, building cabins and a palisade wall that they named Fort Mandan in honor of their hosts, who supplied them with food in exchange for goods.

Among the Indians they met there was Sacagawea, a Shoshone woman believed to have been born in the Rocky Mountains and kidnapped in 1800 by Hidatsa Indians. Later she married French Canadian fur trader Toussaint Charbonneau. As she spoke Shoshone and Hidatsa, and Charbonneau spoke Hidatsa and French, Lewis and Clark hired them both as interpreters. On April 7, 1805, the party set off west, Sacagawea carrying her infant son, Pomp, on her back. As it turned out, her presence was invaluable to the expedition, not only as an interpreter but as a pacifying influence on Indians who had never seen a white man before: In Native culture, a war party never traveled with a woman, especially not one with a baby.

The original Fort Mandan was destroyed by fire, and the remains were lost, but a full-scale replica was built in 1972 amid riverbank cottonwoods near the location of the original fort. In 1997, the interpretive displays were added, and today it's open to the public year-round, its rough furnishings and supplies mirroring those of the expedition's members during their winter residence.

In Washburn, the Lewis & Clark Interpretive Center includes a complete historical recounting of the expedition, with Indian artifacts, including a 30-foot hand-hewn dugout canoe, a

The Lewis & Clark Interpretive Center tells the story of the legendary expedition via replicas and dioramas.

buffalo robe you can try on, and a replica of the cradleboard in which Sacagawea carried her son. The Bergquist Gallery displays the works of Swiss watercolorist Karl Bodmer, who from 1832 to 1834 traveled the American West. Bodmer's paintings are considered among the most important visual records of the North American Plains tribes in the early 19th century, before the effects of American expansionism and imported diseases began to take their toll.

A few miles upriver, Knife River Indian Villages National Historic Site preserves the ruins of several Indian villages, including Sacagawea's home. The site contains village remains going back thousands of years, as well as a reconstruction of a Hidatsa earth-lodge, a museum and visitors center, and 11 miles of trails.

WHERE: 40 miles northwest of Bismarck. *Lewis and Clark Trail info:* nps.gov/lecl. **FORT MANDAN AND LEWIS & CLARK INTERPRETIVE CENTER:** Tel 877-462-8535 or 701-462-8535; fortmandan.com. **KNIFE RIVER INDIAN VILLAGES:** Tel 701-745-3300; nps.gov/knri. **BEST TIME:** 3rd full weekend in June for Lewis & Clark Days in Washburn.

Frank Lloyd Wright and Buffalo Nights

BARTLESVILLE

Oklahoma

When Frank Lloyd Wright died in 1959, he had designed over 1,000 buildings, with some 532 built (400 of which still stand), including the fabled Guggenheim Museum in New York City (see p. 184). His legacy included just one skyscraper, and serious lovers of architecture have long been coming to this small prairie city to behold Price Tower, Wright's elegantly streamlined 19-story high-rise. Converted into a hotel, it is the ultimate mecca of modernism.

Built in 1956 as corporate headquarters for the H.C. Price Pipeline Company, Price Tower embodies Wright's ideal of a skyscraper surrounded by open space. It has many beautiful but practical features, such as the signature green copper louvers to provide shade from the hot prairie sun. The Inn at Price Tower now occupies six of the upper floors, with 19 modern guest rooms recently refurbished and honoring the Wright aesthetic.

Bartlesville is hometown to Frank Phillips, the ultra-successful oilman who founded Phillips Petroleum. You can visit his imposing 1909 neoclassical mansion to get a remarkably intimate look at the life of an extremely wealthy family back in 1930 (when the home was last decorated).

For fun, Phillips and his wife entertained some of the country's brightest stars (Rudy Vallee and Will Rogers visited) at their lodge at Woolaroc, a 3,700-acre fantasy retreat just outside Bartlesville. Named for the woods, lakes, and rocks found so abundantly in the rolling landscape, Woolaroc was created from the 1920s to the 1940s, and has all been preserved as it was: The free-roaming herd of buffalo are descendants of those brought here in 1926.

Wright called his 221-foot-tall skyscraper "the tree that escaped the crowded forest."

In 1929, Phillips started a museum at Woolaroc. It is a curious hodgepodge of shrunken heads from Ecuador, one of the world's finest collections of Colt firearms, a great array of Western art, including six mural-size paintings by William R. Leigh, and all the bronze statues that once lined the road to oil baron E.W. Marland's fabulous mansion (see p. 649). Enjoy one of the Phillipses' favorite meals, a barbecue sandwich made with Woolaroc bison.

Arrive at or leave Bartlesville by way of one of the country's most dramatic drives, due west on Highway 60 toward Ponca City. It passes through the Osage reservation and along the Nature Conservancy's Tallgrass Prairie Preserve, at 39,000 acres the largest protected remnant of this distinctly American ecosystem and a refuge for free-roaming buffalo. It's easy to imagine Indians on horseback, or cowboys moving cattle toward a distant horizon.

INN AT PRICE TOWER: Tel 877-424-2424 or 918-336-4949; pricetower.com. *Cost:* from $145. **FRANK PHILLIPS HISTORIC HOME:** Tel 918-336-2491; frankphillipshome.com. *When:* Wed–Sat. **WOOLAROC:** Tel 888-WOOLAROC or 918-336-0307; woolaroc.org. **TALLGRASS PRAIRIE PRESERVE:** Tel 602-273-8494; nps .gov/tapr. **BEST TIME:** June for the OK Mozart Festival in Bartlesville.

"Queen of the Prairie," Preserved

GUTHRIE

Oklahoma

Guthrie sprang out of the prairie dust when Congress opened the Oklahoma Territory to settlers in the 1889 Land Run. Prosperous and nicknamed "Queen of the Prairie," Guthrie soon became the territorial capital and

then state capital in 1907, and city founders constructed eclectic, picturesque Italianate and Romanesque buildings worthy of that prestigious distinction. But when Oklahoma City snatched away the title of state capital in 1910, the city slipped into a deep sleep, inadvertently preserving its Victorian architectural legacy.

It is now the largest contiguous district on the National Register of Historic Places, covering 1,400 acres, extending 400 blocks, and containing 2,169 buildings.

Chief among them are the two- and three-story brick buildings downtown, the finest designed by Belgian-born architect Joseph

Foucart and featuring showy details such as minarets, stone finials, towers, and large arched windows.

Guthrie was once home to the Banjo Hall of Fame (which has since moved to Oklahoma City), but the instrument remains a popular pastime here. There's picking aplenty to be had at October's Oklahoma International Bluegrass Festival, organized by three-time national fiddle champ Byron Berline, who still performs at his Double-Stop Fiddle Shop and Music Hall.

Take a guided tour of the city's architectural apogee, the outlandishly grand Guthrie Scottish Rite Masonic Temple—one of the world's largest. Built at an eyebrow-raising cost of $2.6 million during the oil boom of the 1920s, a time when almost every man in town was a Mason, the entrance to the neoclassical building boasts sixteen 70-foot-high limestone columns, and it's even more lavish inside the massive complex.

Stay in one of the town's B&Bs, in highest demand when the Pollard Theatre, a year-round professional theater, is mounting *A Territorial Christmas Carol*, a frontier version of the Dickens classic, and a longtime, much-loved tradition in these parts.

Guthrie's historic buildings are replete with Victorian architectural details.

WHERE: 30 miles north of Oklahoma City. *Visitor info:* Tel 800-299-1889 or 405-282-1947; guthrieok.com. **DOUBLE-STOP FIDDLE SHOP:** Tel 405-282-6646; doublestop.com. **GUTHRIE SCOTTISH RITE MASONIC TEMPLE:** Tel 405-282-1281; guthriescottishrite.org. *When:* tours Mon–Fri. **GUTHRIE B&Bs:** guthrieinns.com. *Cost:* from $120. **POLLARD THEATRE:** Tel 405-282-2800; thepollard.org. *Cost:* $25 for *A Territorial Christmas Carol.* **BEST TIMES:** mid-Apr for Oklahoma 89er Celebration; 1st weekend in Oct for the Oklahoma International Bluegrass Festival (oibf.com); Dec for Guthrie Territorial Christmas Celebration.

Where Cowboy Culture Lives On

CATTLEMEN'S RESTAURANT & STOCKYARDS CITY

Oklahoma City, Oklahoma

W hen cattlemen and cowboys come into town, they head straight for Stockyards City Main Street, a retail district smack in the center of the city, chock-full of saddleries and Western-wear clothing stores.

It's right next to the Oklahoma National Stockyards, the world's largest stocker/feeder market, where every Monday and Tuesday you can watch live cattle being auctioned, a spectacle where millions of dollars change hands with the nod of a head.

For the uninitiated, cattlemen are the men who own the livestock (cowboys are the hired hands) and, their business dealings done, they stop at Cattlemen's Restaurant, the consummate Western steak house where USDA Prime beef is slowly aged and hand-cut—never frozen. The most popular cuts are rib eye quickly broiled over hot charcoals and served in a salty jus with homemade Parker House rolls. The T-bone is called the "Presidential Choice" because President George H. W. Bush ordered it when he dined here. Adventurous palates can start with a plate of lamb fries—the deep-fried testicles of lambs. Delicately flavored and meltingly tender, they can taste pretty good if you don't know what you're eating. House-made coconut cream pie is the dessert of choice.

The original 1910 café is popular for breakfast, but the dinner crowd likes the 1960s-era South Dining Room. Settle into a red vinyl booth, riding a little low from the bulk of the generations of beef-lovers before you, and enjoy the backlit wall-size panorama, a garishly tinted photograph of two gentlemen ranchers herding Black Angus beneath a radiant blue sky. One of them is Gene Wade, who won the place in a craps game in 1945 and ran it until 1990.

Directly across the street is Langston's Western Wear, Oklahoma's oldest Western-wear store and the very first stop on any cowboy's shopping spree. Oklahoma has more horses per capita than any other state, and Langston's is piled high with Wrangler jeans as well as a dizzying selection of boots and oversize belt buckles.

Oklahoma City also has more horse shows than any other city in America, and Stockyards City Main Street is at its best and busiest during competitions like the American Quarter Horse Association World Championship Show. Drawing competitors from around the world, the show features real-life cowboy skills like cutting, a two-and-a-half-minute battle of wills where horses (and their riders) have to keep a single cow away from the herd.

WHERE: Stockyards City Main Street, 1305 S. Agnew Ave. Tel 405-235-7267; stockyards city.org. **OKLAHOMA NATIONAL STOCKYARDS:** Tel 405-235-8675; onsy.com. **CATTLEMEN'S RESTAURANT:** Tel 405-236-0416; cattlemens restaurant.com. *Cost:* dinner $40. **LANGSTON'S:** Tel 800-658-2831 or 405-235-9536; langstons. com. **BEST TIME:** 1st 2 weeks in Nov for American Quarter Horse Association World Championship Show (aqha.com).

How the Wild West Was Tamed

NATIONAL COWBOY & WESTERN HERITAGE MUSEUM

Oklahoma City, Oklahoma

The Old West comes to life down to the last vivid detail at this salute to cowboy culture. A distant train whistle punctuates the tinny melody of a saloon's player piano in Prosperity Junction, the moody re-creation of an early 1900s cattle town just after dusk. Kerosene lanterns light the livery stable, illuminating a plaque's good advice for stagecoach passengers: Don't pomade your hair before the journey, it will collect dust.

The museum's American Cowboy Gallery follows the evolution of the ranching industry in the West, starting with the nattily dressed Spanish *vaqueros* of colonial times who taught cowboys the skills, if not the sartorial flair, they began honing in Europe in the late 1500s, and ending in the 20th century. A large collection of clothing, boots, bridles, saddles, and ropes will expand your knowledge about cowboy fashion and how it varied from region to region.

In the Western Performers Gallery, a 1950s matinee theater plays grainy movie clips that demonstrate the sway the West has always exerted on Hollywood's—and the world's—imagination. Within a replica 1950s rodeo arena, the American Rodeo Gallery tells the

The End of the Trail *(1915) by James Earle Fraser is a highlight of the museum.*

story of the gritty, dangerous lives of bronc busters and bull riders and the history behind the West's truly indigenous sport. There's a good permanent collection of Western artists, including a significant group of paintings and sculpture by Charlie Russell and Frederic Remington. A focal figure is the highly recognizable piece *The End of the Trail,* an 18-foot plaster sculpture of a lone, defeated Indian on his weary horse, created for the 1915 Panama-Pacific International Exposition in San Francisco.

If you've got a hankering for some real cowboy grub, you'll have to wait for the museum's annual Memorial Day event, the Chuck Wagon Gathering & Children's Cowboy Festival, when crews of ranch hands rustle up cowboy food—brisket, beans, and sourdough biscuits baked in Dutch ovens buried in coals in the ground—and serve it off chuck wagons in a grassy field at the bottom of Persimmon Hill.

WHERE: 1700 NE 63rd St. Tel 405-478-2250; nationalcowboymuseum.org. **BEST TIME:** late May for Chuck Wagon Gathering & Children's Cowboy Festival.

On the Powwow Trail

RED EARTH NATIVE AMERICAN CULTURAL FESTIVAL

Oklahoma City, Oklahoma

Oklahoma is home to 39 federally recognized tribes, more than any other state. It's an unmatched cultural wealth that manifests itself every summer, when you can find a powwow—and its attendant colorfully costumed dancers in full regalia—almost every weekend. Consider yourself lucky if your first introduction to a powwow is at the Red Earth Native American Cultural Festival. It includes a large juried art show and market where you can buy paintings, pottery, beadwork, basketry, and jewelry—reason enough for many to go. But there's no doubt that most of the 30,000 visitors come to see some of the country's most gifted and accomplished Native American dancers.

Visitors get easily swept up in the drumming, singing, and dancing. There are countless styles of dance, each mesmerizing in its own way. Men's Northern Traditional, the original dance of the Northern Plains, depicts a warrior challenging an enemy and uses buckskin and natural colors in the costuming. The fast-paced, neon-colored Men's Fancy Dance is the showiest and most athletically demanding, usually performed by boys and young men. And there's no mistaking the popularity of the Tiny Tots division, children age five and under who learn to dance as soon as they walk—it's not just proud parents beaming in the audience.

Bring a lawn chair to smaller powwows that are held on the open plains or in wooded groves, often on tribal lands. You may not see the polished level of showmanship of the Red Earth Festival at these local powwows, but they have a traditional, authentic community feel, and can be often more interesting for that very reason. And you are always welcome.

Other places to explore Indian culture include the Cherokee Heritage Center in Tahlequah, where an outdoor living exhibit called Diligwa offers an authentic experience of Cherokee village life circa 1710. In the museum, a permanent Trail of Tears exhibit tells how the Five Civilized Tribes were forcibly relocated from the Southeast to Oklahoma in the mid-1800s. Anadarko's annual American Indian Exposition in August is where Plains tribes show off their cultural traditions and the princesses who will represent them for the year, proving that, for all the hardships they suffered, it was never really the end of the trail. Indian traditions live on vibrantly here.

WHERE: Cox Convention Center in downtown Oklahoma City. Tel 405-427-5228; red earth.org. *When:* early June. *Powwows info:* powwows.com. **CHEROKEE HERITAGE CENTER:** Tahlequah. Tel 888-999-6007 or 918-456-6007; cherokeeheritage.org. **AMERICAN INDIAN EXPOSITION:** Anadarko. Tel 580-678-1282. *When:* early Aug.

An Oil Baron's Prairie Palace

MARLAND ESTATE MANSION

Ponca City, Oklahoma

A veritable Hearst Castle of the Plains, the Marland Estate Mansion is a lavish 55-room villa built from 1925–28 for an astounding $5.5 million. That was just a sliver of the massive fortune of E. W. Marland, a Pittsburgh native who came to Ponca City in 1908 in search of oil and was rewarded with a stupendous find on an allotment of land leased from a Ponca Indian called Willie Cries-for-War. It was the start of an era when Oklahoma was at the epicenter of the world's biggest oil discoveries; at one point in the 1920s, Marland personally controlled 10 percent of the world's oil. Awash in money and inspired by the Renaissance Davanzati Palace in Florence, the oil baron gathered artisans from all over the world, including a master Italian muralist responsible for all the ornately painted ceilings throughout the mansion.

Marland's luck ran out when he borrowed money from the wily eastern banker J.P. Morgan; he lost both his company and his palace not long after the paint was dry. Today, many of the furnishings have been returned, and it's easy to imagine the extravagant balls and lively fox hunts Marland enjoyed here, however briefly, with his scandalously wed second wife, Lydie (his adopted daughter and his first wife's niece). Marland's first home in Ponca City, a 22-room white stucco mansion known as Marland's Grand Home, holds a large oil painting of a Marland fox hunt and memorabilia from the once world-renowned 101 Ranch and Wild West Show.

Ponca City is famous for two colossal bronzes. Commissioned by Marland and unveiled in 1930, *The Pioneer Woman* by Bryant Baker pays tribute to women's role in settling the West. In 1996, the city unveiled a 22-foot bronze of *Standing Bear*, the great Ponca tribal leader who in 1879 was the first to successfully argue in court that Indians are actually "persons" under the law. The surrounding 63-acre park commemorates the Indian removals following the Civil War, when tribes like the Ponca and Osage were forced to leave their homelands and relocate to this area.

After lunching on meaty pork ribs and unsurpassed homemade onion rings at Blue Moon Restaurant, a Ponca City institution, head downtown to the Ponca City Library, a 1935 brick building with an impressive collection of Western and Asian art. Nearby, the beautifully restored Poncan Theatre is a 1927 beauty where Oklahoma's most famous son, Will Rogers, once twirled his lasso.

WHERE: 106 miles north of Oklahoma City. *Visitor info:* Tel 866-763-8092 or 580-765-4400; poncacitytourism.com. **MARLAND**

The Marland Estate Mansion contains 10 bedrooms, 12 bathrooms, 7 fireplaces, and 3 kitchens.

ESTATE MANSION: Tel 800-422-8340 or 580-767-0420; marlandmansion.com. **MARLAND'S GRAND HOME:** Tel 580-767-0427; marland grandhome.com. **PIONEER WOMAN MUSEUM:** Tel 580-765-6108; pioneerwomanmuseum.com. **STANDING BEAR MEMORIAL PARK:** Tel 580-762-1514; standingbearpark.com. **BLUE MOON:** Tel 580-765-0065. *Cost:* rib dinner $13. **PONCA CITY LIBRARY:** Tel 580-767-0345; poncacity library.com. **PONCAN THEATRE:** Tel 580-765-0943; poncantheatre.org. **BEST TIMES:** 1st weekend in June for the Herb Festival; 3rd weekend in Aug for the 101 Ranch Rodeo; last weekend in Sept for the Standing Bear Powwow.

World's Greatest Collection of Art Devoted to the American West

GILCREASE MUSEUM

Tulsa, Oklahoma

An unsurpassed repository for the best of the Old West, the Gilcrease Museum is the lasting legacy of a one-eighth Creek Indian who struck it rich when oil was found on his 160-acre allotment 20 miles south of Tulsa.

Thomas Gilcrease started his own oil company in 1922 and spent his profits gleefully amassing the world's largest collection of fine art, artifacts, and archives devoted to the American West (some 300,000 items, all told, if you count every last arrowhead, manuscript, and piece of pottery).

Buying great Western art at a time when few others were interested, Gilcrease quickly built a major collection that included the iconic oil painting *Black Hawk and His Son Whirling Thunder* by John Wesley Jarvis, 18 of the 22 different Frederic Remington sculptures, and a remarkable group of works by

Charlie Russell and Thomas Moran, whose paintings helped make the case to America that Yellowstone was worth protecting.

The depth and breadth of Gilcrease's taste outstripped his ability to pay, however, when the price of oil declined precipitously in the 1950s. Rather than sell off a single piece, he deeded the entire collection to the city of Tulsa, which approved a $2.25 million bond issue to cover his debts. Gilcrease put his oil revenue toward museum maintenance until the bond was repaid; he died, debt-free, in 1962.

Long known for its magnificent oil paintings, the Gilcrease offers equal riches in its vast artifact collections, previously available only to scholars. Now the public can browse the razor-sharp Aztec obsidian blades used for human sacrifice, richly beaded Cheyenne moccasins, or 2,700-year-old effigy ceramics from western Mexico by randomly opening glass-covered drawers down in the Kravis Discovery Center.

Oil money is also behind Tulsa's other world-class collection, the Philbrook Museum of Art, an ornate 72-room Italian Rennaissance villa from the 1920s that was once the home of oilman Waite Phillips. (His brother Frank made a fortune up in Bartlesville; see p. 644.) When Waite and his wife decamped to California in 1938, they gave Tulsa their fabulous home for use as a new arts center. Its collection includes fine Italian Renaissance and Baroque paintings, 20th-century Native American art, and an important Hopi collection.

With money and civic pride in unlimited supply, a proliferation of art deco masterpieces from the 1920s to 1940s were built throughout Tulsa to remind the world of the town's (now nostalgic) status as "Oil Capital of the World."

GILCREASE MUSEUM: 1400 N. Gilcrease Museum Rd. Tel 888-655-2278 or 918-596-2700; gilcrease.org. *When:* closed Mon. **PHILBROOK MUSEUM OF ART:** Tel 918-749-7941; philbrook.org. *When:* closed Mon.

A portrait of Buffalo Bill is one of countless paintings in the Gilcrease collection.

The Nation's First Wildlife Preserve

WICHITA MOUNTAINS WILDLIFE REFUGE

Oklahoma

Rugged islands of ancient rock surrounded by a sea of grass, the Wichita Mountains are the nation's first big-game wildlife preserve. The buffalo still roam here, as do the elk and herds of Texas longhorns. Prairie dogs bark high-pitched warnings at your approach. It's a magical landscape of timeless beauty where you can drive, hike, rock climb, bike, camp, and even bushwhack through one of the few mixed-grass prairies in the country to have escaped the plow.

Deeply moved by a letter from great Comanche Chief Quanah Parker bemoaning the destruction of buffalo herds (fewer than 1,000 animals were left), President Theodore Roosevelt named the Wichita Mountains a national wildlife preserve in 1907. Fifteen bison were returned to the plains (from the New York Zoological Society, ironically), and in the 1920s the endangered Texas Longhorn cattle joined them on the 60,000-acre refuge. Numbers for both are now so high that there's an annual roundup and auction to keep the refuge from being overgrazed. The buyers are usually ranchers or sometimes Indian tribes who want to return buffalo to their own lands.

Give yourself plenty of time to enjoy some 15 miles of hiking trails and drive to the top of Mount Scott. The range's highest peak at 2,464 feet, it offers broad views of lakes dotting the boulder-studded grasslands below.

Don't leave these parts without a Longhorn "Meersburger" from the Meers Store, a ramshackle piece of Americana serving Oklahoma's —some say America's—best burger. Owners Joe and Margie Maranto keep their own herds of grass-fed Longhorns just down the road, and then grind the beef themselves because Joe's daddy was a butcher, and that's the way you do it. The half-pound Meersburger—served only with mustard—is so big it comes in an aluminum pie pan and is quartered just so you can pick it up.

Nearby in Lawton, the famous warrior Geronimo is buried in an Apache cemetery in an evocative corner of Fort Sill. Geronimo was the daring leader of the last Indian fighting force to formally surrender to the U.S., back in 1886. Because he fought against such daunting odds and held out the longest, he was the most famous—and feared—Apache of all. Wayfarers pay tribute to him by leaving a coin on his monument, a cobblestone pyramid topped with a proud eagle.

WHERE: 15 miles northwest of Lawton; junction of routes 49 and 115. Tel 580-429-3222; fws.gov/refuge/Wichita_Mountains. **MEERS STORE:** Tel 580-429-8051; meersstore.com. *Cost:* Meersburger $7. **GERONIMO'S GRAVE:** Tel 580-581-3460; discovermgp.org. **BEST TIMES:** spring and fall for weather; Sept–Oct for bison and Longhorn auctions at the Refuge.

Nature's High Drama

BADLANDS NATIONAL PARK

South Dakota

To the Lakota Sioux, who controlled this part of the Dakotas before the white man arrived, they were the *mako shika*, "the bad lands." To the French-Canadian fur trappers who came later, they were *les mauvaises terres à traverser*, "bad lands to travel across." But in 1935, the great architect Frank Lloyd Wright came here and described what he saw with an artist's eye: "an indescribable sense of mysterious elsewhere . . . [an] endless supernatural world more spiritual than earth but created out of it."

Once upon a time this area rested under an inland sea, and once upon another time it was a lush forest full of animal life; but despite the fossilized richness that lies beneath the surface, it's the "bones of the Badlands" themselves that draw us. Sculpted by 75 million years of sedimentation and erosion, 243,000 acres are crammed full of cones, ridges, buttes, gorges, gulches, pinnacles, and precipices in an eerily sparse yet breathtakingly beautiful landscape. Some formations rise more than 1,000 feet into the sky, while in other places the forces of erosion have, over thousands of years, brushed away the surface to reveal band upon band of stratified mineral deposits, weaving through the ridges and ravines like nature's brushstrokes.

You can explore the park up close and in depth on a day or overnight hike, from a short quarter-mile loop to the little-used 10-mile Castle Trail to an unmarked cross-country trek. Or you can see and experience the majesty from your car on the 31-mile Badlands Loop, which provides an ample eyeful of nature's theatricality, especially at dawn, dusk, and just after a rainfall, when the interplay of light and shadow on the earth is most poetic.

American Indians lived on this land for 11,000 years, but they were forced onto reservations when white homesteaders began arriving in the late 19th century. As their situation grew desperate, many became followers of the Paiute prophet Wovoka, who

preached that by adhering to virtuous principles and performing a "Ghost Dance" he'd seen in a dream, the Indians' traditional way of life would be restored. As the movement grew, fearing that the dancers' religious fervor could be an incitement to war, the government sent in the troops. In December 1890, a band of Sioux dancers was taken into custody by the Seventh Cavalry. While they were camping at Wounded Knee Creek, a scuffle between a soldier and an Indian escalated into a wholesale slaughter in which at least 150 Indians were killed, many of them women and children. Today a simple memorial marks the site, approximately 45 miles south of the park, off Route 27.

WHERE: 80 miles southeast of Rapid City. Tel 605-433-5361; nps.gov/badl. **BEST TIMES:** spring and fall for weather. If you crave solitude, come in winter.

Badlands National Park contains the world's richest fossil beds, which date to between 25 and 35 million years ago.

Where the Buffalo Roam

CUSTER STATE PARK

South Dakota

The Lakota called them *tatanka*, the great buffalo that once migrated freely through the American prairie, influencing almost every aspect of the Plains Indians' lives. At one time, more than 60 million bison roamed

North America, but overhunting and a government policy of extermination decimated the herds. By 1893, there were fewer than 1,000

left in the whole country; now, there are approximately half a million.

Named for one of the most famous Indian

fighters in the American Indian Wars (see p. 618) and dedicated to buffalo preservation, Custer State Park covers 71,000 acres adjacent to Mount Rushmore and the Crazy Horse Memorial (see p. 657). One of the world's largest publicly owned buffalo herds lives here, some 1,300 strong. Each October, the park's annual Buffalo Roundup gives a sense of what it must have been like to see one of the great herds stampeding across the prairie when the country was young. Thousands of visitors arrive for the Roundup to watch cowboys on horseback (and rangers in pickups) bring the herds to corral. The accompanying three-day Buffalo Roundup Arts Festival brings in artists and craftspeople, traditional entertainers perform throughout the day, and hungry crowds gather for the popular one-day Chili Cookoff.

Bison can be viewed year-round as they range through the park. Mid-July through August is rutting season, while springtime sees the birth of new calves. Viewing is especially good on the 18-mile Wildlife Loop Road. You might also spot elk, coyotes, prairie dogs, eagles, and hawks along with pronghorn, white-tailed deer, and mule deer. Spectacular views can also be enjoyed on Needles Highway, a 14-mile scenic route named for the needle-like granite spires that jut from the ground, and Iron Mountain Road which takes you up to Rushmore.

In a beautiful mountain valley near the

The American buffalo is the largest land mammal in North America.

park's eastern border is the seven-room stone-and-pine State Game Lodge. It was built in 1920, and in 1927 the lodge served as President Calvin Coolidge's Summer White House. You can stay in Coolidge's room, but less pricey accommodations are also available in adjacent motel units and rustic cabins. Experience the local wildlife by heading out on one of the lodge's buffalo jeep safaris into the park's backcountry for up-close bison viewing.

WHERE: 20 miles south of Mount Rushmore. Tel 605-255-4515; gfd.sd.gov/state_parks. **STATE GAME LODGE:** Tel 888-875-0001 or 605-255-4772; custerresorts.com. *Cost:* from $165. *When:* early May–early Oct. **BEST TIME:** late Sept or early Oct for the Buffalo Roundup.

Last Resting Place of "Wild Bill" Hickok

DEADWOOD

South Dakota

Established during the 1876 gold rush, Deadwood was a magnet for get-rich-quick prospectors and the kinds of businesses where they could lose those riches quick: bars, brothels, dance halls, and gambling houses.

The latter is what brought James Butler, aka "Wild Bill," Hickok to town. Famous as a

quick-draw artist, stagecoach driver, and scout for George Custer, Hickok had enlarged his myth as sheriff of Hays City and Abilene, Kansas, and cemented it with a stint in "Buffalo Bill" Cody's Wild West Show. On August 2, 1876, little more than a month after he arrived in Deadwood, Hickok was shot in the back of the head as he played poker in Saloon No. 10, by a boastful no-account named Jack McCall. The cards that fell from his hand—pairs of black aces and eights—have been known ever since as the "dead man's hand."

Located in the northern Black Hills, the town today looks much as it did in the 1880s, owing to preservation and gambling initiatives. Today, scores of gaming establishments line the streets, and block after block of restored Victorian buildings have earned the town a place on the National Register of Historic Places. On Main Street during the summer there are multiple daily reenactments of the murder of Wild Bill, and a play, *The Trial of Jack McCall*, takes place Monday–Saturday in summer at the Masonic Temple. You can pay your respects to Wild Bill at his grave in the Mount Moriah Cemetery. (Martha Jane Canary, aka "Calamity Jane," is buried in the next plot.) Elsewhere in town, the Adams Museum is a repository of Deadwood and Black Hills history.

The Midnight Star Casino, owned by actor Kevin Costner, is the home of Jakes, considered one of the best restaurants in South Dakota. One mile

north of town, an exhibition called "Tatanka: Story of the Bison" is the actor's real pet project. The indoor-outdoor interpretive center explores the relationship between the Plains Indians and the great bison herds, and displays include a traditional encampment, art gallery, and theater.

Some of the most beautiful scenes in 1990's *Dances with Wolves* were filmed in Spearfish Canyon, which runs west of Deadwood.

WHERE: 35 miles north of Mount Rushmore. *Visitor info:* Tel 800-999-1876 or 605-578-1876; deadwood.org. **TRIAL OF JACK McCALL:** Tel 605-578-1876. *When:* summer. **ADAMS MUSEUM:** Tel 605-578-1714; deadwoodhistory.com. *When:* closed Sun–Mon in winter. **JAKES ATOP THE MIDNIGHT STAR:** Tel 800-999-6482 or 605-578-1555; themidnightstar.com. *Cost:* dinner $50. **TATANKA:** Tel 605-584-5678; storyofthebison.com. *When:* mid-May–Sept. **BEST TIME:** fall for foliage.

The well-preserved streets of Deadwood give visitors the impression that they've traveled back to the 1880s.

Little Town on the Prairie

LAURA INGALLS WILDER COUNTRY

DeSmet, South Dakota

Laura Ingalls was born in Wisconsin and lived in Kansas, but the quiet town of DeSmet, South Dakota, can rightfully claim its place as the centerpiece of her life story. It was here that her family finally settled in 1879, here that she became a teacher at age 15, here that she met and married Almanzo Wilder and gave birth to their daughter, Rose.

The series of Little House books, which Ingalls Wilder wrote between 1932 and 1943, are American classics, depicting America's frontier heritage and the important role women played in opening up the West. Today, visitors to DeSmet can see the sites that became the inspiration for many of the books, including *By the Shores of Silver Lake*, *The Long Winter*, *Little Town on the Prairie*, and *These Happy Golden Years*.

In town, the Surveyors' House was the Ingalls's first home when they moved to DeSmet. Nearby is a replica of the Brewster School, where Laura once taught, plus the Discover Laura! learning center where kids can dress in period costume and get a hands-on experience of frontier life, picking vegetables from a garden, playing checkers, or collecting eggs. A few blocks to the west, the white-shingled Ingalls Home was the last residence of Laura's parents. Both are buried in the local cemetery, along with Laura's sisters Mary, Carrie, and Grace.

Just south of town, the Ingalls Homestead is the site of Charles Ingalls's land claim. A replica of the original house shows how the family lived in the 1880s, while a reconstructed "dugout" house shows how the family lived during their years in Walnut Grove, Minnesota. On the grounds are the five cottonwood trees that Charles Ingalls planted for his wife and four daughters. Visitors can take a covered-wagon ride to the Little Prairie School, where kids can get experience learning, 19th-century–style. For several weeks each summer, actors in the Laura Ingalls Wilder Pageant re-create scenes from her books as the sun sets on the prairie.

DeSmet is the westernmost stop on the Laura Ingalls Wilder Historic Highway, which snakes through the Midwest, linking sites associated with the Little House books. Other notable stops include Laura's Home in Mansfield, Missouri (where she lived from 1894 until her death in 1957, and where she wrote the series). Laura is buried there.

WHERE: 95 miles northwest of Sioux Falls. **DISCOVER LAURA:** Tel 800-880-3383 or 605-854-3383; discoverlaura.org. *When:* daily, June–Aug; closed Sat–Sun, Sept–May. **INGALLS HOMESTEAD:** Tel 800-776-3594 or 605-854-3984; ingallshomestead.com. *When:* daily, late May–early Sept; call for spring and fall hours. **LAURA INGALLS WILDER PAGEANT:** Tel 800-880-3383 or 800-776-3594; desmet pageant.org. *When:* Fri–Sun nights in July.

Corny Beyond Belief

THE CORN PALACE

Mitchell, South Dakota

While western South Dakota is the very picture of the American West, the eastern part of the state is solid Midwestern farm country, where corn is king—and a king, of course, has got to have a castle. In 1892,

the town of Mitchell built its first Corn Palace as a home for the Corn Belt Exposition, a showcase of agricultural strength. The current building, a Moorish fantasy reminiscent of old Atlantic City theaters, is the palace's third incarnation, dating from 1921. At first glance it appears not quite of this world, and certainly not of South Dakota, with its decorative columns and arabesque minarets, but closer inspection reveals that the Corn Palace is very much a product of its place. The huge murals around its exterior are mosaics composed entirely of corn, grains, and local grasses—thousands and thousands of bushels of them. It's a tradition that goes back to the very first palace, and has been repeated annually ever since, with South Dakota artists creating designs that reflect some aspect of the state's life or history. Lit nightly in summer, the

The Corn Palace, with its distinctive Moorish-style domes and minarets, is in its third incarnation.

outdoor murals become a giant bird feeder from the moment of their creation—one of the main reasons new ones have to be made every year. Inside, displays explain how the murals are created, and a number of murals from past years are preserved, including those of noted Yanktonai Sioux artist Oscar Howe, once the artist laureate of South Dakota.

The Palace is also a multipurpose arena seating more than 3,000 for shows, circuses, basketball games, and other events. And each Labor Day weekend it's the site of the Corn Palace Festival, featuring a carnival, crafts, food booths, and entertainers such as Willie Nelson, Glen Campbell, and REO Speedwagon.

WHERE: 75 miles west of Sioux Falls; 604 North Main St. Tel 866-273-CORN or 605-996-8430; cornpalace.com. *When:* closed Sat–Sun, Nov–April. **BEST TIMES:** Murals are begun in spring and completed by late summers; late Aug for the festival and optimal mural viewing (cornpalace.com).

The Black Hills: Holy Land of the Sioux

MOUNT RUSHMORE & CRAZY HORSE

South Dakota

For the generation that saw it born, Mount Rushmore was the symbol of American optimism after the triumph of WWI. For many who grew up in the 1950s and '60s, it became a symbol of the family road trip. And for American Indians of any generation, it's a complicated symbol of broken treaties and loss.

Conceived in 1924 by Danish-American sculptor Gutzon Borglum, the great sculptures on Rushmore were to be a "Shrine of Democracy" that would use the presidents' images to trace the country's history, from its birth (Washington) through its early growth (Jefferson), preservation (Lincoln), and robust

development in the 20th century (Teddy Roosevelt). Work on the monument began on October 4, 1927, and ended 14 years later, on October 31, 1941. When the granite dust cleared, Rushmore had been transformed forever, with four enormous faces, six stories high, peering into the Black Hills.

Though America hailed Borglum's great achievement (completed by the sculptor's son,

Lincoln, after his father's death), the work was a slap in the face to South Dakota's Lakota people, to whom *Paha Sapa* (the Black Hills) was a sacred place that figured prominently in their creation stories. An 1868 treaty had deeded the land to the Sioux "in perpetuity," but their ownership lasted only six years. When gold was discovered in the area, the U.S. government reclaimed the land. In 1876, when the government ordered all Lakota bands onto reservations, the great chiefs Crazy Horse, Sitting Bull, and Gall organized a resistance that eventually destroyed the Seventh Cavalry in General George Custer's Last Stand at the Little Bighorn (see p. 618). But the Sioux's victory was short-lived: In less than two years, Crazy Horse was dead, and their fate was sealed.

Gutzon Borglum and 400 workers sculpted the impressive 60-foot busts of the former U.S. presidents between 1927 and 1941.

In 1939, as the faces of the presidents were emerging from the granite, the Sioux began planning their own memorial, inviting Boston-born sculptor Korczak Ziolkowski to carve the image of Crazy Horse into another Black Hills mountain, 17 miles southwest of Rushmore. Work finally began in 1947 on Ziolkowski's grand vision: Unlike the sculptures at Rushmore, which are carved onto just one side of a peak, Crazy Horse would be sculpted in the round, the great chief sitting astride a horse, his arm outstretched. The memorial would also be massive, measuring 563 feet high and 641 feet long, utterly dwarfing Rushmore. (His arm alone is longer than a football field.)

Such a thing takes time and effort. Following his death in 1982, Ziolkowski's family has carried on with the work. Today, with several million tons of rock blasted away from the mountain, Crazy Horse's head, arm, and the top of his horse's head are in various states of completion. A final completion date is impossible to predict, but, as the project's motto says, "Never forget your dreams."

MOUNT RUSHMORE: 25 miles southwest of Rapid City. Tel 605-574-2523; nps.gov/moru. **CRAZY HORSE:** Tel 605-673-4681; crazyhorse memorial.org. **BEST TIMES:** summer evenings for illumination ceremony of Rushmore and for the Crazy Horse "Legends in Light" multimedia laser light show; 1st weekend in June for the 10K Crazy Horse Volksmarch, an organized hike up the Crazy Horse mountain.

Vroom, Vroom!

STURGIS MOTORCYCLE RALLY

Sturgis, South Dakota

For folks who like bikes, there's no place like Sturgis, a small town (population 6,800) that annually hosts the biggest motorcycle rally in America. Historians trace the event back to 1936, when Clarence "Pappy" Hoel established an Indian motorcycle franchise in town and founded the Jackpine Gypsies Motorcycle Club. Two years later the club held the first Black Hills Motor Classic, with nine participants and a small audience. Today the rally—known to most as just Sturgis—attracts well over half a million people every year for a week of bike shows, concerts, races, demos, group rides, camaraderie, and plain old partying. Attendees run the gamut from those who live the Harley life to CEOs who put on their leathers only on weekends. Hundreds of vendors sell clothing, accessories, food, and drink, and tattoo artists do a brisk business. It's like Mardi Gras with chrome, though things have quieted down some since the good old days, when it was fairly common to see naked people riding down Main Street. The average attendee is in his mid-forties, and it's not uncommon to see baby strollers among the hogs.

Yes, there's a good deal of drinking (Budweiser is a major sponsor, and bobbing for free beer in a bucket of ice water is a tradition at the Dungeon Bar); yes, there's a lot of rock 'n' roll (recent concerts have included ZZ Top, Kid Rock, Alice Cooper, and the Guess Who); and campgrounds like the Buffalo Chip (site of many of the concerts) get pretty wild, but Sturgis isn't all just a big party. Outside town, the scenic byways of the Black Hills National Forest are some of the most gorgeous anywhere,

and legions of riders head to Mount Rushmore and the Crazy Horse Memorial (see p. 657), and beyond. Back in town, bike buffs explore the Sturgis Motorcycle Museum and Hall of Fame. And lest we forget that bikers are all big romantic softies at heart, each year Sturgis's county courthouse issues more than 100 marriage licenses during bike week. Ain't love grand?

WHERE: 24 miles north of Rapid City. Tel 605-720-0800; sturgismotorcyclerally.com. **BUFFALO CHIP CAMPGROUND:** Belle Fourche. Tel 605-347-9000; buffalochip.com. *Cost:* 1-week rally pass from $355 per person, includes campsite, facilities use, and access to all concerts on the campground. Day passes from $30, depending on the day's concert. *When:* The 1-week rally starts the 1st Mon after 1st complete Aug weekend.

Bikes line the streets during the Sturgis Motorcycle Rally.

"Free Ice Water" in the Middle of Nowhere

WALL DRUG STORE

Wall, South Dakota

Like the Kardashians, Wall Drug is famous for being famous. It all started back in 1931, when Ted and Dorothy Hustead bought a small drugstore in a small town on the edge of the South Dakota Badlands (see p. 652).

Dorothy's father described Wall as "just about as godforsaken as you can get," but it suited the young couple.

Fast-forward four years, to the middle of the Great Depression. In the middle of nowhere, with business flat and no prospects in sight, Dorothy tried to nap away a hot July day but was kept awake by the sound of traffic on the nearby highway. It was then that she experienced her eureka moment: If you promise free ice water, the people will come. And come they did, even before Ted had finished planting the first signs along Highway 16A. The following year the Husteads had to hire extra help to manage the crowds. Ted made the next logical leap: The more signs you put up, the more people will come.

So Ted made *lots* of signs. During WWII, a friend put up signs in Europe advertising the distance to Wall Drug. Soon GIs were writing, asking for more signs, slapping them all over the continent and beyond. Advertising in the London Underground and other seemingly illogical places followed, but who can argue

The kitschy Wall Drug Store is packed to the rafters with interesting artifacts and souvenirs.

with success? Today, Wall Drug has been transformed from the only pharmacy within 6,000 square miles to one of the biggest tourist attractions in South Dakota, pulling in 2 million annual visitors. It sprawls over 76,000 square feet of Western-themed floor space, selling everything from hand-tooled cowboy boots to camping gear, horse liniment, and shelf upon shelf of Wall Drug souvenirs. A cowboy orchestra plays like clockwork every 15 minutes, hundreds of Western paintings and artifacts line the walls, and if you're hungry you can grab a buffalo burger at the 520-seat restaurant and wash it down with a glass of French wine. Ice water is still free, and the vibe is still good old-fashioned Western hospitality, as testified by the locals who sometimes sit around all day enjoying the nickel cups of coffee and homemade doughnuts. If you like, you can get in on the joke that made Wall famous: Anyone who asks for it will get a free Wall Drug sign, as long as they promise to display it and send back a snapshot of it on location. The walls of Wall are lined with these photos. Who knew that it's only 10,728 miles from the Taj Mahal to Wall Drug?

WHERE: 52 miles southeast of Rapid City; 510 Main St. Tel 605-279-2175; walldrug .com. **BEST TIMES:** spring and fall for weather.

Scenic Byways over the Wyoming Horizon

BIGHORN MOUNTAINS & THE MEDICINE WHEEL

Wyoming

The Bighorn Mountains rise unexpectedly out of the plains, a soaring, crag-crowned plateau with high-elevation lakes, deep canyons, and waterfalls, and one of the most mysterious archaeological formations

in North America: the Medicine Wheel, an ancient American Indian sacred and ceremonial

site. Three roads climb and switchback across the Bighorns, each road gorgeous enough to have been designated a national scenic byway. With that triple-whammy stamp of approval, don't expect anything subtle about this unusual mountain range, a massive block of limestone and granite pushed up like an enormous molar from the plains.

The Bighorn Scenic Byway (Highway 14) climbs from rangeland, up through pine forests, quickly reaching subalpine meadows at the range's crest, all dominated by rough peaks and dizzying outcrops reaching over 13,000 feet. Near the highway's summit is Burgess Junction and a Forest Service visitors center, where in summer you'll face two choices.

The first option is to continue on Highway 14, dropping down from the summit through the dramatic red-cliffed Shell Canyon, named for 550-million-year-old shell fossils (some of the earliest crustacean fossils ever found) discovered in this valley.

The second route down from Burgess Junction is the summer-only Highway 14A, the Medicine Wheel Passage Scenic Byway, alleged to be the most expensive stretch of road in the U.S. (it was an engineering feat to wedge the road into such extreme gradients, so drivers must be prudent, and large or heavy vehicles should avoid this road). As the byway crosses the summit plateau, a side trail leads toward the Medicine Wheel. This 80-foot-wide wagon wheel of stone is over 700 years old, with 28 rock spokes radiating out from a central hub and six smaller rock cairns arranged around the rim. Experts disagree on its traditional purpose, but modern-day American Indians still come here for ceremonies.

The Cloud Peak Skyway (Highway 16) charts a more southerly passage through the Bighorns, along an old wagon road that passes vintage cabin resorts and campgrounds, some by Meadowlark Lake, a lovely tree-lined lake ringed by regal

peaks. At the foot of the Bighorns off Highway 14, where the plains roll up to meet the Shell Valley, the century-old Flitner Ranch spreads across 250,000 acres. When this fourth-generation ranch decided to open its 1,200-head cattle operation to guests in the 1990s, the Flitner family built a "hideout" with upscale guest cabins, a commanding central lodge, and gourmet meals. What they didn't change was the authentic nature of the ranch itself. While you may choose to fish, hike, or ride trails through the foothills and prairie badlands, you can also join the ranch hands in honest, unvarnished ranch work such as cattle wrangling and calf branding.

WHERE: Bighorn National Forest is 65 miles east of Cody. *Visitor info:* Tel 307-674-2600; fs.usda.gov/bighorn. **SCENIC BYWAYS INFO:** wyomingtourism.org/thingsto-do/parks-and-nature/scenic-byways. *When:* byways open year-round, except for Hwy. 14A, which is generally open late May–mid-Oct. **HIDEOUT LODGE & GUEST RANCH:** Shell. Tel 800-354-8637 or 307-765-2080; thehideout.com. *Cost:* 4 nights from $1,985 per person, includes meals, lodging, and on-premises activities. *When:* open mid-Mar–early Nov. **BEST TIMES:** June–Sept for weather; June for wildflowers; July and Aug for on-site interpreters at the Medicine Wheel.

Shell Falls carries churning water through the canyons of Bighorn National Forest.

Wild Mustangs in Canyon Country

BIGHORN RIVER CANYON

Wyoming

The Bighorn River flows north through Wyoming ranch country, a blue ribbon coursing between irrigated fields and dusty cattle pastures. Then, as it approaches the Montana border, the Bighorn begins to trench deeply

through an uplift of limestone, cutting one of the grandest canyons in the northern U.S. The river's Yellowtail Dam, 45 miles north in Montana, backs up magnificent Bighorn Lake through over 70 miles of this ruggedly beautiful canyon, with sheer bluffs rising to 2,500 feet above the surface. The area is relatively untrammeled, but its strikingly dramatic landscapes, recreational opportunities, fascinating history, and unusual wildlife—the nation's first wild mustang preserve is adjacent to the canyon—make it a treasure awaiting discovery.

The 68,000-acre Bighorn Canyon National Recreation Area, established in 1966, preserves the canyon and straddles the northern Wyoming and southern Montana borders, with visitors centers in Fort Smith, Montana, and in Lovell, Wyoming. However, in Montana the recreation area is surrounded by the 2-million-acre Crow Indian Reservation, to which non-tribal members have very limited access.

Wyoming's south district has the most dramatic views onto the canyon, particularly at Horseshoe Bend, where a wide expanse of the lake passes into Bighorn Canyon to the north, and at Devil Canyon, where sheer 1,000-foot-high cliffs tower above the lake. The park road also crosses into the 31,000-acre Pryor Mountains Wild Horse Range, where one of America's last herds of wild mustangs runs free. In the mid-1960s, public concern became focused on about 200 wild horses living in the Pryors, a vestige of larger herds that once roamed the remote areas of the West. In 1968, the Secretary of the Interior established the first-of-its-kind preserve along the Montana-Wyoming border.

These herds represent a genetically unique population, closely related to original European breeds brought over by 16th-century Spanish explorers. Identify them by their unusual coloring and markings, particularly dark stripes on the back and zebra-like stripes on the legs. You can usually spot wild mustangs in their stallion-led herds along the park road, but for those with a high-clearance vehicle, the meadows of the Pryor Mountains—a range

There's no shortage of dramatic scenery at Bighorn Canyon.

of low, greatly eroded fault blocks that rise just west of Bighorn Canyon—are a more memorable place to see them.

WHERE: Lovell is 45 miles northeast of Cody. *Visitor info:* Tel 307-548-7552; lovell chamber.com. **BIGHORN RECREATION AREA:** Tel 307-548-5406; nps.gov/bica. **PRYOR MOUNTAINS WILD HORSE RANGE:** Lovell. Tel 406-896-5013; blm.gov/mt/st/en/fo/billings_ field_office/wildhorses.html. **BEST TIME:** May–June for warm but not hot weather, wildflowers, and mustang foals.

The Daddy of All Rodeos

CHEYENNE FRONTIER DAYS

Cheyenne, Wyoming

The Cowboy State's capital city was once nicknamed Hell on Wheels, and during the annual ride-'em-cowboy Frontier Days you'll understand why. The rodeo and its surrounding celebration of all things Western was first held in 1897, a mere 15 years after William F. Cody, aka "Buffalo Bill," created the rodeo tradition with his traveling Wild West Show. Today, it's a no less vital ten-day carnival of rodeos, wild-horse races, marching bands, concerts, inter-tribal Indian dancing, a chuckwagon cook-off, and a parade that's been led by some memorable names over the years—Buffalo Bill himself in 1898, and an enthusiastic Teddy Roosevelt in 1910. The event's rollicking, can't-be-contained atmosphere extends to its famous free pancake breakfasts, at which up to 40,000 guests consume more than 100,000 flapjacks (cooked on military ranges, though not really mixed in a cement truck, as legend has it), 475 gallons of syrup, and 520 gallons of coffee.

In the burgeoning world of rodeo, Frontier Days is known as "The Daddy of 'em All," and for good reason. Frontier Days brings more than 250,000 visitors to Cheyenne every year, many decked out in their finest Western wear, plus more than 1,200 of the toughest cowboys and cowgirls from across the nation.

If you have a hankering for more genteel pursuits, Frontier Days has a more sophisticated side. For more than 35 years, the celebration has included an art show and sale featuring the work of dozens of Western and wildlife artists, carvers, and Navajo weavers. Cheyenne's Victorian opulence is on display today in the stretch of 17th Street known as "Cattle Baron's Row." To experience the magnificent residential architecture at length and in detail (think ornate woodwork, exquisite stained glass, and

It's nonstop entertainment during the rodeo at Frontier Days.

period decor) and to indulge like a gentleman cattle baron from another age, come for tea or stay the night at Nagle Warren Mansion B&B, situated in the meticulously restored home of a former governor and U.S. senator.

WHERE: 100 miles north of Denver, CO; Arena at Frontier Park. Tel 800-227-6336 or 307-778-7200; cfdrodeo.com. *Cost:* rodeos from $18; concert tickets from $26. *When:* 10 days in late July. **NAGLE WARREN MANSION B&B:** Tel 800-811-2610 or 307-637-3333; naglewarrenmansion.com. *Cost:* from $155. **BEST TIME:** Wed for an aerial performance by the Thunderbirds U.S. Air Force drill team.

Paean to a Great Showman, and Old West Gateway to Yellowstone

CODY

Wyoming

W illiam F. "Buffalo Bill" Cody was one of the most famous men of the late 19th century—literally a legend in his time—after parlaying his experience as a Pony Express rider, fur trapper, gold miner, and Army scout into a highly profitable Wild West show. Like some of today's boldfaced names, he was caught up in real estate speculation—including a scheme to create an agricultural and tourism center just west of then brand-new Yellowstone National Park (see p. 676).

Today Cody is one of the premier tourist towns in Wyoming, famed for its Old West atmosphere, its rodeos and shoot-'em-up entertainment, and its high-end Western art scene.

The top attraction in Cody's namesake town is the 300,000-square-foot Buffalo Bill Center of the West, one of the nation's most comprehensive collections of Western Americana, and since 2008 an affiliate of the Smithsonian. A complex of five different museums and a research library, the center includes thousands of artifacts and works of art. One of the museums focuses on Cody and his life, another on the natural history of Yellowstone's ecosystem, and another features a collection of more than 4,000 vintage firearms and weapons. Many favor the Whitney Gallery of Western Art—a collection of paintings and sculpture by artists ranging from Frederic Remington and Charlie Russell to contemporary painters. Also fascinating is the Plains Indian Museum, a showcase of regional Native culture.

Cody also serves as the eastern gateway to Yellowstone National Park, just an hour to the west. Teddy Roosevelt called the road there "the most scenic 50 miles in the U.S." As Highway 14/16/20—also called the Buffalo Bill Cody Scenic Byway—climbs from Cody toward Yellowstone, it follows the North Fork Shoshone River through an astounding landscape of volcanic spires and cliffs, intermixed with ponderosa pine forests and sagebrush, and promises substantial wildlife sightings.

During summer, Cody is alive with travelers passing to and from Yellowstone, and the town erupts with enough festivals and events to make ol' Buffalo Bill blush. Cody Nite Rodeo, held nightly in summer, pits broncos and bulls against cowboys; the rodeo season climaxes the first four days of July, at the world-famous Cody Stampede, one of the West's top rodeos. In mid-June, the Plains Indian Powwow is a celebration of American Indian culture with singing and dancing competitions, plus lots of food and crafts booths.

During the summer months, there's also free nightly entertainment on the steps of the Irma Hotel (once owned by Buffalo Bill himself): a mock shootout between the good and bad guys, all in ten-gallon hats. Built in 1902 and named after Cody's daughter, the Irma has hosted famous personalities including Frederic Remington, Annie Oakley, and Calamity Jane. Today, it still boasts wall-to-wall Western charm—you'll want to swagger in for a steak or a drink at the hotel's elaborate cherrywood bar (a personal gift from Queen Victoria to Buffalo Bill). The antiques-rich rooms here don't offer the latest in ultramodern amenities, but if you upgrade to a suite (perhaps Buffalo Bill's own private suite—just avoid the 1970s motel rooms out back) you will enjoy a night of authentic Western atmosphere.

The Buffalo Bill Center of the West offers a crash course on life in the Old West.

WHERE: 214 miles northwest of Casper. *Visitor info:* Tel 307-587-2777; codychamber .org. **BUFFALO BILL CENTER OF THE WEST:** Tel 307-587-4771; centerofthewest.org. **BUFFALO BILL CODY SCENIC BYWAY:** wyomingtourism .org. **CODY NITE RODEO AND STAMPEDE:** Tel 307-587-5155; codystampederodeo.org. *When:* June–Aug; July 1–4 for Stampede. **PLAINS INDIAN POWWOW:** centerofthewest .org. *When:* mid-June. **IRMA HOTEL:** Tel 800-745-IRMA or 307-587-4221; irmahotel.com. *Cost:* from $132.

Monumental Encounter of the Igneous Kind

DEVILS TOWER

Wyoming

An enormous monolith visible for miles around the relatively flat and featureless landscape of northeastern Wyoming, Devils Tower exerts such a hypnotic pull that tribes of the northern plains consider it sacred and

Steven Spielberg had aliens land atop it in *Close Encounters of the Third Kind*. Tales about its origins—in lore of the Lakota, Kiowa, Cheyenne, and other early inhabitants of the region—differ in details, but the essence of the story is that it arose to protect seven sisters pursued by a bear. The bear's claw marks are the striations in the rock face, and the sisters, thrust into the sky, became the Pleiades (a star cluster also known as the Seven Sisters). Geologists posit quite a different account: It is an igneous intrusion, the hardened remnant of magma that erupted into softer sedimentary soils, which have long since eroded away.

The rock is the center of the 1,347-acre Devils Tower National Monument, the first national monument in the country. It has

Climbers test their skills on Devils Tower's vertical rock walls.

become a magnet for climbers, who have mapped out more than 200 routes to the scrubby acre-and-a-half at the summit, 867 feet above the base. (A voluntary climbing ban is observed in June out of respect for Native American ceremonies.) The park includes 7 miles of trails, including a paved 1.3-mile trail through the ponderosa pine forest around the tower itself. It is a prime spot for watching birds and other wildlife, including deer and prairie dogs—and yes, some insist you might catch a glimpse of a UFO, too.

WHERE: 62 miles northeast of Gillette. Tel 307-467-5283; nps.gov/deto. *When:* year-round; visitors center open daily. **BEST TIME:** May–June for weather and wildflowers.

Horse Heaven

BITTERROOT RANCH

Dubois, Wyoming

Fifty wild, mountainous miles from Yellowstone, Bitterroot Ranch sits in a remote valley flanked by the Shoshone National Forest on one side and a 52,000-acre game and fish wildlife refuge on the other. Among the 50 states in the U.S., Wyoming ranks 50th in population, with only five people per square mile. You'll have no reason to question those glorious statistics here.

Mel and Bayard Fox own and operate this 1,300-acre rider's paradise with a dozen hand-hewn log cabins, some a century old, scattered along the trout stream that runs through it. The magnificent Arabians they breed and train here, plus prize specimens selected from elsewhere, make up a herd over 140 strong kept exclusively for the use of their 30 guests. The high horse-to-rider ratio ensures that mounts can be changed frequently, so they're fresh and ready to go throughout the season.

Visitors can take riding lessons or take part in cattle drives; trails wind through extremely varied terrain ranging from sage-brush plains and rocky gorges to badlands and alpine meadows, and snowcapped mountains are usually in view. Guests are immersed in a wilderness setting within minutes, in the competent hands of guides who know it intimately. Riders are expertly matched with horses and assembled into groups with similar skills; for the experienced there's even a cross-country course with more than 70 jumps.

It's not necessarily all horses, all the time here. Non-equestrians may hike, fish, or just relax, and kids can meet the lambs, foals, and other animals on Bitterroot's family farm. Evenings feature some of the finest and freshest eating in the area. The quaint tourist town of Dubois, 26 miles away, offers shops and galleries, and square dancing in the summer. It's also home to the National Bighorn Sheep Interpretive Center, thanks to the country's largest herd of bighorns, which roam the mountains above the town.

WHERE: 85 miles east of Jackson; 1480 East Fork Rd. Tel 800-545-0019 or 307-455-2354; bitterrootranch.com. *Cost:* from $1,920 (off-peak), from $2,400 (peak) per person per week, double occupancy, all-inclusive. *When:* May–Sept. **NATIONAL BIGHORN SHEEP INTERPRETIVE CENTER:** Tel 307-455-3429; bighorn.org. **BEST TIMES:** June–July for Technicolor carpets of blooming wildflowers; Sept for glorious golden aspen.

Most guests at the Bitterroot Ranch come for horseback riding in incomparable surroundings.

The West's Most Scenic Mountains

GRAND TETON NATIONAL PARK

Wyoming

Craggy, glacier chiseled, and rising up to 7,000-plus feet above the floor of Wyoming's Jackson Hole Valley (itself about 6,400 feet above sea level), the dramatic peaks of Grand Teton National Park win America's topographical beauty pageant as the most photogenic of them all. With no foothills to mar the view, the Tetons completely dominate the skyline with a grandeur that's starkly primeval—and irresistible to Ansel Adams students: These are some of the most photographed vistas in the national park system.

The Tetons are the youngest mountains in the Rockies and constitute a relatively small park area of 310,000 acres—one-sixth the size of neighboring Yellowstone (see p. 676).

The valleys of the Teton range were rich hunting grounds for neighboring Plains Indians. When French Canadian trappers moved to the high valleys in search of beaver pelts in the early 19th century, some lonely Gallic soul gave the three largest Teton peaks their lasting nickname—*les trois tétons* translates, straightforwardly enough, as "the three breasts." Early homesteaders found the winters inhospitable and the growing season short, but it didn't take long for enterprising landowners to realize that marketing the beauty of the area to "dudes" provided the best hope of making a living. Guest ranches have a long tradition here; many, such as the handsome and venerable Lost Creek Ranch, go back to the 1920s. The lodging and dining at Lost Creek are deluxe, a precise mix of rustic and refined. The riding program will turn even a greenhorn into a cowhand and there's no better place to relax than the ranch's new full-service spa.

As a fifth-generation family-owned operation, Triangle X Ranch offers the same Western hospitality and gorgeous setting with a more laid-back atmosphere. Guests get their own log cabin and a choice of outdoor adventures such as great fly-fishing or rafting on the Snake River, which winds through the property.

At the foot of the range, glacial advance gouged a string of deep, cold sapphire blue lakes, of which Jenny Lake is among the most beautiful and most visited. The popular Jenny Lake Lodge, one of the park's nicest and best situated, originated as a dude ranch accommodating the eastern effetes who came west to rough it. The elegant lodge is often booked a year in advance by those who don't care to rough it one bit. Above all else, don't miss dinner in the lodge's timbered dining hall, where the food, amazingly, matches the views.

The largest lake, Jackson Lake, is 15 miles long, with cruises to Elk Island and its western shore, where the mountains thrust up from the valley floor. Guided float trips meander down a calm stretch of the Snake from Deadman's Bar to Moose, while a 45-mile loop drive from Moose via Moran Junction presents much of the same spectacular scenery without leaving terra firma.

WHERE: 12 miles north of Jackson. Tel 307-739-3300; nps.gov/grte. **LOST CREEK RANCH:** Tel 307-733-3435; lostcreek.com. *Cost:* cabins

The Teton Range, a branch of the Rockies, is endlessly photogenic, with rugged peaks reaching as high as 13,000 feet.

from $5,600 (off-peak), from $6,700 (peak) per week, double occupancy, all-inclusive. *When:* June–Sept. **TRIANGLE X RANCH:** Tel 307-733-2183; trianglex.com. *Cost:* cabins from $1,820 per person per week (off-peak), from $2,130 (peak), includes meals and activities. **JENNY LAKE LODGE:** Tel 307-733-4647; gtlc.com. *Cost:* from $700. *When:* early May–early Oct. **BEST TIMES:** July–Aug for warmest weather; Sept for fall foliage and fewer crowds.

Wyoming's Hometown for Cowboy Chic

JACKSON

Wyoming

"There are two places I love: Africa and Wyoming," wrote Ernest Hemingway, and judging from a sustained boom in Wyoming tourism, many people concur with at least half of his sentiment. The town of Jackson, one of the art, recreation, and lifestyle capitals of the New West, is a major draw in Wyoming, having evolved from a former fur-trading cow town into a bustling tourist center that borders on the cosmopolitan: Just take a stroll through the lobby of the Amangani, the exquisite U.S. representative of the luxury hotel chain Aman Resorts (see p. 670). While the scenic 48-mile-long Jackson Hole area ("hole" is what settlers called a high, enclosed mountain valley) continues to fill with trophy homes and gated communities for celebrities, seasonal nouveau riche residents, and the Lear-Jet-erati, Jackson itself retains a spirited Western character and encourages an egalitarian mix of ski bums, the moneyed elite, gung ho hikers and climbers, and even a real Wyoming cowboy or two.

Jackson's ground zero is Town Square, a tree-lined park with four entry arches made from thousands of elk antlers. Surrounding the square are many of Jackson's top bars, restaurants, boutiques, and dozens of art galleries; Jackson is particularly noted for its blue-chip Western art, and its September art festival turns the town on its ear. Drop by timeworn hangouts like Bubba's Bar-B-Que and the Million Dollar Cowboy Bar on the Town Square, where local folks have filled the huge saloon since the day it opened in 1937. The Silver Dollar Bar and Grill in the historic Wort Hotel boasts 2,032 silver dollars embedded in its bar, a lively crowd, and enjoyable bonhomie.

Whatever you may think of Jackson's ongoing popularity, there's no denying that the influx of new money elevated the quality of food and lodging in this mountain town. One of the first to arrive was the Spring Creek Ranch, where elegant town houses and log cabins are scattered about a 1,000-acre wildlife sanctuary, sitting high above the Jackson Hole valley with panoramic views. The ranch's acclaimed restaurant, The Granary, specializes in wild game and regional dishes such as elk medallions.

Down in town, the Rusty Parrot Lodge and Spa is a modern version of a traditional log-and-stone lodge, combining woodsy and inviting informality with Teton-chic comfort. Regional cuisine and fresh seafood at the lodge's Wild Sage Restaurant are top-notch. The lodge's Body Sage Spa, one of the city's first, remains one of its best. For a taste of refined Rocky Mountain cuisine, take a seat at the Snake River Grill, right on Town Square in an intimate dining room with a double-sided fireplace and log walls. The sophisticated menu focuses on dishes

that reflect Wyoming traditions—fresh trout, grass-fed beef, buffalo, and elk—with stylish preparations that deliciously tweak the mountain-man ethos.

Of course, Jackson's true glory is location, location, location. Within range of some of America's most exalted scenery, including Grand Teton National Park's lofty peaks, which rise just to the north (see p. 667); a day trip away from Yellowstone (see p. 676); and minutes away from some of the West's most challenging skiing (see p. 671), Jackson offers stellar opportunities to fill your day. Jackson Hole's twisting Snake River, one of the country's cleanest, is beloved by anglers and rafters. From May to late September, nearly 20 outfitters offer white-water and float trips down Wyoming's largest river. Long-established dude ranches offer Old West–style recreation—an hour north of Jackson, at the Heart Six Guest Ranch, trail rides, float trips, stream fishing, and rodeos are the main attractions in summer. In winter, guests explore a virgin wonderland aboard snowmobiles and enjoy the solitude of the snowbound Rockies before returning to their cozy cabins.

One of the area's unmatched pleasures is a visit to the 25,000-acre National Elk Refuge, the winter home for thousands of migrating elk, the largest herd in North America. You'll first start to hear them bugle in the fall during mating season, and from mid-December through March you can get up-close glimpses

Old wooden sidewalks and Western attractions line Jackson's Town Square.

of them via a horse-drawn sleigh ride offered by the Fish and Wildlife Service.

WHERE: 275 miles northwest of Salt Lake City, UT. *Visitor info:* Tel 307-733-3316; jacksonholechamber.com. **SPRING CREEK RANCH:** Tel 800-443-6139 or 307-733-8833; springcreekranch.com. *Cost:* from $180 (off-peak), from $360 (peak); dinner at The Granary $60. **RUSTY PARROT LODGE AND SPA:** Tel 800-458-2004 or 307-733-2000; rustyparrot.com. *Cost:* from $225 (off-peak), from $465 (peak); dinner at Wild Sage Restaurant $65. **SNAKE**

RIVER GRILL: Tel 307-733-0557; snakeriver grill.com. *Cost:* dinner $65. **HEART SIX GUEST RANCH:** Tel 888-543-2477 or 307-543-2477; heartsix.com. *Cost:* from $110 per person per night (off-peak), from $2,200 per person per week (peak), includes meals and activities. **NATIONAL ELK REFUGE:** Tel 307-733-9212; fws.gov/refuge/national_elk_refuge. *When:* mid-Dec–Mar. **BEST TIMES:** late May for Old West Days weekend; June–Sept for best weather; the 10-day Fall Arts Festival in mid-Sept features hundreds of top Western artists.

East Meets West

AMANGANI

Jackson, Wyoming

Perched high above the lush Snake River valley, eye-to-eye with the awesome peaks of the Grand Teton range (see page 667), the luxurious and beautifully designed resort hotel Amangani is the most exclusive of Jackson's many upscale lodgings. Built of Oklahoma sandstone, Douglas fir, cedar, and redwood, Amangani is cut into the flank of East Gros Ventre Butte at an elevation of 7,000 feet—this is the view of eagles. Entirely distinctive, with 40-foot-high picture windows and a cliffside infinity swimming pool heated year-round, the resort also blends into and reflects the colors and contours of the landscape like a natural extension of the Rockies themselves.

Amangani (which means "peaceful home" in a mixture of Sanskrit and Shoshone) was the first U.S. outpost of the upscale Aman Resorts, a Singapore-based chain of luxury hotels in unique and dramatic locales across 20 countries. Aman's design for its Rocky Mountain property is, like its name, a beguiling mix of Eastern aesthetic and Western cool. It has the stone and wood accents of a traditional mountain lodge, but with a sleek, minimalist touch that reveals a soaring sense of spirit. Each of the 40 suites in the three-story complex shares the astounding views of jagged peaks and meadowlands below—vistas available not just from the balcony or floor-to-ceiling windows, but also from each room's shower and deep soaking tub.

Amangani's health center and spa has a full selection of offerings, including hot stone massages and classes in yoga and tai chi. Many spa treatments can be scheduled alfresco at the cliffside pool and terrace overlooking Jackson Hole. Your eyes can continue to feast—along with your remaining senses—in the Grill, Amangani's elegant dining room, where fresh local ingredients are transformed into a nouveau mountain fare.

WHERE: 5 miles west of Jackson; 1535 N. East Butte Rd. Tel 877-734-7333 or 307-734-7333; aman.com. *Cost:* from $750 (off-peak), from $1,180 (peak); dinner at the Grill $75. **BEST TIMES:** late May for Old West Days weekend; late Sept for film festival (jhfestival.org); July 4th for Jackson's Music in the Hole Concert.

SKIING JACKSON HOLE

Jackson Hole, Wyoming

Many ski resorts crow about their steep slopes and deep powdery snow, but the phrase "steep and deep" must have been coined at Jackson Hole Mountain Resort in the Grand Tetons (see p. 667). The snow here is abundant and fine, and the trails, with a stunning total vertical drop of 4,139 feet down the east face of 10,450-foot Rendezvous Mountain, are long and varied. Ski or ride almost straight downhill for 3,000 feet on the Hobacks run, but don't forget to take in the genuinely breathtaking views from the top first. And blue-run skiers needn't shy away—Jackson Hole also has outstanding intermediate skiing, such as the chivalrously named Apres Vous Mountain run.

Mosey on back to the town of Jackson (see p. 668) or hang around Teton Village at the base of the resort and swing by the forever popular Mangy Moose, a boisterous bar in a big, barnlike structure just south of the tram. Try their signature buffalo meat loaf, and stay late for live music and Western swing dancing. Of the handful of lodgings in Teton Village, the slopeside location of the Teton Mountain Lodge can't be beat. Owned by an ex-ski bum, it blends Western warmth and flat-out luxury, making it a perfect year-round base to explore the area's riches.

Just over the divide from Jackson Hole and enjoying a lower profile and far fewer skiers, Grand Targhee Ski Resort extends across two mountains (one of which is devoted almost entirely to snowcat skiing, where runs are accessed by snowmobiles) on the western slopes of the Tetons above Driggs, Idaho. Receiving full-blast winter storms and averaging a whopping 500 inches (40 feet) of light, dry powder a year, it's frequently cited as having some of the most (and best) snow in the U.S., making it one of skidom's Holy Grails.

JACKSON HOLE MOUNTAIN RESORT: Tel 888-333-7766 or 307-733-2292; jacksonhole.com. *Cost:* lift tickets $109. *When:* Dec–mid-Apr. **MANGY MOOSE:** Teton Village. Tel 307-733-4913; mangymoose.net. *Cost:* dinner $40. **TETON MOUNTAIN LODGE:** Teton Village. Tel 855-318-6669 or 307-201-6066; tetonlodge.com. *Cost:* from $159 (off-peak), from $399 (peak). **GRAND TARGHEE SKI RESORT:** Tel 800-827-4433 or 307-353-2300; grandtarghee.com. *Cost:* lift tickets $75. *When:* Dec–mid-Apr. **BEST TIMES:** Jan–Mar for skiing. The Grand Teton Music Festival brings classical concerts to Teton Village July–Aug (gtmf.org).

Steep trails await expert skiers and snowboarders at Jackson Hole Mountain Resort.

Hot Springs, Pools, and Fishing Holes in Ranch Country

SARATOGA

Wyoming

I n some areas of Wyoming, the Old West isn't really that old—the low-key, courtly ways of the rancher and cowboy still provide the rhythm of daily life. Saratoga is one such place, one of Wyoming's most alluring small towns,

on the edge of the prairies and backed up against the foothills of the Snowy Range Mountains. A town with a deep sense of Western history in a stunning, big-as-all-outdoors setting, Saratoga got its start when hot water—lots of it, bubbling to the surface in natural springs beside the North Platte River—caught the attention of settlers. A town had already taken hold beside these hot springs pools when an early booster decided that the fledgling community needed to think big, and in 1884 the town was renamed Saratoga after the upscale mineral water resort town in New York State (see p. 203). Unsurprisingly, East Coast moneyed gentry seeking to "take the waters" didn't suddenly beat a path to remote southern Wyoming—and instead, Saratoga became the main trade town for cattle ranchers in the upper North Platte valley.

Today, Saratoga's famous hot springs are diverted into the so-called Hobo Pool, a large municipal soaking pool with an average temperature of 117°F that's been free to all 24/7 since the Great Depression. When you weary of the pool's steaming temperatures, slip into the adjacent North Platte, where the hot pool waters mingle with the river's cooler flows.

The North Platte is more than just a lovely spot for a soak: The river drops down through the canyons of the nearby Medicine Bow range (reached by the Snowy Range Scenic Byway, linking Saratoga to Laramie via the 10,847-foot Snowy Range Pass) and slows along the cottonwood-lined banks of Saratoga, where both brown and rainbow trout snap hungrily at

hand-tied flies. Along this fabled blue-ribbon stretch of river, there are more than 2,500 trout per mile, all grown naturally without stocking from hatcheries.

Saratoga's town center retains its frontier trappings. The 1915 Union Pacific Railroad Depot now houses the Saratoga Museum, with exhibits on the town's history, and the 1893 redbrick Wolf Hotel is still in service. Have a seat on the front porch and watch the world go by, or treat yourself to a ranch-hand-size prime rib in the small, casual restaurant.

The more modern Saratoga Resort & Spa just outside town is a solid choice, with a 9-hole golf course, spa, and hot mineral springs, including private tepee-covered soaking pools. Get back in the saddle at the area's finest property, Lodge & Spa at Brush Creek Ranch, an old-time working cattle ranch that offers horseback riding, cattle driving, river floats, archery, and a host of other outdoor activities. A luxury, Orvis-endorsed property, sitting on 30,000 pristine acres, BCR also offers guided fly-fishing on private streams and local blue-ribbon rivers.

WHERE: 80 miles west of Laramie. *Visitor info:* Tel 307-326-8855; saratogachamber.info. **SARATOGA MUSEUM:** Tel 307-326-5511. *When:* late May–Sept. **WOLF HOTEL:** Tel 307-326-5525; wolfhotel.com. *Cost:* from $85; dinner $30. **SARATOGA RESORT & SPA:** Tel 800-594-0178 or 307-326-5261; saratogaresortandspa .com. *Cost:* from $149 (off-peak), from $769 (peak). **LODGE & SPA AT BRUSH CREEK RANCH:** Tel 307-327-5284; brushcreekranch

.com. *Cost:* from $750 (off-peak), from $1,100 (peak) per person per day, includes meals and activities. *When:* mid-May–Oct. **Best time:** 3rd weekend in Aug for the official Wyoming Microbrewery competition and Taste of the West chili cook-off (saratogachamber.info).

A Ranching Capital of the Old West

SHERIDAN

Wyoming

S heridan's the kind of town that could be a cowboy open-air museum if it weren't so full of life—and it always has been. With the towering Bighorn Mountains standing sentinel in the west and prairie rolling to the east,

Sheridan was in the right place when the range opened for cattle grazing in the 1880s, and later, when strip mines unearthed the massive coal deposits of the nearby Powder River Basin. The railroad arrived in 1892, providing a way in for prosperous gentlemen ranchers from Britain and the East—who set a refined standard not often found in the West, then or now—and a way out for grass-fattened beef, and a few decades later, coal.

The city's early affluence and sophistication, combined with rugged ranch charm, still define Sheridan. Take polo, for instance—not exactly a typical Marlboro Man sport, but played just south of town at the Big Horn Equestrian Center, home of the oldest polo club west of the Mississippi (introduced by early English cattle barons).

The Sheridan Inn, reopened as a 22-room inn in 2015 after a total renovation, was originally modeled after a Scottish hunting lodge and considered the finest hotel between Chicago and San Francisco when it opened in 1893. Known as the "House of 69 Gables" for its abundant dormer windows, the Open Range Restaurant operates on the inn's main floor—it's a great place for lunch, a cold beer, and a wander around the very Western lobby to peruse old photos.

Sheridan's Main Street, lined with

beautifully maintained redbrick-and-sandstone storefronts that sprouted up during the late 1800s heyday, is now a curious mix of old-fashioned saloons, upscale art galleries, cowboy-chic home decor boutiques, and Western clothing stores. If you're beginning to like the look of pearl-snap shirts and boot-cut jeans, here's the chance for you (and the horse you rode in on) to cowboy up at King's Saddlery, a town fixture since the 1940s. This local saddle maker has been providing saddles, bridles, saddle blankets, ropes, spurs, and tack to both international equestrians and local cowhands for generations. Walk to the back of the store, past a station where saddle makers sit hand-tooling leather, to King's Western Museum, a fascinating collection of

Farms nestled in the scenic Bighorn foothills exemplify Sheridan's rural charm.

erstwhile saddles and saddle-making equipment, Indian artifacts, and mementos from old Western films.

Dude ranches are another part of Sheridan's heritage: Two of the oldest, most respected and laid-back guest ranches in the U.S. are found in the Bighorn foothills. The oldest is Eatons' Ranch on Wolf Creek; its roots go back to 1879. This 7,000-acre ranch is the genuine article—a time-honored, family-oriented outfit with handsome old ranch buildings, cozy log cabins, and over 220 horses.

The nation's second-oldest guest ranch is south in the community of Saddlestring: the HF Bar, another easygoing dude ranch that's long on Western tradition but short on regimented structure. For a week, you'll call a vintage log cabin home, get your own horse, and have the freedom to explore 7,500 acres of Bighorn valleys and foothills. The meals are delicious, and anglers will appreciate the Orvis fly shop.

WHERE: 130 miles south of Billings, MT. *Visitor info:* Tel 307-673-7121; sheridan wyoming.org. **BIG HORN EQUESTRIAN CENTER:** Tel 307-673-0454; thebhec.org. *When:* polo matches Sun in summer. **SHERIDAN INN:** Tel 307-674-2178; sheridaninn.com. *Cost:* from $139 (off-peak), from $189 (peak). **OPEN RANGE RESTAURANT:** Tel 307-675-1152; open rangerestaurant.com. *Cost:* dinner $40. **KING'S SADDLERY:** Tel 307-672-2755; kingssaddlery .com. *When:* closed Sun. **EATONS' RANCH:** Tel 800-210-1049 or 307-655-9285; eatonsranch .com. *Cost:* from $210 per person (off-peak), from $230 per person (peak), includes meals and ranch activities. *When:* open June–Sept. **HF BAR RANCH:** Tel 307-684-2487; hfbar .com. *Cost:* $300 per person per day, includes meals and activities. *When:* open late May–Sept. **BEST TIMES:** June–Sept for weather; mid-July for Sheridan PRCA Rodeo (sheri danwyorodeo.com); early Sept for Don King Days "Old West" rodeo plus polo tournament.

Ghostly Birthplace of Women's Suffrage

SOUTH PASS CITY

Wyoming

South Pass was the magic portal between the American East and West in the mid-1800s, a natural gap in the Continental Divide through which settlers could guide their covered wagons and dream of a new life on the other side.

Although the Rockies pass was high (7,550 feet), the approaches were gentle and wide, allowing a nearly level route between the Atlantic and Pacific watersheds. Nearly a half-million pioneers rumbled across the West on the 19th century's Oregon, California, and Mormon trails, and all of them traversed the South Pass.

When prospector Henry Reedal discovered gold here in 1867, rip-roaring South Pass City grew up overnight to address the needs of prospectors and the cardsharps, dance-hall girls, and merchants who fed off them. Within

a year, it boasted a bustling downtown, with six general stores, two breweries, five hotels, dozens of saloons, and a population of 4,000, making it then the largest settlement in Wyoming. But the deposits depleted quickly, and the prospectors rushed off toward the next glittering stream. By 1872, the town was all but abandoned.

Today, South Pass City, a state historic site and one of the most intact frontier ghost towns in the American West, has been carefully restored. Many of the town's original buildings are open for viewing, including saloons, cabins, a general store, and a small mine. In summer, the dusty streets and boardwalks bustle with actors and merchants in period costumes; you may even get a chance to hone your gold-panning skills. Just down the road, the old mining town of Atlantic City is a degree or two less of what you'd call a ghost town, with a few more services, such as the atmospheric Atlantic City Mercantile, an excellent place for a steak dinner or a good burger in 19th-century digs.

Perhaps the most remarkable thing about South Pass is its role in women's suffrage. When Wyoming's territorial government first met, South Pass saloon keeper and territorial representative William H. Bright introduced a women's suffrage bill. It passed and was signed into law in 1869, making Wyoming the first state or territory granting women the vote, 51 years before the 19th Amendment to the U.S. Constitution secured this right for women throughout the nation. South Pass City also boasts the first female justice of the peace. In 1870, Esther Hobart Morris was appointed by the Sweetwater County Commissioners as justice of the peace for South Pass City, effectively making her the first woman judge in the world.

WHERE: 177 miles west of Casper. Tel 307-332-3684; southpasscity.com. *When:* site grounds open year-round, weather permitting; exhibit buildings and visitors center open mid-May–Oct. **ATLANTIC CITY MERCANTILE:** Atlantic City. Tel 307-332-5143. *Cost:* dinner $35. **BEST TIME:** last weekend in July for Gold Rush Days, with old-time music, costume contests, and a baseball tournament.

Wyoming's Rocky Mountain High

WIND RIVER COUNTRY

Wyoming

The Wind River Mountains are Wyoming's highest and most rugged range, stretching along the Continental Divide for 100 miles of high-altitude splendor, holding all but one of Wyoming's 15 tallest peaks, including the loftiest, 13,804-foot Gannett Peak. Considered by many to be the top backcountry hiking and climbing destination in Wyoming, the Wind River Mountains offer 700 miles of trails to high-country lakes, alpine meadows, glacier-carved cirques, and towering granite pinnacles. Three different wilderness areas protect the Wind River high country, with turretlike alps visible for over 100 miles from the state's sagebrush rangeland. The range's most popular destination is the Cirque of the Towers, a semicircle of 12,000-foot crags around Lonesome Lake at the headwaters of the North Fork Popo Agie River. It's not a magnificence to be taken for

The rugged Titcomb Basin is one of many exhilarating hiking spots in Wind River high country.

granted; reached by a strenuous 17-mile back-country trail, the Cirque can only be accessed through the 10,800-foot Jackass Pass.

Most travelers settle for more distant views of the Wind River Mountains. The Centennial Scenic Byway, which extends from Dubois to Moran Junction near Grand Teton National Park (see p. 667) and south to Pinedale in the Green River valley, essentially rings the northern Wind River Mountains, offering a "best of" tour of Wyoming's mountain land-scapes. Between the 1820s and '40s, the Green River valley was a center of fur-trapping activity, and mountain men gathered in the Pinedale area for "rendezvous," at which trappers, local Indians, and early trad-ers exchanged furs, bought supplies for the coming season, and socialized. Each July, the Green River Rendezvous re-creates the high spirits of an 1830s encampment with music, lectures, and buffalo burgers, plus a pageant that brings together grizzled enthusiasts who play mountain men, Native Americans, mis-sionaries, and other characters of the early West.

The eastern flanks of the Wind River Mountains drain into the Wind River, which flows southwest through range- and farmland before veering north and cutting a dramatic canyon through the Owl Creek Mountains. The Wind River Canyon, with walls that rise 2,500 feet, capturing 2.9 billion years of geo-logic history, is just wide enough for two-lane Highway 20 on one side and a rail line on the other. Once through its canyon, the river flows directly north to Thermopolis, a ranching town with a difference. At Hot Springs State Park is one of the world's largest hot springs, where 135°F 2,575-gallon-per-minute waters are funneled to three separate indoor and outdoor spa facilities. The pastel-colored deposits left by the mineral-laden water warrant a visit, best seen at a series of natural formations called the Rainbow Terraces. Paved walkways here extend across centuries' worth of sedi-ment, vividly colored by algae, plankton, and trace minerals.

WHERE: Pinedale is 75 miles south of Jackson. Tel 307-739-5500; fs.usda.gov/btnf. **CENTENNIAL SCENIC BYWAY:** wyomingtourism .org. **GREEN RIVER RENDEZVOUS PAGEANT:** Pinedale. Tel 307-367-2242; meetmeonthe green.com. *When:* 2nd weekend in July. *When:* open mid-June–Sept. **HOT SPRINGS STATE PARK:** Thermopolis. Tel 307-864-2176; wyoparks.state.wy.us. *When:* indoor pools, daily; outdoor pools, May–Sept. **BEST TIMES:** June–Sept for weather; July for wildflowers.

Nature's Extravagant Showcase

YELLOWSTONE NATIONAL PARK

Wyoming

Established in 1872, Yellowstone National Park is the world's oldest and perhaps most famous national park, known worldwide for its geysers and geothermal pools. The largest of America's national parks outside Alaska,

Yellowstone crosses volcanic plateaus and heavily forested peaks, containing 2.2 million acres of steaming hot springs, crystalline lakes, and thundering waterfalls. Of course, this natural glory is no secret. With close to 4 million visitors a year—the vast majority visiting between June and September—the park's popularity may mean that summertime visitors can see more RV bumpers than buffalo. This doesn't mean that summer visits to this beloved park aren't worth it; just come expecting plenty of company.

Geothermal curiosities such as Old Faithful and the Norris Geyser Basin are just the beginning of Yellowstone's beguilements. The park offers incredible natural diversity and abundant wildlife, together with postcard-perfect vistas. The Grand Canyon of the Yellowstone River, 24 miles long and up to 1,200 feet deep, begins at the river's thundering 308-foot Lower Falls; bear and bison roam the grassy meadows of the Hayden Valley; elk linger near the hot springs terraces at Mammoth; some 330 bird species flit from spruce to fir; and gray wolves, reintroduced to the park in 1995 after being almost eradicated in the 1930s, hunt in the Lamar Valley.

One highlight of a summer visit may be a stay at the Old Faithful Inn. The huge lodge-pole pine edifice, designed in rugged Craftsman style, is right next to its namesake geyser, which sends a spray of steaming water up to 184 feet into the air every 60 to 110 minutes. The recently renovated 1904-built inn (possibly the world's largest log building) set the fashion for all the great lodges of the national park system back in its day. The rooms are somewhat spartan, but take a seat in the inn's grandly evocative log-and-stone lobby, anchored by a massive four-sided fireplace rising more than 90 feet; it's guaranteed to make your heart soar.

In the off-season, Yellowstone seems less like a park and more like nature itself. This is when you realize that the real tension here is not about traffic or crowded campgrounds, but about what's brewing beneath the earth's crust. The park's countless geysers and the bubbling mud pools, hissing fumaroles, and hot springs act as pressure valves, releasing the heat and steam that build up below the ground. Together they make up the world's largest geothermal system (75 percent of the earth's geysers are found here in Yellowstone), remnants of a tumultuous volcanic past that

Crowds gather to witness Old Faithful erupt thousands of gallons of boiling-hot water.

Rudyard Kipling described as "the uplands of Hell."

Winter is the serene season in Yellowstone. Only one entrance, from Gardiner, Montana, remains open to vehicles as far as Mammoth Hot Springs, while the park's other entrances are open to cross-country skiers and snowshoers, as well as to guided tours on snowmobiles and snowcoaches (vanlike vehicles with ski runners and snowmobilelike treads). Snowcoaches also run deep into the park to Old Faithful Snow Lodge & Cabins. Completed in 1999, this is the newest Yellowstone lodge, and with winter accommodations and dining, it's the perfect base for snowshoeing, ice-skating, snowmobiling or cross-country skiing.

Only 1 percent of visitors to Yellowstone venture beyond 3 miles of the park's paved highways, regardless of the season. Yellowstone is a big place, so that a quiet communion with nature is never more than a short walk away.

Beautiful Yellowstone National Park is home to more than 3,900 bison.

WHERE: There are 5 entrances: 3 in Montana and 2 in Wyoming. Tel 307-344-7381; nps.gov/yell. *When:* most park roads open Apr–early Nov; north entrance (Gardiner, MT) is open year-round. **OLD FAITHFUL INN:** Tel 307-344-7311; yellowstonenationalpark lodges.com. *Cost:* from $115 with shared bath, from $175 with private bath. *When:* mid-May–mid-Oct. **OLD FAITHFUL SNOW LODGE & CABINS:** Tel 307-344-7311; yellowstone nationalparklodges.com. *Cost:* cabins from $104. *When:* May–mid-Oct, and mid-Dec–Feb. **BEST TIMES:** May–mid-June and Sept–mid-Oct for nice weather without the crowds. Old Faithful is especially striking in the autumn; cross-country skiing is exceptional in winter.

FOUR CORNERS AND THE SOUTHWEST

ARIZONA • COLORADO •
NEVADA • NEW MEXICO •
TEXAS • UTAH

CANYON DE CHELLY

Arizona

Owned by the Navajo Nation, one of 22 tribes that live in Arizona, Canyon de Chelly (pronounced de-SHAY) exudes a quiet magic and spirituality that inspired mythology scholar Joseph Campbell to call it "the most sacred place on Earth." Navajo families tend farms and orchards on the fertile bottom of this canyon system, and herds of sheep and goats graze in the shadows of stone towers. Around A.D. 1150 the Ancestral Puebloans began building multistoried masonry dwellings in caves and recesses in the sandstone cliffs. Abandoned by 1300 due to drought, they are the oldest known houses in the U.S., and—paired with the canyon's special beauty—the principal attraction of this 130-square-mile monument.

Most of the canyon bottom is off-limits to visitors to protect the privacy of the Navajo who live here. Part of the vast Navajo tribal lands (see p. 689), it is considered one of its holiest sites: Aside from one steep trail to the bottom, you'll have to go on an organized vehicle tour in the company of a Navajo guide to enter the gorge.

The region's name comes from the misspelling and mispronunciation of the Navajo word *tseyi* (pronounced say-ee), meaning "rock cavern," and what a canyon it is: Soaring cliffs glowing pink, yellow, and orange are cut by the cottonwood-lined Rio de Chelly, here and there decorated with ancient pictographs and petroglyphs. Near the park visitor center, one mile east of Chinle, you'll find the Thunderbird Lodge on the site of a trading post built in 1896. You can still buy fine Native American jewelry, crafts, and Navajo rugs, and eat Native American dishes in the popular all-day cafeteria. Sign up for one of their shake-and-bake jeep tours, named for the bumpy road and summer heat.

The paved 18-mile North Rim Drive follows the Canyon del Muerto (Canyon of the Dead), named for a prehistoric burial ground found in 1882. Across from the Antelope House ruins is Navajo Fortress Rock, where Navajo people hid from U.S. troops in 1863 after the government ordered the tribe moved to a barren reservation in eastern New Mexico.

If your time is limited, opt for the 16-mile South Rim Drive, which offers even more remarkable views from places like the Tseyi Overlook and the Junction Overlook. The White House Overlook is the only place you're allowed to visit the canyon bottom without a guide; take the steep but short trail a mile down to White House Ruin, the remains of an 80-room dwelling believed to have been inhabited between A.D. 1070 and 1300 and the largest ruins in the canyon. Spider Rock Overlook is the last stop on the South Rim Drive and one of the most spectacular. Kids thrill to know that Spider Woman, who Navajo

Canyon de Chelly is one of North America's longest continuously inhabited areas.

say taught their ancient tribes to weave, still lives on top of the stark pinnacle that rises 800 feet from the canyon floor.

Where: Chinle is 170 miles northeast of Flagstaff. Tel 928-674-5500; nps.gov/cach. **How:** Canyon de Chelly Unimog Tours offers Navajo-guided half-day tours of the canyon bottom in off-road vehicles. Tel 928-349-1600; canyondechellytours.com. *Cost:* $83. **Thunderbird Lodge:** Tel 800-679-2473 or 928-674-5842; thunderbirdlodge.com. *Cost:* from $70 (off-peak), from $100 (peak). **Best time:** May–Oct for weather and canyon conditions.

Drama, Golf, and Relaxation in the High Desert

Boulders Resort & Spa

Carefree, Arizona

From a distance it's hard to pick out the buildings of Boulders Resort & Spa among the jumble of house-size granite rocks that give the place its name. Quail, javelinas (skunk pigs), and cottontail rabbits wander among 160 adobe-style casitas the same colors and contours as their ancient surroundings in the Sonoran Desert. Fine local art, skylights, and fireplaces decorate the main lodge, and many of the 61 villas (one-, two- and three-bedroom versions are available) are set along the championship world-class golf courses that are arguably the resort's biggest draw: The emerald green fairways of two Jay Morrish–designed courses stand out against the arid terrain.

The Boulders Spa offers a wealth of choices that will leave you absolutely glowing with health, from the recessed circle of the

Covering 1,300 acres of the Sonoran Desert, Boulders Resort & Spa is nestled amid 12-million-year-old rock formations and towering cacti.

entryway inspired by Native American kivas to the outdoor labyrinth, which draws on the tradition of Hopi medicine wheels. The spa offers 33,000 square feet of wellness options including a full workout center, aerobic room, and a swimming pool with lap lanes to pass an idyllic afternoon. Enjoy a Turquoise Wrap, Sage Detox, or other signature experiences.

Private lessons and weekly clinics are available on the eight tennis courts, and El Pedregal, Boulders' popular marketplace, offers interesting art, apparel, and dining. Sign up for rock climbing or a desert hike with a naturalist guide. Mountain biking attracts the intrepid, while early risers enjoy hot-air ballooning to watch the desert come alive. Opt for a jeep tour in the late afternoon to catch the desert's changing colors or the unmatched spectacle of them all: an all-day excursion to the Grand Canyon (see p. 685).

Tool into town, whimsically named Carefree (with street names like Don't Worry Lane), but be back in time for dinner at Palo Verde, one of the hotel's six restaurants and cafés. With dishes like cascabel chili seared prawns with sweet corn and truffle tamale on the menu, it serves contemporary Southwest specialties indoors or on a patio overlooking the sixth fairway and duck pond.

WHERE: 13 miles north of Scottsdale; 34631 N. Tom Darlington Dr. Tel 800-488-9009 or 480-488-9009; theboulders.com.

Cost: casitas from $179 (off-peak), from $345 (peak); dinner at Palo Verde $70. Greens fees from $65 (off-peak), from $285 (peak). **BEST TIMES:** Nov–May, with a moonlight concert series Apr–June. Desert flowers and cacti bloom in early spring.

Land of Wild West Legends

COCHISE COUNTY

Arizona

John Wayne once said about the West: "The very words go straight to that place of the heart where Americans feel the spirit of pride in their Western heritage." Nowhere is that sentiment more alive than in the county named

for the infamous chief of the Chiricahua Apache tribe feared for his raids on white settlements. Comprising 6,219 square miles of southeastern Arizona, as big as Rhode Island and Connecticut combined, Cochise County is filled with ghost towns and lively tourist centers among rocky mountain ranges, all of it little changed from a century ago.

On October 26, 1881, a blaze of 30 gunshots fired in 30 seconds at a livery stable earned the town of Tombstone a firm spot in Wild West infamy. A raucous mining town founded in 1879, Tombstone exploded as a total of $37 million in silver was mined here. After the mines flooded, its population collapsed. Today the "Town Too Tough to Die" rebrands itself as a tourist attraction, drawing on its rowdy heritage.

Visit the O.K. Corral, where the famous gunfight is reenacted daily, and then stop by Big Nose Kate's Saloon, built in 1881, for an icy beer and a sandwich. Don't miss The Bird Cage Theater, now a museum but once a local nightspot where "soiled doves" plied their trade in 14 velvet-draped cribs suspended from the ceiling, and Enrico Caruso and Sarah Bernhardt performed.

Bisbee, in the mouth of Tombstone Canyon 24 miles south, is a historic mining town that in

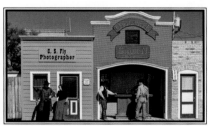

Costumed performers reenact Tombstone's Gunfight at the O.K. Corral, the most legendary shootout in the history of the Wild West.

the early 1900s was the biggest city between St. Louis and San Francisco. More than 3 million ounces of gold, 8 billion ounces of copper, as well as silver, lead, and zinc were extracted from the nearby hillsides (the mines weren't shut down until 1975), and nearly 50 saloons and bordellos along Brewery Gulch kept cowboys and miners entertained. Today Bisbee has been restored into an eclectic art town full of galleries, restaurants, and small hotels. Stay at the Bisbee Grand Hotel and soak up the atmosphere in its historic saloon as you enjoy a Copper City Ale made right here in town.

Cochise Stronghold was the final refuge of the Apache leader who was never defeated in battle but eventually turned himself in to the U.S. Army. Located in the Dragoon Mountains, it is a gorgeous area of granite peaks and forests within the Coronado National Forest, an hour's drive north of Tombstone. The Cochise Stronghold Retreat, with a wide shady porch and stargazing from the hot tub at night, is the place to stay as you explore the remote Chiricahua National Monument and hike through the outlandish rock formations in the Chiricahua Mountains, a place the early settlers called "a wonderland of rocks."

WHERE: Tombstone is 70 miles southeast of Tucson. *Visitor info:* explorecochise.com. **O.K. CORRAL:** Tombstone. Tel 520-457-3456; ok-corral.com. *When:* gunfights staged daily at noon, 2 P.M., and 3:30 P.M. **BIG NOSE KATE'S SALOON:** Tombstone. Tel 520-457-3107; bignosekates.info. *Cost:* dinner $15. **BIRD CAGE THEATER:** Tombstone. Tel 800-457-3423 or 520-457-3421; tombstonebirdcage.com. **BISBEE GRAND HOTEL:** Tel 800-421-1909 or 520-432-5900; bisbeegrandhotel.com. *Cost:* from $99. **COCHISE STRONGHOLD RETREAT:** Pearce. Tel 877-426-4141 or 520-826-4141; cochisestrongholdretreat.com. *Cost:* from $189. **CHIRICAHUA NATIONAL MONUMENT:** Willcox. Tel 520-824-3560; nps.gov/chir. **BEST TIMES:** spring and fall, as summer can get very hot; late May for Wyatt Earp Days; 3rd weekend in Oct for "Helldorado Days" (tombstonehelldoradodays.com).

Gateway to the Grand Canyon

FLAGSTAFF

Arizona

The city closest to the South Rim of the Grand Canyon is a lively, historic place named for a flagpole erected by settlers at the foot of the San Francisco Mountains on July 5, 1876. "Flag" quickly became a railroad town—over 100 trains still roar through the center of the city, where the tracks parallel a section of old Route 66 (see p. 745), every day. Located at an elevation of 7,000 feet, Flagstaff was the world's first "Dark Sky City" for its commitment to low light levels at night.

The Museum of Northern Arizona holds 5 million Native American artifacts, natural science specimens, and fine art pieces. Ancient pottery, modern native silver work and paintings, and changing exhibits make this an ideal place to get an overview of the area's history and cultures. In 1894, astronomer Percival Lowell founded Lowell Observatory above Flagstaff atop Mars Hill, where he made most of the calculations that led to the discovery of Pluto in 1930.

An 1894 home, transformed into a Craftsman bungalow in 1907, is now a luxurious B&B called The Inn at 410. Soak up Southwestern hospitality in any of the ten distinctive rooms and suites, some with fireplaces. Spend an evening at the nearby Museum Club, built in 1931 on old Route 66, with five pine trees supporting the ceiling. The locals call it the Zoo Club, perhaps because of all the taxidermy decorating the walls or perhaps because things get crazy every weekend when there's live country music, with some nights given over to country dancing lessons.

Flagstaff has plenty of outdoor activities to choose from, starting with its 50-mile urban trails system. Hiking and mountain bike trails lace the foothills of the San Francisco Mountains. Even better, no fewer than three national monuments are within half an hour's drive. Ruins dating to the 12th and 13th centuries peek from the walls of a sandstone gorge in Walnut Canyon National Monument, while the remains of three cultures—including a multistory pueblo—fill Wupatki National Monument. Along the same loop road is Sunset Crater Volcano, which erupted in the 11th and 12th centuries; the landscape of red and black volcanic cones stands in stark contrast to the flat surrounding desert.

WHERE: 144 miles north of Phoenix. *Visitor info:* Tel 800-379-0065 or 928-213-2951; flagstaffarizona.org. **MUSEUM OF NORTHERN ARIZONA:** Tel 928-774-5213; musnaz.org. **LOWELL OBSERVATORY:** Tel 928-233-3212; lowell.edu. **THE INN AT 410:** Tel 800-774-2008 or 928-774-0088; inn410.com. *Cost:* from $180. **MUSEUM CLUB:** Tel 928-526-9434; themuseumclub.com. **WALNUT CANYON MONUMENT:** Tel 928-526-3367; nps.gov/waca. **WUPATKI MONUMENT:** Tel 928-679-2365;

The Lowell Observatory's Slipher Building houses a blink comparator, the machine used to identify Pluto.

nps.gov/wupa. **SUNSET CRATER MONUMENT:** Tel 928-526-0502; nps.gov/sucr. **BEST TIMES:** late spring–early fall. The Museum of Northern Arizona hosts four Heritage Festivals: Zuni (Memorial Day weekend); Hopi (July 4th weekend); Navajo (early Aug); and Hispanic Celebraciones de la Gente (late Oct).

Natural Wonder of the World

GRAND CANYON

Arizona

Few things in this world produce such awe as one's first glimpse of the Grand Canyon. "It will seem as novel to you," wrote a mesmerized John Muir, "as unearthly in color and grandeur and quantity of its

architecture as if you found it after death, on some other star." The mile-deep chasm carved by the Colorado River is 277 miles long and up to 18 miles wide in places—creating vast and unobstructed views as you look down upon the ancient multihued gorge. Most of the 5.5 million visitors per year head to the South Rim, about an hour's drive north of Flagstaff (see previous page). Here you'll find the main visitors center, a cluster of shops, and six lodges led by the grand old El Tovar, the park's main man-made wonder. Built by Hopi craftsmen in

1905 of native limestone and Oregon pine logs, it is considered the crown jewel of all the other national park lodges, offering edge-of-the-world views and the best food in the park.

Guided mule rides go down to Plateau Point and back in a day, or you can ride or hike the Bright Angel Trail 9.3 miles to Phantom Ranch (a no-frills lodge with dorm rooms by the river, the only accommodations below the rim). The more scenic South Kaibab Trail gets less foot traffic. Even the easy and mostly paved Rim Trail is hardly taxing but with views that will leave you breathless. The canyon's North Rim, a 210-mile drive from Flagstaff (although only about 10 to 12 miles away from the South Rim as the crow flies), is less visited though no less awe-inspiring. It's also 1,000 feet higher and therefore cooler. The stone-and-log Grand Canyon Lodge here, built in 1937, has a collection of cabins that are usually booked a year in advance. As on the South Rim, many short trails lead to various overlooks, and the North Kaibab trail runs 14 miles down to Phantom Ranch.

Two hundred and fifty driving miles west of the South Rim in the Hualapai Indian Reservation is the exhilarating 70-foot glass-bottomed Grand Canyon Skywalk, which juts out 4,000 feet above the canyon floor.

The best way to get a more intimate view of the canyon is to raft through it on the Colorado River. Options include white-water rafts or dories, and the trip can take 5 to 18 days. Either way it's one to tell the grandkids about, as you explore ruins in side canyons, swim in waterfalls, and brave rapids that can reach Class V.

Where: South Rim is 80 miles north of Flagstaff. North Rim is 210 miles north of Flagstaff. Tel 928-638-7888; nps.gov/grca. **El Tovar:** Tel 888-297-2757 or 303-297-2757;

grandcanyonlodges.com. *Cost:* from $217. **Grand Canyon Lodge:** Tel 877-386-4383; grandcanyonforever.com. *Cost:* from $148 for cabins. *When:* mid-May–mid-Oct. **Mule rides:** South Rim. Tel 888-297-2757 or 303-297-2757. *Cost:* from $133 per person for 3-hour ride. *When:* year-round. North Rim. Tel 435-679-8665. *Cost:* $80 per person for half-day trip. *When:* mid-May—mid-Oct. **Skywalk:** grandcanyonskywalk.com. **River rafting:** Contact O.A.R.S. Tel 800-346-6277 or 209-736-4677; oars.com. *Cost:* from $2,379 per person for 5 days. *When:* Apr–Oct. **Best times:** Mar–early May and Sept–Oct to avoid summer heat and crowds.

The Grand Canyon is over a mile deep in places, revealing nearly 2 billion years of our planet's history.

A Cultural Island Out of Time

Hopi Tribe

Arizona

Encircled by the much larger Navajo Nation (see p. 689), the Hopi Tribe is a sovereign nation in northeast Arizona (sometimes referred to as Hopiland) consisting of 12 ancient villages and a handful of more recent

settlements spread across three high, narrow mesas. Tribe members have lived in a few of these villages for well over 800 years, making them some of the oldest continually inhabited settlements in North America.

Adobe buildings on the edge of 600-foot-high flat-topped mesas give the reservation a strong sense of history, and the tribe—with 7,812 members living here (with an additional 7,000 living off the reservation)—is one of the most traditional in the country. Visitors are welcome to Hopitutskwa, the Hopi ancestral lands, but they're expected to behave with respect, and photography or recording of any kind are strictly prohibited at all times.

The main mesas are named First, Second, and Third Mesa from east to west, the direction from which Spanish explorers first approached them. On First Mesa is the town of Sichomovi, founded in 1750 by residents of nearby Walpi, a cliff village known for fine pottery and katsina dolls. The views from here are endless. Second Mesa is the center of tourism and is the location of Hopi Cultural Center, a small complex with a crafts museum, a modest motel, and a restaurant that serves traditional dishes such as *noqkwivi*, a stew of hominy and mutton. Next door is the Hopi Arts and Crafts Silvercraft Cooperative Guild, where artisans have been training to make silver jewelry and katsina figures since 1949.

Third Mesa is home to the modern Hopi government seat in Kykotsmovi. Up on top is Old Oraibi, established in A.D. 1100 and arguably the oldest continuously inhabited community in the U.S. Visiting this windswept collection of stone and cinder-block buildings is like stepping back centuries, despite the occasional satellite dish. With permission you are free to wander about the streets. Weaving plaques and baskets of multicolored wicker are the local specialties.

The Hopi ceremonies are highly complex, and only some are open to the public, while others require a personal invitation from a tribe member. One of the best ways to experience Hopiland is on a private tour with a tribe member who will lift the veil on a number of the Hopi's religious beliefs, which have stayed remarkably pure over the millennia.

WHERE: Kykotsmovi is 95 miles northeast of Flagstaff. **THE HOPI TRIBE:** hopi-nsn.gov. **HOPI CULTURAL CENTER:** Second Mesa. Tel 928-734-2401; hopiculturalcenter.com. *Cost:* rooms from $115; lunch $15. **HOW:** tours led by Hopi guide Gary Tso, tel 928-206-7928. *Cost:* full-day tours, including lunch, transportation, and entry fees, $300 for 2 people. **BEST TIMES:** spring and fall, and during ceremonies open to the public (contact Hopi Cultural Center).

Man-Made Sea of the Southwest

LAKE POWELL

Arizona and Utah

Imagine the Grand Canyon and then fill it with water. That is Lake Powell— the second largest man-made lake in the country, whose turquoise waters shimmer like a mirage in the red rock country of northern Arizona and

southern Utah. Page, its gateway town, started as a housing camp in 1957 for workers building the 710-foot-high Glen Canyon Dam, which plugged a narrow span of the Colorado River to form the lake. You can join free tours from Carl Hayden Visitor Center that take you down inside the dam to see the gigantic turbines that generate power for states across the West.

Measuring 186 miles long and creating some 2,000 miles of shoreline, Lake Powell is one of the country's finest houseboat destinations. The dramatic red cliff walls let onto 96 canyons of all sizes, as well as countless inlets and sandy beaches, many of which are accessible only by boat. Houseboats are available for rent at Wahweap Marina, and are the most enjoyable way to experience the far and hidden corners of the lake. For the ultimate land-based stay, it's an easy 15-minute drive to Amangiri, the exquisite 34-suite, 600-acre property owned by the famously high-service Asia-based Amanresorts. Amangiri's kitchen serves up delicious, locally sourced American Southwest cuisine.

On the southern edge of the lake is Rainbow Bridge, called *nonnozhoshi*, or "the rainbow turned to stone," a site of deep spiritual significance to the Navajo. At 290 feet high and 275 feet across, it is nearly as tall as the Statue of Liberty. If the water's level is low,

Lake Powell is named after John Wesley Powell, an American Civil War veteran who explored the Colorado River in 1869.

boaters can pull up within a short hike of the span, which stands in its own tiny national monument.

Page also sits on the edge of the Navajo Nation (see next page). A short drive from town is Antelope Canyon, 120 feet deep and only yards wide in spots. The most visited canyon in the Southwest, its rust-colored curves, softly lit by narrow shafts of light, are a photographer's dream, particularly around high noon. The hike there is short and easy but is allowed only with a licensed Navajo guide.

WHERE: Page is 130 miles north of Flagstaff. *Visitor info:* Tel 928-645-9496; visitpagelakepowell.com. **HOUSEBOATS:** for houseboat rentals at Wahweap Marina and other lake info, contact Lake Powell Resorts & Marinas, tel 888-896-3829 or 928-645-2433 (Wahweap Marina); lakepowell.com. *Cost:* houseboat (sleeps 8) from $3,717 for 5 nights in summer. **AMANGIRI:** Tel 877-695-3999 or 435-675-3999; aman.com. *Cost:* $1,500. **ANTELOPE CANYON NAVAJO TOURS:** Tel 928-698-3384; navajotours.com. *Cost:* $40. **BEST TIMES:** June–Oct for water sports; Apr, June, and Oct–Nov for fishing. Hottest and busiest months are July and Aug.

The American West Written in Stone

MONUMENT VALLEY

Arizona and Utah

J ust over 13 miles north of the Arizona border, Highway 163 runs straight as an arrow south toward the silent stone monoliths of Monument Valley. The flat-bottomed valley itself is a park administered by the Navajo Nation,

where tribe members still live and farm among the skyscraper-size sandstone buttes and towers that soar from the plain of sagebrush scrublands.

To the Navajo all of *Tse'bii' nidzisgai* ("The Valley Within the Rocks") is sacred. It's special to Hollywood, too, since countless classic

Westerns have been filmed here. Get an introduction to the area's celluloid history at Goulding's Lodge and Trading Post, established in 1924 by trader Harry Goulding and his wife "Mike," and the only lodge actually located in Monument Valley. It was Goulding who convinced director John Ford that the local scenery would make the ideal mythic backdrop for his movies about the West. Ford and John Wayne filmed movie after movie here, from *Stagecoach* (1939) to *Fort Apache* (1948) and more. Goulding's original trading post has been turned into a museum chock-full of movie memorabilia and historic artifacts. Next door is a spotless 62-room hotel with private balconies that promise spectacular views. Today's restaurant once served as the movie set for Ford's 1949 classic *She Wore a Yellow Ribbon.* A more recent arrival is the Navajo-owned and -run View Hotel, aptly named for the inspiring vistas from its 95 rooms.

A highly scenic (and very rough) 17-mile dirt loop road runs from the visitors center past starkly eroded buttes and sculpted spires with telling names such as the Totem Pole, the Mittens, and Elephant Butte. Some of the most awe-inspiring monuments to nature, they capture the light at various times of the day, and have transfixed artists and visitors alike for centuries. Allow at least an hour for the drive—also great on mountain bikes—to drink it all in. This is sacred land, and the only way you can wander off the road to explore (on foot, in a jeep, or on horseback) is in the company of a Navajo guide. Arrange to be in the valley at sunset, and you'll

The deep red formations of Monument Valley create one of the most famous vistas in the Southwest.

feel as if you just stepped into a classic '40s Western as the closing credits roll.

WHERE: on Utah-Arizona border 170 miles northeast of Flagstaff. *Visitor info:* Tel 928-871-6647; navajonationparks.org. **HOW:** Sacred Monument Tours, tel 435-727-3218; monumentvalley.net. *Cost:* horse, jeep, and hiking tours from $75. **GOULDING'S LODGE:** Tel 435-727-3231; gouldings.com. *Cost:* from $75 (off-peak), from $225 (peak). **THE VIEW HOTEL:** Tel 435-727-5555; monumentvalley view.com. *Cost:* from $100. **BEST TIMES:** late afternoon, sunset, or during a full moon; spring and fall when weather is cool (due to high altitude) and crowds are smaller.

Native Heart of the Southwest

NAVAJO NATION

Arizona, New Mexico, and Utah

The largest Native American reservation in the country covers over 27,000 square miles—roughly the size of West Virginia—in northeastern Arizona and smaller adjoining parts of Utah and New Mexico. A world

unto itself, the Navajo Nation is large enough to contain the smaller Hopi Tribe (see p. 686) and world-famous sights such as Monument Valley (see previous page) and Canyon de Chelly National Monument (see p. 681), with vast land to spare. It is home to some 300,000 plus tribal members (the largest tribe in the

country) who are spread thinly across the mountains, high desert, and rivers of *Diné Bikéyah*, as the Navajo call their homeland. Some still live in the traditional ways, farming or herding sheep, horses, and cattle, and conducting ceremonies in eight-sided buildings called hogans.

Gallup, New Mexico (see p. 739), is the commercial center for the Navajo people, but Window Rock, Arizona, is Navajo Nation's governmental and administrative hub. Here you'll find the tribe's council chamber and police headquarters, as well as a small zoo and the Navajo Nation Museum, Library, and Visitor Center, with displays on tribal history. In September Window Rock hosts the Navajo Nation Fair and Rodeo, the largest gathering of its kind in the Navajo Nation, with livestock shows, powwows, nightly performances, and the crowning of Miss Navajo Nation. On the way in or out of town, stop by the Hubbell Trading Post, known for its Navajo, Hopi, and Zuni crafts, artisans, and quite a variety of Navajo rugs (with weavers on site). The trading post today is more a living museum than a store, continuing its traditional role as a place for meeting people and exchanging news.

Tuba City, Arizona, is one of the most diverse communities on the reservation, with many Anglo and Hopi residents as well as Navajo tribal members. It sits in one of the most eye-catching stretches of the Painted Desert, and is home to the historic Tuba Trading Post, a two-story showroom established in 1905 that's one of the best places to shop for jewelry and other crafts. Come if you can in October for the Western Navajo Fair, with music, dancers, a parade, and car shows.

Between Tuba City and Monument Valley on Highway 160 is the turnoff for little-visited Navajo National Monument, which protects three of the most impressive "Anasazi" ruins

in the Southwest. The stunning 160-room Keet Seel cliff dwellings are a difficult 17-mile round-trip hike from the visitors center, but the trip is well worth it; it's like having part of Mesa Verde (see p. 716) to yourself.

WHERE: Window Rock is 27 miles northwest of Gallup, NM. *Visitor info:* Tel 928-810-8501; discovernavajo.com. **NAVAJO NATION MUSEUM:** Window Rock. Tel 928-871-7941; navajonationmuseum.org. *When:* closed Sun. **NAVAJO NATION FAIR AND RODEO:** Window Rock. Tel 928-871-6478; navajonationfair.com. *When:* 1 week in early Sept. **HUBBELL TRADING POST:** Ganado. Tel 928-755-3475; nps.gov/hutr. **TUBA TRADING POST:** Tuba City. Tel 928-283-5441. **WESTERN NAVAJO NATION FAIR:** Tuba City. Tel 928-283-3284. *When:* 4 days in Oct. **NAVAJO NATIONAL MONUMENT:** Tel 928-672-2700; nps.gov/nava. **WHERE TO STAY:** Experience Hopi, tel 928-283-4500; experiencehopi.com. *Cost:* from $140. **BEST TIMES:** during festivals; spring and fall for weather.

Those who live on the Navajo territory have created a unique blend of both traditional and modern ways of life.

Superlative Collection of Native Arts and Culture

HEARD MUSEUM

Phoenix, Arizona

A Spanish Colonial–style mansion built by Phoenix settlers Dwight and Maie Heard in 1929 now houses perhaps the premier collection of Native American art and culture in the country. Step through the distinctive arches and colonnades to enter 130,000 square feet of exhibit space, enough to house a Navajo hogan (an eight-sided ceremonial structure), along with a staggering collection of pottery, paintings, textiles, and an enormous number of Hopi katsina figurines that represent the variety of spirits of the Hopi and Zuni religions.

In all, there are over 40,000 artifacts, ranging from historic works to pieces made by living artists, including members of Arizona's 21 federally recognized tribes. The museum grounds are delightfully landscaped with sculptures, and an outstanding museum shop sells high-quality crafts bought directly from Native artisans.

As part of its mission to support Native artists and educate the public about their cultures, the Heard hosts many annual events, starting with the World Championship Hoop Dance Contest in February, when Native dancers from the U.S. and Canada compete for

The Heard Museum's courtyard promises a serene respite, with fountains, sculptures, and beautiful landscaping.

the title. The Heard Museum Guild Indian Fair and Market, in March, has been drawing enthusiastic crowds since 1958.

HEARD MUSEUM: 2301 N. Central Ave. Tel 602-252-8840; heard.org. **BEST TIMES:** Mar for Indian Fair & Market; Apr for Katsina Doll Marketplace; Nov for Mercado de las Artes; Dec for Holidays at Heard.

A Desert Oasis Where Golf Is King

VALLEY OF THE SUN

Phoenix and Scottsdale, Arizona

With over 200 golf courses and more than 300 days of sun on average annually, the greater Phoenix metropolitan area—known more poetically as the Valley of the Sun—has become one of America's most popular winter destinations. With its unmatched combination of exceptional golf, stunning desert scenery, and luxurious accommodations, the Valley is without equal in the country. Lovingly manicured fairways (surrounded by cacti and desert scrub), lake-size swimming pools, and towering palm trees are ringed by jagged mountains and random rock formations seemingly from the dawn of time.

Many resorts and courses are concentrated in and around Scottsdale, the more thoroughly upscale community 31 miles long and 11 miles wide, to the east of Phoenix. Outstanding golf facilities cement Scottsdale's reputation as golfing mecca of the U.S. Troon North is home to the two top-ranked daily fee courses in the state: the Monument course, designed by Tom Weiskopf and Jay Morrish, and Weiskopf's Pinnacle course. Perhaps the state's best examples of desert courses, they are considered highly challenging for golfers of all levels. The Grayhawk Golf Club has the Tom Fazio–designed Raptor course and the Talon course, designed by David Graham and

Gary Panks and famous for its "risk-reward" 13th hole, nicknamed "Heaven or Hell." Both have hosted PGA Tour tournaments.

In addition to the courses at the Boulders (see p. 682) and the Phoenician (see p. 694), a host of first-class resorts and hotels in the Valley cater to golfers and nongolfers alike. The JW Marriott Scottsdale Camelback Inn Resort & Spa, opened in 1936 at the base of Mummy Mountain, has two championship 18-hole courses and 453 guest rooms and suites, some with sundecks and private pools, and a highly regarded spa with lots of fitness classes included in your stay.

The Valley of the Sun has long been considered the golf capital of the Southwest.

Set in the foothills of Pinnacle Peak, the Southwest-styled Four Seasons Resort Scottsdale at Troon North offers guests priority use of the adjacent Troon North courses and boasts lavish adobe casitas, each with its own terrace and some with private plunge pools. Stick around for weekend brunch at Proof, an American canteen.

Still graced by royal palms and tiled fountains, The Fairmont Scottsdale Princess has transformed its palacio look into a sleek, chic environment. One of its two courses, the TPC Scottsdale, is home to the Waste Management Phoenix Open, the best-attended golf tournament in the world with 600,000 attendees. The resort's top-notch Well & Being Spa and a water playground for the kids will keep the whole family happily engaged. La Hacienda is the area's top-rated Mexican restaurant, while Michael Mina's Bourbon Steak features only the finest cuts.

At Phoenix's Royal Palms Resort and Spa, a historic estate at the foot of Camelback Mountain, guests can choose from 117 rooms or casitas gathered in small clusters, and dine at T. Cook's. The Wigwam is the only resort in the area with three championship golf courses, including the classic Gold and Patriot courses, both designed by Robert Trent Jones Sr. Two- and three-day golf schools let you hone your game.

The state's largest infinity pool and the unparalleled Asian-inspired Sanctuary spa are part of the Sanctuary on Camelback Mountain, set on lushly terraced acres with breathtaking vistas across Paradise Valley. Secluded casitas (some with outdoor soaking tubs) are the most sumptuous of its 98 accommodations. Camelback is the highest mountain in Phoenix; take the Summit Trail for the finest views around.

TROON NORTH GOLF CLUB: Scottsdale. Tel 480-585-7700; troonnorthgolf.com. *Cost:* greens fees from $109 (off-peak), from $175 (peak). **GRAYHAWK GOLF CLUB:** Scottsdale. Tel 480-502-1800; grayhawkgolf.com. *Cost:* greens fees from $80 (off-peak), from $225 (peak). **CAMELBACK INN:** Scottsdale. Tel 800-24-CAMEL or 480-948-1700; camelbackinn .com. *Cost:* from $199 (off-peak), from $399 (peak); greens fees from $59 (off-peak), from $189 (peak). **FOUR SEASONS RESORT:** Scottsdale. Tel 480-515-5700; fourseasons .com/scottsdale. *Cost:* from $195 (off-peak), from $529 (peak). **FAIRMONT SCOTTSDALE PRINCESS:** Scottsdale. Tel 800-344-4758 or 480-585-4848; fairmont.com/scottsdale. *Cost:* from $199 (off-peak), from $599 (peak); dinner at La Hacienda $45; dinner at Michael Mina's Bourbon Steak $80. **ROYAL PALMS:** Phoenix. Tel 800-672-6011 or 602-840-3610; royal palmsresortandspa.com. *Cost:* from $180 (off-peak), from $540 (peak); dinner at T. Cook's $70. **Wigwam Golf Resort & Spa:** Litchfield Park. Tel 623-935-3811; wigwamresort.com. *Cost:* from $199 (off-peak), from $365 (peak); greens fees from $64 (off-peak), from $135 (peak). **Sanctuary on Camelback Mountain:**

Paradise Valley. Tel 855-245-2051 or 480-948-2100; sanctuaryoncamelback.com. *Cost:* from $289 (off-peak), from $599 (peak). **Best times:** fall–spring (June–Aug can hit triple-digit temperatures, but prices are lower); 1st week in Feb for the Waste Management Open (wmphoenixopen.com).

The Best of Small-Town Arizona and a Wild Rodeo to Boot

Prescott

Arizona

This small town belies the Arizona stereotype of scorpions crawling in the sandy shadows of tall cacti. With a tree-shaded central plaza and nearby streets lined with Victorian architecture, Prescott (rhymes with biscuit) has a rich 150-year history and a good sense of fun, with beautiful forests, Granite Dells, mile-high mountains, and a small-town ambience.

Over 20 saloons and houses of pleasure once flourished along "Whiskey Row" on Montezuma Street, catering to miners who flocked to the mountains in search of gold. Check out The Palace at #120: It's the oldest saloon in Arizona, and its honky-tonk music on weekends will set your feet tapping. The Sharlot Hall Museum showcases Prescott's history with ten exhibit buildings, including the historic Governors Mansion and the oldest log cabin in the state. The Phippen Museum, founded by and named for the artist who helped form the prestigious Cowboy Artists of America organization, displays a first-rate selection of Western art in changing shows.

In late June or early July, Prescott Frontier Days features The World's Oldest Rodeo (since 1888), rounded out by a dance and parade. During the rodeo, pray for a cancellation at the Hassayampa Inn. Opened as a luxury hotel in 1927 when Prescott was the bustling territorial capital, it's been lovingly restored with 67 guest rooms and the elegant

Every summer, locals dress in period clothing to celebrate Prescott Frontier Days.

Peacock Room for very good dining. And there's usually someone tickling the ivories in the hotel's welcoming art nouveau piano bar on weekends, just like the old days.

Where: 100 miles north of Phoenix. *Visitor info:* Tel 800-266-7534 or 928-445-2000; visit-prescott.com. **Sharlot Hall Museum:** Tel 928-445-3122; sharlot.org. **Phippen Museum:** Tel 928-778-1385; phippenartmuseum.org. *When:* closed Mon. **Frontier Days Rodeo:** Tel 928-445-3103 (office)

or 928-445-4320 (tickets); worldsoldestrodeo .com. *When:* 7 days in late June–early July. **HASSAYAMPA INN:** Tel 800-322-1927 or 928-778-9434; hassayampainn.com. *Cost:* from $89 (off-peak), from $119 (peak); dinner $45. **BEST TIMES:** late May for the Phippen Museum Art

Show and Sale; June for Sharlot Hall Museum Folk Arts Fair and for Bluegrass Festival (prescottbluegrassfestival.org); late June/early July for Frontier Days; July for Prescott Indian Art Market; Aug for the Arizona Cowboy Poets Gathering (azcowboypoets.org).

A Desert Palace with Royal Golf

THE PHOENICIAN

Scottsdale, Arizona

With a spectacular setting hugging the south side of Camelback Mountain, a level of service unparalleled in the Valley of the Sun (see page 691), and perfectly manicured gardens that Alice in Wonderland would love, The Phoenician is considered the "granddaddy" of luxury resorts in and around Phoenix. Marble, crystal, and formal furniture abound, giving this palatial resort the feel of a private club. It doesn't hurt that the resort also has its own multimillion museum-quality art collection, well worth a self-guided audio tour. Oversize guest rooms and suites in the main buildings (there are also more than 100 casitas) are decorated with leather headboards and other fine furnishings, while the spacious bathrooms gleam with Italian marble. The exclusive Canyon Suites is a 60-room boutique "resort within a resort" whose amenities include daily complimentary wine tasting. Guests can soothe mind and body at the resort's Centre for Well-Being, a two-level spa and adjacent salon whose extensive menu encourages you to come and hand yourself over. Full weight-training and aerobic facilities offer classes in everything from yoga to Zumba, and 24 treatment rooms await therapy sessions using plants and minerals from the surrounding desert. After a private wellness consultation, enjoy a few laps in the resort's signature pool lined with mother-of-pearl tiles, or relax with a guided meditation session in the skylit atrium. A guided hike on Camelback Mountain takes you into the natural world with panoramic views of the valley.

Golf leads the activities of choice at the Phoenician, and with three sets of nine holes spread out over 110 lush acres, most guests are happy never to leave the premises. Swimming pools—eight, to be precise—include an exclusive pool at The Canyon Suites. A 165-foot waterslide and a SURGE splash pad for kids are at the center of endless days of entertainment at the "Funicians" Kids Club (mornings start with koi feeding at Necklace Lake). Of

The Phoenician's inviting pool evokes a desert oasis.

the 11 tennis courts, 10 are lit for nighttime action, and a 2-acre cactus garden is planted with 250 exotic species from around the world.

Diners need look no farther than the posh J&G Steakhouse created by Jean-Georges Vongerichten and featuring prime meats and global seafood, matched with wines from a celebrated list overseen by a master somme-lier. The nightly live jazz goes well with magi-cal views of the city at sunset. Il Terraza is known for its Sunday brunch, and Relish Burger Bistro, overlooking the golf courses,

boasts their signature Kobe-style burgers with prickly pear relish. For a unique experience, sign up for a Tee Box dinner, where you're shuttled by golf cart to an elegant meal on the course beneath a canopy of stars.

WHERE: 9 miles north of the Phoenix air-port; 6000 E. Camelback Rd. Tel 480-941-8200; thephoenician.com. *Cost:* from $169 (off-peak), from $499 (peak); dinner at J&G Steakhouse $70. **BEST TIMES:** early spring for blooming desert flowers and cacti; Nov–May to avoid desert heat.

Frank Lloyd Wright Goes West

TALIESIN WEST AND ARIZONA BILTMORE

Scottsdale, Arizona

America's most famous architect described the idea behind Taliesin West, the winter campus of the school of architecture that bears his name, as "a look over the rim of the world." The 500-acre complex was begun when Frank Lloyd Wright purchased land at the foot of the McDowell Mountains in 1938—five years after he and his wife had founded an architectural apprenticeship program named after their Spring Green, Wisconsin, home, Taliesin (see p. 586). Wright was drawn to the Sonoran Desert, its "clear sun-drenched air" and the "stark geometry of the mountains." Drawing on this natural beauty, he and his stu-dents built theaters, living quarters, an archi-tectural studio, and a drafting room, adding and tweaking buildings for over 20 years. (Wright spent his winters here until his death in 1959.)

The design of Taliesin West earned universal praise for its subtle interplay of light, color, and indoor and outdoor space, and is considered one of Wright's most significant works. Striking ter-races, walkways, and gardens surround build-ings with distinctive low ceilings and stone walls. Today master-level architecture students live here for three to five years, studying and working in an environment that couldn't be more inspiring. Visitors may choose from a variety of tours, from a one-hour overview to a three-hour behind-the-scenes tour.

Wright's influence carries on into down-town Phoenix, where the world-famous Arizona Biltmore, a Waldorf-Astoria Resort, echoes his distinctive touch. Opened just before the stock market crashed in 1929, the Biltmore was designed by Albert Chase McArthur, a Wright draftsman who used blocks cast from desert sand in 34 different geometric patterns. From the palm-lined entrance drive to the tricycle-borne room ser-vice, it's much cheerier than many high-end hotels tend to be, though no less luxurious. Guests are welcomed next door at the two 18-hole golf courses, the Adobe and the Links, and the resort spa, with everything from organic and vegan treatments to cutting-edge noninvasive skin therapies. Of its eight pools, the Catalina Pool is straight out of classic Hollywood, built when Chicago chewing-gum king William Wrigley owned the place. It was Marilyn Monroe's favorite and the place where Irving Berlin penned "White Christmas." Wright's, the resort's signature restaurant, specializes in fresh, local ingredients elegantly prepared and served with a celebrated wine list. Devoted Wright-heads will also want to visit Paolo Soleri's Arcosanti, a visionary experimental community 70 miles north of Phoenix, in which Wright's former student fused architecture and ecology into the earth-friendly concept of "arcology."

TALIESIN WEST: Cactus Rd. and Frank Lloyd Wright Blvd. Tel 480-627-5340; franklloydwright.org. **BILTMORE:** Phoenix. Tel 602-955-6600; arizonabiltmore.com. *Cost:* from $159 (off-peak), from $399 (peak); dinner at Wright's $75. **ARCOSANTI:** Mayer. Tel 928-632-7135; arcosanti.org. **BEST TIME:** Nov–Apr for weather.

Perhaps the Most Beautiful Place in the Country

SEDONA AND RED ROCK COUNTRY

Arizona

As if sculpted in crimson stone, the City of Sedona and its red rock towers stand tall against pine green hillsides and a cerulean sky. Getting there from Flagstaff is half the fun; State Route 89A through Oak Creek Canyon takes you past monoliths and refreshing swimming holes in the creek itself.

Sedona's specialness goes beyond the surface. The Yavapai Apache tribe consider this area to be sacred, and seven supposed energy vortexes in the vicinity draw spiritualists and would-be shamans for their healing and cleansing properties. Author Zane Grey used it as the attention-stealing backdrop of his 1924 classic *The Call of the Canyon*, and Hollywood made the local scenery famous in dozens of Western films. Outdoor enthusiasts can explore by foot on over 100 day-hiking trails, or mountain bike on hundreds of miles of dirt roads and single-track. Other options include hot-air ballooning and tours in distinctive pink jeeps, while the summer heat (moderated only somewhat by the city's 4,500-foot altitude) drives many toward the slick natural water chute and wading at Slide Rock Canyon State Park, right in town.

Others choose to explore the high-end shops and galleries, over 80 of which are in the Tlaquepaque Arts & Crafts Village, a re-created Mexican village complete with leafy trees, a plaza, and restaurants with outdoor seating. (It's across the street from the Center for the New Age, offering guided vortex tours and psychic readings.) The contemporary Chapel of the Holy Cross, another spiritual must-see, was built into the living rock 200 feet above the valley, with great views from the front, which forms a huge cross.

Sedona is also known for some of Arizona's most luxurious lodgings, starting with the world-famous Enchantment Resort (see next page), but a host of less pricey accommodations make Sedona a place begging you to stay far beyond the typical weekend. The Lodge at Sedona is an intimate, wellness-leaning B&B with 3 acres of gardens and an outdoor meditative labyrinth built of local river stones. Garland's Lodge is a comfy 1930s hotel known for its food. Lush gardens and orchards surround the 17 phone- and TV-free cabins, some with fireplaces. At the Amara Creekside Resort, guests can avail themselves of spa treatments or just enjoy the red rock views from poolside. The Casa Sedona is yet another charming selection, an award-winning B&B with rose-tinted walls and 15 rooms decorated with the work of local artists.

WHERE: 120 miles north of Phoenix. *Visitor info:* Tel 800-288-7336 or 928-282-7722; visitsedona.com. **PINK JEEP TOURS:** Tel 800-873-3662 or 928-282-5000; pinkjeep tourssedona.com. **SLIDE ROCK CANYON STATE PARK:** Tel 928-282-3034; azstateparks.com/parks/slro. **CENTER FOR THE NEW AGE:** Tel 888-881-6651 or 928-282-2085; sedonanew agestore.com. **CHAPEL OF THE HOLY CROSS:** Tel 928-282-4069; chapeloftheholycross.com. **THE LODGE AT SEDONA:** Tel 800-619-4467 or 928-204-1942; lodgeatsedona.com. *Cost:* from $219. **GARLAND'S LODGE:** Tel 928-890-4023; garlandslodge.com. *Cost:* from $225. *When:* closed late Nov–mid-Mar. **AMARA CREEKSIDE**

Built into a thousand-foot solid red rock wall, the physical construction of the Chapel of the Holy Cross was an engineering feat.

RESORT: Tel 855-324-1313 or 928-282-4828; amararesort.com. *Cost:* from $199 (off-peak), from $319 (peak). **CASA SEDONA:** Tel 800-525-3756 or 928-282-2938; casasedona.com. *Cost:* from $209. **BEST TIMES:** spring and fall for weather; late Feb for Sedona International Film Festival (sedonafilmfestival.com).

Bliss Among the Red Rocks

ENCHANTMENT RESORT

Sedona, Arizona

Only a ten-minute drive from downtown Sedona (see previous page), the Enchantment Resort and Mii amo, a destination spa, sit at the mouth of dazzling Boynton Canyon, surrounded by red stone spires. At 4,500 feet (and thus not subject to the desert's ovenlike summers), the 70-acre resort blends perfectly with the area's fabled high-desert scenery. It is an ancient, peculiarly eroded landscape that varies from pink and orange to sienna and vermilion, depending on the day's mood and the sun's position. Enchantment proposes to be your cocoon in this environment—to lavish upon you exquisite offerings in food, accommodations, and recreation until you choose to return to the real world.

Boynton Canyon is a particularly beautiful example of the many box canyons that slice the rosy scenery near Sedona. Overlooking the resort is a set of stone spires said to be one of Sedona's revitalizing energy vortexes—electromagnetic fields that ancient Native Americans considered sacred. Every one of the resort's sumptuous Southwest-themed rooms and suites has an outdoor deck for basking in the sun and soaking up the dramatic surroundings. Suites boast log-beamed ceilings, beehive fireplaces, soaking tubs, and in some, full kitchens and outdoor gas grills.

Using your kitchen for more than coffee might not make much sense when you can dine at the Che-Ah-Chi Restaurant, with the best views of any restaurant in town: You can watch the sun set or see the moon rise over rust-colored cliffs as you tuck into some of the finest cooking in Sedona. More informal but no less exceptional dining is available at the Tii Gavo restaurant and Mii amo Café. Fresh seasonal and local ingredients are used at all three.

Enchantment guests can choose from many other pastimes, such as wine tastings and star-gazing. Follow any of the trails for mountain bikers and hikers up the canyon or take a guided nature walk with a U.S. Forest Ranger.

The hotel's affiliated Mii amo Spa is a classically Southwestern experience, specializing in treatments inspired by Native American and other healing traditions. It excels in metaphysical treatments, such as psychic massage, aura-soma color readings, and energy work to take you on a journey within. There are also hard-to-find offerings, such as watsu, neuro-muscular therapy, and Thai massage, along with the usual roster of spa treatments. Don't miss a session in the Crystal Grotto, a meditation room with a skylight in its domed ceiling. Mii amo has its own gorgeous rooms with

private patios, a health-conscious restaurant, and indoor and outdoor pools.

WHERE: 120 miles north of Phoenix; 525 Boynton Canyon Rd. Tel 888-250-1699 or 928-282-2900; enchantmentresort.com. *Cost:* from $325 (off-peak), from $425 (peak); dinner at Che-Ah-Chi $70; dinner at Tii Gavo $40. **MII AMO SPA:** Tel 888-749-2137 or 928-203-8500; miiamo.com. *Cost:* spa treatments from $160; all-inclusive 3-night packages from $2,850 per person (off-peak), from $3,330 (peak), single-occupancy, includes 2 spa treatments per day (6 total). **BEST TIMES:** spring and fall for weather.

Enchantment Resort is nestled between the dramatic red walls of Boynton Canyon.

Art and History near the Mexican Border

TUBAC

Arizona

Thirty miles north of the Mexican border, this city of just over 1,000 is one of Arizona's largest arts communities. Originally a Pima Indian village, it became a mission, farm, and ranch in 1691 and later a Spanish presidio

(or garrison) in 1752 after a bloody revolt by the Pima Indians. The first European settlement in the future Arizona went through periods of abandonment and plenty, and was reborn yet again with the arrival of its first art school in 1948.

Today a diverse artistic scene draws visitors from around the Southwest to browse more than 100 shops, studios, and galleries, many of which are owned and operated by the artists themselves. Start at the Tubac Center for the Arts, a Spanish Colonial building hosting art shows and music performances. In February the Tubac Festival of the Arts is a juried show featuring 175 arts and crafts booths with artists from across the country.

The museum and crumbling adobe walls at the Tubac Presidio State Historic Park offer a taste of the city's venerable past as the oldest settlement in Arizona. At the nearby Tumacácori National Historical Park, the gorgeous San Jose de Tumacácori Mission church has been partly restored. A 30-mile drive away is the Buenos Aires National Wildlife Refuge, where 117,500 acres of grassland, marsh, and streams are home to an amazing variety of birdlife.

One of the nicest and most relaxing destinations in the Southwest can be found at the Tubac Golf Resort & Spa set on the historic 500-acre Otero Ranch. The still-intact 18th-century family hacienda and the well-regarded Stables Ranch Grill on the site of the original stables both enjoy beautiful panoramas of the Tumacácori and Santa Rita Mountains. Bing Crosby was involved with the creation of the grassy 27-hole championship golf course, bordered by old-growth cottonwoods and mesquites. Hollywood returned when Kevin Costner chose to film *Tin Cup* here in 1966. The small but highly regarded spa features Southwest-inspired products that show up in treatments such as the Desert Flower Indulgence and the Spanish Sage Sports Massage.

WHERE: 48 miles south of Tucson. *Visitor info:* Tel 520-398-2704; tubacaz.com. **TUBAC CENTER FOR THE ARTS:** Tel 520-398-2371; tubacarts.org. **TUBAC PRESIDIO:** Tel 520-398-2252; azstateparks.com/parks/tupr. **TUMACÁCORI PARK:** Tel 520-377-5060; nps.gov/tuma. **BUENOS AIRES NATIONAL WILDLIFE REFUGE:** Arivaca. Tel 520-823-4251; fus.gov/refuge/buenos_aires. **TUBAC GOLF RESORT & SPA:** Tel 520-398-2211 or 800-848-7893; tubacgolfresort.com. *Cost:* rooms from $129 (off peak), from $189 (peak); green fees from $36; dinner at Stables $45. **BEST TIMES:** early Feb for Tubac Festival of the Arts; Oct–May for weather; 3rd weekend in Oct for Anza Days cultural celebration.

Colorful, handmade ceramics are featured at many of Tubac's art galleries.

Cacti, Roadrunners, and a Desert Dude Ranch

TUCSON AND TANQUE VERDE

Arizona

A deep sense of history pervades Tucson, Arizona's second-largest city (population 526,000), which is almost exactly as old as the U.S. itself. Surrounded by jagged, arid mountains, it's the epicenter of southeastern

Arizona's distinctive cowboy-and-cactus landscape, and there's nowhere better to become a part of it than at the Tanque Verde Ranch.

Sprawling across 60,000 acres in the desert foothills of the Rincon Mountains, this dude ranch was originally a horse-and-cattle spread in 1868. Guests can go hiking or mountain biking, play tennis or relax by the two pools, but most come here for the horseback riding through the rugged desert. This is one of Arizona's largest stables, with a herd of over 150, so it's impossible not to find the match for you. There are also guided nature walks through the desert, evening lectures about geology or flora and fauna, barbecues under the stars with live music, and an adobe spa. Children's programs keep the little buckaroos busy, too. Multiday packages include "Harmony with Horses" and "Women of the West," and luxurious rooms and adobe casitas, many with fireplaces and patios, encourage extended stays.

Make time for a visit to the Arizona-Sonora Desert Museum, an exceptional natural history museum, zoo, and botanical garden all rolled up into one on the western edge of Tucson. About 85 percent of it is outdoors, including enclosures populated by some of the desert's most elusive species, from mountain lions to black bears and Mexican wolves. Watch for otters and beavers in the Riparian Corridor, and meet rattlesnakes and Gila monsters face-to-face indoors. Just north of the museum is the western unit of Saguaro National Park, named

for the cacti seen in Roadrunner cartoons and innumerable Westerns. Hiking trails lace through the hills and canyons here and in the larger eastern unit on the opposite side of the city. The park is especially known for its bird-watching; keep an eye out for curve-billed thrashers, Gambel's quail, and cactus wrens.

Tucson has a tricultural population: Hispanic, Native American, and Anglo. Only 60 miles north of the border, it has its fair share of Mexican restaurants and promotes itself as the "Mexican Food Capital of the U.S." The Cafe Poca Cosa is an impressive showcase for chef-owner Suzana Davila's creative dishes inspired by different regions of her native Mexico.

WHERE: Tucson is 115 miles southeast of Phoenix. *Visitor info:* Tel 800-638-8350 or 520-624-1817; visittucson.org. **TANQUE VERDE:** Tel 800-234-3833 or 520-296-6275; tanqueverderanch.com. *Cost:* from $400 (off-peak), from $600 (peak), all-inclusive. **ARIZONA-SONORA DESERT MUSEUM:** Tel 520-883-2702; desertmuseum.org. **SAGUARO NATIONAL PARK:** Tel 520-733-5153; nps.gov /sagu. **CAFE POCA COSA:** Tel 520-622-6400; cafepocacosatucson.com. *Cost:* dinner $30. **BEST TIME:** Nov–Apr for weather.

World-Class Wellness Centers

CANYON RANCH AND MIRAVAL

Tucson, Arizona

The gorgeous Santa Catalina Mountains are home to two of the country's most interesting and transformative luxury wellness resorts, with distinct approaches to making sure you go home better off in mind, body, and spirit.

Canyon Ranch was at the cutting edge of spas when it opened on 150 acres of a former dude ranch in 1979, and it still sets the standard for excellence. Its team of physicians and registered nurses have unrivaled expertise in preventive medicine, integrative medicine, and healthy lifestyle change. Add to that exercise

physiologists, licensed therapists, nutritionists, dietitians, and spiritual wellness experts, and you can improve your life in almost every direction. Just as at the equally well-equipped sister facility in the Berkshires (see p. 56), there is a seemingly endless roster of activities, from Pilates to photography hikes, golf school to culinary classes, and expert lectures on resiliency, healthy sleep, and the science of weight loss. Specially focused weeks at the self-contained "Life Enhancement Center" include brain health, spiritual renewal, and women's journey to wisdom. The goal is that you'll take the benefit of the vacation home with you.

Set in nearly 400 acres of serene desert, nearby Miraval has won fans like Oprah Winfrey and Dr. Oz with its emphasis on challenging yourself to achieve personal growth. With a small group of other people and sensitive leaders, you can walk a desert tightrope, jump off a 25-foot pole, let go of a rope and swing from a height of 35 feet—then discuss your feelings with your group. It's also famous for the Equine Experience, where you're shown how to groom a horse and then left to do it yourself. Master therapists here create their own unique treatments at the Life in Balance Spa, highly regarded for the excellence of its treatments. You can also meet the farmer who supplies all the spa's produce and eggs, and help harvest honey with the beekeeper.

Tucked away in the Santa Catalina Mountains, Canyon Ranch creates the perfect atmosphere for rejuvenation.

Canyon Ranch: 8600 Rockcliff Rd., Tucson. Tel 800-742-6494 or 520-749-9000; canyonranchdestinations.com. *Cost:* 3-night all-inclusive package from $2,600 (off-peak), from $3,646 (peak), double occupancy; includes $450 treatment allowance. **Miraval Resort:** 5000 E. Via Estancia Miraval, Catalina. Tel 800-232-3969 or 520-825-4000; miravalresorts.com. *Cost:* from $399 (off-peak), from $699 (peak) per person per night, includes meals, and most fitness classes, lectures, and programs.

Birthplace of the Arizona Guest Ranch

WICKENBURG

Arizona

Wandering the cactus-stubbled hills between Phoenix and the Grand Canyon, Prussian prospector Henry Wickenburg struck gold here in 1863. His discovery set off a rush: The town that bears his name grew so fast that just three years later it missed becoming the territorial capital by only three votes. Over 80 mines soon dotted the hillsides, and Wickenburg became known far and wide as one of the richest areas in the territory. This golden moment inevitably played out, and in the 1920s and '30s Wickenburg reinvented itself as the "dude ranch capital of the world."

Today only two guest ranches survive from the glory days, but they still offer a ride through landscape you've seen in countless Westerns.

This homey, unassuming town of 6,600 has held on to the general store and its Jail Tree, where prisoners were chained for all the public to see. The Desert Caballeros Western Museum focuses on the region's history and culture, and Western art. Paintings by Frederic Remington and Charlie Russell hang near prehistoric stone tools and Navajo blankets, and dioramas depict Henry Wickenburg's famous Vulture Mine, which produced more gold than any other mine in Arizona. Vulture City is now a well-preserved ghost town, which you can tour on Saturday mornings.

The Rancho de Los Caballeros is an upscale resort set on 20,000 acres of an old working ranch that still retains Old West touches like Mexican tiles and whitewashed walls. Beginner, intermediate, and advanced rides go out twice a day (except Sunday) and expert hands pair you with the right horse for your skill level. It's also known for its championship golf course and a spa where the saddle-sore can be restored. Other activities at the family-friendly resort include jeep tours, trap

A wrangler leads a trail ride at Rancho de Los Caballeros.

and skeet shooting, and guided hikes through the desert. The bright, busy dining room is the finest in the area, and guests are required to dress for dinner. Other evenings promise serenading cowboys and cookouts under the stars.

Not far away is the Flying E Ranch, a dude and working cattle ranch operating since 1946. Guests pay extra for riding, so you can ride as little or as much as you want, from an hour or two to a full day roaming the ranch's 20,000 scenic acres. Guests enjoy traditional ranch activities or sign up for themed visits like the Wanna Be a Cowgirl Weekend, Gold Rush Days, and the old-timey Ranch Christmas. Evening events are impromptu—you might find square dancing in the barn or cowboy poetry around the campfire.

WHERE: 60 miles northwest of Phoenix. *Visitor info:* Tel 800-942-5242 or 928-684-5479; outwickenburgway.com. **DESERT CABALLEROS WESTERN MUSEUM:** Tel 928-684-2272; westernmuseum.org. **VULTURE MINE:** vultureminetours.com. *When:* Sat, late-Oct–early May. **RANCHO DE LOS CABALLEROS:** Tel 800-684-5030 or 928-684-5484; ranchodeloscaballeros.com. *Cost:* from $395, includes meals and activities for two (off-peak). Activities additional during peak season. *When:* mid-Oct–mid-May. **FLYING E RANCH:** Tel 928-684-2690; flyingeranch.com. *Cost:* from $330, includes all meals; riding extra. **BEST TIMES:** Nov–May to avoid summer heat; mid-Feb for Gold Rush Days; mid-Nov for Bluegrass Festival; early Dec for Cowboy Christmas Poetry Gathering.

The High Life: Glamour and Glorious Skiing

ASPEN

Colorado

Strip away its ultrarich celebrity veneer and Aspen shines as one of the country's best places to ski, with no fewer than four mountains cheek to cheek. Add in a funky ski town with a year-round scene, where you can rub elbows with the latest Hollywood boldfaced names before tackling world-class bumps, and you'll realize why Aspen is such a special place. It's a walking town, with excellent restaurants and galleries every few steps and an unbeatable après-ski bar scene to boot. Gingerbread houses from the city's heady mining-town years of the late 19th century may be out of the average visitor's price range, but the peerless views of the Rockies are free.

Aspen's four mountains offer more than 5,500 skiable acres, and all are linked by free shuttle service and transferable lift tickets. Snowmass is the biggie, with 3,342 acres of wide-open groomed runs perfect for families. Aspen Mountain, "Ajax" to locals, is a challenging peak that rises to 11,000 feet and offers steep, bumpy runs practically into downtown. Many locals consider Aspen Highlands a favorite for the hikes into steep Highland and Olympic bowls. Finally, Buttermilk is rated the best in the country for beginners, although it hosts extreme skiers and snowboarders during the ESPN Winter X Games.

Aspen also has some of the highest-rated ski lodges in the country. Start with the Little Nell, the only ski-in/ski-out lodge on Aspen Mountain and a snowball's throw from the Silver Queen gondola, the longest single-stage gondola in the world. The elegant rooms in the chalet-style hotel come complete with chocolates and bedtime storybooks, and the staff is gracious to a fault. Its unpretentious Element 47 restaurant pays tribute to silver, the precious metal that first put Aspen on the map.

Aspen Mountain has 76 ski trails on 673 skiable acres and a vertical drop of 3,267 feet.

In town, the Hotel Jerome is a former silver mining hotel that opened in 1889 and is now the epitome of ski town sophistication. The stylish Western decor blends historically inspired furnishings with modern comfort in all 93 rooms. The hotel's historic J-Bar is still among the best places in town for people-watching and nightlife.

You won't go hungry in town, with options that range from jammin' bars to world-class cuisine. But head out of the fray to Krabloonik Mountain Dining and Dog Sledding, a log cabin on Snowmass named for the previous owner's lead sled dog (it's Eskimo for "Big Eyebrows"). Repeat visitors come for the succulent wild game and dogsled rides into the quiet woods.

Aspen also lays claim to the title of Festival Capital of the Rockies—though Telluride (see p. 722) might have something to say about that. A year-round roster of cultural events climaxes with the classical Aspen Music Festival, the Aspen Santa Fe Ballet, and Jazz Aspen Snowmass, with year-round programming and two huge festivals featuring Motown legends, country rockers, and major jazz performers in June and again around Labor Day.

WHERE: 200 miles southwest of Denver. *Visitor info:* Tel 800-670-0792 or 970-920-1940; aspenchamber.org. **ASPEN SNOWMASS:** Tel 800-525-6200 or 970-925-1220; aspensnow mass.com. *Cost:* lift tickets with access to all 4 ski areas, $149. *When:* ski season, late Nov–mid-Apr. **THE LITTLE NELL:** Tel 855-920-4600 or 970-920-4600; thelittlenell.com. *Cost:* from $550 (off-peak), from $1,125 (peak). **HOTEL JEROME:** Tel 855-331-7213 or 970-920-1000; hoteljerome.aubergeresort.com. *Cost:* from $375 (off-peak), from $765 (peak). **KRABLOONIK:** Snowmass Village. Tel 970-923-3953. *Cost:* dinner $70. **MUSIC FESTIVAL:** Tel 970-925-9042; aspenmusicfestival.com. *When:* late June–late Aug. **ASPEN SANTA FE BALLET:** Tel 970-925-6098; aspensantafeballet.com. *When:* Feb–Mar. **JAZZ ASPEN SNOWMASS:** Tel 970-920-4996; jazzaspen.org. *When:* 3 days in late June and 3 days in early Sept. **BEST TIME:** Dec–Mar for skiing.

A Dark and Precipitous Gorge

BLACK CANYON OF THE GUNNISON NATIONAL PARK

Colorado

Travelers who've been to the Grand Canyon (see p. 685) and think they've seen all the Southwest has to offer when it comes to massive gorges have a surprise waiting in south-central Colorado. The Black Canyon of the Gunnison is a crack in the Colorado Plateau half a mile deep yet astonishingly narrow—just 40 feet across at one point called the "Narrows"—with the raging Gunnison River as its floor. It takes its name from the limited sunlight that penetrates its depths, its eternal shadows evoking a somber, almost religious mood.

The entire canyon stretches for 53 miles, but it's the 14-mile section from Gunnison to Montrose that was elevated to national park status in 1999. At 30,385 acres, it is one of America's smallest national parks, and you know what they say about gifts in small packages. The 2,250-foot Painted Wall is the tallest vertical wall in the state, where dark expanses of gneiss and schist plunge headlong to the river's edge. This is the revered realm of rock climbers as well as peregrine falcons, the fastest birds in the world.

The 7-mile South Rim Drive runs from Tomichi Point to Warner Point, passing overlooks with signs explaining the canyon's unique geology. A number of short, easy trails lead through pine, juniper, and oak to overlooks on both rims, but getting to the bottom is a more serious undertaking. The trails to the river aren't long (none over 3 miles), but they each drop at least 1,600 feet, making routes like the Long Draw the toughest and steepest three-hour mile you've ever hiked. Anglers willing to make the trek will find some of the best brown and rainbow trout fishing in these Gold Medal Waters. For a less strenuous tour, hop aboard a half-day raft trip with Three Rivers Outfitting upstream from the park. It offers a quiet family-friendly float with Class I through III rapids on the Gunnison and Taylor Rivers, and a range of cabins. While inside the park, beware: This stretch of the wild Gunnison is considered one of North America's premier kayak challenges and is for experts only.

The Ute Indian Museum & Ouray Memorial Park in Montrose holds exhibits on the culture of western Colorado's original inhabitants. It's located on the original homestead site of the famous leader of the Uncompahgre band of Ute, Chief Ouray; he dwelled here until his death in 1880, shortly before the government forced his tribe to migrate. Besides its comprehensive collection of native rugs, historic photos, and household artifacts, the museum offers classes in traditional crafts such as weaving and beadwork.

WHERE: Gunnison is 200 miles southwest of Denver. Tel 970-641-2337; nps.gov/blca. **When:** Rim roads are closed in winter. **THREE**

At its deepest section, the canyon has a depth of 2,722 feet.

RIVERS RESORT & OUTFITTING: Tel 888-761-3474 or 970-641-1303; 3riversresort.com. *Cost:* $55 for half-day raft trip. *When:* May–Oct.

UTE INDIAN MUSEUM: Montrose. Tel 970-249-3098. *When:* Closed Sun. **BEST TIME:** May–June for peregrine falcon nesting.

Real Colorado, Real Skiing

BRECKENRIDGE

Colorado

The county seat of Summit County, Breckenridge is Colorado's recreation wonderland and also its oldest and largest community. Less pretentious than many of the state's mining-camps-turned-ski-towns, Breckenridge nestles in the Blue River Valley at the foot of the Tenmile Range, and is nearly synonymous with the ski resort that towers above. It has more than 200 restaurants, bars, and shops to keep visitors entertained, and more than 250 restored Victorians fill its National Historic District. Walking tours are offered by the Breckenridge Heritage Alliance, illustrating how the town flourished from the gold that was dredged in these hills until the 1940s.

The Breckenridge Ski Resort covers five mountains—Peaks 5, 7, 8, 9, and 10—with a vertical rise of 3,400 feet. Its 2,908 acres include four terrain parks, a 22-foot superpipe, the highest chairlift in North America, family-friendly slopes, and a world-class ski and snowboard school. Breckenridge was one of the first resorts in Colorado to allow snowboarders and now has one of the country's best snowboard parks, the Freeway Terrain Park and Pipe. Once known for its groomed beginner and intermediate slopes, it has expert skiers flocking here as more challenging terrain has been made accessible (more than 50 percent of its trails are rated expert and advanced).

With an elegant, rustic vibe, the Mountain Thunder Lodge is perfectly situated between the gondola (to Peaks 7 or 8) and the shops and eateries that flank Main Street. Studios, and one-, two-, and three-bedroom condos are perfect for those staying for more than a night

The ski resort's Peak 8 looms over lit-up downtown Breckenridge.

or two. If you're in town at the end of January, be sure to watch the International Snow Sculpture Championships, where artists from around the world carve astounding creations out of 20-ton blocks.

Things don't stop in the summer in Summit County. The Breckenridge Golf Club is the only 27-hole municipal course in the world laid out by Jack Nicklaus. Mountain bikers carry their wheels uphill on chairlifts, and hikers and horseback riders revel in the fact that 80 percent of the county is designated National Forest. Boaters and anglers head to the 3,300-acre Dillon Reservoir and the Gold Medal fishing stream of the Blue River.

WHERE: 80 miles west of Denver. *Visitor info:* Tel 888-251-2417; gobreck.com. **BRECKENRIDGE SKI RESORT:** Tel 800-789-SNOW or 970-453-5000; breckenridge.com. *Cost:* lift tickets $164. *When:* Nov–Apr. **MOUNTAIN THUNDER LODGE:** Tel 855-822-5045; breckresorts.com. *Cost:* from $289. **BRECKENRIDGE GOLF CLUB:** breckenridgegolfclub.com. *Cost:* greens fees $67 (off-peak), $117 (peak). **BEST TIMES:** mid-Nov–late Apr for skiing; Jan for Ullr Fest; 5 days in late Jan for International Snow Sculpture Championships; mid-July–mid-Aug for Breckenridge Music Festival (breckenridge musicfestival.com).

The Cowboy Life, Revisited

THE COLORADO RANCH EXPERIENCE

Colorado

C olorado's dude ranches range from top-end to family-run operations, many of them world-famous and some kept out of the spotlight. Whether you want to ride horses, soak in a hot tub, shoot skeet, or just relax on the porch as the sun sets over awesome panoramas, it's all here for the asking.

A short drive from Rocky Mountain National Park (see p. 720), the C Lazy U Ranch is the state's consummate upscale, family-oriented dude ranch named for the shape of the meandering path cut by Willow Creek across the 8,500-acre property. The main lodge features a grand piano often in use, a big stone fireplace appreciated even during summer nights, and a front porch with amazing mountain views. Next door is the patio house with an outdoor swimming pool fed by a natural spring, and exercise and game rooms. Horses play a big role—there's riding on miles of hoof-worn trails or in a 12,000-square-foot indoor arena. In summer you can also choose from tubing, paddleboats, basketball, tennis, Western cookouts, and square dances. In winter you can hop in the hay wagon to help feed the horses, ice-skate on the pond, learn how to cross-country ski, go for a sleigh ride, or go sledding—the vast holdings of this family-owned ranch are one big playground.

With a more subdued and exclusive ambience, Dunton Hot Springs is a low-profile destination that's hard to find and even harder to leave after you've experienced its solitude and rare beauty. A restored 19th-century ghost town north of Durango (see p. 712) on the west fork of the Dolores River, it has evolved from an 1895 camp for miners and trappers to an opulent resort hidden behind an authentically weathered facade. Guest cabins are unique hand-hewn log and wooden buildings (and three tepees) tucked into 1,600 acres situated in the midst of blissful Rockies splendor. The yoga/massage studio was once a Pony Express

Once you pass through this ranch's gate, kick-back fun and gorgeous views await.

stop, and Butch Cassidy spent a winter in what is now the breakfast room. Go horseback riding, fly-fishing, or helicopter skiing, or spend the day in nearby Telluride (see p. 722) and be back "home" in time for a hot rocks massage and a soak in the mineral springs. The free-standing bathhouse is the resort's jewel, and one of the cabins has the 103°F geothermal waters piped directly into its tub. The food and wine list is startlingly excellent for a middle-of-nowhere ghost town. (Ask about the organic ice cream made with peaches from a local farm.)

Those visiting Steamboat Springs will find an idyllic ranch experience north of town in Clark at either of two luxury options, the well-known Home Ranch (see p. 722) or its friendly competitor, the Vista Verde or "Green View." A working ranch since the 1930s, the Vista Verde evolved into a hunting and fishing camp and eventually a luxury resort when Peggy and Jerry Throgmartin bought it in 2006. Peggy

now runs the ranch with the help of a wonderful family of can-do staff, and she can often be found popping in at meals—a delicious highlight every day—to check on guests. The lodge rooms are huge and sumptuous, and the more rustic cabins are named after local peaks. There are rides and horse clinics as well as a plethora of off-ranch activities, from hot-air ballooning in the summer months to dogsledding in the winter.

C LAZY U RANCH: Granby. Tel 970-887-3344; clazyu.com. *Cost:* $340 per person, 2-night minimum, all-inclusive (off-peak); from $400 per person, all-inclusive (peak). **DUNTON HOT SPRINGS:** Dolores. Tel 970-882-4800; duntonhotsprings.com. *Cost:* cabins from $700 per night, all-inclusive (off-peak); from $900 (peak). **VISTA VERDE RANCH:** Tel 800-526-7433 or 970-879-3858 vistaverde.com. *Cost:* from $1,295 per person, all-inclusive, for 3 nights (off-peak); from $3,975 per person, all-inclusive, for 7 nights (peak).

Grande Dame of the Rockies

THE BROADMOOR

Colorado Springs, Colorado

It was a clever stroke indeed to have John D. Rockefeller Jr. and his party sign the guest register at this superlative resort hotel the day it opened in 1918. Although they allegedly checked out almost immediately, driven away by the

smell of fresh paint, the Broadmoor has maintained the highest standard of excellence ever since. Entrepreneur Spencer Penrose created the resort around the same time he built the toll road up nearby Pikes Peak (see p. 719) for a then mind-boggling quarter-of-a-million-dollar investment. Intending to compete with the Cog Railway, he then bought the railway, too.

The Broadmoor occupies 5,000 magnificently landscaped acres at the foot of Cheyenne Mountain, with Italianate architecture set off by pink stucco and palazzo-style

towers. The main building features the Old World opulence of a marble staircase and fountain, hand-painted ceilings, and Italian tile. The hotel has a larger distinguished collection of Western art and its assortment of restaurants, lounges, bars, and cafés feed the eye and palate. The culinary possibilities are excellent: from the exquisite French menu of the elegant Penrose Room and the Italian-style Ristorante Del Lago to the informal Golden Bee, a gloriously old-fashioned bar (with an excellent wine list).

Three world-class championship golf courses—designed by Robert Trent Jones Sr., Jack Nicklaus, and Donald Ross—coupled with the sheer beauty of the Rocky Mountains, make this a golfer's dream destination. Of the three pools, one measures 11,000 square feet at the north end of private Cheyenne Lake and comes complete with waterslides and private cabanas. Seven courts (two of which are covered) make up the tennis complex, known for its outstanding tennis camps. Families come for the wide range of outdoor activities, including horseback riding, falconry, fly-fishing, and white-water rafting. Couples gravitate toward private lakeside rooms and two-at-a-time Swedish massages in the resort's top-notch spa.

Colorado Springs has lots of other historical and recreational options, making it one of the state's most popular destinations. Home to Colorado College, the University of Colorado at Colorado Springs, the U.S. Air Force Academy, and the ProRodeo Hall of Fame & Museum of the American Cowboy, it also has a downtown central park and plaza as charming as any in the state.

Where: 75 miles south of Denver; 1 Lake Ave. Tel 855-634-7711 or 719-623-5112; broadmoor.com. *Cost:* from $400 (off-peak), from $525 (peak); dinner at the Penrose Room $84; dinner at Ristorante Del Lago $40. **Best times:** 4th of July for celebration and fireworks; May–Oct for weather.

The Broadmoor enjoys a prime location by the triple-peaked Cheyenne Mountain.

Hiking the Backbone of North America

CONTINENTAL DIVIDE TRAIL

Colorado, Montana, Idaho, Wyoming, and New Mexico

America's longest and most rugged National Scenic Trail, the King of Trails follows the wandering spine of the Rocky Mountains from Canada to Mexico, tracing the dividing line between the Atlantic and Pacific watersheds. Over 3,100 miles of high peaks, mountain meadows, and high desert, the Continental Divide Trail (CDT) threads the nation's wildest backcountry, crossing 25 National Forests, 21 Wilderness Areas, and three National Parks in five western states. It's been a work in progress since the 1960s, and the "trail" is a mixture of defined trail, cross-country travel, dirt, and paved road walking. Raw, wild, remote, and unfinished, the trail will require an experienced backpacker's skill. Together with the Appalachian Trail (see p. 332) and the Pacific Crest Trail (the focus of the bestselling book *Wild* by Cheryl Strayed), the CDT (the highest altitude of the three) forms the Triple Crown of long-distance hiking.

Numerous through-hikers complete the entire trail every year, while those without a five-month hole in their schedules can embark on shorter trips in every state—in particular Colorado, which offers plenty of easy access.

Starting in the north, the CDT runs for 980 miles through Montana and southeastern Idaho, crossing Glacier National Park (see p. 620) and skirting the 22-mile, 1,000-foot-high Chinese Wall in the enormous Bob Marshall Wilderness (see p. 617). Entering Wyoming, the trail passes Old Faithful geyser and Shoshone Lake in Yellowstone National Park (see p. 676) and hits the Wind River Range as it runs 550 miles to the Colorado border. The 770-mile New Mexico segment is the least mountainous, crossing lava fields and stretches of desert mountains before hitting the Mexican border.

In Colorado, the CDT traverses 800 miles of stunning, remote high-mountain scenery, running contiguous with the popular Colorado Trail for over 100 miles. Here almost the entire stretch of the CDT is on national forest land. The route stays above 11,000 feet for almost

70 miles, and reaches the trail's highest point at Grays Peak, at 14,270 feet. Most of the backcountry is good enough for mountain bikers. The two easiest access points for shorter hikes are near Steamboat Springs (see p. 721) and Wolf Creek Pass near Pagosa Springs. Near Denver, the Front Range Segment touches the edge of Rocky Mountain National Park (see p. 720) and the Indian Peaks Wilderness. In the San Juan Mountains Segment to the south, the wild Weminuche Wilderness sees a good number of trekkers. You can't go wrong with views that are never anything less than breathtaking, in every sense of the word.

WHERE: 3,100 miles from Canada to Mexico along the Continental Divide. **CONTINENTAL DIVIDE TRAIL COALITION:** Tel 303-996-2759; continentaldividetrail.org. **BEST TIME:** In Colorado, the snow-free season on the CDT is typically late June–early Oct.

Mountain Biking and Extreme Skiing in a Historic Town

CRESTED BUTTE

Colorado

Like many places in Colorado, this charming ski town in the Gunnison National Forest began as a mining camp in the 1880s but survived longer than most, thanks to the discovery of coal nearby. Crested Butte's

downtown is one of Colorado's largest National Historic Districts; Elk Avenue is chock-full of renovated and whimsically painted Victorian saloons, bordellos, and general stores in a style that's refreshingly and decidedly (for the moment) unchic. Add to that a wealth of outdoor activities available in every season, some of the most challenging downhill skiing in the Rockies, as well as a friendly and quirky populace of 1,519, and this out-of-the-way place is well worth the trip. Its remote location means no crowds and no weekend traffic. This could very well be Colorado's best-kept secret.

In the late 1970s Crested Butte was one of the original mountain biking towns, and fattire bikers are still drawn by legendary trails like the 30-mile "401" ride from the old mining town of Gothic past Emerald Lake. In summer you can take the ski lift up Mount Crested Butte to access hair-raising downhill trails, while old mining roads wind through the national forest in every direction. The legendary Pearl Pass that crests at 12,700 feet is only for the experienced and confident. Crested Butte hosts the original Bike Week in late June. Hiking, climbing, horseback riding, rafting, kayaking, and fishing are other summer options, and the unrivaled display of columbine and Indian paintbrush has earned the town the title "Wildflower Capital of Colorado" and spawned a special festival held in their honor every July.

Once the snow starts falling, things really take off. Free shuttles run the 3 miles from town to the Crested Butte Mountain Resort and some of the steepest lift-served terrain in North America, with a separate trail guide for double-black-diamond runs. The mountain

Mountain bikers enjoy lush displays of wildflowers in summer.

hosts the National Extreme Skiing and Snowboarding Championships every winter, utilizing 550 ungroomed acres for experts only. (If you're not a hot dog, don't worry—there are plenty of cruiseworthy trails for beginners and intermediates.)

Crested Butte's Evolution Bike Park has 30 miles of trails for everyone, from beginners to all-out cliff jumpers. Relax at Lodge at Mountaineer Square just steps from the ski lifts, hiking, and biking.

WHERE: 228 miles southwest of Denver. *Visitor info:* Tel. 855-631-0941 or 970-349-6438; cbchamber.com. **CRESTED BUTTE RESORT:** Tel 877-547-5143 or 970-349-2211; skicb.com. *Cost:* lift tickets $108. *When:* ski season Nov–early Apr. **LODGE AT MOUNTAINEER SQUARE:** Tel 970-349-4000; skicb.com. *Cost:* from $159 (off-peak), from $252 (peak). **BEST TIMES:** late Feb for U.S. Extreme Freeskiing Championship; late Jan for Fat Bike World Championship; June for CB Bike Week; July for wildflowers; Sept for foliage.

Art, Opera, and an Awesome Red Rock Amphitheater

DENVER'S CULTURAL SCENE

Denver, Colorado

I t's hard to compete with the views of the Rocky Mountains, but the Denver Art Museum is up to the challenges. Founded in 1893 and designed in the 1970s by the famous Italian architect Gio Ponti, the seven-story structure is faced

with over a million shimmering gray tiles. And if you can keep your eyes off of the gorgeous views, you'll agree that the collection is every bit as dazzling.

The museum is famous worldwide for its collection of Native American arts, representing over a hundred tribes in the U.S. and Canada and spanning more than 2,000 years. The pre-Columbian and Spanish Colonial collections are equally superb, and the American

West collection includes paintings by Frederic Remington, George Catlin, and Albert Bierstadt. Its Asian art collection, ranging from Japan to India, is the only one of its kind in the Rockies, and works by Calder, Degas, Picasso, Rodin, and Georgia O'Keeffe are on exhibit. Families love it for its many child-friendly offerings, including activity-filled backpacks to carry around the museum and the Discovery Library. The Palettes restaurant does a good job of serving up food that aspires to its environs.

In the fall of 2006 the museum nearly doubled in size with the opening of the $90 million, 14,000-square-foot Frederick C. Hamilton Building, designed by Daniel Libeskind, the Polish-American architect well known for his museum designs around the world. Large galleries for traveling exhibitions, a rooftop sculpture garden, and an indoor auditorium are part of the distinctive, angular design—Denver's most distinctive building by far.

Denver has become the cultural beacon of the American West. At its center is 16th Street Mall, a mile-long pedestrian mall designed by I. M. Pei. Nearby is the mammoth Denver Performing Arts Complex, with over 10,000 seats in ten performance spaces. It includes the new Ellie Caulkins Opera House, home to the Colorado Symphony and host to ballet, opera, and Broadway-style productions.

Denver outdid itself when creating the unmatched Red Rocks Amphitheatre, one of the most stunning venues for outdoor summer performances in the country. The natural acoustics are excellent, and the color and formations of the natural amphitheater created by cinnamon-colored rocks is the essence of Colorado's good looks. The setting is pure magic and sell-out performers from the Beatles (1964) to the world's finest symphonies have graced its stage.

The latest facet of Denver's cultural scene is not art-related—the legal marijuana industry is drawing new crowds and adding to the city's unique character.

DENVER ART MUSEUM: Tel 720-865-5000; denverartmuseum.org. *When:* closed Mon. **DENVER PERFORMING ARTS COMPLEX:** Tel 720-865-4220; artscomplex.com. **RED ROCKS AMPHITHEATRE:** Morrison. Tel 720-865-2494; redrocksonline.com. *When:* May–Sept.

The Denver Art Museum is the only completed design in the U.S. by renowned Italian architect Gio Ponti.

The Napa Valley of Beer

GREAT AMERICAN BEER FESTIVAL

Denver, Colorado

The U.S. has always been beer-crazy, but it wasn't until the mid-1980s that brewpubs took off and beer lovers everywhere began enjoying hand-crafted bottles of suds with bold flavors and imaginative names.

No state encapsulates this love affair better than Colorado, which ranks third in the U.S. in its abundance of microbreweries and brewpubs. Coors, established in Golden (see p. 714) by German immigrants in 1873, has grown to become the largest single brewery facility in the world.

Denver's first permanent structure was said to have been a saloon: The Mile High City now boasts 52 craft brewers, and the region between Denver, Boulder, and Fort Collins is so renowned for its brews that it's called the "Napa Valley of beer." For one weekend in the fall it boasts the best selections on earth during the Great American Beer Festival, a New World Oktoberfest that gathers representatives from the nation's best breweries to tap over 3,800 different kinds of beer—enough to get it listed in *Guinness World Records*. Winning a medal at GABF is the ultimate trophy for craft brewers across the nation. Brewer's tables and beer-cooking demonstrations keep even the teetotalers happy.

If you fancy yourself a connoisseur or wannabe, visit the Wynkoop Brewing Company, Colorado's oldest brewpub. It's unpretentious but proud of its various microbrews; tour the brewing

There's plenty to go around at this popular festival.

facilities or play a few rounds of pool. There are good beer-and-food pairings available, or head on over to the Buckhorn Exchange, Denver's original steak house. Colorado Liquor License No. 1 is on display over the 140-year-old bar where Buffalo Bill once quenched his thirst.

Fort Collins, 65 miles north of Denver, holds the largest outdoor brewing festival in the state, the Colorado Brewers Festival in June. The local Anheuser-Busch brewery and their world famous team of Clydesdales is one of the city's top tourist draws.

GREAT AMERICAN BEER FESTIVAL: Tel 888-822-6273 or 303-447-0816; greatamerican beerfestival.com. *Cost:* from $65 per session. *When:* late Sept–early Oct. **WYNKOOP BREWING COMPANY:** Denver. Tel 303-297-2700; wynkoop .com. *Cost:* lunch $12. **BUCKHORN EXCHANGE:** Denver. Tel 303-534-9505; buckhorn.com. *Cost:* dinner $65. **COLORADO BREWERS FESTIVAL:** Fort Collins. Tel 970-484-6500. *When:* last weekend in June. **ANHEUSER-BUSCH BREWERY TOURS:** Fort Collins. Tel 970-490-4691; budweisertours.com.

A Young-at-Heart Mountain Town

DURANGO

Colorado

66 I t's out of the way and glad of it," cracked Will Rogers. Nestled in the Animas River Valley between the desert and the San Juan Mountains, Durango is not all that inaccessible these days and draws lots of folks for

its irresistible mix of history and activity. This railroad town of 17,600 residents, founded in 1881, is known for its wealth of outdoor offerings, its proximity to Mesa Verde National Park (see p. 716), and its restored railroad through the mountains to Silverton (see p. 717) that you might remember from its hair-raising robbery scene in *Butch Cassidy and the Sundance Kid*.

Students attending Fort Lewis College give Durango an upbeat air and keep dozens of ski,

mountain bike, and camping stores in business. The Purgatory Resort has 1,360 skiable acres and 91 trails on Purgatory Mountain and bragging rights to more sunshine than any other ski resort in Colorado. Kayakers tackle Class I through III rapids on the Animas River, which flows right through the center of town (more thrilling rapids are not far away). To top it off, Durango is known as one of the hottest mountain biking towns in the West, starting with its hosting of the first-ever Mountain Bike National Championships in 1990, now held annually around the country. Hundreds of miles of trails wander through the nearby hills. The 12-mile Dry Fork Loop on the edge of town connects to the statewide Colorado Trail.

Mosey on over to the Strater Hotel and step into a time machine. Wild West legends Bat Masterson and Butch Cassidy both stayed at this handsome four-story redbrick Victorian hotel, built in 1887. Louis L'Amour wrote a few of his Western novels while checked into room 222 or sitting in the Diamond Belle Saloon, still the town's hot spot after all these years. Live ragtime music wafts from the bar, decorated with crystal chandeliers and plush velvety curtains. Adjacent to the Strater is the Mahogany Grille restaurant, where the Chocolate Avalanche dessert is reason enough to come for dinner. Locals stave off winter cabin fever during Snowdown, Durango's wild winter celebration, complete with kayak races in the snow.

The Durango & Silverton Railroad follows the twists and turns of San Juan Mountains' steep cliffs.

The biggest draw for all ages is the Durango & Silverton Narrow Gauge Railroad. In operation since 1882, it once took mining supplies, workers, and precious minerals to and from Silverton. Now it carries tourists along the 45-mile route across narrow bridges spanning roaring white-water canyons along a 3,000-foot ascent. A full day of exhilarating fun awaits those who sign up for the Soaring Tree Top Adventures, the longest zip-line course of its kind (and appropriate for all ages). The package includes round-trip train passage in a special first-class car, a gourmet lunch, and a lot of group bonding.

Durango is also the most common starting point for the San Juan Skyway, which crosses five mountain passes. The 236-mile loop heads through the beautiful San Juan Mountains north to the Million Dollar Highway between Silverton and Ouray (see p. 717) before circling back via Telluride (see p. 722), Rico, and Stoner.

WHERE: 336 miles southwest of Denver. *Visitor info:* Tel 800-463-8726 or 970-247-3500; durango.org. **PURGATORY RESORT:** Tel 800-525-0892 or 970-247-9000; purgatoryresort.com. *Cost:* lift tickets $85. *When:* Nov–Apr. **STRATER HOTEL:** Tel 800-247-4431 or 970-247-4431; strater.com. *Cost:* from $109 (off-peak), from $180 (peak). **DURANGO & SILVERTON RAILROAD:** Tel 888-872-4607 or 970-247-2733; durangotrain.com. *Cost:* from $89 roundtrip. *When:* May–Oct. **BEST TIMES:** last weekend in Jan for Snowdown; early Oct for Durango Cowboy Gathering.

An Old-Fashioned Spa Town and Fairy Caves

GLENWOOD SPRINGS

Colorado

For centuries the Ute Indians, first inhabitants of this part of western Colorado, knew about the natural hot springs that still bubble to the surface. They came to heal their wounds and take the vapors in the natural saunas of nearby caves. Whites arrived in the 1880s after the discovery of gold and silver nearby, and the "spa in the Rockies" was born. European royalty came to take the waters, Hollywood discovered it, Teddy Roosevelt designated the local Hotel Colorado "Little White House of the West." Today Glenwood Springs has preserved the air of an old-fashioned spa town with easy access to great skiing (Aspen and Vail are both within an hour's drive; see pp. 702 and 723) and has the distinction of being the burial place of Wild West legend Doc Holliday.

The Utes called the local hot water pools Yampah, or Big Medicine Springs. The town claims that the main pool, at 405 by 100 feet, is the largest mineral hot springs pool in the world. It holds 1,071,000 gallons of water maintained at 90°F and is big enough to fit a diving area and lanes for lap swimming. There's also a smaller pool that is slightly hotter (104°F). Massages, facials, and cleansing

Glenwood's hot springs pool offers two blocks of swimming area.

sweats are available next door at the Yampah Spa and Vapor Caves, the only natural geothermal steam baths in North America. Glenwood Springs' newest hot spot is Iron Mountain Hot Springs, with 16 soaking pools along a curve in the Colorado River.

East of Glenwood Springs is Glenwood Canyon, a deep, 15-mile gorge carved by the Colorado River. At the western end of the canyon is kitschy Glenwood Caverns Adventure Park, where you can ride European-style gondolas up 4,300 feet to Glenwood Caverns and Historic Fairy Caves. Once promoted as the Eighth Wonder of the World, the caverns are filled with fantastical natural formations and are one of the few places in the country where you can go spelunking at over 7,000 feet. Choose from a moderate half-mile, one-hour guided tour or the more challenging three-hour "wild tour" (be ready to crawl on your stomach). Also in Glenwood Canyon are the starts of a number of trails, including Hanging Lake Trail (2.4 miles round trip), a popular hike that climbs a side canyon past numerous falls to a hauntingly gorgeous little green pool.

Where: 157 miles west of Denver. *Visitor info:* Tel 970-945-6580; visitglenwood.com. **Hotel Colorado:** Tel 800-544-3998 or 970-945-6511; hotelcolorado.com. *Cost:* from $99 (off-peak), from $145 (peak). **Yampah Spa:** Tel 970-945-0667; yampahspa.com. **Iron Mountain Hot Springs:** Tel 970-945-IRON; ironmountainhotsprings.com. **Glenwood Caverns Adventure Park:** Tel 800-530-1635 or 970-945-4228; glenwoodcaverns.com.

Living Reminders of Mining History

GOLD CIRCLE TOWNS

Golden, Idaho Springs, and Georgetown, Colorado

A handful of mining camps just west of Denver flourished with the Colorado Gold Rush of 1859. Today they make a charming driving circuit with great scenery and a hefty dose of pre-statehood Colorado history.

Golden, once the territorial capital, hosts the Colorado School of Mines and the Coors Brewing Company, founded in 1873 by 26-year-old Adolph Coors (originally Kohrs), which offers free guided tours of its facility as well as tastings. Golden is also home to the Buffalo Bill Museum and Grave, which preserves the memory of Bill Cody, who was born in Iowa in 1846 and became a Pony Express rider, cavalry scout, and ardent promoter of his touring Wild West Show. The small museum is full of Indian artifacts and Western memorabilia he collected, and the ride up to its location on Lookout Mountain alone is worth the trip.

Visit the old-fashioned town of Golden to see "Where the West Lives!"

The nearby picturesque Victorian village of Idaho Springs boomed when a major gold vein was found here. Look for the largest waterwheel in the state under Bridal Veil Falls across from City Hall, and try your hand at panning for gold at the Argo Gold Mine and Mill, which processed over $100 million worth of ore in its heyday when gold was $18–$35 an ounce. Southwest of Idaho Springs, the 49-mile Mount Evans Scenic and Historic Byway climbs 7,000 feet in just 28 miles before reaching Mount Evans Peak, at 14,265 feet.

Founded in 1864, Georgetown has preserved the narrow streets and Victorian buildings it had when it was "The Silver Queen of the Rockies." It brims with history, from the 1868 stone jail to the Hotel de Paris, built by a Frenchman during the silver mining boom and now a museum administered by the Colonial Dames of America. The Guanella Pass Scenic Byway winds for 22 miles along an old wagon route. Views of 14,278-foot Grays Peak and 14,275-foot Torreys Peak are possible year-round, and keep an eye out for bighorn sheep that sometimes create traffic jams.

WHERE: Golden is 15 miles west of Denver. *Visitor info:* Tel 866-674-9237 or 303-567-4660; clearcreekcounty.org. **COORS BREWING COMPANY:** Golden. Tel 800-642-6116 or 303-277-2337; coors.com. *When:* closed Tues–Wed. **BUFFALO BILL MUSEUM AND GRAVE:** Golden. Tel 303-526-0744; buffalobill.org. *When:* daily, May–Oct; closed Mon, Nov–Apr. **ARGO GOLD MINE AND MILL:** Idaho Springs. Tel 303-567-2421; historic argotours.com. **HOTEL DE PARIS MUSEUM:** Georgetown. Tel 303-569-2311; hoteldeparis museum.org. *When:* daily May–Sept; weekends Oct–Dec; by reservation Jan–Apr. **BEST TIME:** In the fall, Guanella Pass is one of the best places in the state to see the turning of the aspen leaves.

North America's Tallest Sand Dunes

GREAT SAND DUNES

Colorado

The Rocky Mountain State is famous for its alpine peaks, tumbling rivers, forested hillsides, and snowy winter vistas. What you don't expect to find here, a thousand miles from the ocean, are sand dunes. But in the south-central part of the state, there they are, up to 750 feet high, the tallest in North America. The shifting light paints them in different hues: gold, pink, tan, even blue.

Over 30 square miles of dunes have been shaped by the prevailing westerly winds streaming through the San Luis Valley. The 13,000-foot-high Sangre de Cristo Mountains act like a giant catcher's mitt, collecting sand deposited by creeks flowing out of the San Juan Mountains over the millennia. The recently established Great Sand Dunes National Preserve includes some of the highest peaks in the Rockies, alpine lakes, forests, wetlands, and tundra in addition to the dazzling dunes.

The snow-covered Sangre de Cristo Mountains rise above the Great Sand Dunes.

In other desert parks in the West you have to worry about leaving tracks, but not here: The wind will erase them within a day, sometimes within hours. There aren't any trails on the dunes themselves, so you're free to play Lawrence of Arabia for an afternoon or longer. It's not always that easy hiking—but the views from the tops of the highest dunes are worth it. (Stick to the ridges for easier going.) Foot and horse trails in the mountainous preserve climb to Medano Lake at 11,500 feet, as well as 11,380-foot Music Pass, with great views of Music Mountain (13,355 feet) and Tijeras Peak (13,604 feet). Keep hiking northwest from the pass to reach Upper and Lower Sand Creek Lakes in a magnificent alpine setting.

Of course, this is Colorado, so it was only a matter of time before someone tried to ski the dunes. Sandboarding, as this Sahara-meets-Steamboat pastime is called, is usually done on old snowboards and saucers on these lengthy slopes. It's an odd sight to see cars pull into the parking lot here with skis attached to the roof.

Where: 169 miles southwest of Colorado Springs. Tel 719-378-6399; nps.gov/grsa. **Best times:** mornings in spring and fall (afternoons can be windy).

Awe-Inspiring Cliff Dwellings in Desert Canyons

MESA VERDE

Colorado

L ocated in the area known as the Four Corners, where Colorado, New Mexico, Arizona, and Utah meet, Mesa Verde is the only national park in the U.S. devoted exclusively to archaeology: One glance at the intricately

constructed multistory homes in the rocky cliffs shows why. With close to 5,000 known archaeological sites, it's the largest such preserve in the U.S.

Members of the Ancestral Puebloan culture (sometimes still referred to as the Anasazi) that

flourished here between A.D. 600 and 1300 created astounding masonry buildings in alcoves in the canyon walls. Storage rooms and kivas, circular underground chambers, accompanied the living quarters. Many of the alcoves face south, allowing them to capture precious sunlight in winter and avoid the summer glare. Residents grew corn, beans, and squash using dryland farming techniques and left behind pottery painted with delicate geometric designs.

Descendants of Mesa Verde Ancestral Puebloans include the Hopi in Arizona and the 19 Rio Grande pueblos of New Mexico. Though well known to the neighboring Ute Mountain tribe, the empty dwellings went mostly unnoticed until local ranchers stumbled on them in 1888. The area was declared a park in 1906, and since then a handful of the 600 or so cliff dwellings in its 52,000 acres have been stabilized and opened to the public.

Cliff Palace, the jewel of the park, had over 150 rooms occupied by about 100 people at its peak. You'll have to get a ticket for a ranger-led tour of this and Balcony House, which requires climbing ladders and crawling through a 12-foot-long tunnel, the most challenging in the park. Both are on Chapin Mesa, as is Spruce Tree House (temporarily closed to the public at press time), with 130 rooms and eight kivas. Wetherill Mesa, named for the ranching family that first discovered and popularized the ruins, sees less traffic; here you'll find Long House, the park's second largest, open only to ranger-led tours.

The 6-mile Mesa Top Loop Road passes a number of interesting spots with easy access, including Cliff dwellings and overlooks. The only place to stay in the park is the modest Far View Lodge, where the restaurant offers pretty good Southwestern fare and a number of rooms have private porches and great views. They say that on a clear day you can see all four states that make up the Four Corners.

WHERE: 35 miles west of Durango. Tel 970-529-4465; nps.gov/meve. *When:* park open year-round, but certain sites open only Apr–Oct. **FAR VIEW LODGE:** Tel 800-449-2288 or 970-564-4300; visitmesaverde.com. *Cost:* from $110. *When:* late Apr–Oct. **BEST TIMES:** Apr–June and late Aug–Oct for fewer crowds; late May–early Sept for Wetherill Mesa; late May for annual Country Indian Arts Culture Festival; winter for cross-country skiing on the park's unplowed roads.

The Cliff Palace, the largest cliff dwelling in North America, was abandoned by A.D. 1300.

Mines and Mountains in Little Switzerland

MILLION DOLLAR HIGHWAY

Ouray and Silverton, Colorado

Nowadays the million dollars that it took to build this road isn't such a big deal, but in 1884, when the supply route connecting the tiny mining outposts of Ouray and Silverton was completed, that was a hefty sum.

The short but breathtaking road winds over the ore-rich San Juan Mountains, through tunnels, past waterfalls, and along the edge of wheel-clutching drop-offs. It is the spectacular highlight of the 236-mile San Juan Skyway, itself a gorgeous multiday drive through the alpine scenery north of Durango (see p. 712).

Start at the town of Silverton, connected to Durango by a historic narrow gauge railway (see p. 713) that is certainly the most entertaining way to get here. Among the lofty peaks are glimpses of the mines that once yielded gold, silver, zinc, lead, and copper until the last big mine closed in 1991. Now the town booms when wintertime visitors grab their skis and head to its simple but revered Silverton Mountain, and summertime tourists pour into town for its undeniable Old West atmosphere. Gunfights are authentically staged during the summer months when train riders briefly fill the town before getting back on board for the return to Durango. A local brass band plays old-time favorites. Silverton's most impressive throwback to bygone days is the red sandstone Wyman Hotel and Inn, with antiques-filled guest rooms and unusually sophisticated restaurant fare for a town whose population hovers around 630.

North of Silverton, the road becomes progressively steeper and more convoluted. Eight of the 23.5 miles to Ouray are considered the Million Dollar Highway proper, the brainchild of Otto Mears, who built supply roads to Colorado mining towns in the late 19th century. The historic toll road crosses Red Mountain Pass (11,018 feet) near rust-colored Red Mountain, a collapsed volcano that gave up $750 million worth of gold, silver, and other minerals. Mining ghost towns and log cabins dot the alpine scenery.

The last section through the narrow Uncompahgre Gorge, with its tunnels and waterfalls, is the most impressive, bringing you out above the archetypal Victorian mining town of Ouray, named for the great Ute chief and earnestly promoted today as "the Switzerland of America" (you'll see why when you visit Yankee Boy Basin). Mount Sneffels (14,157 feet) rises to the west of town in the center of its own wilderness area. Ouray is the perfect base to explore this gorgeous area: Strike off on the 6.2-mile round-trip hike to Oak Creek Overlook and a perfect lunch spot 2,400 feet above the trailhead, or, closer to town, let the crashing

The Million Dollar Highway cuts a scenic path through the densely forested San Juan Mountains.

Box Canyon Falls be your destination. Off-road enthusiasts arrive by the hundreds in September to drive over 500 miles of dirt roads through some spectacular scenery during the annual rally, earning Ouray the title "Jeeping Capital of the World." Jeep-rattled bones can be pampered at the sulfur-free Ouray Natural Hot Springs Pool, which promises a 96°F soak. The St. Elmo Hotel is an 1898 landmark with nine rooms that ooze historic charm. A mainstay for guests of the Victorian hostelry is the Bon Ton Restaurant next door specializing in Italian-influenced fare and understandably proud of its menu and extensive wine list that has won a whole cluster of awards.

WHERE: runs from Silverton (48 miles north of Durango) to Ouray (70 miles north of Durango). *Visitor info:* Tel 800-752-4494 or 970-387-5654; silvertoncolorado.com. **WYMAN HOTEL:** Silverton. Tel 800-609-7845 or 970-387-5372; thewyman.com. *Cost:* from $145. **OURAY NATURAL HOT SPRINGS POOL:** Tel 970-325-7073; ourayhotsprings.com. **ST. ELMO HOTEL AND BON TON RESTAURANT:** Durango. Tel 970-325-4951; stelmohotel.com. *Cost:* from $119 (off-peak), from $154 (peak); dinner $40. **BEST TIMES:** Jan for ice climbing at Ouray Ice Festival; summer for alpine flowers and scenery; Sept for Ouray Jeep Jamboree.

Where America the Beautiful Began

PIKES PEAK

Colorado

Colorado has the highest mean elevation of any state, with more than 1,000 Rocky Mountain peaks over 12,000 feet and a remarkable 54 peaks that tower above 14,000 feet, called "the 14'ers." But the state's most famous peak is not its highest—that would be Mount Elbert, at 14,433 feet the highest in the entire 1,800-mile swath of the Rockies and the second highest in the contiguous U.S. By far the most familiar of them all is Pikes Peak, at 14,115 feet just a smidgen lower, proudly jutting out of the plains above Colorado Springs. Named for explorer Zebulon Pike, who led the first nonnative attempt on the summit in 1806, the windy peak of pink granite inspired him to write in his journal after failing, "I believed no human being could have ascended to its pinical [sic]." The mountain became a symbol of the Gold Rush during the 19th century, when the slogan "Pikes Peak or Bust!" showed the determination of travelers heading west.

There are many ways to reach the top of "America's Mountain" today. Most direct is the 19-mile toll road, which crosses forests and tundra to reach the expansive view that is said to have inspired Katharine Lee Bates to write "America the Beautiful" after a wagon ride to the top in 1895. Every year the Pikes Peak International Hill Climb (the second oldest auto race in the U.S.) sees drivers and motorcyclists race up the road to the peak around hairpin curves without guardrails. Its other famous race to the top is nonmotorized—the Pikes Peak Marathon. Participants follow the Barr Trail, which offers the greatest base-to-base summit climb in the state as it gains over 7,815 feet in 13.3 miles.

The Pikes Peak Cog Railway, which opened in 1891, offers the same thrill without all the work. The Swiss-made railcars haul passenger cars up a 9-mile track with grades up to 25 percent past deep gorges, frothing streams, and stunning vistas. The trip includes a stop at the top for its arresting 360-degree views. On a clear day you can see the myriad peaks of the Rockies, and Denver, almost 70 miles away.

Nestled at the base of the landmark mountain is the lovely Victorian town Manitou Springs, named for the nine mineral springs that gave nearby Colorado Springs its name. The Cliff House at Pikes Peak is a Queen Anne Victorian built in 1873 on the site of an old stagecoach stop attracting guests who came for the mineral springs. "Celebrity suites" with two-person spa tubs bear the names of the famous guests who have stayed there, including Thomas Edison, Teddy Roosevelt, and Clark Gable. Dinner is the main event here, offering expertly prepared old favorites and wines from a celebrated cellar that augments the hotel's acclaim.

Admire the otherworldly sandstone formations in the Garden of the Gods.

Close by is the Garden of the Gods, a 1,335-acre regional park full of bizarre but beautiful rock formations of eroded red sandstone. Motorists can follow the road that loops around, through, and past such oddities as the Siamese Twins, the Three Graces, and Kissing Camels.

WHERE: 76 miles south of Denver. *Visitor info:* Tel 800-525-2250 or 719-685-5894; pikespeak.com. **COG RAILWAY:** Tel 719-685-5401;

cograilway.com. *Cost:* from $38 round-trip. *When:* May–early Mar. **THE CLIFF HOUSE:** Manitou Springs. Tel 888-212-7000 or 719-785-1000; thecliffhouse.com. *Cost:* from $145 (off-peak), from $199 (peak). **GARDEN OF THE GODS:** Tel 719-634-6666; gardenofgods.com. **BEST TIMES:** late June for the Broadmoor Pikes Peak International Hill Climb (ppihc.com); late Aug for the marathon (pikespeakmarathon.org).

A Natural High

ROCKY MOUNTAIN NATIONAL PARK

Colorado

Within 415 square miles and crossing three distinct ecosystems, Rocky Mountain National Park encapsulates everything that makes America's stony backbone special. Sparkling alpine streams, high-altitude glacial lakes, dense forests, and rugged peaks galore—the towering Long's Peak stands at 14,259 feet—are all part of Colorado's natural crown jewel. Most of the 3.5 million visitors who come every year start at the picture-perfect mountain town of Estes Park, 3 miles from the park's eastern edge. From here the

The park's rugged mountains and grassy meadows are home to a herd of about 3,000 elk.

only route through the park is the Trail Ridge Road, offering 48 miles of two-lane astonishment as it follows an old Indian path across the Continental Divide. Threading through a mountainous wonderland, it tops out at 12,183 feet before reaching Grand Lake, the park's western entrance.

In between are over 350 miles of hiking trails that lead to the park's splendid backcountry of meadows, surging streams, and waterfalls, and some of the park's 50 lakes. Bear Lake, served by a shuttle bus in season, is a popular starting point for the highly scenic trail to Emerald Lake; the hiking route to Glacier Gorge and the don't-miss Mills Lake Trail start nearby. The Continental Divide Trail (see p. 708), one of the country's most important long-distance treks, threads the park from north to south. Wildlife abounds, from elk, moose, and bighorn sheep (the park's unofficial emblem) to the elusive mountain lions, bears, and coyotes, and different wildflowers bloom every month from May through August.

While there aren't any accommodations inside the park, Estes Park is home to the Stanley Hotel, inspiration for Stephen King's 1977 classic *The Shining* (at the end of the season King and his wife Tabitha were the only guests in the hotel, and the entire book came to him while staying in room 217). This grand 1909 lodge (ask for a renovated room) sits on a promontory overlooking town and has historic ambience (including a ghost expert on staff—ask him about room 418) and sweeping views of Lake Estes. A more intimate experience awaits at the Romantic RiverSong Inn, with ten rooms set among 26 acres of pines and spruces. The amiable innkeepers are authorized to marry anyone interested; give it some thought during your outdoor massage by the mountain stream.

Where: Estes Park is 70 miles northwest of Denver. Tel 970-586-1206; nps.gov/romo. *When:* park, year-round; Trail Ridge Rd., late May–mid-Oct. **The Stanley Hotel:** Estes Park. Tel 800-976-1377 or 970-577-4000; stanleyhotel.com. *Cost:* from $239 (off-peak), from $329 (peak). **Romantic RiverSong Inn:** Estes Park. Tel 970-586-4666; romanticriver song.com. *Cost:* from $199. **Best times:** 4th of July for an old-fashioned celebration at the Stanley Hotel; July for Estes Park's Rooftop Rodeo and Parade (rooftoprodeo.com); mid-Sept–mid-Oct for elk viewing. Mid-June–mid-Aug is the park's busiest season.

Birthplace of Skiing in Colorado with an Old West Flair

STEAMBOAT SPRINGS

Colorado

T he place where it all started was named in the 1860s by French fur trappers who thought a hot spring near the Yampa River sounded like a steamboat coming up the river. The town of Steamboat Springs (population 12,088) began as a summer resort, but with the opening of Howelsen Hill in 1915 it became one of the first ski destinations in the state and the oldest in continuous operation. Equal parts ranching community and Ski Town, U.S.A. (its trademarked moniker), Steamboat built its main street wide to accommodate cattle drives. It's the hometown of more Winter Olympics athletes than any other place in the country, including Billy Kidd, the 1964 slalom silver medalist (the first American male to win an Olympic medal in alpine skiing). Now Steamboat's Director of Skiing, Kidd gives free pointers when he's on the slopes wearing his Stetson hat and trademark grin.

Steamboat sits at 6,732 feet in the Yampa River Valley, surrounded by the Medicine Bow/Routt National Forests and two wilderness areas, one of which rises to just over 12,000 feet. In addition to Howelsen Hill, with 4 lifts, 17 alpine trails, and 9 Nordic trails, there's the

Steamboat claims a total of 2,965 acres of skiable terrain, and its vertical rise of 3,668 feet is the third highest in Colorado.

much larger Steamboat Ski Resort 3 miles from town. Six peaks topped by 10,568-foot Mount Werner make up the resort where the term Champagne Powder was coined (and trade-marked); its much-ballyhooed eiderdown-soft snow is some of the best in the world. It's a friendly place void of day-tripping crowds, and you might easily find yourself alone on a tree run like Shadows or Twilight. With plenty of easy and intermediate terrain, and its pioneer-ing of kid-friendly programs, this is an American beauty everyone can enjoy.

It's no surprise that there are over 150 min-eral springs in the area, starting with the Old Town Hot Springs, which offers outdoor mineral pools, two 230-foot waterslides, and an aquatic climbing wall. Seven miles from town are the Strawberry Park Hot Springs, where you can enjoy 104°F springs in a more natural setting, camp, stay overnight in rustic cabins, and sit in an in-water massage called watsu.

The Steamboat Grand Hotel sits across from the resort gondola, and has a deluxe spa. But to better explore the cowboy life, head 18 miles out of town to Clark and the Home Ranch, a luxury dude ranch where haut moun-tain cuisine is served at communal tables and sweeping mountain views are just the start; choose between horseback riding and soaking in the private hot tub on your aspen-shaded porch, or repair indoors to your tastefully fit-ted lodge room, cabin, or bunk house which sleeps a family of six.

At the nearby Vista Verde Ranch, a well-known luxury contender, you'll feel more cat-tle baron than cowpoke (see Colorado Ranch Experience, p. 706).

WHERE: 156 miles northwest of Denver. *Visitor info:* Tel 970-879-0880; steamboat chamber.com. **HOWELSEN HILL:** Tel 970-879-8499. *Cost:* lift tickets from $25. *When:* ski sea-son Nov–Mar. **STEAMBOAT SKI RESORT:** Tel 800-922-2722 or 970-879-6111; steamboat .com. *Cost:* lift tickets from $149. *When:* ski season late Nov–early Apr. **OLD TOWN HOT SPRINGS:** Tel 970-879-1828; oldtownhotsprings .org. **STRAWBERRY PARK HOT SPRINGS:** Tel 970-879-0342; strawberryhotsprings.com. *Cost:* rooms from $70. **STEAMBOAT GRAND HOTEL:** Tel 970-871-5500; steamboatgrand.com. *Cost:* from $99 (off-peak), from $259 (peak). **HOME RANCH:** Clark. Tel 970-735-0750; homeranch.com. *Cost:* from $635 per night, 2-night minimum, all-inclusive (off-peak); from $6,960 per week, 7-night minimum, all-inclusive (peak). **BEST TIMES:** Jan–Feb for skiing; early Feb for Winter Carnival; late June–early July for wildflowers; early July for Hot Air Balloon Rodeo.

Epic Scenery and Skiing Second to None

TELLURIDE

Colorado

Start with one of the best-preserved silver mining towns in the state and perhaps the prettiest setting in the Rockies. Add an outstanding ski resort, season with a year-round roster of dazzling festivals and diversions, and you

have the truly unique place called Telluride. It all makes for a charming, interesting mix, with bluegrass fans mingling with celebrities like Oprah and Ralph Lauren fleeing the glitz of Aspen. Restored Victorian homes and chic boutiques stand in the shadow of steep moun-tains that rise from the edge of town. Things have definitely changed since Butch Cassidy robbed his first bank here in 1889.

A lot of folks rave about the summer's

stellar possibilities for hiking in these parts. But most are here for the skiing, and few go away disappointed. The Telluride Ski Resort has 18 lifts serving more than 2,000 skiable acres, including some of the steepest mogul fields you've ever seen, though the mountain's 147 trails offer plenty of opportunities for beginner and intermediate skiers. On a crystalline day, the aptly named See Forever, an intermediate run, boasts views as far as the red rock country near Moab (see p. 796).

A free 12-minute gondola ride, called "the most beautiful commute in America," connects the town with the European-style Mountain Village, full of luxury condos, shops, and restaurants. This is where you'll find the Peaks Resort & Spa, whose mineral pools and spa treatments will recharge you for the slopes tomorrow. Families love the two-story waterslide. Locals congregate downtown at places like the mining-era Last Dollar Saloon and the Fly Me to the Moon Saloon, with live music and what rumor says is a spring-loaded dance floor to put an extra bounce in your step.

Telluride has also successfully branded itself as the Festival Capital of the Rockies. Mountainfilm kicks things off in late May, and the Bluegrass Festival happens in June, followed by the diverse musical roster of the Jazz Celebration in early August. September brings another film festival, this one described by the late Roger Ebert as "like Cannes died and went to heaven," as well as the beer-and-music festivities of Blues & Brews later the same month. With so many events held here,

Spring in Telluride affords excellent hiking and jogging opportunities in the surrounding mountains.

the townsfolk understandably welcome the Telluride Nothing Festival.

WHERE: 111 miles north of Durango. *Visitor info:* Tel 888-605-2578 or 970-728-3041; visit telluride.com. **TELLURIDE SKI RESORT:** Tel 800-778-8581 or 970-728-6800; tellurideski resort.com. *Cost:* lift tickets $122. *When:* ski season late Nov–early Apr. **PEAKS RESORT:** Tel 888-696-6734 or 970-728-6800; thepeaks resort.com. *Cost:* from $189 (off-peak), from $349 (peak). **MOUNTAINFILM:** Tel 970-728-4123; mountainfilm.org. *When:* 4 days in late May. **BLUEGRASS FESTIVAL:** Tel 800-624-2422; bluegrass.com/telluride. *When:* 4 days in mid-June. **JAZZ CELEBRATION:** Tel 970-728-7009; telluridejazz.org. *When:* 3 days in early Aug. **FILM FESTIVAL:** Tel 510-665-9494; telluride filmfestival.org. *When:* 4 days in early Sept. **BLUES & BREWS FESTIVAL:** Tel 866-515-6166; tellurideblues.com. *When:* 3 days in mid-Sept. **BEST TIMES:** spring–fall for weather; June–Sept for cultural events.

Powder Bowls and Perfect Snow

VAIL

Colorado

The largest single ski resort in North America has over 10 square miles of skiable terrain—and what terrain it is. From manicured trails on the front side to the seemingly endless majesty of the world-famous Back Bowls,

Vail has something for everyone. The town itself, built in the 1960s, lacks the character of other Colorado ski towns, but visitors are here for the skiing, and for that they have one of the world's top five resorts. Vail possesses 31 lifts, including the biggest, fastest set of high-speed detachable quads on one mountain.

Seven natural bowls filled with dry, fluffy powder stretch over 7 miles wide on the backside of the mountain—a good-size resort in themselves. The Blue Sky Basin offers 645 more acres of gladed runs (and no groomed trails) in the wilderness, a quieter and more isolated experience.

Vail is also home to the Colorado Ski and Snowboard Museum Hall of Fame. Peruse a collection of artifacts and memorabilia from Colorado's 140-year history of skiing.

The deluxe Lodge at Vail, a Rock Resort, has the best slopeside location in town (and a steak house, Elway's, owned by former Denver Bronco John Elway). Another good choice

Vail boasts three distinct areas for skiers: four terrain parks, seven bowls, and more than 5,000 acres for freeriding.

is the Sonnenalp Hotel in Vail Village. A full-service spa, a riverside pool, and 127 rooms and luxury suites create an atmosphere of Old World charm that might have you wondering how it is you woke up in the Alps.

Beaver Creek Resort is close enough to Vail to ski one in the morning and the other in the afternoon. Beaver Creek offers 150 trails across three mountains. It brings to mind a sheltered town in the Alps. The Ritz-Carlton Bachelor Gulch, named for a group of old fogeys who settled here in the early 1900s, centers on a grand timber lodge designed like those in Yellowstone and Yosemite. The ski-in/ski-out place has plenty of fireplaces to keep it cozy and a 21,000-square-foot spa with three rock-lined grottoes and a river hot tub to keep its guests happy.

WHERE: 100 miles west of Denver. **VAIL MOUNTAIN RESORT:** Tel 800-842-8062 or 970-476-9090; vail.com. *Cost:* lift tickets $175. **COLORADO SKI AND SNOWBOARD MUSEUM:** Tel 970-476-1876; skimuseum.net. **LODGE AT VAIL:** Tel 888-328-1005 or 970-429-5044; lodgeatvail.rockresorts.com. *Cost:* from $139 (off-peak), from $464 (peak). **SONNENALP:** Tel 866-284-4411 or 970-476-5656; sonnenalp.com. *Cost:* suites from $265 (off-peak), from $510 (peak). **BEAVER CREEK:** Tel 800-842-8062 or 970-476-9090; beavercreek.com. *Cost:* lift tickets from $175. **RITZ-CARLTON BACHELOR GULCH:** Avon. Tel 800-241-3333 or 970-748-6200; ritzcarlton.com. *Cost:* from $199 (off-peak), from $549 (peak). **BEST TIME:** ski season mid-Nov–early Apr.

Party Arty

BURNING MAN

Black Rock City, Nevada

Don't worry if you can't find Black Rock City on a map. It exists for only a few short days—erected on a playa, a dried-up lake bed, in the middle of the scorching Nevada desert. But for its self-proclaimed citizens, it is its own universe and the place they consider home. It is the setting for Burning Man, a weeklong art project/installation/festival that celebrates art, survival, and life—and the opportunity for some 65,000 fierce individualists to go crazy.

The first "Man" was burned on a beach in San Francisco by friends Larry Harvey and Jerry James on June 21, 1986. What started as an act of "radical self-expression" soon evolved into a participatory event that outgrew its original northern California location. In 1991, the organizers moved to the wide-open isolation of Nevada's Black Rock City, and a tradition was born. Every year, creative, free-spirited souls, hippies, artists, punks, bikers, and dreamers descend on the playa and erect their temporary city. And then they have at it, trying to outdo last year and each other. There's art, art, and more art, throughout the theme camps, on the vehicles, and even on the flamboyantly embellished bodies of the participants. There are bicycles made to look like dinosaurs, evil clowns, nudie shows, goddess offerings.

Each year the festival has a theme (such as 2015's Carnival of Mirrors). But at the end of the day, anything goes—provided you adhere to the cooperative community spirit (Black Rock City works strictly on the barter and volunteer system) and you don't harm the environment. Anything you need—from shelter to water to food to art supplies—must be brought in or bartered for. In between, you can do what you like. And boy, do they ever. This is not for the prudish or nervous; some wild stuff goes on in the desert night. And yet participants, many of whom go year after year, report very little other than kindness, silliness, and great inspiration.

The peak (though it takes place on the penultimate night) is the burning of the "Man," a four-story wooden figure erected with great care, only to be destroyed in an act of sacrifice and acknowledgment of the fleetingness of art and life itself. Then the Tribe of the Burning Man returns to what clansmen call the "default world," already planning for next year.

WHERE: 120 miles north of Reno. Tel 415-TO-FLAME; burningman.com. *Cost:* from $390, includes entrance fee and a campsite. *When:* late Aug–early Sept.

Where Have All the Cowboys Gone?

COWBOY CULTURE

Nevada

The American cowboy is the very symbol of American spirit, strong and proud. Embodied on the silver screen by everyone from John Wayne and Alan Ladd to Clint Eastwood and Robert Duvall, he is the essential masculine hero figure. Today's Wild, Wild West is not so wild anymore, and in Nevada you have to drive past miles of strip malls and gigantic casinos to find the last vestiges of the cowboy. But cowboy culture is alive and kicking in Las Vegas during the National Finals Rodeo—the World Series and Rose Bowl of rodeos and the largest event of its kind in the world. Selling to standing-room-only crowds since the '70s, the NFR attracts some 170,000 people over 10 days (with more than 8 million tuning in on TV) as the top 15 competitors in each of professional rodeo's seven events (saddle bronc riding, bull riding, bareback riding, calf roping, team roping, steer wrestling, and barrel racing) compete for prize money in excess of $10 million. Meanwhile, clubs and concert halls fill with the best country-and-western performers, and you'll see big hats and big belt buckles on folks four-deep at the blackjack tables.

The Reno Rodeo is one of the feeder events for the NFR, held every June in "the biggest little city in the world," since 1919 (the oldest rodeo is in Prescott, Arizona; see p. 693). Reno's event, though not as attention-grabbing as the Vegas finals, has an authentic vibe; most of the competitors, and much of the audience, come from Nevada, Wyoming, Idaho, and Montana. It features all the riding and bronc bustin' you'd expect, plus a carnival, drill team competitions, an Xtreme Bulls event, and a cattle drive.

Poetry has helped keep cowboy mythology alive, hence the National Cowboy Poetry Gathering, a get-together that originated in 1985 and now boasts more than 6,000 out-of-town participants during a weeklong celebration of the rural American West. Held in Elko, 290 miles northeast of Reno, in late January or early February—the only time cowboying really slows down—it may well be one of the most famous poetry gatherings in the world. Featuring readings, musical jamborees, storytelling, films, photography, food, and cowboy poets from many countries, the gathering pays homage to the culture and the people who created it, and has spawned dozens of such events throughout the U.S. and Canada.

NATIONAL FINALS RODEO: Las Vegas. nfr experience.com. *Cost:* from $64. *When:* for 10 days, from the 1st Fri in Dec. **RENO RODEO:** Tel 775-329-3877. *Cost:* from $13. *When:* 2nd and 3rd weeks of June for 8–10 days. **COWBOY POETRY GATHERING:** Elko. Tel 888-880-5885 or 775-738-7508; westernfolklife.org. *When:* about 1 week in late Jan or early Feb.

Heaven on Earth

LAKE TAHOE

Nevada and California

The stunning alpine Lake Tahoe is known as the Jewel of the Sierra. Its deep sapphire blue water surrounded by the soaring, snowcapped mountains forms a postcard vista that leaves visitors convinced of a higher power.

It is one of the largest (192 square miles and boasting its own Coast Guard), deepest (only Oregon's Crater Lake is deeper; see p. 870), and, at 6,229 feet, highest lakes in America.

Covering more than 17,520 skiable acres along both sides of the Nevada and California border, the Lake Tahoe region is best known as one of the nation's premier ski destinations, with more resorts and terrain than any other on the continent. Seven skiing and snowboarding resorts offer world-class accommodations and runs that range from bunny hills to those requiring Olympian skills, all enhanced by an average annual snowfall that ranks among the deepest in the world and 44 weeks of sunshine a year (see Skiing Northern California, p. 859). A beauty for all seasons, Lake Tahoe is also a destination for all interests. Gambling aficionados will find several major resort-hotel-casinos on the Nevada side, including Montbleu Resort Casino and Spa and Harrah's. But few will resist getting outdoors to explore what proves to be one big photo opportunity.

The tourist industry is not exaggerating when it speaks of "the most beautiful drive in America," the 25-mile Lake Tahoe–East Shore Drive (Highways 50 and 28 between Stateline and Incline Village) that winds along the footprint of the lake with water vistas on one side and mountain views on the other.

Those in shape should park the car and take to the Tahoe Rim Trail, a 165-mile-long, 24-inch single-track trail that encircles the entire lake (it can be accessed at 16 different points). Whether you're on foot, horseback, or mountain bike, it's one of the most beautiful lakeside excursions anywhere. Those who manage to do the whole thing (all at once or in sections) can join the 165 Mile Club, and be rewarded with a patch, a certificate, and a shout-out in the club's book and website.

WHERE: 187 miles northeast of San Francisco. *Visitor info:* Tel 530-541-5255; tahoeinfo.com. **TAHOE RIM TRAIL:** tahoerimtrail.org. **WHERE TO STAY:** Resort at Squaw Creek, Olympic Valley, CA. Tel 800-327-3353

or 530-583-6300; squawcreek.com. *Cost:* from $254. **BEST TIMES:** Nov–Feb for skiing; July and Aug for finest summer conditions.

Lake Tahoe is picture-perfect from every angle.

The Four Queens of Las Vegas

BELLAGIO, WYNN LAS VEGAS, CAESARS PALACE, AND THE MIRAGE

Las Vegas, Nevada

Picking one fabulous hotel in a sea of fabulous hotels is a little like picking a favorite card from the deck of fifty-two. Forced to narrow it down, you'll find that what remains is royalty—the most grand, most delirious, most wonderfully archetypal Las Vegas casino resorts to make any monarch proud.

The Bellagio Hotel and Casino remains the indisputable queen of diamonds, an imposing Italianate palazzo named after its storied namesake on Lake Como, floating here on its own 8.5-acre man-made lake. It somehow manages to be over-the-top yet dwells within the bounds of good taste—something of a rarity in a city that is a paean to glitz and glam. With more than 3,000 sumptuously furnished guest rooms, one of the largest casinos in town, and some of the best restaurants in the city, it was the most expensive hotel ever constructed at the time it was built,

with a price tag exceeding $1.6 billion. You will forget you are in a desert when you see the outdoor Fountains of Bellagio, more than 1,200 water cannons choreographed to create a liquid ballet, the best free show in town.

The queen of clubs is typified by Wynn Las Vegas: Staying here (or at its sister hotel, Encore) makes you feel like part of an exclusive members-only society. Steve Wynn, the hotel impresario who built Bellagio, added another billion to his previous record and came up with this sensually curved bronze skyscraper looming large over its neighbors. Packed with every luxury imaginable, from high-tech-gadget–embellished rooms and a bevy of elegant restaurants, it even boasts its own man-made mountain and a fountain that empties into a 3-acre lake. A highlight of its countless amenities is Wynn Golf and Country Club, boasting a Tom Fazio–designed course. Right on the Las Vegas Strip, the course is restricted to very lucky hotel guests.

Caesars Palace has everything a gaudy Las Vegas hotel should have in (a queen of) spades. Originally built in 1966, it has had several billion dollars' worth of upgrades and additions that have kept its profile high and polished enough to keep up with the newcomers, turning what was once a kitschy Roman wonderland into a gleaming, well, palace.

Finally, the queen of hearts goes to The Mirage Hotel and Casino for its special place in the zeitgeist of Las Vegas. Also built by Steve Wynn and setting a new standard for Vegas hotels, its white-and-gold towers soar from the desert like the oasis evoked by its name. It is an escapist property, with a lush indoor rain forest of lagoons and waterfalls and palm trees soaring 60 feet beneath a glass dome. Where else would you expect to find one of Las Vegas's signature attractions, a faux volcano that erupts every 15 minutes? When the Mirage arrived on

Bellagio (left) and Caesars Palace (right) are two of Las Vegas's most renowned hotels.

the scene in 1989, it changed everything for Las Vegas, and none of the other queens would exist today without it.

BELLAGIO: Tel 888-987-6667 or 702-693-7111; bellagio.com. *Cost:* from $159 (off-peak), from $239 (peak). **WYNN LAS VEGAS:** Tel 888-320-9966 or 702-770-7123; wynnlasvegas.com. *Cost:* from $209 (off-peak), from $399 (peak). **CAESARS PALACE:** Tel 866-227-5938 or 702-731-7110; caesars.com. *Cost:* from $132 (off-peak), from $249 (peak). **THE MIRAGE:** Tel 800-374-9000 or 702-791-7111; mirage.com. *Cost:* from $99 (off-peak), from $179 (peak). **BEST TIMES:** Apr or Oct for weather.

Putting the Awe Back in Awesome

CIRQUE DU SOLEIL

Las Vegas, Nevada

For some years now, the Canadian performance troupe Cirque du Soleil has been transforming the age-old concept of big-top circus acts, elevating it to a new level of entertainment. Cirque du Soleil was founded in 1984 by

Montreal street performers Guy Laliberté and Daniel Gauthier. Mixing traditional circus components with dramatic visual artistry and eliminating animal acts entirely, the pair began a series of unique traveling shows that grew steadily in popularity. But it was in 1993,

with the opening of the show *Mystère*, that Cirque du Soleil rocketed into another dimension of success. Las Vegas is now home to seven permanent, multimillion-dollar Cirque productions that take the original Cirque concept ever higher, thanks to no-expense-spared production values and the potential these specially built theaters guarantee.

Expect eye-popping sets, evocative (and occasionally perplexing) performance-art pieces, plus a wide array of extraordinarily talented acrobats, aerialists, and gymnasts from around the globe. Any of the heady concoctions produces gasps, laughs, and even tears, sending audiences to the exits feeling exhilarated and enhanced: Such is the value of watching performers do the well-nigh impossible.

In *O*, acts of all kinds take place in, around, and above a 1.5-million-gallon water tank, from diving to synchronized swimming and beyond, creating a montage of floating carousel horses, otherworldly characters, and surreal beauty.

KÀ breaks the mold by giving masterful physical feats a context via a full-blown story line of young twins born in ancient Asia and separated by tribal wars. They attempt to find each other as they swim through raging seas, scale steep mountainsides, swing through jungles, and fly through the skies. The staging borders on epic, with a massive rotating, tilting, and telescoping platform providing a variety of backdrops for a series of martial-arts battles in the style of *Crouching Tiger, Hidden Dragon*.

For "another side of Cirque du Soleil" check out *Zumanity*, the first adult-themed cabaret-style production at the New York–New York Hotel & Casino. You must be 18 to attend this "human zoo," presented in an intimate theater where you can buy sofa tickets for two.

LOVE, a blend of Cirque du Soleil magic and Beatles music at The Mirage, and *Michael Jackson: One* at Mandalay Bay are two of the latest productions.

MYSTÈRE: Treasure Island. Tel 800-944-7444 or 702-894-7722; treasureisland.com. *Cost:* from $75. *When:* Sat–Wed. **O:** Bellagio. Tel 888-488-7111 or 702-693-7111; bellagio.com. *Cost:* from $99. *When:* Wed–Sun. **KÀ:** MGM Grand. Tel 877-880-0880 or 702-531-3826; mgmgrand.com. *Cost:* from $75. *When:* Sat–Wed. **ZUMANITY:** New York–New York Hotel & Casino. Tel 866-606-7111 or 702-740-6815; newyorknewyork.com. *Cost:* from $69. *When:* Fri–Tues. **LOVE:** Mirage. Tel 800-963-9634 or 702-792-7777; mirage.com. *Cost:* from $101. *When:* Thurs–Mon. **MICHAEL JACKSON: ONE:** Mandalay Bay. Tel 877-632-7400 or 702-632-7580; mandalaybay.com. *Cost:* from $69. *When:* Fri–Tues. **BEST TIMES:** anytime except Dec and early Jan, when the shows generally take several weeks off.

KÀ is unique among Cirque du Soleil shows for its fully developed narrative, blending circus acts with more traditional storytelling.

Vegas Food Is Haute, Haute, Haute!

DINING IN LAS VEGAS

Las Vegas, Nevada

Long gone are the days when Las Vegas dining consisted of cheap buffets of uninspired foods to fuel another round at the slot machines. Now no celebrity chef's empire is complete without a presence in the Vegas arena, usually ensconced in an over-the-top, budget-be-damned showcase. When multi-Michelin-starred chef extraordinaire Joel Robuchon sets up shop, you know the Vegas food scene has not only arrived but is taking on all comers. True, the celebrity chefs aren't always, or even often, physically present in their Vegas kitchens, but they all maintain long-distance eagle-eyed control and have confidently placed superb chefs in their stead. The result: Dining in Vegas is as good as anywhere in the nation—some say the best.

Guy Savoy has long been considered a high priest of French cuisine, and while the tasting menus at his eponymously named restaurant at Caesars Palace are not cheap, they raise the bar of dining in Vegas to quasi-perfection. Hubert Keller's Fleur in Mandalay Place offers global small plates (such as beef tartare tacos, smoked duck terrine, and rock shrimp gnocchi) that are sophisticated but unintimidating. At Costa di Mare in Wynn Las Vegas, you can dine outdoors in a cushy cabana by the lake-style fountain. Chef Mark LoRusso specializes in basic grilled Italian seafood, using fish that is flown in daily from the Mediterranean.

If your credit cards aren't yet maxed out, try any of these top restaurants: the multi-course prix-fixe wonders prepared nightly by Julian Serrano (and yes, this chef is in the kitchen!) as you dine under the gaze of the Picassos that give his restaurant its name (Picasso, at Bellagio); the two exquisite restaurants by the Michelin-starred chef Joel Robuchon (L'Atelier de Joel Robuchon and Joel Robuchon, both in the MGM Grand); or the perfect French bistro food deftly prepared at Thomas Keller's Bouchon (in the Venetian).

What about those buffets? They're still there, and thanks to Vegas's upscale dining trend, better than ever. In fact, they often nail a two-thumbs-up rating for quality (and awesome quantity). The uncontested champion is the Buffet at Wynn, a thoughtful, artful atrium with everything from Kansas City-style barbecue to jerk chicken and five kinds of seviche. And unlike most Vegas buffets, it's actually worth saving room for dessert, with an active pastry chef on the premises turning out unexpected treats like mini floating islands and light-as-air madeleines. The runner-up is Le Village Buffet, at Paris, where stations represent regions of France (such as Burgundy and Provence) with an impressive array of dishes to match. Made-to-order crepes and Bananas Foster promise a grand finale at the Brittany dessert station.

Guy Savoy: Caesars Palace. Tel 702-731-7286; caesars.com. *Cost:* $210. **Fleur:** Mandalay Place. Tel 702-632-7200; hubert keller.com. *Cost:* $65. **Costa di Mare:** Wynn Las Vegas. Tel 877-321-9966 or 702-770-3305; wynnlasvegas.com. *Cost:* dinner $85. **Buffet at Wynn:** Tel 702-770-3340; wynn lasvegas.com. *Cost:* dinner $39. **Le Village Buffet:** Paris Las Vegas. Tel 702-946-7000; caesars.com. *Cost:* dinner $31.

From Highbrow to Lowbrow and Everything in Between

Las Vegas Culture

Las Vegas, Nevada

Defining "culture" in Las Vegas requires a paraphrase of the adage: It's not easy to say what it is, but you'll know it when you see it. The days of nonstop tackiness are waning, as some of the cheese factor is replaced with honest-to-goodness art and sophistication. But the visitor in the mood for some classic American kitsch or a slice of naughty indulgence needn't look far.

Those seeking high-minded pursuits can try one of the many art galleries and museums dotting the city. Visit the Bellagio Gallery of Fine Art to see a small but top-drawer collection featuring some of the finest of fine art. Step out of casino-fueled bustle into a serene enclave where rotating

The Bellagio Gallery of Fine Art displays several paintings by Impressionist masters.

shows include works by masters such as Renoir, Degas, and Picasso. The Neon Museum's goal is to collect, preserve, and exhibit iconic Las Vegas signs, and this museum's outdoor space known as The Neon Boneyard has some doozies. Guides explain the evolution of the art from the 1930s to the present.

The classic "showgirl" experience is alive and well in Vegas, evolving into a rebirth of burlesque. Not that the traditional shows, replete with sparkly costumes, big headdresses, and bare breasts, have disappeared. Of a number of clubs featuring scantily clad ladies strutting their stuff, the best are Absinthe at Caesars Palace, equal parts

cabaret and circus with aerial and acrobatic entertainment, and the high-energy and relatively more wholesome Pin Up at the Stratosphere. Their noble attempt to transcend the strip club factor by keeping the naughtiest body parts covered while still ramping up the titillation factor results in far more sophisticated productions and classier dames.

Visitor info: Tel 877-VISIT-LV or 702-892-7575; visitvegas.com. **Bellagio Gallery of Fine Art:** Tel 888-488-7111 or 702-693-7871; bellagio.com. **Neon Museum:** Tel 702-387-6366; neonmuseum.com. **Absinthe:** Tel 800-745-3000; absinthevegas.com. **Pin Up:** Tel 702-380-7777; stratospherehotel.com. **Best times:** Aug and Dec for smaller crowds.

Where Megawatt Crass Marries Nouveau Class

THE LAS VEGAS STRIP

Las Vegas, Nevada

The 4-mile stretch of Las Vegas Boulevard known as the Strip is the world capital of glitter, festooned with pleasure palaces, quick-hitch wedding chapels, and cheap all-you-can-eat buffets—and, of course, it's alive with

gambling, anytime, any kind, and everywhere. This is where Bugsy Siegel laid down the law

and the Rat Pack laid down the style; where Howard Hughes hid out and where Elvis made his last stand. But, maybe sadly, all that is changing. The tacky wackiness is slowly ceding ground to top-of-the-line luxury, defined more by marble and earth tones than faux-crystal chandeliers and neon.

The good news is the metamorphosis is gradual and much of the Strip is still all about brashness. Take a drive (preferably with the top down and Sinatra blasting) and soak in the sights and the possibilities of its flashy parade of iconic hotels-cum-casinos: Luxor is the hulking black pyramid with a replica of the Sphinx out front and even more oversized Egyptian embellishments inside. Giant bronze lions guard the entrance to the MGM Grand, the third largest hotel in the world, with more than 6,800 rooms and a sprawling casino. Yes, Virginia, that is a roller coaster barreling at 70 mph through the Big Apple skyline at New York–New York. And, *oui*, Virginia, that is a half-scale copy of the Eiffel Tower at Paris Las Vegas. Gondolas run through canals both in front of and inside the Grand Canal Shoppes of the Venetian, and crowning it all is the Stratosphere, the tallest observation tower west of the Mississippi at more than 1,000 feet, with controlled freefall sky jumps from the 108th floor.

Venture past the theoretical northern border of the Strip to find the vestiges of the tacky Las Vegas of yore, including miles of hitching

The neon lights of the Las Vegas Strip are especially dazzling at night.

posts like the busy Little Chapel of the Flowers, which, along with the more than three dozen other Strip chapels, account for over 80,000 marriages every year.

It's all dazzling and unabashedly artificial, a 24/7 place where only the money is real and if the crowds in the casino are too big at 2 A.M., that just means one thing: It's time to go shopping. You gotta love this place.

Visitor info: Tel 877-VISIT-LV or 702-892-0711; lasvegas.com. **Best time:** June–Aug is hot, but offer the best hotel rates.

Man-Made Water Wonders in the Desert

Hoover Dam, Lake Mead, and Lake Las Vegas

Near Las Vegas, Nevada

Several of the most popular and scenic destinations in this rugged and arid corner of southwest Nevada involve water and were made by man, not nature. Hoover Dam has long been considered one of the greatest engineering marvels of the 20th century, an icon of modernist architecture. Built between 1931 and 1936, and named after Herbert Hoover, who was instrumental in its creation, the massive 726-foot gravity-arch dam (the second-highest in the U.S.) harnessed the Colorado River. In doing so it provided the irrigation, electricity, and flood control that helped create the population boom of the American Southwest. Restrictions may limit what visitors see and do at the dam, but it's still one of those sights that takes your breath away. Just try peering over the edge.

The construction of the dam created the second man-made wonder directly behind it—Lake Mead. Backing up more than 100 miles behind the dam, it is the largest man-made lake in the U.S. and as a national recreation area encompasses nearly 1.5 million acres. It is a paradise for lovers of recreation and nature, with boating, skiing, fishing, hiking, camping, and some of the most beautiful flora and fauna anywhere in the country. The northern arm of Lake Mead is bordered by the Valley of Fire State Park, a dramatic moonscape created by erosion of the highly oxidized landscape over a couple millennia, leaving behind alien and wholly unexpected rock formations in blazing, fiery colors. Highway 169 is known as the Valley of Fire Highway and offers eye-riveting vistas from the comfort of your air-conditioned vehicle.

Another far smaller dam was built between 1988 and 1991 on a tributary feeding into Lake Mead, creating Lake Las Vegas. Most of its allure centers on the respected championship golf courses and the mini-oases that surround the lake and its picturesque marina. Where scorched desertscape once sprawled not long ago, impeccable homes now blend with luxe resort accommodations, pampering spas, high-end shopping, and the prerequisite casino. It has everything you might want from a Las Vegas visit—without the hectic hustle.

WHERE: 17 to 35 miles southeast of Las Vegas. *Hoover Dam info:* Tel 702-494-2517; usbr.gov/lc/hooverdam. *Lake Mead info:* Tel 702-293-8990; nps.gov/lake. *Lake Las Vegas info:* lakelasvegas.com. **BEST TIMES:** Apr–May and Sept–Oct for weather.

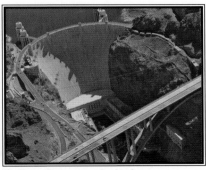

The Hoover Dam was completed in five years, two years ahead of schedule.

The Biggest Little City in the World

RENO

Nevada

Believe it or not, Reno used to be the biggest gambling destination in the world. But then a little town called Las Vegas took off, and Reno became more of an afterthought in the minds of people bent on spending their nest egg at a craps table. Too bad, really, because while Reno may not have the glitz and glamour of Las Vegas, neither does it have the high prices, snobbery, and the crushing crowds.

Sprawling across the foothills of the majestic Sierra Nevada mountain range and with the snow-fed Truckee River flowing through its center, Reno certainly beats Las Vegas when it comes to scenic vistas. And downtown hews more closely to a "swingers" hipster vibe than anything you can find on the Strip these days. There are more than a dozen major hotel-casinos along Virginia Street, many with brand names like Harrah's, Circus-Circus, Atlantis, Nugget, and the Sand's. Each comes with the typical gaming amenities one would expect to find in a Nevada casino, often with lower limits and lower prices for everything from the hotel rooms to dinner.

Without the roller coasters or headline shows that draw the crowds in Vegas, Reno goes out of its way to offer the kinds of events, festivals, and attractions that are more closely associated with small-town America. You'll find a satisfying arts district along the river; several major museums, including the Nevada Museum of Art and the Fleischmann Planetarium and Science Center; film and theater festivals; and cultural events, including an annual Basque Festival celebrating the legacy, food, and music of the early settlers from that region of Spain.

In general Reno is a much friendlier, more laid-back place than Las Vegas, allowing for a more relaxed getaway that still provides plenty to see and do. Find out why the town calls itself the "Biggest Little City in the World."

WHERE: 447 miles northwest of Las Vegas. *Visitor info:* Tel 800-FOR-RENO or 775-827-7600; visitrenotahoe.com. **NEVADA MUSEUM OF ART:** Tel 775-329-3333; nevadaart.org. *When:* closed Mon–Tues. **FLEISCHMANN PLANETARIUM AND SCIENCE CENTER:** Tel 775-784-4812; planetarium.unr.nevada.edu. **BEST TIME:** July for the Basque Festival (renobasqueclub.org).

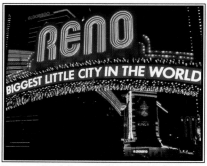

Downtown Reno's famous arch over Virginia Street

Surreal Sand Dunes, Airpower, and Atomic History

WHITE SANDS NATIONAL MONUMENT

Alamogordo, New Mexico

One of the stranger sights in a state full of oddities fills the Tularosa Basin, just west of Alamogordo: the world's largest field of gypsum sand dunes (most desert sands are composed of quartz), blinding white and ringed by the San Andres and Sacramento mountains. The snow-colored dunes cover 275 square miles of the Chihuahuan Desert, and are constantly changing as they are moved by the steady southwest winds.

A large part of the dune field is a national monument, with a visitors center and an

8-mile scenic Dunes Drive. Walk ten minutes from the road in just about any direction, and suddenly all you can see are chalk-white dunes, some as high as 60 feet, mountains shimmering on the horizon, and the blue bowl of sky. No wonder aliens chose nearby Roswell to visit (see p. 744). More adventurous visitors can hike farther into the backcountry to camp.

One of the best ways to see the dunes is in moonlight. The road is kept open for bicyclists on one full-moon night each in the spring and fall, when the dunes glow as if lit from within, and ranger-led full-moon hikes take place from May through October. Since the monument is sandwiched between the army's White Sands Missile Range and the Holloman Air Force Base, strange shapes soar overhead quite often.

Another singular site awaits at the northern end of the missile range. At 5:30 A.M. Mountain War Time on July 16, 1945, the skies over the sand dunes were lit by a new sun, as the world's first atomic bomb test went off. The Trinity Site, marked by a stone tower, historical photos, and the casing from the "Fat Man" bomb (dropped on Nagasaki) is now open to the public twice a year. Trinitite—desert sand fused into greenish glass—can sometimes be

spotted, but is still radioactive and must not be picked up. Visitors can stand on the very spot where Manhattan Project scientists from nearby Los Alamos (see p. 742) ushered in the end of WWII and the beginning of the Atomic Age. Concerned about radiation? You receive three times as much during a typical coast-to-coast airline flight as you will during a one-hour visit here.

WHERE: 209 miles south of Albuquerque. Tel 505-679-2599; nps.gov/whsa. **TRINITY SITE:** wsmr.army.mil/PAO/Trinity/Pages/Home .aspx. *When:* 1st Sat in Apr and Oct. **BEST TIMES:** full-moon nights year-round; early morning or early evening for summer hikes.

The wind creates beautiful ripple patterns on the dunes of White Sands National Monument.

The Friendly Skies

ALBUQUERQUE INTERNATIONAL BALLOON FIESTA

Albuquerque, New Mexico

A t roughly the size of a house, the average hot-air balloon is mighty impressive. Now imagine more than 500 of them all around you, slowly inflating and lifting off into the sky like the preamble to the

world's biggest birthday party. This is the Albuquerque International Balloon Fiesta, the world's largest hot-air balloon rally. It's

impossible not to get swept away by the color and excitement, even if it is near dawn and freezing cold.

Held every year since 1972, the Balloon Fiesta draws more than 950,000 people, who wander among the balloons on the 80-acre launch field and chat with the pilots as they prepare for liftoff. Nearly every morning of the ten-day event sees a dawn patrol—selected balloons launch before sunrise, glowing like giant lightbulbs—a little later comes a mass ascension of all the balloons, a wondrous two-hour polychromatic spectacle. Some pilots compete in events such as key-grabs (which involves fetching a set of keys from the top of a tall pole) and distance competitions, and two mornings feature Special Shape Rodeos, when balloons in fanciful forms such as mushrooms, witches, cows, and stagecoaches are launched. Arrive early—perhaps 5:30 A.M. on weekends—to beat the ever-growing crowds, and feel like you're 12 years old again.

Learn more about the technology and history of the sport at the Anderson-Abruzzo Albuquerque International Balloon Museum. There's a tethered balloon ride out back, but if you just have to get up in the air for real, Rainbow Ryders offers balloon rides year-round.

Another option for gaining altitude is the Sandia Peak Tram, which at 2.7 miles long is billed as the world's longest tramway. It runs from the northeast corner of the city to 10,378 feet at the top of the Sandia Mountains, with a panorama overlooking northern New Mexico. At the top of the tram you can hike on trails

The hundreds of balloons rising during one of the fiesta's mass ascensions is truly a sight to behold.

above the precipitous west face of the granite-topped range. Grab a bite at the High Finance Restaurant and Tavern, where you can enjoy a prime rib sandwich and local microbrew with your view.

Where: Balloon Fiesta Park. Tel 888-422-7277 or 505-821-1000; balloonfiesta .com. *When:* 9 days in early Oct. **Balloon Museum:** Tel 505-768-6020; balloonmuseum .com. *When:* closed Mon. **Rainbow Ryders:** Tel 800-725-2477 or 505-823-1111; rainbow ryders.com. *Cost:* balloon rides $195, includes continental breakfast and champagne toast; from $325 during Fiesta. **Sandia Peak Tram:** Tel 505-856-7325; sandiapeak.com. **High Finance Restaurant:** Tel 505-243-9742. *Cost:* lunch $20.

Ancients, Aliens, and Six Old Soreheads

Aztec

New Mexico

The Navajo Indians called the spot Totah, "the place where the three rivers meet," referring to the junction of the La Plata, Animas, and San Juan Rivers. Today, the most interesting destination in this fertile northwest corner of New Mexico is a town where visitors are greeted with a sign that reads, "Welcome to Aztec: Home to 6,800 Friendly People and 6 Old Soreheads."

Named—incorrectly, by the early Anglo settlers—after the supposed builders of pre-Columbian ruins on its outskirts, this quirky town is now the home of Aztec Ruins National Monument, where you can explore 400 meticulously constructed rooms around an open plaza by means of a half-mile paved trail. The ruins were built and occupied between A.D. 1100 and 1300 by the Ancestral Puebloans, and boast the largest reconstructed Great Kiva of its kind (over 40 feet in diameter), a partially buried ceremonial chamber lit by shafts of sunlight and full of the spirits of the people who walked here 900 years ago.

Many buildings in Aztec's downtown area were built in the Victorian style near the turn of the 20th century. One of the Four Corners' most

The Great Kiva at Aztec Ruins National Monument was probably used for communal activities and ceremonies.

unusual overnight experiences lies 12 miles southwest of Aztec near the town of Farmington: Kokopelli's Cave B&B offers comfortable lodgings in a man-made one-bedroom cave 70 feet below ground. Originally intended to be a geologist's office, it includes a waterfall-style shower, a flagstone hot tub, and a replica kiva. Supremely comfortable, the 1,700-square-foot space is more like a spacious apartment including a living room and a modern kitchen.

The state that spawned the Atomic Age also seems to have a corner on alien sightings. Although not as famous as Roswell (see p. 744), Aztec did supposedly witness a UFO crash near town in 1948. A 9-mile Alien Run mountain bike trail leads up Hart Canyon to the alleged site.

And who are those soreheads? Every year money is raised for community projects, and the six residents who raise the most are honored in a parade during Aztec Fiesta Days in June.

WHERE: 180 miles northwest of Albuquerque. *Visitors info:* Tel 505-334-9551; aztecnm.com. **AZTEC RUINS NATIONAL MONUMENT:** Tel 505-334-6174; nps.gov/azru. **KOKOPELLI'S CAVE B&B:** Tel 505-860-3812; kokoscave.com. *Cost:* from $280, 2-night minimum. *When:* closed Dec–Feb. **BEST TIME:** June for Aztec Fiesta Days.

Underground Wonder in the Chihuahuan Desert

CARLSBAD CAVERNS

Carlsbad, New Mexico

One of the world's most complex and astounding—and easily accessible—cave systems winds beneath the Guadalupe Mountains in southeastern New Mexico. Carlsbad Caverns National Park contains more than 119

known caves, all formed when sulfuric acid dissolved the surrounding limestone.

Aboveground, this corner of the state has the stark, unforgiving beauty of the northern Chihuahuan Desert. Beneath the surface,

though, is another universe entirely. Take the steep walkway down 750 feet through the natural entrance to reach the Big Room, one of the largest underground chambers on the planet, large enough to hold six football fields with room to spare. (You can also reach the Big Room by elevator, a ride that evokes a journey-to-the-center-of-the-earth sensation.) From here a mile-long trail winds past speleotherms—that's "cave formations" to the uninitiated—resembling soda straws, curtains, totem poles, lily pads, or simply stone that flowed like water or draped like

silk. Many have colorful, descriptive names, from the Rock of Ages to the Painted Grotto. Subdued lighting adds to the unearthly effect.

If you're in the mood for something a little more adventurous, take a ranger-guided tour of some of the other "wild" caves in the park. The Left Hand Tunnel tour is moderately difficult, a candlelit lantern tour through an undeveloped section of the cave on unpaved trails. Trips to grottos such as Spider Cave are the most strenuous and involve stooping, climbing, wading across pools, and

Along with stalagmites and stalactites, the caverns have formations that resemble draperies, soda straws, and popcorn.

even crawling on your stomach through tight passages. Access to Lechuguilla Cave is limited to researchers and exploration teams, who have descended 1,604 feet into it and mapped 138 miles of passages, establishing it as the fifth longest cave in the world and the deepest limestone cave in the country.

Another Carlsbad treat happens nightly from spring to fall: the mass exodus of hundreds of thousands of Brazilian free-tailed bats from the natural mouth of the cave. They leave in a whirring dark cloud silhouetted against the setting sun, off for a frenzied night of insect hunting. If you're a chiroptophobe, this is not for you, but visitors who aren't afraid of bats will want to come for the pre-launch ranger talks, where you'll learn that the animals are hardly threatening and very beneficial to the ecosystem. Bat fans old and new can even adopt a bat at the visitors center to raise money for their study and conservation.

WHERE: 304 miles southeast of Albuquerque. Tel 575-785-2232; nps.gov/cave. **GUIDED CAVE TOURS:** Tel 877-444-6777 or 575-785-3137; recreation.gov. **BAT FLIGHT INFO:** Tel 575-785-3012. **BEST TIMES:** Bat flights happen May–Oct, but are best in Aug–Sept.

Railroads and Rafts in the New Mexico Mountains

CUMBRES & TOLTEC SCENIC RAILROAD

Chama, New Mexico

Pine-covered hillsides, alpine peaks, and one of the highest railroad summits in the West are all part of the Cumbres & Toltec Scenic Railroad, which winds its steam-powered way across the scenic New Mexico–Colorado border north of the small town of Chama.

The Denver and Rio Grande Railroad arrived in Chama in 1881, turning the riverside town into a lumber and mining center and a transportation hub for the northern part of the New Mexico Territory. Today the Chama spur still chugs to (and from) Antonito, Colorado, offering one of the country's prettiest and most authentic Old West train experiences. It stands as perhaps the finest example of what once was a vast network of remote Rocky Mountain railways and of the engineering challenges that had to be overcome to create them.

At 64 miles one-way (the return is by bus), the trip is the longest narrow gauge train route in the U.S. Climb aboard for the 6½-hour journey back in time, stopping midway for lunch at Osier. The 3-foot-wide train tracks were built narrower than the standard in order to hug the sheer sides of Toltec Gorge, 600 feet above Rio Chama, and pass through two tunnels and over a 137-foot trestle. At Cumbres Pass, at 10,015 feet the highest point in the U.S. used by scheduled passenger trains, you chug past Windy Point, from which you can see the Chama Valley below in all its pastoral glory, surrounded by the densely wooded Rio Grande, Carson, and Santa Fe National Forests.

The quiet and unassuming town of Chama itself, with a population not much higher than 1,000, is chock-full of gift shops and B&Bs. Head out of town to the rustic 21-room Lodge at Chama, with 36,000 private acres of untrammeled nature, including alpine lakes and rivers that offer nirvana to anglers. Southwest of town, paddle on the Rio Chama as it flows through a 1,500-foot-deep canyon

lined with red cliffs and sage-covered grasslands on its way to join the Rio Grande. Declared a National Wild and Scenic River, it is an easy, popular white-water run.

Where: 106 miles north of Santa Fe. Tel 888-286-2737 or 575-756-2151; cumbres toltec.com. *Cost:* $95 round-trip, includes lunch. *When:* Sat–Thurs, late May–late Oct. **The Lodge at Chama:** Tel 575-756-2133; lodgeatchama.com. *Cost:* from $290 per person, all inclusive. **Rafting:** Far Flung Adventures, Taos. Tel 800-359-2627 or 575-758-2628; farflung.com. *Cost:* 1-day trip $115. *When:* Apr–early Sept. **Best times:** mid-May–Aug for fishing and wildlife ranch tours at the Lodge; late May–early June for high water rafting; June–Sept for fishing; July–Aug for lower water rafting and warmer weather.

The Cumbres & Toltec Scenic Railroad is a living artifact of railroad history and engineering.

Gateway to Indian Country

GALLUP

New Mexico

Although it's located outside the reservation boundary, Gallup is the most important commercial center of the Navajo Nation, the largest Indian reservation in the continental U.S. Covering 27,000 square miles of

Arizona, New Mexico, and southern Utah, the reservation has over 300,000 inhabitants. Once an important railroad and coal-mining

hub, Gallup has rebranded itself as Indian Capital of the World, and boasts a host of trading posts, pawnshops, and art galleries specializing in crafts made by the Navajo, Hopi, and Zuni tribes, who collectively make up 40 percent of the local population.

A classic neon-lit stretch of Main Street was once part of the legendary Route 66 (see p. 745). The downtown area near the Santa Fe Train Depot is full of venerable stores such as Richardson's Trading Company, open since 1913. Browse Navajo turquoise jewelry, hand-woven sheep wool rugs, Hopi katsina figures, intricately painted pottery, and thousands of other items, then stop by the nearby Gallup Cultural Center for the best overview of the area's Native American heritage. Continue your education about the area's early inhabitants and their heritage, with a visit to the ruins of nearby Chaco Canyon (see p. 743).

You can complete the frontier experience by joining yesterday's stars of the silver screen and booking a room at the El Rancho Hotel on Route 66. Built in 1936, it is a shrine to

Native Americans dress in traditional costumes for the Gallup Inter-Tribal Indian Ceremonial.

Hollywood's golden age of Westerns, when it served as a home away from home for stars such as Kirk Douglas (here to film *Ace in the Hole* in 1951) and Ronald Reagan (*The Bad Man* in 1940), as well as Gene Autry and Mae West, to name but a few. Signed photos line the hallways of this National Historical Site, and Native crafts, mounted deer heads, and a gigantic geode fill the lobby. Rooms are Western-rustic and the 49er Lounge is the perfect setting for a beer.

None other than Will Rogers called the Gallup Inter-Tribal Indian Ceremonial, held since 1922, the "Greatest American Show." Every August, members of 15–20 tribes come together for parades, powwows, rodeos, art displays, and the crowning of the Ceremonial Queen. The ceremonial dance costumes alone are worth the trip. Many balloonists prefer Gallup's Red Rock Balloon Rally in December to the more crowded Albuquerque event (see p. 735); the scenery is prettier and the winds easier to navigate.

WHERE: 140 miles west of Albuquerque. *Visitor info:* Tel 800-380-4989 or 505-722-2228; gallupnm.gov. **RICHARDSON'S TRADING COMPANY:** Tel 505-722-4762; richardson trading.com. **CULTURAL CENTER:** Tel 505-863-4131. *When:* closed Sat–Sun. **EL RANCHO HOTEL:** Tel 505-863-9311; elrancho hotel.com. *Cost:* from $113. **INTER-TRIBAL INDIAN CEREMONIAL:** Tel 505-863-3896; theceremonial.com. *When:* 5 days in Aug. **RED ROCK BALLOON RALLY:** redrockballoon rally.com. *When:* 1st weekend in Dec.

Living History

INDIAN PUEBLOS OF NEW MEXICO

New Mexico

The 19 Pueblo communities of New Mexico are the descendants of the Ancestral Puebloans, who lived in the arid Four Corners region five centuries ago. Arriving from Mexico, Spanish pioneers found them living in well-defined settlements and so named them "Pueblo," which means "village" in Spanish.

Today, New Mexico's Pueblo tribes are spread along the river between Albuquerque and Taos, with a few to the west such as Zuni and Acoma. Many of the adobe buildings that line the dusty streets of these towns were built hundreds of years ago, and pickup trucks and televisions are often the only signs of modernity. Some villages are more traditional than others; some residents of Taos Pueblo (see p. 753) and Acoma Pueblo still live without running water or electricity.

Acoma Pueblo, the "Sky City," sits atop a sheer-walled sandstone mesa an hour west of Albuquerque. Perched 367 feet above the desert floor, it is a walled village of some 250 adobe structures, believed to have been inhabited since the 12th century. Only 50 or so of the tribe's 4,800 members reside here year-round but many return for holidays. The best time to visit is September 2, the feast day celebrating this Pueblo's patron saint San Esteran.

All Pueblos welcome visitors, including during some festivals, which occur nearly every month. You'll see traditional dances celebrating the harvest or the feast day of one of the many Catholic saints absorbed into the animistic Pueblo worldview. The evocative scenes are complete with colorful ceremonial costumes, chanting, and drums, but photography or recording is usually not allowed.

A good place to start your exploration of New Mexico's Pueblo tribes is the Indian Pueblo Cultural Center in Albuquerque, owned and

An adobe dwelling at the Acoma Pueblo

operated by the 19 Pueblos. It includes a large museum of Pueblo culture, demonstrations by Native artists, and traditional dances every weekend. Albuquerque also hosts the Gathering of Nations Powwow in late April, the largest annual gathering of Native Americans in the world. A kaleidoscopic event of swirling sound and color, it brings together representatives of more than 700 tribes, including Cherokee, Pueblo, Sioux, and Seminole who arrive from across the U.S. and Canada to practice, teach, and exchange tribal traditions. The three-day event features an Indian Trader's Market powwow, dancing, singing, and drumming competitions, and the crowning of Miss Indian World.

Acoma Pueblo: 67 miles west of Albuquerque. *Visitor info:* Tel 800-747-0181 or 505-552-7861; acomaskycity.org. **Cultural Center:** Albuquerque. Tel 800-766-4405 or 505-843-7270; indianpueblo.org. **Gathering of Nations Powwow:** Albuquerque. Tel 505-836-2810; gatheringofnations.com. *When:* 3 days in late Apr. **Best times:** Sep 2 for San Esteran feast at Acoma Pueblo; Dec 24–25 for dances, processions, and mass at Pueblo.

The Other (and Original) Vegas

Las Vegas

New Mexico

I t may not have roulette wheels or sequin-studded showgirls, but New Mexico's Las Vegas does have an alluring Old West atmosphere and enticing outdoor offerings—and a visit here won't break the bank. In its heyday, this quiet city at the eastern slopes of the Sangre de Cristo Mountains was one of the most important in the Rocky Mountains West, a bustling stopover on the Santa Fe Trail from Missouri, as well as host to a veritable who's who of Wild West legends. Wyatt Earp, Doc Holliday and his girlfriend Big Nose Kate Elder, and Jesse James all frequented town, as did lesser-known desperados such as Hoodoo Brown, Cock-Eyed Frank, and Handsome Harry the Dancehall Rustler. Legendary sheriff Pat Garrett once escorted Billy the Kid in handcuffs across the main plaza for a short stint in the local jail.

The city's history can be sensed in the central plaza with its gazebo shaded by great old trees. The handsome three-story Plaza Hotel was and still is the pride and joy of Las Vegas. Built in 1882 in the typical style of the West's railroad hotels, it was considered the best around in its day. A night in one of the hotel's Victorian-styled rooms goes well with a drink in Byron T's Saloon downstairs. In all, more than 900 buildings are on the National Register of Historic Places. Adobe structures built by the Spanish in the 16th century stand side by side with the fancier brick buildings of the 19th century. Many of the latter are still owned and lived in by descendants of the original builders, while others have become B&Bs, restaurants, galleries, and antiques stores.

Teddy Roosevelt's famous First U.S. Volunteer Cavalry Regiment, better known as the Rough Riders, chose Las Vegas as the site for their first reunion, held at the Plaza Hotel in 1899. Today the City of Las Vegas Museum and Rough Rider Memorial Collection displays mementos of the action they saw in Cuba during the Spanish-American War in 1898, including the famous charge up San Juan Hill, as well as more than 1,500 photographs, tintypes, and stereoviews dating back to 1880.

A short drive from town is the Las Vegas National Wildlife Refuge, a favorite destination for birders, who have logged more than 270 avian species. The refuge is comprised of 8,672 acres of grasslands, marshes, ponds, and canyons at the ecologically rich intersection of the Great Plains, the Rocky Mountains, and the Chihuahuan Desert.

WHERE: 68 miles east of Santa Fe. **PLAZA HOTEL:** Tel 505-425-3591; plaza hotellvnm.com. *Cost:* from $99. **CITY OF LAS VEGAS MUSEUM:** Tel 505-426-3205; lasvegas museum.org. **LAS VEGAS NATIONAL WILDLIFE REFUGE:** Tel 505-425-3581; fws.gov/refuge/ las_vegas. **BEST TIMES:** dusk and dawn in spring and fall for birding.

Birthplace of the Atomic Age

LOS ALAMOS

New Mexico

One of the most pivotal cities in the history of the 20th century sits on the Pajarito Plateau, sandwiched between the beautiful Jemez Mountains and the Rio Grande Valley. Along with its enviable setting, Los Alamos

("The Cottonwoods") offers a fascinating backstory that has not ended; to this day, there is more brainpower per capita in the city than just about anywhere else in the country.

Until WWII, Los Alamos was just a sleepy mountain town at 7,320 feet. Chosen in 1942 by J. Robert Oppenheimer for its remoteness—in case anything went wrong—the city became a key location of the ultra-secret Site Y of the Manhattan Project, which resulted three years later in the world's first atomic bomb.

Today the Los Alamos National Laboratory is one of the world's leading scientific research institutions, with plenty of top-secret areas and high-tech projects ranging from hydrogen fuel cells to supercomputers. It employs some 11,000 people in a space that covers 36 square miles. But even visitors without security clearances can visit downtown's Bradbury Science Museum (named after the man who succeeded Oppenheimer, and run by Los Alamos National Laboratory). The exhibits on the lab's wartime roots share space with interactive science displays on radiation, lasers, and the human genome, and an actual 5-ton "Little Boy" nuclear bomb like the one dropped on Hiroshima.

A casing for the B61 nuclear bomb is on display at the Bradbury Science Museum.

Scientists couldn't ask for a lovelier place to live while they probe the secrets of the universe. The eastern edge of the stunning Jemez Mountains forms the remains of a gigantic volcano that once stood higher than Mount Everest when it erupted nearly a million years ago.

Within an hour's drive lies the Valles Caldera National Preserve, a gorgeous reserve inside the 13-mile-wide collapsed volcanic crater. You can hike through the pines and junipers to natural hot springs above the town of Jemez Springs (see p. 751).

The area's first inhabitants date back far earlier than the Manhattan boys. Nearby Bandelier National Monument preserves thousands of archaeological sites spread across 33,000 acres of high-desert wilderness laced with trails. One of the most visited sites is Alcove House in Frijoles Canyon near the visitors center, where precipitous pine ladders lead up to fascinating cavelike cliff dwellings 140 feet above the canyon floor, inhabited from A.D. 1100 to 1500. If you are less adventuresome, you can admire the breathtaking view from among the cottonwoods on the valley floor.

WHERE: 35 miles north of Santa Fe. **BRADBURY SCIENCE MUSEUM:** Tel 505-667-4444; lanl.gov/museum. **VALLES CALDERA:** Tel 575-829-4100; vallescaldera.gov. **BANDELIER NATIONAL MONUMENT:** Tel 505-672-3861; nps.gov/band. **BEST TIMES:** May–June, Aug–Oct.

Ruins of an Ancient Metropolis

CHACO CULTURE NATIONAL HISTORICAL PARK

Nageezi, New Mexico

The remnants of what was once the hub of an important and thriving culture fill a remote, arid valley in northwestern New Mexico. It's hard to believe that this barren spot once teemed with thousands of people, but the finely built ruins of four-story structures show otherwise. Some 4,000 cultural sites fill the Chaco Culture National Historical Park, which covers 53 square miles of unforgiving desert that once was fertile and flourishing.

Chaco Canyon served as the ceremonial and political hub of the Anasazi (or Ancestral Puebloan) culture from roughly A.D. 850 to 1250, when a number of monumental "great houses" were built of stone using increasingly sophisticated masonry techniques. By 1050, Chaco was the ceremonial, administrative, and economic center of the San Juan Basin. Dozens of great houses in the Chaco Canyon were connected by roads to more than 150 others throughout the region. A trading network extending to the Pacific and southern Mexico may have brought seashells and tropical birds in exchange for pottery and turquoise.

Like many archaeological sites in the Southwest, Chaco experienced a massive, sudden population decline near the end of the 13th century, thought to have been caused by a

Twenty Puebloan groups in New Mexico, as well as the Hopi in Arizona, claim Chaco as their ancestral homeland.

combination of drought and overpopulation. By 1300, Chaco was almost entirely deserted. Many historians believe that the inhabitants drifted away to more hospitable areas, and that their descendants are today's Southwest Indians.

It's the combination of grandeur and emptiness that gives the ruins such otherwordly appeal. Some have been partially restored, others left undisturbed. Take the 9-mile paved Canyon Loop Road, the only one in the park, to Pueblo Bonito, Chaco's most famous great house. A steep trail leads to an overlook above the D-shaped complex, which at its peak had about 600 rooms and dozens of kivas, or round ceremonial chambers, covering three acres. You can enter the ruins themselves to see the intricate stonework on the walls up close, but to fully experience the buildings' size and haunting splendor, view them from above at sunrise or sunset.

Chetro Ketl, Pueblo del Arroyo, Tzin Kletzin, and Casa Rinconada are other giant ruins along or near the road, each impressive for its size and meticulous construction. Four backcountry hiking trails, open from sunrise to sunset, lead past ancient farming terraces, prehistoric stone staircases, and rock art panels, one of which is thought to depict a supernova visible in 1054. Frequent night-sky programs at the park's small observatory help you learn more about the brilliant stars above Chaco.

WHERE: 165 miles northwest of Albuquerque. Tel 505-786-7014; nps.gov/chcu. **BEST TIMES:** spring and fall for weather; Apr–Oct for Night Sky programs.

Out of This World

ROSWELL

New Mexico

Who knows what actually crashed to earth near the sleepy city of Roswell that early July night in 1947? Local ranchers described finding pieces of purple metal inscribed with strange hieroglyphics;

the *Roswell Daily Record* and the Associated Press reported the recovery of "flying discs"; and the U.S. Army announced a spaceship had crashed, then said it was a weather balloon and stonewalled further discussion.

Nevertheless, in the decades since "the incident," this midsize city in southeastern New Mexico has become synonymous with Unidentified Flying Objects and their purported crews, embellished with rumors of alien autopsies and abductions and government cover-ups. Roswell's notoriety has spawned movies, TV shows, conferences, and the International UFO Museum and Research Center downtown, where budding ufologists and conspiracy theorists can peruse celestial paintings, models of alien spacecraft, and some of the thousands of books written about the subject. There's an endearing earnestness to the place— where else can you buy crop-circle earrings, green alienhead mugs and potholders, and the book *Talking to Extraterrestrials* all in one place?

Two aliens mug for the camera at the annual Roswell UFO Festival.

Every July 4th weekend, the annual Roswell UFO Festival features lectures, workshops, and abduction panels, along with lighthearted costume contests, fireworks, and a parade down Main Street. The infamous Hangar 84, where the government stored the debris from the mysterious crash, is occupied by a working company, so it is no longer open to the public.

On a more serious note, the Roswell Museum and Art Center displays an excellent collection of New Mexico fine art, including 71 Pueblo-related sketches by Peter Moran, and modernist works from the Santa Fe and Taos art colonies. Also on exhibit, in homage to this city's self-anointed role as the cradle of America's space industry, is a special collection of early rockets and engines created and developed by Robert Goddard. The father of modern rocket science, he lived and worked here for 12 years beginning in the 1930s. The attached Robert H. Goddard Planetarium is the second largest in the state, with shows on Mars and screenings of the original *The War of the Worlds* film.

WHERE: 200 miles southeast of Albuquerque. **INTERNATIONAL UFO MUSEUM:** Tel 575-625-9495; roswellufomuseum.com. **ROSWELL UFO FESTIVAL:** roswellufofestival .com. *When:* July 4th weekend. **ROSWELL MUSEUM:** Tel 575-624-6744; roswellmuseum .org.

Get Your Kicks on America's Mother Road

ROUTE 66

New Mexico

There's no road more embedded in the psyche of America than Route 66, the "Mother Road" of song and legend. Commissioned in 1926, the 2,451-mile route led Dust Bowl refugees and beatniks to California and spawned an unparalleled profusion of neon and drive-in Americana in eight states from Chicago to Los Angeles. Steinbeck and Kerouac wrote about it (in *The Grapes of Wrath* and *On the Road*, respectively), Bobby Troup sang about it ("Get Your Kicks on Route 66"), and there was even a TV series about it (*Route 66* premiered in 1960 with George Maharis and Martin Milner and catchy theme music by Nelson Riddle).

Although it was gradually replaced as a travel corridor by the interstate highways and officially decommissioned in 1984, "America's Main Street" retains its hold on the national imagination. From the birthplace of the corn dog (Springfield, Illinois) to the Grand Canyon, this National Scenic Byway still touches on much that defines America, from kitsch to natural wonders.

While portions of the route are gone, either subsumed by the interstates or crumbled into dust, you can still drive 85 percent of the original road by car. New Mexico's section parallels, and often disappears beneath, I-40. The flatter eastern section starts at Glenrio, 44 miles east of Tucumcari. Stop at the Dinosaur Museum at Mesalands Community College in Tucumcari, home of the world's largest collection of bronze skeletons (created at the school's own foundry), and spend the night at the classic and super-friendly Blue Swallow Motel, built in 1939. Don't miss Tom Coffin's huge sculpture *Roadside Attraction* at the west end of town; it resembles a chrome tail fin with glowing red taillights.

In Santa Rosa, 60 miles west, take a dip in the cool, clear waters of the Blue Hole, one of many natural sinkholes nearby, and stop to ogle the classic cars at the Route 66 Auto Museum. From here, the road once curved north to hit Santa Fe before heading south again to Albuquerque. Eighteen miles of Albuquerque's Central Avenue, once part of Route 66, is still lined with classic neon signs and '50s architecture, including diners and motels with assertive signs (note the bronco rider advertising the El Don Motel).

Fill up your tank and keep heading west to Gallup, commercial hub of the nearby Navajo reservation and the self-proclaimed Capital of Indian Country, where Route 66 still serves as Main Street. It's lined with neon signs, of course, as well as the largest concentration of trading posts and galleries selling Native American crafts in the state (see p. 739).

Route 66 Federation: Tel 909-336-6131; national66.org. **Dinosaur Museum:** Tucumcari. Tel 575-461-3466; mesalands.edu/community/dinosaur-museum. *When:* closed Sun–Mon. **Blue Swallow Motel:** Tucumcari. Tel 575-461-9849; blueswallowmotel.com. *Cost:* from $75. **Route 66 Auto Museum:** Santa Rosa. Tel 575-472-1966.

A Fiesta for All Seasons

Markets of Santa Fe

Santa Fe, New Mexico

On the north side of Santa Fe's historic central plaza sits the Palace of the Governors, the oldest continually occupied public building in the U.S., dating from 1610 and the early days of Spanish colonization from northern Mexico. Outside the Palace's distinctive front portico, specially authorized Native American artisans from 47 communities throughout the state display their creations as part of the Portal Program. On display are a wide variety of local crafts—turquoise and silver jewelry, paintings and sculpture, weavings and pottery—and as a bonus you'll learn something about the history and design of your purchase directly from its creator.

Santa Fe holds some of its most popular events in the plaza. Every August, the City

Different cranks into high gear for its Indian Market, the largest happening of its kind in the U.S. It draws more than 700 Native artists who display their crafts in booths spread across 14 square blocks around the plaza and nearby streets, a magnet for shoppers, collectors, and gallery owners from around the world. Everyone is welcome to shop or just watch the costumed Native dance and dress competitions. Complete the experience by visiting the Museum of Indian Arts & Culture. Just before Indian Market comes Spanish Market (a second, similar Spanish Market is held in early December at the Sweeny Convention Center). A vibrant scene, with booths, food, and music on and around the plaza, the focus here is on New Mexico's Iberian heritage. Hundreds of juried local Hispanic artists display and sell handmade furniture, tinwork, pottery, retablos, woodcarvings, textiles, and more.

September's Fiesta de Santa Fe, the oldest continual celebration in the United States, has its roots in the peaceful reconquest of New Mexico by the Spanish in 1692, after an Indian revolt drove out European settlers for over a decade. It's an exuberant time of parades, mariachi concerts, masses, crafts fairs, and lots of local entertainment that kicks off with Zozobra, a more recent celebration in which a 50-foot effigy of "Old Man Gloom"—symbolizing the travails of the past year—is burned in Fort Marcy Park. Hosted by the Museum of International Folk Art, July's International Folk Art Market is the largest of

its kind in the world, drawing outstanding artisans from Armenia to Zimbabwe.

Conveniently close to the plaza lies one of the best of the city's growing number of upscale hostelries. The excellent Rosewood Inn of the Anasazi, named after the ancestral Puebloans who once occupied this region (see p. 740), is worth visiting just for its decor. The welcoming areas are decorated with flagstone floors and massive cacti, and an impressive collection of handwoven rugs and baskets, pottery, and artwork. The attention to detail and warm environment continues in the lobby's award-winning Anasazi Restaurant, a standout in a city that offers some pretty stiff competition.

VISITOR INFO: Tel 800-777-2489 or 505-955-6215. **PALACE OF GOVERNORS PORTAL PROGRAM:** Tel 505-476-5100; palaceof thegovernors.org. *When:* closed Mon, Nov–Apr. **INDIAN MARKET:** Tel 505-983-5220; swaia.org. *When:* 2 days in late Aug. **MUSEUM OF INDIAN ARTS & CULTURE:** Tel 505-476-1269; miaclab.org. *When:* closed Mon, Nov–Apr. **SPANISH MARKET:** Tel 505-982-2226; spanishcolonial.org. *When:* 1 week in late July/early Aug and 1st weekend in early Dec. **FIESTA DE SANTA FE:** Tel 505-913-1517; santafefiesta.org. *When:* early Sept. **INTERNATIONAL FOLK ART MARKET:** Tel 505-992-7600; folkartalliance.org. *When:* early July. **INN OF THE ANASAZI:** Tel 888-767-3966 or 505-988-3030; rosewoodhotels.com. *Cost:* from $205 (off-peak), from $315 (peak); dinner $60.

Glorious Arias in a Glorious Setting

SANTA FE OPERA

Santa Fe, New Mexico

Founded in 1957, the groundbreaking Santa Fe Opera is famed for the wide variety and high quality of its productions, from masterworks like *Madama Butterfly*, which kicked off the first season, to world premieres like Jennifer

Higdon's *Cold Mountain* in 2015. It consistently attracts world-class conductors, directors, and singers—and the audiences who love them—so reserve your seats in advance.

Set on a hilltop just north of Santa Fe, with a nearly 360-degree view of the Jemez and Sangre de Cristo mountains and the high desert in between, the adobe opera house was built in 1998. It is open on the sides and capped by two upward-sweeping arcs of roof designed to trace the acoustic reflections of sound from the stage to the audience. The opera is also known for its

The roof of the Santa Fe Opera was designed to enhance acoustics.

Apprentice Program for Singers, which helps budding vocalists make the transition into professional life and is considered one of the most prestigious in the world.

Come if you can for opening night, launched by a gala celebration and marked by posh tailgate parties in the parking lot, with champagne and catering by some of the city's best restaurants. As for attire, jeans and cowboy boots are just as acceptable as tuxedos.

Las Palomas Inn, a favorite haunt of both performers and operagoers only three blocks from Santa Fe's historic plaza, is owned by Neil Rosenshein, a well-known tenor for the Metropolitan Opera, who discovered the property years ago while in town to perform in *The Barber of Seville*. The Inn offers 63 Santa Fe–style studios and one-bedroom casitas with wood-beam ceilings, kiva fireplaces, and hand-woven rugs. An outdoor fireplace keeps things cozy when the temperature drops at night.

Where: 7 miles north of Santa Fe. Tel 800-280-4654 or 505-986-5900; santafeopera.org. *Cost:* tickets from $35. *When:* July–Aug. **Las Palomas Inn:** Tel 855-982-5560 or 505-982-5560; laspalomas.com. *Cost:* from $109 (off-peak), from $169 (peak).

The Unique Flavor of the Southwest

Santa Fe's Southwest Cuisine

Santa Fe, New Mexico

While some might vote for spectacular sunsets, red rock scenery, or the vibrant blend of contemporary and ancient cultures, there's nothing quite as emblematic of the Southwest as its food. One bite of a blue-corn chicken enchilada covered with a piquant blend of red and green chiles, washed down with a Silver Coin margarita and followed by a fluffy sopaipilla pastry, and you're hooked. You might end up like relocated natives who have care packages full of chiles shipped from home to satisfy their cravings.

America's oldest living indigenous cuisine is, like the Southwest itself, an intriguing blend of traditions: blue corn, beans, and squash from Native Americans; tomatoes, chiles, and barbecue from Mexico; wheat and rice introduced by the Spanish and Anglo settlers. Spices are used liberally but tastefully, especially chili powder. Chiles are a cornerstone, and over 200 kinds—from mild to wild—are cultivated in Mexico and the Southwest. New Mexico is the country's largest grower and consumer, and the official state question—"Red or green?"—accompanies every order. ("Christmas" is the local lingo for both.)

Although Southwestern cooking ranges in style from Mexico to Colorado, Santa Fe's has proven to be on the vanguard, with eateries that are just plain outstanding. An early source of culinary fanfare was world-renowned chef and cookbook author Mark Miller, who, more than anyone, put the local cuisine on the national radar. In 1987 he teamed up with Eric Di Stefano to launch the Coyote Café in Santa Fe, the city's first internationally recognized restaurant showcasing distinctive regional cooking. When it's warm, head for the open balcony of the Coyote Café's Rooftop Cantina on the second floor, where the less expensive menu is just as delicious. Just down the road from Coyote Café is the small and cheerful Café Pasqual, which draws a crowd of loyal patrons with dishes that blend Old Mexican, New Mexican, and Asian flavors.

Another great way to sample Santa Fe cooking is at the Santa Fe Wine & Chile Fiesta in late September. The region's premier food and wine event pairs sample dishes from dozens of local restaurants with the glories of nearly 100 American wineries. Cooking demonstrations, guest chef luncheons, and seminars are also on the schedule, and it all culminates in the Grand Tasting at the Santa Fe Opera, overlooking the fall colors in the Sangre de Cristo Mountains.

Alternatively, master the flavors of the City Different at the Santa Fe School of Cooking, where the classes, taught by some of the city's finest chefs, end in remarkable meals enjoyed by everyone. Even if you aren't a cook, stop by the vibrant Santa Fe Farmers Market in the railyard area. It is the largest farmers market in the state, with more than 150 vendors hawking fruit, flowers, spices, chiles, vegetables—you name it, it's there.

COYOTE CAFÉ: Tel 505-983-1615; coyote cafe.com. *Cost:* dinner at Café $65, Rooftop Cantina $30. CAFÉ PASQUAL: Tel 800-722-7672 or 505-983-9340; pasquals.com. *Cost:* $45 dinner. SANTA FE WINE & CHILE FIESTA: Tel 505-438-8060; santafewineandchile.org. *Cost:* events from $75. *When:* late Sept. SANTA FE SCHOOL OF COOKING: Tel 800-982-4688 or 505-983-4511; santafeschoolofcooking.com. *Cost:* classes from $40. SANTA FE FARMERS MARKET: Tel 505-983-4098; santafefarmers market.com. *When:* Sat year-round.

A Painter's Love Affair with the Southwest

GEORGIA O'KEEFFE TRAIL

Santa Fe and Abiquiu, New Mexico

"The colors are different up there," Georgia O'Keeffe wrote of the Land of Enchantment. Although a Midwesterner who for years found her inspiration in New York City, she has long been considered New Mexico's most famous artist. Her first visit to the state came in 1929, and O'Keeffe moved to the little town of Abiquiu permanently in 1949, three years after the death of her husband, the acclaimed photographer Alfred Stieglitz. Her simplified, refined canvases portrayed her adopted land in a way no one had done before, and her sensual images—usually instantly recognizable as hers—include animal bones, clouds, and, most famously, large-scale flowers.

Despite the O'Keeffe effect, Abiquiu remains a small village in the Old World mold with about 575 residents. It lies within a land grant dating to 1754, one of the last of its kind still owned by residents, many of whom are artists who make Abiquiu a quiet hotbed of the arts. If you're spending the night, stay at the Abiquiu Inn, with Southwest-themed rooms and private casitas and a fountain in the courtyard.

O'Keeffe divided her time between Abiquiu and nearby Ghost Ranch, whose stark vistas the artist recorded, creating what she called "the wideness and wonder of the world as I live in it." The ranch is now an education and interfaith retreat center run by the Presbyterian Church. They offer seminars on topics ranging from spirituality to science and art, and welcome day-trippers for O'Keeffe landscape walks and trail rides. Accommodations are basic yet comfortable, and the views can't be beat.

Don't miss Santa Fe's Georgia O'Keeffe Museum, the most popular art museum in the state. Its collection of more than 3,000 works, including 140 oil paintings, is the world's largest permanent collection of the artist's work. The museum also offers tours of her home and studio in Abiquiu. Not far away, the New Mexico Museum of Art also displays a number of her works, along with those of other artists involved in the Taos and Santa Fe art communities.

WHERE: Abiquiu is 48 miles northwest of Santa Fe. **ABIQUIU INN:** Tel 888-735-2902 or 505-685-4378; abiquiuinn.com. *Cost:* from $120. **GEORGIA O'KEEFFE TOURS:** Tel 505-685-4539; okeeffemuseum.org. *When:* tours Mar–Nov by appointment on Tues, Thurs, and Fri. **GHOST RANCH:** Tel 877-804-4678 or 505-685-1000; ghostranch.org. *Cost:* 3-night Georgia O'Keeffe immersion from $595, all-inclusive. **GEORGIA O'KEEFFE MUSEUM:** Santa Fe. Tel 505-946-1000; okeeffemuseum .org. **NEW MEXICO MUSEUM OF ART:** Santa Fe. Tel 505-476-5072; museumofnewmexico.org. *When:* closed Mon.

Aquatic Elixirs

HOT SPRINGS AND SPAS

Santa Fe and Northern New Mexico

New Mexico is brimming with places to indulge the pleasure of soaking in hot water, from natural sandy-bottom pools deep in the woods to spas that seem more Kyoto than Four Corners. One of the latter can be found

in the pine- and juniper-covered hills above Santa Fe, at Ten Thousand Waves, a well-known and much-loved Southwest version of a Japanese hot spring resort. It is a longtime favorite whose peaceful, down-to-earth ambience and wooden outdoor pools, both private and shared, promise to treat both your body and your mind. Those elemental joys, available year-round, are especially welcome in the

winter on the way back from a hard day of skiing. Aesthetically spare Zen-style rooms invite you to spend the night, and a full menu of spa treatments offers everything from a deep-stone massage to a Japanese Organic Facial Massage.

An hour north of Santa Fe is Ojo Caliente Mineral Springs, one of the oldest health resorts in North America. Ancestors of today's

Pueblo Indians once considered these natu-rally heated waters sacred, as did the Anglos who followed them, seeking relief from aches and disease near the turn of the 20th century. Eleven pools are filled with different types and combinations of waters containing iron, soda, lithium, sodium, and arsenic. The Mission Revival–style adobe hotel built here in 1916, now listed on the National Register of Historic Places, houses the Artesian Restaurant, deco-rated with historic photographs. Don't miss the mud pool—it's fun in warm weather (spread it on, let it dry, and wash it off—your skin never felt so soft).

If you prefer your hot springs au naturel (in all senses of the words), head to Jemez Springs, where the surrounding forests are filled with naturally heated springs containing over 20 minerals and gases. Just north of town are the Spence Hot Springs. It takes about ten minutes to hike from the road to the rough stone pools, which offer wonderfully hot water (95–105°F) and inspiring views of the hills, particularly at sunset—and it's free.

Ten Thousand Waves: Tel 505-982-9304; tenthousandwaves.com. *Cost:* rooms from $209 (off-peak), from $249 (peak); shared tubs $25 per person. **Ojo Caliente Mineral Springs:** Ojo Caliente. Tel 800-222-9162 or 505-583-2233; ojospa.com. *Cost:* rooms from $149; mineral springs from $20 per person. **Spence Hot Springs:** Jemez Springs. Tel 575-829-3535; fs.usda.gov. **Best times:** fall, winter, and spring.

A Real Find—the Quiet Kind

SILVER CITY

New Mexico

S ilver City is overshadowed by more stylish Santa Fe (see p. 746) and funkier Taos (see p. 753), but it is one of New Mexico's gems. Rich in history, surrounded by 3 million acres of the wild Gila National Forest, and with

a population of just 10,273, it's small enough to be both friendly and manageable, and has been dubbed one of America's "10 coolest towns."

The city's historic downtown architecture evokes its Victorian heyday as a mining cen-ter—silver was discovered in them thar hills in 1870—in what was once Apache country. Western history buffs can take a self-guided tour through the early years of one of New Mexico's most infamous native sons: William Bonney, aka Henry McCarty, aka Billy the Kid. He grew up here, and you can see his boyhood home, the hotel where he washed dishes and waited tables, and the jail (now a warehouse) from which he escaped at age 15 by climbing the chimney.

Sitting on its own 178 acres just outside of town, the Bear Mountain Lodge was built as a ranch school in 1928. This comfortable 11-room getaway is known throughout the Southwest as a

A full moon rises over the Santa Rita Copper Mine just east of Silver City.

mecca for outdoor enthusiasts who like their creature comforts. It's particularly known for its bird-watching, and riders bring their bikes and horses to explore the trails. For a Santa Fe–style meal, check out Diane's Bakery & Café: You'll be thrilled with just about anything here, from home-baked green chile cheddar toast for breakfast to the perfectly prepared grilled rib eye with southwestern dry rub and spicy buckshot butter.

Take New Mexico Highway 15 north 44 miles to Gila Cliff Dwellings National Monument, which preserves examples of the cragside homes of the area's original inhabitants who lived here in the late 1200s. The people of the Mogollon culture grew corn, squash, and beans and lived in natural caves that they made homelike with walls and roof beams. Five of the caves contain the ruins, about 42 rooms altogether. They sit in the middle of the country's first designated wilderness area, a gorgeously rugged expanse of forested hills and naked rocky peaks. Hiking trails abound and there are natural hot springs among the trees nearby, where you can soak and contemplate life as a troglodyte.

Where: 236 miles southwest of Albuquerque. **Bear Mountain Lodge:** Tel 575-538-2538; bearmountainlodge.com. *Cost:* from $160. **Diane's:** Tel 575-538-8722; dianesrestaurant.com. *Cost:* dinner $50. **Gila Cliff Dwellings:** Tel 575-536-9461; nps .gov/gicl. **Best times:** late spring–early fall.

Touching the Heavens

THE VERY LARGE ARRAY & *THE LIGHTNING FIELD*

West of Socorro, New Mexico

O ut on the high desert plains of west-central New Mexico, the sky is the biggest natural feature, so the most interesting view is often upward. It's fitting, then, that two major structures have been built west of Socorro with the same general theme—the intersection of sky and earth—but with radically different methods and motivations.

Science fiction buffs will recognize the giant radio antennas of the Very Large Array (VLA) from the movie *Contact;* it's where the astronomer played by Jodie Foster first hears alien signals. It's easy to imagine voices from other worlds as you stand on the barren Plains of San Agustin, surrounded by 27 huge white dishes. Each is 82 feet in diameter and weighs 230 tons; together in a Y-shaped formation, they act as a single dish 22 miles across, one of the premier astronomical radio observatories in the world. At its highest resolution, the array can pick out a golf ball from 100 miles, allowing astronomers to watch galaxies spin and planets form in the far reaches of space. The VLA is also used for atmospheric and weather studies and to track satellites.

The radio antennas of the Very Large Array act in concert with each other.

Sixty miles west of the VLA lies Walter De Maria's *The Lightning Field*, a famous outdoor art installation consisting of 400 polished stainless steel poles erected in a grid 1 mile by 1 kilometer. The poles average 20 feet, 7½ inches in height, and are carefully placed so their tips describe a flat plane over the uneven ground. De Maria is well known for thought-provoking large-scale art installations, including a room in a New York City gallery filled 22 inches deep with dirt (see p. 183).

The only way to visit *The Lightning Field* is to make advance reservations and spend the night in a comfortable but spare cabin on the site. If you're very lucky, you may see lightning hit one of the rods, but more likely you'll simply watch the interplay of light and shadow as the sun moves across the sky, and stay up late pondering art, life, and what our limited views of the heavens say about our place in the universe.

VERY LARGE ARRAY: 130 miles southwest of Albuquerque. Tel 575-835-7000; vla.nrao .edu. *When:* self-guided tours daily; guided tours offered the first Sat of every month. **WALTER DE MARIA'S *THE LIGHTNING FIELD:*** 150 miles southwest of Albuquerque. Tel 505-898-3335; lightningfield.org. *Cost:* $150 per person (off-peak), $250 per person (peak), includes accommodations for up to 6 people and vegetarian dinner. *When:* May–Oct.

The Quintessential New Mexico Town

TAOS

New Mexico

If one town had to sum up an entire state, Taos would come close. On the scrubby plain between the Rio Grande gorge and the stark ramparts of the Sangre de Cristo Mountains, it is artsy, outdoorsy, rugged yet genteel, and definitely funky. D. H. Lawrence described it as "a state of mind." The town's curious and alluring mix of galleries and trinket shops, historic sites and mobile homes, ski bums, Pueblo Indians, and multimillionaires captures the Land of Enchantment in a nutshell.

Start your reconnaissance at the 17th-century central plaza, then swing by one of the city's many small museums, maybe stopping en route to peruse some of the dozens of high-quality art galleries—with a population of 5,731, Taos is said to be home to more than 1,000 artists and musicians. With one of the country's best ski resorts 18 miles outside of town (see next page), and challenging white-water runs on the Rio Grande nearby, you're looking at a resort town that pretty much has it all.

There are lots of lodging options, but Palacio de Marquesa is one of the most elegant, with seven rooms that pay homage to the women of Taos, including Martha Reed and Millicent Rogers. Just a few blocks from the busy plaza, this quiet oasis has earned kudos for its sophisticated sleek lines, in-room spa treatments, and hot tub under the stars, making it a showcase of southwestern elegance.

Continuously occupied for more than a millennium, the multistoried adobe complex of Taos Pueblo, just north of town, is straight out of a faded tintype—particularly in the winter, when it's covered with snow and fireplace smoke drifts into the sky. About 150 of the tribe's 1,900 members live here without electricity or running water, much as their ancestors did. (The others live in more conventional homes on the 99,000 acres that make up the pueblo.) Taos is the northernmost of New Mexico's 19 pueblos (see p. 740) and you are welcome to stroll about, shopping for fry bread, silver jewelry, and mica-flecked pottery from artisans' homes. The pueblo has numerous feast days, but try to visit during the

The ancient Taos Pueblo is made entirely of adobe—earth mixed with water and straw.

important Taos Powwow in July or the feast day of San Geronimo in September.

On the way to or from Santa Fe, the "High Road" to Taos (New Mexico Highway 76 and New Mexico Highway 518) is much prettier and more interesting than the busier route along the Rio Grande (New Mexico Highway 68). The slower, winding High Road passes through wonderfully scenic hills and a number of villages straight out of Old Mexico, with old adobe churches and residents who speak more Spanish than English.

WHERE: 70 miles northeast of Santa Fe. *Visitor info:* Tel 575-758-1028; taospueblo .com. **PALACIO DE MARQUESA:** Tel 855-846-8267 or 575-758-4777; visittaos.com. *Cost:* from $209, includes dinner. **BEST TIMES:** winter and early spring for skiing; late spring–fall for hiking and rafting; July for Taos Powwow (taospueblopowwow.com); late Sept for San Geronimo Day.

A Powderhound's Dream

TAOS SKI VALLEY

New Mexico

It's world-famous for its mind-bogglingly steep high-alpine, high-adventure terrain—51 percent of which is rated expert—as well as its top-ranked ski school. There are no gondolas, no ski-and-be-seen scene to speak of, and snowboarders weren't allowed until 2008. It gets the same number of sunny days per year as it does inches of glorious powder snow—more than 300, on average. Small, intimate Taos Ski Valley, high in the mountains above the high-end ski-bum town of Taos, has long been a powderhound's dream, and in 2015 it celebrated its 60th year.

People come here for serious runs down some of the best terrain in the West. Hard-core skiers travel from far and wide to hike the final climb to the summit and ski the chutes of Highline. Fifteen lifts serve 110 trails, with a total vertical drop of 3,281 feet from Taos' iconic Kachina Peak at 12,481 feet (Kachina has one of the highest chairlifts in North America). The Ernie Blake Snowsports School, named after the Swiss-German immigrant who founded the ski area in 1955, boasts talented instructors and is repeatedly rated one of the best in the country as a result. No wonder aspiring shredders and hot-dog skiers flock to Taos.

For a standout place to stay, even in the increasingly high-end clime of Taos, try El Monte Sagrado, which effortlessly proves that a resort can be both environmentally sensitive and full-blown luxurious. After a day of powder shots, relax in the Living Spa, an eco-friendly healing retreat, and follow that up with dinner at the hotel's De la Tierra restaurant, which consistently receives glowing honors from critics and patrons alike for its regional and seasonal American cuisine. To top off a superb evening's repast, drop by the Anaconda Bar, the only spot in town that resembles an après-ski scene.

WHERE: 18 miles northeast of Taos. Tel 866-968-7386 or 575-776-2291; skitaos.org. *Cost:* lift tickets $86. *When:* ski season late Nov–early Apr. **ERNIE BLAKE SNOWSPORTS SCHOOL:** Tel 866-968-7386. *Cost:* from $70 for a group lesson. **EL MONTE SAGRADO:** Tel

Enthusiasts come to Taos Ski Valley for the 1,294 skiable acres.

855-846-8267 or 575-758-3502; elmonte sagrado.com. *Cost:* from $199 (off-peak), from $299 (peak); dinner at De la Tierra $40.

Where's the Beef?

CENTRAL TEXAS BARBECUE

Austin and environs, Texas

Texas barbecue is so good, you really shouldn't bother with barbecue sauce, and some places don't even serve it, believing that it distracts from the exquisite flavors. What many consider the best Texas barbecue around

is found in the middle of the state, often in towns such as Austin, which has German, Polish, and Czech roots, where the pit-masters learned from their grandpas the secrets of smoking meat with pecan, oak, and hickory wood. Beef is king here, and the most popular is beef brisket.

Sausage is a specialty in these parts, too, but you'll never find anything resembling the grocery store variety. Smoked sausage in and around Austin and the Hill Country has a coarse texture and resonates with that smoke infusion. Tender pork ribs are another favorite, and a few places have a wide selection of other meats such as pork shoulder, cabrito—even bologna.

One of Austin's venues of choice is the Iron Works BBQ, an old tin building near the state capital, the University of Texas campus, and the party corridor known as Sixth Street. Favorite

picks here include oak-smoked brisket, spicy sausage, chicken, smoked turkey, pork ribs, and beef ribs. But the Iron Works is only the tip of the iceberg. If you drive about 20 miles south of the city to the crossroads of Driftwood, you'll find the landmark known as The Salt Lick BBQ. Packing in road-trippers and locals every day since 1969, this stone-house country retreat is most popular for its family-style evening meals, guaranteed to fill you up with platters of pork ribs, beef brisket, and smoked sausage, along with potato salad, coleslaw, and pinto beans.

Roughly 30 miles southeast of Austin, the town of Lockhart is home to Kreuz Market, begun as a modest German meat market in 1900. Today's version is in a barnlike structure, but you still get your food piled on butcher paper, and you won't mind the absence of sauce one bit. Beef brisket and tender pork shoulder are the prime picks, with jalapeño sausage, boneless beef prime ribs, spare ribs, and pork chops among other mouthwatering choices. About 35 miles northeast of Austin, the town of Taylor is home to Louie Mueller Barbecue, where the walls are deeply stained from over a half-century's worth of wood smoke, and the plain sausage, jalapeño sausage, and pork ribs are phenomenal. Don't be surprised if the meat-cutters offer you a sampling to savor while you wait in line.

In Llano, 75 miles northwest of Austin, Cooper's Old Time Pit Bar-B-Que remains the favorite of George W. Bush and countless other devotees. When you approach the front door, stop at one of the giant pits out front and choose your smoked meats, which include sausage, pork ribs, pork chops, chicken, goat,

sirloin steak, brisket, and beef ribs. Inside, pick up cole slaw and potato salad, serve yourself some beans and barbecue sauce, then find a seat at one of the long picnic tables. Roll up your sleeves and enjoy.

IRON WORKS BBQ: Austin. Tel 512-478-4855; ironworksbbq.com. *Cost:* sampler plate $17. **THE SALT LICK BBQ:** Driftwood. Tel 512-858-4959; saltlickbbq.com. *Cost:* family-style dinner $25. **KREUZ MARKET:** Lockhart. Tel 512-398-2361; kreuzmarket.com. *Cost:* dinner $16. **LOUIE MUELLER BARBECUE:** Taylor. Tel 512-352-6206; louiemueller barbecue.com. *Cost:* lunch $12. **COOPER'S OLD TIME PIT BAR-B-QUE:** Llano. Tel 325-247-5713; coopersbbq.com. *Cost:* lunch $12. **BEST TIMES:** mid-Mar to coincide with South by Southwest (sxsw.com); late Mar–May for wildflower viewing.

Taking Care of Body and Soul

LAKE AUSTIN SPA RESORT

Austin, Texas

O nce a funky country cousin to luxury properties like the Boulders (see p. 682) and Canyon Ranch (see p. 700), with a distant past as both a nudist colony and camp for bronco busters and rodeo clowns,

Lake Austin Spa Resort in the Hill Country (see p. 786) is respected today as one of the country's premier destination spas.

The resort makes the most of its waterfront location: All 40 of its charming country-style rooms are laid out in single file along an arbor-lined walkway facing the lake. A yoga deck extends out over the glass-green water, and the indoor exercise studio has a picture window with views of its mirror-calm surface and densely wooded opposite shore. You can hydro-bike, kayak, scull (two-handed rowing), stand-up paddle, or even take private classes from a pro water-skier, and when you're ready to relax, head out on a sunset cruise. There are plenty of

nonaquatic activities, including Pilates-based core work, the TRX circuit workout (used by Navy Seals to increase strength and endurance), tai chi, spinning, and kickboxing.

Don your spa sandals and fluffy robe and shuffle on over to the magnificent 25,000-square-foot LakeHouse Spa, built from native yellow limestone and decorated with award-winning quilts from the Texas State Fair. You might opt for indigenous treatments like the Gifts of Our Garden experience, based on therapeutic herbs from the resort's garden, mixed with shea butter, sea salts, and essential oils. Lake Austin is also known for alternative treatments, such as a Manaka Tapping treatment for the needle-phobic that uses rhythmic tapping with tiny wooden mallets to open up the body's energy pathways.

The dining room's menu may sound fancy, featuring lamb loin with smoked eggplant, cilantro-cauliflower couscous, and beet relish, but the casual atmosphere is not. The screened windows open onto the lake, and with just 65 guests at full capacity, it's easy for people traveling alone (usually women) to mingle. Finish the day on your room's little porch, taking in the scent of rosemary bushes, the wind rustling in the magnolia leaves, and the sparkle of the lake under the moon.

WHERE: 23 miles northwest of Austin; 1705 S. Quinlan Park Rd. Tel 800-847-5637 or 512-372-7300; lakeaustin.com. *Cost:* from $1,720 per person for 3 nights, double

Start the day with a kayak adventure on the glassy water of Lake Austin.

occupancy, includes meals and classes (spa treatments à la carte). **BEST TIMES:** spring and fall for weather; spring for great heron nesting season; 1 week of every month for the Culinary Experience, and a year-round program featuring noted authors.

Letting the Good Times Roll

AUSTIN'S LIVE MUSIC SCENE

Austin, Texas

Although it's the seat of state government and home to one of the largest universities in the nation, Austin's soul really comes from its music. Laid-back and fun-loving, the city bills itself as the Live Music Capital of the World and boasts more than 250 venues offering everything from rockabilly to Tejano, from no-names to Texas giants like Willie Nelson, Lyle Lovett, Spoon, and Los Lonely Boys.

No surprise, then, that the city's famous South by Southwest Music and Media Festival (aka "SXSW") is one of the biggest music showcases anywhere, a gathering of more than 2,000 music hopefuls yearning to become the next big thing. If you're a music lover looking for the new and edgy, make every effort to get your tickets and lodging months in advance. If you're in town at another time, get tickets to a studio taping of the renowned *Austin City Limits*, a PBS television favorite since 1976.

Or, you could hit the clubs. Austin's year-round music nerve center is on Sixth Street and in the Warehouse District immediately south of it, where rock 'n' roll, blues, jazz, country, and R&B emanate from beer joints housed in stone-and-brick Victorian buildings. This is where you'll find the world-renowned Antone's, Austin's "Home of the Blues"; the Continental Club, an old-time bar that books the top country and swing bands in Austin (with jazz upstairs in the gallery); the Broken Spoke, Texas's premier two-step dance hall; and both Stubb's Bar-B-Q and Threadgill's Old No. 1, each beloved for great food and great music.

SOUTH BY SOUTHWEST: Tel 512-467-7979; sxsw.com. *Cost:* festival admission from $650.

When: 10 days in mid-Mar, with music for the last 5 days. **AUSTIN CITY LIMITS:** Tel 512-475-9077; acltv.com. *When:* tapes in spring and summer and as needed. **ANTONE'S:** Tel 512-814-0361; antonesnightclub.com. **CONTINENTAL CLUB:** Tel 512-441-2444; continentalclub.com/austin.html. **BROKEN SPOKE:** Tel 512-442-6189; brokenspokeaustintx.net. **STUBB'S BAR-B-Q:** Tel 512-480-8341; stubbsaustin.com. **THREADGILL'S OLD NO. 1:** Tel 512-451-5440; threadgills.com. **BEST TIMES:** mid-Mar for SXSW; 3-day weekends Sept–Oct for *Austin City Limits* Music Festival with more than 130 bands.

John Legend is one of many world-class names who have played SXSW.

Madcap Merriment in the Capital City

THE AUSTIN FESTIVAL SUBCULTURE

Austin, Texas

While it's best known for its music, Austin is also beloved for its quirky culture. It's on full display throughout the year with plenty of fun and funky festivals. In the spring, there's Eeyore's Birthday Party, begun in 1963 by a University of Texas English professor and continued through the 1970s by Austin's hippie-dippy residents, who brought their favorite party favors to honor the pessimistic donkey of A. A. Milne's Winnie the Pooh stories. Before long the gathering became a fund-raiser for numerous nonprofit groups, drawing celebrants to Pease Park for one long Saturday each April for costume contests, games, face-painting and temporary tattoos, musical jam sessions and giant drum circles, and maypoles. In May, folks yuk it up downtown at the annual Pun-Off World Championships. Assembled in Brush Square, behind the O. Henry Museum, an 1891 cottage that was once home to the renowned short story scribe, Pun-Off competitors vie in two events: Punniest of Show, in which contestants deliver 90 seconds of their best prepared puns and wordplay on a selected theme; and Punslingers, which requires improvisational quipping and punning on randomly selected topics.

From spring through fall, you'll find locals and visitors gathering at dusk on the Congress Avenue Bridge, just south of downtown, to watch the stunning sight of 1.5 million Mexican free-tailed bats—the largest urban bat population in the nation—taking flight. The creatures are headed out in search of supper, which consists of up to 30,000 pounds of insects each night. When the colony heads out to feed one Saturday evening in August, the Bat Fest sees it off with live music, arts and crafts vendors, and food and drinks, all on the bridge, which is closed to traffic for the party. **EEYORE'S BIRTHDAY PARTY:** Tel 512-448-5160; eeyores.org. *When:* last Sat in Apr. **PUN-OFF WORLD CHAMPIONSHIPS:** Tel 512-472-1903; punoff.com. *When:* Sat in early May. **BAT FEST:** Tel 512-327-9721 x16; roadwayevents.com (click on Bat Fest). *When:* 3rd Sat in Aug.

Duding It Up in the Cowboy Capital of the World

BANDERA

Texas

Bandera, the Cowboy Capital of the World, sits along the bucolic Medina River in the western reaches of Texas Hill Country (see p. 786). It has earned its nickname honestly—with a tradition of producing championship rodeo competitors, holding rodeos on weekends from June through early September, and offering city slickers a choice of nearly a dozen dude ranches, including some on working cattle spreads.

Founded as a camp and mill for producing cypress shingles, Bandera (population 850) is one of the oldest Polish communities in the nation, its roots going back to 11 families who arrived in 1855 to help work the mill. The beautiful church they built in 1876, St. Stanislaus, is the second oldest Polish church in the U.S. and sits on a hill at Cypress and 7th Street, not far from Main Street, where shops sell all the gear you'll need on a ranch: jeans, boots, a good hat, and a really big belt buckle.

Saturday afternoons from March through mid-November offer Cowboys on Main, a street party sponsored by Bandera's Frontier Times Museum Living History Project and featuring a chuck wagon, strolling cowboy singers, trick-roping demonstrations, and a trick horse at work. Year-round, there's also live music at bars such as Arkey Blue's Silver Dollar, a saloon established in the 1930s with a sawdust floor and great honky-tonk atmosphere.

The Dixie Dude Ranch is a family favorite, a 725-acre working ranch offering horseback riding, bonfires, campfire sing-alongs, hayrides, and visits to a historic Range War cemetery, plus noncowboy pastimes like swimming, hiking, fishing, horseshoes, and volleyball. Lodging is in rustic but comfortable cabins, in the main lodge, or in the bunkhouse.

Life revolves around horses at Hill Country Equestrian Lodge, a 275-acre ranch where you can take one-on-one riding lessons from an expert or bring your own horse for long, quiet rides in the adjacent Hill Country State Natural Area, a secluded, 5,500-acre retreat with wonderful birding and 40 miles of multiuse trails. At night, you can hunker down in the lodge's private cedar and limestone cabins or suites, play cards, and sit on your porch and watch the sun drop past rocky hills covered with juniper, oak, and mesquite.

WHERE: 54 miles northwest of San Antonio. *Visitor info:* Tel 800-364-3833; banderacowboycapital.com. **ARKEY BLUE'S:** Tel 830-796-8826. **DIXIE DUDE RANCH:** Tel 800-375-9255 or 830-796-7771; dixiedude ranch.com. *Cost:* from $145. **HILL COUNTRY EQUESTRIAN LODGE:** Tel 830-796-7950; hillcountryequestlodge.com. *Cost:* from $198. **BEST TIMES:** Feb–May and Sept–Nov for weather; Sat afternoons, Mar–Nov for Cowboys on Main; June–early Sept for weekend rodeos.

Cowboy and cowgirl sightings are commonplace in the small town of Bandera.

Last Frontier of the Lone Star State

BIG BEND NATIONAL PARK

Texas

Deep in the southwest corner of Texas lies one of the nation's better kept secrets. Big Bend National Park is both one of the largest and least-visited U.S. national parks outside of Alaska, encompassing 800,000 acres, miles from the nearest town, and rising from a river elevation of 1,800 feet up to some 8,000 feet into the rough, dry Chisos Mountains. From the park's canyon clifftops you can see hundreds of miles into Mexico, and on 150-plus miles of hiking trails you can immerse yourself in the gloriously wild flora and fauna of the Chihuahuan Desert. In the Chisos Basin you'll find the Chisos Mountain Lodge, with basic but comfortable rooms and a simple restaurant. Several trails take off from here, including the famous Lost Mine Trail. The most serious hikers should look southeast of the basin to trails in Mariscal Canyon. About 3 miles upriver from Rio Grande Village, Hot Springs was a resort in the 1920s and still makes a good place to soak your feet before or after a hike.

Rafting the Rio Grande is more soft adventure than hard-core thrill, but great fun nonetheless, heading through Santa Elena, Boquillas, and Castolon canyons. You can book rafting trips at outfitters 28 miles away in Terlingua (population less than 100), where 20,000 rowdy celebrants show up each November for the Terlingua Chili Cookoff—actually, two dueling cook-offs that take place simultaneously in and around town. If you feel the need to take refuge from the festivities, try the nearby Lajitas Golf Resort. Originally a crusty little town with a saloon and trading post, Lajitas functioned for over a century as a jumping-off point for people

The volcanic Chisos Mountains jut dramatically out of the sedimentary plains.

escaping the real world—today it boasts a complete little desert oasis with great restaurants, 101 beautifully appointed rooms, a magnificent swimming pool, stables, an 18-hole golf course, a spa, and an airport with a fleet of Lear jets. A less extravagant (but still impressive) option is the Gage Hotel, a 1927 railroad hotel that remains a lovely example of Old West hospitality, with 45 comfortable rooms in a number of original buildings and a newer adobe wing, some with fireplaces and parlors.

WHERE: Park headquarters is 329 miles southeast of El Paso. Tel 432-477-2251; nps.gov/bibe. **CHISOS MOUNTAIN LODGE:** Tel 877-386-4383 or 432-477-2291; chisosmountainslodge.com. *Cost:* from $140. **RAFTING:** Far Flung Adventures. Tel 800-839-7238 or 432-371-2633; bigbendfarflung.com. *Cost:* 1-day trips from $145. **TERLINGUA CHILI COOKOFF(S):** abowlofred.com and casichili.net. *When:* 1st Wed–Sat in Nov. **LAJITAS GOLF RESORT:** Tel 877-LAJITAS or 432-424-5000;

lajitasgolfresort.com. *Cost:* from $200. **Gage Hotel:** Marathon. Tel 800-884-4243 or 432-386-4205; gagehotel.com. *Cost:* from $218.

Best times: Feb–Apr and Sept–Oct for the weather; 1st Sat in Nov for judging at the Terlingua chili cook-offs.

A Spectacular Crack in the High Plains

PALO DURO CANYON STATE PARK

Canyon, Texas

Way up north in the Texas Panhandle, where the roads appear to stretch across a vast, baked nothingness called the Llano Estacado, is a giant gap in the ground known as Palo Duro ("hard wood"). Formed by the Prairie Dog Town fork of the Red River, the magnificent canyon is roughly 120 miles long, 20 miles wide, and 800 feet deep, and was presumably named for the proliferation of mesquite and juniper trees that cling to the rust- and ocher-colored cliffs. Humans have lived in the canyon for about 12,000 years—first nomadic hunters, then Apache, and later Comanche and Kiowa peoples—but in 1874 a U.S. Cavalry unit forcibly removed the Indians to Oklahoma. Two years later, cattlemen moved in.

The best way to explore this generous gift of nature is to roam around 29,000-acre Palo Duro Canyon State Park, filled with fragrant sumac trees and Indian blanket wildflowers. The 6-mile round-trip Lighthouse Trail takes you through the canyon to the park's signature geological formation, a towering shale and sandstone pinnacle. You can hike it or ride it, either on bike or horseback (the latter available through the park's Old West Stables). Keep an eye out for resident wildlife, including roadrunner, coyote, and the western diamondback rattlesnake. A scenic road also makes the park accessible to drivers. For rustic accommodations, book one of the park's rock cabins, built by the Civilian Conservation Corps in 1933: There are three rim-side, and four Cow Camp Cabins. On summer evenings at the canyon's Pioneer Amphitheater, the outdoor musical *TEXAS* tells the story of pioneer farmers and ranchers, Native Americans, and their historic struggles. While you're in the neighborhood, be sure to check out the Panhandle-Plains Historical Museum, the largest history museum in the state, which explores the cultures that have helped make Texas legendary. In all, there are about 8,000 pieces of fine and decorative art, including 700 works by Frank Reaugh, "the dean of Texas painters," famous for his illustrations of West Texas cattle drives.

In Palo Duro, you can catch sight of hoodoos—oddly shaped stone pillars formed by erosion.

Where: 30 miles south of Amarillo. *Visitor info:* Tel 806-488-2227; paloduro canyon.com. *Cost:* cabins from $60. **OLD WEST STABLES:** Tel 806-488-2180. *When:* open mid-Mar–Oct. **TEXAS:** Tel 806-655-2181; texas-show.com. *Cost:* tickets from $17.

When: June–mid-Aug. **PANHANDLE-PLAINS MUSEUM:** Canyon. Tel 806-651-2244; panhandleplains.org. **BEST TIMES:** Mar–June and Sept–Nov for the nicest weather.

Mission Control and the Blast-Off! Theater

SPACE CENTER HOUSTON

Clear Lake, Texas

On July 20, 1969, when Neil Armstrong touched down on the moon and uttered some of the most famous words of the 20th century—"Houston, Tranquility Base here. The Eagle has landed"—the people on the receiving end of that call were right here at NASA's Johnson Space Center. Named for native son President Lyndon B. Johnson and opened in 1961, the center is the site of Mission Control, the iconic earthbound tether of all U.S. manned missions. It's where the first astronauts were quarantined after returning from the moon, where the first moon rocks brought back to Earth are stored, and where many of the great technological artifacts left from the first decades of America's space program have found a home.

The official visitor site at Johnson Space Center, Space Center Houston employs dozens of state-of-the-art exhibits, hands-on activities, and films to help you explore the legend and lore of the great beyond. The five-story screen of the Space Center Theater shows the film *Journey to Space* while the Blast-Off! Theater offers visitors a simulation of a real space launch. On the NASA Tram Tour, you'll visit Mission Control itself, plus Rocket Park, home to rockets used in the earliest days of the space program. In the Astronaut Gallery you can see an astounding collection of space suits, while Living in Space illustrates the complications of living in a microgravity setting, with volunteers helping to show how even eating or sleeping in space poses challenges.

Fascinating to both kids and parents, Space Center Houston is a true family attraction, so it is very convenient that the town of Kemah, which has grown up as a family entertainment polestar on the Galveston Bay shore, is only 12 miles away. The birth of the Kemah Boardwalk in the 1990s brought to the region boating opportunities, theme park–style rides, a gas-powered train, a water garden, small boutiques, art galleries, cafés, a winery, live music, and a multitude of seafood restaurants and bars. Don't miss the Aquarium restaurant, with its 50,000-gallon home for numerous species of fish, sharks, and stingrays.

A retired Saturn rocket is on display at the Space Center.

WHERE: 24 miles southeast of downtown Houston; 1601 NASA Pkwy. Tel 281-244-2100; spacecenter.org. **KEMAH BOARDWALK:** Tel 877-AT-KEMAH; kemahboardwalk.com. **BEST TIMES:** Thurs in May, June, and July for Kemah's Rock the Dock concert series.

Cultural Jewels in Big D

THE DALLAS ARTS DISTRICT

Dallas, Texas

The Dallas Arts District is the largest contiguous arts district in the U.S., 19 blocks of museums, galleries, performance spaces, and parks in downtown Dallas that are the centerpiece of the city's cultural life. One of the newer arrivals devoted to the study, preservation, and exhibition of modern sculpture, the Nasher Sculpture Center is a 55,000-square-foot oasis of both art and nature. Within the starkly modern building designed by renowned architect Renzo Piano resides the stunning collection amassed over more than four decades by Dallas philanthropist and developer Raymond Nasher and his late wife, Patsy—more than 300 pieces including works by Rodin, Picasso, Miró, Matisse, Serra, Calder, and Degas, among others. Unfolding from the building proper is a 1.5-acre lush green garden rimmed with stone walls surrounding a bevy of sculptures.

Next door stands the Edward Larabee Barnes–designed Dallas Museum of Art, a treasure trove of American masterpieces from the likes of Wyeth and O'Keeffe; more contemporary works by Warhol, Pollock, and Rothko; European art from Renoir, van Gogh, Cézanne, and Monet; and magnificent works from Africa, Asia, and the Pacific. A block away, the Crow Collection of Asian Art represents an exemplary assemblage of scrolls, paintings, metal and stone works, plus large architectural items like a sandstone facade from an 18th-century home in India.

A 2012 addition to the district is the Perot Museum of Nature and Science, a boldly modern structure designed by Thom Mayne and his firm Morphosis Architects. Encompassing 180,000 square feet, the museum's 11 permanent exhibit halls transport visitors across time and space to explore the birth of our solar system, experience an earthquake, and come face-to-face with a *Tyrannosaurus rex.*

NASHER SCULPTURE CENTER: Tel 214-242-5100; nashersculpturecenter.org. *When:* closed Mon. **DALLAS MUSEUM OF ART:** Tel 214-922-1200; dallasmuseumofart.org. *When:* closed Mon. **CROW COLLECTION:** Tel 214-979-6430; crowcollection.org. *When:* closed Mon. **PEROT MUSEUM:** Tel 214-428-5555; perotmuseum.org. **BEST TIME:** 1st and 3rd Sat of the month for the docent-led Arts District Architecture Walking Tour (thedallasartsdistrict.org).

The Dallas Museum of Art is a treasure trove of paintings by the masters of various periods.

Texas-Size Pampering

DELUXE HOTELS OF DALLAS

Dallas, Texas

Dallas has become adept at spoiling its guests to a fault, a habit that may have begun when the Adolphus Hotel opened downtown in 1912. A baroque landmark built by beer baron Adolphus Busch, it still feels like a royal palace, its public areas hung with Flemish tapestries and ornately framed artwork, and its lobby dominated by a Victorian Steinway once owned by the Guggenheim family. Repair to any of the 422 exquisite guest rooms and suites, or to the hotel's magnificent French Room restaurant, with its elaborate chandeliers and ceilings painted with clouds. Shoppers love the proximity to the flagship Neiman Marcus store, one easy block away, which has been doing business since 1907.

In the nearby Uptown neighborhood, the Rosewood Mansion on Turtle Creek has been a favorite among boldface guests—from members of U2 and the Rolling Stones to every sitting president—since the hotel opened in 1981, and is a popular venue for celebrity weddings. Built as an addition to the 1925 Sheppard King Mansion on a small hill overlooking lovely Turtle Creek, the hotel includes 143 spacious guest rooms and a small but enticing swimming pool. The rich and elegant Mansion Restaurant, which occupies the historic home, has a long tradition as one of the city's most popular dining rooms. A few blocks away, Uptown got a dose of chic with the recent arrival of the exceptionally popular Hotel ZaZa. The darling of young and glamorous celebrities, the Mediterranean-style boutique hotel offers 169 rooms and suites, a number of them named to reflect their design theme, like "Out of Africa" and "Shag-a-Delic." The on-site ZaSpa is spectacular (with treatments like the Rock Star! hot stone massage), and the Dragonfly restaurant and Poolside at ZaZa shine with eclectic but gratifying menus and cocktails.

THE ADOLPHUS: Tel 800-221-9083 or 214-742-8200; hoteladolphus.com. *Cost:* from $179. **ROSEWOOD MANSION ON TURTLE CREEK:** Tel 888-767-3966 or 214-559-2100; mansiononturtlecreek.com. *Cost:* from $330. **HOTEL ZAZA:** Tel 800-597-8399 or 214-468-8399; hotelzaza.com/dallas. *Cost:* from $270 (off-peak), from $349 (peak). **BEST TIME:** early Dec for Christmas decorations and the Dallas Children's Health Holiday Parade at the Adolphus.

Tragedy of a Nation

SIXTH FLOOR MUSEUM

Dallas, Texas

On November 22, 1963, President John F. Kennedy was assassinated while driving in a motorcade through Dealey Plaza in Dallas. The events of that fateful day shook the nation, and the museum dedicated to Kennedy's presidency and assassination ensures that we never forget their impact. Among the exhibits are enlarged police and news photographs, media coverage, and documents that give you a look at the preparations and planning for JFK's trip to Dallas, as well as the social and political developments of the period and President Kennedy's career. Of significant interest are the 6th-floor window through which 24-year-old Lee Harvey Oswald is said to have fired his rifle; views of Dealey Plaza and the motorcade route; and a film incorporating broadcasts and film footage from the day of the assassination through the funeral in Washington, D.C. The four official investigations into the assassination and conspiracy theories are detailed as well. An excellent audio tour that includes clips from historic broadcasts and interviews with eyewitnesses is available in seven languages, including an English-language version for children.

Allow time to walk around Dealey Plaza National Historic Landmark District, where at almost any hour and in every kind of weather you'll see visitors wandering the sidewalks along

The Sixth Floor Museum's southerly windows offer Dealey Plaza views, but the sniper's nest itself, kept as it was on November 22, 1963, is restricted from access.

the president's motorcade route. Just a block east is the John F. Kennedy Memorial Plaza, completed and dedicated in 1970 after Dallas philanthropist Stanley Marcus convinced famed architect Philip Johnson to design the cenotaph. Starkly dramatic, the "open tomb" sits adjacent to the spectacular Old Red courthouse and remains a special place for reflection.

WHERE: 411 Elm St. Tel 214-747-6660; jfk.org.

Country Comes to the City

THE STATE FAIR OF TEXAS

Dallas, Texas

For three weeks each autumn, Dallas becomes home to all Texans: ranchers, home cooks, rodeo junkies, professionals, gridiron fans, and music lovers, all of whom converge on the city for the great State Fair of Texas.

Staged just east of downtown in the beautiful 277-acre spread of art deco buildings known as Fair Park, the State Fair represents a grand tradition begun in 1886. It's one of the nation's largest such gatherings, pulling in millions of attendees each year, all of whom get a hearty welcome from the newly rebuilt Big Tex (the 1952 original burned in a 2012 electrical fire), a 55-foot mechanical cowboy with size 96 boots and a 95-gallon hat who waves at visitors and

offers a drawling "Howdy, folks!" Many guests coming to the fair do so for one of the two successive Saturdays on which college football grudge matches are held at the Cotton Bowl: the State Fair Classic between Grambling University and Prairie View A&M, followed by the Red River Rivalry between the universities of Texas and Oklahoma. Throughout the fair, four music stages welcome stars such as Jerry Jeff Walker, The Beach Boys, and the Dixie

Chicks. Each night, there's the Starlight Parade, led by a vintage Greyhound bus, complete with more than 15 lighted floats, stilt walkers, giant puppets, and a band playing classic hits.

Other big draws include the Auto Show, showcasing the next year's vehicles and fancy pickup trucks; a classic car corral; daily cooking contests; the ever-popular pig races and corn-

The State Fair of Texas is one of the most highly attended fairs in the country.

dog-eating contests; and, of course, the Midway, offering carnival games, thrill rides, and food booths. Among the more than 70 rides is the 212-foot Texas Star, the tallest Ferris wheel in Texas. More than a few people come each year to eat the beloved Fletcher's corny dogs, famous since 1942, along with a heart-stopping number of other fried goodies, including chicken fried lobster, beer-battered buffalo, fried pork ribs, fried popcorn balls, and fried Oreos.

While you're in Fair Park, take time to explore its museums, halls, and memorials, including the beautiful Hall of State, home to the Dallas Historical Society; the African American Museum, which has an exceptional folk art collection; and Texas Discovery Gardens. **WHERE:** 3921 Martin Luther King Jr. Blvd. Tel 214-565-9931; bigtex.com. *When:* 24 days from late Sept–mid-Oct. **FAIR PARK:** Tel 214-426-3400; fairpark.org. *Cost:* State Fair season pass, $40.

From Fine Art to Cowgirls

COWTOWN'S CULTURAL DISTRICT

Fort Worth, Texas

Thanks to the generosity of Fort Worth's cattle barons, oil magnates, and cotton kings, this easygoing town—nicknamed the place "where the West begins"—is the proud home not only of a huge cowboy quarter

(see next page) but also of one of the nation's largest cultural quarters. Scarcely a five-minute drive west from downtown, the Cultural District claims six world-renowned Western, classic, and modern art museums, not to mention the Will Rogers Memorial Center and its world-class equestrian facilities.

The Modern Art Museum of Fort Worth is the nation's second largest contemporary art museum behind New York's MoMA (see p. 182) in terms of total gallery exhibit space. Designed by Japan's celebrated modernist architect Tadao Ando and opened in 2002, this contemporary

masterpiece in stone, glass, and steel includes works by Pablo Picasso, Mark Rothko, Robert Rauschenberg, Andy Warhol, Roy Lichtenstein, and Robert Motherwell. Don't pass up a chance to have lunch at Café Modern, and get a table overlooking the sparkling pond.

A few feet away, the magnificent Kimbell Art Museum, named for a local philanthropic family, has long been known as one of the richest privately endowed museums in the nation, hosting some of the most important exhibitions traveling the U.S. in a breathtaking Louis Kahn–designed structure with a Renzo Piano–

designed pavillion added in 2013. In addition to its considerable Asian art collection, the Kimbell also includes works by Titian, El Greco, Rubens, Rembrandt, Goya, Cézanne, Matisse, Mondrian, and Picasso. From the Kimbell, walk past a reflecting pool and alongside a lush green lawn to reach the Amon Carter Museum of American Art, named for the creator of the *Fort Worth Star-Telegram.* Housed in a thrilling design by celebrated architect Philip Johnson, the wide-ranging permanent collection includes works by Georgia O'Keeffe, Alfred Stieglitz, Winslow Homer, Eliot Porter, Charlie Russell, and Frederic Remington.

Inside the Tex-Deco building is the National Cowgirl Museum and Hall of Fame, the first facility to tell the story of the women who helped shape the history and culture of the American West. You can hear the voices of these women, see films in two theaters, and take a simulated bucking bronco ride. Adjacent to the Cowgirl is the Fort Worth Museum of Science and History, which incorporates the Cattle Raisers' Museum,

a planetarium, an Imax theater, a children's museum, and dinosaur exhibits.

Check out any of the myriad horse shows hosted at the Will Rogers Memorial Center, like midwinter's Fort Worth Stock Show and Rodeo. There are more than 30 rodeo events during the stock show's three weeks, plus a Western parade, an extreme bull-riding competition, and a celebrity goat-milking contest.

MODERN ART MUSEUM: Tel 866-824-5566 or 817-738-9215; themodern.org. *When:* closed Mon. **KIMBELL ART MUSEUM:** Tel 817-332-8451; kimbellart.org. *When:* closed Mon. **AMON CARTER MUSEUM OF AMERICAN ART:** Tel 817-738-1933; cartermuseum.org. *When:* closed Mon. **NATIONAL COWGIRL MUSEUM:** Tel 800-476-3263 or 817-336-4475; cowgirl.net. **FORT WORTH MUSEUM OF SCIENCE AND HISTORY:** Tel 817-255-9300; fwmuseum.org. **WILL ROGERS MEMORIAL CENTER:** Tel 817-392-7469; willrogersmemorialcenter.com. **BEST TIME:** mid-Jan–early Feb for the Fort Worth Stock Show and Rodeo (fwssr.com).

Ride 'em, Cowboy!

STOCKYARDS NATIONAL HISTORIC DISTRICT

Fort Worth, Texas

Some 130 years ago, the legendary 800-mile Chisholm Trail passed through Fort Worth, where cowpokes would rest up from arduous months pushing cattle from south Texas up to northern markets, spending their hard-earned

wages on hot food, strong whiskey, and felicitous companionship.

Today, ol' Cowtown is awash in places glorifying that particularly vivid period of the state's misspent youth. The best is the Fort Worth Stockyards National Historic District, covering 98 acres on the city's north side, a top livestock market when it opened in 1889. The Stockyards Championship Rodeo, with events including

bull riding, team roping, barrel racing, and calf roping, is held every Friday and Saturday night and some Sundays at the Cowtown Coliseum, which also serves as home to Pawnee Bill's Wild West Show, a historical reenactment of the early 1900s original. Across the street, the Texas Cowboy Hall of Fame fills one of the district's original horse and mule barns with videos, trophies, saddles, and photographs of honored cowboys and cowgirls, as well as 60 perfectly restored wagons, carriages, and sleighs, some of which date to the 1700s.

Board a century-old train bound for the nearby historic town of Grapevine on the Grapevine Vintage Railroad in Stockyards Station. Restaurants, gift shops, and art galleries fill the nooks and crannies of the station, and right next door is the Stockyards Visitor Information Center, where you can sign up for several guided walking tours offered daily. Another event to catch is what's thought to be the world's only twice-daily urban cattle drive, in which a team of cowpokes in period costume pushes a herd of longhorns along the rough brick Exchange Avenue.

Mosey on in to the White Elephant Saloon for a cold Lone Star longneck, live country music, and two-step dancing. Across the street, Booger Red's Saloon is a fine place for sittin' a spell (on saddle-shaped bar stools)

The Stockyards, on Exchange Avenue and near the White Elephant Saloon, is likely the most photographed spot in Fort Worth.

while waiting for a table at the adjacent H3 Ranch steak house. Both are just off the lobby of the Stockyards Hotel, circa 1907. The hotel itself is the best in the area, a comfortable, authentic place where Bonnie and Clyde hid out. The most famous of all the dancin'-and-drinkin' spots is Billy Bob's Texas, the world's largest honky-tonk. Housed in what was once an open-air barn for cattle, Billy Bob's hosts big-name musicians, from David Allen Coe to Willie Nelson. Inside are a general store, dozens of bars, a restaurant, and an indoor arena for professional bull riding.

The Red Steagall Cowboy Gathering, a three-day festival in October, keeps the cowboy way of life alive and accessible with Western swing music, ranch rodeo action, cowboy poetry, an authentic chuck-wagon competition, and a cowboy trading post.

Where: 130 E. Exchange Ave. Tel 817-624-4741; fortworthstockyards.org. **Stockyards Rodeo:** Tel 817-625-1025; stockyardsrodeo.com. **Cowboy Hall of Fame:** Tel 817-626-7131; texascowboyhalloffame.org. **Grapevine Vintage Railroad:** Tel 817-410-3185; grapevinetexasusa.com/trains. **Stockyards Visitor Center:** Tel 817-624-4793. **White Elephant Saloon:** Tel 817-624-8273; whiteelephantsaloon.com. **H3 Ranch:** Tel 817-624-1246; h3ranch.com. **Stockyards Hotel:** Tel 817-625-6427; stockyardshotel.com. *Cost:* from $199. **Billy Bob's Texas:** Tel 817-624-7117; billybobstexas.com. **Best time:** last weekend in Oct for Red Steagall Cowboy Gathering (redsteagallcowboygathering.com).

Lone Star Bavaria in the Texas Hill Country

FREDERICKSBURG

Texas

For several decades, Fredericksburg has been a popular place to enjoy German-style beer gardens, menus laden with brats and schnitzel, and shops selling beer steins—all of which makes no sense at all unless you know the region's history: In 1829, postal clerk Johann Friedrich Ernst lit out from Germany after having allegedly embezzled money. The first German to settle in Texas, he encouraged his countrymen to follow. In 1846, Fredericksburg became one of the first German towns that made up Texas's German Belt. Today, nearly 20 percent of Texas's population claims pure or partial German ancestry.

Fredericksburg is the jewel in Texas's Teutonic crown, offering German festivals like Oktoberfest (with continuous oompah music and polka contests) and the Christmas celebration known as Weihnachten. More than 300 inns and B&B lodgings and an infusion of art galleries, restaurants, design studios, and vineyards have added a new level of sophistication in recent years. The area is also a hikers' paradise, with the aptly named pink granite Enchanted Rock highlighting a 1,643-acre state natural area just to the north.

Hoffman Haus is a compound of old and new structures (including an old log cabin, a bunkhouse, and an old barn, all beautifully repurposed) nestled in a quiet neighborhood just a block from the hustle and bustle of downtown. The 14 supremely comfortable rooms, suites, and houses are tucked in amid 5 acres of lawns and gardens, and each has its own soothing style.

For a decidedly more rustic ambience, check into the Chuckwagon Inn, parts of which date back to 1850 when it was a dairy farm. Here, Old Texan detail meets with modern day amenities and a mouthwatering breakfast. Outside of town, the Rose Hill Manor is a

Stone houses built by early German immigrants can be found throughout Fredericksburg.

plantation-style B&B with wide wraparound porches on both floors and traditional-style furnishings. Nearby wine-tasting destinations include the award-winning Becker Vineyards.

For still more German heritage, check out the nearby towns of New Braunfels, Comfort, and Boerne. Each is filled with historic buildings housing shops, cafés, and inns, and can be seen on an easy day trip from Fredericksburg, Austin, or San Antonio.

Where: 78 miles west of Austin. *Visitor info:* Tel 888-997-3600 or 830-997-6523; visit fredericksburgtx.com. **Hoffman Haus:** Tel 830-997-6739; hoffmanhaus.com. *Cost:* from $135 (off-peak), from $165 (peak). **Chuckwagon Inn:** Tel 830-990-2777; chuckwagoninn.com. *Cost:* from $169. **Rose Hill:** Tel 830-644-2247; rose-hill.com. *Cost:* from $199. **Becker Vineyards:** Tel 830-644-2681; beckervineyards.com. **Best times:** Apr for bluebonnets and other wildflowers; 1st weekend in Oct for Oktoberfest; late Dec for Weihnachten.

Sandcastle Architecture and Victorian Splendor

GALVESTON

Texas

For one afternoon on the first weekend of June, architects, engineers, and contractors from across Texas step away from their drafting tables and come to the island city of Galveston's East Beach. They work in teams of

5 to 20 people for five hours, using elaborate design systems to create incredibly intricate, complex buildings and sculptures . . . all entirely out of sand. In the three decades since the Houston chapter of the American Institute of Architects first hosted its annual Sandcastle Competition, the seaside bash has grown to include more than 60 teams, all competing for fun and bragging rights. Some of the creations are simply hilarious, most are amazingly clever, but the old-fashioned sandcastle is rare. Pop culture plays a big role in many themes, with standouts like *Downton Crabby* and *Sandy Warhol: The Marilyn Faces.*

There is plenty of draw besides sand castles, of course—like Galveston's Victorian charm. The richest town in the Southwest during the cotton boom of the late 19th century, the city (population around 50,000) enjoys 32 miles of beaches, plus magnificently restored mansions, heritage museums dedicated to everything from the railroad to offshore drilling, and a restored wharfside historic district known as the Strand, containing one of the nation's largest collections of restored Victorian-era iron-front commercial buildings.

Wander over to the piers to tour the elegant 1877 ship *Elissa* at the Texas Seaport Museum, then head to the Pier 21 Theater to see a 30-minute multimedia documentary called *The Great Storm,* which details the devastating

AIA Sandcastle Competition judges consider originality, artistic execution, technical difficulty, and more to determine the "Gold Bucket" winner.

1900 hurricane that killed 8,000 residents and nearly leveled the town. Visit Moody Gardens and its three pyramids for any of its wonderland offerings: a 1.5-million-gallon aquarium, a rain forest, science and discovery activities, 3-D and special effects theaters, and a luxury hotel and spa.

Soak in more of Galveston's history by touring some of the eye-popping mansions (such as the ornate 1892 Bishop's Palace, cited by the American Institute of Architects as one of America's 100 most important buildings), or take a walking tour through the 50-block East End Historic District, the city's old silk-stocking neighborhood. Take a bike ride along the Galveston Seawall, a 10-mile granite barrier erected after the great 1900 storm to protect the city. Clustered along the seawall, waterside on the vintage piers, and throughout the Strand, Galveston's restaurants serve some of the freshest Gulf shrimp, snapper, oysters, and crab you'll ever taste, with the guarantee of a gorgeous sunset. At the Saltwater Grill, seafood is prepared in minutes in super-hot, steam-fed boiling kettles, one serving at a time. Afterward, head down the block for a musical or a play at the Grand 1894 Opera House.

WHERE: 50 miles southeast of Houston. *Visitor info:* Tel 888-425-4753 or 409-797-5144; galveston.com. **SANDCASTLE COMPETITION:** Tel 713-520-0155; aiasandcastle.com. *When:* 1st Sat in June. **TEXAS SEAPORT MUSEUM:** Tel 409-763-1877; galveston.com/texasseaportmuseum. **PIER 21 THEATER:** Tel 409-763-8808; galvestonhistory.org. **MOODY GARDENS:** Tel 800-582-4673; moodygardens.com. **BISHOP'S PALACE:** Tel 409-762-2475; galveston.com/bishopspalace. **SALTWATER GRILL:** Tel 409-762-3474; saltwatergrill.com. *Cost:* dinner $40. **GRAND 1894 OPERA HOUSE:** Tel 409-765-1894; thegrand.com. **BEST TIMES:** Feb–Mar for Galveston's Mardi Gras (mardigrasgalveston.com); 1st weekend in June for the AIA Sandcastle Competition; 1st weekend in Dec for the British-themed Dickens on the Strand holiday celebration (dickensonthestrand.org).

The Dance Halls of the Hill Country

GRUENE

Texas

If you really want to understand the heartbeat of Texas music, you've got to scoot your boots across the well-worn floors of the legendary Hill Country dance halls, beginning in the tiny hamlet of Gruene (pronounced *green*).

Gruene Hall is the busiest and most evocative of these halls, as well as the oldest continuously operating one in the state since 1878. It all goes back to those early days, when farming and ranching families would come to town for market, gossip, and Sunday church, then live it up at the local dance hall before another week of hard work. Real music fans and families continue to show up at this historic landmark to drink, dance, and take in some real good music, whether it be country, polka, folk, or zydeco.

Sitting to one side of Gruene Hall is the century-old Gristmill, once a working mill and now a favorite Texas dining spot with live music, good margaritas, and solid fare like a half-pound Guadalupe chopped steak with spicy Tex-Mex queso, onions, and jalapeños. On the other side is the Gruene Mansion Inn, a Victorian wedding cake built in 1872 for the town's founder, Henry D. Gruene. The mansion, along with its old barns, corn crib, and carriage house, has been transformed into a 31-room inn on the Guadalupe River. Antiques shops, boutiques, a general store, and galleries spread out in all directions, while hours of watery fun are within easy reach on the Guadalupe River, a favorite for inner-tubing and rafting.

Other legendary dance halls are located nearby, all set amid the ancient live oaks, cacti, and rampant wildflower meadows for which this reach of central Texas is known. In Helotes, the John T. Floore Country Store opened in 1942 and has seen performances by

Small in size but big in prestige, Gruene Hall is a rite of passage for country musicians following in the footsteps of George Strait and Merle Haggard.

legends like Hank Williams, Patsy Cline, Elvis Presley, Willie Nelson, and Merle Haggard. The Luckenbach General Store dates back to 1849, when it opened as a combination saloon and trading post, gaining fame as a country hot spot in the 1970s, when legends like Willie Nelson, Waylon Jennings, and Jerry Jeff Walker performed here. About 50 miles southwest of Austin, Twin Sisters Hall opened in 1879 and offers lots of local color, generally featuring pickers and singers from nearby towns such as Boerne and Blanco.

WHERE: 37 miles northeast of San Antonio. *Visitor info:* Tel 830-629-5077; gruenetexas .com. **GRUENE DANCE HALL:** Tel 830-606-1281; gruenehall.com. **GRISTMILL:** Tel 830-625-0684; gristmillrestaurant.com. *Cost:* dinner $28. **GRUENE MANSION INN:** Tel 830-629-2641; gruenemansioninn.com. *Cost:* from $195.

FLOORE'S: Helotes. Tel 210-695-8827; liveat floores.com. **LUCKENBACH GENERAL STORE:** Luckenbach. Tel 830-997-3224; luckenbach texas.com. **TWIN SISTERS HALL:** Blanco. Tel 830-833-5773; twinsistersdancehall.com.

BEST TIMES: 2nd Sun each month for Gruene Hall's gospel brunch; 10 days over the first 2 weekends in Nov for Wurstfest (wurstfest.com), a giant version of Oktoberfest in New Braunfels.

Houston's Choicest Steaks

PAPPAS BROS. STEAKHOUSE

Houston, Texas

Even as the Houston food scene evolves to incorporate more global trends, many Houstonians proudly maintain that nothing beats a big ol' juicy steak. For the quintessential Texas steak house experience, legions have long headed to Pappas Bros., a Houston tradition for over two decades. The Pappas brothers in question—Chris and Harris—are grandsons of an enterprising Greek restaurateur who immigrated from the Old Country to Texas in 1897 to launch a restaurant empire now spanning seven states. The two Pappas Bros. locations in Texas remain the standouts (and the Galleria-area original location is still the favorite of many), offering classic Texas hospitality and exceptional food.

All of the beef at Pappas Bros.—corn-fed, USDA Prime grade cuts of the highest rating—comes from a single source to maintain tight control. The beef is dry-aged in-house for 28 days to develop the fullest flavor. The same attention to detail is paid to the rest of the menu, including Colorado lamb, fresh seafood, sauces, desserts, and sides (consider starting your meal with grilled bacon-wrapped scallops or fresh Gulf oysters on the half shell). Several pastry chefs are on hand to create decadent desserts, like warm peach cobbler with ice cream and maple-glazed pecans, and the wine menu wins gold medals from *Wine Spectator*.

WHERE: 5839 Westheimer Rd. Tel 713-780-7352; pappasbros.com *Cost:* dinner $85. *When:* closed Sun.

The Grandest Yee-haw of All

HOUSTON LIVESTOCK SHOW AND RODEO

Houston, Texas

If you arrive in H-town between late February and mid-March, you'd better show up in boots and a ten-gallon hat, pardner. That's because the world's largest rodeo and livestock show will be in full swing, with a hootin'-'n'-hollerin' good time for all. Held in the 300-acre NRG Park, the centerpiece of this hoedown is Rodeo Houston, one of the nation's richest such events, with more than 2 million spectators coming to see the best cowboys and cowgirls competing for championship titles in bareback bronco riding, bull riding, tie-down roping, saddle bronco riding, steer wrestling, and team roping that will send them to the national finals. There's also Women's Professional Rodeo Association barrel racing—an extremely popular sport in which riders race their horses in a cloverleaf pattern around three barrels, vying for the shortest time.

On the livestock side of the show, 30,000 exhibitors (some as young as third grade) come from around the state and nation to show the cattle, sheep, horses, rabbits, and other critters they raise on their ranches. Capping the excitement are the livestock auctions and a donkey-and-mule competition featuring the popular mule pull, donkey snigging (aka log dragging), and the "Ear of the Year" awards, going to the donkey and mule with the widest ear-span measure. It's all for a good cause, of course: The entire show is a charity that benefits young competitors, with $400 million paid for scholarships and other research and educational programs since 1957.

After the rodeo ends each night, recording stars take the stage at the 71,500-seat NRG Stadium for concerts that would get top billing anywhere—past performers include George Strait, Trisha Yearwood, Melissa Etheridge, Kenny Chesney, Alan Jackson, and Keith Urban. If that weren't enough, the World's Championship Bar-B-Que Contest takes place the weekend prior to the start of the livestock show and rodeo in the NRG Park parking lot. For three full days, wood smoke from hundreds of portable pits suffuses the air for miles around as more than 250 teams compete for trophies in the best brisket, chicken, and pork spare ribs categories. Prizes are awarded for the most unique pit, most colorful gimmicks, cleanest setup, and even the best recycling program.

Where: NRG Center, 8334 Fannin St. Tel 832-667-1000; hlsr.com (includes info on the World Championship Bar-B-Que Contest). *Cost:* from $18 for rodeo tickets; $15 for Bar-B-Que Contest; concert prices vary. *When:* 3 weeks late Feb–Mar.

An Eclectic Collection of Texas Treasures

Houston's Art Museums

Houston, Texas

Widely esteemed as one of the finest private museums in the United States, the Menil Collection contains some 17,000 objects amassed by the late legendary Houston arts patron Dominique de Menil and her husband, John. Opened in 1987 in a simple but elegant low-rise building designed by Italian architect Renzo Piano, the museum is suffused with natural but skillfully filtered Texas light, and the free admission and lack of audio guides make for a very low-key, intimate experience, just as Dominique intended.

In many ways, the Menil's vision is the broadest among America's great small museums. At its heart is the justly famous Surrealism collection, with works by Man Ray, Duchamp, and Max Ernst, and one of the world's best collections of Magritte. The Menil is also rich in other 20th-century European artists, such as Picasso, Matisse, Giacometti, and Rodin. Across the street, an annex comprises nine galleries of the work of the artist Cy Twombly, a favorite of the de Menils.

Elsewhere in the museum district, the Museum of Fine Arts Houston is home to a vast collection that includes canvases by Rembrandt, Van Gogh, Monet, Picasso, and Matisse, as well as one of the largest photography collections in the country. Must-see sites on the MFAH campus include the original neoclassical Caroline Wiess Law Building, dating to 1924, and additions by Mies van der Rohe that house the 20th- and 21st-century art, installations of Oceanic art, Asian art, Indonesian gold artifacts, and pre-Columbian and sub-Saharan African artworks. The Audrey Jones Beck Building displays antiquities, European art, and American

The entrance to the Menil Collection is both unassuming and welcoming.

art in 28 galleries, while the Lillie and Hugh Roy Cullen Sculpture Garden is an urban oasis with works by some of the best-known sculptors of the 19th and 20th centuries, including Henri Matisse and Alexander Calder.

For something utterly different, make time to see the offbeat Orange Show Center for Visionary Art. Created by Houston postal worker Jeff McKissack between 1956 and 1980, the Orange Show is an architectural wonder of balconies, catwalks, arenas, and exhibits made from a wide assortment of materials—including gears, mannequins, tiles, and tractor seats—all honoring its namesake citrus fruit. Since McKissack's death in 1980, the Orange Show site has been preserved by arts patrons ranging from Dominique de Menil herself to Texas boogie-rockers ZZ Top, and remains a haven of contemporary art with programs that foster the inventive spirit and make art accessible to the public.

MENIL COLLECTION: Tel 713-525-9400; menil.org. *When:* closed Mon–Tues. **MFAH:** Tel 713-639-7300; mfah.org. *When:* closed Mon. **ORANGE SHOW:** Tel 713-926-6368; orangeshow.org. *When:* closed mid-Dec–early March. **BEST TIME:** 2nd weekend in April for the Orange Show's Art Car Parade, which features more than 250 extraordinary vehicles.

Elegant Grace and Spooky Waters

JEFFERSON & CADDO LAKE

Texas

Oozing vintage Southern charm, tiny Jefferson lies in the northeast corner of Texas only moments from the Louisiana state line. A well-preserved Civil War town, Jefferson was once the Lone Star State's version of

New Orleans: one of the most important river ports in Texas from the 1840s to the 1870s, rivaling Galveston's.

There's an appreciation for languid living among its 2,000 residents, and you'll find

yourself slowing down simply to admire the brick streets and gaze in the windows of the numerous antiques shops. Or you can take it all in on a narrated riverboat, vintage train, or historic homes tour. If you find yourself parched and craving a cool lemonade or an ice-cream soda, lucky for you, they're both served at the old-fashioned fountain inside the century-old Jefferson General Store, which also sells homemade pralines, lemon drops, aprons, pocketknives, paddleball games, and books on local history. Visit the history museum inside the old Federal courthouse, where exhibits include Civil War artifacts, vintage weapons, and papers of Republic of Texas hero and president Sam Houston.

With an abundance of charming B&Bs, there are plenty of places to stay, but the vaunted 15-room Excelsior House, a gracious 1858 inn where several presidents have slept, is one of those rare genteel places where everyone feels welcome, and many folks come to Jefferson primarily to stay here. Breakfast is a memorable experience, thanks to the inn's famous Plantation Breakfast with don't-miss orange blossom muffins.

About 15 miles from town, Caddo Lake, a magnificent 26,800-acre expanse of water, is distinguished by its seven-centuries-old cypress trees draped with heavy curtains of Spanish moss for a haunting, ethereal effect. Lest you get lost amid the baffling network of spooky sloughs and canals (and possibly surprise an alligator or two in the process), solicit the help of a Caddo Lake State Park ranger, who can point you to tour operators and canoe rentals, as well as to ten cabins built in the

1930s by the Civilian Conservation Corps (CCC). On the lake's shore, the quirky town of Uncertain offers fishing camps, lakeside cabins, camping supplies, a beer store or two, and plenty of folks with good stories to tell.

WHERE: 166 miles east of Dallas. *Visitor info:* Tel 888-467-3529 or 903-665-2672; jefferson-texas.com. **JEFFERSON GENERAL STORE:** Tel 903-665-8481; jeffersongeneral store.com. **JEFFERSON HISTORICAL MUSEUM:** Tel 903-665-2775; jeffersonmuseum.com. **EXCELSIOR HOUSE:** Tel 800-490-7270 or 903-665-2513; theexcelsiorhouse.com. *Cost:* from $135. **CADDO LAKE:** Tel 903-679-3351; tpwd .texas.gov/state-parks/caddo-lake. *Cost:* cabins from $75. **BEST TIMES:** 1st weekend in May for the Annual Pilgrimage Tour of Homes; first 2 weekends in Dec (Thurs–Sat) for the special candlelight Christmas homes tour (jeffersoncandlelight.com).

A small wooden windmill whirls outside Jefferson General Store.

Music Along the Scenic Guadalupe River

KERRVILLE FOLK FESTIVAL

Kerrville, Texas

Since 1972, the central Texas Hill Country has come alive each summer for the 18-day celebration of music known as the annual Kerrville Folk Festival. The longest-running musical festival of its sort in the nation,

the shindig brings more than 30,000 guests from around the globe to Quiet Valley Ranch,

just 9 miles south of the small resort town of Kerrville and 25 miles from Fredericksburg (see p. 768). Setting it apart from similar gatherings is the festival's blend of traditional folk, blues, jazz, country, bluegrass, and acoustic rock musicians and those aspiring talents who want to learn more from the experts. Over the years, more than 1,500 artists have taken the festival's stages, including Judy Collins, Janis Ian, and Peter Paul & Mary, plus then-emerging (and now well-known) talents such as Lyle Lovett, Mary Chapin Carpenter, Lucinda Williams, and Nancy Griffith.

There's more to the festival than the evening performances, however: You'll find impromptu jam sessions throughout the campgrounds any time of the day or night, plus kids' special activities and concerts, songwriting classes, music industry seminars, bike rides through the Hill Country, canoe trips on the lovely Guadalupe River, and the New Folk Competition for newcomers to the folk music scene. A second festival takes place over Labor Day weekend: The three-day Kerrville Fall Music Festival, dubbed "Little Folk," brings together music, great wines and beers from Texas vintners and brewers, and camping. Concerts are scheduled for afternoons and evenings, and afternoon seminars pair savory foods with local drink picks.

If you hit Kerrville, which has a population of just over 22,500, at other times of year, head to the bucolic Guadalupe River, a gentle, jade-colored ribbon that cuts through town and then meanders into the magical countryside, offering great opportunities for fly-fishing, tubing, canoeing, kayaking, and birding. You can also enjoy the area's scenery from a saddle by booking a trail ride at places like the legendary 40,000-acre Y.O. Ranch, settled in 1880 by one of Kerrville's pioneer families. In addition to its ongoing cattle operations, the ranch offers lodging in period cabins and bus tours of the ranch lands, which are populated by exotic animals from around the world, such as the blackbuck antelope of India and the East African oryx.

WHERE: 66 miles northwest of San Antonio. *Visitor info:* Tel 800-221-7958 or 830-792-3535; kerrvilletexascvb.com. **KERRVILLE FOLK FESTIVAL/FALL MUSIC FESTIVAL:** Tel 830-257-3600; kerrvillefolkfestival.org. *Cost:* tickets from $25. *When:* late May–mid-June (Folk Fest), and early Sept (Fall Music Fest). **BOATING:** Kerrville Kayak and Canoe, tel 830-459-2122; paddlekerrville.com. **Y.O. RANCH:** Mountain Home. Tel 844-835-3222 or 830-640-3222; yoranchheadquarters.com. *Cost:* from $225 per person, includes meals; riding $80 per hour.

Western Luxury in the Chinatis

CIBOLO CREEK RANCH

Marfa, Texas

Set in the hulking Chinati Mountains in a region called the Trans-Pecos (see p. 778), Cibolo Creek Ranch is one of the most historic and unusual retreats you'll find in all the Southwest. Named for the mythic Seven Cities of Cibolo (sought by gold-seeking 16th-century Spanish conquistadors), the 30,000-acre resort began as a ranch with three adobe forts founded by Milton Faver in 1857. In the early 1990s, Houston businessman John Poindexter bought the forts and the green, stream-fed ranchlands and spent four years upgrading the property. Today, the forts, now elegantly modernized, form the foundation for a luxury getaway.

The combination of quiet Chihuahuan Desert majesty and sublime digs provides myriad ways to recuperate from whatever life throws at you. Take a horse for an early-morning ride, lounge beside the lovely pool, or doze in a hammock, dreaming of your next exquisite meal. You can hike or bike in the mountains or simply explore the small museum tucked between the twin towers of El Cibolo, the original building. There, you'll find hundreds of volumes of Southwestern history and a wealth of artifacts recovered from the ranch.

Before dinner, rest up in your peaceful room, one of 22 in the main building, where the floors are paved in thick Saltillo tiles and handcrafted Mexican furniture is comple-mented by Talavera pottery and antique brass lamps. It takes mere seconds to drift

A cowboy rides across the open prairies surrounding Cibolo Creek Ranch.

off beneath goose-down comforters, with fra-grant piñon wood ablaze in your own small fireplace. At dinner, sit down to a feast of pork loin in guava and plum sauce or chicken with almond mole. Afterward, guests may gather at a giant firepit beside the large, spring-fed pond, under a stunning canopy of stars.

If you seek real seclusion, you'll want to book yourself into one of the resort's more remote lodgings. Thirty minutes away from the main site is the 19th-century fort La Cienega, where five guest rooms offer fire-places, hammocks, fabulous kitchens, and dining and living rooms. Another five rooms are located in an adjoining hacienda. La Morita, the most remote fort (about 45 minutes from the main site), is a single cottage with a queen bed and a sitting room, all served by oil lamps, a gas-log stove, and mountain breezes.

WHERE: 33 miles south of Marfa. Tel 866-496-9460 or 432-229-3737; cibolocreek ranch.com. *Cost:* from $350; dinner $75. **BEST TIMES:** Feb–Apr and Sept–Nov for most com-fortable weather.

Maximal Sky, Minimal Art

MARFA

Texas

In 1971, minimalist artist Donald Judd headed west from New York in search of a place to create and permanently house his increasingly large-form sculptures. West of the Pecos he found the quiet town of Marfa and, in 1979,

the Fort D. A. Russell, a decommissioned mili-tary base where he created the Chinati Foundation, one of the country's finest exhibi-tion spaces for contemporary installation art. Named for the nearby mountain range, the foun-dation emphasizes works in which the art and the surrounding landscape are intimately linked, with a permanent collection containing pieces by Judd and 11 like-minded artists,

including Don Flavin and Claes Oldenburg. The centerpiece, Judd's *100 Untitled Works in Mill Aluminum*, 100 aluminum rectangles, cre-ates startling effects through a combination of light and space. Outside, *15 Untitled Works in Concrete* uses the region's daytime light as its medium, with a half-mile of 16-by-8-foot hollow concrete blocks creating a slowly changing dis-play of shadow and light amid the prairie grass.

Because of the Chinati Foundation, a cottage industry for conceptual art has developed in Marfa, a town of about 1,800 that began as a railroad watering stop in the early 1880s. In the town center, restaurants catering to the area's ranchers coexist with arts bookshops, while the Thunderbird motel, a 1950s original, has been redesigned to fit the new art aesthetic, blending minimalism with retro. For more traditional digs, the restored Hotel Paisano dates from 1930 and was used as both set and lodging for James Dean's last movie, *Giant*, in the 1950s.

East of town, the so-called Marfa Mystery Lights were one of Marfa's claims to fame before Judd arrived, flickering sporadically along the horizon after sundown for no known reason. The nearby McDonald Observatory (see below) opens up other horizons of its own at regularly scheduled evening star parties.

WHERE: 194 miles southeast of El Paso. *Visitor info:* Tel 432-729-4772; marfachamber .com. **CHINATI FOUNDATION:** Tel 432-729-4362; chinati.org. *When:* closed Mon–Tues. **THUNDERBIRD:** Tel 432-729-1984; thunder birdmarfa.com. *Cost:* from $160. **HOTEL PAISANO:** Tel 866-729-3669 or 432-729-3669; hotelpaisano.com. *Cost:* from $109. **BEST TIME:** early Oct for the annual Chinati Weekend, a free 2-day festival of art, music, and lectures.

On Top of the World in the Trans-Pecos

THE MOUNTAINS OF WEST TEXAS

Texas

The arid but ruggedly beautiful Trans-Pecos region of West Texas comprises four remote mountain ranges that extend from the bottom of the Rocky Mountain system at the New Mexico state line to Big Bend National Park (see p. 760) and the Mexican border. Begin exploring in the north amid the forests, meadows, and cliffs of lonely, exquisite Guadalupe Mountains National Park. Home to 8,749-foot Guadalupe Peak—Texas's tallest—this range of dramatic rock formations was actually a vast underwater limestone reef 250 million years ago. Climbers will need six to eight hours to hike the steep but well-marked Guadalupe Peak Trail to "the top of Texas," where you can sign a register to prove you made it. Among the 80 miles of park trails are the 5- to 7-mile round-trip McKittrick Canyon Trail (following a pretty stream to sites like the historic Pratt Lodge); the strenuous 8.4-mile Permian Reef Trail (offering excellent views into McKittrick Canyon); and the Marcus Overlook Trail (a moderate climb with steep, dramatic views).

Balmorhea State Park, 136 miles south, is an oasis fed by the beautiful San Solomon Springs that once served buffalo, Native Americans, and pioneer families. Channeled into an enormous 1.75-acre pool, more than 15 million gallons of natural spring waters rush in daily and stay at 72° to 76°F. The pool, the two wooden bathhouses, and the adobe-brick San Solomon Spring Courts Motel were constructed by the Civilian Conservation Corps (CCC) during the Great Depression.

Just to the south, the peaks of the Davis Mountains were formed by volcanic activity 35 million years ago. In the range's northern sector, you'll find the Limpia Canyon Primitive Area, with 7 miles of backcountry trails for hardcore campers, or take in the views from the leisurely 75-mile drive that passes nine scenic roadside parks and the McDonald Observatory. Among the world's leading centers for astronomical research, it sits beneath some of the darkest night skies in the continental United States and offers daily public viewing programs and star parties on some evenings. Spend the night at nearby Indian Lodge, a 39-room hotel built by the CCC in the 1930s in Southwestern Native American Pueblo style, with 18-inch adobe walls and hand-carved cedar furniture. Fort Davis National Historic Site, one of the nation's best-preserved cavalry forts, is a short drive or an 8-mile round-trip hike from the hotel. At the fort's museum, you can learn more about the illustrious Buffalo Soldiers, the legendary black troops known for their bravery and toughness.

Healing waters burble up from a 20,000-year-old geothermically heated aquifer in Chinati Hot Springs just east of the little hamlet of Ruidosa, making it the perfect place to appreciate the third range, the Chinati Mountains. You can soak in the outdoor hot tub, take sunrise hikes or bike rides in the desert, and rest up in modest cabins near the cottonwood-lined creek.

From Ruidosa, point yourself eastward along the spectacularly scenic River Road, following the Rio Grande toward Big Bend National Park and the final set of West Texas peaks, the Chisos Mountains, rising above the Chihuahuan Desert.

WHERE: from about 110 miles east of El Paso to about 325 miles southeast of El Paso. **GUADALUPE MOUNTAINS NATIONAL PARK:** Tel 915-828-3251; nps.gov/gumo. **BALMORHEA STATE PARK:** Toyahvale. Tel 432-375-2370; tpwd.texas.gov/state-parks/balmorhea. *Cost:* rooms at San Solomon Courts from $75. **DAVIS MOUNTAINS STATE PARK:** Fort Davis. Tel 432-426-3337; tpwd.texas.gov/state-parks/davis-mountains. **MCDONALD OBSERVATORY:** Tel 877-984-7827 or 432-426-3640; mcdonald observatory.org. **INDIAN LODGE:** Tel 432-426-3254; tpwd.texas.gov/state-parks/indian-lodge. *Cost:* from $95. **CHINATI HOT SPRINGS:** Presidio. Tel 432-229-4165; chinatihotsprings.net. *Cost:* from $85. **BEST TIMES:** Oct–Apr for weather, scenery, and nature at Guadalupe and Balmorhea; Mar–Oct for weather at Davis; Feb–Apr and July–Nov for weather at Chinati; for viewing at the McDonald Observatory, avoid full moons.

Mescalero Apache Indians made the harsh Guadalupe Mountains their home until they were forced onto reservations in the 19th century.

The World Capital of Fine Feathered Friends

THE GREAT TEXAS BIRDING TRAIL

Rockport, Lamar, and Mission, Texas

They say everything's bigger in Texas, and this holds true even for bird-watching. With over 500 native and migratory bird species—more than half the species recorded in North America—found along what's become known as the Great Texas Coastal Birding Trail, the state is known for some of the best birding in the world and was the first to introduce such a viewing trail. Running along the

Gulf Coast, the trail encompasses 42 separate birding loops that can be driven or hiked; more than 300 marked birding sites with boardwalks, observation decks, and special bird-friendly landscaping; and a number of state and national refuges, home to tanagers, warblers, buntings, hummingbirds, orioles, and Texas specialties like the ringed king-fisher, the green jay, and the great kiskadee.

The trail is divided into three sections, designated the Upper, Central, and Lower Texas Coast. Along the Central Coast, you'll find possibly the most famous of all Texas birding sites, the Aransas National Wildlife Refuge, winter home to the world's only natural flock of whooping cranes—the largest birds in North America, standing nearly 5 feet tall and with a 7-foot wingspan. From mid-October through March, you can observe more than 300 of them feeding in the marshes during daylight hours, emitting their distinctive loud trumpeting calls.

You can see a few crane families by climbing the refuge's observation tower, or stay at the Habitat Vacation Cabins, a peaceful, secluded property bordering the refuge, and kayak over to see them from the water. Or book a crane-watching trip in Rockport, a booming resort town immediately north of Corpus Christi, where you'll find seaside beach houses for rent and million-dollar manses serving as second homes for well-heeled Texans.

Follow the Lower Coast trail to the end of the line at the headquarters of the World Birding Center in Bentsen–Rio Grande Valley State Park. The 760-acre center offers a beautiful bird and butterfly habitat with walking trails, a two-story hawk observation tower, two bird blinds, rustic campsites, and an impressive visitors center with bird education displays.

WHERE: 500 miles along the Texas Gulf Coast from Beaumont to Laredo. *Trail info:* Tel 800-792-1112 or 512-389-4800; tpwd.texas.gov/huntwild/wild/wildlife-trails-old/coastal. *Rockport visitor info:* Tel 800-242-0071 or 361-729-6445; rockport-fulton.org. **ARANSAS WILDLIFE REFUGE:** Lamar. Tel 361-286-3559; fws.gov/refuge/Aransas. **HABITAT VACATION CABINS:** Lamar. Tel 361-790-3732; txhabitat.com. *Cost:* $110. **WORLD BIRDING CENTER:** Mission. Tel 956-584-9156; worldbirdingcenter.org. **BEST TIMES:** Oct–Mar at the Aransas Refuge for whooping cranes and birding in general; June–Aug for butterflies at Bentsen–Rio Grande Valley State Park.

Texas Capital of Vintage Shopping

ROUND TOP ANTIQUES FAIR

Round Top, Texas

In the rolling countryside halfway between Houston and Austin, there's a crossroads called Round Top whose whopping year-round population of 90 belies the fact that twice a year the place attracts tens of thousands to the Round Top Antiques Fair. Held in late March or early April and then again in late September or early October, the 15-day fair takes over a 30,000-square-foot barn, two enormous tents, and a historic dance hall. Whether you're hunting furniture, art, hardware, china, linens, jewelry, or your own quixotic *objet du désir*, it'll probably be here by the wagonload.

At other times, things are pretty quiet around here, and that's just fine with everyone who loves Round Top. The earliest settlers were plantation owners who set down roots in 1826, and by the late 1840s German immigrants were building homes in the area. Many of these early cabins, schoolhouses, commercial buildings, and churches have been restored and relocated to the center of town in such places as Bybee Square (where they're now occupied by artisan shops, an art gallery, a coffeehouse, and antiques shops) and Henkel Square, with its housewares, gift and bookshops, and archival collections.

Smart antiques browsers book a room months in advance or stay in nearby towns such as Brenham, Fayetteville, or La Grange. One of the more delightful accommodations is The Prairie by Rachel Ashwell just outside town. Here you can choose from an assortment of cottages crafted from vintage barns, log cabins, and guesthouses, each restored and outfitted with period Texana furnishings, luxury bedding, and front porches or terraces with a view. When you're hungry, wait as long as it takes for a table at Royers Round Top Café, by far the most popular place for lunch and supper in town. Royers is famous for its grilled pork tenderloin topped with a peach-and-pepper glaze, beef tenderloin filet so tender you can cut it with a fork, and cheese and jalapeño grits served with Cajun spicy shrimp. Since pie is Royers's true claim to fame, consider the Pie Sampler: four slices (from an assortment including chocolate chip, pecan, peach, buttermilk, and strawberry rhubarb) on a platter with Amy's vanilla ice cream on top.

WHERE: about 73 miles east of Austin. *Visitor info:* Tel 888-368-4783 or 979-249-4042; roundtop.org. *When:* beginning 15 days before the 1st full weekends in Apr and Oct. **THE PRAIRIE:** Tel 979-836-4975; theprairie byrachelashwell.com. *Cost:* from $195 (off-peak), from $275 (peak). **ROYERS ROUND TOP CAFÉ:** Tel 877-866-PIES or 979-249-3611; royersroundtopcafe.com. *Cost:* dinner $35. **BEST TIMES:** late Mar–early Apr and late Sept–early Oct for the antiques fairs and great weather; Mar–Apr for bluebonnet season.

The Shrine of Texas Liberty

THE ALAMO & THE MISSIONS TRAIL

San Antonio, Texas

A site of great bloodshed and bravery, the Alamo was at one time the greatest symbol of freedom in the nation, and it remains an iconic element of Texas independence. Founded near the San Antonio River in 1718, the mission was catapulted to fame in 1836 during the Texas Revolution, when 200 Texan defenders held off President Santa Anna's 2,000-strong Mexican army for 13 days. The end finally came on March 6, 1836, when Santa Anna took the mission and killed almost everyone inside. While the loss was devastating, the long battle gave Texas Commander-in-Chief Sam Houston a chance to gather soldiers and supplies farther east, which he used six weeks later to stop Santa Anna's march across southeast Texas, leading to Texas's independence. Were it not for the Alamo, the memory of men like Davy Crockett and Jim Bowie—who joined the fight for independence and died in the process—would not have seeped into our national myth.

You might have seen one of the Alamo movies, but that doesn't measure up to seeing the surprisingly small place in real life, and experiencing the true heart and soul of San Antonio. Preface your visit by walking around the corner to the Rivercenter to see the IMAX movie *Alamo: The Price of Freedom*, then visit the Alamo Cenotaph, a marble-and-granite sculpture on the plaza in front of the mission, carved with the images and names of the 180-plus Alamo heroes who lost their lives. The 5-acre Alamo complex itself comprises the mission building; the Long Barrack Museum, which

Originally named San Antonio de Valero, the Alamo served as a Spanish mission for 70 years before it was secularized in 1793.

contains Texas history and revolution exhibits; and the lush, beautiful Alamo Gardens.

The Alamo was one of five area missions settled on or near the San Antonio River in the 1700s by Franciscans to prevent the French in Louisiana from expanding into Spanish territory. The Alamo's four remaining sister missions lie south of downtown along the river, forming San Antonio Missions National Park. The most popular stop along the Mission Trail is Mission San José, called Queen of the Missions. Established in 1720, it still serves as a parish church and is a photographer's dream, with its myriad stone walls, granary, bastions, and beautiful 1782 church building. Sunday noontime's bilingual mariachi mass is a must-do San Antonio experience.

The Alamo: 300 Alamo Plaza. Tel 210-225-1391; thealamo.org. **Missions National Park:** Tel 210-932-1001; nps.gov/saan. **Best times:** Mar 2 for Texas Independence Day at the Alamo; Mar 6 for Dusk at the Alamo; mid- to late Dec for *Los Pastores*, a Mexican folk play at Mission San José.

A Lively Oasis in a Multicultural Town

River Walk

San Antonio, Texas

Way back when, Mark Twain and Will Rogers both rated San Antonio as one of America's most outstanding cities. Today Twain would recognize the city's historic showpiece, the Alamo (see previous entry), but not its

second most visited attraction, the historic downtown River Walk, a lively flagstone esplanade that wends for 3 miles amid tropical foliage along both banks of the lazy, narrow San Antonio River. Originally funded in 1939 by the Depression-era Works Progress Administration, it is lined with lively sidewalk cafés, open-air restaurants, shops, and hotels, and it has greatly expanded in recent years to include 15 miles of hiking and biking trails along the river.

At the prettiest of the river's many horseshoe bends you'll find the Omni La Mansión del Rio. Originating as a Spanish-influenced 19th-century boys' school, it was reborn in 1968 as an elegant respite of cool courtyard fountains and old-world ambience, with most rooms overlooking the river. Its Las Canarias Restaurant is one of River Walk's most distinguished. Directly across the river is its sister property, Mokara, with sumptuous but understated interiors, rooms with river views, and a highly polished staff. Its 17,000-square-foot spa is one of the city's most luxurious, with a rooftop pool and café. On the hotel's river level, Ostra is a superb seafood restaurant with a spectacular stone-and-glass oyster bar. For more casual fare, head upriver to Boudro's for a prickly pear margarita and smoked shrimp enchiladas. Anchoring the northerly reach of the River Walk in the culinary and cultural hub of the Pearl District, Hotel Emma is another excellent lodging choice, with 146 stylish and industrial-elegant rooms housed within the impressive Mission-style walls of a 19th-century brew house.

The River Walk is a special pleasure at night and on weekends, but two periods are particularly wonderful: the Christmas season, when 250,000 twinkling lights illuminate its vintage facades and bridges and light the way for traveling barges of carolers; and late April, when the whole city stops for the Fiesta San Antonio (see below). At any time of year, arrive early for the narrated Rio San Antonio Cruise. You can take a dinner cruise, too, or take in an opera, flamenco show, or *ballet folklorico* performance from a seat on the grass tiers at the open-air Arneson River Theater. It's on the river next to La Villita, the original city settlement and now a compound of art galleries and shops.

RIVER WALK: Tel 210-227-4262; thesanantonioriverwalk.com. **MANSIÓN DEL RIO:** Tel 888-444-OMNI or 210-518-1000; lamansion .com. *Cost:* from $179 (off-peak), from $250 (peak); dinner at Las Canarias $55. **MOKARA:** Tel 888-444-OMNI or 210-396-5800; mokara hotels.com. *Cost:* from $270 (off-peak), from $350 (peak); dinner at Ostra $50. **BOUDRO'S:** Tel 210-224-8484; boudros.com. *Cost:* dinner $40. **RIVER CRUISES:** Tel 800-417-4139 or 210-244-5700; riosanantonio.com. **HOTEL EMMA:** Tel 210-448-8300; thehotelemma.com. *Cost:* from $325 (off-peak), from $375 (peak). **ARNESON RIVER THEATER:** Tel 210-207-8610. **BEST TIMES:** late Apr for Fiesta San Antonio (fiesta-sa.org); Christmas season for lights.

Shops, restaurants, trees, and walkways line the banks of the narrow San Antonio River.

A Capital of Latino Culture in the Southwest

SAN ANTONIO'S HISPANIC HERITAGE

San Antonio, Texas

Your visit will be a charmed one if you land in the Alamo City in the latter half of April, when its vibrant pitch crescendos during the ten-day Fiesta San Antonio. Begun as a parade in 1891 to honor the heroes of the Alamo (see p. 781) and the Battle of San Jacinto, the fiesta's centerpiece extravaganza remains the Battle of the Flowers Parade but includes more than 100 events across the city. Among the most delightful is the four-night celebration called Night in Old San Antonio, when more than 85,000 participants gather to dance, eat, drink, and watch traditional performance groups in 15 themed areas honoring different immigrant heritages.

Even if you're not blessed with a visit to San Antonio (and never, ever say "San Antone") during Fiesta, you can still indulge yourself in the city's rich Hispanic heritage. El Mercado, or Market Square, is the largest Mexican market outside Mexico, with stalls selling pottery, jewelry, blankets, leather goods, and papier-mâché decorations; and mariachi bands and folk dancers promising entertainment. Grab a pan dulce from the bakery case or a plate of superb green-chile enchiladas at the renowned Mi Tierra Café, open since 1941 and serving customers 24 hours a day.

A walk through San Antonio's downtown will take you to the exquisite San Fernando Cathedral, originally founded in the 1730s. From there, head to the beautiful San Antonio Museum of Art to visit the Nelson A. Rockefeller Center for Latin American Art, which holds a collection that spans 4,000 years and includes work by pre-Columbian civilizations, Spanish Colonial artisans, and 20th-century masters such as Diego Rivera.

Listed on the National Register of Historic Places, the Aztec Theatre returned to its original 1926 glory when it reopened in 2014 with a new state-of-the-art sound system. Inside its magnificent three-story lobby, the Aztec's eye-popping three-ton chandelier—restored by the grandson of the theater's original designer—dominates the tableau.

A few blocks away, work continues on the lovely 1949 Alameda, once the largest Spanish-language theater in the U.S. The 2,400-seat movie palace is slated to become a center for Latino arts and culture. Watch for bilingual offerings of first-rate opera, film, dance, theater, concerts, and Broadway productions here.

Just south of downtown you'll find the Guadalupe Cultural Arts Center, dedicated to preserving and promoting Chicano, Latino, and Native American art and culture. Wind up your visit at the University of Texas at San Antonio's Institute of Texan Culture, which tells the stories of the many ethnic and cultural groups that make up the fabric of the Lone Star State.

Fiesta San Antonio: Tel 877-723-4378 or 210-227-5191; fiesta-sa.org. *When:* 10 days in late Apr. **Market Square:** Tel 210-207-8600; marketsquaresa.com. **Mi Tierra Café:** Tel 210-225-1262; mitierracafe.com. *Cost:* dinner $25. **San Antonio Museum of Art:** Tel 210-978-8100; samuseum.org. *When:* closed Mon. **Aztec Theatre:** Tel 210-812-4355; azteetheatre.com. **Guadalupe Cultural Arts Center:** Tel 210-271-3151; guadalupeculturalarts.org. **Institute of Texan Culture:** Tel 210-458-2300; texancultures.com. **Best times:** late Apr for Fiesta San Antonio; May 5 for Cinco de Mayo; mid-May for Tejano Conjunto Music Festival at the Guadalupe Cultural Arts Center; early June for the Texas Folklife Festival (texancultures.com/festivals_events/texas_folklife_2016).

Mexican Food for Gringos and Purists

TEXAS COMFORT FOOD

San Antonio, Texas

No self-respecting Texan would be caught dead eating Mexican food anywhere outside the state lines—except maybe in Mexico. An American regional cuisine that combines northern Mexican peasant food with

Texas cowboy favorites, Tex-Mex got its start from Tejanos, who cooked up a mix of Mexican and Spanish dishes. In the 1880s, the famous San Antonio Chili Queens sold tacos, tamales, and chili con carne in the town's Military Square, but the food didn't get its current moniker until the 1940s. To eat the very best Tex-Mex, go to its San Antonio origins, where true Texas heritage is served on a plate in places like Mi Tierra in Market Square (see previous page).

Whereas Tex-Mex is characterized by fajitas and heavier, cheesier creations, foods from Mexico's interior tend to display more nuances and layering of flavors that reflect the refined preparation processes from various regions of the country. San Antonio offers a number of fine places to sample such artfully wrought dishes, starting with El Mirador, a festive place just south of downtown, serving unforgettable dishes like red snapper crusted in crushed tortilla chips, served atop tomatillo-corn salsa, yellow rice, and green vegetables. Other seafood treasures include the lobster taco with spinach and the shrimp-stuffed poblano chile. Alternatively, for a beautiful garden setting and a taste of all Mexican food worlds, head to La Fogata, where favorites include marinated pork with squash and corn; chile relleno stuffed with spicy beef, almonds, and green olives; and chicken in mole sauce.

El Mirador: Tel 210-225-9444; elmirador restaurant.com. *Cost:* dinner $20. **La Fogata:** Tel 210-340-1337; lafogata.com. *Cost:* dinner $25. **Best times:** May 5 for Cinco de Mayo; late May weekend for the Return of the Chili Queens festival; Sept 16 for Diez y Seis (Mexican Independence Day); Sept 15–Oct 15 for Hispanic Heritage Month.

The extensive menu at La Fogata includes the signature Sopa de Tortilla.

Sandy Pleasures and Historic Ranchlands

SOUTH TEXAS GULF COAST

Texas

Life was relatively simple for the Indians who originally roamed the windswept shores, grassy dunes, and mesquite-clustered prairies of Texas's 367-mile Gulf Coast, and that idyll remains on North Padre Island, the longest undeveloped barrier island in the world. The 65-mile Padre Island National Seashore can be found here, where it's not uncommon to be the only one leaving footprints in the sand. Between June and September, you can even witness the release of endangered sea turtle hatchlings from here into the Gulf of Mexico.

The South Texas coast harbors a healthy respect for history and the wonders of nature, too. On Corpus Christi's bayfront (reached by driving inland across the John F. Kennedy Causeway), you can tour the mighty USS *Lexington*, a WWII aircraft carrier that's now a floating naval museum. You're likely to find a sailboat regatta in progress in the bay, plus windsurfers taking advantage of the impressive breezes that blow here year-round.

Less than an hour southwest of Corpus lies the renowned King Ranch, founded in 1853 by riverboat captain Richard King. At 825,000 acres, the spectacular spread is larger than the state of Rhode Island and is one of the largest privately owned ranches in the world. You can see the ranch on guided bus tours, and it's a primary birding destination along the Great Texas Coastal Birding Trail (see p. 779). Be sure to visit the adjacent town of Kingsville, for the small but worthy King Ranch Museum.

From Kingsville, it's 141 miles south to South Padre Island, a beach town that lies at the far end of the Queen Isabella Memorial Bridge, the second longest bridge in Texas at nearly 2.4 miles. On the island, you can ride horses on the beach, visit a sea turtle rehabilitation center, max out your credit cards at the shopping malls, or zip down slides and chutes and float the Rio Aventura at the 25-acre Schlitterbahn Beach Waterpark. Dozens of restaurants and bars await on the island, of course, but if you don't want to carouse with 250,000 high school and college kids, steer clear during spring break, mid-March through mid-April.

Although South Padre Island is renowned for its many tourist amenities, it's easy to find a quiet stretch of beach.

Padre Island National Seashore: 31 miles southeast of Corpus Christi. Tel 361-949-8069; nps.gov/pais. **King Ranch:** Kingsville. Tel 361-592-8055; king-ranch.com. *When:* Bus tours daily. Most nature tours Oct–Mar. **King Ranch Museum:** Kingsville. Tel 361-595-1881. **South Padre Island:** Tel 800-767-2373 or 956-761-6433; sopadre.com. **Best times:** early Feb for South Padre Island's Kite Fest (spikitefest.com); early Sept for Ruff Rider Regatta (ruffrider.net); Oct–May for weather; early Oct for Sandcastle Days (sandcastledays.com); Nov, the weekend before Thanksgiving for Ranch Hand Festival in Kingsville.

Wild for Flowers: Lady Bird's Legacy

TEXAS HILL COUNTRY

Texas

Growing up in the verdant forests of the East Texas region called the Piney Woods, little Claudia Taylor could no more have foreseen that she'd become the nation's First Lady than anticipate that she would change the way Americans view their highway roadsides. But Lady Bird Johnson ("pretty as a lady bird," as her childhood nursemaid said) did both. During her husband's time in the White House, Lady Bird threw her energy into preserving the countryside and promoted the Highway Beautification Act, thereby planting wildflowers along highway shoulders and limiting the visual pollution of billboards.

Visitors to the Hill Country will thank her for this, as it is a veritable blanket of wildflowers from March through much of summer, although April is typically the peak. Follow the two-lane roads that twist and climb through scrubby hills covered with prickly pear cactus and bluebonnets (the state flower) and valleys blanketed in pink evening primrose, bright yellow black-eyed Susans, and reddish purple Mexican hats—all alongside ancient juniper, mesquite, and live oak. In the Hill Country's upper reaches, you'll find festivals every spring weekend in the tiny towns of Burnet, Kingsland, Marble Falls, and Buchanan Dam, all clinging to the Highland Lakes, a 150-mile-long string of six sparkling lakes formed by the Colorado River.

After LBJ left office in 1969 and the couple settled at their ranch outside Austin, Lady Bird's passion for wildflowers only grew. Some 300 miles from the humble house where she grew up, she founded the National Wildflower Research Center (now called the Lady Bird Johnson Wildflower Center) to foster preservation and reintroduction of native plants in landscaping. Visitors can roam the 279-acre grounds, take in 700 plant species, attend classes and festivals, buy wildflower seeds, and find out where to see some of the best floral patches in Texas.

Forty-eight miles west of Austin, the historic LBJ Ranch, part of the Lyndon B. Johnson National Historical Park, lies on the Pedernales River between the tiny twin towns of Stonewall and Johnson City, as does the LBJ State Park

and Historic Site, where living history programs re-create a pioneer farmstead. In Johnson City proper, you can visit LBJ's boyhood home, or drive to Austin and visit the wonderful Lyndon Baines Johnson Library and Museum, with both traveling and permanent exhibits.

WILDFLOWER CENTER: Austin. Tel 512-232-0100; wildflower.org. **LBJ NATIONAL HISTORICAL PARK:** Johnson City. Tel 830-868-7128; nps.gov/lyjo. **LBJ STATE PARK:** Stonewall. Tel 830-644-2252; tpwd.texas.gov/state-parks/lyndon-b-johnson. **LBJ LIBRARY:** Austin. Tel 512-721-0200; lbjlibrary.org. **BEST TIMES:** Apr for peak flower viewing and festivals; weekdays to avoid crowds.

The Wildflower Center works to protect the 200 at-risk native Texas plant species—including aquatic plants—by banking endangered seeds and propagating rare species.

Wonderland of Stone Sculptures

ARCHES NATIONAL PARK

Utah

"This is the most beautiful place on earth," wrote American author, essayist, and environmental advocate Edward Abbey in *Desert Solitaire*. Every year more than a million awestruck visitors nod in silent

agreement: Utah's most famous park is an extraordinary place. Just a short drive from Moab (see p. 796), Arches contains more than 2,000 natural arches whose salmon-colored

sandstone has been sculpted by the inexorable forces of water, ice, and gravity. The magnificent vistas combine cacti and petrified sand dunes with the oft-snowcapped La Sal

Mountains, so named by early Spanish explorers who thought they looked as if they had been sprinkled with salt.

Many visitors along the 18-mile scenic drive are content to admire the view through the windshield, but it's well worth it to get out and explore on foot. Balanced Rock, a 3,577-ton boulder that looks as if it could be toppled by a stiff wind, is close to the road, as are the Windows, a pair of huge arches that dwarf hikers. Each arch is different from the next; many are so thin and fragile it's a wonder they stand at all. The don't-miss 3-mile hike to famous Delicate Arch, Utah's

Because of its distinctive shape, Delicate Arch was known by local cowboys as the "Chaps" and the "Schoolmarm's Bloomers."

unofficial state symbol, begins at Wolfe Ranch, a one-room cabin built by a Civil War veteran in 1898. (You might recognize some of the Hollywood-worthy scenery as one of the locations for the classic 1991 film *Thelma & Louise*.)

Past the crazy pastels of Salt Valley is the Fiery Furnace, a sandstone labyrinth that, despite its name, actually stays cooler in the summer than the surrounding desert. The way to explore these is on a ranger-led hike. At the end of the scenic drive is the trailhead for another great hike, Devils Garden, and the turnoff for the park's best 4WD adventure. The 7-mile path leads past eight major arches, including the impossibly thin Landscape Arch, the park's largest at 290 feet across.

For idyllic lodgings, nothing in the area matches Sorrel River Ranch, set directly on the banks of the Colorado River a half-hour away. This plush but informal 160-acre property offers an exciting slate of outdoor activities, including a stableful of horses and a full-service spa. Views of the red cliffs of Castle Valley create a setting so beautiful it's almost surreal.

WHERE: 5 miles north of Moab. Tel 435-719-2299; nps.gov/arch. **SORREL RIVER RANCH:** Tel 877-317-8244 or 435-259-4642; sorrelriver.com. *Cost:* from $359 (off-peak), from $489 (peak). **BEST TIMES:** spring and fall. Summer can get very hot.

Rivers, Canyons, and a Monument to the Four Corners

BLUFF & THE SAN JUAN RIVER

Utah

Restored sandstone pioneer homes set among huge old cottonwoods make up the tiny and friendly town of Bluff, with a population of just 258. It was settled in 1880 by exhausted Mormon pioneers sent south from Salt Lake City by Brigham Young. Today it's an unusually liberal enclave for conservative southern Utah and prides itself on being home to many artists, writers, and artisans, as well as offering plenty of options for exploring—on land and afloat—the history- and canyon-rich country that stretches in every direction.

Set on the sinuous San Juan River, Bluff has become a center for desert river rafting. A one-to five-day raft trip on the canyon-lined stretch of river between Bluff and Mexican Hat (see p. 795) will give you a chance to visit the ancient ruins and petroglyphs along the way. Wild Rivers Expeditions offers some of the best river rafting. Fun for the whole family, the trips are led by guides who point out and interpret American Indian sites such as the 250-foot-long Butler Wash Petroglyph Panel. Explore on land with Far Out Expeditions, which offers day hikes and truck-supported overnight trips to see the rock art and ruins that abound nearby, as well as accommodations in a historic home.

At the foot of the Navajo Twins, a pair of stone formations on the northern edge of town, stop by the Cow Canyon Trading Post, or pay a visit to the larger Twin Rocks Trading Post with a selection of quality mementos and a popular restaurant that's one of the most reliable in the area.

Bluff is the closest town to the Four Corners Monument, marked by a concrete platform more or less in the middle of nowhere. The monument, a tiny Navajo park, sits at the intersection of Utah, Arizona, Colorado, and New Mexico, the only place in the U.S. where four states meet. You can kiss across state lines or play interstate Twister ("Right hand Arizona . . ."), and Native vendors sell hand-made jewelry and crafts. You're also not far from one of the country's most iconic Wild West locations, Monument Valley (see p. 688), the bulk of which falls within the state of Arizona.

Where: Bluff is 334 miles south of Salt Lake City. **Wild Rivers Expeditions:** Tel 435-672-2244; riversandruins.com. *Cost:* 1-day raft trips from $175 per person. *When:* Mar–Oct. **Far Out Expeditions:** Tel 435-672-2294; faroutexpeditions.com. *Cost:* day trips from $295 per person; rooms from $95. **Cow Canyon Trading Post:** Tel 435-672-2208. **Twin Rocks Trading Post:** Tel 435-672-2341; twinrocks.com. *Cost:* lunch $14. **Best times:** May–Oct.

Whimsical Sculptures Frozen in Time

Bryce Canyon National Park

Utah

The thousands of multihued limestone hoodoos (odd-shaped pillars of rock formed by erosion) rising from the eastern edge of the Paunsaugunt Plateau were thought by the Paiute Indians to be the petrified remains of the

"legend people," turned to stone for their evil ways and frozen in time forever by a vengeful god. To Mormon settler Ebenezer Bryce, who settled here in 1876, the natural amphitheater was "a helluva place to lose a cow." To 1.5 million visitors every year, Bryce Canyon is a veritable fantasyland, where whimsical spires of endless shades and sizes change by the minute as the clouds and sun slide overhead.

The formations come in every possible hue of white, pink, red, and purple; just wait a minute as the light shifts, and it can all change before your eyes.

The park itself isn't very big—at only 56 square miles—but it's a gem. The views from the rim at 9,100 feet are astonishing, especially at sunrise, since much of the canyon faces east. You can take the easy 38-mile (round-trip) scenic drive following the park's rim, or opt to hike among the formations and on any of the 60 miles of trails. There are short walks like the Queen's Garden (2 miles) and longer trails like Fairyland Loop (8 miles); or head down to Wall Street and ponder its towering "skyscrapers." From Fairyland to Bryce Point, the Rim Trail skirts the edge for

The view of Bryce Canyon, with its thousands of hoodoos, is quite striking.

6 miles. This route is particularly breathtaking on cross-country skis in winter, when you'll feel as if you have the magical place to yourself.

The venerable Lodge at Bryce Canyon was built a short distance from the rim by the Union Pacific Railroad Company in the 1920s. The main lodge of ponderosa timbers and native sandstone has just 4 guest rooms along with 40 cabins and 70 motel rooms on the grounds, plus a lively dining room where you can get a pretty good meal.

In the morning head out on Highway 12, known for 112 of the prettiest driving miles in the country. This "All American Road" (the highest designation in the national highway system) peaks at almost 1,000 feet and drops you off at Capitol Reef National Park (see next page) and Torrey, its gateway town.

BRYCE CANYON NATIONAL PARK: 260 miles south of Salt Lake City. Tel 435-834-5322; nps.gov/brca. **THE LODGE AT BRYCE CANYON:** Tel 877-386-4383 or 435-834-5361; brycecanyonforever.com. *Cost:* from $192. *When:* Apr–Oct. **BEST TIMES:** The altitude keeps things cool in summer; the park is almost deserted in winter, except during the mid-Feb Bryce Canyon Winter Carnival.

Nature-Carved Heart of the Colorado Plateau

CANYONLANDS NATIONAL PARK

Utah

U tah's largest national park packs so many reasons to visit into 527 square miles that it's divided into three districts—four, if you count the Green and Colorado Rivers that slice it all in a big watery Y. From the high

tablelands of the Colorado Plateau to the dizzying depths of river-carved canyons, Canyonlands encapsulates nearly everything that makes the Southwest such a special place: challenging hiking trails, roiling white water, ancient rock art and prehistoric dwellings, plentiful desert life, and some of the most astounding views you'll ever see.

The Island in the Sky district, in the cup of the Y, is the district closest to Moab (see p. 796) and, with some 20 miles of paved road, the most accessible by car. The White Rim Road provides an additional 100 miles of dirt

road—heaven for mountain bikers and 4WD adventurists. Around every turn are sublime vistas over hundreds of miles of unique canyon country, with its river gorges, distant mesas, and mountain ranges. The Needles district to the southeast takes its name from its distinctive red-and-white striped sandstone spires; it's also home to a number of impressive arches, including the 150-foot-tall Angel Arch, and abundant archaeological sites. This is the best section for hiking and camping, with many excellent trails for day hikes and overnight trips.

The Maze district, reached by a long drive

through the city of Green River and southwest on Highway 24 toward Hanksville, is the most remote part of the park. If you have a tough 4WD vehicle and at least three days free, you can find yourself in country so rugged that the outlaw Butch Cassidy once successfully hid here from the law. A small detached part of the Maze called Horseshoe Canyon is easier to access (only 30 miles of dirt road and a 7-mile hike from Highway 24) and contains some of the most outstanding rock art in the Southwest: dozens of larger-than-life figures stretching along a 300-foot-long rock panel called the Great Gallery, painted by prehistoric Indians known as the Archaic People.

The Green and Colorado Rivers, which cut through the park, offer everything from peaceful flat-water floats to raging white water in Cataract Canyon below their confluence. River access is

generally from Moab, where many river tour companies offer guided tours and boat rentals.

WHERE: Island in the Sky District entrance is 30 miles southwest of Moab. *Visitor info:* Tel 435-719-2313; nps.gov/cany. **BEST TIMES:** spring and fall for all districts.

A "high desert," Canyonlands experiences very hot summers, cold winters, and less than 10 inches of rain each year.

Canyons and Fruit Trees in a Historic Eden

CAPITOL REEF NATIONAL PARK

Utah

With a fraction of the name recognition of Utah's more famous parks, Capitol Reef National Park, the second largest of the state's "Mighty Five," is a relatively unknown gem. Long and narrow,

it follows the Waterpocket Fold, a 100-mile rust-red wrinkle in the earth's crust, and is home to a historic settlement, countless narrow canyons, and some of the most surreally beautiful rock formations in the Southwest.

Highway 24 cuts across the northern part of the park along the banks of the Fremont River, which has given birth to an

Dramatic rose-colored cliffs rise behind an old barn at Capitol Reef National Park.

oasis of green in the unforgiving desert landscape. Mormon settlers planted fruit trees in Fruita, the "Eden of Wayne County," in the 1880s, about the time Butch Cassidy and his fellow outlaws were hiding out in nearby canyons. Today the orchards are maintained by the National Park Service, and visitors are welcome to pick apples, apricots, peaches, and other fruits in season. The small historic district holds a one-room schoolhouse and farmstead as well, where settlers once grew vegetables, alfalfa, and sorghum.

South of Fruita, the park's only other paved road, the Scenic Drive runs 18 miles past the Egyptian Temple, an unmistakable stone landmark. The pavement ends at Capitol Gorge, once the only way vehicles could cross the Waterpocket Fold, where you can see the petroglyphs made by the Fremont people, who lived here from A.D. 600 to 1300, and the names of the pioneers who came after them and carved their names into the canyon wall nearby. Capitol Gorge also leads to some of the park's most spectacular views, which can be seen without leaving the comfort of your air-conditioned car. Visitors with 4WD vehicles can reach Muley Twist, a popular hike through a narrow, sinuous canyon.

The park's gateway town of Torrey counts only a few hundred residents, but it does have two outstanding places to eat. The Capitol Reef Inn & Café uses locally grown produce in its excellent restaurant, and you can also spend the night in its homey Southwest-style rooms filled with handmade furniture. And to augment the surprise of great eating in this edge-of-nowhere region, make sure you drop in to the uninspired-looking Café Diablo, which offers a jazzed-up menu of Southwest fare including honey and red chile–glazed salmon with black bean croquettes. You'll want to stay another day just for the rich homemade ice cream.

Where: 220 miles south of Salt Lake City. Tel 435-425-3791; nps.gov/care. **Capitol Reef Inn & Café:** Torrey. Tel 435-425-3271; capitolreefinn.com. *Cost:* rooms from $64; lunch $15. **Café Diablo:** Torrey. Tel 435-425-3070; cafediablo.net. *Cost:* dinner $40. **Best times:** spring and fall for weather.

The Real Jurassic Park

DINOSAUR NATIONAL MONUMENT

Utah and Colorado

It's a park to make Spielberg proud, with not only one of the world's largest concentrations of dinosaur bones from the Late Jurassic Period ever discovered, but also white-water rafting wild enough to make the most jaded action-film fan squeal. Dinosaur National Monument straddles the Utah-Colorado border, with 210,000 acres of some of the roughest and most gorgeous canyons and mountains in the American West.

Twenty miles east of Vernal, Utah, is the Quarry Exhibit Hall (accessible only from the Utah side), the destination for most day visitors to the 329-square-mile monument. More than 1,500 bones of the so-called "terrible lizards" that lived here 150 million years ago have been exposed on a 150-foot rock face. You'll see the remains of the meat-eating *Allosaurus*, the long-necked *Apatosaurus* (previously known as *Brontosaurus*), and the smaller "bird robber," *Ornitholestes*. Full-size dinosaur replicas round out the displays, with depictions of how these fascinating animals moved and lived.

To the east, at the Canyon Area Visitor Center near the town of Dinosaur, Colorado, you can watch a video about the park and follow a short nature trail into the high desert. Better yet, take the ultrascenic 31-mile (one-way) "Journey Through Time" drive north on Harpers Corner Road. It ends at the start of a strenuous but worthwhile 1-mile hike (one-way) from Harpers Corner Trail to a knee-weakening overlook 2,300 feet above Echo Park, where you'll see the 1,000-foot Steamboat Rock rising above the confluence of the Yampa River, the last free-flowing tributary of the Colorado, and the Green River.

One of the best ways to see this magnificent country is by water, and the monument is as popular for its rafting as for its prehistoric skeletons. Along with one-day trips, you can also choose from a multitude of multiday adventures: the three- to five-day trip with Class III rapids down the Green River, starting at the Gates of Lodore (which 19th-century explorer John Wesley Powell described as "a mountain drinking a river") and ending at Split Mountain Campground near the Dinosaur Quarry; or the four- to five-day trip with Class IV rapids down the Yampa from Deerlodge Park to Split Mountain. Both offer a journey through canyons older than time where you just might find yourself watching out for a *Diplodocus*.

WHERE: Vernal is 172 miles east of Salt Lake City. Tel 435-781-7700; nps.gov/dino. **HOW:** O.A.R.S. Raft Trips. Tel 800-346-6277 or 209-736-4677; oars.com. *Cost:* all-inclusive

trips from $929 per person for 4 days. *When:* late May–early Sept (Green River); May–early July (Yampa River). **BEST TIMES:** Sept and Oct for weather, as summer is hot and spring can be muddy.

A hiker studies ancient petroglyphs in Dinosaur National Monument.

The Last Blank Spot on the U.S. Map

GRAND STAIRCASE-ESCALANTE NATIONAL MONUMENT

Utah

This most recent addition to Utah's plentiful protected lands came by proclamation of President Bill Clinton in 1996. Bigger than the state of Delaware, these nearly 3,000 square miles contain enough geological

wonders, desert life, and solitude to earn the nickname American Outback. The huge expanse of red-orange canyons, cliffs, rivers, and high-desert plateaus is divided into three distinct regions from west to east: the Grand Staircase, a series of gigantic, colorful steps rising a total of 3,500 feet; the Kaiparowits Plateau, the monument's vast, remote center, known for paleontology and prehistoric human relics; and the Escalante Canyons, a complex network of interconnecting gorges converging on the Escalante River, the last major river to be "discovered" in the Lower 48 by European settlers in 1872.

The easiest access to this isolated region is off Highway 12 between Bryce Canyon National Park (see p. 789) and Boulder. The road itself is a stunner, and near the town of Escalante it connects with the Hole-in-the-Rock road, a dirt track into the heart of the Escalante Canyons blazed by courageous Mormon pioneers over a century ago. In dry weather it's good enough for most vehicles, at least far enough (26 miles) to reach the trailheads for Coyote Gulch, one of the monument's most popular destinations for hiking and backpacking. Short, narrow slot canyons with names like Spooky and Peek-a-Boo branch off the main gulch. Unlike most national monuments, almost all this vast area is undeveloped, and options for overnight backpacking trips abound in the larger canyons nearby, where it's likely you won't see another soul. (It's a very good idea to check in with one of the four visitors centers before heading out to the monument, as travelers often underestimate the rigors of desert exploring.)

In Boulder, a remote speck on the map on Highway 12 is the Boulder Mountain Lodge, an inviting getaway out in the middle of nowhere. The building abuts a private waterfowl sanctuary, and gourmands travel for hours to dine at the attached Hell's Backbone Grill, serving organic Southwest–Pueblo Indian cuisine that's both unfussy and innovative—and pretty remarkable even if you don't consider where you are.

Where: 278 miles south of Salt Lake City. Tel 435-644-1200; ut.blm.gov/monument. **Boulder Mountain Lodge:** Tel 800-556-3446 or 435-335-7460; boulder-utah.com. *Cost:* from $115 (off-peak); from $135 (peak). **Hell's Backbone Grill:** Tel 435-335-7464; hellsbackbonegrill.com. *Cost:* dinner $50. **Best times:** spring and fall, since summer temperatures can be over 100°F.

Sandstone formations make up the Grand Staircase's Devil's Garden.

The Greatest Snow on Earth—and Tons of It

Alta and Snowbird

Little Cottonwood Canyon, Utah

Driving up Little Cottonwood Canyon, which climbs 3,600 feet in 6 dramatic glacier-cut miles, it's easy to see why powderhounds consider it some of the best ski terrain on earth. It's not just any snow that blankets these peaks—it's the legendarily light Utah powder, and a remarkable average of 500 inches falls on Alta and Snowbird every year. Welcome to Powder Paradise.

Snowbird Ski and Summer Resort is a newer, high-tech contrast to Alta's old-school atmosphere. Snowbird was cofounded by mountaineer, visionary, and environmentalist Dick Bass, the first person to climb the highest peak on all seven continents; he sold his stake to Ian Cumming in 2014 and died a year later. Snowbird features an aerial tram that can zip 120 people from 8,100 feet to 11,000 in about eight minutes. The emphasis here is on families (there are some "family only" ski zones), the unparalleled conditions, and the spectacular scenery. Parents love the ski-in/ski-out Cliff Lodge's après-slopes amenities—a spa with over 30 treatments, and updated rooms with Tempurpedic beds. The rooftop Aerie Restaurant offers views as distracting as the menu.

Alta, one mile up-canyon, is Utah's oldest resort, and prides itself on its sense of tradition and lack of pretension. Alta calls itself a "skiers' mountain," which means it's one of the few resorts left in the country that still prohibits snowboarders, and skier numbers are sometimes capped on busy days. Folks still talk of the record-breaking 748 inches of snow that fell here in 1981–82, but even an average year's snow is exceptional, covering 2,220 skiable acres laced by 116 runs. Of five base lodges, the family-owned ski-in/ski-out Alta Lodge has been open the longest. The funky, low-key inn was opened by the Denver & Rio Grande Railroad in 1940 and is practically a museum of ski memorabilia. Dining includes "joiner" tables, and the camaraderie of the patrons is infectious. The hotel's Sitzmark Club is a classic ski bar that's a throwback to its founding days.

WHERE: 25 miles southeast of Salt Lake City. **SNOWBIRD SKI & SUMMER RESORT:** Tel 800-232-9542 or 801-933-2222; snowbird .com. *Cost:* Cliff Lodge from $119 (off-peak), from $250 (peak). Lift tickets from $98; AltaSnowbird pass $114. *When:* ski season mid-Nov–May. **ALTA SKI AREA:** Tel 801-359-1078;

alta.com. *Cost:* lift tickets $89. *When:* ski season mid-Nov–mid-Apr. **ALTA LODGE:** Tel 800-707-2582 or 801-742-3500; altalodge.com. *Cost:* rooms from $94 (off-peak), includes breakfast, from $235 (peak), includes breakfast and 4-course dinner. **BEST TIMES:** Jan–early Mar for best ski conditions; every Sat–Sun from mid-Aug–mid-Oct for Snowbird's well-known Oktoberfest.

Skiers at Snowbird and Alta enjoy expansive vistas of Little Cottonwood Canyon.

Valley of the Gods and the Ancients

MEXICAN HAT AND CEDAR MESA

Utah

You gotta love a place called Mexican Hat. Nestled deep in the canyon country of south-central Utah, this tiny crossroads whose population hovers around 30 doesn't have a lot to see, but nearby are enough outdoor temptations and unusual sights to hold you captive for weeks. It's hard to miss the distinctive rock formation that gives this former mining center its name, but it is the forest of giant rock formations just to the north called the Valley of the Gods that is a real knockout. A 17-mile dirt road loops through the rock towers, which resemble a Monument Valley in miniature at the foot of Cedar Mesa and act as a prelude to the real thing (Monument Valley rises 20 miles to the south on the Utah-Arizona border; see p. 688). Book way in advance at the very special Valley of the Gods B&B, a historic stone ranch house with just four guest rooms and a great view of the stunning Red Rock country from any seat on the 75-foot-long front porch.

Closer to town is Goosenecks State Park, overlooking a 1,000-foot-deep series of tight turns (hence the park's name) carved into the desert by the San Juan River. It took 300 million years for the river to weave a stretch of 6 serpentine miles that progresses just 1.5 linear miles in the direction of the Colorado River. An upstream stretch of the San Juan from the town of Bluff makes a great three-day rafting trip (see p. 788).

Adventurous hikers couldn't ask for a better region to explore than Cedar Mesa. From Mexican Hat, drive north up the white-knuckle curves of the Moki Dugway, a dirt switchback road climbing 1,100 feet in 3 miles onto the mesa. This high, wide plateau is covered with pines and junipers and cut by numerous canyons chock-full of reminders of the Ancestral Puebloans, who made their

Moki Dugway Road leads to Bears Ears buttes, considered a sacred site by Native Americans.

home here some 1,000 years ago. The Kane Gulch Ranger Station is the starting point for the popular 23-mile loop into Grand Gulch and Bullet Canyon, a veritable adventure past prehistoric paintings and caves containing centuries-old stone residences. Owl and Fish Creek Canyons to the east make another popular overnight loop, and Johns Canyon and Slickhorn Canyon are also great hikes, with some moderate scrambling and route-finding involved, following in the footsteps of the Ancestral Puebloans.

WHERE: 359 miles south of Salt Lake City. **VALLEY OF THE GODS B&B:** Tel 970-749-1164; valleyofthegodsbandb.com. *Cost:* from $175. **GOOSENECKS STATE PARK:** Tel 435-678-3348; stateparks.utah.gov/parks/goose necks.htm. **CEDAR MESA:** Tel 435-587-1500; blm.gov/ut/st/en/fo/monticello/recreation/places /cedar_mesa.htm. **BEST TIMES:** spring and fall for weather.

Utah's Adventure Nexus

MOAB AND RED ROCK COUNTRY

Utah

The adventure-travel epicenter of the canyon country is a surprisingly small town. But even with a population of just over 5,000, Moab boasts enough great-outdoors options—plus epic movie-worthy scenery to match—to justify a town ten times its size. The city started as a Mormon settlement named for a Biblical kingdom in 1855, and went through a phase as a uranium boomtown in the 1950s. Moab's latest incarnation began in the 1980s, when proponents of a nascent sport called mountain biking discovered that the endless miles of colorful slickrock were perfect for fat-tired fun.

Moab has off-road trails galore, from easy spins to challenging single-track loops. The granddaddy of them all is the punishing 10-mile Slickrock Trail, a kind of rite of passage for serious bikers—but starting with a shorter practice loop to get a feel for the naked sandstone is strongly recommended. The city's unique location, in a narrow green valley split by the Colorado River, has made it known for prime river-rafting as well. Numerous local outfitters such as Tag-a-Long Expeditions will guide you down white water on the Colorado or the nearby Green River. They'll also arrange self-guided trips in backcountry solitude on 120 miles of flat water in nearby Canyonlands National Park (see p. 790).

But it was Moab's ideal location that sealed its fate—it's an easy ten minutes from Arches

National Park (see p. 787) and less than an hour from Canyonlands National Park. Hiking trails and astounding views fill both, and rough dirt tracks and prospectors' roads left over from the area's mining days have helped make Moab one of the most famous destinations in the country for 4WD enthusiasts, or "jeepers" as they're known locally, who arrive in droves for Jeep Safari on Easter weekend. On a more refined note, September brings the strains of chamber music, jazz, and traditional music to the red rocks during the world-renowned Moab Music Festival. Then it's wild fun again when fat-tire fans gather at the end of October for the Moab Ho Down Mountain Bike Festival and Film Fest.

Among the growing number of places to hang your hat, try the centrally located Gonzo Inn for the touch of retro 1970s charm it brings to this old mining town, complete with a pool that beckons your slickrock-weary body.

Where: 234 miles southeast of Salt Lake City. *Visitor info:* Tel 800-635-6622 or 435-259-8825; discovermoab.com. **Tag-a-Long**

Expeditions: Tel 800-453-3292 or 435-259-8946; tagalong.com. *Cost:* day trips from $56; 4-night Green River trips $850. **Gonzo Inn:** Tel 800-791-4044 or 435-259-2515; gonzo inn.com. *Cost:* from $174. **Best times:** spring and fall for weather; Easter weekend for Jeep Safari (rr4w.com); 1st 2 weeks in Sept for the Moab Music Festival (moabmusicfest.org); late Oct for Moab Ho Down Mountain Bike and Film Festival (moabhodown.com).

Moab is mecca for mountain bikers who come for its many scenic and challenging trails.

One Big Ski Treat Extraordinaire

Park City Skiing

Park City, Utah

Interstate 80 shoots east of Salt Lake City through the mountains toward Park City, Utah's lively and sophisticated ski epicenter. A century-old mining town, today it is world-famous for hosting the yearly movie-star-studded Sundance Film Festival (see p. 801).

In 2015, Park City Mountain Resort and Canyons Resort combined to create the largest single ski and snowboard resort in the United States. With over 7,300 skiable acres, over 300 trails catering to beginners and experts alike, 41 lifts, eight terrain parks, one superpipe, and one minipipe, Park City is now officially considered a world-class mountain destination. It's no surprise that the resort is the training spot of choice for U.S. ski and snowboard Olympic teams.

Comfortable and convenient lodging can be found at the Hotel Park City, a classic Rockies lodge updated with a Ralph Lauren aesthetic and 100 luxury suites, a full-service spa, and views of the slopes from the massive windows of Ruth's Chris Steak House. For dining at a height, stop by Lookout Cabin, boasting Rocky Mountain cuisine and glorious views of the Wasatch Mountains.

The destination of choice for those seeking the country's top-drawer ski experience is

Deer Valley, unquestionably Utah's most elegant resort since its opening a quarter of a century ago. Its four summits—the highest 9,570 feet—were home to the slalom, mogul, and aerial events of the 2002 Olympic Games. Deer Valley doesn't allow snowboarders (the other two resorts do) and provides impeccably groomed cruising runs, with two of skidom's best hotels nearby. The chic but unpretentious Norwegian-themed Stein Eriksen Lodge is known for a host of pampering amenities that include a spa, dozens of cozy fireplaces, and the award-winning Glitretind restaurant. A friendly rival is the château-style, 20-room Goldener Hirsch Inn, with European-style service and Austrian antiques.

Park City Mountain Resort is the largest ski resort in the country.

Relive the 2002 Winter Olympics at the 389-acre Utah Olympic Park 5 miles west of town, where sports fans go for a shot at the Olympic bobsled track, six Nordic jumps, a 750,000-gallon training pool for practicing freestyle aerials, plus ziplines, tubing, and two museums to round out the facilities.

Where: 30 miles east of Salt Lake City. *Visitor info:* parkcity.com. *When:* Ski season runs from late Nov–Apr. **Park City Mountain Resort:** Tel 888-226-7667 or 435-649-8111; parkcitymountain.com. *Cost:* lift tickets $122. **Hotel Park City:** Tel 888-999-0098 or 435-200-2000; hotelparkcity.com. *Cost:* from $254 (off-peak), from $685 (peak). **Deer Valley:** Tel 800-424-3337 or 435-649-1000; deervalley.com. *Cost:* lift tickets $120. **Stein Eriksen Lodge:** Tel 800-453-1302 or 435-649-3700; steinlodge.com. *Cost:* from $250 (off-peak), from $720 (peak); dinner at Glitretind $50. **Goldener Hirsch Inn:** Tel 800-252-3373 or 435-649-7770; goldenerhirschinn.com. *Cost:* from $179 (off-peak), from $539 (peak). **Olympic Park:** Tel 435-658-4200. *Cost:* winter bobsled rides $175. *When:* bobsled rides, Jan–Mar. **Best time:** late Jan in Park City for the Sundance and Slamdance Film Festivals (slamdance.com).

The Art of Land, Water, and Time

SPIRAL JETTY

Rozell Point, Great Salt Lake, Utah

Spiral Jetty, created by the artist Robert Smithson, is an unusual work of art constructed from the earth, far from the confines of a museum or gallery. In 1970, Smithson traveled to the Great Salt Lake, where he hired contractor

Bob Phillips and his earthmoving equipment. In little more than a week, they constructed an enormous stone earthwork that curled like a fiddlehead fern out from the shoreline, framed by waters dyed wine red by millions of tiny brine shrimp. Fifteen hundred feet long, 15 feet wide, and constructed from 6,650 tons of black basalt rock and earth, *Spiral Jetty* is said to be one of the few works of art visible from space—when it's visible at all.

And therein lies the problem—or the mystique. When Smithson constructed this earthwork, the waters of the lake were unusually low because of a protracted dry spell. A year later they began to rise, and submerged the work for most of the next 30 years. In 2002, following three years of drought, the jetty reemerged completely transformed, its black rocks encased in gleaming white, icelike salt crystals. Debate persists on whether Smithson (who died in a plane crash in 1973) would have celebrated or mourned his work's transformation. Interestingly, his writings show how central decay and change were to his artistic vision.

The New York–based Dia Art Foundation (which acquired the work in 1999) is working with the Great Salt Lake Institute and the Utah Museum of Fine Arts as part of its ongoing stewardship of this iconic work. Check its status before making your pilgrimage. Walk the jetty's curving path to its center, seeing it the way it was meant to be seen, its size and bulk reduced to a fragile tendril in the water, dwarfed by the desert landscape and the waters all around.

WHERE: Access to *Spiral Jetty* is through the Golden Spike National Historic Site, 90 miles north of Salt Lake City. *Visitor info:* Dia Art Foundation in NYC, tel 212-989-5566; diaart.org. **BEST TIMES:** during periods of low water.

Mormon Mecca

TEMPLE SQUARE

Salt Lake City, Utah

"This is the place," declared Brigham Young, leader of the Church of Jesus Christ of Latter-day Saints (LDS), when he first gazed across the bleak Salt Lake Valley in July 1847. Young had led 148 fellow believers from Nauvoo, Illinois (see p. 498), where they had been persecuted and driven out for their beliefs, ending with the arrest and mob killing of the church's founder, Joseph Smith, in 1844. Under the leadership of Young, the valley turned into a thriving city and is now the epicenter of one of the world's fastest-growing religions. Sixty percent of Utahns are Mormon, and of the creed's more than 15 million believers, more than 9 million live outside the U.S.

The very heart of this community and of Salt Lake City is Temple Square, a 10-acre plot laid out within days of the settlers' arrival to house the church administration buildings and Young's personal residence. Enter the square through wrought-iron gates on the south, west, or north side, where enthusiastic young guides offer free tours in any of 40 languages.

Young selected the location for the Salt Lake Temple and laid the cornerstone himself in April 1853. It took 40 years to build the temple, which has over 253,000 square feet of floor area. Mammoth quartz monzonite blocks were brought from Little Cottonwood Canyon 20 miles away. A 14-foot statue of the angel Moroni tops the tallest of six spires, 210 feet above Temple Square. The interior, where the First Presidency and the Quorum of the Twelve Apostles meet weekly, is open only to LDS church members in good standing.

The famous Mormon Tabernacle Choir has its home in a distinctive dome-shaped building on the west side of Temple Square. It was built in the 1860s and seats 12,000. Its organ—with 11,623 pipes, 147 voices (tone colors), 206 ranks (rows of pipes), and five keyboards—is considered one of the finest in the world. The huge instrument is a fitting match for the near-perfect acoustics of the building itself, which your guide may demonstrate by dropping a pin onstage that you can hear in the back rows, 170 feet away. The Grammy-winning 360-member all-volunteer choir performs Sunday mornings and rehearses on Thursday evenings when they are not traveling the world.

WHERE: 50 North Temple St. Tel 801-240-4872; templesquare.com. **SALT LAKE TEMPLE:** Tel 801-240-2640. **MORMON TABERNACLE:** Tel 801-240-4150. **BEST TIMES:** Sun mornings and Thurs evenings for Tabernacle music (mormontabernaclechoir.org); late Nov–Dec for Christmas lights, a life-size Nativity, and nightly music performances.

Pampering Spas and Outdoor Action in Utah's Dixie

ST. GEORGE

Utah

The largest and fastest-growing town in southern Utah sits between hills of red sandstone and the winding Virgin River, a beautiful area of the state aptly dubbed Color Country. Its proximity to a number of national and state parks (not to mention Las Vegas, right over the Utah-Nevada border; see p. 727), and its year-round pleasant weather has given it the reputation as a Four Corners playground.

The area's idyllic climate was the very reason "Utah's Dixie" was founded in 1861 by Mormon families sent by Brigham Young to grow cotton (unsuccessfully). The church leader eventually established his own winter home here, and in 1877 the gleaming white St. George Temple was dedicated; it's the first Mormon temple in the West (Salt Lake City's was not yet completed), and the oldest active Mormon temple in the world. Only church members can go inside, but visitors can admire the grounds and the building, impressively lit at night, and are welcome to visit the St. George Utah Temple. The "jewel in the desert" is a beautiful example of craftsmanship and artisanal detail.

St. George also has two destination spas for outdoor enthusiasts who want to be pampered in a dramatic natural setting. Both feature top-notch health-conscious restaurants, accommodations that honor the Southwest aesthetic, and the myriad activities of the surrounding area. The Red Mountain Resort prides itself on its hiking program, with everything from beginner strolls to endurance hikes through nearly 7,000 acres of red cliffs and canyons at the adjacent Snow Canyon State Park. The Green Valley Spa and Resort also starts the day with morning hikes, and has a range of wellness programs, including weight loss and stress relief. It also has specialized tennis and golf instruction. Both spas benefit from St. George's dozen golf courses, only one of which is private. Thespian pursuits make an appearance at Utah's impressive summertime Shakespeare Festival in nearby Cedar City.

WHERE: 300 miles southwest of Salt Lake City. **ST. GEORGE UTAH TEMPLE:** Tel 435-673-3533. *When:* tours Mon–Sat. **RED MOUNTAIN RESORT:** Tel 877-246-4453 or 435-673-4905; redmountainresort.com. *Cost:* from $265 per person, all inclusive. **GREEN VALLEY SPA AND RESORT:** Tel 800-237-1068 or 435-628-8060; greenvalleyspa.com. *Cost:* from $295 per person, all inclusive. **BEST TIME:** late June–Sept for the Utah Shakespeare Festival (bard.org).

Redford's Own Award-Winning Production

SUNDANCE

Utah

B y 1969, riding high on the success of *Barefoot in the Park*, actor Robert Redford had bought 5,000 acres in beautiful Provo Canyon southeast of Salt Lake City, where he then filmed *Jeremiah Johnson* in 1972. Today the 5,000-acre mountain community is known as both an intimate, all-season resort and North America's premier showcase for independent films.

Sundance Resort is an unobtrusive alternative to the larger Park City Mountain Resort nearby (see p. 797), a picture-perfect grouping of rustic but elegant cabins in the craggy shadow of 12,000-foot Mount Timpanogos, the highest point in Utah's Wasatch Range. Set among old-growth pines, the small area (450 skiable acres) offers four lifts, 42 runs, and a drop of 2,150 vertical feet, along with an excellent 16-mile network of trails for cross-country skiing and snowshoeing. The mountaintop Bearclaw's Cabin provides some Oscar-worthy views.

The emphasis at Sundance is on the environment and the arts; Redford's "small is better" vision of less development and more preservation is reflected in environmentally friendly building techniques and conservation efforts. When guests are not exploring outdoors, they can take classes in pottery, painting, and drawing, or enjoy the Native American–inspired treatments at the Spa at Sundance. The rustic-elegant Tree Room dining room is the resort's venue of choice: cozy, candlelit, and decorated with Native American artwork and objects from Redford's private collection. The centerpiece of the informal Owl Bar is the 1890s rosewood bar frequented by Butch Cassidy's Hole-in-the-Wall Gang and shipped here from Wyoming.

Sundance is more often associated with the film festival held here and (mostly) at Park City, 37 miles north, every January. Redford began the Sundance Institute in 1981 to encourage the development of independent filmmakers, playwrights, and artists. Since then the annual film festival it spawned has become the leading event of its kind anywhere, with ten days of parties, receptions, panel discussions, and—oh yes—screenings of independent films. Ski bums and struggling artists rub elbows with movie stars and celebrities.

WHERE: 53 miles southeast of Salt Lake City. Tel 800-892-1600 or 801-225-4107; sundanceresort.com. *Cost:* lift tickets from $65; rooms from $199 (off-peak), from $315 (peak); dinner at Tree Room $65. *When:* ski season mid-Dec–early Apr. **SUNDANCE FILM FESTIVAL:** Tel 801-328-3456; sundance.org/festival. *Cost:* tickets $20, multiple-pass packages from $500. *When:* 10 days in late Jan. **BEST TIMES:** late Jan for the film festival; 1st week in June for the Intermountain Cup Mountain Bike Race.

Sundance Film Festival draws nearly 50,000 attendees to Sundance and Park City each year.

Heaven Set in Stone

ZION NATIONAL PARK

Utah

The oldest and perhaps most beautiful of Utah's five national parks—and that's saying a lot—was named for an ancient Hebrew word meaning "sanctuary." Entering Zion Canyon for the first time, it's easy to see why,

even if it is hard to believe that it was the pretty little Virgin River that carved these 1,000-foot walls of delicately hued sandstone. Some of the largest chunks of rock you've ever seen also awed 19th-century Mormon settlers, who gave them names like Angel's Landing, the Court of the Patriarchs, the West Temple, and the Great White Throne.

The Zion–Mount Carmel Highway (Highway 9) crosses the southern edge of the park, passing west from an expanse of slickrock through a pair of stone tunnels to Zion Canyon itself. You'll have to park to enter the canyon's true heart, since the Zion Canyon Scenic Drive is open only to the free shuttle buses from mid-March through October.

The 229-square-mile park is laced with trails, starting with short paved walks in the dramatic chasm of Zion Canyon. If the Grand Canyon is all about standing at the rim and looking down, here inspiration comes to those who travel along the bottom and look (or hike) up. Adventurous hikers tackle Angel's Landing, which climbs 1,500 feet in just a mile, ending on top of a rock outcropping so steep you'll often see rock climbers inching up beneath you. Zion is also known for its slot canyons, and few miss the 16-mile Zion Narrows, where hikers splash up or down the shallow waters of the Virgin River. Parallel cliffs soar 1,000 feet overhead, only 20 feet apart in places. In the Kolob Canyons, the westernmost section of the park, a 14-mile trail (round-trip) leads to 287-foot Kolob Arch, the second largest freestanding arch in the world.

The only lodging in the park itself is the Zion Lodge in Zion Canyon, restored to its original rustic 1924 appearance. Utah red mountain trout is just one reason to check out the lodge's excellent Red Rock Grill, with immense windows looking onto the surrounding rockscape. Across the road is the start of the popular Emerald Pools Trail that leads through forests to three basins fed by small waterfalls and kept a deep, rich green by algae.

WHERE: 307 miles southwest of Salt Lake City. Tel 435-772-3256; nps.gov/zion. **ZION LODGE:** Tel 888-297-2757 or 303-297-3175; zionlodge.com. *Cost:* rooms from $189; dinner at Red Rock Grill $35. **BEST TIMES:** spring and fall.

Angel's Landing is ringed on three sides by the river below, with inspiring views in both directions along the canyon.

WEST COAST

CALIFORNIA •
OREGON •
WASHINGTON

A Town That Changed How America Eats

BERKELEY & CHEZ PANISSE

California

A fiercely independent city of local bookstores and cafés where everything is political (even eating), this leafy suburb across the bay from San Francisco was at the heart of the sixties' antiwar efforts (when it was called "The People's Republic of Berkeley"). But for all the passionate demonstrations, the town's most lasting influence probably emanates from Alice Waters's legendary Chez Panisse, the restaurant that helped create "California cuisine," turn San Francisco into one of America's best restaurant cities (see p. 849), and change the way America eats.

The high priestess of the Northern California food cult since 1971, Alice Waters made "fresh, seasonal, and local" the mantra of American chefs (and many home cooks as well) who aspire to create seriously good food. Inspired by a trip through France, the idealistic New Jersey native and UC Berkeley grad opened a restaurant that became known for its extraordinary ingredients—organically and locally grown vegetables just out of the garden, fruit right off the branch, and fish straight from the sea. In a time of iceberg lettuce and flavorless tomatoes, the idea was revolutionary. Waters helped champion mesclun salad, domestic goat cheese, and heirloom tomatoes, but beyond the bold new flavors was a message: Eating is an agricultural act, with social and ecological consequences.

A neighborhood bistro named after a character in Marcel Pagnol's 1930s film trilogy, the redwood-paneled Chez Panisse is snugly aristocratic, and tables can be hard to book. (They say even President Clinton was initially turned down when the employee who took the call from *Air Force One* didn't believe the reservation was really for the president.) The pinnacle of foodie destinations, Chez Panisse serves prix-fixe menus (Monday's menu has three courses and Tuesday through Saturday there are four). Some 60 local farms supply the kitchen, inspiring every aspect of the meal. Upstairs, the lively, more informal Café at Chez Panisse offers the same pristine ingredients in a less expensive à la carte menu.

To experience a less white-linen side of Berkeley, walk along Telegraph Avenue between Bancroft and Dwight Avenues, where incense burning at the outdoor craft stalls mingles with the aromas of coffee and curries, lending the street the feel of an international bazaar. Dozens of ethnic restaurants, including Indian, African, Japanese, Thai, and Korean, offer great lunch options for under $10. Book lovers will find independent bookstores such as Moe's, and Caffe Mediterraneum, a literary landmark; Beat poet Allen Ginsberg is said to have penned part of his epic poem "Howl" here.

At the University of California at Berkeley, founded in 1868, highlights include Sproul Plaza, where Mario Savio ignited the Free Speech Movement and antiwar protests in the '60s; the Campanile, a 307-foot Italianate tower with panoramic views; the new Berkeley Art Museum and Pacific Film Archive, with a vast art collection and an archive of over 17,000 films; and the Lawrence Hall of Science, a hands-on museum with interactive exhibits for kids of any age.

WHERE: 10 miles northeast of San Francisco. **CHEZ PANISSE:** Tel 510-548-5525 (restaurant) or 510-548-5049 (café); chezpanisse .com. *Cost:* prix-fixe dinner at restaurant from $75 Tues–Thurs, $125 Fri–Sat; dinner at café

$50. **MOE'S:** Tel 510-849-2087; moesbooks .com. **CAFFE MEDITERRANEUM:** Tel 510-549-1128; caffemed.com. **UNIVERSITY OF** **CALIFORNIA AT BERKELEY:** Tel 510-642-5215; berkeley.edu. **LAWRENCE HALL OF SCIENCE:** Tel 510-642-5132; lawrencehallofscience.org.

9021—Oh!

BEVERLY HILLS

California

S wimming pools! Movie stars! The mystique of Beverly Hills loomed large in the world's collective imagination long before Julia Roberts's character in *Pretty Woman* had a troublesome shopping experience along famously chic

Rodeo Drive. Though the city is less than 6 square miles, its graceful Spanish buildings, wide palm-tree–lined streets, mammoth mansions, and wildly expensive stores leave a bigger-than-life impression.

Surrounded by Los Angeles on three sides and West Hollywood to the east, Beverly Hills is its own independent city with A-list residents who can easily afford to breeze in and out of the high-priced boutiques, rack up a small fortune on their black American Express cards, and disappear into gated residences. Its commercial heart is the three-block-long "Golden Triangle" (bounded by Santa Monica Boulevard, Wilshire Boulevard, and Rexford Drive). Here you'll find Rodeo (that's pronounced Ro-DAY-oh) Drive

Rodeo Drive is known as one of the most exclusive shopping districts in the world.

and such big-ticket jewelers as Tiffany & Co. and Harry Winston, plus every imaginable designer, from Armani to Zegna. If you aren't feeling flush enough to even window-shop, the city offers a charming 40-minute trolley tour. The wealth and glamour of the area's golden age can still be found in the opulent Greystone Mansion and Estate, built by the Doheny oil family in 1928. The residence and the lush 18.3-acre park and gardens that surround it are a popular location for commercials, television, and films. The Paley Center for Media (sister of a museum by the same name in New York City) is a shrine to how most Beverly Hills residents made their fortunes. Visitors can request a favorite show from a collection of more than 160,000 programs covering 100 years, and view it in a private cubicle.

While you're in the neighborhood, nosh at Nate 'n Al, the favorite deli and hangout of old-timers like Groucho and Doris Day. Don't be afraid to pry stories out of the staff; every waitperson and almost every patron has a tale, and most of them will share it gladly.

WHERE: 10 miles west of Los Angeles. *Visitor info:* Tel 800-345-2210 or 310-248-1015; lovebeverlyhills.com. **TROLLEY TOURS:** Tel 310-285-1128; beverlyhills.org/exploring/trollytours. **GREYSTONE PARK:** Tel 310-285-6830; beverlyhills.org/exploring/greystonemansiongardens. **PALEY CENTER FOR MEDIA:** Tel

310-786-1000; paleycenter.org. *When:* closed Mon–Tues. **NATE 'N AL:** Tel 310-274-0101; natenal.com. *Cost:* lunch $20. **BEST TIME:** May for blooming jacaranda trees.

Along El Camino Real

CALIFORNIA MISSION TRAIL

California

O n July 16, 1769, Father Junípero Serra, accompanied by a scraggly, depleted band of Spanish soldiers and missionaries, erected a brushwood shelter and founded the Mission San Diego de Alcala. It was the first of

21 Franciscan missions established along the coastal route dubbed El Camino Real (Spanish for "The Royal Road"), extending from what we now know as San Diego north to Sonoma. Combining spiritual and military ends, these outposts, designed to convert and conquer the natives, are a cornerstone of California history, culture, and architecture. They are considered among the most beautiful buildings in the state and some of the most historically significant in the country. Father Serra, who personally established the first nine missions, died in 1784 at Mission San Carlos Borromeo in Carmel (see p. 810) and is buried beneath the sanctuary floor. He was canonized by Pope Francis in 2015.

If you're considering paying a visit to some of the missions, you'll have to make some tough choices, since virtually all of them hold individual appeal. The mission in Santa Barbara (see p. 854), with its distinctive twin bell towers, was founded in 1786. Its treasures include paintings, statues, and a unique Abalone-encrusted Chumash altar dating to the 1790s. Carmel's San Carlos Borromeo dates back to 1771 and was home to the first library in California (a collection of 200 books); it was visited in 1987 by Pope John Paul II, who came to beatify Father Serra. It's hard to pass up the stunning mission in San Juan Capistrano, which is equally famous for the migrating swallows that return annually to build their mud

nests around March 19 (St. Joseph's feast day). Mission San Buenaventura, which is located in Ventura, between Los Angeles and Santa Barbara, still looks largely the way it did when it was constructed, between 1792 and 1809.

WHERE: from San Diego to Sonoma; missionsofcalifornia.com. **SANTA BARBARA MISSION:** Tel 805-682-4713; santabarbaramission.org. **SAN CARLOS BORROMEO:** Carmel. Tel 831-624-1271; carmelmission.org. **MISSION SAN JUAN CAPISTRANO:** San Juan Capistrano. Tel 949-234-1300; missionsjc.org. **SAN BUENAVENTURA MISSION:** Ventura. Tel 805-643-4318; sanbuenaventuramission.org. **BEST TIMES:** at Mission San Juan Capistrano, mid-Mar for migrating swallows; Sat evenings June–Aug for Music Under the Stars summer concerts; early Dec for Christmas celebration at the Mission.

The Mission at Santa Barbara was the tenth of the California missions established by the Spanish Franciscans.

Rafting the American, Yuba, and Kern Rivers

CALIFORNIA WHITE WATER

California

S pilling down the western slope of the Sierra Nevada at breakneck pace, the American, Yuba, and Kern rivers offer some of the most exhilarating white-water rafting anywhere in the world. The sheer slope of the mountains translates into wild rides through Class III, IV, and V rapids, with lots of rocks to dodge and narrow channels to pass through. Guided trips (recommended for all but the most highly experienced rafters) of five or six people promise you and your boatmates an emotional journey through the tumultuous rapids that can take you from fear to profound joy in just a few hours.

Three hours east of San Francisco, the American is the easiest of the three rivers despite its big, crashing, roller-coaster waves. The boulder-strewn South Fork (also known as Gold Rush River) is the most famous and most popular of the river's three forks, a Class III intermediate river that can truly exhilarate with its sheer drops at Troublemaker and Satan's Cesspool. More skilled or adventurous rafters can run the North and Middle forks of the American, which traverse the steeper mountains at higher elevations with many Class IV rapids. Farther north is the more demanding Yuba River, a Class IV+ run where you're either in a rapid or on the brink of one the entire day. The Lower section is doable for the adventurous first-timer, though beware the aptly named Maytag, a steep set of rapids that can flip you around (or be bypassed on foot). The upper Yuba, a Class V gauntlet of churning white water and steep drops, is for white-water veterans only.

At the southern end of the Sierra Nevada range is the Kern River, one of the nation's "Wild and Scenic Rivers" (an official designation for the country's most beautiful undammed rivers). This jewel runs 60 miles through the heart of Sequoia National Forest, offering everything from mild waves to wild rides. Most popular is the two-day trip on the Lower Kern, which tumbles inside a narrow granite canyon through a series of adrenaline-pumping Class IV rapids. During late spring and early summer, the Upper Kern offers a heart-stopping series of four rapids that takes only a couple of hours. Another two- or three-day trip down the Forks of the Kern, one of America's most challenging and starkly beautiful rivers, hurtles through some of the steepest and most frightening Class V rapids one could ever hope to survive. Last but certainly not least, the Tuolumne and Merced rivers near Yosemite (see p. 862) combine the thrills of California's white water and the scenic beauty of the state's river canyons.

WHERE: The put-in for the South Fork American is 40 miles east of Sacramento; the Yuba is 210 miles northeast of San Francisco; and the Kern is 153 miles northeast of Los Angeles. **How:** O.A.R.S. (tel 800-346-6277; oars.com) for the American, Merced, and Tuolumne. Whitewater Voyages (tel 800-400-7238 or 760-376-1500; whitewatervoyages.com) and Kern River Outfitters (tel 760-376-3370; kernrafting.com) for the Kern only. *Cost:* 1-day trips on the American from $125, 1-day on the Tuolumne from $228; 2-day Lower Kern trips from $350; 3-day Forks of the Kern from $749. *When:* Apr–Oct. **BEST TIME:** May–June, when water is high and crowds are low. Avoid busy weekends on the South Fork American.

From Boomtowns to Jumping Frogs

CALIFORNIA'S GOLD COUNTRY

California

The discovery of gold at Sutter's Mill on the American River in 1848 set in motion the greatest migration of people in the Western hemisphere and shaped the history of the soon-to-be state of California. By 1849, news had reached the East Coast that there was gold in the foothills of California's Sierra Nevada, and the Gold Rush was on. Almost overnight, dozens of Wild West towns—complete with saloons, bordellos, and general stores—sprang up throughout Gold Country, sending the state's population soaring from 15,000 to more than 300,000 by the 1850s.

The best starting point is the place where that first nugget was found, at Marshall Gold Discovery Historic Park. Located on the South Fork of the American River near Coloma, the park features a realistic replica of Sutter's sawmill and the chance to rent equipment for some do-it-yourself panning. Nearby is the town of Placerville, called "Hangtown" in the early 1850s for its definitive form of justice. Over in Calaveras County is the once rough-and-tumble town of Angels Camp, made famous by Mark Twain's short story "The Celebrated Jumping Frog of Calaveras County." Bronze plaques are embedded in the sidewalk, dedicated to the winners of a frog-jump contest held the third weekend in May.

Called Deer Creek Dry Diggins when it was just a mining camp, Nevada City is perhaps the most interesting of the Mother Lode towns, with a compact downtown that looks like a timeworn set from a Wild West movie. Gaslights made from original 1800s molds light up Broad Street, where the historic Nevada Theatre and charming Emma Nevada House are located. Built in 1856 as the childhood home of opera star Emma Nevada, the six-room inn is an easy walk to the town's shops and restaurants.

Near the top of California's Central Valley, Sacramento, the state capital, was once the terminus for the Pony Express (see p. 457). Don't miss the domed state capitol building; the California Railroad Museum, which displays 21 restored locomotives; and the scenic riverside district of Old Sacramento. For lodging that fits the time, stay on the *Delta King*, a 1927 paddleboat transformed into a permanently moored hotel in Old Sacramento.

WHERE: Gold Country runs along State Hwy. 49, roughly 140 miles east of San Francisco. *Calaveras County visitor info:* Tel 800-225-3764 or 209-736-0049; gocalaveras .com. *Nevada City visitor info:* Tel 530-265-2692; nevadacitychamber.com. **MARSHALL GOLD DISCOVERY STATE PARK:** Coloma. Tel 530-622-3470; parks.ca.gov. **EMMA NEVADA HOUSE:** Nevada City. Tel 530-265-4415; emmanevadahouse.com. *Cost:* from $169 (off-peak), from $195 (peak). **RAILROAD MUSEUM:** Sacramento. Tel 916-323-9280; csrmf.org. *DELTA KING:* Sacramento. Tel 800-825-5464 or 916-444-5464; deltaking.com. *Cost:* from $150. **BEST TIMES:** early Jan for Nevada City's Wild & Scenic Film Festival (wildandscenic filmfestival.org); 3rd weekend in May for Calaveras County Fair and Jumping Frog Jubilee (frogtown.org); July for the California State Fair in Sacramento (castatefair.org); Sept for World Gold Panning Championships in Placerville and Coloma Gold Rush Live; Oct for Gold Rush Day in Angels Camp.

Art Galore and Natural Splendor

CARMEL-BY-THE-SEA

California

The tree-lined streets of the pretty, prosperous, and pampered town of Carmel-by-the-Sea are filled with art galleries (100 and counting), gift shops, and cafés next to a crescent of beautiful, white sandy beach.

With its rounded tower and Moorish accents, the 1771 Carmel Mission is one of the state's most beautiful and served as the headquarters for the entire mission system in California (see p. 807).

This seaside village is still one of the world's loveliest collaborations between man and nature, where groves of live oaks, pines, and Monterey cypress meet the fine white sand of the beach. Its magical natural light inspired artists and writers to flock here from the turn of the 20th century, and many of its 3,850 residents are still professional artists (though millionaires and second-home owners made inroads long ago). The village's ongoing beauty is due in part to the foresight of city officials who, in 1929, passed an ordinance declaring Carmel to be "a residential city," thus keeping business and commerce in check. Strict zoning means: no house numbers, no traffic lights, no neon signs, no billboards, and no parking meters.

Carmel Mission was one of the most important California missions in the late 18th century.

Its most famous resident, Clint Eastwood, fell in love with the area in the 1950s and now lives in nearby Carmel Valley. Elected mayor in 1986, Eastwood's presence still lingers in town: He used to own downtown's most popular pub, the Hog's Breath Inn (you can still get a Dirty Harry Burger) and rescued the historic Mission Ranch Inn, a former seaside dairy farm just outside town, from condo developers. The inn has old-fashioned accommodations within an 1850s farmhouse, converted bunkhouse, barn, and cottages, and the old creamery was reimagined as a restaurant and lounge.

For sheer luxury, nearby Bernardus Lodge is a lushly landscaped romantic retreat, complete with its own small vineyard and spa (featuring wine-inspired treatments like body scrubs using crushed grapeseeds). Its 57 rooms and suites are huge and luxuriously appointed and its fine-dining restaurant, Lucia, serves some of the best food around.

WHERE: 120 miles south of San Francisco. *Visitor info:* Tel 800-550-4333 or 831-624-2522; carmelcalifornia.com. **CARMEL MISSION:** Tel 831-624-1271; carmelmission.org. **HOG'S BREATH INN:** Tel 831-625-1044; hogsbreath inn.net. *Cost:* lunch $30. **MISSION RANCH INN:** Tel 800-538-8221 or 831-624-6436; mission ranchcarmel.com. *Cost:* from $140. **BERNARDUS LODGE:** Carmel Valley. Tel 831-658-3400; bernarduslodge.com. *Cost:* from $325 (off-peak), from $495 (peak); dinner $55. **BEST TIMES:** mid-May for Carmel Art Festival (carmelart festivalcalifornia.com); mid-July–early Aug for Carmel Bach Festival (bachfestival.org).

DEATH VALLEY NATIONAL PARK

California

Located in the northern reaches of the Mojave Desert, Death Valley National Park enjoys the dubious distinction of being the lowest, driest, and hottest spot in America, with scorching summers that can reach 125°F—and in 1913 topped out at 134°F. Its fearsome name draws folks from all over the world. What strikes them is not just the area's brutality but its spectacular and varied beauty, with parched Deadman Pass and Dry Bone Canyon standing in contrast to the dramatic hills and mountains, such as 11,049-foot Telescope Peak. Under the desert sun, more than 1,000 species of plants and 440 species of animals life are indigenous to this desiccated land (with just 2 inches of rain a year), with many found nowhere else on earth.

Death Valley is actually not a valley at all, but a plate of crusty salt flats that has been steadily dropping between two mountain ranges that are slowly rising and sliding apart. Within the long, narrow park confines (140 miles from one end to the other, about the size of Connecticut), one of the most popular sights is Artist's Palette, where mineral deposits have caused swaths of red, pink, orange, purple, and green to color the hills. Others include Zabriskie Point, with its views of wrinkled hills and perfectly sculpted Sahara-like sand dunes. Find the dead-end road that leads to the mile-high (and aptly named) Dante's View, from which you can see 360 degrees for 100 miles on a clear day, taking in both the highest and lowest points in the Lower 48: Mount Whitney, at 14,494 feet, and Badwater, at 282 feet below sea level. Look familiar? Scenes from the original *Star Wars* (1977) were filmed here.

The park's most peculiar happenings take place on the flat, dry lakebed of Racetrack

A rock leaves a mysterious trail on Racetrack Playa.

Playa, where boulders weighing as much as 700 pounds sometimes move hundreds of yards, leaving trails in the dried mud surface as testimony. Scientists have recently determined that a combination of shifting ice sheets and wind cause the movement during certain times of the year.

Air-conditioned cars and luxury inns have improved on the experience that led 19th-century pioneers to give the valley its name. At the heart of the Furnace Creek Resort, the 66-room, 1927 stone and adobe Mission-style Inn at Furnace Creek is a veritable oasis of spring-fed swimming pools and palm gardens, with an 18-hole golf course and a desert sky filled with a sea of stars thrown into the bargain. The 224-room Ranch at Furnace Creek is a more family-friendly option.

Farther south is Joshua Tree National Park, 800,000 acres of high desert whose most prominent feature is the distinctive and ubiquitous Joshua tree, festooned with creamy white blossoms from February to late March. (Mormon pioneers believed the limbs of the trees resembled the upraised arms of Joshua leading them to the promised land.) Joshua Tree is one of the most popular rock-climbing areas in the country, with more than 8,000 established routes, ranging from friendly bouldering to immensely challenging cliffs. Desert Hot Springs, named for its wealth of natural hot springs, has many resorts but only at Two Bunch Palms (legend has it) did Al Capone come to soothe his nerves. Sink into the unusually pure mineral water that comes out of the earth at 148°F but is cooled for two different tubs in the palm-shaded grotto, one a soothing 99°F, the other still toasty at 104°F.

WHERE: 120 miles northwest of Las Vegas. *Visitor info:* Tel 760-786-3200; nps.gov/deva.

FURNACE CREEK RESORT: Tel 800-236-7916 or 760-786-2345; furnacecreekresort.com. *Cost:* the Inn from $389; the Ranch from $239. *When:* mid-Oct–mid-May. **JOSHUA TREE NATIONAL PARK:** Tel 760-367-5500; nps.gov/jotr. **TWO BUNCH PALMS:** Desert Hot Springs. Tel 800-472-4334 or 760-329-8791; two bunchpalms.com. *Cost:* from $200 (off-peak), from $300 (peak). **BEST TIMES:** Oct–May for weather; early spring for wildflowers; dawn and late afternoon for the visual power and play of light.

Alternative Big Sur and a Southern Cousin

ESALEN, TASSAJARA, AND THE ASHRAM

California

Most of the movements in America considered either enlightened or loopy (from yoga to meditation to crystals) were pioneered in California—and nowhere more than in the mountains, canyons, and seaside retreats of Big Sur (see p. 836). Ground zero for these cultural changes is Esalen Institute, a 120-acre healing retreat synonymous with New Age consciousness, Eastern mysticism, and self-awareness since it was founded in 1962 as part of the human potential movement, a response to the repressive 1950s. Aldous Huxley, British author of the science-fiction classic *Brave New World*, was an early teacher here. Its sulfur-rich natural hot springs, which circulate into hot tubs built into the cliffs so near the ocean you can watch whales spouting, have been drawing people (including the now-extinct tribe of Esselen Indians) for centuries. (These days, nudity is the norm.)

More than 17,000 people come each year to Esalen's pristine oceanfront setting to transform themselves through hundreds of workshops in meditation, massage, yoga, psychology, ecology, spirituality, art, and music. Esalen's famous oceanfront massages are set in a large outdoor treatment room with ocean views and open-air ceilings that let the roar drift in and over your body.

If Esalen keeps you busy with workshops, the greatest attraction of the nearby Tassajara Zen Mountain Center is doing nothing (though they have workshops, too). Located deep in a canyon at the end of a formidable 14-mile road, Tassajara was founded in 1967, the first residential Zen training monastery outside Japan.

The guest cabins have no phones or electricity (kerosene lamps provide light), no hot water, and no showers or tubs. (All bathing is done in the gender-segregated communal showers and Japanese-style baths, fed by sulfur hot springs.) Join black-robed monks for 5:50 A.M. sitting meditation (called *zazen*) or sleep in—it's your call.

The Ashram, farther south toward L.A., provides a week-long transformative ordeal for a dozen people. Ashram alums include Oprah Winfrey and Amber Valleta, who have suffered along with mere mortals in days that include mandatory 16-mile hikes through the Santa Monica mountains, along with yoga, meditation, and much-appreciated daily massages. Most guests opt for a small private bedroom, but all share bathrooms. The payoff? Losing weight and gaining the feeling that you can do anything.

WHERE: Big Sur is 150 miles south of San Francisco. **ESALEN:** Big Sur. Tel 831-667-3000; esalen.org. *Cost:* weekend workshops from $730 (standard dorm bed), includes meals. **TASSAJARA ZEN MOUNTAIN CENTER:** Jamesburg. Tel 888-743-9362 or 415-475-9362; sfzc.org/tassajara. *Cost:* dorms from $122; cabins from $243 per person, double occupancy, includes meals; day-use passes $32. *When:* late Apr–mid-Sept. **THE ASHRAM:** Calabasas. Tel 818-222-6900; theashram.com. *Cost:* $5,000 per person for 6 nights, all-inclusive. **BEST TIMES:** spring and fall for weather.

A Tale of Two Spas

GOLDEN DOOR AND CAL-A-VIE

Escondido and Vista, California

Workaholics can disconnect from their laptops and cell phones and reconnect with their minds and bodies at either of Southern California's top spa destinations, among the best in the country. The better known of the two is the venerable Golden Door, which set a spa gold standard with its week-long all-inclusive retreats. Established in 1958 as the first wellness destination to combine nascent American fitness concepts with European body treatments, it consistently ranks among the best anywhere and has long been a top choice for Hollywood A-listers like Nicole Kidman and well-heeled denizens. Inspired by centuries-old ryokan-style Japanese inns, the oasis of rejuvenation is set on 600 decidedly Zen acres complete with Japanese meditative sand gardens, elevated wooden paths, and koi ponds. It serves a mere 40 guests in private rooms, usually all women, but men and coeds occasionally take over the place throughout the year. Activities range from the physically healing, such as a hike at sunrise or a yoga class in a hilltop pavilion, to the guiltlessly indulgent: an in-room massage and breakfast in bed. For all meals served here, many ingredients come from their 5 acres of gardens and magically combine the best of health and flavor. Whatever your preferred path to a healthful new you, an unheard-of staff-to-guest ratio of four to one helps guarantee your every goal.

The inviting grounds of Golden Door are well suited to meditative walks.

The newer Cal-A-Vie looks like a luxurious village in Provence, complete with a 400-year-old chapel and vineyard. Its 440 acres include 32 villas and an 18-hole golf course used by guests, who enjoy the same super-pampering staff-to-guest ratio as the Golden Door, not to mention spectacular views of California hills from every corner. Beautifully furnished accommodations are adorned with 18th-century French country antiques and toile. In addition to enough spa treatments to melt the most wound-up minds and muscles, the resort promotes fitness through 150 fitness classes and a fitness pavilion loaded with enough contraptions to work off a lifetime's worth of holiday dining binges. Like the Golden Door, it has all-inclusive rates—even providing workout clothes—but Cal-A-Vie offers shorter packages for those who can't disappear for a week at a time.

GOLDEN DOOR: 30 miles north of San Diego. Tel 866-420-6414 or 760-744-5777; goldendoor.com. *Cost:* $8,850 per person per week, all-inclusive. **CAL-A-VIE:** 40 miles north of San Diego. Tel 888-373-8773 or 760-945-2055; cal-a-vie.com. *Cost:* from $4,550 for 3 nights, all-inclusive. **BEST TIME:** Sept–May for weather.

Healing Waters from the Earth's Depths

HOT SPRINGS OF NORTHERN CALIFORNIA

California

Long before there were modern spas there were hot springs—mineral-rich waters heated by the earth's interior and considered to have healing properties. Immersion in hot springs is one of the oldest health treatments known to man, and Northern California is unusually rich in this natural resource. Native Americans enjoyed the hot springs here, and after them the Victorians, who built resorts around—and sometimes on top of—them.

The old-style hot springs experience can

Treatments at the Osmosis Spa include an enzyme tea ritual in a meditation room overlooking the Japanese garden.

be found at Vichy Springs in Ukiah, a 160-year-old California State Historic Landmark named after the renowned spring in France. Famed for its naturally warm and carbonated "Champagne" baths, which flow into the original outdoor stone tubs, Vichy Springs has lured such legendary guests as Mark Twain and Jack London. Most of the rooms on the property are simple ranch style, but there are two rustic cottages that date from 1852.

Just north of California's wine country, Harbin Hot Springs is the birthplace of "Watsu" (short for water shiatsu), a massage that takes place in warm waist-deep water with a therapist who takes your body through a series of passive stretches that would be hard to achieve on dry land. Fire destroyed most of the buildings in 2015, but rebuilding is underway so that people can once again soak in the natural spring pools at this nonprofit retreat and workshop center, take yoga classes, and join other birthday-suited bathers on the sunny wooden deck.

Before Napa Valley was known for its wines (see p. 833), the town of Calistoga was famous for its mud baths. Submerge yourself in a tub of 100 percent pure local volcanic ash mixed with thermal mineral water—an experience that is either loved (spa junkies) or hated (claustrophobes beware). With modest bungalow accommodations on a property dotted with palm and olive trees, Indian Springs is just one of the many Calistoga destinations offering mud baths. At the ultra-luxurious Calistoga Ranch, a sleek, romantic hideaway with 50 cedar-shingle guest lodges, find rejuvenation in The Auberge Spa, where body scrubs and a honey-based massage supplement a good long soak in the mineral pool outdoors.

In western Sonoma County's hamlet of Freestone, a day spa called Osmosis offers a hard-to-find Japanese enzyme dry bath. In the Japanese garden with rock-lined paths and a koi-filled pond, a kimono-clad bath attendant will bury you in a dry "bath" of cedar, rice bran, and enzymes, which seems to grow warmer during the 20-minute session. Afterward enjoy a blanket wrap during which you listen to "meta-music" designed to "balance the left and right spheres of your brain." It may be Japanese-inspired, but this is California.

Vichy Hot Springs Resort: Ukiah. Tel 707-462-9515; vichysprings.com. *Cost:* from $215; day use of tubs and grounds $55. **Harbin Hot Springs:** Middletown. Tel 707-987-2477; harbin.org. Check website for updates on the rebuilding. **Indian Springs:** Calistoga. Tel 707-942-4913; indiansprings calistoga.com. *Cost:* from $259 (off-peak), from $359 (peak); mud baths $75. **Calistoga Ranch:** Calistoga. Tel 855-942-4220 or 707-254-2800; calistogaranch.aubergeresorts .com. *Cost:* lodges from $845; private bath $90. **Osmosis:** Freestone. Tel 707-823-8231; osmosis.com. *Cost:* enzyme bath for 2 with blanket wrap, $89 per person. **Best times:** spring and fall for weather.

The California Riviera

La Jolla

California

Just 15 miles north of central San Diego, the area loosely known as the California Riviera lures vacationers with its 17 miles of gorgeous sandy coves sheltered by dramatic cliffs. Such a stunning natural endowment is offset by the ritzy-but-casual small town of La Jolla ("the jewel"), packed with fancy shops, restaurants, and enough resorts and accommodations to satisfy everyone from the sun worshiper to the golfer to the honeymooner.

It doesn't hurt that it's always beach season here, with a temperate clime that's eternally conducive to outdoor play. A stroll down the town's main strip reveals its dual personality, where shops ask Rodeo Drive prices from a clientele clad in casual beach attire. Life centers around the coastal treasures such as La Jolla Cove, the most photographed niche of town that's also its most popular swimming area (and boasting a growing number of sea lions). This most coveted view is enjoyed by the iconic and recently rejuvenated "Pink Lady," the Mediterranean-style La Valencia Hotel and its bluff-top position, where guests once included Hollywood film stars of the 1930s and '40s. The nearby University of California San Diego takes full advantage of the seaside setting as the site of the renowned Scripps Institute of Oceanography and the Birch Aquarium. Surfing is big here, and there are even all-girl surf lessons at the Surf Diva Surf School, where a two-day clinic attempts to turn a landlubber lady into a modern-day Gidget.

Golfers around the world know La Jolla as the home of the celebrated Torrey Pines Golf Course, host of the PGA's Farmers Insurance Open each January and February. Past champions such as Tom Watson, Jack Nicklaus, and Tiger Woods have considered these links heaven, with views of the ocean from many holes. The Lodge at Torrey Pines, a Craftsman wonder overlooking the course, is a natural choice whether you're a golfer or not (the extensive spa easily distracts golf widows). It is the ultimate base from which to explore the Torrey Pines State Natural Reserve: 2,000 acres of unspoiled coastline laced with miles of hiking trails, at the hotel's border.

Theater buffs can build a stay around the acclaimed La Jolla Playhouse—founded in 1947 by Gregory Peck, Dorothy McGuire, and Mel Ferrer. The Playhouse has earned an international reputation for launching productions, such as *Jersey Boys*, that go on to become acclaimed Broadway hits, and has won a Tony Award for Outstanding Regional Theater.

If La Jolla begins to feel all too precious, it needn't. Stop in at George's at the Cove, a local institution where cove views are matched by consistently great cuisine and a bill that won't break the bank. It gets even better upstairs on a splendid rooftop terrace, where the million-dollar sunset comes free with dinner.

WHERE: 15 miles north of San Diego. **LA VALENCIA:** Tel 858-454-0771; lavalencia.com. *Cost:* from $349. **SURF DIVA SURF SCHOOL:** Tel 858-454-8273; surfdiva.com. *Cost:* $165 for 2-day clinic. **TORREY PINES GOLF COURSE:** Tel 877-581-7171 or 858-581-7171; torreypines golfcourse.com. *Cost:* greens fees from $100 (nonresident). **THE LODGE AT TORREY PINES:** Tel 888-826-0224 or 858-453-4420; lodgetorrey pines.com. *Cost:* from $425 (off-peak), from $600 (peak). **TORREY PINES STATE NATURAL RESERVE:** torreypine.org. **LA JOLLA PLAYHOUSE:** Tel 858-550-1010; lajollaplayhouse.org. *Cost:* tickets from $20. *When:* May–Nov. **GEORGE'S:** Tel 858-454-4244; georgesatthecove.com. *Cost:* dinner $45. **BEST TIMES:** fall and spring for weather.

Because La Jolla Cove is part of an ecological reserve, no harm may be done to any plant or animal within it.

Life Imitates Art

THE FESTIVAL OF ARTS

Laguna Beach, California

The Pageant of the Masters is an extraordinary bit of theater. Set in the charming artists colony and coastal community of Laguna Beach, it is part of California's oldest art show, The Festival of Arts, held each summer

since 1932. The unique pageant is an annually changing selection of masterpiece paintings and sculptures meticulously re-created and depicted live onstage—motionless (or nearly motionless) *tableaux vivants* of Botticellis and Seurats— every night of the festival. Since real people take the place of the figures showcased in the original works, everything is in "life-size" detail. It's a remarkable sight, enriched by explanations of exactly how more than 500 volunteers construct the sets, costume and prepare the "actors," and compose the scenes before revealing the finished product. Running concurrently is the formerly "alternative,"

Re-creating masterpiece paintings such as this one onstage is a festival favorite.

now well-established, Sawdust Festival, a charming collection showcasing over 200 local artists in booths arranged across a sawdust-covered canyon hillside.

Not to be missed is Laguna itself. One of a number of seaside jewels strung together by the Pacific Coast Highway (Laguna's Main Street), the formerly funky, sleepy seaside community has morphed into an expensive and bustling town. Galleries are open regularly and at their most festive on First Thursday Art Walks, held once a month.

For accommodations, consider the ocean-front Montage Resort & Spa, which offers breathtaking ocean views from every point of its 30-acre bluff-top setting. The local love affair with art is obvious here, with works by contemporary and early 20th-century artists filling the Arts and Crafts–inspired interior. Its seaside spa is one of the finest in the state, and its signature restaurant, Studio, serves modern French cuisine with California influences.

WHERE: 50 miles southeast of Los Angeles. **PAGEANT OF THE MASTERS AND FESTIVAL OF THE ARTS:** Tel 800-487-3378 or 949-497-6582; foapom.com. *Cost:* Pageant tickets from $15. *When:* July–Aug. **SAWDUST FESTIVAL:** Tel 949-494-3030; sawdustartfestival.org. *When:* late June–late Aug; 5 weekends between Thanksgiving and Christmas. **MONTAGE RESORT:** Tel 866-271-6953 or 949-715-6000; montagehotels.com/lagunabeach. *Cost:* from $495 (off-peak), from $595 (peak). **BEST TIMES:** July–Aug for Pageant of the Masters; off-season for pleasant weather and fewer crowds.

The Last of Her Kind

THE *QUEEN MARY*

Long Beach, California

Book a cabin aboard this grand old art deco ship, or come for just a few hours of fantasy travel—a visit here takes you back to a time when travel was a decadent pleasure to be savored. Though she no longer leaves the

harbor (she's been docked here since 1967), your imagination will instantly embark upon an old-world journey the minute you board the classic luxury liner known as the *Queen Mary*.

Commissioned by Cunard Steamship Co., the *Queen Mary* made her maiden voyage in 1936, and remains a stunning piece of engineering to this day. Totaling 1,019 feet in

length, 181 feet from keel to the top of her foremost smokestack, and weighing in at over 81,000 gross tons, the deco beauty made 1,001 transatlantic crossings before retiring in 1967. During that time she served four years of war duty, carrying more than 765,000 military personnel, including Winston Churchill. Today, she remains elegant inside and out, with a sleek lobby and 346 original first-class staterooms (total capacity was just under 2,000 passengers), including art deco built-ins and rich wood accents. Much has been written about the ship's ghost population: Sign up for one of the tours to find out more about the paranormal activity that carries on today.

During her stint as a WWII troopship, the Queen Mary *sometimes carried as many as 16,000 men in a single voyage.*

You don't have to spend the night to experience this throwback to the golden era of travel. Pay a modest admission and take a self-guided tour to learn about the legendary era of the *Queen*; pay a little more for a behind-the-scenes tour; or arrive in early evening for cocktails at the elegant Observation Bar, or dinner at one of the four restaurants. The aptly named Grand Salon, the ship's original first-class dining room, is the setting for the famous Sunday Champagne Brunch with a live harpist and buffet extravaganza.

WHERE: 25 miles south of Los Angeles. Tel 877-342-0738 or 562-435-3511; queen mary.com. *Cost:* admission from $27, waived for those dining; staterooms from $149 (off-peak), from $189 (peak). **BEST TIMES:** various annual events on board, including a New Year's Eve bash.

The Happiest Place on Earth

DISNEYLAND AND DISNEY'S CALIFORNIA ADVENTURE

Anaheim, California

In 1955, when filmmaker Walt Disney opened up his eponymous amusement park, promoted as the world's first family-oriented mega–theme park and hotel, it was dubbed "Walt's Folly." Today, it is hard to imagine the world without this little place called Disneyland—and the global spin-offs it has spawned.

The park has come a long way since Walt's time, when everything could be experienced in one long, sunny California day. The original park is now a vast resort, brightly proclaiming itself "The Happiest Place on Earth," and requires multiple days to fully explore. It includes two theme parks (Disneyland and the newer Disney's California Adventure), a shopping and entertainment area (Downtown Disney), and three hotels.

The cast of Disney characters that roams the park, stopping for hugs and posing for photos, is still one of the greatest attractions for younger visitors. Lines can be long, so if you're being selective, make sure to include Pirates of the Caribbean, one of the longest and best rides in the park. It's full of the animatronic imagery and storytelling that made this the gold standard of amusement parks. Ditto the Haunted Mansion. Thrill-ride enthusiasts can get their roller-coaster fix at Hyperspace Mountain, while Fantasyland offers sweeter, more whimsical rides like Alice in Wonderland, where riders hop a caterpillar down into Wonderland. A major 14-acre expansion based on *Star Wars* is scheduled for a 2018 unveiling.

Guests enter Disney's California Adventure, located across from the entrance plaza, through the newly designed Buena Vista Street reminiscent of L.A. in the 1920s. New attractions include Toy Story Mania, World of Color, and The Little Mermaid. Kids prefer the amusement park–style rides on the Paradise Pier or the unpredictable splashes from the Grizzly River Run. Take the little kids on the *Bug's Life*–themed Heimlich's Chew-Chew to join that Teutonic caterpillar as he chomps his way around.

Though Anaheim was once little more than orange orchards, Disney's presence lured a number of other attractions here. Restaurants in the Downtown Disney district include Ralph Brennan's Jazz Kitchen, which serves straight-out-of–New Orleans dishes of Cajun-Creole flair in an ambience redolent of the French Quarter. Conveniently located just opposite the theme park's ticket booth is the outpost of L.A.'s famed La Brea Bakery, which offers terrific sandwiches on their artisanal bread, plus a host of sweets. The best treat for theme park enthusiasts beyond Disneyland itself is a stay at Disney's Grand Californian Hotel & Spa, modeled after Yosemite's landmark hotel (see p. 863). It's a perfect homage to the Arts and Crafts movement, with its cavernous yet homey six-story lobby complete with an enormous river-rock, wood-burning fireplace big enough to walk into. The hotel doesn't disappoint with the surprisingly sophisticated Napa Rose restaurant, which will have you believe you're dining somewhere in California's fabled wine country.

WHERE: 30 miles southeast of Los Angeles. **DISNEYLAND/CALIFORNIA ADVENTURE:** Tel 800-225-2024 or 714-781-4565; disneyland.disney.go.com. *Cost:* 2-day ticket $172 (ages 3–9), $185 (ages 10 and up). **RALPH BRENNAN'S JAZZ KITCHEN:** Tel 714-776-5200; rbjazzkitchen.com. *Cost:* lunch $35. **LA BREA BAKERY:** Tel 714-490-0233; labreabakery.com. *Cost:* lunch $20. **GRAND CALIFORNIAN HOTEL & SPA:** Tel 714-635-2300; disneyland.disney.go.com. *Cost:* from $379; dinner at Napa Rose $45. **BEST TIMES:** Sept–May for weather; middle of the week to avoid the long lines.

Once Ramshakle, Now a Global Destination

DOWNTOWN LOS ANGELES

Los Angeles, California

L ong perceived as a completely different city than its more glamorous, informal, and beachy neighbors to the west, downtown Los Angeles was little more than a business destination that became a ghost town after 5 P.M.

However, exceptional attractions have sprouted up in the recent past, making for an easy (if sometimes hilly) half-day walking tour. The Walt Disney Concert Hall is the sparkling centerpiece and architectural landmark courtesy of celebrated architect Frank Gehry. It's an undulating mass of shiny steel that billows like a galleon ship at full sail, and the permanent home of the Los Angeles Philharmonic, which takes advantage of state-of-the-art acoustics that came with its $274 million-plus price tag. Included in the complex, along with a small café and an arty gift shop, is the acclaimed Patina, one of L.A.'s finest restaurants (see p. 824). It's all part of the Music Center, which includes three more theaters across the street:

the Dorothy Chandler Pavilion (former home of the Academy Awards), the Ahmanson Theater, and the Mark Taper Forum, where some of Los Angeles's exceptional and unjustly overlooked theater scene occurs. (The Tony and Pulitzer winner *Angels in America* was developed here.)

Just two blocks away is the Cathedral of Our Lady of the Angels, opened in 2002 as the seat of the Archbishop of L.A. It is an unconventional and austere structure considered by many to be a stunning example of modern ecclesiastical architecture and by others to be uninspired and ungainly. To honor the ethnic melting pot of Los Angeles, the welcoming Madonna is deliberately multiracial. She was created by local sculptor Robert Graham, who also designed the Great Bronze Doors that incorporate 40 pre-Christian symbols. Frequent

With its postmodern design, the Walt Disney Concert Hall is an example of architectural deconstructivism.

organ recitals fill the airy space with the sound of the 42-ton instrument's 6,019 pipes.

Two blocks south of the Music Center is the Museum of Contemporary Art (MOCA) Grand Avenue, which collects, presents, and interprets art from 1940 to the present in all media. Significant retrospectives are frequently held here. Several blocks away is The Geffen Contemporary at MOCA, which holds rotating shows. The city's newest contemporary art museum, The Broad, opened in 2015 in an eye-catching honeycombed building that has further secured the city's reputation as a cultural destination.

Try the modern Mexican food at Border Grill, one of three locations featuring a menu by Mary Sue Milliken and Susan Feniger, the chef duo known as the "Too Hot Tamales." This fun, casual venue is lively with an appreciative crowd who come for the fresh margaritas and updated classics.

WALT DISNEY CONCERT HALL: Tel 323-850-2000; musiccenter.org. **OUR LADY OF THE ANGELS:** Tel 213-680-5200; olacathedral.org. **THE MUSEUM OF CONTEMPORARY ART:** Tel 213-626-6222; moca.org. *When:* closed Tues. **THE BROAD MUSEUM:** Tel 213-232-6200; thebroad.org. **BORDER GRILL:** Tel 213-486-5171; bordergrill.com. *Cost:* dinner $35. **BEST TIME:** Oct–May for walking weather.

Six Feet of Separation

GRAVEYARDS OF THE STARS

Los Angeles, California

Go ahead: Admit your visit to Los Angeles won't be complete without seeing a celebrity. If you're not picky about whom or how, there is one guaranteed way to get within 6 feet of a genuine superstar. The cemeteries

of Southern California are filled with some of Hollywood's biggest icons, who, although inaccessible in life, now welcome any and all visitors to drop by and pay homage.

Hollywood Forever, formerly known as Hollywood Memorial Park, is a slightly Gothic graveyard with an abundance of artistic and curious markers and a fitting view of the

"Hollywood" sign in the distance. Find out who's resting beneath a marble replica of the Pioneer Rocket or the oversize bronze replica of a guitar-wielding Johnny Ramone. Drop in for tours, weekend concerts, and quirky events, including a colorful Day of the Dead celebration in late October or early November, with over a hundred homemade folk art altars, food, music, and folklore. Summer weekend movie screenings against the wall of a mausoleum also draw crowds. Among the dearly departed are Rudolph Valentino (note lipstick prints on his marble tomb), Cecil B. DeMille (who lies facing Paramount, his old studio), and Douglas Fairbanks Senior and Junior.

The more sterile but even more luminary-filled Pierce Brothers Westwood Village Memorial Park is oddly located in the center of a cluster of office buildings near UCLA. It's a small place but boasts perhaps the biggest star in the galaxy, Marilyn Monroe. If you drop by on August 5, the anniversary of her death, you'll see the floral tributes that cover the area near her wall vault. In a wall nearby are the ashes of Truman Capote. Delightful longtime collaborators Jack Lemmon, Walter Matthau, and Billy Wilder are all within a few feet of each other, while out in the center grassy area are Natalie Wood, Frank Zappa, Roy Orbison (the latter two in unmarked graves), and many more.

The two Forest Lawn cemeteries at Glendale and Hollywood Hills are more parklike and expansive, and downplay their famous occupants—a curious thing, since they were designed to encourage people to see cemeteries as places to visit. At the Glendale location, along with some bad statuary and rolling green hills, is the tucked-away, tiny bronze grave marker for Walt Disney. George Burns and Gracie Allen are together again in a mausoleum, as are Carole Lombard and Clark Gable. In Forest Lawn Hollywood Hills, you'll find Liberace (in a disappointingly sedate tomb) and nearby Andy Gibb, while the Nelsons—Ozzie, Harriet, and Ricky—are reunited in a bittersweet family plot.

Plan a do-it-yourself tour by tapping into the website findagrave.com, or better yet, sign up with the highly entertaining and obsessively informed Scott Michaels and his three-hour Dearly Departed tour around town, which includes driving past the hotels where John Belushi, Whitney Houston, and Janis Joplin died. It really brings it all alive.

Hollywood Forever: Tel 323-469-1181; hollywoodforever.com. **Pierce Brothers Westwood Village Memorial Park:** Tel 310-474-1579. **Forest Lawn Glendale:** Tel 888-204-3131 or 323-254-3131; forestlawn .com/glendale. **Forest Lawn Hollywood Hills:** Tel 800-204-3131 or 323-254-3131; for estlawn.com/hollywoodhills. **Dearly Departed Tours:** Tel 855-600-3323 or 323-825-0040; dearlydepartedtours.com. *Cost:* $48.

Where America Reinvents Itself

HOLLYWOOD

Los Angeles, California

After show-biz pioneers Cecil B. DeMille and Jesse Lasky were drawn to the climate-blessed West Coast in 1913, Hollywood ceased being a real place and became a concept, a glittering Tinseltown synonymous with glamour and ambition. However, it has long been true that the only stars you are now likely to see on Hollywood Boulevard (premieres aside) are those embedded in the sidewalk.

Known as the Walk of Fame, the pathway honors more than 2,500 legends of film, television, radio, theater, and recording art, and runs along Hollywood Boulevard from La Brea Avenue to Vine Street where it turns left and heads down to Sunset Boulevard.

But Hollywood is currently in the midst of a Times Square–like revival, with new attractions that are actually luring highbrow locals and celebrities to an area that for decades has been known as gritty and rife with riffraff and cheap tourist shops. A major catalyst of the upgrade and an anchor of the neighborhood is the Hollywood & Highland Center, a stylish complex and shopping mall that pays homage to its surroundings with whimsical tributes to Hollywood's heritage, such as a red-carpet–like pathway embedded with quotes from industry insiders. Its centerpiece is the Dolby Theatre: Take a guided tour and get a behind-the-scenes view of the 3,400-seat theater designed as the permanent home for the Academy Awards.

From here, it's an easy walk to TCL Chinese Theatre (formerly Grauman's), a movie palace of a bygone era built to impress. This historic landmark still shows new releases (in IMAX since 2013) and regularly hosts premieres, but it's most visited for its fabulous Asian design and an impressive collection of handprints and footprints of some of Hollywood's best-known stars from 1927 to the present. Of the nearly 200 imprints, look for those of Mary Pickford, Elizabeth Taylor, Frank Sinatra, and Marilyn

Brave children peer into the mouth of the Jaws *shark replica at Universal Studios.*

Monroe. Other prints lean toward the odd: Jimmy Durante's nose, George Burns's cigar, Betty Grable's legs, and R2D2's wheels.

While many of the major studios are located elsewhere (such as Studio City in the San Fernando Valley), filmmaking has been going on at nearby Paramount since the 1920s, and you can experience it through an intimate tour of the sound stages and backlot, with sets from celebrated films. But for the best glimpse of how movies are made, head over the Hollywood Hills to Universal Studios in Universal City. Though it's been a working studio for decades, it has become a major tourist destination thanks to its popular tour of the world's largest television and movie studio. Suitable for the whole family, skeptics included, the tour includes special effects experiences like King Kong 360 3-D, visits to famous film and TV sets, and tales of the amazing world of filmmaking. A recent addition to Universal Studios is an immersive journey through the world of The Walking Dead.

Whether you'll actually have a star-sighting during your tour is questionable. But some spots around town have relatively decent odds. One such place is the historic Hollywood Roosevelt Hotel. A celebrity hangout for 90 years, and host to the first Academy Awards in 1929, the hotel has had a full-blown face-lift, and its high-beamed art deco lobby, decorated swimming pool by David Hockney, and smartly redone bars are all star attractions.

And don't forget to look for that famous "Hollywood" sign. The 50-foot-high sign was placed atop Mount Lee in the Hollywood Hills in 1923 as part of a promotion for a real estate development called Hollywoodland. The last syllable was removed when the city of Los Angeles took over the land. The 450-foot-long landmark that remained was demolished in 1978 after a termite infestation and arson, and completely rebuilt of concrete and steel. The best view is from Sunset Boulevard and Bronson Avenue: Get your cameras out!

WHERE: 6 miles northeast of downtown Los Angeles. *Visitor info:* Tel 323-469-8311; hollywoodchamber.net. **HOLLYWOOD &**

HIGHLAND CENTER: hollywoodandhighland .com. DOLBY THEATRE: Tel 323-308-6300; dolbytheatre.com. TCL CHINESE THEATRE: Tel 818-977-1569; tclchinesetheatres.com. *Cost:* movies $23. PARAMOUNT STUDIOS: Tel 323-956-1777; paramountstudios.com. UNIVERSAL STUDIOS HOLLYWOOD: Universal City. Tel 800-UNIVERSAL; universalstudioshollywood .com. *Cost:* tours $95. HOLLYWOOD ROOSEVELT HOTEL: Tel 323-466-7000; thehollywoodroos evelt.com. *Cost:* from $299. BEST TIME: mid-June–mid-Sept for the outdoor Hollywood Bowl's concert season, which includes hosting the L.A. Philharmonic (hollywoodbowl.com).

Everything Old Is New Again

L.A.'s CULINARY CLASSICS

Los Angeles, California

L.A.'s motto is "Out with the old, in with the new"—except when it comes to Tinseltown dining establishments, where historical character commands respect and patronage. Scandia, Chasen's, and The Brown Derby are no longer, but Musso & Frank Grill remains. This wood-paneled, red-leather-booth icon is one of the town's oldest joints, a Hollywood hot spot that has been the place to get classic steak house fare and classic martinis since 1919—served by waiters who just might have been working on opening day. Industry types and lookers-on order from a defiantly retro menu: grilled calf's liver, shrimp Louie salad, grena-dine of beef, and six different kinds of potatoes.

Older still, the casual, sawdust-on-the-floors Philippe the Original opened in 1900 and claims to have invented the French Dip sand-wich in 1918. Regardless of the assertion's validity, this landmark order-at-the-counter joint surely perfected the art, with delicious thinly sliced beef (pork, ham, turkey, and lamb are options) sandwiched in a halved French roll and accompanied by a savory dipping sauce of meat juices. Breakfast's cinnamon-dipped French toast gives you a reason to return.

In the Fairfax area, experience L.A.'s diversity at the vibrant Farmers Market, the city's favorite outdoor dining bazaar. A land-mark since the Depression, the charming and weathered maze of stalls, shops, grocers, and casual alfresco eating spots lures longtime locals and fresh-faced celebrities alike. Favorites include classic pies at Du-Par's, fresh seafood creations at the Gumbo Pot, and caffeine at Bob's Coffee and Doughnuts, an aspiring-screenwriter haunt. Nearby, Pink's hot-dog shack has been serving perfect dogs for nearly as long. Paul and Betty Pink opened it in 1939 and you can still order a hot dog drowned in Betty's secret chili sauce—it's one of 40 "dogs" on the menu. But today the park-ing lot is filled with Jaguars and Mercedes, and there's almost always a line.

This is a town that takes its sushi very seri-ously. From small neighborhood restaurants that serve fish so fresh it's practically flopping on the plate, to chic hot spots frequented by a glamorous crowd, sushi joints here are abun-dant. The most famous shrine to raw seafood belongs to superchef Nobu Matsuhisa, who has outposts across the country. His longtime res-taurant Matsuhisa featured a menu that was a master's manifesto of exquisite sushi and inno-vative cooked dishes served in an unremark-able venue. In 2006, Chef Matsuhisa moved his restaurant a few blocks south. Now called Matsuhisa Beverly Hills, the chef's menu con-tinues to be delicious and groundbreaking, and the restaurant will no doubt remain a must-stop on the foodie circuit. Less expensive and larger, but rightly popular, is the always busy Sushi Gen, while Kanpai ("Cheers" in Japanese) is known for its pristine sushi and late-night hours, as well as tempura and ramen options and a choice of 20 sakes.

MUSSO & FRANK GRILL: Tel 323-467-7788; mussoandfrank.com. *Cost:* dinner $50. **PHILIPPE THE ORIGINAL:** Tel 213-628-3781; philippes.com. *Cost:* lunch $8. **FARMERS MARKET:** Tel 323-933-9211; farmersmarketla.com. **PINK'S:** Tel 323-931-4223; pinkshollywood.com. *Cost:* chili dog $5. **MATSUHISA BEVERLY HILLS:** Tel 310-659-9639; nobumatsuhisa.com. *Cost:* dinner $75. **SUSHI GEN:** Tel 213-617-0552. *Cost:* dinner $40. **KANPAI:** Tel 310-338-7223; kanpai-sushi.net. *Cost:* $30.

From Holes in the Wall to the High Life

L.A.'S CULINARY STANDOUTS

Los Angeles, California

Thanks to the unique combination of beach, city, celebrities, and micro-communities from virtually every nationality in the world, L.A. has everything a great food town needs, from four-star dining rooms to holes-in-the-wall to all the options in between.

Book a coveted table at downtown's Patina, where outstanding French-inspired cuisine is overseen by celebrity chef Joachim Splichal. Like many top toques, Splichal has myriad restaurants, but this is his flagship, moved from West Hollywood years ago to a more modern locale in downtown's Music Center (see p. 819), a cluster of theaters that makes a deliciously cultural evening a breeze.

L.A.'s current food has been heavily shaped by the genius of Nancy Silverton, prolific baker, pastry chef, cookbook author, chef, restaurateur, and entrepreneurial business-woman. Nancy co-founded La Brea Bakery in 1989, which changed the game for artisanal bread in America (she sold it in 2001), and the seminal Campanile restaurant (closed in 2012). She later partnered with NY-based food moguls Mario Batali and Joe Bastianich to open Osteria Mozza. An overnight L.A. institution inspired by a mozzarella-themed eatery she had discovered in Rome, "Mozza" serves up excellent pastas and out-of-the-ordinary Italian fare. Other collaborations followed: the meat-driven Chi Spacca next door, and the unpretentious Pizzeria Mozza with delicious slices.

Beverly Hills (see p. 806) is the perfect backdrop for José Andrés's inventive cooking, a blend of tradition and fantasy that flawlessly fits the SoCal zeitgeist. The Bazaar, located in the splashy SLS Hotel, features a playful Philippe Starck-designed dining room and a diverse menu boasting straight-from-Seville-style tapas along with more avant-garde offerings—all vividly flavorful and beautifully prepared.

A staple with the discerning dining set, Lucques (the name of the chef's favorite French olive, pronounced "Luke") is a chic brick-walled space with a pleasant ivy-covered patio. The eclectic Cal-Med menu is small, often the unpredictable result of what chef Suzanne Goin, formerly of Campanile, found at the farmers market that morning. The prix-fixe "Sunday Supper" has become a popular tradition and true bargain.

While these restaurants can stand proudly with some of the finest in the country, some of the best tasting food for the best price can be found in small ethnic joints. There are over 200 different languages spoken in the county, and you can savor the flavor of their homelands within a 2-mile stretch of Hollywood Boulevard. The roasted chicken with pungent garlic sauce at Middle Eastern–style Zankou is so popular it now counts a long list of fervent devotees since opening its first of eight locations in 1984. The Hollywood neighborhood of Thai Town knows no shortage of solid eateries. Many chefs regularly rank Jitlada as their go-to option, claiming the epic range of spicy Southern Thai specialties to be as authentic as any found in Southeast Asia. Thai Town sits side by side with the small area

loosely dubbed Little Armenia. Drop in to Sahag's Basturma to try a sandwich made of the spicy Armenian cured beef (also called pastirma) that gives this grocery store its name and has kept the fans coming since 1987.

Patina: Tel 213-972-3331; patinagroup.com. *Cost:* 3-course tasting menu $79. **Osteria Mozza:** Tel 323-297-0100; mozza-la.com. *Cost:* dinner $70. **The Bazaar:** Tel 310-246-5555; sbe.com. *Cost:* dinner $60. **Lucques:** Tel 323-655-6277; lucques.com. *Cost:* dinner $50. **Zankou:** Tel 323-882-6365; zankouchicken.com. *Cost:* lunch $10. **Jitlada:** Tel 323-667-9809. *Cost:* $30. **Sahag's Basturma:** Tel 323-661-5311. *Cost:* lunch $6.

Luxury Havens Where Everyone's a Star

L.A.'s Diva Hotels

Los Angeles, California

Located in a ritzy, lush canyon just minutes from busy L.A. intersections, the Hotel Bel-Air is one of the city's finest and most exclusive temporary addresses. Since 1946, the 12-acre refuge with its flowering native and

subtropical flora has been *the* spot for stars to seek respite and anonymity. It's not just the no-camera policy and subtle service that keeps them coming. Everything about this recently reimagined place is quietly exquisite, while relaxed. Shaded pathways meander past swan-dotted ponds to hideaway Mission-style bungalows. Former guest Marilyn Monroe's bungalow has been transformed into a state-of-the-art gym, and La Prairie Spa meets every relaxation and beauty need amid 12 acres of gardens. The sterling restaurant serves one of the best Sunday brunches in town; air-light lemon pancakes with fresh raspberries are a menu fixture.

The Beverly Hills Hotel is a friendly rival, even more venerable and flashy. Anchored at the corner of a sweeping curve of Sunset Boulevard since 1912, the towers of the "Pink

Palace" grace the cover of the Eagles' seminal *Hotel California* album. Though it's no longer the shade of Pepto-Bismol pink depicted on the record, it's still a standout. This grande dame has everything a rich, fashionable traveler could wish for, from a showy pool scene complete with

Bette Davis, Jimmy Stewart, Judy Garland, and Grace Kelly were all once guests at the Hotel Bel-Air.

coveted cabanas to rooms and bungalows with butler service and walk-in closets, some boasting more square footage than the average home. The forever-popular Polo Lounge has long been the place where Old Hollywood makes and breaks its deals, while the hotel gardens brim with various palms and exotic blooms that smell of jasmine and bergamot.

Another famous historic favorite, the Chateau Marmont is set directly in the center of the Sunset Strip action. A gorgeous rambling and romantic venue built in 1929 and today run by hotelier Andre Balazs, it's a reliable top pick for young celebrities who prefer the casual, incognito atmosphere and apartmentlike guest rooms. Secluded bungalows are even larger,

each with furnishings and style straight out of a film noir flick. The place's reputation for discretion even in the face of outrageous star behavior (such as Jim Morrison's drunken saunter across its rooftop and John Belushi's fatal overdose) hasn't changed since the days studio boss Harry Cohn told William Holden and Glenn Ford, "If you must get into trouble, do it at the Marmont."

HOTEL BEL-AIR: Tel 800-650-1842 or 310-472-1211; dorchestercollection.com. *Cost:* from $595 (off-peak), from $645 (peak). **THE BEVERLY HILLS HOTEL:** Tel 800-650-1842 or 310-276-2251; dorchestercollection.com. *Cost:* from $565 (off-peak), from $745 (peak). **CHATEAU MARMONT:** Hollywood. Tel 323-656-1010; chateaumarmont.com. *Cost:* from $450.

Culture Among the Stars

THE MUSEUMS OF L.A.

Los Angeles, California

Masterpiece of famed architect Richard Meier, the 110-acre, six-building Getty Center was 14 years and $1 billion in the making when it opened in 1997 as a modern Acropolis, perched atop a Santa Monica mountain

ridge, looking out over L.A. to the Pacific. Designed to house the ever-expanding Getty art collection and a library of more than 1 million books, the hilltop citadel is a work of art itself in gleaming off-white travertine marble and glass. Inside, soaring galleries rely heavily on natural light and are interspersed with courtyards, fountains, connecting walkways, and windows that frame views of the Robert

The Getty Center's curving glass walls create a sense of openness and fluidity between indoor and outdoor space.

Irwin–designed gardens and the urban sprawl beyond. Van Gogh's *Irises* and five Cézannes (including his *Still Life with Apples*) are the Getty's magnets to the masses, offset by its esoteric specialty collections, from Renaissance to Impressionism and 18th-century European decorative arts.

A side trip to Pacific Palisades reveals the original Getty Museum, now known as Getty Villa. The Pompeii-inspired home was commissioned from afar by the expat American oil billionaire Jean Paul Getty. It was completed two years before his death in 1976, and although he never visited it, he chose to be buried there. It was designed on an ancient Roman model, with meticulously styled gardens and fountains, and today it houses the Getty's superb collection of Greek, Roman, and Etruscan antiquities.

For over half a century, the city's other cultural claim has placed it in the nation's highest ranks: the massive collection of the Los Angeles County Museum of Art, considered the most comprehensive in the West. Just a sampling of its 130,000 possessions is displayed, dating from antiquity to the present. Its strengths include Asian, Latin American, and Islamic art. In the Pavilion for Japanese art, the collection of Japanese Edo paintings is said to be rivaled only by that of the emperor of Japan and is one of the few buildings outside of Japan strictly dedicated to Japanese art.

Next door is the enthralling La Brea Tar Pits, where dire wolves, saber-toothed cats, and mammoths were trapped between 10,000 and 40,000 years ago. Excavations go on to this day. Nearly 400 species of mammals, birds, and fish—many of them now extinct—fell victim, and scores of fossilized remains can be seen in the museum.

GETTY CENTER: Tel 310-440-7300; getty .edu. *When:* closed Mon. **GETTY VILLA:** Pacific Palisades. Tel 310-440-7300; getty.edu. *When:* closed Tues. **LOS ANGELES COUNTY MUSEUM OF ART:** Tel 323-857-6000; lacma.org. *When:* closed Wed. **LA BREA TAR PITS:** Tel 323-934-PAGE; tarpits.org.

Winding Street of Dreams

SUNSET BOULEVARD

Los Angeles, California

The freeways put a stop to Sunset Boulevard's status as Los Angeles's main artery, but that's a good thing—all the less traffic for you on this iconic 22-mile boulevard, a fantastic drive that moves you from one end of town to the other with great views and sightseeing along the way. Immortalized in the 1950 film classic *Sunset Boulevard*, it's not the jaw-dropping route of the Pacific Coast Highway (see p. 836), but as you wend your way along its curves, you will encounter a little bit of every piece of the crazy quilt that is Los Angeles. From the palm trees to the stark looming mountains, from ethnic enclaves to the manicured perfection of Beverly Hills, from star-spotting to sites of scandal, all the way to the shimmering finale of the Pacific Ocean, Sunset offers a moving tour and taste of Los Angeles's elusive magic.

Sunset Boulevard starts in downtown L.A., not far from Olvera Street, the oldest extant street in Los Angeles, which includes a bustling 19th-century marketplace where you can fuel up for your drive with fine Mexican food. From there it heads west through craggy Echo Park (home to Dodger Stadium), cutting and curving through the hills of newly hip Silver Lake before flattening out through Hollywood's shabby and chic sections. At the corner of Vermont and Gower, glance up at the hills on your right for a good view of the iconic "Hollywood" sign and the sparkling art deco jewel that is Griffith Observatory (a supporting player in *Rebel Without a Cause* and recipient of a complete face-lift funded in part by *Star Trek*'s Leonard Nimoy). Take a right on Vine if you want to head to the sights of Hollywood Boulevard. Otherwise, continue on Sunset through the stretch from Laurel Canyon Boulevard to Doheny Drive, which is known as the "Sunset Strip." Even if you don't see the street signs, you can't miss it. Just look for the giant billboards, clubs, cafés, and pretty people. Check out Sunset Plaza, a short strip of costly shops and eateries, plus often lots of well-known faces enjoying both.

The independent city of Beverly Hills (see p. 806), almost entirely surrounded by Los Angeles, begins at Doheny. The landscaping is more groomed and the homes are much larger the minute you cross into the tony 90210 area code. The pink celebrity haunt Beverly Hills Hotel (see p. 825) is on this stretch of Sunset, while a right turn up Benedict Canyon will take you to one of the sites of the Manson murders, though the actual house has been torn down. At the corner of Beverly Glen, Los Angeles proper returns with the leafy green and extremely exclusive Bel Air neighborhood. Turn left down Kenter Avenue if you want to see the site of the murder of Nicole Simpson, O. J. Simpson's ex-wife. Continue west on Sunset to enter the upscale but still family-oriented neighborhood of Pacific Palisades, home to its share of bold-faced names. At Mandeville Canyon, you might want to start singing a Beach Boys tune—you are nearly at the ocean.

WHERE: from downtown L.A. west to the Pacific. **BEST TIMES:** avoid rush hour.

Sun, Sand, and Shopping

SANTA MONICA & VENICE

California

This is the prototypical California beach moment: You're in your shorts and flip-flops, standing on a sidewalk with palm trees and clear blue sky overhead. Scantily clad nubile young things zip past on bikes and Rollerblades. Nearby, gently breaking Pacific Ocean waves lap onto the glistening sandy shore. Across the street a café overflows with tanned patrons, shaded by a canopy of bougainvillea. And you think, "It's January."

Welcome to Santa Monica. An incorporated city since 1907, bounded by lumbering Los Angeles on one side and the big blue ocean on the other, L.A.'s most beachy community is no longer the sleepy, shambling, relaxed resort town it once was. But the flat streets of Santa Monica are still perfect for walking, jogging, biking, or taking in the sun once the morning fog lifts.

The Third Street Promenade, once a somewhat shabby outdoor mall—also one of the first in the country—is now the very model of "new" urban spaces, and one of Southern California's favorite gathering places with its shops, cafés, and movie theaters. While undeniably a pleasant place to stroll, you'll also want to head to historic Santa Monica, well preserved and at its best at the world-famous Santa Monica Pier. A beloved institution since 1909, it boasts a collection of classic carnival rides, seashell souvenir shops and, best of all, a genuine 1930s all-wooden merry-go-round that's likely to be familiar to anyone who has seen *The Sting*. The upscale boutiques along Montana Avenue provide frequent opportunities for celebrity sightings, while the highly touted farmers market on Wednesdays and Saturdays brings out all the local amateur and professional chefs (some of

Santa Monica Pier's Pacific Park features 12 rides, including a large Ferris wheel, popular for its spectacular views of the Pacific.

whom put on special cooking demonstrations), searching out the best in organic, seasonal produce in colors and varieties you didn't know existed.

If you'd rather have your food prepared, and in a manner nothing less than *divino*, search out the tony Italian cuisine at Valentino, where legendary host-owner Piero Selvaggio treats his customers like long-lost family and the 1,200-selection wine list is acclaimed as one of the best in the United States. Back on the beachfront and within sight of the pier is the delightful Shutters on the Beach, one of just two hotels in Santa Monica positioned directly on the beach rather than across the street. One of the most alluring accommodations in the area, it manages to combine the casual Cape Cod resort look (all rooms have balconies that open to let in the sound of the ocean) with all the luxurious amenities its VIP guests have come to expect, including a spa and seaside meals at One Pico Coast.

Just a stroll south of Santa Monica is the still funky, oddball, and delightful beach community of Venice, founded in 1905 by Abbott Kinney, who envisioned a Venice-of-America. Kinney designed it to include canals and Italian architecture and imported authentic gondolas, long since gone. Though the canals still exist, they're not nearly as noteworthy as the city's famed 1.5-mile long Venice Beach boardwalk, a wide,

paved promenade that runs alongside the white sand beaches. This was the epicenter of L.A.'s 1960s hippie scene, and much of that bohemian vibe lingers still. With its inexpensive cafés and stalls selling T-shirts, sunglasses, and temporary tattoos, it's a carnival of humanity where street performers, skateboarders, Rollerbladers, bums, bikini-clad babes, and classic Southern California freaks are perpetually on parade. The area's long-famous weight lifters' mecca, Muscle Beach, is still pumping up young Ahhh-nuld wannabes. Those in-the-know line up for take-away at Jodi Maroni's Sausage Kingdom or stroll Venice's Main Street, a stimulating seven-block mix of shops, both fabulous and quirky.

WHERE: 15 miles west of Los Angeles. **SANTA MONICA PIER:** Tel 310-458-8901; santa monicapier.org. **FARMERS MARKET:** Tel 310-458-8712; smgov.net/portals/farmersmarket. **VALENTINO:** Tel 310-829-4313; valentinossanta monica.com. *Cost:* dinner $75. **SHUTTERS ON THE BEACH:** Tel 310-458-0030; shuttersonthe beach.com. *Cost:* from $625. **VENICE BEACH:** venicebeach.com. **MUSCLE BEACH:** Tel 310-399-2775; musclebeach.net. **JODY MARONI'S:** Tel 310-822-5639; jodymaroni.com. *Cost:* hot dog $4. **BEST TIME:** summer for free concerts on Thurs nights at the pier and Pacific waters warm enough for swimming, but also the biggest crowds.

Coastal Bluffs, Pounding Surf, and Galleries Galore

MENDOCINO

California

Perched on tawny bluffs and surrounded on three sides by crashing surf, the impossibly quaint Northern California town of Mendocino is among the state's top coastal destinations. Settled in the 19th century by Maine fishermen, Mendocino looks so much like a New England village, with white clapboard houses, a lofty church, and public gardens, that it was used as the location for the Maine village in the 1980s TV series *Murder, She Wrote.*

Since the 1950s, Mendocino has been a magnet for artists, who came for the inspiring views and affordable rents. Those cheap studios have vanished, but the town, lined with one-of-a-kind galleries, remains a haven for artists, food lovers, and those who come to visit any of the dozens of nearby vineyards. At the MacCallum House, a restored 19th-century inn, Chef Alan Kantor prepares eco-friendly market seafood and beef from the local Niman Ranch in the homey gourmet restaurant while, a few blocks away, Café Beaujolais serves up seafood bouillabaisse and Petaluma duck two ways. You might check into the historic Joshua Grindle Inn, which features fireplaces in many rooms, or continue down the coast to Albion, where the Albion River Inn lures guests with breathtaking views and a fine restaurant.

It's just a short walk to the coastal headlands and beaches. Tide-pooling here is a delight: You'll find sea anemones, starfish, and hermit crabs. December to March is prime time for whale-watching, as great gray whales swim from their summer homes near Alaska to winter feeding grounds off the coast of Mexico.

Within a few miles of Mendocino are wondrous state parks, including Van Damme, Russian Gulch, and Jug Handle State Natural Reserve, where you can hike inland into the "pygmy forest" full of cypress trees stunted by poor soil. Railroad fanciers head to Fort Bragg or Willits to ride the Skunk Train 20 miles to Northspur and back—you'll smell the sooty engines before you see them, hence the name.

With occasional whistles as it chugs through tunnels, over bridges, and past open meadows, the Skunk Train has followed the coastal Redwood Route since 1885.

WHERE: 155 miles north of San Francisco. *Visitor info:* Tel 707-961-6300; mendocinocoast .com. **MacCallum House:** Tel 800-609-0492 or 707-937-0289; maccallumhouse.com. *Cost:* from $160; dinner $60. **Café Beaujolais:** Tel 707-937-5614; cafebeaujolais.com. *Cost:* dinner $50. **Joshua Grindle Inn:** Tel 707-937-4143; joshuagrindlemendocino.com. *Cost:* from $169. **Albion River Inn:** Albion. Tel 800-479-7944 or 707-937-1919; albionriverinn.com. *Cost:* from $195; dinner $50. **Whale-watching:** Telstar Charters, tel 707-964-8770; goocean fishing.com. **Jug Handle, Van Damme, and Russian Gulch state parks:** parks.ca.gov. **Skunk Train:** Fort Bragg. Tel 707-964-6371; skunktrain.com. *Cost:* $59. **Best times:** Dec–Mar for whale-watching (mendowhale.com); May–Sept for warmer weather.

A World-Class Aquarium and "Steinbeck Country"

MONTEREY PENINSULA

California

Mother Nature worked overtime on the rugged Monterey Peninsula, a surf-and-wind-sculpted wonder of cliff-lined beaches, sandy dunes, rocky shores, and deep ocean bays. Pacific Grove (aka Butterfly Town, U.S.A.,

famous as the resting stop for migrating monarch butterflies) and Carmel-by-the-Sea (see

p. 810) are big attractions, but the old fishing town of Monterey, forever immortalized by

Nobel Prize–winning novelist John Steinbeck, remains the peninsula's biggest draw. Every September, it hosts the Monterey Jazz Festival, a huge three-night affair that attracts more than 500 greats from around the world and is the oldest ongoing jazz festival in the nation.

Once famous for whaling and sardine canning, Monterey was also California's first capital and retains more than 40 buildings built before 1850. Today, Monterey's most popular attraction is the world-class Monterey Bay Aquarium on Cannery Row, the alley of sardine canneries that thrived in downtown Monterey in the 1930s and '40s and the setting for Steinbeck's 1945 novel *Cannery Row*. The hard-luck world he describes has vanished (most of the canneries closed by mid-century due to overfishing), replaced by shops and restaurants that make for an enjoyable stroll.

The Monterey Bay Aquarium's largest exhibit is Open Sea, where diverse aquatic species cohabitate behind a 90-foot window.

Closely modeling a natural environment, the Monterey Bay Aquarium is home to 550 species of marine animals, including sharks, penguins, and a dazzling rainbow of fish. Curious sea otters (rescued and unable to survive in the open ocean) cavort in a land-and-sea exhibit, while nearby, a comical crew of African penguins dive into chilly waters. Then there are the mesmerizing jellies, fantastic works of living aquatic art, displayed to reveal their brilliant colors. Check into the Old Monterey Inn, a beautifully renovated half-timbered Tudor built in 1929, with a handful of rooms and an enchanting cottage.

Nearby Salinas and its surrounding landscape (sometimes referred to as "Steinbeck Country") was the birthplace and early home of Steinbeck, best known for his 1939 classic *The Grapes of Wrath*, which chronicled the hardships of migrant workers in California during the Depression. Here you'll find the National Steinbeck Center's exhibits linking his life with his literature, and frequent showings of films based upon his novels. Two blocks west is the Steinbeck House, an 1897 Queen Anne Victorian where Steinbeck was born. You can enjoy a light lunch, or request a docent-led tour.

WHERE: 120 miles south of San Francisco. *Visitor info:* Tel 888-221-1010; seemonterey .com. **MONTEREY JAZZ FESTIVAL:** Tel 888-248-6499 or 831-373-3366; montereyjazzfes tival.org. *Cost:* from $51. *When:* 3rd weekend in Sept. **MONTEREY BAY AQUARIUM:** Tel 831-648-4800; montereybayaquarium.org. **OLD MONTEREY INN:** Tel 800-350-2344 or 831-375-8284; oldmontereyinn.com. *Cost:* from $199 (off-peak), from $319 (peak). **NATIONAL STEINBECK CENTER:** Salinas. Tel 831-796-3833; steinbeck.org. **STEINBECK HOUSE:** Tel 831-424-2735; steinbeckhouse.com. *Cost:* $20. **BEST TIME:** early May for the Steinbeck Festival.

The Ne Plus Ultra of Golf Courses

PEBBLE BEACH

California

Considered by many to be the most thrilling, beguiling, and breathtaking golf course on the face of the earth, Pebble Beach's ocean-hugging links are sacred ground for golfers. Jack Nicklaus said of this spectacular (and wildly expensive) spot, "If I had only one more round to play, I would choose to play it at Pebble Beach."

Now part of a trio of championship courses that includes Spyglass Hill and The Links at Spanish Bay, Pebble Beach opened in 1919. In the late 1940s, crooner Bing Crosby brought his pro-am tourney here, the "clambake" that evolved into the AT&T Pebble Beach National Pro-Am, played on Pebble, Spyglass, and the nearby Poppy Hills courses during the second weekend of February. Tiger Woods, Phil Mickelson, Vijay Singh, and other top golfers join such celebrities as Clint Eastwood (now a part-owner of Pebble Beach) for the vaunted pro-amateur tourney.

The refined elegance of the Lodge at Pebble Beach offers the ultimate in holy-grail golfing convenience. Its 161 rooms have working fireplaces, and many skirt the right flank of Pebble's 18th fairway, within earshot of the Pacific's crashing waves. Also hugging the coastline is the more modern Inn at Spanish Bay, with 269 palatial rooms that feature antique furniture and splendid marble showers.

Nongolfers can enjoy the area's beauty on the legendary 17-Mile Drive, a private toll road connecting Monterey (see p. 830) to its peninsular neighbor Carmel (see p. 810). A microcosm of the coastline's romantic beauty, dotted with ocean-sprayed outcroppings where harbor seals and sea lions laze, the winding drive also takes in man-made marvels like multimillion-dollar mansions.

For classic-car lovers, the Pebble Beach Concours d'Elegance in August is one of the world's finest car shows—originally a sideshow to the Pebble Beach Road Race, which was moved after a fatal accident in 1956 involving a Ferrari and a pine tree ("Too much car and not enough race course," it was observed). Feast your eyes on the most rare, valuable, and beautiful cars in the world—Rolls-Royce Phantoms from the '30s, racing Jaguars from the '50s, and Lamborghinis from the '60s.

WHERE: 6 miles southwest of Monterey. Tel 800-877-0597 or 831-624-3811; pebble beach.com. *Cost:* greens fees for Pebble Beach $495; for Spyglass Hill $395; for The Links at Spanish Bay $280. Rooms at the Lodge at Pebble Beach from $815; Inn at Spanish Bay from $695. **CONCOURS D'ELEGANCE:** Tel 831-622-1700; pebblebeachconcours.net. *Cost:* $375. *When:* 3rd weekend in Aug. **BEST TIMES:** Feb for the AT&T Pebble Beach National Pro-Am; Sept–Oct for weather.

Volcanic Energy and Spiritual Power

MOUNT SHASTA

California

"When I first caught sight of Mount Shasta over the braided folds of the Sacramento Valley," wrote naturalist John Muir in 1874, "my blood turned to wine, and I have not been weary since." A colossus of four

volcanic cones, the highest rising 14,179 feet above the flats of upper Northern California, Mount Shasta is the crown jewel of the Cascades, a snowcapped peak that is one of the state's most beautiful landmarks, visible from as far as 100 miles away.

Considered a place of great spiritual power by Native Americans and New Agers, Mount Shasta (in a 38,200-acre designated wilderness located within the larger 2.1-million-acre Shasta-Trinity National Forest) draws mountain climbers looking to summit. Its eight glaciers and a base-to-summit elevation gain of 11,000 feet (one of the highest in the world) qualifies it as a mountaineering peak that requires crampons and an ice ax, but beginners in good shape can usually make it up in 12 hours, with an overnight stay on the way. The fast way down is glissading—sliding on your behind, using an ice ax to control your speed. It may sound easy, but injuries are common.

Nearby scenic Shasta Lake, California's third-largest lake after Lake Tahoe (see p. 726) and the Salton Sea, is home to one of the state's largest populations of bald eagles (and a substantial collection of vacationing houseboaters). From there, Highway 299 takes you through lush pine forests to the otherworldly landscape of Lassen Volcanic National Park, with its steaming cauldrons of turquoise pools, belching mud pots, and scalding hot springs. Towering 2,000 feet over the beguiling landscape is Lassen Peak, which last erupted in 1915 and fumed until 1921. The most charming place to stay is the Drakesbad Guest Ranch, right inside the park. Despite a rustic, homespun ambience—most of its pine-paneled guest rooms are lit by kerosene lanterns—rooms are sometimes booked months in advance, often by those who have been returning for generations. At Castle Crags State Park, granite spires shoot 6,000 feet above sea level and the Sacramento River and Pacific Crest Trail wend their way through the landscape, providing unparalleled fishing, swimming, and hiking.

WHERE: 280 miles northeast of San Francisco. *Mount Shasta Ranger Station:* Tel 530-926-4511; fs.usda.gov. **LASSEN VOLCANIC NATIONAL PARK:** Tel 530-595-4480; nps.gov/lavo. **CASTLE CRAGS STATE PARK:** Tel 530-235-2684; parks.ca.gov. **HOW:** Shasta Mountain Guides offers guided ascents and gear. Tel 530-926-3117; shastaguides.com. *Cost:* 2-day hikes from $695. *When:* May–Aug. **DRAKESBAD GUEST RANCH:** Chester. Tel 530-529-1512; drakesbad.com. *Cost:* from $295, includes meals. *When:* June–early Oct. **BEST TIMES:** summer for hiking Shasta and exploring Lassen; early Oct for fall colors.

America's Most Famous Wine Region

NAPA VALLEY

California

Packed in shoulder-to-shoulder along a narrow 35-mile valley bounded by two mountain ranges, American winemaking's greatest and most famous names are all found in the verdant Napa Valley. Three hundred-plus wineries lie along Highway 29 and the more scenic Silverado Trail in what is considered the epicenter of American wine, food, and fine living (an additional 450 wineries blanket the Sonoma region; see p. 860). The sunny days, cool nights, long growing season, and well-drained soil caught the eye of winemakers as early as 1858, but disasters like phylloxera (root-destroying insects) and later Prohibition left growers more interested in almonds and fruit trees. Its modern revival as a world-class wine region began in the 1960s, when pioneers like Robert Mondavi devoted themselves to producing superb cabernet sauvignons that could stand up to the greats of France. And a culinary tradition to equal the wines has since sprung up in the small towns along Highway 29, including the restaurant lauded by many as America's finest, the French Laundry (see p. 863).

Crowd-pleasing wineries include power-house Robert Mondavi Winery in Oakville for one of the best and most extensive tours; Inglenook (formerly Niebaum-Coppola), owned by filmmaker Francis Ford Coppola, for its expansive wine offerings and stunning restored historic grounds; Yountville's Domaine Chandon for its sparkling wines and expansive Tasting Lounge with food; and Sterling Vineyards for its broad selection and tram-accessed valley views. But don't overlook the little gems, like Schramsberg, with excellent sparkling wine and appointment-only tastings and tours of hand-dug caves, and Swanson Vineyards, where tastings are limited to eight guests and include finger foods in an intimate, vibrant Salon.

Sterling Vineyard's cabernet vines yield the grapes that go into its esteemed Napa Valley Cabernet Sauvignon.

For a multisensory experience (and eliminating concerns about designated drivers) hop aboard the Napa Valley Wine Train, which runs from Napa to St. Helena, past countless vineyards. Enjoy the scenery and dine hand-somely during the three-hour, 36-mile journey aboard restored 1915-era Pullman Cars.

Develop your palate at The Culinary Institute of America (CIA) at Copia, an 80,000 square foot complex with a 280-seat theater, a 100-seat demo kitchen, two restaurants, class-rooms, and exhibition spaces. Visitors can enjoy programs focused on food and wine, res-taurants, special events, a public museum, and cooking classes. Many visitors come for the day, but to truly appreciate all Napa's offerings, stay awhile. The Meadowood Resort is one of the finest choices, with an old-money feel in the rambling main lodge and cottage-like suites scattered in the hills above and the acclaimed restaurant. Rooms are at their most precious the first week of June during the Napa Valley Wine Auction, a lavish three-day swirl of parties, wine tastings, dinners, and the auction at Meadowood, the world's most soi-gné charity wine event.

Smaller and more intimate, Auberge du Soleil is a luxury property perched on a 33-acre hillside dotted with olive trees. Its sunny one- and two-bedroom suites have private terraces overlooking the vine-studded valley, offering

the same heavenly views as its celebrated Restaurant at Auberge du Soleil. For lunch and dinner, the list of favorites is endless: Mustard's Grill in Yountville; Terra, known for chef Hiro Sone's innovative cuisine; and the French Laundry's more relaxed sister restaurant, Bouchon, in Yountville, featuring classic bistro fare. Housed in the historic Napa Mill complex on the banks of the Napa River, Celadon's style of "global comfort food" is best enjoyed in their lovely courtyard.

Believe it or not, there's more to the valley than food and wine. It's beloved by joggers and cyclists for its undulating country roads, spa junkies for its famed mud baths (see p. 815), and just about everyone for its warm, sunny days, laid-back country air, and scenic drives.

WHERE: 50–70 miles north of San Francisco. *Visitor info:* napavalley.com. **ROBERT MONDAVI WINERY:** Oakville. Tel 888-766-6328 or 707-226-1395; robertmondaviwinery.com. **INGLENOOK:** Rutherford. Tel 707-968-1100; inglenook.com. **DOMAINE CHANDON:** Yountville. Tel 888-242-6366 or 707-944-2280; chandon .com. **STERLING VINEYARDS:** Calistoga. Tel 800-726-6136 or 707-942-3345; sterlingvineyards .com. **SCHRAMSBERG:** Calistoga. Tel 800-877-3623 or 707-942-4558; schramsberg.com. **SWANSON VINEYARDS:** Rutherford. Tel 707-754-4018; swansonvineyards.com. **NAPA VALLEY WINE TRAIN:** Napa. Tel 800-427-4124 or 707-253-2111; winetrain.com. *Cost:* from $129, includes lunch. **The Culinary Institute of America at Copia:** Napa. enthusiasts.ciachef.edu/copia. **Meadowood:** St. Helena. Tel 877-963-3646 or 707-531-4788; meadowood.com. *Cost:* from $500 (off-peak), from $750 (peak). **Auberge du Soleil:** Rutherford. Tel 800-348-5406 or 707-963-1211; aubergedusoleil.com. *Cost:* from $675 (off-peak), from $800 (peak); 3-course tasting menu $110. **Mustard's Grill:** Yountville.

Tel 707-944-2424; mustardsgrill.com. *Cost:* dinner $60. **Terra:** St. Helena. Tel 707-963-8931; terrarestaurant.com. *Cost:* 4-course tasting menu $85. *When:* closed Tues–Wed. **Bouchon:** Yountville. Tel 707-944-8037; thomaskeller.com. *Cost:* dinner $60. **Celadon:** Napa. Tel 707-254-9690; celadonnapa.com. *Cost:* dinner $55. **Best times:** 1st week of June for the 3-day Napa Valley Wine Auction (auctionnapavalley.org); summer for the Mondavi Summer Concert Series.

Real-Life Shangri-la

Ojai

California

When filming *Lost Horizon* in 1937, Frank Capra was looking for a sunny paradise to be Shangri-la, the mythical land of eternal youth. He chose the mystical, oak-covered Topa Topa Mountains that ring Ojai (pronounced OH-high), a Spanish Colonial-style village north of Los Angeles. The ancient Chumash Indians (whose word for "the nest" gives the town its name) revered it as a place of healing, and over the years it has drawn many spiritual seekers like the East Indian philosopher J. Krishnamurti, who moved here in 1922. Sunsets, when the mountains take on a warm, rosy cast known as the Pink Moment, are its most special time.

The downtown's picture-perfect signature is its tall stucco and red-tiled bell tower, one of many similar buildings commissioned in the 'teens and '20s by Edward Libbey, a Toledo glass magnate

Ojai's post office bell tower was inspired by the famous campanile in Havana, Cuba.

who wintered here. Libbey was also the impetus for what is now the most perfect place to stay, the 220-acre Ojai Valley Inn & Spa. In 1923 he built a private Spanish-style clubhouse and 18-hole golf course, designed by George C. Thomas Jr. to be one of the country's most beautiful and challenging golf experiences, with scenic vistas and sharp angles. At the far end of the resort, cars are banned to maintain the peace of a walled 31,000-square-foot Spa Village, complete with 50-foot bell tower and outdoor courtyard with fountain and fireplace. Inside, the spa offers impeccable services that include a Himalayan warm salt stone therapy and detox massage.

Artists, writers, and craftsmen are thick on the ground in Ojai. Unleash your creativity under their tutelage in the spa's Artist's Cottage and Apothecary, which offers classes in watercolors, drawing, herbal wreaths, silk scarf painting, and custom-blending aromatherapy scents. The Nickelodeon set (ages 4–12) stays busy at Camp Oak, a kid's program that includes outdoor adventures, arts and crafts, and campfire fun. Maravilla, the inn's fine dining venue, features prime steaks, chops, and fresh seafood complemented by the chef's garden-grown and local Ojai ingredients.

A very different experience can be had right in the midst of Ojai's downtown buzz at the Oaks at Ojai, one of the first health and wellness spas in the country (many say it was the inspiration behind the first Canyon Ranch that opened in Tucson, AZ, in 1979). Known for its high spirits and low prices, the Oaks has a loyal clientele who keep coming back to burn calories, condition the heart, and lose weight on 1,200 calories a day. The Oaks is located in the historic 1918 El Roblar Hotel, whose exterior has been restored to its original Spanish Colonial style. While most of the rooms are simple, five luxury suites have been added and the unusual (for a spa) downtown

location is a great part of its charm. Between the aqua-toning class and the Ojai Olive Oil Body Soufflé, stroll along Ojai Avenue's arcade of boutiques, art galleries, and ice cream parlors. If you buy a cone, you won't be the first Oaks patron to do so. Paradise pardons all.

WHERE: 33 miles east of Santa Barbara. **OJAI VALLEY INN & SPA:.** Tel 855-697-8780 or 805-646-1111; ojairesort.com. *Cost:* from $400 (off-peak), from $600 (peak); greens fees from $180. **THE OAKS AT OJAI:** Tel 800-753-6257 or 805-646-5573; oaksspa.com. *Cost:* from $260 per person (double occupancy), includes meals and classes, 2-night minimum. **BEST TIMES:** spring and fall for weather; early June for Ojai Music Festival (ojaifestival.org) and Ojai Wine Festival (ojaiwinefestival.com); second weekend in Oct for Ojai Studio Artists Tour (ojaistudioartists.org); early Nov for Ojai Film Festival (ojaifilmfestival.com).

America's Dream Drive

THE PACIFIC COAST HIGHWAY AND BIG SUR

California

Known by those not from these parts as Route 1, the Pacific Coast Highway is America's dream drive, offering stunning coastal views along almost all of its twisting dramatic route from California's northern border with

Oregon (where it joins with Route 101) to its southern boundary with Mexico. Most of the two-lane PCH runs through gorgeously isolated terrain, and frequent turnouts and vista points provide ample opportunity to soak in the coast's rare and astounding natural beauty. You can head south from L.A. to San Diego, or take the traditionalist's route north to San Francisco and even beyond, past the 19th-century fishing-town-turned-artists-colony of Mendocino (see p. 829).

From the heart of L.A. head west to Santa Monica then follow the coast to Malibu, where

you'll already feel a world away. Seventy miles up the road, you'll skirt the environs of Santa Barbara (see p. 854) at the base of the dramatic Santa Ynez mountains. Farther north, the fabled PCH begins to unfurl at its most majestic, carving an awesome ribbon of highway 500 to 1,000 feet above the roaring Pacific. Extolled as America's road trip extraordinaire, the wild and rugged 90-mile stretch from the Hearst Castle at San Simeon (see p. 853), past Big Sur and on to the Monterey Peninsula (see p. 830) is the uncontested high point.

Bounded by the rugged Santa Lucia Mountains to the east and the Pacific to the west, Big Sur remains a remote wilderness and natural masterpiece. "A place of grandeur and eloquent silence" is how Henry Miller, the author of *Tropic of Cancer*, described his adopted home. Virtually inaccessible before the PCH was built with the help of prison labor and New Deal funds, Big Sur saw more tourism and second homes when the highway finally opened in 1937. Its beauty drew writers and artists like Miller, whose books and photographs can be explored at the Henry Miller Memorial Library, and alternative thinkers, some of whom later helped found Esalen Institute (see p. 812).

Many natural treasures await just off the Pacific Coast Highway.

Fiercely protected by its 1,500 residents, Big Sur has a dramatic loneliness about it, with angry ocean breakers on one side and a narrow curving road that snakes along the edge of the mountains. Pfeiffer State Beach is breathtaking—in fact, there's precious little around here that's not. Stop to take it all in with a drink or dinner at the well-known Nepenthe, with its outdoor patio suspended 800 feet above the surf. Big Sur's stunningly sited Post Ranch Inn, perched 1,200 feet above the Pacific, is a window to vast vistas of dramatic ocean and mountains on clear days. Even when the coast is fogged in, this place breathes romance, with wood-burning stoves and indoor spa tubs in all 39 rooms. On the other side of the highway, the Ventana Big Sur is a friendly competitor offering the same casual luxury and middle-of-nature feel. An infinitely more affordable slice of Big Sur can be yours with a reservation at Deetjen's Big Sur Inn. A sweet place to sleep since the 1930s, the cabinlike rooms offer classic old-fashioned comfort, from antiques to woodstoves to beds with linen sheets. Equally loved is the inn's restaurant, where locals gossip each morning over bottomless cups of coffee and hearty breakfasts.

WHERE: Big Sur is 140 miles south of San Francisco. **HENRY MILLER LIBRARY:** Tel 831-667-2574; henrymiller.org. **NEPENTHE:** Tel 831-667-2345; nepenthebigsur.com. *Cost:* dinner $50. **POST RANCH INN:** Tel 888-524-4787 or 831-667-2200; postranchinn.com. *Cost:* from $775 (off-peak), from $825 (peak). **VENTANA BIG SUR:** Tel 800-628-6500 or 831-667-2331; ventanainn.com. *Cost:* from $480 (off-peak), from $750 (peak). **DEETJEN'S:** Tel 831-667-2377; deetjens.com. *Cost:* from $125 (shared bath), from $185 (private bath). **BEST TIMES:** spring and early fall for sunny, clear weather; Dec–Feb for whale-watching.

Playground of the Stars

PALM SPRINGS

California

Palm Springs' history is rife with celebrity guests, but the arid climate first attracted visitors for health reasons: The Desert Inn, founded in 1909, began as a tuberculosis sanitarium. But by the 1930s the area had evolved into an oasis for the rich and famous, becoming a booming resort town in the post-WWII years. It lured such names as Sinatra, Hope, and Liberace as well as a growing stream of increasingly mobile middle-class vacationers and residents. The Desert Inn has since closed, but today Palm Springs is reinventing itself, attracting VIPs with first-class accommodations, dining, and shopping, while Hollywood's young glitterati and gay and lesbian vacationers discover its agreeable winter clime. The treasure chest of mid-century modern aesthetics has become a recharged magnet, and many of the landmark homes and hotels from that era are spotlighted and toured during the annual Modernism Week every February. If modernism is your thing, the style-conscious Avalon Hotel is the place to stay during your visit.

Swimming, sunbathing, golfing, and tennis are still the pastimes of this desert oasis. Upscale resorts with world-class golf courses and spas have proliferated both here and in neighboring Rancho Mirage and Palm Desert, and several Indian casinos are within easy driving distance for those who care to roll the dice. Here in town, simple pleasure can be found by taking a ride on the aerial tramway, the steepest cable car in the U.S. It soars to the top of Mount San Jacinto for breathtaking 360-degree desert views at 8,516 feet.

More than anything, a Palm Springs visit should involve lounging by a kidney-shaped

With around 30 courses, the neighboring city of Palm Desert is often called the "World's Golf Capital."

pool—especially when summer temperatures routinely hit 110°F. To take a day of dipping and reading poolside to the ultimate Hollywood-style heights, you can rent Frank Sinatra's former Twin Palms home, a spectacular example of mid-century architecture located in the heart of Palm Springs' former Movie Colony. It's 4,500 square feet of Ol' Blue Eyes memories (check out the crack in the sink made when Sinatra threw a Champagne bottle at Ava Gardner), including four bedrooms, seven bathrooms, and a piano-shaped pool. Or go the romantically swank route by renting the home where Elvis Presley honeymooned with Priscilla in 1967. It's even got a circular bedroom fit for a king.

More traditional romance can be found at two of Palm Springs' most characterful inns. The lovely Willows Historic Palm Springs Inn, the honeymoon choice for Carole Lombard and Clark Gable, is a 1920s Mediterranean villa with eight sumptuous suites tucked into the hillside of Mount San Jacinto. The Korakia, the dreamy Moroccan-inspired 1920s former home of an artist, is an oasis of simple rooms with flowing white curtains and a mix of exotic antiques.

Where: 107 miles east of Los Angeles. *Visitor info:* Tel 800-347-7746 or 760-778-8418; visitpalmsprings.com. **Avalon:** Tel 760-320-4117; avalonpalmsprings.com. *Cost:* from $170 (off-peak), from $340 (peak). **Aerial Tramway:** Tel 888-515-TRAM or 760-325-1391; pstramway.com. *Cost:* $25. **Twin Palms:** Tel 877-318-2090; sinatrahouse.com. *Cost:* from $1,950 (off-peak), from $2,600 (peak). **Elvis Honeymoon House:** Tel 760-322-1192; elvishoneymoon.com. *Cost:* from $1,800 per night, 2-night minimum. **The Willows Historic Palm Springs Inn:** Tel 800-966-9597 or 760-320-0771; thewillowspalmsprings.com. *Cost:* from $375. *When:* closed June–Aug. **The Korakia:** Tel 760-864-6411; korakia.com. *Cost:* from $209 (off-peak), from $309 (peak). **Best times:** early Jan for the Palm Springs International Film Festival (psfilmfest.org); Feb for Modernism Week (modernismweek.com); Oct–Apr for weather.

A Rose Is a Rose Is a Rose

PASADENA

California

F ounded in 1873 by migrants from the Midwest, Pasadena remains in many ways a relatively bucolic, prim foothills suburb that feels at least a few states away from nearby Los Angeles in pace and personality. But every year on New Year's Day it moves to the No. 1 spot on the country's radar—with its televised Tournament of Roses Parade and Rose Bowl football game.

First held in 1890, the parade is one of California's favorite and most celebrated annual events, when the million people lining the 5.5-mile route along Orange Grove and Colorado Boulevards are far outnumbered by the quantity of flowers used to decorate the brilliantly colored and exotically aromatic floats. Later

The Rose Parade features many elaborate floats, like this one inspired by ancient Egypt.

that afternoon, the Rose Bowl game, the first-ever national post-season collegiate football game in 1902 and therefore known as the "Grandaddy of Them All," is a part of the Bowl Championship Series. Less well known but also fun is the area's *other* spectacle, the Doo Dah Parade. Since 1978, a ragtag gang of eccentrics, disruptors, and merrymakers like the Flying Baby Naptime Aerialists and Carpool DeVille (a drivable 1969 convertible hot tub) have shambled down part of Colorado Boulevard, spraying onlookers with Cheez Whiz, while the crowd throws tortillas. It's anti-organization and very much pro-laughter.

For the rest of the year, visitors to Pasadena are drawn to the Norton Simon Museum (its interior was designed by Frank Gehry), one of the country's best private collections, exemplary in both Impressionist and classical art. A remarkable roster includes works by Degas, Kandinsky, and Rembrandt; Goya's *The Disasters of War* and Picasso's *Woman with a Guitar*; and one of the world's greatest collections of Southeast Asian sculpture and painting. The other jewel in Pasadena's crown is the Huntington Library, Art Collections, and Botanical Gardens, a 207-acre hilltop Italianate estate initially built by the eponymous railroad and real estate magnate to be his private residence. Its world-class collection includes a Gutenberg Bible on vellum from the 15th century and the First Folio edition of William Shakespeare's plays, published seven years after his death. Gainsborough's *Blue Boy* is complemented by Sir Thomas Lawrence's *Pinkie*. Head outside for the astoundingly large and lush botanical gardens, some parts of them so authentically Japanese that Hollywood filmed scenes here for *Memoirs of a Geisha*. Enjoy a moment's respite at the museum's much-loved tearoom where terraces overlook the Rose Garden and its 1,200-variety display.

WHERE: 15 miles northwest of Hollywood. **TOURNAMENT OF ROSES:** parade begins at corner of Green St. and Orange Grove Blvd., ends at Villa St. Tel 626-449-4100; tournamentof roses.com. *Cost:* parade seating from $35; Bowl game tickets from $150. *When:* Jan 1. **NORTON SIMON MUSEUM:** Tel 626-449-6840;

nortonsimon.org. **HUNTINGTON LIBRARY AND GARDENS:** San Marino. Tel 626-405-2100; huntington.org. *Cost:* high tea $31 (reservations required; tel 626-683-8131). **BEST**

TIMES: balmy off-season Sept–Apr; 2nd Sun of every month for the Rose Bowl Fleamarket; Nov for the Pasadena Doo Dah Parade (pasadenadoodahparade.info).

San Francisco's Backyard Wilderness

POINT REYES NATIONAL SEASHORE

California

Point Reyes National Seashore's coastal wilderness is so dramatically juxtaposed to San Francisco's urban landscape that it's hard to believe the oceanfront area is just an hour's drive from the city. Stretching 30 miles along the rugged Marin County coastline, this 71,000-acre preserve of pine forests, canyons, meadows, and dunes is the only national seashore on the West Coast and one of the Bay Area's most spectacular treasures, drawing hikers, whale-watchers, solitude seekers, and birders. (Nearly 490 varieties of birds have been spotted here, including the threatened snowy plover and northern spotted owl.)

It's a prime spot for wildlife-watching. In early fall, tule elk bugle and rut (males going rack to rack to determine who gets the girl) near Tomales Point and, in late winter and

spring, enormous elephant seals spar for females on the beach near Chimney Rock. Migrating gray whales can sometimes be spotted in winter from the 1870 landmark Point Reyes Lighthouse, a working lighthouse until 1975. Point Reyes offers 150 miles of hiking trails, including the mostly flat 8-mile Bear Valley trail which ends with gorgeous coastal views before looping back, and the Earthquake Trail, a paved loop which runs along the famous San Andreas fault that leveled San Francisco in 1906.

Many of Point Reyes's gloriously pristine beaches are accessible only by trail, but picturesque Limantour Beach is reachable by car. Point Reyes's gateway villages are loaded with good shops and restaurants, including specialists in the region's most famous delicacy, barbecued oysters—and not just any oyster but the *Crassostrea gigas*, a large, fleshy, succulent Pacific oyster ranging in size from a half-dollar to the palm of your hand. You'll find the delicacy at dozens of restaurants, markets, seaside shacks, and oyster farm picnic areas, but The Marshall Store, Olema Farm House, and Tony's Seafood are three of the best known. Hog Island Oyster Company in Marshall, just north of Point Reyes, is a

Climb to a vantage point to see breathtaking seashore views and, in winter, maybe a whale or two.

working farm (you can ask for a tour) and a prime spot for shucking fresh oysters and dining alfresco. Gloriously restful nights can be found at Manka's, a rustic 1910 hunting and fishing lodge in the town of Inverness with ten rooms and two cabins restored to their full Arts and Crafts glory. Just south of Point Reyes, Muir Beach is one of the region's most charming tiny seaside villages, the perfect place to watch sunsets from a driftwood-strewn cove. Stay in one of the tastefully sedate rooms at the Pelican Inn, modeled after an English country inn with traditional pub fare like bangers and mash and shepherd's pie.

WHERE: 42 miles north of San Francisco. Tel 415-464-5100; nps.gov/pore. **THE MARSHALL STORE:** Marshall. Tel 415-663-1339; themarshallstore.com. *Cost:* 6 raw oysters $15. **OLEMA FARM HOUSE:** Olema. Tel 415-663-1264; point reyesseashore.com/dine. *Cost:* a dozen oysters $32. **TONY'S SEAFOOD:** Marshall. Tel 415-663-1107. *Cost:* 6 oysters on the half shell $13. **HOG ISLAND OYSTER COMPANY:** Marshall. Tel 415-663-9218; hogislandoysters.com. **MANKA'S LODGE:** Inverness. Tel 415-669-1034; mankas .com. *Cost:* from $215; prix-fixe dinner $75 (Sat only). **MUIR BEACH:** muirbeach.com. **THE PELICAN INN:** Muir Beach. Tel 415-383-6000; pelicaninn.com. *Cost:* from $215. **BEST TIMES:** May–mid-June and Sept–Oct for clear skies and uncrowded trails; Dec–Mar for whale-watching.

The Giants That Built the West

REDWOODS OF NORTHERN CALIFORNIA

California

O ften cloaked in misty fog, the great coast redwood trees stretch for 40 miles along California's northern coast with a majestic presence that makes these trees feel not just alive, but aware. Looming more than

350 feet above the forest floor, coast redwoods are the world's tallest trees (the giant sequoias in Sequoia and Kings Canyon national parks south of here are shorter but more massive; see p. 858) and unfortunately for them, make ideal lumber, since they are naturally resistant to both termites and rot. Only 5 percent of the mighty redwoods that once hugged the coast between Oregon and Big Sur survived the loggers who arrived in the 1850s. Men came in search of gold, but found the real money in lumber, as redwoods built the boomtowns of the West, including the Nob Hill mansions of San Francisco.

Coast redwoods grow so tall because of the temperate climate, rich soil, fire resistance, lack of natural enemies, large amounts of rain,

The climate and weather systems of Northern California provide the perfect conditions for these dizzyingly tall trees.

and summer fog that accounts for up to one-fourth the precipitation the redwoods need to become mysterious gray giants. While the average age of the trees here is 500 to 700 years, they can live to be 2,000 years old.

The scenic 31-mile-long Avenue of the Giants, which runs along a section of old Highway 101 through Humboldt Redwoods State Park, is the largest remaining contiguous old-growth of coastal redwoods in the world. Crescent City is the gateway to the Redwood National and State Parks farther north. Here, you'll find these ancient giants wherever there are groves such as Lady Bird Johnson, an easy mile-long loop that wends its way through the towering redwoods. Serious hikers who can handle the 800-foot drop in elevation (and who have a permit, due to restricted parking) can make the 1.6-mile trek to the Tall Trees Grove.

A midway stop between Humboldt in the south and Redwood National and State Parks in the north is Ferndale, a 1,400-person hamlet chock-full of Victorian houses, galleries, bookshops, and 1950s-style soda fountains. About a half hour outside of town, lumberjack-size appetites are satisfied at Samoa Cookhouse in Eureka. Dating to the 1890s, it is the last surviving lumber camp–style cookhouse in the West.

WHERE: Orick, the gateway in the south, is 314 miles north of San Francisco; Crescent City, near the Oregon border, is the northern gateway. Tel 707-465-7335; nps.gov/redw. *Humboldt County visitor info:* Tel 800-346-3482 or 707-444-6634; redwoods.info. **SAMOA COOKHOUSE:** Samoa. Tel 707-442-1659; samoacookhouse.net. *Cost:* dinner $17. **BEST TIMES:** mid-May–mid-Oct, when rain is rare; mid-May–mid-June for rhododendron blooms.

Not Just a Walk in the Park

BALBOA PARK AND THE SAN DIEGO ZOO

San Diego, California

B alboa Park is the heart of San Diego—more or less geographically and certainly metaphorically. A spectacularly verdant 1,200-acre recreational area set aside in 1868, it's the largest cultural park in the country. Here you can find stunningly beautiful Spanish-Moorish buildings constructed for the 1915 Panama-California Exposition, now home to 15 museums, including the San Diego Air & Space Museum and The San Diego Museum of Art. The former gives a fine overview of aviation history, from hot-air balloons to the space race. The latter has one of the grandest entrances along El Prado, the park's main thoroughfare, and boasts exemplary collections of Spanish works, 19th- and 20th-century European art (with an emphasis on drawings by Toulouse-Lautrec) and Asian art, which is the

museum's largest holding. Also worth exploring is the Museum of Photographic Arts, where you can admire works by Ansel Adams, Edward Weston, and Margaret Bourke-White. Though not quite as lofty as its neighbors, the San Diego Model Railroad Museum is too cute to pass up—and it boasts the largest operating model railway display in the world. Drop by to see miniature versions of California's railways.

The most visited resident of Balboa Park is the world-famous San Diego Zoo. Dating back to 1916, and more parklike than a traditional zoo, it set the standard for zoos around the world with its well-tended grounds, up-to-the-minute approach to exhibits, and wildlife conservation. Every corner of the park is gorgeous, clean, and expansive enough to almost make you feel happy for the 3,500 rare and endangered animals representing 650 species who call these 100 acres home. One of the most popular exhibits is the giant pandas, including the adorable Xiao Liwu, born in 2012. Other popular residents are the Sumatran orangutans and Indonesian siamangs who live peaceably together, and their next-door neighbors, two troops of western lowland gorillas.

Koala bears are among the hundreds of species on display at the sprawling San Diego Zoo.

If you can't get your fill of animals, the San Diego Safari Park, a 30-mile drive from here, transports you to the vast plains of Africa. A monorail takes you through some of the 1,800-acre park where hundreds of different species are left to roam and mingle much as they would in the wild (though predators like lions and cheetahs are kept separate). Far more commercial and twice as wet is Seaworld San Diego, one of California's most visited tourist attractions. The aquatic theme amusement park is perhaps the world's largest; the marquee lists the cast of dolphins, otters, walruses, and sea lions, who all perform daily.

BALBOA PARK: Tel 619-239-0512; balboapark.org. *When:* park open daily; museums vary. **SAN DIEGO ZOO:** Tel 619-231-1515; sandiegozoo.org. *Cost:* $40 (ages 3–11), $50 (ages 12 and up). **SAN DIEGO SAFARI PARK:** Tel 760-231-1515; sdzsafaripark.org. *Cost:* $40 (ages 3–11), $50 (ages 12 and up). **SEAWORLD SAN DIEGO:** Mission Bay. Tel 800-257-4268 or 619-226-3901; seaworldparks.com. *Cost:* from $69 (all ages). **BEST TIMES:** cooler months and early or late in the day for more active zoo animals.

By the Sea, by the Sea

HOTEL DEL CORONADO

San Diego and environs, California

Famous for hosting 14 presidents as well as for its role in *Some Like It Hot*, the Hotel Del Coronado is a captivating and elegant "Grand Lady by the Sea," a timeless beachfront escape that recalls the grand old resorts of yesteryear.

Built in 1888, the National Historic Landmark is situated on the "island" (really a peninsula) of Coronado in the middle of San Diego Bay. Sitting like a Victorian wedding cake, it stands sentinel over an impressively pristine mile and a half of spectacular white beach, its red turrets a stunning contrast to the sand and shore.

Inside, many of the spacious, detailed public areas of "The Del" are right out of a bygone era. The Del's guest rooms have been upgraded to today's luxury standards with a soothing color palette, rich textiles, and luxurious beds, many with ocean views and balconies. Accommodations in the original Victorian building offer a modern take on antique charm, while those in the Tower and Cabana buildings are more contemporary beach-chic.

You can stay in one of the private cabanas on the beach (where Marilyn Monroe stayed when filming *Some Like It Hot*). Onetime San Diego social figure Wallis Simpson is rumored to have met her future husband here in 1920. She went on to become the Duchess of Windsor and change the course of British history. (Her former home, the Windsor Cottage, is now part of The Del property and is available for visits by guests of the Beach Village, a cluster of 18 waterfront rooms and suites that is a new and exclusive addition to the resort.) Pay them homage by dining in the world-famous Crown Room for Sunday brunch.

Behind the beautiful blue waters and landmark resort is Coronado, a simple yet very chic village of little California bungalows and shops along Orange Avenue. Walking here is a quiet pleasure, but if you need a bit more excitement, you can head across the soaring Coronado Bay Bridge into San Diego's historic Gaslamp Quarter. Once a rather seedy section of town, the neighborhood has undergone an extreme makeover, including restoration of its 19th- and early-20th-century buildings, which now

hold a variety of restaurants and clubs. The area has become even more popular as a recreation destination with the addition of Petco Park, a retro-style baseball stadium that is home to the San Diego Padres. The combination of sunshine, sea views, and America's favorite pastime leaves little for sports fans to desire.

WHERE: 1500 Orange Ave. Tel 800-468-3533 or 619-435-6611; hoteldel.com. *Cost:* rooms from $329 (off-peak), from $425 (peak); brunch at Crown Room $93. *San Diego visitor info:* Tel 619-232-3101; sandiego.org. *Gaslamp Quarter visitor info:* Tel 619-233-5227; gaslamp.org. **PETCO PARK:** Tel 619-795-5000; sandiego.padres.mlb.com. *When:* Apr–Sept. **BEST TIMES:** Dec for Christmas lights; late Dec–mid-Mar for whales migrating north from Baja California in Mexico.

Hosting guests like Charlie Chaplin, Babe Ruth, and Bill Clinton, the Hotel Del Coronado has long been a favorite of the rich and famous.

A Trip to the Rock

ALCATRAZ ISLAND

San Francisco, California

An icon of American criminal culture and history, Alcatraz ("the Rock") was perhaps America's best-known prison from 1934 to 1963, when it housed such notorious criminals as Al Capone, Robert "Machine Gun"

Kelly, and Robert "The Birdman" Stroud (who looked nothing like Burt Lancaster from the 1962 movie, and was not allowed to keep birds there, like he had at Leavenworth, Kansas). Located on a rocky outcropping jutting out of

San Francisco Bay, the maximum-security prison was considered escape-proof because of the sheer cliffs and choppy, bone-chilling waters. (Of the 36 who tried to escape, 23 were caught, 6 were shot and killed, and 2 drowned.

Five more are presumed to have drowned.) Reachable by a 1.5-mile ferry trip, Alcatraz today is part of the National Park Service, and also promises spectacular views of the city, thousands of roosting seabirds, and extraordinary gardens from the time Alacatraz was the first military fortress on the West Coast.

Named for the brown pelicans, or *alcatraces*, that nested here when Spanish explorer Juan Manuel Ayala noted the island in 1775, Alcatraz was closed in 1963 because it was far more expensive to operate than other prisons—even fresh water had to be brought in by boat—and sewage from 250 inmates and 60 Bureau of Prisons families was polluting the bay. Native American activists occupied the island for 19 months starting in 1969, making it a milestone in the Red Power Movement. Today Alcatraz is a popular must-do day trip: Take the audio tour (complete with sounds of cell doors slamming, guards shouting orders, and prisoner interviews) or enter a solitary confinement cell and let someone close the door, leaving you in utter silence and darkness—just long enough to welcome the sense of relief when you see light again.

A few miles north is Angel Island, a lushly forested state park with a rich history as an immigration center. From 1910 until 1940, Angel Island was the Ellis Island of the West, processing thousands of immigrants annually,

Isolated Alcatraz Island is home to the West Coast's first and oldest operating lighthouse.

of whom 97 percent came from China. Today, the island's 5 miles of paved roads and even more trails invite hikers and bikers to explore forests and the summit of Mount Livermore, with its 360-degree panorama of San Francisco, Marin County, and the East Bay.

Visitor info: Tel 415-561-4900; nps.gov/alca. *When:* daily, but closes in extreme weather when ferries can't run. **How:** Alcatraz Cruises offers ferries from San Francisco's Pier 33, tel 415-981-7625; alcatrazcruises.com. *Cost:* from $31. **Angel Island:** Tel 415-435-5390; parks.ca.gov/angelisland. **How:** Angel Island–Tiburon Ferry, tel 415-435-2131; angelislandferry.com. *When:* daily in peak season, limited schedule in winter. Blue & Gold ferries depart for Angel Island from Pier 41, tel 415-773-1188; blueandgoldfleet.com. **Best times:** Apr–June and Sept–Oct for weather.

A City's Oasis and an Engineering Marvel

GOLDEN GATE PARK AND THE GOLDEN GATE BRIDGE

San Francisco, California

One of the country's greatest city parks, rivaling New York's Central Park in beauty and in importance (see p. 166), Golden Gate Park is a magical place where American bison, Dutch windmills, and towering redwoods rub shoulders with star attractions like the Japanese Tea Garden and the world-class de Young Museum (see p. 847). Carved out of sand dunes known as the "outside lands" when it was conceived in 1870, Golden Gate Park is a long, rectangular 1,017-acre urban oasis of forests, meadows, footpaths and, yes, roads, though many are closed to traffic on Sundays and holidays, when cyclists, walkers, and in-line skaters own the park's thoroughfares with gleeful abandon.

The American Society of Civil Engineers proclaimed the Golden Gate Bridge to be one of the modern wonders of the world.

A seemingly endless number of destinations lie within the park, like the magnificent domed Conservatory of Flowers, the radiant crystal palace from 1879 that was modeled on London's Kew Gardens. It is the oldest building in the park and the last remaining wood-frame conservatory in the country, with an astounding array of orchids. Another early feature, and one of the park's most popular destinations, is the Japanese Tea Garden, an enchanting landscape of small ponds, arching bridges, perfect miniature pagodas, and bonsai trees first created in 1894 for a world's fair, the California Mid-Winter International Exposition. (Its caretaker from 1895 to 1925, Makoto Hagiwara, is said to have invented the fortune cookie in 1909.) The 70-acre San Francisco Botanical Garden at Strybing

Arboretum, one of the country's great public gardens, features some 6,000 plants and a redwood grove. Nearby is the California Academy of Sciences, which includes Steinhart Aquarium, Morrison Planetarium, and the Natural History Museum.

Just north of the park, traverse the majestic 1.7-mile-long Golden Gate Bridge for an exhilarating, wind-blasted walk and an enthralling panorama that takes in the bay, the undulating profile of the city, and the Marin headlands. One of the world's most beautiful bridges, the graceful orange structure opened to great fanfare in 1937, linking San Francisco to Marin County and making possible the growth of suburban communities. An engineering marvel whose 4,200-foot central span set a record for suspension bridges unchallenged for 27 years (it was eclipsed by New York's Verrazano Narrows in 1964), the Golden Gate Bridge is not named for its color (an "international orange" chosen to make the bridge more visible in fog) but for the Golden Gate Strait it crosses.

WHERE: Golden Gate Park is loosely bounded on the east by Stanyan St., on the north by Fulton Ave., on the west by the Great Highway, and to the south by Lincoln Way. *Visitor info:* Tel 415-391-2000; sanfrancisco travel.com. **BEST TIMES:** early spring for cherry blossoms in Japanese Tea Garden; Sun for car-free wandering; weekdays for less crowded visits to park museums and Japanese Tea Garden.

Foodie Paradise on the Waterfront

THE SAN FRANCISCO FERRY BUILDING

San Francisco, California

The crossroads of all things delicious, the historic San Francisco Ferry Building is a place to congregate and worship the region's culinary delights at shops, restaurants, and some 100 outdoor market stalls that make up the country's finest farmers market. The imposing 1898 structure with its signature clock tower has long been the hub for ferries arriving from Sausalito, Tiburon, Larkspur, Vallejo, and Alameda, but was reimagined as a food mecca after the earthquake of 1989. The quake so damaged the Embarcadero Freeway (an eyesore obscuring the waterfront) that it had to be demolished, opening up sweeping views of the East Bay. After $110 million and four years of remodeling, the refurbished Ferry Building opened in 2003.

Inside, people marvel at the high-vaulted halls, packed with the European-style "stalls" that are a showcase for Northern California's legendary food purveyors: Marin County's Cowgirl Creamery, Berkeley-based Acme Breads, and Prather Ranch Meat Company, headquartered in Siskiyou County, to name just a few. At the outdoor farmers market, food-lovers jostle for crimson strawberries, grass-fed steaks, and Indian-summer tomatoes, particularly on Saturday, when crowds can reach the thousands.

It's just as seductive to feast at restaurants like the Slanted Door, where Charles Phan serves inspired Vietnamese fare like gorgeously light cellophane noodles with fresh Dungeness crabmeat, and melt-in-your-mouth shaking beef—cubed filet mignon with watercress, red onion, and lime sauce. Traci Des

Jardins of Jardiniere fame has a sunny taqueria called Mijita, and its crispy Baja-style fish tacos and queso fandido with chorizo are every bit as good as homemade. For a taste of nearby Tomales Bay (see p. 840), stop by the Hog Island Oyster Company. Throw back a few freshly shucked mollusks and you'll understand why they sell over 3.5 million a year.

The beautiful waterfront Embarcadero rims several miles of the city's edge. On a sunny day, as century-old streetcars pass by (on the F line to Fisherman's Wharf), you can see clear across the bay to Oakland. The Hotel Vitale, just a block from the Ferry Building, is done up in restrained color schemes so you'll keep your eye on the dramatic Bay Bridge views. Walk southbound and you'll end up at the stunning AT&T Ballpark where the San Francisco Giants play so close to the water that a slugger's homer can land in the bay.

WHERE: on the Embarcadero at the foot of Market St. Tel 415-983-8030; ferrybuilding marketplace.com. *When:* farmers market open Tues, Thurs, and Sat, year-round. **HOTEL VITALE:** Tel 888-890-8688 or 415-278-3777; jdvhotels.com. *Cost:* from $269. **SAN FRANCISCO GIANTS AT&T BALLPARK:** Tel 415-972-2000; sanfrancisco.giants.mlb.com. *When:* games Apr–Sept. **BEST TIMES:** summer and fall for the biggest selection at the farmers market and best weather.

A City's Cultural Showpieces

SAN FRANCISCO'S ART MUSEUMS

San Francisco, California

It took a good many years to see any bright side to the destruction caused by the 1989 earthquake in the Bay Area. But if ever there was a silver lining, it can be found in the de Young Museum, which started in 1895 as an outgrowth

of a world's fair held in Golden Gate Park (see p. 845). After the fair closed, the collection of curiosities housed in a pseudo–Egyptian

Revival building (complete with images of Hathor, the cow goddess) evolved into the West Coast's foremost museum of the art of the Americas, Oceania, and Africa. In addition to its traditional strengths, the de Young has strong holdings of sculpture and American art dating to the 17th century, including Edward Hopper and Grant Wood. The earthquake so gravely damaged the museum that it had to be razed, but what has risen in its place is a $200 million avant-garde beauty. Designed by famed Swiss architectural firm Herzog & de Mueron, the angular copper-clad building will take on a green patina with time.

A pair of concrete sphinxes stand guard by the entrance to the de Young museum.

As befits a city where over a third of the population claims Asian and Pacific Islander heritage, the Asian Art Museum is the country's largest museum devoted to Asian art (and many believe it the city's finest museum). Much of its 18,000-piece collection (including its celebrated gilt bronze Buddha from A.D. 338, the oldest-known Chinese Buddha in the world) was donated in the 1960s by Avery Brundage, a Chicago industrialist who envisioned San Francisco as a great center of Asian culture. In its new home, a 1917 Beaux-Arts building, natural light floods in through angled skylights installed by Gae Aulenti, the Italian designer who turned a Paris train station into the acclaimed Musée d'Orsay. The dazzling collection spans 6,000 years of works from China, Japan, Korea, India, Afghanistan, Thailand, Myanmar (Burma), Turkey, and the Philippines, and explores three main themes—the development of Buddhism, how trade and pilgrimage led to cultural exchange, and how Asian artists influenced one another.

Rounding out the city's trio of museums with new homes is San Francisco's Museum of Modern Art (SFMOMA), founded in 1935 as the first museum on the West Coast devoted solely to modern and contemporary art. In 1995 it moved into its new building designed by Swiss architect Mario Botta, located in SoMa (the South of Market neighborhood) across from the urban-cool Yerba Buena Gardens. In 2009–2010, the remarkable offer of a 100-year loan of 1,100 works by 185 artists from the Doris and Donald Fisher Collection was the incentive behind the expansion of Botta's building with a 10-story architectural statement by Norwegian firm Snøhetta. A true game changer for the city, the new SFMOMA reopened after a three-year closure as the largest modern and contemporary art museum in America with an additional 3,000 new works donated or acquired for its permanent collection.

DE YOUNG: Tel 415-750-3600; deyoung .famsf.org. *When:* closed Mon. **ASIAN ART MUSEUM:** Tel 415-581-3500; asianart.org. *When:* closed Mon. **SFMOMA:** Tel 415-357-4000; sfmoma.org. *When:* closed Wed.

From China (and Vietnam and Japan) with Love

SAN FRANCISCO'S BEST ASIAN RESTAURANTS

San Francisco, California

Chinese residents have been an important part of San Francisco's identity since they first arrived with other treasure seekers in the great Gold Rush of 1849. Recruited in the 1860s to build the railroads and later work the fields, Chinese immigrants overwhelmingly arrived from Guangdong Province (now called Guangzhou) in the south, just across the water from Hong Kong. They brought their complex, rich Cantonese cuisine with them, as well as a fondness for dim sum (literally translated as "so close to the heart"), essentially a large range of hors d'oeuvres traditionally enjoyed in restaurants for breakfast and lunch.

In the heart of the heavily Asian Richmond district, Ton Kiang is arguably the city's favorite dim sum restaurant. During brunch and lunch (the restaurant opens by 9:30 A.M. on weekends and is packed soon afterward), young waitresses roll carts laden with these delicious treats, the best-known of which is fluffy white barbecue-pork buns. Indulge in shrimp and spinach dumplings, shrimp-stuffed crab claws, pot stickers, and egg custard rice cakes.

In more recent years San Francisco has been a magnet for immigrants from Southeast Asia, particularly Vietnam, the Philippines, and Thailand, and this new wave has naturally brought their food ways with them. Down the street from Ton Kiang is La Vie, a Vietnamese restaurant many locals feel has food (minus the view) to match the chic Slanted Door at downtown's Ferry Building (see p. 846). With wonderful clay pot dishes, imperial rolls, and a beef fondue that diners cook at their tables in a broth of lemongrass and ginger, a meal at La Vie becomes an aromatic feast.

On the other side of Golden Gate Park in the teeming Sunset district is Pho Phu Quoc, known to locals as PPQ, one of the city's go-to choices for Vietnamese noodle soup (pho). The house specialty is the beef version, which features a variety of cuts cooked in the boiling broth. Atmosphere may be lacking, but the low price more than makes up for it.

You can have exceptional raw-fish feasts if you head across the Golden Gate Bridge to the elegantly casual and cramped Sushi Ran in Sausalito. For 30 years, this unpretentious institution has been offering deliciously fresh seafood along with artistically prepared cooked dishes.

Ton Kiang: Tel 415-752-4440; tonkiang .net. *Cost:* lunch $20. **La Vie:** Tel 415-668-8080. *Cost:* lunch $20. **Pho Phu Quoc:** Tel 415-661-8869; ppqsf.com. *Cost:* big bowls of pho from $8. **Sushi Ran:** Sausalito. Tel 415-332-3620; sushiran.com. *Cost:* dinner $40.

A Feast for the Senses

San Francisco's Finest Restaurants

San Francisco, California

San Francisco may be a smaller culinary universe than New York City or Los Angeles, but there is more attention to honest cooking, less dependence on evanescent trends, and (perhaps most important) access to the staggering profusion of top-quality ingredients from Northern California—organic fruits and vegetables, local cheeses, pasture-raised beef, lamb and pork, famous Hog Island oysters, and olive oils. When accompanied by wines from America's greatest vineyards in nearby Napa and Sonoma (see pp. 833 and 860), it guarantees unparalleled dining.

The Bay Area became a must-stop on the food-lover's tour in the 1970s with the opening of

Chez Panisse in nearby Berkeley (see p. 805). Today competition is fierce, but food-loving locals keep a whole starry constellation of fabulous restaurants aloft. At Restaurant Gary Danko you'll find exceptional California cuisine made with local ingredients and French technique: glazed oysters with Osetra caviar, salsify, and lettuce cream; pan-seared beef filet with potato gratin, Swiss chard, and Bordelaise butter; and luscious lemon soufflé cake with crème fraîche panna cotta and raspberry sorbet. At Michael Mina, located in the historic Westin St. Francis Hotel in Union Square, guests who order from the three-course dinner menu can select three mini renditions of some courses.

Coi (pronounced kwa) is the antiquated French word for "tranquil," and the Coi restaurant is just that: an oasis of serenity that sets the tone for an evening of exceptional gastronomy in an intimate 48-seat space. Brightly flavored, forward-thinking food is full of the *terroir* of Northern California created by new chef Matthew Kirkley. His ever-changing tasting menu reflects his minimalist style, utilizing the best and freshest ingredients available. This is cooking of great distinction, in which even the simplest foods sing with flavor.

Quince is set amid elegant digs on Jackson Square, with passionate chef Michael Tusk creating impeccable daily-changing tasting menus. Influenced by Northern Californian as well as French and Italian cuisines, this restaurant delivers—but save this sophisticated experience for a very special occasion when both the expectations and budget are high.

Options that are more casual and unassuming abound. Given San Francisco's flower-power underpinnings, it's not surprising that the city is home to excellent vegetarian restaurants, where "gourmet," "delicious," and "vegan" can be uttered in the same breath. At the much loved Pacific Heights restaurant-with-a-view called Greens, executive chef and cookbook author Annie Somerville is both a pioneer and a legend in the world of vegetable-based cuisine. The global menu follows the seasons with lots of surprises thrown in. Al's Place is not officially

vegetarian per se, but vegetables are featured front and center. A sampling of the now famously intense french fries had the food world claiming Aaron London (hence AL) was a genius. It's a basic restaurant that feels like a neighborhood find, with a compact menu whose simplicity belies London's creativity.

A host of other local favorites include Nancy Oakes's Boulevard, with its modern French-American cuisine and breathtaking views of the Bay Bridge; Anne and Craig Stoll's Delfina, with hearty and deeply satisfying Tuscan fare in the Mission District (their simple signature dish of spaghetti with plum tomatoes has been on the menu since the beginning); and the stylish long-time favorite Zuni Café on Market Street, where the regional French and Italian menu changes daily and the bar is abuzz with the city's glitterati.

GARY DANKO: Tel 415-749-2060; gary danko.com. *Cost:* 5-course menu $119. **MICHAEL MINA:** Tel 415-397-9222; michaelmina.net. *Cost:* 3-course tasting menu $125. **COI:** Tel 415-393-9000; coirestaurant.com. *Cost:* 12-course tasting menu $155. **QUINCE:** Tel 415-775-8500; quincerestaurant.com. *Cost:* 9-course menu $198. **GREENS:** Tel 415-771-6222; greens restaurant.com. *Cost:* 4-course tasting menu $58. **AL'S PLACE:** Tel 415-416-6136; alsplacesf .com. *Cost:* $45. **BOULEVARD:** Tel 415-543-6084; boulevardrestaurant.com. *Cost:* dinner $70. **DELFINA:** Tel 415-552-4055; delfinasf .com. *Cost:* dinner $50. **ZUNI CAFÉ:** Tel 415-552-2522; zunicafe.com. *Cost:* dinner $50.

Award-winning chef Annie Somerville samples the dishes of the day at Greens.

Fortune Cookies, Cracked Crab, and Cable Cars

SAN FRANCISCO'S GREAT NEIGHBORHOODS

San Francisco, California

S an Francisco is the city Americans fantasize about, sing about, leave their heart in, a place of myth and magic on par with Paris and Venice. One of California's greatest native writers, John Steinbeck (see p. 831), called it

"a golden handcuff with the key thrown away." With a stunning waterfront setting that rivals Rio de Janeiro's and just 850,000 inhabitants, it is America's most livable great city, and its fascinating mosaic of ethnic neighborhoods is one of its most charming features.

In Chinatown you'll hear more Cantonese and Mandarin than English, and find the same authentic grit and bustle of the alleys of Hong Kong. Enter that exotic world through the green-roofed, pagoda-style "Dragon's Gate" that opens onto Grant Avenue, the city's oldest street. At Portsmouth Square, you may find people practicing tai chi or a crowd of men immersed in gambling games. Wander Stockton Street's back alleys to see butchers, fishmongers, Chinese herb shops, and a fortune cookie factory on Ross Alley. Bring your own fortunes and they'll fold them into freshly made cookies right before your eyes.

Look for small eating places packed with Chinese patrons, such as the R&G (try their lichee martinis). If you don't mind sharing a long table with other tourists, try a longtime city favorite, House of Nanking, known for its noodles. Don't be surprised if the waiter tells you what to order—and don't hesitate to follow his advice.

Walk a few blocks to enter North Beach, characterized by alfresco café tables, the aromas of garlic and freshly ground coffee, and European accents. It's perfect for strolling, and Telegraph Hill offers some of the best

City Lights served as an intellectual hub of the Beat movement in the 1950s.

vistas in town, particularly from the top of 210-foot-high Coit Tower.

Explore café culture at City Lights, the bookstore founded in 1953 by poet Lawrence Ferlinghetti and Peter D. Martin. City Lights served as a launching pad for Jack Kerouac, Allen Ginsberg, and other Beat Generation writers and remains an institution of progressive literature and poetry today.

Fisherman's Wharf, the famous waterfront tourist destination, has long been the spot San Franciscans love to avoid (though as the rest of the city gets slicker they're coming around to its nostalgic charm). Join the teeming humanity eating freshly cracked Dungeness crab in season and fish-and-chips from the dockside stalls, and take in the stunning view of the Golden Gate Bridge (see p. 845) or Alcatraz (see p. 844). Top it off with a chocolate sundae at Ghirardelli Chocolate Company in Ghirardelli Square or an Irish coffee at the Buena Vista, which claims to have perfected the drink in 1952. Leave time for a cable car ride, one of San Francisco's most beloved icons and one of the few national historic landmarks that moves. A throwback to the late 1800s, when they were the best transportation up and down the 43 hills of America's most topographically endowed city, the cars still bustle along at a constant 9.5 miles per hour. Don't leave town without hopping aboard.

Visitor info: Tel 415-391-2000; san francisco.travel. **R&G Lounge:** Tel 415-982-7877. *Cost:* dinner $35. **House of Nanking:** Tel 415-421-1429; houseofnanking.net. *Cost:* dinner from $25. **City Lights Bookstore:** Tel 415-362-8193; citylights.com. **Ghirardelli Square:** Tel 415-775-5500; ghirardellisq.com. **The Buena Vista:** Tel 415-474-5044; the buenavista.com. **Best times:** May–June and Sept–Oct for weather and to avoid crowds.

Where SLO Town Meets the Sea

SAN LUIS OBISPO & MORRO BAY

California

The small town of San Luis Obispo is one of central California's friendliest, most compelling, and charming small towns. The quaint college town (Cal Poly is here) is the perfect base for antiques shopping or for visits to the booming Central Coast wine country known for its Rhône blends, heritage zinfandels, pinot noirs, and chardonnays. Fill your day with a visit to the pretty Mission San Luis Obispo de Tolosa founded in 1772 by Father Junípero Serra (see p. 807), or biking, hiking, golfing, or just plain strolling around what's known as "SLO Town." Sample the famed local barbecue (there's no place like Mo's, according to the local devotees), and sample your way through the four-block-long evening farmers market every Thursday on Higuera Street where barbecues and entertainment start at 6 P.M.

The Madonna Inn has nothing to do with the Material Girl of the same name, but is just as outrageous, with 110 kitschy themed rooms like Caveman, made of solid rock and decorated with waterfall and animal prints. Some say the Madonna is a sly parody of nearby Hearst Castle (see next page), the ultimate Xanadu of excessive materialism, and certainly it's a sight to behold—especially the famously whimsical restrooms.

Neighboring Morro Bay, 15 miles to the north, is a lovely complement to San Luis Obispo. Famed for its natural wonders, its most notable attraction is Morro Rock, ambitiously nicknamed the "Gibraltar of the Pacific." An imposing dome protruding out of the shallows like something in a James Bond movie, Morro Rock is surrounded by a cove

The 581-foot-tall gumdrop-shaped Morro Rock is believed to be 20 million years old.

and estuary with a stunningly rich habitat for birds, fish, and sea mammals (including impressively chatty elephant seals).

WHERE: 220 miles north of Los Angeles. *Visitor info:* Tel 805-781-2777; visitslo.com. **MO'S SMOKE-HOUSE BBQ:** Tel 805-544-6193; mosbbq.com. *Cost:* full slab $23. **MADONNA**

INN: Tel 800-543-9666 or 805-543-3000; madonnainn.com. *Cost:* from $199. **MORRO BAY:** Tel 805-255-1570; morrobay.org. **BEST TIMES:** Thurs for farmers market; late July–early Aug for the San Luis Obispo Mozart Festival (festivalmozaic.com); early fall in wine country for grape harvest.

A Paean to Exuberant Wealth

HEARST CASTLE

San Simeon, California

O ne of the most influential men of the 20th century, publishing titan William Randolph Hearst was larger than life, so it's fitting that his home is, too. In 1919, W.R. (as he was known to his friends) inherited 250,000 acres of ranchland along a striking and desolate section of the California coast and set about building "a little something." By 1947, that something turned out to be a 165-room Mediterranean Revival–style spectacle that remains unparalleled in its combination of opulence, grandeur, and excess. It is one of the last great examples of America's Gilded Age, an over-the-top paean to a lifestyle long gone.

Designed by renowned architect Julia Morgan and built over the course of 28 years (although never officially completed) atop what Hearst would call "La Cuesta Encantada" (The Enchanted Hill), it's characterized by 58 bedrooms, 41 fireplaces, exuberantly adorned swimming pools, and a dizzying collection of art and antiques obsessively amassed by Hearst during his lifetime. With his inexhaustible funds, Hearst would scour the auction houses of New York City, buying entire rooms from a French medieval castle here, a 15th-century Renaissance villa there. In its heyday the estate included the world's largest private zoo (wild descendants of the zebras still roam the grounds) and private airstrip, and was the getaway playground for Hollywood legends such as Marion Davies (his mistress

Hearst Castle's Neptune Pool is encircled by ancient Greek colonnades and sculptures and filled with fresh mountain water.

for over three decades), Charlie Chaplin, Bette Davis, and Cary Grant. The fantasy estate—and Hearst himself—was the inspiration behind Xanadu, the pleasure palace of the haunted hero in *Citizen Kane*, Orson Welles's 1941 masterpiece.

Today the lavish memorial to one man's wealth is now officially known as Hearst San Simeon State Historical Monument (Hearst himself would refer to it as "the ranch"). A variety of tours offer the chance to walk in the footsteps of revelers past. The Grand Rooms Tour is recommended for first-timers, who can view an introductory movie and see splendid social rooms on the ground floor of the opulent Casa Grande main house. The Evening Tour allows visitors to stroll the grounds at night, with staff dressed in 1930s attire. Hearst entertained an ever-changing roster of high-profile guests but was known for his strict rules of behavior. Guest David Niven was often chastised for drinking in his room.

Hearst Castle covers the hillside above the tiny coastal town of San Simeon, but most visitors will prefer spending time in the relaxed, exceedingly charming artists community of Cambria, located 6 miles south. Though the center of town is only a few blocks long, diversity can be found by meandering the historic and country-elegant East Village and the newer, more touristy West Village. Drop by the Sow's Ear restaurant for comfort food in a tiny cottage that is both warm and romantic. If you're staying the night, revel in the small-town country-coastal vibe at the J. Patrick House, a charming two-story log cabin B&B complete with wood-burning fireplaces, fluffy duvet covers, and bedtime milk and cookies.

WHERE: 211 miles south of San Francisco. Tel 800-444-4445; hearstcastle.com. **THE SOW'S EAR:** Cambria. Tel 805-927-4865; thesowsear.com. *Cost:* dinner $45. **J. PATRICK HOUSE:** Cambria. Tel 800-341-5258 or 805-927-3812; jpatrickhouse.com. *Cost:* from $195. **BEST TIMES:** winter for the smallest crowds; Christmas, when the castle is extravagantly decorated.

Low-Key Enclave of the Rich and Famous

SANTA BARBARA

California

In the 1920s, the Hollywood elite "discovered" this oak-dotted seaside paradise where the lush Santa Ynez Mountains cascade down to white sandy shores and the glistening Pacific beyond. Now it's known as the American Riviera, and the famous and humble alike have continued to discover Santa Barbara's many charms ever since. And there are many, from its natural wonders to its quaint historic downtown and destination restaurants. Town buildings largely keep to the area's red-tiled Spanish heritage, making a Main Street shopping spree a notably picturesque endeavor. But it's worth detouring off the main drag to take in the region's most notable structural highlights, specifically the historic hilltop mission, founded in 1786, rebuilt in 1812 and 1925 after earthquakes, and so beautiful it is dubbed the Queen of the Missions (see p. 807), as well as the 1929 Spanish Moorish–style courthouse, known as one of the country's most spectacular public buildings.

Just 30 miles north you can sip exceptional wines within the lush Santa Ynez Valley (see p. 857), or you can head east of downtown Santa Barbara to rub elbows with the rich and famous residing in ritzy and reclusive Montecito. Stay in Santa Barbara and you may run into famous residents such as Oprah or Kevin Costner at one of the vaunted dining locales. Roll up your sleeves for one of the city's best-known dining haunts, La Super-Rica, a street-corner shack selling soft tacos. Many a foodie has made a day trip up to Santa Barbara just for the pleasure of these divine tacos and tamales. The late, great (and local resident) Julia Child was a regular.

Should you plan to spend the night and want to experience the area at its most luxurious, Santa Barbara and its environs have you covered. Follow the lead of celebrities and head to San Ysidro Ranch, an exclusive 500-acre resort that was formerly a working ranch and citrus grove. This rustic-chic hideaway tucks private bungalows along a hillside creek and tree-lined paths, and houses the world-class Stonehouse restaurant in a century-old farmhouse. The gorgeous, understated home-away-from-home has played host to every type of star, perhaps most famously to John and Jacqueline Kennedy for their honeymoon (ask for their suite). Check into any of the 41 classic

The Santa Ynez Mountains rise beyond the coastal city of Santa Barbara.

bungalows, many with wood-burning fireplaces and decks with sweeping views of the Channel Islands, and order a tiny bowl of chilled berries by the pool from the attentive staff, or indulge in an in-room spa treatment while your dog receives a pet massage.

In contrast to the intimate ranch is the expansive—yet equally lavish—Bacara Resort and Spa. Here the Mediterranean-style beach-side rooms are strung along a hillside dipping down to the sea. The real draw is the knockout setting—perched before the ocean, three infinity pools, and enough spa treatments and athletic pursuits to keep the overstressed of the world coming back for more.

WHERE: 90 miles north of Los Angeles. *Visitor info:* Tel 805-966-9222; santabarbara ca.com. **SANTA BARBARA MISSION:** Tel 805-682-4713; santabarbaramission.org. **LA SUPER-RICA TAQUERIA:** Tel 805-963-4940. *Cost:* lunch $8. **SAN YSIDRO RANCH:** Tel 805-565-1700; sanysidroranch.com. *Cost:* from $845. **BACARA RESORT:** Tel 855-968-0100 or 805-968-0100; bacararesort.com. *Cost:* from $450. **BEST TIMES:** early Aug for Old Spanish Days Fiesta (sbfiesta.org); every Sun for waterfront arts and crafts show.

---

26 Miles Across the Sea

SANTA CATALINA ISLAND

California

Just 26 miles from the coast of Southern California, the jewel-like island of Santa Catalina seems worlds away from the bustling urban sprawl of Los Angeles. It was first purchased and developed by William Wrigley

(of chewing gum fame) in 1915, as a popular resort destination for movie stars and Hollywood folks seeking weekend escapes. Today, it's still an oasis that recalls a simpler time and a glimpse of what undeveloped Southern California once looked like. Its tiny town of Avalon—the only real town on the island—is

characterized by Spanish 1920s architecture and a sprinkling of little touristy trinket shops. It backs up to what is essentially one big nature preserve covering 88 percent of the island, deeded to Catalina Island Conservancy by Wrigley, where feet, bikes, golf carts, and a trolley are the only means of transportation.

Avalon's stand-out building is the glamorous 1929 Casino. Never actually a gambling place, it was a ballroom frequented by Catalina's early visitors and jumped with the music of every big band of the 1930s and '40s. The ornate art deco landmark features a movie theater, and each month it honors its heritage when an organist plays its historic instrument; it's also the venue for October's important jazz festival. There's little more to do in the town than catch a movie and meander the shops. Take a hike or an inland tour (the latter is the only way visitors are allowed to explore most of the island's interior), or try zip-lining. Yes, those are bison you see

The stylish Catalina Casino is the island's premier entertainment destination.

grazing, descendants of those brought over in the 1920s when Westerns were filmed here.

For a glimpse of life at the top, head up to the former Wrigley mansion that sits 350 feet above town, now the Inn on Mt. Ada. Built in 1921, and named after Wrigley's wife, the grand Georgian Colonial estate entertained the likes of Calvin Coolidge, Warren Harding, and the then Prince of Wales in its heyday. You can join the ranks of dignified guests by reserving one of the mansion's six sun-soaked bedrooms with ocean or harbor views (the very reason Wrigley chose this site), many with fireplaces. At press time, the inn is closed for renovations, with a reopening scheduled for spring 2017.

Where: 26 miles from San Pedro. *Visitor info:* catalinachamber.org. **How:** Catalina Express ferry from San Pedro, Long Beach, and Dana Point, tel 800-613-1212; catalina express.com. *Cost:* roundtrip from $750. The Island Express helicopter flight, tel 800-228-2566 or 310-510-2525; islandexpress.com. *Cost:* roundtrip from $250. **The Inn on Mt. Ada:** Tel 877-778-9395 or 310-510-2030; visitcatalinaisland.com. *Cost:* from $545 (off-peak), from $615 (peak). **Best time:** Oct for the Jazz Trax Festival (jazztrax.com).

A Classic Beach Town with a Boardwalk and Surfer Vibe

SANTA CRUZ

California

This Northern California surfing town's Giant Dipper roller coaster has been a beloved draw for its Beach Boardwalk since it was built in 1924. Overlooking a classic stretch of perfect California beach, the wooden-

beam-supported coaster is located on a wonderfully old-fashioned boardwalk that claims to be the last genuine beachfront amusement park in California. (Southern California's Santa Monica Pier is on a pier, after all.) Along its wide and bustling stretch you'll find thrill rides, like Double Shot, which drops riders from a

125-foot-high perch straight to the ground, and timeless attractions like the endearing 1911 Looff carousel with its original Ruth & Sohn band organ—and all the corn dogs and saltwater taffy you can eat.

Santa Cruz (which means "Holy Cross" in Spanish) identifies just as much with its longtime surf culture. Locals maintain that this town, and not rival Huntington Beach, is the "real" Surf City, U.S.A. They may try to conceal the identity of their favorite surf spots, but the secret's out. Among the favorite beaches: Cowell's for the long and gentle waves favored by beginners; Pleasure Point, where more advanced surfers ride larger waves; and the challenging and dangerous Steamer Lane, with some of the best surfing waves in the world. About 30 miles north is the world-renowned but treacherous surf spot Mavericks, where waves can top 80 feet after a winter storm. Big wave surfers live for the competition held here in February when conditions are favorable.

Santa Cruz's Steamer Lane (known as "The Lane") is an experienced surfer's paradise.

At the minute but interesting Santa Cruz Surfing Museum, housed in a historic lighthouse, photos depict the Hawaiian royalty who first surfed in Santa Cruz in 1885. The nearby University of California at Santa Cruz has perhaps the most beautiful of all UC campuses, with cathedral-like groves of redwood trees and winding trails that are ideal for an afternoon stroll.

It's an easy and lovely trip to nearby Natural Bridges State Beach, named for its ocean-carved archways and known for its monarch butterflies, and Big Basin Redwoods State Park, with its skyscraping redwoods and silvery waterfalls, which gush after spring rains.

WHERE: 74 miles south of San Francisco.

Visitors info: Tel 800-833-3494 or 831-425-1234; santacruz.org. **BEACH BOARDWALK:** Tel 831-423-5590; beachboardwalk.com. *When:* daily Apr–early Sept; off-season schedule varies. **SURFING MUSEUM:** Tel 831-420-6289; santacruzsurfingmuseum.org. *When:* Thurs–Mon. Open Wed in summer. **HOW:** Richard Schmidt's Surf School. Tel 831-423-0928; richardschmidt.com. *Cost:* $90 per person for 2-hour group class. **UC SANTA CRUZ:** ucsc.edu. **BIG BASIN REDWOODS STATE PARK:** Tel 831-338-8860; parks.ca.gov/bigbasin. **BEST TIMES:** winter for whale migration and watching surfers ride huge breakers; Jan–Feb for annual surfing competition; Aug for Cabrillo Festival of Contemporary Music; mid-Oct–mid-Feb for monarch butterflies.

Sideways Through Vineyards

SANTA YNEZ VALLEY

Santa Ynez, California

Some of California's finest wines are grown, produced, bottled, swirled, and sipped in the 50-some wineries in and around the Santa Ynez Valley. The idyllic setting nestled in the hillside just north of Santa Barbara (see p. 854) and inland from the glistening Pacific has five distinct viticultural areas that make it one of the most diverse wine regions in the country.

Before its latest 15 minutes of fame in the 2004 movie *Sideways*, the Santa Ynez Valley was known as the locale of President Ronald

Reagan's western White House ranch in the '80s and later as the site of Michael Jackson's Neverland compound. But even before that, tourists driving the California coastline discovered a bounty of roadside attractions, most notably the Danish-themed village of Solvang. Windmills, half-timbered houses, and great bakeries were cornerstones of this borderline kitsch but undeniably cute town founded in 1911 by Danish immigrants.

Rustic destinations include the Alisal Ranch, an old-time 10,000-acre resort-ranch favored for its two 18-hole golf courses and horseback riding on 50 miles of trails; the lively one-of-a-kind Cold Spring Tavern, a romantic restaurant and former 1860s stagecoach stop serving game, burgers, and other hearty meat dishes; and man-made Lake Cachuma and its resident bald eagles.

Fess Parker, who made his fame and fortune in the 1950s as the TV star portraying Daniel Boone, opened a winery and hotel before his death in 2010. Stay at Fess Parker's Wine Country Inn & Spa resort in Los Olivos, a nice, old-fashioned country town and good base for touring the wine country, including four tasting rooms owned by Fess's children and granddaughter. Have dinner at the nearby Hitching Post II, a fantastic spot famous for its excellent local beef, barbecued over open flames using red oak, pairing beautifully with the restaurant's highly regarded Hitching Post wines.

WHERE: 290 miles north of Los Angeles. *Visitor info:* visitsyv.com. **ALISAL GUEST RANCH:** Solvang. Tel 800-425-4725 or 805-688-6411; alisal.com. *Cost:* from $525, includes breakfast and dinner for two. **COLD SPRING TAVERN:** Tel 805-967-0066; cold springtavern.com. *Cost:* dinner $45. **FESS PARKER'S:** Los Olivos. Tel 800-446-2455 or 805-688-7788; fessparkerinn.com. *Cost:* from $265 (off-peak), from $395 (peak). **HITCHING POST II:** Tel 805-688-0676; hitchingpost2 .com. *Cost:* dinner $55. **BEST TIMES:** Mar for Taste of Solvang; Dec for Julefest in Solvang (solvangusa.com).

Awe in the Land of Giants

SEQUOIA AND KINGS CANYON NATIONAL PARKS

California

Home to ancient groves of giant sequoia, towering granite peaks, and the tallest mountain in the Lower 48 states, Sequoia and Kings Canyon National Parks, located in central California on the western flank of the Sierra Nevada range, are truly the land of behemoths. Only one road, the Generals Highway, loops through the parks. But stay in your car and you'll miss the grandeur of the experience: feeling yourself to be a small and humble creature at the ankles of the giant sequoias, the world's largest living things.

Legendary naturalist John Muir described these massive trees as "the most beautiful and majestic on earth." Sequoias achieve their size because they grow quickly over a long lifetime, and they live so long because a 6-to-8-inch-thick armor of bark protects them from both insects and fire. (They do have one weakness—a shallow root system—and the main cause of death is toppling.) Created in 1890 to prevent logging, Sequoia was declared the second national park in the U.S. (Yellowstone was the first, in 1872; see p. 676); adjoining Kings Canyon was added in 1940. Because Sequoia and Kings are more remote than nearby Yosemite (see p. 862), they're much less crowded, and give visitors the priceless feeling they've really gotten away from it all.

The mountaintop plateau of Giant Forest, with its thousands of giant sequoias, has always been the heart of Sequoia National Park. The Redwood Mountain Grove is the largest of the world's 75 majestic groves, 29 of them located in the park, and each pervaded by a mystic quiet that one has to experience to fully appreciate. The General Sherman, the largest tree in the world by volume, is 2,500 years old, 275 feet high, and has a circumference of 103 feet. Benches invite you to sit and contemplate its

A hike along the picturesque 0.8 mile Big Trees trail is an easy way to see the sequoias up close.

mass—the trunk alone weighs nearly 2.8 million pounds, with its first branch beginning 130 feet above the ground.

Other attractions include Mount Whitney, at 14,494 feet the tallest peak in the continental U.S.; the hiking trails of Mineral King, past waterfalls and lakes; the road through Kings Canyon, a beautiful U-shaped glacial ravine with granite pinnacles; and Crystal Cave, one of the 200 caves in the park, and the only one you can tour. A 50-minute tour led by a guide brings alive the eons of time it took to form these fantastical shapes.

Tucked away in the midst of such natural grandeur is rustic Wuksachi Lodge; at 7,200 feet, it's one of the highest resorts in the central Sierra. Crafted of cedar and stone and located deep in the Giant Forest area, the lodge has many rooms with spectacular views of the High Sierra. Come in the winter for cross-country skiing or snowshoeing in the awesome silence of these gentle giants.

Where: 260 miles southeast of San Francisco. Tel 559-565-3341; nps.gov/seki. **Crystal Cave:** explorecrystalcave.com. *When:* Mar–mid-Oct. **Wuksachi Lodge:** Sequoia National Park. Tel 866-807-3598 or 801-559-4948; visitsequoia.com. *Cost:* from $109 (off-peak), from $225 (peak). **Best times:** late spring until Sept–Oct for finest weather; June–July for wildflowers.

Sun and Deep Snow on the High Sierra

Skiing Northern California

California

Say "California" and most people think sun and surf . . . but skiers think sun and snow, some 400 glorious inches of it each winter, frequently deposited in 2-to-3-foot dumps on the western slopes of the Sierra Nevada mountains,

followed by long stretches of brilliant California sunshine. Most of California's ski resorts are centered around Lake Tahoe

(see p. 726), the 22-mile-long, 12-mile-wide sapphire-hued glacial lake that straddles the state line between California and Nevada and is ringed by snowcapped granite peaks. Lake Tahoe has the greatest concentration of ski resorts anywhere in the country and offers something you'll get nowhere else—thrilling views of the country's largest alpine lake as you speed down the mountainside.

Squaw Valley is the best-known of the Tahoe resorts, made famous as the host of the 1960 Winter Olympic Games (the first to be televised) and more recently, the birthplace of extreme skiing. Squaw is as raw as it comes, with daredevil skiers and so many GoPro-toting cinematographers recording the action that it's known as "Squallywood." Alpine Meadows is favored by locals as a low-key alternative—a lot of mountain without the attitude. Smaller, with a down-home feel, Alpine Meadows features a string of wide-open bowls with phenomenal expert terrain, stunning views of Lake Tahoe, and no crowds.

Heavenly Mountain Resort has the most breathtaking views of the lake (it feels like you could ski straight into it), a tremendous variety of runs, and great glade skiing, with mighty pines and firs spaced so far apart you can pick your own line and ski it like a natural slalom course. Right on the California-Nevada state line, Heavenly is the only resort where you can ski in two states—and gamble après ski on the Nevada side.

Northstar-at-Tahoe is the most family-friendly resort, with easy cruising on milder terrain, wide-open glades, and famously patient instructors. Snowboarders can enjoy a Superpipe, Halfpipe, and seven terrain parks.

A skier makes a daunting jump from a cliff on Mammoth Mountain.

A hundred miles to the south, the sprawling monolith called Mammoth Mountain is a favorite of Southern California skiers and snowboarders. Its massive Superpipe and terrain parks are rated among the best in the country. One of Mammoth Mountain's most attractive features is its long ski season—into May, and even June in big snow years.

Squaw Valley Alpine Meadows: near Tahoe City, 200 miles northeast of San Francisco. Tel 800-403-0206 or 530-583-6985; squawalpine.com. *Cost:* lift tickets $139. **Heavenly Mountain Resort:** South Lake Tahoe. Tel 800-432-8365 or 775-586-7000; skiheavenly.com. *Cost:* lift tickets $125. **Northstar-at-Tahoe:** Truckee. Tel 800-466-6784 or 530-562-1010; northstarcalifornia.com. *Cost:* lift tickets $130. **Mammoth Mountain:** Mammoth Lakes. Tel 800-626-6684 or 760-934-2571; mammothmountain.com. *Cost:* lift tickets $135. **Best times:** ski season is Nov–May, but best snow is late Dec–Mar.

Elegant Pinot Noirs and Chardonnays Amid Stunning Scenery

Sonoma County

California

There is no place on earth like Sonoma County when it comes to sheer beauty, and few can rival it for fine-wine diversity. Home to towering redwood trees, pristine forests, and the meandering Russian River, Sonoma

("Valley of the Moon") is bordered by the rocky Pacific coastline to the west and the Mayacamas Mountains and the Napa Valley (see p. 833) to the east. Lusher, greener, and decidedly cooler than Napa, Sonoma is known for producing California's best chardonnays and pinot noir (the notoriously finicky grape that makes France's esteemed Burgundies), which love the cool, foggy mornings that come courtesy of the Pacific. Sonoma's 450 wineries are spread out over the county's 1,768 square miles, with big names like Kendall-Jackson and not-so-well-known ones (though names like Kistler turn wine lovers' heads) and tasting rooms that are more laid-back. Unlike Napa, Sonoma has managed to hold on to its humbler forms of agriculture, with fertile orchards, vegetable farms, and outstanding producers of olive oil, lamb, and cheese. Traveling is a delight through this rural landscape, and many find the picturesque towns of Healdsburg, Sonoma, and Sebastopol to be more uniquely charming than those of the Napa Valley.

Green and gold Sonoma Valley is the county's most popular destination, and many visitors never get beyond it. Its oldest and most famous city is Sonoma, centered around a shady, grassy central plaza with good shopping, small restaurants, and a historic adobe mission—the last to be built in California, back in 1823. A couple of miles northeast of the plaza is another piece of history, Buena Vista Winery, established in

Sonoma County has 16,000 acres of chardonnay vineyards, making it the area's leading varietal.

1857 by Agoston Haraszthy, a Hungarian immigrant and one of the first in California to plant the European vinifera varieties that now make the fine wines.

Fairmont Sonoma Mission Inn and Spa has been the region's best-known and most luxurious place to stay since the signature pink mission-style inn was built in 1927. Oprah Winfrey, Harrison Ford, and Tom Cruise are all said to have passed through its baronial reception hall. This 226-room property with a 40,000-square-foot spa is one of a handful of resorts to have its own hot springs, which flow 1,100 feet below the inn at 135°F.

Nearby in the tiny country town of Glen Ellen is Gaige House, the intimate wine-country inn of your dreams. Originally built in the late 1800s for a butcher with shops in San Francisco and Kenwood, this Queen Anne Victorian home is now one of the region's finest B&Bs, with a sophisticated design aesthetic, including Zenlike spa suites inspired by Kyoto's ancient ryokan inns.

Hike the landscape beloved by Jack London, author of *The Call of the Wild* and *White Fang*, at the 1,400-acre Jack London State Historic Park, where he lived from 1905 until his death in 1916. In northern Sonoma's Russian River Valley, Healdsburg is the center of the action, with a historic town square flanked by inviting shops and cafés such as the always-packed Downtown Bakery and Creamery. Close to the square, Les Mars Hotel's limestone and wrought-iron exterior and 17th- and 18th-century antiques evoke the Old World inns of France, but with 21st-century amenities that make for the town's finest overnight address. The young chef at the helm of the always full Valette restaurant is a hometown son of Healdsburg, and culls the finest from local farmers, winemakers, and artisans to create the quintessential wine-country experience. Healdsburg's 1881 Madrona Manor sets the standard for Victorian elegance with nine luxurious rooms in the main house, with suites and cottages in historic buildings surrounded by stunning gardens.

WHERE: Sonoma is 45 miles north of San Francisco. *Visitor info:* Tel 800-576-6662 or 707-522-5800; sonomacounty.com. **BUENA VISTA WINERY:** Sonoma. Tel 800-926-1266; buenavista.com. **FAIRMONT SONOMA MISSION INN & SPA:** Sonoma. Tel 866-540-4499 or 707-938-9000; fairmont.com/sonoma. *Cost:* from $209 (off-peak), from $349 (peak). **GAIGE HOUSE:** Glen Ellen. Tel 800-935-0237 or 707-935-0237; gaige.com. *Cost:* from $275. **JACK LONDON STATE HISTORIC PARK:** Glen Ellen. Tel 707-938-5216; jacklondonpark.com.

DOWNTOWN BAKERY: Tel 707-431-2719; downtownbakery.net. **LES MARS HOTEL:** Healdsburg. Tel 707-433-4211; hotellesmars.com. *Cost:* from $405 (off-peak), from $540 (peak). **VALETTE:** Tel 707-473-0946; valettehealdsburg.com. *Cost:* dinner $60. **MADRONA MANOR:** Healdsburg. Tel 707-433-4231; madronamanor.com. *Cost:* from $235 (off-peak), from $385 (peak). **BEST TIMES:** spring for wildflower season; 2nd weekend in Sept for Russian River Jazz and Blues Festival (russianriverfestivals.com) in Guerneville; fall for harvest season.

A High Sierra Gem

YOSEMITE NATIONAL PARK

California

"No temple made with hands can compare with Yosemite," wrote naturalist John Muir, the conservationist whose work led to the founding of Yosemite National Park in 1890. Most of the park's natural attractions have become icons of the American landscape, immortalized by the photographs of Ansel Adams. Who doesn't recognize the bald image of Half Dome, Yosemite's 8,839-foot trademark peak? Or El Capitan, the largest single granite rock on earth, rising 3,000 feet from the valley floor (twice the size of the Rock of Gibraltar) and drawing rock climbers from all over the world? Venture deeper into the park and visit the magnificent Yosemite Falls, the highest on the continent at 2,425 feet.

Millions converge in high season on this temple of nature, most heading for the star attractions and awesome beauty of the mile-wide, 7-mile-long Yosemite Valley, cut by the Merced River and guarded by sheer granite cliffs and domes, rising 2,000 to 4,000 feet from the valley floor. Avoid the park's notorious summertime people-jams by exploring the backcountry—the wilder 95 percent of the 1,190-square-mile park.

Yosemite's 750 miles of trails, ranging from easy day hikes to challenging overnight trips, can be covered by horse, mule, or on foot. One of the most popular is the moderately strenuous Mist Trail, offering a close-up view of 317-foot Vernal Fall and the 594-foot Nevada Fall. The most ambitious hikers tackle some or all of the 211-mile John Muir Trail, which travels end-to-end through three

The 750,000-acre park features thousands of lakes and ponds and 1,600 miles of streams.

national parks—Yosemite, Kings Canyon, and Sequoia (see p. 858)—along the backbone of the Sierra Nevada. Named for the founder of the Sierra Club, the trail was created between 1915 and 1938 and runs from the summit of Mount Whitney in the south (see p. 859) to the Yosemite Valley in the north.

For those who prefer to remain in the car, the park offers 214 miles of paved roads. (Head to Glacier Point for spectacular views of the valley below.) Or experience Northern California's great white-water rafting on the Merced River, where rafters can find Class III or IV rapids over a 28.3-mile stretch, or on the Tuolumne River, just outside the park, which offers over 18 miles of scenic Class III or IV rapids (see p. 808).

The Majestic Yosemite Hotel (formerly the Ahwahnee is a 1927 showpiece of stone and native timber with heart-stopping views. Inside, Native American motifs blend with massive chandeliers that look like they were meant for a castle and fireplaces large enough to walk into.

South of Yosemite, Château du Sureau is an enchanting ten-room European-style country inn where the crackling fires and attentive staff just might spoil you for staying anywhere else. Its acclaimed restaurant, Erna's Elderberry House, where a six-course tasting menu changes daily, draws foodies the way El Cap lures climbers.

WHERE: 165 miles east of San Francisco. *Park info:* Tel 209-372-0200; nps.gov/yose. **JOHN MUIR TRAIL:** for reservations, permits, and trail conditions, tel 916-285-1846; pcta .org. **THE MAJESTIC YOSEMITE:** Tel 209-372-1407; travelyosemite.com/lodging/the-majestic-yosemite-hotel. *Cost:* from $458. **CHÂTEAU DU SUREAU:** Oakhurst. Tel 559-683-6860; chateausureau.com. *Cost:* from $385; prix-fixe dinner $135. **BEST TIMES:** late spring for waterfalls. Reserve early for the Ahwahnee's Christmas Bracebridge dinner.

Where Food Is Art in the Napa Valley

FRENCH LAUNDRY

Yountville, California

Justifiably known as one of the top restaurants in the world, the French Laundry is not just another super-expensive Michelin-three-star dining experience. It's culinary theater, and the drama begins the moment you try to snare one of the coveted and very limited reservations. Competition from neighboring restaurants here in the Napa Valley is fierce (see p. 833), but at the French Laundry you're bound to have one of the most glorious gourmet experiences of your life.

The modestly formal scene, set within intimate dining rooms or in the beautiful flower-filled garden, is subtle enough not to steal attention from the stars of the show: every dish that makes up chef-owner Thomas Keller's nine-course tasting menu. Gorgeously sculpted and dramatically delivered by a perfectly polished waitstaff, Keller's astounding presentations are invariably finished at the table with a precious drizzle, sprinkle, or spoonful of something fabulous.

The showmanship is impressive, and the flavor combinations and creative use of the finest ingredients are extreme too, in the best possible way. Menu classics include "Oysters and Pearls" (a light yet decadent sabayon of pearl tapioca with Malpeque oysters and white sturgeon caviar) and the poached Alaskan king crab with toasted pine nuts, nasturtium leaves, and Holland white asparagus "Vichyssoise."

Virtually everything on the menu is no more than a few heavenly bites, but belt buckles still get loosened a notch or two thanks to the richness of the meal. Even exquisite desserts are followed by fruit, ice cream, chocolate, and candies. The staff's timing is perfect, so one's appetite and spirits never flag until, sadly, it is time to leave after having experienced a spectacle made of nine edible one-act wonders.

WHERE: 60 miles north of San Francisco; 6640 Washington St. Tel 707-944-2380; thomaskeller.com/tfl. **COST:** 9-course tasting menu $310. **HOW:** reservations taken starting 2 months to the calendar day. **BEST TIME:** If you're in town, drop by in the morning and leave your name in case of cancellations; it sometimes works—especially on rainy days.

In the 1920s, the restaurant's building was used as a French steam laundry, hence the name.

Much Ado About Ashland

OREGON SHAKESPEARE FESTIVAL

Ashland, Oregon

"Gentles, perchance you wonder at this show; but wonder on, till truth make all things plain," wrote William Shakespeare about the magic of theater—abundantly on display each year at the Oregon Shakespeare Festival (OSF), the largest and longest-running celebration of the Bard in America. Today, upwards of 400,000 theater lovers come to Ashland each year to attend performances at the festival's three venues, including the outdoor Elizabethan Theatre, which seats 1,200 and is fashioned after a 17th-century English theater. The Tony Award–winning festival, which has staged performances in Ashland since the 1930s, is home to the biggest rotating repertory theater in the country. The festival's success unquestionably derives from the excellence of its productions, but is aided too by the charm of Ashland, a small, colorful city 15 miles north of the California border that has become the cultural—and gastronomic—center of southern Oregon.

While the festival repertory here is rooted in Shakespeare, it also features revivals and contemporary theater from around the world. In addition to 11 plays presented annually, from mid-February through October, there are also backstage tours, lectures and discussions led by actors and scholars, and alfresco concerts of Renaissance music and dance.

Ashland's main streets buzz with well-heeled shoppers and youthful bohemians. From the town's central plaza, lovely Lithia Park winds up along Ashland Creek; park trails meander for miles past swans, picnickers, and declaiming thespians, and there are day trips galore in the mountainous region of southern Oregon, from visits to nearby vineyards to skiing at Mount Ashland in the white months.

Of Ashland's dozens of historic B&Bs and small inns, the Peerless Hotel is a favorite. Built in 1900 as a railroad workers' boardinghouse, the beautifully updated Peerless now offers tastefully appointed rooms with luxurious comforts. These take a backseat to the eponymous restaurant next door, one of the best in town. An inventive cuisine fashioned from the bounty of local farms and ranches is paired with an award-winning wine list heavy with Oregon's finest.

The grand Elizabethan Theatre presents Shakespeare in a venue reminiscent of London's original Globe Theatre—but here, the "groundlings" sit in comfort.

WHERE: 285 miles south of Portland. Tel 541-482-4331; osfashland.org. *Cost:* tickets from $30. *When:* Feb–Oct. **PEERLESS HOTEL & RESTAURANT:** Tel 541-488-1082 (hotel), 541-488-6067 (restaurant); peerlesshotel.com. *Cost:* from $92 (off-peak), from $174 (peak); dinner $45. **BEST TIMES:** May–Oct for weather; July 4th for live music, a food and crafts fair, an old-fashioned parade, and fireworks.

An Enclave of History and Art at the Columbia's Mouth

ASTORIA

Oregon

From its perch above the mouth of the Columbia River, Astoria has seen more history flow by than any other city in the Pacific Northwest. Established in 1811, Astoria is the oldest U.S. settlement in the American West, and offers two centuries' worth of frontier and maritime history. It also boasts the kind of scruffy charm that draws in painters and writers, and this onetime center of seafaring now serves as an artists retreat.

The Lewis and Clark expedition (see p. 643) literally put Astoria on the map. The mouth of the Columbia was the western terminus of the Corps of Discovery's journey, and they built Fort Clatsop—their encampment for the tough winter of 1805–06—just south of the future city. At the National Park Service's fort replica, living history interpreters lead tours through the stockaded encampment, demonstrating such frontier skills as leather tanning and flintlock marksmanship.

Astoria itself was born just five years later when American fur traders working for John Jacob Astor established Fort Astoria in his name, on a rocky ledge above the Columbia. With its auspicious position at the mouth of the West's largest river, Astoria grew wealthy through trade and fishing. Sea captains built magnificent trophy homes overlooking the river. Many of these flamboyant Victorian mansions, which cling to the steep hillsides behind downtown, have been painstakingly restored and afford incredible views of the high-arching Astoria Bridge. At over 4 miles, it is North America's longest continuous truss bridge, connecting Astoria to Washington State. To glimpse the period's grandeur, tour the ornate Queen Anne showcase built in 1885 by Captain George Flavel, now a museum. Stay at the Hotel Elliott, built in the Roaring '20s and recently refurbished; it is Astoria's most sophisticated downtown hotel.

The former salmon canning center of the West Coast, Astoria's waterfront isn't the bustling fishing hub that it once was, but there's still a sufficient fishery to supply the city's restaurants with the freshest catch imaginable. Don't be fooled by the scrappy facade of the Columbian Café: Chef-owner Uriah Hulsey secures the best of locally caught fish to serve in his tiny, vividly painted diner. While the decor is the epitome of Oregon funkiness, come here for first-class food, especially at dinner.

Astoria's long fishing and seafaring history is the focus of the not-to-be-missed Columbia River Maritime Museum along the waterfront. The breadth of the museum's collections is remarkable, from scrimshaw to harpoons, from the history of Pacific lighthouses to the evolution of boat design. Huge windows overlook the Columbia, an appropriate backdrop for viewing the museum's classic fishing vessels and other historic watercraft.

WHERE: 95 miles northwest of Portland. *Visitor info:* Tel 503-325-6311; travelastoria .com. **FORT CLATSOP:** Tel 503-861-2471; nps.gov/lewi. **CAPTAIN GEORGE FLAVEL HOUSE MUSEUM:** Tel 503-325-2203. **HOTEL ELLIOTT:** Tel 877-EST-1924 or 503-325-2222; hotelelliott.com. *Cost:* from $131 (off-peak), from $219 (peak). **COLUMBIAN CAFÉ:** Tel 503-325-2233. *Cost:* dinner $40. *When:* closed Tues. **COLUMBIA RIVER MARITIME MUSEUM:** Tel 503-325-2323; crmm.org. **BEST TIMES:** June–Oct for weather; 3rd weekend in June for Scandinavian Midsummer Festival; early Aug for the Astoria Regatta.

Scottish Links on the Oregon Coast

BANDON DUNES GOLF RESORT

Bandon, Oregon

Even before golf came to town and turned things around, Bandon was a little different from Oregon's other coastal towns, equal parts practical and artsy, rustic and refined. Bandon is known for both its cheese factory (many Oregonians claim Bandon's cheddar is superior to that made at the larger and better-known factory up the coast in Tillamook; see p. 876) and its cranberries. Lots of cranberries. Bandon sits on a particularly beautiful piece of coastline littered with offshore monoliths and haystack rocks; you'll find it's enough to come just for the sunsets.

When the Bandon Dunes Golf Resort was built in 1999, it catapulted small Bandon into the national spotlight. Designed by Scotsman David McLay Kidd, the first 18-hole links-style course gained a reputation among avid golfers as one of the best and most challenging in America. Bandon Dunes now boasts four links-style 18-hole courses, plus a par-3, 13-hole short course, and The Punchbowl, a 100,000-square-foot putting course. Bandon's position on the coast means that there are exquisite views from every hole, and the sand hills, gorge, and wind-swept fairways are as much like Scotland as any place you'll find on this side of the Atlantic. Bandon Dunes is also known for its no-carts policy—players either carry their clubs or hire caddies, which gives golfers a chance to really savor the beauty of the course.

Though it may be possible to spend every waking hour on the greens, travelers seeking a break should take some time to walk Bandon's beaches, and then venture about 25 miles south to Cape Blanco to see its photogenic white-washed lighthouse. It's an especially beautiful and little visited stretch of the coast. It was once famous as the westernmost point in the Lower 48 until that title was given over to Cape Flattery in Washington. It now settles for being the westernmost point in Oregon.

WHERE: 235 miles south of Portland.

Visitor info: Tel 541-347-9616; bandon.com. **BANDON DUNES GOLF RESORT:** Tel 888-345-6008 or 541-347-4380; bandondunesgolf.com. *Cost:* greens fees from $100 ($75 for resort guests) (off-peak), from $290 ($245 for hotel guests) (peak). Rooms from $120 (off-peak), from $250 (peak). **CAPE BLANCO STATE PARK:** Tel 800-551-6949 or 541-332-2973; oregon stateparks.org. **BEST TIMES:** July–Sept for weather; Sept for Bandon Cranberry Festival.

Premier Skiing on Oregon's Sunny Side

BEND & MOUNT BACHELOR

Oregon

Just east of Oregon's chain of volcanic Cascade peaks is the rapidly growing city of Bend, a four-season haven for skiers, hikers, anglers, and refugees from the rainy side of the mountains. The mountains snag most of the clouds rolling in from the west and wrest the moisture from them, leaving an annual accumulation of about 460 inches of snow on nearby 9,065-foot Mount Bachelor. With a vertical drop of 3,365 feet and a network of cross-country ski and snowshoe trails to fill out the fun-in-the-snow scene, it's no wonder that Mount Bachelor Ski Area is considered the biggest and the best skiing in the Pacific Northwest.

Convenient lodging can be found at Tetherow Resort, offering sophisticated rooms and suites and an acclaimed 18-hole golf course. In summer, the nearby Deschutes River is one of the state's best rivers for white water, and although this is not the wildest stretch (that's north of Bend), rafting here makes for a mighty exciting introduction to the sport.

Bend's old commercial center has in recent years been revivified with smart shops, galleries, and good restaurants. It's easy to spend several hours here chatting in a coffeehouse or browsing through bookstores. Parks stretch along the Deschutes through the downtown area, making it a lovely spot to stroll or picnic.

The 87-mile-long Cascade Lakes Highway starts in Bend and passes Mount Bachelor as it loops back to Highway 97 near La Pine, packing in some of the best scenery in Oregon's Cascades. Once the winter snows have melted (sometimes as late as June), this road leads to some of Oregon's best hiking trails, including the trailhead for a nontechnical but challenging

Mount Bachelor was named by early explorers for the way it stands apart from other Cascade peaks, but its popularity today makes it anything but isolated.

summertime climb up 10,358-foot South Sister, a volcanic peak at the edge of the Three Sisters Wilderness Area.

Directly south of Bend, Highway 97 passes through National Forest Service's Newberry National Volcanic Monument, a showcase of volcanic features, including lava tubes, obsidian flows, lava cast forests, and cinder cones. The Lava Lands visitors center provides information and exhibits on the geology, wildlife, and archaeology of these eerie volcanic landscapes, with information on hikes and scenic drives. Farther south, seasonal paved roads ascend the slopes of Newberry Crater, the centerpiece of this otherworldly landscape, leading to astonishing vistas above Paulina Lake and East Lake, both nestled within a volcanic caldera.

Where: 175 miles southeast of Portland. *Visitor info:* Tel 800-800-8334 or 541-389-8799; visitcentraloregon.com. **Mount Bachelor Ski Area:** Tel 800-829-2442 or 541-382-2442; mtbachelor.com. *When:* Dec–Apr. *Cost:* lift tickets from $84. **Tetherow Resort:** Tel 541-388-2582; tetherow.com. *Cost:* from $233 (off-peak), from $352 (peak). **Three Sisters Wilderness Area:** Tel 541-225-6300; fs.fed.us/r6/willamette. **Newberry National Volcanic Monument:** Tel 541-593-2421; fs.fed.us/visit/destination/newberry-national-volcanic-monument-0. **Best times:** Jan–Feb for skiing or boarding; early Aug for hiking.

A Quaint Spot on a Rugged Coastline

Cannon Beach

Oregon

Cannon Beach's setting is undeniably spectacular. Four miles of pristine beach hemmed in by thickly forested headlands are accented by immense rock formations (such as the iconic Haystack Rock, a 235-foot thumb of rock rising from the beach) and home to numerous seabirds, while the Coast Range provides a steep green backdrop. In addition to its dramatic natural attributes, Cannon Beach offers cozy B&Bs, luxury inns, good food, and an arty, sophisticated atmosphere that's pleasantly at odds with the surging Pacific. It's no surprise that Portlanders have been making their second homes here for almost a century.

Despite its burgeoning tourist trade over the past several decades, Cannon Beach retains its weathered-shingle seaside charm, with none of the outsize development that often blights beach towns. The town's quiet good taste is exemplified by the Stephanie Inn, an ocean-front boutique inn that's arguably the most romantic getaway on the Oregon coast. The guest rooms are supremely comfortable, each

The looming Haystack Rock can be reached by foot during low tides; resident tidepool creatures and nesting birds are protected by its Marine Garden status.

with a fireplace and balcony, and the dining room serves up-to-date Northwest Cuisine. Pray for bad weather, maybe a little winter storm-watching, and the excuse of never leaving the folds of the inn's cozy embrace.

Just north of town, Ecola State Park and Tillamook Head offer hiking trails with dramatic ocean vistas that take in Cannon Beach and Haystack Rock. Tillamook Lighthouse sits offshore on a 100-foot sea stack, a reminder of the treacherous seas responsible for Cannon Beach's name: When the U.S. survey schooner *Shark* wrecked in 1846, a portion of her deck with an iron cannon attached washed up here.

Cannon Beach hosts a number of popular festivals throughout the year but the most celebrated event is Sandcastle Day in mid-June, when everyone is ten years old again. The beach fills with all sorts of fanciful sculpture and architecture, some of it improbably huge, much of it surprisingly good. Castles are the perennial favorite of sand sculptors, but you'll also see sand dragons, mermaids, and complex creations complete with embedded human beings—until the next high tide arrives and carries the sculptures away, leaving the humans behind.

WHERE: 80 miles west of Portland. *Visitor info:* Tel 503-436-2623; cannonbeach.org. **STEPHANIE INN:** Tel 855-977-2444 or 503-436-2221; stephanie-inn.com. *Cost:* from $325 (off-peak), from $459 (peak); dinner $75. **BEST TIMES:** Jan–Mar for storm-watching; Apr for the Kite Festival; mid-June for Sandcastle Day; Nov for the Stormy Weather Arts Festival.

A Majestic Cleft Through the Cascade Volcanoes

THE COLUMBIA RIVER GORGE

Oregon and Washington

The Columbia River's enormous 80-mile-long gorge through the Cascade Mountains is one of the most dramatic destinations in the Pacific Northwest, so breathtaking that in 1986 Congress designated it the first of America's

National Scenic Areas. The mile-wide river, flanked by volcanic sentinels Mount Hood (in Oregon; see p. 874) and Mount Adams (in Washington), flows beneath banded basalt walls rising 3,000 feet. Waterfalls tumble from the gorge's edge, cascading hundreds of feet to meet the river. All this beauty—plus excellent hiking trails and world-class windsurfing—is just an hour from Portland.

This awe-inspiring chasm—scoured by a series of Ice Age flash floods—has long been more than a scenic wonder: The only sea-level passage through the Sierra and Cascade ranges, for centuries it has also served as a major transportation corridor. For millennia, Native peoples traveled through the gorge to trade and fish. The Corps of Discovery, led by Meriwether Lewis and William Clark, also passed through the gorge in 1805–06 on its epic journey to the Pacific (see p. 643). The gorge was also the final challenge to pioneers on the 2,000-mile Oregon Trail, which between 1843 and 1860 brought an estimated 53,000 settlers to the Northwest. In 1916, the Historic Columbia River Highway, a marvel of mountain road engineering, opened the gorge to automobile traffic. Although much of this route has been subsumed by fast-moving I-84, remnants of the winding roadway (now Highway 30) remain and are by far the best routes for exploring the gorge.

The town of Hood River, the hub of the gorge, is known in the world of sports as the windsurfing capital of America. Stiff prevailing winds and the Columbia's strong river currents combine to create a kind of wind tunnel that makes for legendary windsurfing and kite-surfing conditions. South of the city, above the pear and apple orchards of the Hood River Valley, the massive glaciered peak of Mount Hood rises to fill the horizon, a perfect postcard image of Oregon. In the 1910s, a rail line ran up the Hood River Valley to bring out lumber and later

A 1.2-mile hiking trail climbs to the top of Multnomah Falls.

transported the valley's rich bounty of fruit. The Mount Hood Railroad now carries day-trippers between Hood River and Parkdale on vintage Pullman railcars.

West of Hood River, a segment of the Historic Columbia River Highway climbs along the nearly sheer basalt cliffs, which serve as backdrop for the greatest concentration of waterfalls in North America. The most spectacular of all is Multnomah Falls, the tallest in Oregon and the second highest year-round waterfall in the U.S. (after Yosemite Falls in California; see p. 862), with a total drop of 642 feet.

Riverboat cruises aboard the *Columbia Gorge* sternwheeler depart from the town of Cascade Locks, offering modern-day travelers a chance to see the river from the viewpoint of early pioneers. Lindblad Expeditions offers longer river trips on the Columbia and Snake rivers aboard a 70-person boat departing from Portland, accompanied by noted historians and naturalists.

WHERE: 56 miles east of Portland. **MOUNT HOOD RAILROAD:** Hood River. Tel 800-872-4661 or 541-386-3556; mthoodrr.com. *Cost:* day trip from $30. *When:* closed Jan–May. *COLUMBIA GORGE STERNWHEELER:* Cascade Locks. Tel 800-224-3901 or 503-224-3900; portlandspirit .com. *Cost:* from $28. *When:* daily May–Oct. **LINDBLAD EXPEDITIONS:** Tel 800-397-3348 or 212-261-9000; expeditions.com. *Cost:* from $4,750 per person, double occupancy, for 7-day trip, includes lodging and meals. **WHERE TO STAY:** Columbia Gorge Hotel, Hood River, tel 800-345-1921 or 541-386-5566; columbia gorgehotel.com. *Cost:* from $119 (off-peak), from $269 (peak). **BEST TIME:** May–Oct for weather.

From Volcanic Fury, a Rugged Beauty

CRATER LAKE NATIONAL PARK

Oregon

Most visitors are drawn to Crater Lake by its perfect jewel-like beauty. But for the geologically minded, rather than being a place of awesome splendor, Crater Lake is a place of catastrophic legacy. Oregon's oldest national park had its beginnings about 7,700 years ago when a phenomenal eruption caused the massive Mount Mazama (thought to have been about 12,000 feet high) to collapse in on itself. The resulting 6-mile-wide caldera slowly filled with water, eventually reaching 1,949 feet deep, making it the nation's deepest lake.

The cold, calm, and exceptionally clear water doesn't fill the caldera all the way to its rim; from the crater's edge, it's anywhere from 507 feet to 1,980 feet down to the water. A very steep mile-long trail on the lake's north side leads down to the shore, where hikers can board a tour boat (the only boat aside from research vessels permitted on the lake) and cruise to Wizard Island, a perfect cone-shaped extrusion formed when lava seeped up from the lake's bottom.

The 33-mile Rim Drive encircles the 21-square-mile lake and offers an eyeful for motorists, hikers, and bicyclists. In winter, heavy snowfall closes the road, and it becomes a breathtaking place to cross-country ski.

Construction on Crater Lake Lodge began in 1909, but because of the very short building season, the lodge was only partially finished when it opened six years later. Over the years,

The summit of Wizard Island is 760 feet above lake level, high enough that it is often snowcapped.

the lodge was alternately renovated and upgraded, then allowed to deteriorate as finances dictated. A huge push in the 1990s brought it to its present renovated, and finally complete, rustic elegance. The Great Hall's huge stone fireplace, Craftsman-style furniture, and broad picture windows framing the cobalt blue of the lake are all in the tradition of the other great national park lodges and make it the finest in the Pacific Northwest.

Get the big picture of the Cascades' fierce past on the 500-mile Volcanic Legacy Scenic Byway, which starts at the park and heads south past the town of Klamath Falls into California, where it skirts Mount Shasta and terminates just south of Mount Lassen.

WHERE: 77 miles northeast of Medford. Tel 541-594-3000; nps.gov/crla. *When:* park open year-round; Rim Drive late June–mid-Sept, depending on snowfall; boat tours July–mid-Sept. **CRATER LAKE LODGE:** Tel 888-774-2728 or 541-594-2255; craterlakelodges.com. *Cost:* lake-view from $219. *When:* mid-May–mid-Oct. **VOLCANIC LEGACY BYWAY:** volcanic legacybyway.org. **BEST TIMES:** July–Aug for weather. Wildflowers peak briefly in mid-July.

A Plant and Animal Fossil Bonanza

JOHN DAY FOSSIL BEDS NATIONAL MONUMENT

Dayville, Oregon

Don't come to the John Day Fossil Beds National Monument looking for dinosaur bones. What you'll find instead, here in dry, remote east-central Oregon, is one of the world's most extensive and unbroken fossil records

of the post-dinosaur Cenozoic Era, the Age of Mammals and Flowering Plants. The monument is composed of three distinct units separated by as much as 85 miles and featuring fossils of early flowering plants, animals (including ancient camels, buffalo-size pigs, and bear-

dogs), and spectacularly colorful rocks formed millennia ago by drifts of ancient volcanic ash. The fossils of over a hundred different animal species have been found in the monument. While the world-renowned fossil sites more than justify this road trip, you'll also enjoy the spectacular but little-visited ranch country of the John Day River valley, with step-sided canyon walls resembling ancient ziggurats.

The John Day fossil beds were laid down between 25 and 40 million years ago, when this area was a coastal plain with a tropical climate. Then a period of extensive volcanism commenced, producing clouds of ash and mudflows that buried entire ecosystems in a matter of hours, like a plant and animal Pompeii. The cycle recurred over millions of years; life would return to the area, and again be buried beneath the residue of distant eruptions. Locked in stone, these fossil remains awaited the mightily erosive John Day River to unlock their story.

The monument's Clarno Unit is closest to Portland and just southwest of the small town of Fossil. The Clarno formations are studded with fossilized logs, seeds, and nuts and have eroded into distinctive, sheer white palisades topped with spires and turrets of stone.

Visit the monument's popular Painted Hills Unit late in the afternoon when the angle of the light intensifies the gold, red, and black bands on the hills, left by drifting volcanic ash some 33 million years ago. There are no fossils here, just an age-old landscape now weathered into soft, striped mounds of vivid hues. Not only are the hills themselves almost sensuously beautiful, but in the springtime they're covered with a blanket of wildflowers.

The monument's third unit, the Sheep Rock, has both fossil beds and a visitors center. Hike the Blue Basin trail, where intensely blue-green rocks tower, and lizards and the

The Painted Hills are known for their mesmerizing colors.

occasional rattlesnake contrast with fossil replicas of various animals—including a saber-toothed tiger and a miniature horse—that lay as they were found in this formation.

Towns here are few and far between but have their special charms. Particularly worth a visit is the Kam Wah Chung & Co. Museum in the town of John Day. At the time of eastern Oregon's 1860s gold rush, John Day had more Chinese than white settlers, and this small stone building was a de facto community center, medical clinic, opium parlor, and general store for the settlers, and today is the most interesting small-town historical museum in Oregon.

WHERE: The Clarno Unit is 152 miles southeast of Portland. To visit all 3 units involves a drive of 121 miles. Tel 541-987-2333; nps.gov/joda. **WHERE TO STAY:** Hotel Condon, Condon. Tel 800-201-6706 or 541-384-4624; hotel condon.com. *Cost:* from $100. **KAM WAH CHUNG & CO. MUSEUM:** John Day. Tel 541-575-2800; oregonstateparks.org. *When:* open May–Oct. **BEST TIME:** late Apr–May for comfortable hiking and wildflowers in the Painted Hills.

Quintessential Pacific Northwest R&R

SALISHAN SPA AND GOLF RESORT

Gleneden Beach, Oregon

Woodsy, naturally elegant, laid-back, romantic, Salishan Spa and Golf Resort is the Pacific Northwest's longtime favorite destination resort, famed equally for the quality of its links-style golf course and its superlative dining room. Built in the 1960s on 250 acres overlooking Siletz Bay, Salishan preserves the natural beauty of the forest and coast by integrating the resort into its setting—in its time a revolutionary concept. Local wood and stone were used for the homes, lodge, and spa—bringing the outside in—and the golf course is landscaped with indigenous plantings. Salishan's par-71 golf course follows the flow of the land, winding through dunes and forests and by the shores of the bay. There is also a full-service spa (you'll long remember the fireside massage), tennis courts, and a heated indoor swimming pool popular with kids and golf widows.

Built of local cedar and scattered around the wooded property, the resort's 21 villas are separated by wooden walkways and bridges, and a romantic sense of seclusion prevails. Each room has a fireplace, original Northwest art, and oversize windows and balconies to take in the views. Most guests have a favorite spot at Salishan: the Dining Room, with some of the most acclaimed fare in Oregon. This is classic Pacific Northwest cuisine at its peak—rich in fresh fish and seafood, ranch beef and lamb from the area, plus a cornucopia of local berries, nuts, and cheeses. And then there's the wine cellar. Estimates of the cellar range between 10,000 and 15,000 bottles—no one seems to know for sure—so finding the perfect wine to complement the evening's menu (perhaps a rare Oregon pinot noir from their prizewinning collection) should be a delight.

WHERE: 95 miles southwest of Portland; 7760 Hwy. 101 N., Gleneden Beach. Tel 800-452-2300 or 541-764-3600; salishan.com. *Cost:* from $159 (off-peak), from $185 (peak); greens fees from $59 (off-peak), from $99 (peak). **BEST TIMES:** July–Oct for weather. Nearby Lincoln City has 3 well-known annual kite festivals, the largest on the last weekend in June (oregoncoast.org).

With hiking trails, private beach access, and a woodsy setting, Salishan is fully immersed in nature.

Where the Cultural Beat Goes On

JACKSONVILLE AND THE BRITT FESTIVALS

Jacksonville, Oregon

The oldest settlement in southern Oregon, Jacksonville began as a gold rush boomtown and thrived as an 1860s trade hub and county seat with handsome commercial buildings and elegant Victorian homes. Then, like many a town in the American West, it became a backwater when the mainline railroad passed it by in the 1890s.

Jacksonville languished for decades until preservationists' efforts earned its entire downtown a rare National Historic Landmark

District designation in 1966—one of only a handful in the nation. Today, handsomely preserved Jacksonville is both a working community and an open-air architectural museum, and its Italianate courthouse is the museum of the Southern Oregon Historical Society. In the center of town, the Jacksonville Inn, built in the gold rush days of the 1860s using brick and gold-flecked mortar, is one of the state's oldest buildings to house an inn. The inn's restaurants, with patio dining during the summer months and extensive wine lists, have each won a clutch of international awards.

Jacksonville's most celebrated citizen, the acclaimed photographer Peter Britt, first came west in 1852 as a Swiss immigrant in search of gold with just $5 in his pocket. He eventually opened Oregon's first winery and the first photographic studio west of the Rockies, and when he died in 1905 he had chronicled a half-century of history. His name is carried on by the Britt Festivals, a summer-long binge of outdoor concerts held since 1963 on land he once owned. The core of the festival takes place over three weeks in August and attracts world-class performers, from jazz to blues and the performing arts.

Where: 223 miles south of Portland. *Visitor info:* Tel 541-899-8118; jacksonville oregon.org. **Southern Oregon Historical Society Museum:** Tel 541-773-6536; sohs .org. *When:* closed Mon–Tues. **Jacksonville Inn:** Tel 800-321-9344 or 541-899-1900; jacksonvilleinn.com. *Cost:* from $159; dinner $60. **Britt Festivals:** Tel 800-882-7488 or 541-773-6077; brittfest.org. *Cost:* tickets from $32. *When:* mid-June–mid-Sept.

Specialty shops, galleries, and coffeehouses inhabit historic downtown Jacksonville's landmark buildings.

Oregon's Highest Peak

MOUNT HOOD

Oregon

"Mount Hood is in full view . . . rising at every turn, solitary, majestic, awe inspiring, the ruling spirit of the landscape." So wrote naturalist John Muir about the Cascade peak closest to Portland. It is the state's highest, and its silhouette is almost iconic for Oregonians. Winter or summer, this glacier-clad 11,249-foot volcano exerts a mighty pull. Many visitors to Portland take a day trip to Mount Hood—which reaches into the sky like a mighty incisor—and some make it a vacation destination.

Campers may claim that a tent tucked into a forested glade is the best place to stay on Mount Hood, but those looking for creature comforts among the mountain wilderness will check in at Timberline Lodge. Built during the Depression by unemployed craftspeople hired by the Works Progress Administration, Timberline is the very model of rustic Northwest Craftsman design, with handmade furniture in the lodge rooms, handwoven curtains, and newel posts hewn from giant logs.

The lodge's Cascade Dining Room is considered the best on the mountain.

This is also where you'll begin the 41-mile Timberline Trail for a summertime trek encircling the mountain. There's even summertime skiing at Timberline Ski Area—head for Palmer Lift reaching up to more than 8,500 feet, making it the mountain's highest; it stays open nearly year-round for skiing and snowboarding on its vast glacier. Timberline is just one of the mountain's five ski areas, with Mount Hood Meadows being the largest and most visited because of its varied territory and network of trails. For the country's largest lighted nighttime ski area, visit Mount Hood SkiBowl, the closest of them all to Portland.

Many summer visitors come to hike the dormant volcano (moderate experience is enough to get you to the top, making it the most climbed major peak in the U.S.) or to hike to the many waterfalls or clear lakes, with eyes cast down to enjoy wildflowers (even orchids) and up to catch sight of the top of Mount Hood. In summer, there's no better reflecting pool than Trillium Lake, just south of the mountain, which captures a perfect image of the peak—and serves as a wonderful swimming pond for dusty hikers along the Cascade's crest.

Hike some of the easy trails southeast of Mount Hood for gorgeous views, or wait in nearby Portland for clear weather, when "the mountain is out."

WHERE: 60 miles east of Portland. *Visitor info:* Tel 503-622-5560; mthood.info. **TIMBERLINE:** Tel 800-547-1406 or 503-272-3311; timberlinelodge.com. *Cost:* from $135; dinner $55; lift tickets from $66. *When:* ski season late Nov–early Aug. **MOUNT HOOD MEADOWS:** Tel 503-337-2222; skihood.com. *Cost:* lift tickets $74. *When:* late Nov–Apr. **SKIBOWL:** Tel 800-SKIBOWL or 503-272-3206; skibowl.com. *Cost:* lift tickets $50. *When:* late Nov–Apr. **BEST TIMES:** Jan–Mar for skiing or boarding; late July–early Sept for hiking; July–Aug for wildflowers.

The Pacific's Coastal Masterpiece

THE OREGON COAST

Oregon

Sculpted by the turbulent, pounding waves of the Pacific, Oregon's 362-mile coastline is one of nature's masterworks. Thanks to a farsighted state government in the 1910s, the entire length of the coast in Oregon was set aside as public land, which has left most of it, especially in the central and southern regions, nearly undeveloped.

For one of the most awe-inspiring road trips in America, follow U.S. Route 101 and the western edge of the continent from north to south. Begin at the northern outpost of Astoria, the richly historic city where the Columbia River flows into the Pacific (see p. 865). At Cannon Beach, northern Oregon's most beautiful seaside village (see p. 868), sandy beaches stretch for miles, interrupted by massive basalt sea stacks such as the iconic 235-foot Haystack Rock. Route 101 stays close to the coast, traversing river valleys and climbing up over the flanks of mountains that reach to the Pacific. The view from Neahkahnie Mountain, where the road edges around 700-foot cliffs that drop into the surging Pacific, is of wide-open seascape—on a clear day, you can see 50 miles.

At Tillamook, home to dozens of dairies and the famed Tillamook Cheese Factory, the highway tucks inland, passing forests and dairy and artichoke farms, before rejoining the Pacific at Lincoln City, just north of Oregon's beloved Salishan Spa and Golf Resort (see p. 872).

Newport is the central Oregon coast's largest city, a hardworking seaport dominated by a high-arching bridge. The Oregon Coast Aquarium, once home to the orca Keiko (of *Free Willy* film fame) and one of the coast's top attractions, provides a fascinating glimpse into the northern Pacific's sea and intertidal life (a favorite resident is the octopus with a 20-foot span). Or encounter Oregon's aquatic life in the wild—at Newport's harbor, join a whale-watching tour and journey out into the Pacific where gray whales breach and spout as they pass between their winter and summer feeding grounds. About 20,000 pass by here each year, and when the numbers are dense, you don't even have to leave shore to watch. Newport's quirky Sylvia Beach Hotel (named for the American owner of the Shakespeare and Co.

bookstore in Paris during the 1920s and '30s) is the coast's most unusual refuge—a hotel dedicated to book-lovers. Its 20 guest rooms (don't expect TV or wi-fi) are decorated to evoke the spirit and work of various authors, including Agatha Christie, Colette, and Mark Twain. Even nonguests should book at the hotel's well-regarded Tables of Content restaurant: Hope for the ubiquitous fresh oysters for which Newport is widely known.

South of Yachats (pronounced YA-hots) is the most rugged stretch of the Oregon coast, where ancient volcanoes and lava flows meet the Pacific. Towering 830 feet above the roiling waters, Cape Perpetua is one of the area's highest points, in every sense of the word, with scenic lookouts and hiking trails. Just south is Heceta Head Lighthouse, probably the most photographed spot in all Oregon. This stark white, functioning lighthouse on a rocky headland 205 feet above the Pacific is jaw-droppingly dramatic. The beautifully maintained 1894 lighthouse keeper's home is one of the very few in the U.S. that is open as a B&B. The breakfasts enjoy a certain fame, as does the resident ghost. The nearby Sea Lion Caves is another natural wonder—a natural sea grotto, the largest in the country, populated by smelly, shrieking sea lions. A 208-foot elevator descends into the sea cave, where you can watch hundreds of Steller's sea lions clambering onto rocks, jockeying for position, and letting loose mighty roars (bulls can weigh more than a ton).

South of Florence, the Oregon Dunes, among the largest oceanfront sand dunes in the world, extend along the coast for over 40 miles. Hiking trails explore this unusual ecosystem, linking scrub forests, small lakes, and some 27,200 acres of mighty, ever-shifting dunes, some measuring up to 500 feet high.

From Charleston south to the California border, the beaches are increasingly flanked by high cliffs and craggy teeth of rock, home to rookeries of puffins, penguinlike murres, and wheeling gulls. Human comforts are not abandoned, however. Bandon, one of the most charming towns along the coast (see p. 866), is equal

The Heceta Head Lighthouse—also serving as a B&B—is the brightest light on the Oregon coast, with a beam reaching some 21 miles out into the ocean.

parts New Age retreat and golf mecca. The state's most famous river, the fast-flowing Rogue, meets the Pacific at Gold River; just upstream is an excellent lodge and opportunities for unmatched fishing and exhilarating jet-boat trips on the river's surging rapids (see p. 880).

Drive off into the sunset, as Route 101's final stretch in Oregon keeps getting more and more beautiful. Just 6 miles above the California border, Brookings basks in Oregon's "banana belt": Mild winter temperatures enable palm trees to grow in this pleasant harbor city, and wild azaleas bloom every year in late May. But this is also home to the northernmost range of the West's giant coast redwoods, more commonly associated with northern California.

WHERE: from Astoria, 95 miles northwest of Portland, to Brookings, 318 miles south of Portland. *Visitor info:* Tel 888-OCVA-101 or 541-574-2679; visittheoregoncoast.com. **TILLAMOOK CHEESE FACTORY:** Tillamook. Tel 503-815-1300; tillamook.com/cheese-factory. **OREGON COAST AQUARIUM:** Newport. Tel 541-867-3474; aquarium.org. **SYLVIA BEACH HOTEL:** Newport. Tel 888-795-8422 or 541-265-5428; sylviabeachhotel.com. *Cost:* from $120; dinner $28. **HECETA HEAD LIGHTHOUSE B&B:** Yachats. Tel 866-547-3696 or 541-547-3696; hecetalighthouse.com. *Cost:* from $133 (off-peak), from $209 (peak). **SEA LION CAVES:** Tel 541-547-3111; sealioncaves.com. **OREGON DUNES:** Reedsport. Tel 541-271-3611. **BEST TIMES:** Mar–May for whale-watching; June–Sept for warmer weather; fall and winter for seal viewing at Sea Lion Caves; winter months for storm watching.

Let 'er Buck!

PENDLETON ROUND-UP

Pendleton, Oregon

Even on its most placid days, one senses that Pendleton isn't afraid of a party. Eastern Oregon's largest city, Pendleton sits at the foot of the Blue Mountains, where rolling cattle ranch country meets the Umatilla Indian Reservation, the state's second largest. Rowdiness has a long tradition here: One of the city's best attractions is a tour of the 1890s "underground"—a subterranean network of opium dens, card rooms, jail cells, speakeasies, and shady businesses that thrived beneath the streets in days when gold was discovered in the nearby mountains.

But all this seems pretty tame when mid-September rolls around and the town breaks loose for the Pendleton Round-Up, held every year since 1910. During this weeklong celebration, the streets are lined with vendors selling everything from cowboy hats to tattoos. The bars and restaurants burst at the seams, strains of live country-and-western music drift down the streets, and lodgings are booked months in advance. Cowboys, real and urban, come from far and wide to this well-known event in the rodeo world, one of the largest and oldest in North America.

The four-day rodeo itself—with bronco busting, calf roping, and barrel racing—is the Round-Up's centerpiece, but there are many other diversions. The temporary Indian tepee encampment behind the rodeo grounds is where tribal members from around the Northwest come to meet, socialize, and sell handmade arts and crafts. Visit the Round-Up Hall of Fame museum under the grandstands, and then quench your thirst at the Let 'er Buck Room, which is, for these few days a year, perhaps the wildest bar in Oregon. At night, the Happy Canyon Pageant, long a fixture at the Round-Up, depicts the opening of the West in a series of vignettes, with strutting cowboys and traditional Umatilla dancing.

The Umatilla Reservation is home to three confederated tribes: the Cayuse, Umatilla, and Walla Walla. For a deeper look at their culture, visit the Tamástslikt Cultural Institute, a few miles northeast of downtown, which focuses on the impact the Oregon Trail and the pioneer settlements had on the indigenous peoples of this region. Or, for those who are still in party mode, the nearby tribal Wildhorse Casino Resort offers a chance to bankroll the next vacation.

In between Round-Up events, fill a few good hours with a visit to the Pendleton Woolen Mills, a fixture since 1909. Take the short, informative factory tour to see the famous blankets being made and shop the outlet store for good values. One venue in town not to miss is Virgil's at Cimmiyotti's, an old-fashioned saloon and steak house with excellent beer and a few unexpected new options like jambalaya and delicious crab cakes.

WHERE: 208 miles east of Portland. *Visitor info:* Tel 541-276-7411; pendletonchamber .com. **PENDLETON UNDERGROUND TOURS:** Tel 541-276-0730; pendletonundergroundtours .org. *When:* tours Mon–Sat, Mar–Oct; call for winter schedule. **PENDLETON ROUND-UP:** Tel 800-457-6336 or 541-276-2553; pendleton roundup.com. *When:* mid-Sept. **TAMÁSTSLIKT CULTURAL INSTITUTE:** Tel 541-966-9748; tamastslikt.org. **PENDLETON WOOLEN MILLS:** Tel 541-276-6911; pendleton-usa.com. *When:* free mill tours Mon–Fri. **VIRGIL'S:** Tel 541-276-7711; virgilsatcimmiyottis.com. *Cost:* dinner $40. **BEST TIME:** On Fri of Round-Up week, catch the 9 A.M. Westward Ho! Parade through Pendleton's downtown.

Party Time in the Microbrew Capital of the Nation

OREGON BREWERS FESTIVAL

Portland, Oregon

"Beervana": that's a word you hear bandied about at the Oregon Brewers Festival, the big beer party held every July since 1988 in Portland's Tom McCall Waterfront Park. It may refer to the festival itself, hailed by many as the finest crafts beer festival and the largest of its kind in the nation, or to Portland, an exceptionally beer-friendly town with more microbreweries and brewpubs than any other city in the world.

More than 100 brewers from around the world fill grassy Waterfront Park, the city's front yard spread out along the Willamette River. Festive it is, with good grub from local restaurants and live music that will transport you back to your campus days, though the beer back then never tasted this good.

If the crowded festival scene is not your cup of tea, spend time touring the city's countless local brewpubs. It won't take long to realize why Portland is the only logical choice to host a major beer festival. Starting in the mid-1980s, microbreweries and brewpubs began opening in the city at a dizzying rate, touting an independent and small-is-beautiful ethos. Entrepreneurial beer gurus founded BridgePort (Oregon's oldest), Widmer, and Portland Brewing, all getting their starts around the same time and flourishing still—these popular brews are widely distributed across the West. The McMenamin brothers started brewing beer while in college and now have 65 pubs in Oregon and Washington. Many of the McMenamin operations are housed in revitalized, funky, and sometimes historic buildings; the county's former poor farm, a movie palace, and even a century-old grade school are reincarnated as microbrew pubs (and sometimes lodging) that promise "the McMenamin experience." Smaller operations, such as Hair of the Dog, which brews rich, quasi-chocolaty beers, have cultlike followings. And for a real Portland experience, hang out on the dog-friendly back patio of the Lucky Labrador, housed in an old sheet-metal warehouse just over the Hawthorne Bridge from downtown.

Of course, not everyone in Portland has forsaken international or national brands for locally made hoppy ales. At Nick's Famous

Coney Island, a low-key outpost of blue-collar Americana in the otherwise deeply alternative Hawthorne neighborhood, you can get a frosty Heidelberg on tap to go with their famed Coney-style hot dogs.

Where: Tom McCall Waterfront Park. Tel 503-778-5917; oregonbrewfest.com. *When:* last full weekend in July. **Bridgeport Brewpub:** Tel 503-241-3612; bridgeportbrew .com. **Widmer:** Tel 503-281-2437; widmer brothers.com. **Portland Brewing:** Tel 503-228-5269; portlandbrewing.com. **McMenamin:** mcmenamins.com. *Cost:* lodging from $75. **Hair of the Dog:** Tel 503-232-6585; hair ofthedog.com. **Lucky Labrador:** Tel 503-236-3555; luckylab.com. **Nick's Famous Coney Island:** Tel 503-235-3008; nicks famousconeys.com.

The City of Roses, a Paradise for Green Thumbs

Portland's Public Gardens

Portland, Oregon

Here's a little-known fact: The world's most spectacular gardens are found within the USDA's climatic Zone 8, the climate that Portland shares with most of the British Isles, much of France, northern Italy, and large areas

of Japan—in short, the world's best gardening zip codes. Combine this favorable gardening climate (characterized by four definite seasons but mild winters) with the incredibly fertile soils of Portland, at the base of the Willamette Valley (see p. 883), and you've got a city where—literally—everything's coming up roses.

In the months of glorious (and dry) weather between late spring and early autumn, Portland's infamously dreary winter rainy season seems like a modest price to pay for a gardener's paradise. Evidence of the city's mild climate, plentiful rain, and sunny summers is everywhere, from world-famous public

gardens owned by Portland Public Parks (which manages 200 parks in Portland

There are around 300 Japanese gardens in the world outside Japan, but Portland's is considered one of the most authentic.

encompassing over 10,000 acres, including 5,000-acre Forest Park, the largest urban wilderness park in the country) to neighborhoods where many residents forgo the traditional front lawn in favor of lush jungles of both familiar and unusual plants. The city's gardens reflect something of the spirit of Portland itself: vibrant, eclectic, creative, and outdoorsy. This nonconformist individualism is practically Portland's civic ethos, and along with an endearingly scruffy funkiness, it gives this city—Oregon's largest—its particular charm.

Portland has been called the "City of Roses" at least since the Lewis & Clark Centennial exhibition in 1905, when roses lined 200 miles of the young city's streets. The holy of holies for enthusiasts is the International Rose Test Garden in Washington Park, in downtown Portland's West Hills. Established in 1917, it boasts more than 7,000 rosebushes representing over 550 varieties (most are new hybrids being tested before marketing) in a magnificent 5-acre location, with a spectacular view across the city toward Mount Hood. Its June Rose Festival is considered by many to be the city's biggest celebration.

Rhododendrons also thrive in Portland's moist and mild climate, and the Crystal Springs Rhododendron Garden in southeast Portland features more than 2,000 rhododendrons and azaleas in a gorgeous setting with spring-fed waterfalls, streams, and lakes.

Reflecting the city's Pacific Rim location are two of the finest examples of Far Eastern garden traditions outside Asia. A stone's throw from the International Rose Test Garden, Portland's renowned Japanese Garden offers five formal garden types in 5.5 serene acres, with a teahouse and koi-filled ponds. Unveiled in 2000, the Lan Su Chinese Garden occupies an entire downtown block at the edge of Chinatown and is the largest of its kind outside China. It was built by artisans from Portland's sister city Suzhou, which shares a similar climate and is also famous for its gardens—hundreds of years older, perhaps, but no more inspiring.

Forest Park: Tel 503-823-4492. **International Rose Test Garden:** Tel 503-823-3636; portlandoregon.gov/parks. **Crystal Springs Rhododendron Garden:** Tel 503-771-8386. **Japanese Garden:** Tel 503-223-1321; japanesegarden.com. **Lan Su Chinese Garden:** Tel 503-228-8131; lansugarden.com. **Best times:** May for the wisteria blooming in the Japanese Garden; late May for peak bloom at the Rhododendron Garden; June for heaviest bloom at the Rose Test Garden and the month-long Portland Rose Festival (rosefestival.org).

A River of Legend and Beauty

THE ROGUE RIVER

Oregon

Y ou won't be the first to discover the dramatic beauty of southern Oregon's Rogue River—but at least you'll be in good company. Zane Grey, Teddy Roosevelt, and Herbert Hoover journeyed here in the early 1900s to enjoy the rustic comforts of Rogue-side fishing lodges. With the advent of Hollywood, such stars as John Wayne, Clark Gable, Bing Crosby, and Carole Lombard came to the Rogue for a bit of backcountry R&R. Meryl Streep even battled the Rogue's white water as she trained for her splashy 1994 thriller, *The River Wild*. Clearly the Rogue is a river with star power.

From its beginnings on the flanks of Crater Lake (see p. 870) to its entry into the Pacific at Gold Beach, the Rogue charts an impetuous westward course through the lower left-hand corner of Oregon. From its Cascade Range headwaters, the river plunges through lava canyons and dense forests, then, after slowing in an arid pear-growing valley near Medford, cuts a precipitous path through the crenellated Coast Range. This portion of the Rogue, preserved in the Wild Rogue Wilderness Area, is one of the most legendary white-water rivers in the U.S. Within its canyon, the river drops sharply through a 34-mile series of chutes and chasms, providing an adrenaline-pumping three-day white-water adventure of Class III and IV rapids. As it nears the Pacific, the river slows and broadens. Flanked by dense coastal forest, this majestic stretch of the Rogue draws outdoorsmen of another sort who come for fantastic fishing: Chinook salmon and fighting steelhead are the prize.

Which of the Rogue's multiple personalities you'll get to know depends on where you test the waters. Just east of Grants Pass, the beloved Weasku Inn (as in "We ask you in") sits on the banks of the Rogue amid towering pine and fir trees. The handsome log lodge, originally built in 1924, was a favorite of Hollywood celebrities, and its woodsy charm and warm welcome are still potent. A complete renovation left the rustic elegance of its lodge rooms and riverfront cabins intact.

Near the mouth of the river at Gold Beach, just 7 miles from the Pacific, is the Tu Tu' Tun Lodge (with the accent on the second syllable), a sophisticated retreat for anglers or anyone seeking a tranquil escape and one of Oregon's best-loved getaways. Fishing is excellent on the lower reaches of the Rogue, and Tu Tu' Tun Lodge will set you up with a guide to help you catch your limit. Looking for something more exhilarating? Powerful jet boats depart from the lodge dock and head upstream, reaching the edge of the Rogue's wilderness canyon boundary before bouncing through rapids back to the lodge.

Rogue River is known for some of the country's best white-water rafting in an extraordinary setting.

The fun is extensive, but equally attractive are Tu Tu' Tun Lodge's gracious hospitality and acclaimed restaurant. Meals here are sumptuous, celebrating the bounty of the nearby river, ocean, and forests. In the evening, guests gather for hors d'oeuvres on the terrace before adjourning to the candlelit dining room, perhaps to enjoy fresh wild Chinook salmon with fruit jalapeño salsa and popovers, a lodge specialty. The rooms are spacious, many with water-view decks, some with fireplaces and outdoor soaking tubs, all with a restrained elegance that merges effortlessly with the serene woodlands.

WHERE: Grants Pass is 60 miles north of the California border. **RAFTING:** Rogue Wilderness Adventures. Tel 800-336-1647 or 541-479-9554; wildrogue.com. *Cost:* 3-day trip with camping $829; 3-day trip with lodge accommodation $1,069. **WEASKU INN:** Grants Pass. Tel 800-493-2758 or 541-471-8000; weasku.com. *Cost:* from $279. **TU TU' TUN LODGE:** Gold Beach. Tel 800-864-6357 or 541-247-6664; tututun.com. *Cost:* from $150 (off-peak), from $255 (peak); dinner $55. **BEST TIMES:** The height of the rafting season is late July; Chinook salmon fishing season peaks in Oct.

High, Wide, and Lonesome

STEENS MOUNTAIN & MALHEUR NATIONAL WILDLIFE REFUGE

Oregon

O regon's southeast corner, on the edge of the Great Basin Desert, is a dramatic land of extremes. It is archetypal American West, with vast, arid, underpopulated stretches of sagebrush, coyotes, and barbed wire.

Rising above this austere landscape is spectacular Steens Mountain, a 30-mile-long uplifted fault block nearly 10,000 feet high at its peak. Its broad west flank, marked by huge glacier-cut valleys, rises gradually through aspen groves and alpine meadows, whereas the east face drops precipitously to the alkali flats of the Alvord Desert nearly a mile below. Wild horses, pronghorn antelopes, and bighorn sheep roam the mountain, which is also home to sage grouse and golden eagles, while rare Lahontan trout can be found in tiny glacier-scoured Wildhorse Lake.

Stretched along the base of Steens's west side is the Malheur National Wildlife Refuge, a major stop for migratory birds on the Pacific Flyway and a birding mecca of the Northwest. Over 320 species visit the refuge—waterfowl, shorebirds, songbirds, and raptors—most drawn by the oasis of lakes, streams, and marshes in the otherwise parched region, remnants of Ice Age lakes.

At the southern end of the refuge is Frenchglen, with the small middle-of-nowhere 1920s-era Frenchglen Hotel, popular among travelers (especially bird-watchers) for its simple charms, Western ambience, and warm hospitality. The dining room's hearty family-style dinner is popular with nonguests as well. Frenchglen is also the starting-off point for the 66-mile Steens Mountain Loop Road,

a summer-only scenic byway that passes through portions of the Malheur refuge and ascends to the mountain's crest, where the panorama across southeastern Oregon is nothing less than spectacular.

WHERE: Frenchglen is 318 miles southeast of Eugene. **MALHEUR NATIONAL WILDLIFE REFUGE:** Princeton. Tel 541-493-4222; fws.gov/refuge/malheur. **FRENCHGLEN HOTEL:** Frenchglen. Tel 541-493-2825; oregonstate parks.org. *Cost:* from $75. *When:* mid-Mar–Nov. **STEENS MOUNTAIN LOOP ROAD:** Road conditions, tel 541-573-4400. **BEST TIMES:** Apr–May and Sept–Oct for birding and mild weather.

Verdant Kiger Gorge exemplifies Steens Mountain's valleys, which, cut by glaciers rather than rivers, are U-shaped instead of V-shaped.

OREGON COUNTRY FAIR

Veneta, Oregon

S orry you never really embraced your inner hippie? Then save the second weekend in July for the Oregon Country Fair, a one-of-a-kind countercultural arts and crafts fair heavy with great music, good food, and exhibits on how

to live in harmony with the earth. The Oregon Country Fair grew out of the hippie movement that thrived in nearby Eugene, home to the University of Oregon, and it quickly gained its reputation as a cross between Woodstock, a circus, a love-in, and a New Age pilgrimage site. Volunteers plan year-round for this one fleeting and much-awaited weekend in July, when 45,000 like-minded artists and free-thinkers from around the world gather to celebrate, listen to music, and get happy.

The three-day fair is held among a labyrinth of forested trails next to the Long Tom River west of Eugene and features more than 900 artisans, over 20 stages (madcap vaudeville acts are a Country Fair specialty), and some 70 food booths. Several times each day, a whimsical parade winds through the

shaded fairgrounds, with stilt walkers, jugglers, "country fairies," and whirling dancers (booths can supply costumes and masks to help you blend in). This is also one of the largest juried crafts fairs in the world, and the excellent live entertainment on and off stage makes this an exuberant event for just about anybody with an adventurous spirit—former flower child or not.

Despite its freewheeling nature, the fair is entirely drug- and alcohol-free and is family-friendly for those who don't mind seeing lots of happy folks not always fully clothed.

WHERE: 13 miles west of Eugene. Tel 541-343-4298; oregoncountryfair.org. *Cost:* $25. Tickets must be bought in advance at Tickets West; tel 800-325-7328 or 503-224-8499; ticketswest.com. *When:* 2nd weekend in July.

WILLAMETTE VALLEY

Oregon

B eginning in the 1840s, the Oregon Trail funneled thousands of settlers into the Willamette Valley ("That's Will-AM-ette, dammit!"), many of them farmers drawn by the fertile soil that massive Ice Age floods had poured

into the valley millennia earlier. With abundant water and ideal growing conditions—warm, dry summers and ample rain the rest of the year—the area from Eugene to Portland

became a phenomenally productive agricultural center.

However, wine grapes have since transformed the culture of the Willamette Valley. In the 1960s a few maverick winemakers defied the conventional wisdom that the northerly climate was too marginal for wine grapes. They introduced vineyards to the valley and spawned a booming industry that has put Oregon prominently on the viticulture map. Pinot noir is the unconditional leader, though pinot gris and chardonnay thrive here as well.

Route 99W, the main road through Yamhill County—the heart of northern Oregon's wine country—is frequently clogged with traffic, but the back roads, winding through vineyards and oak groves, are ideal for bicycling or a lazy drive. Many wineries operate tasting rooms, and most are open daily in summer and on weekends in winter. You can also explore the valley's bounty through the wine lists of the area's growing number of small, excellent restaurants.

Driving north to south through the heart of the valley, the first small town you'll find is Newberg—home of Rex Hill Vineyards, whose tasting room and museum both warrant a stop. Here you'll also find the area's most sophisticated accommodations at The Allison Inn & Spa, enveloped in 35 acres of gardens and vineyards. Another excellent facility is Ponzi Vineyards in Sherwood, one of the pioneers of top-shelf Oregon pinot noirs.

Don't miss the area's top dining room at the Joel Palmer House, created by the celebrated Jack Czarnecki, a truffle- and mushroom-hunting chef whose award-winning restaurant has been a regular destination for food pilgrims since 1966.

Oregon Trail pioneers flocked to Willamette Valley for agricultural opportunities; today its growing importance attracts oenophiles.

WHERE: Newberg is 15 miles southwest of Portland. *Visitor info:* Tel 503-228-8336; oregonwine.org. **REX HILL VINEYARDS:** Newberg. Tel 503-538-0666; rexhill.com. **ALLISON INN & SPA:** Newberg. Tel 877-294-2525 or 503-554-2525; theallison.com. *Cost:* from $350. **ARGYLE WINERY:** Dundee. Tel 503-538-8520; argylewinery.com. **PONZI VINEYARDS:** Sherwood. Tel 503-628-1227; ponziwines.com. **JOEL PALMER HOUSE:** Dayton. Tel 503-864-2995; joelpalmerhouse.com. *Cost:* 3-course tasting menu $55. **BEST TIMES:** Memorial Day weekend and Thanksgiving weekend for special tastings at boutique wineries otherwise closed to the public; the International Pinot Noir Celebration in McMinnville in late July (ipnc.org); Jan for the Oregon Truffle Festival.

Northern Outposts of Culture and Recreation

BELLINGHAM & MOUNT BAKER

Washington

Tucked into the far northwest corner of Washington, only 18 miles shy of the Canadian border, Bellingham is a handsome and appealing old seaport perched on a series of hills overlooking busy Bellingham Bay and the forested San Juan Islands (see p. 896). Rising behind the city is Mount Baker, crowned with glaciers and hornlike peaks. Add to this great location the youthful high spirits of 15,000 Western Washington University students, a hip cultural scene, and easy access to Vancouver, British Columbia (see p. 1047), less than an hour to the north, and you've got one of the Pacific Northwest's most vital and enjoyable small cities.

While downtown Bellingham has broad, tree-lined avenues and handsome redbrick storefronts, the Fairhaven neighborhood to the south is where you'll find galleries, coffee bars, bookstores, and tempting restaurants. Overlooking Fairhaven's busy commercial harbor, the distinctive Chrysalis Inn is a European-style hotel with sleek and comfortable rooms, all with fireplaces and window seats. The Chrysalis Spa provides soothing relaxation after exploring Fairhaven's many diverse stores; dinner at the inn's Keenan's at the Pier combines fine wine, contemporary cuisine, and views onto the island-sprinkled bay.

Immediately south of Fairhaven, 12th Street turns into 21-mile-long Chuckanut Drive (aka Highway 11), a highly scenic route built in 1913 to link Bellingham to the Skagit Valley (see next page) via a mountainous headland. In places, the roadway is chiseled out of sheer sandstone, with waterfalls tumbling down from the forests above and the swirling waters of Samish Bay pulsing at the base of cliffs. If such stirring seascapes should lead you to thoughts of seafood, pull in at the famed Oyster Bar on Chuckanut Drive, its deck and dining room overlooking Samish Bay and the San Juan Islands. It's been in business since the 1920s ("the oysters that we serve today slept last night in Samish Bay" is its longtime slogan).

Rising directly behind Bellingham is Mount Baker, a stunning 10,781-foot volcanic peak that's Bellingham's all-season recreational mecca. The 58-mile scenic Mount Baker Highway (Highway 542) leads from Bellingham past mighty fir forests and misty waterfalls to vista points at Picture Lake, whose postcard-perfect Mount Shuksan view is rumored to be the most photographed peak in the world. The road ends at Artist Point, elevation 5,140 feet, where the colossal white face of Mount Baker fills the sky. Snowfalls here are prodigious: Mount Baker holds the world record (an astonishing 95 feet in winter 1998–99). Skiers and snowboarders flock to the Mount Baker Ski Area, and in summer, the peak is a magnet for hikers and climbers—one of the most accessible glacial summits in the Lower 48.

WHERE: 90 miles north of Seattle. *Visitor info:* Tel 360-671-3990; bellingham.org. **CHRYSALIS INN:** Tel 888-808-0005 or 360-756-1005; thechrysalisinn.com. *Cost:* from $229; dinner $55. **OYSTER BAR:** Bow. Tel 360-766-6185; theoysterbar.net. *Cost:* dinner $55. **MOUNT BAKER SKI AREA:** Tel 360-734-6771; mtbaker.us. *Cost:* lift ticket $58. *When:* Nov–Apr. **BEST TIMES:** Jan–Mar for skiing; June–Sept for warm weather; July for the Bellingham Festival of Music (bellinghamfestival.org).

Bellingham's 1892 Old City Hall is now a museum.

SEMIAHMOO RESORT

Blaine, Washington

Just south of the Canadian border—and 45 minutes south of Vancouver—at the tip of a spit reaching out into Drayton Harbor, the Semiahmoo Resort Golf and Spa is home to two challenging and astoundingly beautiful golf courses. Each of the resort's courses, the Semiahmoo Golf and Country Club and the Loomis Golf Trail Club, has individually been rated the top public course in the state of Washington in recent years, making this a prime destination for serious golfers. The Semiahmoo course, designed by Arnold Palmer, puts its generous fairways in a natural tree-lined setting. Loomis Trail is known for its enormous Tudor-style clubhouse and the course's abundance of water—a system of canals and lakes means that every hole has a water feature.

This award-winning 212-room oceanfront resort is named for the Native people who lived on the coast of Washington and British Columbia and who today form British Columbia's Semiahmoo First Nation. Built on the site of a former salmon cannery, the resort boasts an atmospheric oyster bar and stylish lounge housed in the former packing area. It's located on a 1,000-acre wildlife preserve that reaches almost to Canada, with scenic paved bike and jogging paths. Golf widows can enjoy Semiahmoo Resort's full-service European spa or go salmon fishing or beachcombing. Exploring Drayton Harbor by sea kayak is a special adventure for bird-watchers, as the waters surrounding Semiahmoo Resort are ranked among the top birding areas on the West Coast—herons, cormorants, belted kingfishers, and a host of other shorebirds all make the preserve their home.

WHERE: 110 miles north of Seattle; 9565 Semiahmoo Pkwy. Tel 360-318-2000; semiahmoo.com. *Cost:* from $139 (off-peak), from $199 (peak); greens fees from $35 (off-peak), $70 (peak). **BEST TIME:** July–Oct for salmon fishing.

LA CONNER & THE SKAGIT VALLEY

Washington

La Conner, just north of where the Skagit River reaches Puget Sound, is a classic Northwest waterfront village, with a long and rich history, a thriving arts scene, and a beautiful maritime setting. La Conner has benefited from well-timed neglect. The little farming and seafaring village got its start in the 1860s, when settlers began building dikes to channel the Skagit. Little changed in this handsome, slumbering town until the mid-20th century, when La Conner's well-maintained and stylish

Victorian architecture and pretty harbor became a magnet for artists and writers such as Morris Graves, the noted Northwest painter, and Tom Robbins, author of *Even Cowgirls Get the Blues*. Soon, boutiques, fine inns, excellent restaurants, and antiques shops took up residence.

Much of La Conner's bustling business district faces onto sculpture-lined First Street, which parallels the Swinomish Channel, the narrow waterway separating the mainland from Fidalgo Island. For art lovers, the top stop is the Museum of Northwest Art, a spacious and coolly elegant exhibition space that features a permanent collection of contemporary works by Pacific Northwest artists, revolving exhibits by regional artists, and an excellent gift shop filled with local crafts.

Facing onto the Swinomish Channel is the appealing La Conner Channel Lodge, the town's only waterfront hotel. Oyster & Thistle Restaurant and Pub, located across the street in the lodge's sister property La Conner Country Inn, serves up the town's most sophisticated cuisine, melding the bounty of local farms and seafood from local fishermen with urbane European finesse.

The rich farmland around La Conner is some of the most productive in Washington and the most beautiful crop by far is spring bulbs. This is one of the nation's primary sources of tulip bulbs; in fact, more acreage is

Farmers cultivate acres and acres of tulips for their bulbs—the blooms' saturated color is a happy by-product for sightseers.

under tulip cultivation here than in Holland. April's Skagit Valley Tulip Festival draws nearly half a million people to the valley for a variety of art shows, street fairs, and parades—though most come just to drive or cycle the back roads and take in the amazing display of color.

WHERE: 60 miles north of Seattle. *Visitor info:* Tel 888-642-9284 or 360-466-4778; lovelaconner.com. **MUSEUM OF NORTHWEST ART:** Tel 360-466-4446; monamuseum.org. **LA CONNER CHANNEL LODGE:** Tel 888-466-4113 or 360-466-1500; laconnerlodging.com. *Cost:* from $139 (off-peak), from $219 (peak). **OYSTER & THISTLE RESTAURANT AND PUB:** Tel 360-766-6179; theoysterandthistle.com. *Cost:* dinner $55. **BEST TIMES:** Apr for bulb blooms and the Skagit Valley Tulip Festival (tulipfestival.org); June–Oct for weather; early Nov for the 3-day Art's Alive festival.

A Bit of Bavaria in the Cascades

LEAVENWORTH

Washington

With its spectacular setting on the eastern slope of Washington's Cascade Range, the town of Leavenworth would hardly seem to need a fanciful theme. But back in the 1960s, when the local economy took a nosedive, locals felt the need to drum up tourist business beyond what came from the typically frugal backpackers headed up Icicle Creek in the Washington Cascades. So the logging town of Leavenworth began its transformation into a little Bavaria. The Cascades were a pretty good stand-in for the Alps, and the makeover was successful—even though it is obviously faux alpine, the half-timbered buildings, painted flower boxes, carved wooden beams, and gabled roofs are quite attractive, even charming. In fact, at night when the entire town is outlined by

Crowds gather in Leavenworth every Saturday evening in December for the ceremonial lighting of the village's holiday decorations.

millions of tiny lights and a stray snowflake dances in the mountain air, you might fancy yourself to be in Bamberg. Festivals are a part of life in Leavenworth, and summer weekends sometimes provide an opportunity for the local dirndl-and-lederhosen set to polka through the streets to the accompaniment of accordions. You may even catch the scent of schnitzel and strudel.

You can expect a lovely meal at the elegant Mozart's Restaurant, where many of the dishes have a German or Austrian influence and can be enjoyed in the ambiance of a cozy European bistro. But it's downstairs, at the more casual Andreas Keller (*keller* means "cellar") that you'll be immersed in real *gemütlichkeit*. There's an accordionist here, and a wide array of sausages and German beer and the feeling that everyone is going to burst into song.

For many, the town's biggest charms are still its surroundings. Head up Icicle Road to the 3.5-mile Icicle Gorge loop trail for a view of cascading waterfalls and verdant Douglas fir forests. The trail brushes against the edge of the Alpine Lakes Wilderness Area, a haven for backpackers and rock climbers, and offers up some of the most beautiful mountain scenery in the state—and that's saying something.

A mile up Icicle Creek from Leavenworth, the stylish and comfortable Run of the River Inn & Refuge is a good place to settle into a

balcony swing and watch wildlife. With river-rock-lined hot tubs, stone fireplaces, and handmade pine furniture, each of the inn's six suites and a small cabin combines woodsy warmth and the luxury of a venerable mountain lodge.

During the winter, the 12 guest rooms of the Mountain Home Lodge, a modern but homey backcountry retreat with rustic Northwest touches, make a great base for exploring 20 miles of cross-country skiing or snowmobile touring. Wintertime access to the lodge, located on a secluded 20-acre meadow overlooking the Cascades, is via the lodge's snowcat or 4WD van. Meals are included in winter rates, and the sensation that you're snowbound here is a lovely one: The lodge is known as much for its excellent food as for its cozy, tranquil accommodations.

WHERE: 155 miles northeast of Seattle. *Visitor info:* Tel 509-548-5807; leavenworth .org. **MOZART'S RESTAURANT:** Tel 509-548-0600. *Cost:* dinner $40. **ANDREAS KELLER:** Tel 509-548-6000; andreaskellerrestaurant.com. *Cost:* dinner $30. **RUN OF THE RIVER:** Tel 800-288-6491 or 509-548-7171; runoftheriver.com. *Cost:* from $235. **MOUNTAIN HOME LODGE:** Tel 800-414-2378 or 509-548-7077; mthome.com. *Cost:* from $755 (summer), from $370 (winter; includes all meals). **BEST TIMES:** Jan–Mar for cross-country skiing; mid-May for Maifest;

late June for the Leavenworth International Accordion Celebration. There's no better spot in the Northwest to celebrate Oktoberfest, held in Oct (leavenworthoktoberfest.com).

Cape Cod of the Pacific Coast

LONG BEACH PENINSULA

Washington

Billboards on the Long Beach Peninsula, the thin sand spit stretching north from the Columbia River mouth, remind motorists that this 28-mile beach is the world's longest. Not that size matters—the Long Beach Peninsula offers one of the most unusual marine environments along the Pacific Coast, with fascinating history and unfussy beach towns that invite visitors to slow down and taste the oysters. Bivalves are big business here: On the west, the long arm of the peninsula is pounded by the Pacific, but to the east is Willapa Bay, a shallow river basin perfect for growing some of the most succulent oysters on the West Coast. And to those who know their seafood, these oysters are primo.

There's lots of family fun here, too. The small beach resort towns of Seaview and Long Beach are busy in summer with multiple-generation vacationers, and the strand bustles with carnival-like activity. Both towns have long pedigrees, dating from the 1880s, when Portland families journeyed up the Columbia River by steamboat to summer on the beach. A few lodgings from this era remain and have been beautifully restored, including the Shelburne Inn, built in 1896 as a stagecoach inn. The entire building is a jewel of late 19th-century craftsmanship and has been carefully preserved and refurbished with period fixtures—and outfitted with modern comforts for 21st-century guests. The inn's cozy restaurant is a showcase of Northwest cuisine.

Long Beach is noted worldwide for its mid-August kite festival, so it was just a matter of time before someone opened a kite museum here. Kites have been used for scientific research, aerial photography, mail delivery, and reconnaissance—as well as for amusement—for centuries. The whole story's here at the World Kite Museum and Hall of Fame, along with 1,300 examples that include the largest, smallest, rarest, and wackiest.

Much of the quiet Willapa Bay is preserved as a wildlife sanctuary. Bird-watching, cranberry and oyster harvesting, and gracious dining occupy the time of residents and visitors. Both Nahcotta and Oysterville are centers for modern oyster production, but while Oysterville has more history (the entire town has been placed on the National Register of Historic Places and might well be the area's prettiest), Nahcotta has the Pickled Fish, a hip and casual restaurant/lounge on the top floor of the modern waterfront Adrift Hotel. Expect the finest and freshest the coastline has to offer.

WHERE: 120 miles northwest of Portland. *Visitor info:* Tel 800-451-2542 or 360-642-2400; funbeach.com. **SHELBURNE INN:** Seaview. Tel 360-642-2442; theshelburneinn.com. *Cost:* from $149; dinner $55. **WORLD KITE MUSEUM:** Tel 360-642-4020; kitefestival.com. **PICKLED FISH:** Tel 360-642-2344; pickledfish.com. *Cost:* dinner $35. **BEST TIMES:** June–Sept for weather; July for Sand Castle Competition in Long Beach; 3rd weekend in Aug for the Washington State International Kite Festival (kitefestival.com).

Unparalleled Cross-Country Skiing

THE METHOW VALLEY

Washington

Just east of Washington's North Cascades (see p. 893), the wide and mountain-flanked Methow (MET-how) Valley is known for its world-class cross-country skiing. In fact, with 130 miles of classic and ski-skate trails, the valley has one of North America's largest networks of groomed Nordic trails. And then there's the climate: East of the Cascade rain shadow, the skies are often clear and sunny here, and the snow is much lighter and dryer than that on Washington's western slopes, making it a winning destination for Nordic skiers.

In the Methow, cross-country has become a lifestyle, and a number of comfortable lodges cater to skiers' needs. The Freestone Inn, located on a ranch near the town of Mazama, has easy access to the trail network (with a number of trails paralleling the beautiful Methow River) and provides rentals, a guide service, and accommodations in cabins, large family lodges, and well-appointed lodge rooms.

Fifteen miles east of Mazama is Winthrop, a larger town with a Western-themed downtown. With a mix of galleries, antiques stores, and Western-style home decor shops, it's a destination in its own right.

There's only one really great place to stay in these parts: the luxurious Sun Mountain Lodge, just southwest of Winthrop. Its mountaintop perch affords views of the Methow Valley and the Cascade Mountains, and its interior holds handsome furniture made by local artisans. This rusticity adds counterpoint to the lodge's sophisticated service; it boasts an excellent dining room with breathtaking views from every angle. Skiers have the lodge's 3,000 acres all to themselves.

If you don't need pampering on your ski outing, consider Rendezvous Huts, a circuit of five backcountry huts in the Methow's least-visited area near Rendezvous Mountain. These cozy cabins (which sleep up to eight) are no-frills but comfortable—with a kitchen, sleeping loft, and plenty of firewood—and are a welcome sight at the end of a blissful day of skiing. If you're feeling like a splurge, pay a bit extra to have your food and gear brought in ahead by snowmobile.

WHERE: in summer, 193 miles from Seattle via SR 20; in winter, 243 miles from Seattle via I-5 and Wenatchee. **METHOW TRAILS:** Tel 509-996-3287; methowtrails.com. *When:* Nov–Mar. **FREESTONE INN:** Mazama. Tel 800-639-3809 or 509-996-3906; freestoneinn.com. *Cost:* from $199 (off-peak), from $245 (peak). **SUN MOUNTAIN LODGE:** Winthrop. Tel 800-572-0493 or 509-996-2211; sunmountainlodge.com. *Cost:* from $195 (off-peak), from $285 (peak). **RENDEZVOUS HUTS:** Tel 800-442-3048 or 509-996-8100; rendezvoushuts.com. *Cost:* from $175 a night for exclusive use of a cabin, or from $35 per person per night. **BEST TIMES:** Dec–Mar for cross-country conditions; mid-Feb for Winthrop's Snowshoe Softball Tournament (winthropwashington.com).

Ranch horses feed on hay in snowy Methow Valley.

Sentinels of Fire and Ice

MOUNT RAINIER NATIONAL PARK & MOUNT ST. HELENS

Washington

T wo of North America's mightiest and most explosive volcanoes, slumbering Mount Rainier and smoldering Mount St. Helens, stand side by side in the Cascade Range of volcanic mountains that extends from Canada to Northern California. Capped by 25 glaciers, 14,410-foot Mount Rainier is the highest and iciest volcano in the lower 48 states, and the tallest mountain in the Northwest. Often shrouded in clouds, its massive snowy dome towers over nearby Seattle and Tacoma, acting as a giant weather gauge. When it is in view, the locals simply say, "the mountain is out." With over 260 miles of trails and just two hours from Seattle, no other mountain invites such convenient exploration for Puget Sound residents.

In summer, a scenic drive from the popular Nisqually entrance of Mount Rainier National Park winds past waterfalls and old-growth forests to Paradise (5,400 feet), home of the mountain's most beautiful wildflower meadows and about as close as you can get to a glacier without crampons. To the east at 6,400 feet, the barren Sunrise viewpoint—all tundra, glaciers, and mountain goats—offers the biggest mountain views from the highest trails in the park. Heavy snowfall closes most roads in winter, bringing cross-country skiers and snowshoers. Two historic lodges provide dining and accommodations. The bustling 121-room Paradise Inn is the nicer of the two, with incredible mountain views and a mountain-man's Sunday Brunch. The smaller and quieter National Park Inn is down-slope in woodsy Longmire, with a front veranda where guests gather to swap trail information.

Only 35 miles south of Mount Rainier as the crow flies is Mount St. Helens (8,363 feet),

Mount St. Helens is part of the Cascade Volcanic Arc, which encompasses several major volcanoes and more than 4,000 volcanic vents.

an active volcano where you can witness the destructive forces of nature up close on a day trip. On May 18, 1980, this once quiet, beautifully symmetrical mountain with a fishing resort tucked away on Spirit Lake was devastated by a huge eruption of superheated steam. The volcano's top 1,300 feet were obliterated in a cataclysmic blast—with the equivalent force of 21,000 atomic bombs—that flattened 150 square miles of forests, triggered landslides and boiling mudflows, and fumed a 15-mile-high cloud of ash and rock into the air at speeds of 500 miles an hour. In the end, 59 people were killed in the blast, and a pall of volcanic ash drifted as far east as Saskatchewan. In 2004, a smaller explosion reawakened the possibility of another major eruption, and geologists keep a close eye on domes growing inside the crater.

Scenic Truman Highway (State Route 504) climbs up to Johnston Ridge Observatory, just 5 miles shy of ground zero, with a spectacular view of the sometimes smoking crater. In early summer a carpet of pink and violet flowers spreads across the desolate blast zone—life is returning to the once-devastated landscape.

WHERE: The Nisqually entrance to Mount Rainier National Park is 90 miles south of Seattle. **MOUNT RAINIER:** Tel 360-569-2211; nps.gov/mora. *When:* July–Sept; Nisqually entrance open year-round. **PARADISE INN AND NATIONAL PARK INN:** Nisqually entrance at Paradise and Longmire. Tel 360-569-2275; mtrainierguestservices.com. *Cost:* from $122. *When:* Paradise Inn closed mid-Oct–mid-May. **MOUNT ST. HELENS:** Tel 360-449-7800; fs.usda .gov/mountsthelens. *When:* Johnston Ridge Observatory, May–Oct; other facilities, year-round. **BEST TIMES:** June–early July for Mount St. Helens' wildflowers; July–Aug for Mount Rainier's wildflowers.

A Native American Pompeii

THE MAKAH MUSEUM

Neah Bay, Washington

At the far northwestern tip of the Olympic Peninsula, a long and increasingly winding cliffside road leads to Neah Bay, the leading town of the Makah Indian Reservation, a 27,000-acre holding for the Makah tribe's 2,400 members. This beautiful natural harbor on the Strait of Juan de Fuca, watched over by looming totem poles, has for centuries been home to the Makah, one of the great seafaring peoples of the native Pacific Northwest. Expert hunters, the Makah paddled large dugout canoes into the surging Pacific in pursuit of gray whales. The meat of the enormous sea mammals was used for food; the bones and other body parts were turned into tools; and the oil was both consumed and traded to other tribes.

That so much is known of precontact Makah life is the result of a tragic accident: Around 500 years ago, a massive mudslide on the western coast of the Olympic Peninsula engulfed part of a Makah village called Ozette. The surviving Ozette villagers—about 500 people lived there—were unable to retrieve anything from the buried village, and the site remained undisturbed for centuries. In the 1970s, another lashing Pacific storm exposed some timbers and artifacts from the old village. A passing hiker noticed the remains, contacted the tribe and archaeologists, and excavation of Ozette—the American Pompeii—began.

The astonishingly complete remains of the 16th-century Ozette village are now on display at the Makah Museum in Neah Bay. Excellent displays interpret the many objects found at the site—including a full-size replica longhouse and four cedar dugout canoes—illustrating the day-to-day life of the ancient people. The sophistication of the tribe's early life is exemplified by the refinement of their carving and basketry. To leave the museum and find oneself in the same environment where the ancient Makah spirit lives on produces a profound respect.

WHERE: 75 miles west of Port Angeles. *Visitor info:* makah.com. **MAKAH MUSEUM:** Tel 360-645-2711; makahmuseum.com. *When:* daily, year-round. **BEST TIME:** Makah Days, 3 days in late Aug, with a parade, traditional dancing, singing, and food (makah.com/ activities/makah-days).

The American Alps

NORTH CASCADES NATIONAL PARK

Washington

The mountains of North Cascades National Park are so thoroughly alpine in character—with more than 300 glaciers, countless snowfields, steep-sided valleys, icefalls, and cirque-cradled lakes—that John Muir labeled them the "American Alps." Part of a vast complex of National Park Service– and U.S. Forest Service–administered public lands where the rocky spine of the Cascade Range abuts Canada, the park is at the heart of some of the most remote and rugged land in the American West.

Only one road, the dramatic, summer-only North Cascades Highway (State Route 20), climbs up and over the high country of the park complex, linking the lake-filled Skagit Valley on the west to the more arid eastern uplands. But what a road! One of the most scenic mountain routes in the U.S., the North Cascades Highway provides teasing glimpses of the backcountry, the little-trammeled province of distance hikers and climbers.

On the park's western approach, Newhalem is the jumping-off point for hiking and rafting and fishing the Skagit River; the visitors center here explains the park's natural and cultural history. As it climbs to the east, the North Cascades Highway crests two passes, the 4,855-foot Rainy Pass and, 5 miles to the east, 5,477-foot Washington Pass.

Another entry to the park is by ferry up Lake Chelan, a 50-mile-long lake that stretches from the base of the North Cascades to the barren scrubland of central Washington. A major fishing and boating playground, glacier-dug Lake Chelan is almost 1,500 feet deep, making it the third-deepest lake in the U.S. (only Crater Lake and Lake Tahoe are deeper; see pp. 870 and 726). While the eastern end of Lake Chelan offers lovely beaches and summer resorts, the most unusual adventure here is the ferry ride from the town of Chelan to the village of Stehekin, at the isolated southern edge of the park. This tiny community, with just 100 year-round residents, supports several lodges, including the North Cascades Lodge at Stehekin, a year-round modern lakeside hotel complete with a marina and restaurant. You'll enjoy comfort—and near-complete solitude.

WHERE: 140 miles northeast of Seattle. *Visitor info:* Tel 360-854-7200; nps.gov/noca. *When:* SR 20 is usually completely open from mid-Apr–Oct and, from the west, is open to 14 miles beyond the visitor center year-round. **LADY OF THE LAKE FERRIES:** Chelan. Tel 509-682-4584; ladyofthelake.com. **NORTH CASCADES LODGE AT STEHEKIN:** Tel 509-682-4494; lodgeatstehekin.com. *Cost:* from $128. **BEST TIMES:** early Feb for the Upper Skagit Bald Eagle Festival in Newhalem (skagiteagle .org); July–Sept for weather.

Lake Ann, one of the many crystalline pools dropped into this craggy range, lies near the North Cascades Highway.

A Walk on Washington's Wild Side

OLYMPIC NATIONAL PARK

Washington

The remote and rugged Olympic Peninsula juts into the Pacific from the western flank of Washington State, its moatlike isolation allowing for the development of a natural and human history all its own. At the center of the peninsula is 1,400-square-mile Olympic National Park, a preserve of rare, primordial ecosystems that has garnered the park the rare dual designation of World Heritage Park and International Biosphere Reserve.

A quick visit to the park is nearly impossible: This is a vast and subtle area, suffused with a mystical spirit. Only one road, Highway 101, rings the park, and few penetrate the interior, which means that many of the best and most spectacular sights are reserved for long-distance walkers who trek across the mountainous interior or coastal trails.

The northern entrances to the park are the most popular. Beginning at sea level at Port Angeles, the 17-mile Hurricane Ridge Road climbs 5,000 feet into the Olympic peaks, where trails wind through extensive wildflower meadows, and vistas open to the rugged crags and glaciers of 7,980-foot Mount Olympus, the park's highest peak. Also easily reached from the north is Lake Crescent, a deep blue, fjordlike lake favored for boating, swimming, fishing, and picnicking. Cedar-sided Lake Crescent Lodge, built in 1915, is a well-loved family destination with rustic lodge rooms, cottages, and an atmospheric dining room (nonguests are welcome).

The western slopes of the park receive the full brunt of Pacific storms—annual rainfall here is measured in yards. This heavy precipitation, coupled with mild temperatures and dense summer fog, provides perfect conditions for temperate rain forests (unique in the contiguous U.S.), such as the primeval moss-bearded woodlands in the Hoh River valley.

The longest wilderness coastline in the Lower 48, the 57-mile Olympic Coastal Strip is accessed by roads at only a few points. Otherwise, this expanse of rock and sand belongs to hardy backpackers who negotiate the tides, beaches, and treacherous headlands on foot. This is some of the most rugged and picturesque coastline anywhere; sea stacks and islands parade out into the pounding surf, often capped by miniature forests.

At the southern edge of the Olympic Coastal Strip, Highway 101 briefly joins the shoreline. Above a rocky, wave-dashed cove sits the Kalaloch Lodge (CLAY-lock). From the back of the handsome lodge, a staircase leads from a gazebo (good for whale-watching) down the cliffs to a protected, pristine beach. With its fine dining restaurant, comfortable accommodations in the main lodge and cabins, and dramatic setting, the Kalaloch Lodge is easily the most civilized point along this wilderness coast.

Although only the northern shore of Lake Quinault is in the park (the lake itself is

Avalanche lilies bloom along Hurricane Ridge in Olympic National Park.

administered by the Quinault tribe), the misty spirits of the Olympic forests make themselves felt in this steep mountain valley, with towering trees and totem poles alike. The lake's quiet isolation is perfectly captured by the woodsy 1926 Lake Quinault Lodge, with a spacious wood-paneled lobby, massive fireplace, and comfortably old-fashioned rooms.

WHERE: 79 miles west of Seattle. Tel 360-565-3130; nps.gov/olym. **LAKE CRESCENT LODGE:** Tel 360-928-3211; olympicnational parks.com. *Cost:* from $189; dinner $50. *When:* May–mid-Oct. **KALALOCH LODGE:** Forks. Tel 866-662-9928 or 360-962-2271; thekalalochlodge.com. *Cost:* from $186; dinner $50. **LAKE QUINAULT LODGE:** Quinault. Tel 888-896-3818 or 360-288-2900; olympic nationalparks.com. *Cost:* from $119 (off-peak), from $209 (peak); dinner $45. **BEST TIME:** June–Oct for weather.

A Victorian Seaport Reborn

PORT TOWNSEND

Washington

One of the best-preserved Victorian-era seaports in the western U.S., Port Townsend looks across deep blue Admiralty Inlet, dotted with sailboats and ferries, to Whidbey Island (see p. 904) and on to the white-glaciered mass of Mount Baker (see p. 884). Port Townsend was established in 1851, quickly becoming the premier city on Puget Sound and a major center of trade during the era of sailing ships. Much of what you see today can be traced to the frenzy of commercial development in the 1880s, when the town had plans to become the most important shipping port on the West Coast. But Port Townsend's boom went bust when the railroad passed them by, and the once-bustling seaport was all but deserted by 1895.

Today, the handsome downtown district has been reborn, with block after block of elaborate storefronts lining the harbor, and the residential area uptown along the bluff is rich with ornate mansions. One of the most flamboyant, the 1889 Ann Starrett Mansion, was built by the town's leading contractor as his wife's wedding gift. The Queen Anne Victorian home is now a beautifully restored hotel, with lavish period appointments, a spiral staircase, and a four-story tower complete with frescoes.

Just north of downtown is Fort Worden, a 1902 military fortification turned state park. The commanding officer's quarters is open for tours, and a barracks serves as the Puget Sound Coast Artillery Museum, telling the story of early Pacific coastal fortifications. The fort's old blimp hangar has been converted into a performance theater, often used for music and arts events by Centrum, the community's very active performance arts organization.

West of Port Townsend along the Olympic Peninsula coastline is the Dungeness Spit, a sandy arm extending 5.5 miles into the Strait of Juan de Fuca, with the 1857 Dungeness Lighthouse at its tip. The longest natural sand hook in the U.S., it's now part of Dungeness National Wildlife Refuge and a marvelous place to hike and get a closer look at the marine environment of the northern coast. Watch for seals bobbing offshore.

But mention Dungeness and who doesn't think of the area's most famous denizen, the Dungeness crab, the Pacific Northwest's great seafood delicacy. None of the passionate local purveyors in this area should go unsampled, especially the cozy Alder Wood Bistro. Chef

Gabe and his wife Jessica have created an immediately popular spot that showcases the bounty of the Olympic Peninsula. A wood-fired oven produces excellent pizzas and breads, as well as their signature mussels (fried oysters are also a crowd pleaser).

WHERE: 45 miles northwest of Seattle via the Bainbridge Island ferry. *Visitor info:* Tel 360-385-2722; enjoypt.com or ptguide.com. **ANN STARRETT MANSION:** Tel 800-321-0644 or 360-385-3205; starrettmansion.com. *Cost:* from $105. **FORT WORDEN STATE PARK:** Tel 360-344-4400; fortworden.org. **PUGET SOUND COAST ARTILLERY MUSEUM:** Tel 360-385-0373; coastartillery.org. *When:* late May–early Sept. **CENTRUM:** Tel 360-385-3102; centrum .org. **DUNGENESS NATIONAL WILDLIFE REFUGE:** Sequim. Tel 360-457-8451; fws.gov/refuge/dungeness. **ALDER WOOD BISTRO:** Sequim. Tel 360-683-4321; alderwoodbistro.com. *Cost:* $50. **BEST TIMES:** June–Sept for weather; mid-Sept for the Port Townsend Wooden Boat Festival (nwmaritime.org) and for Historic Homes Tours (ptguide.com).

Washington's Ferry Land

THE SAN JUAN ISLANDS

Washington

In the northwest corner of Washington State, the waters of Puget Sound, the Strait of Georgia, and the Strait of Juan de Fuca mingle, forming the Salish Sea, home to the forested, rock-faced San Juan Islands, whose landscapes range from tightly folded mountain peaks to rolling moors and farmland. Although the San Juan archipelago contains more than 750 islands scattered across 10,000 square miles of Pacific waters, only 170 are named, only about 40 are inhabited, and only four are served by Washington State Ferries.

Despite their proximity to Seattle, the islands have significantly better weather (due to the Olympic Mountains' rain shadow) and have remained relatively undeveloped, retaining their bucolic charm. Three have plentiful inns, resorts, and facilities, and each has its own distinct character. Lopez is the most rural, with fields and pastures stretching across its central plateau. With few hills and friendly drivers—it's one of those places where everyone waves hello to one another—Lopez is a great island to explore on two wheels.

Many consider Orcas Island the most beautiful. It is the largest, rockiest, and most mountainous, nearly divided into halves by the intruding waters of East Sound. From the top of 2,409-foot Mount Constitution in rugged Moran State Park, the views stretch from Mount Rainier in the south to Mount Baker and north to Vancouver in British Columbia. Stay at the historic Rosario Resort and Spa, whose centerpiece is the 1906 waterfront mansion built by a onetime Seattle mayor, or spend the night in a yurt and sun yourself au naturel on the private, clothing-optional beaches of Doe Bay Village Resort. Much of the delight of staying at the bluff-top 11-room Inn at Ship Bay is the proximity to its acclaimed restaurant, considered by many to deliver the island's best and most creative Pacific Northwest cuisine.

If your sweet spot is somewhere in between, Turtleback Farm Inn strikes the balance between refinement and rural charm. The inn is a working farm set on 80 acres of meadows, woods, and duck ponds, with lodging in both the beautifully restored green clapboard farmhouse, dating back to the late 19th century, and in the new

Orchard House, which overlooks apple trees and the crest of Mount Wollard. Your fondest memory may be of breakfast, and the lovely owners Susan and Bill, who welcome guests as family.

San Juan Island is the second largest of the islands, the most distant from the mainland, and the only one boasting an incorporated town, Friday Harbor. A bustling port, with ferries, sailboats, and cruisers to-ing and fro-ing, it's also the center for kayak trips—the San Juans are noted worldwide for excellent sea kayaking—and for whale-watching. Three resident pods of orcas, one of the highest concentrations anywhere, call these chilly waters home—*Free Willy* was filmed in the San Juans—as do seals and porpoises. Learn more about the San Juan marine ecosystem at the Whale Museum, a one-of-a-kind facility that helps support local whale research. Friday Harbor's nicest spot for a memorable getaway is Friday Harbor House, a contemporary boutique hotel with spacious, art-filled rooms, sweeping views of the marina, and an excellent dining room with—naturally enough—a seafood-focused menu.

WHERE: 90 miles north of Seattle. *Visitor info:* Tel 888-468-3701 or 360-378-9551; visit sanjuans.com. **WASHINGTON STATE FERRIES:** Anacortes. Tel 206-464-6400; wsdot.wa.gov/ferries. **ROSARIO RESORT AND SPA:** Eastsound, Orcas Island. Tel 800-562-8820 or 360-376-2222; rosarioresort.com. *Cost:* from $99 (off-peak), from $169 (peak). **DOE BAY RESORT &**

Tiny Patos Island is part of the San Juan Islands National Monument, created by President Obama in 2013.

RETREAT: Olga, Orcas Island. Tel 360-376-2291; doebay.com. *Cost:* yurts from $48 (off-peak), from $125 (peak). **INN AT SHIP BAY:** Tel 877-276-7296; innatshipbay.com *Cost:* rooms from $150; dinner $60. **TURTLEBACK FARM INN:** Eastsound, Orcas Island. Tel 800-376-4914 or 360-376-4914; turtlebackinn.com. *Cost:* from $100 (off-peak), from $125 (peak). **WHALE MUSEUM:** Friday Harbor, San Juan Island. Tel 360-378-4710; whalemuseum.org. **FRIDAY HARBOR HOUSE:** Friday Harbor, San Juan Island. Tel 866-722-7356 or 360-378-8455. fridayharborhouse.com. *Cost:* from $168 (off-peak), from $315 (peak); dinner $55. **BEST TIMES:** late Apr for the Tour de Lopez bicycling event (lopezisland.com); June–Sept for sighting orcas; early Sept for the Deer Harbor Wooden Boat Rendezvous on Orcas (deerharborwoodenboats.org).

The Gastronomic Heart of Seattle

PIKE PLACE MARKET

Seattle, Washington

Not all roads in Seattle lead to Pike Place Market, but it sure feels that way. Follow your stomach and you're sure to wind up at this Seattle institution. The market was first created in 1907—making it the oldest continuously operating farmers market in the U.S.—so farmers could sell directly to customers, eliminating the middleman. Today, this always busy, always freewheeling marketplace is as noted for its upbeat theatricality as for its unending display of fish and produce market stalls.

The market sits at the edge of bluffs overlooking the Seattle waterfront—views from west-facing market cafés are some of the best in the city—and extends across seven city blocks, filling 11 multilevel buildings with 500 vendors and countless visitors daily. Though the heart of the market remains its wondrous food and produce, there's a lot more than eats for sale in this assemblage of shops, stalls, and warrenlike underground arcades. You'll find everything from magicians' supplies, antique political buttons, and ethnic clothing to wind-up toys. In addition, the North Arcade teems with craftspeople selling all manner of handmade products, and coffeehouses galore. The market is also home to some of Seattle's best-loved restaurants and watering holes, many of them tucked into narrow Post Alley.

The circuslike atmosphere is underscored with buskers, street entertainers, and the spectacle of fishmongers tossing whole salmon across the counters while shouting "low-flying fish!" for the amusement of passersby. Spot prawns (Northwest shrimp), halibut, geoduck clams, and oysters from a variety of Northwest bays all chill under mountains of shaved ice. It's a crowded, sometimes crazy scene, all part of the market's timeless charm.

In addition to luxurious guest rooms with views over the market and Elliott Bay, the

Pike Place Market is famous for its countless vendors, including fish-throwing fishmongers.

small, European-style Inn at the Market offers light meals and a wine bar at the informal Café Campagne. The restaurant, which opened in 1994, bills itself as a classic Parisian brasserie, and its food and drink frequently receive local accolades. A longtime favorite, Etta's Seafood Restaurant is a valentine to lovers of fish and seafood, with oysters on the half shell, not-to-be-missed Dungeness crab cakes, and smoked sake salmon. For this (and a bevy of other delights such as Dahlia Lounge, Palace Kitchen, Serious Pie, and Lola) you can thank local restaurateur extraordinaire Tom Douglas.

WHERE: info booth and principal entrance at First Ave. & Pike Pl. Tel 206-682-7453; pikeplacemarket.org. **INN AT THE MARKET:** Tel 800-446-4484 or 206-443-3600; innatthemarket.com. *Cost:* from $275 (off-peak), from $350 (peak). **CAFÉ CAMPAGNE:** Tel 206-728-2233; cafecampagne.com. *Cost:* dinner $35. **ETTA'S:** Tel 206-443-6000; tomdouglas.com. *Cost:* dinner $50.

More Than a Room with a View

SEATTLE CENTER

Seattle, Washington

Seattle's iconic Space Needle offers visitors a place to dine and catch a panoramic view, soaring high above Seattle Center, the city's rec room. It also symbolizes Seattle to the world, and it provides an idiosyncratic

look at the future from nearly half a century in the past. The structure, which today looks

decidedly *Jetsons*-inspired, is 605 feet tall—plus almost an inch when it expands on a hot day—and was built for the 1962 World's Fair. If you dine at SkyCity, revolving just beneath the 520-foot-high observation deck, the elevator ride is free (otherwise it's $23), but be forewarned that the restaurant is pricey (you're paying for the million-dollar view).

At the base of the Space Needle, the amorphous, Frank Gehry–designed Experience Music Project is one of the many ambitious undertakings through which Microsoft cofounder Paul Allen has transformed his hometown. Originally conceived as a tribute to Jimi Hendrix, another native son, EMP grew into a state-of-the-art rock museum hosting exhibits, concerts, and even an interactive studio where you can live out the fantasy of strumming your Stratocaster onstage in front of 10,000 screaming fans. The EMP building also contains the Science Fiction Museum.

There's much, much more to the 74-acre Seattle Center: three theaters; the new eye- and ear-catching McCaw Hall, the venue of the Seattle Opera and Pacific Northwest Ballet; KeyArena; the Children's Museum; the Pacific Science Center; and one end of the 1962 Monorail. The city's most celebrated new attraction is the Chihuly Garden and Glass, a celebration of the incomparable glass art created by Dale Chihuly, yet another Washington-born luminary (see p. 903).

Architecture buffs will want to stray farther into downtown to take in some of the other landmark buildings that have given the cityscape a cutting-edge look. They include the acoustically excellent Benaroya Hall, for the Seattle Symphony; the Robert Venturi–designed Seattle Art Museum; and the Seattle Mariners' Safeco Field, one of the country's landmark new ballparks. The most audacious of the city's newer structures is Rem Koolhaas's Seattle Public Library, a light-filled temple of books recalling Victorian London's Crystal Palace.

WHERE: between Denny Way & Mercer St., and 1st & 5th Aves. N. Tel 206-684-7200; seattlecenter.com. **SPACE NEEDLE:** Tel 800-937-9582 or 206-905-2100; spaceneedle.com. **EXPERIENCE MUSIC PROJECT:** Tel 206-770-2700; empmuseum.org. **CHIHULY GARDEN AND GLASS:** Tel 206-753-4940; chihulygardenandglass.com. **BEST TIME:** early Sept for the huge arts festival Bumbershoot (bumbershoot.org).

The soaring Space Needle can be seen through the windows of the Chihuly Garden and Glass.

Wired on the Sound

SEATTLE'S COFFEE CULTURE

Seattle, Washington

With 3.5 coffee shops for every 1,000 citizens, Seattle has the greatest concentration of coffeehouses in the country, which underscores a key element of Seattle's reputation: The city is awash in caffeine.

In a remarkably short time—the world's first Starbucks opened here in 1971—coffeehouses have become the social and community centers of the Emerald City, where you go on dates, take the kids, listen to music, sit with your laptop, finish your great American novel, or meet your friends. In Seattle, you'll find coffee shops attached to everything from Laundromats to barbershops, cinemas to strip clubs.

Coffee beans don't grow in these parts, but there are a few good reasons for Seattle's emergence as the world coffee capital. A warm, legal stimulant is just the thing to take the edge off the Pacific Northwest's long and dismal wet winters, and the city's large and relatively affluent population demands good coffee in dizzying variety all day long—it's not just for breakfast anymore.

There's also the influence of a little coffee shop, named after a character in *Moby Dick*, that turned into an internationally big (well, huge) deal: The original Starbucks began in Pike Place Market (see p. 897) as a plain-Jane, unremarkable coffee shop but, having awakened a coffee revolution, has been opening everywhere else since—there are now more than 21,000 Starbucks retail operations on the planet—and counting. Still in business, that

first location attracts Starbucks pilgrims from all over the world.

There are plenty of other Starbucks shops in Seattle, but there are also lots of more funky and unique indie coffeehouses. The Capitol Hill area is home to many, including Espresso Vivace, renowned for its devotion to perfection in coffee, and the art deco Victrola Coffee, which hosts live music and art shows. In the Maple Leaf neighborhood, Cloud City offers a kids' area, a dollar-a-cup honor bar, and an emphasis on wireless connectivity. If you're after no-nonsense coffee and loads of food to go with it, head to famous, funky 24-hour Beth's Café, home to the he-man's 12-egg omelette.

ORIGINAL STARBUCKS: Tel 206-448-8762; starbucks.com. **ESPRESSO VIVACE ROASTERIA:** Tel 206-860-2722; espressovivace.com. **VICTROLA COFFEE:** Tel 206-624-1725; victrola coffee.com. **CLOUD CITY COFFEE:** Tel 206-527-5552; cloudcitycoffee.com. **BETH'S CAFÉ:** Tel 206-782-5588; bethscafe.com. *Cost:* 12-egg omelette from $17.

A Tribute to the Bounty of the Pacific Northwest

SEATTLE'S SEAFOOD RESTAURANTS

Seattle, Washington

Seattle's vibrant culinary culture is an embarrassment of riches, with an inspiring bounty of fresh fruits and vegetables, local meats, and top-notch wines. Not surprisingly, though, it's seafood that rules here. The quiet bays

and estuaries of Puget Sound are rich with oysters and Dungeness crabs, while the waters of the Pacific yield tuna, halibut, cod, and rockfish. The fast-flowing and nutrient-rich waters of the Strait of Juan de Fuca and the San Juan Islands are home to succulent Manila clams, small but delicious swimming scallops, and spot prawns—with firm, sweet flesh, they are

the top choice for Pacific shrimp. Watch menus for fresh razor clams—6-inch-long bivalves with a wonderfully mild and nutty flavor—considered by many Northwesterners as the Pacific's greatest and most delicious gift.

The city's most famous waterside eatery is Ray's Boathouse, a Seattle classic 15 minutes from downtown, where you'll find shorts and sandals upstairs on the popular summertime deck, and a more refined eatery downstairs, all with the city's best view of Shilshole Bay. This is your Seattle Moment: Watch the sun go down over Puget Sound and the towering Olympic Mountains while enjoying straightforward, unfussy, incredibly fresh fish such as the grilled black cod marinated in sake. Stunning views and excellent seafood are also on the menu at another Seattle institution, Canlis, which looks out over Lake Union just north of downtown Seattle. Atypically formal for Seattle—you won't be seated if you're in jeans—it's the kind of place where people splurge for special occasions. Canlis features renowned steaks, stellar service, and a mind-bending wine list 2,000 selections long.

Down on the waterfront, tourists and locals mix at busy Elliott's Oyster House, which includes among its many varieties of seafood a dazzling selection of oysters. The lounge offers a happy hour at the 21-foot-long oyster bar, your chance to taste the best of the Northwest— rare native oysters from Olympia, Willapa Bay oysters from southwest Washington's Long Beach Peninsula (see p. 889), and up to two dozen other choice local bivalves.

The constant buzz at The Walrus and The Carpenter is testimony to this neighborhood spot's wild popularity. Most come to eat piles of fresh local oysters while enjoying the friendly

Ray's Boathouse serves delicious and beautifully presented fresh fish.

and casual atmosphere. Or visit Shiro Kashiba, whose superb sushi is widely regarded as the best in the city. If at all possible, go to Shiro's in the fall when he's also serving matsutake mushrooms; get there early, seat yourself at the bar, and submit yourself to the master.

RAY'S BOATHOUSE: Tel 206-789-3770; rays.com. *Cost:* dinner $65. **CANLIS:** Tel 206-283-3313; canlis.com. *Cost:* 3-course dinner $85. **ELLIOTT'S OYSTER HOUSE:** Tel 206-623-4340; elliottsoysterhouse.com. *Cost:* dinner $65. **THE WALRUS AND THE CARPENTER:** Tel 206-395-9227; thewalrusbar.com. *Cost:* dinner $55. **SHIRO'S:** Tel 206-443-9844; shiros.com. *Cost:* dinner $35. **BEST TIMES:** late summer and early fall for local salmon; Dec–Feb for fresh razor clams.

A Boat Trip to Native America

TILLICUM VILLAGE

Seattle, Washington

From Pier 55 in downtown Seattle, you can travel 8 miles by boat and end up a world away from the clatter and bustle of the big city. Blake Island, a state park in Puget Sound, is not accessible by car or, for that matter,

by public ferry. For most visitors, the best way to get there is on a boat tour that includes a visit to Tillicum Village, a replica Native

American village built to display the rich culture of Puget Sound indigenous peoples. Guests at Tillicum Village are welcomed to a clearing in the forest and a cedar longhouse for a traditional Northwest Indian salmon bake and a dance performance that incorporates masks, myths, and customs of Northwest coastal tribes. After the meal, there's time for a short hike on the 475-acre island (there are even a few beaches) before catching the boat back to the Seattle waterfront.

Although today's Tillicum Village dates only from 1962, when it was built for the Seattle World's Fair, Blake Island has provided home and shelter to native tribes such as the Suquamish of Puget Sound for thousands of years. Legend has it that Blake Island was the birthplace of Chief Seattle, who led the Suquamish when the first white settlers arrived in the area in the 1850s and who urged peaceful coexistence between the settlers and the natives. That didn't stop the federal government from relocating the tribe to a reservation an hour outside Seattle. Chief Seattle's sentiments from an 1854 address to Washington's territorial governor have become an environmental movement creed: "This we know; the earth does not belong to man; man belongs to the earth. This we know. All things are connected like the blood which unites one family. All things are connected."

WHERE: 8 miles west of downtown Seattle on Blake Island. Tours leave from Pier 55 in Seattle, tel 888-623-1445 or 206-623-1445; tillicumvillage.com. *Cost:* Tillicum Village tour, dinner, dance performance, and boat ride $88; tour without dinner $45. *When:* daily, late May–Sept. **BEST TIME:** During summer, tours are frequent and weather is generally good.

Location, Location, Location

SALISH LODGE & SPA

Snoqualmie, Washington

This four-story luxury lodge perched on the brink of a cliff overlooking the misty plumes of Snoqualmie Falls will seem familiar to those who recall the 1990s TV series *Twin Peaks*. Exterior shots of the lodge and falls may have helped set the scene for the dark David Lynch thriller, but there's nothing ominous about this superb hotel and spa in one of the Pacific Northwest's most spectacular locations. This synthesis of dramatic natural beauty and sophisticated comfort explains Salish Lodge's well-deserved popularity: It's both a special occasion romantic getaway and a mountain retreat with great access to recreation.

The first lodge at this unique site was established in 1916 as a wayside inn for early automobile travelers. The mighty fireplace from that early lodge still dominates the handsome, wood-beamed Dining Room, the lodge's formal restaurant, which offers both elaborate four-course breakfasts and Northwest cuisine for dinner. Its views match Chef Matt Heikkila's seasonal creations and the lodge's 1,700-bottle wine list. The decor of the guest rooms retains a pleasantly casual atmosphere, with original local art and Native American crafts, wood-burning fireplaces, goosedown comforters, and large whirlpool tubs. The award-winning Spa at Salish Lodge is one of the best in Washington, with a subtle Asian ambience and a full menu of treatments, services, and therapies for pampering and relaxation.

WHERE: 30 miles east of Seattle; 6501 Railroad Ave. Tel 800-272-5474 or 425-888-2556; salishlodge.com. *Cost:* from $239; dinner $75. **BEST TIME:** May–Oct for weather.

The Art Glass Capital of the Northwest

THE MUSEUM OF GLASS

Tacoma, Washington

Tacoma has been transformed by the arrival of glass. Led by the efforts of a native son, acclaimed glass artist Dale Chihuly, this Puget Sound city is home to the dynamic and unusual $48 million Museum of Glass, which opened in 2002. One of the most striking features of a visit to the museum is the Chihuly Bridge of Glass, a colorfully glowing 500-foot-long pedestrian overpass that spans an expressway and links the museum to the Washington State History Museum and downtown Tacoma. Indoors, large galleries show off a wide range of glass art, including blown and fused glass. But the heart of the museum is the Hot Shop, a 90-foot-tall, 100-foot-wide amphitheater where visitors can watch teams of artists blowing glass. Unless you've been to the thousand-year-old glass furnaces on Venice's island of Murano (where Chihuly studied with the masters), you most likely have never seen anything like this.

Chihuly is one of the world's greatest contemporary glass artists, and his work is prominently and proudly displayed throughout his hometown. In 1971 he founded the Pilchuck Glass School, 50 miles north of Seattle, which is credited with transforming glass—previously used mostly for utilitarian or decorative purposes—into a medium of artistic expression both bold and delicate. In 2012, The Chihuly Garden and Glass opened in Seattle at the foot of the Space Needle (see p. 899). Chihuly's blown-glass sculptures defy the everyday experience of glass: Infused with lush color and sensual textures, these pieces extend the traditional notion of "glass-ness" into a whole new realm of beauty.

Just a short walk from the museum, the city's long-standing Tacoma Art Museum will also be of interest to fans of Chihuly's work. While not as flashy as the Museum of Glass, it has a substantial collection of early Chihuly pieces, plus many fine works in glass and other media from Northwest artists.

WHERE: 30 miles south of Seattle; 1801 Dock St. Tel 866-468-7386 or 253-284-4750; museumofglass.org. *When:* daily, late May–early Sept; closed Mon–Tues rest of year. **TACOMA ART MUSEUM:** Tel 253-272-4258; tacomaartmuseum.org. *When:* closed Mon.

So Nice They Named It Twice

WALLA WALLA

Washington

It wasn't that long ago that Walla Walla was best known to outsiders, insofar as it was known at all, as the source of a certain sweet onion. That changed when Army Reserve buddies Gary Figgins and Rick Small established, respectively,

Leonetti Cellar and Woodward Canyon Winery, laying the foundation of a wine industry that has transformed the small city (population 31,800) and the surrounding region in a scant quarter-century. Almost overnight, it seemed, Washington was producing world-class cabernet sauvignon and merlot, and growing numbers of vintners were having equal success with such varieties as syrah, viognier, and tempranillo. Walla Walla's name came from American Indians in the region, meaning "many waters," but increasingly it means "many wines" to tourists: The city now boasts more than 100 wineries, and it remains the focal point of a vibrant wine region that extends nearly to Yakima.

Washington's emergence as a winemaking titan has been sudden. In 1970, there were only two wineries in the state, and now it is the second largest wine producer in the U.S., after California, with over 850 wineries and over

Walla Walla's remoteness creates a certain esprit de corps among its vintners.

50,000 acres under wine grape cultivation. In contrast with neighboring Oregon, whose top wineries are on the cool slopes of the Willamette Valley, perfect for pinot noir (see p. 883), Washington's top terroirs are in the state's eastern deserts, where burly red wine grapes thrive in the baking heat. Not long ago Northwest wines were a novelty, but today they are setting the pace for their respective varietals, and while some Northwest wines are distributed across the U.S., much of the best is very limited in quantity and never makes it out of the region.

Chefs and inn-keepers invariably follow where winemakers go, and in newly luxurious Walla Walla—"the town so nice they named it twice," as the Chamber of Commerce likes to say—they're sometimes to be found in the same location. The Whitehouse-Crawford Restaurant, where chef Jamie Guerin revolutionized local dining in 2000, is next door to the barrel room of the Seven Hills Winery, and both the ambitious Abeja Winery and the gracious Inn at Abeja are located in a gorgeously restored early 20th-century farmstead with seven suites and cottages.

Where: 92 miles south of Spokane. *Visitor info:* Tel 509-525-0850; wwvchamber.com or wallawallawine.com. **Whitehouse-Crawford Restaurant:** Tel 509-525-2222; whitehouse crawford.com. *Cost:* dinner $50. **Inn at Abeja:** Tel 509-522-1234; abeja.net. *Cost:* from $295. *When:* closed Jan–Feb. **Best times:** 1st full weekend in May for Spring Release Weekend (wallawallawine.com.); mid-June for the Sweet Onion Festival (sweetonions.org).

An Island for Artists

WHIDBEY ISLAND

Washington

In marked contrast to densely populated "Pugetopolis" of mainland suburban Seattle, the islands of Puget Sound remain mostly rural, with quaint and quiet bayside towns interspersed with fields and forest. Low-lying and verdant,

Whidbey Island is just 30 miles north of downtown Seattle and is the tonic that revives the weary urban soul. It retains a slow-paced rural sensibility, offering refuge to farmers, artists, and well-heeled urban refugees alike. The island makes an excellent weekend getaway, and for visitors short on time a very pleasant stand-in for the more distant San Juan Islands (see p. 896).

The historic towns and old military forts of Whidbey Island—at 45 miles, it is one of the longest islands in the U.S.—also open a window onto Puget Sound's maritime past. The island's ports were important centers between the 1850s and 1900, when ships were the region's primary mode of transport. Only after rail lines and highways linked mainland cities did the islands become backwaters. More recently, Whidbey Island's well-preserved Victorian-era towns have been transformed by art galleries, boutiques, and fine inns, and the area's beautiful land and seascapes are unequaled: Vistas of white sails, deep green forests, and azure waters reward you at every bend, often surmounted by the snowcapped peaks of the Olympic and Cascade mountains.

Langley is a charming little village overlooking Saratoga Sound and the tip of Camano Island. Its old town center, with vintage false-front shops and an air of prosperous quaintness, is known as an artists' enclave. In such an unassuming town it is surprising to find one of the Northwest's most luxurious and

"Do nothing here" is Whidbey Island's official slogan, but activities like hiking, sailing, and fishing are available just in case.

romantic hideaways, the Inn at Langley. This modern four-story lodge, set on a bluff above the sound with 180-degree seafront views, has the tranquility of a venerable country inn, with just the right touch of urban sophistication. The inn's renowned restaurant (with its unforgettable, weekends-only multiple-course, three-hour dinner) focuses on the finest flavors and ingredients of the Northwest.

WHERE: 30 miles north of Seattle. *Visitor info:* Tel 360-221-6765; visitlangley.com. **INN AT LANGLEY:** Tel 360-221-3033; innatlangley .com. *Cost:* from $225 (off-peak), from $325 (peak); multi-course prix-fixe dinner $145. **BEST TIMES:** June–Sept for weather; mid-Sept for Langley's Djangofest celebrating the late hot club jazz guitarist Django Reinhardt (djangofest.com).

Wine Country in Suburban Seattle

WOODINVILLE WINERIES & THE HERBFARM

Woodinville, Washington

If you're looking to experience the genteel burnish of Washington State's Wine Country lifestyle, you don't need to make the journey to Walla Walla (see p. 903). A day trip to Seattle's eastern suburbs is all it takes. Over 90 wineries string through Woodinville, though many of the grapes for the area's wines come from the hot, arid districts of southeastern Washington, particularly between Yakima and Walla Walla.

The two giants of Woodinville-area wine are Columbia Winery, the state's oldest producer of premium wine (since 1962), and Château Ste. Michelle, the state's largest winemaker and winner of numerous international awards. Both offer tastings, tours, and wine sales out of opulent buildings. The beautiful Château Ste. Michelle's 105-acre park-like property was the private estate of a lumber baron in the early 1900s.

If wine's not your thing, Woodinville rolls out the barrel with some of Washington's finest beers from Redhook Ale Brewery, one of Seattle's first microbreweries. Micro no longer, the brewery offers tours and tastings at its Woodinville location, as well as great pub food at the Forecasters Public House. The wineries and brewery are all on the same street (several smaller wineries are also within walking distance), making this a favorite day trip from central Seattle, particularly to catch live music concerts at Château Ste. Michelle's outdoor amphitheater in warm weather months.

But gastronomes think of Woodinville as one thing: the hallowed destination of the famed Herbfarm Restaurant. A new location has doubled its seating capacity, but reservations are still coveted for the lavish, single seating, nine-course meals created by Chef Chris Weber. Every dish features local foods at the peak of their season, richly enhanced with herbs and paired with wine. For much of the year, the Herbfarm's gardens and farm supply the restaurant with a bounty of produce, bolstered by specialty growers and producers who provide wild mushrooms, heritage fruits, handmade cheeses, and rare treasures such as Oregon truffles and Montana caviar. The 26,000-bottle cellar represents one of the world's most noted collections of Oregon and Washington wines.

Stay at the Willows Lodge, located adjacent to the Herbfarm. A lovely blend of the rustic and contemporary, its sumptuous suites, full-service spa, 5-acre gardens, and luxury amenities offer very civilized comfort away from Seattle's hubbub. The lodge's Barking Frog dining room features award-winning Northwest bistro fare, paired with local wines and beers.

WHERE: 20 miles northeast of Seattle. **COLUMBIA WINERY:** Tel 855-374-9463 or 425-488-2776; columbiawinery.com. **CHÂTEAU STE. MICHELLE:** Tel 800-267-6793 or 425-488-1133; ste-michelle.com. **REDHOOK ALE BREWERY:** Tel 425-483-3232; redhook.com. *Cost:* dinner $20. **HERBFARM RESTAURANT:** Tel 425-485-5300; theherbfarm.com. *Cost:* 9-course prix-fixe dinners, including wines, from $179 per person. **WILLOWS LODGE:** Tel 877-424-3930 or 425-424-3900; willowslodge .com. *Cost:* from $260; dinner $60. **BEST TIME:** mid-June–late Sept for the Château Ste. Michelle's concert series.

ALASKA
AND
HAWAII

The Last Great Race on Earth

THE IDITAROD

Anchorage, Alaska

Starting from Anchorage each March and ending 8 to 15 days later in Nome, the Iditarod is one of the great endurance tests in sport, with competitors from around the globe mushing sled dogs across 1,150 miles of snow in

temperatures as low as 40 below zero. No wonder it's been called "The Last Great Race on Earth."

The Iditarod Trail began as a mail and supply route from Seward to Nome for gold miners. In 1925 one of its legendary dog teams, led by the great Balto, became national heroes after rushing diphtheria serum to epidemic-stricken Nome. The route was revived for racing in 1973, and today an average of 75 mushers and their teams come from as far away as Norway, Japan, and Russia to compete for a share of the $700,000-plus purse. It's the largest spectator event in Alaska, with crowds showing up for the pre-start party and camping out along the trail. The course record is currently held by John Baker, who won in 2011 with a time of 8 days, 18 hours, 46 minutes, and 39 seconds.

To get into the race yourself as an "Iditarider," place a bid for a spot on one of the mushers' sleds for the first 11 miles (the auction begins in October, with winning bids sometimes as high as $7,000). The remote fly-in Winterlake Lodge, sits directly on the trail and offers handsome guest cabins and the opportunity to traverse the trail with the lodge's team of 24 Alaskan huskies. The dinner menu is as remarkable as the wintry surroundings, with daily cooking classes and special culinary weekends scheduled throughout the year.

If you are visiting Alaska during the summer or fall, stop by the Iditarod Trail Sled Dog Race Headquarters near Wasilla, where you can watch videos about the race, view trophies, and see adorable sled dog puppies. In summer, you can also take a short cart ride pulled by sled dogs.

WHERE: headquarters in Wasilla, 40 miles north of Anchorage. Tel 907-376-5155; iditarod.com. *When:* early Mar. **IDITARIDERS AUCTION:** Tel 800-566-SLED or 907-352-2212. *When:* early Oct–Jan. **WINTERLAKE LODGE:** Finger Lake checkpoint. Tel 907-274-2710; within thewild.com. *Cost:* $4,840 per person for 3 nights, includes air transfer to/from Anchorage, meals, and activities. **IDITAROD TRAIL SLED DOG HEADQUARTERS:** Wasilla. Tel 907-376-5155; Iditarod.com. *Cost:* dog cart rides $20. *When:* May–Sept.

Each Iditarod team has 12 to 16 sled dogs, most of which are huskies bred for speed and endurance and who show extreme loyalty to the musher.

A Little Portion of Our Planet Left Alone

THE ARCTIC NATIONAL WILDLIFE REFUGE

Alaska

As conservationist Margaret Murie told Congress in 1959, arguing for the creation of the Arctic National Wildlife Refuge, "I feel so sure that, if we are big enough to save this bit of loveliness on our earth, the future citizens of Alaska and of all the world will be deeply grateful. This is a time for a long look ahead." She was right, of course, about both the importance of preserving the land and the future's appreciation of a place that remains preciously, absolutely wild. That protection is not guaranteed, however: With suspected oil deposits in the region, talk of opening it up for drilling has persisted for more than three decades.

Only about 1,200–1,500 people make the trek here every year, but that's not the point: Unlike the vast majority of the country's public lands, ANWR's mission is to put the sanctity of wilderness ahead of the needs of human visitors. Though the reserve measures about 19 million acres, there are no visitor centers, no campgrounds, no roads, and no trails. People who come here have to know what they're doing, but they're rewarded for their effort with access to utterly unspoiled wilderness that encompasses alpine and coastal tundra, coastal lagoons and salt marshes, rolling taiga uplands, 18 major rivers, and seemingly endless stands of birch, spruce, and aspen.

The four highest peaks of the Brooks Range are here, as are most of its glaciers, and the land supports an animal population that includes brown, black, and polar bears; the second largest caribou herd in Alaska; and over three dozen other species of land mammals, 42 fish species, and 200 species of birds.

A polar bear mother and cub wrestle playfully in the snow.

There are no known introduced species living in the refuge today, and people are almost absent. Even the area's Native population—a mix of Inupiat Eskimos and Athabascans from the interior—live only on the reserve's borders. This is what they meant by "undisturbed nature."

WHERE: north of the Arctic Circle in northeast Alaska. Tel 800-362-4546 or 907-456-0250; fws.gov/refuge/arctic. **HOW:** Arctic Treks (tel 907-455-6502; arctictreksadventures.com) and Arctic Wild (tel 888-577-8203 or 907-479-8203; arcticwild.com). Both offer guided backpacking and canoeing trips in the refuge. *Cost:* from $3,900 for 7-day trip, includes air transfer from Fairbanks and meals. **BEST TIME:** June–Aug, when temperatures are moderate and the sun is out 24/7.

Starry, Starry Nights in the Alaskan Interior

THE NORTHERN LIGHTS

Chena Hot Springs, Alaska

Ninety-three million miles away, a huge explosion on the sun's surface sends a rush of charged protons and electrons into space. A few days later they collide with earth's magnetic field and atmosphere, releasing energy that appears as bands of red, green, and sometimes blue light, traveling down the magnetic field lines toward the surface—and thus we have the northern lights, aka the aurora borealis, that light up the dark winter nights.

John Muir had a more poetic take: "Gazing into the starry sky and across the sparkling bay, magnificent upright bars of light in bright prismatic colors suddenly appeared, marching swiftly in close succession along the northern horizon. . . . Sense of time was charmed out of mind and the blessed night circled away in measureless rejoicing enthusiasm." The northern lights have that kind of effect on people. They're awed, struck by a sense that the sky they've looked at all their lives holds great mysteries. The aurora, said Muir, is "the most glorious of all the terrestrial manifestations of God."

The Chena Hot Springs Resort, outside Fairbanks, is particularly blessed as a viewing spot for aurora borealis activity. Located 60 miles beyond the city's ambient light, the 1,940-acre resort was opened in 1905 by a rheumatic prospector and his brother and has been a getaway spot ever since, its waters touted for their curative powers. You can't help but feel buoyed sitting in a natural outdoor rock lake as the lights dance right above your head, or in a Snow Coach bound for a nearby ridge for unobstructed views.

The resort's low buildings are set among the trees in a bowl of fir-covered mountains, with accommodations that range from yurts to newer hotel-like buildings (day visitors are also welcomed). Also on the grounds is America's only year-round ice museum—its vaulted rooms, Stoli Ice bar, gallery, and wedding altar all carved entirely out of ice. Outside, the soaking is the best of any Alaska hot spring, whether in the rock lake or hot tub, or you can head to their indoor pool. Other activities range from snowshoeing and dogsled rides in winter to canoeing and fishing in summer, with massage and flightseeing year-round.

The Alaska Railroad's Aurora Escape train is also a magnificent way to explore the state (see p. 914). It operates a year-round 365-mile journey from Anchorage to Fairbanks, making a stop on the outskirts of Denali National Park (see p. 912) and offers great views of the mountains, scenery, and wildlife, with informative and entertaining commentary.

WHERE: 60 miles northeast of Fairbanks. **CHENA HOT SPRINGS:** Tel 907-451-8104; chena hotsprings.com. *Cost:* yurts from $65, rooms

The aurora borealis gets its name from the Roman goddess of the dawn, Aurora, and the Greek god of the north wind, Boreas.

from $209. **BEST TIMES:** Northern lights viewing is best near the equinoxes (in late Sept and Mar) or during dark nights (from 10 P.M.–2 A.M.) Sept–Mar. Feb for the Yukon Quest International Sled Dog Race (yukonquest.org); Mar for World Ice Art Championships in Fairbanks.

The Great One

DENALI NATIONAL PARK AND PRESERVE

Alaska

For centuries, the Athabascans of central Alaska looked up at this 20,310-foot mountain and called it Denali, "the great one." Then, in 1896, businessman-turned-gold-prospector William Dickey rechristened it in honor of President William McKinley, who hailed from Ohio and had never set foot in Alaska. That's never sat well with a lot of Alaskans. The move to officially rename the mountain Denali took place in 2015. But whatever you call the mountain, its grandeur transcends any language.

The tallest peak in North America, Denali is the primary attraction of Denali National Park and Preserve, but it's not the only draw. Visitors return from the 6-million-acre park with tales of the grizzlies, wolves, caribou, moose, and golden eagles they sighted. And then there are the views, sweeping vistas of subarctic tundra and taiga, glaciers and deeply gouged valleys, and a good number of massive mountain peaks that almost compete with the Great One.

Touring and tent camping are controlled to protect the park's fragile ecology. There's only one 92-mile road, of which only the first 15 miles are paved, and vehicular traffic past the 15-mile point is limited to buses and official vehicles. Summer brings long northern days, with 16 to 20 hours of light in which to take in the scenery. For an upstairs view, a number of operators offer plane or helicopter flightseeing excursions. For a more in-depth, active experience, you can stay at Camp Denali and North Face Lodge, sister properties located in the heart of the park that accommodate 36 guests each. Founded in 1951 by homesteaders on the not-yet-designated national parkland, the camp offers rustic cabins with shared bath and shower facilities a five-minute walk away, while the renovated lodge has small but well-appointed rooms with private bathrooms. Both offer a dining room with a North Country menu, an idyllic location near Wonder Lake, and breathtaking views of the Alaska Range. Naturalist guides lead hikes suitable for all ages to explore the backcountry and offer evening educational programs.

Despite previous attempts, the first successful ascent of Denali's main summit was not made until 1913.

Alternative options that blend an untouched wilderness sanctuary with comfortable digs are few (and similarly pricey). Denali Backcountry Lodge is a friendly competitor when Camp Denali and North Face Lodge get booked months in advance. It is owned by Alaska Denali Travel, who can also place visitors in any of the more affordable lodgings at Denali Park Village at the park's entrance. Reputable and established, Alaska Denali Travel also helps visitors maximize the Denali experience with a list of exciting activities to choose from, including flightseeing, dogsledding, gold panning, jeep tours, guided hiking, and rafting.

DENALI NATIONAL PARK: 237 miles north of Anchorage. Tel 907-683-9532; nps.gov/dena.

When: park road closed Oct–Apr. **TOURS:** Alaska Wildland Adventures. Tel 800-334-8730 or 907-783-2928; alaskawildland.com. *Cost:* $4,695 for a 7-day lodge-based, all-inclusive tour. *When:* June–mid-Sept. **FLIGHTSEEING:** Denali Air. Tel 907-683-2261; denaliair.com. *Cost:* from $315. *When:* May–mid-Sept. **CAMP DENALI:** Tel 907-683-2290; campdenali.com. *Cost:* from $1,725 per person, double occupancy, for 3-night stay, all-inclusive. *When:* June–early Sept. **ALASKA DENALI TRAVEL:** Tel 855-359-9142; alaskadenalitravel.com. *Cost:* Denali Backcountry Lodge from $529 per person, double occupancy, all-inclusive. *When:* mid-May–mid-Sept. **BEST TIMES:** June for wildflowers and birding; Aug–Sept for autumn foliage.

North to Alaska!

DRIVING THE ALASKA HIGHWAY

Fairbanks to Dawson Creek, British Columbia

I t began in panic: On December 7, 1941, when Japan bombed Pearl Harbor, American military planners looked at a map and saw the long sweep of Alaska's Aleutian Islands extending like a bridge down into the Pacific,

only 1,000 miles from Japan. If the Japanese were to gain a foothold in Alaska, they feared, the continental U.S. could be invaded by land.

Mobilization was swift. By March 1942, the U.S. Army Corps of Engineers had begun work on a supply road that would connect the U.S. and Canadian road systems to Fairbanks, a distance of 1,520 miles. With engineers working just ahead of the bulldozers, the Alaska–Canada Military Highway ("Alcan" for short) was completed in only eight months.

Postwar, engineers have worked almost continuously to improve conditions that initially included 90-degree turns, 25 percent grades, and loose gravel virtually guaranteed to spit up and crack your windshield. Today, though extreme weather requires near-constant maintenance work, the two-lane highway is

almost entirely paved—a significant inroad on America's last frontier.

The road begins officially in Dawson Creek, in northeastern British Columbia, about 825 miles north of Seattle. The Canadian portion of the highway is particularly spectacular, crossing the Canadian Rockies past gorgeous Muncho Lake; going through the town of Watson Lake with its signpost forest (72,000 strong, pointing to every place under the sun); zipping past Whitehorse (the Yukon's largest town) and Kluane Lake (its largest lake) in the Kluane National Park Reserve; then crossing the border into Alaska for the final 500-mile push (200 to Delta Junction and 300 to Fairbanks). Along the way, you'll pass scores of snowcapped mountains and ice fields, lakes mirroring an endless sky, and miles of wilderness—plus museums, gold rush sites, and innumerable hiking, fishing, and canoeing opportunities. All told, the drive takes a minimum of seven to ten days.

Fairbanks is not Alaska's prettiest town, but it's a hub for exploration of Alaska's Interior. The four-day World Eskimo-Indian Olympics is held here in the summer, when more than 400 Native athletes and dancers from around the U.S. and Canada compete in traditional sports. Started in 1961, the event has grown to more than 50 games, plus dance competitions, displays and sale of Native crafts, Native foods, and the crowning of the Miss World Eskimo-Indian Olympics Queen.

In Fairbanks, you can catch the 12-hour Alaska Railroad trip south to Anchorage, stopping at Denali National Park along the way (see p. 912). Expansive picture windows and outdoor viewing areas let you marvel at the scenery and wildlife without worrying about keeping an eye on the road, and tour guides (one per car) are on hand June through August to clue you in on what you're seeing. They even stop for bear sightings.

WHERE: 1,520 miles from Dawson Creek, BC, to Fairbanks. *Highway info:* themilepost .com. **WORLD ESKIMO-INDIAN OLYMPICS:** Fairbanks. Tel 907-452-6646; weio.org. *When:* mid-July. **ALASKA RAILROAD:** Tel 800-544-0552 or 907-265-2494; alaskarailroad.com. *Cost:* $189 (off-peak), $236 (peak). *When:* daily mid-May–mid-Sept; less frequently off-season. **BEST TIMES:** May for wildflowers; June–Aug for weather; late June for Midnight Sun Festival in Fairbanks; Sept for fall colors, but beware of iffy weather.

A sign marks the beginning of the world-famous Alaska Highway.

Hiking and River Trekking in America's Last Great Wilderness

GATES OF THE ARCTIC & NOATAK

Alaska

There was a time not too long ago when a person could travel west and be all alone in total wilderness—no trails to guide their way, no jets overhead, and no sign of humanity anywhere in sight. Those days are long gone throughout most of the Lower 48, but up here the contiguous Gates of the Arctic National Park and Noatak National Preserve represent one of the world's largest areas of protected and utterly pristine wilderness.

The 8.5-million-acre Gates of the Arctic National Park was always intended to remain wild, with a poetic mandate that it provide "opportunities for visitors to experience solitude." That it does: On any given day, there are likely to be fewer than 50 visitors—which means they each have 164,000 acres all to themselves. With no trails, you're completely immersed in the stern mountains, vast tundra, and wide, sweeping valleys, which in summer bloom with a profusion of wildflowers. Several Athabascan and Inupiat subsistence communities survive here, but you'll find far more animals than humans, including musk ox, wolves, brown and black bears, thousands of migrating caribou, and more than 145 species of birds.

Gates of the Arctic and Noatak, just to the west, offer two of America's best wilderness float trips, on the 350-mile Kobuk River and 400-mile Noatak. From Walker Lake in the park's southern section, the Kobuk is navigable for its entire length, with a few short stretches of rapids that can reach Class V. Tracking the south side of the Brooks Range and connecting with a series of small lakes, it flows westward through Kobuk Valley National Park before joining the Chukchi Sea at Kotzebue Sound.

To the north, the Noatak is the largest unaltered, mountain-ringed river basin in America, preserving 330 miles of officially designated Wild and Scenic River. From headwaters just north of Walker Lake, on the slopes of Mt. Igikpak, the mostly Class I and Class II river flows around the northern side of the Brooks, passing through broad, sloping valleys and high-walled canyons before turning south to Kotzebue Sound. It's one of the most elemental river experiences in North America.

Bettles, population 63 and 35 miles north of the Arctic Circle, is a wise choice for a base. The rustic Bettles Lodge is open year-round, which means a wintertime promise of the northern lights.

WHERE: 200 miles northwest of Fairbanks. GATES OF THE ARCTIC: Tel 907-692-5494; nps.gov/gaar. NOATAK: Tel 907-442-3890; nps.gov/noat. HOW: Arctic Treks (tel 907-455-6502; arctictreksadventures.com) and Arctic Wild (tel 888-577-8203 or 907-479-8203; arcticwild.com) both offer backpacking and canoeing trips in Aug–Sept. *Cost:* from $5,400 for 8-night canoe trip. BETTLES LODGE: Tel 907-692-5111; bettleslodge.com. *Cost:* $1,140 per person for 2-night stay, includes meals and air transfer from Fairbanks. BEST TIMES: July–Aug for warmer temperatures and caribou viewing; Sept–Mar for spectacular aurora borealis activity.

First-Class Skiing and Sky-High Dining

THE ALYESKA RESORT

Girdwood, Alaska

Alaska really is the last vestige of America's frontier, so the term "deluxe hotel" is sometimes a relative term—except when the accommodations in question are the Alyeska. Opened as a ski resort in 1959, the hotel didn't come into its own until the Japanese Seibu Corporation took over in 1980 and built the luxurious Alyeska Prince. A high-style château that sits in a gorgeous valley surrounded by miles of spruce trees, it is framed by the vast bulk of 3,939-foot Mount Alyeska that looms behind it.

Just 40 miles from Anchorage along the scenic Seward Highway that skirts the Turnigan Arm Waterway, the Alyeska (an Aleut word meaning "great land of white to the east") sits near the funky town of Girdwood in the Chugach Range. Inside, a million board feet of cherrywood paneling link the guest rooms and the public areas, which include a lobby with riveting mountain views and a stunning indoor pool under a wooden A-frame ceiling. Outside, more than 1,600 acres of slopes offer skiing and snowboarding for all abilities. Heli-skiing is also available, as are snowshoeing, cross-country skiing, dogsledding, and flightseeing. In summer, the resort offers glacier and trail hiking, white-water rafting, salmon and halibut fishing, and bear viewing, plus access to the 18-hole, par-72 Anchorage Golf Course, where during summer you can play from 4:30 A.M. till after midnight.

In the evening, ride the aerial tramway up the mountain for dinner or drinks at the sumptuous Seven Glaciers Restaurant. Its view—possibly the best at any U.S. ski resort—inspired its name: On a clear day, you really can see seven glaciers while sampling from a menu that focuses on Alaskan seafood and game.

WHERE: 40 miles south of Anchorage. Tel 800-880-3880 or 907-754-2111; alyeskaresort .com. *Cost:* from $139 (off-peak), from $319 (peak); lift tickets from $60; dinner at Seven Glaciers $70. **SEWARD HIGHWAY:** themilepost .com. **BEST TIMES:** Mar for winter daylight and highest average snowfall; June for constant daylight and the driest weather.

The Making of the World, Right Before Your Eyes

GLACIER BAY NATIONAL PARK

Alaska

At the far northern end of Alaska's Inside Passage (see next page), Glacier Bay is like a time-lapse photo of our world being born. Its stones, which endured beneath as much as 4,000 feet of ice for thousands of years, still bear the deep grooves left by glaciers that only started retreating in the 19th century. Its soil is now rising at more than an inch a year as it recovers from all that weight. Flora and fauna are also returning, with forests clustered at the bay's entrance but becoming more and more sparse the farther you penetrate, following the slowly receding ice. Humpback whales arrive in great numbers each summer to feed on the bay's bounty, while bears, moose, and mountain goats mine the shoreline.

The 3-million-acre park extends some 65 miles from Icy Strait to the northern tip of Tarr Inlet, with 11 tidewater glaciers pouring down from the mountains like the frozen rivers they really are. In the western arm of the bay, the Reid, Lamplugh, Margerie, Johns Hopkins, and Grand Pacific glaciers are all approached regularly by cruise ships, though the Park Service limits the number of vessels in the bay on any given day.

For those who want more than a quick day-visit on a cruise, the park-run Glacier Bay Lodge sits right at the entrance to the park, while a 10-mile drive down the road brings you to the welcoming Gustavus Inn, a former homestead and farm. Both the lodge and inn can arrange day trips into the park by foot, boat, or mountain bike, though the most personal way to see the bay may be by sea kayak, either on your own or on a guided expedition.

WHERE: Park entrance is 95 miles northwest of Juneau. Tel 907-697-2230; nps.gov/glba.

Experience Glacier Bay leisurely by kayak or boat.

When: visitor center open May–Sept. **GLACIER BAY LODGE:** Tel 888-229-8687 or 907-264-4600; visitglacierbay.com. *Cost:* from $245. *When:* late May–Sept. **GUSTAVUS INN:** Gustavus. Tel 800-649-5220 or 907-697-2254; gustavus inn.com. *Cost:* $225 per person, double

occupancy; day cruise $225. *When:* May–Sept. **KAYAKING:** Glacier Bay Sea Kayaks for rentals (tel 907-697-2257; glacierbayseakayaks.com; from $40 for half-day). **BEST TIMES:** Services in winter are extremely limited; May and June get the least rain; July and Aug are warmest.

Another Land Made of Water

SAILING THE INSIDE PASSAGE

Alaska

T he Inside Passage is like a red carpet to the 49th state, stretching through some 500 miles of Southeast Alaska, from near British Columbia's Queen Charlotte Islands in the south to Skagway in the north. More than two

dozen mainstream ships sail through this island-studded southeast region each summer, carrying a full third of all visitors to Alaska. And that's not even counting the long-distance year-round state ferries, known as the Alaska Marine Highway.

The big draw is wilderness, with snow-capped mountains and deep rain forests stretching as far as the eye can see. Glacier Bay (see previous page) has the most name recognition of Southeast's wild areas, but it's hardly alone. In Tracy Arm Fjord, mile-high mountains rise right from the waterline, striped by falls of meltwater from the peaks. Near the

fjord's forked end, the waters can become almost impassably choked with ice, which calves off the twin South and North Sawyer glaciers by the ton. Some bergs are as big as your ship, while others are only large enough to accommodate a sunbathing harbor seal.

Farther to the south, Misty Fjords National Monument is a primordial place, its 2.3 million acres of wilderness accessible via a series of narrow fjords—so narrow that only small ships can enter. Hemlock and spruce forests crowd the waterline, backed by 3,000-foot cliffs, with an almost ever-present mist providing the area's name and its otherworldly, Tolkienesque atmosphere.

And everywhere there's wildlife, from the bald eagles soaring overhead to the brown and black bears feeding on salmon at the water's edge. The stars of the show are undoubtedly the whales, especially the giant humpbacks that feed and play in the region's cold waters each summer.

Tucked into all that nature are the towns. Sitka, midway up Southeast, is the region's prettiest (see p. 923), while southernmost Ketchikan may be its most touristy. Farther north lies Juneau, Alaska's easygoing capital city, with its hilly downtown, its mountaintop

Cruising the Inside Passage affords the chance to see majestic humpback whales up close.

hiking trails, and nearby Mendenhall Glacier (see next entry). Skagway, to the east of Glacier Bay, is a charming, well-preserved gold rush town that now mines tourists' wallets instead. Admire the 19th-century architecture, then grab a trail map and walk into the hills, or ride the historic narrow-gauge White Pass and Yukon Route Railroad to the 2,865-foot summit of White Pass.

Ships operating in Alaska range from megacruisers carrying more than 2,500 passengers (the biggest player is *Princess* with more than 3,000 passengers), down to 60-passenger expedition ships. The megaships offer cheaper rates, but the small ships can sometimes reach places inaccessible to larger ships and offer the better experience of real Alaska, often concentrating on natural areas and smaller, less-visited towns. For a more budget-friendly experience, the Alaska Marine Highway ferries afford a kind of Eurail adventure along the coast, letting you stop for days at a time in different towns.

Where: Most cruise ships sail from Vancouver, Anchorage, or Seattle. **How:** One small-ship operator to try is Lindblad Expeditions (tel 800-EXPEDITION or 212-261-9000; expeditions.com). Regent Seven Seas Cruises offers a more luxurious experience on a 490-passenger vessel (tel 844-473-4368 or 732-335-3251; rssc.com). *Cost:* from $650 per person per day, double occupancy, for small ships; from $800 per person per day on larger ships. *When:* Cruises run May–Sept. **State ferries:** Tel 800-642-0066 or 907-465-3941; state.ak.us/amhs.wpyr.com. **Railroad:** Tel 800-343-7373. *Cost:* from $119 roundtrip. **Best times:** May–June is driest; July–Aug is warmest; May and Sept have the lowest rates and smallest crowds.

A Bird's-Eye View on the Passage of Time

HELICOPTER GLACIER TREKS

Juneau, Alaska

Every year, thousands of people come to Alaska specifically to see glaciers, watching from sea level as they calve off huge icebergs. Yes, it's impressive, but what is truly awesome is the other 99.9 percent of those glaciers, the part that snakes up, up, up into the mountains, far out of sight.

Glaciers are born in the high altitudes, where temperatures never exceed freezing. When snow falls, it compacts the snow below it, eventually building up such pressure that the bottom layers turn to dense ice. All that ice spreads out into an ice field, and when its edge finds a valley heading downhill, it starts to flow like a very, very slow-moving river—.000005 miles per hour slow. In Juneau, for example, it takes 250 years for ice born in the Juneau Icefield to travel the length of the Mendenhall Glacier to Mendenhall Lake, 12 miles below.

Take to the air to experience Alaska's inaccessible glacial treasures.

Visitors who stare at the ice face, waiting for bergs to crack off into the water, witness only the final moments of that long voyage.

Located 13 miles north of downtown, Mendenhall is a major tourist destination, but you'll have it (or one of the other Juneau-area glaciers) almost to yourself if you sign up for a helicopter trek. You'll spend about half an hour following the great flow of ice into the mountains, witnessing its full immensity before landing on the surface for a walkabout. Sign up for a more strenuous trip and you may spend four or more hours climbing in rugged terrain, descending ice walls, and exploring glacial pools and ice caves. Get down on your knees to drink from one of the many streams flowing along the ice surface, or peer down into a bottomless blue crevasse, your hands resting on ice that may have formed when George Washington was president.

WHERE: 600 miles southeast of Anchorage. **HOW:** North Star Trekking caters to small groups, spending 1 to 4 hours on the ice (tel 907-790-4530; northstartrekking.com). *Cost:* from $359, includes equipment. *When:* May–Sept. **WHERE TO STAY:** Pearson's Pond Luxury Inn and Adventure Spa, tel 888-658-6328 or 907-789-3772; pearsonspond.com. *Cost:* from $239 (off-peak), from $399 (peak). **BEST TIME:** May–June tends to be the driest and sunniest.

A Sportsmen's Paradise in Anchorage's Backyard

THE KENAI PENINSULA & PRINCE WILLIAM SOUND

Alaska

Sitting right across a narrow channel from metropolitan Anchorage, the nature-packed Kenai Peninsula is like a movie trailer of Alaska highlights: incredible fishing, hiking, and kayaking opportunities; prolific wildlife;

and, on its eastern coast, stunning Prince William Sound with its dozens of glaciers.

From Anchorage, it's only 100 miles by car to Cooper Landing on the Kenai River, where fishermen stand shoulder to shoulder during heavy runs, pulling in some of the world's biggest salmon. Keep going another 120 miles and you're in the artsy town of Homer, a small town (population 5,000) that fancies itself both a cultural and fishing hub. Drop into Homer's landmark Salty Dawg Saloon, an old trapper's hut where tourists hoist their beers with local fishermen and cannery workers. The best halibut grounds in Southcentral lie just an hour out to sea.

From Homer, a kayak trek or boat trip across gorgeous Kachemak Bay provides glimpses of terns, puffins, cormorants, and hundreds of resident sea otters. On the bay's distant shore, the town of Halibut Cove sits on pilings above the water, its art galleries and houses connected by boardwalks. The charming Saltry Restaurant offers a wooded location and great seafood dinners, via a water taxi from Homer. Just to the south, the enchanting fly-in Kachemak Bay Wilderness Lodge is the ultimate escape-cum-classroom, where six luxurious private cabins blend into the landscape. Some guests come to fish, others to explore the wilderness in the company of staff naturalists, others for the Dungeness crab, salmon, and halibut, all prepared to perfection. For more intimacy, book the lodge's Loonsong Mountain Lake Chalet, a private retreat with two bedrooms, a network of hiking trails, a mountain lake, and a Finnish sauna.

On the eastern edge of the Kenai, the towns of Seward (named for the secretary of state who purchased Alaska from Russia in 1867) and Whittier serve as jumping-off points not only for dozens of cruise ships but for more elemental exploration. From Seward, sightseeing boats take you out to Kenai Fjords National Park, where waves and tectonic forces have carved the coast into a rugged natural cathedral filled with whales, seabirds, waterfalls, and brown bears. From Whittier and Valdez, boats and kayaks head out for day trips onto Prince William Sound, full of wooded islands, tidewater glaciers, and wildlife.

WHERE: beginning about 50 miles southeast of Anchorage. *Visitor info:* Tel 907-262-5229; kenaipeninsula.org. **SALTY DAWG SALOON:** Homer. Tel 907-235-6718; saltydawg saloon.com. **SALTRY RESTAURANT:** Halibut Cove. Tel 907-399-2683; halibut-cove-alaska .com. *Cost:* dinner $45. **KACHEMAK BAY WILDERNESS LODGE:** China Poot Bay. Tel 907-235-8910; alaskawildernesslodge.com. *Cost:* $2,100 per person for 2 nights, includes meals

and activities; Loonsong $1,800 for 3 nights. **KAYAKING IN HOMER:** True North Kayak. Tel 907-235-0708; truenorthkayak.com. *Cost:* guided day trips from $160. *When:* May–Sept or Oct. **KENAI FJORDS TOURS:** Seward. Tel 877-777-4051 or 907-224-8068; kenaifjords.com. *Cost:* from $89. *When:* May–Sept. **KAYAKING ON PRINCE WILLIAM SOUND:** Prince William Sound Kayak Center, Whittier. Tel 877-472-2452 or 907-472-2452; pwskayakcenter.com. *Cost:* day tours from $189. *When:* May–Sept. **BEST TIMES:** May and Sept for smaller crowds.

Steller sea lions lounge on Prince William Sound.

Bear Viewing in Paradise

KODIAK ISLAND & THE KATMAI COAST

Alaska

For bear lovers, there is no better place than Kodiak National Wildlife Refuge or nearby Katmai National Park. The second-largest island in the U.S. after Hawaii's Big Island, Kodiak is sufficiently separated from the

mainland that Kodiak bears are considered a distinct type within the brown bear family, noticeably larger (owing to their protein-rich diet) than their cousin the grizzly. About 3,500 Kodiak browns live on the island, mostly within the 1.9-million-acre refuge, which

encompasses a full two-thirds of Kodiak's landmass. In spring, they tend to favor the high country, but beginning in mid-June visitors can see them fishing in the island's hundred-plus rivers and streams. As there are no roads in the refuge, you'll need to hire a boat or floatplane to take you in. You can come as part of an organized bear-viewing trip, but you can also be dropped off at one of the eight forest service cabins (available by lottery) or at remote fishing spots on Kodiak's rivers and lakes. Along with the wildlife, you'll find rich rain forests, a craggy coast of wide bays, glacially carved valleys whose green summer coat rivals Ireland's, a mild maritime climate, and a genial main town with reminders of its history as Russia's first permanent settlement in North America.

On the mainland, across a 30-mile channel, the bear viewing is even better at the Katmai National Park and Preserve, where planes from Kodiak may travel to watch bears dig for clams in the tidal flats. Away from the coast, the main focus is on the Brooks River, where as many as 50 browns can be seen at a time during the peak sockeye salmon season. Three viewing platforms are set up within walking distance of the Brooks Lodge, the most comfortable accommodations in the park. In addition to bear viewing, the lodge offers plenty of opportunity for fly-fishing.

WHERE: About 290 miles southwest of Anchorage. **KODIAK NATIONAL WILDLIFE REFUGE:** Tel 888-408-3514 or 907-487-2600; fws.gov/refuge/kodiak. *Cost:* cabins $45. **KATMAI NATIONAL PARK:** Tel 907-246-3305; nps.gov/katm. **BROOKS LODGE:** Tel 800-544-0551 or 907-243-5448; katmailand.com. *Cost:* 3-night air/lodging package, $1,836 per person, double occupancy. *When:* June–Sept. **BEST TIMES:** July–mid-Aug for bear viewing and salmon fishing in Kodiak; July and Sept in Brooks River. Salmon runs vary year by year but typically occur June–Sept.

Just to Say You've Been There

NOME

Alaska

N ome is almost synonymous with "the middle of nowhere," though in fact it's really the *edge* of nowhere: on the coast of the Bering Sea, equidistant from the Russian border and the Arctic Circle, and a whole lot farther from everything else. People began coming here in 1899 after three lucky Swedes discovered gold on Anvil Creek, and within a year the city hosted a full third of Alaska's non-Native residents. Large-scale mining ended in the 1980s, but individual panners still live in tents along the beach, hoping for the next big strike. Wander through the dirt streets and take in the frontier ambience. A fire in 1934 destroyed many of the old buildings, but there's still a string of rough-and-tumble saloons (and a sign marking where Wyatt Earp's saloon stood in 1899), a platform that's the official end-point of the annual Iditarod race (see p. 909), and a few shops that sell art from nearby Native villages.

Living here apparently gives people an off-kilter sense of humor. In March, the monthlong Iditarod celebration includes the six-hole par-41 Bering Sea Ice Golf Classic, in which competitors walk out onto the frozen sea to hit orange golf balls off old shotgun shells, aiming for Astroturf greens. If the ice has broken up by June, bathers can brave the 40°F water of the annual Polar Bear Swim—or they can wait a few months, put their bathtub on wheels, and compete in the Labor Day Bathtub Race down Front Street. Each team must finish with a bar of soap, towel, bath mat, and at least ten gallons of water; the winners get to keep the "Miss Piggy & Kermit Taking a Bath" trophy for a year.

Outside town, Nome's 350 miles of roads make it the jumping-off point for exploring the area's amazing subarctic wilderness. Drive 30 miles north on the Nome-Teller road to reach the awesomely beautiful and incredibly undervisited Kigluaik Mountains. This is real wilderness, but many of its most scenic vistas can nevertheless be viewed on long day-hikes, or even from the road.

Another 40 miles will take you to the Native village of Teller, population 247. You'll be rewarded with spectacular scenery along the way (plus a chance to see some of Seward Peninsula's 8,000 reindeer) and friendly people and good craftwork when you arrive. Farther north, beyond the road system, the 2.7-million-acre Bering Land Bridge National Preserve is some of America's most remote and little-visited national parkland, offering wilderness trekking in a harsh landscape full

of lava flows, tundra, and granite spires. In the other direction, southeast along the coast of Norman Sound, the Unalakleet River Lodge is a living dream for fly-fishers, with room for only 14 guests and more than 100 miles of fishable water. Nights are spent nestled into the warm, woody, hilltop lodge, offering a view of the Unalakleet Valley below and gourmet meals served near its stone fireplace.

WHERE: 540 miles northwest of Anchorage. *Visitor info:* Tel 907-443-6555; visitnomealaska .com. **BERING LAND BRIDGE PRESERVE:** Tel 800-471-2352 or 907-443-2522; nps.gov/bela. **UNALAKLEET RIVER LODGE:** Tel: 800-995-1978 or 907-624-3031; unalakleet.com. *Cost:* 7-night package $5,300 per person, double occupancy, includes meals and guided fishing. *When:* mid-June–mid-Sept. **BEST TIMES:** Mar for Iditarod events; mid-June for Polar Bear Swim; summer for fishing and weather.

A Wildlife Shangri-la, Remote as Timbuktu

THE PRIBILOF ISLANDS

Alaska

Once volcanic mountain peaks on a 1,000-mile grassland steppe that stretched from Siberia to Alaska, the Pribilofs became islands at the end of the last ice age, when melting glaciers caused the oceans to rise. So cut off were these peaks, some 300 miles from the Alaskan mainland, that stranded wooly mammoths survived here for some 3,500 years after their species became extinct on the mainland.

Russian navigator Gavriil Pribilof discovered the uninhabited islands in 1786, while searching for fur seal breeding grounds. He struck the mother lode: St. Paul and St. George (the two largest islands, along with smaller Otter Island, Walrus Island, and Sea Lion Rock) are the summer pupping grounds for 800,000 Northern Pacific fur seals, the greatest such concentration in the world. The commercial seal trade, worked by transplanted Aleut laborers

under Russian and then American control, continued on the islands until 1985, when pressure from animal rights groups scaled it back to a subsistence harvest for Natives.

Today, you can see thousands of seals at their rocky seaside rookeries, the male beachmasters roaring, the smaller females belching, and the babies mewling—while nearby some of the islands' 2.5 million seabirds build their cliff nests, circle overhead, or fish in the frigid Bering waters. Experts typically count the Pribilofs among the top birding sites in the United States (if not the world), with nearly 254 species either in residence or passing through on their migrations. Tufted and horned puffins, common and thick-billed murres, crested auklets, red-faced cormorants, and northern fulmars are common, and 82 percent of the red-legged kittiwakes in North America choose the Pribilofs for their nesting ground. Because of the islands' proximity to Siberia, Asian species are commonly sighted as well. On land, you may spot arctic blue fox or one of the islands' secretive reindeer, while harbor

In summer, St. Paul's volcanic terrain is coated in green grass.

seals breed on Otter Island and Steller sea lions haul out on St. Paul and Walrus Island.

Representing the vast majority of the islands' human population, the 572 Aleut residents make up the largest remaining Aleut population on earth. They survive in an environment that is exceedingly harsh. Volcanic and treeless, the Pribilofs are constantly hounded by winds, rain, and heavy fog, though summer's comparative warmth brings lush green grasses and more than 100 species of wildflowers.

Where: in the Bering Sea, 750 miles southwest of Anchorage. **How:** Most visitors arrive by tour, arranged through St. Paul Island Tours, tel 877-424-5637 or 907-278-2312; alaskabirding.com. *Cost:* from $2,329 for 3-day tour, includes transportation from Anchorage and shared accommodations. *When:* May–mid-Sept. **Best time:** late June–July, when seabird chicks are abundant, fur seal pups are active, and the islands are greenest.

A Treasure Trove of Colonial Russian and Tlingit History

SITKA

Alaska

K nown in the early 19th century as the "Paris of the Pacific," Sitka is the least touristy large town on the Alaskan Panhandle, with 9,000 residents and a rich history that encompasses its days as a center of Tlingit Indian

culture and the capital of Russian America. Sitka preserves both of its heritages in one of the prettiest settings in the region, surrounded by mountains and facing the vast sweep of the Gulf of Alaska.

The rich, powerful Kiksadi Tlingit clan occupied land at the head of Sitka Sound for centuries, but in 1799 Alexander Baranof, manager of the Russian-American Company, arrived to establish a fort, expand his fur-trading operation, and consolidate Russia's territorial claims. Faced with subjugation, the Tlingit attacked the fort in 1802 and killed

almost everyone inside. Two years later Baranof returned with reinforcements, forcing the tribe to make way for the new colonial city of Novoarkhangelsk (New Archangel).

The Russian Orthodox St. Michael's Cathedral sits at the very center of town. Designed and built by Bishop (now Saint) Innocent Veniaminov in the 1840s, it's full of icons and paintings from the period and has a congregation composed mostly of Native Alaskan peoples. Nearby, the Russian Bishop's House, run by the National Park Service, features a museum of Sitka history and several restored residential rooms. Furniture built by the Renaissance-man bishop is on display, as is his private chapel. Down the road, the Sitka National Historical Park preserves the battleground where the Tlingit and Russians waged their bloody fight, which you can learn more about at the park's interpretive center. You can also walk the haunting forest trail lined with totem poles.

Back in town, performances by the Sheetka'Kwaan Naa Kahidi Dancers and the New Archangel Dancers help preserve the town's dual heritage. Other sites worth exploring include Castle Hill, where Russia ceremonially transferred Alaska to the U.S. in 1867, and where the first U.S. flag was raised on Alaska soil, and the Sheldon Jackson Museum of Native arts.

WHERE: 150 miles southwest of Juneau. *Visitor info:* Tel 907-747-5940; sitka.org. **RUSSIAN BISHOP'S HOUSE AND SITKA NATIONAL HISTORICAL PARK:** Tel 907-747-0110; nps .gov/sitk. **DANCE INFO:** sitkatours.com and newarchangeldancers.com. **SHELDON JACKSON**

Snow caps the dome of St. Michael's Russian Orthodox Cathedral.

MUSEUM: Tel 907-747-8981; museums.alaska .gov/sheldon_jackson. **WHERE TO STAY:** Otter's Cove B&B, tel 907-747-4529; ottercovebandb .com. *Cost:* from $140 (off-peak), from $175 (peak). **BEST TIMES:** May and Sept for smaller summer crowds; early Nov for the annual Sitka Whale Festival (sitkawhalefest.org).

There's Gold in Them Thar Hills!

HIKING THE CHILKOOT TRAIL

Skagway, Alaska

In 1896, prospectors discovered gold in a tributary of Canada's Klondike River, and thousands of starry-eyed men started dreaming of wealth. Trouble was, they had to go to Alaska to get it, setting out on the 33-mile Chilkoot Trail bound for the Yukon—and that was a bit more than most of them bargained for. Though it's only 16.5 miles from the old supply town of Dyea to the Canadian border, the Chilkoot rises some 3,600 vertical feet through the coastal mountains, with 2,300 of those feet inside a short 7-mile stretch. By itself that was manageable for a determined gold-seeker, but Canada's mounted police required that everyone entering their territory carry an entire year's worth of provisions. This forced prospectors to take an incremental route, carrying a portion of their supplies to a drop spot and then returning to Dyea for more, all the while numbed by temperatures that could fall to 50 below zero. The process often took as many as 20 trips, and once it was completed they still had to make the long trek to the goldfields.

Today hikers can re-create that tortured march in three to five days. Pick up your trail permits in nearby Skagway, then catch a taxi-van 9 miles north to Dyea—or what's left of it, since nearly everyone vacated by 1903. From there, you have an easy start through coastal forest. Even though the terrain is rough and often muddy, you might start to feel cocky—that is, until you look up and see the huge wall of granite rising in front of you. Beyond Sheep Camp, the forests thin out until you're in high alpine terrain, and by the time you reach the Scales—where the miners' goods were once weighed—you'll know exactly why so many of those miners just chucked it all and went home. From here you don't even have a trail to follow until you're past the summit; it's just "up." Take heart: From the top you hike down through beautiful boreal forest and on to Lake Bennett. There's not much there now, but during the gold rush there was a restaurant called the Arctic, run by entrepreneur Fred Trump, Donald Trump's grandfather.

WHERE: Dyea is 111 miles northwest

of Juneau. *Hiking info:* Tel 907-983-9200; nps.gov/klgo. *Cost:* permits $20 (U.S. side only), $55 (entire trail). **How:** Dyea-Chilkoot Trail Transit provides shuttle service to hikers (tel 907-617-7551). *Cost:* $15 per person one-way. **BEST TIMES:** Trail is generally free of snow mid-July–mid-Aug, though this is also the busiest season; mid-Aug–late Sept has wetter weather and colder temperatures, but hiking conditions generally remain good.

Though physically taxing, the Chilkoot Trail rewards those who persevere with stunning views of the Alaskan wilderness.

Deep Powder, Steep Slopes . . . and No Tracks

HELI-SKIING IN THE CHUGACH MOUNTAINS

Valdez, Alaska

S tretching east to west just above Prince William Sound (see p. 919), the 300-mile Chugach Range is perfectly positioned between warm air from the Pacific and arctic air from the Alaskan interior, which mix together to make

snow—lots of snow. It's the kind of fine, dry, deep powder that skiers dream about, and when layered over almost unlimited runs of 3,000 to 5,000 vertical feet across 2,500 square miles of empty, pristine slopes, it's some kind of heaven for advanced to expert skiers only. The town of Valdez is the hub of backcountry skiing in the Chugach, home to numerous operators, guides, and extreme skiing competitions. The average annual snowfall in town is 325 inches, and in

the Thompson Pass area, outside town, 900 inches isn't uncommon. Valdez Heli-Ski Guides and Alaska Backcountry Adventures both offer guided Chugach heli-skiing, with skiers able to choose as much or as little adventure as they want, from full-day six-run programs to weeklong packages. Small groups of four to five skiers and professional guides head by helicopter to mountains that match the group's level of experience. It's all about fast, hard skiing, with the average run lasting up to an hour and the average guest completing six to

The Chugach Mountains offer skiers spectacular views of glaciers.

ten difficult runs a day. With daylight in springtime often stretching until 10 P.M., you have all the time you need.

WHERE: 120 miles east of Anchorage. **VALDEZ HELI-SKI:** Tel 907-835-4528; valdez heliskiguides.com. *Cost:* 3-day packages $4,629; weeklong packages $10,806, includes lodging. *When:* late-Feb–early May. **ALASKA BACKCOUNTRY ADVENTURES:** Tel 907-835-5608; alaskabackcountry.com. *Cost:* full-day packages $1,000; weeklong packages from $7,000, includes lodging. *When:* Mar–Apr. **BEST TIMES:** Feb–Mar for the deepest powder, though days are shorter and colder; Apr–May for longer days and a mix of powder and corn snow.

The Heavyweight Champ of National Parks

WRANGELL-ST. ELIAS NATIONAL PARK

Alaska

Imagine a wilderness bigger than Vermont and Rhode Island put together, but where fewer than 250 visitors show up most days. Imagine further that it's connected to another enormous stretch right across the Canadian border

(Kluane National Park), forming one of the largest internationally protected ecosystems on the planet. That's Wrangell-St. Elias, the largest of the U.S. National Parks and the only binational World Heritage Site on the globe.

Located a day's drive east of Anchorage where the Chugach, Wrangell, and St. Elias ranges converge, the park is home to 9 of the continent's 16 tallest mountains, as well as the largest collection of glaciers in North America. At 18,008 feet, Mount St. Elias is the second-highest peak in the U.S. (after Denali, see p. 912), while 14,163-foot Mount Wrangell is one of the continent's largest active volcanoes.

Hikers can choose from short, marked day-trails near the visitor center or unmarked multi-day routes that reach remote lakes, valleys,

glaciers, and abandoned mountainside copper mines. Rafters and kayakers can run the 77-mile route down the Copper River from the village of Chitina to the Gulf of Alaska, passing through some of the park's harshest terrain. Visitors with more horsepower than stamina can explore the rugged McCarthy Road, a 61-mile gravel drive from Chitina through the heart of the park, full of great hiking, camping, wildlife-watching, and fishing opportunities. Four miles beyond the end of the road, accessible via shuttle, the old company town of Kennecott preserves some 40 mine-owned buildings in various stages of restoration. The ghost town is considered the best remaining example of an early 20th-century copper mining operation. Five miles down the road, McCarthy is a more active town with restaurants, lodgings, and other visitor services. Beyond the remote southeast corner of the park and accessible only by air and ferry, the small town of Yakutat is notable for exceptional salmon and halibut fishing as well as (believe it or not) surfing.

In the heart of the park, a hundred miles from anything and accessible only by bush plane, the family-run Ultima Thule Lodge is all about the outdoors, plus niceties like a wood-fired sauna bathhouse, a dozen log cabins with balconies, and a dining hall serving local salmon and fresh-picked organic greens. All activities are included, with decisions about the day's schedule made over breakfast. Options include bush plane flightseeing (landing on glaciers, mountaintops, and ocean beaches), hiking through untracked valleys and tundra, fishing, rafting, wildlife viewing, climbing, and incredible skiing. There's even a 50-dog kennel, where guests can learn the ropes and take out a dogsledding team. Unlike many of Alaska's deep-country lodges, Ultima Thule is open year-round.

WHERE: park visitor center at Copper Center, 190 miles northeast of Anchorage. Tel 907-822-5234; nps.gov/wrst. **HOW:** St. Elias Alpine Guides (tel 888-933-5427 or 907-544-4445; steliasguides.com) offers guided rafting trips and glacier trekking. *Cost:* from $295 per person for 1-day rafting trip; $1,250 per person for 4-day trek. For surfing in Yakutat, Icy Waves Surf Shop, tel 907-784-3226; icywaves.com. **ULTIMA THULE LODGE:** Chitina. Tel 907-854-4500; ultimathulelodge.com. *Cost:* $1,925 per person per night, all-inclusive. **WHERE ELSE TO STAY:** Kennicott Glacier Lodge, tel 800-582-5128 or 907-258-2350; kennicottlodge.com. *Cost:* from $195. *When:* mid-May–mid-Sept. The McCarthy Lodge and Ma Johnson's Hotel, tel 907-554-4402; mccarthylodge.com. *Cost:* from $229. *When:* mid-May–Sept. **BEST TIMES:** mid-Apr–mid-June and mid-Aug–early Oct for surfing; May–June for red salmon fishing on Copper River. The McCarthy Road is passable to most vehicles mid-May–mid-Sept, which are also the best months for weather.

The abandoned mining city of Kennecott affords a glimpse into the 20th-century copper industry.

Birth of an Island

HAWAII VOLCANOES NATIONAL PARK

Big Island, Hawaii

Born of violent underwater eruptions and shaped by a million years of pounding waves, driving rain, and occasional earthquakes, Big Island is the youngest and largest of the 1,500-mile-long Hawaiian archipelago (measuring 93 by 76 miles, it's about the size of Connecticut). The island, a miracle of diversity, contains 11 of earth's 13 climate zones—from lush tropical rain forests to desolate, black lava deserts to arctic tundra. Its beaches offer white, black, and even green shades of sand.

The island's most prominent features are its five volcanoes; the largest, Mauna Kea, extends from sea level to 13,796 feet. View these primitive forces in the 330,000-acre Hawaii Volcanoes National Park, a journey back into the creation of earth, where deep, smoldering calderas hiss, smoky black pit craters belch out sulfur fumes, multihued cinder cones provide the backdrop for miles of charcoal-colored flows, and lava tubes cut their way through the junglelike prehistoric subway tunnels. Kilauea Volcano, the world's most

Lava enters the ocean along the coastline of the Big Island.

active and the park's biggest draw, has been spewing 2,000°F molten lava almost continuously since 1983. According to ancient legend, Pele, goddess of the volcano, searched the entire Hawaiian island chain before settling in Kilauea's Halemaumau Crater, and today she continues to create land through daily eruptions.

From the visitor center on the north rim, follow Crater Rim Drive, an 11-mile loop that circles the summit, traverses a desert, and winds through a native rain forest. Sites along the way include Kilauea Caldera, a 2.5-mile-wide, 500-foot-deep pit; the Sulphur Banks and Steam Vents, where an active volcano emits trails of smoke and steam; and Pele's home, Halemaumau Crater. Depending on volcanic activity, there may be opportunities for viewing active lava flows; check with rangers at the visitor center about where and how. At night the streaming lava glows like an incandescent ribbon on the flank of the mountain.

Where: 30 miles southwest of Hilo. Tel 808-985-6000; nps.gov/havo. **Where to stay:** The 1846 newly renovated Volcano House (the only hotel within the park), tel 808-441-7750; hawaiivolcanohouse.com. *Cost:* from $185. **Best times:** Apr–May and Sept–mid-Dec, during the off-season; the week after Easter for the Merrie Monarch Festival in Hilo (see next page).

From Mangoes to Mangosteen, a Cornucopia of Exotic Food

HILO FARMERS MARKET

Hilo, Big Island, Hawaii

The sun is just a bright orange line on the eastern horizon, and already more than 200 vendors have set up stands with red heart-shaped anthuriums, Hawaiian sweet corn, green seaweed, pale purple orchids, white pineapples, fiery red lychees, and hundreds of other products at the Hilo Farmers Market, the best in the state. The alluring smell of just-baked bread wafts through the air, mixed with the aroma of traditional Hawaiian *lau lau* (pork, chicken, or fish steamed in ti leaves).

This is the place for an epicurean adventure into the diverse culinary cultures of Hawaii. The selection changes constantly, but it's always fresh, appealing, and reasonably priced. You'll also find seafood, including ahi, *opihi* (limpets), and dried fish, as well as crafts and clothing. The market is open Wednesday and Saturday with vendors selling their flowers, produce, and baked goods from sunrise to about 4 P.M.—or as they say in casual Hawaiian fashion, from dawn 'til it's gone.

After exploring the market, visit some of the area's museums. The Lyman Museum features exhibits focused on Hawaii's natural history, while the 1839 Mission House next door, the oldest wood-frame house on the island, offers a glimpse of the lives of the New England Congregationalist missionaries who built it. The Mokupapapa Discovery Center for Hawaii's Remote Coral Reefs allows visitors to experience a part of Hawaii they're unlikely to see for themselves, the reef ecosystem of the state's far northwest islands. The Pacific Tsunami Museum houses artifacts and exhibits of the devastating "walls of water" that struck Hilo in 1946 and 1960; survivors of those catastrophes are among the museum's volunteers.

There's also the 12-acre Pana'ewa Rainforest Zoo, the only natural (outdoor) tropical rain forest zoo in the U.S. Gardens abound in Hilo—not surprising, given that the city gets nearly 130 inches of rain per year—and among them is the largest formal Japanese garden outside Tokyo, the 30-acre Liliuokalani Gardens on the waterfront. After you take in the sights, you can grab dinner at one of the city's many and varied restaurants; one of the best has long been the Hilo Bay Café, which serves adventurous Pacific Rim cuisine with great views.

WHERE: Kamehameha Ave. at Mamo St. Tel 808-933-1000; hilofarmersmarket.com. *When:* Wed and Sat. **LYMAN MUSEUM AND MISSION HOUSE:** Tel 808-935-5021; lyman museum.org. *When:* closed Sun. **MOKUPAPAPA DISCOVERY CENTER:** Tel 808-933-8180; papahanaumokuakea.gov. *When:* closed Sun–Mon. **TSUNAMI MUSEUM:** Tel 808-935-0926; tsunami.org. *When:* closed Sun–Mon. **PANA'EWA RAINFOREST ZOO:** Tel 808-959-9233; hilozoo .com. **HILO BAY CAFÉ:** Tel 808-935-4939; hilobaycafe.com. *Cost:* dinner $40. **BEST TIME:** sunrise on Sat for the best selection at the market.

The Olympics of Island Dance

MERRIE MONARCH HULA FESTIVAL

Hilo, Big Island, Hawaii

E very year, starting on Easter Sunday for a week, the generally quiet town of Hilo fills with visitors, and hotels as far away as Volcano, 30 miles to the south, swell to capacity. The town's festive mood is due to the annual

Merrie Monarch Festival, Hawaii's largest and most prestigious hula competition. A gorgeous display of performance and pageantry, the fete features intense competitions among the best hula *halau* (schools) from the islands and the

U.S. mainland, with hundreds of dancers and musicians participating. Festival highlights also include the Miss Aloha Hula solo competition and separate female and male halau competing in both *kahiko* (ancient) and *'auana* (modern) styles. There's also a day-long ho'olaule'a (party) at the civic auditorium, and the entire week becomes a joyous celebration of Hawaiian culture, with music, food, and arts and crafts.

The "Merrie Monarch" of the festival's name was Hawaii's last king, David Kalakaua, an enthusiastic patron of the arts who led the revival of the hula and other cultural traditions during his reign from 1874 to 1891. The dance and its accompanying chants (mele), said to have semi-divine origins, communicated history, genealogy, and prayers through the generations before Protestant missionaries introduced a writing system in the 1820s. Those same missionaries regarded the hula as a heathen practice; abetted by Queen Ka'ahumanu, a Christian convert, they suppressed it for a half-century.

First held in 1964 to help Hilo's slumping economy and morale recover from a disastrous tsunami four years earlier, the Merrie Monarch Festival helped spark a revival of Hawaiian culture that began in the 1970s. For decades until 1978, it was illegal to teach Hawaiian as the primary language, but today there are 21 Hawaiian-language immersion programs in schools across the state, educating some 2,000 children. In Hilo itself, the state's Hawaiian Language College is the only college in the U.S. offering a master of arts degree in an indigenous language.

WHERE: The main hula competitions are held at the Edith Kanaka'ole Stadium. Tel 808-935-9168; merriemonarch.com. *Cost:* $35 for 3 nights. *When:* the week beginning with Easter Sun (Mar or Apr). **WHERE TO STAY:** Book a year in advance for the 5-room historic Shipman House B&B in Hilo. Tel 808-934-8002; hilo-hawaii.com. *Cost:* from $219. **BEST TIMES:** Thurs for the crowning of Miss Aloha Hula; Fri for the hula *kahiko* (ancient) competition; Sat for the hula *'auana* (modern) competition.

A Place of Refuge

Pu'uhonua o Honaunau

Honaunau, Big Island, Hawaii

In ancient Hawaii, death was the penalty for breaking a *kapu* (law), but offenders who somehow eluded the chief's warriors could find safety at a *pu'uhonua*, or place of refuge. One of these, Pu'uhonua o Honaunau National Historic Park, is located on the coast south of Kailua-Kona in Honaunau, and in wartime it offered sanctuary to defeated warriors as well as women and children. The 420-acre park is home to the nearly 500-year-old Great Wall. Ten feet high, 1,000 feet long, and 17 feet thick, the wall circumscribes the pu'uhonua proper; outside it lies a complex of archaeological sites, including temple platforms, royal fishponds, and reconstructed thatched huts. The restored temple, Hale o Keawe Heiau, built in 1650 as the burial site of King Kamehameha I's ancestor Keawe, is located along the wall. The temple holds the bones of 23 ancient Hawaiian chiefs—an old Hawaiian belief held that the bones of high-ranking chiefs and powerful warriors carried their *mana*, or spiritual power.

Start your visit with an orientation in the amphitheater, and then take a self-guided tour through the royal grounds. Along the way you'll discover temple sites; a canoe landing featuring koa-wood canoes guarded by carved statues; the stone remains of Hawaiian games such as *konane,* similar to checkers; the royal fishponds; and the pu'uhonua itself. In addition, the park has hands-on demonstrations of Hawaiian culture, including poi-pounding and canoe-making; an oceanside picnic area, shaded by coconut palms; a beach for swimming and snorkeling; tide pools to explore; and from December to April, offshore sightings of green sea turtles and humpback whales.

WHERE: 22 miles south of Kailua-Kona. Tel 808-328-2326; nps.gov/puho. **BEST TIMES:** late June or early July for the Hawaiian Cultural Festival; early Sept for the Queen Liliuokalani Outrigger Canoe Race.

Totems watch over the Hale o Keawe Heiau temple at Pu'uhonua o Honaunau National Historic Park.

Only the Strong Survive

THE IRONMAN TRIATHLON

Kailua-Kona, Big Island, Hawaii

It started as a bet in 1978, when Navy Commander John Collins and his buddies were arguing over which athletes were more fit: swimmers, runners, or cyclists. To settle the dispute, Collins proposed holding a one-day competition that included Honolulu's three most difficult races—the 2.4-mile Waikiki Rough Water Swim, the 112-mile Around O'ahu Bike Race, and the 26.2-mile Honolulu Marathon; the winner would be called "Iron

"Swim 2.4 miles! Bike 112 miles! Run 26.2 miles! Brag for the rest of your life."—John Collins

Man." That first year, just 15 people showed up at Waikiki Beach for the event, 12 finished, and Gordon Haller became the first Ironman, with a time of 11 hours, 46 minutes, 58 seconds. By 1981, more than 300 people signed up to test their mettle, far too many for urban O'ahu, so the race was moved to the then-rural Big Island, where it still takes place. Today, some 100,000 athletes from around the world compete in qualifying races for 2,000 starting positions. Most of the competitors, who range in age from 18 to 80, race just for the T-shirt that proclaims "Ironman Finisher," but the top athletes vie for $650,000 in prize money and lucrative endorsements. As of 2015, the course record is an astonishing 8:03:56, set by 2011 winner Craig Alexander, from Australia.

The best view of the start is on the Kailua Bay seawall. Although the starting gun doesn't go off until 7 A.M., the cherished seawall seats are filled by 5 A.M. Once the swimmers are off, head for the intersection of Palani Road and Kuakini Highway to see the bikers embark on their 112-mile round-trip to the town of Hawi at the tip of the Big Island. At the transition area on the Kailua Pier, by the King Kamehameha Kona Beach Hotel, competitors begin the 26.2-mile run. The best viewing is at the finish line, again at the seawall along Alii Drive, where the winners finish around 3 P.M.

WHERE: start and finish at Kailua Bay and Pier on Alii Drive. Tel 813-868-5940; ironman.com. *When:* Sat closest to the full moon in Oct. **WHERE TO STAY:** King Kamehameha Kona Beach Hotel. Tel 888-236-2427 or 808-329-2911; konabeachhotel .com. *Cost:* from $159 (book a year in advance for Ironman reservations). **BEST TIMES:** around 3 P.M. for the top finishers; just before the midnight cutoff for the most poignant finishing moments.

The Kingdom's Capital

HISTORIC KAILUA-KONA

Kailua-Kona, Big Island, Hawaii

The oceanside tourist town of Kailua-Kona, located at the base of 8,271-foot Hualalai Volcano and known for its sport fishing, is also one of Hawaii's most significant historic sites. It was here in 1812 that Kamehameha I established the capital of the Kingdom of Hawaii, after his 1785–1810 campaign to unite the islands. At Kamakahonu, a sacred spot at the tip of Kailua Bay, he restored the centuries-old temple Ahu'ena Heiau and dedicated it to Lono, the god of peace and prosperity. Today the compound, on the grounds of the King Kamehameha Kona Beach Hotel, measures just a third of its original size but still features an imposing 'anu'u (oracle tower) clad in white tapa cloth and several ki'i akua, carved representations of temple gods.

The year after Kamehameha's death in 1819, the compound witnessed a momentous event: The late king's son Liholiho sat down to dine with his mother, Kamehameha's principal queen, breaking not just the *kapu* that forbade women and men to eat together, but the entire kapu system of restrictions that had governed religious and social life for centuries. Into the resulting spiritual void sailed Christian missionaries. Liholiho welcomed them in and the generous spirit that came to define Hawaiian culture, gave the strangers land next to his own sacred compound. There they built Hawaii's first Christian church, Mokuaikaua Church, which today still stands about 100 yards from the Ahu'ena Heiau; its 112-foot steeple is the tallest man-made structure in Kailua-Kona.

Across the street from Mokuaikaua Church, Hulihe'e Palace, built in 1838 and used for years as a summer residence for royalty, occupies a site overlooking the bay. Now run by the Daughters of Hawaii, the regal mansion offers a window on the lifestyle of Hawaii's ruling classes.

WHERE: the grounds of King Kamehameha Kona Beach Hotel. Tel 888-868-5940 or 808-329-2911; konabeachhotel.com. *When:* guided tours Mon–Fri. **MOKUAIKAUA CHURCH:** Tel 808-329-0655. **HULIHE'E PALACE:** Tel 808-329-1877; huliheepalace.com. **HOW:** Historic Kailua Walking Tour, tel 808-323-3222; kona historical.org. **BEST TIME:** one varying Sun of each month, when the Hulihe'e Palace hosts concerts dedicated to a Hawaiian monarch.

Hawaiian Feast Under the Stars

GATHERING OF THE KINGS LUAU

Kohala Coast, Big Island, Hawaii

Most commercial luau extravaganzas are pale shadows of the grand Hawaiian feasts traditionally held to mark auspicious occasions, but the Gathering of the Kings luau at the Fairmont Orchid is smaller, more intimate, and more authentic. This is the show where locals bring their mainland visitors, both for the performance and the food.

As the shadows lengthen and the drums begin to sound, this oceanside setting is the ideal place to witness the timeless rituals of the luau, in the exact location where ancient kings once feasted. Kalahuipua'a, the "gathering place for chiefs," dates back to A.D. 1200 when it was a celebratory site for ancient Hawaiian royalty. Thousands of petroglyphs carved into nearby lava flows illustrate their ocean journeys of long ago. The ceremony itself presents the historic journey of the Polynesian people through a fusion of traditional Polynesian and modern choreography and music. The high-energy show incorporates fire dancers, stilt warriors, and a bevy of swaying, grass-skirt-clad beauties.

Offsite, preparations for a traditional luau feast get underway in the morning with the lighting of a mesquite-wood fire in the *imu*, an underground earthen oven; a few hours later a whole pig is lowered into it, to cook slowly throughout the afternoon. The *imu* yields over 200 pounds of succulent, shredded *kalua pua'a* (roast pork). It is the highlight of the evening's vast array of traditional luau fare from around Polynesia, including *ahi poke* (raw tuna with seaweed, onion, and spices); a medley of seafood with taro leaves and coconut cream sauce; roast chicken with charred papaya and mango glaze; and lomi-lomi salmon (salt-cured and topped with Maui onions and tomatoes). Mango and coconut cream cake and macadamia nut tarts end the meal on a sweet, tropical note, while Kona beer keeps the libations local and spirits high.

Sprawled across 32 acres of oceanfront, the Fairmont Orchid is a jewel along the Big Island's sunny Kohala Coast. Chic guest rooms and suites are just minutes from the hotel's protected white sand beach, the Spa Without Walls, a 10,000-square foot swimming pool complex, 36 holes of golf, and miles of beachfront hiking trails. Native Hawaiians serve as cultural guides to the area's rich history and appear on the beachfront for the sunset torch lighting ceremony and the ritual blowing of the pū (conch shell).

The Fairmont's Gathering of the Kings luau is open to nonguests and held on Saturday evenings only. Other outstanding Big Island luaus are held more frequently. The Royal Kona Resort luau offers a full *imu* ceremony, and at the Waikoloa Beach Marriott Sunset Luau, you'll find a mix of traditional and contemporary Polynesian cuisine and dance from across the South Pacific.

WHERE: 1 North Kaniku Drive. **GATHERING OF THE KINGS:** Tel 866-482-9775 or 808-326-4969; eventsbyislandbreeze.com. *Cost:* luau $109. *When:* Sat. **FAIRMONT ORCHID:** Tel 800-257-7544 or 808-885-2000; fairmont.com/orchid. *Cost:* from $329 (off-peak), from $419 (peak). **ROYAL KONA LUAU:** Tel 866-482-9775 or 808-329-3111; royalkonaluau.org. *Cost:* luau $91. *When:* Mon–Wed and Fri. **WAIKOLOA BEACH MARRIOTT SUNSET LUAU:**

Tel 808-886-6789; sunsetluau.com. *Cost:* luau $102. *When:* Wed and Sat. **Best times:** 1st weekend in Mar for the Great Waikoloa Ukulele Festival (waikoloabeachresort.com).

A Night in Old Hawaii

TWILIGHT AT KALAHUIPUA'A

Big Island, Hawaii

As a sienna-colored sun sinks slowly into the darkening cobalt waters of the Pacific, the haunting drone of a conch shell pierces the air, calling all to assemble. In the distance, the alpenglow on majestic Mauna Kea fades from fiery red to hazy purple and finally to inky black as the full moon rises over the mountain's shoulder. This is the setting for "Twilight at Kalahuipua'a," a monthly Hawaiian cultural celebration. Its special location is the grassy oceanside lawn of the Eva Parker Woods Cottage, a modest 1920s structure on a small spit between the Kalahuipua'a fishponds and the Pacific at Mauna Lani Resort. (Eva Parker was the great-granddaughter of Parker Ranch founder John Parker; see p. 941.) The unscripted event recalls another time in Hawaii, when family and neighbors would gather in yards and on porches to sing, dance, and "talk story." Each month features guests ranging from famous Hawaiian entertainers to virtually unknown local *kupuna* (elders), all of whom meet to perpetuate the art of traditional storytelling, accompanied by plenty of music and dance. Unlike resort luau with their spectacle and pageantry, this is a casual gathering permeated by the spirit of aloha.

Begun in the late 1990s, Twilight at Kalahuipua'a occurs on the Saturday closest to the full moon. Things get underway at least an hour before the 5:30 P.M. start, when hotel guests and people from across the island begin arriving with picnic baskets, mats, coolers, and babies. A sort of oceanside pre-music tailgate party takes place with *kama'aina* (local resident) families and visitors sharing their plate lunches, sushi, and beverages. The man behind these magical events is the serene, soft-spoken Daniel Akaka Jr., who serves as Mauna Lani Resort's historian. "The spirit of the Twilight at Kalahuipua'a is *ho'okipa*, sharing hospitality by giving," he says. "We want to share our culture, our music, and our dance."

WHERE: 30 miles north of Kailua-Kona; Mauna Lani Resort, Mauna Lani Dr. Tel 808-885-6622. **WHERE TO STAY:** Mauna Lani Bay Hotel, tel 800-367-2323 or 808-885-6622; maunalani.com. *Cost:* from $399. Or the Fairmont Orchid, tel 800-257-7544 or 808-885-2000; fairmont.com/orchid. *Cost:* from $329. **BEST TIME:** To get a good seat at Twilight at Kalahuipua'a, plan to arrive by 4:30 P.M.

An audience listens intently as locals tell a story from the porch of the Eva Parker Woods cottage.

The Big Island's First Temple of Tourism

MAUNA KEA RESORT

Kohala Coast, Big Island, Hawaii

T he year was 1960. Laurance S. Rockefeller, grandson of industrialist John D. Rockefeller, was touring the Big Island when he spotted a long, crescent-shaped white-sand beach called Kauna'oa, bordered by two distinct lava points and facing a bay frequented by fishermen. By 1965, he had built a luxury hotel on the spot, creating Hawaii's first resort destination. The hotel, the Mauna Kea Beach, is now the cornerstone of the Mauna Kea Resort, a complex of over 1,800 acres that also includes the Hapuna Beach Prince Hotel ("The Prince") on another spectacular white sand beach just to the south. The resort features two championship golf courses, the Mauna Kea course, designed by Robert Trent Jones Sr. on the ancient oceanfront lava flow, and the newer Hapuna course, designed by Arnold Palmer and Ed Seay. With a 13-acre, 11-court tennis park, the resort is also a top tennis destination, and guests can take to the turquoise water for swimming, snorkeling, scuba diving, kayaking, fishing, and whale-watching.

Today's affluent guests aren't the first to treasure this place: Long ago it was a recreation spot for the island's *ali'i*, or royalty and nobility. Next door to the resort is Pu'ukohola Heiau National Historic Site, where in 1791 Kamehameha I built the sacred *heiau* whose name means "temple on the hill of the whale," a project meant to incur the favor of the war god Ku in advance of Kamehameha's successful campaign to unite the islands. The temple stands 224 by 100 feet, with three narrow terraces on the seaside and an amphitheater with views down the hills and onto the ocean.

WHERE: 32 miles north of Kailua-Kona. Tel 866-977-4589; princeresortshawaii.com. **MAUNA KEA BEACH HOTEL:** Tel 808-882-7222 (golf 808-882-5400). *Cost:* from $375; greens fees $275 ($235 for resort guests). **HAPUNA BEACH PRINCE HOTEL:** 808-880-1111 (808-880-3000 for golf). *Cost:* from $225; greens fees $150 ($130 for resort guests). **PU'UKOHOLA HEIAU:** near Kawaihae Harbor. Tel 808-882-7218; nps.gov/puhe. **BEST TIME:** Sept for the Aloha Festival Poke Contest at the Hapuna Beach Prince Hotel.

Aquatic Playground

KONA COAST

Big Island, Hawaii

T he serrated Kona coast on the west side of the Big Island is a marine playground par excellence. In Hawaiian, *kona* means "leeward" (as opposed to *ko'olau*, "windward"); two nearly 14,000-foot volcanoes, Mauna Kea (see p. 937) and Mauna Loa, shield this part of the island from northeasterly winds. A dry climate and calm waters prevail 350 days a year. Geologically speaking, the island is relatively young, and its underwater topography is dramatic, with cliffs, caves, canyons, lava tubes, arches, and pinnacles. Fascinating in themselves, these features also serve as diverse habitats for a wide range of marine life, from technicolor tropical reef fish and moray eels to sea turtles and huge pelagic predators.

Snorkelers and scuba divers come to this garden of Neptunian delights to swim with angelfish, puffer fish, darting wrasses, brilliant yellow tangs, and the occasional dolphin. If you are a beginner, Kahalu'u Beach Park is an excellent place to start, as much of the protected cove is only 3 feet deep—if you get tired or nervous, just stand up. More experienced snorkelers have plenty of other places to choose from, including White Sands Beach, Kekaha Kai State Park, Ho'okena, and Honaunau. Several establishments offer exhilarating night dives for up-close experiences with enormous manta rays.

Kona's calm waters also make it ideal for sea kayaking, which allows a sea-level view of the coastline and often the wildlife; December to April is the best time to see Hawaii's winter visitors, humpback whales. Beginners can practice in the calm area of the lagoon at Kailua Bay or in the protected waters of Kealakekua Bay. The Kona coast is renowned worldwide for its big-game fishing, with

A variety of marine life awaits divers along the Kona Coast, including green sea turtles.

"granders" (Pacific blue marlin weighing more than 1,000 pounds) reeled in every year from the fleet of high-tech sport fishing boats based in Honokohau Harbor.

SNORKELING: Kahalu'u Beach Park. *How:* Snorkel Bob's, tel 808-262-7725; snorkelbob .com. **KAYAKING:** Kailua Bay at Kailua-Kona. *How:* Aloha Kayak, tel 808-322-2868; alohakayak.com. *Cost:* from $99 for an afternoon tour, includes equipment; from $60 for half-day kayak rental. **FISHING:** Honokohau Harbor. *How:* Charter Desk at Honokohau Marina, tel 888-566-2487 or 808-326-1800; charterdesk.com. *Cost:* from $95 for a shared half-day charter. **BEST TIMES:** June–Sept for fishing; 5 days in late July or early Aug for the Hawaii International Billfish Tournament (hibtfishing.com). Avoid Jan–Feb for snorkeling, as the water can be choppy with poor visibility.

Java from the Lava

KONA'S COFFEE BELT

Big Island, Hawaii

Weather conditions on the Hualalai and Mauna Loa Volcanoes—hot, sunny mornings, humid afternoons with rain showers, mild nights— make their slopes perfect for growing coffee. For this reason, a 20-mile stretch of land, from Holualoa to Kealakekua, is known as the Kona Coffee Belt and is home to some of the world's most prized beans.

In 1828 an American missionary, Samuel Ruggles, planted the first coffee in Kona. Within a decade, it was being grown commercially, and before long earned a reputation for high quality. Mark Twain concurred in his (1866) *Letters from Hawaii*, "I think Kona Coffee has a richer flavor than any other." By the beginning of the 20th century, Kona had over 6,000 acres in coffee, spread out among family farms of a few acres apiece, mostly leased by Japanese immigrants who had emigrated to work on the island's sugar plantations. Today, after a century of boom and bust, the Kona bean grows on 600 farms covering around 3,500 acres. Hawaii remains the only U.S. state with a commercial coffee crop.

One of the best places to explore the Kona Coffee Belt is in the little village of Holualoa, just off the two-lane Mamalahoa Highway above Kailua-Kona. Nestled amid a lush, tropical landscape, this funky upcountry hamlet is a two-block cluster of brightly painted, tin-roofed plantation shacks, an old-fashioned general store, several art galleries, and coffee trees in everyone's backyard. In February and March, the branches are covered in the jasmine-and-orange-scented blossoms known as "Kona Snow"; in late summer, they're laden with cherry-red fruit. As you might expect, the village also has a terrific coffee shop, the Holualoa Café, where you can linger over the freshly brewed local java.

About 10 miles to the south, in the village of Captain Cook, the Kona Historical Society's Kona Coffee Living History Farm offers a taste of early 20th-century coffee country life. Guided tours of the 5.5-acre working farm cover the orchards, the 1925 six-room farmhouse, the Japanese bathhouse, the *kuriba* (pulping mill) and the *hoshidana* (drying platforms). Die-hard coffee enthusiasts will want to visit in early November during the ten-day Kona Coffee Festival, held at multiple locations throughout the Coffee Belt, with dozens of events including a picking contest, cupping competition (blind tasting judged by experts), art exhibits, farm tours, and even a Miss Kona Coffee pageant.

WHERE: 20 miles between Holualoa and Kealakekua. **HOLUALOA CAFÉ:** Tel 808-322-2233. **KONA COFFEE LIVING HISTORY FARM:** Captain Cook. Tel 808-323-3222; kona historical.org. *When:* closed Sat–Sun. **BEST TIME:** early Nov for the annual Kona Coffee Festival (konacoffeefest.com).

At Bay View Farm, a worker dries coffee beans in the Kona sun.

Where the Hawaiian Gods Dwell

THE MAUNA KEA SUMMIT

Mauna Kea, Big Island, Hawaii

To the ancient Hawaiians, the snow-covered summit of Mauna Kea ("White Mountain") was where the gods lived. To astronomers, the 13,796-foot mountain, with its close-to-the-equator location and unusually clear, pollution-free skies, is the best place on earth to see the stars. It's the world's tallest mountain when measured from its base on the sea floor, and its peak is home to the world's largest telescope—but even naked-eye stargazing here is fantastic.

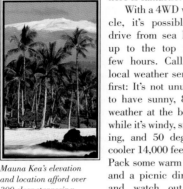

With a 4WD vehicle, it's possible to drive from sea level up to the top in a few hours. Call the local weather service first: It's not unusual to have sunny, 80°F weather at the beach while it's windy, snowing, and 50 degrees cooler 14,000 feet up. Pack some warm gear and a picnic dinner, and watch out for signs of altitude sickness, which is com-

Mauna Kea's elevation and location afford over 300 clear stargazing nights per year.

mon. The steady climb takes you by the rolling pastureland of Parker Ranch (see p. 941), up the Saddle Road and through lava fields that resemble a desolate moonscape. At 9,200 feet is the Onizuka Visitor Information Station,

named in memory of Hawaii's fallen astronaut, Ellison Onizuka, who died in the 1986 explosion of the space shuttle *Challenger.* The center offers telescopes, lectures, and terrific educational exhibits. (Plus, it's an ideal spot to stop and acclimate to the altitude before pressing onward.) The information center offers a nightly stargazing program that begins with the showing of a documentary followed by a star tour, using the station's telescopes, of the celestial objects visible at the time.

It's a mere 6 miles from the center to the top, but with an elevation gain of 5,000 feet, it takes about 30 to 45 minutes in low gear, engine whining all the way. Arrive at the summit before sunset to wander around the colony of observatories, where 11 nations have set up 13 of the world's most sophisticated telescopes for deep space exploration. **WHERE:** 70 miles east of Kailua-Kona. *Visitor info:* Tel 808-961-2180; ifa.hawaii .edu/info/vis. **HOW:** Mauna Kea Summit Adventures, tel 888-322-2366 or 808-322-2366; maunakea.com. 8-hour guided tour in a 4WD van. *Cost:* $204, includes use of Celestron telescopes and dinner. **BEST TIMES:** avoid Nov–Mar, when inclement weather can shut down the Summit Road.

Temple of Human Sacrifice

MO'OKINI LUAKINI HEIAU

North Kohala, Big Island, Hawaii

Accsording to Hawaiian legend, from sunset to sunrise one night 1,500 years ago, some 18,000 *po'e li'ili'i* ("little people") passed huge stones in a 14-mile line from the Pololu Valley to a wind-pummeled hilltop on the

Kohala Coast. They stacked the stones around a 250-by-125-foot area, which became the Mo'okini Heiau, a sacrificial temple, a National Historic Landmark, and Hawaii's greatest sacred site. Enclosed by sturdy walls—raised by later additions to as high as

15 feet—the temple was dedicated to the war god Ku and reserved for the island's *ali'i nui,* or ruling chiefs, for prayer, fasting, and human sacrifices on a stone altar.

Many Hawaiians still give a wide berth to the macabre mysticism of the place, which was off-limits to commoners until the current *kahuna nui* (high priestess), Momi Mo'okini Lum, lifted the restriction in 1978; she rededicated the temple to the children of the world, as a place where they can learn the values and traditions of the Hawaiian people. Some who journey to this revered spot admit to feeling an inexplicable, ethereal presence, and being near the altar is said to stir even the most unflappable visitor. Some bring flowers or a homemade lei as an offering to the spirits of this ancient and mysterious site.

Just 1,000 yards from Mo'okini Heiau is the birthplace of Kamehameha I, the great warrior-king, who unified the Hawaiian archipelago into the Kingdom of Hawaii early in the 19th century. According to legend, he was born in 1758, under Halley's Comet (the local ruler at the time, Alapa'i, had been warned by one of his *kahuna*—priests—that a fiery celestial light would signal the coming of a "chief killer") and was taken to Mo'okini Heiau for his birth rituals.

For many people, a visit to Mo'okini Luakini Heiau is a deeply spiritual experience.

He continued to worship there until rebuilding the temple of Pu'ukohola Heiau, near Kawaihae (see p. 935); the two powerful temples were the spiritual base for his fight to unite the isles.

WHERE: about 50 miles from Kailua-Kona. Tel 808-961-9540. *When:* closed Wed. **BEST TIME:** Nov for Children's Day, when hundreds of schoolchildren come to learn about Hawaiian culture.

Rock Art of Ages

PUAKO PETROGLYPH ARCHAEOLOGY DISTRICT

Big Island, Hawaii

For a taste of the mysteries of Hawaii's past, pack your sense of awe and head for the seemingly desolate lava field just north of the Mauna Lani Resort as the sun is waning and the shadows are long. There along the

Ka'eo Trail, incised drawings cover the rust-colored lava as far as the eye can see—some 3,000 of them, the highest concentration of petroglyphs in the state and among the highest in the world. Who made them and what they mean are unknown: They may be records of history and legend, artworks, or boundary markers. Some historians and archaeologists claim the petroglyphs were the focus of ritual and ceremonial activities, while others argue

they were cues for storytellers, but the drawings themselves offer nothing more than their simple and enigmatic forms.

Of the numerous petroglyph sites on the Big Island, Puako is distinguished by the variety of the carvings, which include basic T figures, with vertical lines for torsos and horizontals for arms; more elaborate family groups clearly depicting men, women, and children; people of high rank; a fisherman catching a fish; as well as dogs, turtles, canoes, fish hooks, and fertility symbols. Small wonder that experts are so divided over the meaning and origins. By contrast, other petroglyph sites are devoted to specific subjects: A site near the Kings Shops in the nearby Waikoloa Beach Resort, for example, is devoted especially to birthing symbols, while one three miles north of the former Kona Village Resort in Kaupulehu features voyaging symbols, including sails, kites, figures with fishing lines and hooks, and transformational figures combining human and animal forms.

One thing we do know about the petroglyphs is that there are many threats to their continued existence: natural forces, from wind and rain to fire, floods, and lava flows; plants such as kiawe trees that can lift rocks and destroy the carvings; and, of course, man. Taking rubbings or moldings of the petroglyphs was once considered harmless, but now it's emphatically discouraged. Today, the only

Human figures are among the many symbols found in the Puako Petroglyphs.

way to capture a petroglyph is with a camera.

Puako Petroglyphs: 30 miles north of Kailua-Kona, off Hwy. 19. **Waikoloa Petroglyphs:** Waikoloa. Tel 808-886-8811. *When:* guided tours, Thurs–Sat. **Best times:** early morning or late afternoon, when the low sun heightens the contrast between carvings and lava surface.

Of Discovery, Death, and Dolphins

KEALAKEKUA BAY

South Kona, Big Island, Hawaii

On January 18, 1778, two "floating islands" filled with *haole* (foreigners) sailed into Hawaii, changing it forever. They were HMS *Resolution* and HMS *Discovery*, and the man at the helm was 50-year-old Captain James Cook,

the first European to chart much of the Pacific. The following winter, Cook sailed from Kauai down the Hawaiian island chain and anchored at Kealakekua Bay, on the southern Kona Coast of the Big Island. Here he was greeted by thousands of islanders, who lined the shore and paddled up to his ships in canoes. Ancient chants had foretold the coming of the god Lono, and many historians believe that Cook was honored as a deity. He arrived during the annual celebration of Makahiki, a post-harvest thanksgiving season in Lono's honor, and was welcomed. Cook set sail in early February but

was forced to return a week later when a ship's mast broke in stormy seas. The timing couldn't have been worse: The peaceful season of Lono had passed, and it was now the season of the war god Ku. The Hawaiians had already supplied Cook with much of their harvest, and relations soured. The theft of one of the boats led to a skirmish, in which the great navigator was struck on the back of the head and killed. In 1874, Cook's countrymen erected a 27-foot white obelisk at the northern end of the bay, on a small patch of land that remains British-owned. You can get to it via a rugged 2.5 mile trail from Napo'opo'o Road, or more easily by boat from across the bay.

Today, it's not Cook's legacy that brings most visitors here, but rather the teeming life in Kealakekua Bay's underwater park and marine preserve, one of Hawaii's best snorkeling and diving locations. It's home to abundant populations of tropical fish, coral reefs, sea turtles, octopus, and visiting spinner dolphins that lend a magical note. Calm conditions prevail all but a few days out of the year, and the turquoise water is warm and clear, with visibility up to 100 feet.

WHERE: 16 miles south of Kailua-Kona. **HOW:** Fair Wind Snorkeling and Diving Adventures, Kailua-Kona. Tel 800-677-9461 or 808-322-2788; fair-wind.com. *Cost:* from $79 for 3-hour snorkeling trip, includes

equipment. **BEST TIMES:** Storms often brew in Jan and Feb; morning snorkel cruises have the best conditions.

From diving and snorkeling tour boats you can witness the natural wonders and marine life of Kealakekua Bay.

Where the Paniolos Roam

PARKER RANCH

Waimea, Big Island, Hawaii

S itting tall in the saddle between the Kohala Mountains and Mauna Kea, the Parker Ranch is the home of the *paniolo*, the Hawaiian cowboy. It's among the oldest U.S. ranches, founded in 1847 by one of Hawaii's earliest Anglo

immigrants, and at over 150,000 acres it's also among the largest, stretching from sea level to 7,000 feet and occupying a vast swath of the Big Island's northwest corner. Founder and patriarch John Parker came to the islands by jumping ship in 1809 as a 19-year-old New England sailor. He became a trusted friend of Kamehameha I, who hired him to shoot some of the thousands of maverick cattle that had become a nuisance in the Kohala area. Before long, Parker married the daughter of a high-ranking chief, and salt beef became the island's top export—a dynasty and an industry had been born. In the 1830s, *vaqueros* from California, then part of Mexico, were brought in to teach riding and roping skills to their Hawaiian counterparts, who became known as

paniolos (from the Hawaiian pronunciation of "español"). The Mexicans also brought guitars and thus sparked the musical tradition that would ultimately result in the distinctively Hawaiian *ki ho'alu*, or "slack-key," style.

The Parker Ranch still has a cattle operation, producing 14 million pounds of beef annually, but it has also branched out into real estate. A number of visitor attractions have been cut back, but you can still tour two historic Parker Ranch houses in the small town of Waimea. Mana Hale is the two-story koa-wood cabin built by the original John Parker, and it stands next to the grander Puuopelu Manor House, which was purchased by John Parker II and served as the family home until the 1990s. The horseback rides once so popular here are no longer offered, but for a similar experience, head on over to Paniolo Adventures at the nearby 11,000-acre Ponoholo Ranch, which boasts the island's second largest cattle herd after the Parker Ranch.

If you work up an appetite at the ranch, you're in the right place: Merriman's Restaurant, one of the island's most renowned, is only 1.5 miles away in Waimea. Peter Merriman, who helped to pioneer Hawaiian regional cuisine in the 1980s, serves up signature dishes such as kalua pig quesadillas and wok-charred ahi, and the place is regularly packed. Look for his newer outposts in Kauai and Maui.

Where: 50 miles north of Kailau-Kona. Tel 808-885-7655; parkerranch.com. *When:* Mon–Fri. **Paniolo Adventures:** Tel 808-889-5354; panioloadventures.com. *Cost:* $99 for a 2.5-hour guided ride. **Merriman's Restaurant:**

Waimea. Tel 808-885-6822; merrimanshawaii .com. *Cost:* dinner $70. **Best times:** 4th of July Horse Races and Rodeo; early Dec for annual Holiday Tree Lighting Event.

For horseback riding, visit Ponoholo Ranch, which boasts 11,000 acres with stunning coastal views.

Birthplace of Kings

WAIPI'O VALLEY

Big Island, Hawaii

A Garden of Eden dense with tropical fruit trees, a smattering of taro farms, lofty waterfalls, rolling surf, and a beach of black sand, Waipi'o Valley is an alluringly scenic stop on a tour of the Big Island. It's also the setting for key episodes in Hawaiian mythology and history; the bones of many *ali'i* (royalty) rest in ancient burial caves in the cliffs above this "Valley of Kings," and the dreaded night marchers, ghost armies of Hawaii's fallen warriors, were said to emerge from the *Lua-o-Milu,* the land of the dead, through a doorway at the valley's mouth. At the turn of the 17th century, an enormous *heiau* (temple) stood here, along with vast aqueducts and ingenious aquaculture ponds, which supported a population of 40,000 governed by a complex political-religious structure. Once the very center of Hawaii, Waipi'o witnessed royal betrayal, human sacrifices, and tsunamis over the centuries. Today,

it's a sleepy, peaceful place with fewer than 50 residents and dozens of wild horses.

Every day, from the time the sun lights up the 6-by-1-mile valley, a continuous stream of cars makes the almost 7-mile side trip from the Mamalahoa Highway to the Waipi'o Valley Overlook, perched on the side of the cliff. Many visitors come just to drink in the majestic view and take photos, others linger to explore the nearby postcard-quaint villages of Kukuihaele and Honoka'a, with their one-of-a-kind shops, inviting eateries, and charming B&Bs, or to head down into the valley. You can hike along old mule paths running past historic sites and gorgeous scenery, or take horseback trips with guides versed in the valley's long, rich history. Several spectacular waterfalls mark white stripes on the steep, jungled valley walls, including the 1,200-foot Hi'ilawe Falls, Hawaii's tallest, and Nanaue Falls, the serene pool at the base of which, so the legend goes, was home to a mythical man-shark. Partially buried in the mud about 150 yards from the beach is a random scattering of stones, part of the once great Paka'alana heiau, a royal compound as well as a place of refuge.

Access to the sand beach is limited by the steep road into the valley, a brake-burning 25 percent grade that can be attempted only in a 4WD vehicle. Or head off in the direction of Hilo, following the beautiful 50-mile drive along the Hamakua Coast.

WHERE: 50 miles north of Hilo. **HIKING:** Hawaiian Walkways offers the Black Sand Beach Hike, tel 808-322-2255; gowaipio.com. *Cost:* $175. **RIDING:** Waipi'o Na'alapa Trail Rides conducts 2.5-hour tours on horseback,

The Hi'ilawe waterfall is just one of Waipi'o's beautiful cascades.

tel 808-775-0419; naalapastables.com/waipio .html. *Cost:* $94. **WHERE TO STAY:** A historic 1932 former plantation home, now the five-room Waipi'o Wayside B&B Inn, tel 800-833-8849 or 808-775-0275; waipiowayside.com. *Cost:* from $125.

Frolicking in the Autumn Mist

HANALEI & PRINCEVILLE RESORT

Kauai, Hawaii

The most dazzling beaches in Hawaii are strung out like jewels in a necklace along 7 miles of Kauai's north shore. One of the finest and most famous is Hanalei Beach, where Puff the Magic Dragon frolicked in the autumn mist

in the 1962 hit by Peter, Paul, and Mary. Hanalei is the archetypal Hawaiian beach paradise, featured in countless travel posters: razor-straight cliffs, laced with ribbonlike waterfalls, tower some 4,000 feet in the background as gentle waves roll in to the golden sands of half-moon Hanalei Bay. The place owes some of its natural beauty to its age: An ancient sunken valley that indents the coast a full mile inland, it runs 2 miles end to end, with coral reefs on either side and a patch of coral in the middle. Protected from the strong

currents that make waters dangerous elsewhere on the north shore, in winter and spring the bay is Kauai's surfing central, with a wide variety of breaks that attract everyone from beginners to experts. Swimming is excellent year-round (especially in summer, when Hanalei Bay is as placid as a lake), and thanks to a sunken ship that belonged to the early 19th-century King Liholiho, the bay is popular with divers, too.

Just west of here is Lumahai Beach, an idyllic crescent of luxuriant sand framed by lush vegetation and lava-rock cliffs, where Mitzi Gaynor washed Rossano Brazzi right out of her hair in the 1957 classic *South Pacific.* Nearby, the National Tropical Botanical Garden's Limahuli Garden sits at the foot of steepled cliffs. Spread over 1,000 acres of tropical valley, the garden is noted both for its beauty and for its focus on the conservation of Hawaii's indigenous plant species.

Dramatic vistas are the backdrop to the luxurious St. Regis Princeville Resort at Hanalei. Set into the side of a cliff overlooking Hanalei Bay, the hotel is built in tiers leading down the bluff, with the lobby entrance on the ninth floor, the beach down at the bottom of the elevators, and 251 breezy guest rooms in between. On the grounds is the Makai Golf Club, one of the state's largest and most challenging golf destinations, with four different courses designed by Robert Trent Jones Jr. Just three miles away is the tiny town of Hanalei, full of appealing boutiques, restaurants, and inns, and the Wai'oli Mission House, a time capsule preserving mid-19th-century Hawaii. Built in 1836 for New England missionaries, the two-story house has a lava-rock chimney and koa-wood furniture.

HANALEI BEACH: 30 miles from Lihu'e.

At the Princeville Hotel, relax in a hammock overlooking Hanalei Bay.

LIMAHULI GARDEN: Haena. Tel 808-826-1053; ntbg.org. *When:* Tues–Sat. **ST. REGIS PRINCEVILLE:** Tel 866-716-8140 or 808-826-9644 (golf, 808-826-1912); stregisprinceville .com. *Cost:* rooms from $505; greens fees from $239. **WAI'OLI MISSION HOUSE:** Hanalei. Tel 808-245-3202. *When:* closed Mon, Wed, Fri, and Sun. **BEST TIMES:** summer, when the north shore beaches are generally calm; winter for surfing.

A Bird's-Eye View of the Garden Isle

KAUAI BY HELICOPTER

Kauai, Hawaii

The oldest of the main Hawaiian islands, lush and timeless Kauai is essentially a single massive volcano rising 3 miles from the ocean floor. Two-thirds impenetrable, it has provided a scene-stealing vision of tropical paradise for many Hollywood movies and TV shows, including *Jurassic Park, Blue Hawaii, King Kong,* and *Fantasy Island.* More rain falls here than in the rest of Hawaii—Kauai is known in Hawaiian lore as the birthplace of the rainbow—and it's so extravagantly covered with flowers and dense vegetation that it seems like one vast botanical garden, thus the nickname "The Garden Isle." The people here, who make up just about 4 percent of Hawaii's population, live a mostly rural and old-time Hawaiian life, in which natural beauty is the focus and small-scale development is the norm. County ordinance even requires that no building be taller than a coconut tree.

You can drive around the accessible parts of Kauai—it's only about 30 miles across at its widest—in just a few hours, but the only way to take in the natural drama of the whole island is via helicopter. Blue Hawaiian has been the Cadillac of helicopter tour companies for over a decade, with an elite crew of pilots and a first-rate fleet including sleek Eco-Star copters—featuring an unrivaled viewing area, comfort, and quiet. The 50-minute flights go from Hanapepe Valley to Manawaiapuna, also known as "Jurassic Park Falls," then on to some of Kauai's most beautiful sites: the Bali Hai Cliffs; the pristine blue waters of Hanalei Bay and the St. Regis Princeville area (see p. 943); Olokele Canyon; and Waimea Canyon, the dramatically, ruggedly beautiful "Grand Canyon of the Pacific" (see p. 947). From there, most of the flights follow the towering, deeply carved cliffs

of the Na Pali Coast (see below), one of Hawaii's most stunning landscapes. Weather permitting, you can even fly to the 5,148-foot Mount Wai'ale'ale—with an average yearly rainfall of over 460 inches, it's one of the two wettest spots on earth—and descend into its crater, where waterfalls plunge thousands of feet down steep walls nearly a mile high.

Blue Hawaiian Helicopters: Lihu'e Airport. Tel 800-745-2583 or 808-245-5800; bluehawaiian.com. *Cost:* $239 per person. **Best time:** Nov–Mar are the rainiest months.

Fly among the clouds to view the grandeur of Kauai.

Hiking Through Eden

THE NA PALI COAST

Kauai, Hawaii

The Na Pali ("the cliffs") Coast is the Hawaii of your dreams, 16 miles of vibrant green valleys with nearly vertical walls and thundering waterfalls plunging into the sea from cliffs as high as 4,000 feet. Hawaii's last true

wilderness where no road will ever cross, it is protected as the Na Pali Coast State Park, whose 6,500 acres hug the northwest shore of Kauai between Ke'e Beach and Polihale State Park. You can view this magnificent piece of Eden by helicopter (see above) or boat, but the best way to experience the thickly jungled shore at the base of its craggy palisades is on foot.

Even fit, seasoned hikers find a challenge in the narrow, strenuous Kalalau Trail, an ancient 11-mile footpath that winds along

imposing cliffs through the Hanakapi'ai, Hanakoa, and Kalalau valleys—a remote, spectacular region that's home to long-plumed tropical birds, golden monarch butterflies, and many of Kauai's rare and endangered plant species. The hike all the way to the end of the trail at Kalalau Beach is both gorgeous and grueling, so hikers are advised to spend two full days on the way in, stopping often to admire the view, swim, pick fruit, and revel in the experience. Note, though, that the sometimes precipitous heights aren't for those who suffer from vertigo.

The golden-red sands of Ke'e Beach, at the trailhead, lie at the foot of sheer volcanic cliffs and are a favorite of swimmers, snorkelers, divers, and kayakers. The 2-mile stretch of the Kalalau Trail from here is a popular, moderately difficult day hike that climbs from sea level to 400 feet in the steep first mile, then descends to sea level at Hanakapi'ai Beach, which has sand in summer, but just rocks when the winter waves roll in. The trail here is narrow and often

Na Pali Coast stretches 16 miles along the northwest side of Kauai.

so crowded that the hike takes up to two hours one-way. Bear in mind also that Hanakapi'ai is not a swimming beach—the undertow and rip currents are fierce, and there are no lifeguards. If you've got energy, you can continue along a 2-mile inland trail from the beach to Hanakapi'ai Falls, a 120-foot cascade.

On the other side of the wilderness from Ke'e is Polihale State Park, home to Hawaii's biggest beach—17 miles long and as wide as three football fields. Located on the remote, extreme western end of Kauai (and lacking any kind of facilities), it's an exceptionally beautiful spot, snuggled up at the base of the Na Pali cliffs and offering one of the best places on Kauai for watching the sunset. The park includes ancient Hawaiian *heiau* (temples) and burial sites, views of the neighboring islands of Ni'ihau and Lehua Rock, and the famed Barking Sands Beach, where your footsteps make a sound like squeaking snow.

WHERE: 36 miles northwest of Lihu'e. *Kauai State Park info:* Tel 808-274-3444; dlnr.hawaii.gov/dsp. **How:** Liko Kauai Cruises offers snorkeling and sightseeing trips, tel 808-338-0333; liko-kauai.com. *Cost:* $150 for 4-hour trip. **BEST TIME:** Apr–Oct for weather.

Sunny Beaches, Hawaiian Gardens, and Moaning Lizards

PO'IPU BEACH

Kauai, Hawaii

A t the center of Kauai's sunny southern coast is Po'ipu Beach Park, a legendary beauty spot famous for its gardens and glamorous resorts, as well as for its surfing, snorkeling, diving, and kayaking. Technically,

Po'ipu Park comprises two beaches naturally divided by Nukumoi Point, a kind of sandbar known as a tombolo. On one side, a rocky outcrop protects a sandy-bottom pool that's perfect for children, and on the other side lies open ocean for swimmers, snorkelers, and surfers. Everyone loves this place, so expect a

crowd—especially on weekends, when local families come and stay for hours to picnic on the green lawn fronting the beach.

West of the beach, in the Lawa'i Valley, are two world-class horticultural attractions run by the National Tropical Botanical Garden, which also operates Limahuli Garden on Kauai's North

Shore (see p. 944). The 252-acre McBryde Garden boasts the world's largest ex situ collection of native Hawaiian plants, many of which are rare and endangered, plus many specimens from elsewhere in the tropics. The Allerton Garden occupies more than 100 adjacent acres, where Hawaii's Queen Emma lived in the 1860s; it includes the historic house, exquisite formal features, and a tropical fruit orchard planted as a victory garden. Nearby is Spouting Horn, a pair of blowholes in a lava outcrop. When swells steamroll into the south shore, one sprays like a geyser, while the other makes a loud moaning sound. According to legend, this coastline was once guarded by a giant female *mo'o*, or lizard, who ate anyone who dared come into her domain. A man named Liko, who wanted to fish in the area, threw a spear into her mouth, then escaped under the lava shelf and out one of the holes. The mo'o was trapped in the lava tube, and the sound of Spouting Horn is said to be her cries of hunger and pain.

For a luxury room, check into the 50-acre Grand Hyatt Kauai, a classically handsome low-rise resort with lavishly landscaped grounds, an open-air Anara spa, 1.5 acres of saltwater swimming lagoons, dozens of tennis courts, and a championship golf course designed by Robert Trent Jones Jr. Of the resort's numerous restaurants and cafés, Dondero's is widely regarded as the best Italian restaurant on the island.

WHERE: 12 miles west of Lihue. **ALLERTON/ MCBRYDE GARDENS:** Tel 808-332-7324; ntbg .org. *Cost:* Allerton $45; McBryde $30. *When:* Allerton Garden via daily tours only; McBryde Garden daily. **GRAND HYATT KAUAI:** Tel 808-742-1234; kauai.hyatt.com. Golf, tel 808-742-8711; poipubaygolf.com. *Cost:* from $510; greens fees $250 ($180 for hotel guests). **BEST TIMES:** Mar for the daylong Prince Kuhio Celebration of the Arts; July for the weeklong Koloa Plantation Days (koloaplantationdays .com); July–Sept for greatest variety at the botanical gardens.

Grand Canyon of the Pacific

WAIMEA CANYON AND WAIMEA TOWN

Kauai, Hawaii

Ten miles long, more than a mile across, and over 3,500 feet deep, Waimea Canyon is one of Kauai's most awe-inspiring sights. Dubbed "The Grand Canyon of the Pacific" by Mark Twain, the cavernous gorge was carved by the Waimea River, which channels heavy rainfall from Mount Wai'ale'ale through lava flows that filled in a depression where a part of the island collapsed catastrophically 4 million years ago. The rich palette of ocher, russet, and amber, the colors of the weathered rock, is enhanced in places by vivid green vegetation and the occasional striking white stripe of a waterfall. You can take in the view from above via helicopter (see p. 944) or at scenic overlooks—such as the Waimea Canyon Lookout on Waimea Canyon Road, or the 3,336-foot-high Puu Hina Hina Lookout 3 miles beyond—or from ground level at 1,866-acre Waimea Canyon State Park.

In Waimea Canyon and its neighbor to the north, Koke'e State Park, there's a vast network of hiking trails snaking through some 6,200 acres of rain forest. Short hikes offer views of the stunning landscape and encounters with native plants, trees, and birds, while long, often strenuous hikes lead to the base of the canyon, where you can immerse yourself in a place that bears the marks of all the lava flows, earthquakes, and torrential storms that have shaped it. Koke'e Park's streams offer seasonal trout fishing, and from its scenic vistas you can see the privately owned island of Ni'ihau, also known as the "Forbidden Isle," 17 miles distant.

Low-key Waimea (population 1,787), the original capital of Kauai, is the town closest to the Canyon. With dogs napping in the dusty

From the Waimea Canyon Lookout, see a waterfall cascade over the canyon's ancient volcanic rock.

street and residents sitting on wide porches watching the traffic go by, it seems to be a town that time forgot, and it's a great place to relax and wander, taking in the historic buildings. The town's claim to fame is that Captain James Cook made the first European contact with Hawaii here in 1778, dropping anchor at a sleepy village of grass shacks before sailing down to the Big Island (see p. 940).

The only accommodations of note are the Waimea Plantation Cottages, 61 restored century-old workers' homes that were relocated to a lovely beachside coconut grove. Every cozy cabin has been remodeled with a modern kitchen; the rattan and wicker furniture and fabrics from the 1930s, when sugar was king on Kauai, lend an old-time plantation atmosphere. Each has a furnished lanai, some with views of the ocean.

WHERE: 32 miles west of Lihu'e. **WAIMEA CANYON AND KOKE'E STATE PARKS:** hawaiistate parks.org/parks/kauai. **WAIMEA PLANTATION COTTAGES:** Tel 800-716-6199 or 808-338-1625; waimeaplantation.com. *Cost:* from $195. **BEST TIME:** May–Oct for weather.

From Pineapples to Posh Hotels

THE LANA'I COAST

Lana'i, Hawaii

Hawaii's most secluded island, tiny unhyped Lana'i was once the state's largest pineapple plantation, with field after field of red-dirt Dole pineapple groves producing 8 percent of the world's total crop. The island's new role

as a tourist destination was sealed in the 1990s when it was taken over by entrepreneur David Murdock, whose Castle & Cooke Resorts, LLC, owned 98 percent of Lana'i. Murdock suspended pineapple planting and built two superplush hotels, the Four Seasons Resort Lanai and the Lodge at Ko'ele (see next page). Both changed hands in 2012 when billionaire Larry Ellison, the head of Oracle,

bought the entire island with intentions of totally renovating both luxury properties. They sit 8 miles and many worlds apart on the otherwise largely empty island, which is home to only 3,100 people. Indoors, guests are spoiled to an almost unheard-of degree, but the great outdoors remain unspoiled, with few cars, no traffic lights, and no helicopters overhead to interrupt the Pacific Isle fantasy.

The Four Seasons Resort Lanai quietly reopened in February 2016 following a total face-lift that promoted it to one of Hawaii's finest. Reimagined as a breezy pleasure palace, it offers 268 guest rooms and suites spread amid waterfalls, streams, fishponds, and dense tropical gardens. It occupies the headland of idyllic Hulopo'e Bay, where crystal waters and perfect, palm-shaded white sand beaches are excellent for swimming and snorkeling (visited frequently by spinner dolphins and humpback whales). This beach is also a marine preserve, where no fish can be taken from the pristine waters and no boats can anchor. The natural drama extends to its renowned 18-hole Jack Nicklaus–designed Signature Manele Golf Course, located on the cliffs above Hulopo'e with some of the most riveting ocean views in all of Hawaii and open to resort guests only. The resort's private-club atmosphere and panoply of amenities have made it a magnet for such luminaries as Bill and Melinda Gates, who tied the knot here.

Lana'i isn't just for the rich and powerful. The 141-square-mile island is accessible via small commuter planes or the ferry from Maui just 9 miles away. If you're just coming for a day, rent a 4WD and go exploring. Out on the north shore, the rugged, colorful, rock-strewn Garden of the Gods is considered a sacred site by the Hawaiians: The area's red, orange, ocher, and yellow hues are at their most mysteriously beautiful in the early morning or just before sunset.

VISITOR INFO: Tel 800-947-4774 or 808-565-7600; gohawaii.com/en/lanai. **HOW:** Island Air (tel 800-652-6541; islandair.com) offers 25-minute flights from Honolulu or from Kahului, Maui. *Cost:* from $180 round-trip. The Expeditions Lahaina/Lana'i Passenger Ferry (tel 808-661-3756; go-lanai.com) offers a 45-minute ride from Lahaina, Maui, to Manele Bay. **FOUR SEASONS RESORT LANAI:** Tel 800-321-4666 or 808-565-2000 (golf, 800-321-4666 or 808-565-2222); fourseasons .com/lanai. *Cost:* from $975; greens fees $375 (unlimited play). **BEST TIMES:** 1st weekend in July for the Pineapple Festival, featuring some of Hawaii's best musicians; late Sept or early Oct for the Aloha Festival celebrating Hawaiian culture.

The rocky Lana'i coast is perhaps best experienced at sunset.

A Plush Resort and a Plantation Town

THE LODGE AT KO'ELE & LANA'I CITY

Lana'i, Hawaii

The Lodge at Ko'ele overlooks Lana'i City from the cool, wooded upland district of Ko'ele at the center of Lana'i Island. Managed by the Four Seasons group, it is one of the island's two ultra-luxury properties (together with The Four Seasons Resort Lana'i) purchased in 2012 by billionaire Larry Ellison (see previous entry). The lodge sits 1,700 feet above sea level among towering pine- and eucalyptus-covered hills, with views of green pastures, grazing horses, and the odd wild turkey, and is scheduled to be closed until early 2017 for a complete renovation.

Among the main attractions at the resort is its championship golf course designed by Greg Norman, a stunning layout with sweeping views. The sibling resorts share an exotic sense of remoteness, as if this distant, underdeveloped island had not yet entered the 21st century, despite the modern, up-to-the-minute amenities.

The island's only other hotel option to speak of is the Hotel Lana'i, a historic landmark built in 1923 to house Dole executives and now a modest but charming bungalow-style inn. The 11-room hotel sits at the heart of town amid parklike gardens and offers low-key luxury, with additional cottages and lanai-style rooms scattered around the property. The hotel's Lanai

A gazebo overlooks a pond on the Lodge at Ko'ele's manicured grounds.

City Grille offers fresh Pacific Rim small-plates dining with live music on weekends.

Lana'i City itself looks like a 1930s film set. Built in 1924 as a pineapple plantation company town and still the only town on the 13-by-18-mile island, it's laid out around Dole Park Square, a picturesque village center bordered by tall pines and plantation buildings housing a couple of general stores and a handful of boutiques and art galleries. Neat, square blocks radiate outward, lined with modest tin-roofed homes painted in a rainbow of colors. Lana'i City also offers the homegrown Lana'i Art Center, where top artists from across Hawaii teach arts including ceramics, painting, and woodworking.

The town also serves as a jumping-off point for one of Hawaii's toughest hikes, the 13-mile (round-trip) Munro Trail, an all-day trek up the narrow, winding ridge trail that runs across Lana'i's razorback caldera rim to the top of the island's highest peak, 3,370-foot Lana'ihale. On a clear day, you can see the islands of O'ahu, Molokai, and Maui from the top, as well as the peaks of the Big Island off in the distance.

VISITOR INFO: Tel 800-947-4774 or 808-565-7600; gohawaii.com/en/lanai. **LODGE AT KO'ELE:** Tel 800-321-4666 or 808-565-4500; fourseasons.com/lanai. **HOTEL LANA'I:** Tel 808-565-7211; hotellanai.com. *Cost:* from $175; dinner $55. *When:* dining room closed Mon–Tues. **LANA'I ART CENTER:** Tel 808-565-7503; lanai art.org. **BEST TIME:** summer, since Lana'i City's 1,600-foot elevation means winters can be chilly.

Tee Time at the Oasis

THE GOLF RESORTS OF WAILEA AND MAKENA

Maui, Hawaii

Just four decades ago, Wailea was a dusty, barren area covered by an impenetrable scrub of thorny *kiawe*. Today, after a multimillion-dollar deal that pumped in water from the rainy forests across the island, plus billions more in high-end building and landscaping, this part of Maui's South Shore is a veritable oasis. Spread over 2 miles of palm-fringed gold coast, the destination resort area has everything: warm, sunny weather nearly every day; sandy beaches sloping into fish-filled waters; luxury hotels and shopping; and Wailea's greatest claim to fame, world-class golf.

Wailea, a virtual golf mecca, features three of Maui's best courses: the beginner-friendly Blue Course, designed by Arthur Jack Snyder; the championship Gold Course, designed by Robert Trent Jones Jr.; and Jones's slightly more player-friendly Emerald Course. You can play them all from any of the area's best hotels—which offer every creature comfort imaginable. The Grand Wailea Resort was one of Hawaii's first resorts and spas and is still one of its most lavish. It boasts an opulent 50,000-square-foot spa and an astounding water park with waterfalls, slides, and nine pools—it's kid heaven. The Four Seasons Resort Maui at Wailea, a Hawaiian seaside palace, features another top spa, pampering service, and a branch of the famous Spago restaurant chain. At the Fairmont Kea Lani Maui, an all-suite luxury hotel, there are private 2,000-square-foot beach villas, each with its own plunge pool and designer kitchen.

Golf aside, the next biggest draws in Wailea are golden sand Wailea Beach and crescent-shaped Ulua Beach. A couple of miles to the south, Makena is home to two more Jones-designed golf courses and the Makena Beach & Golf Resort, luxurious if remote, with an atrium garden and a koi-filled waterfall stream. Must-see beaches nearby: palm-fringed, sandy Maluaka Beach and 3,300-foot-long (and 100-foot-wide) Big Beach, also known as Oneloa ("long sand").

WHERE: 12 miles south of Kahului Airport. WAILEA GOLF CLUB: Tel 888-328-MAUI or 808-875-7450; waileagolf.com. Cost: greens fees from $240 ($199 for Wailea hotel guests). GRAND WAILEA RESORT: Tel 800-888-6100 or 808-875-1234; grandwailea .com. Cost: from $459. FOUR SEASONS RESORT MAUI: Tel 800-311-0630 or 808-874-8000; fourseasons.com/maui. Cost: from $569. FAIRMONT KEA LANI MAUI: Tel 866-540-4456 or 808-875-4100; fairmont.com/kea-lani-maui. Cost: from $449. MAKENA RESORT: Makena. Tel 800-321-6284 or 808-874-1111; makenaresortmaui.com. Cost: from $259. BEST TIMES: 4 days in June for the Maui Film Festival (mauifilmfestival.com); Nov–Apr for whale-watching.

House of the Sun

HALEAKALA VOLCANO

Maui, Hawaii

Who's to argue with the local saying *Maui no ka oi*—"Maui is the best." The "Valley Isle" is named after the Polynesian demigod, who, after having plucked all the Hawaiian islands up out of the sea, decided to make this, the most beautiful one, his home. Nothing beats the views of and from the hulking mass of 10,023-foot Haleakala (House of the Sun), whose dormant volcanic crater, 2,600 feet deep and 21 miles around, is the largest in the world—so big that the island of Manhattan could fit inside. Annually, more than 1.5 million visitors follow a must-do tradition and make the 3 A.M. ascent through the cool upcountry landscape to Haleakala's lofty peak to watch a sunrise that Mark Twain called "the sublimest spectacle I ever witnessed." Just ascending the mountain is an experience in itself; it's the only place in the world where you can drive from sea level to over 10,000 feet in just 38 miles. The two-hour trip snakes through three different climate zones along the way and offers magnificent views of the island's lush sugarcane and pineapple plantations, as well as some of Maui's 81 accessible beaches along its famous 120-mile shoreline.

Kamaʻlioʻi is one of the volcanic cinder cones inside the massive Haleakala crater.

At the headquarters of the 34,000-acre park, you can get info on Haleakala's geological wonders and maybe catch a glimpse of Hawaii's state bird, the endangered nene, or Hawaiian goose. On the road, don't miss the Leleiwi Overlook, the first place to get a glimpse of the moonscape inside the crater. Another overlook, the Kalahaku, offers up-close views of the rare silversword, which grows only on Haleakala

and the Big Island. A striking plant with silvery succulent foliage, it takes as long as 50 years to reach flowering stage, at which point it throws up a tall stalk of hundreds of sunflower-like maroon flower heads, sets seed, and dies.

At the summit, you get a full view of the crater and also, in the distance, the summit of Mauna Kea on the Big Island (see p. 937). Tour operators offer hiking trips that take you down into the crater, and several companies operate bike tours that start from the park boundary and require little pedaling.

Where: 40 miles southeast of Kahului Airport. Tel 808-572-4400; nps.gov/hale. **Hiking:** Hike Maui (tel 808-879-5270; hikemaui.com) offers a strenuous full-day hike in Haleakala Crater. *Cost:* $179. **Biking:** Maui Downhill (tel 800-535-BIKE or 808-871-2155; mauidownhill.com) offers a sunrise safari bike tour. *Cost:* from $189. **Where to stay:** The historic plantation-era Hale Hoʻokipa Inn, Makawao, tel 877-572-6698 or 808-572-6698; maui-bed-and-breakfast.com. *Cost:* from $125. **Best times:** either sunrise (which can be crowded) or sunset (when you can practically have the place to yourself); May–Sept for warmest weather.

Hawaii's Most Famous Byway

Hana Highway

Maui, Hawaii

Besides the Crater Road to Haleakala's summit (see above), Maui's other famous road show, and one of the Pacific's most scenic, is the narrow, corkscrew Hana "Highway" on the island's lush, isolated northern coast.

Beginning at the laid-back former sugar-plantation town of Paʻia, the 50-mile drive takes two to four hours, climbing and dropping among some 617 curves, crossing 59 one-lane bridges, and passing dozens of waterfalls and vistas before reaching the quiet, old-fashioned, eye-blink town of Hana (see next page). Bring a

picnic lunch, stop and swim in mountain streams fed by waterfalls, take lots of photos to show the folks back home, and smell the flowers. Some travelers who hurry to get to Hana wonder what all the fuss is about when they arrive; it's about the journey and the incredible display of nature along the way.

Pa'ia is Maui's "coolest town," known for its charm, galleries, and the forever-packed Mama's Fish House, a casual restaurant that now offers lodging in a clutch of tropical cottages. Your first stop just outside of town should be at Ho'okipa ("hospitality") Beach Park, one of the greatest windsurfing spots on the planet. If it's winter and the surf's up, detour left off the Hana Highway at Hahana Road, where the famous surf site known as Jaws features offshore waves that can reach heights of 60 feet or more. There's no beach here and the road going down is rough, so most are content to watch from cliffs above. Highly experienced surfers sometimes take off from nearby Maliko Gulch, riding on the back of a Jet Ski to a perfect spot from which to catch the monster waves.

Back on the highway, stop at Twin Falls, or at Puohokamoa Falls farther along the road, to experience the much calmer waters of a waterfall pool, and stretch your legs at the Waikomoi Ridge Trail for an easy three-quarter-mile loop through eucalyptus and bamboo. Great picnic places include Kaumahina State Wayside Park and Pua'a Ka'a State Wayside Park, where a short path leads to accessible swimming holes and waterfalls. The Ke'anae Arboretum features native and introduced trees, as well as traditional Hawaiian plants used in food and medicine. Nearby is the Ke'anae Peninsula, where taro fields dot the landscape, fishermen line the shoreline, and the Ke'anae Congregational Church has been standing since the missionaries arrived in 1860.

There are no gas stations until Hana so fill up your gas tank and drive with *aloha* (i.e., drop the aggressive mainland road manners). There will be traffic on the barely one-and-a-half lane road, so yield to oncoming cars at the one-lane bridges, and remember that locals can drive this road in their sleep, so let them pass.

WHERE: 50 miles from Pa'ia (6 miles east of Kahului Airport) to Hana town. **MAMA'S FISH HOUSE:** Pa'ia. Tel 800-860-HULA or 808-579-9764; mamasfishhouse.com. *Cost:* dinner $60; rooms from $250. **BEST TIMES:** Leave early in the morning, and plan to stay overnight in Hana. Avoid the 2nd Sat in Sept, when hundreds of runners take to the Hana Highway in the Hana Relays.

Hana Highway hugs Maui's lush, green coast, with exquisite views of the Pacific.

Hawaii of Yesteryear

HANA

Maui, Hawaii

In a timeless setting of natural beauty, surrounded by dense rain forest, with tumbling waterfalls, clear azure pools, and white, red, and black sand beaches within minutes of each other, the tiny village of Hana (population 1,250) is a throwback to the Hawaii of yesteryear. At the end of the serpentine Hana Highway (see above) and nestled next to the shoreline and the bay of the same name, this stronghold of local culture is home to a high percentage of native Hawaiians, as well as a place to get away from it all and connect with nature. Here you can luxuriate on one of Maui's most dramatic beaches: Hamoa Beach, a large, crescent shape at the base of 30-foot black lava sea cliffs.

Hana offers a dozen inviting inns and B&Bs, but its main attraction is the unique Travaasa Hana, the island's most exclusive hideaway, founded in 1946. A cluster of hillside cottages on 66 secluded acres sloping down to a rugged seacoast, Travaasa Hana is an ideal romantic getaway, with spacious, airy rooms, bleached-wood floors, and sweeping views of the ocean. It also features one of Maui's best spas, two pools, and the open-air Preserve Kitchen and Bar, whose cuisine showcases local in-season ingredients.

Three miles from the center of town, at mile marker 32 off the Hana Highway, oceanside Wai'anapanapa State Park invites visitors to explore an ancient 6-mile trail past green naupaka shrubs, a forest of lauhala trees (used in local weaving), and coastal formations such as blowholes, sea arches, and caves. One striking and anomalous feature is the tide pool of Wai'anapanapa Cave, which turns bloodred in spring. According to legend, this is where the jealous chief Ka'akea killed his wife, Princess Popo'alaea. (The more prosaic scientific explanation attributes the color to the hatching of millions of 'opae'ula, a small red shrimp.) Farther down the road past the park, in the National Tropical Botanical Garden's 472-acre Kahanu Garden (home of the world's largest collection of breadfruit cultivars), you'll find the extraordinary temple known as Pi'ilanihale Heiau, the largest intact *heiau* in Hawaii and a masterpiece of masonry. Begun around 1200, it measures 340 by 425 feet, with walls 50 feet tall and 10 feet thick. On the other side of Hana lies the eastern end of Haleakala National Park, at Ohe'o Gulch in Kipuhulu. Also called the "Seven Sacred Pools," this awe-inspiring area has some 24 waterfalls and pools, descending the mountain like stair steps into the cobalt blue water of the Pacific.

WHERE: 50 miles southeast of Kahului Airport. **HOTEL TRAVAASA HANA:** Tel 888-820-1043 or 808-359-2401; travaasa.com/hana. *Cost:* from $450. **WAI'ANAPANAPA STATE PARK:** dlnr.hawaii.gov/dsp. **KAHANU GARDEN:** Tel 808-248-8912; ntbg.org. *When:* closed Sat–Sun. **HALEAKALA NATIONAL PARK:** Tel 808-572-4400; nps.gov/hale. **BEST TIME:** late Apr for the East Maui Taro Festival (tarofestival.org).

They're Ba-ack!

HUMPBACK WHALE NATIONAL MARINE SANCTUARY

Maui, Hawaii

Humpback whales are Hawaii's largest visitors, and when they come, they come in force. Nearly half of the entire North Pacific population of humpbacks, estimated at 21,000, spend the winter months here, the majority arriving by December and staying until late March or early April. Measuring some 45 feet long and weighing 40 to 45 tons, the humpbacks migrate from their summer feeding grounds off Alaska, arriving in the warm, shallow Hawaiian waters to mate and calve—and fascinate human visitors. To protect these magnificent leviathans, in 1992

Congress established the Hawaiian Islands Humpback Whale National Marine Sanctuary, one of 14 such national marine sanctuaries, in five areas around the state. Nearly half the sanctuary's 1,400 square miles lies in the channel between Maui and the neighboring islands of Lana'i and Molokai; smaller portions are located off the north shore of Kauai, the Big Island's Kona coast, and the north and southeast coasts of O'ahu.

Breaching is considered by many to be a social activity of whales.

If you're in Maui during the winter, you can book a cruise on a whale-watching boat, hop a ferry to Molokai (see p. 959) or Lana'i (see p. 948), or simply scan the horizon. Calm conditions offer sightings of whales slapping their huge tails on the surface or breaching—leaping completely clear of the water, one of nature's more wonderfully playful spectacles. The best places for whale-watching from land are Olowalu Reef outside of Lahaina and McGregor Point near Ma'alaea (both on the Honoapi'ilani Highway); the Wailea Resort area (where there's a telescope provided as a public service by the sanctuary); and the 360-foot cinder cone of Pu'u Olai in Makena (at the northern end of Big Beach or Oneloa Beach, off South Makena Road), where you can spot whales for miles.

To learn more about humpback whales, head to the Hawaiian Islands Humpback Whale Sanctuary Education Center in Kihei, with exhibits, artifacts, and displays on whales, turtles, Polynesian canoe-making, and other related subjects. The center also hosts a monthly lecture series featuring whale researchers and other marine science professionals, as well as specialists in Hawaiian culture.

WHERE: off the shores of Maui, Lana'i, and Molokai, plus parts of Kauai, the Big Island, and O'ahu. **HOW:** The nonprofit Pacific Whale Foundation (tel 800-942-5311 or 808-879-8811; pacificwhale.org) offers catamaran cruises and snorkel tours from Ma'alaea and Lahaina harbors. **HAWAII HUMPBACK WHALE EDUCATION CENTER:** Kihei. Tel 808-879-2818; hawaiihumpbackwhale.noaa.gov. *When:* closed Sat–Sun. **BEST TIMES:** Nov–Mar for whale migration; mid-Feb for The Maui Whale Festival (mauiwhalefestival.com).

Luxury Links, Fantastic Food

KAPALUA RESORT

Maui, Hawaii

Across the island and worlds away from the small-town life and thick rain forest of eastern Maui is the sun-drenched, beach-blessed northwest coast. One of the area's top destinations, the 22,000-acre Kapalua Resort, encompasses residential developments, luxury accommodations, restaurants and shops, and golf galore. With five bays, the property's beaches are a big draw, especially the secluded D. T. Fleming Beach Park and Kapalua Beach, with perfect conditions for swimming, snorkeling, and kayaking. At the heart of the resort, on a knoll in a dramatic setting between these two sandy stretches, sits the Ritz-Carlton Kapalua Hotel. The developers' original plan was to build the hotel on the beach, like most of Maui's luxury hotels, but construction revealed hundreds of ancient burial sites in the sand. The hotel was relocated to the top of the hill, which became a plus: The views are nothing short of spectacular.

Surrounding the Ritz-Carlton are 36 holes of championship golf on two courses, making it one of the world's regularly short-listed golf resorts. It includes the Bay Course (designed by Arnold Palmer and Francis Duane); and the Plantation Course (designed by Ben Crenshaw and Bill Coore), the site of the PGA Tour's Hyundai Championships every January. The resort is also home to the Kapalua Golf

Despite the resort's popularity, secluded spots can be found among its five bays and picturesque beaches.

Academy, one of the best golf schools in Hawaii.

In recent years, Kapalua has also become a culinary attraction for its many well-known restaurants: Pineapple Grill Kapalua, where Asian and Pacific Rim ingredients fuse into culinary masterpieces; Sansei Seafood Restaurant and Sushi Bar, where Maui chef D. K. Kodama devised his distinctive marriage of Japanese and western delicacies; and Plantation House Restaurant, known for its 360-degree view and its Hawaiian-Mediterranean menu.

WHERE: 30 miles northwest of the Kahului Airport. Tel 800-527-2582 or 808-665-5400; kapalua.com. **RITZ-CARLTON KAPALUA:** Tel 800-542-8680 or 808-669-6200; ritzcarlton .com. *Cost:* from $450. **GOLF COURSES AND ACADEMY:** Tel 877-KAPALUA or 808-669-8044; golfatkapalua.com. *Cost:* greens fees from $219 (from $199 for hotel guests); golf school from $435 per half-day. **PINEAPPLE GRILL:** Tel 808-669-9600; cohnrestaurants .com/pineapplegrill. *Cost:* dinner $55. **SANSEI:** Tel 808-669-6286; sanseihawaii.com. *Cost:* dinner $60. **PLANTATION HOUSE:** Tel 808-669-6299; theplantationhouse.com. *Cost:* dinner $65. **BEST TIME:** 4 days in mid-June for the Kapalua Wine and Food Festival (kapaluawineandfoodfestival.com).

History and Gustatory Pleasure in a Former Whaling Capital

LAHAINA

Maui, Hawaii

Nestled between the West Maui Mountains and the cobalt blue waters of the Pacific, Maui's western coast is home to the colorful 19th-century whaling village of Lahaina, which now concentrates on excursions to

watch the whales its sailors once tried to harpoon. In 1820, when whaling thrived and ships lined the Lahaina Roadstead, King Kamehameha moved the royal capital from Kailua-Kona to here, where it remained until

Honolulu assumed the mantle in 1845. By 1860, sugar had taken over as the driver of the island's economic engine, a position it held for more than 110 years. Today tourism is the big kahuna, with visitors thronging Lahaina's walkable streets, lined with art galleries, trendy cafés, restaurants, and shops, after a day at Ka'anapali Beach.

The town's heritage lives today through the Historical Walk, which includes 20-plus sites marked with plaques and noted on an easy-to-follow map. Among the main sites are the 1836 Baldwin Home, built for the first missionary to Lahaina; the Old Lahaina Courthouse, now housing the Lahaina Heritage Museum and art gallery; and the plantation-style Pioneer Inn, built in 1901 and still accepting guests today as a Best Western. There's also the Old Prison, where whalers who refused to return to their boats at sunset were confined, and Hawaii's biggest banyan tree, planted in 1873 to mark the 50th anniversary of Lahaina's first Christian mission. Only 8 feet tall when planted, it now reaches more than 60 feet high, has 12 major trunks, and covers more than a full acre's worth of park near the courthouse.

Lahaina has also made a name for itself in the state's culinary world, with a growing number of renowned restaurants. The stylish Lahaina Grill offers unique Pacific Rim cuisine, and French-born and -trained chef Gerard Reversade combines Gallic traditions with local ingredients at Gerard's, housed in the exceptionally charming 18-room Plantation Inn. For cultural entertainment there's 'Ulalena, a sort of Hawaiian version of Cirque du Soleil

Today Lahaina's harbor is dotted with whale-watching boats, a popular choice among visitors.

that tells the story of Hawaii in chant, song, original music, acrobatics, and dance.

WHERE: 22 miles west of Kahului Airport. **BALDWIN HOME AND OLD LAHAINA COURTHOUSE:** Tel 808-661-3262; lahainarestoration.org. **PIONEER INN:** Tel 800-457-5457 or 808-661-3636; pioneerinnmaui.com. *Cost:* from $180. **LAHAINA GRILL:** Tel 808-667-5117; lahainagrill.com. *Cost:* dinner $75. **GERARD'S:** Tel 808-661-8939; gerardsmaui.com. *Cost:* dinner $64. **PLANTATION INN:** Tel 800-433-6815 or 808-667-9225; kbhmaui.com/plantation-inn. *Cost:* from $180. **'ULALENA:** Tel 808-865-7900; ulalena.com. *Cost:* from $60. *When:* closed Sun, Wed, and Sat. **BEST TIME:** Halloween—also known as the "Mardi Gras of the Pacific."

Feasting and Dance: A Night of Aloha

OLD LAHAINA LUAU

Lahaina, Maui, Hawaii

For most Hawaiians, luau are rich traditional feasts held by families and churches; for visitors, they're often uninspired commercial clichés produced by hotels. The nightly Old Lahaina Luau stands apart: intimate, genuine, and suffused with the spirit of aloha, it's widely recognized as Maui's best. After visitors are greeted with leis and libations, they can wander about the 1-acre villagelike oceanside site, chatting with local residents working on traditional Hawaiian crafts. As evening comes, the cooks uncover the *imu*, or earthen oven, and remove the traditionally prepared pig and

According to myth, the hula was born when Pele (the goddess of fire) asked her sister, Laka, to dance for her.

vegetables. A conch shell calls everyone to dinner; chairs are available, but guests can opt to sit on lauhala mats, as the old Hawaiians did. The menu features both customary luau dishes: *kalua* (roast pork), *lau lau* (pork wrapped in luau leaf), poi, and *ahi poke* (marinated raw tuna), as well as stir-fried vegetables, steak, fresh island fruit, and assorted desserts. After dinner there's a beautiful program of dance and chant, presented in an informative and spellbinding narrative.

The presenters of the Old Lahaina Luau also offer the Feast at Lele, a combination fine dining–luau event with a broader experience of Pacific Island culinary and performing arts. It takes place at another oceanside spot, with white-clothed, candlelit tables set on the sand, where waiters serve a five-course dinner of foods from around the Pacific, including kalua pig from Hawaii, braised short ribs from New Zealand, and grilled mango ginger chicken from Tahiti. Entertainment features colorful costumes, songs, chants, drumming, and dances from across the islands.

WHERE: 22 miles west of the Kahului Airport. Tel 800-248-5828 or 808-667-1998; oldlahainaluau.com. *Cost:* $115. **THE FEAST AT LELE:** Tel 886-244-5353 or 808-667-5353; feastatlele.com. *Cost:* $125.

A Diver's Garden in the Sea

MOLOKINI

Maui, Hawaii

Midway between Maui's south shore and the uninhabited island of Kaho'olawe is the tiny islet of Molokini. Viewed from Maui, the islet looks like the partial wall of a collapsed volcanic crater. Up close,

you discover that below the 150-foot wall, in a semicircular crater, there exists an underwater park teeming with coral life and reef fish. You can glimpse enormous, graceful manta rays here, as well as colorful schools of butterfly fish,

spotted puffer fish, and moray eels hiding in the crannies of the rubble. Big cauliflower corals cling tenaciously to the wall of the crater, which is dotted with crevices that provide homes for lobsters, crabs, octopuses, and several species of the fascinating, sometimes psychedelically colored nudibranchs, or sea slugs. Scuba divers love the deep side of the islet, where they can descend as far as 350 feet and see pelagic fish (big tuna, mahi-mahi, jack trevally, and wahoo) cruise by, as well as schools of dolphins and an occasional shark. At greater depths, divers can spot rare black-coral trees.

In the morning hours, when Maui's 10,000-foot Haleakala Volcano acts as a wind block, Molokini is a hive of sail- and powerboats carrying snorkelers and divers. Marine park status makes it illegal to take anything, fish or coral, from the waters. Above the surface, Molokini is a bird sanctuary, so stepping ashore is forbidden—not that that would be easy since the rock wall falls directly into the shallow inlet cove. There are neither beaches nor much of anything else save the only man-made structure on the island, a navigational aid known as the Molokini Light.

WHERE: 5 miles off Maui's southwest coast. **HOW:** Trilogy Charters (tel 888-225-

The partially exposed volcanic crater wall of Molokini is shaped like a crescent moon.

MAUI or 808-874-5649; sailtrilogy.com) sails catamarans out of Ma'alaea Harbor and a marine naturalist leads guests on a snorkel tour. *Cost:* $129 for half-day, includes equipment. **BEST TIME:** morning, before the trade winds pick up around noon.

Timeless Hawaii

THE FRIENDLY ISLE OF MOLOKAI

Hawaii

Blessed with lush vegetation and carved by eons of pounding waves and driving rain that produced the world's tallest sea cliffs and some of Hawaii's longest waterfalls, Molokai is Mother Nature's wild and uninhibited work of

art and one of Hawaii's least developed places. Fewer than 7,500 people live on the 10-by-38-mile island, a great many of them native Hawaiians who maintain a traditional lifestyle—fishing, hunting, and otherwise living from the land. You won't find traffic lights or fast-food restaurants here, so come to relax and recharge by spending your days hiking, kayaking, fishing, snorkeling, walking on stretches of pristine white sand beaches, or just chilling out in a hammock.

The east side of the island—mostly lush tropical forest and a coast lined with sandy coves—betrays few or no signs of tourism. The sleepy main town of Kaunakakai lies in the center of the island's south side and—with the exception of a few B&Bs—is the location of the island's only place to stay: the Hotel Molokai, a well-situated Polynesian classic since 1968.

Isolated on the north side of the island is the dramatically beautiful Kalaupapa Peninsula, a small tongue of land surrounded on three sides by the ocean and on the fourth by forbidding cliffs, where Father Damien, a young Belgian priest, arrived in 1873 to minister to natives stricken with Hansen's disease (leprosy), until his death from the disease 16 years later. Today the peninsula is a National Historic Park, where a few lepers still reside voluntarily (it ceased being a leper colony in 1969), and it can only be visited with permits and by guided tours. There is no ferry service to Kaluapapa. Visitors must arrive by charter flights, which are included in the cost. Stops include Father Damien's St. Philomena Church, a museum/crafts shop in the village, and Judd Park on the Kalawao side, overlooking sea cliffs and waterfalls, dramatic ocean rock formations, and crashing surf. Visitors get here on foot (a strenuous hike, especially on the return), by small plane, or by mule. The Molokai Mule Ride begins at the top of 1,700-foot sea cliffs, which the sure-footed mules traverse slowly through 26 switchbacks.

WHERE: 9 miles northwest of Maui. **HOTEL MOLOKAI:** Tel 877-553-5347 or 808-660-3408; hotelmolokai.com. *Cost:* $180. **KALAUPAPA NATIONAL HISTORIC PARK:** Tel 808-567-6802;

Of Hawaii's eight principal islands, the 260-square-mile Molokai is one of the smallest.

nps.gov/kala. **HOW:** Father Damien Tours arranges charter air service, permits, and tours. Tel 808-349-3006; fatherdamientours.com. *Cost:* $298. **MOLOKAI MULE RIDE:** Kualapu'u. Tel 800-567-7550 or 808-567-6088; muleride .com. *Cost:* $199, includes guided tour permit and lunch. **BEST TIME:** 3rd Sat in May for the Molokai Ka Hula Piko (kahulapiko.com), a weekend celebration of the hula, at various sites on the island's western tip.

A Legendary Repository of Polynesiana

BISHOP MUSEUM

Honolulu, O'ahu, Hawaii

O'ahu ("the gathering place") has been a magnet for tourists at least since the days of Hawaii's last kings, and it's easy to see why when you consider the daily rainbows that arch over its 125 beaches, the thundering waterfalls that cascade into crystal blue lagoons, and the perfect waves that roll steadily to shore. Today the 600-square-mile island is Hawaii's urban center, state capital, nightlife and shopping mecca, commercial and culinary hub, and cultural hot spot. For the greatest repository of Hawaiian history and lore, spend a few hours at Honolulu's newly refurbished Bishop Museum, designated the Hawaii State Museum of Natural and Cultural History and further distinguished as the largest in the state and one of the finest in the Pacific. It was founded in 1889 by Charles Reed Bishop in honor of his late wife, Princess Bernice Pauahi Bishop (the great-granddaughter of King Kamehameha I and the last descendant of the royal Kamehameha lineage). The multibuilding museum contains the world's greatest collection of royal Hawaiian family heirlooms, natural and cultural artifacts from Hawaii and across the Pacific (from Papua New Guinea and New Zealand to Easter Island), and a high-tech 16,500-square-foot Science Adventure Center specializing in oceanography, biodiversity, and volcanology. It even has its own man-made volcano, and in the state-of-the-art

The Bishop Museum is the largest museum in Hawaii.

planetarium visitors can learn how ancient voyagers navigated the Pacific using the stars.

The core of the museum's collection is Princess Pauahi's own collection of artifacts and royal family heirlooms, which she asked be displayed in a museum "to enrich and delight" the people of Hawaii. With a host of items added since its opening, the museum is jam-packed with acquisitions—from insect specimens and ceremonial spears to calabashes and old photos of topless hula dancers, plus the last grass shack in Hawaii, pre-industrial Polynesian art, and even the 50-foot skeleton of a sperm whale. Museum programs include workshops in Hawaiian crafts, such as lei making, feather working, and quilting, on a regular basis.

WHERE: 5 miles from Waikiki; 1525 Bernice St. Tel 808-847-3511; bishopmuseum .org. **BEST TIMES:** Wed–Sat evenings for the Museum After Dark program.

Ascending an Island

DIAMOND HEAD

Honolulu, O'ahu, Hawaii

O f all the state's volcanoes, the one that symbolizes Hawaii most famously is Diamond Head, an ancient volcanic cone rising at the end of Waikiki Beach to create a timeless image, especially under a night sky full of stars

and a glowing full moon. In olden days, when it was known as Le'ahi (the shape of the crater rim resembles the brow of an *ahi*, or tuna), Diamond Head was considered a sacred spot: Hi'iaka, sister of the fire goddess Pele, was said to have named it, and King Kamehameha offered human sacrifices at a temple on the crater's western slope. Early Hawaiians built fires on the top as a navigational aid for canoes traveling along O'ahu's south shore, a function now provided by the Diamond Head Light, built in 1917. The name "Diamond Head" dates to the 1800s, when British sailors digging around

in the crater found what they thought were diamonds. They rushed into Honolulu with their newfound treasure, only to discover that the "diamonds" were really worthless calcite crystals—but the name stuck.

Visitors can reach the 760-foot summit of Honolulu's number one landmark on foot, via a relatively short (1.5-mile roundtrip) but steep walking path. The round-trip takes about an hour and a half, and the stunning 360-degree views of O'ahu—and on a clear day, Molokai and Maui—are well worth it. With keen eyes (or binoculars), you might even spot the occasional whale. The trail begins at the Diamond Head Crater parking lot and proceeds uphill along a paved walkway with handrails. You'll pass old gun emplacements and tunnels, a legacy of Diamond Head's use as part of the military's Pacific defense network. Several steps take you up to the top observation post on Point Le'ahi. About half the path is paved or made into stairs, but even though it's not wilderness, visitors should be prepared with good walking shoes and plenty of water. And expect to see legions of other hikers—this is one of the most popular walks in all Hawaii. Early risers make it to the top in time for sunrise, and then—if it's Saturday morning—head down to the popular KCC Farmers Market, located at Kapi'olani Community College, for breakfast.

WHERE: 3 miles east of Waikiki. Tel 808-587-0300; hawaiistateparks.org/parks/oahu.

Diamond Head crater offers an unparalleled 360-degree view of O'ahu and the surrounding area.

KCC FARMERS MARKET: htbf.org. *When:* Sat 7:30–11 A.M. **BEST TIME:** Sunrise or early morning, to beat the heat and people traffic.

Snorkeling Where Only Royalty Once Swam

HANAUMA BAY

Honolulu, O'ahu, Hawaii

For a first-time snorkeler in tropical waters, it might seem like a psychedelic dream: A cloud of black-masked raccoon butterfly fish in brilliant yellow flitters by, followed by a swarm of black-and-white Hawaiian damselfish

Hanauma means "curved bay" in the Hawaiian language.

hovering close to their favorite coral head, while parrot fish in green, yellow, and orange dart in and out. Welcome to O'ahu's most popular snorkeling spot, Hanauma Bay Nature Preserve, with its Hollywood-perfect 2,000-foot crescent-shaped beach bordered by palm trees. Once a volcanic crater, now breached by the sea, Hanauma used to be the exclusive beach of the royal families and the place where the sport of uma (hand-wrestling) was performed, but today visitors arrive every day by the thousands. They're drawn by the gorgeous white sand beach, shallow water near the shoreline, and more than 100 different species of abundant marine life. Fish identification charts sold in local shops will help the uninitiated ID the hawk, surgeon, trigger, file, puffer, trunk, and other fish living in these calm, warm waters.

Most snorkelers explore close to shore, in the safe 10-foot-deep inner bay, which is almost always crowded. Serious scuba divers go farther out, shooting "the slot" through the reef's edge to get to turbulent Witch's Brew cove and braving strong currents in 70-foot depths at the bay mouth to see coral gardens, turtles, and sharks. Hanauma Bay is a conservation district, so you cannot touch, take, or feed any marine life here. Before putting a toe in the water, visitors are guided through

the $13 million, 10,000-square-foot Marine Education Center, which houses a variety of marine exhibits and a seven-minute orientation video about the Marine Life Sanctuary. Rent fins, masks, and snorkel equipment at the beach, jump in, and enjoy the underwater wonder of it all.

WHERE: 10 miles east of Waikiki. Tel 808-396-4229; gohawaii.com/en/oahu. *When:* closed Tues. **How:** A shuttle beach bus runs frequently from Waikiki to Hanauma Bay (tel 808-848-5555; thebus.org). **BEST TIME:** early, about 8 A.M., on weekday mornings to avoid crowds and parking problems.

Hawaii's Past, on the Streets of Its Capital

HISTORIC HONOLULU

O'ahu, Hawaii

Hawaii is both an isolated archipelago and a crossroads of civilization, with a fittingly rich history. That history lives in Honolulu, and not just in a museum or in the state archives. It's there in a voyaging canoe at

Honolulu Harbor, reminding every passerby of the oceangoing Polynesians who discovered the islands 1,500 years ago. It's there in the landmark Kawaiaha'o Church, a reminder of the profound impact of the missionaries who brought Christianity in the early 19th century. And it's there in the handsome 'Iolani Palace, the last home of the Hawaiian monarchy and subsequently the seat of government of the Republic, Territory, and finally State of Hawaii, until a new capitol building was constructed behind it in 1969.

The city's—indeed, the island's—most visited historical site is Pearl Harbor (see p. 969). But there are older sites closer to the heart of downtown that illustrate the island's rich heritage, dating back to the early 19th century. In 1820, Christian missionaries arrived from America's East Coast to convert a people they considered heathen. The Mission

'Iolani Palace is the only royal palace in the U.S.

Houses Museum preserves three of their historic buildings, restored with period furnishings. Across the street stands the New England–style Kawaiaha'o Church, the first permanent Christian church in the islands. Finished in 1842 after five years of collaboration between the missionaries and Hawaiians (who were ordered to work by King Kamehameha III), the church was built with 14,000 coral blocks—each weighing 1,000 pounds—taken from the offshore reefs. Part of Sunday's 9:00 A.M. service is conducted in the Hawaiian language.

Perhaps the saddest reminder of history for many Hawaiians is the 'Iolani Palace, an extraordinary four-story structure in Italianate Hawaiian Renaissance style and the only royal palace located in the U.S. Built by King David Kalakaua between 1878 and 1882 at a cost of $360,000 (an amount that nearly bankrupted the Hawaiian kingdom), it was the first electrified building in Honolulu—it even beat the White House and Buckingham Palace to the punch. The last of Hawaii's rulers to occupy the palace was Queen Lili'uokalani, who was overthrown by U.S. Marines on January 17, 1893, ending the Hawaiian monarchy. Today the palace galleries include exhibits of the crown jewels, ancient feathered cloaks, and the royal china. Facing the royal palace is Ali'iolani Hale, intended as a royal residence but today used as the home of Hawaii's supreme court. Before it stands a statue of the beloved King Kamehameha in regal costume, his arms outstretched.

MISSION HOUSES MUSEUM: Tel 808-447-3910; missionhouses.org. *When:* closed Sun–Mon. **KAWAIAHA'O CHURCH:** Tel 808-469-3000. **'IOLANI PALACE:** Tel 808-522-0832; iolanipal ace.org. *When:* closed Sun. **BEST TIME:** weekend closest to June 11 for the King Kamehameha Celebration (kamehamehafestival.org).

Plate Lunch, Poke, and a Side of Spam

HONOLULU FOR FOODIES

O'ahu, Hawaii

Honolulu's hundreds of restaurants range from flagships of celebrity chefs to humble dives where ethnic cuisine is cheap and plentiful. The dining scene here is as exciting as that of any major American city, thanks to Honolulu's diversity and place at the crossroads of the Pacific: Within a couple of blocks you can find a superb sushi bar, a top-notch steak house, a lunch counter serving spicy Filipino delicacies, a local-style plate-lunch wagon, a classic American diner, and an upscale exemplar of Hawaiian regional cuisine.

It wasn't long ago that few foodies would deign to use "Hawaiian" and "cuisine" in the same sentence. But in the early 1990s, a band of creative local chefs married fresh Hawaiian ingredients with a variety of traditions to produce cross-cultural fusions—Euro-Asian and Indo-Pacific cooking. A revered figure in Hawaiian regional cuisine, Alan Wong still works his magic at his eponymous restaurant that opened in 1995 and its more casual branch, the Pineapple Room. He combines tastes from all the ethnic groups of Hawaii with the organic, seasonal ethic of California cuisine to create signature dishes such as macadamia-coconut-crusted lamb chops with Asian ratatouille.

Wonder chef Roy Yamaguchi created Roy's, Hawaii's biggest success story, with a string of more than two dozen restaurants from Japan to Pebble Beach. The original site, a hectic, fun spot at Hawaii Kai, opened in 1988. One of three in Honolulu, it still serves Yamaguchi's signature blackened island ahi with spicy soy mustard butter. George

Roy's restaurant boasts a menu of inventive seafood, artistically presented.

Mavrothalassitis, a James Beard Award winner and another of the original group of chefs who gave birth to Hawaiian regional cuisine, combines Hawaiian style with influences from his native France. His well-known Honolulu bistro, Chef Mavro, introduced the trend of serving wine pairings with each course.

Hawaii's culinary revolution continues with a crop of young chefs (many who trained under the early trailblazers), pop-ups, food trucks, and farmers markets like the KCC Farmers Market at the foot of Diamond Head (see p. 961)—one of 200-plus throughout the state. Hawaii's "local food" fills out the culinary spectrum with cultural hybrids like plate lunches, *poke*, and shave ice. The plate lunch usually comes from a lunch truck and consists of fried meat or fish, "two scoops rice," plus a macaroni salad, a sprinkling of julienned cabbage, and the possibility of *poke* (pronounced po-KAY), cubed raw fish seasoned with onions and seaweed. For dessert, the ultra-simple culinary creation known as shave ice is the island version of a snow cone, only served with shaved instead of crushed ice. Matsumoto Shave Ice, on Kamehameha Highway in Haleiwa, serves it with dozens of flavors, from coconut to guava to pickled mango.

A deliciously authentic representation of local food is the unassuming 'Ono Hawaiian Foods, a dive on the outskirts of town featuring island dishes you've likely never heard of—such as sweet *haupia* pudding made of coconut milk—as well as that old-time Hawaiian favorite, Spam. Along with Guam and Saipan, Hawaii accounts for the greatest per-capita consumption of Hormel's "spiced ham." Spam *musubi*, a popular snack, is a sushi-style combination of Spam, rice, and seaweed. You can find all manner of variations at the city's annual Spam Jam Festival.

ALAN WONG'S: Tel 808-949-2526; alanwongs.com. *Cost:* dinner $60. **THE PINEAPPLE ROOM:** Tel 808-945-6573; alanwongs.com. *Cost:* dinner $50. **ROY'S:** Hawaii Kai. Tel 808-396-7697; roysrestaurant.com. *Cost:* dinner $70. **CHEF MAVRO:** Tel 808-944-4714; chefmavro.com. *Cost:* dinner $75. **MATSUMOTO SHAVE ICE:** Haleiwa. Tel 808-637-4827; matsumotoshaveice.com. *Cost:* $3. **'ONO HAWAIIAN FOODS:** Tel 808-737-2275; onohawaiianfoods.com. *Cost:* lunch $20. **BEST TIME:** April for Spam Jam (spamjamhawaii.com).

A Jam-Packed Cultural Stir-Fry

HONOLULU'S CHINATOWN

O'ahu, Hawaii

As the sun's rays first cross over the Ko'olau Mountains, Honolulu's diminutive, five-by-three-block Chinatown awakens with a riot of sounds, smells, and colors. The dialects of at least half a dozen different Asian countries fill the air, as vendors set up their wares in open markets. A heady mixture of smells wafts through: pungent dried herbs, aromatic blends of different ethnic breakfasts, fragrant blooming lei flowers, and burning incense. The dawn illuminates the area's unique architecture and dramatic colors. By 9 A.M., crowds have filled the sidewalks. They move not with the slow gait common in more laid-back parts of Hawaii, but with the hurried steps of bargain-hunters, the swift shuffle of early morning shoppers pulling their already overflowing carts, and the purposeful strides of businesspeople talking loudly on cell phones. The only people to pause are wide-eyed tourists trying to assimilate the rapid assault on their senses.

Honolulu's Chinatown has a history of constant change and an ability to rise phoenixlike and redefine itself. Chinese were first brought to Hawaii from Guangdong Province beginning in 1855 as indentured laborers for the sugarcane and pineapple plantations. When their contracts were up, the immigrants looked around for better work, and many of them opened small shops and restaurants in the area around River Street, which soon prospered and by 1870 had become known as Chinatown.

The area has twice burned to the ground, in 1886 and in 1900—the second time because fires set to destroy bubonic-plague-infected houses got out of hand and burned the entire 40 acres. Chinatown not only rebuilt each time, but also continued to thrive. By the 1930s, tourists poured into the exotic area. A decade later, during WWII, sailors flocked to Chinatown in search of pool halls, tawdry bars, and good-time girls. Today, Chinatown is home to an eclectic mix of cultures, from Chinese to Vietnamese. Visitors come to bargain for jade and antiques, worship in incense-filled temples, pick up high-quality/low-priced leis, or eat authentic ethnic cuisine.

Food is central to the Chinatown experience, with everything for the East Asian kitchen—homemade noodles, fresh herbs, seafood, live poultry, you name it. A plethora of restaurants dishes up pho, pad thai, dim sum, and a myriad of other delights; a long-standing local favorite, Little Village Noodle House, offers such delicacies as super-fresh clams in lemongrass sauce and crispy pan-fried beef from its extensive menu. Chinatown goes all out for Chinese New Year, holding several big celebrations including the Narcissus Festival, with its queen pageant, cooking demonstrations, and cultural fair.

WHERE: 4 miles from Waikiki. **LITTLE VILLAGE NOODLE HOUSE:** Tel 808-545-3008; littlevillagehawaii.com. *Cost:* dinner $15. **BEST TIME:** Jan or Feb for Chinese New Year.

The World's Most Famous City Shoreline

WAIKIKI BEACH

Honolulu, O'ahu, Hawaii

It used to be a swamp—its name, which means "spouting water," comes from the springs that fed the taro patches and fishponds—but Waikiki also had a 2-mile crescent of sand, plenty of sunshine, and perfect waves rolling

into shore. So in the early days, after Honolulu became the capital of the Kingdom of Hawaii in 1845, the royalty wisely chose to build their beach homes on Waikiki.

At the turn of the next century, Moana

Hotel (today, part of the Moana Surfrider) was the first hotel to be built on Waikiki Beach—it was considered cutting-edge because not only did each room have a private bathroom, but the hotel also had a telephone, an unheard-of luxury at the time. In 1906, the Hawaii Board of Health called Waikiki "dangerous and unsanitary" because of its swarms of mosquitoes, and ordered the swamp drained. By the early 1920s, the Ala Wai Canal had been built, the former swamplands drained, and the Royal Hawaiian Hotel was constructed on the site of a former royal beach house. The "Pink Palace of the Pacific" is an institution beloved since it opened in 1927, and today it remains true to its time, though carefully updated.

Just after statehood in 1959, when newly introduced jets were bringing visitors to the 50th state, builders usurped the rest of Waikiki Beach, resulting in today's side-by-side

A retreat for Hawaiian royalty in the past, Waikiki Beach continues to be a place for idyllic relaxation.

cornucopia of tropical resort hotels. In fact, Waikiki even ran out of sand and for a couple of decades had to import it from Molokai, across the channel, to spread over the world-famous beach. It worked, and Waikiki still ranks as one of the world's best urban beaches.

Today the sumptuous, intimate beachside Halekulani ("House Befitting Heaven") is the premier hotel on O'ahu, and one of the best in the U.S., a 5-acre oasis of elegance that first opened in 1917. For the most romantic (and expensive) dining in town, visit its La Mer restaurant, whose superb preparation of fresh fish and island ingredients reinterprets the tenets of classic French cuisine. Downstairs, the hotel's less formal oceanfront Orchids dining room has a famous Sunday brunch offering more than 200 dishes served buffet style, and draws as many Hawaiian families as visitors.

WHERE: Waikiki Beach is bordered by the Ala Wai Canal and Diamond Head. **MOANA SURFRIDER:** Tel 866-716-8112 or 808-922-3111; moana-surfrider.com. *Cost:* from $257. **ROYAL HAWAIIAN:** Tel 866-716-8110 or 808-923-7311; royal-hawaiian.com. *Cost:* from $300. **HALEKULANI HOTEL:** Tel 800-367-2343 or 808-923-2311; halekulani.com. *Cost:* from $495; dinner at La Mer $110; dinner at Orchids $80.

A One-Stop Trip Around the Pacific

POLYNESIAN CULTURAL CENTER

La'ie, O'ahu, Hawaii

The Pacific is vast, but you can experience its islands, its people, and its culture in a single day without leaving O'ahu. The Polynesian Cultural Center, a kind of living museum, details the lifestyles, songs, dance,

costumes, and architecture of seven Pacific islands—Fiji, Aotearoa, Marquesas, Samoa, Tahiti, Tonga, and Hawaii—in recreated villages scattered throughout a 42-acre park. Visitors travel through the outdoor museum by

foot or in canoes on a man-made freshwater lagoon, visiting villages "inhabited" by native students from Polynesia who attend the La'ie campus of Brigham Young University. Operated by the Mormon Church, the park also features a variety of stage shows celebrating the music, dance, history, and culture of Polynesia, and a luau every evening. Just beyond the center is the Hawaii Temple of the Church of Jesus Christ of Latter-day Saints; completed in 1919, it was the first Mormon temple outside the continental U.S.

Since the 1970s, Hawaii has experienced a resurgence and revival of native Hawaiian culture. Not only is the Hawaiian language taught in public schools, but there has also been a renaissance in traditional Hawaiian arts—including weaving *lahaula* (the straw-like leaf of the hala tree), making the bark cloth known as *tapa*, building canoes, and navigating by the stars—in myriad programs, including the annual statewide celebrations known as the Aloha Festivals, which feature events ranging from an annual parade to a royal ball.

The biggest interest has been in hula, with a proliferation of *halau* (schools) teaching the ancient dance. The best way to experience this renaissance is to attend one of Hawaii's many hula competitions. In June and July, top dancers from around the world travel to Honolulu to compete at the King Kamehameha Hula Competition, the Prince Lot Hula Festival, and the Queen Lili'uokalani Keiki Hula Competition, which features some 500 children from across the state.

The Polynesian Cultural Center hosts elaborate luau shows.

Where: 35 miles north of Waikiki; 55-370 Kamehameha Hwy. Tel 800-367-7060 or 808-293-3333; polynesia.com. *Cost:* general admission $60. *When:* closed Sun. **Aloha Festivals:** Statewide. Tel 808-923-2030; alohafestivals.com. *When:* Sept–Oct. **King Kamehameha Hula Competition:** Honolulu. Tel 808-745-3000; oha.org/events. *When:* 3rd weekend in June. **Prince Lot Hula Festival:** Honolulu. Tel 808-839-5334; mgf-hawaii.org. *When:* July. **Queen Lili'uokalani Keiki Hula Competition:** Honolulu. Tel 808-521-6905; kpcahawaii.com. *When:* July. **Best time:** mid-May for the World Fire-Knife Dance Championships and Samoan Festival at the Polynesian Cultural Center.

Big Waves, Big Kahunas

NORTH SHORE SURFING

O'ahu, Hawaii

Ever since Hawaiians revived the ancient practice of surfing a century ago, and especially after Duke Kahanamoku—Olympic gold-medal swimmer and the original "Big Kahuna"—popularized it from Australia to California,

riding the waves has been the quintessential Hawaiian sport. For surfers and spectators alike, there's no place like the 6-mile stretch of

O'ahu's North Shore from Hale'iwa to Sunset Beach, where in winter monster swells from Pacific storms rush unimpeded toward reef breaks. This area of deserted beaches, spiky cliffs, and lush vegetation becomes a scene of death-defying thrill rides, as elite surfers come to test themselves against waves four to six stories tall. Cars, from prosaic rentals to sparkling BMWs to rusty pickups and kid-filled SUVs, line up bumper-to-bumper along the road to Waimea Bay, Sunset, and the fabled Banzai Pipeline off Ehukai Beach Park, taking throngs to see nature at its wildest. Only the very best surfers even attempt to enter the water when the big waves come, and those who manage to ride these gargantuan swells appear as fragile thumbnail figures on a raging backdrop.

It's hard to believe that during the summer months, from April to October, these same tumultuous waters settle to a flat calm, inviting swimmers, kayakers, snorkelers, divers, and fishermen to come out to play. Hale'iwa, officially designated a historic, cultural, and scenic district, thrives in a time warp going back to 1899, when sugarcane king Benjamin Dillingham built a 30-mile railroad to link his Honolulu and North Shore plantations. Dillingham also opened a Victorian hotel overlooking Kaiaka Bay and named it Hale'iwa, or "house of the frigate bird," the tropical seabird often seen here. The hotel and railroad are both gone, but Hale'iwa still draws visitors with its blend of funky old town and upscale boutiques, and those in the know now book at the modest but perfectly situated Ke Iki Beach Bungalows.

The local tradition for a trip to the North Shore includes stopping at one of the shrimp trucks, located around Hale'iwa or Kahuku on the Kamehameha Highway, selling farm-raised North Shore shrimp. The menu usually offers shrimp prepared spicy, garlic, Cajun, coconut, buttered, lemon, or just plain, and most trucks have picnic tables alongside. Giovanni's Shrimp Truck claims to have been the first truck to serve the delicious fare, but Kahuku Famous Shrimp has a more extensive shrimp menu plus squid, shrimp and steak, and shrimp and vegetable stir-fry. The trucks generally show up before noon and stay until about sunset, when the last surfers head home.

WHERE: Hale'iwa is 28 miles northwest of Honolulu. **KE IKI BEACH BUNGALOWS:** Tel 866-638-8229 or 808-638-8229; keikibeach.com. *Cost:* from $100. **GIOVANNI'S SHRIMP TRUCK:** Kahuku. Tel 808-293-1839. *Cost:* $13. **KAHUKU FAMOUS SHRIMP:** Kahuku. Tel 808-389-1173. *Cost:* $12. **BEST TIMES:** mid-Nov–mid-Dec for Van's Triple Crown of Surfing (vanstriplecrown ofsurfing.com); Nov–Mar for biggest waves.

O'ahu's North Shore is a world-renowned place for surfers and bodyboarders to test their skills.

Remember . . .

PEARL HARBOR

O'ahu, Hawaii

O n a sunny Sunday morning, December 7, 1941, hundreds of Japanese planes appeared over the island of O'ahu and began bombing the U.S. Navy's Pacific fleet, the bulk of which was docked in Pearl Harbor.

Ninety minutes later, 2,403 Americans had been killed and over 1,000 wounded. Nearly half died on the 608-foot battleship USS *Arizona*, which sank in nine minutes without firing a shot after its forward ammunition magazines exploded catastrophically, taking 1,177 sailors and marines to their deaths. The attack crippled the fleet, severely damaging or destroying 12 warships; destroyed 188 aircraft, representing nearly all the planes on nearby air bases; and catapulted the U.S. into WWII.

More than 20 years later, in 1962, the USS *Arizona* memorial opened to the public, its bone-white rectangular structure spanning the middle portion of the sunken ship, which lies untouched and rusting just a few feet below the surface. A trip to Hawaii's most visited site is a somber, poignant event, as you step from the ferry—the only access—into the shrine-like space, peer over the side toward the sunken ship, and begin to notice the spots of oil that still bubble up from her tanks to the surface, between 2 and 9 quarts a day, like a dark shadow of blood. At the far end, a memorial marble wall includes the names of all

The USS Arizona *memorial's design has a peak at each end with a sag in the center, representing America's initial defeat and ultimate victory in WWII.*

those killed on the *Arizona*, along with those of surviving crewmen who later chose to have their ashes interred with their comrades in the sunken ship.

At the opposite end of Battleship Row, where eight ships were moored together off Ford Island on that grim day, sits the 58,000-ton battleship USS *Missouri*, which served as part of the force that carried out bombing raids over Tokyo and provided firepower in the battles of Iwo Jima and Okinawa. While the nearby *Arizona* represents the beginning of American involvement in the war, the *Missouri* represents its end, as it was on the deck of this great ship, the last battleship the Navy ever built, that the war finally came to an end with the signing of the Japanese surrender on September 2, 1945. Visitors are shuttled to Ford Island on military-type buses while listening to a 1940s-style radio program (complete with news clips, wartime commercials, and music). Once aboard the ship, you watch an informational film and are then free to explore on your own or take a 60-minute guided tour. The last stop on the tour of Hawaii's role in the war is the slender 311-foot USS *Bowfin*, one of only 15 WWII submarines still in existence today. You can go below decks on this famous submarine—nicknamed the "Pearl Harbor Avenger" for its successful attacks on the Japanese—and see how its 80-man crew lived during wartime.

WHERE: 11 miles from Waikiki. **HOW:** Various tours offered (including Waikiki pick-up/drop-off) from $40 (pearlharboroahu.com). **BEST TIMES:** mornings for smaller crowds; Dec 7th for the anniversary of the attack.

CANADA

—

EASTERN CANADA

WESTERN CANADA

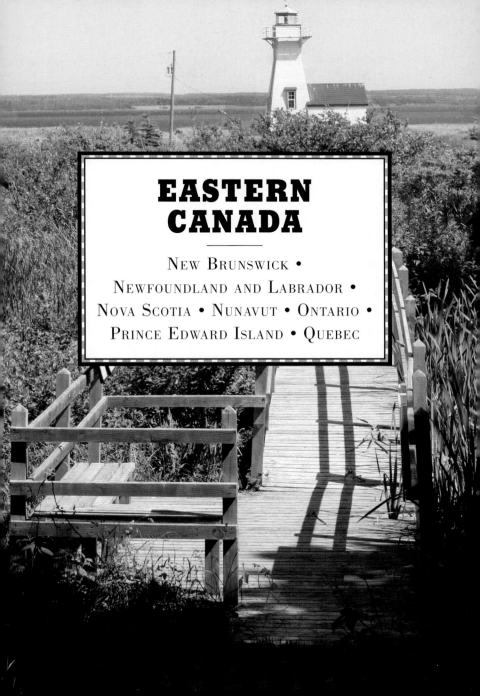

EASTERN CANADA

New Brunswick •
Newfoundland and Labrador •
Nova Scotia • Nunavut • Ontario •
Prince Edward Island • Quebec

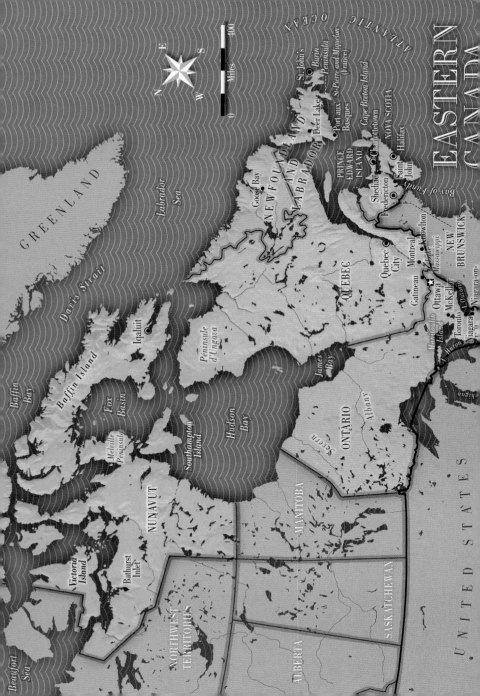

Music, Culture, and Lobsters on New Brunswick's Northern Shore

FESTIVALS ALONG THE ACADIAN COAST

New Brunswick

Ⓘn the 1750s, when the British deported French Acadian settlers from Nova Scotia and the lower mainland of New Brunswick, some fled north to the coastline of the Gulf of St. Lawrence, where they reestablished farms and fishing villages. Many settled along this long stretch of sandy beachfront, barrier islands, and coastal wetlands known today as the Acadian Coast, where French Canadian joie de vivre is manifest in a summer's worth of festivals.

Maritime Canada has long been renowned for succulent lobsters and the summertime festivals that celebrate them. The largest of both are at the fishing town of Shediac, at the base of New Brunswick's Acadian Coast. With down-home events and lots and lots of just-caught lobsters to eat, this is one of New Brunswick's best-loved summer events with over 50,000 gastronomic devotees of *Homarus americanus* gathering in early July for four days to devour several tons of lobster.

Self-appointed Lobster Capital of the World, Shediac also has the largest lobster in the world—the 50-ton, 36-foot-long statue at the town entrance that seems more sci-fi monster than tempting crustacean, and just a little scary if you happen upon it by chance.

North of Shediac, sandy beaches and grassy dunes front the warmest coastal waters north of Virginia—stretching past Kouchibouguac National Park and Miramichi Bay. At the end of the Acadian peninsula, two islands point out into the Gulf of St. Lawrence. The larger of the two is Île Lamèque (Lamèque Island), whose sleepy fishing village of Petite Rivière de l'Île is transformed in late July by the week-long Lamèque International Baroque Music Festival. Many recitals and concerts take place in the early 20th-century Church of Sainte-Cécile, a brightly painted wooden structure with perfect acoustics.

Just west of the islands, on the protected Baie des Chaleurs (which translates as "bay of warmth" for the very temperate waters found here) is the cultural heart of traditional French Acadian culture: the picturesque beachside town of Caraquet. You can spend hours wandering the 100 acres that make up the Village Historique Acadien and its 45 buildings dating from 1770 to 1890, brought here from across the region to illustrate the history and heritage of the Acadian people. But it is Caraquet's 15-day *Festival Acadien* or Acadian Festival, the largest cultural event in French Acadian Canada, that puts this town on the map. Devoted to promoting and supporting

For their own version of Mardi Gras, Tintamarre festival-goers don elaborate masks, face paint, and costumes.

Acadian culture, the festival brings in hundreds of Francophone bands and musicians to play at various venues in Caraquet, while the *Festival acadien de poésie* is a showcase for French Canadian writers, poets, and playwrights. Besides exhibitions of visual arts and special concerts and storytelling events for children, one unique event is the Tintamarre, an ancient celebration on August 15, the Acadian national holiday. Literally translated, "tintamarre" means "loud racket," and so it is. Thousands of merrymakers march through Caraquet, making as much noise as possible with anything they can get their hands on—pots, pans, shakers, drums, tin cans, and whistles—and waving the *stella maris*, the tricolor-and-gold-star Acadian flag.

WHERE: Shediac is 108 miles/175 km northeast of Saint John. **SHEDIAC LOBSTER FESTIVAL:** Tel 506-532-1122; shediaclobster festival.ca. *When:* early July. **LAMÈQUE INTERNATIONAL BAROQUE MUSIC FESTIVAL:** Tel 506-344-3261; festivalbaroque.com. *When:* last week of July. **VILLAGE HISTORIQUE ACADIEN:** Caraquet. Tel 506-726-2600; villagehistorique acadien.com. *When:* June–mid-Oct. **ACADIAN FESTIVAL:** Caraquet. Tel 506-727-2787; festival acadien.ca. *When:* Aug 1–15.

A Marine Wonder of the World

BAY OF FUNDY

New Brunswick

The Bay of Fundy boasts the world's highest tides, rising as much as 48 feet in six hours—more than 22 times greater than the average tide in open seas. With every tide, 100 billion tons of water enters or exits the bay, equal to the daily discharge of all the world's freshwater rivers. These massive flows create a series of unique environments. The hard, rapid tides have sculpted the bay's cave-pocked coastline, where huge boulders have been reduced to fantasy shapes, and they churn up nutrients to feed one of the world's richest marine ecosystems. It is all best observed at Fundy National Park, established in 1948 to protect 80 square miles of coastline and forested mountains on the bay's New Brunswick coast.

So dramatic is the difference between low and high tide that, at the park's Alma Beach, almost three-quarters of a mile of tidal flats are exposed at low tide. Then, when the water comes rushing back in, it produces a roar at midtide called "the voice of the moon." The bay's vast intertidal zone is a fascinating showcase of marine species, especially for feeding shorebirds—for them these mudflats are like a huge buffet dinner. Ten miles east of the park at Mary's Point, the Bay of Fundy Hemispheric Shorebird Reserve is one of the top bird-watching destinations in the area, with over 250 documented species.

In the park, hiking opportunities abound, with over 60 miles of trails traversing the coastline and forested backcountry. For experienced hikers, the Fundy Circuit is a 30-mile network of seven linked trails that traverse valleys, forest, and wilderness coastline along the bay, requiring three to five days to complete.

Twenty-four miles northeast of the national park, the Hopewell Rocks are a kind of natural sculpture garden filled with tide-carved rock monoliths jutting from the sand. Some have sprouted mini-forests on their summits, giving them a dramatic yet whimsical look—hence their popular moniker, "the flowerpots." Local

Mi'kmaq legend has it that the boulders were once men, who were enslaved by angry whales and turned to stone when they tried to escape.

Perhaps the best way to experience the Bay of Fundy is by sea kayak. FreshAir Adventure's half-day guided tour offers an adventure in natural history as it explores the dramatic coastal cliffs, sea caves, and hidden beaches swallowed twice daily by the cycle of tides. You may also see right whales—the bay has the largest population of these endangered sea mammals anywhere. Your guide will also keep an eye on the tide table—you don't want to be stranded once the tides change.

Fundy National Park's headquarters has interpretive activities and numerous sports options, including golf, tennis, and a saltwater swimming pool. Within walking distance of the nearby village of Alma, the elegant Cliffside Suites offers spacious rooms and cottages, all with views of the bay, from a peaceful and secluded perch above the village.

Those wanting to explore the bay by car can take the scenic Fundy Coastal Drive stretching from St. Stephen to Aulac. This enjoyable 5-hour route takes in great stretches of natural beauty and some lovely towns as well—don't miss the 19th-century seaside village of St. Andrews (see next page).

WHERE: Park headquarters at Alma is 84 miles/135 km northeast of Saint John. **FUNDY**

The Bay of Fundy's high tides have sculpted the Hopewell Rocks into unique formations.

NATIONAL PARK: Tel 506-887-6000; pc.gc.ca/fundy. **HOPEWELL ROCKS:** Hopewell Cape. Tel 877-734-3429 or 506-734-3429; thehopewellrocks.ca. *When:* mid-May–mid-Oct. **FRESHAIR ADVENTURE:** Alma. Tel 800-545-0020 or 506-887-2249; freshairadventure.com. *Cost:* from US$52/C$69 for half-day guided kayak tour. **CLIFFSIDE SUITES:** Alma. Tel 866-881-1022 or 506-887-1022; cliffsidesuites.com. *Cost:* from US$82/C$109. *When:* mid-May–mid-Oct. **BEST TIMES:** a new or full moon for the most dramatic tides; mid-July–mid-Sept for peak bird migration; July–Sept for best kayaking weather; Sept–Oct for foliage and whale-watching.

Like a World Unto Itself

GRAND MANAN ISLAND

New Brunswick

A craggy sentinel at the Bay of Fundy's mouth (see previous page), Grand Manan Island is surrounded by some of the world's most turbulent waters. The cliff-faced island's isolation is more than just

an accident of the tides, however. On Grand Manan, nature, history, and tradition combine to make this tiny enclave—just 21 miles long,

with a population of only 2,500—an outpost of a seafaring lifestyle long bypassed elsewhere. For many visitors, however, Grand Manan's greatest draw is its wildlife. The island is considered one of Canada's top birding destinations; no less an authority than John James Audubon journeyed here in 1831 to study.

More than 360 bird species have been identified on Grand Manan and surrounding islets, with 131 species breeding and nesting here, the rest passing through on their long migrations. The boat journey to Machias Seal Island, the outermost of the Grand Manan archipelago and a bird sanctuary maintained by the Canadian Wildlife Service, is nearly mandatory. The southernmost nesting site of the North Atlantic puffin, the island is also home to an abundance of razorbills, terns, eiders, guillemots, and storm petrels—and to one of eastern Canada's last staffed lighthouses. Sea Watch Tours, out of tiny Seal Cove Village, is authorized to land tour boats on Machias Seal Island; during the 11-mile journey to the island, watch for humpback and finback whales, seals, and porpoises grazing in the herring-rich waters.

The island offers comfortable lodging and good food but is still very rooted to the age-old rhythms of the sea. At tiny fishing villages perched above the surging tides, wooden docks bustle as fishermen unload lobster, haddock, and cod. The rough-edged charm hooks even the unprepared.

Today, the best and most atmospheric lodging on Grand Manan is North Head's family-run Inn at Whale Cove, overlooking the sea and offering B&B rooms in a gray-shingled 1816 farmhouse and several cottages (one once owned by author Willa Cather) scattered around a 10-acre meadow. The inn's dining room offers sophisticated preparations of local fish and seafood that still adhere to the island's unpretentious ways.

WHERE: 20 miles/32 km from the New Brunswick mainland; accessible only by ferry. *Visitor info:* Tel 888-525-1655 or 506-662-3442; grandmanannb.com. **HOW:** Grand Manan Island Ferry offers year-round service to North Head from the mainland's Black Harbour; coastaltransport.ca. **SEA WATCH TOURS:** Seal Cove Village. Tel 877-662-8552 or 506-662-8552; seawatchtours.com. *Cost:* US$85/C$113. *When:* mid-June–mid-Aug. **INN AT WHALE COVE:** North Head. Tel 506-662-3181; whalecovecottages.com. *Cost:* from US$110/C$150, dinner US$30/C$40. **BEST TIMES:** Apr–July for birding; early Aug for Rotary Festival, with music and activities across the island.

An Affluent Historic Seaport

ST. ANDREWS BY-THE-SEA

New Brunswick

The charming village of St. Andrews flourished as Canada's first seaside resort and remains one of the Maritime Provinces' most delightful destinations. Situated on the mouth of the St. Croix River, about 30 miles from the Maine border, St. Andrews was settled in 1783 by American loyalists who chose not to join the revolution against Great Britain. Much of the town's architectural unity is due to these affluent New Englanders, some of whom dismantled their homes in the U.S. and barged them here for reassembly (a few still stand today). The beauty of St. Andrews' location—on a protected bay spangled with islands—later made it a favorite summer playground for the wealthy and fashionable at the turn of the 20th century. Many of the town's imposing estates and resorts date from this prosperous era.

Historic Water Street parallels the bay and is lined with tasteful shops, boutiques, and sophisticated art galleries. The bustling harbor offers whale-watching trips (with bald eagles, porpoises, and seals along for good measure), guided kayak tours, and ferry rides to nearby islands. If you'd prefer terra firma, walking tours of the historic district are available (with ghost walks offered on summer nights), and the gorgeous Kingsbrae Garden offers 27 acres of formal plantings and woodland trails. Plan your day to have tea here in the Garden Café, or treat yourself to a sumptuous dinner at Savour in the garden, where views of the lush lawns reach down to the bay.

The choice of aristocratic accommodations is no less impressive. The grandest option is the Tudor-style, 223-room Algonquin Resort, which reopened in 2014 after a $30-million face-lift. Built in 1889, the hilltop dowager's turrets and red tile roof might convince you that you've woken up on the other side of the Pond. The Algonquin's seaside golf course was redesigned in 2000 and now ranks among Canada's finest, while its spa features indulgent beauty treatments and fitness facilities.

More intimate lodging is available at Kingsbrae Arms, built in 1897 as a "cottage-style" manor house and later converted into a sumptuous country house hotel. All ten rooms and suites are decorated with infallible good taste and unending attention to detail, with fireplaces and lovely balcony views of the bay or the neighboring Kingsbrae Garden (one lucky room sees both). The resident owners are lovely, service is regal, and the dining, while casual, is world-class.

WHERE: 83 miles/133 km south of Fredericton. *Visitor info:* Tel 506-529-5120; townofstandrews.ca. **KINGSBRAE GARDEN:** Tel 866-566-8687 or 506-529-3335; kingsbrae garden.com. **ALGONQUIN RESORT:** Tel 855-529-8693 or 506-529-8823; algonquinresort.com. *Cost:* from US$105/C$139 (off-peak), from US$172/C$229 (peak). **KINGSBRAE ARMS:** Tel 506-529-1897; kingsbrae.com. *Cost:* from US$412/C$549. **BEST TIMES:** June–July for perennial garden blooms; June–Sept for weather; late Aug–mid-Sept for whale-watching; late Sept–early Oct for foliage.

A Viking Colony in Canada

L'ANSE AUX MEADOWS

Newfoundland and Labrador

66 "Give a land a good name so that men would want to go there," was reportedly the policy of Norse explorers such as Leif Erikson. Which goes a ways in explaining why the name "Vinland" (or "land of grapes")

was given to the 11th-century Viking colony at the northern tip of Newfoundland's Great Northern Penninsula—the oldest European settlement yet discovered in North America, now preserved and reconstructed as L'Anse aux Meadows National Historic Site. This highly significant spot had historians rethinking the early chapters of European expansion once it was determined that Vikings had settled on these shores centuries before the arrival of Christopher Columbus and John Cabot.

According to the ancient Norse sagas, almost 1,000 years ago Vikings set sail from Greenland across the Atlantic, discovering a green, fertile land they called Vinland for the wild grapes growing there (the fruit most probably was some other berry—grapes do not grow at this latitude). The sagas relate that the Vikings established a settlement in this new land to which numerous Norse explorers returned over the course of years.

Such was the information that propelled Norwegian archaeologists Helge and Anne Ingstad in the 1960s to search eastern North America for evidence of Viking settlements. At the northernmost tip of Newfoundland, on a protected bay called L'Anse aux Meadows, the Ingstads uncovered what the sagas had reported: the remains of a Viking colony from the 11th century.

The Ingstads excavated the site, as did Parks Canada later, discovering that the

Costumed actors re-create Viking life at the rebuilt camp.

L'Anse aux Meadows community comprised a number of sod and timber building complexes, each with a dwelling and workshops. The colony supported up to 135 men and women, and was used for an undetermined number of years as a base for cutting timber, hunting, and exploring the unknown Vinland wilderness.

The settlement—the terminus of a highly scenic 304-mile Viking Trail, aka Hwy 340—has been partly reconstructed by Parks Canada. The visitors center displays many of the artifacts discovered there and screens a film about the Ingstad excavation. The rebuilt camp is the real highlight, where you can explore the interior of an 11th-century Viking compound in the company of a trained guide who helps bring it all alive, and interact with actors in period dress as they demonstrate Viking skills such as blacksmithing and weaving.

WHERE: 268 miles/431 km north of Deer Lake. **L'ANSE AUX MEADOWS:** St-Lunaire-Griquet. Tel 709-623-2608; pc.gc.ca/meadows. *When:* June–mid-Oct. **VIKING TRAIL:** Tel 877-778-4546 or 709-861-2288; vikingtrail.org. **WHERE TO STAY:** The rustic Valhalla Lodge in Gunners Cove has great views. Tel 877-623-2018 or 709-754-3105; valhalla-lodge.com. *Cost:* from US$90/C$120. *When:* mid-May–Sept. **BEST TIME:** July–Sept for weather.

Microcosm of a Country's Seafaring Past

BONAVISTA PENINSULA

Newfoundland and Labrador

As remote as Newfoundland seems today, it was once one of North America's primary gateways to European trade and exploration. The Bonavista Peninsula—a rocky and thickly wooded thumb extending roughly

70 miles into the North Atlantic from the island's eastern face—has seen European arrivals perhaps since 1497, when John Cabot (aka Giovanni Caboto, the Italian-born explorer sailing for the English Crown) made landfall in

this vicinity (although the exact spot is debated). Cabot's reports of cod-rich waters brought Portuguese, French, and English fishing fleets to the peninsula, and by 1700, fishing villages had grown along its craggy harbors.

The tiny fishing communities that ring Trinity Bay on the peninsula's southern shores were once a hub of European culture in Canada—in fact, the hamlet of Trinity, with a year-round population today of 200, was once larger than the Newfoundland capital of St. John's and today is the peninsula's most popular spot. Historic homes and commercial buildings crowd around Trinity's once-busy harbor. Around 50 of the village's original structures are preserved, today housing shops, B&Bs, restaurants, and cafés. In summer the Rising Tide Theatre group effectively turns the entire village into a stage for the Trinity Pageant. In this peripatetic production, the audience follows actors through the streets as they present episodes of Trinity history with the village itself as backdrop.

From here it's about 50 miles to the tip of the peninsula and the village of Bonavista, which offers even more edge-of-the-world remoteness. Among other historic homes and structures, the Ryan Premises National Historic Site is a series of period seafront buildings that present the last word on the once mighty cod fishing industry. In Bonavista harbor is an exact replica of the *Matthew*, the ship that brought Cabot and his crew to North America. Tour the boat and imagine the claustrophobia the crew must have felt during a 35-day Atlantic crossing.

At Cape Bonavista, 4 miles outside town, and the end of the road between here and Europe, stands the Cape Bonavista Lighthouse. This vividly striped lighthouse was placed in service in 1842, and although now defunct, you can visit and hear tales of a lighthouse keeper's

Puffins are seabirds but they breed in colonies on land, often on rocky cliffs.

life from costumed docents. From the top, look for a puffin colony that is often visible on a nearby promontory. If you gaze into the watery distance, you might see massive icebergs and a departing whale-watching boat.

WHERE: 125 miles/200 km northwest of St. John's. *Visitor info:* Tel 709-466-3845; newfound landlabrador.com. **RISING TIDE THEATRE:** Trinity. Tel 888-464-3377 or 709-464-3232; risingtidetheatre.com. *When:* mid-June–early Oct. **RYAN PREMISES:** Tel 709-468-1600; pc.gc .ca/ryanpremises. *When:* mid-May–mid-Oct. **MATTHEW:** Tel 877-468-1497 or 709-468-1493; matthewlegacy.com. *When:* mid-May–Sept. **CAPE BONAVISTA LIGHTHOUSE:** Tel 709-468-7444. *When:* mid-May–early Oct. **WHERE TO STAY:** The 33-room Fishers' Loft Inn, Port Rexton, tel 877-464-3240 or 709-464-3240; fishersloft.com. *Cost:* from US$75/C$99 (off-peak), from US$105/C$140 (peak). *When:* May–Oct. **BEST TIME:** June 24–25, the date of John Cabot's landfall, for the Discovery Celebrations.

A Toute Petite Bit of France

ST-PIERRE AND MIQUELON

French Territories off Newfoundland

Who knew that you could see France from North America? The archipelago of St-Pierre and Miquelon is a French territory, a negligible fraction of that country's once huge colonial holdings in North America.

Between 1713 and 1814, these barren, wind-swept islands—which lie just 18 miles from Newfoundland's Burin Peninsula—passed back and forth between France and Britain no fewer than six times. In the end, they remained in French control, and today these tiny islands are solidly French and proud of it.

France fought to retain control of St-Pierre and Miquelon because of their location near the Grand Banks, legendary fishing grounds for cod. Though the once enormously prolific fisheries of the Grand Banks are now sadly depleted, the villages on St-Pierre and Miquelon are still bustling fishing ports.

St-Pierre, the archipelago's largest center (with a population of 6,000), can be reached by air or via ferry from Fortune, on Newfoundland's Burin Peninsula. Arriving is a jolt—although the landscape and the vividly colored wooden houses are similar to that of other rocky islands throughout the Maritimes, this is definitely not Canada. Settled largely by Breton, Norman,

During the 1880s St-Pierre's port was one of the liveliest in North America.

and Basque fishermen, St-Pierre is resolutely French, with good bistros and brasseries and shops selling French wine at European Union prices. Don't forget that these islands are French in other ways too—euros are the currency, the electricity is 220 volts, and the guys with the *kepis* and guns are gendarmes.

Apart from the novelty of being on French soil in North America, the main sights to see in St-Pierre are the Heritage Museum, which relates the history of this remote fishing colony of France, and the Pointe Aux Canons Lighthouse with distinctive red and white stripes and a battery of cannons standing guard at the mouth of St-Pierre harbor. Flanked by cafés, bakeries, bars, and municipal buildings, Place Charles de Gaulle is the center of the town.

If you can't get enough of these Gallic islands, guided boat excursions also lead to even more remote sites on the cliff-lined island of Miquelon and the truly remote, now deserted island of Île aux Marins.

WHERE: 18 miles/29 km southwest of Newfoundland's Burin Peninsula. *Visitor info:* Tel 5-08-41-02-00; tourisme-st-pierre-et-miquelon.com. **WHERE TO STAY:** Nuits Saint-Pierre, St-Pierre. Tel 5-08-41-20-27; nuits saintpierre.com. *Cost:* US$105/€95. **ST. PIERRE FERRY:** Passengers only. Tel 855-832-3455 or 709-832-3455; saintpierreferry.ca. *Cost:* US$70/C$93 roundtrip. *When:* ferries between Fortune and St-Pierre daily from mid-July–early Sept. Otherwise check website. **HERITAGE MUSEUM:** Tel 5-08-41-58-88; musee-heritage.fr. *When:* daily, July–Aug; closed Sun, Sept–June.

Primordial Landscapes at the Continent's Edge

GROS MORNE NATIONAL PARK

Newfoundland and Labrador

Eastern Canada's most renowned hiking and adventure destination is a place of immense splendor and geological uniqueness. Gros Morne National Park, along Newfoundland's rugged Great Northern Peninsula, is a larger-than-life area of stunning beauty with a rich natural and cultural heritage so unlike that found almost anywhere else in North America. Roughly translated as "the big gloomy," the term "Gros Morne" refers to the park's barren, mist-draped peaks and remote fjords that can bring on a mild case of melancholy even on a sunny day.

The southern region of the park is a great place to start your exploration. Tour boats ply Trout River Pond, once a sea fjord, now a 9-mile-long lake in a steep cliff-lined glaciated valley. One of the park's indisputable highlights is the rugged massif called the Tablelands, which expose rocks from the earth's interior. Mantle rocks such as this are usually found only deep below the surface, and have such an unusual chemistry that few plants can survive on their otherworldly orange-brown terrain. You can experience this fascinating environment on the Trout River Pond Trail, on the challenging 10-mile Green Gardens Trail, or by taking a guided hike on the 2.5-mile Tablelands Trail.

Explore coastal sections of the park for the combination of rugged cliffs, sandy beaches, and small, hardworking fishing villages that continue to operate as they have for generations. To the north, coastal lowlands bordering the Gulf of St. Lawrence are covered with expanses of boreal forest and bog. Inland regions are dominated by the wilderness plateau of the Long Range Mountains and a series of glacier-carved fjord-lakes. Walkers will enjoy the challenging day hike up Gros Morne, the park's highest peak at 2,644 feet and the second highest in Newfoundland, with

spectacular views of the park. Western Brook Pond is among the park's most popular stops, a landlocked glacial fjord that offers travelers a combination of trails and boat trips. It is located less than a half-hour's drive north of Rocky Harbour—location of a regional visitors center and the six-room waterfront Candlelight B&B. While in the area, don't miss the Anchors Aweigh musical show, three hours of Newfoundland fun and a local institution.

WHERE: The park entrance at Wiltondale is 186 miles/300 km from Port aux Basques. Tel 709-458-2417; pc.gc.ca/grosmorne. *When:* Most park facilities and services are available late May–mid-Oct. **CANDLELIGHT B&B:** Rocky Harbour. Tel 877-458-3147 or 709-458-3147. *When:* open May–Oct. *Cost:* from $US85/ C$115. **BEST TIMES:** June, when the rhododendrons are in bloom; July–Aug for hiking and wildlife; June–Sept for the Gros Morne Theatre Festival (theatrenewfoundland.com); Sept and early Oct for foliage.

The unique terrain of Gros Morne National Park includes bogs, forests, and mountains.

At the Edge of the Earth

FOGO ISLAND

Newfoundland and Labrador

This far-flung and until recently forgotten island off the northeast coast of Newfoundland was home to some of Canada's oldest European outports—temporary fish camps that dotted the coast of Atlantic Canada and survived by salting and drying cod for export and trading lumber, seal oil, and furs. The Europeans flocked here for waters reputedly so rich in fish that when John Cabot arrived in 1497, he had only to drop a weighted basket into the water to pull up a haul of cod.

Eleven of these outports still exist today on Fogo, with names like Seldom, Little Seldom, Tilting, and Joe Batt's Arm, but the government-mandated Cod Moratorium of 1992 sounded the death knell for their subsistence fishing economies. The island's population today hovers between 2,000 and 3,000.

Zita Cobb, one of Canada's richest women, created the extraordinary Fogo Island Inn in 2013 to immediate international buzz, with the goal of revitalizing her community's local culture and redirecting the island's fate. Its 29 luxurious but unpretentious suites feature floor-to-ceiling, wall-to-wall windows and pale natural materials, with bright, locally crafted furniture, quilts, and hooked rugs. The inn's dining room is unlike anything else in Fogo, offering sophisticated takes on culinary traditions using fresh local ingredients.

Cobb also kick-started Fogo Island Arts, a contemporary art program with gallery space and residencies for international artists drawn to Fogo's ethereal light and serenity.

In the middle of Joe Batt's Arm, Quintal House Heritage Guest Home is a welcoming B&B in a restored house from the mid-1800s, and right next door is the friendly and casual Nicole's Café, the best spot in town for fish and chips, chowder, and lots of local gossip.

WHERE: 280 miles northwest of St. John's. **HOW:** ferry from Farewell. Tel 855-621-3150; tw.gov.nl.ca/ferryservices. **FOGO ISLAND INN:** Joe Batt's Arm. Tel 709-658-3444; fogoisland inn.ca. *Cost:* suites from US$850/C$1,175. **QUINTAL HOUSE:** Joe Batt's Arm. Tel 709-658-7829; quintalhouse.ca. *Cost:* from US$97/C$130. **NICOLE'S CAFÉ:** Joe Batt's Arm. Tel 709-658-3663; nicolescafe.ca. *Cost:* 3-course dinner $55. **BEST TIMES:** mid-Aug weekend for the Brimstone Head Folk Festival, a celebration of traditional Newfoundland music (brimstone headfestival.com); Apr–Aug for watching the icebergs moving south.

Centuries Old But Young at Heart

ST. JOHN'S

Newfoundland and Labrador

Newfoundland's capital, St. John's—founded in 1583, the oldest city established by the British in North America—stands in stark contrast to outlying regions of the province. Much of the island's hinterland is somber, a wilderness of windswept rock, moor, and plunging coastline, with human outposts few and remote. St. John's, on the other hand, is a colorful city of muscle and vitality, with a bustling sense of purpose and youthfulness. About half of the island's 500,000 residents live in or near St. John's, and visitors find it to be a good base for exploring the Avalon Peninsula (don't miss the much photographed Cape Spear Lighthouse, the island's iconic symbol located on the continent's most easterly point). With the 2005 opening of The Rooms—the city's most important cultural facility—St. John's has an impressive showcase for its long, compelling history and artistic traditions.

The architecture of The Rooms is boldly innovative and has been the dominant structure of the skyline since its arrival. The three structures are designed to resemble the traditional tall, steep-roofed codfish-curing warehouses called "rooms" that cluster along the shores of the island's old fishing villages (for centuries Newfoundland was the leading supplier of salt cod in the world). Each of the institutions brought together at The Rooms—the Provincial Archives, Art Gallery, and Museum Divisions— is housed in a separate four-story "room" structure but is joined at ground level by a central glass arcade.

Newfoundland's cod fishing industry shut down in the 1990s, but cod—and seafood in general—remains at the center of a growing culinary movement. Book a table at Bacalao (the name given to salt cod throughout the Mediterranean), a trailblazing restaurant that helped reintroduce innovative Newfoundland cuisine.

St. George Street is the town's main drag, lined with other great eating options, pubs, and bars. It's a five-minute walk to Murray Premises, one of the city's most historic landmarks. Once a fish-packing warehouse, it now houses restaurants and boutiques, as well as the Murray Premises Hotel.

THE ROOMS: Tel 709-757-8090; the rooms.ca. *When:* daily, June–mid-Oct; closed Mon, mid-Oct–May. **BACALAO:** Tel 709-579-6565; bacalaocuisine.ca. *Cost:* US$41/C$55. **MURRAY PREMISES HOTEL:** Tel 866-738-7773 or 709-738-773; murraypremiseshotel.com. *Cost:* from US$150/C$195. **BEST TIMES:** late July–early Aug for the George Street Festival; early Aug for the Newfoundland and Labrador Folk Festival.

Nova Scotia's Bastion of History

ANNAPOLIS ROYAL

Nova Scotia

Nova Scotia's broad, orchard-filled Annapolis River Valley was once known as "Canada's breadbasket," so rich was the bounty of the land. Little surprise, then, that this fertile valley saw some of the earliest European

settlement—and warfare—in North America as Europe's empire builders acted out their conflicts on the banks of the important Annapolis River.

In 1605, French colonists under the leadership of Samuel de Champlain established Port-Royal Habitation, a fortified trading post at the mouth of the wide Annapolis River. Life at the fringes of the known world was harsh for the French settlers, but they responded with good spirits, establishing l'Ordre de Bon Temps (Order of Good Cheer) as a social and dining club—another first for North America. The decadent good times didn't last, however, as British forces destroyed the Habitation in 1613. The French rebuilt an even more grandly fortified Port-Royal a few miles upriver.

However, in 1710, Port-Royal fell to another British siege, and shortly thereafter Port-Royal was rechristened as Annapolis Royal in honor of Queen Anne. In 1755, the British began the expulsion of the Acadians from their land (see p. 989), scattering the French pioneers elsewhere, including Louisiana (see p. 434) and the colonies of New England.

This long history is evident everywhere in Annapolis Royal. The village itself retains its vintage charm, with narrow, tree-lined streets, stunning gardens, and historic houses overlooking the waterfront. With numerous structures dating from the early 18th century (including the 1708 DeGannes-Cosby House, the oldest wooden home in Canada), the sense of the living past is profound and real. The old fort is now maintained as Fort Anne National Historic Site. In addition to visiting the Officer's Quarters Museum, join the candlelight tours of the fort's graveyard, offered on summer nights.

The Annapolis Royal Historic Gardens are exceptional—17 acres of plantings, highlighted by a rose garden with 2,000 bushes. Three miles from the village is Port-Royal National Historic Site, a painstaking replica of the imposing 1605 Habitation. Costumed interpreters demonstrate the skills and tools used by the French settlers and relate tales of the Bon Temps club, when high-living 17th-century revelers sat down to savory banquets of delicacies such as beaver tail or moose nose.

WHERE: 122 miles/197 km west of Halifax. *Visitor info:* Tel 902-532-5454; annapolisroyal .com. **PORT-ROYAL:** Tel 902-532-2898; pc.gc .ca/portroyal. *When:* mid-May–mid-Oct. **FORT ANNE:** Tel 902-532-2397 or 902-532-2321; pc.gc.ca/fortanne. *When:* June–Sept (grounds open year-round). **WHERE TO STAY:** The Queen Anne Inn, tel 902-532-7850; queenanneinn .ns.ca. *Cost:* from US$74/C$99 (off-peak), from US$90/C$119 (peak). *When:* Apr–Oct. **BEST TIME:** mid-Aug for Annapolis Royal ARTS Unleashed.

Atlantic Canada's Most Scenic Drive

THE CABOT TRAIL

Cape Breton Island, Nova Scotia

66 I have traveled the globe. I have seen the Canadian and American Rockies, the Andes and the Alps and the Highlands of Scotland: But for simple beauty, Cape Breton outrivals them all." So said Alexander Graham Bell,

who summered and worked here for 35 years.

As it juts north between the Atlantic Ocean and the Gulf of St. Lawrence, Nova Scotia's Cape Breton Island becomes increasingly mountainous and barren. Cape Breton Highlands National Park protects much of the island's northern tip, a sometimes melancholy landscape of windswept mountains and deep river canyons, with a blustery coastline of plunging cliffs and sandy beaches. This remote area of Cape Breton wasn't even served by automobile until the 1930s, when roads finally edged across the island's spine to join Chéticamp on the west and Cape Smokey on the east. This route, which became known as the Cabot Trail, linked isolated communities previously accessed only by boat or winter dog team and is now considered to be one of the world's great drives.

The 184-mile-long Cabot Trail follows the picturesque, craggy coastline around the 365-square-mile national park, passing centuries-old French Acadian and Scottish fishing villages, wooded valleys, and viewing points from which you can often spot finback and pilot whales. The route crosses the island's central plateau between Pleasant Bay and Cape North—a striking moorland, with stunted old-growth hardwood forests and tundralike meadows. The park's 26 hiking trails are also popular, especially the Skyline Trail, a 5-mile loop full of bluff-top sea views.

The most scenic highlight might be the 27-mile stretch between Chéticamp and Pleasant Bay. Chéticamp is a centuries-old Acadian village of just 1,000 folks, and is the heart of the French-speaking culture on the island. Main Street boasts a pub, a bakery, a museum, and a restaurant serving traditional sea-based specialties. Pleasant Bay (population 350) offers a whale interpretive center and whale-watching trips on fishing boats when sightings are just about guaranteed. You can expect to see everything from humpback, fin, and minke to pilot and northern right whales.

On the island's east coast (predominantly settled by Highland Scots; see below), the village of Ingonish Beach is the park's eastern gateway and the largest of its holiday destinations. It is home to the Keltic Lodge Resort & Spa, a gleaming-white red-roofed Tudor-style destination exceptionally situated on a spit of

Black Brook is one of many scenic beaches along Cape Breton Island's rugged coastline.

land so narrow it feels like an island. The views are a knockout, and the lodge is welcoming and nicely worn without being threadbare, and offers unusually good dining. With gorgeous ocean views, the nearby Highlands Links is a quirky gem and is widely considered one of Canada's must-play golf courses.

WHERE: 175 miles/282 km northeast of Halifax. *Visitor info:* Tel 800-565-0000 or 902-425-5781; novascotia.com. **CAPE BRETON HIGHLANDS NATIONAL PARK:** Tel 902-224-2306; pc.gc.ca/capebreton. *When:* open year-round, but park services available mid-May–mid-Oct. **CAPT. MARK'S WHALE & SEAL CRUISE:** Tel 888-754-5112 or 902-224-1316; whaleandsealcruise.com. *Cost:* US$35/C$45. *When:* June–mid-Oct. **KELTIC LODGE:** Ingonish Beach. Tel 800-565-0444 or 902-285-2880; kelticlodge.ca. *Cost:* from US$140/C$187 (off-peak), from US$182/C$243 (peak); includes dinner and breakfast. *When:* mid-May–Oct. **HIGHLANDS LINKS GOLF COURSE:** Ingonish. Tel 800-441-1118 or 902-285-2600; highlandslinksgolf.com. *Cost:* greens fees from US$61/C$81 (off-peak), from US$77/C$103 (peak). *When:* June–Oct. **BEST TIME:** Sept for fall foliage and nice weather, with fewer crowds and less traffic.

A Wee Bit of the Old Country Transplanted West

EXPLORING "NEW SCOTLAND" ON CAPE BRETON ISLAND

Nova Scotia

The craggy hills, precipitous coastline, and slender lakes of Cape Breton Island must have looked just like home to the Scottish immigrants who streamed into Nova Scotia (Latin for "New Scotland") between 1770 and 1850, but who could have foreseen that its isolation would preserve an island of Gaelic culture into the 21st century? With the only native Gaelic-speaking population outside Scotland and Ireland and a thriving Celtic music and art scene, Cape Breton preserves its Gaelic heritage with passion.

A glance at a map of Cape Breton shows names—Glencoe, Dundee, Inverness, Dingwall —that are redolent of places the early Scots settlers left behind. Today's heartland of Gaelic culture runs in a swath through the center of Cape Breton, particularly the Mabou Highlands and lakes and channels that make up Bras d'Or Lake, a major boating destination.

Overlooking St. Ann's Bay, the Gaelic College of Celtic Arts and Crafts is North America's only school devoted to the study and preservation of the Gaelic language and Celtic arts and culture. *Ceilidh* (pronounced kaylee) is the word for a traditional Gaelic social gathering which involves lots of music, singing, and dancing. Check the college's summertime schedule for an impressive host of these and other events that promise a good dose of all-around fun for visitors and locals alike. Kitchenfest is one of the most ambitious, drawing the best fiddlers from across the island and offering delicious local foods. The college's Great Hall of Clans museum provides a year-round chance to view the history of the Great Migration, the exodus of the Scottish people for the New World.

At Iona, on Bras d'Or Lake, is the Highland Village Museum, a living history museum set high on a mountainside overlooking Barra Strait. A self-guided trail winds up the side of a hill to a series of ten historic buildings, including a crofter's hut, farmhouse, blacksmith forge, school, and church that chronicle the life and times of the Scottish immigration to Nova Scotia. If you think you can trace your Scottish roots back to Nova Scotia, their genealogy center is the place to try. The Highland Village hosts Scottish concerts on its outdoor stage throughout the summer.

The Black House at the Highland Village Museum represents a common mid-19th-century Gaelic home.

Don't miss the coast-hugging hills around Mabou (population 400), another bright outpost of Scottish culture. Gaelic language is still taught at Mabou's high school, and the Red Shoe Pub, a former grocery store, is one of the best venues in which to enjoy frequently scheduled and impromptu live Celtic music and a pint of ale. Pick up some CDs of local recording artists to play as you tool around the back roads of the island. Just north of town in the forests near Glenville is the Glenora Inn and Distillery, Canada's only single malt whiskey distillery. The distillery offers full Scottish hospitality, including tours that let you sample a "wee dram," a pub frequently alive with local Cape Breton music, and a dining room with regional specialties. If the drams are not so wee and you don't want to drive, there are comfortable guest rooms in the adjacent inn or in new log chalets with fireplaces, Jacuzzis, and lovely views that will convince you you've woken up somewhere in the misty highlands of Scotland.

It is not surprising that local folks wait until October, when the summer tourists have gone home, to host the islandwide nine-day Celtic Colours festival, a full-fledged celebration of all things Gaelic, the largest of its kind in North America. There's plenty of music, workshops on folklore and history, and over 300 artists from around the Celtic world; it's as if the first Scots landed just yesterday.

WHERE: 175 miles/282 km northeast of Halifax. **GAELIC COLLEGE OF CELTIC ARTS AND CRAFTS:** St. Ann's. Tel 902-295-3411; gaelic college.edu. *When:* Great Hall of the Clans open Mon–Fri, mid-May–early Oct; closed mid-Oct–mid-May. **HIGHLAND VILLAGE MUSEUM:** Iona. Tel 902-725-2272; highlandvillage.nova scotia.ca. *When:* June–mid-Oct. **RED SHOE PUB:** Mabou. Tel 902-945-2996; redshoepub .com. **GLENORA INN AND DISTILLERY:** Glenville. Tel 800-839-0491 or 902-258-2662; glenora distillery.com. *Cost:* from US$105/C$140. *When:* early May–late Oct. **BEST TIMES:** late June–early July for 8-day Kitchenfest; 9 days in Oct for the Celtic Colours International Festival (celtic-colours.com).

Picture-Perfection on Nova Scotia's South Shore

CHESTER

Nova Scotia

A t the base of island-dotted Mahone Bay is the historic seafaring village of Chester, with colorful clapboard homes and fishing warehouses clustered above a bustling harbor. This is poster-perfect Nova Scotia as the tourism authorities would have you imagine. Settled in the 1750s, Chester and its idyllic location soon caught the attention of more than fishermen: By the mid-1800s the wealthy elite from Halifax began to build exclusive homes on the hills above the bay. Chester became a favorite seaside colony and later a haven for artists, socialites, and the yachting set even as it retained the hardscrabble vigor of its fishing fleets. Main Street snakes along the bay and is lined with waterfront galleries, boutiques, and cafés.

The harbor is always busy with yachts and sailboats—Chester remains one of the most popular boating destinations in Nova Scotia. Little wonder, as it's even more eye-catching from offshore. Things come to an annual climax in August with Chester Race Week, Atlantic Canada's largest regatta.

If you've left your yacht at home or missed the August hoopla, jump on the next passenger ferry to the nearby Tancook Islands. They offer unmatched views of Chester and the bay, along with the chance to wander quiet country lanes in an idyllic atmosphere that gives you the peaceful sense of being lost in time.

WHERE: 50 miles/80 km west of Halifax. *Visitor info:* Tel 902-275-4616; vic.chester chamber.ca. **WHERE TO STAY:** Atlantica Oak Island Resort, tel 800-565-5075 or 902-627-2600; atlanticaoakisland.com. *Cost:* from US$86/C$115 (off-peak), from US$134/C$179 (peak). **BEST TIMES:** June–Sept for weather; Aug for Chester Race Week.

Chester epitomizes the Nova Scotia lifestyle.

Evangeline and the Acadian Expulsions

GRAND PRÉ & WOLFVILLE

Nova Scotia

T he expansive vista over Grand Pré—a broad green peninsula flanked by the sea and distant, cliff-sided hills—today seems bucolic, even serene. In the 1750s, however, Grand Pré (French for "large meadow") was the scene of violence and great sadness, as British soldiers forced the resident French farmers and villagers into exile during the Deportation of the Acadians. Like historic battlefields, Grand Pré exerts a ghostly power over the visitor: For descendants of the French Acadian diaspora, the site of Grand Pré is a haunted place; for others, it is a sanctuary for quiet reflection.

Grand Pré was founded in 1682, with French colonists building an extensive dike system along the shores of Minas Basin, converting and taming the salt marshes into fertile farmland. By 1750, over 2,000 settlers lived here, making it the largest single village in Acadia, the name given to French colonies in Atlantic Canada. In 1755, with the British and French preparing for the Seven Years' War in Europe, the British governor in Halifax saw the French-descended Acadians as a threat. When the Acadians refused to take an oath of allegiance to the British crown, the governor confiscated their property and ordered the deportation of the entire French population. Villages were burned to the ground. Before the year was over, more than 6,000 Acadians from the region were deported to other British colonies in North America. Many wound up in Louisiana—land then held by the British—where the Acadian refugees became known as Cajuns (see p. 434). Henry Wadsworth Longfellow immortalized the deportations in his epic poem *Evangeline: A Tale of Acadie*, which is set in Grand Pré and tells the story of the Acadian deportations and the forced separation of young Evangeline and her fiancé, Gabriel.

A bronze statue of the fictional Evangeline Bellefontaine stands outside a stone memorial church with exhibits on the deportation and struggles of the Acadians. The grounds have retained their formal gardens, with 14 land-scaped acres where the razed village once stood.

With the abandoned farmlands open for resettlement, a British community, Wolfville, grew up adjacent to Grand Pré. Now at the center of a major orcharding and winegrowing region, it is one of Nova Scotia's most charming towns, with stately elms and beautiful Victorian homes lining leafy streets. Downtown is especially lovely, with unique shops and fine restaurants. Acadia University has nearly as many full-time students (3,500) as there are residents in Wolfville, which keeps the town lively.

WHERE: 56 miles/90 km northwest of Halifax. *Visitor info:* Tel 902-542-7000; wolfville.ca. **GRAND PRÉ NATIONAL HISTORIC SITE:** Tel 866-542-3631 or 902-542-3631; pc.gc.ca/grandpre. *When:* grounds open year-round; exhibits closed mid-Oct–mid-May. **WHERE TO STAY:** Tattingstone Inn, Wolfville, tel 800-565-7696 or 902-542-7696; tatting stone.ns.ca. *Cost:* from US$73/C$98 (off-peak), US$96/C$128 (peak). **BEST TIMES:** summer for weather; late July for Acadian Day (grand-pre.com).

Vibrant and Historic Seaport

HALIFAX WATERFRONT & THE CITADEL

Nova Scotia

Despite its pedigree as the oldest British city in Canada, Halifax is a youthful, high-energy place—a beautifully preserved seaport overlaid with more than a touch of bohemia. The area's dramatic setting induced

British General Edward Cornwallis to establish an army and naval base here in 1749: With a deep, protected harbor, the site was easily defended from a hilltop garrison. Under the vigilance of this stone-walled Citadel, Halifax quickly grew into a thriving seaport. Today, terraced into the steep hillside between the historic waterfront and the lofty Citadel is downtown Halifax, where, in a mix of old and new, beautiful historic buildings stand next to soaring towers of glass.

The Citadel's massive, star-shaped masonry fortification took 28 years to build.

The waterfront is the oldest part of the city, with many structures dating back to the turn of the 19th century. At its heart is the Historic Properties, an extensive 4-acre restoration that has converted many centuries-old wharves and warehouses into shops, museums, and restaurants, making this a lively area for exploring and people-watching on sunny afternoons, when it can seem that everyone in Halifax has come here to play hooky. Right on the waterfront is the Maritime Museum of the Atlantic, the city's signature museum, with fascinating exhibits on Halifax's seafaring past, the 1912 *Titanic* disaster (many rescue and salvage operations were based out of Halifax, and 150 of the 2,000 victims are buried here), and the tragic Halifax Explosion of 1917, when two warships collided in Halifax harbor, detonating tons of TNT and killing nearly 1,700.

From the waterfront, zigzag the nine blocks up through the heart of Halifax, passing beautifully maintained Victorian storefronts, modern shopping areas, 18th-century churches, and a former military Grand Parade ground that's now a park. At the crest of the bluff is the Citadel, the enormous star-shaped defensive fort established to protect Halifax from invasion. The fortifications are very impressive—complete with defensive ditches, granite ramparts, a musketry gallery, a powder magazine, and signal masts. Equally impressive are the views over Halifax and the second-largest natural harbor in the world. There was no sneaking up on this place. Now operated by Parks Canada, the Citadel features guided tours of the fort and a living history program: Don't be surprised if strangers in kilts and ostrich-plume hats approach and start talking about the past.

Of Halifax's many fine hotels, the small and charming Halliburton House preserves the relaxed feel of a classy country inn. Built in 1809 as a grand home for the Nova Scotia Supreme Court's first chief justice, Halliburton House offers handsome rooms in three town house–style buildings connected in the back by a flowering courtyard. The attention to detail and the intimate, romantic ambience continues in the hotel's Stories Restaurant, whose limited but innovative menu has made it one of the city's favorites.

WHERE: 265 miles/426 km from Saint John. *Visitor info:* Tel 877-422-9334 or 902-422-9334; destinationhalifax.com. **HISTORIC PROPERTIES:** Tel 902-429-0530; historic properties.ca. **MARITIME MUSEUM OF THE ATLANTIC:** Tel 902-424-7490; maritimemu seum.novascotia.ca. *When:* daily; closed Mon, Nov–Apr. **HALIFAX CITADEL:** Tel 902-426-5080; pc.gc.ca/halifaxcitadel. **HALLIBURTON HOUSE:** Tel 902-420-0658; thehalliburton .com. *Cost:* from US$97/C$129 (off-peak), from US$119/C$159 (peak); dinner at Stories US$41/C$55. **BEST TIMES:** late June–mid-July for the Nova Scotia International Tattoo, a vibrant celebration of Canadian patriotism (nstattoo.ca); last weekend in July for the Halifax International Buskerfest (buskers.ca).

A Colonial Town Perfectly Preserved

LUNENBURG

Nova Scotia

I n the 1750s, lured by the prospect of free land, nearly 1,500 Protestant German, Swiss, and French pioneers set sail from Europe under protection of the British Crown to establish a colony on the coast of Nova Scotia. With them

was a set of town plans drawn up by the London-based Board of Trade and Plantations. As part of their agreement with their British sponsors, the colonists would use these plans to impose a pre-designed "model town" onto the wilderness.

The Lunenburg Colony survived and prospered as a fishing and well-known shipbuilding center. Little change came to its Old Town and waterfront—with the result that, two and a half centuries later, this tiny coastal hamlet is in near pristine condition, minimally different from its 18th-century beginnings. Dignified homes and buildings have been beautifully maintained, and the streets of the Old Town still follow the original town plan, with accommodations for the unexpected steep hills they found upon arrival. In recognition of Lunenburg's extraordinary level of preservation—70 percent of its homes and structures are from the 18th and 19th centuries—the United Nations has declared Lunenburg's

entire Old Town district a UNESCO World Heritage Site.

While it's fascinating to wander the picturesque streets, with colorful Victorian and Georgian houses marching up the hillside from the bay, the heart of the village remains the waterfront. The sprawling Fisheries Museum of the Atlantic combines an aquarium of local sea life with exhibits on the history of Lunenburg's seafaring past. Moored off the museum wharf (and part of its operation) are a number of historic ships you can tour. They were built right here in Lunenburg, including a replica of the legendary 1921 racing schooner *Bluenose* that you might recognize from the back of the Canadian dime.

The bustling harbor is filled with fishing boats (scallop fishing is still an important industry) and a surprising number of both new and old wooden tall ships, which call here for repair, ship-fitting, or provisions. You can catch the spirit of Lunenburg's wooden boat heritage aboard the *Eastern Star*, a 48-foot wooden ketch that offers tours of Lunenburg harbor. Setting out with the sails snapped taut and the hull cleaving the water, you'll relive the days when sailing ships ruled the seas and Lunenburg was one of colonial North America's most important ports of call.

WHERE: 62 miles/100 km southwest of Halifax. *Visitor info:* Tel 902-634-8100; explorelunenburg.ca. **FISHERIES MUSEUM:** Tel 866-579-4909 or 902-634-4794; fisheries museum.novascotia.ca. *When:* daily, May–Oct; closed weekends, Nov–Apr. **EASTERN STAR:**

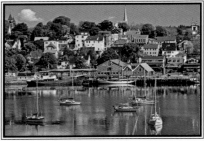
Fishing and marine-related industries have been central to Lunenburg for over 200 years.

Tel 877-386-3535 or 902-634-3535. *When:* June–Oct. **WHERE TO STAY:** Boscawen Inn and McLachlan House, tel 800-354-5009 or 902-634-3325; boscawen.ca. *Cost:* from US$71/C$95. **BEST TIME:** 3 days in early Aug for Lunenburg Folk Harbor Festival.

Safari in the Extreme North

ARCTIC WATCH WILDERNESS LODGE

Somerset Island, Nunavut

N unavut is Canada's newest territory, formally created in 1999 as a homeland for the Inuit people. It is also the largest of Canada's territories and provinces—approximately the size of Western Europe—but has a population of only 32,000. Few people travel this far north, but those who do experience the subtle yet powerful beauty of the remarkable landscape and witness the reawakening of life that is the arctic summer, when 24-hour daylight ignites a kaleidoscope of wildflowers and a veritable safari of animals migrate here for the warmer weather months.

The ideal launching pad for Nunavut adventures is the Arctic Watch Wilderness Lodge, owned and operated since 2000 by renowned polar explorers Richard Weber and Josée Auclair. With 16 comfortable private cabins equipped with thick, warm duvets and fresh water drawn from the Cunningham River, Arctic Watch offers an environment that easily approaches luxury in this remote corner of the world. The lodge's main complex houses a lounge, a library, and a museum center, displaying regional artifacts such as 42-million-year-old fossils and traditional Inuit clothing. The kitchen and dining room delight guests with locally-sourced, Canadian-inspired gourmet meals, such as sous vide pork tenderloin in a mushroom truffle cream sauce.

The main draw of Arctic Watch is inarguably its exceptional location. Situated along Cunningham Inlet on Somerset Island— Canada's 12th largest—the lodge is ideally positioned for exploration and memorable wildlife encounters. The Cunningham River is part

Beluga whale sightings are just one of countless wildlife encounters visitors can expect on Somerset Island.

of the annual migration path for beluga (or white) whales, and in summer some 2,000 of them congregate here in these relatively warm waters to nurse their young and molt their skin. The lodge is just a 15-minute walk from their favorite meeting place (a nearby tower offers a bird's-eye vantage). Small in size (3–20 feet) and very vocal, belugas are related to the peculiarly tusked "unicorn" whale known as the narwhal, which can also be seen in these waters. But it's not just about the whales: a rich variety of arctic species can be spotted on land, including polar bears, caribou, arctic foxes and hares, snowy owls, and lemmings, among others. And at this latitude—more than 50 percent of Nunavut's landmass is above the Arctic Circle—sightings are enjoyed during long days of ethereal light.

Arctic Watch now partners with polar specialists Quark Expeditions to offer jam-packed eight- to ten-day Discovery Programs through-out the summer months that bring visitors face-to-face with the magic of life on the tundra. Highlights include hiking and ATV rides, fishing, kayaking in Cunningham Inlet among the whales, a trip to Gull Canyon (a unique micro-ecosystem favored by visiting peregrine falcons), and a journey to an ancient site at Cape Anne, where the Thules, the ancestors of the Inuits, built homes of giant prehistoric bow-head whalebones. In the evenings, Richard Weber, the world's most traveled North Pole explorer, offers riveting lectures on his own fascinating arctic expeditions.

WHERE: 1,000 miles north of Yellowknife, the capital of the Northwest Territories. **ARCTIC WATCH WILDERNESS LODGE:** Somerset Island. Tel 819-923-0932; arcticwatch.ca. *How:* Quark Expeditions, quarkexpeditions .com. *Cost:* 8-day Arctic Watch Discovery programs from US$6,000/C$7,800 per person double-occupancy, from US$9,000/C$11,700 single-occupancy, all-inclusive. The 4.5-hour charter flight from Yellowknife to the lodge's private air strip and return is included. *When:* Arctic Watch open late-June–Sept. **BEST TIME:** July–mid-Aug for whale-watching.

Canoes, Wolves, and the Great North Woods

ALGONQUIN PROVINCIAL PARK

Ontario

The cry of a loon across a misty lake, a wolf's howl at sunset, paddling through a string of lakes to reach a remote log lodge—these experiences of the Canadian frontier are found today at Algonquin Provincial Park,

a sanctuary of nature just three hours but worlds away from Toronto or Ottawa. Algonquin, one of Canada's largest provincial parks—stretching across 3,000 square miles of wilderness forest and lakeland—is traversed by just one road. The Algonquin backcountry is paradise for paddlers and is one of Canada's top canoeing destinations. The canoe is about the only means of exploring Algonquin's watery wonderland, where more than 2,500 lakes and more than 1,240 miles of designated canoe routes converge. With lake pouring into lake, experienced paddlers can plan a leisurely multi-day trip through the heart of Algonquin, or, with a few short portages, complete a loop circuit through the wilds.

When a wolf pack comes within range of the park's southern corridor, rangers offer evening "public wolf howls," one of the highlights of a late summer trip to the park. With large crowds in attendance in an outdoor amphitheater, park naturalists howl to the wolf pack and the audience awaits a response from the pack. There's nothing more spine-tingling than hearing the cries of wolves echoing across the lakes and lonely hills under a black, star-filled sky.

At the backcountry's edge, nestled in deep forest, is Arowhon Pines, a historic lodge resort at the edge of Little Joe Lake. The Kates family established Arowhon Pines in the 1940s, when they built the original six-sided log-and-stone lodge right on the lake's edge, and have been running it ever since.

With a massive three-story stone fireplace at its center, the lodge serves as the dining room, famous across Ontario for its fresh ingredients expertly prepared, friendly and excellent service, and extraordinary sunset views. Log cabins are scattered around the lakefront, decorated with pine furniture and rustic Canadiana, and some feature stone fireplaces. Arowhon Pines is like summer camp for families, with activities galore on the lake (sailing, canoeing, stand-up paddleboarding) and on terra firma (follow extensive walking trails along the lake shore). **WHERE:** 167 miles/270 km north of Toronto. **ALGONQUIN PROVINCIAL PARK:** Tel 705-633-5572; algonquinpark.on.ca. **PUBLIC WOLF**

HOWL: Tel 705-633-5572. *When:* Thurs in Aug and early Sept, when an accessible pack of wolves is located, and when weather permits. **AROWHON PINES:** Huntsville. Tel 416-483-4393 (winter), 705-633-5661 (summer); arowhonpines.ca. *Cost:* from US$165/C$220 per person per day, all-inclusive. *When:* June–mid-Oct. **BEST TIMES:** spring for trout fishing; May–June for moose viewing; July–Aug for long days and warm temperatures; Sept for foliage.

Festival Towns on the Grand River

ELORA & FERGUS

Ontario

In the midst of rolling Ontario farmland, the Grand and Irvine rivers converge at the charming village of Elora. Their combined waters drop as a roaring falls into the Elora Gorge, a narrow limestone chasm with rock walls over 70 feet high. The gorge was sacred to the indigenous Iroquois Indians, who believed the shadowy depths provided an abode for spirits. In the 1830s, the cave-riddled gorge reminded early European settlers of the famed Ellora caves in India, and the name—slightly misspelled—stuck. Today, it's mostly high spirits that fill Elora Gorge Park, as hikers explore trails along the cliff edge, and kayakers and canoeists run river rapids below. Follow the locals who know the best way to see the gorge, and rent inner tubes from park concessionaires at the base of the falls to run the Grand River white water. It's a laughing, splashing affair, offering a duck's-eye view of the 2-mile-long gorge, its shoreside wildlife, and mysterious caves.

The countryside around the Elora Gorge is some of the most enchanting around. The village of Elora, dubbed by local tourism officials as the most beautiful in Ontario, was established in the 1830s when a Scottish pioneer harnessed the Grand River falls for a mill, and a sturdy market town grew up along the riverbanks to serve the needs of local farmers.

Elora's beautiful village center is remarkably intact, including the original 1870 grist mill. Handsome mid-19th-century brick and stone buildings that now house galleries, cafés, sweet shops, and inns fill out the town. Elora bustles during July's three-week Elora Festival, one of Canada's most heralded summer music events.

Just 2 miles upriver from Elora, the town of Fergus was also settled by Scottish immigrants. Beginning in the 1830s, these Gaelic newcomers quarried local limestone to build handsome homes and commercial buildings in old country style. A century and a half later, over 250 of Fergus's original stone structures from the 1850s and earlier are still in use, lending a handsomely uniform ambience to the small town, a magnet for artists and urban refugees.

There's no doubting the town's authentic Scottish roots in August, when the Fergus Scottish Festival and Highland Games opens with a skirl of bagpipes from more than 40 clans who come from across North America. "Enjoy Scotland Without the Airfare" its posters proclaim. In addition to highland dancing and piping competitions, the games also feature the Professional Scottish Athletic Championship, in which brawny, tartan-clad athletes from around the world flex their muscle in traditional "heavy events" such as caber and hammer tossing. During the festival lots of traditional fiddle, harp, and accordion music fills the town's pubs and halls, and competitions include those grade schoolers determined to keep their rich heritage alive.

WHERE: 62 miles/100 km west of Toronto. *Visitor info:* Tel 519-846-9841; elora.info. **ELORA GORGE PARK:** Tel 519-846-9742; grandriver.ca. *When:* May–mid-Oct. **WHERE TO STAY:** Breadalbane Inn, Fergus, tel 888-842-2825 or 519-843-4770; breadalbaneinn .com. *Cost:* from US$67/C$90 (off-peak), from US$98/C$130 (peak). **BEST TIMES:** 3 weeks in July for the Elora Festival (elorafestival.ca); mid-Aug for Fergus Scottish Festival (fergus scottishfestival.com).

Where the Great Spirit Dwells in Lake Huron

MANITOULIN ISLAND

Ontario

According to legend, the Great Spirit Gitchi Manitou of the Odawa people inhabited a vast, lake-filled island along the northern shore of Lake Huron, where deep hardwood forests cloak rocky uplands and fingers of water curl far inland. A mystical presence still fills today's Manitoulin Island—whether it's the quiet reverence of the island's many First Nations communities, the New Age sensibilities of the island's young artists and back-to-the-earth freethinkers, or the simple contentment of vacationing families who return to the island's many lakefront resorts year after year.

The largest freshwater island in the world, 100-mile-long Manitoulin seems more water than land. The island contains almost 100 lakes of its own—the largest is over 30 miles long—and some have islands themselves. Needless to say, fishing, boating, and water sports (including the local hobby of cardboard boat racing) are the magnets for many visitors. Sailing is especially popular between Manitoulin and the mainland, where more than 2,000 islands rise above the waters of the North Channel. There is also great hiking: the 3–4 hour Cup and Saucer Trail is considered one of Ontario's best.

However, to truly experience the spirit of Manitoulin, explore quiet island backroads by bicycle. Choose a network of smaller roads and rural lanes connecting villages and resorts in the island's bucolic center, where farmlands and forests fill the gaps between inland lakes.

WHERE: 330 miles/531 km northwest of Toronto. *Visitor info:* Tel 705-368-3021; manitoulintourism.com. *When:* mid-June–Sept. **BEST TIME:** 1st weekend in Aug for the Wikwemikong Cultural Festival (wikwemikong heritage.org), eastern Canada's oldest First Nations Powwow.

A lighthouse keeps watch over the rocky shores of Manitoulin Island.

Lake Ontario's Rustic-Chic Island

PRINCE EDWARD COUNTY

Ontario

A fertile, 270-square-mile island brimming with vineyards, organic farms, and over 500 miles of sandy beaches and shoreline, Prince Edward Island has become a natural magnet for a vibrant community of artists, chefs, and food lovers in recent years. A short two-hour drive east of metro Toronto, "The County" (as it is simply called) boasts plenty of distinctive redbrick Georgian architecture that dates from the late 18th century, when Loyalist settlers from the Thirteen Colonies moved here to escape the newly-founded United States. Their well-preserved villages are now a striking backdrop to The County's burgeoning arts and culinary scene.

Almost no point on the island is more than an hour's drive from another, which means that you're never far from a glass of wine. With a climate moderated by the waters of vast Lake Ontario, Prince Edward County has over 40 wineries. Visit Norman Hardie Winery to sample excellent pinot noir and chardonnay wines, best enjoyed alongside the winery's crusty wood-fired pizza while lounging on the vineyard-view patio.

The island's lodging scene was jolted awake in 2015 with the opening of the 13-room Drake Devonshire Inn. It's more relaxed than its Toronto cousin, the upscale Drake Hotel (see p. 1007), but with a fashion-forward rustic sensibility. The dining room is the island's best, with inventive farm- and lake-to-table cooking. For something more low-key, consider the Merrill Inn, an elegant country hotel with wall-to-wall antiques, beautifully appointed guest rooms, and a dining room with refined, locally sourced Mediterranean cuisine.

WHERE: 126 miles/200 km east of Toronto. *Visitor info:* prince-edward-county.com. **NORMAN HARDIE WINERY:** Tel 613-399-5297; norman hardie.com. *When:* open daily, April–early Dec; closed Sun, Jan–Mar. **DRAKE DEVONSHIRE INN:** Tel 844-898-3338 or 613-399-3338; drake devonshire.ca. *Cost:* from US$183/C$229 (off-peak), from US$263/C$329 (peak); dinner US$40/C$50. **MERRILL INN:** Tel 866-567-5969 or 613-476-7451; merrillinn.com. *Cost:* from US$128/C$160 (off-peak), from US$172/C$215 (peak); dinner US$44/C$55. **BEST TIMES:** early June for the Great Canadian Cheese Festival in Picton (cheesefestival.ca); mid-Aug for the PEC Jazz Festival (pecjazz.org).

The Greening of the Canadian Shield

GOLFING MUSKOKA

Ontario

M uskoka is so rocky that, until recently, even golf greens had trouble taking root. Just two hours north of Toronto, Muskoka sits at the southern edge of the Canadian Shield, the vast granite plateau that Ice Age glaciers scraped clean of topsoil, exposing the underlying stone. Too rocky to farm, the Muskoka region boomed as a resort destination beginning in the 1880s and '90s, when Gilded Age millionaires journeyed to the area's lakes (the region boasts over 1,600) for summer lakeside holidays. The Muskoka region grew famous for its lovely scenery, hardwood forests, boating, and resort living—but not for golf. With a couple of exceptions, the ubiquitous granite outcrops made building golf courses a difficult and expensive proposition.

That changed in 1990 with the opening of Deerhurst Highlands Golf Course. Rather than view the exposed granite as an obstacle, course architects Robert Cupp and Thomas McBroom embraced it. The result is a highly acclaimed and challenging course that uses rock ledges, cliffs, walls, and outcrops, adding a strategic and aesthetic element to the play. Suddenly, Muskoka took off as a golfing destination, and a bevy of new courses were designed to make the most of the distinctive landscape. Today, Muskoka is one of Canada's top golfing destinations, and its trademark granite is a selling point—in fact, one of the area's most renowned courses, in its early years named Best New Course in Canada, is simply called The Rock. Choose among the region's more than 15 golf courses, or contact the Muskoka Golf Trail, which designs mix-and-match golf and resort packages.

While championship golf may be relatively new to Muskoka, quality resorts aren't.

Deerhurst is one of Muskoka's earliest, originally built in 1896, and one of the region's most popular destinations for both couples and families. With updates and expansions it remains as impressive as ever. Spread across 760 acres of woodlands and waterfront, it offers a near-endless array of diversions, facilities, and amenities, from boating and swimming to horseback riding, hiking, and cross-country skiing in winter. Its Shizen Spa offers an extensive selection of soothing treatments, like Hydradermie facials and European-Rose Body Mud wraps, in case you overdo it.

Deerhurst is also famed for its nightly song-and-dance stage show—a Muskoka tradition for the last two decades. Singer Shania Twain grew up hereabouts and got her start at the resort (she was also married here).

WHERE: 140 miles/225 km north of Toronto. *Visitor info:* Tel 800-267-9700 or 705-689-0660; discovermuskoka.ca. **DEERHURST RESORT AND HIGHLANDS GOLF COURSE:** Tel 800-461-4393 or 705-789-6411; deerhurst resort.com. *Cost:* from US$82/C$109 (off-peak), US$180/C$239 (peak); greens fees from US$105/C$140. *When:* resort, year-round; golf, May–Oct. **THE ROCK:** Minett. Tel 866-765-ROCK or 705-765-7625; therockgolf.com. *Cost:* greens fees from US$56/C$75 (off-peak), from US$67/C$89 (peak). *When:* May–Oct. **MUSKOKA GOLF TRAIL:** golftrails.ca/muskoka. **BEST TIMES:** July–Sept for weather. The Huntsville Festival of the Arts (huntsvillefestival .on.ca) is year-round, but July is the highlight, with events almost nightly.

A Thunderous Beauty

NIAGARA FALLS

Ontario and New York State

"It would be more impressive if it flowed the other way," Oscar Wilde supposedly quipped of Niagara Falls, revealing a sangfroid that few can muster when viewing the vast and thundering falls in the Niagara River, by volume the largest waterfalls in North America. Straddling the U.S.-Canada border, Niagara Falls draws water from four of the five Great Lakes and flings it down 20 stories at the rate of 42 million gallons a minute. Almost a mile wide in total, the falls are divided by islands into three sections: the 1,060-foot American Falls, which includes a small section called Bridal Veil Falls, and the larger, 2,600-foot Horseshoe Falls on the Canadian side.

Niagara Falls are the most powerful waterfalls in North America.

Western society first became aware of the falls in 1678 when Jesuit missionary Louis Hennepin grew curious about the roar he heard in the distance and followed it to its source, writing Niagara's first tourist account. Almost three centuries later, Marilyn Monroe and Joseph Cotten headed this way in the falls' namesake film, in the process establishing the falls as an iconic honeymoon destination.

Although both the U.S. and Canadian sides of the falls are well worth visiting, the best views, including nighttime illumination, are from the beautifully manicured flower gardens that line the Canadian side. However, to get up-close-and-personal with the falls, visit Niagara Falls State Park in New York, where there are several locations, including Prospect Point, Luna Island, Terrapin Point, and the Three Sisters Islands, that allow visitors to stand within a few feet of the raging rapids and at the brink of the falls.

A classic way to view Niagara Falls is from aboard the *Maid of the Mist*, a sturdy 600-passenger boat that's the tenth in a same-name line of craft since 1846, safely taking passengers right into the maelstrom at the base of Horseshoe Falls. You'll be very glad of the plastic raincoats they issue at boarding—they only augment the school-trip atmosphere, and let you get a little wet anyway.

For a different though still drenching view, take the Journey Behind the Falls tour, on the Canadian side, which descends via elevator through 150 feet of rock to a series of man-made tunnels that provide a view from behind the cascading water. On the U.S. side, the Cave of the Winds tour leads visitors to the base of the Bridal Veil Falls. Donning souvenir raincoat and sandals, walk along a series of decks and stairs to the Hurricane Deck, just 20 feet from the base of the pounding waters.

The Canadian side of the falls offers better facilities—nightclubs, restaurants, upscale hotels, and an IMAX theater for the next-best experience of the falls' wonder. But the primary man-made attraction here is the 2.5-million-square-foot Niagara Fallsview Casino Resort, which in addition to gaming offers a variety of dining options, from deli to fancy venues meant to pamper high rollers, lovely rooms with the best views of the falls, and nighttime illumination shows.

WHERE: 82 miles/132 km southeast of Toronto. *Ontario visitor info:* Tel 800-563-2557 or 905-356-6061; niagarafallstourism.com. *New York visitor info:* Tel 877-325-5787 or 716-282-8992; niagara-usa.com. **MAID OF THE MIST:** Tel 716-284-8897 (New York); maidofthemist.com. *When:* May–mid-Nov. **JOURNEY BEHIND THE FALLS:** Tel 877-642-7275; niagaraparks.com. **CAVE OF THE WINDS:** Goat Island. Tel 716-278-1796; niagarafallsstatepark.com. *When:* late May–Oct. **NIAGARA FALLSVIEW CASINO RESORT:**

Tel 888-325-5788 or 905-374-6928; fallsview casinoresort.com. *Cost:* from US$105/C$139.
BEST TIMES: Apr–Nov for Niagara-on-the-Lake's annual Shaw Festival (see below); mid-May–Aug for Fireworks Fri and Sun at 10 P.M.; Nov–early Jan for winter Festival of Lights.

Charm and Culture in Wine Country

NIAGARA-ON-THE-LAKE

Niagara-on-the-Lake, Ontario

Leave the thunder of Niagara Falls behind you (see p. 998), and follow the road that leads to an entirely different world, far from the conga line of tour buses and the big business of honeymooning. Just north of the falls is the lovely little 19th-century town of Niagara-on-the-Lake, one of the prettiest in Canada and all these years happily existing in the shadow of its world-famous neighbor.

Niagara-on-the-Lake is best known as home to the acclaimed Shaw Festival, one of the largest and most successful theater festivals in North America. John Simon, writing in *New York* magazine, called it "the best repertory theater on the continent." Dedicated to presenting the works of George Bernard Shaw and his contemporaries and new works about Shaw's life, the festival fills three theaters with a dozen or more plays each season, from early April to November.

Niagara-on-the-Lake is filled with elegant historic homes (many now exclusive B&Bs), Victorian storefronts, wine shops, beautiful parks and gardens, and the mixed-use Niagara Parks Garden Trail, for walkers and cyclists, that hugs the Niagara River. The Prince of Wales Hotel and Spa, a grand and beautifully restored Victorian hotel, presides over the center of town. Exuding the sophistication and refinement of a bygone era (replete with a lovely tea room), it also promises all the comforts of the 21st century, with lavishly decorated rooms and a number of eating options, the standout being the Escabèche Restaurant for its excellent haute French dining.

More than a festival town, Niagara-on-the-Lake is also, along with the neighboring communities of St. Catharines, Jordan, and Vineland, at the heart of the Niagara wine region. The Niagara Peninsula, a neck of land that separates Lake Erie from Lake Ontario, is the largest viticultural area in Canada. This area shares the same latitude as Tuscany and the border area of France and Spain, and the microclimate of the Niagara Peninsula further adds to its winegrowing potential, as its position between two huge bodies of water moderates extremes in both winter and summer temperatures. More than 46 classic European grape varieties are now grown in Ontario, but it's ice wine—a honey-sweet dessert wine made after freezing temperatures concentrate the sugars in grapes purposefully left to hang on the vine—that is the region's most sought-after.

The Niagara Peninsula is home to more than 80 wineries. Most are open year-round and welcome visitors with tasting rooms and winery tours, and a growing number promise an excellent meal as well. Top wineries to visit include Peller Estates; Inniskillin Wines (whose barn may—or may not—have been designed by Frank Lloyd Wright); Château des Charmes; and Vineland Estates Winery, housed on a former Mennonite homestead.

One of Ontario's top country hotels, the Inn on the Twenty, can be found in the small town of Jordan and is a welcoming and convenient base for touring the wine country. The inn's structure was once a sugar warehouse; a stylish renovation has kept the vintage detail while infusing the 27 suites and facilities with lots of charm—and it includes a spa with plenty of treatments for both men and women. Foodies come for the reputation of the farm-to-table cuisine and fine wines found in the inn's acclaimed dining room.

WHERE: 80 miles/128 km south of Toronto. *Visitor info:* Tel 905-468-1950; niagara onthelake.com. **GEORGE BERNARD SHAW FESTIVAL:** Tel 800-511-7429 or 905-468-2172;

shawfest.com *Cost:* tickets from US$26/C$35. *When:* Apr–Nov. **PRINCE OF WALES HOTEL:** Tel 888-669-5566 or 905-468-3246; vintage-hotels.com. *Cost:* from US$134/C$179 (off-peak), from US$233/C$310 (peak); dinner at Escabèche US$48/C$50. **WINE COUNTRY ONTARIO:** Tel 905-684-8070; winesofontario .org. **INN ON THE TWENTY:** Tel 800-701-8074 or 905-562-5336; innonthetwenty.com. *Cost:* from US$119/C$159 (off-peak), from US$195/C$259 (peak); dinner US$41/C$55. **BEST TIMES:** mid-Jan for the Niagara Icewine Festival (grapeandwine.com); Sept for the Niagara Wine Festival.

The Civic Heart of Canada

PARLIAMENT HILL

Ottawa, Ontario

Before a stalwart stone hall, regiments of red-coated ceremonial guards present arms and march in stiff formation to their posts, accompanied by the beat of drums and the blast of bagpipes. You are forgiven a moment of spatial disorientation, but you're not in London. The Changing of the Guard at Ottawa's Parliament Hill is a colorful reminder of Canada's continuing place in the British Commonwealth.

Ottawa has come a ways since 1857, when Queen Victoria named the muddy lumber town as capital of the new and united Province of Canada, which joined the former colonies of French-speaking Lower Canada (now Quebec) and English-speaking Upper Canada (now mostly Ontario).

Today, Ottawa is a vital, fascinating city, full of the pomp and beauty of a world capital. High on a bluff above the Ottawa River, Parliament Hill is the political epicenter of Canada. Rising above manicured grounds are three massive, castlelike buildings surmounted by towers and steep, verdigris copper roofs. The Centre Block, containing the

chambers of the House of Commons and the Senate, is the largest, with a single campanile rising high above the structure's two wings. Known as the Peace Tower, the campanile stands over 300 feet tall, and was completed in 1927 to commemorate Canada's 60,000

At the Centre Block of Parliament Hill, the Peace Tower stands 303.5 feet tall.

dead in WWI; it's now dedicated to all Canadians who have given their lives for their country. The tower houses a carillon, a set of 53 bells sounded from a keyboard. In July and August, one-hour carillon concerts take place at 11 A.M. weekdays; the rest of the year, there are 15-minute concerts at noon on most weekdays. An elevator runs to the Peace Tower's observation deck, with fantastic views over the parliamentary precinct and the Ottawa River. Free guided tours of the Centre Block are offered daily (though not all areas may be available when Parliament is in session). Visitors can also attend debates in the House of Commons, with its soaring stained-glass windows, and in the Senate Chamber, an ornate hall ringed with murals.

Flanking the Centre Block are the oldest buildings on Parliament Hill—the East and West Blocks, built in the 1860s in High Victorian Gothic style. The East Block first housed the offices of the British governor general and the Privy Council, and later, the Canadian prime minister. In summer, four grandly furnished offices—preserved in 1870s finery—are open to visitors. The West Block, containing parliamentary offices, is closed to the public.

In addition to the Changing of the Guard, Parliament Hill's grandeur is on display during the summer's Sound and Light Show. The Parliament buildings are the stately backdrop for a dazzling multimedia show that blends music, projected images, and shimmering light effects to reflect the "Spirit of Canada."

Visitor info: Tel 866-599-4999 or 613-992-4793; parl.gc.ca. **Changing of the Guard:** 10–10:30 A.M. daily, late June–late Aug (weather permitting). **Sound and Light Show:** early July–mid-Sept (weather permitting); 1 bilingual presentation nightly. **Best time:** mid-May for the Canadian Tulip Festival that brings millions of blooms, plus arts and crafts fairs and live music.

Celebrating the Canadian Winter

Winterlude & the Rideau Canal

Ottawa, Ontario

If nature gives you snow and ice, then celebrate the joys of winter. That's exactly what Canada's capital city does each February during Winterlude, since 1979 Ottawa's paean to skating, family activities, and fun in the snow.

More than 650,000 visitors show up every year for the celebration, which includes a whole host of events: a winter triathlon (skiing, skating, and running), a hot stew cook-off, figure-skating performances, and evening entertainment. In Gatineau's Jacques-Cartier Park (north of Ottawa, across the river), Snowflake Kingdom is the world's largest snow playground—complete with a snow maze—while Ottawa's Confederation Park is the site of the Crystal Garden International Ice-Carving Competition, with pros and amateurs each having their own contests. The National Snow Sculpture Competition is a crowd favorite that displays giant works prepared by professional snow sculptors from each province and territory.

The centerpiece of Winterlude is the Rideau Canal, built in the 19th century as a military route linking Montreal to Kingston. During the winter, 5 miles of its length are groomed for skating and serve as Winterlude's main drag. During the rest of winter the canal doubles as an ice thoroughfare—and possibly the world's longest naturally frozen ice rink. During the week, it fills with businesspeople commuting by skate between home and office and schoolchildren zipping along carrying lunch boxes. On weekends the pace is more leisurely, with skaters making frequent stops at food concessions for hot chocolate, beavertails (wedges of deep-fried dough covered with cinnamon sugar), and maple syrup on shaved ice.

If you're looking for a place to hang your skates or at least grab a cup of tea, the imposing Fairmont Château Laurier remains the finest hotel in the nation's capital. Built in 1912, at the site where the Rideau Canal meets the Ottawa River, the Laurier offers a historic castlelike setting, handsome furnishings, old-world service, and one of the most European hotel experiences this side of the Atlantic.

WINTERLUDE INFO: Tel 844-878-8333 or 613-239-5000; canadascapital.gc.ca/winter lude. *When:* 1st 3 weekends in Feb. **FAIRMONT CHÂTEAU LAURIER:** Tel 613-241-1414; fair mont.com/laurier. *Cost:* from US$209/C$279 (off-peak), from US$225/C$299 (peak).

The impressive Fairmont Château Laurier presides over the Rideau Canal's extensive skateway.

The Bard—and More—on Canada's River Avon

THE STRATFORD FESTIVAL

Stratford, Ontario

"The play's the thing," according to Shakespeare—a philosophy that has guided the highly acclaimed Stratford Shakespeare Festival of Canada since the early 1950s, when Stratford-born journalist Tom Patterson established a summer theater festival in this scenic and historic city that carries the appropriate name. Now the largest classical repertory theater in North America, the festival offers over a dozen productions yearly, from mid-April through late October. In addition to world-class productions of Shakespeare, it mounts a broad range of plays—from classics to cutting edge—on its four stages. Recent productions span ancient Greek tragedy, Molière, and the great dramas of the 20th century. The festival also revives the best in comedy, operetta, and musical theater, and regularly stages world-premiere productions by contemporary Canadian and international playwrights. Visitors can also attend a full program of Fringe events, including concerts, discussions, and readings.

The stars come out for the Stratford Shakespeare festival. Its first production—

Richard III in 1953—headlined Alec Guinness, and international artists of the stage, cinema, and TV have followed.

Quite apart from the city's dynamic thespian activity, Stratford is a charming and romantic place to visit. The downtown core is a well-preserved bastion of ivy-covered Victorian storefronts centered on a market square, with excellent antiques stores, bookshops, and art galleries. Diners are also lucky—the Stratford Chef's School, one of Canada's top culinary institutes, ensures a

The Stratford Festival staged a humorous rendition of Molière's The Hypochondriac.

steady stream of newly minted talent for the city's many restaurants. Call ahead for reservations at the Revival House, a deconsecrated Baptist church built in 1873, with an original cuisine to match the unique setting, or climb upstairs to The Chapel, a gastro pub popular for light lunches and dinner.

With ten quirkily individual but luxurious guest rooms in three historic 19th-century homes and a carriage house, the Three Houses Inn perfectly captures Stratford's sophistication and good-natured sense of high drama. The very stylish decor partakes equally of whimsy and refined good taste, while breakfasts have the festive spirit of a dinner party.

WHERE: 93 miles/149 km west of Toronto; 55 Queen St. Tel 800-567-1600 or 519-273-1600; stratfordfestival.ca. *Cost:* tickets from US$38/C$50. *When:* mid-Apr–late Oct. **REVIVAL HOUSE:** Tel 519-273-3424; church restaurant.com. *Cost:* dinner US$41/C$55. **THREE HOUSES INN:** Tel 519-272-0722; the threehouses.com. *Cost:* from US$169/C$225. **BEST TIMES:** July–Aug for the peak of the theater festival; late July–mid-Aug for live chamber music, opera, jazz, and contemporary music at the Stratford Summer Music Festival (stratfordsummermusic.ca).

Canadian Art—Past, Present, and Future

ART GALLERY OF ONTARIO

Toronto, Ontario

Major changes helped secure the future of the Art Gallery of Ontario (AGO), long known as one of North America's finest art museums. A 2008 project called Transformation AGO, added more than 10,000 new works of art to the permanent collection and 97,000 square feet of gallery space. AGO now holds what is arguably Canada's best collection of visual art—some 90,000 works in total, and an impressive space of 583,000 square feet.

Transformation AGO was triggered in 2002 when Kenneth Thomson, a leading Canadian art collector and businessman, donated nearly 2,000 works from his private collection to the museum.

To accommodate the additions and bring

the museum into the 21st century, the AGO engaged renowned Toronto native Frank Gehry, the architectural genius behind global projects such as the Guggenheim Museum Bilbao. The expansion includes a four-story tinted titanium-and-glass-faced wing overlooking Grange Park and a 600-foot-long glass and wood facade with 450 feet of sculpture gallery visible from the street.

Founded in 1900, the AGO now has more than 90,000 works in its collection.

The museum's significant European collection includes works by Tintoretto, Brueghel, Rembrandt, Renoir, Degas, Picasso, Gauguin, and van Gogh, while its contemporary collection includes pieces by Andy Warhol, Robert Smithson, Gerhard Richter, and Claes Oldenburg.

The Canadian collection represents more than half the museum's holdings, with works ranging from before Confederation to the present day—including 19th-century landscapes and scenes of early Canadian life by artists such as Cornelius Krieghoff and Lucius O'Brien. Also marvelous are pieces by the Group of Seven and their contemporaries, early 20th-century Canadian artists whose work celebrates the country's natural splendor. The collection of Inuit art is one of the finest in Canada.

In 1974, British sculptor Henry Moore was moved when the citizens of Toronto pitched in to purchase his sculpture *The Archer* for their new city hall after legislators had refused to provide funds. As a result, he donated more than 800 works—bronzes, woodcuts, lithographs, etchings, plasters, and drawings—to the museum, which now maintains the world's largest collection of his art.

WHERE: 317 Dundas St. W. Tel 416-979-6648; ago.net. *When:* closed Mon.

Canada's Oldest and Largest Public Market

ST. LAWRENCE MARKET

Toronto, Ontario

St. Lawrence Market in Toronto's Old Town district is Canada's oldest and largest, a focal point where food and history have intersected for over 200 years. A public market has stood on these grounds since 1803, though in those days it was an altogether rowdier experience, with livestock mingling with haberdashers and soup merchants, and the occasional public flogging taking place as a public reminder.

Over the course of the next century, three different market buildings grew up to serve the public. The South Market, a soaring redbrick structure dating from 1904, hosts over 120 vendors selling the freshest seafood, fruits and vegetables, specialty meats and dairy products, spices, baked goods, and ethnic foods, as well as high-quality arts and crafts.

The North Market, relocated since 2015 to an adjacent temporary structure pending completion of a new market building in 2018, is open on Saturdays for a bustling farmers market featuring produce direct from local Ontario purveyors. On Sundays, this same market space switches gears and becomes a popular antiques and flea market with over 80 vendors offering a vast array of furniture, art, collectibles, and other treasures. The third market building, the St. Lawrence Hall from 1850, is currently used as an office and event space.

Of course, you can buy more than just ingredients for dinner at St. Lawrence—a number of bakeries and food stalls offer delicious snacks to go. Don't leave the market without sampling the classic peameal bacon sandwich from the South Market's Carousel Bakery—perfectly cooked Canadian-style loin bacon piled on a house-made Kaiser roll, lashed with mustard. It's a Toronto favorite, and on Saturdays, the Carousel sells more than 2,600 of them!

WHERE: at the intersection of Front St. East and Jarvis St. Tel. 416-392-7219; stlawrencemarket.com. *When:* South Market open Tues–Sat; North Market Farmers Market Sat only; Antiques Market Sun only. **CAROUSEL BAKERY:** Tel 416-392-7219. *Cost:* peameal bacon sandwich US$5/C$7. **BEST TIMES:** Check the market web site for year-round cooking lessons and other food events.

Temples of Canadian Culture

ROYAL ONTARIO MUSEUM & HOCKEY HALL OF FAME

Toronto, Ontario

Canada's largest museum of natural history and human culture, the Royal Ontario Museum (ROM) opened to the public in 1914. Since then, the institution has grown immensely, both in size of collection and also in scope. With over 6 million objects in its collections, today's ROM preserves an overview of natural history from the dawn of time, and the arts and artifacts of human cultures from around the world. The exhibits are diverse and fascinating, ranging from a remarkable selection of Chinese art, a wing dedicated to European decorative arts, dinosaur skeletons, a Canadian heritage gallery, and a whole lot more. Kids love the Bat Cave, a walk-through miniature replica of Jamaica's St. Clair cave, with 800 very lifelike bats darting about.

Given such a broad mandate and a burgeoning collection, it's no wonder the museum outgrew its original exhibition space. A major revitalization restored the museum's former buildings to their period glory and built a new,

The Hockey Hall of Fame was founded in Kingston, Ontario, in 1943, relocating to its current Toronto location in 1958.

architecturally daring structure, which added 300,000 square feet of new and renovated space to the museum. The new structure, the Michael Lee-Chin Crystal, designed by Daniel Libeskind, is in the form of a multifaceted crystal, creating unusual architectural forms that offer terrific views over downtown Toronto's Bloor Street. The added exhibition space, which opened in 2007, allows the museum to display Egyptian mummies, medieval armor, and displays on Canadian history, as well as never-before-seen collections and many museum favorites from the past.

For insight into a whole other sort of Canadian culture, visit the Hockey Hall of Fame, a shrine to the nation's most popular sport. This C\$35 million facility devotes 60,000 square feet to exhibits on the history of hockey,

the great Canadian hockey rinks, and the sport's most legendary players. The Stanley Cup, professional hockey's top prize, also resides here—hockey fans stand in line to have their photo taken with it. Most exciting are the interactive exhibits: Ever wonder what if feels like for a goalie to face a shooter like Wayne Gretzky? Simulator games allow you to suit up and tend goal against video images of legendary hockey stars, while sponge pucks are fired at you at speeds up to 70 mph. Many Canadians profess that you'll never understand the country until you understand hockey—here's the perfect window into the national psyche.

ROYAL ONTARIO MUSEUM: 100 Queen's Park. Tel 416-586-8000; rom.on.ca. **HOCKEY HALL OF FAME:** 30 Yonge St. Tel 416-360-7765; hhof.com.

Hollywood Glam on Lake Ontario

TORONTO INTERNATIONAL FILM FESTIVAL

Toronto, Ontario

B egun in 1976, the Toronto International Film Festival (TIFF) is a relative upstart in the film festival circuit. However, as the top film festival in North America and widely considered to be second only to Cannes on the

world stage, offering more than 300 films from over 60 countries, the festival is now regarded by many filmmakers as the premier platform for launching new films.

Toronto's reputation as a center of cinema doesn't derive just from its increasingly must-attend festival. Canada in general and Toronto specifically have become Hollywood North, where U.S. filmmakers come to make films more cheaply than in California.

The festival, held in early to mid-September, began as an assemblage of films from other festivals, a "festival of festivals," but quickly became a showcase for film premieres,

idiosyncratic retrospectives, and the introduction of international films to North America.

For ten intensive days, the films are screened in 11 different venues in downtown Toronto. The presence of so many filmgoers, Hollywood executives, and movie stars in a relatively compact area makes for a real *People*-magazine-goes-to-the-carnival atmosphere. Rooms at the brand new 55-story Four Seasons are harder to come by than Oscars, while the smaller design-aware Drake Hotel serves as the perennial crossroads for Toronto's creative types. Trendy bars and restaurants in town report sightings of Nicole, Leo, Penelope, and Reese all in the course of one air-kissed evening.

WHERE: various venues in Toronto. Tel 416-599-8433; tiff.net. *Cost:* from US$19/ C$25 for individual tickets. **FOUR SEASONS:** Tel 416-964-0411; fourseasons.com/toronto. *Cost:* US$440/C$585. **DRAKE HOTEL:** Tel 866-372-5386 or 416-531-5042; thedrake hotel.ca. *Cost:* from US$170/C$225. *When:* 10 days in early–mid-Sept.

Island Birthplace of Canada

CHARLOTTETOWN

Prince Edward Island

P rince Edward Island's (PEI) capital, Charlottetown, is a delightful small city with a deep sense of history enlivened with a youthful spirit and postcard looks. With a beautiful waterfront location and an abundance of handsome 19th-century redbrick structures and shady squares, Charlottetown is PEI's one true hub—it's the economic, governmental, cultural, and shopping center of the province. With a population of 35,000, however, it feels more like a well-heeled and friendly small town.

On a protected harbor and between the mouths of two rivers, the city was established as a port in the 1760s and maintains a distinct seafaring atmosphere. The waterfront, with Peake's Wharf at its center, is a lively place to visit, with its brick warehouses converted to shops, restaurants, nightclubs, and open-air cafés. Above the waterfront, the old town center is more stately, with Georgian-era homes and storefronts lining the narrow cobbled streets. Wander up Great George Street, lined with old churches, majestic maples, and trim brick homes, for an especially evocative glimpse of Old Charlottetown. Several of the historic buildings on this street are part of The Great George, a unique set of lodging options with a variety of guest rooms that range from stylishly modern to traditionally authentic and a young, house-proud staff.

Charlottetown is called the Cradle of Confederation and served as the Philadelphia of Canada; this is the place where the Fathers of Canadian Confederation met in 1864 to discuss unifying the country. Take a crash course on events leading up to (and following) confederation at the waterfront Founders Hall. Province House was the site of the meeting, and today you can visit the Confederation Chamber and several other rooms, all restored to appear as they did in the 1860s.

Adjacent to Province House is the Confederation Centre of the Arts, PEI's top performing arts center and home to the Charlottetown Festival, which offers four theatrical productions each summer, including the perennial favorite *Anne of Green Gables— The Musical* (see next page).

Most of PEI's original settlers came from Ireland, Scotland, England, and France, and today you can hear their descendants playing traditional Celtic and Acadian music at any of the summertime festivals or at a number of places in Charlottetown, including the Irish Hall and the Olde Dublin Pub. Charlottetown celebrates its renowned fishing heritage during September's PEI International Shellfish Festival, one of the largest in the Atlantic provinces. Those prized Malpeque oysters shipped worldwide taste twice as sweet here just plucked from the bay in the midst of the revelry.

Where: 210 miles/341 km east of Fredericton, NB. *Visitor info:* Tel 800-955-1864 or 902-629-1864; discovercharlottetown.com. **The Great George:** Tel 800-361-1118 or 902-892-0606; thegreatgeorge.com. *Cost:* from US$108/C$144 (off-peak), from US$172/C$229 (peak). **Founders Hall:** Tel 800-955-1864 or 902-368-1864; foundershall.ca. *When:* daily May–Oct; check website for off-season

hours. **Province House:** Tel 902-566-7050; pc.gc.ca/provincehouse.   **Charlottetown Festival:** Tel 800-565-0278 or 902-566-1267. *When:* June–Oct. **PEI International Shellfish Festival:** Tel 866-955-2003 or 902-566-2549; peishellfish.com. *When:* 3rd weekend in Sept. **Irish Hall:** Tel 902-566-3273. **Olde Dublin Pub:** Tel 902-892-6992. **Best time:** June–Sept for summer weather.

The Land of Anne and Sandy Beaches

PRINCE EDWARD ISLAND NATIONAL PARK

Prince Edward Island

Along the northern shores of Prince Edward Island (PEI), deep bays intrude into a pastoral landscape of rolling hills and fields. White steeples dot small villages, and prim farmsteads are flanked by grazing sheep and orchards. This corner of PEI doesn't just *look* storybook, it is storybook: This is the bucolic setting of *Anne of Green Gables*, Lucy Maud Montgomery's famed 1908 novel of a spunky, red-haired orphan girl coming of age in turn-of-the-20th-century rural PEI. The inspiration for the setting of *Anne* (and the seven books in the series that followed) was Green Gables House, the farm belonging to cousins of Montgomery's grandfather and now preserved for all to enjoy as part of Prince Edward Island National Park. Montgomery, who was born in the area in 1874, set her novels amid the area's rich beauty. Translated now into 36 languages and adapted multiple times into films, the book has fan clubs around the world and draws countless visitors annually to the island and its many Anne-related sights. Cavendish is the area's most-visited town and is on the touristy side, with every other shop dedicated to Montgomery and her adolescent creation while a kitschy theme park called Avonlea Village re-creates scenes and characters from the books.

Prince Edward Island National Park is more than just Anne's Land, though. The park also protects 25 miles of the island's north-central coast, a unique maritime shoreline of sand spits, dunes, islands, and beaches plus coastal wetlands and forests.

For convenient accommodations, there are bright, simple cabins right next to Gables

Established in 1876, the active New London Rear Range Lighthouse sits at the mouth of the harbor across from the lovely Cavendish beach.

House at the Green Gables Cottages, but for more atmosphere, the Kindred Spirits Inn is a fine country hotel with antiques-decorated rooms and suites and an outdoor pool. An easy drive away, Dalvay-by-the-Sea National Historic Site and Heritage Inn is a more evocative choice, especially for visitors seeking access to the beaches. Built in 1895 as a grand summer "cottage" by Alexander MacDonald, a business partner of John D. Rockefeller, and now administered by the park, this seaside Victorian mansion has been a summer resort since the 1930s, offering a TV-free environment, 25 simple, bright guest rooms, 3 cottages, and an old-timey restaurant serving fine cuisine.

WHERE: Cavendish is 24 miles/39 km from Charlottetown. **PARK:** Tel 902-672-6350; pc.gc.ca/pei. **GREEN GABLES HERITAGE HOUSE:** Cavendish. Tel 902-963-7874; pc.gc.ca/greengables. *When:* May–Oct. **AVONLEA VILLAGE:** Cavendish. Tel 902-963-3050; avonlea.ca. *When:* mid-June–mid-Sept. **GREEN GABLES COTTAGES:** Cavendish. Tel 800-965-3334 or 902-963-2722; greengablescottages.com. *Cost:* from US$52/C$69 (off-peak), from US$86/C$115 (peak). *When:* June–mid-Sept. **KINDRED SPIRITS INN:** Cavendish. Tel 902-963-2434; kindredspirits.ca. *Cost:* from US$64/C$85 (off-peak), from US$79/C$105 (peak). **DALVAY-BY-THE-SEA:** Dalvay. Tel 902-672-2048; dalvaybythesea.com. *Cost:* from US$150/C$199. *When:* June–Sept. **BEST TIMES:** July–Aug for the weather; mid-Sept–late Oct for foliage.

Exploring Canada's Island Province

TOURING PEI's BACK ROADS

Prince Edward Island

Canada's smallest province, Prince Edward Island (PEI) is a low-lying, richly agricultural island rising in the Gulf of St. Lawrence. Midway in size between Rhode Island and Connecticut, PEI is as pastoral as a picture book, with tiny towns set among rolling green hills. Its self-reliant lifestyle was nurtured by isolation—for centuries, ferries were the only link to the mainland. Even once the island was connected to the New Brunswick mainland by the 9-mile Confederation Bridge in 1997, the feel remained more sheep pasture than rat race.

Three officially designated driving routes showcase the island's best features. Points East Coastal Drive heads northeast from Charlottetown (see p. 1008), following the coastline of Kings County. It winds through green fields and dozens of small rural hamlets with views onto the Gulf of St. Lawrence and, in clear weather, Nova Scotia's Cape Breton (see p. 987). Here in bucolic Kings County, the well-known Inn at Bay Fortune is its own destination.

The rambling oceanfront property was originally built in 1910 as the summer home of a Broadway playwright and later served as an ersatz artists colony. Today with new innkeepers at the helm, it's one of the most comfortable and atmospheric places to stay on PEI, where guests have the option of staying in 15 rooms dispersed between the main house and the tower. The Fireworks restaurant is one of the most noteworthy in PEI, having earned a clutch of stars from guidebooks and much attention from national press. Chef Michael Smith offers innovative, intensely regional cuisine that captures the essence of PEI.

Central Coast Drive is probably the most traveled (and most commercial) route, as it passes the north shore's PEI National Park and destinations related to L. M. Montgomery and her novel *Anne of Green Gables*. (see p. 1009). But there are lots of other alluring vignettes along the way, such as in the small fishing village of North Rustico, whose weathered Fisherman's Wharf restaurant has tanks holding 40,000 pounds of lobster—guess what's for dinner?

North Cape Coastal Drive, around the west coast, is even more rural, passing lighthouses, fishing villages, and a group of houses in Cap-Egmont made entirely of recycled bottles. Plan your trip to coincide with the Summerside Lobster Festival in mid-July, which features lobster suppers, music, a parade, a spelling bee, and cardboard boat races.

Follow the red clay road to discover PEI's hidden corners.

Get even closer to the rural heart of PEI on the Confederation Trail, a 170-mile rails-to-trails shared-use hiking and biking path running the length of the island. The trail makes it easy to walk from village to village, or inn, and it's even more popular as a bicycling path. Hearty cyclists can make the trip from one end of the pastoral island to the other in three days, with nights spent at inns or provincial park campgrounds. MacQueen Island Tours offers bike rentals, plus guided, unguided, and custom tours along the Confederation Trail and other rural routes on PEI.

WHERE: 337 miles/542 km from Bangor, ME. *Visitor info:* Tel 800-463-4734 or 902-437-8570; tourismpei.com. **INN AT BAY FORTUNE:** Tel 888-687-3745 or 902-687-3745; innat bayfortune.com. *Cost:* from US$113/C$150, 5-course prix-fixe dinner US$60/C$80. *When:* mid-May–mid-Nov. **FISHERMAN'S WHARF RESTAURANT:** North Rustico. Tel 877-289-1010 or 902-963-2669; fishermanswharf.ca. *When:* mid-May–mid-Oct. *Cost:* lobster dinner US$25/C$34. **CONFEDERATION TRAIL:** tourismpei.com/pei-confederation-trail. **MACQUEEN ISLAND TOURS:** Charlottetown. Tel 800-969-2822 or 902-368-2453; macqueens.com. **BEST TIMES:** June–Aug for hiking and biking; mid-July for Summerside Lobster Festival (summerside lobsterfestival.com); 1st weekend in Aug for the Highland Games in Eldon.

Wilderness Grandeur in the Newport of the North

CHARLEVOIX

Quebec

An hour northeast of Quebec City along the north shores of the St. Lawrence River, Charlevoix is an area of astonishing natural beauty. The land is rugged, with forests of fir, cedar, and spruce edging into farmland

and the banks of the river rising into rock-faced cliffs. This is such a unique mix of environments and history that UNESCO recognized it in 1989 as a World Biosphere Reserve, the first time a populated area was so named.

Although the first French traders arrived here in the 1670s, it was in the next century, after the English began driving the French Acadians from the Maritime Provinces, that Charlevoix was truly settled. Charlevoix's beauty began to attract travelers, and during the Gilded Age of the late 1800s, a summer influx of wealthy American families began requiring ever more opulent resorts. The Charlevoix villages known collectively as Murray Bay (in French, La Malbaie and Pointe-au-Pic) were the nexus of this "Newport of the North."

The cliff-top Fairmont Le Manoir Richelieu has stood above the St. Lawrence since 1899 (the current structure was built after a fire in 1928). This castlelike 405-room hotel

Charlevoix's dramatic landscape includes rolling terrain, fjords, headlands, and bays.

perfectly captures Charlevoix's blend of quiet countryside charm, wilderness grandeur, and world-class resort life. In addition to sumptuous guest rooms, a tunnel connection to the Casino de Charlevoix, a pampering spa, and a number of dining choices, it is the great outdoors that has long lured most guests. The area's summertime visitors enjoy myriad opportunities for hiking, biking, golf, kayaking, whale-watching, and canoeing at two nearby national parks. For the less wilderness-minded, the resort's golf club offers 27 scenic holes of golf on a bluff above the river.

In the white months, the region's deep snowfalls lure snowmobilers, downhill and Nordic skiers, and dogsledders, while ice-skaters glide and twirl at the hotel's river-facing rink. It's just a minute's ride to the hotel's nearby neighbor, the tranquil and charming Auberge des Falaises, where guests can expect the same breathtaking views of the St. Lawrence River from some of the balconied rooms, the glassed-in restaurant, and the spa's heated pool and two outdoor Jacuzzis.

Where: 50 miles/80 km northeast of Quebec City. **Le Manoir Richelieu:** La Malbaie. Tel 800-441-1414 or 418-665-3703; fairmont.com/richelieu. *Cost:* from US$127/C$169 (off-peak), from US$172/C$229 (peak). **Auberge des Falaises:** Tel 800-386-3731 or 418-665-3731; aubergedesfalaises.com. *Cost:* from US$88/C$117 (off-peak), from US$185/C$247 (peak). **Best times:** May–Oct for outdoor activities and whale-watching; Dec–Mar for skiing and snowmobiling.

Following the Food Trail in Southern Quebec

THE EASTERN TOWNSHIPS

Quebec

Quebec's Eastern Townships are a rich agricultural area of wide valleys and low mountains (the northern extension of the Appalachians) snuggled between the St. Lawrence River and the borders of Maine, New Hampshire, and Vermont. This area was initially settled by British loyalists who moved here in the 1770s and '80s after fleeing the newly independent U.S. The land is some of Quebec's most beautiful, with dozens of tiny 19th-century villages and resorts nestling among fields and orchards, glacial lakes, and majestic mountains.

The landscape is not just for viewing, it's for savoring. The heart of the Eastern Townships, a lovely area of rolling hills and valleys known as Brome-Missisquoi, serves as the breadbasket of Quebec, providing many of the traditional foods that lend a French *je ne sais quoi* to fine cuisine in Montreal and Quebec City. More than 70 winemakers, farmers, maple syrup producers, beekeepers, cheese makers, cider brewers, and other producers of fresh local food products open their properties to visitors.

Throughout the region, sheltered valleys produce microclimates where wine grapes and orchards flourish. The village of Dunham is at the center of "la Route des Vins"—a circuit of over 20 wineries that's also a popular cycling route. Artisanal cheeses are another local specialty, none more revered than the award-winners made by the small community

of monks at the Abbey of St. Benoit-du-Lac, on Lake Memphremagog. Daily vespers are sung in Gregorian chant and you can spend a night or two, which the monks welcome.

The lovely village of Knowlton (part of Lac Brome township) is a center of regional gastronomy, with many fine restaurants and food producers (as well as antiques shops, boutiques, and art galleries). Its real claim to fame, however, is its duck farms. This region is one of North America's leading producers and for several weeks in late September to early October, Knowlton celebrates the annual Duck Festival, which brings together the skills of local winemakers and chefs in a grand culinary showcase.

WHERE: Knowlton is 60 miles/97 km southwest of Montreal. *Visitor info:* Tel 800-355-5755 or 819-820-2020; easterntownships .org. **ABBEY OF ST. BENOIT-DU-LAC:** Tel 819-843-4080; st-benoit-du-lac.com. **WHERE TO STAY:** Auberge & Spa, West Brome. Tel 888-902-7663 or 405-266-7552; awb.ca. *Cost:* from US$141/C$188. **BEST TIMES:** July–Sept for weather; several weeks in Sept–Oct for Knowlton Duck Festival and village harvest festivals.

Nordic Skiing and Year-round Beauty in Ottawa's Backyard

GATINEAU PARK

Gatineau, Quebec

This is your dream: gliding silently through snowbound forests of spruce and fir, across frozen lakes and icy river channels to a remote wood-fire-warmed hut or lodge. And the next day? Do it again, another day of deep snow, deep woods, and another hut even deeper in the woods. Gatineau Park is one of North America's top cross-country ski and snowshoeing destinations, with nearly 124 miles of groomed trails forming a network throughout the park's 142 square miles—all just minutes from downtown Ottawa (see p. 1002).

Wedge-shaped Gatineau Park stretches from the city of Gatineau (formerly called Hull) up a series of lake-filled valleys flanked by rolling, snow-catching hills. For day skiers, the park's nine shelters along the ski trails offer tables for lunch and a chance to warm up by woodstoves. But, for a real North Woods adventure, ski deep into the forest to spend a night or two in the park's dozen backcountry ski cabins, four-season tents, or yurts (large, cozy tentlike structures fashioned after traditional cloth-sided dwellings in Central Asia) —all with bunk beds and woodstoves for cooking and heating. The cabin at Brown Lake also offers the comforts of modern electrical appliances. After an exhilarating day of skiing or snowshoeing through a snow-filled forest, it's an unparalleled experience to spend a winter night in a toasty fire-warmed cabin on the edge of a quiet frozen lake.

If you like your backcountry ski adventure with a little more comfort, try the Wakefield Mill Inn, a heritage 1838 stone mill that's been refurbished into a delightful country inn

Created in 1938, Gatineau Park is known for its network of cross-country ski trails, but it also offers snowshoeing, and in summer, hiking, biking, and swimming.

spanning a waterfall on La Pêche River. It is Gatineau Park's only traditional lodging choice, and an excellent one. The inn is close to the park's trail network, and makes a delightful departure point or destination for expeditions into the park. Rooms are all unique—some with original stone walls, others within the old grain silo, some overlooking a 28-foot waterfall and others in the Eco River Lodge, which incorporates the original 1840's miller's house—and are beautifully furnished with modern comforts and rural Quebecois charm. The restaurant offers excellent cuisine derived from deep-rooted French and Quebec traditions, updated with contemporary flair and local organic ingredients. After a massage in the inn's spa, relax in the spectacular outdoor hot tub at the base of the waterfall—ideal for après-ski bliss.

In warm weather months 78 miles of trails promise great bird-watching, hiking, and biking. In summertime, visitors enjoy picnics and a swim in the park's pristine lakes.

WHERE: 6 miles/10 km north of Ottawa. *Visitor info:* Tel 866-456-3016 or 819-827-2020; ncc-cnn.gc.ca. *Cost:* cabins, tents, and yurts, from US$17/C$22 per person per night. **WAKEFIELD MILL INN:** Tel 819-459-1838; wakefieldmill.com. *Cost:* from US$150/C$199. **BEST TIME:** mid-Jan for Ski-Fest, with cross-country skiing, snowshoeing, and family fun.

Eastern Canada's Top Ski Area

MONT TREMBLANT RESORT

Quebec

Mont Tremblant, North America's second-oldest ski resort (after Idaho's Sun Valley; see p. 604) sits atop the highest peak (3,001 feet) of Quebec's Laurentian Mountains. Established in 1939, the venerable resort underwent more than just a face-lift in the 1990s when Intrawest, the corporation that also owns Whistler Blackcomb Resort in British Columbia (see p. 1062), poured nearly a billion dollars into development and upgrades. The result is an all-season destination resort, often ranked the No. 1 ski area in eastern North America, with 49 miles of trails (broken up into 96 runs) attracting skiers from around the world.

The mountain receives more than 150 inches of snow in winter, and a full 47 percent of its trails are classified advanced and expert, including the daunting double-black-diamond Dynamite, with its 42-degree incline, the steepest in eastern Canada. Nonskiers can try dogsledding and evening sleigh rides that come complete with storytelling and hot chocolate. But Mont Tremblant (French for "trembling mountain") is known for more than its slopes. At the mountain's base lies Mont Tremblant Village, alive with countless bars, restaurants, and shops. This pedestrian-only area is designed to resemble Quebec City's historic district, right down to its cobbled streets, wrought-iron balconies, and tin roofs. Le Shack, located on the St.-Bernard Plaza, is one of Tremblant's popular après-ski spots, with a nonglitzy feel that's shared by the whole resort.

The ski-in/ski-out Fairmont Mont Tremblant, built in 1996, sits just above the village. Harmoniously integrated into its natural setting, Fairmont Mont Tremblant has the feel of a country inn on a grand scale, with a fitness center, indoor-outdoor swimming pools year-round, three outdoor hot pools overlooking the ski slopes, and a European-style spa. At Windigo Restaurant, chef Eric Beaupré brings traditional French techniques to natural local products. Mont Tremblant is as busy in summer as in winter, with families attracted to the region's hiking, water sports, mountain biking, and other outdoor activities. The village edges up to the busy Lake Tremblant, with two world-class 18-hole golf courses, the par-71 Le Diable and par-72 Le Géant, that are arguably Quebec's best.

WHERE: 75 miles/121 km north of Montreal. Tel 888-738-1777 or 514-764-7546; tremblant.ca. *Cost:* lift tickets US$63/C$84; greens fees from US$59/C$79 (off-peak), from US$89/C$119 (peak). *When:* ski season mid-Nov–mid-Apr; golf season May–mid-Oct. **FAIRMONT MONT TREMBLANT:** Tel 819-681-7000; fairmont.com/tremblant. *Cost:* from US$164/C$219 (off-peak), from US$217/C$289 (peak). **BEST TIMES:** Dec–Mar for ski conditions; summer and fall for music festivals.

Mont Tremblant Resort has 96 marked trails, including an exhilarating trail that's almost 4 miles long.

A Music Extravaganza of International Proportions

MONTREAL INTERNATIONAL JAZZ FESTIVAL

Montreal, Quebec

As the largest such music celebration in the world, the ten-day Montreal International Jazz Festival is the highlight of Montreal's festival-packed summer (see next page). In the entertainment district anchored by the

Place des Arts, Montreal's grand concert hall, 15 concert halls and ten outdoor stages present 1,000 concerts and activities, two-thirds of them free. A festival atmosphere transforms the city, with the long summer evenings enlivened

More than 2 million attend the Montreal International Jazz Festival each year to witness extraordinary jazz performers.

by high spirits and the thrill of the moment.

Held annually since 1979, the festival attracts an audience of 2 million music lovers, and brings together some 3,000 world-class musicians from more than 30 countries who fill the city with jazz as well as blues, reggae, and Latin and African music. Recent years have shown participation by internationally renowned performers ranging from such jazz stalwarts as Wynton Marsalis and Tony Bennett, to k.d. lang, Diana Krall, Norah Jones, Santana, and Keith Jarrett, with visits by France's Orchestre National de Jazz and George Thorogood thrown in for good measure.

WHERE: various venues in downtown Montreal. Tel 855-299-3378 or 514-871-1881; montrealjazzfest.com. *When:* late June–early July.

Fireworks, Film, and a Good Laugh

MONTREAL'S SUMMER FESTIVALS

Montreal, Quebec

Although similar in size and prosperity to a number of other large urban centers, Montreal has a unique, buoyant spirit. This city loves a festival, as its reputation as Canada's "capital of festivals" makes clear.

By far the most important on the roster is the Montreal International Jazz Festival, one of the world's biggest and best (see previous page). Fast on its heels and starting out with a bang—quite literally—is the Montreal International Fireworks Competition lighting up the city's skies from mid-June through July. National teams of fireworks designers from around the world send off their biggest, newest, and most revolutionary creations into the Montreal night to the accompaniment of brilliant musical arrangements. Founded in 1985, the event draws around 3 million spectators annually. The culmination of the festival—the largest of its kind in the world—is the awarding of the gold Jupiter, the festival's top prize

and the highest achievement in the pyrotechnics industry.

In late August and early September, the World Film Festival brings together more than 400 international films. Founded in 1977, the designation as a "world" festival is taken seriously, with entries from more than 80 countries and a growing number of them world premieres.

The Just for Laughs Festival is the world's largest and most prestigious comedy event. Each July, more than 1,700 comedians from 19 countries come to Montreal for the two-week festival, cracking up audiences at over 2,000 shows and performances (many of them are in English).

Other standouts of Montreal's summer lineup include Les FrancoFolies de Montréal, celebrating French music from around the world; and the Festival Nuits d'Afrique, promoting music of the African diaspora with indoor and outdoor concerts that really get the city in party mode.

WHERE: various venues around Montreal. *Visitor info:* Tel 800-230-0001 or 514-844-5400; tourism-montreal.org. **INTERNATIONAL FIREWORKS COMPETITION:** Tel 418-692-3736; lesgrandsfeux.com. *When:* mid-June–July, usually on Sat evenings. **WORLD FILM FESTIVAL:** Tel 514-848-3883; ffm-montreal.org. *When:* 12 days in late Aug–early Sept. **JUST FOR LAUGHS FESTIVAL:** Tel 888-244-3155 or 514-845-3155; hahaha.com. *When:* 2 weeks in mid-July. **LES FRANCOFOLIES DE MONTREAL:** Tel 855-372-6267 or 514-876-8989; francofolies.com.

The pyrotechnics of the Montreal International Fireworks Competition are considered the best in the world.

When: 10 days in mid-June. **FESTIVAL NUITS D'AFRIQUE:** Tel 514-499-9239; festivalnuits dafrique.com. *When:* 13 days in mid-July.

Dining Par Excellence in Montreal

TOQUÉ!

Montreal, Quebec

Since 1993, chef Normand Laprise has presided over the kitchen at Toqué!, almost unanimously acclaimed as Montreal's top contemporary French restaurant. Then, in 2004, Toqué! up and moved from its original spot into

a new location between downtown and its former venue in Vieux-Montréal. The new, coolly chic dining room is much quieter and less crowded than the previous, but the cuisine remains as excellent as ever.

With the philosophy of showcasing Quebec products and using only the freshest regional and seasonal foods to best reveal their natural textures and tastes, Laprise was on the cutting edge when he first opened Toqué! The menu is constantly changing, reflecting the long-standing relationships Laprise has built with local farmers, artisanal cheese makers, fruit growers, and fishermen who provide him with the freshest and rarest raw materials. A seasonal menu

may include Nova Scotia princess scallops with olive oil, yellow pepper juice, and strawberry mousse. Laprise also offers a special tasting menu, seven courses designed to be eaten as a series of taste and textural discoveries. Even with food this special, the service is friendly and unpretentious. It's little wonder that Laprise has been credited with single-handedly raising the standard of food in Montreal, and then taking it a little further.

WHERE: 900, Place Jean-Paul-Riopelle. Tel 514-499-2084; restaurant-toque.com. *Cost:* dinner US$68/C$90; 7-course tasting menu US$92/C$122. *When:* lunch Tues–Fri, dinner Tues–Sat.

VIEUX-MONTRÉAL

Montreal, Quebec

Montreal got its start in 1642, when a group of French missionaries led by Paul de Chomedey arrived by river and set up camp, intent on converting the local Iroquois to Christianity. By 1759, after the British defeated the French for the rule of Canada, Montreal was centered along a narrow stretch of headland above the busy port on the St. Lawrence River. Today, this is Montreal's old city center, better known as Vieux-Montréal or Old Montreal, and despite over 250 years of British rule and the influence of *anglais*-speaking Canada and the United States all around, it remains a bastion of French diaspora culture—in its architecture, its cuisine, and its palpable joie de vivre.

For much of the 20th century, the historic buildings and cobblestone streets of Vieux-Montréal slumbered in disrepair. Today, after being rediscovered and renovated as a hot spot of nightlife, café culture, and tourism, Vieux-Montréal preserves its 18th- and 19th-century atmosphere so well that it's commonly used by American and Canadian film crews as a stand-in location for Europe.

Place Jacques-Cartier is the epicenter of Montreal's summer life, with its street performers, cafés, flower merchants, and a line of horse-drawn calèches offering carriage rides back in time. Place d'Armes is another popular gathering spot, with views onto some of the city's most beautiful and historic sites, including the 1824 Basilica of Notre Dame, with its stunningly rich interior, and the adjacent Sulpician Seminary, Montreal's oldest building, dating to 1685. Rue St-Paul is Montreal's oldest, a winding street lined by gaslights and early 19th-century storefronts, many now housing art galleries and boutiques. Along the riverfront, the Vieux Port has been transformed from a gritty warehouse district into a

Exposed limestone and brick buildings line the streets of Vieux-Montréal, one of the oldest urban neighborhoods in North America.

promenade full of parks, exhibition spaces, skating rinks, and playgrounds.

A Montreal splash of opulence can be had at the Hotel Le St-James, an 1870 former merchant's bank of exceptional architecture reincarnated as a very posh gentlemen's-club–like boutique hotel. For a fraction of the price, check in at the always popular Hotel Épik, a former fur warehouse built in 1723, now converted into a delightful B&B whose ten rooms—with their stone walls, beamed ceilings, polished wood floors, and traditional Quebecois furniture—are veritable time machines, but with all the modern comforts.

For a quick bite, head north of the Old Quarter and join *tout Montréal* at L'Express, one of the most popular spots in town for authentic French bistro fare and atmosphere.

WHERE: bounded on the north by Rue St-Antoine, on the south by the St. Lawrence River, and on the east and west by Rue Berri and Rue McGill; vieux.montreal.qc.ca. **HOTEL**

LE ST-JAMES: Tel 866-841-3111 or 514-841-3111; hotellestjames.com. *Cost:* from US$320/C$425. **HOTEL ÉPIK:** Tel 514-842-2634; epikmontreal.com. *Cost:* from US$105/C$140 (off-peak), from US$135/C$180 (peak).

L'EXPRESS: Tel 514-845-5333. *Cost:* dinner US$30/C$40. **BEST TIMES:** Feb–Mar for the High Lights Winter Festival (montrealhighlights.com); mid-June–early Sept for summer festivals (see p. 1016); June–Sept for weather.

Lake Life, à la Québec

LAKE MASSAWIPPI

North Hatley, Quebec

The beautiful Lake Massawippi, a narrow, 10-mile-long glacier-dug lake flanked by dense hardwood forests, is nestled among the hills of Quebec's Eastern Townships (see p. 1012) and the border of New England. At the turn of the 20th century, the lake was a favorite vacation destination for wealthy families seeking a break from summer ennui, providing the kind of swimming, boating, and fishing holidays that induce sepia-toned memories of the Good Old Days. The beauty of its autumn colors was no less irresistible. Today, Lake Massawippi (an Abenaki name meaning "deep waters") is still an idyllic place, seemingly far from the stress of modern life, with friendly small lakeside resorts, gallery-filled villages, fine golf courses, and excellent restaurants, all exuding an inimitable mix of Quebecois charm and New England culture.

At the north tip of Lake Massawippi is North Hatley, a charming village built in the New England style, with tree-lined streets, white picket fences, and brightly painted clapboard homes. When train lines linked North Hatley to the cities of the U.S. East Coast in the 1880s, America's captains of industry built grand lakefront estates here as summer retreats. Today many of these imposing homes have been converted to small boutique hotels and country inns.

Built in 1899, Manoir Hovey is reminiscent of George Washington's Mount Vernon, with a broad, white-columned veranda. It sits amid 25 hillside acres and features English-style gardens sloping down to two small lake beaches.

The inn's 37 guest rooms (many with fireplaces and balconies) are sumptuously furnished in a style that blends discreet luxury with rustic coziness. The wood-beamed carriage house is now a comfortable country pub pouring local ales and ciders. Diners can enjoy award-winning Quebecois fine dining and the acclaimed wine cellar on the garden terrace or beside the inn's fireplace.

At the southern end of Massawippi, in the town of Ayer's Cliff, Ripplecove Hotel & Spa sits directly on the lake, a testament to its beginnings as a 1940s fishing resort. In its modern incarnation, Ripplecove is the most hotel-like of the Massawippi inns, focusing in summer on golf, water sports, tennis, hiking, and horseback riding, and in winter on alpine and cross-country skiing. The 31 rooms and

The wooded shores of Lake Massawippi are ablaze with color in autumn.

two cottages are uniformly warm, cozy, and charmingly decorated, about half with fireplaces, balconies, and whirlpools.

WHERE: 100 miles/161 km southeast of Montreal. *Visitor info:* Tel 800-355-5755 or 819-820-2020; easterntownships.org. **MANOIR HOVEY:** Tel 800-661-2421 or 819-842-2421; manoirhovey.com. *Cost:* from US$113/C$150

(off-peak), from US$188/C$250 (peak). **RIPPLECOVE HOTEL & SPA:** Ayer's Cliff. Tel 800-668-4296 or 819-838-4296; ripplecove .com. *Cost:* from US$140/C$186 (off-peak), from US$202/C$268 (peak). **BEST TIMES:** June–Sept for fishing and boating; July for North Hatley Antique Show; 1st week in Oct for foliage.

Celebrating Winter's Chill

CARNAVAL DE QUÉBEC

Quebec City, Quebec

In winter's midst—partly in defiance, partly in celebration—Quebec City springs to life during the Quebec Winter Carnival (Carnaval de Québec), with over two weeks of music, parades, winter sports, and high spirits serving as

Quebec City's Mardi Gras. The world's largest winter carnival—the event attracts more than a million festivalgoers—owes some of its feistiness to a traditional beverage called the Caribou, a mixture of brandy, vodka, sherry, and port, though there are plenty of events that cater to the whole family.

Presiding over the carnival is Bonhomme, a snowmanlike creature who serves as festival mascot, master of ceremonies, and mythical resident of the Ice Palace, an enormous castle built entirely of snow and ice near the Quebec Parliament building. A high point of the

Teams from around the world give life to blocks of snow at the International Snow Sculpture event.

carnival is the snow sculpture competition at Place Loto-Québec, while from the ramparts of Dufferin Terrace, adults and children whiz down icy chutes on toboggans. The narrow streets of Vieux-Québec ring with the musher's cries as La Grande Virée dogsledding competition circles the city, and after downing a few fortifying Caribous, hardy Quebecois engage in the annual Snow Bath by stripping down to their Speedos in front of a raucous outdoor crowd and diving into a snowdrift. Even more daring is the annual canoe race in which paddlers race across the ice-choked St. Lawrence River.

While all Vieux-Québec hotels put on a festive air, there's no more appropriate place to make reservations than the Hôtel de Glace, a 32,000-square-foot hotel constructed each winter of ice and snow. (It is the only Ice Hotel in North America, created annually since 2001.) Located on the outskirts of Quebec City, the hotel offers 44 guest rooms and suites, and includes a wedding chapel, a Nordic-style spa with hot tubs and sauna, plus a bar and nightclub—all fashioned anew each year from 12,000 tons of snow and 400 tons of ice. Admittedly, it's not an overnight choice for everyone, but at least make time to visit for a tour, and perhaps have something cool to drink—in an ice glass, of course—at the Ice Bar.

QUEBEC WINTER CARNIVAL: Tel 866-422- 7628 or 418-626-3716; carnaval.qc.ca. *When:* late Jan–early Feb. **HÔTEL DE GLACE:** Quebec City. Tel 877-505-0423 or 418-623-2888; hoteldeglace.com. *Cost:* from US$120/C$159 per person, double occupancy. *When:* early Jan–late Mar.

Old France in the New World

VIEUX-QUÉBEC

Quebec City, Quebec

Once capital of New France and a fur-trading empire that stretched west to the Rocky Mountains, Quebec City is one of the oldest European settlements in North America, and the continent's only walled city north of Mexico. Perched on Cap Diamant, a rocky promontory above the St. Lawrence River, Quebec City was established in 1608 by French explorer Samuel de Champlain. The walls of Vieux-Québec (Old Quebec) didn't stop the British troops of General James Wolfe, who took the city after a two-month siege in 1759, ending France's colonial aspirations in eastern North America.

Quebec City reflects its French birthright in thousands of ways, both obvious and subtle: cobbled streets with outdoor cafés, slate-roofed stone houses, patisseries, and an attitude toward life that's at once studied and playful. Vieux-Québec is divided into the Haute-Ville and Basse-Ville (upper and lower towns), designations that are now simply geographic but were once economic and strategic. Haute-Ville is the fortified city that occupies the crest of Cap Diamant. At the base of Cap Diamant, on the banks of the St. Lawrence, was Basse-Ville, lined with warehouses and other necessities of the river trade.

Filled with old-world atmosphere, Haute-Ville is best explored on foot. Winding, hilly streets lined by vintage stone houses and chic boutiques give onto leafy public squares, with glimpses of the St. Lawrence in the distance.

Housed in a 1677 home, the well known restaurant Aux Anciens Canadiens is a wise bet for classic Quebecois preparations in a highly

Situated on Cap Diamant, the historic Fairmont Le Château Frontenac has some of the best views in town.

atmospheric setting. The Citadel occupies the highest crag of Cap Diamant, a still-militarized fortification constructed by the English against U.S. invasion during the War of 1812. From the Terrasse Dufferin view-point, take the Escallier Casse-Cou (the aptly named Breakneck Stairs) or the funicular to Basse-Ville, the old port district. The center of life in Basse-Ville is Place Royale, the city's public market area since the 17th century.

Without a doubt the best place to spend the night is the Fairmont Le Château Frontenac, fresh from a massive 2014 renovation. Designed in the style of a Loire Valley château and looking as if it has stood here forever, it was built in 1893 by the Canadian Pacific Railway on the highest point in town. Outside, it's all stone-and-brick turrets, green copper roofs, and dormered windows, while inside its labyrinthine corridors lead through various wings—with 611 guest rooms and suites in all—built over a hundred-year span with total stylistic consistency. Book an odd-numbered room in the main tower for a view of the St. Lawrence River, or an even-numbered room for a panorama of the city's rooftops—probably the most European vista this side of Paris.

VISITOR INFO: Tel 877-266-5687 or 514-873-2015; bonjourquebec.com. **AUX ANCIENS CANADIENS:** Tel 418-692-1627, auxanciens canadiens.gc.ca. *Cost:* dinner US$52/C$70. **FAIRMONT LE CHÂTEAU FRONTENAC:** Tel 866-540-4460 or 418-692-3861; fairmont.com/frontenac. *Cost:* from US$150/C$199 (off-peak), from US$223/C$299 (peak). **BEST TIMES:** late Jan–early Feb for Carnaval de Québec (see p. 1020); 11 days in mid-July for the Festival d'été de Quebec; July–Sept for best weather.

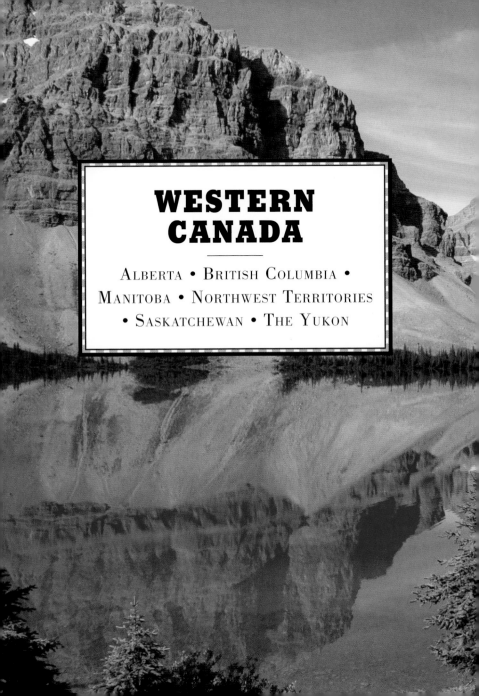

WESTERN CANADA

Alberta • British Columbia •
Manitoba • Northwest Territories
• Saskatchewan • The Yukon

The Canadian Rockies' Top Destination

BANFF NATIONAL PARK

Alberta

Summon a mental image of the Canadian Rockies: towering, glacier-clad peaks; turquoise blue lakes; grand, castellated hotels; and ambling moose, bear, and mountain sheep. The vision's reality is Banff National Park,

the very archetype of Canadian wilderness, and one of several federal and provincial parks that form the Rocky Mountain Parks World Heritage Site, one of the largest protected areas in the world. Banff was Canada's very first national park, incorporated as a tiny 10-square-mile parcel in 1885 and now grown into a 2,564-square-mile giant that's one of the top tourist destinations in Canada. Banff's most famed beauty spot, jaw-droppingly dramatic Lake Louise (see next page) is just one of many stunning sights and recreational destinations in this beloved park.

In fact, Moraine Lake, 8 miles south of Lake Louise, is considered by many to be the most beautiful of all. Certainly it's a much less crowded, less commercialized experience than Lake Louise; you might even find yourself alone on the hiking trail that skirts the sapphire lake's north shore beneath soaring 10,000-foot peaks.

No visitor should bypass the Icefields Parkway (see p. 1027), one of the world's most spectacular mountain roads, linking Lake Louise and Jasper Townsite, 142 miles to the north. The park also offers more than 80 maintained hiking trails, including a trail up Johnston Canyon that passes between 100-foot cliffs and climbs through the mists of seven waterfalls on its way to a series of emerald pools known as the Inkpots. In winter, Banff is renowned for skiing, with three ski areas within half an hour of Banff Townsite, and Nakiska Resort—site of the downhill ski events for the 1988 Winter Olympics—just outside the park near Kananaskis.

Ringed by massive mountain blocks carved into craggy, finlike peaks, few towns in the world can boast a more primordial and stunning setting than Banff Townsite. Banff is both cosmopolitan and stylish—surprising, considering its wilderness location. Exclusive shops along Banff's bustling streets vie for the attention of international shoppers, while excellent restaurants address the needs of hungry hikers and consumers alike.

The Fairmont Banff Springs Hotel stands in princely splendor along the Bow River, a testament to the expansive vision of the Canadian Pacific Railroad. This amazing structure—built in 1888 to resemble a fortified Scottish castle—is one of Canada's most famous hotels, with remarkable views, beautifully furnished rooms, and indulgent service (a staff of 1,200 will fulfill your every wish). Its Stanley Thompson golf course is one of Canada's best, and the luxurious Willow Stream Spa is regularly ranked as Canada's top spa.

Dramatic mountain peaks are reflected in the still water of Moraine Lake at sunrise.

Where: 80 miles/129 km west of Calgary. Tel 403-762-1550; pc.gc.ca/banff. **Ski Banff Lake Louise Sunshine:** Tel 855-335-8837 or 403-762-4561; skibig3.com. *Cost:* lift tickets from US$79/C$105. *When:* ski season late Dec–early Apr. **Nakiska Resort:** Tel 800-258-7669 or 403-591-7777; skinakiska.com. *Cost:* lift tickets from US$58/C$77. **Fairmont Banff Springs Hotel:** Tel 866-540-4406 or 403-762-2211; fairmont.com/banffsprings. *Cost:* from US$300/C$399 (off-peak), from US$443/C$589 (peak). **Best times:** Jan–Mar for best skiing; late Jan–early Feb for Winterfest; mid-July–mid-Aug for the Banff Summer Arts Festival (banffcentre.ca); Sept–Oct for foliage; late Oct–early Nov for the Banff Mountain Film and Book Festival (banffcentre.ca).

A Jade Green Lake and a Fairy-Tale Castle

Lake Louise

Banff National Park, Alberta

Their fame and gorgeousness are inextricable—Lake Louise, a jade green lake surrounded by towering, glacier-hung peaks, and the Fairmont Château Lake Louise, the legendary luxury-hotel-cum-storybook-castle that sits by its side, keeping a watchful eye on this scene of primordial beauty. The lake and the hotel are equally stunning, and in their juxtaposition of wilderness and sophistication, they come close to epitomizing Canada itself. Located within Banff National Park (see previous page), renowned for its untouchable beauty, they are its exclamation point.

The lake sits at the base of the Continental Divide, in a basin trenched by Ice Age glaciers. A vestige of that ancient frozen bulldozer remains as Victoria Glacier, hanging

Lake Louise, created by ancient glaciers, is gloriously beautiful year-round.

just above the lake's western shore. From here, glacial stream water tumbles into the lake, carrying with it finely ground minerals, which refract in sunlight to create the lake's brilliant and almost eerie blue-green hue.

One of Canada's most beloved hotels and possibly the greatest of the Rocky Mountain hotels, the Fairmont Château Lake Louise stands like a palace on the edge of the lake, its Edwardian profile punctuated by turrets rising into the crisp mountain air. The vast, high-ceilinged lobby is filled with carved chandeliers, liveried attendants, and a cosmopolitan crowd of travelers from around the world. With more than 550 handsomely furnished rooms, Château Lake Louise doesn't pretend to be a cozy lakeside cottage: It's a vibrant and happily contained community, replete with seven restaurants and dining areas (head to The Fairview Room for formal dining or to the Walliser Stube Wine Bar for the best cheese fondue in the Rockies).

In winter the hotel is more tranquil, as horse-drawn sleighs deliver guests up to the hotel steps, and ice-skating parties gather on the lake. The extravagantly photogenic Lake Louise Ski Area—with the deserved reputation as the most scenic ski resort in North America—offers a mix of novice, intermediate, and advanced terrain and a range of activities for the whole family, from dogsledding to ice-skating and torchlight ski parades at dusk.

Where: 35 miles/56 km northwest of Banff Township. **Fairmont Château Lake Louise:** Tel 800-441-1414 or 403-522-3511; fairmont.com/lakelouise. *Cost:* from US$240/C$319 (off-peak), from US$472/C$669 (peak). **Ski Lake Louise:** Tel 877-956-8473 or 403-522-3555; skilouise.com. *Cost:* lift tickets US$69/C$92. *When:* Dec–Apr. **Best times:** Jan–Mar for skiing; late Jan for the International Ice Carving Competition; July–Sept for nice summer weather but largest crowds.

A Truly Spectacular Mountain Road

The Icefields Parkway

Banff and Jasper National Parks, Alberta

The two unofficial capitals of the Canadian Rockies, the towns of Banff and Jasper, bookend the Icefields Parkway, one of the world's most scenic roadways. This broad, well-maintained highway links together one extravagantly beautiful vista after another—craggy peaks topped with glaciers, massive waterfalls, turquoise green lakes flanked by deep spruce and fir forests. Though most visitors to Banff and Jasper National Parks (see pp. 1025 and 1034) drive the 142-mile Icefields Parkway, veteran cyclists can experience this dramatic top-of-the-world landscape on two wheels. Considering that this is a mountain highway, the gradients are mostly gentle, and in-shape cyclists should encounter no problems as they pedal this once-in-a-lifetime route.

Though it's possible to plan your own tour between Banff and Jasper, signing on with a local cycling outfitter offers lots of advantages. Longtime operators Canusa Cycle Tours offers six-day tour packages that include guides, a support vehicle and trailer, and all meals and accommodations en route. Average mileage is a gentle 30 miles per day, a leisurely pace that allows plenty of time to stop for photographs, explore the landscape, and watch for wildlife, such as elk, mountain sheep, and bears, commonly seen along the parkway. Best of all, your gear is transported ahead to the next

The parkway, one of Canada's most scenic, was completed in 1940 and is primarily a two-lane highway.

overnight stop, so all you need to carry with you is a jacket, water bottle, and camera.

Leaving Banff, the tour explores back roads up to Lake Louise, then continues through deep forests up to glittering Bow Lake, below Crowfoot and Bow Glaciers, and then over Bow Summit. Descending into the drainage of the Mistaya and North Saskatchewan Rivers, the parkway passes more eerily green lakes (the color is the result of glacier-ground minerals suspended in the water) and alpine landscapes before beginning the route's one big climb, up to 6,676-foot Sunwapta

Pass. Here, at the very crest of the continent, the icy tendrils of the Columbia Icefield come into view. Covering more than 200 square miles, the Columbia Icefield—the largest nonpolar ice cap in the world—is the source of rivers flowing to the Pacific, Arctic, and Atlantic oceans. Cyclists here can trade steeds to explore the face of a glacier that measures 2,500 feet thick; massive all-terrain Ice Explorers with special balloon tires travel onto the ice fields, a frozen world of centuries-old ice cleft with deep crevasses. From Sunwapta Pass, cyclists can relax—it's all down-hill along the Sunwapta and Athabasca Rivers to Jasper, past two spectacular waterfalls and wildlife-rich meadowlands. After a night in Jasper, exhilarated cyclists hop a ride in the sup-port van as it retraces the route back to Banff.

WHERE: between Banff and Jasper National Parks. *Visitor info:* icefieldsparkway .ca. *When:* open year-round but all services closed Oct–May. **CANUSA CYCLE TOURING:** Tel 403-993-0063; canusacycle.ca. *Cost:* 6-day fully supported tour from US$1,240/C$1,650. *When:* July–early Sept. **BREWSTER ICE EXPLORERS:** Tel 866-606-6700 or 403-762-6700; brewster.ca. *Cost:* US$41/C$55. *When:* mid-Apr–mid-Oct. **BEST TIME:** Aug–Sept for best chances of dry and sunny weather.

The Wild West, Canada-Style

CALGARY STAMPEDE

Calgary, Alberta

Calgary gets wild during its world-famous stampede, with lots of whooping, hollering, good-natured yellin', beer drinking, and Wild West cavorting. Rodeos have been a part of Calgary summers since 1886, a few short years after the city was founded as a western outpost for the Royal Canadian Mounted Police.

The Calgary Stampede is now the world's largest, richest, and most prestigious rodeo, with more than 400 of the world's elite rodeo contestants entered in six major events, competing for a total prize topping C$2 million. For ten days in July, more than 1.3 million visitors attend Stampede events, which include lots more than traditional rodeo roping and riding. Music performances, parades, a Western art showcase, a carnival and midway, and native powwow dance competitions are a few of the back-to-back spectacles that take over the city.

But the heart of the Stampede is the rodeo. North America's top cowboys and cowgirls gather in Calgary for competition in bareback, saddle bronc, and bull riding; tie-down rop-ing; steer wrestling; and barrel racing, all woven through with traditional rodeo clown acts and music. One of the Stampede's most unique competitions is the Chuckwagon Race (aka the GMC Rangeland Derby), in which old-time Western cook wagons—not exactly built for speed or grace—contend for the fast-est time around the track in a fury of dust and pounding hooves.

With prize money totaling US$20,000, the first Calgary Stampede in 1912 was the richest rodeo competition in North America and remains so today.

To keep in the spirit of the city's historic tradition, make your hotel reservations at the Fairmont Palliser, built in 1914, just two years after the first official Stampede was held. You'll feel like one of the cattle barons who hung his hat at this oasis of genteel civility, with a classic columns-and-marble lobby, luxurious guest rooms, and a palpable sense of period grandeur. Be sure to enjoy the selection of Alberta beef in the Rimrock Restaurant, with its authentic Canadiana decor, right down to the hand-tooled leather wall panels.

WHERE: Stampede Park. Tel 800-661-1767 or 403-269-9822; calgarystampede .com. *Cost:* rodeo tickets from US$30/C$40; chuckwagon races and evening show tickets from US$42/C$56. *When:* 10 days in mid-July. **FAIRMONT PALLISER:** Tel 800-441-1414 or 403-262-1234; fairmont.com/palliser. *Cost:* from US$202/C$269; dinner at Rimrock Restaurant US$44/C$55.

Riding Canada's Steel Spine

THE CANADIAN ROCKIES BY TRAIN

Alberta

A rail trip through the Canadian Rockies figures on every train enthusiast's short list of once-in-a-lifetime experiences, providing some of the most awe-inspiring scenery imaginable. Traveling by train through the Rockies is easy on your eyes, but also easy on your nerves—free of the frustrating RV traffic that frequently clogs park roadways in the summer months. Instead, enjoy long stretches of exquisite wilderness that seem almost completely unpopulated—Alberta, a Texas-size province, has the population of Philadelphia.

When the railroad builders first crossed Canada in 1886 ("an act of insane recklessness," the papers wrote), they did more than just bring in settlers: They also opened up western Canada to tourism by creating lavish hotels in the wilderness and romanticizing the Rockies. "If we can't export the scenery," declared William Cornelius Van Horne, the first president of the Canadian Pacific Railroad, "we'll import the tourists."

More than a century later, the Canadian Rockies are still one of Canada's top tourism draws, and there are several great rail options for exploring this massive and inspiring country. VIA Rail, Canada's national passenger rail network, offers a year-round northerly passage through the Canadian Rockies as part of *The Canadian*'s three-day, 2,769-mile trip between Toronto and Vancouver. It passes through Jasper National Park (see p. 1034), over the Continental Divide, and by the Canadian Rockies' highest peak, Mount Robson, which juts up to 12,972 feet. An excellent option is to change trains at Jasper to *The Skeena*, which travels west to Prince Rupert and the Pacific Coast ferries along the Inside Passage. In winter, VIA Rail's Snow Train packages offer passengers special transportation in vintage stainless steel railcars, accommodations, and ski packages to Jasper from all points along *The Canadian*'s route.

The seasonal *Rocky Mountaineer*, the largest privately owned passenger rail service in North America, is deservedly popular for its two-day (and longer) train journeys to or from Vancouver and Jasper, Banff, or Calgary. All travel is during daylight hours, so you won't miss a single scenic wonder. You'll also spend the night in comfortable hotels in Kamloops, not in a jostling railcar. Glass-domed observation cars provide horizon-to-horizon views of ancient glaciers, snowcapped peaks, roaring waterfalls, and tranquil mountain lakes. The *Rocky Mountaineer* also offers service between Whistler (see p. 1062) and Jasper via Prince George, as well as between Vancouver and Whistler from its classy Vancouver station and to or from Seattle and Vancouver. All these lines open up various options for loop rail journeys during warm-weather months in the Rockies and the Northwest.

VIA RAIL: Tel 888-842-7245 or 514-871-6000; viarail.ca. *Cost:* 3-day Toronto–Vancouver sleeper berths from US$987/C$1,313 (off-peak), from US$1,315/C$1,750 (peak) per person, double occupancy. *When:* year-round; Snow Train packages Nov–Apr. *ROCKY MOUNTAINEER VACATIONS:* Tel 877-460-3200 or

Witness the beauty of Canada on a train ride through the rugged Canadian Rockies.

604-606-7245; rockymountaineer.com. *Cost:* all-inclusive 2-day tour from US$1,265/C$1,682 per person, double occupancy. *When:* mid-Apr–mid-Oct and select departures in Dec. **BEST TIMES:** Jan–Mar for skiing; Sept and Oct for weather and smaller crowds.

Fascinating Repository of Prehistoric Life

ROYAL TYRRELL MUSEUM

Drumheller, Alberta

The Royal Tyrrell Museum, with one of the the world's most extensive collections of dinosaur fossils and exhibits on prehistoric life, stands amid eastern Alberta's Red Deer River badlands, a haunting landscape of

dun-colored buttes and prairies that were once at the swampy, prehistoric crossroads of Cretaceous Era life. Some 65 to 70 million years ago, eastern Alberta lay at the verge of vast inland seas where countless creatures swam the shallow waters or stalked the coastal plains and marshes, following life's eat-and-be-eaten cycle. Over millions of years, plant and animal remains were deposited in sediments and preserved as coal and fossils. Fast-forward several millennia, when 19th-century geologists began to explore Alberta's prairies for coal deposits. They found much more than just coal: They also discovered some of the world's best dinosaur fossil beds.

The modern, high-tech Royal Tyrrell Museum is far more than a dusty collection of skeletons. It brings dinosaurs back to life through innovative exhibits and hands-on displays that will fascinate anyone interested in natural history. The museum's main gallery, a vast 47,000-square-foot showcase, displays dozens of reassembled dinosaurs, some emerging from the rock in which they were found, many others posed in lifelike dioramas depicting the natural environment of their time along with marine and flying reptiles. Interspersed with the fossils are computerized exhibits that explain natural selection, climate change, and extinction—the entire story of life on earth is retold in the museum. You can also watch technicians at work in a laboratory preparing fossils and visit the Cretaceous Garden, featuring 600 species of living plants similar to those that existed in the Red Deer valley 72 million years ago.

The North Dinosaur Trail, an hour's loop drive that radiates from Drumheller, lets you explore Alberta's badlands by car. Or for real hands-on involvement, the museum also offers many outdoor field programs exploring the fossil-rich landscape, including guided hikes, participation in digs, fossil casting, and summer day camps that let kids—and the parents who happily tag along—be paleontologists for the day or week.

Where: 90 miles/145 km northeast of Calgary. Tel 403-823-7707; tyrrellmuseum.com.

Where to stay: Jurassic Inn, tel 888-823-3466 or 403-823-7700; canaltahotels.com. *Cost:* from US$124/C$165. **Best time:** May–Sept for outdoor field programs.

Royal Tyrrell Museum's Dinosaur Hall features nearly 40 mounted dinosaur skeletons.

Offbeat Theater and Performance on the Prairies

EDMONTON INTERNATIONAL FRINGE THEATRE FESTIVAL

Edmonton, Alberta

Every August, Edmonton gets turned on its ear when it hosts North America's largest fringe theater festival, one of the most colorful and entertaining happenings anywhere. The Edmonton International Fringe Theatre Festival takes over Old Strathcona, a historic Edmonton neighborhood near the University of Alberta, and offers a dizzying selection of theatrics and performance amid a nonstop street party atmosphere. Originating in 1982, the festival has continued to grow larger and more popular, attracting theater companies and performing artists from around the world who play to an audience of more than 600,000. Only Edinburgh's Fringe Festival in Scotland is bigger.

Old Strathcona is Edmonton's hippest area, where students, artists, and alternative-lifestyle types come to hang out, but the Fringe Festival transforms even this bastion of youthful energy. The festival has 40 different venues, indoors and out, offering more than 1,600 individual performances during the 11-day run. It's nonstop theater: On any given day, there are over 100 performances, and when one show ends, another begins on the same stage. Projects that the festival can't accommodate are encouraged to BYOV—Bring Your Own Venue—that is, create their own theater spaces (and any street corner will do). In addition to the hubbub of actors and theater, the Fringe Festival also hosts food and crafts booths, beer tents, and innumerable buskers and street performers.

Not every production is life-changing, but hunting out the gems is part of the fun. Performances include drama, comedy, musicals, puppetry, fire artistry, poetry—you'll find everything from an audience-participation *Macbeth* to a one-man *Lord of the Rings* to a musical version of *Reefer Madness*. **FRINGE FESTIVAL:** Tel 780-448-9000; fringetheatre.ca. *Cost:* tickets from US$10/ C$13 (although many performances are free). *When:* 11 days in mid-Aug. **WHERE TO STAY:** Fairmont Hotel Macdonald, tel 800-441-1414 or 780-424-5181; fairmont.com/macdonald. *Cost:* from US$217/C$289 (off-peak), from US$269/C$349 (peak).

Go Western on a 19th-Century Homestead

BREWSTER'S KANANASKIS GUEST RANCH

Exshaw, Alberta

I f your mind wanders to more southern locales like Wyoming or Montana when the word "guest ranch" comes up in conversation, think again—and think Alberta. This sweeping expanse of land, every bit as gorgeous as its neighboring Rockies just west of here, has been ranch country for well over a century. Of the numerous dude ranches offering Old West hospitality and lifestyle, Brewster's Kananaskis Guest Ranch is one of the oldest and best.

There's a long, rich history between the Brewster family and nearby Banff National Park (see p. 1025). After the Banff Springs Hotel was established in 1888, the Brewsters provided milk from their farm homestead just outside park boundaries to hotel guests. They were the first to lead guided pack trips into the park's backcountry, and as Banff grew in popularity in the early 20th century, so did the family's involvement.

In 1923, the family transformed their original 1880s farm into a guest ranch, offering cowboy wannabes horseback vacations in the surrounding wilderness. After six generations, the Brewster family is still running the picture-perfect 2,000-acre guest ranch where the Bow River exits the Rockies through a steep decline.

With this stunning setting, you'll want to get outdoors and go Western. Visitors are offered a variety of horseback rides along the river, plus multiday pack trips to backcountry cabins. In addition to horseback adventures, the guest ranch offers its own 18-hole golf course, river rafting, and canoe trips, plus access to myriad possibilities for hikers and anglers. There's not much that can't be arranged, and with a smile. For groups hankering for some Western entertainment, the Brewsters offer rodeos, western barbecues, live country music, and that traditional cowboy favorite—sitting around the campfire. If you think that sounds a little bit hokey, just look at the faces of the three-generation families who come back here year after year.

The Brewsters no longer offer overnight lodging or scheduled meals at the Ranch, but modern western-style accommodations are offered at the supremely comfortable Brewster Mountain Lodge half an hour west in Banff.

WHERE: 32 miles/52 km east of Banff. Tel 800-691-5085 or 403-673-3737; kananaskis guestranch.com. *Cost:* horseback rides from US$60/C$80; greens fees US$40/$C59. *When:* June–Sept. **BREWSTER MOUNTAIN LODGE:** Tel 888-762-2900 or 403-760-7505; brewster mountainlodge.com. *Cost:* from US$120/C$159 (off-peak), from US$184/$C245 (peak). **BEST TIME:** last weekend in July for the Canmore Folk Music Festival (canmorefolkfestival.com).

A Tribute to Plains Indian Culture

HEAD-SMASHED-IN BUFFALO JUMP INTERPRETIVE CENTRE

Fort MacLeod, Alberta

For over 5,500 years, Plains Indians gathered to hunt American bison, commonly referred to as buffalo, at a windswept site in southern Alberta. Because their lifestyle was so dependent on hunting buffalo, they developed numerous techniques. The most sophisticated method was the buffalo jump, in which thunderous herds of buffalo were stampeded off cliffs and then butchered for their meat, hides, and horns. Here, where the foothills of the Rocky Mountains meet the prairies, natural conditions and geologic features combined to create a perfect buffalo jump—and the interpretive center and museum you'll find here today is an invaluable window to the culture and ways of the Plains Indians.

A Blackfoot tepee on display at the Centre

Head-Smashed-In Buffalo Jump Interpretive Centre is one of the oldest and best-preserved jumps in the world, designated a World Heritage Site by UNESCO in 1981. It is just one part of an extensive communal hunting complex that included Native encampments and meat-processing areas plus a network of sophisticated drive lanes used to direct the herds toward the cliffs.

For the First People of the Great Plains, the bison was the staff of life. The hide provided tepee coverings and leather for moccasins; the flesh was eaten fresh in season and preserved for later consumption. The bones were used to create a number of tools, and dried manure was used in campfires. Even the dried tail was used, as a flyswatter.

The five-level Head-Smashed-In Buffalo Jump Interpretive Centre is built into the slope bordering the jump's sandstone cliff. Trails lead to the top, with staggering views across the prairies and to the Rockies, shimmering in the distance. May through October, on the first Saturday of the month, hike the ancient drive lanes with a Blackfoot guide and hear stories of how the Plains people hunted the mighty buffalo. On Wednesdays in July and August the plaza is filled with the music and dancing of some of the best dancers and drum groups in Blackfoot country.

The center includes exhibits on the natural plains ecosystem and the culture of the Blackfoot, who dominated these prairies until the near-extermination of the buffalo, in the 1880s. More than 600 Blackfoot—a quarter of the tribe's population at the time—died of starvation during the winter of 1884, after the buffalo had been eliminated from the plains. About 15,000 Blackfoot now live in reservations that straddle the border of Montana and Alberta.

WHERE: 104 miles/167 km south of Calgary. Tel 403-553-2731; history.alberta.ca/headsmashedin. **BEST TIMES:** mid-May–mid-Sept for weather; June 21 is National Aboriginal Day with special Blackfoot entertainment, storytelling, and events.

All Adventure, All the Time

JASPER NATIONAL PARK

Alberta

An outdoors lover's dream come true, Jasper National Park has more of a recreational focus than Banff National Park, its magnificent neighbor to the south (see p. 1025). As Canada's largest mountain park, Jasper ropes in more than 4,200 square miles of towering peaks, broad lake-filled valleys, and dense forests of spruce and fir, so there's a lot of room to play, and it's year-round fun. In summer, you'll want to get out and raft some roiling white water, saddle a horse for a trail ride, or canoe a mirror-still mountain-ringed lake. Luckily, a small army of outfitters is here to make your every outdoor dream come true.

Hiking opportunities abound, with trails snaking through narrow Maligne Canyon and beyond, and rafting trips are available on the mighty Athabasca and Sunwapta rivers. Many trails are also open to mountain bikers, making this a popular park for fat-tire adventurers. Angling on Maligne Lake (the largest of the Rockies' glacier-fed lakes) can be heaven, while the Miette Hot Springs offer soaks in outdoor pools, surrounded by forest and mountains. During the snowy months, snowshoeing, ice-skating, and skiing at Ski Marmot Basin are but a few of the temptations. Marmot offers some of the least crowded slope conditions in the Rockies, drawing in-the-know snowboarders and skiers looking for some alone time.

Fortunately, there's nothing rugged about creature comforts in Jasper. The village was born as a railway town, and instead of Banff's upscale shoppers, you'll find outdoors folks who look as if they just spent the afternoon rafting or snowshoeing. The park's most exclusive destination by far is Fairmont Jasper Park Lodge. This venerable resort resembles an idealized summer camp, with lodgings ranging from comfortable all the way to sumptuous in

Athabasca Falls is a must-see 80-foot waterfall 19 miles south of Jasper, and is easily accessed via the Icefields Parkway.

a wide mix of cabins, chalets, and cottages in a woodsy 900-acre lakeside setting. The lodge's Stanley Thompson golf course makes it a perennial choice as Canada's No. 1 golf resort. It offers ten excellent dining rooms and bars; the Moose's Nook Northern Grill is a favorite for inventive Rocky Mountain cuisine featuring local fish, game, and regional specialties in a setting of rustic elegance, accompanied by outstanding wines from the nearby Okanagan Valley (see p. 1042).

WHERE: 178 miles/287 km north of Banff. Tel 780-852-6176; pc.gc.ca/jasper. **SKI MARMOT BASIN:** Tel 780-852-3816; skimarmot.com. *When:* ski season late Nov–early May. *Cost:* lift ticket US$67/C$89. **FAIRMONT JASPER PARK LODGE:** Tel 800-441-1414 or 780-852-3301; fairmont.com/jasper. *Cost:* from US$195/C$259 (off-peak), from US$406/C$540 (peak); greens fees from US$149/C$199 (US$112/C$150 for guests); dinner at Moose's Nook US$56/C$75. **BEST TIMES:** Jan–Mar for snow sports; July–Sept for hiking.

The Park with Million-Dollar Views

WATERTON LAKES NATIONAL PARK

Alberta

Waterton Lakes National Park butts up against the U.S.-Canada border, beyond which spreads Glacier National Park in Montana to the south (see p. 620): Together they form the massive Waterton-Glacier International Peace Park. Waterton is famous for its string of deep lakes shimmering beneath the Continental Divide's jagged peaks, and for its stunning vistas—all the products of Ice Age glaciers. An excellent way to view the park's monumental landscape is on the Waterton Inter-Nation Shoreline Cruise, an excursion boat that leaves from the tiny hamlet of Waterton Park and plies Upper Waterton Lake to Goat Haunt, right over the border in Montana's Glacier National Park. Paddling and kayaking is also a great way to explore the otherwise vertical landscapes. Cameron Lake, at the end of the scenic Akamina Parkway, offers boat rentals and a sheltered spot for canoeing, while the more lively water of Upper Waterton Lake—the deepest lake in the Canadian Rockies—is better for experienced paddlers. Grizzly bears frequent the shores of Cameron Lake (in Glacier National Park), and viewing these magnificent, though sometimes ferocious, creatures from the safety of a boat is smart—and a top park experience.

Waterton was one of Alberta's first tourist destinations—in fact, the golf course here is one of the oldest in the province—and venerable lodges and hotels lend the village the air of a civilized wilderness outpost. The park boasts breathtaking scenery at every turn, but its grandest view belongs to the Prince of Wales Hotel, built on a bluff above the lake in 1926 by the Great Northern Railroad. Take tea in the parlor, but spend the night at the Waterton Lakes Lodge, a contemporary resort complex offering large, comfortable rooms, a woodsy New West decor, and a host of welcome health club facilities.

WHERE: 164 miles/264 km south of Calgary. Tel 403-859-5133; pc.gc.ca/water ton. **WATERTON INTER-NATION SHORELINE CRUISE:** Tel 403-859-2362; watertoncruise .com. *When:* May–mid-Oct. **PRINCE OF WALES HOTEL:** Tel 403-859-2231; glacierparkinc .com. **WATERTON LAKES LODGE:** Tel 888-985-6343 or 403-859-2150; watertonlakes lodge.com. *Cost:* from US$60/C$80 (off-peak), US$120/C$159 (peak). *When:* mid-Apr–mid-Nov. **BEST TIMES:** Jan–Mar for cross-country skiing; July–Sept for hiking.

The Prince of Wales Hotel enjoys one of many extraordinary vistas in Waterton Lakes National Park.

HOLLYHOCK

Cortes Island, British Columbia

To reach Hollyhock—Canada's leading educational retreat center—by car from Vancouver requires three different ferries and takes at least six hours to travel just 100 miles (as the spirit flies). But once you reach

Cortes Island and arrive at this world-famous 48-acre community devoted to progressive thought and action, it doesn't feel remote. Hollyhock has long attracted some of the top intellectuals, writers, artists, and activists from around the world, and is an important locus for people dedicated to issues of the spirit, environment, and social growth. Located above a sandy beach amid dense fir and cedar forests, Hollyhock is a marvelous place to find inspiration and to enjoy nature's beauty.

Hollyhock had its beginnings in the late 1960s, when the retreat offered Gestalt therapy. A group of friends and fellow thinkers bought the property in the 1980s and expanded its offerings to include an ever-widening array of programs and workshops. Today, visitors come to Hollyhock for retreats on subjects as varied as memoir writing, holistic healing for pets, Metta Vipassana meditation, studies in

chant and shamanic ritual, and programs on ecology activism. However, Hollyhock also offers family vacations focused on use of the facilities (hot tubs, beach swimming, hiking, and morning yoga and stretching), plus gourmet organic meals and the option to join in classes, guided kayak trips, or bodywork sessions. For many return visitors, the other guests are a prime draw, and a regular community of familiar faces returns annually, whether to teach or attend programs, or for some simple R&R of the body and soul.

WHERE: 100 miles/161 km north of Vancouver. Tel 800-933-6339 or 250-935-6576; hollyhock.ca. *Cost:* from US$147/C$196 per person, double occupancy, includes all meals; workshops, programs, kayaking extra. *When:* Mar–Nov; programs and workshops from May–mid-Oct. **BEST TIMES:** July–Sept for weather; late July for Cortes Island Music Festival.

Powder Snow Capital of Canada

KICKING HORSE MOUNTAIN RESORT

Golden, British Columbia

Want to get a little high for dinner? And tread where only mountain goats dare to dine? Eagle's Eye Restaurant is Canada's highest-elevation restaurant—a soaring glass and timber lodge at the very crest of the

Purcell Range. Massive windows overlook the Columbia Valley, the main spine of the Canadian Rockies, and the jagged Selkirk Mountains. Located on a rocky summit 7,700 feet above sea level, Eagle's Eye is reached via a 11,266-foot gondola ride in just 12 breathtaking minutes. It is a unique place for lunch or dinner—chef Alain Soret is known for his Rocky Mountain cuisine which blends French influences and local ingredients to create food that is as elevated as the landscape. And do what you have to do to nab either of the two luxury guest suites, for the inimitable sensation of waking up on top of the world.

The restaurant is just one newsworthy element of Kicking Horse Mountain Resort, a four-season ski and summer activities destination high above the small alpine town of Golden. The ski area also has the third-greatest vertical drop in the Canadian Rockies—4,133 feet (surpassed by Whistler's at 5,020 feet; see p. 1062). Speedy lifts take skiers to elevations as high as 8,033 feet at the summit of Blue Heaven, opening up the kind of high-elevation terrain once reserved for heli-skiers, a sport that was, by the way, born in these very mountains in the 1960s (see p. 1040).

However, it's the quality of Kicking Horse snow that has caught the attention of serious skiers and snowboarders. Climatic patterns provide the right mixture of moist high-level air and super-dry, low-level air to create massive falls of perfect powder, and the resort's excellent snow retention has earned Purcell Powder world renown as "the champagne of powder."

In summer, mountain bikers ride Canada's longest lift with their two-wheeled steeds while below some of the best white-water rafting in the Rockies awaits.

WHERE: 84 miles/135 km northwest of Banff. Tel 866-754-5425 or 250-439-5425; kickinghorseresort.com. *Cost:* from US$127/ C$169; lift tickets US$68/C$90. *When:* ski season mid-Dec–mid-Apr. **EAGLE'S EYE RESTAURANT:** Tel 256-439-5413. *Cost:* lunch US$19/C$25, dinner US$45/C$60; *When:* closed late Sept–early Dec and mid-Apr–late May. **BEST TIMES:** Jan–Mar for skiing; June for rafting.

Floating Beauties Full of Charm and Great Country Inns

THE GULF ISLANDS

British Columbia

The rural Gulf Islands archipelago is a laid-back haven for celebrities, back-to-the-earth ecofarmers, artists, and travelers seeking quiet back roads and stunning maritime beauty. These forested, rock-faced islands—

almost 100 of them, each with its own unique character—lie sprinkled between mainland Vancouver and Vancouver Island in the Strait of Georgia. Relatively undeveloped, the Gulf Islands are rustic but not undiscovered and are known for their impressive and ever-growing choice of classy country inns, B&Bs, and culinary outposts, some of western Canada's best. Spend a day kayaking the islands' rugged and otherwise inaccessible coastline (populated by bald eagles, seals, sea otters, and innumerable shorebirds) and return to an evening of expertly prepared regional cuisine and sumptuous accommodations. And with much of the area now protected by the Gulf Islands National Park Reserve, the wildlife, natural beauty, and resources of this marvelous archipelago will be preserved forever.

Five of the Gulf Islands are easily reached on BC Ferries, from Tsawwassen on the mainland or Swartz Bay on Vancouver Island. Salt Spring Island is the largest, with 82 miles of ragged coastline and a population of 10,000. The main town, Ganges, sits on a protected cove filled with bobbing sailboats and is known as a thriving artists colony as well as the "Organic Gardening Capital of Canada." Get a taste of the local bounty at the boisterous Salt Spring Saturday Market held in Ganges' Centennial Park. Delightfully incongruous to the setting is Hastings House Country Estate, a stately English manor and one of the country's most exclusive luxury hideaways (see next page).

The coast of Galiano Island is distinguished by unusual sandstone formations.

Galiano is a long string bean of an island whose cliff-lined southern reaches drop straight into the churning waters of Active Pass. Full of getaways where you can check your hat, it is a Vancouver favorite for an island getaway. Galiano Oceanfront Inn and Spa is a charming escape on Sturdies Bay, located above a private beach with views onto the boat harbor and a distant lighthouse.

Across the busy waters of Active Pass is Mayne Island, once an agricultural center known for apples, tomatoes, and sheep farms. The island's relaxed, eco-friendly atmosphere is perfectly captured by the Mayne Island Resort, comprised of rooms in the main lodge built in 1912. Villas with private decks, and a cluster of waterfront cottages—all promising ocean views and relaxation.

The highlight of the Pender Islands—two rural islands joined by a short bridge—is the beautifully situated Poet's Cove Resort and Spa. Just a mile north of the U.S.-Canada border, this marina and resort on Bedwell Harbour is the popular port of call for pleasure boats passing between the two countries. Overlooking the busy marina, the large wood-beamed resort features elegant guest rooms, spacious two- and three-bedroom cottages, and villas scattered along the forested headland. This is the perfect spot for days of kayaking, whale-watching, or sailing, followed by

massage treatments at the spa and alfresco dining on the terrace.

Almost half of Saturna Island is now protected in Gulf Islands National Park Reserve. Pair the island's pristine beauty with the cozy, low-key Saturna Lodge and you've got the best of both worlds—a supremely comfortable small inn with six stylish rooms overlooking a rock-lined bay, each named after a wine produced at the local Saturna Island Vineyard and several decorated with local artists' work.

WHERE: between Victoria and Vancouver in the Strait of Georgia. *Visitor info:* Tel 250-754-3500;vancouverisland.travel/regions/gulf-islands. **BC FERRIES:** Tel 888-BCFERRY or 250-386-3431; bcferries.com. **SALT SPRING SATURDAY MARKET:** saltspringmarket.com. *When:* Apr–Oct. **GALIANO OCEANFRONT INN AND SPA:** Tel 877-530-3939 or 250-539-3388; galianoinn.com. *Cost:* from US$150/C$199 (off-peak), from US$187/C$249 (peak). **MAYNE ISLAND RESORT:** Tel 866-539-5399 or 250-539-3122; mayneislandresort.com. *Cost:* from US$107/C$139 (off-peak), from US$122/C$159 (peak). **POETS COVE RESORT AND SPA:** South Pender Island. Tel 888-512-7638 or 250-629-2100; poetscove.com. *Cost:* from US$131/C$175 (off-peak), from US$297/C$395 (peak). **SATURNA LODGE:** Saturna Island. Tel 866-539-2254 or 250-539-2254; saturna.ca. *Cost:* from US$109/C$145. *When:* closed Jan–Feb. **BEST TIME:** Apr–Oct for best weather.

An English Manor with a Pacific View

HASTINGS HOUSE
COUNTRY HOTEL

Salt Spring Island, Gulf Islands, British Columbia

Of the dozens of islands that make up the Gulf Islands archipelago in the Strait of Georgia between Vancouver and Victoria (see p. 1037), Salt Spring Island is the largest and most developed. But it is still a world apart for the urbanites who flock here, especially if they have booked at the Tudor-style Hastings House, an exemplary luxury retreat and spa perched above the town of Ganges amid 22 lush acres of flowering English gardens and towering Douglas firs.

One of western Canada's most exclusive hideaways, Hastings House Country Hotel has a long history, and each of its historic buildings has had its individual era and style preserved into a curious mix of luxury-level accommodations. Reserve a room in the old plank barn for example: Totally transformed from the inside out, it now houses a set of wonderfully quirky, elegant suites and an intimate spa. There's nothing rustic about the Hayloft suite except the comfortable, Canadian country-style furniture and the high, gabled ceiling. The original Hudson's Bay Company trading post has been transformed into a two-room garden cottage complete with French doors that open onto a lawn where sheep graze and deep views look down to the sea. The 19th-century farmhouse has been converted into two-story suites, complete with a friendly ghost (or tales of one).

The rural estate's centerpiece is the imposing Manor House, courtesy of English-born former owners, who in the 1930s built a home to resemble the centuries-old Sussex country manse they were forced to leave behind. The Manor House features two elegant suites, plus the renowned Manor Dining Room, which offers some of the best dining in Canada. Dinner here, overlooking lavender gardens and the sea, is the romantic, let's-dress-for-dinner highlight of a stay at Hastings House. Meals are prepared with ingredients harvested from the inn's gardens and orchards and pulled from the islands' fish-rich waters and fertile farmland—try the Local Salt Spring Island lamb; it's justly famous.

HASTINGS HOUSE: 160 Upper Ganges Rd. Tel 800-661-9255 or 250-537-2362; hastingshouse.com. *Cost:* from US$320/C$425; 4-course dinner US$94/C$125. *When:* closed January. **BC FERRIES:** from Tsawwassen on mainland, and Swartz Bay and Crofton on Vancouver Island. Tel 250-386-3431; bcferries.com. **BEST TIME:** Apr–Oct for weather.

The inviting Sussex-style Manor House offers luxurious lodging overlooking the peaceful Ganges Harbour.

High-Altitude Nirvana in Remote Backcountry

HELI-SKIING
AND HELI-HIKING

British Columbia

J ust west of the continent-dividing Canadian Rockies rise waves of mountains:
The Cariboo, Monashee, Selkirk, and Purcell ranges are unknown to many,
but famed to fans of high-mountain hiking and powder skiing. These remote
ranges are short on traditional mountaintop resorts, but their heavy snowfalls and breathtaking scenery make them irresistible year-round destinations to adventurers. There are no ski lifts on most (there are barely any roads) but getting to the mountaintop has never been so easy—or exhilarating.

Canadian Mountain Holidays (CMH) solved that logistical problem beginning in 1965 by ferrying in skiers and outdoor enthusiasts aboard its fleet of helicopters. Today, CMH operates 12 comfortable backcountry lodges perched at about 4,000 feet in the majestic heights of southeastern British Columbia. The lodges, which are fully modern and very comfortable despite their isolation,

Helicopters offer access to remote, high-elevation mountains in Southeastern British Columbia.

each accommodate only 40-some guests at a time, guaranteeing individual attention and service while offering exclusive access to a wilderness area half the size of Switzerland—all without a chairlift (or chairlift line) in sight.

The challenges of high-country skiing require at least strong intermediate to advanced skills, but the rewards are generous. In the course of one mind-boggling powder-filled week, helicopters set skiers down for 8 to 15 different runs per day, all on snow uncrossed by another human's tracks. The preferences and skills of the individual—and the expert guides' and pilots' consideration of weather and snow conditions—determine the day's adventure. Meanwhile, back at the lodge, skiers can depend on mountain-man breakfasts and epicurean dinners, with a massage to make your day that much more perfect.

As soon as the snows melt, heli-tourist thoughts turn to summer hiking and trekking. The high country is transformed into a primordial world of alpine wildflowers, creaking glaciers, rivulets, and monumental views of dozens of snowcapped mile-high peaks. Five of the lodges remain open, enticing adventurers to remote and rarely visited backcountry for hiking, mountaineering, and climbing. Some heli-hiking ambles are gentle enough to accommodate four-generation family groups, but others require some technical climbing skill and mountaineering training, which guides can provide.

WHERE: Trips originate in Calgary or Kamloops. **CANADIAN MOUNTAIN HOLIDAYS (CMH):** Tel 800-661-0252 or 403-762-7100; canadianmountainholidays.com. *Cost:* 7-day ski trips all-inclusive (with equipment) from US$5,545/C$7,379 per person, double occupancy; 3-night hiking trip from US$2,110/ C$2,806 per person, all-inclusive. Transportation (2- to 6-hour road trip from Calgary or Kamloops, followed by a 10-minute helicopter ride to any of the 12 mountain lodges) is included. *When:* ski trips Dec–Apr; hiking trips early July–late Sept. **BEST TIMES:** Jan–Feb for best ski conditions; Dec and Apr for low-season ski trip rates; mid-July–Aug for hikes among the wildflowers.

A Duffer's Paradise at the Columbia River Headwaters

GREYWOLF GOLF COURSE

Invermere, British Columbia

The southwest corner of British Columbia is a top destination for golfers with a long attention span. Between Cranbrook and Radium Hot Springs, a distance of 87 miles, there are 12 championship-level golf courses, many consistently rated among Canada's best. The reason this area is popular for building courses (many of them in the last 25 years) becomes clear as you gaze at the skyline. Here, at the headwaters of the Columbia River, the broad lake-filled valley is surrounded by the saw-toothed Canadian Rockies and the glaciered Purcell Mountains. Until recently, the valley floor was open ranch land, so the new golf courses have had plenty of room to limber up, stretch out—and then work in some kinks.

Of the many excellent courses in the area, perhaps the most notable is Greywolf Golf Course at Panorama Mountain Resort, at the edge of the canyon-cut Purcells just west of Invermere. Canadian course architect Doug Carrick designed Greywolf to offer spectacular mountain vistas from every hole, making it nearly impossible to keep your eye on the ball. "Cliffhanger," Greywolf's signature hole, requires a carry of between 140 and 200 yards over a canyon onto a rocky crag that forms an "island" green with steep vertical drops on the front, left, and back. With dramatic beauty and challenges like this, it's no wonder

Greywolf was named best new Canadian course by *Golf Digest* magazine when it opened in 1999. For lodging, Panorama offers over 500 rooms, including the Gold Premium Condos just above the Panorama Springs Hot Pools. Six other top-rated courses are within a 40-minute drive.

In winter, Panorama Mountain Resort focuses on skiing: With a 4,019-foot vertical drop and nearly 3,000 patrolled acres, it has more than 120 trails, serviced by nine lifts. It has all the trappings of a great resort, including a much acclaimed ski school, but it never gets crowded—one of its many pluses.

WHERE: 183 miles/295 km west of Calgary. Tel 888-473-9965 or 250-341-4100; greywolfgolf.com. *Cost:* greens fees from US$75/C$99 (off-peak), from US$105/C$139 (peak). *When:* May–early Oct. **PANORAMA MOUNTAIN RESORT:** Tel 800-663-2929 or 250-342-6941; panoramaresort.com. *Cost:* from US$126/C$168; lift tickets US$66/C$88. *When:* early Dec–mid-Apr for ski season; mid-May–mid-Oct for golfing. **BEST TIMES:** Jan–Mar for skiing; July–Oct for golfing; Oct for foliage.

Bliss in the Wilderness on the Edge of the Map

NIMMO BAY RESORT

British Columbia

The adventure begins as the helicopter whisks you away, soaring above the islands of Queen Charlotte Strait, nosing toward the craggy, glaciered peaks of the Coast Mountains on the largely unsung western coast of Canada.

Your destination is Nimmo Bay Resort, an 18-guest wilderness retreat carved into this remote corner of Great Bear Rain Forest. No roads lead to Nimmo Bay; at this pocket-size enclave of luxury and ecological stewardship, guests experience the serenity of a verdant waterfront paradise with opportunities for action-packed adventures in the primordial wilderness—all far from the rigors and disruptions of modern life.

Nimmo Bay Resort was a pioneer in using helicopters for adventure tourism, and the resort's private helicopter is the conveyance for a series of thrilling "heli-ventures"—ascending 6,000 feet up and over ancient rain forests to the toe of a glacier for a gourmet mountaintop picnic hike; flying to a small Kwakiutl Indian village surmounted by totem poles; or heading to the area's pristine rivers and streams for catch-and-release fishing. For a less lofty day, guests can begin the morning with a massage or yoga session, then go beachcombing for shells and driftwood, or get a seal's-eye view of the bay during a guided sea kayaking trip.

At the end of the day's adventure, return to the resort's nine elegantly furnished, cedar-paneled chalets, built on stilts above a fjord-like bay. The dining room competes with Vancouver's best: locally grown organic produce, fish and shellfish pulled each morning from neighboring bays, paired with wines from around the world.

Owners Craig and Deborah Murray and their children have built the resort into a wilderness paradise after almost a quarter century of hard work and dedication. Once written off as eccentric dreamers, they now hold the gold standard to which all others aspire.

WHERE: 200 miles/322 km north of Vancouver. Tel 800-837-4354 or 250-956-4000; nimmobay.com. *Cost:* numerous packages available; 3-night package from US$3,778/C$5,025 per person; includes meals, activities, and transfer from Port Hardy to Nimmo Bay (helicopter rides extra). *When:* May–Oct. **BEST TIMES:** Aug–Oct for fishing; May–July for most other activities.

The Napa Valley of Canada

THE OKANAGAN VALLEY

British Columbia

To early settlers of central British Columbia, this steep and craggy valley with a number of interconnected lakes (*okanagan* is the Salishan word for "lake") must have seemed barren and forlorn. With less than 12 inches of rain a year and summer temperatures that can spike up to 100°F/38°C, the Okanagan Valley effectively comprises a glacial lake flanked by desert. But this landscape holds a secret—just add water to create a fruit-growing oasis. With irrigation, the narrow arid valley was transformed from desert to an orchardist's paradise: Today, you'll see roadside farm stands selling cherries, apricots, plums, pears, peaches—and especially apples.

Although French missionaries first planted wine grapes in Kelowna in the 1860s, it wasn't until a century later that modern winemaking took root in the Okanagan Valley. Today, with more than 8,600 acres in wine grape production and over 120 wineries (150, if you include the small artisanal operations), the dry yet fertile valley is Canada's second-largest wine-producing area (after the Niagara region in Ontario; see p. 1000), with wines very similar to nearby Washington State's in power and finesse (see p. 903). Like California's Napa Valley 40 years ago (see p. 833), the Okanagan remains relatively unknown outside Canada. It is a wine success story slowly being written.

The Okanagan's winegrowing area begins immediately north of the U.S.-Canada border at Osoyoos and extends along the lake-filled valley to Vernon, a distance of 118 miles. Kelowna—a bustling city of 106,000 that essentially straddles Okanagan Lake—is the valley's most sophisticated destination for dining and lodging and is central for tasting expeditions into wine country. Over a dozen wineries are within a half-hour's drive of Kelowna, so ask for local recommendations and set out (or let Okanagan Wine Country Tours do the driving so you can sample to your palate's content). Wineries not to miss include Quails' Gate Estate—try its pinot noir and chardonnay in the tasting room or at their Old Vines Restaurant, with alfresco dining and views over vineyards and Okanagan Lake. Mission Hill Family Estate Winery was one of the first serious vineyards on board, established in 1981. Its handsome, upscale $40 million winery looks like a cross between a Tuscan hill town and a French monastery. The tasting room offers award-winning chardonnay, merlot, ice wine, and the estate's signature Bordeaux-inspired Oculus. Terrace, Mission Hill's restaurant, offers light regional cuisine paired with estate wines.

Where there's good wine there's always good food, and Kelowna has become a chef's playground. See what's cooking at RauDZ Regional Table, known for some of the most exciting and stylish dining in town. Its excellent local wine list and regionally sourced cuisine are prepared with contemporary savvy by chef-owner Rod Butters, who is one of Kelowna's better-known and most innovative chefs. One of the area's most characterful lodgings is the lakeside Hotel Eldorado. Of its 55 all-unique rooms, some of the best, appointed entirely with antiques, are the suites that have balconies and views of the lake. You just might spot Ogopogo, the lake's own "Loch Ness monster," especially after a day spent tippling.

WHERE: Kelowna is 245 miles/395 km east of Vancouver. *Visitor info:* Tel 800-663-4345 or 250-861-1515; tourismkelowna.com. **OKANAGAN WINE COUNTRY TOURS:** Tel 866-689-9463 or 250-868-9463; okwinetours.com. *Cost:* from US$87/C$115 for a 3-hour tour. **QUAILS' GATE:** Kelowna. Tel 800-420-9463 or 250-769-4451; quailsgate.com. *When:* wine

The Okanagan Valley is Western Canada's oldest and principal grape-growing region.

tasting and Old Vines Restaurant, May–Oct. *Cost:* dinner US$38/C$50. **MISSION HILL WINERY:** Westbank. Tel 250-768-7611; mission hillwinery.com. *Cost:* lunch US$30/C$40. **RAUDZ REGIONAL TABLE:** Kelowna. Tel 250-868-8805; raudz.com. *Cost:* dinner US$49/

C$55. **HOTEL ELDORADO:** Kelowna. Tel 250-763-7500; hoteleldoradokelowna.com. *Cost:* from US$98/C$130 (off-peak), from US$209/C$279 (peak). **BEST TIMES:** May–Oct for weather; early Oct for the Wine Festival throughout Okanagan Valley (thewinefestivals.com).

A Dream Float Through B.C.'s Coastal Archipelago

CANADA'S INSIDE PASSAGE

Port Hardy to Prince Rupert, British Columbia

The misty islands and rugged fjords of British Columbia's Pacific coast are nearly inaccessible to all but fishing vessels and private yachts. To glimpse the region's fabled coastal rain forests, towering mountains, and abundant

marine wildlife—a wealth of orcas, porpoises, seals, and bald eagles—many travelers join the cruise ships that travel the Inside Passage, a protected navigational channel squeezed between coastal islands and the mainland from north of Vancouver Island to Alaska (the Alaskan stretch promises a different experience; see p. 917). While a cruise ship tour of the Inside Passage is a wonderful way to experience this coastal wilderness, alternatives that require less money and less time can easily be added onto a loop trip around British Columbia with a little advance planning. And the results can be just as rewarding.

The dramatic waters of Canada's Inside Passage are accessible by cruise ship or ferry.

BC Ferries operates a regularly scheduled car and passenger ferry between Port Hardy on the northern tip of Vancouver Island and Prince Rupert, B.C.'s northernmost coastal city. This 274-mile route negotiates the Inside Passage, following the same route as Alaska-bound cruise ships. Make this 15-hour journey in midsummer, when days are very long at this northern latitude, and nearly the entire sailing is in daylight (the ferry sets sail at 7:30 A.M.).

From Port Hardy, the ferry initially crosses open sea before entering the actual Inside Passage north of Bella Bella. As the ferry slips behind mountainous islands, the passage between them and the mainland is very narrow—often less than a mile wide. The scenery is extraordinarily dramatic: Black cliffs drop thousands of feet directly into the channel, notched with hanging glacial valleys and fringed with forests. Powerful waterfalls shoot from dizzying heights into the sea. Eagles float along thermal drafts, and porpoises cavort in the ferry's wake. Even in poor conditions (the weather is very unpredictable here), this is an amazing trip.

From mid-June to mid-September, the ferry makes the journey north one day, returning south the next (the rest of the year, the Port Hardy–Prince Rupert service runs overnight;

the service gradually drops to one trip per week in midwinter). Although the ferry doesn't offer the luxury of the average cruise ship, it does provide a cafeteria, snack bar, and buffet-style dining.

Arriving in the mainland fishing port of Prince Rupert, travelers will discover the city is not the end of the road but rather is a gateway to more travels in the north. The *Northern Adventure* is just one leg in a series of fascinating loop tours around the Pacific Northwest. From here, VIA Rail trains and the Yellowhead Highway head east to Prince George and Jasper (see p. 1034). Alaska Marine Highway ferries stop in Prince Rupert on their way north to

Alaska and BC Ferries leave here for the even more remote and mystical Haida Gwaii (see next page). Once infected by the lure of the north, you'll want to see it all.

WHERE: Port Hardy is 312 miles/504km north of Victoria on Vancouver Island. *Visitor info:* Tel 800-663-8843 or 250-561-0432; hellobc.com. **BC FERRIES:** Tel 888-223-3779 or 250-386-3431; bcferries.com. *Cost:* Port Hardy to/from mainland Prince Rupert, foot passenger one-way from US$89/C$119 (off-peak), from US$152/C$202 (peak); car one-way US$195/C$259 (off-peak), US$346/C$460 (peak). **BEST TIMES:** June and July for the longest days; Aug–Sept for weather.

A Queen City Built from Silver

NELSON

Kootenay Valley, British Columbia

Born as a silver-mining boomtown in the 1880s, Nelson is perhaps the most vibrant and attractive town in the British Columbian interior—and its artiest. With a population of 10,000, Nelson claims more artists

and craftspeople per capita than any other city in Canada.

The scenery here is a work of art in itself. Nelson sits on a shelf of land above the West Arm of Kootenay Lake, a three-pronged, glacier-trenched body of water with over 310 miles of shoreline and depths of 650 feet that are legendary for trout fishing (the world's largest strain of rainbow trout, the Gerrard, tops 20 pounds in these pristine waters). Rising high above it all are the 10,000-feet Selkirk Mountains, dense with fir and cedar forests.

In terms of architectural heritage, Nelson came of age at a great time. At the turn of the 20th century, Nelson was the third-largest city in British Columbia and promoted itself as the "The Queen City." Flush with mining wealth, the townsfolk built a very impressive inventory of ornate late-Victorian and Queen Anne–style

structures. The gracious town center is still intact, with an eclectic mix of boutiques, galleries, outdoor gear stores, and an abundance of coffeehouses and restaurants with flamboyant storefronts.

Just north of the city is 124-square-mile Kokanee Glacier Provincial Park, one of BC's oldest parks, with 53 miles of hiking trails leading to over 30 high-elevation lakes below the glaciered face of 9,032-foot Grays Peak. After a day on the trail, stop by Ainsworth Hot Springs for a therapeutic soak. A flood of 117°F natural mineral water spills from a rocky cleft on the Kootenay Lake shoreline, where the water is diverted into a modern 27,000-gallon soaking pool and—for an experience that will tantalize the adolescent explorer in you—also into a series of natural limestone caves, where another 18,000 gallons of hot mineral water awaits in a well-lit subterranean labyrinth.

In winter, Nelson is a magnet for in-the-know powder hounds. The Whitewater Ski Resort has some of the best snow conditions in Western Canada, due to its cradled location in a natural snow-catching bowl below an escarpment of 8,000-foot peaks. Average snowfalls are 40 feet of pure powder. But Whitewater isn't just for snow bunnies. In fact, 90 percent of the 81 runs are rated More Difficult to Expert.

In a Canadian city with a rich history, you'd expect a grand downtown hotel, and in Nelson, that's the Hume, a beautifully preserved 1898 hotel with a fresh update ensuring the latest in comfort while maintaining vintage charm. The All Seasons Café was a pioneer of seasonal and regional cooking when it opened in 1995, and it's still a friendly and relaxed spot to sample the bounty of local mushrooms, fruit, meat, fish, and vegetables, all prepared with a Mediterranean flourish.

Where: 150 miles/241 km north of Spokane, Washington; nelson.ca. **Kokanee Glacier Provincial Park:** env.gov.bc.ca/bcparks. **Ainsworth Hot Springs:** Tel 250-229-4212; hotnaturally.com. *Cost:* US$10/C$12. **Whitewater Ski Resort:** Tel 800-666-9420 or 250-354-4944; skiwhitewater.com. *Cost:* Lift tickets US$59/C$71. **Hume Hotel:** Tel 877-568-0888 or 250-352-5331; humehotel.com. *Cost:* from US$111/C$139 (off-peak), from US$151/C$189 (peak). **All Seasons Café:** 250-352-0101; allseasonscafe.com. *Cost:* US$40/C$50. **Best times:** mid-Apr for the weeklong Kootenay Festival of the Arts (kootenayfestivalofthearts.ca); early Aug for the 3-day Shambhala Music Festival, 23 miles south of Nelson in Salmo River Ranch, a showcase of live electronic dance music (shambhalamusicfestival.com).

The Galapagos of Canada

Haida Gwaii

British Columbia

The remote and little-known Haida Gwaii (formerly known as the Queen Charlotte Islands) are the homeland of the Haida people, and an incredibly rich preserve of biological diversity. Situated 80 nautical miles off the coast of British Columbia and long isolated, this 150-island archipelago has evolved its own endemic species and subspecies of flora and fauna: From black bears to deer mice, many of the animals differ genetically from their mainland cousins. Considered by many to be the Pacific Northwest's "Galapagos Islands," Haida Gwaii is home to an estimated 1.5 million nesting seabirds, a quarter of British Columbia's population of peregrine falcons, and major runs of salmon. About 6,000 people live on the islands, mostly on northerly Graham Island, and about half of them are Haida.

The islands' deep forests and protected bays have been home to the Haida for more than 10,000 years. Legendary seafarers, they were masterful carvers of totem and house poles, masks, and other ceremonial objects. After contact with European explorers, the Haida were decimated by smallpox and other diseases, and their once magnificent villages were deserted and left for the forest to reclaim.

To protect the islands' unique human and natural history, the Canadian government in conjunction with the Council of the Haida Nation has preserved the southern portion of

Moresby Island, the second largest in the archipelago, as Gwaii Haanas National Park Reserve and Haida Heritage Site. The parkland is primordial and beautiful, dominated by giant old-growth cedar, spruce, and hemlock, completely untouched by modern logging, but the most interesting areas—the abandoned Haida villages—are accessible only by boat. For most people, just about the only way to visit the park is by arranging to join a guide or outfitter on a multiday kayaking or boating excursion. The veteran park-sanctioned outfitter Butterfly Tours offers eight-day kayaking tours appropriate for both novice and experienced kayakers, which visit abandoned villages plus the island's rugged outer coastline. Or consider one of Butterfly Tours' eight-day "mothership" excursions, in which an 80-foot motorized sailboat serves as a floating base camp for day kayak explorations. At the end of the day, kayakers return to the ship for gourmet meals and the comfort of private, heated staterooms.

WHERE: 80 miles/129 km west of Prince Rupert. Sandspit (Moresby Island) is a 2-hour flight north of Vancouver. *Visitor info:* Tel 250-559-8050; gohaidagwaii.ca. **HOW:** BC Ferries,

Many Haida totem poles can be seen in their original location in Ninstints, a village in the South of Gwaii Haanas.

tel 250-386-3431; bcferries.com. **GWAII HAANAS NATIONAL PARK:** Tel 250-559-8818; pc.gc.ca/gwaiihaanas. **BUTTERFLY TOURS:** Sandspit. Tel 604-740-7018; butterflytours .bc.ca. *Cost:* 8-day kayak and tenting tours to Gwaii Haanas from US$1,940/C$2,580. *When:* July–Aug. *Cost:* 8-day Mothership Cruise from US$3,158/C$4,200. *When:* June. **BEST TIMES:** July–Sept for weather; early Aug for the Edge of the World Music Festival in Tlell (edgefestival.ca).

The Culinary Crossroads of Vancouver

GRANVILLE ISLAND PUBLIC MARKET

Vancouver, British Columbia

Like a maze of plenty, the Granville Island Public Market is the epicenter of Vancouver's burgeoning food scene. This warehouselike structure, located on the waters of False Creek in a redeveloped former industrial area and

tucked away beneath the Granville Street Bridge as if an afterthought, is a veritable cornucopia of the Northwest's best. Stalls sell local fruit, vegetables, flowers, just-caught fresh fish and seafood, local meats and sausages, farm-made cheeses, pastries and still warm baked goods,

and wines from the province's vineyards—the cream of British Columbia's crop. Come early and catch the city's top chefs working the market to secure the freshest produce and sweetest fruits. Part of the palpable excitement of the market is its bustling ethnic diversity—better than anywhere, the market's food court reflects the cross-pollination of Canada's most ethnically diverse city. Like Vancouver writ small, the market's buyers and sellers resemble a culinary League of Nations, with chefs and farmers gathered here to share the incredible bounty of local land and sea. It's hard to imagine the existence of Vancouver's flourishing food scene without the passion of those who fill this 50,000-square-foot marketplace.

Granville Island Public Market is a great place to provision a picnic, find a unique food or gift, rediscover culinary curiosity, or assail your senses. At the very least, grab a coffee and a croissant and step out onto the docks fronting the market. Here, musicians strum and buskers

With no chain stores allowed, this public market is a showcase of the region's bounty.

perform, while the young and athletic zip by on bikes and Rollerblades. From the waterfront, the urban core of Vancouver rises across the narrow bay, and water taxis zip to and from various downtown stations.

Granville Island, technically a peninsula, offers much more than the public market. Next door is Emily Carr Institute, British Columbia's top school of art, design, and media. Visit its student gallery or any of the dozens of artists' studios and galleries that fill warehouses around the institute. Not surprisingly, with the market close at hand, a number of fine small restaurants have also crowded onto the island, along with theaters and nightclubs. And in the midst of this arty bohemia stands a small offbeat boutique hotel on the water's edge—the Granville Island Hotel, an enjoyable False Creek ferry ride away from downtown.

PUBLIC MARKET: 1689 Johnston St. (under the south end of the Granville St. Bridge). Tel 604-666-6655; granvilleisland.com. **GRANVILLE ISLAND HOTEL:** Tel 800-663-1840 or 604-683-7373; granvilleislandhotel.com. *Cost:* from US$157/C$209 (off-peak), from US$199/C$265 (peak). **BEST TIMES:** Weekends can be very busy, a scene you'll either want to experience or to avoid.

Northwest Native Art and Modern Architecture

MUSEUM OF ANTHROPOLOGY

Vancouver, British Columbia

Rising from a cliffside meadow above the Strait of Georgia's churning waters, the Museum of Anthropology at the University of British Columbia houses one of North America's leading collections of Northwest Native art. The focus of the museum is the phantasmagorical carvings of British Columbia First Nation artists: towering totem poles; squat tree-trunk sculptures of ravens, whales, and bears; and intricately colored masks of cedar and feathers. The haunting figures and artifacts are both historical—many of the carvings formerly served as house poles at remote coastal villages—and contemporary, as traditional wood-carving remains an active art form in many Native communities.

The Pacific Northwest was a rich homeland

for precontact Native North Americans, allowing for the growth of highly developed cultural and artistic traditions. Native artists created sophisticated carvings to represent clan myths, relate creation stories, and portray the supernatural creatures of Native religion.

The cliff-top building created to house the MOA is as dramatic as the art it holds. Designed by Canadian architect Arthur Erickson, the award-winning museum is a soaring, light-filled space that seems less a storehouse of artifacts than a brooding house of spirits. From the 50-foot windows of the Great Hall, carved creatures and totem poles stare out across the forests and waters like waiting deities, while in the Rotunda, the massive yellow cedar sculpture *Raven and the First Men* by the late Haida artist Bill Reid is a potent expression of pagan wonder.

Adjacent to the museum is an outdoor sculpture garden, including a number of memorial and mortuary poles, plus re-creations of

A Musqueam house post from one of the Northwest Coast First Nations

19th-century Haida village structures that blend perfectly into the woodland setting.

WHERE: 11 miles/18 km west of downtown Vancouver on the campus of the University of British Columbia. Tel 604-822-5087; moa .ubc.ca. *When:* daily, late Jan–mid-Oct; closed Mon, mid-Oct–late Jan.

An Urban Oasis—a Rarity and a Treasure

STANLEY PARK

Vancouver, British Columbia

One of Vancouver's true glories and North America's third-largest urban park, the 1,000 green acres of Stanley Park occupy the northern edge of downtown Vancouver, on a wooded peninsula extending into Burrard Inlet.

The parklands were set aside in 1886 and dedicated by Lord Stanley, governor general of Canada, preserving this vast stretch of dense cedars, Douglas firs, and lakes, all linked by shaded trails and quiet drives. Stanley Park is just moments from the core of busy Vancouver, making it an idyllic retreat on sunny summer days, when joggers, bikers, skateboarders, and picnickers take to the park for fresh air and time with the great outdoors.

For the best first impression, take the Seawall Promenade, a 5.5-mile paved walking

and biking path along the circumference of the park. Walking briskly, it's easy to circumnavigate the park in two hours (less if you rent a bike from a park concessionaire), though if you build in time to leisurely visit various sites, stop for coffee or a picnic, or simply relax and take in the extraordinary views, it's best to allow a full afternoon (Stanley Park shuttle buses also make a circuit of the park on Stanley Park Drive).

The southern part of the park, nearest downtown, is the most developed. Trails lead to alfresco theater spaces, the city's formal rose gardens, public art, a visitors center, and incredible vistas of downtown Vancouver over a busy yacht-filled marina. Toward the eastern edge of the park is a grouping of totem poles, carved in the late 1900s by Squamish artists whose ancestors once occupied these lands. The park's

Established in 1886, Stanley Park was Vancouver's first park; more than 120 years later it remains a place of respite minutes from downtown.

northernmost tip is Prospect Point, with views of North Vancouver, Coast Range peaks, and the soaring Lions Gate Bridge. The west side of the park provides stunning sunset views over Vancouver Island, and between Third Beach and Second Beach—both popular with children and sunbathers—is the Teahouse in Stanley Park, a lovely spot for a casual lunch or dinner.

The Vancouver Aquarium, the largest in Canada, occupies a shady corner of Stanley Park. With more than 160 separate aquatic displays spread over 100,000 square feet, this vast underwater zoo houses more than 50,000 aquatic animals in re-created habitats. For many, the highlight of a visit is the acrobatic demonstrations of the marine mammals, including dolphins, sea lions, and beluga whales.

WHERE: just north of downtown Vancouver. *Park info:* Tel 604-873-7000; vancouver parks.ca. **TEAHOUSE IN STANLEY PARK:** Tel 604-669-3281; vancouverdine.com. *Cost:* dinner US$34/C$45. **VANCOUVER AQUARIUM:** Tel 604-659-3474; vanaqua.org. **BEST TIMES:** mid- to late May for rhododendrons; July–Sept for weather; Dec for Bright Nights, when a million twinkling lights transform the park.

Eastern Roots in Canada's West

DR. SUN YAT-SEN CLASSICAL CHINESE GARDEN

Vancouver, British Columbia

Canada prides itself on its multiculturalism, a fascinating mosaic of peoples and customs that finds its apogee in Vancouver, home to the largest Chinese population of any city outside Asia. The first Chinese immigrants

arrived to work the 1858 gold rush and later the railroads, and as their numbers grew, the Chinese created and settled into their own Vancouver community. The massive influx of Hong Kong Chinese in the 1980s and '90s only underscored what had been apparent for

over a century—the great affinity that exists between China and Vancouver. Its ever-expanding Chinatown is one of the largest and most vibrant Asian enclaves in North America. Just east of downtown Vancouver is a real Chinese market and business district; nearly all signs are in Chinese, and storefronts are filled with hanging ducks, bales of dried fish, exotic fruits, and unlikely looking medicinal potions.

An island of calm in this otherwise frenetic community is the Dr. Sun Yat-Sen Classical Chinese Garden, a 2.5-acre complex on the neighborhood's edge and the first full-scale classical Chinese garden ever built outside China. Completed in 1986, the garden is designed in the style of Suzhou, Vancouver's sister city, famed for over 700 years for its exquisite gardens.

The Sun Yat-Sen garden (named after the founder of China's first republic) is an exquisite re-creation of a typical 14th-century Ming garden, a walled oasis filled with horticultural and man-made treasures. Its complex network of corridors and courtyards seems like an intricately chambered jewel box, a pocket-size otherworld. A team of 52 Suzhou artisans and horticulturists spent over a year building the garden, and almost everything was brought from China, including the pagoda roof tiles, the naturally sculpted rocks, the worn pebbles that

The meticulously designed garden offers a serene escape from bustling Vancouver.

create the mosaics covering the winding pathways, and the bat-shaped bronze door handles. Don't miss the complimentary volunteer-led tours that provide perspectives on this and other aspects of Chinese culture, life during the Ming Dynasty, architecture, horticulture, and the art of feng shui.

CHINESE GARDEN: Carrall St. between Pender St. and Keefer St. Tel 604-662-3207; vancouverchinesegarden.com. *When:* daily, May–Oct; closed Mon, Nov–Apr.

Epicureans Celebrate the Northwest's Bounty

VANCOUVER'S BEST RESTAURANTS

Vancouver, British Columbia

O ne of the world's most cosmopolitan cities, with a rich mix of overlapping cultures, Vancouver is wedged between the chilly waters of the Pacific, the farmlands of the Fraser River valley, and misty mountains whose

meadows abound with wild mushrooms and berries.

There's no better way to explore the city than through its cuisine, and no more enjoyable way to savor the bounty of Vancouver's natural setting than at the following restaurants, each renowned for instilling world-class cuisine with a real sense of locale and season.

Tojo's is a bright and popular restaurant

and longtime institution named for its revered chef-owner, Hidekazu Tojo, said to have invented the California roll. Specialties reflect the changing seasons, but tuna and wild salmon are perennial favorites, consumed at the rate of 300 pounds and 200 pounds, respectively, every week. The waters around Vancouver are rich with king, coho, sockeye, chum, and pink salmon, and Tojo gets his hands on the very best, maintaining an unwavering commitment to fresh local ingredients. The most coveted seats are at the convivial *omakase* ("in the chef's hands") counter, where menus are banned and the chef prepares the freshest, most original dishes— sushi and sashimi plus some cooked items— in season. At the center of it all is the beaming and energetic master, Tojo, who performs his magic with the precision of a surgeon and the faintest Vegas swagger.

Hidekazu Tojo has an uncanny skill for selecting the best and freshest fish.

West Restaurant offers a contemporary reinterpretation of classic regional cuisine. In a sleek, jewel-box-like dining room along fashionable South Granville Street, executive chef Quang Dang performs a kind of kitchen alchemy, transforming pristine local ingredients into novel dishes packed with flavor and artful style. For the complete experience, book a "chef's table" in the kitchen, order from one of three multicourse tasting menus (land, sea, or vegetarian based), and marvel as the masterfully trained kitchen professionals perform their own version of dinner theater.

The restaurant is known for both an impressive wine list as well as creative cocktails from an award-winning mixologist.

West shares an owner with another Vancouver institution, the consistently acclaimed Blue Water Café, long regarded as Vancouver's premier seafood restaurant. The menu's perennial crowd-pleasers include the famous three-tiered seafood towers and expansive raw bar, sablefish specials, Dungeness crabs, and the signature braised short ribs, one of many carnivore options that prove the kitchen knows its way around meat. The Yaletown restaurant, housed in a handsomely converted 100-year-old warehouse, owes much of its renown to Chef Frank Pabst, highly respected as a leader in sustainable and responsible dining. He has impeccable skill with seafood and a firm focus on the West Coast, while also incorporating Western European and Eastern Asian influences. An extensive wine list has a comprehensive selection of British Columbia's best vintages, plus notable selections from California and Italy.

Tojo's: Tel 604-872-8050; tojos.com. *Cost:* 5-course *omakase* dinner US$60/C$80. **West Restaurant:** Tel 604-738-8938; westrestaurant.com. *Cost:* dinner US$65/C$85; tastings from US$78/C$99. **Blue Water Café:** Tel 604-688-8078; bluewater cafe.net. *Cost:* US$80/C$101.

One-of-a-Kind European Elegance

WEDGEWOOD HOTEL

Vancouver, British Columbia

Perennially ranked one of the highest in the world for its quality of life, Vancouver is also one of North America's most cosmopolitan cities, and still proud of its role as host city to the 2010 Winter Olympics. The city

offers a fascinating mosaic of cultures, prominently on display along Robson Street, one of downtown Vancouver's busiest shopping

districts. Just a few steps from the bustling throngs and boutiques on Robson is the Wedgewood Hotel, an island of elegance and splendor—and the best spot in the city to sample Vancouver's famed urban finesse.

Originally built as a residential hotel at the turn of the 20th century and later thoroughly gutted and remodeled, the Wedgewood differs markedly from the anonymous business hotels that otherwise populate downtown Vancouver. The luxurious and beautiful boutique hotel was the consummate vision of Eleni Skalbania, a hospitality dynamo who served as chief designer, contractor, and

From the moment you step through the door of the Wedgewood, you will be immersed in Old World luxury.

entrepreneur, and today it is operated by her daughter Elpie Marinakis Jackson.

While the foyers and public spaces are awash with European opulence, the guest rooms are furnished with understated style and comfort. The family's private collection of art and antiques adds to their sophistication, making each room personalized. The rooms are large, and some have fireplaces and all offer balconies, some with views over the magisterial Vancouver Art Gallery and the Law Courts, one of Vancouver's architectural gems.

As the hotel's many return guests will attest, the Wedgewood isn't just about good looks. The service level is exemplary— with an impressive guest-to-staff ratio. The hotel's spa is widely considered one of Vancouver's top day spas, while the Bacchus restaurant is known for its brilliant menu.

Where: 845 Hornby St. Tel 800-663-0666 or 604-689-7777; wedgewoodhotel.com. *Cost:* from US$194/C$248; dinner at Bacchus US$56/C$75. **Best times:** late June–early July for the Vancouver International Jazz Festival (coastaljazz.ca); mid-July for the Vancouver Folk Music Festival (thefestival.bc.ca).

Wildness and Wilderness on the North Pacific Coast

PACIFIC RIM NATIONAL PARK

Vancouver Island, British Columbia

The remote western flank of Vancouver Island forms a primordial tableau of dense forest and rugged mountains deeply bitten by steep-sided fjords. Large sections of the area's coastal rain forests, islands, and broad sandy beaches are preserved as the Pacific Rim National Park Reserve, established in 1971 as Canada's first marine park. This three-unit maritime wilderness is hallowed ground for ecotourists, long-distance hikers, and sea kayakers. The famous West Coast Trail is hailed by the Sierra Club as one of the most spectacular and challenging hikes on the continent.

From May through September each year, intermediate and experienced hikers arrive from all over the world to follow the 47-mile track, which was initially designed as a rescue trail for shipwrecked sailors along the otherwise inaccessible coastline between Port Renfrew and Bamfield. The five- to seven-day journey, which involves fording rivers, climbing cliffs, traversing rope bridges, and slogging along miles of wilderness beachfront, is for many the hike of a lifetime.

At the mouth of Barkley Sound is the park's second unit, centered on the Broken Group Islands. The rocky shoreline was once known by mariners as the Graveyard of the Pacific for the ferocious winter storms that hit these craggy headlands, but yesterday's tragedy is today's tourist destination, as these sunken vessels provide a number of historic shipwrecks for scuba divers to explore. Diverse and plentiful marine life is also a major draw: Kayakers explore the archipelago to view sea lions, bald eagles, and pods of whales.

Access to the Broken Group Islands is somewhat limited (outfitters in Bamfield and Ucluelet lead kayak tours), though passengers on the MV *Lady Rose* and MV *Frances Barkley*, packet freighters that deliver mail and supplies to remote fishing and logging communities along Alberni Inlet and Barkley Sound, pass by this watery wilderness. The only transport in this otherwise roadless outback area of Vancouver Island, these Port Alberni–based freighters also convey sightseers on their day-long delivery circuit past tiny waterfront settlements, cliff-lined islands, and heavily wooded mountains. There's no better way to catch a glimpse of daily life in this remote maritime corner of British Columbia.

The park's third unit is its most accessible, the 9-mile curve of Long Beach, some 500 yards wide at low tide. Broken here and there by rocky outcrops and groves of cedar and Sitka spruce, the beach is popular in summer, when the area enjoys sunny weather and mild breezes. Families gather to build sand castles and stroll along the strand, wet-suited surfers brave the still-cold waters, and hikers can explore woodland and coastal trails.

Winter brings a different kind of beach experience: Exposed to the full fury of north Pacific winter storms, with howling winds, sheets of rain, and crashing 20-foot waves, the Long Beach section of the park is home to the curious Northwest pastime of winter storm-watching, best done from a number of surprisingly luxurious inns and hotels in the small coastal towns of Tofino (see next page) and Ucluelet that bookend the park. Just north of the park boundary and perched on Cox Bay is Long Beach Lodge Resort. A favorite of design magazines that praise its sensitive design and respect for the environment, the luxury inn is the quintessence of the island's rugged beauty. Visitors enjoy First Nations art, handsomely appointed beachfront and forest rooms, secluded cottages, and the excellent Great Room with an oversize fireplace and regional dining at its best.

WHERE: west coast of Vancouver Island. Tel 250-726-3500; pc.gc.ca/pacificrim. *Cost:* West Coast Trail hiking permit US$95/C$127. *When:* West Coast Trail open May–late Sept; the rest of the park open year-round. **LADY ROSE MARINE SERVICES:** Tel 800-663-7192 or 250-723-8313; ladyrosemarine.com. *Cost:* round-trip between Port Alberni and Bamfield US$59/C$78; round-trip between Port Alberni and Ucluelet US$62/C$82. **LONG BEACH LODGE RESORT:** Tel 877-844-7873 or 250-725-2442; longbeachlodgeresort.com. *Cost:* rooms from US$150/C$199 (off-peak), from US$210/C$279 (peak). **BEST TIMES:** June–July for warm weather and long days; Nov–Feb for storm-watching.

Outfitters offer kayak tours of the ecologically rich Broken Group Islands.

Summer Home of Orcas

STUBBS ISLAND WHALE-WATCHING

Vancouver Island, British Columbia

Separating Vancouver Island from the cedar-covered coast of British Columbia, Johnstone Strait near Telegraph Cove is seasonal home to the world's largest concentration of orcas (killer whales): Roughly 150 inhabit these waters from late June into the winter months before heading south. The orcas have good reason to gather here. The confines of Johnstone Strait force migrating salmon into a narrow channel, which means easy hunting and an all-you-can-eat fresh fish buffet to an orca. The area also features "rubbing beaches" where orcas scoot along on their bellies on shallow beds of gravel to rub barnacles from their hides. Although tour boats aren't allowed to disturb the orcas at their grooming, they can visit nearby areas and watch from a distance.

Stubbs Island Whale Watching operates one 60-foot and one 40-foot Coast Guard–certified vessel, with hydrophones that allow passengers to eavesdrop on the whales' haunting melodies and other communications. With a curiosity that matches the visitors', the whales often approach the boats, which have become familiar to them over the company's quarter-century-plus years of cruising (and with a 90 percent success rate of sightings). Identified by their scars, white "saddle patch" markings, and the shapes of their flukes, the whales are natural show-offs, slicing through these calm waters, diving and surfacing to the viewers' delight.

WHERE: Telegraph Cove is 250 miles/ 402 km north of Victoria. Tel 800-665-3066 or 250-928-3185; stubbs-island.com. *Cost:* US$75/C$99. *When:* late May–mid-Oct. **BEST TIME:** July–Sept during salmon runs.

Orcas often spyhop (similar to treading water).

A Luxury Oasis at the Pacific's Rim

WICKANINNISH INN AND TOFINO

Vancouver Island, British Columbia

You wouldn't expect to find one of the country's top-ranked hotels on the edge of a rocky promontory, hours from the nearest urban center. Yet the Wickaninnish Inn, a rustically elegant and highly sophisticated inn surrounded by beaches, old-growth forest, and the surging Pacific on Vancouver Island's untamed west coast, is consistently rated among the world's best, and one of the very finest in North America. Nature was extravagant when it created the Long Beach section of Pacific Rim National Park (see p. 1053), which is just to the south, and the Wickaninnish Inn is that rare modern structure that blends harmoniously with the glories of its natural surroundings.

Built of local cedar, stone, and glass, the hotel is like a natural extension of the landscape. The interior is filled with light and thoughtfully chosen objects, from the dramatic high-ceilinged lobby with Northwest Native carvings and the warmth of the stone fireplace, to the large and luxurious guest rooms, each with ocean views, floor-to-ceiling windows, and private balconies close enough to the sea that guests hear the waves while relaxing beside the fireplace—or in the window-side soaker tub.

To capture the sheer drama of the location, visit during winter's "storm watch" months, when howling winds, sheets of rain, and crashing 20-foot Pacific waves nearly engulf the inn. Don't miss the Northwest specialties at the inn's Pointe Restaurant or its 240-degree views. The in-house Ancient Cedars Spa offers a selection of body treatments, which along with long walks on Chesterman Beach will help guests keep in shape and de-stressed. And service? With a guest-to-staff ratio of 2.5 to 1, you'll feel like rusticating royalty.

Just to the north, the little seafaring village of Tofino is a quirky, unpretentious place that

The Wickaninnish Inn is the perfect base for exploring Vancouver Island's dramatic west coast.

thrives on contrasts—it's both lively and relaxed, and young, buff ecotourism outfitters rub shoulders with grizzled fishermen, while upscale European tourists share tables with tattooed, back-to-the-earth surfer dudes. With the tang of the sea in the air and a busy harbor filled with fishing boats and Zodiacs, Tofino (population around 1,900) manages at once to feel like the edge of the earth and the center of the universe.

WHERE: 206 miles/332 km northwest of Victoria. Tel 800-333-4604 or 250-725-3100; wickinn.com. *Cost:* from US$225/C$300 (off-peak), from US$390/C$520 (peak); dinner at the Pointe US$49/C$65. **BEST TIMES:** 10 days in March for Pacific Rim Whale Festival, when some 20,000 gray whales migrate north; 1st weekend in June for the Tofino Food and Wine Festival; July–Sept for weather; Dec–Mar for storm-watching.

Tented Opulence in Coastal Outback

CLAYOQUOT WILDERNESS RESORT

Vancouver Island, British Columbia

The small ecotourism resort town of Tofino is literally the end of the road on Vancouver Island's wild west coast—unless you've got reservations at the Clayoquot Wilderness Resort. At this ultra-premium resort, accessible only by floatplane or water taxi from Tofino, there's no roughing it allowed, even if your lodging is a tent. Against a backdrop of pristine coastline and primordial forest on Vancouver Island, the eco-safari camp is located within the fragile Clayoquot Sound Biosphere reserve, a wilderness so lush and exotic and so dense with wildlife that *National Geographic* deemed it an upside-down rain forest. Inspired by the late 19th-century Great Camps, this unique enclave promises indulgent pampering while treading gently in a little-visited Eden.

Twenty roomy prospector-type white canvas tents, with wooden floors, beautifully furnished with Adirondack-style furniture, Oriental rugs, rich fabrics, antiques, and otherworldly comforts, serve as guest rooms and suites. The lounge tent and games tent offer visitors a taste of upscale safari life; all are connected by cedar boardwalks along the water's edge. The heart of the resort is the stylish log dining room, with a towering double-sided fieldstone fireplace, outdoor lounge, and showpiece open kitchen

attended by chef Ryan Orr, a master of Pacific Northwest cuisine.

The camp is surrounded by verdant coastal wilderness, and the resort offers unparalleled access to both guided and unguided recreation, including horseback riding, whale- and bear-watching, hiking, ocean and river fishing, and kayaking. Or your day's adventure may be finishing that book you've been meaning to read, or being alone with your thoughts in a primal setting you once only dreamed about.

You may not be able to wind down any further, but wander by the cluster of spa treatment tents nonetheless for a massage or a revitalizing soak in an outdoor wood-fired hot tub, under the stars.

WHERE: 15 minutes east of Tofino by floatplane. Tel 888-333-5405 or 250-266-0397; wildretreat.com. *Cost:* 3-night minimum, from US$3,571/C$4,750 per person, double occupancy, includes floatplane transfer from Vancouver, meals, activities, and a massage. *When:* mid-May–Sept. **BEST TIMES:** May–Sept for fishing; Aug–Sept for weather.

A Pacific Island's Epicurean Heartland

COWICHAN VALLEY

Vancouver Island, British Columbia

One of Canada's most temperate agricultural areas, the Cowichan Valley is Vancouver Island's food basket—a veritable cornucopia of artisanal food production all nestled in a green and buoyantly fertile landscape. Rent a car for a drive past abundant farms, orchards, vineyards, dairies, cideries, and other outposts of gastronomy—sampling along the way, of course.

Duncan is the valley's main trading center, and its bustling, year-round Saturday farmer's market is a showcase for the valley's fruits, vegetables, fish and seafood, and local meats. Browse the displays of charcuterie, baked goods, cheese, honey, jam, and preserves, and

pick out a picnic's supply of edible and drinkable wonders. Then head for the hills south of Duncan where over a dozen vineyards roll out across the slopes. Averill Creek Vineyard's perfect location allows pinot noir and pinot gris grapes to ripen to perfection in a maritime climate. If it's lunchtime, consider Merridale Estate Cidery, with a tasting room for hard apple and pear cider and a bistro dining room centered around a massive fieldstone fireplace.

The valley ends at Cowichan Bay, a small but vital fishing port facing the summits of Salt Spring Island, with epic vistas from the village's restaurants and lodgings. Right on the harbor, the Masthead Restaurant was built in 1863 as a waterfront hotel; it's now the Cowichan Valley's top choice for locally sourced fine dining, served in a light-filled dining room overlooking the fishing boats that may have apprehended your catch of the day. Rising above the bay, Dream Weaver B&B has wraparound porches and rocking chairs to take in the view. Though it sports the gabled majesty of a Victorian manse, in fact the Dream Weaver is recently built, with just three large modern guest suites—and no squeaky floors.

WHERE: Duncan is 38 miles north of Victoria; tourismcowichan.com. **DUNCAN FARMER'S MARKET:** Tel 250-732-1723; duncanfarmersmarket.ca. **AVERILL CREEK VINEYARD:** Tel 250-709-9986; averillcreek.ca. *When:* open daily in summer, weekends-only in winter. **MERRIDALE ESTATE CIDERY:** Tel 250-743-4293; merridalecider.com. **MASTHEAD RESTAURANT:** Tel 250-748-3714; themastheadrestaurant.com. *Cost:* dinner US$44/C$55. **DREAM WEAVER B&B:** Tel 888-748-7689 or 250-748-7688; dreamweaverbedandbreakfast.com. *Cost:* from US$100/C$125 (off-peak), from US$108/C$135 (peak).

Raising Regional Cuisine to an Art Form

SOOKE HARBOUR HOUSE

Sooke, Vancouver Island, British Columbia

It doesn't look like the site of a revolution. On a quiet wooded promontory overlooking the Strait of Juan de Fuca and the distant Olympic Mountains sits a tidy white 1929 clapboard inn that has long played a leading role in changing how we eat and think of food today. Sinclair and Fredrica Philip's Sooke Harbour House is justly known as one of North America's foremost hotel restaurants for authentic regional cuisine, and has been a leader in placing fresh and resolutely local ingredients at the forefront of today's best cooking.

The Sooke Harbour House dining room features inventive and delicious cuisine prepared from the freshest sources: just-caught fish and seafood from the waters off the hotel and produce and meats from local organic farms. With 400 varieties of rare and unusual herbs, edible flowers, and organic vegetables, the inn's lovingly tended garden's bounty is used liberally and innovatively in the menu's ever-changing, one-of-a-kind dishes. For connoisseurs, the four-course gastronomic menu features delicacies like seared halibut cheek with Dungeness crab and roast venison loin dusted with wild rose petals. Served in a candlelit dining room overlooking the rocky coastline, these delicious repasts are complemented by a list of more than 2,000 wines, 40 of them served by the glass.

Sooke Harbour House has culinary treasures inside and out—the building's grounds include a special organic garden of edible plants, herbs, and flowers.

Sampling the stellar wine selection becomes twice as enjoyable when you needn't journey far to any of the inn's serene yet unpretentious guest rooms, each offering ocean views and uniquely decorated with antiques and original West Coast art. All rooms have wood-burning stone fireplaces, and most have whirlpools for two, positioned to enjoy the gorgeous views.

Sooke Harbour House offers a tour of their organic edible flower gardens with one of the staff gardeners, who will also be happy to explain how locally harvested seaweed is used in the inn's specialty spa treatments and in evening meals.

WHERE: 23 miles/37 km west of Victoria; 1528 Whiffen Spit Rd. Tel 800-889-9688 or 250-642-3421; sookeharbourhouse.com. *Cost:* from US$150/C$199 (off-peak), from US$247/ C$329 (peak), includes breakfast and packed lunch; 4-course prix-fixe dinner US$60/C$80.

Splendorous and World-Famous Gardens

BUTCHART GARDENS

Victoria, Vancouver Island, British Columbia

It all started as a gaping hole in the ground. Cement tycoon Robert Butchart exhausted the limestone quarry near his Saanich Peninsula home in 1904, but one person's 50-foot-deep abandoned pit is another's gardening challenge.

Butchart's wife, Jennie, had the quarry filled with topsoil and gradually landscaped the deserted eyesore into the magnificent Sunken Garden. By 1908, the Butcharts had created a Japanese garden, later adding an Italian garden on the site of their former tennis court. A few years later, a fine rose garden replaced the family vegetable patch. Word spread quickly of Mrs. Butchart's amazing green thumb, and by the 1920s some 50,000 visitors were coming each year to visit the Butcharts' private gardens.

Now extending across 55 acres, the Butchart Gardens, still family-run, today is Canada's most-visited private attraction, drawing almost a million visitors a year. Over a million bedding plants in some 900 varieties are planted throughout the gardens to ensure uninterrupted bloom from March through October. Not for the faint of heart, the midsummer display is absolutely riotous, with the gardens transformed by thousands of strands of twinkling lights. Spring is another colorful time to visit, when 300,000 tulips, daffodils, hyacinths,

Each season at Butchart Gardens promises a beauty all its own.

and other bulbs are in bloom. Fall and winter present a more subdued landscape, but it's an opportunity to enjoy the quiet and appreciate the underlying architecture of the gardens and indoor displays. A small ice-skating rink has been added to take your mind off the warm-weather spectacle you're missing.

From the first weekend in July until September, a variety of musical entertainments are offered on outdoor stages in the evenings. On summer Saturday evenings the immensely popular fireworks display is followed by a pipe-organ concert. Throughout the year, the Dining Room Restaurant—located in Benvenuto, the Butcharts' original home—serves traditional afternoon tea in the fall, with lunch and dinner served in season.

WHERE: Brentwood Bay (14 miles/23 km north of Victoria), 800 Benvenuto Ave. Tel 250-652-5256; butchartgardens.com. **DINING**

ROOM: Tel 250-652-8222. *When:* tea service Oct–late Dec; lunch daily, May–Sept; dinner daily, mid-June–mid-Sept and Dec–early Jan. *Cost:* dinner US$38/C$50. **BEST TIMES:** Mar–Apr for spring bulbs; May–June for rhododendrons and azaleas; mid-June–early Sept for evening magic; July–Sept for roses and summer annuals; July–Aug for fireworks every Sat; Oct for fall colors; Dec–Jan for Christmas lights.

Outpost of Old World Charm

THE FAIRMONT EMPRESS

Victoria, Vancouver Island, British Columbia

The word "palatial" was created to describe landmarks like the Fairmont Empress—larger than life, shaped by marvelous architecture, and filled with a sumptuous refinement of detail. The city, named after Queen Victoria, Empress of India, was the first European settlement on Vancouver Island. When it became the capital of British Columbia in 1868, an appropriate hotel befitting its new status was needed; that did not arrive until 1908. Designed by Francis Rattenbury, who also designed the Parliament buildings just across the way ten years earlier, the Empress is one of Canada's most beloved hotels.

The Empress rises imposingly over Victoria's Inner Harbour, a grand lodging with the style and furnishings of another, more gracious era, but with all the comforts and conveniences of a modern luxury hotel. Over the years, the ivy-covered Fairmont Empress has become the very symbol of Victoria, the most British of Canada's cities, and a beautifully preserved showcase of Edwardian-era architecture.

For most visitors, taking afternoon tea at the Empress is a Victoria tradition. While sitting in the opulent Tea Lobby, partake of the hotel's secret Tea at the Empress blend served in fine William Edwards china, accompanied by freshly baked raisin scones served with Devon-style double-clotted cream and strawberry preserves. You won't be thinking about dinner anytime soon.

If tea is not your thing, there's no better spot for a fortifying beverage than the richly atmospheric Bengal Lounge, with colonial furnishings and leather wingback chairs redolent of a London gentlemen's club; the huge wall-mounted tiger skin was donated by the King of Siam. The Bengal Lounge's curry buffet is a favorite for those seeking a bit of spice and raj recollection. If you prefer to experience the full force of Northwest cuisine, reserve a table in the regally decorated Empress Room, the hotel's deservedly acclaimed dining room with tapestried walls and refined service.

For the classic Fairmont Empress experience, reserve a Harbourview Suite or Fairmont Gold Room, which offer sumptuous decor and magnificent views over the Inner Harbour, downtown Victoria, and the Parliament buildings. In addition to every other amenity known to purveyors of luxury, the hotel also offers Willow Stream spa, a well-known therapeutic and beauty treatment center.

WHERE: 721 Government St. Tel 866-540-

4429 or 250-384-8111; fairmont.com/empress. *Cost:* from US$144/C$192; tea from US$40/C$53; dinner at Bengal Lounge US$26/C$34; dinner at Empress Room from US$56/C$75. **BEST TIME:** mid-June–Aug for various music festivals in Victoria.

Showcase of Region's Natural and Human History

ROYAL BRITISH COLUMBIA MUSEUM

Victoria, Vancouver Island, British Columbia

The Royal British Columbia Museum sits between two of Victoria's most famous landmarks, the beloved Fairmont Empress Hotel (see previous page) and the British Columbia Parliament Building, but offers more history than either. Bypassing world history to focus on the importance of this intriguing niche of the globe, the museum is considered one of the best regional museums anywhere. Its three galleries focus on British Columbia's natural environment, its settlement history, and the rich art and culture of its First Nations peoples.

Visitors follow a time line of the province's history, from the Ice Age (the 10-foot woolly mammoth is a guaranteed hit with children) to its mining and fishing heyday. An excellent exhibit features a partial re-creation of George Vancouver's ship the HMS *Discovery*, in which the English sea captain explored the Northwest Pacific Coast in the 1790s. The natural history gallery contains many lifelike dioramas illustrating the province's broad range of wildlife and flora.

Perhaps most compelling, and always the most visited, is the First Peoples Gallery, which details the history and culture of the region's several distinct coastal nations. These cultures reached their zenith in the late 18th century, when European traders began making incursions into the Northwest. However, contact with the Europeans' diseases, to which the Native population had little resistance, decimated them. The museum's displays of hand-carved masks, ceremonial garb and headdresses, decorative accessories and textiles, and iconic totem poles bring to life vibrant Native cultures dating back thousands of years.

Directly behind the museum is Thunderbird Park, with a thicket of towering totem poles carved by 20th-century Native artists. On-site wood-carvers occasionally demonstrate their age-old skills. A genuine ceremonial longhouse stands beside the totem poles, reserved for traditional First Nations gatherings.

WHERE: 675 Belleville St. Tel 888-447-7977 or 250-356-7226; royalbcmuseum.bc.ca. **BEST TIME:** early Aug for Victoria's First Peoples Festival.

A full-size woolly mammoth welcomes you to the Royal British Columbia Museum.

WHISTLER BLACKCOMB SKI RESORT

British Columbia

The giant twin peaks of Whistler and Blackcomb, just 75 miles north of Vancouver on the stunning Sea-to-Sky Highway, comprise North America's largest ski and snowboard destinations, regularly rated No. 1 by countless polls and magazines. Its hosting of the 2010 Winter Olympic games is yet another measure of the high regard these slopes inspire. Talk about Whistler Blackcomb, and one speaks in superlatives.

In part, the numbers do the talking: Whistler Blackcomb has a vertical mile of drop; 8,100 acres of skiable terrain (that's 2,400 acres more than the largest U.S. resort); more than 200 marked trails, 16 massive alpine bowls, an unfathomable 38 feet of snowfall per year; and a ski season that runs from late November through May (with summer skiing on Blackcomb mid-June through August). Runs are both lengthy (the longest is 7 miles) and dramatically set, with renowned views from an impressively developed lift system, reason enough for skiiers to come from as far away as Moscow and Japan. The very size of Whistler Blackcomb allows the million-plus annual visitors to enjoy alone-with-nature runs on their personal favorite trails—it never really feels crowded.

Whistler Blackcomb's 37 ski lifts can transport 69,939 skiers an hour to mountain peaks above the clouds.

Whistler Blackcomb has acquired a cult reputation with advanced and extreme skiers and snowboarders, but in truth the resort offers something—and lots of it—for everyone. Over half the trails are rated intermediate, and cross-country skiers can glide along 18.5 miles of groomed trails in Lost Lake Park. Other winter activities include dogsledding, snowshoeing, and ice-skating. Thrill-hungry skiers can also take advantage of guided heli-skiing or snowcat skiing on more remote and challenging mountains near Whistler.

The runs on Whistler and Blackcomb peaks are linked at their base by the Tyrolean-style, pedestrian-only Whistler Village, with café-lined plazas, boutiques, over 170 restaurants and après-ski watering holes, and accommodations—some grand and others swank and intimate.

The Four Seasons Resort is among Whistler's finest hotels, a spare, très elegant monument to refinement in a town with its share of faux alpine homeyness. Its urbane good taste extends to the oversize guest rooms, decorated in wood and cool earth tones, all with fireplaces, balconies, and soaker tubs. With 13 treatment rooms, the Spa at Four Seasons Resort is Whistler's largest and most luxurious, with a heated outdoor pool and three whirlpool baths that fill half the hotel courtyard. Whistler Blackcomb's best ski-in/ski-out property, however, is the grand, gabled Fairmont Chateau Whistler, a resort-within-a-resort at the base of

Blackcomb Mountain. With 550 luxury-level rooms it's not exactly intimate, but it's the place to ski and be seen. The Wildflower Restaurant's acclaimed local seafood is reason enough to check in, as are superlative Asian and Ayurvedic spa treatments that are nirvana for après-ski weariness. As the season turns, Fairmont Chateau Whistler effortlessly segues into a summertime playground, with rafting, hiking, horseback riding, and the 18-hole Robert Trent Jones Jr. course that is one of Canada's most beautiful, with three other fine courses lying within striking distance.

WHERE: 75 miles/120 km north of Vancouver. *Visitor info:* Tel 800-766-0449 or 604-967-8950; whistlerblackcomb.com. *Cost:* 3-day lift tickets from US$246/C$327. *When:* ski season Nov–May. **FOUR SEASONS:** Tel 888-935-2460 or 604-935-3400; fourseasons.com/whistler. *Cost:* from US$224/C$299 (off-peak), from US$262/C$349 (peak). **FAIRMONT CHATEAU WHISTLER:** Tel 800-606-8244 or 604-938-8000; fairmont.com/whistler. *Cost:* from US$192/C$255 (off-peak), from US$247/C$329 (peak); dinner US$49/C$65; greens fees US$75/C$99 (off-peak), US$120/C$159 (peak). **BEST TIMES:** Jan–Mar for skiing; mid-July for Whistler Music & Arts Festival; early Nov for Cornucopia, Whistler's annual food and wine celebration.

A Place of Awe and Wonder

YOHO NATIONAL PARK

British Columbia

Yoho National Park's name derives from a Cree expression of awe and wonder—an apt summation of the marvels found here on the steep western face of the Rockies. In fact, the park's towering peaks, hidden jewel-colored glacial lakes, and thundering waterfalls are relatively undisturbed compared to the tourism juggernauts of Banff and Jasper National Parks just east in neighboring Alberta (see pp. 1025 and 1034). It's quieter here, despite eye-riveting scenery, outstanding even in the gorgeous Canadian Rockies.

Much of Yoho's 507 square miles lies in the drainage of Kicking Horse River, which gathers the glacial waters along the Continental Divide before plunging to meet the Columbia River at Golden, B.C. The river's steep descent makes it popular with white-water rafters; with near-constant Class III and IV rapids, the Kicking Horse is one of the most exciting white-water destinations in Canada. Local outfitters provide guided day trips to both the river's more gentle upper reaches, and the adrenaline-pumping chutes and drops that attract rafting enthusiasts

The Takakkaw Falls are fed by the Daly glacier.

from around the world. In just two hours you can splash through 14 sets of rapids ranging from Class II to IV with evocative names like "Shotgun," "Table Saw," "Roller Coaster," and "The Last Waltz."

The park's visitor center at Field will introduce you to more than 250 miles of well-kept hiking trails, and backcountry destinations such as remote aquamarine Lake O'Hara and its historic wilderness lodge. The lake is well known among hikers and outdoor enthusiasts for its stunning setting and the network of trails (some strenuous) radiating into the high alpine neverland with top-of-the-world views. A popular short hike leads to a viewpoint and picnic area overlooking Takakkaw Falls, Canada's second highest (after 1,443-foot Della Falls on Vancouver Island), with a total drop of 1,250 feet. Its name comes from the Cree word meaning "wonderful," which it certainly is. Like the park's many other cascades, Takakkaw is most voluminous in early summer, when melting snow and ice provide ample runoff.

Seven miles northwest of Field is glacier-fed Emerald Lake, the largest in the park and named for the peculiar color that astonished those who first happened upon it in 1882. It is another of Yoho's most popular destinations, a perfect place for hiking, canoeing (which is not allowed on Lake O'Hara), and horseback riding. From the Emerald Lake Lodge, strike out on a gentle 90-minute trail around waters that reflect the jagged peaks surrounding the lake. Lakefront cottages with balconies overlooking the water are the park's best accommodations, but even they can feel not removed enough during the busy summer months. Visit in the off months (the lodge stays open year-round), when the lake can be even more magical, if that's possible.

WHERE: 130 miles/209 km west of Calgary. Tel 250-343-6783; pc.gc.ca/yoho. **HOW:** for rafting on Kicking Horse River, Alpine Rafting, tel 888-599-5299 or 250-344-6778; alpinerafting.com. *Cost:* half-day trips from US$71/C$95, full-day trips from US$94/C$125. *When:* mid-May–mid-Sept. **LAKE O'HARA LODGE:** Tel 250-343-6418 or 403-678-4110 (off-season); lakeohara.com. *When:* mid-June–early Oct and late Jan–early Apr. *Cost:* from US$500/C$665. **EMERALD LAKE LODGE:** Tel 800-663-6336 or 403-410-7417; crmr.com. *Cost:* from US$119/C$159 (off-peak), from US$300/C$399 (peak). **BEST TIMES:** Jan–Mar for cross-country skiing; mid-July–mid-Aug for hiking; Sept–Oct for foliage.

Kings of the Tundra in the Far North

POLAR BEAR SAFARI

Churchill, Manitoba

Polar bears are among the largest of all terrestrial predators, some weighing in at 1,500 pounds. While they are generally solitary creatures, many of the polar bears that live in the Hudson Bay area during the mild summer months congregate along its southern shores near the port town of Churchill, and patiently wait until the ice floes form again—their means of hunting seals. This is the polar bear capital of the world, where expectant bears come to their maternity dens to bear their young. If the chance to see roving polar bears in their native habitat isn't enough, the late-fall night skies are frequently pulsing with the dancing lights of the aurora borealis.

The Churchill denning area, one of the largest in the Arctic, was placed under the protection of Wapusk National Park in 1996, and travelers are permitted to visit these sites only by joining authorized tour groups. In a separate protected area that is more accessible from Churchill, Natural Habitat Adventures takes small groups into the vast and empty tundra in the comfort (and safety) of a massive polar rover with the hopes of spotting young males engaged in play-fight and solitary adults lumbering across the tundra in a lethargic state of walking hibernation.

Nearly 1,000 polar bears call the Hudson Bay area home.

Although polar bear viewing takes place in fall, the arctic summer brings a brief but astonishing display of flora and wildlife to the tundra. Summer trips to Churchill, a town with fewer than 1,000 inhabitants, allow you to journey onto Hudson Bay or along the coast—under nearly 24-hour daylight—in search of beluga whales, caribou, and seals, or to join a birding trip focused on the more than 200 species of rare arctic waterfowl and shorebirds.

You can't reach Churchill by road; most travelers fly in from Winnipeg, but VIA Rail offers passenger rail service between Winnipeg and Churchill year-round (a 36-hour journey each way). It's a great way to observe the changing landscapes of northern Canada's countless lakes, forests, and vast tundra.

WHERE: 630 miles/1,014 km north of Winnipeg. **WAPUSK NATIONAL PARK:** Tel 888-773-8888 or 204-675-8863; pc.gc.ca/wapusk. **NATURAL HABITAT ADVENTURES:** Tel 800-543-8917 or 303-449-3711; nathab.com. *Cost:* 6- and 7-day fall polar-bear-viewing trips from US$4,432/C$5,895 per person, includes charter flights to/from Winnipeg and Churchill; 7–9 day summer excursions from US$3,756/C$4,995, includes round-trip transportation to/from Winnipeg. *When:* polar-bear-viewing trips, mid-Oct–mid-Nov; summer excursions July–mid-Aug. **VIA RAIL:** Tel 888-842-7245 or 514-871-6000; viarail.ca. *Cost:* round-trip coach (no sleeper) fare Winnipeg–Churchill from US$875/C$1,164 for two; round-trip with double-occupancy sleeper, US$2,003/C$2,664.

Forests High Above the Prairie

RIDING MOUNTAIN NATIONAL PARK

Manitoba

Amid the rolling grain fields and plains of southern Manitoba, sharp, forested hills rise like islands above the prairies. In fact, the steeply buckled uplands of Riding Mountain National Park were once literally islands. This jagged ridge blocked the western advance of Ice Age glaciers and when the glaciers melted, forming vast lakes, the escarpment stood above the waters, creating outposts of Ice Age flora and fauna. Riding Mountain National Park is unique in the wide variety of ecosystems it embraces: Within 1,158 square miles, the park includes expanses of boreal (northern) forest more typical of subarctic latitudes; a band of eastern hardwood forest; huge meadows of fescue grasslands; and lakes, marshes, and river-bottom wetlands. Wildlife now found nowhere else on the surrounding prairies also call the park home; it includes over 260 species of birds, as well as moose, wolf, elk, coyote, lynx, black bear, and bison.

The park offers over 250 miles of hiking and mountain biking trails leading to backcountry lakes and vistas, plus more unusual destinations, such as a deserted WWII prisoner of war camp, which held 450 Germans captured in North Africa from 1943 to 1945. At the time, the area was considered so remote that the camp didn't even need walls or fences

to contain the prisoners. The park's center is the village of Wasagaming, located on Clear Lake, a popular destination for swimming, fishing, and boating. The best of the village's comfortable lodges is Elkhorn Resort Hotel, with large rooms and chalets, a great steak house restaurant, and an archetypal Canadian bar, with a huge stone fireplace and fish mounted on log walls. Elkhorn offers a wide range of warm-weather activities including tennis, hiking, mountain biking, and even scuba diving in summer. White months present opportunities for snowshoeing, cross-country skiing, dogsledding, and a recuperative treatment at the resort's spa, appreciated anytime of year.

WHERE: 154 miles/248 km northwest of Winnipeg. Tel 204-848-7275; pc.gc.ca/riding. **ELKHORN RESORT HOTEL:** Tel 866-355-4676 or 204-848-2802; elkhornresort.mb.ca. *Cost:* from US$75/C$100 (off-peak), from US$117/C$155 (peak). **BEST TIMES:** Jan–Mar for cross-country skiing; June–Sept for hiking and boating.

A Wintertime Celebration of Western Canada's French Heritage

FESTIVAL DU VOYAGEUR

Winnipeg, Manitoba

From the late 17th century to the early 19th century, French fur traders and explorers called *voyageurs* canoed the continent's waterways, from Montreal to the Pacific Ocean, from the Arctic Ocean to the Mississippi River.

These Men of the North, as they called themselves, were the first Europeans to settle in Canada. As expert woodsmen, canoe handlers, and hunters, they were widely respected for their skills and hard work but were even better known for their joie de vivre under the harshest conditions. When a group of voyageurs got together, particularly at the annual gathering called the Rendezvous, the fiddle would come out and all the pent-up energy of a full year's

work was released in singing, dancing, and merrymaking—and in the unrestrained consumption of food and drink, usually of the fortifying kind.

The Festival du Voyageur, the largest winter festival in western Canada, is held every February in the streets and halls of St. Boniface, Winnipeg's French Quarter. Dating back to 1783, when it began as a fur trappers' hub, today it is the largest French-speaking community in western Canada. The festival vividly recaptures the spirit of a fur traders' rendezvous during a ten-day celebration of food, song, dance, and the joys of all things winter. It takes place at Fort Gibraltar, a recreation of a North West Company fur-trading fort from 1815. Within the walls of the trading post are large heated tents dedicated to musical events, great quantities of food, crafts fairs, and other entertainment. The festival is especially noted as a showcase for traditional music, with internationally recognized fiddling and jigging competitions.

In other parts of the festival grounds, performers in historic garb sing traditional songs and tell tales of adventure. It wouldn't be a festival of French culture without food and drink, and traditional delicacies such as *poutine*—fried potatoes topped with cheese and gravy—are served up with warm hospitality. One favorite spot for a drink is Sur le Bar'd'la Rouge, a "snow bar" where all the fixtures—including the pool table and shuffleboard—are made of ice. And there's straight-up winter fun for the kids, like a snow maze and a snow slide in the crisp winter air.

WHERE: Voyageur Park, St. Boniface. Tel 204-237-7692; festivalvoyageur.mb.ca. *When:* 10 days in mid-Feb. **WHERE TO STAY:** Fort Garry Hotel, tel 877-596-3046 or 204-942-8251; fortgarryhotel.com. *Cost:* from US$119/C$159.

Fishing the Lakes of Arctic Canada

YELLOW DOG LODGE

Duncan and Graham Lakes, Northwest Territories

Anglers, imagine this: a fly-in fishing adventure with wilderness solitude, pristine waters, and trophy-size lake trout and northern pike to complete a too-good-to-be-true scenario. Unfortunately, the not-so-dreamy component

of a fishing holiday at a remote northern lake has often been the lodge itself—sometimes no more than a set of weather-beaten cabins that puts the rough back in roughing it. However, a new generation of Canadian fishing lodges is set to prove that you don't need to give up on comfort and fine food as you fish the lakes of the little-visited Northwest Territories.

Just 20 minutes north by floatplane from Yellowknife, the territorial capital, Yellow Dog Lodge is an exemplar of this new breed of backcountry destinations. On Pilote Point, which sits on a rocky divide between Duncan and Graham lakes, Yellow Dog seamlessly blends the features of a high-toned ecotourism resort and a traditional fishing camp. During the long summer days, guided day hikes take guests past mossy bogs, across trickling ponds, and through the taiga, the boreal forest of spruce and fir that covers the rocky barrens. From canoes and kayaks, guests can explore the lakeshore and view wildlife—moose, beaver, and nesting waterfowl all make a home in this aqueous landscape. In winter, when the lodge will open on special request, the frozen lakes become highways for snowmobiles, and the silent snow-filled forests invite exploration with snowshoes and Nordic skis. With zero light pollution, the pulsing, multicolored aurora borealis puts on a fantastic display in the fall and winter sky.

But fishing remains the focus at Yellow Dog Lodge. Fishing guides will help ensure even amateurs a chance to catch that big one in the deep, pure crystal clear waters of glacier-trenched Duncan Lake. There's also seasonal fly-fishing for Arctic grayling, a colorful trout relative with an outsize dorsal fin that gives a good, hard fight with lots of high, twisting jumps.

The comforts of Yellow Dog Lodge are the reward for a long recreation-filled day in the arctic backcountry. Perched above the lake on a rocky outcrop, the lodge provides snug guest rooms, while private chalets extend along a pristine waterfront. The lodge's food is a point of pride and expression of passion. Owners Kathy and Gordon Gin are excellent hosts and fine cooks, and lodge meals—served family-style in the cozy dining room or, in warm weather, on the lakeside patio—are jubilant occasions that combine great food and convivial conversation. The wood-fired hot tub offers anglers and hikers a chance to relax weary muscles before another perfect day of adventure in the Canadian Arctic.

WHERE: 30 miles/48 km north of Yellowknife. Tel 403-668-9936; yellowdoglodge .ca. *Cost:* 2-night packages from US$1,285/ C$1,709 per person, double occupancy, includes all meals, lodging, use of equipment, and round-trip transportation from Yellowknife. *When:* closed Oct–May. **BEST TIMES:** Jan–Apr for winter sports; June–late Sept for fishing; Oct–Mar for northern lights.

Where the Great Plains Meet the Great North Woods

PRINCE ALBERT NATIONAL PARK

Saskatchewan

A secluded world of forest-ringed lakes and rich with wildlife, Prince Albert National Park in Saskatchewan is a million acres of nearly roadless wilderness, and a paddler's and hiker's paradise. The terrain is astonishingly varied, beginning at the upper verge of the great Canadian prairies and moving into the dense woodlands of the north. The hilly landscape is dotted with ponds and trenched by cold streams, and at the heart of the park is a series of large glacier-gouged lakes, linked by meandering rivers. In fact, more than 30 percent of the park's surface is water, making a canoe or kayak a perfect way to navigate and explore this boreal Eden.

Because of its size and the fact that it straddles two major ecosystems, the park is home to a wide range of animal species, including lynx, black bear, and gray wolf. The park is also the habitat for one of the world's largest colonies of nesting white pelicans, and has one of Canada's few free-roaming plains bison herds. It's true Canadian backcountry, but because the park is on the edge of the prairies, it's easy to get to—you can use the family car to visit this piece of the outback.

You don't need the skills of a *voyageur* to explore the park. CanoeSki Discovery Company offers a selection of multiday canoe adventures into the heart of the wilderness. The trips, led by naturalists and certified canoeing guides, include tours especially for families and birders. Some include excursions to the cabin of author and conservationist Grey Owl, an Englishman who was adopted by the Ojibwa and spent seven years living on Ajawaan Lake. A number of canoe trips depart from Kingsmere Lake, including the gentle one- to two-day Bagwa route and the arduous four- to seven-day Bladebone route with numerous and lengthy portages. In winter, the company offers cross-country skiing excursions into the park's southern woodlands.

The park's headquarters and visitor center is in the town of Waskesiu Lake, which offers a full range of services, including very comfortable rooms and enjoyable meals at the Hawood Inn, a handsome wooden lodge with a serene backwoods atmosphere just steps from the beach.

WHERE: 149 miles/240 km north of Saskatoon. Tel 306-663-4522; pc.gc.ca/prince albert. **CANOESKI DISCOVERY COMPANY:** Tel 306-653-5693; canoeski.com. *Cost:* in-park canoe packages including overnight trips from US$330/C$440. **HAWOOD INN:** Tel 877-441-5544 or 306-663-5219; hawood.com. *Cost:* from US$59/C$79 (off-peak), from US$99/C$132 (peak). **BEST TIMES:** Jan–Mar for cross-country skiing; June–Sept for canoeing and hiking.

Historic Home of Canada's Finest

ROYAL CANADIAN MOUNTED POLICE TRAINING ACADEMY

Regina, Saskatchewan

I t's hard to believe that Saskatchewan's capital, Regina—now a prosperous and progressive city with beautiful historic buildings and gleaming office towers—literally began as a pile of bones. The first European settlement on these fertile prairies was called "Pile O' Bones" for the large stacks of buffalo bones assembled on the banks of Wascana Creek by Cree hunters (who reasoned that buffalo herds would not leave the land that contained the bones of their buffalo ancestors).

In 1882, two events changed Pile O' Bones forever: The Canadian Pacific Railroad passed through on its way to the Pacific, linking this tiny collection of tents and shacks to the rest of Canada. Then the Royal Canadian Mounted Police (the RCMP, or Mounties) made the settlement—grandly renamed Regina (Latin for "queen") for Queen Victoria—its headquarters. With the protection of the Mounties, Regina quickly grew from a railroad settlement to the capital of the vast Northwest Territories, which then included both Saskatchewan and Alberta and all points north.

Today the link between the RCMP and Regina is stronger than ever. The RCMP Training Academy, just west of downtown and referred to simply as "the Depot" by locals, has served for over a century as the agency's primary training facility for new recruits. Guided tours of the academy and historic non-denominational chapel are offered after the Sergeant Major's Parade, held weekdays at

As a federal, provincial, and municipal policing body, the RCMP is unique in the world.

12:45 P.M., when trainee Mounties in full red and gold regalia strut their stuff on parade grounds (in winter or inclement weather, the parade is held in the Drill Hall). On July 1 and successive Tuesday evenings through mid-August, the Mounties also enact the Sunset Retreat Ceremony, an exciting 45-minute display of horsemanship accompanied by bagpipe and bugle bands. Also at the Depot is the C$40 million RCMP Heritage Centre, designed by renowned Canadian architect Arthur Erickson. It relates the compelling, colorful history of the Mounties via exhibits and interactive media. From its earliest days of horseback patrols across an untamed land, the RCMP has been one of Canada's most recognizable symbols, and the Heritage Centre displays an extensive collection of historical material and artifacts.

To gain more insights into the life and times of frontier Saskatchewan and the early days of the Mounties, time your visit to Regina to coincide with a performance of the long-running *The Trial of Louis Riel*, by John Coulter. Mounted each summer at the Royal Saskatchewan Museum, the play is drawn from courtroom transcripts of Regina's most famous trial. Louis Riel was a leader in the 1880s Northwest Rebellion, when the mixed-race Métis people, the offspring of French trappers who had intermarried with Native women, clashed with incoming settlers protected by the Mounties. After a series of armed conflicts between the Métis and the Mounted Police, the final episode of the rebellion was played out in Regina in 1885, when Métis leader Louis Riel, after a long trial, was hanged for treason. *The Trial of Louis Riel* captures the compelling drama of two cultures in conflict, addressing issues of religion, language, race, justice, and prejudice on the Canadian frontier.

Where: 160 miles/257 km south of Saskatoon. Tel 306-522-7333; rcmpheritage centre.com. **Where to stay:** Hotel Saskatchewan, tel 888-236-2427 or 306-522-7691; marriott.com. *Cost:* from US$147/C$195. *The Trial of Louis Riel:* Tel 306-728-5728; rielcoproductions.com. *When:* Thurs–Sat, mid- to late July. **Best times:** July–mid-Aug for the Mounties Sunset Retreat Ceremony; early Aug for Queen City Ex, Regina's big summer arts festival (thequeen cityex.com).

Native Prehistory on the Northern Plains

WANUSKEWIN HERITAGE PARK

Saskatoon, Saskatchewan

A round 6,000 years ago, as Ice Age glaciers retreated from the plains of southern Canada, Native Americans first stood on the bluffs above the South Saskatchewan River, at the place that would be known as Wanuskewin. Over the millennia, successive Native cultures passed through Wanuskewin, each leaving tantalizing clues of ancient ways and lives. On this same windswept ridge now stands Wanuskewin Heritage Park, a magnificent interpretive center at the hub of 19 separate archaeological sites that step across time from the post–Ice Age era to the 19th century.

Wanuskewin, a term from the Cree language meaning "seeking peace of mind," was central for Northern Plains Indian bison hunting. The 300-acre area contains virtually every type of archaeological feature common to the precontact Northern Plains, all within walking distance of each other. Trails lead from the interpretive center across the prairie and into the Opimihaw Valley, linking remains such as tepee rings (circles of stone that once held down the buffalo-skin walls of tepees), stone cairns that early hunters used to guide herds of stampeding bison, and a boulder alignment or medicine wheel, which may have played a role in early spiritual practices. Wanuskewin also contains two bison jumps, the cliffs over which early hunters stampeded herds of buffalo in order to slaughter them.

The visitors center, built in the form of a vast tepee, explores the history and culture of

A dancer in traditional Ojibwa (Chippewa in the U.S.) Nation clothing

Northern Plains peoples, with a broad collection of artifacts and tools, interactive displays, and a fascinating collection of contemporary Indian art. In summer, First Nations dancers, resplendent in feathers and colorful costumes, perform ancient, rhythmic dances to the sound of drums and singing in the center's outdoor amphitheater. The visitors center's cafeteria lets you sample traditional foods such as bison, bannock, Saskatoon berry pie, and muskeg bush tea.

Wanuskewin Heritage Park is just minutes north of Saskatoon, a pleasant city with deep agrarian roots yet a youthful vibe due to the University of Saskatchewan's 20,000 students. Downtown is dominated by the Delta Bessborough Hotel, a historic riverside fantasy built in the style of a turreted French château. Originally constructed in the 1930s by the Canadian National Railway as its showcase in western Canada, the Delta Bessborough remains just that.

Where: 3 miles/5 km north of Saskatoon. Tel 306-931-6767; wanuskewin.com. **Delta Bessborough Hotel:** Tel 888-236-2427 or 306-244-5521; marriott.com. *Cost:* from US$153/C$200. **Best time:** 10 days in late July and early Aug for the PotashCorp Fringe Festival (25thstreettheatre.org).

Catching Gold Fever in the Klondike

Dawson City

The Yukon

In 1896, the cry went up: Gold! Three prospectors panning for nuggets on a remote tributary of the Yukon River had discovered gold, and lots of it. Word of the Klondike gold fields quickly spread, and the lure of easy riches drew

men and women from every corner of the world. By 1900, Dawson City, just 165 miles south of the Arctic Circle, counted more than 30,000 inhabitants (thousands of them living in tents), a boomtown if ever there was one.

While some early prospectors made easy fortunes, many other Stampeders eked out livings without ever holding a pan, working as merchants, cardsharps, bankers, saloonkeepers, and dance hall girls. By the 1910s, most of the easily panned gold had been harvested and industrial dredging replaced prospecting. More than US$360 million in gold had been shipped out.

However, unlike many gold rush towns in the Yukon, Dawson City refused to die. It served as capital of the Yukon Territory until 1953, when the torch was passed to Whitehorse, and with its solid core of late Victorian hotels, saloons, false-fronted stores, and all manner of private residences from mansions to miner's shacks, it has become one of western Canada's most fascinating open-air museums.

Dawson retains the air of a turn-of-the century frontier town, with many buildings preserved by Parks Canada.

Dawson City today has a year-round population of 1,300 (with the entire territory of Yukon ringing in at 34,000 and more than half living in Whitehorse). Much of the town is protected by Parks Canada, which has done a masterful job of preserving and restoring the remaining frontier structures, most of which are still open for business. The park service offers walking tours, with stops to view a replica of novelist Jack London's log cabin (he would later return home to California and write *The Call of the Wild*) and to hear actors recite the verses of Robert Service, whose many poems, such as "The Cremation of Sam McGee," immortalize the Klondike spirit. The SS *Keno*, built in 1922 and just one of the hundreds of riverboats that once linked Dawson City to the outside world, is now permanently moored to the Yukon River docks.

In summer, stroll along the boardwalks under the midnight sun and listen to traditional Yukon fiddle tunes drifting from barrooms. Honky-tonk piano and dancing girls provide the entertainment at Diamond Tooth Gerties Gambling Hall, Canada's northernmost casino. Several vintage hotels are in operation, authentically old but comfortably up-to-date. One of the most unusual is Bombay Peggy's Victorian Inn and Pub. Built in 1900 as the town brothel, it's a stylish inn now, peddling hospitality of a more reputable kind.

WHERE: 333 miles/537 km north of Whitehorse. **KLONDIKE NATIONAL HISTORIC SITES:** Tel 867-993-7200; pc.gc.ca/klondike. **DIAMOND TOOTH GERTIES:** Tel 867-993-5525; dawsoncity.ca. **BOMBAY PEGGY'S VICTORIAN INN AND PUB:** Tel 867-993-6969; bombaypeggys.com. *Cost:* from US$135/C$179. **BEST TIMES:** Feb for the Yukon Quest dogsled race (yukonquest.com), which runs between Fairbanks, Alaska, and Whitehorse, Yukon, stopping for a mandatory 36-hour layover in Dawson City; June–mid-Sept for long summer days and Parks Canada sites; mid-Aug for Discovery Days celebrating the finding of Klondike gold.

SPECIAL INDEXES

ACTIVE TRAVEL AND ADVENTURE •
CULINARY EXPERIENCES •
FIRST-RATE HOTELS, RESORTS,
AND SPAS • FOR THE CULTURALLY
MINDED • GLORIOUS NATURE •
GREAT GOLF • LOVELY BEACHES
AND GETAWAY ISLANDS •
SCENIC DRIVES, TRAIN TRIPS, AND
CRUISES • SPORTS FANS, TAKE NOTE
• TAKE THE KIDS •
WINDOWS ON THE PAST

SPECIAL INDEXES

For additional information, please refer to the General Index starting on page 1119.

MEMORABLE MEALS

REGIONAL SPECIALTIES AND HIGHLIGHTS

First-Rate Hotels, Resorts, and Spas

Alaska & Hawaii

Canada

For the Culturally Minded

ARTS CENTERS AND FESTIVALS

BOOKSTORES

CULTURAL CENTERS AND FESTIVALS

DANCE, DANCE FESTIVALS

FOLK ART AND FESTIVALS

LITERARY EXCURSIONS

MUSEUMS

Alaska & Hawaii

Canada

Four Corners and the Southwest

MUSICAL JOURNEYS

NATIVE AMERICAN CULTURE

Great Golf

Scenic Drives, Train Trips, and Cruises

Sports Fans, Take Note

BASEBALL

BOXING

EQUESTRIAN SPORTS

FOOTBALL

HOCKEY

MARATHON AND TRIATHLON

MOTOR SPORTS

MOUNTAIN BIKING

RODEOS

Take the Kids

This list features activities of specific interest to children. Many other family-friendly destinations, such as national parks and beaches, can be found in other special indexes and in the general index (p. 1119).

Alaska & Hawaii

Canada

Four Corners and the Southwest

Windows on the Past

COWBOYS AND THE AMERICAN WEST

HISTORIC DISTRICTS

HISTORIC SITES AND INSTITUTIONS

LIVING HISTORY

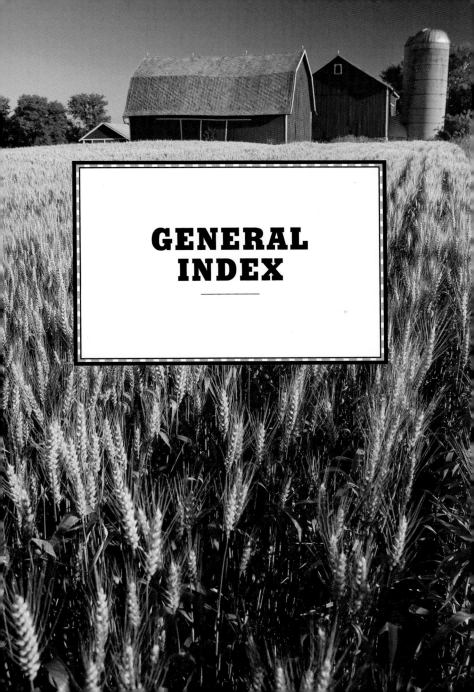

GENERAL INDEX

GENERAL INDEX

NOTE: In the General Index, readers will find proper names listed alphabetically, as well as categories such as Casinos and Powwows. Categories such as dining and sports are cross-referenced to the special index on that subject. Please note that items in SMALL CAPS refer to main topics.

The Special Indexes, found on pages 1073–1118, include the following categories:

- ACTIVE TRAVEL AND ADVENTURE, including hiking, biking, fishing, skiing, snowboarding, boating, horseback riding, and more
- CULINARY EXPERIENCES, including destination restaurants, food festivals, wineries, breweries, distilleries, and more
- FIRST-RATE HOTELS, RESORTS, AND SPAS, plus B&Bs, inns, and lodges
- FOR THE CULTURALLY MINDED, featuring museums, performances, literary pilgrimages, music and arts festivals, concert halls, and bookstores
- GLORIOUS NATURE, including gardens, national parks, nature centers, wildlife encounters, wilderness preserves, birding, and natural wonders
- GREAT GOLF, featuring America's best courses and golf trails
- LOVELY BEACHES AND GETAWAY ISLANDS, including seashores, lakeshores, and secluded isles
- SCENIC DRIVES, TRAIN TRIPS, AND CRUISES, featuring byways, rail tours, and sightseeing voyages
- SPORTS FANS, TAKE NOTE, including ball parks, race tracks, and Halls of Fame
- TAKE THE KIDS, featuring activities of specific interest to children
- WINDOWS ON THE PAST, including living history, museums, historical institutions, military history, and restored private homes.

A

Abbey of St. Benoit-du-Lac, Que., 1013

Abbot's Lobster in the Rough, Conn., 7

Abeja Winery, Wash., 904

Abe's Barbecue, La., 436

Abiel Smith School, Mass., 38

Abilene, Kans., 609

Abingdon, Va., 233–34

Abiquiu, N.Mex., 749–50

Abita Mystery House, La., 420

Abita Springs, La., 419–20

Abraham Lincoln Birthplace, Ky., 410

Absinthe, Nev., 731

Abyssinian Baptist Church, N.Y., 177

ACADIA NATIONAL PARK, Maine, 20–21

ACADIAN COAST, FESTIVALS ALONG, N.B., 975–976

ACADIAN CULTURAL CENTER, La., 420, 421–22

Acadian Festival, N.B., 975–76

accommodations, overnight (by region)

Alaska & Hawaii

Alyeska Resort, Alaska, 915–16

Bettles Lodge, Alaska, 915

Brooks Lodge, Alaska, 921

Camp Denali, Alaska, 912

Chena Hot Springs Resort, Alaska, 911

Fairmont Kea Lani Maui, Hawaii, 951

Fairmont Orchid, Hawaii, 933

PHOTO CREDITS

Unless otherwise specified, copyright on the works reproduced lies with the respective photographers, agencies, and museums. Despite extensive research, it has not always been possible to establish copyright ownership. Where this is the case, we would appreciate notification.

FRONT COVER AND SPINE: Arnaldo Jr/Fotolia.

BACK COVER AUTHOR PHOTO: **Gabrielle Revere** (gabriellerevere.com).

TABLE OF CONTENTS: p. iii Cosmo Condina/Getty Images; p. vii Batos/fotolia; p. viii james_wheeler/fotolia; p. ix Extreme Sports Photo/Alamy Stock Photo.

NEW ENGLAND: **Alamy Stock Photo:** p. 8 Ira Berger; p. 16 AugustSnow; p. 24 John Van Decker; p. 29 Stock Connection Blue; p. 31 Aurora Photos; p. 34 Mira; p. 36 Bill Bachmann; p. 37 Randy Duchaine; p. 38 Brian Jansen; p. 49 Robert Harding; p. 52 Danita Delimont; p. 57 JTB Media Creation, Inc.; p. 61 Jon Arnold Images, Ltd.; p. 62 Marianne A. Campolongo; p. 65 Version One; p. 67 Aurora Photos; p. 72 Erin Paul Donovan; p. 77 Look Die Bildagentur der Fotografen; p. 78 EcoPhotography.com; p. 79 Pat & Chuck Blackley; p. 81 Mira; p. 91 RosalreneBetancourt 7; p. 92 George Robinson; p. 95 Edwin Remsberg; p. 101 Robert Harding. © **Cate Brown 2015:** p. 88. **Fotolia:** p. 5 alex9500; p. 13 f11photo; p. 14 jiawangkun; p. 18 Bill Perry; p. 26 Chee-Onn Leong; p. 39 david9039; p. 51 nfsphoto; p. 79 Chee-Onn Leong; p. 83 demerzel21; p. 106 crin. **Getty Images:** p. 32 Lonely Planet Images; p. 41 J. Rogash/Getty Images Sport; p. 47 John Coletti; p. 58 Kim Grant/Lonely Planet Images; p. 76 Boston Globe; p. 80 John Elk III/Lonely Planet Images; p. 86 Douglas Manson; p. 98 Christian Aslund; p. 110 Denis Jr. Tangney. **Shutterstock:** p. 21 Vladimir Ivanov; p. 46 CO Leong; p. 75 Robert Manley.

Courtesy Photos: p. 3 Gabriel Loughlin Photography/Cambridge Office of Tourism; p. 9 Robert Benson/Westport County Playhouse; p. 10 Foxwoods; p. 17 Mike Franzman/Louis' Lunch; p. 20 Grace Hotels Limited; p. 23 Sugar Loaf; p. 35 David Troup/Farnsworth Museum; p. 43 Isabella Stewart Gardner Museum; p. 63 Zoran Orlic/Mass MoCA; p. 65 Robert Deschene/Salem Witch Museum; p. 70 Ralph Morang/Canterbury Shaker Village; p. 84 The Chanler; p. 89 Al Forno; p. 92 Twin Farms; p. 94 Catamount Trail; p. 96 Grafton Inn; p. 99 Rob Bossi/Okemo; p. 103 Jumping Rocks Photography/Rabbit Hill Inn; p. 105 Marshall Webb/Shelburne Farms.

MID-ATLANTIC: **age fotostock:** p. 131; p. 221 russellkord.com; p. 263 Dennis MacDonald. **Alamy Stock Photo:** p. 114 Ian Dagnall; p. 119 Brian Cahn/ZUMAPRESS.com; p. 121 Philip Rink Jr.; p. 122 Vespasian; p. 124 National Geographic Image Collection; p. 125 Tom Uhlman; p. 129 incamerastock; p. 137 Sandra Baker; p. 141 Robert K. Olejniczak; p. 142 Randy Duchaine; p. 146 Patti McConville; p. 149 Danita Delimont; p. 150 James Schwabel; p. 152 Danita Delimont; p. 154 Bob Elam; p. 155 Mira; p. 157 Zuma Press, Inc.; p. 159 Pegaz; p. 164 nobleIMAGES; p. 176 age footstock; p. 177 Johnny Stockshooter; p. 179 Patrick Batchelder; p. 183 Peter Barritt; p. 185 Richard Green; p. 187 Sandra Baker; p. 191 Marmaduke St. John; p. 193 Zoonar GmBH; p. 202 Philip Scalia; p. 204 Danita Delimont; p. 205 DOD photo; p. 213 brt COMM; p. 214 dpa picture alliance; p. 219 H. Mark Weidman Photography; p. 220 Randy Duchaine; p. 223 Bastiaan Slabbers; p. 227 RosaIreneBetancourt; p. 229 Jon Bilous; p. 234 Pat & Chuck Blackley; p. 237 Tim Mainiero; p. 239 Danita Delimont; p. 240 Visions of America, LLC; p. 242 catnap; p. 246 Visions of America, LLC; p. 248 SuperStock; p. 252 Gregory/Photri Images; p. 253 Pat & Chuck Blackley; p. 261 Nick Jene; p. 262 Michael Ventura; p. 267 Prisma Bildagentur AG; p. 272 Chuck Pefley; p. 280 Danita Delimont. **Fotolia:** pp. 111, 117 SeanPavonePhoto; p. 163 biegles; p. 166 Bokicbo; p. 168

stine1online; p. 170 SeanPavonePhoto; p. 174 venemama; p. 192 Bastos; p. 199 romanslavik.com; p. 207 pabrady63; p. 209 demerzel21; p. 224 Samuel Borges; p. 251 garytog; p. 257 lunamarina; p. 260 marcorubino; p. 264 SeanPavonePhoto; p. 268 Kevin Tietz; p. 270 Calado; p. 271 f11photo; p. 273 sborisov. **Getty Images:** p. 123 Richard L'Anson; p. 130 Cosmo Condina; p. 133 Laura S. Kicey; p. 135 amana productions inc; p. 144 Marie Hickman/Photolibrary; p. 188 Lonely Planet Images; p. 195 Siegried Layda/ Photographer's Choice; p. 250 Jaap Hart/E+; p. 254 Dixie D. Vereen/The Washington Post; p. 277 Jeff Swensen; p. 278 Danita Delimont. **Shutterstock:** p. 118 Wendy Farrington; p. 127 Geoffrey Kuchera; p. 169 Sean Pavone; p. 182 Andrew McDonough; p. 196 littleny; p. 197 CristinaMuraca; p. 203 Cheryl Ann Quigley; p. 222 Benjamin F. Haith; p. 233 Paul S. Wolf; p. 236 Robert Strain; p. 249 Jeremy R. Smith Sr.; p. 255 Matt McClain.

Courtesy Photos: p. 113 Kevin Fleming/Southern Delaware Tourism; p. 115 Ashley Schroeder/Fantail Photography/Hagley Museum; p. 116 Robert Leitch/Winterthur; p. 128 Historic St. Mary's City; p. 138 Woolverton Inn; p. 139 John Gallino/Ryland Inn; p. 148 Corning Museum of Glass; p. 165 Jim Smith Photography/Mohonk Mountain House; p. 184 The Solomon R. Guggenheim Museum, New York. Photograph: David Heald©SRGF, NY.; p. 211 Larry Albee/Longwood Gardens; p. 216 Visit Bucks County; p. 228 Abby Warhola/The Andy Warhol Museum; p. 244 Omni Homestead Resort; p. 258 Lee Stalsworth/Smithsonian Institution; p. 259 Sam Kittner/Newseum; p. 266 James Di Loreto/Smithsonian Institution; p. 275 Josh Saul/ Mountain Stage; p. 276 Stephen Brightwell; p. 279 Pamela R. Withrow/Lewisburg Carnegie Hall; p. 285 Oglebay Resort; p. 286 Greenbrier Resort.

SOUTHEAST: **Alamy Stock Photo:** p. 295 Jon McLean; p. 298 Images-USA; p. 305 Cal Sport Media; p. 317 Nadia Mackenzie; p. 318 Efrain Padro; p. 323 Tim Gartside USA America; p. 326 Katherine Andriotis; p. 332 Pat & Chuck Blackley; p. 337 Danita Delimont; p. 342 SuperStock; p. 350 Jennifer Wright; p. 352 Wesley Hitt; p. 353 Cyrille Gibot; p. 357 Danita Delimont; p. 360 Ron Chapple Stock; p. 380 Planetpix; p. 382 George Oze; p. 385 Ian Dagnall. **Fotolia:** p. 303 Wimbledon; p. 307 Maisna; p. 327 SeanPavonePhoto; p. 336 Doug Pieper; p. 346 SeanPavonePhoto. **Getty Images:** p. 287 Walter Bibikow/age footstock; p. 294 Richard Cummins/Lonely Planet Images; p. 304 Photo Researchers; p. 373 Christian Science Monitor; p. 378 John Elk/Lonely Planet Images. **Shutterstock:** p. 306 Tomasz Szymanski; p. 321 FloridaStock; p. 354 Hank Shiffman; p. 359 John Ray Upchurch; p. 362 Forrest L. Smith, III; p. 365 Jill Lang; p. 366 Mitchell Franklin; p. 368 Keith Murphy; p. 369 Ishbukar Yalilfatar; p. 387 Rob Huntley.

Courtesy Photos: p. 289 Carol M. Highsmith Archive/Library of Congress; p. 290 Bellingrath Gardens; p. 292 Doug Richardson/W.C. Handy Festival; p. 301 Amelia Island Tourist Development Council; p. 309 Dolphin Research Center, Grassy Key, Florida, dolphins.org; p. 310 Little Palm Resort and Spa; p. 315 MCH Messe Schweiz (Basel) AG; p. 325 The Breakers Palm Beach; p. 330 Milledgeville-Baldwin Convention and Visitor's Bureau; p. 333 Porter McLeod/Anthfest; p. 334 Flying Biscuit Café; p. 339 Greyfield Inn; p. 340 Lamar Bates Photography/Dahlonega-Lumpkin County Chamber & Visitors Bureau; p. 343 Jekyll Island Club; p. 344 Cassie Wright Photography; p. 355 ExploreAsheville.com; p. 358 Omni Grove Park Inn; p. 364 Donnie Roberts/The Dispatch/Barbecue Festival; p. 370 Fearrington Village; p. 374 Old Salem Museum and Gardens; p. 379 Historic Charleston Foundation; p. 384 ©Julia Lynn Photography/Spoleto; p. 386 Kiawah Island Golf Resort.

MISSISSIPPI VALLEY: **Alamy Stock Photo:** p. 389 Sean Pavone; p. 391 Buddy Mays; p. 401 JTB Media Creation, Inc.; p. 402 Danita Delimont; p. 408 Stephen Saks Photography; p. 413 Cal Sport Media; p. 421 Stephen Saks Photography; p. 423 John Elk III/Lonely Planet Images; p. 426 Nikreates; p. 428 Flirt; p. 430 Andy Levin; p. 432 Philip Scalia; p. 435 Hemis; p. 439 Andre Jenny; p. 441 Don Smetzer; p. 445 Cindy Hopkins; p. 447 age footstock; p. 452 Danita Delimont; p. 455 Philip Scalia; p. 461 RosaIreneBetancourt 3; p. 466 Martin Thomas Photography; pp. 469, 470 ZUMA Press, Inc.; p. 471 Philip Scalia; p. 472 Flirt; p. 473 Danita Delimont; p. 474 Stephen Saks Photography; p. 475 Brian Jannsen; p. 477 The TN Collection; p. 480 Norman Barrett. **Associated Press:** p. 478 Alyson Wright/Chattanooga Times Free Press. **Fotolia:** p. 462 f11photo. **Getty Images:** p. 398 Richard Cummins/Lonely Planet Images; p. 403 Richard L'Anson/ Lonely Planet Images; p. 409 Richard Cummins/Lonely Planet Images; p. 411 Lexington Herald-Leader; p. 422 John Elk/Lonely Planet Images; p. 425 Neil Setchfield/Lonely Planet Images; pp. 434, 449, 450, 453, 454 John Elk/Lonely Planet Images; pp. 465, 468 Richard L'Anson/Lonely Planet Images. **Newscom:** p. 442 Gayle Harper/DanitaDelmont.com. **Shutterstock:** p. 405 Melissa Caudill; p. 427 Gennady Stetsenko.

Courtesy Photos: p. 393 Brian Chilson/King Biscuit Blues Festival; p. 395 Visit Hot Springs; p. 400 Arkansas Department of Parks and Tourism; p. 415 © H & B; p. 417 National Corvette Museum; p. 419 louisiananorthshore.com; p. 424 Mickey Delcambre/Shadows-on-the-Teche; p. 433 louisiananorthshore.com; p. 436 Austin Britt/Shack-Up Inn; p. 458 St. Joseph Visitors Bureau, stjomo.com; p. 459 Anheuser-Busch; p. 463 Chattanooga Convention & Visitors Bureau; p. 464 VisitFranklin.com; p. 476 Museum of Appalachia.

THE MIDWEST: age fotostock: p. 505 Bob Harr. **Alamy Stock Photo:** p. 481 RosaIreneBetancourt 3; p. 483 Steve Skjold; p. 489 Ian Dagnall; p. 490 Nikreates; p. 491 Jason Lindsey; p. 492 ZUMA Press, Inc.; p. 497 Philip Scalia; p. 500 imageBROKER; p. 502 Jason Lindsey; p. 508 Cal Sport Media; p. 512 Ron Buskirk; p. 515 Stephen Saks Photography; p. 521 John Elk III; p. 524 Andre Jenny; p. 526 Danita Delimont; p. 528 dpa picture alliance; p. 534 Jim West; p. 542 aaronpeterson.net; p. 545 Images-USA; p. 550 America; p. 552 age fotostock; p. 553 CC; p. 556 Tribue Content Agency, LLC; p. 557 Greg Ryan; p. 563 Russel Kord; p. 564 Steven Russell Smith; p. 566 age fotostock; p. 570 Tom Till; p. 580 Danita Delimont; p. 582 Chuck Eckert. **Fotolia:** p. 503 Wirepec; p. 535 SNEHIT; p. 548 AMB-MD Photography; p. 549 wildnerdpix. **Getty Images:** p. 488 Lonely Planet Images; p. 525 Lou Jones/Lonely Planet Images; p. 533 Corinne J. Humphrey/Lonely Planet Images; p. 555 John Elk/Lonely Planet Images; p. 561 Chicago Tribune; p. 562 Holly Hildreth; p. 575 Matt Anderson Photography. **Shutterstock:** p. 495 Jenny Solomon; p. 507 W. Shane Dougherty; p. 523 Bartosz Wardzinski; pp. 536, 538 Michael G. Smith; p. 540 photogeek; p. 541 Brian Morrison; p. 551 Michael J. Thompson; p. 572 Kenneth Sponsler; p. 585 Ryan Mulhall.

Courtesy Photos: p. 494 Taste of Chicago; p. 501 Illinois Historic Preservation Agency; p. 513 Elkhart County Convention and Visitors Bureau; p. 517 Iowa State Fair; p. 518 NPS Photo; p. 520 Iowa Tourism Office; p. 530 Grayling Regional Chamber of Commerce; p. 531 Dean Van Dis/Frederick Meijer Gardens; p. 539 Marshall Area Chamber of Commerce; p. 546 Grand View Lodge; p. 559 Terri Campbell/Camp Washington Chilli; p. 560 Cincinatti Flower Show; p. 574 Canoe Bay; p. 577 Kohler Co; p. 583 Green County Tourism; p. 587 Taliesin Preservation, © Jack Whaley.

GREAT PLAINS: Alamy Stock Photo: p. 589 NaturalLight; p. 594 Paul Harris; p. 596 SuperStock; p. 598 NatPar Collection; p. 601 Steve Bly; p. 603 BLM Photo; p. 610 B. O'Kane; p. 615 Michael DeFreitas (bottom), Blaine Harrington III (top); p. 617 David Cobb; p. 622 Greg Vaughn; p. 625 Allen Russell; p. 627 Stock Connection Blue; p. 628 Danita Delimont; p. 634 John Oeth; p. 637 Wayne Lynch; p. 641 Danita Delimont; p. 644 Witold Skrypczak; pp. 645, 646 Danita Delimont; p. 650 BA LaRue; p. 661 Clint Farlinger; p. 662 franzfoto.com; p. 663 Richard Ellis; p. 675 Aurora Photos; p. 677 Jordi Elias Grassot. **Fotolia:** p. 604 knowlesgallery; p. 611 Michael Vorobiev; p. 614 davidmarx; p. 653 naughtynut; p. 654 wollertz; p. 668 Rob. **Getty Images:** p. 599 Stephen Saks/Lonely Planet Images; p. 605 Glenn Van Der Knijff/Lonely Planet Images; p. 612 Tim Fitzharris/Minden Pictures; p. 619 Lonely Planet Images; p. 631 Joel Sartore/National Geographic; p. 642 Stephen Saks/Lonely Planet Images; p. 651 Dea Picture Library/ De Agostini; pp. 655, 660, 665 Richard Cummins/Lonely Planet Images; p. 666 Lonely Planet Images; p. 669 Richard Cummins/Lonely Planet Images; p. 673 Flash Parker. **Shutterstock:** p. 592 Weldon Schloneger; p. 613 Jennifer Leigh Selig; p. 620 Pierdelune; p. 623 Christopher; p. 633 Chad Bontrager; p. 657 Peder Digre; p. 658 Michael J. Thompson; p. 659 Tracey Stearns; p. 678 Gene Vaught.

Courtesy Photos: p. 616 Museum of the Rockies; p. 626 Montana Book Festival; p. 630 Evan McGlinn; p. 639 Kari L. Barchenger/International Peace Garden; p. 640 Fargo Kiwanis; p. 648 National Cowboy and Western Heritage Museum; p. 667 Jeff Vanuga Photography/Bitterroot Ranch; p. 671 Jackson Hole Mountain Lodge.

FOUR CORNERS AND THE SOUTHWEST: age fotostock: p. 754 Walter Bibikow. **Alamy Stock Photo:** p. 683 Ian Dagnall; p. 685 Brian Green; p. 693 ZUMA Press, Inc.; p. 699 Dennis Frates; p. 702 RosaIreneBetancourt 4; p. 703 Tetra Images; pp. 705, 711 Efrain Padro; p. 715 Stephen Saks Photography; p. 716 K. Philip Harrison; p. 720 Nicholas Henderson; p. 723 Aurora Photos; p. 728 Jan Butchofsky; p. 731 Dave G. Houser; p. 738 YAY Media AS; p. 740 Yaacov Dagan; p. 741 Steve Hamblin; p. 743 Jim West; p. 755 ZUMA Press, Inc.; p. 759 Amar and Isabelle Guillen—Guillen Photo; p. 766 Steve Hamblin; p. 768 Nikreates; p. 769 David R. Frazier Photolibrary, Inc.; p. 774 Ian Dagnall; p. 775 Anne Rippy; p. 777 Prisma Bildagentur AG; p. 786 Danita Delimont; p. 801 Rob Crandall. **Fotolia:** p. 679 Frankix; pp. 681, 686 kojihirano; p. 688 SNEHIT; p. 689 Pixelshop; p. 704 Zack Frank; p. 718 SNEHIT; p. 719 SUDIO 1ONE; p. 727 Mariusz Blach; p. 732 littlestocker; p. 733 davey_photo; p. 735 Sigen Photography; p. 744 eunikas; p. 752 Joe Gough; p. 760 Rusty Dodson; p. 761 Brian Scantlebury; pp. 782, 783 f11photo; p. 788 dfikar; p. 790 James Insogna; p. 791 Scott Prokop; p. 802 ericurquhart. **Getty Images:** p. 690 Dallas Stribley/ Lonely Planet Images; p. 698 Innerflux/E+; p. 710 David Epperson/Moment; p. 714 Walter Bibikow; p. 721 Ron Dahlquist/Corbis Documentary; p. 737 Karl Lehmann/Lonely Planet Images; p. 739 John Elk/Lonely Planet Images; p. 751 Alan Dyer/Stocktrek Images; p. 758 Tim Mosenfelder; pp. 779, 793 Witold Skrypczak/ Lonely Planet Images; p. 794 Lonely Planet Images; p. 796 Witold Skrypczak/Lonely Planet Images; p. 797 Per Breiehagen/Photographer's Choice; p. 798 Erik Isakson. **Shutterstock:** p. 697 coral; p. 713 David Gaylor; p. 717 Theresa Martinez; p. 728 Charles Zachritz; p. 734 Karin Hildebrand Lau; p. 736 David James; p. 745 Kathy Burns-Millyard; p. 762 Mark Scott; p. 791 Tomasz Szymanski.

Courtesy Photos: p. 682 Boulders Resort & Spa; p. 691 Heard Museum; p. 692 Visit Pheonix; p. 694 The Phoenician; p. 701 Canyon Ranch; p. 706 Molly Johnson/C Lazy Ranch; p. 708 The Broadmoor; p. 712 © Brewers Association; p. 724 Jack Affleck, Vail Resorts; p. 748 Robert Godwin for the Santa Fe Opera; p. 757 Lake Austin Spa & Resort; p. 763 Dallas Museum of Art; p. 765 Sixth Floor Museum; p. 770 AIA Houston; p. 771 Jeff Wilson/Greune Dance Hall; p. 785 Jennifer Whitney/La Fogata; p. 787 Tim Turner/ Lady Bird Johnson Wildflower Center, The University of Texas at Austin; p. 795 Matt Crawley/Snowbird.

WEST COAST: **age fotostock:** p. 822 Super Stock. **Alamy Stock Photo:** p. 806 Ian Dagnall; p. 807 Gary Corbett; p. 830 Lee Foster; p. 835 Visions of America, LLC; p. 837 Jon Bilous; p. 839 David Zanzinger; p. 848 Clive Sawyer; p. 851 Patrick Batchelder; p. 860 Design Pics Inc.; p. 864 California Dreamin; p. 867 Jesse Kraft; p. 871 Bill Gozansky; p. 874 Russ Bishop; p. 879 Dennis Frates; p. 881 Lee Foster; pp. 882, 884 Dennis Frates; p. 885 Danita Delimont; p. 890 David A. Barnes; p. 894 Inge Johnsson; p. 897 Purestock; pp. 904, 905 Danita Delimont. **Fotolia:** p. 810 Melastmohican; p. 826 NING RUAN; p. 838 Jeff; p. 840 Mark Rasmussen; p. 841 wildnerdpix; p. 846 luciano mortula; p. 852 bcfotos; p. 855 sborisov; p. 862 Sarah Fields; p. 870 efaah0; p. 891 jpldesigns. **Getty Images:** p. 816 Woods Wheatcroft; p. 817 David Peevers; p. 834 Wes Walker/Lonely Planet Images; p. 850 The Washington Post; p. 856 Hiroyuki Matsumoto; p. 857 Rick Gerharter; p. 859 Neale Clark; p. 861 Rachid Dahnoun; p. 893 John Elk II/Lonely Planet Images; p. 899 Don Bartletti/LA Times. **Shutterstock:** p. 803 Heather L. Jones; p. 818 Rodolfo Arpia; p. 828 Celso Diniz; p. 845 Adam Tinney; p. 853 seanlean; p. 868 Ronald Sherwood; p. 872 David MacFarlane; p. 875 James R. Hearn; p. 876 md8speed; p. 888 Natalia Bratslavsky; p. 898 Poul Costinsky.

Courtesy Photos: p. 813 © Jan Joan Vanderschuit/Golden Door Spa; p. 814 Osmosis Spa; p. 820 Los Angeles Philharmonic Association; p. 825 Bel-Air Hotel; p. 831 © Monterey Bay Aquarium, photo by Randy Wilder; p. 843 Ken Bohn/San Diego Zoo; p. 844 Hotel Del Coronado; p. 865 David Cooper/Oregon Shakespeare Festival; p. 873 Salishan Spa & Golf Resort; p. 887 Tulip Town; p. 901 Ray's Boathouse & Café.

ALASKA & HAWAII: **age fotostock:** p. 914 SuperStock; p. 917 Stuart Westmorland. **Alamy Stock Photo:** p. 909 Tribune Content Agency LLC; p. 910 Design Pics Inc.; p. 918 RosaIreneBetancourt; pp. 920, 923, 926 AccentAlaska.com; p. 928 John De Mello; p. 931 Douglass Peebles Photography (top), National Geographic Creative (bottom); p. 936 WaterFrame; pp. 938, 940 Design Pics Inc.; p. 941 Andre Seale; p. 943 Alvis Upitis; p. 949 Dennis Frates; p. 956 David Olsen; p. 957 Rick Strange; p. 958 Tim McGuire Images, Inc.; p. 959 Douglas Peebles Photography; p. 961 Craig Ellenwood; p. 963 Ellen Isaacs; p. 967 Chad Ehlers; p. 968 Jose Gil; p. 969 Extreme Sports Photo. **Fotolia:** p. 911 karrapavan; p. 912 Galyna Andrushko; p. 916 sorincolac; p. 927 bennymarty; p. 945 peteleclerc; p. 946 nstanev; p. 948 MNStudio. **Getty Images:** p. 907 Kim Grant/Lonely Planet Images; p. 924 Ernest Manewal/Lonely Planet Images; p. 937 Ann Cecil/ Lonely Planet Images; p. 939 Karl Lehmann/Lonely Planet Images; p. 944 Kim Grant/Lonely Planet Images; pp. 952, 953 Karl Lehmann/Lonely Planet Images; p. 965 Ann Cecil/Lonely Planet Images. **Shutterstock:** pp. 955, 960 Hiroyuki Saita; p. 962 Lisa Hoang (top), Patrick Hannon (bottom); p. 970 Bryan Busovicki.

Courtesy Photos: p. 925 NPS photo; p. 934 Mauna Lani Bay Hotel & Bungalows; p. 942 "Paniolo Adventures" Big Island, Hawaii; p. 950 Peter Vitale/Four Seasons.

EASTERN CANADA: age fotostock: p. 982 Targa; p. 996 Henry Georgi. **Alamy Stock Photo:** p. 975 canadarian; p. 980 All Canada Photos; p. 981 Rolf Hicker Photography; pp. 983, 987, 991 All Canada Photos; p. 1003 Brownstock; p. 1005 Prisma Bildagentur; p. 1006 Pietro Scozzari; pp. 1011, 1014 All Canada Photos; p. 1015 Andre Jenny; p. 1016 Blaine Harrington III; p. 1018 Per Anderson; pp. 1019, 1021 Danita Delimont. **Fotolia:** p. 977 onepony; p. 999 filtv. **Getty Images:** p. 988 Emily Riddell/Lonely Planet Images; p. 989 shaunl/E+; p. 992 Rolf Hicker; p. 1012 Jean du Boisberranger; p. 1020 Glenn Van Der Knijff/Lonely Planet Images. **Shutterstock:** p. 973 V.J Matthew; p. 1001 John Czenke; p. 1009 V.J Matthew; p. 1017 Vladimir Eremin.

Courtesy Photos: p. 993 Nansen Weber/Quark Expeditions; p. 1004 Don Dixon/Stratford Festival.

WESTERN CANADA: age fotostock: p. 1033 John E. Marriott. **Alamy Stock Photo:** p. 1026 eye35.pix; p. 1027 GALA Images; p. 1031 John Elk III; p. 1035 Robert Harding; p. 1038 All Canada Photos; p. 1040 Buddy Mays; p. 1043 GALA Images; p. 1044 Bubby Mays; p. 1047 Gunter Max; p. 1048 Robert Harding; p. 1049 Klaus Lang; p. 1050 Michael Wheatley; p. 1051 Digital-Fotofusion Gallery; p. 1054 All Canada Photos; p. 1055 Rolf Hicker Photographer; p. 1056 Blaine Harrington III; p. 1508 Chris Cheadle; p. 1061 John Elk III; p. 1062 Gunter Marx; p. 1069 Robert McGouey; p. 1072 Gary Cook. **Fotolia:** p. 1025 james_wheeler; p. 1034 elena_survorova; p. 1063 james_wheeler. **Getty Images:** p. 1039 Rhonda Gutenberg; p. 1071 Jeff Greenberg/UIG. **Shutterstock:** p. 1023 Nelson Sirlin; p. 1028 Clive Watkins; p. 1030 Natalia Bratslavsky; p. 1059 Allen Furmanski; p. 1065 Keith Levit.

Courtesy Photos: p. 1052 Leila Kwok/Tojo's; p. 1053 Wedgewood Hotel & Spa.

Special Indexes: p. 1073 karrapavan/Fotolia.

General Index: p. 1119 Image Studios/Getty Images.

And please check out:

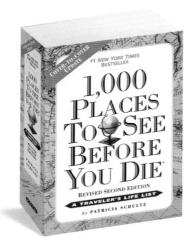

It's the world's bestselling travel book with over 3.3 million copies in print. And it's better than ever, in a new full-color edition that's more informative, more experiential, more budget-friendly. There are 600 full-color photographs. Over 200 entirely new entries, 28 new countries. In all, 1,000 places guaranteed to inspire and amaze, with each entry expanded to include suggestions for places to stay, restaurants to visit, festivals to check out, best times to visit, plus the nuts and bolts: prices, websites, and phone numbers. The world is calling. Time to answer.

LEARN MORE AT 1000PLACES.COM.